The Handbook of
APPLIED EXPERT SYSTEMS

Edited by
Jay Liebowitz

CRC Press
Taylor & Francis Group
Boca Raton London New York

CRC Press is an imprint of the
Taylor & Francis Group, an **informa** business

Preface

PREAMBLE

Over the years, the expert systems field and community have grown tremendously worldwide. As the field has matured, expert systems are being developed and deployed in a myriad of applications. To help the expert systems practitioner, educator, manager, and student become better acquainted with expert systems, a need exists for the *Handbook of Applied Expert Systems*.

We are very proud of this *Handbook*, and we hope it will serve as the key reference for expert systems, especially from an applied viewpoint. The handbook covers both technologies and applications associated with expert systems. This handbook would never have been possible without the scholarly contributions of over 40 chapter authors from close to 20 nations. As Editor, I gratefully acknowledge their important support, as well as that from the reviewers. I also would like to thank up front Ron Powers, Cindy Carelli, Chuck Rogan, and the CRC Press staff for undertaking this project. I am very pleased to have CRC Press publish this handbook, as they are probably the leader in handbook publishing. I would also like to thank Bob Miranda, Sheila Bergman, the World Congress on Expert Systems regional chairs, George Washington University, James Madison University, and the U.S. Army War College for their encouragement and interaction throughout the years. And, of course, without my family's support (Janet, Jason, Kenny, Mazel, and my parents), I would not have had the energy and wisdom to complete this project.

Over the past 6 years, there have been some interesting trends in expert systems activity worldwide (Liebowitz, 1991, 1994, 1996; Zarri, 1991; Lee et al., 1991, 1996; Suen, 1991; Cantu-Ortiz, 1991; Liebowitz et al., 1996). An excellent indicator in gaining a global perspective on expert systems technology, applications, and management has been through chairing or co-chairing the World Congress on Expert Systems (International Society for Intelligent Systems, 1996).

In order to gain an appreciation for worldwide expert system activities over the past six years, the World Congress on Expert Systems serves as an excellent sampling of applied (mostly) papers in expert systems technology and applications.* About 800 papers from more than 45 countries have been presented at the three World Congresses on Expert Systems. The next sections will highlight some of the major global expert system trends and activities, based upon an analysis of the first three World Congresses on Expert Systems.

WORLDWIDE EXPERT SYSTEMS APPLICATIONS

The 1st World Congress on Expert Systems showcased some of the leading expert systems work being used worldwide. The quality of the operational expert systems was outstanding. Applications ranged from using expert systems for blast furnace control at Fukuyama Works in Japan or expert systems for elevator design at Japan's Mitsubishi Electric Corporation to using expert systems for strategic management support in Germany. The variety of expert systems work being conducted was quite evident at the Congress. Applications ranged from employing expert systems to schedule crews in Portuguese railways to sheep reproduction management in Australia to hurricane damage assessment in the Caribbean to modeling a black teenager on subjects of teenage pregnancy, drug, and alcohol abuse.

---

* Adapted from Liebowitz, J. 1997. "Worlwide Perspectives and Trends in Expert Systems." *AI Magazine*, 18(2); 115–119; with permission of AAAI Press.

The Congress also had sessions on representative expert systems in various geographic regions throughout the world. In the Far East, expert systems were highlighted in the steel, electromechanical, power, automobile, oil, paper, airline, construction, and investment industries. In Europe, expert systems work was described in Germany, Spain, France, and the U.K. The following trends were noted: expert systems, are being used chiefly for the heavy industries in Germany and a wave of interest in fuzzy logic is rapidly growing in Germany; the United Kingdom remains conservative in its development and deployment of expert systems and foreign investment, particularly Japanese, is quite evident in the expert systems companies in the U.K.; in France, a trend of mergers and acquisitions within the expert systems field continues; in Spain, a great need exists to provide the transfer of expert systems technology out of the university labs and into industry. Other sessions on representative expert systems in Mexico, the Caribbean, eastern Europe, Scandinavia, Canada, Australia, South America, and Africa were held. It was apparent that there is growing interest in expert systems technology and applications in these regions.

In the 2nd Congress in Lisbon, a worldwide outlook on expert systems activities and trends was gained. In the Pacific Rim, notably Japan, Korea, Hong Kong, and Singapore, expert systems activity was steadily growing in 1994. Even though Japan was in the midst of a recession then, high technology projects (including expert systems) were still being funded. The typical funding for a corporate expert systems project in Japan in 1994 was $100,000–$500,000. Korea, Hong Kong, and Singapore were rapidly growing countries for expert systems development. In Korea, expert systems are being used in shipbuilding, telecommunications, finance, and engineering. Singapore, through the National University of Singapore, is very active in AI/expert systems development, including projects in interactive multimedia and AI development, case-based reasoning, and intelligent information retrieval.

Europe and Scandinavia are actively pursuing expert systems, intelligent systems, hybrid systems, and knowledge technology. The ESPRIT program is probably the major source of funds for expert systems projects in Europe. Most of the European countries are engaged in expert systems projects, but some countries like Portugal are lagging behind somewhat. In Scandinavia, expert systems are being applied to the fishing, shipping, oil, and engineering industries. In the Netherlands, knowledge technology is gaining in popularity and usage.

In the U.S. in 1994, expert systems were being deployed through such terms as hybrid intelligent systems, integrated systems, business process reengineering, business process automation, and knowledge technology, among others. The expert systems field was fairly healthy in the U.S. in 1994, even though funding for expert systems research had declined over recent years. Many corporations are using expert systems as a strategic advantage. Others are using expert systems as a value-added feature. As we continue to move toward knowledge technology and management, expert systems will play a major role.

Developing countries such as Mexico, Thailand, Egypt, and others are also becoming involved with expert systems development and deployment. Agriculture, manufacturing, medicine, and engineering are popular domains for expert systems in these developing nations.

In the 3rd Congress in 1996, chaired by Prof. Jae Kyu Lee of the Korea Advanced Institute of Science and Technology (KAIST), there were a number of expert/intelligent system techniques that echoed throughout the Congress. These included data mining, hybrid systems, machine learning, intelligent database systems, intelligent agents, fuzzy expert systems, model-based reasoning, neural networks, genetic algorithms, multimedia expert systems, and case-based reasoning. Business, financial, medical, engineering, manufacturing, environmental, agricultural, energy, retailing, transportation, and other expert system applications were covered during the Congress (the 4th World Congress on Expert Systems, under the chairmanship of Professor Francisco Cantu-Ortiz of ITESM, is scheduled for March 16–20, 1998 in Mexico City).

ANALYSIS OF WORLD CONGRESS' EXPERT SYSTEMS APPLICATIONS

In reviewing the expert system application areas of papers accepted for the first three World Congresses on Expert Systems, the following can be observed:

- The leading expert system applications worldwide, in order, are: engineering/manufacturing (35%), business (29%), medicine (11%), environment/energy (9%), agriculture (5%), telecommunications (4%), government (4%), law (3%), and transportation (1%).
- From papers accepted for the 3rd World Congress in 1996, the leading business global expert system applications are, in order: finance, production management, general management, accounting/auditing, marketing/sales, electronic commerce, international business, and human resource management.
- From papers accepted for all three Congresses, the following trends appear:
  - Business: sizable increase in expert system applications (29–41%)
  - Engineering/Manufacturing: steady increase in expert system applications
  - Agriculture: decrease (7–4%)
  - Medicine: increase (7–21%)
  - Environment/Energy: sizable increase (2–13%)
  - Telecommunications: stable (around 4–5%)
  - Transportation: stable (around 3–4%)
  - Law: decrease (around 3%)
  - Government: decrease (around 5%)

EXPERT SYSTEMS TECHNOLOGY

The 1st Congress was full of sessions that dealt with the integration of expert systems with conventional and new technologies. It appeared that the "hot" technologies associated with expert systems were case-based reasoning, object-oriented programming, interactive multimedia, and neural networks. There were also several sessions on the use of fuzzy logic throughout the world. Interest in fuzzy logic seems to be increasing worldwide, with the U.S. lagging behind in sponsored research in fuzzy logic.

Several researchers stressed that expert systems in the future should possess increased power and decreased complexity. Increased power will be in the form of large knowledge bases, integration with other systems, and the use of packages of methods. Decreased complexity will be in the building and maintenance of expert systems (knowledge acquisition tools, machine learning) and in "using" the expert system (customizable systems, "invisible" systems, designed for specific problems/person-role, place). Others stressed the gap between the AI theorist and the expert systems practitioner.

In the 2nd Congress in Lisbon, much focus was placed on knowledge sharing and the need for furthering research and applications in this area. The idea that expert systems are merely islands needs to be greatly expanded into developing the bridges and covering the water between the islands. Other selected trends emerged from this 2nd Congress:

- Expert/intelligent systems are becoming more widespread, and are being developed and used for a myriad of tasks at varying levels of maturity.
- Hybrid systems, knowledge technology, fuzzy logic, business process automation, and interactive multimedia are the popular buzz words.
- Real-time expert systems, expert scheduling systems, and expert diagnostic systems are gaining in popularity and usage.
- The management of expert systems technology and the legal implications of using or misusing expert systems are still not as strongly considered by developers and managers as they should be.

- Embedded expert systems (i.e., the raisin in the bread phenomenon) are gaining momentum in usage.
- The developing countries are becoming more interested in expert systems/AI technology by using shells to develop expert systems.

In the 3rd Congress, knowledge acquisition still looms as a major stumbling block in expert systems development. Some interesting ways of improving the knowledge acquisition process were using genetic algorithms (GA) to weed out the "bad" rules, using simulated breeding (GA-based) and inductive learning to develop decision rules from questionnaire survey data, and developing a framework to assess the impact of culture on knowledge acquisition methods.

Besides knowledge acquisition, another important area that was stressed during the 3rd Congress dealt with intelligent scheduling and constraint-based programming. One project called GUESS (Generically Used Expert Scheduling System) (Liebowitz et al., 1996) was discussed, a project using an object-oriented, constraint-based, AI toolkit approach for performing scheduling. Other intelligent scheduling papers described the use of genetic algorithms for job shop and project management scheduling applications. A constraint-based approach, using CHIP, has also been developed (as a prototype) for airplane gate assignment for Korean Air. Other uses for constraint logic programming involved resource allocation problems (such as for personnel, vehicles, slots, and timetabling).

Another emerging topic emphasized in the 3rd Congress dealt with intelligent agents and their use on the Web and for electronic commerce. A workshop on "AI on the Web" was held during the 3rd Congress, as well. It may turn out that the "killer application" for expert systems and AI is intelligent search engines and browsers for the Web. For electronic commerce, a need exists in applying AI technology for intelligent customer and vendor agents, inter-agent communications methods as related to AI in electronic commerce, and the like. KAIST in Korea has established a research center focusing on intelligent systems in electronic commerce.

ANALYSIS OF EXPERT SYSTEM TECHNOLOGIES BASED UPON THE THREE WORLD CONGRESSES

In reviewing the accepted papers relating to expert system technologies and their percentages of the expert system technology totals, the following trends can be summarized:

- Steady increase:
    Genetic algorithms (1–5%)
    Intelligent and multiple agents (1–5%)
    Model-based reasoning (1–4%)
    Hybrid expert systems (around 6%)
- Stable:
    Distributed expert systems (around 4%)
    Fuzzy expert systems (around 16%)
    Knowledge acquisition (around 6%)
    Knowledge sharing (around 2%)
    Machine learning (around 3%)
    Neural networks (around 4%)
    AI with Quantitative Techniques (around 3%)
    Verification and validation (around 6%)
    Expert system tools (around 3%)
    Case-based reasoning (around 4%)
    Knowledge base management (around 2%)
    Multimedia expert systems (around 4%)
    Expert system interfaces (around 3%)

- Steady decrease:
  Uncertainty management (7–4%)
  Other (miscellaneous)

MANAGEMENT OF EXPERT SYSTEMS

The 1st Congress had several sessions that addressed the management of expert systems programs and projects. It was evident that the technology may not be the stumbling block in expert systems applications, but the *management* of the expert systems technology is just as, if not more, important. The need for proper institutionalization of the expert systems technology was emphasized. There were several sessions that addressed the need for standards or guidelines in expert systems development, integration, and usage.

At the 3rd Congress, knowledge management was a topic of widespread discussion. Knowledge management (Liebowitz and Wilcox, 1997) looks at continual, incremental improvement, whereas business reengineering is more of a one-time "shock treatment" for the organization. Presenters at the Congress were emphasizing the need to use knowledge management techniques and companies need to consider knowledge asset management. Most chief executive officers realize the strategic importance of knowledge in their organization, but don't have metrics to determine its "knowledge asset's" size and how to value knowledge.

Lastly, sessions on "explanation of expert systems" at the 3rd Congress suggested that explanations may not be as important as some believe. Several studies indicated that commercial users may not need it (this was pointed out by a medical expert system application in the U.K.). However, there are mixed views as others feel that explanation is necessary for maintaining the expert system.

SUMMARY

From the data surveyed from the first three World Congresses on Expert Systems, it appears that the "applied" expert systems market is healthy, but growing slowly. Figures from the March 1996 Intelligent Software Strategies report indicate the 1995 North America knowledge-based systems tool and consulting market is about $258 million (which accounts for about 71% of the AI market), and has grown from the 1994 figures. Durkin (from the University of Akron), in his catalog of expert system applications, estimates the number of expert systems being around 12,500 (which includes an estimate of company proprietary expert systems).

There is stable to steady growing interest in expert systems technology and applications, but the research dollars to support and advance the state-of-the-art in expert systems seems to be declining. In order to further advance this field, and the intelligent systems field in general, more work needs to be done to address the research issues at hand (Liebowitz and Letsky, 1997). Recently, the General Accounting Office and one of the House Congressional Subcommittees have shown interest in further exploring the use of expert systems in our government and US society as a whole. Perhaps, with reaching these strategic decision makers, the expert systems field will get the recognition it so richly deserves.

REFERENCES

Liebowitz, J. (Ed.) (1994), *Worldwide Expert System Activities and Trends*, Cognizant Communication Corp., Elmsford, NY.
Liebowitz, J. (Ed.) (1991), *Operational Expert System Applications in the United States*, Pergamon Press, Oxford, England.
Zarri, G.P. (Ed.) (1991), *Operational Expert System Applications in Europe*, Pergamon Press, Oxford, England.

Lee, J.K., R. Mizoguchi, D. Narasimhalu, and D. Yeung (Eds.) (1991), *Operational Expert System Applications in the Far East*, Pergamon Press, Oxford, England.

Suen, C. (Ed.) (1991), *Operational Expert System Applications in Canada*, Pergamon Press, Oxford, England.

Cantu-Ortiz, F. (Ed.) (1991), *Operational Expert System Applications in Mexico*, Pergamon Press, Oxford, England.

Liebowitz, J. (Ed.) (1991), *Proceedings of the 1st World Congress on Expert Systems*, Pergamon Press, Oxford, England.

Liebowitz, J. (Ed.) (1994), *Proceedings of the 2nd World Congress on Expert Systems*, Cognizant Communication Corp., Elmsford, NY.

Lee, J.K., J. Liebowitz, and Y.M. Chae (Eds.) (1996), *Proceedings of the 3rd World Congress on Expert Systems*, Cognizant Communication Corp., Elmsford, NY.

Liebowitz, J. (Ed.) (1996), *Hybrid Intelligent Systems*, Cognizant Communication Corp., Elmsford, NY.

Liebowitz, J. et al. (1996), *The Explosion of Intelligent Systems in the Year 2000*, International Society for Intelligent Systems/Cognizant Communication Corp., Elmsford, NY.

Liebowitz, J. (Ed.) (1990–present), *Expert Systems with Applications: An International Journal*, Pergamon Press/Elsevier Science, Oxford, England.

International Society for Intelligent Systems, *The World Congress on Expert Systems*, P.O. Box 1656, Rockville, MD 20849.

Liebowitz, J., V. Krishnamurthy, I. Rodens, A. Liebowitz, S. Baek, and J. Zeide (1996), *Final Report: A Generic Expert Scheduling System Architecture and Toolkit*, American Minority Engineering Corporation, Prepared for NASA Goddard, Kensington, MD, March 31.

Liebowitz, J. and L. Wilcox (Eds.) (1997), *Knowledge Management and Its Integrative Elements*, CRC Press, Boca Raton, FL.

Liebowitz, J. and C. Letsky (1996), *Developing Your First Expert System CD ROM*, CRC Press, Boca Raton, FL.

Contributors

Mark R. Adler
SystemSoft Corp.
Natick, MA

Barbro Back
Turku School of Economics
  and Business Administration
Turku, Finland

Amelia Baldwin
Florida International University
  School of Accounting
Miami, FL

Thomas J. Beckman
Internal Revenue Service
Washington, DC

Paul L. Bowen
University of Queensland
  Department of Commerce
Brisbane, Australia

Bernt A. Bremdal
Bremdal Technology Services
Vettre, Norway

Carol Brown
Oregon State University
  College of Business
Corvallis, OR

Chae Young Moon
Yonsei University
  Graduate School of Health Science
  and Management
Seoul, Korea

Chaomei Chen
Glasgow Caledonian University
  Department of Computer Studies
Glasgow, UK

Timothy Paul Darr
University of Michigan
  Department of Electrical Engineering
  and Computer Science
Ann Arbor, MI

Jefferson T. Davis
Clarkson University
  School of Business
Potsdam, NY

Robert de Hoog
University of Amsterdam
  Department of Social Science Information
Amsterdam, The Netherlands

Jasbir S. Dhaliwal
National University of Singapore
  Centre for Management of Techology
Kent Ridge, Singapore

John Durkin
The University of Akron
  Department of Electrical Engineering
Akron , OH

Clive L. Dym
Harvey Mudd College
  Department of Engineering
Clairmont, CA

Roar Arne Fjellheim
Computas AS
Sandvika, Norway

Thomas P. Galvin
U.S. Army War College
  Center for Strategic Leadership
  Science and Technology Division
Carlisle Barracks, PA

Linda Gammill
Oregon State University
  College of Business
Corvallis, OR

Randy G. Goebel
University of Alberta
  Computing Science
Edmonton, AB, Canada

Asunción Gómez-Pérez
Campus de Monte Gancedo, SN
Madrid, Spain

Peter Grogono
Concordia University
  Department of Computer Science
Montreal, PQ, Canada

Alan Gunderson
Spring Street Software
Eagle River, AK

Patrick R. Harrison
U.S. Naval Academy
  Computer Science Department
Annapolis, MD

George Hluck
Corning, Inc.
Corning, NY

Joseph G. Kovalchik
U.S. Naval Academy
Annapolis, MD

Jae Kyu Lee
Korea Advanced Institute of Science
  and Technology MIS Department
Seoul, Korea

Sang-Kee Lee
Seoul, Korea

Jay Liebowitz
The George Washington University
  School of Business Management
Washington, DC

Yihwa Irene Liou
University of Baltimore
Baltimore, MD

Lean Suan Ong
National University of Singapore
  Institute of Systems Science
Kent Ridge, Singapore

Dhiraj K. Pathak
Glaxo Wellcome
Research Triangle Park, NC

Juan Pazos Sierra
University Politecnica de Madrid
  Department of Artificial Intelligence
Madrid, Spain

David S. Prerau
DPC
Chestnut Hill, MA

Roy Rada
Washington State University
  Department of Computer Studies
Pullman, WA

Ahmed A. Rafea
Central Laboratory for Agricultural Expert Systems
Giza, Egypt

James M. Ragusa
University of Central Florida
Titusville, FL

Alan Sangster
Queen's University at Belfast
  School of Management
Belfast, UK

Peter Smith
University of Sunderland
Sunderland, UK

Ming Tan
GTE Labs
Waltham, MA

I. B. Türkşen
University of Toronto
  Department of Mechanical and Industrial Engineering
Toronto, ON, Canada

Tibor Vámos
Hungarian Academy of Sciences
  Computer and Automation
  Research Institute
Budapest, Hungary

Anca Vermesan
Det Norske Veritas Research
  Division of Technology and Products
Hovik, Norway

Mark Wallace
Imperial College
  William Penney Laboratory
London, UK

Gen'ichi Yasuda
Nagasaki Insitute of Applied Science
  Department of Mechanical Engineering
Nagasaki, Japan

Gian Piero Zarri
EHESS-CAMS
Paris, France

Contents

Critical Technologies Associated with Expert Systems

Section B: Selected Expert Systems Applications

Engineering-Related Expert Systems

Section A
Expert Systems Technology

Part I
Expert System Development Process

1 Methodologies for Building Knowledge Based Systems: Achievements and Prospects

Robert de Hoog

CONTENTS

1. INTRODUCTION

Since knowledge-based systems (KBSs) became a commercially viable solution to real-life problems in the beginning of the 1980s, increasing attention is paid to ways to develop them in a systematic fashion, just as ordinary information systems. Just as the latter, early KBSs suffered from serious delays in delivering, disappointing functionality, and appreciable problems in maintenance. The code-and-fix approach, so typical for research laboratories from which they evolved, simply could not stand up to the harsh reality of operational environments and intransigent users. Not surprisingly, the first guidelines for developing KBSs appeared in the middle 1980s and the heyday's of tailored methodologies fell somewhere in the late 1980s and early 1990s. The goal of this chapter is to give a bird's-eye overview of this development[1]. It should be stressed from the beginning, however, that there is no claim to completeness. The blooming of methodologies and methods (this distinction will be discussed in Section 1.2) in the period under study precludes this. Additionally, it will be argued that there are only a few methodologies as they are going to be defined in the next section. This rules out the need for a comprehensive overview of methodologies that do not qualify as such in my definition. In Sections 3 and 4, some of these will be mentioned briefly, but the selection is rather arbitrary, based on my necessarily limited insight in the literature. Section 5 devotes more attention to full-fledged methodologies as they are defined in Section 2. In Section 6, some prospects for KBS-specific methodologies in the future are sketched.

This chapter could have been stuffed with tens or even hundreds of references to books, papers in journals, and conference proceedings that mention something about methodology. This author has chosen not to do so. First, it would make the chapter almost unreadable. Second, what matters most, to the author at least, are not the details but the general line of development from which we

---

[1] Earlier examples of reviews comparable to this one are Inder and Filby (1991), Hilal and Soltan (1991), and Hilal and Soltan (1993).

can derive insights for the future. Third, most references would only have a curiosity value, because of all the proposals, methods, techniques, methodologies, and so forth, only a few have made some impact and even fewer survive in daily use.

2.   WHAT'S A METHODOLOGY?

Throughout the literature, confusion reigns about several terms that occur frequently in the context under consideration. Words like method, technique, instrument, and methodology are often used indiscriminately. To clarify my point of view, a definition is given of some of these terms in a way that seems to hang together. These definitions, however, are idiosyncratic. They are not universally known, let alone adopted. As this is not the place to discuss these issues, it will be assumed that they are useful in making distinctions that matter.

In its original meaning, a methodology refers to *knowledge about methods*. This immediately implies that though methodology and methods are in the same domain, they are not the same. The former clearly is some kind of meta-knowledge if we assume that methods also contain knowledge. The next question to answer is about the nature of this (meta)knowledge. It seems to be different from the kind of knowledge we encounter in most scientific theories, which are mostly about causal relations ("laws of nature") that hold in a particular domain. Probably nobody will argue that methodological knowledge is in the same class. What is commonly understood to be methodological knowledge is "know what," "know-how," and "know when." These "knows" are *normative* or *prescriptive*: they don't *describe* a state of the world, but prescribe how a sensible agent should act to achieve a certain goal. Therefore, the quality of prescriptive knowledge is not whether it enables you to "predict" or "explain" something, but whether you have achieved the goal. Additional criteria may come in here, like speed and cost. The bottom line for any prescription is that it should improve goal achievement over "unaided" behavior.

Prescriptive statements may differ greatly in preciseness. For example, the prescription "work hard" is rather imprecise if the goal is to become rich. In the same vein, shouting "faster" to a runner trying to beat a world record will generally not be of great help (though the motivating power of such exhortations should not be underestimated). At the other end of the spectrum, we come across very detailed specification about what, how, and when. Anybody who has submitted a funding proposal to major funding agencies has experienced the myriad prescriptions one has to follow about how and when to submit. Not following them usually misses the goal: the proposal will be rejected before it has been judged. The most restrictive prescriptions we know are computer algorithms, which leave no room for interpretation by the agent (the computer). Methodological knowledge of the type we are discussing here, will clearly fall between these two extremes. If it's too general, it will most of the time not be of great help; if it's too specific, it will suffer from very limited applicability and a high vulnerability to slightly different contexts.

To pull these notions together, the *methodological pyramid*[2] introduced by Wielinga et al. (1994) is a convenient way to characterize what is involved in a methodology (see Figure 1).

The **world view** top layer of the pyramid refers to the principles and assumptions that underlie the methodology. They often include the goal(s) that is being served. The **theory** layer elaborates these principles and assumptions and forms the core of the knowledge in the domain of the methodology. **Methods and techniques** operationalize the content of the theories, the main "how" part of it. **Tools** are computerized instances of methods and techniques in the previous layer. Being computerized often requires additional use knowledge attached to them. The use layer represents the touchstone of a methodology. It will reveal shortcomings in the prescriptions provided by the layers above, which will lead to revisions in the different components of the methodology. From

---

[2] The metaphor of a "pyramid" is not chosen accidentally. Most methodologies rely on a limited number of key principles, which in turn spawn more elaborate theories that can be operationalized in a set of methods/techniques, which can be implemented in different tools and used by a large number of users.

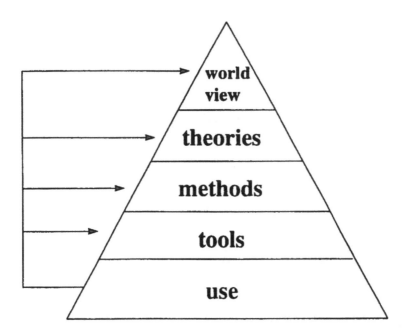

FIGURE 1   The methodological pyramid.

the arrows in Figure 1 it can be gauged that the higher in the pyramid an arrow ends, the more serious the repercussions for the methodology are. If the methodology hangs together, a change in its assumptions and principles will propagate through the pyramid, leading to major modifications.

The pyramid depicted in Figure 1 can be illustrated by means of a well-established and fairly complete example. In the social sciences there has been for many decades a concern about how to conduct "proper" research. The dominant definition for "proper" refers to the goal of obtaining time, location, and observer-independent knowledge: that is, knowledge that can be generalized, not unlike the "laws of nature." Without going into the philosophical merits of these goals, it can be said that for more than three-quarters of a century, a systematic methodology in the sense of Figure 1 has been developed that can assist and guide the researcher in achieving these goals. To the world view principles mentioned above, a few more are added that are mainly borrowed from statistics (e.g., uncertainty). These principles have spawned an extensive set of theories (prescriptive statements) about conducting research. Some are based on statistics, for example sampling theory and inferential statistics; others are based on more general theories about human behavior (e.g., response biases). Almost all theories became embodied in methods and techniques that operation-alize the theories (e.g., how to draw a random sample, how to phrase questions to avoid response bias) and, in particular, the ones based on statistics are now widely available in computerized tools (e.g., SPSS™, but also tools for designing experiments). This body of knowledge has grown over the years based on feedback from use. The discovery that not all variables that are interesting in social science have well-defined statistical distributions has led to the incorporation of nonpara-metric statistics in the theory and subsequently in the methods and tools. An example of a major addition to the world view is the notion that not always all hypotheses are equally likely, which is the cornerstone of classical statistics. This led to including Bayesian statistics in the methodology, thus increasing the scope and applicability of the methodology.

Besides the coverage of the levels of the methodological pyramid, the *scope* of the methodology is another important aspect to consider. With scope is meant the range of activities included in a methodology. Building a KBS is not a one-dimensional affair; it encompasses a wide range of problems and tasks running from organizational factors to low-level coding in a programming/devel-opment language.

Based on the methodological pyramid and the scope, the approaches appearing in the literature can be placed into three general classes:

1. *Boxes-and-arrows* approaches. These approaches are characterized by the fact that they are mainly limited to giving a kind of "life-cycle" consisting of boxes, denoting developing activities, and arrows linking these activities, to generate a sequence. What these approaches lack is a detailed specification of the "how" of the boxes. That is, there are no methods, techniques, or tools provided. However, they cover most of the activities normally seen as important in developing KBSs, albeit in a very general way. They are broad and shallow.

2. *Focused* approaches. These limit themselves to one or a few methods and techniques that cover part of the work to be done. Within certain bounds they can be seen as "mini methodologies": in their limited scope they sometimes cover all levels of the pyramid. Being focused on a limited number of activities, they are narrow and deep.

3. *Full-fledged* methodologies, providing support for all levels in the pyramid. As we shall see in Section 5, these come in two strands:
   - Methodologies for conventional systems design with "KBS oriented" additions
   - Methodologies specially designed for KBS development
   Claiming to cover all levels of the pyramid and including all important aspects of KBS development, they can be seen as broad and deep.

Before starting the survey of these classes of approaches, it must be emphasized that the methodological pyramid and the derived classification do not imply a value judgment. Though it may seem that "more is better," this cannot be proven to be true in general. From experience with methodologies for the development of conventional systems, we know that a "bad" methodology in the hands of an experienced person may turn into a "good" one, while a "good" methodology may be spoiled by the incompetence of a user. Just as shouting "faster" may sometimes help the runner, boxes-and-arrows may sometimes help the developer.

In more general terms, it is extremely difficult to judge the value of a methodology in an objective way. Experimentation is of course the proper way to do it, but is hardly feasible because there are too many conditions that cannot be controlled. Moreover, nobody will in practice pay for building the same KBS twice with different approaches. Introducing an experimental toy problem will violate the basic assumption behind the need for a methodology: a complex development process. So, of necessity, the notion of "achievement" will be limited mainly to reported use in practice. Though it could be an interesting research project, investigating the relation between use of a methodology and "success" of a KBS is outside the scope of this chapter.

3.   BOXES-AND-ARROWS APPROACHES

One of the earliest examples in the literature is that of Buchanan et al. (1983). As the book in which this paper appears is from the dawn of the commercial uptake of expert systems, it has exerted a considerable influence. Figure 2 reproduces Buchanan et al.'s approach.

Gradually this has been extended into what has come to be called the "Expert Systems Development Life Cycle"[3] or ESDLC, which by minor or major variations have been modified conventional systems development approaches. The dominant variant is the *waterfall approach*,

---

[3] The name "cycle" seems to be wrong, because there is not much "cyclical" in the development of information systems. However, the name has caught on, probably because it is derived from the notion of the product life cycle, which is also not cyclical. This one could be derived from the human life cycle, which can be cyclical if reproduction takes place. (Un?)fortunately, information systems don't reproduce (yet?).

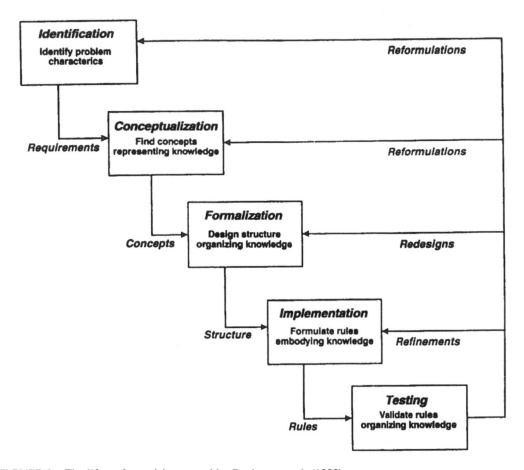

FIGURE 2   The life cycle model proposed by Buchanan et al. (1983)

though sometimes (see, e.g., Khan, 1992) references are made to prototyping and even spiral-model approaches derived from the work of Boehm (1988).

As has already been said in the introduction, it is impossible to track all the proposals that have been made over the last 15 years in this area. In the U.S., the major effort seems to have been in the area of mapping the expert systems life cycle to existing standards for conventional software engineering (e.g., DoD-Std-2167A), which resembles the approach described in Section 5 of linking with existing methodologies for conventional systems. To summarize these efforts it seems sufficient to take one of the most recent books about building KBSs (Awad, 1996) as an example[4]. The life cycle given in this book is depicted in Figure 3.

Though the world view behind approaches like the one in Figure 3 is rarely made explicit, a few of them can be inferred from the properties of Figure 3:

- The main focus of development is on *tasks*; if one succeeds in carrying out the tasks prescribed, it will increase the quality of the resulting KBS.
- Tasks must be carried out in a more or less *fixed sequence* that does not depend on the context.

---

[4] The book by Stefik (1995) is another example. He also modifies the life cycle model of Buchanan et al. (1983) and devotes approximately 15 of the more than 800 pages to methodology issues (though the book abounds with methods and techniques).

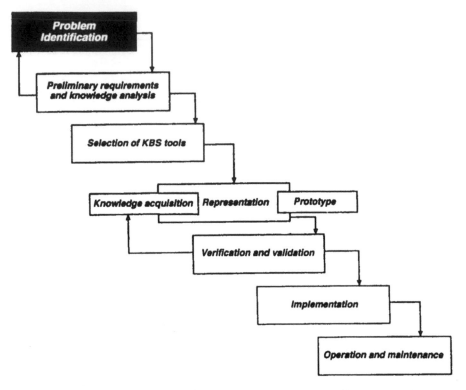

FIGURE 3 A recent example of a waterfall model variant of Figure 2 (from Awad, 1996).

- *Think before you build;* you cannot start programming before you have done a proper and complete analysis.
- *Limited "backtracking"*; as in all waterfall approaches, the developer is not supposed to go back to all activities completed before

Variants of this approach mostly will exhibit the following modifications:

- Different names in the boxes. This may either reflect another way to carve up the development tasks or just semantic disagreement.
- More or less boxes. An important problem is the grain size of the tasks. The coarser the grain size, the fewer boxes, the finer the more. Ultimately, the finer the grain size, the closer the tasks come to a "how" description of the task, which is equivalent to a method or a technique.
- More arrows pointing to previous tasks. The strong linear development path implied by the waterfall model quite often needs modification. This can be achieved by adding arrows to tasks that have already been carried out, increasing the iterating nature of the approach. Note that more arrows of this type don't violate the basic world view that to execute a task you should at least have executed its predecessor once.

Given the abundance of schemes of the type depicted in Figure 3 and the intractability of their possible development into the other two classes, it is impossible to make any definite statement about what they have achieved. From the superficial review of the literature reported in Section 6 it appears that boxes-and-arrows approaches have been used most frequently for building KBSs.

4.   FOCUSED APPROACHES

Doing away with the claim that they cover all aspects of the KBS development process, the approaches in this class limit themselves to one or a few activities and try to support them in depth. The focus chosen most frequently is the long-standing problem, identified first by Buchanan et al. (1983), of the knowledge acquisition bottleneck. Extracting the knowledge from the expert was seen to be the major time and effort consuming activity, quite unlike what was the case in conventional systems development[5]. Additionally, there was the concern for the maintainability of the KBS, as it became clear that large unstructured rule bases were extremely difficult to modify.

Broadly spoken, the knowledge acquisition bottleneck problem was attacked in three ways:

- Trying to *model* the expertise using knowledge acquisition (KA) methods and techniques like protocol analysis, interviewing, case reviewing, concept sorting/laddering, etc., employing a knowledge engineer.
- Transfer of the knowledge from the expert *directly* into a KBS using appropriate expertise transfer methods and techniques.
- Providing a *domain tailored environment,* which is applicable to a well-defined and limited area of expertise or is bound to a *specific method.*

The first path has been taken mainly in Europe. One of the earliest automated support tools in this area was the KEATS system (Motta, et al., 1988). Later, two ESPRIT Projects [ACKnowledge and VITAL (Shadbolt et al., 1993)] were active in this area. Also, the KADS-I project was mainly concerned with knowledge acquisition, though some initial work was done for broader coverage. Both ACKnowledge and VITAL produced a coherent set of knowledge acquisition methods and techniques, including repertory grids, protocol analysis methods, laddering, sorting, etc., as well as libraries of generic templates of expertise models (mostly derived from KADS-I). Both VITAL and ACKnowledge have contributed to the PC-PACK® tool marketed by ISL in the U.K. KADS-I fed into KADSTool® marketed by ILOG in France. Though precise numbers are hard to come by, there seems at least to be a modest market for tools of this type.

The second path is most visible in the work of John Boose on the Expertise Transfer System and the AQUINAS environment (Boose et al., 1989). This approach strives to eliminate the knowledge engineer as the intermediary between expert and coding. The idea is that the expert can directly enter his expertise in a kind of "workbench" that relies heavily on repertory grid and cluster algorithms for translating expertise into executable code. The main difference between this approach and the one described above, is the lack of an explicit modeling effort. One could argue that the format prescribed by the repertory grid is a kind of model, or at least a structure that facilitates knowledge acquisition. It seems that most experience with this approach has been gained in the U.S. and Boeing in particular. Spread to Europe has been hindered by the prevailing preference for the modeling approach. Work in this area has not progressed much since the early 1990s. It could be eclipsed somewhat by the growing popularity of machine learning techniques since the early 1990s. As these techniques follow the same strategy as AQUINAS, bypass the knowledge engineer and modeling, they are in obviously in competition in particular when a case base is available.

The third and last path is based on the idea that knowledge acquisition works best when it stays as close as possible to a specific domain. The SALT system (Marcus and McDermott, 1989) relied on a specific problem solving method (propose and revise) and could be used for all domains in which this method is implicitly or explicitly employed by experts. The sequel to this work is

---

[5] It is difficult to establish whether this observation was ever really true. To people like DeMarco (1982) requirements analysis and correct specification, if done well, just as important and time consuming in conventional systems development as knowledge acquisition is in KBS development.

the PROTÉGÉ-II system (Musen, 1989), which instead focuses on task-specific tools that enable the experts to communicate in their familiar domain-specific terms and concepts. Work on this approach is still progressing, though the major thrust is in the academic community (see Rothenfluh et al., 1996).

A fairly complete overview of the work and the results in this area can be found in a special issue of the *International Journal of Human-Computer Studies* (1996).

Before moving to the next section, a word about KBS development environments like ART, KEE, AionDS, etc. Sellers of these tools would probably hold that they also have at least a methodological flavor because they provide tools and techniques for building KBSs. Though this may be true, the author still sees them primarily as programming languages, albeit sophisticated ones. To make a comparison: in methodologies for conventional information systems building, this would be equivalent to calling PASCAL, SMALLTALK, DELPHI, or any other programming language a "methodology," though they certainly are tools. One could even argue that the sense of having a methodology at all lies in keeping analysis, specification, and design as much as possible apart from a commitment to a particular programming language. No existing methodology (e.g., Yourdon, Martin, SDM, or JSD) has ever made such a commitment.

5.   FULL-FLEDGED METHODOLOGIES

As soon as softwarehouses working in the area of conventional software development sensed the commercial uptake of expert systems, they entered the market by profiling themselves as competitors through their methodologies. These were mostly the same they also used for developing conventional systems, with an added "KBS-specific" component, mostly focused on knowledge acquisition and representation. As their methodologies were full-fledged, in the sense that they covered all levels of the pyramid and were of a broad scope, they automatically possessed a KBS methodology. As most of them were to a greater or lesser extent of the waterfall type described in Section 3, they shared the world view underlying this approach, though they differed in theories and methods[6]. In particular in Europe, these methodologies were seen to be proprietary to a company and the KBS methodology carried the name of the original with some kind of "AI," "KBS" or "Expert Systems"-like extension to it. In including KBS-specific elements, they relied heavily on advances made in R&D in the focused approaches described in Section 4. Some companies even started subsidiaries in the AI market, but most of these have disappeared by now. In general, for most softwarehouses, it turned out to be difficult to dress up in new clothes, a situation aggravated by the lack of qualified personnel because knowledge acquisition called for different skills than those possessed by most computer scientists and programmers. It can be safely stated that from this area not much new was added to the KBS development process not already known or developed elsewhere. From that angle, the short-lived nature of these methodologies is not surprising. In the wake of the disappointment with KBS benefits that overtook the initial optimism in the early 90s, building a KBS is just a particular brand of systems development in general, which occasionally occurs when things cannot be solved with conventional techniques. Thus, the need for profiling through proprietary KBS specific methodologies gradually faded away.

Of the full-fledged methodologies only a few are entirely KBS specific. The most complete and best known is the CommonKADS methodology, the product of two consecutive R&D projects funded by the European Community under the ESPRIT program. This is not the place to elaborate extensively this wide ranging methodology. The reader is referred to Schreiber et al. (1994) for a concise overview. Apart from being full-fledged, the interesting point in CommonKADS is its

---

[6] In the 1980s, most conventional methodologies were not supported by computerized tools. However, this changed in the 1990s. Starting with rather simple drawing tools for data flow and entity-relation diagrams, they grew by including more and more activities from the life cycle. One of the most comprehensive computerized development environments on sale in Europe is the S(ystems) D(evelopers) W(orkbench), marketed by Cap Gemini.

farewell to waterfall like approaches, and opting instead for a fully objectives and risk driven development approach, which owes much to the work of Boehm. Thus, the methodology also includes its own peculiar project management approach. To give its flavor, the CommonKADS worldview is summarized below:

- Knowledge acquisition requires knowledge modeling.
- Parts of expertise can be caught in generic libraries which can be reused.
- KBS development should take place by building models as the main products.
- Organizational issue should be part of the methodology.
- The development process must be supported by a flexible, configurable approach, based on the analysis of objectives and risks.

The theory layer of the pyramid is embodied in the six models and their templates making up the CommonKADS model suite. These models are:

- **The organization model.** The organization model addresses issues concerning the socio-organizational environment of the KBS. It contains several views on the organization or part of the organization that enables the people involved to identify problems areas where KBSs could be fruitfully introduced, but also areas where problems can arise when an actual system is put into operation.
- **The task model.** The task model is a specification of how an organizational function can be achieved by means of a number of tasks, with a focus on knowledge-intensive tasks. This is achieved by means of a task decomposition. Furthermore, there is a description of a number of important properties of tasks like inputs and outputs, capabilities needed to carry out the task, task frequency, etc. For one or more knowledge-intensive tasks, the required expertise is modeled in the expertise model.
- **The agent model.** This model describes the important properties and capabilities of agents[7] that perform tasks in the context of the KBS. This information is important for deciding about the task assignment in the new situation. It also models the communication capabilities of agents, important inputs for the communication model.
- **The expertise model.** This is a central model in the CommonKADS methodology as it is one of the main components that distinguishes KBS development from conventional system development. It contains a specification of the problem-solving expertise required to carry out the expert's task. The structure of this model is three layered: the domain layer, the inference layer, and the task layer (not to be confused with the task model).
- **The communication model.** The communication model is devoted to an issue that is frequently overlooked in KBS development: the interaction with the user and other software systems (e.g., databases). It only covers man-computer and computer-machine communication and not man-man communication even if it is relevant for the context of the KBS.
- **The design model.** The bridge to actual implementation of the system is provided by the design model. This consists of a description of the computational and representational techniques that must be used for building and running the KBS.

In addition, there are several libraries that can be used by the developer to shortcut the work. These also promote reuse over projects. The CommonKADS Workbench marketed by ISL from the U.K. is the powerful, though somewhat erratic, embodiment of the tools layer. Figure 4 shows the control window for the CommonKADS Workbench.

---

[7] The term "agent" refers to any entity that can carry out a task. Thus, an agent can be a human, but also a computer or another machine.

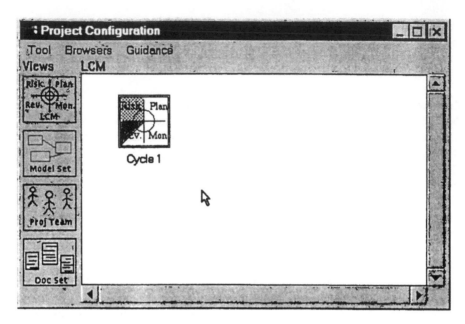

FIGURE 4   Main control window of the CommonKADS Workbench.

Figure 4 shows the four main aspects that play a role in the methodology:

- the life cycle approach LCM (project management) as a sequence of Risk, Plan, Monitor and Review
- the model set, to be developed in the project
- the people working in the project
- the documents to be generated during the project

Not shown is the Library which can be accessed from the "Guidance" menu item.

CommonKADS is the sequel to KADS, which was wholly developed in the eighties. Therefore many ideas originated in KADS are incorporated in the focused approaches and the full-fledged methodologies which KBS specific grafts. In particular the library of generic expertise tasks as can be found in Breuker et al. (1988) and elaborated in Breuker and van de Velde (1994), has been frequently (re)used. It could be that this library is ultimately the most frequently used product of the entire KADS endeavor.

The COMMET methodology (Steels, 1990; 1993) has not been widely published. It is based on the theory that three major components make up a knowledge level description of expertise: the model perspective, the task perspective, and the method perspective. These perspectives are refined in a "spiral" movement. The COMMET approach is supported by a workbench described in Steels (1993). However, the move to operational use has been mainly limited to Belgium and there was never a commercially available version of the COMMET workbench.

Though not sailing under the flag of a methodology, the book by Prerau (1990) comes fairly close to the methodology definition of Section 2. Though the world view is not stated explicitly, the sequence of phases that Prerau describes is of the familiar waterfall type. But the support for carrying out these phases as presented in the majority of the chapters is, most of the time, very KBS specific.

6.   PROSPECTS

Though reading the future is a difficult and hazardous thing to do, the author will conclude this chapter with some reflections on the past and the future.

The past can probably best summarized by investigating how much attention the knowledge-based systems/expert systems community has paid to methodologies. To investigate this topic, the author made an analysis of two main sources of publications concerning expert systems:

- The journal *Expert Systems*, founded in 1984, is an example of a journal with a definitely practical interest, which is combined with two or three "in-depth" articles in every issue. As the journal has maintained this approach as well as its layout for 13 years, it is particularly suited for a comparative analysis. The analysis covered Volumes 2 through 13 (3).
- The Proceedings of three consecutive *World Congress on Expert Systems*™ Conferences held in 1991, 1994, and 1996 (Liebowitz, 1991; 1994; Lee et al., 1996). As these congresses are not "AI" congresses and are strongly focused on the practical aspects of developing KBSs, they can be seen as another major forum for dissemination of expert systems related results.

All articles and papers in these sources were analyzed[8] for references to methodologies and classified the "hits" in two groups:

1. Papers describing the development of an (operational) expert system, that pay explicit attention to the way it was developed, most of the time referring to a life cycle approach (*application papers* in Tables 1 and 2).
2. Papers mainly or wholly devoted to describing or discussing methodologies as defined in Section 2. In this category are also included papers that did not cover the complete life cycle, but only the major part of it (e.g., knowledge acquisition and design-development, *full papers* in Tables 1 and 2.)

Together these sources provide a base of approximately 900 papers in the area of expert systems, which probably is still a moderate sized sample of all papers ever written about this topic. However, given the practical orientation of the two sources it can be argued that this base will more or less correctly reflect the trend in the field concerning the attention paid to methodologies.

In Table 1 the results for *Expert Systems* can be found. As this journal has maintained its size and composition over the period studies, there is no need to compute percentages.

As can be seen from Table 1, 31 papers appeared paying attention to methodologies, equally distributed between the two categories (this is almost 20% of all papers that appeared in the period studied). The peak year is 1990 and taken together, 1990, 1991, and 1992 account for almost 50% of all methodology-oriented papers. In later years, the numbers return to their pre-1990 values. This seems to corroborate the notion that the methodology heyday's fell somewhere in the early 1990s.

Table 2 gives the results for the *World Congress on Expert Systems*™ proceedings. As the number of papers in the Proceedings (N) is different over the years studied, percentages are computed for comparisons.

From Table 2 it is clear that there is a drop in absolute numbers between 1991 and 1996 of papers referring to methodologies. In percentages, 1994 is the peak year. As this conference was

---

[8] Unfortunately, one could not rely on the abstracts, due to the confusion about terminology. Many papers referred to "methodologies," which in terms of the classification presented in Section 2 are techniques or methods.

TABLE 1
Methodology-Related Papers in *Expert Systems*, 1985–1996

Year	Application papers	Full papers
1985	1	0
1986	2	0
1987	0	1
1988	1	2
1989	0	1
1990	3	4
1991	1	2
1992	3	1
1993	1	1
1994	1	2
1995	1	0
1996 (3 issues)	1	2
Total	*15*	*16*

held in January 1994, most papers must have been written in late 1992 or early 1993. This is in line with the trend in Table 1, showing a peak in the early 1990s. Again, there is a clear decline in numbers and percentage in 1996.

Tentatively, the conclusion is that there seems to be a decline in interest in general methodological issues in KBS development. Expert systems are becoming increasingly absorbed in overall system development and will be subject to methodologies and life cycle approaches used for conventional information systems. Consequently, in the opinion of this author, there will be less and less room for very KBS-specific methodologies, notwithstanding the theoretical and practical merits they have. This is not to say that all efforts in this area were wasted. Given the peculiar nature of some aspects of KBS development, there will be a niche for products of the focused approach type. Also, modeling efforts and modeling languages developed in the framework of methodologies will quite likely survive their originating methodologies. The risky nature of many expert systems projects have contributed to the increasing importance of risk analysis in systems development in general and boosted risk driven approaches pioneered by Boehm in the mid-1980s.

Looking back on the last 15 years, a familiar curve can be discerned. This is the technology adoption curve (or for this chapter better named "technology interest curve") depicted in Figure 5 below (taken from Rogers, 1983).

TABLE 2
Methodology-Related Papers for *World Congress on Expert Systems™*

Year	Applications	Full papers	% of total # of papers
1991 (N = 348)	8	21	8.3
1994 (N = 217)	10	14	11.0
1996 (N = 182)	7	6	7
Total	*25*	*41*	*8.8*

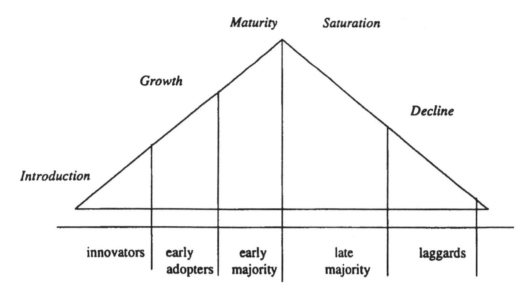

FIGURE 5 Technology adoption curve.

In terms of interest in and impact of ES/KBS methodologies, it appears that the period 1987 to 1990 covers the *Introduction* and *Growth* stages; the period 1991 to 1993, the *Maturity* stage; and the period from 1994 onward, the *Saturation* and *Decline* stages.

As methodologies for KBS development are "technologies" just like all others, it is to be expected in the end that they follow the route of all others. Disappointing though this must seem to all who spent considerable effort in this area, it is a comforting thought that this is exactly how "progress" is commonly defined.

Of course, all work in the area of methodologies for KBS-development will stop in the future. However, it seems not too risky to predict that the days of encompassing KBS specific methodologies are over. Progress will mainly continue in the area of the focused approaches described in Section 1.4 with emphasis on:

- Knowledge modeling and knowledge reuse
- Automated knowledge acquisition, including machine learning techniques
- Integration with related fields like (very large) databases

The wider perspective seems that ideas developed for KBS methodologies could also feed into the emerging field of knowledge management. This still lacks a coherent and consistent "view" on what it precisely stands for. As developing KBSs can be seen as an example of a knowledge management action operating on crucial aspects of knowledge like availability and maintainability, there is a need for fine-tuning methods and techniques for knowledge management with methods and techniques (and methodologies) for KBS development. The first outline of this is evidenced in Wiig (1995) who incorporates KBSs as important elements of knowledge management and also in van der Spek and de Hoog (1995) who borrow ideas and concepts from the CommonKADS methodology.

REFERENCES

Awad, E.M. (1996). *Building Expert Systems.* West Publishing Co.

Breuker, J. and W. van de Velde (Eds.) (1994). *CommonKADS Library for Expertise Modelling.* IOS Press.

Breuker, J.A., B.J. Wielinga, M. van Someren, R. de Hoog, A.T. Schreiber, P. de Greef, B. Bredeweg, J. Wielemaker, J.P. Billault, M. Davoodi, and S. Hayward (1987). *Model Driven Knowledge Acquisition: Interpretation Models.* ESPRIT Project P1098 Deliverable D1 (task A1), University of Amsterdam and STL Ltd.

Boehm, B.W. (1988). "A spiral model of software development and enhancement". *IEEE Computer,* May, p. 61–72.

Boose, J.H., D.S. Shema, and J.M. Bradshaw (1989). "Recent progress in *Aquinas*: A knowledge acquisition workbench". *Knowledge Acquisition,* 1, p. 185–214.

Buchanan, B.G., D. Barstow, R. Bechtal, J. Bennett, W. Clancey, C. Kulikowski, T. Mitchell, and D.A. Waterman (1983). "Constructing an Expert System". In: Frederick Hayes-Roth, Donald A. Waterman, and Douglas B. Lenat (Eds.), *Building Expert Systems.* Addison Wesley, p. 127–167.

DeMarco, T. (1982). *Controlling Software Projects.* Yourdon Inc., New York.

Expert Systems. Vol. 2–Vol 13(3).

Hilal, D.K. and H. Soltan (1991). "A suggested descriptive framework for the comparison of knowledge based system methodologies", *Expert Systems.* Vol. 8, 2, p. 107–113.

Hilal, D.K. and H. Soltan (1993). "Towards a comprehensive methodology for KBS development". *Expert Systems,* Vol. 10, 2, p. 75–81.

Inder, R. and I. Filby (1991). *Survey of Knowledge Engineering Methods and Supporting Tools.* AIAI-TR-99, presented at BCS SGES Workshop on KBS Methodologies, London, December 1991.

International Journal of Human-Computer Studies, Vol. 44, 3–4, (1996).

Khan, A.F. Umar (1992). "Managing knowledge-based systems development using standard life-cycle techniques". In: Efraim Turban and Jay Liebowitz (Eds.), *Managing Expert Systems,* Idea Group Publishing, Harrisburg, PA, p. 120–160.

Lee, J.K., J. Liebowitz, and Y.M. Chae (1996). *Critical Technology. Proceedings of the Third World Congress on Expert Systems.* Cognizant Communication Corporation.

Liebowitz, J. (Ed.) (1991). *Expert Systems World Congress Proceedings,* Vol. 1–4. Pergamon Press.

Liebowitz, J. (Ed.) (1994). *Moving Toward Expert Systems Globally in the 21st Century.* Cognizant Communication Corporation.

Marcus, S. and J. McDermott (1989). "SALT: A knowledge acquisition language for propose-and-revise systems". *Artificial Intelligence,* 39, p. 1–37.

Motta, E., M. Eisenstadt, K. Pitman, and M. West (1988). "Support for knowledge acquisition in the Knowledge Engineer's Assistant (KEATS)". *Expert Systems,* Vol. 5, 1, p. 6–27.

Musen, M.A. (1989). *Automated Generation of Model-Based Knowledge-Acquisition Tools.* Morgan-Kaufmann.

Prerau, David S. (1990). *Developing and Managing Expert Systems.* Addison Wesley.

Rogers, E.M. (1983). *Diffusion of Innovations.* The Free Press, 3rd ed.

Rothenfluh, T.E., J.H. Gennari, H. Eriksson, A.R. Puerta, S.W. Tu, and M.A. Musen (1996). "Reusable ontologies, knowledge acquisition tools, and performance systems: PROTÉGÉ-II solutions to Sisyphus-2". *International Journal of Human-Computer Studies,* Vol. 44, p. 303–332.

Schreiber, Guus, Bob Wielinga, Robert de Hoog, Hans Akkermans, and Walter van de Velde (1994). "CommonKADS: A comprehensive methodology for KBS development". *IEEE Expert,* 9, 6, p. 28–37.

Shadbolt, N., E. Motta, and A. Rouge (1993). "Constructing knowledge based systems". *IEEE Software,* November, p. 34–38.

Spek, R. van der, and R. de Hoog (1995). "A framework for a knowledge management methodology". In: K. Wiig, *Knowledge Management Methods.* Schema Press, Arlington, TX, p. 379–396.

Steels, L. (1990). "Components of expertise". *AI Magazine,* 11(2), p. 29–49.

Steels, L. (1993). "The componential framework and its role in reusability". In: J.-M. David, J.-P. Krivine, and R. Simmons (Eds.), *Second Generation Expert Systems.* Springer Verlag, p. 273–298.

Stefik, M. (1995). *Introduction to Knowledge Systems.* Morgan Kaufmann.

Wielinga, B.J., A. Th. Schreiber, and R. de Hoog (1994). "Modelling perspectives in medical KBS construction". In: P. Barahona and J.P. Christensen (Eds.), *Knowledge and Decisions in Health Telematics.* IOS Press.

Wiig, K.M. (1995). *Knowledge Management Methods.* Schema Press, Arlington, TX.

2 Expert System Technology: Knowledge Acquisition

Yihwa Irene Liou

CONTENTS

1. INTRODUCTION

Since Artificial Intelligence (AI) was introduced in the early 1970s, the goal of AI scientists has always been to develop computer programs that can think and solve problems as intelligently as human experts. Expert systems are computer programs that use domain-specific knowledge to emulate the reasoning process of human experts. It was not until the late 1970s that AI scientists realized that the problem-solving power of a computer program mainly derives from the knowledge it possesses rather than the inference mechanism it employs.

Knowledge acquisition is the process of extracting, structuring, and organizing knowledge from several knowledge sources, usually human experts so that the problem-solving expertise can be captured and transformed into a computer-readable form. Knowledge is the most important component of expert systems. The captured knowledge forms the basis for the reasoning process of an expert system. Without explicitly represented knowledge, an expert system is no more than a computer program.

The increasing complexity of expert systems applications dictates the involvement of many experts in building those systems. Collaborative knowledge acquisition is broadly defined as the process of collaboratively extracting problem-solving expertise from a team of experts. The collective expertise enables an expert system to incorporate more comprehensive domain knowledge so that it may function more effectively than an expert system that was built from an individual expert's knowledge.

The process of assimilating the expertise of several experts into an expert system is not easy, particularly when these experts are trained in different disciplines. The differences not only appear in problem-solving strategies taken by each expert, but also appear in what heuristic is applied to solve the problem. Furthermore, the difficulty arises because of the communications barriers among experts and between experts and the knowledge engineer(s). How to facilitate the knowledge acquisition process involving multiple experts becomes a major challenge to knowledge engineers.

There are three primary concerns of the knowledge acquisition task: the involvement of appropriate human resources; the employment of proper techniques to elicit knowledge; and a structured approach to performing the knowledge acquisition task. We discuss these three areas in the following sections.

2. PEOPLE ISSUES

Identifying appropriate domain experts and involving proper people in the knowledge acquisition process is critical to the success of knowledge acquisition. Those who are involved in the knowledge acquisition process include: (1) domain experts who have had years of experience working in the application domain; (2) knowledge engineers who possess technical skills in eliciting knowledge, representing knowledge, and implementing expert systems; and (3) users and managers.

2.1. SELECTING DOMAIN EXPERTS

By analyzing the domain and the problem characteristics, it is possible to pinpoint sources of expertise. This is a joint responsibility of managers of the organization, users of the target system, and knowledge engineers. Attributes that should be considered when selecting domain experts include:

1. *Domain expertise, experience, and reputation* — The experts chosen should have expertise and experience in the specific aspect of the domain for the target expert system. Practicing experts, who are currently active in domain tasks, are the domain experts who should be identified. Leading experts are recognized by their colleagues and clients. The reputations of the experts are sometimes the major determinant of the credibility of a deployed expert system. It is also helpful to select experts with some background or interests in AI and expert systems.
2. *Personal characteristics and attitudes* — Domain experts not only should have skills in the domain but also should have skills in communicating their knowledge, judgment, and experience and the methods they use to apply these to a particular task. Other desirable attributes include a sense of humor, being a good listener, a sense of commitment, cooperativeness, patience, being easy to work with, persistence, and honesty.
3. *Availability* — The most common problems in knowledge acquisition are caused by time demands on an "already-busy" expert. Therefore, management's commitment of experts' time to a project should be secured. If problems with access are anticipated, an individual should not be selected as the primary expert regardless of his/her experience and characteristics.

2.2. SINGLE VS. MULTIPLE EXPERTS

An expert system development project may utilize one expert or a number of them as the primary source of domain expertise. The use of a single expert is sometimes preferred, but there are many cases in which it is useful or necessary to utilize multiple experts. There are four primary problems with knowledge acquisition from a single expert: (1) difficulty in allocating adequate time by a key individual in the organization, that may create a bottleneck in the expert system development process; (2) personal bias, that may affect the performance of the system; (3) limitation to a single line of reasoning, that may affect the usefulness of a system, since expert systems that are developed based on a single, perhaps narrow, line of reasoning do not emulate most real-life decision making;

and (4) incomplete domain expertise, that may affect the performance of a system (McGraw and Harbison-Briggs, 1989). The first problem may create a bottleneck in the expert system development process. If only one expert is the sole knowledge source for the expert system, it is very difficult to acquire a sufficient amount of his or her time. This is not because of an unwillingness to cooperate with the knowledge engineer, but because of other commitments and the fact that knowledge acquisition is so time-consuming. Depending upon the availability of such an individual can delay a project's progress. Personal bias, which constitutes the second problem, may affect the performance of the system. The third problem affects the usefulness of a system, since expert systems that are developed based on a single, perhaps narrow, line of reasoning do not emulate most real-life decision making. Furthermore, with attempts to apply expert systems technology to more sophisticated problems, restricting the knowledge acquisition activity to a single expert could result in incompleteness of the system.

Experts by definition are "very knowledgeable about only a small subset of the tasks in the domain." As expert systems become more and more complicated and the domains become more complex, the required expertise is most likely to reside in not one but a team of experts. A designated primary expert is needed when multiple experts are utilized (Prerau, 1990).

Incorporating the expertise of a team of experts provides the following positive effects on the resulting expert system: (1) it assures that the knowledge base can be complete; (2) it improves the likelihood of obtaining specialized knowledge in subdomains of the problem; (3) it increases the quality (i.e., reliability and consensus among experts) of the acquired knowledge; (4) it assures that the facts that are included in the knowledge base are important ones; (5) it enhances understanding of the domain knowledge through discussion, debate, and exchange of hypotheses between members of the expert team; and (6) it encourages interactions among experts and creates a synergy such that the acquired group knowledge is greater than the sum of the individual's knowledge.

When multiple experts are involved in the development process, knowledge acquisition sessions can be flexibly designed. First, it is not necessary that all experts be present at the same time in one place throughout the acquisition process. Advanced information technology such as group support systems can be used to facilitate interactions with experts, not only in face-to-face meetings but also in meetings conducted in dispersed locations. Second, interactions among experts can create a synergy such that the acquired group knowledge is greater than the sum of the individual's knowledge (Liou, Weber, and Nunamaker, 1990). However, the involvement of multiple experts increases the complexity of the knowledge acquisition process and makes an already difficult task even more complicated. Two factors contribute to this complexity. One factor involves the difficulty of merging each individual expert's knowledge structures into one group knowledge structure that provides the underlying problem-solving expertise of the expert system. This involves resolving conflicts between various problem-solving approaches and reasoning processes. The other factor involves the difficulty of the generation of group knowledge that does not reside in any one individual expert but evolves as a result of the group interaction. A group support system has been proven to be useful and effective to ease these difficulties when acquiring knowledge from multiple experts (Liou, 1992).

2.3. ROLE OF KNOWLEDGE ENGINEER, END-USERS, AND MANAGERS

A knowledge engineer is the individual responsible for structuring and constructing an expert system. The literature reveals diverse perspectives on the qualifications and responsibilities of the knowledge engineers, that include leading and managing the project, defining the problem domain, selecting hardware/software, acquiring and representing knowledge, implementing the expert system, interacting with users and managers, preparing technical documentation, verifying and validating the system, training users, operating and maintaining the initial system, and providing advice for further extension and updates (Prerau, 1990). Knowledge engineers should have some mastery of the domain to identify the type of knowledge that is required. They should be able to conceptualize and analyze the problem, to employ various knowledge acquisition techniques, and to communicate and work with other people.

Users and managers should be involved in the knowledge acquisition task, especially in the planning stage where decisions of problem scope are made and in the verification stage where the prototype system is evaluated. The problem scope should be jointly determined by a group of people that includes domain experts, users, managers, and knowledge engineers. Domain experts provide a subjective perspective of what the system can do for users, while users provide a broader perspective of how the system may be able to help them. Managers provide strategic guidelines as to what should and should not be included in the system. Knowledge engineers can assess technical feasibility. One individual, such as the manager, can of course decide the scope of the system based on policies and the needs of the organization. However, systems that involve users in the development process tend to be more acceptable to the users when they are delivered.

3.   KNOWLEDGE ACQUISITION TECHNIQUES

The approach used for knowledge acquisition determines both the quality of knowledge and the amount of effort required for its acquisition, so the technique selected greatly affects the performance of the expert system and the resources required for its development. The growing recognition of the importance of knowledge acquisition has resulted in the development of various techniques, methodologies, and tools for automated knowledge acquisition. This section reviews techniques used in psychology and social sciences for revealing expert knowledge structures and processes. Techniques that involve the concept of machine learning (e.g., induction), neural networks, simulation, web-based knowledge acquisition, and automated knowledge acquisition tools designed for specific applications are not discussed in this chapter (see Cox, Al-Ghanim, and Culler, 1995; Osyk and Vijayaraman, 1995 for neural-based knowledge acquisition).

Many knowledge acquisition techniques and tools have been developed. Each technique has its strengths and limitations. How well a knowledge engineer can utilize them will depend on his/her selection of appropriate techniques and tools, which in turn determine the quality of knowledge acquired, the amount of effort needed, and the skills required.

Interviewing is the most commonly used method in requirements elicitation for analysis and design of information systems. It is also widely used in eliciting knowledge from domain experts for expert systems development (Olson and Rueter, 1987). In general, there are two forms of interviewing. The basic form involves question-answer sessions between the knowledge engineer and the expert. These free-form or unstructured interviews are usually started by the engineer's asking "How do you solve this problem?" Follow-up questions usually reflect further explanation or clarification of some points that the expert has made. The process is fairly unstructured. A distinct advantage of free-form interviews is that knowledge engineers can elicit unanticipated information.

However, there are difficulties with this technique. First, as people become more experienced at performing certain tasks, they become less aware of the cognitive processes involved in their performance. They cannot explicitly describe their reasoning process step by step. Second, there are certain biases and fallibilities in human reasoning. When reasoning about the entire sequence, people tend to anchor on items that occur early in a sequence. People see what they expect to see. When asked to describe their reasoning process and problem-solving methods, experts tend to provide reconstructed versions of their reasoning and omit some components that may be important to solve the problem because they assume them to be obvious and explicit. Moreover, experts may get tired and become bored with repeating what to them seems to be obvious information. People do not talk in complete sentences. Speech is marked by phrases, asides, "ers," etc. Neither the expert nor the knowledge engineer knows at the time which parts of the dialogues are important. Consequently, all details of the interviews must be recorded, transcribed, and analyzed. This makes knowledge acquisition a tedious and time-consuming process.

Structured interviewing, a more effective form of the interviewing technique, is goal-oriented. It forces organization of the communications that take place between a knowledge engineer and experts. The structure provided by clearly stated goals reduces the interpretation problems inherent in free-form (e.g., unstructured) interviews and allows the knowledge engineer to prevent the distortion caused by domain expert subjectivity. This technique is more effective because it forces the domain expert to be systematic in attending to interview tasks. Empirical evidence has shown that the structured interviewing technique improves the efficiency and effectiveness of knowledge acquisition, and can be applied to knowledge acquisition from multiple experts. When this technique is used, experts either fill out a set of carefully designed questionnaire cards or answer questions raised by the knowledge engineer, making use of an established domain model of the business decision-making activity to capture the subjective and qualitative aspects of decision making. Questionnaires can be particularly useful in discovering the objects of the domain, in uncovering relationships, and in determining uncertainties.

Observations, an obvious way of discovering how an expert solves a real problem, involves observing how he or she does it. This technique allows an expert to work in the accustomed environment without interruptions by the knowledge engineer and gives the knowledge engineer insights into the complexities of a problem. One important decision that must be made before employing this technique is how the expert's performance is to be recorded. One easy way is for the knowledge engineer to observe and take notes. The other alternative is to videotape the problem-solving process. A major limitation of this technique is that the underlying reasoning in an expert's mind is usually not revealed in his or her actions.

Protocol analysis, usually referred to as "thinking aloud," is a form of data analysis that has its origin in clinical psychology. When employing this technique, a knowledge engineer describes a problem scenario and asks an expert to talk about his or her thinking process while solving the problem. Experts find it much easier to talk about specific examples of problems than to talk in abstract terms. The "thinking aloud" process is videotaped and analysis of it is based on transcripts. Once the transcripts are produced, protocols must be analyzed based on a systematic breakdown of the information to produce a structured model of the expert's knowledge. The goal is to identify the kinds of objects that the expert sees, the attributes of those objects, the relationships among those objects, and the kind of inferences drawn from these relationships. The advantage of this technique is that the transcripts describe specific actions and rationales as the expert thinks through and talks about the decision-making process. There is no delay between the act of thinking of something and reporting it.

Protocol analysis is not appropriate for all kinds of tasks. Some of the tasks that are suitable include various puzzles, elementary logic problems, chess strategy, binary-choice sequence prediction, concept identification for the induction of various logical and sequential concepts, various understanding tasks, and those tasks for which verbalization is a natural part of thinking. However, the validity and applicability of pure "thinking aloud" protocols in verbally complex situations has been questioned by many researchers.

Repertory grid analysis, which had its origin in Kelly's personal construct theory (1955), aims at gaining insights into the expert's mental model of the problem domain. It involves an initial interview with an expert, a rating session, and analyses that cluster both the objects and the traits on which the items were rated. In the initial interview, the expert is asked to identify some objects in the domain of expertise. After a set of objects has been identified, the expert is asked to compare three of these objects at a time, in each case naming a trait that two of the objects possess but the other does not. The expert is then asked to identify an opposite of that trait. The expert further provides a scale to rate the importance of the traits. The same process is repeated until all the objects have been compared and traits to differentiate them identified. In the rating session, these objects are rated according to the traits identified and scales assigned. At any stage the expert can add more objects or traits or alter entries in the grid. In this way the process heightens his or her awareness of how he or she views the problem. Once the rating grid has been established, a computer program can be used to cluster the objects and cluster the traits.

This technique is useful in extracting subjective data, but there are a number of difficulties associated with its use. First, unless the number of objects in the problem domain is small, an enormous number of comparisons need to be made. Second, it is not always easy to identify traits that differentiate objects. It sometimes takes a long time to make just one comparison and, as a result, the process becomes very time-consuming.

4.   TECHNIQUES FOR COLLABORATIVE KNOWLEDGE ACQUISITION

As the size and complexity of expert systems increase, many experts and several knowledge engineers are needed in the knowledge acquisition process of an expert system project. Techniques described above may be employed in collaborative knowledge acquisition by interviewing (or observing) a team of experts one at a time. The "serial" knowledge acquisition process causes the following problems. (1) It is a lengthy and time-consuming process. (2) Problem-solving strategies and the knowledge used by experts may conflict with each other. Knowledge engineers should not assume that they have sufficient knowledge in the domain to try to solve these conflicts, which must be resolved by the individual experts through several iterations. (3) Experts do not have chances to stimulate each other's thinking to surface the underlying knowledge they use. (4) The integration of problem-solving expertise acquired from individual experts into a knowledge base is still needed even if there is no conflict among experts' opinions. The missing links of various expertise in the domain have to be acquired from the experts themselves.

Brainstorming is a group method for developing ideas and exploring their meaning. It promotes the identification of a number of considerations related to a problem domain. It is designed to stimulate thinking and generate ideas in such a way that each individual may develop his or her train of thought or expand upon other individuals' thinking. Interactions in the form of exchanging thoughts are encouraged to enrich the outcome of the group process. Brainstorming also can be used to help experts and knowledge engineers discover areas that require special attention in the problem-solving process. With multiple experts working as a team, brainstorming can help prevent immediate confrontation, reduce inhibited behavior, and resolve conflicting views.

To use the brainstorming technique for knowledge acquisition, a stimulus must be introduced to domain experts. This takes the form of a question, a statement, or a problem scenario. For instance, a brainstorming stimulus might be "describe specific steps in a consultation session." Each participant (i.e., domain expert) of the brainstorming session suggests one idea in response to the question by writing it on a piece of paper or entering it into a computer file. These suggestions are then randomly assigned to participants, who are asked either to follow the same train of thought or come up with new ideas. The process is repeated until the rate of idea generation slows down to a threshold rate and the pool of ideas is collected. At this point the process moves on to analyze and organize these ideas.

An electronic form of the brainstorming technique has been used in group sessions to define a problem scope, to identify possible solutions, and to develop a heuristic classification scheme. This technique provides a useful tool for acquiring knowledge from multiple experts. Conflicts can be identified and resolved during the brainstorming session and interactions among experts create a synergy of expertise.

Nominal Group Technique (NGT) is a method for structuring small group meetings that allows individual judgments to be pooled effectively and used in situations where there is uncertainty or disagreement about the nature of a problem and possible solutions. This technique is helpful in identifying problems, exploring solutions, and establishing priorities. It typically includes four steps: (1) silent generation of ideas in writing; (2) round-robin recording of ideas; (3) serial discussion of the list of ideas; and (4) voting. This problem-solving procedure reduces negative effects (i.e., nonparticipation, conflicts) that may be triggered by face-to-face interaction among team members. In a collaborative environment, such as a GDSS, the Idea Organization tool facilitates the first three steps of the NGT. A voting tool completes the fourth step. Knowledge engineers have found that a combination of group interaction and the Nominal Group Technique enhances the creativity and quality of the resulting solutions.

The Delphi technique uses a series of questionnaires to aggregate the knowledge, judgments, or opinions of experts (usually anonymous) to address complex problems. Individual contributions are shared with the whole group by using the results from each questionnaire to construct the questionnaire for the next round. One of Delphi's principal uses has been to make future projections and forecasts. It can also be used to identify goals and objectives, generate possible alternatives, establish priorities, reveal group values, gather information, and educate a respondent group. By keeping individuals separated and maintaining their anonymity, the Delphi technique reduces the influence of potentially dominant people, prevents the undue influence of the personalities of certain individuals and allows strangers to communicate effectively. It also allows for the participation of more people than could interact effectively in a group and prevents unproductive disagreements. Delphi is useful whenever it is desirable to have pooled judgment and when experts are geographically dispersed. This technique has been used to facilitate an expert system development project for target industry analysis. A hypermedia-based Delphi tool has also been developed for knowledge acquisition (Wolstenholme and Corben, 1994).

Focus group interviews is a technique developed in marketing research. It involves conducting intensive discussions of a team of consumers to generate ideas for new products or explore consumer reaction to new product concepts. The interviews are conducted by a moderator and consist of three stages: (1) establish rapport with the group, structure the rules of group interaction, and set objectives; (2) attempt to provoke intense discussion in relevant areas; and (3) attempt to summarize the groups' responses to determine the extent of agreement.

In the context of knowledge acquisition, a knowledge engineer, as the moderator, conducts a group meeting with a team of experts discussing the problem-solving strategies. The moderator must perform the difficult task of "guiding" the discussion into the relevant areas while exerting minimal influence on the content of the discussion. The interaction process induced by the group situation produces a number of potential advantages: (1) Snowballing — Each individual is able to expand and refine his/her opinions in the interactions with the other members. (2) Stimulation — A group interview situation is more exciting and offers more stimulation to participants than a standard-depth interview. (3) Security — The security of being in a crowd encourages some members to speak out when they otherwise would not. (4) Individuals are not under any pressure to make up answers to questions.

This technique can be used in conjunction with the structured interviewing technique to force organization of the communications that take place between a knowledge engineer and experts. The structure provided by goals reduces the interpretation problems inherent in unstructured interviews and allows the knowledge engineer to prevent the distortion caused by domain expert subjectivity. It is more effective because it "forces the domain expert to be systematic in attending to interview tasks." However, the moderator can introduce biases in the interview by shifting topics too rapidly, verbally or nonverbally encouraging certain answers, failing to cover certain areas, and so forth. In addition, the interviews are usually taped and transcribed for further analysis, which can be very time-consuming.

The voting technique emphasizes on finding a compromised solution to a problem. It involves presenting a problem to domain experts and encouraging each member to vote on alternative solutions to the problem. Alternatives are ranked and rated by the group of experts. It is effective only if each expert who participates in the team feels that his or her views and opinions have been heard. It is also vital that each expert has a commitment to the group decision though he or she may have some reservations. Even when one best answer may not be agreed upon by the team, this technique can significantly contribute to knowledge-based systems development efforts.

It can be used in defining problem scope, identifying alternate solutions, and soliciting proper solutions. For the technique to be effective, the knowledge engineer must be aware of the possible effects of status, rank, or experience differences among the domain experts.

Group Repertory Grid Analysis is a group version of the repertory grid analysis technique. It attempts to represent the domain expert's problem-solving knowledge in repertory grids, which allow experts to rate or judge a solution according to its level of a problem-solving trait. A domain expert uses repertory grids to enter knowledge by means of a rating grid. This grid displays problem solutions that have been elicited from the domain expert, which serve as column headings within the grid. Constructs (e.g., solution traits) are placed beside the grid's rows. The system elicits constructs by presenting the domain expert with sets of solutions and requesting that the expert discriminate among them. The domain expert then provides each problem solution with a rating that represents how it relates to each trait. Once these initial grids have been constructed, the knowledge engineer analyzes them and refines the knowledge base. This technique can be used in conjunction with the brainstorming technique, using brainstorming to generate solutions and constructs and then using a spreadsheet program to implement the repertory grid. A brainstorming tool can be used to facilitate the interviewing session. A Group Matrix tool can be used to facilitate the rating session. Schuler and colleagues developed the AQUINAS, a repertory-grid-based knowledge acquisition workbench, that can be used for collaborative evaluation.

Group Support Systems (GSS) are computer and communications systems that facilitate a group's communication, coordination, and decision-making process. Techniques such as repertory grid analysis, brainstorming, Nominal Group Technique, Delphi technique, and the voting technique have been implemented in computer programs to facilitate the acquisition of knowledge from multiple experts using a group support system. The six necessary components include: hardware, software, facility, people, procedures, and facilitation.

Benefits derived from using a GSS for knowledge acquisition include: (1) electronic documentation of knowledge; (2) knowledge extraction can be done in parallel from multiple experts; (3) conflicts are addressed during knowledge extraction sessions; and (4) interactions among experts result in an enlarged and enriched domain of expertise.

5.   KNOWLEDGE ACQUISITION METHODOLOGY

McGraw and Harbison-Briggs (1989) pointed out that the lack of structure and organization of knowledge acquisition is one of the impediments to effective knowledge acquisition. It therefore is essential to establish detailed plans for conducting knowledge acquisition sessions. A knowledge acquisition methodology serves as a guide to knowledge engineers in developing these plans. A methodology established to perform the knowledge acquisition task is comprised of four phases: planning for knowledge acquisition, knowledge extraction, knowledge analysis, and knowledge verification. Table 1 summarizes the steps in each phase.

Knowledge Acquisition Planning. The goal of planning, the most important phase of the knowledge acquisition task, is to understand the problem domain, define the problem scope, and identify experts in the problem domain, analyze various knowledge acquisition techniques, and design proper procedures to acquire knowledge. By discussing with experts, the knowledge engineer can identify the characteristics of the problem and comprehend the kind of knowledge required. Knowledge engineers develop proper group process models to acquire knowledge. Existing group support tools are analyzed so that they can be properly employed in the group process. Major steps in this phase include understanding the domain, identifying experts, defining the problem scope, identifying the type of application, analyzing characteristics of the problem, analyzing characteristics of tools and techniques, developing process models, and planning for knowledge acquisition sessions.

Knowledge Extraction. The primary activity of the knowledge extraction phase is to acquire knowledge from experts through a series of knowledge acquisition sessions in a collaborative environment as described. Each session has its own objective; therefore, knowledge engineers may

---

TABLE 1
A Knowledge Acquisition Methodology

Phase	Steps
Planning	Understand the domain
	Identify domain experts and users
	Define the problem scope
	Identify the type of application
	Develop process models
	Plan KA sessions
Extraction	Explain KA approach
	Discuss objectives of KA sessions
	Conduct KA sessions
	Debrief experts
Analysis	Analyze KA session outputs
	Transfer knowledge into representations
Verification	Develop test scenarios
	Verify knowledge with experts

---

apply different tools to support the knowledge acquisition techniques used. During each session, knowledge engineers must explain the session objective, the process and approach to acquiring knowledge, and the expected results. Functionalities of tools, procedures of using them, and the techniques employed are explained to the session participants. Outputs from this phase include heuristic, concepts, or classification structures. These may be captured in an electronic format and require further analysis to be represented in particular schemes.

Knowledge Analysis. The primary task of this phase is to analyze outputs from knowledge extraction sessions. Some of the tools may be used to support analysis activities such as identifying a list of key concepts from the brainstorming results. Heuristic, concepts or classification structures are analyzed and formalized into representations that may be in the form of heuristic rules, frames, objects and relations, semantic networks, and classification schemes. These representations are then transformed into specific representation schemes that are supported by an expert system building tool. This transformation is part of an effort to implement a prototype expert system. This prototype system will be used in the knowledge verification phase.

Knowledge Verification. This phase places emphasis on verifying heuristic, concepts, and classification structures with experts. Formalized representations are presented to the experts. A demonstration of the prototype system to users and experts is also useful. In addition, the validation of knowledge acquisition involves identifying the entities to be measured, the types of evidence to be collected, the criteria to be applied, and the type of comparisons to be made to assess validity. Refinements of represented knowledge can be performed by reexamining acquired knowledge in the analysis phase. If the knowledge base is incomplete, additional knowledge acquisition sessions must be conducted to elicit required knowledge. If knowledge captured in the prototype system does not provide solutions to problems, redesign of the knowledge acquisition sessions may require rethinking of the knowledge acquisition approach as well as procedures and techniques employed. A demonstration of the prototype system to users and experts is also useful. Once the prototype expert system has been approved by the experts, knowledge engineers can continue the development effort by fine-tuning the knowledge representation and user interface. By making the verification of the knowledge base a part of the ongoing knowledge acquisition and review process, expert system developers can minimize the time and money wasted and prevent the development of an inappropriate or useless system.

6. FUTURE TRENDS AND SUMMARY

Knowledge acquisition has been described as a very difficult and time-consuming task that frequently creates a bottleneck in an expert system development effort. There is no single way to avoid the difficulties of knowledge acquisition. However, by identifying the right domain experts, and employing a combination of proper techniques and a structured methodology, we believe that the knowledge acquisition task can be performed more easily as well as more effectively and efficiently than it used to be.

As expert systems become more and more complicated and the problem domains become more complex, the required expertise often resides in not one but a group of experts. Moreover, interaction among experts creates a synergy that results in an enriched and enlarged domain of expertise. These factors all point in the direction of increased use of multiple experts in the expert system development project whenever possible. There is no single knowledge acquisition technique that is the best and most effective; the trend is toward using a combination of techniques that best fit the domain of expertise.

The work of automating the knowledge acquisition process is in progress, but most existing tools have been designed for eliciting knowledge from individuals. The ETS and AQUINAS systems developed by Boose (1989) try to address situations where multiple experts are involved, but they are limited to certain applications. It should be noted that most tools are still in the research and development stage and are available only for in-house use. Nevertheless, the progress in automation of knowledge acquisition is on-going. To be most useful, the focus of this research should be on acquiring the kinds of knowledge that are difficult to acquire manually but for which automated methods are feasible. Research in neural networks and case-based reasoning for knowledge acquisition is another important trend in knowledge acquisition.

The knowledge acquisition methodology described in this chapter was tested in an information center domain where multiple experts were involved in the development of a help service expert system. Positive results indicated the importance of having a methodology and showed the applicability of such a methodology to be used in a group environment. Further efforts to generalize this methodology to test its applicability in other application domains and to incorporate various knowledge acquisition techniques are needed.

The term "knowledge acquisition" usually refers to the acquisition of knowledge for building expert systems. However, acquiring knowledge from a group of people is a ubiquitous activity that can be found in many group tasks such as strategic planning, system design, negotiation, and decision making. For instance, major software design decisions are usually made in face-to-face software design meetings involving users, managers, and system developers. Users have knowledge of how current systems work and requirements of the new systems. Managers know the strategic implications of the new system. System developers can intrigue users and managers by providing them with knowledge of how advanced information technologies can serve them. We may examine many other group works from the knowledge acquisition perspective.

REFERENCES

1. Boose, J.H. (1989). "Using repertory grid-centered knowledge acquisition tools for decision support," *Proceedings of the Twenty-Second Annual Hawaii International Conference on System Sciences*, Vol. III, Kona, HI, January 3–6, 211–220.

2. Cox, Leon D., Al-Ghanim, Amjed M., Culler, David E. (1995). "A neural network-based methodology for machining knowledge acquisition," *Computers & Industrial Engineering*, (29:1–4), September, 217–220.

3. Kelly, G. (1955). *The Psychology of Personal Constructs*, Norton, New York.

4. Liou, Yihwa Irene (1992). "Collaborative knowledge acquisition," *Expert Systems with Applications: An International Journal*, 5:1–13.

5. Liou, Y.I., Weber, E.S., and Nunamaker, J.F. (1990). "A methodology for knowledge acquisition in a group decision support system environment," *Knowledge Acquisition*, (2), 129–144.

6. McGraw, K.L. and Harbison-Briggs, K. (1989). *Knowledge Acquisition: Principles and Guidelines*, Prentice Hall, Englewood Cliffs, NJ.

7. Olson, J.R. and Rueter, H.H. (1987). "Extracting expertise from experts: Methods for knowledge acquisition," *Expert Systems*, (4:3), August, 152–168.

8. Osyk, Barbara A. and Vijayaraman, Bindiganavale S. (1995). "Integrating expert systems and neural nets: Exploring the boundaries of AI," *Information Systems Management*, (12:2), Spring, 47–54.

9. Prerau, D.S. (1990). *Developing and Managing Expert Systems*, Addison-Wesley, Reading, MA.

10. Scott, A. Carlisle, Clayton, Jan E., and Gibson, Elizabeth L. (1991). *A Practical Guide to Knowledge Acquisition*, Addison-Wesley, Reading, MA.

11. Wolstenholme, E. F. and Corben, D. A. (1994). "A hypermedia-based Delphi tool for knowledge acquisition in model building," *Journal of the Operational Research Society*, (45:6), June, 659–672.

3 Knowledge Representation

Tibor Vámos

CONTENTS

> *But I have learnt by trial of mankind*
> *Mightier than deeds of puissance is the tongue*
> Sophocles: Philoctetes, 98-99, Transl.: F. Storr

1. INTRODUCTION

1.1. REPRESENTATION OF KNOWLEDGE: PUTTING THE WORLD INTO COMPUTER

From several points of view, representation of knowledge is the key problem of expert systems and of artificial intelligence (AI) in general. It is not by chance that one of the favorite namings of these products is knowledge-based systems. An expert, either a human or a machine, has her/his/its particular value by her/his/its knowledge. Though knowledge is always related to some special disciplines, professions, and/or experience, knowledge of any art has some generic features that define how this knowledge is acquired, how it can be accessed, and how it can be applied to certain problems that are not totally identical to the earlier acquired cases, i.e., learning, storing, retrieving, and reasoning methods based on knowledge. This circumscription covers somehow the concept of intelligence.

These generic features of knowledge are embodied in representation. A system, human or machine, in the process of learning (respectively input operations) stores the objects, actions, concepts, situations, and their relations in some representation form in the brain, respectively in the computer memory. This stored knowledge is used by retrieval (remembering), combination

3-1

(association), and/or reasoning. If the computer was the same device as the human brain, the representation problem would be a biological and psychological task for achieving the best imitation. This is fortunately or unfortunately not the case; we can use only some analogies, metaphors between the brain and the computer; one should be always very careful as to how far these analogies work. On the other hand, the knowledge of the computer, which is really a directly or indirectly transferred human knowledge, is and should be some approximate copy of the human knowledge, transferred to another representation medium and by that way to another representation form.

Here we can estimate the relevance and difficulty of knowledge representation. Even the human origin is uncertain. The phenomena of the world, like the performance of a mechanical machine, of a living organism, the economy, or social relations are represented in the human brain by the signals of the sensory inputs like vision and touching, and by attaching those to representations of earlier inputs. Philosophy has hopelessly argued for nearly 3000 years over the relation of the world and of the sensory inputs, and other early developmental cognitive phenomena of the human and animal race. Where and how are all these stored, fitted together? Is it the brain only as a biological organism or something more, too, named mind or spirit, that joins this confusion? Here we are, after the sensory representation, only at the second phase of the representation process: the mental one. The third phase is the verbal representation. We experience clearly that the mental representation, e.g., an impression on a traffic situation, of a patient's status or anything else is not the same as the verbal representation. It is different: how we express it for ourselves, communicate with others, put down for a record. Even the nonwritten verbal representation and the written form are slightly different, even if we do not consider the representation means of metacommunication, like gestures, emphasis, pitch, etc.

This verbal representation should be transformed into computer programs, using the basic means of mathematical conceptual apparatus, which is much poorer than the rich human language. How this poverty is to be estimated is the main subject of modern linguistics, *semantics*, knowledge about the meaning of the words, *semiotics* about the general meaning problem of symbols, words included, and *hermeneutics*, the meaning of full texts in different individual, collective representations, like different social, generation, professional groups, or different cultures.

The representation problem is, by that way, a highly complex and highly practical one: by computer representation we try to surpass these dim relations, and get a practically applicable device. In application, we must have steady control over these relations, how the knowledge machine works really in interacting, influencing, governing the processes of reality. By this way the philosophical, biological, psychological, linguistic, and mathematical problems mentioned above receive a very practical relevance.

Our task is the presentation of the computer representation but it can never be detached from the previously exposed problems of representation phases; consequently, though the details of these previous phases are not the subject of this chapter, they will be referred to in all cases where it is unavoidable.

In this mirror, our representation task is a linguistic modeling work, the tool for intelligent actions, that should have:

- Expressive power for unambiguous description of the environment
- Suitability for reasoning in the directions of certain goals
- Efficiency in use for problem solving, like real-time applications

1.2. FUNDAMENTAL TOOLS: VERBAL AND FORMAL MATHEMATICAL METHODS

What are the basic characteristics of our mental representations? The brain collects and stores relevant ensembles of phenomena. These have different names in various disciplines; here, the name *pattern* will be used, with a reference to the analogy of visual patterns. The patterns represent *objects* (any kind, living, not living), *situations* (some coincidences of objects), *actions* of these objects, ourselves included. The actions create new objects, situations, i.e., patterns are remembered as some *sequences* like consecutive frames of a movie. The brain patterns will be discussed later in relation to the pattern representation in computers.

The consecution, sequence of identical patterns, happen with some frequency. What *identical* more precisely means, comes later. This frequency is remembered, too. Certain consecution of certain patterns happens more frequently, sometimes nearly always. This particular pattern dynamics itself emerges as a pattern. These are the patterns of pattern relations, which we call *metapatterns*. The linguistic representation of this metapattern pattern relations developed to be the *logic*. Logical sentences are represented by verbal, formulary, and graphical schemes, i.e., patterns, the variables of the scheme are the original patterns.

The *frequency* issue is much more dubious, just because of the fact that identity and the nature of similarity, their relation to frequency occurrence of these identical or similar patterns is always vague. *Probability* theory and *statistics* are the major representations of these pattern relations, joined with several other *uncertainty* representation philosophies and methods, but all related to the basic impression of frequency of patterns. Representations denying the direct statistical frequency origin return really to the frequency-related memories of pattern impressions. These impressions are weighted by the *relevance* of the experience; this relevance is context dependent and will be a critical estimation issue in knowledge representation for expert systems.

Identity, or more permissively *similarity,* is the most open problem for representations. This is the ever open problem of knowledge, on the one hand, consolidated and canonized by rules, laws, standards, accepted textbooks, professional procedures, on the other hand, ever revised by new patterns, new knowledge. Identity and similarity are based on frequencies of identical or similar pattern consecutions, originally and still now based on relevant effects on changes related to the events and necessities of our life. The verbal representation of these identities and similarities are *concepts.* Conceptual thinking developed different levels, as concepts themselves behaved somehow in a similar way. A multilevel hierarchy of concepts was built where sometimes the higher levels forget completely the original factual patterns but the line can be traced back in most cases. This tracing back on the conceptual level ladder is a very important necessity for expert system representations; they provide the control of logical reasoning and frequency hypotheses of metapattern usage. The antinomies of similarities, *differences,* play a similar role: they provide the bifurcations, other branching, backtracks of the reasoning control.

Now, we are ready with the enumeration of the basic mental and linguistic-philosophical tools of representation. This reference to the origins was important from the practical point of view; the comments on the bottom-up–top-down procedures of conceptual thinking were visible demonstrations of the necessity for progressing in and returning to this theoretical-pragmatic ladder. Unfortunately, these metapatterns were all that was available for representation, a limited scope of representational tools for the unlimited variance of the real world. It was collected in millennia of human development, and only refinements are added, though very delicate ones. This means that representation is always a limited picture, no method can offer the "final" truth, and all the results of representations should be taken care of with continuous critics and checks if they are to work in any new situation.

These tools — logic, frequency relations of uncertainty, conceptual generalizations leading primarily to abstract algebra, and set theories — are the frames of mathematical tools for representation, and these mathematical tools are the direct bridges from verbal to computer representation because of their unambiguously defined character. Mathematical formulae are the representations that can be interpreted by a machine in a straightforward way.

2.   BACKGROUND

2.1.   THE DEVELOPMENT OF LOGIC

The overwhelming means of linguistic representation for relations of objects, actions, patterns, situations, and events were a very early development of human thinking. This line was continued by computer representation, and in a not too different way. This syllogistic-linguistic method was formulized by Aristotle nearly 24 centuries ago, and is continuously being refined so as to be able to express delicate relations of situation patterns. Linguistics, philosophy, mathematics, and recently computer science join these efforts. Those who devote efforts to read the original works of the Greek philosophers, Aristotle, the thinkers of the Megara school and the Stoics, later the Arabic, French, and English authors of the Middle Ages will be surprised at how many ideas can be found there that are considered to be the achievements of computer science and of recent decades only. A new age, starting with Leibniz in the 17th century and followed by the greatest mathematicians and philosophers of the 18th and 19th centuries (like Boole, Frege, and Babbage) led in a direct way to modern developments of logic, to Gödel, Tarski and to the immediate predecessors of computer science, like Turing, Church, Neumann. The Leibnizian line prepared a more precise mathematical notation, representation of different conceptual relations, which could be easily converted into machine representations. The Boolean line prepared the techniques for the manipulation of conceptual formulae, used in practically every basic computer development of calculations.

The latest progress, now bounded with computer science, can be characterized by efforts to bridge the gap between the closed world of classical logic and the open world of reality. The beautiful game of logic could be perfect until it was used for real-life decision support. Every concept was well-defined, unambiguous, suited to the celebrated law of the excluded third (*tertium non datur*). Real life is not like this; it is full of contradictions, ambiguities, changing definitions, and interpretations. After the ancient limitations of logic to certain conditions by *modal logic, intensional logic* considered the interpretations, *nonmonotonic logic* the contradictions, and *situation-, discourse-logic* the personal-social conditions of a communication. Dependency of time was formulated by *temporal logic*, a kind of modality. The concept of different possible worlds, originated from the 17–18th century, received a practical computer representational form. A discussion of these developments follows. Here we mention, among many others, the names of Wittgenstein, Montague, Kripke, and McCarthy. The internal looking problems of logical closeness, provability, computability, and the philosophical mysteries of the infinite and infinitely complex world and worlds are intrinsically related but not solved and possibly never will be. The builder of an expert system designs the knowledge representation with the conscious critics of related compromises.

Chains of concepts and events are represented by the frame idea of Minsky and the semantic nets of Schank, describing scripts of events. The *object-oriented* direction is the most important computer programming representation of those developments.

2.2.   UNCERTAINTY

The science of uncertainty is much younger. Aristotle made a remark that he did not deal with it because it has no science. Really, it was only in the 17th century when the science of uncertainty started, first and long related to dice and card games, and this start defined the ways of thinking about uncertainty until present times, the model of well-defined single events and only the multiplicity of those being uncertain dominated entirely classical probability and its related statistics. Pascal and Leibniz should be mentioned when speaking about origin. Bayes was one of the first to draw relations between uncertainty and logical reasoning.

At the turn of the 19th and 20th centuries, statistical thermodynamics gave a new impulse to the theory by new models of the motion and energy relations of elementary particles. Though Boltzman is more recognized by physics, he can be considered the originator. The story continued with quantum theory.

The edifice of classical probability was nearly completed in the first part of this century by Mises, Kolmogorov, and others. Nearly, because relevant additions are still ongoing, both in statistics and probability, especially related to the theory of information; the key name here is Shannon. The other stimulating application area was economy. In all these latter applications, the behavior of the singular events of the model deviated from the game model; they were uncertain themselves. Applications where human judgement played a relevant role, like in economy, medical diagnosis, social choice opened the eyes onto the contradictions of these judgements contrasted to simple event algebra models. The idea of evidence estimation originates also in the past century; the paper of Venn is considered the first deep presentation of the problem. This was followed by Black, Ramsay, de Finetti, Savage, Wald in the 1930s and 1940s, and later by the school of Tversky in psychology. Subjective probability tried and still makes efforts to integrate these facts of subjective judgement into the framework of classical probability.

Others go further; Dempster and Shafer created a somehow different model for the calculation of combination and propagation of uncertain events. The fuzzy concept of Zadeh formulates a new model of uncertain set memberships and direct transfer of verbal estimations to numerical computer representations. Several other attempts try to bridge classical concepts and all kinds of uncertainties of the reality and our knowledge and expertise. Though many of them try to seclude from the frequency views, this relates only to the reliance on formal statistics. Every human judgement is based on some kind of frequency experience: partly of others, partly their own. For that reason, this remains a hot problem, and probably never to be solved in a final procedural way. Knowledge about the uncertainty of the uncertainty methods is a basic professional and ethical ingredient of all people who design or apply expert systems.

This disciplinary and viewpoint variety reflects also the slowly emerging perception of the very different natures of uncertainty: due to temporary lack of knowledge, not yet succeeded discovery, not computable complexity, subjectivity, conflicting values and interests, imprecision of definitions and measurements, etc.

The best sourcebook of the history of logic until the advent of recent developments is of Kneale and Kneale 1960, the same about uncertainty of Hacking 1975, some later advancements are found in Vámos 1991.

2.3. PATTERNS

Most of the everyday situations are hardly to be represented by logic and the usual ways of uncertainty calculations. As it was mentioned in the introduction, we somehow receive and store coherent impressions that we name patterns, using the visual metaphor. The origin of the pattern idea can be traced back to Plato and further. It always returned at the encounters with the limits of rational thinking, i.e., logic. Scientific investigation started in psychology. In the late 19th century, Ehrenfels coined the German name of shape, appearance, *Gestalt*, for these pattern-related phenomena, yet the field is still investigated mainly by psychology; *scheme* is one of the favorite namings. Cognitive psychology, the psychology of cognition, knowledge acquisition, and brain processing, is a close companion of computer scientists and designers of expert systems.

Mathematical tools for identification, separation, similarity measures of patterns come mainly from statistics, applications of geometrical metaphors (multidimensional, differently shaped, solid objects) and based on that, linear algebra, which is still the most useful tool for separating components of a complex phenomenon.

3.   TECHNIQUES, PRACTICES, AND METHODOLOGIES

3.1.   CONCEPTUAL REPRESENTATION

Concept is a generalization of certain directly experienced objects, phenomena, situations, events. Though Platonistic philosophers believe in the independent existence of concepts (ideas), expert systems cannot apply these metaphysical beliefs; computers which should finally represent some kind of knowledge can start only from the basics, to do anything practical. This means that representation of any kind of knowledge starts with learning and programming of conceptual structures, an attempt to find hierarchies of the subject concerned. Having experienced individual apples and oranges, the concept of a general apple and orange can be built (defined), thereafter the concept of fruits, food, etc. The same way is valid for the conceptualization of body-related phenomena of medical expertise, commodity-related concepts of economy, elementary geometry, material and functional parts of engineering, basic structures of spatial delimitation in architecture, tangible damage in legal practice.

Knowledge engineering, a special branch of expert system design, evokes and helps to learn these conceptual structures inquiring domain experts and other information resources. Each object is characterized by its *attributes*, like shape, color, composition, etc. and *measures* (*values*) of these attributes, qualitative (large, strong, opaque, full) and quantitative in certain well-defined and basic object-originated dimension (like the meter-bar in Paris, or an atomic clock). In building conceptual hierarchy the common features of these characteristics should be accumulated and preserved because the main use of concepts is to provide an easy reference to a greater number of objects, phenomena under the hierarchical structure of the concept. The singular entity should *inherit* these characteristics from the concept and vice versa. Conceptualization is, on the one hand, a shorthand for characterization; on the other hand, a basis for *reasoning*: the first hypothesis for a decision, action is the idea that the same, or at least similar procedure can yield similar effects within the range of a whole conceptual bunch. This latter virtue of conceptual representation hints at the practice of attaching not only attributes and values, but also usual procedures to the representation scheme, like certain checks, medicines, therapies to a certain malady defined on a conceptual level, or a spell checker to the concept of a practical word processor.

The conceptual structure is not too different from any database system, especially not from those sold as intelligent systems, relational databases. Structures programmed in the object-oriented sense bear similar characteristics; for the most part, some of the names of the ingredients are different.

In the object-oriented vernacular the *object* is the bottom concept, that one which is not differentiated further within the system. This means that the chain of definitions and reasoning based on that can start with one particular apple, with the general apple concept or with fruit, according to users' requirements. The next levels of objects are *classes*, within the classes the particular objects are *instances*. The classes and objects have describing, definitional *variables*. Those which characterize a class are the vehicles of the mentioned *inheritance* procedure, one of the keys for reasoning. Objects are embedded into classes, some closer groups of objects into *subclasses*, several coherent classes are embedded in *superclasses*. All of these represent the conceptual hierarchies. For explanation, as used in dictionaries, other terms are used; these are the *metaclasses*. A class or an object can call a procedure, e.g., the program of peeling an apple, or in a general way, any fruit. These are the *methods*. The call is a *message*, and these messages are chosen and combined by *selectors* (Figure 1).

All these are based on the ancient and most simple logical formulae, an object-class relation is defined by the *is_a* junction, the list of definition attributes is collected by practical viewpoints but not very different from those used more than 2000 years ago: quantity, quality, place, time, situation, possession, action, etc. In a more advanced form, this structure is a *frame*; within this frame name, attributes and other ingredients have prefixed places, *slots*; the slot place itself defines

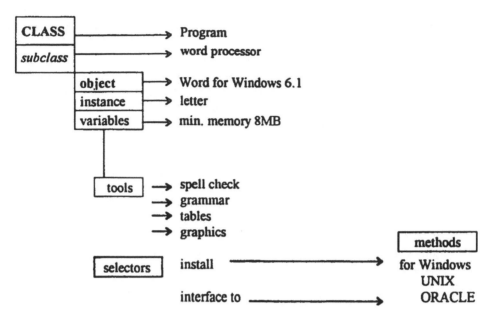

FIGURE 1 Object-concepts-actions.

the route of the input and of the output, i.e., the interpretation, application of the content, makes the user's work easier. *Keys,* used in relational databases, are compositions of attributes that collect the same or similar objects from a larger data (knowledge) base, according to a certain practical objective, e.g., collecting all fruits with removable skin and core.

This very simple and obvious structure of knowledge-database is an essential part of knowledge representation. The accomplishment of such a database in any real life, for a larger scale task is a tremendous professional work and responsibility. Beyond all the usual requirements of large databases, like consistency, possibility and control of multiple use, data integrity, the knowledge base should handle and convert verbal and numerical information. As the most important feature, as emphasized, it should be the basic material for further reasoning. This means that the structure must be available for all further complex reasoning operations, open for appropriate and closed for not applicable reuse, and it must provide a fast, efficient, highly reliable interface both for the user and the inference machine. The conceptual inheritance is a powerful tool for reasoning but multiple embedding always carries the danger of conflicting and not applicable consequences.

The user interface should have attractive, friendly access for non-computer-oriented users, and be an active, stimulating device for knowledge acquisition. Due to these requirements, only professional, well-documented and referenced, supported knowledge base tools are advisable for real-life applications. A careful selection, possibly some previous and extensive tests of the system, are recommended, whether or not it is the best match for the task concerned.

3.2. RELATIONAL REPRESENTATION

Conceptual representation is the main way for putting the patterns of the world into a computer program. The task of concatenation of pattern situations, preparation of the ways of reasoning, inference is the procedural representation of the metapatterns. The essential tool is the *rule*; that is the reason why another name for expert systems is rule-based system. The rule is the first Aristotelian syllogism in the form: *if...then....* The variables of the syllogism are joined by the *and/or* logical connections. The selector *else* points to other cases. This formula is a rule; the rules are sequenced in the succession of logical thinking or pointed at a jump in the sequence (*else→go to*).

The sequencing of the rules, internal and external control of reasoning, offers visual representation by graphs. Object representation with its messages, selectors, is a good basis for graph representation; similarly, the frame has a graph structure.

More complex relations are organized in *nets*. These contain not only the straightforward sequences of logical inference, and some permitted loops for return to check or to try another way if the previously chosen one is not the right solution. Nets are organizations of many returning alternatives, offering ways of multiple interactions, controls, intermediate choices. The complexity of real-life events can be represented in a more flexible way though the net representation and the frame one are not contradictory, they can be connected as this is shown on Figure 2. These nets express the semantic content of the event, situation representing a more or less complete pattern of conceptual generalization. Connecting single objects into a relational entity, these nets are named *semantic* or *conceptual nets*. They usually describe a story or a part of that and, therefore, the verbal correspondent is a *script*. Nodes of a graph are usually objects, the branches represent relations (*is a, part of*), actions. In this latter, important action representational scheme which lends the meaning of the script name, the node-objects are *actors*. The actor-type representation is a relevant emerging concept. We shall come back to that later, discussing different possible worlds of different actors.

The representation scheme is also a guidance for knowledge acquisition, as was mentioned before. Knowledge engineers first clarify the concepts, putting them into an object frame; then the environment of the object in a more elaborated and general frame scheme, and continue the inquiry by representing typical situations, actions, events, drafting synopses, scripts, and putting them into net-like schemes.

Although the basic ideas are very simple, the software quality requirements of the schemes are even higher than in binary graph-organized databases, controlled externally. The multiple loops of the nets, the consequent, unambiguous process of data exchanges, transformations of values, dimensions of those, especially due to the actions on the branches are very sensitive. Because one scheme should cover several individual scripts, this sensitivity is even higher, the automatic operation of concatenations, backtracks, trials on different routes, embedded loops on the net should be unambiguous, the result must be somehow verifiable if the algorithm of the operation delivered the required, feasible solution. The idea of internal control was one of the decisive ones to make the machine procedure more intelligent than the usual, externally controlled databases. Decisions on branching, routings on the graphs, i.e., directions of inference, are made by the algorithm itself in the process of machine solution, instead of the human user (Figure 3). The control can work by decisions on intermediate data and estimation of a best or suitable way to a certain goal. The algorithm should be efficient, applicable in real time interaction with the user on the dedicated computer platform.

All these circumstances advocate for the application of professional tools, shells, which should prove the performance of all these conditions, and offer a wide variety of representations, objects, frames, nets, all programmable and graphically representable, providing guidance and flexibility, automatism and control features simultaneously.

3.3.   REPRESENTATION OF UNCERTAINTY

Logic-based representations have originally binary decision opportunities only, the truth value outcomes *true* or *false* represented with *1* and *0*, respectively. All uncertain possibilities lie between them, and express the measure of uncertainty. All different uncertainty-oriented philosophies, theories, calculation methods do practically the same. This preaches about the common origin of uncertainty estimation, all coming from frequency sensation, should it be hard statistics or weak intuition. The uncertainty of data is attached to that, i.e., to the definition details of an object, the values put into the slots of the frame, the nodes and branches of directed graphs, nets.

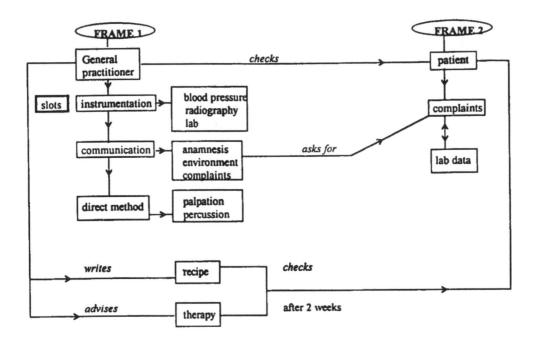

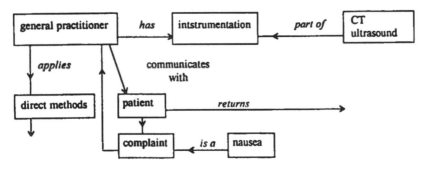

FIGURE 2   Frames and nets.

Fuzzy-type uncertainty measure, expressed in verbal form, is transferred to the same types of numerical representation; the meaning is, on the one hand, a philosophical explanation, beyond the computer representation process; on the other hand, it is a simple look-up table representation attaching the *0* to *1* values to different verbal set membership measures.

The interpretations of the nature of uncertainty, the use of different uncertainty models deviate at *combination, propagation* process. An attempt for a unified graph representation form is the use of probabilistic (uncertainty) networks by Pearl (1988).

The outcome of any uncertainty combination-propagation calculation is used in two ways: the first provides a "certain" resulting value used for decision. *If* two or more different methods or different time medical checks indicate a certain evidence, *then* the resulting evidence will be higher. How high depends on the uncertainty model and the related calculation algorithm. The same is the

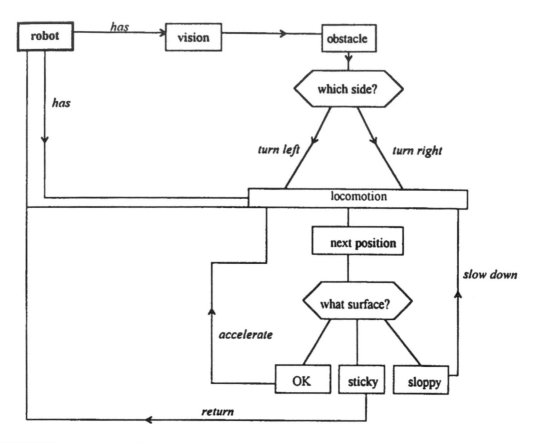

FIGURE 3   Internal control.

case in the multiple evidences of a legal case, a hypothesized outcome of different interventions and situations in economy, etc. This means that the earlier outlined logical structures remain the same, only this outcome chosen in a somehow arbitrary way, is embedded.

The second use of uncertainty combination-propagation results can be useful if different trials are feasible, either in a model calculation or in real life experimentation. In the latter case a typical application is the selection of different medical diagnostic and therapeutical strategies. Led by considerations of least expenses, least possible harm and suffering of the patient, by least risk for the doctor and an unrecoverable deterioration, different strategies can be used with different uncertain but somehow estimable effects, starting from nonintervention to an immediate radical operation, using milder or extremely radical pharmaceutics. In this representation the action branches of a decision tree are taken one after the other according to the resulting uncertainty values. The two types of outcomes are not contradictory, and can apply the same method. The application being different, influences the responsibility, risk-related estimations of the uncertainty values.

As was emphasized, the calculation method of combination-propagation is a basic representation issue, representing the general model of the nature of uncertainty. This very relevant fact is forgotten several times. To make it clear: where reliable statistics are available and the risk of a single decision is not high (moreover, if some experimentation with different possible decisions is possible), the best is a *classical probabilistic model* representation, which is a well-defined model on well-defined, mutually independent events having clear-cut truth values, excluding any intermediate situations. In this case, highly sophisticated estimation methods are available for the distribution of event data, confidence on them, expected failures. Problems of mass production,

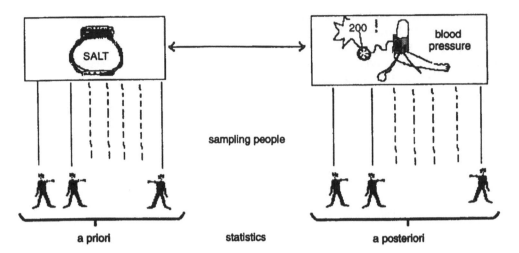

FIGURE 4   Representation of Bayesian inference.

like quality control, are typical examples of application areas. The observations of physical and chemical phenomena also belong to this model usance.

A classic probabilistic-related model is the Bayesian; it concerns certain classes of events within the realm of the total observation. The *Bayesian model* supposes also well-defined classes, reliable sampling methods, and a relevant amount of data for each class. The condition of *independence* belongs also to the model hypothesis. The Bayesian model establishes the well-known relation between a priori and a posteriori estimations, i.e., probability of an effect, if we know the probability of a certain cause, and vice versa, the probability of a cause based on the known probability of an effect (Figure 4). The Bayesian method established relations between *a priori* and *a posteriori* probabilities, i.e., between two events which are cause and consequence-related and vice versa. If

$p(a)$ is the probability estimate of an event (e.g., people salting their food twice higher than the average), and

$p(b)$ the probability of a certain consequence (e.g., people having a high blood pressure), and

$p(b/a)$ the statistics of people who have high blood pressure among those who are excessively salting, then

$p(a/b)$ is the estimate of looking for a cause b in presence of a (e.g., for supposing a habit of excessive salting in a case of high blood pressure) and this will be

$$p(a/b) = \frac{p(b/a)p(a)}{p(b)}$$

If there are many (n) possible reasonings (consequences), the formula for one of them will be modified to:

$$p(a_1/b) = \frac{p(b/a_1)p(a_1)}{\sum_{j=1}^{n} p(a_j)p(b/a_j)}$$

(in our example high blood pressure caused by salting, neurosis, kidney problems, sclerosis, etc.) as a consequence and having a statistics of those singular sets of events. The doctor looks for the cause of the certain symptom, ranking the hypotheses by this formula.

A further extension is updating, i.e., including new data into the existing statistics: If b_1, b_2, ... b_m are different poolings of evidences for b, then

$$P(a_1 \mid b_1 \& b_2 \& b_3 ... \& b_m) = \frac{P(b_1 \& b_2 \& b_3 ... \& b_m \mid a_1)P(a_1)}{\sum_{j=1}^{n} P(a_j)P(_1 \& b_2 \& b_3 ... \& b_m)}$$

This relation is applicable for singular causes and effects within a situation of multiple causes and effects if we have rather reliable data on all hypothetical sampling classes. The double weakness is apparent from the conditions: first, the need for a crisp definition, separation of the singular sampling classes, and second, the requirement of sufficient statistics on all possible classes. Diagnostics, statistical analysis of complex and mass effects, like demographic, diet-related search on medical data, weather research, and research on environmental effects, are typical application fields. Extension of Bayesian concepts, covering a broad field of different representations, like nonmonotonic logic, Dempster-Shafer schemes, etc., is done by the Bayesian nets of Pearl.

A somewhat different model is used by the *Dempster-Shafer* representation. The model has two features: first, it uses a combination calculus of multiplication of each singular observation's confidence with the probability of the phenomenon within the realm of all possible phenomena, and sums up all related results of multiplications. This orthogonal calculation method permits the consideration of all possible combinations of phenomena and causes, respectively (Figure 5).

The method is composed really of two parts: Dempster's rule of combination of evidences and Shafer's application of it for a calculus and philosophy of evidence distribution among certain events and groups of events, events where we have an estimate and those where the chances are completely hidden.

Dempster's rule suggests an orthogonal sum of the estimates in the following way:

$A = (A_1 ... A_n)$ a set of events (symptoms, etc.)
$B = (B_1 ... B_n)$ the other set of the same situation

$m_1(A_i)$, $m_2(B_j)$ are the related estimates; each set of those should be complete $\left(\sum m_i = 1\right)$, then for the combination (intersection) $A_i \cap B_j = S$

$$m(S) = \frac{\sum_{A_i \cap B_j = S} m_1(A_i)m_2(B_j)}{1 - \sum_{A_i \cap B_j = 0} m_1(A_i)m_2(B_j)}$$

The denominator serves for discarding the empty parts of the intersections and for normalization to the measure 1.

The frame of discernment is the totality of events and their combinations within a certain situation (case). The strength of this concept is that it manages combined evidences as, e.g., symptoms that can conclude to more than one disease.

The concept of the frame of discernment permits one to define estimates to all known cases and then combinations and leave the remainder to the whole territory of the unknowns. By combining the different sets of these estimates (different investigations, different witnesses, etc.),

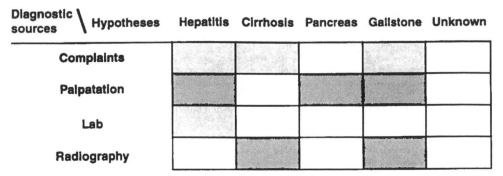

Diagnostic sources \ Hypotheses	Hepatitis	Cirrhosis	Pancreas	Gallstone	Unknown
Complaints					
Palpatation					
Lab					
Radiography					

FIGURE 5   Dempster-Shafer uncertainty representation: orthogonal combinations of information sources and hypotheses on causes.

the uncertainty of the unknown region (remainder of the frame of discernment) decreases gradually. This is the effect of smearing the evidences through the possible cases.

One certain case of evidence (one symptom, one statement of a witness) is a basic probability assignment (the values in the Dempster method), the belief function is the sum of those for a subset of the frame (Bel A). The plausibility function is a complement:

$$Pl(A) = 1 - Bel(A)$$

The other feature is the permission of hypothetical unknown phenomena, and a narrowing procedure of this unknown realm, similar to our investigation procedures in the case of several possible hypotheses and unknown causes or effects. The model yields results for these unknown situations, different from the Bayesian, which distributes the probabilities in an equal proportion if there is no definite probability estimation for those. Several recommendations exist in the literature for establishing bridges between the two models. Another weakness of the model is its deformed behavior in case of marginal probability estimations. The strength of the model excels in cases of multiple combined observations and situations, and in case of human judgement instead of statistical data. Typical application areas are those referred to in the beginning of this section: inference in a complex medical diagnosis or criminal investigation.

The other favorite model is the *fuzzy representation* of Zadeh. The membership estimation of an event, situation in a set of similar cases reflects the pattern metaphor, and simultaneously, the verbal qualification practice of human judgement. The distribution of a membership-judgement class follows also the human practice, we think more in fuzzy way impressions of distribution regions than in the mathematically correct Gaussian-like distribution patterns (Figure 6).

The fuzzy membership value is consciously context-dependent, and has a semantics. The property of attributing this semantics opens the possibility of a direct use for a linguistic interface and for the development of a fuzzy language. The distribution concept of the probability theory has a simplified version by trapezoid- or triangular-like distributions, where the lower and the upper limits of the enclosed area are the *possibility* (resp. *necessity*) limits of the set definition. Combination is somehow relative to the same theoretic solutions and this is not be hance: the problem is for both to get a reliable estimate of uncertain events' coincidence.

In the fuzzy notation $\mu_F(F)$ is the membership function of a set F, i.e., μ_{iF} expresses how the element i is guessed to be belonging to the set F. $\sum \mu_i(F) = 1$ as in any similar uncertainty methods. The membership guess can be expressed by word, e.g., high, low, very cold, hot, etc. Both possibilistic and fuzzy logic are built upon this concept.

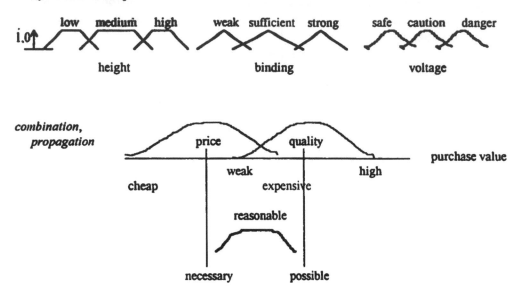

Fuzzy set memberships

FIGURE 6   Fuzzy representation.

Possibilistic logic is concerned with uncertain reasoning where the database is a fuzzy description of a given world.

The fuzzy combination rules:

$$\text{union}: \quad \mu_{\cup} = \max \mu_i$$
$$\text{intersection}: \quad \mu_{\cap} = \min \mu_i$$

for possibility estimation $\pi(u)$ are defined, the degree of possibility that the datum concerned (the height of Mary or the temperature next day at noon) is exactly equal to u by this definition; two further values can be conceptualized, an upper bound named possiblity (Π) and a lower bound, the necessity (N):

$$\Pi = \sup_u \min(\mu(u), \pi(u))$$
$$N = \inf_u \max(\mu(u), 1 - \pi(u))$$

This results in a consciously more subjective classification than any other method claims. The combination-propagation model follows the minimax concepts of game theory, delimiting the outcomes into the possible and necessary extremes. These limits assign rather wide ranges; in practical cases a further fuzzy estimation of the resulting situation is more substantial. The fuzzy representation is useful in all cases where qualitative judgements are common, and not too much more information is available. Similarly, fuzzy representation works well in all cases where the requirement and possibility for more sophisticated methods is not necessary. Fuzzy control is a typical field. Zadeh emphasizes that the fuzzy method has no claim to replace any other, but in many cases it works well and can be applied in combination with others, too.

An important further development of fuzzy-qualitative representation, though not in an acknowledged relation to the fuzzy view, is *qualitative reasoning*, used especially for describing physical processes (Figure 7).

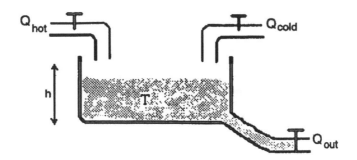

FIGURE 7 Naive physics — qualitative reasoning.

3.4. OPEN WORLD REPRESENTATION

Relational representation of traditional logic is occluded by the *Closed World Assumption,* which includes only a limited number of concepts and relations, and supports the hypothesis that the whole world is explorable in a well-defined way. Uncertainty methods open some windows to the real world of unexplored, unexpected phenomena. This is especially true for the nontraditional uncertainty methods which ignore the hypothesis of excluded middle and of independence of basic events. The price of a more permissive method is the increased softness of their basic model and consequently the inefficiency of reasoning capabilities. From the point of view of logical and mathematical rigor, they are less and less welcome. This used to be the history of all methods beyond the classical probabilistic theory. One of the compromises is that all methods, the fuzzy representation included, can be attached at any instance of an acceptable hypothesis to the relational representation of classical logic. This is the intention of practically all methods concerning an open world: restricting the part of soft representation to the unavoidable limits.

The other way towards the open world of reality is the development of modern logic. It grew out of the *modalities* of classical logic, i.e. the limitations of the validity to certain subjects, interpretation fields. This is done by the different interpretations of the quantifiers (Figure 8). The next, far leading step is a deeper intrusion into the meaning. The *quantifiers* define an external frame for the interpretation, the meaning of the variables, analyzed and interpreted by *intensional logic,* opens every possible interpretation due to the specific usage of the words in different cultures, different ages, different disciplines, different mood, different social environment (Figure 9).

Some readings of Modal Operators

□ A	◇ A	
It is necessarily true that A	It is possibly true that A	Alethic logic
It will always be true that A	It will be sometimes that A	Temporal logic
It ought to be that A	It can be that A	Deontic logic
It is known that A	The opposite of A is not known	Logics of knowledge
It is believed that that A	The opposite of A is not believed	Logics of belief
After every terminating execution of the program, A is true	There is an execution of the program that terminates with A true	Dynamics logic

FIGURE 8 Modal representation. (After A. Thayse, D. Snyers: Languages and logics, in Thayse (Ed.): *From Modal Logic to Deductive Databases,* Chichester: John Wiley, 1989.)

Peter looks for his car

— In the *world* of a certain parking place where automobiles are parking
  * *type* of parking automobiles

— In the *world* of a railway station where railway cars are assigned to the ticket owners
  * *type* of railway cars

— In the *world* of desires where somebody has a lottery ticket, can win a car, and is just looking at the lottery list
  * *type* of lottery prizes

FIGURE 9   Intentional representation.

The open world is full of contradictions. Because not all cases, relations, phenomena are known, one meets new facts in everyday practice, information which is not in strict logical relation with the previous knowledge, cannot be included into the framework of previous definitions. Three ways are used in common practice. The first preserves the earlier knowledge, its frames, structures and recognizes those which could not be fit in as exceptions. The second tries to detach this world of different phenomena by creating other new worlds. The third tries to create a unified new world of renewed concepts and relational hypotheses. The first can be illustrated by the favorite example of *nonmonotonic logic,* the exception of the birds (like the penguin or the oyster) which cannot fly, like the "regular" birds of the northern hemisphere. The second is the case of discovering the viral and bacterial variants of pneumonia or the difference between hepatitis A and B. The third is the case of the Kuhnian new paradigms in science, quantummechanics unifying the theories of the micro and the macroworld, or relativity theory, the Newtonian and the cosmological world. All these have representational methods in modern logic.

Nonmonotonic logic is the conceptual frame of logical relations where some new information is in discord with earlier information; the flow of information does not corroborate the consequence in a monotonic way. Two obvious procedures are at hand: narrowing down the conceptual frame to the extent where no contradiction exists, or the extension of the concept with new rules valid for the exceptions. The first is the *circumscription* of McCarthy, the second is the use of *default rules* of Reiter.

In a system of an open world, not all statements corroborate the previous ones, or those hypotheses or conclusions that are logical antecedents or consequences of these statements. Monotonic logic is created in a closed world where all further statements, data, and facts add to the validity of the previous ones.

Nonmonotonic logic looks at these contradictory sets of statements and attempts to find a consistent way of resolving the situation by adding further new conditions or canceling some old ones.

In classical logic, theorems are results of valid inferences; in nonmonotonic logic, one starts with all inferred statements, whether they are consistent or not. Then in most cases, one starts to find a fixed point, i.e., a minimal set where all statements get a consistent context. A typical paradigm is Tweety the bird, Tweety the penguin. Either we should exclude the penguin from the class of birds or flying should not be a characteristic attribute.

Several methods were developed for restoring consistency, e.g., circumscription and default logic.

Circumscription: "We know some objects in a given class and we have some ways of generating more. We jump to the conclusion that this gives all the objects in the class. Thus, we *circumscribe* the class to the objects we know how to generate."

"It is only a conjecture, because there might be an object such that" a predicate on the object "is not generated in this way." The heuristics of circumscription — when one can plausibly conjecture that the objects generated in known ways are all there are — are completely studied.

Circumscription is not deduction in disguise, because every form of deduction has two properties that circumscription lacks — transitivity and what we may call monotonicity. Transitivity says that 'if *a* is a consequence of *b* and *c* is a consequence of *b*, then *c* is a consequence of *a*. (If snowing, the road is slippery, if slippery then driving is dangerous, consequently if snowing then driving is dangerous.) In realistic cases (circumpscription), driving on snow by a car equipped with tire chains is not dangerous.' Monotonicity says that within a class of statements all further sentences corroborate the statement further." No exception or contradiction occurs. This is not the case in circumscription and generally in *nonmonotonic logic* because we find some exception cases, e.g., our penguin Tweety is a bird that does not fly. The way of circumventing this difficulty is to find a minimum model where all sentences are true (e.g., European birds, cars with standard, low mileage tires, etc.). Nevertheless, "It is not always true that a sentence true in all minimal models can be proved by circumscription. Indeed, the minimal model of Peano's axiom is the standard model of arithmetic and Gödel's theorem is the assertion that not all true sentences are theorems. Minimal models don't always exist, and when they exist, they are not always unique."[1]

Default logic: Default logic is a method for treating nonmonotonic problems. The basic idea is a distinction between general "hard" rules (facts) and their defaults, i.e., those rules which extend the world of the fact by exemptions and irregularities. (All birds fly but penguins do not.) The method is similar to circumscription, the main difference is the theoretically well-formed idea of circumscription's minimal set, related to the fixed point theorems. A weakness of default logic is the arbitrary and occasional nature of the default rules. They cannot be inferred within the system, they can be used for further inference with much caution, and they can yield trivial contradictions.

The general class of default theories is mathematically intractable and that many desirable features of the logic can be obtained only for the class, so-called *normal* default theories, namely, theories in which all defaults have the form:

$$\frac{\alpha(x) : w(x)}{w(x)}$$

Such defaults are extremely common; for example, "Typically, birds fly" would be written:

$$\frac{Bird(x) : Fly(x)}{Fly(x)}$$

without explicating specific conditions $\beta(x)$ under which the inference should be blocked.

While most naturally occurring defaults are normal, the interactions among such defaults lead to anomalous conclusions. For example, suppose we use normal defaults to express the facts that Tweety is a penguin, that penguins are birds, and that birds typically fly but penguins typically do not. We have:

---

[1] The quotations are from McCarthy (1977); the logical formulae are substituted by verbal explanation and examples.

$$W = \{Bird(Tweety), Penguin(x) \supset Bird(x)\}$$

$$D = \left\{ \frac{Bird(x) : Fly(x)}{Fly(x)} \cdot \frac{Penguin(x) : \neg Fly(x)}{\neg Fly(x)} \right\}$$

The theory has two extensions:

$$E_1 = (W \cup Fly(Tweety))$$

and

$$E_2 = (W \cup \neg Fly(Tweety))$$

depending on which default rule is applied first.

In both cases an automatic operating check system is needed for the control of the flow of new information if it really fits into the limited frame of circumscription or can be included into one of the existing default rules. This automatic record keeping and checking system is the *Truth Maintenance System* of Doyle.

A remarkable fact is the application of first-order classical logic for all these purposes of nonmonotonic logic. The necessary logical test of soundness is not different from the usual program test procedures; it can be completed only if the test program covers the whole possible logical graph of inference or better by the resolution principle executing the proof for the impossibility of the negative statement of the system. (All men are mortal — we cannot find a man who was immortal). The complexity of these test procedures is another hint at the advice: do not try to develop specific tools for a real large scale system but use the ones which are developed by professionals of great experience and tested in real-life environments by several well referenced similar applications!

The second mainstream for creating coherent knowledge chunks is the definition of *agents*. Agent can be anything that operates on certain chunks of the "total" knowledge, a person, an enzyme, any process of natural sciences and industry, even time which operates on everything. An agent is in a narrow sense a modality, an external definition how the logic of the system should be interpreted and how it should work, defined by this interpretation. The same case is viewed in a different way by a legal expert agent, who uses the deontic logic modality, and by somebody who has some different cultural beliefs. By this way, different possible worlds are created, a separate world for each agent. In a cooperative process, such as manufacturing a car or building a house, the specialists of each production phase or the machines used for different tasks, the agents in this sense, have own worlds of their own professional knowledge, their task-executing programs. Usually, not only the strongly restricted task-oriented execution program is different, but the entire view. The artist of the interior design has a view about the roles of bricks completely different from a bricklayer.

If the worlds of the different agents can be well separated and well interfaced, no further problem exists, all can be reduced to the methods and their problems discussed earlier. A special type of agent is the system which coordinates different agents; one of the typical representations are the *Blackboard systems* which concentrate on different input agents. They convey various information from various resources, sometimes in various styles. The system's task is to organize the information into a usable structure. The blackboard metaphor is valid only for the nonintelligent part of this task: having a device which can receive many kinds of records. The real problem is the interpretation of the information and creation of rules for putting them into the right place of the object representation, frame, net, etc.

The agents can be supplied with goals, and these goals can create *plans*. An intelligent robot has a goal of reaching and catching an object in an environment where other objects, even other moving robots are present, and the task of the robot is to plan a trajectory which avoids all obstacles and gets to the goal. The goal is usually defined by logical statements on the final situation. The plan is a graph, represented by rules of logic, constraints, i.e., the obstacles are some frame-like representations of their instant locations. The robot task is a general metaphor of any goal-oriented actions satisfying some constraints on the environment. The nature of real environments suggests the understanding of all kinds of open world conditions, nonmonotonicity.

A special kind of method, *autoepistemic logic* was drafted by Stalnaker and Moore for creating different closed worlds for different agents, based on their views, beliefs. The intriguing problem is a belief on the belief of the other agent. The metaphor of the autoepistemic logic procedure is the game with many distorting mirrors, each reflecting the deformed picture of the previous one, and performing some operation on the real object but seen on the last mirror!

The real difficulty is, like in real life, the possible and unforeseeable conflict among the agents resp. their worlds. This is where the knowledge representation joins the disciplines of conflict resolution: decision support, social choice, voting and polling, theories and methods of uncertainty and games. This relation of uncertainty calculations and decision was mentioned before. The *decision support* system which does or advises a choice, a preference of possible conflict resolution should be an integral knowledge part of the expert system. Which conflict resolution procedure should be used, what the previously definable preferences are, these are obvious prerequisite knowledge constituents as this was exemplified by the different possible strategies of medical diagnosis and therapy. An important result of Arrow was the theoretical proof for the non-existence of any finally rational choice in the presence of several rational preferences. This fact is experienced in our everyday life, and it suggests the application of a sophisticated decision support system for seeing pros and cons of alternatives but the final decision is mostly a human responsibility. Knowledge representation should know this, the simplest solution is in any dubious situation a return to a man-machine dialog with the user or with the domain expert.

The third way of creating coherence in knowledge is the creation of new frames, new structures, which is mostly a human learning and ingenuity task, but can be supported also by *machine learning*.

The first-order logic structures behind the various systems permit not only the use of these systems for knowledge acquisition in a conducted domain expert–knowledge engineer dialog but can be a background for learning if information can be fed into the system in a suitable way. In the learning mode of operation not only the previously defined slots are filled in with the new information and according to a prescribed way but a search can be initiated for new structures, such as new relations for a relational database.

The open world is fundamentally represented in *natural language;* this is the reason language is still, and remains for ever, a subject of investigations in human relations. The bridge between natural language and computer representation is, therefore, a basic problem and — as far as it can be approximated — a basic tool for knowledge representation. This is the real blackboard! Syntactical *parsing, semantic analysis* belong to these tools, all achievements of general computer linguistics. These are, therefore, ingredients of every more sophisticated knowledge representation system.

Case-based reasoning can use all these methods of representation. The essential problem is the same as that of human expertize: remembering to a certain similar and some only likely similar cases the expert should decide if the similar decision is applicable or not. The practice of the Anglo-Saxon precedence-based Common Law or of a medical consultant are the best examples. The cases are represented in frames, scripts; the distances to other schemes are mostly defined by fuzzy-like estimations, Bayesian-types of conditional probabilities, distance measures used in clustering problems like the Nearest Neighbor methods. The representation of the singular cases and case prototypes like a given diagnostic pattern or a textbook malady description is the simpler part of the task; the invention of the pertinent similarity measure, definition of its relation to viewpoints (very special modalities) is the real human challenge.

3.5.   CONNECTIVITY, PATTERNS, AND SCHEMES

The most important representation devices of the connectivist-pattern view are the neural nets. The evaluation of pattern-type representations, i.e., the *conceptual clustering* of net images, pattern representations in data files, etc. is a further representation task. Three major methods are available, all in many variations.

The first is the statistical clustering procedure; the most popular one is the *Nearest Neighbor* algorithm which collects the points of nets and data representations which are closer to one or the other density center.

The second group of methods proceeds with the minimization of defining characteristics, such as a minimal word explanation of an event. This happens with the cited geometrical metaphor: the data points create a multidimensional object in a multidimensional space. The *eigendirections*, main axes of these information objects represent the main definitional characteristics, the length of the axes, the relevance of the characteristics. An evaluation decreases the number of these axes, i.e., the definitional characteristics as far as they define somehow the pattern, until they separate it from others.

The third group takes the coded information patterns in the sense of the *information* and *code theory*. The differences in information content, entropy, and the code distances of code representations, e.g. Hamming-distances are the features that define similarities and separations, i.e. representations of conceptual definitions.

3.6.   REPRESENTATIONAL RELATIONS OF FURTHER INTELLIGENT ACTIONS

Representation is a device for the creation and use of intelligent systems such as expert systems. This means that the representation form cannot be separated from the previous and further steps of application, i.e., from knowledge acquisition, inference and explanation of actions. As it was referred to, the choice of knowledge representation forms and methods depend on these applications, and that is the reason advanced shells and toolkits offer various methods.

A typical representation problem for further processing is the application of genetic algorithms. The individual components which should be varied in composition for a feasible solution should be selected by a certain knowledge about the specific problem, e.g. parts of an engine to be assembled in a feasible and most efficient way. The next part of required knowledge is the permitted extent of variations, and finally the fitness algorithm that evaluates the variational generations.

4.   RESEARCH ISSUES

The representation problem is an endless issue because no final solution is under the technological horizon for creating a complete identity of the world and of computer representation. The most ambitious hard advocates of artificial intelligence speak only about the substitution of the human mind, though this is also a dubious expectation. The human mind itself is not the representation body of all possible knowledge, the complexity of the world is much beyond the complexity of the mind.

In the course of representation process the first research task is to find better means for knowledge acquisition. The problem is more rooted in cognitive psychology but the lessons of better human cognition and communication about knowledge are issues to be implemented by the computer representation, especially in the forms of input representation. Icon and other graph representation forms of nowadays common software product were results of earlier computer representation research. This development is only at the beginning; the question how to design flexible, interactive knowledge input interfaces for experts and for non-expert users, for different age groups and cultural environments, for everyday, nearly continuous use or for accidental man-machine communications is still completely open.

The other input-related representation problem is the natural language interface. Natural language contrasted to computer languages contains lexical and semantic ambiguities, sollipsis, i.e., omissions which suppose a background knowledge of the partner and her/his active participation in the discourse, metaphors anticipating the same cultural background of the other side, sentences which are not correct syntactically, jumps in the logical sequence of the subject, uncertain, not well organized references within the text. Verbal communication is understandable within a certain environment which defines the *pragmatics*, i.e., the representation of the communicators and of the communication, considering the situational relativity of the communication, meaning. A reliable and complete understanding of natural spoken language is not either attainable between two persons. The machine solution is farther, though limited results are present, understanding limited subject areas with limited vocabulary, terms, and they can be very helpful in practical applications. The existence of many professional and familiar vernaculars strengthens the need for some common *metalanguages*, metarepresentations, such as the explanation texts of the best dictionaries. A steady progress is ongoing in all these directions.

How central the linguistic issue is, can be felt through the recent efforts of one of the founders and most influential researchers of artificial intelligence, McCarthy. He represents the whole problem in a framework of *speech acts*, i.e., knowledge-based representation of communication among agents. Somehow similar idea is behind Schank's research on *goal-based scenarios*.

The next research issue is the extension and combination of different representation methods. Some higher order logical means expressing embedded knowledge can be more powerful than present first-order logic, straightforward representations. Reasoning based on higher order logic is clumsy, sometimes unsolved. Further combinations of uncertainty methods and logic, their automatic or semiautomatic matching with the most analogous methodological models are future problems.

One of the most promising and fast progressing representation trends is the application of connectivity ideas. This is done in many directions, first of all in hardware. The latest achievements in cellular neural nets provide a several-thousand time faster access to a whole image than any chip before. The image, the pattern can be used as a direct representation of some visual information but also as conceptual structures, entities, similar to the philosophy that was represented in this chapter through the relations of metapatterns and concepts. Physical and programmed links between logic based representations and connectivity-related patterns are emerging. These will help in future development of space and time representation. The human mind's space and time representation history followed somehow in a similar way. A general and automatically given space and time representation can be a frame for most future machine representations; the rapid advancement of multimedia proves this relevant cognitive feature.

5. FUTURE TRENDS, CONCLUSIONS

The general trend of artificial intelligence and related research is a fast unification with all other trends of computer science and practice. Many of the esoteric considerations and imaginative methods of the past are now natural ingredients of the most common products if they were feasible indeed. According to a witty remark: the real successes of science are those which are not noticed anymore but work. This is the relevant trend for a kernel of all software products like representation. The paragraph on input representations outlined the main directions in the interface field. These interface representations are now the hottest problems of practical user-friendliness. The interior representation trend has two parallel and only seemingly diverting directions. On the first, extremely ambitious projects, like the early General Problem Solver or the long dragging Cyc effort try to create very general problem solving, and behind that, try to create very general representation vehicles. On the other second highway, thousands of pragmatic information-, expert systems are born every year for specific use. As it was emphasized, a general, human-like intelligence, and a brain imitating representation scheme is non-existing on the horizon but completely isolated small systems cannot survive too long, and cannot be economical. The necessary integration follows the history of general computing: a few, open-ended operation systems created a frame for free cooperation of an abundance of products. This should be the future of the most successful, open expert system shells, application toolkits. The emerging tools create an environment where the usual task is not related to programming, computational, representational system design but is a steady exercise for domain experts, system analysts, cognitive psychology-oriented knowledge engineers. They all must have a certain general knowledge, but not more, about the interior nature of representation. All further computational work should be executed by the professional toolkit product.

REFERENCES

Brachman, R.J. and Levesque, H.J., Eds., 1985. *Readings in Knowledge Representation*, San Mateo: Morgan Kaufmann.

Collins, A. and Smith, E.E., Eds. 1988. *Readings in Cognitive Science — A Perspective from Psychology and Artificial Intelligence*. San Mateo: Morgan Kaufmann.

Davis, E. 1990. *Representation of Commonsense Knowledge*. San Mateo: Morgan Kaufmann.

Hacking, Ian, 1975. *The Emergence of Probability*. Cambridge: Cambridge University Press.

Lee, J.K., Liebowitz, J., and Chae, Y.M. (Eds.), 1996. *Critical Technology — Proc. of the Third World Congress on Expert Systems*, February 5–9, 1996, Seoul, Korea. New York: Cognizant Communication Corporation.

Kneale, W. and Kneale, M. 1960, 1971. *The Development of Logic*. Oxford: Oxford University Press.

Pearl, J. 1988. *Probabilistic Reasoning in Intelligent Systems: Networks of Plausible Inference*. San Mateo: Morgan Kaufmann.

Russel, W.S.J. and Norvig, P. 1995. *Artificial Intelligence, A Modern Approach*. Englewood Cliffs, NJ.: Prentice Hall.

Vámos, T. 1991. *Computer Epistemology*. Singapore: World Scientific.

Walley, P. 1996. Measures of uncertainty in expert systems. *Artificial Intelligence*, 83: 1–58.

Zadeh, L.A. 1989. Knowledge representation in fuzzy logic. *IEEE Trans. on Knowledge and Data Engineering*, 1 (1): 89–99.

4 Expert System Development Tools

John Durkin

CONTENTS

1. INTRODUCTION

During the past several decades, we have seen expert system technology evolve from a laboratory curiosity into a valuable tool for assisting human decision making. We have witnessed its application over a wide range of tasks: from assisting mine managers with planning mining activities, helping

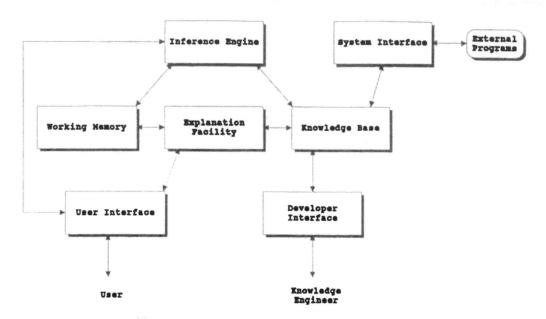

FIGURE 1 Expert system shell architecture.

farmers avoid pest infestations, to controlling life support systems aboard the space station. Many reasons can be put forth to help explain this success story, with one of the better ones centered around the introduction and widespread use of expert system development tools called shells. A *shell* is a programming environment that contains all of the necessary utilities for both developing and running an expert system. Figure 1 shows the architecture of an expert system shell.

- **Knowledge base** contains highly specialized knowledge on the problem area as provided by the expert, and includes problem facts, rules, concepts, and relationships.
- **Inference engine** is the knowledge processor, modeled after the expert's reasoning, that works with available information on a given problem, coupled with the knowledge stored in the knowledge base, to draw conclusions or recommendations.
- *Working memory* contains the facts entered by the user or inferred by the expert system during a consultation.
- **User interface** is the vehicle through which the user views and interacts with the system.
- **Developer interface** is the vehicle through which the knowledge engineer develops the system.
- **Explanation facility** provides explanations on the reasoning of the system.
- **System interface** links the expert system to external programs such as databases, spreadsheets, algorithms, etc., that work in a support role for the system.

We will look at each of these subsystems in more detail later and review some of their more important features to consider when selecting a shell.

In theory, when developing an expert system using a shell, your only major requirement is to place the problem's knowledge in the knowledge base. All the other modules needed to run the system are already there for you. This greatly reduces development time and enables an individual lacking extensive programming experience the opportunity to build the system.

In this chapter we will first look at the history of expert system development tools, including some of the more popular languages. Next we review some of the major types of tools for building knowledge-based systems. We then review the major tool features to consider when selecting a tool, and also look at the results of a survey conducted of expert system developers who were asked to judge the importance of these features. The commercial tool market is also reviewed, where tool sale figures are shown for the last several years. Finally, we consider what the future landscape of the expert system tool market might look like.

2. HISTORICAL OVERVIEW

In 1956, a small group of computer scientists attended a summer workshop sponsored by IBM at Dartmouth College. Their discussion focused on their present research efforts in automatic theorem proving and new programming languages. They also discussed ways that this work might be directed for developing a computer that could simulate human reasoning. This confer ence marked the birth of artificial intelligence (AI).

Following this event, researchers in various countries set out in different directions to develop programs capable of intelligent behavior. Some looked for methods to form the basis of intelligent programs, such as knowledge representation and inferencing techniques, while others took a broader approach and attempted to design general problem solving programs, such as GPS. While this international horse race took many divergent tracks, all projects shared one common point: a basic programming language was used such as LISP or PROLOG.

In the U.S., LISP was the language of choice. Though powerful in its symbolic processing capability, it was found to be difficult to master, giving rise to few LISP programmers who were mainly confined to academic circles. In addition, the many dialects of LISP were the source of migraines for researchers who looked to exchange code. Fortunately, this situation improved in mid-1970s with the introduction of a LISP standard called Common LISP — the aspirin of choice for LISP programmers.

Researchers in the U.K. and Japan adopted PROLOG for developing intelligent programs. It was also the language chosen in Japan for the Fifth Generation effort. Based in a formal well-understood logic, PROLOG offers a language to develop exact deductive programs. Ironicly, it is the exactness of PROLOG that many researchers found too constraining. In addition, like LISP, PROLOG required a disciplined student to master it, thus limiting the number of competent programmers.

Given the complexities of these two languages, AI research was confined principally to the academic world during the 1960s and 1970s, where very few expert systems were built. Also, since these systems were built from scratch, development time was large. Fortunately, an event occurred following the MYCIN project that dramatically changed this situation.

MYCIN (Shortliffe, 1976) was developed at Stanford University to aid physicians in diagnosing and treating patients with infectious blood diseases caused by bacteremia (bacteria in the blood) and meningitis (bacterial disease that causes inflammation of the membrane surrounding the brain and spinal cord). These diseases can be fatal if not recognized and treated quickly. The system was developed during the mid-1970s and took approximately 20 person-years to complete. MYCIN is a rule-based expert system that uses backward chaining and incorporates approximately 500 rules. The system was written in INTERLISP, a dialect of the LISP programming language.

During the work on MYCIN, a large amount of LISP code was written for different modules:

- Knowledge base
- Inference engine
- Working memory
- Explanation facility
- End-user interface

Toward the end of the project, the MYCIN developers realized that because the knowledge on infectious diseases was separate from its control, then the code written for the other modules should be portable to other applications. Bill van Melle (1979) wrote

"One ought to be able to take out the clinical knowledge and plug in knowledge about some other domain."

By removing the knowledge about infectious blood diseases, a system known as EMYCIN (van Melle, 1979) was formed. EMYCIN is a domain-independent version of MYCIN that contains all of MYCIN except its knowledge about infectious blood disease. EMYCIN facilitated the development of other expert systems, such as PUFF (Aikens et al., 1983), an application for the diagnosis of pulmonary problems.

The separation of knowledge from its processing is a powerful feature of expert systems that permits the reuse of existing code and greatly reduces the development time for other systems. For example, PUFF was produced in about 5 person-years, a considerable saving over the 20 person-years required to develop MYCIN. EMYCIN was the forerunner of today's expert system shells.

The value of a shell to greatly reduce expert system development time was quickly recognized by the commercial sector, where the number of shell vendors began to grow rapidly. Following, in short order, was a dramatic increase in the number of developed expert systems. Two surveys of the field underscore this point.

In 1990, along with Brian Sawyer, Harmon published *Creating Expert Systems for Business and Industry* (Harmon and Sawyer, 1990). The book included estimates of the number of developed expert systems between 1985 and 1988. These estimates are shown in Figure 2 along with the result from a 1992 survey (Durkin, 1993). Figure 3 shows the percentage of applications from the 1992 survey that were developed with different software tools. The "other" software category of Figure 3 includes the languages C, Pascal, LOOPS, Fortran, Smalltalk, and Basic. As this figure illustrates, the vast majority of systems have been developed with the aid of a shell.

3.   TYPES OF TOOLS

3.1.   LANGUAGES

As previously mentioned, the dominant languages used for building an expert system have been LISP and PROLOG. OPS has also been popular among rule-based programmers. They remain today the first choice of designers. Recently, C and C++ have also been used for system development.

OPS, Official Production System, has been a very popular choice of expert system developers. OPS is a product of the Instructable Production System Project at CMU back in 1975. The project team was looking for a language that would assist in expert system development. The original version was rule-based and permitted only forward chaining. It was used by John McDermott to create one of the classic expert systems called R1 (later called XCON), to help DEC configure VAX computer systems. Over the years various versions of OPS emerged, the latest being OPS/R2, which supports backward chaining and objects with inheritance. OPS is commercially available from Production Systems Technologies, Pittsburgh, PA. For an excellent historical overview of the evolution of the OPS language, see Forgy (1995).

Using a language provides flexibility. Once you know what features are needed for the system, you can generate the required code. On the down-side, you need to develop the entire infrastructure, including the traditional subsystems such as the inference engine and explanation facility (OPS provides many of the needed facilities). You will also need, obviously, proficiency in the chosen language. As shown in Figure 2, expert system developers have more often turned to shells than languages. A recent survey of the field, one conducted in preparation of a new edition of Durkin (1993), has shown that this trend is increasing. The percentage of systems built using shells has

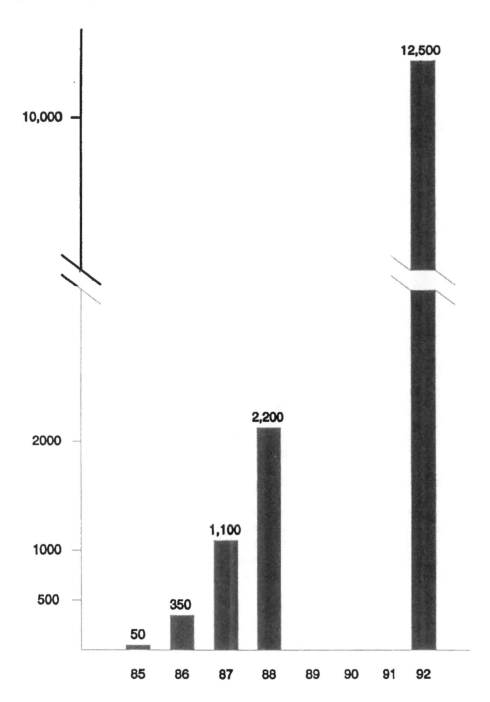

FIGURE 2   Number of developed expert systems per year.

increased slightly over the 1993 figure, while percentages for the languages have all decreased slightly.

3.2.   RULE-BASED TOOLS

Rule-based tools use if-then rules to represent knowledge. These rules are processed through a backward or forward chaining process, or a combination of the two (called bidirectional inference).

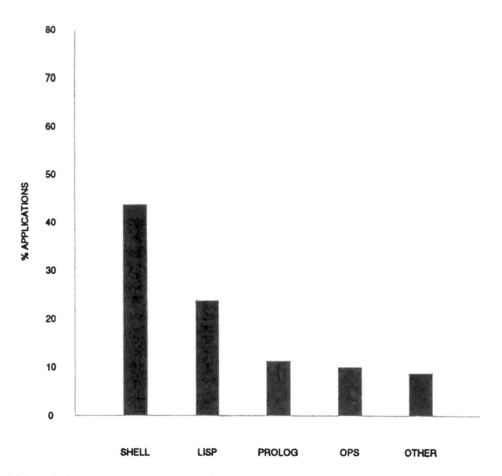

FIGURE 3 Software used in expert system development.

Some tools permit the coding of inexact rules and inexact inferencing, possibly using *confidence factors* and processing methods found in the *certainty theory*, both a product of the work on MYCIN. Some tools permit the coding of rule-sets that act like separate knowledge bases, which can be processed according to the context of the consultation session. These sets act like a committee of experts where they exchange information over a global data location, often called a *blackboard* structure.

During the early 1980s, when commercial tools were first entering the market, most tools were rule-based. Therefore, most developed expert systems to date are rule-based. Even today, rule-based expert system tools remain the first choice of most designers.

3.3.   FRAME-BASED TOOLS

Frame-based tools represent knowledge in frames. Each frame captures descriptive and behavioral information on some object, in slots and methods, respectively. Knowledge processing may be accomplished through an interaction of the frames using a technique such as *message passing*, or through an interaction of frames with a set of rules using a shell that is often referred to as a *hybrid tool*.

Today's frame-based tools share many common points with object-oriented programming. The advantage, however, that these tools have over the base language approach is that they enable the coding of knowledge in a natural symbolic language style versus the more rigid syntax of an object-oriented programming language. Though rule-based tools dominated the 1980s, frame-based ones are dramatically picking up steam during the 1990s. New vendors offering this tool type are entering the market, and ones who provided only rule-based tools are revamping their product to include frame-based methods. Due to the programming power of frame-based systems, this trend should continue.

3.4.   FUZZY LOGIC TOOLS

Fuzzy logic expert system tools represent knowledge in fuzzy rules and fuzzy sets. Fuzzy rules, like ones found in other rule-based systems, are if-then structures. However, they include statements that contain fuzzy variables with corresponding fuzzy values that are represented mathematically in a fuzzy set. It is the term "mathematically" that separates fuzzy logic tools from the symbolic rule-based ones. Processing of these rules relies upon a mathematical approach based in the principles of fuzzy logic.

A fuzzy logic tool is applicable for a problem that is described using vague or ambiguous terms, and where the expert relies on common sense to solve the problem. For example, the expert might state, "When the motor is running *really hot* I decrease the speed *a little*." Fuzzy logic has been used in such application areas as diagnosis and prescription, but it is in the area of control systems where it has really shined. Common sense control rules are usually easy to generate. Also, the fuzzy logic processing of the fuzzy rules and sets, given information about the operation of the system under control, can often produce control performance on the par of a human operator. In addition, fuzzy logic has particular value in control applications where it is difficult or impossible to mathematically model the system to be controlled, a step needed for the development of a traditional control system, such as a PID controller.

3.5.   INDUCTION TOOLS

Induction tools generate rules from examples. They are products of AI research in machine learning. A developer enters a large set of examples from the domain under consideration, where each example contains values for a set of domain features, and a single result characterizing the example. The induction tool then uses an algorithm, such as ID3, to generate a rule or a decision tree. In operation, a user enters information about a current problem and the system then determines the probable result.

An induction tool is an excellent choice if a large set of examples exist characterizing the problem. In addition, even if an expert does not exist who could provide the knowledge needed to develop the expert system, an induction tool can possibly *discover* the necessary knowledge. An extension on this last point shows another plus for this tool. Since the tool can be used without the need of an expert, one can avoid problems associated with knowledge acquisition. An induction expert system can be built relatively quickly, and is easy to maintain by adding/deleting examples or domain features.

3.6.   CASED-BASED REASONING TOOLS

Cased-based reasoning (CBR) tools are somewhat recent additions to the toolbox of the knowledge engineer. In practice, they serve a role similar to induction tools in that they use past experiences (cases) to solve current problems. Given an input specification of a problem, the system will search its case memory for an existing case that matches the input specification. It may find an exact match and immediately go to a solution. Even if an exact match can't be found, the system applies a matching algorithm in order to find a case that is most similar to the input specification.

A CBR tool shares many of the same benefits found in an induction tool, such as being a good choice if a large set of examples exist, and being applicable for a problem where no real expert exists. A case-based expert system can also be built quickly and easily maintained by adding new cases.

3.7.   DOMAIN-SPECIFIC TOOLS

The early shells were general-purpose tools and were offered to address a broad range of problem-solving activities. In many instances, however, it was found that though the tool was fine for one activity (e.g., diagnosis), it was inadequate for another one (e.g., design). To address this situation, the AI community, including both software vendors and researchers, turned their attention to developing domain-specific tools. A domain-specific tool is designed to be used to develop an expert system for a particular problem-solving activity. It provides special features to the developer that are tailored for producing an expert system for the activity. Table 1 shows the typical types of problems addressed by expert system developers (adapted from Hayes-Roth et al., 1983). The following sections describe some of the domain-specific tools developed for most of these activities. Some are commercially available while others were developed by organizations to satisfy their particular needs.

Control. ASIA assists with building real-time control expert systems (Devedzic and Velasevic, 1992). The system is capable of reasoning with external real-time data, using symbolic processing. It was developed at Mihailo Pupin Institute, Belgrade, Yugoslavia.

FAIN, Fast AI shell of Nippon Steel, was developed by Nippon Steel for the design of an expert system for a control application (Wakisaka et al., 1993). The expert system is developed by adding or revising the design specifications in a spiral-up manner. The design document specification suited for the prototyping method is specified and the program is automatically generated from the specification.

G2 is a graphical object-oriented environment for building intelligent process management solutions. Its natural language editor allows users to enter rules, models, and procedures that describe real-time operations. Also available are a number of add-on packages that run on top of G2, including scheduling systems, fuzzy logic, diagnostic packages, genetic algorithms, and neural networks. Typical applications built using G2 include process optimization, real-time quality management, supervisory control, and advanced control using fuzzy logic and neural network techniques. G2 is commercially available from Gensym, Cambridge, MA.

An intelligent control shell for CAD tools was developed that can automatically create a command sequence to control CAD systems using symbolic knowledge of general command flows and nonsymbolic knowledge of the past execution data (Fujita et al., 1994). Users define a model of possible control flows, which are transformed into a state transition graph from which executable

TABLE 1
Types of Problems Solved by Expert Systems

Problem-solving activity	Description
Control	Governing system behavior to meet specifications
Design	Configuring objects under constraint
Diagnosis	Inferring system malfunctions from observables
Instruction	Diagnosing, debugging, and repairing student behavior
Interpretation	Inferring situation description from data
Monitoring	Comparing observations to expectations
Planning	Selecting and sequencing activities according to a set of constraints to achieve a goal
Prediction	Inferring likely consequences of given situations
Prescription	Recommending solution to system malfunction
Scheduling	Assigning resources and times to the set of activities in a plan
Selection	Identifying best choice from a list of possibilities
Simulation	Modeling the interaction between system components

command sequences are inferred. The control system statistically analyzes nondeterministic branches, where a final result is predicted from a current state of a design object, a command history, and the succeeding commands. Then, the most promising command to optimize the design objects is selected and executed. It was developed at NEC Corp., Kanagawa, Japan.

A shell was developed for robotics and flexible manufacturing systems (FMS) applications (Devedzic and Krtolica, 1989). The shell is intended for building and testing knowledge-based systems in various robotics and FMS domains, like design, planning, control, scheduling, routing, diagnostics, etc. The shell can be used for building and testing knowledge-based systems for real-time operation, which is typical for robotics and FMS control tasks. The shell was developed at Mihailo Pupin Inst., Belgrade, Yugoslavia.

Design. DESIGNER assists in general design processes (MacCallum, 1982). A key characteristic in the design of engineering systems is complexity: a designer's task to specify the characteristics of a system, given a set of required functional objectives to be achieved in a given environment. The system works with basic concepts in the design process and applies them to a generic task in order to produce an acceptable design. The system was developed at the University of Strathclyde, Great Britain.

GOES, Graphics-Oriented Expert Shell, is a shell built inside a standard CAD environment (Langley et al., 1995). It is intended to associate logical engineering design procedures with graphical representations, and is particularly useful for managing and documenting large-scale control and automation design activities. GOES operates as an intelligent CASE tool, and eases the task of identifying, assembling, and parametrizing function block subroutines of distributed control systems. It was developed at CMS-CAD Inc., Montreal, Que., Canada.

SATURN is a constraint-system shell that provides knowledge integration and reasoning features suited to supporting concurrent engineering approaches to design (Fohn et al., 1994). SATURN is a logic-based constraint modeling system, tightly coupled with a relational database, and supported by a truth maintenance system. The system was developed at North Carolina State University, Raleigh, NC.

XpertRule Configurator assists in the development of a rule-based expert system for product design. It aids in building the rule-based system for correctly selecting and configuring product components. A user can generate a physical component hierarchy using a graphical configuration tree editor and rule sets associated with different configuration tasks. It is commercially available from Attar Software, Harvard, MA.

Diagnosis. D-IAL, Diagnosis Intelligent Automation Language, assists with the development of manufacturing facility maintenance expert systems (Hori et al., 1992). D-IAL uses the best first-search algorithm and has a plausible reasoning mechanism based on the Dempster-Shafer probability. This plausible reasoning mechanism propagates defect probability in a search tree to maintain the consistency of the defect probabilities. It is written in C so that diagnostic expert systems developed on the shell can operate on workstations and/or personal computers. The system was developed at Mitsubishi Electric Corp., Amagasaki, Japan.

EKO is an object-oriented shell for developing a diagnostic expert system (Ivashchenko et al., 1994). The shell, though providing general features, was developed for use in evaluating the state of hydraulic structures. It contains a database, programs that work with data arriving from sensors, facilities for storing data concerning the state of hydraulic structures, statistical data processing capability, and software for constructing and updating behavioral regression models. EKO has been used to design a computer-based system of diagnostic testing at the Charvak Hydraulic Engineering Center situated 70 km from Tashkent, Russia.

FMEAssit is an expert system development tool to aid in the design of model-based fault diagnosis systems for the Space Station (Carnes and Cutts, 1987). It assists engineers in the complex task of tracking failures and their effects on the system. It was developed using LISP Flavors by Boeing of Huntsville, AL.

HYDRA, Hybrid Reasoning and Knowledge Acquisition Workbench, assists in the development of diagnostic expert systems. It is based on a custom system developed for Daimler-Benz's Mercedes Benz passenger and utility vehicle service centers. HYDRA provides model-based, symptom-failure-oriented, and case-based diagnostic capabilities for diagnosing system failures. HYDRA is commercially available from Itanis International, Pittsburgh, PA.

IDEA is a model-based expert system development tool that assists technicians in identifying component failures in electro/mechanical devices (PC AI, 1990). IDEA employs a model-based reasoning strategy to build and deploy applications, based on the concept that if users know how a device works, as opposed to the way it fails, users can build a diagnostic application. It allows an organization to combine models, graphics, hypertext on-line documentation, linkage to management reporting systems, and traditional decision support into comprehensive diagnostic applications. It runs on IBM ATs and compatibles. The system is commercially available from AI Squared, Chelmsford, MA.

MARPLE is a model-based reasoning tool for producing intelligent diagnostics (Cowles et al., 1990). The system consists of a set of design tools to build application-specific models and rules, and a set of core procedures that run the model and isolate faults. MARPLE was used to implement an expert system for diagnosis of spacecraft power systems. It was developed on the Texas Instruments microExplorer by TRW.

MTK, Model ToolKit, is a model-based reasoning tool that was developed for the design of model-based expert systems (Erickson and Rudokas, 1987). MTK has particular value for building diagnostic expert systems, but can also be used for control applications where a model of the system under control can be defined. It was developed by NASA Ames Research Center and used in the design of TEXSYS, an expert system for controlling the operations of the Space Station's thermal control system. MTK runs on a Symbolics 3670 workstation.

PARAGON is an expert system development tool that interacts with the knowledge engineer to model a satellite (Golden, 1987). The developed system can be used for fault diagnosis using a model-based reasoning approach. PARAGON is generic in that it can be used for modeling other types of systems for fault diagnosis purposes. It was developed by Ford Aerospace of Sunnyvale, California.

PRODE, PROspective Diagnosis Expert, is a shell for building expert systems based on prospective diagnosis (Gini and Sassaroli, 1995). Two kinds of knowledge contribute to modeling the diagnostic process. Failure knowledge expresses cause-effect relations between faults as well as the relations between the result of tests and the "degree-of-belief" about the presence of a fault. Strategic knowledge contains criteria to guide the selection of the appropriate action. A criterion refers to a particular viewpoint (such as the cost of a test or the estimated occurrence of a fault) and its application orders or prunes the set of the actions to take with respect to this viewpoint. Prospective diagnosis evolves acquiring new data to increase the knowledge about the system while the strategic criteria guides in this choice. The inference engine proceeds, alternating data acquisition and focusing, until the most probable cause of the malfunction is found and a repair is executed. PRODE was developed at Politecnico di Milano, Milano, Italy.

TestBench is an environment for creating a diagnostic expert system. It provides four ways to represent knowledge: rules, decision trees, failure hierarchy, and case-based reasoning. The user creates the system using a graphical interface, which includes a tool palette. TestBench also offers a video display window, which can be used to show the user how to perform diagnostic procedures. It is commercially available from Carnegie Group, Pittsburgh, PA.

Instruction. A shell was developed for building intelligent tutoring systems to train medical students in diagnosing patient cases (Reinhardt and Schewe, 1995). The system uses case data and problem-solving knowledge to handle classification problems. The main method of the system is to present case data and to control the student's actions by comparing them to the underlying expert system. The shell was developed at Wurzburg University, Germany.

Interpretation. SSI is a shell for the development of signal interpretation expert systems (Arai et al., 1992). The shell is a product of the design of two expert systems for speech signal processing, where the analysis of the two systems revealed common functions and modules applicable to a wide range of signal interpretation problems. SSI was developed at Osaka University, Osaka, Japan.

Monitoring. PREMON, the Predictive Monitoring system, uses the explicit model of a device to perform real-time monitoring (Doyle et al., 1987). The system has been tested on the partial model of the mirror cooling circuit of the Jet Propulsion Laboratory space simulator. PREMON has three interacting capabilities: (1) causal simulation to generate predictions about the behavior of a physical system; (2) sensor planning to assess the importance of a device's behavior and allocate sensor resources appropriately; and (3) sensor interpretation to verify expected sensor values against actual sensor readings and raise alarms when necessary. The system was developed at NASA Ames Research Center.

RTie is designed specifically for developing real-time expert system applications. It can process several thousand rules per second, thus permitting it to analyze huge amounts of data from different sources. It has particular value in process monitoring applications. A form knowledge entry approach is used for creating rules, classes, and objects. It includes a temporal reasoning ability, where rules can be built to compare past data with current data, enabling trend and statistical processing. RTie is commercially available from Talarian, Mountain View, CA.

Planning. GHOST is a general-purpose planning system in the area of construction (Navin-chandra et al., 1988). It reasons about an object's attributes and relationships between objects to define project activities. GHOST starts with a high-level set of tasks and refines them into subnetworks of more detailed tasks. The system combines object-oriented programming with rule-sets, and employs a blackboard structure.

KBLPS, Knowledge-Based Logistics Planning Shell, assists in the design of an expert system for planning allocation and transportation resource applications. It includes planning algorithms for over-constrained distribution problems, and a decision-centered graphical user interface. In use, KBLPS provides planners with a "what-if" ability to see the impact on changed information on the expected results. Planners are able to cycle through scenarios, breaking resource allocations until the most feasible recommendation is developed. It is commercially available from Carnegie Group, Pittsburgh, PA.

OARPLAN is a general-purpose planning system. It generates project plans using facility object descriptions extracted from the CADD system AutoCad (Darwiche et al., 1989). The system uses an object-oriented product model that employs abstraction hierarchies to produce a plan for structuring the facility. It works within a BB1 blackboard environment.

PIPPA is a general-purpose planning system that has been used to develop plans for manufacturing flight simulators, for construction foundations, and for submitting tenders for furnace installations (Marshall et al., 1987). The system uses a hierarchy of objects and actions, and a set of demons to formulate plans at any level of detail. The system is implemented in RBFS.

SIPEC is a general-purpose planning shell for multiagent planning problems in the area of construction (Kartman and Levitt, 1990). The system uses knowledge based in first principles to derive relationships among activities to order them in the construction plan. SIPEC is integrated with a CADD system to obtain component descriptions.

Scheduling. ESRA is a shell for developing rule-based scheduling expert systems for solving resource allocation problems (Solotorevsky et al., 1994). The designer first describes the scheduling problem as a graph of a constraint satisfaction problem (CSP). The graph is then used to map the problem into a set of rules. ESRA was developed at Ben-Gurion University of the Negev, Beer-Sheva, Israel.

FLES, Fuzzy Logic Expert Scheduler, is an interactive shop floor scheduler that is designed to produce detailed schedules for day-to-day production management (Turksen et al., 1993). The system can produce scheduling assignments over short- or long-term scheduling horizons, or simulate different plant capacity conditions to analyze their effects on future work plans. FLES was developed using Turbo C++ at University of Toronto, Ontario, Canada.

OPTIMUM-AIV is a tool for developing expert systems for planning and scheduling of activities for spacecraft assembly, integration, and verification (AIV) (Arentoft et al., 1991). The system permits the user to form a customized plan to meet specific needs. It consists of a set of software functionalities for assistance in the initial specification of the AIV plan, in verification and generation of the plan, and schedules for the AIV activities. The system is implemented in LISP and was developed at the Computer Resources International, Denmark.

PARR is a C-Based shell designed for scheduling problems (McLean et al., 1991). It was used for scheduling services of the Tracking and Data Relay Satellite System for the Earth Radiation Budget Satellite and the Explorer Platform. The shell offers both frame and rule representation techniques and a blackboard structure. It was developed at the Bendix Field Engineering Corp.

PLANEX is a general purpose planning and scheduling system for the area of building construction (Zozaya-Gorostiza et al., 1989). It uses information on the components of the facility, coded in the industry standard numbering system MASTERFORMAT, to form project activities. The system was developed using KnowledgeCraft.

RPMS, the Resource Planning and Scheduling System, is a general scheduler designed to assist the user in minimizing resource consumption such as time, manpower, and materials (Lipiatt and Waterman, 1985). The system was applied to the space shuttle reconfiguration process for the Johnson Space Center. It was developed by Ford Aerospace.

SURE, Science User, Resource Expert, is a planning and scheduling tool that supports distributed planning and scheduling, based on resource allocation and optimization (Thalman and Sparn, 1990). SURE allows the user to plan instrument activities with respect to scientific goals while maximizing instrument activity with respect to available resources. It is a forward chaining rule-based system. The system was developed using the CLIPS/ADA expert system shell at the University of Colorado.

Simulation. ORBIS, Object-oriented Rule Base Interactive System, is an expert system simulation shell designed to be used in a variety of simulation environments (Evans and Sanders, 1994). These include stand-alone interactive simulations, batch runs for collecting Monte Carlo statistics, and real-time, man-in-the-loop simulations. An ORBIS simulation is composed of two parts, the shell and the application. The shell contains a Simulation Engine, Rule Editor, Dictionary Editor, Object Editor, and Setup Editor, which together provide the basic toolkit for assembling a simulation. The application contains objects, data, algorithms, and rule sets specific to the simulation which serve to generate the desired behavior of the simulation. An important feature of the ORBIS simulation development software is that an expert system, implemented as rule sets, controls simulated objects.

4.   CHOOSING A TOOL

With the large number of expert system development tools commercially available, it is often difficult to choose one for a given application. Fortunately, the subject has been a popular one in the published literature (Reichgelt and van Harmelen, 1986; Citrenbaum et al., 1987; Gevarter, 1987; Freedman, 1987; Press, 1989; Kim and Yoon, 1992; Chang et al., 1992; Rushinek, 1994; Plant and Salinas, 1994; Stylianou et al., 1995). In addition, and in the spirit of the technology as an aid to decision making, even expert systems have been developed to help the effort (Martin and Law, 1988; Daqing et al., 1994).

The next several sections discuss the major shell features to consider when making a selection. The discussion is framed after the expert system architecture shown in Figure 1. We also review the findings of a survey of expert system designers who were asked to rate the importance of various shell features.

4.1. KNOWLEDGE BASE

From a technical perspective, no other factor is more important when selecting a shell than its knowledge base coding facility. This facility defines how you can represent the knowledge (e.g., rules, frames, decision trees). It is also important, however, to consider other knowledge base utilities that may be available, such as inexact reasoning and procedural processing capabilities.

Knowledge representation. Shells for building knowledge-based systems can be classified according to the way they represent knowledge. The most popular categories are: rule-based, frame-based, case examples for induction or CBR, and fuzzy logic. Some shells offer multiple ways of representing knowledge. Before a shell is selected, a study of the problem will usually indicate which shell category is appropriate. This acts as the first major filter when selecting a shell, leaving on-balance only those shells within a selected category to consider further.

Inexact reasoning. One of the trademarks of expert system technology is the ability to solve problems involving uncertain or unknown information, and inexact knowledge. This requires that the expert system be equipped with some inexact reasoning mechanism, such as certainty factors (CF), the Shafer-Dempster method, and in rare occasions a Bayesian approach. Most of the small shells permit the use of CF values for encoding inexact rules and for entering inexact information. Some shells (ironically the larger ones) offer no inexact reasoning methods, and leave the task of developing a method in the hands of the designer — possibly a very difficult task.

Procedural processing capability. In some applications there is a need to write procedural code. Functions might be needed, or in a frame-based system, methods required to support message-passing. Most of the shells, with the exception of frame-based ones, provide limited procedural processing capability. Frame-based shells, particularly the larger ones, usually provide a rich environment for creating procedural code to support the knowledge processing activity.

4.2. INFERENCE AND CONTROL PROCESS

The inference and control mechanisms that a shell provides manipulate the knowledge in the knowledge base in prescribed ways. In theory, this is analogous to the reasoning process in humans. Smaller shells tend to offer limited processing ability, while the larger ones provide a great deal of flexibility to the designer. It is important to have the inference and control strategies available that best match the way the human expert solves the problem.

Chaining. In rule-based programming, backward and forward chaining are the two basic inference techniques used. Some shells offer one or both of these methods, and some even permit the switching between the two during a session to provide bidirectional inferencing. When selecting a chaining method, consider the problem-solving activity to be programmed. For example, backward chaining is a good choice for diagnostic and prescription problems, while forward chaining applies well to design and planning ones.

Agendas. Some shells permit you to define an agenda of activities for the expert system to perform. This agenda might be a series of goals that a backward chaining system is instructed to pursue in a predefined sequence, or, the shell may permit the agenda to be executed in an intelligent fashion, where certain tasks are performed conditionally based on the system's findings. For large applications, having an agenda capability is a big plus.

Meta-rules. A meta-rule describes how other knowledge should be used. It is usually used to direct the processing of the other knowledge into a new area on the basis of discovered information. Typically, the meta-rule begins the processing of a different set of context-related rules. In applications not suited for solely backward or forward chaining, consider the use of meta-rules.

Nonmonotonic reasoning. This type of reasoning allows for changes in the reasoning for changes in a given fact. It not only permits the retraction of the given fact, it also causes the retraction of all other facts that were dependent on the changed fact. This requires that the shell has an additional recording-keeping facility called a *truth maintenance system* (Dolye, 1979).

Nonmonotonic reasoning is valuable in planning, design, or scheduling applications, where newly discovered information would have an impact on the developing product.

4.3.   Explanation Facility

An explanation facility provides a transparency to the expert system's reasoning. This is of particular importance in interactive systems, where the user might want to know *why* a given question is being asked, or *how* the provided result was obtained. Consider, for example, a diagnostic system in the medical domain, where the system's result is a recommended drug to administer to a patient. During the course of the consultation, the user may want to know why certain information is needed, and at the end a rationalization on how the system arrived at the suggested drug. Since the recommended drug is a result of expert judgement, it is easy to see why a user may want to know how the system derived this recommendation before administering the drug.

For the user's needs, most shells provide very poor explanation facilities. Some provide none at all. Those that do, usually simply show the current rule being processed in response to a why query, and a tracing through the processed rules in response to a how query. In general, these types of "computerize" responses are inadequate and difficult for the user to follow. From the designer's perspective, these facilities can be valuable for debugging purposes. For example, if the system's final result is found to be wrong, a trace through the processed rules can often locate an incorrect rule.

4.4.   Developer Interface

The various shells offer different levels of capabilities for the expert system designer to develop and refine the system. The smaller tools usually provide limited development features, while the more sophisticated ones, though more difficult to learn, provide a wider choice of knowledge representation methods, inference techniques, and user interface design alternatives. Various levels of debugging methods are also provided. Some shells also provide extensive on-line help that can greatly assist in system development.

Knowledge base creation. There are two broad ways of creating a knowledge base. Some shells require you to type the entire knowledge base, much in the same way as using a word processor. One advantage with using this approach is that you can print and review the knowledge. Other shells provide an incremental approach, where individual pieces of knowledge are created and added to the knowledge base. To create a rule, for example, the designer might select from a menu a *create-rule* item and be presented with a rule-entry form to be filled out. The advantage of this approach is that the shell aids with system development. However, it can be difficult to determine the new rule's relationship with existing knowledge, unless the shell provides a good rule-browsing utility.

Debugging utilities. Debugging utilities allow the designer to check and debug the system. One of the more common and valuable utilities is *rule-tracing*. Following a session with the system, this utility provides a trace through all of the rules processed, including their processing order and information provided by the user. This trace can uncover problems in the knowledge base when errors occur during system testing. Another valuable utility found in some shells is *incremental compilation*, which allows the designer to compile the knowledge in an incremental fashion. This permits the designer to immediately see any problems with the new knowledge.

On-line help. Having a good manual that provides the instruction needed to build the expert system is obviously a valuable resource for the designer. Some shell vendors have gone a step further and provide system development help on-line. While developing the system, the designer can access this utility to obtain aid in the effort. This aid might simply be in the form of text that provides help on the requested item. In more advanced on-line help utilities, you can paste a template of a knowledge element (e.g., a function) directly into the system, then edit it as needed.

4.5. USER INTERFACE

One of the most critical design issues when developing an expert system, a lesson first learned by the developers of MYCIN, is the importance of accommodating the user by offering an easy-to-use interface, equipped to handle all of the user's requirements. It is, therefore, important to learn of the user's needs and desires before choosing a shell. Some general points to consider are offered in the following paragraphs.

Display type. The early expert systems all relied on a text-based display. Questions were posed to the user in text and answers were provided via keyboard typing or by selecting from a menu. Today, most shells provide a graphical-user-interface (GUI) that permits the user to interact through a point-and-click method. Since most computer users today are more accustomed to a GUI, and computer novices find the interaction more intuitive, a shell offering a GUI is usually preferable.

Information entry. There is a wide range of methods by which the user can enter information into the system. It may be as simple as typing an answer to some question, or as extensive as filling out an entire form. A question might be posed requiring a single answer, or one that permits the user to select multiple answers from a list. Graphical input displays typically available are radio buttons, check boxes, forms, scroll bars, and pushbuttons. Some shells provide limited default ways for entering information, while others permit the designer to choose from a variety of methods while creating the display from scratch.

Information display. The expert system must be able to display its findings to the user. This information might be the final conclusion, or intermediate findings discovered during the session. Typical ways of displaying information are message boxes, value boxes, radio buttons, check boxes, forms, and graphics.

Interface control. The user must always feel in control of the session. This includes an easy way of starting and ending a session, and readily accessible ways of activating needed control during the session. Some shells offer default methods for managing these tasks, while others require the designer to develop the techniques. For a graphical interface, this control is typically done with pushbuttons or a menu-select scheme. A user may also request other special features, such as *save-case* and *what-if*. The save-case feature permits the user to save the context of the present session, either for reporting requirements or for later what-if system testing. The what-if feature allows the user to change an answer to some question from a completed session, in order to see what impact the new answer might have on the final results.

4.6. SYSTEM INTERFACE

The early shells were limited to creating stand-alone expert systems, with no capability of interacting with other programs. Today, most shells offer an open architecture that permits the developed system to share information with external software such as databases, spreadsheets, and procedural programs like C and Fortran. Being able to embed an expert system within an established software environment greatly enhances its applicability and improves its portability between applications.

What software the expert system can interact with, and how this interaction is established, varies widely among the shells. The smaller shells usually have limited access abilities, often only to a certain database or a specific procedural program written in the same language used in the shell development. They may also require the designer to write the code to perform the interaction. The larger shells typically interact with far more programs, and in general, also make the task of establishing the interaction easier, often providing a library of functions to support the effort.

4.7. HARDWARE

The platform on which the expert system will be developed and, if different, where it will be run, is a major consideration when selecting a shell. Overall, the platforms can be divided into four general categories: personal computers, workstations, minicomputers, and mainframe computers.

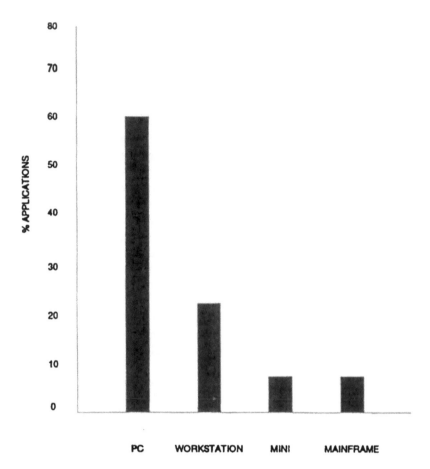

FIGURE 4   Platforms used in expert system development.

The majority of expert systems have been developed on a PC, as illustrated in Figure 4 (Durkin, 1993).

Some vendors offer shells that will run on only one of these platforms. You can expect to find that the smaller tools only run on a PC. The vendors of larger shells often provide versions that can run on different platforms, but charge more for versions that run on the larger ones. This not only provides versatility in selection and portability of the developed software, but also offers an advantage to a company looking to take a low-risk approach to the project. For instance, a cheaper version can be used to develop the expert system on a PC to assess the project's feasibility; then, following successful testing, the more expensive version can then be purchased and the developed system deployed on a larger platform.

4.8.   SUPPORT

Software support is one of those issues that is universally recognized as one of the most important factors when considering a purchase. The level of support can vary appreciably, and often separates a good purchase from a poor one. Points to consider are the provided documentation, example programs, training, and help-desk services.

Documentation. All shells come with a manual that instructs you on how to use the program. Some even provide separate user and reference manuals, which can be helpful. One thing to look for is a manual that has a good index that can lead you to the appropriate section for needed information. A few vendors provide a tutorial that takes you by-the-hand through the process of developing a small system. If done well, this tutorial can quickly get you up-and-running on the software. One point to look for is a tutorial that gradually takes you through the steps of developing a working system, where each step introduces a different feature of the product.

Example programs. Most vendors provide example expert systems that you can review to learn about software coding and to gain insight into how to develop a system. Unfortunately, the number and value of these examples vary considerably. Look for vendors who provide many small examples, where each example demonstrates a different side of the product.

Training. Some vendors provide training for their software. In general, however, it is the vendors of the larger and more expensive tools that provide this service. This training might be offered at the vendor's site, periodically given at geographically selected sites, or in special cases at the buyer's site. For some of the more popular tools, third-party companies offer training on the software.

Help-desk services. Even with the best documentation, you can expect to run into problems where help is needed with the software. To accommodate their clients, some vendors provide a help-desk phone number where, in theory, you can get help. Some of the vendors offer this service free of charge, while others require you to purchase a service contract. If you are lucky, the vendor will provide a toll-free number. If not, you might easily run into a situation where you are put on hold, and are left to mentally calculate your next phone bill as you are entertained by a recording of Barry Manilow.

4.9. Cost

Shell prices range from under $100 to over $50,000. For the most part, you can expect to get more power for more bucks. However, this is not a golden rule and you need to be an educated buyer. As mentioned in the hardware section, you can also expect to spend considerably more for a shell to be run on a large platform such as a mainframe, than for one that runs on a PC. Consider first the technical features of the shell, as previously discussed, to make sure the shell meets your needs. This will filter out many of the tools, leaving a smaller selection. Even here, however, you could be faced with shells having a wide price range. At this point, consider two other factors: licensing and distribution costs.

Licensing costs. Following the shell purchase, you assume a legal responsibility to use the software according to the vendor's licensing agreement. This is the same situation following the purchase of other types of software. Typically, this agreement prohibits the copying of the software and requires that it be used on only one computer. In the event the shell will need to be used on several computers at the same site, purchasing a site license may be the way to go.

Distribution costs. When the shell is used to develop an expert system to be used on other computers, you may need to consider possible distribution costs. Some expert systems can only be run using the original shell. Others can run using a "runtime" version of the shell, which permits the user to run but not modify the system. Some shells provide the ability to produce an executed form of the expert system. Naturally, if you plan to develop an expert system to be sold or used by various parties within your organization, you need to know how the system can be distributed and any distribution costs.

4.10. Ask the Buyers

The prior sections discussed some of the more important features to consider when choosing a shell. How important a specific feature is to a given application is also a point of consideration. One way to determine this is to ask expert system developers.

A survey of close to 300 developers was conducted, where each was given a list of shell features and asked to judge the importance of each feature based on a five-point scale, with 5 representing critical and 1 not important (Stylianou et al., 1995). The questionnaire also asked each developer

TABLE 2
Survey Results of Importance of Shell Features

	Control	Design	Diagnosis	Monitoring	Planning	Prescription
Knowledge base						
Rules	4.0	4.1	3.7	2.6	4.0	4.3
Rule sets	4.2	3.9	3.4	3.0	3.8	3.7
Frames	3.3	3.8	2.9	3.1	3.7	2.5
Induction	3.0	3.1	2.6	2.9	2.5	2.5
Inexact reasoning	3.0	3.6	3.0	2.2	2.8	3.0
Math processing	2.9	4.0	3.1	3.7	3.4	2.9
Inference						
Forward chaining	3.6	4.0	3.9	4.1	4.0	3.6
Backward chaining	4.1	4.0	4.0	3.6	3.8	4.2
Bidirectional chaining	3.3	3.9	3.2	3.5	3.8	3.1
Nonmonotonic reasoning	3.3	3.7	3.0	3.9	3.6	3.0
Explanation facility						
Why and how	3.5	3.9	4.0	3.9	4.3	4.3
Developer interface						
Tracing	3.9	4.0	3.8	4.0	4.2	4.0
Incremental compilation	2.7	3.2	2.8	3.4	3.2	3.1
Knowledge browsing	3.7	3.5	3.2	3.4	3.7	3.5
Customize user interface	3.4	3.8	4.2	3.6	4.0	4.4
Open architecture	3.3	3.4	3.5	3.2	3.7	3.5
User interface						
Saved cases	3.1	3.5	3.3	3.9	3.0	3.5
GUI	2.7	3.5	2.8	3.2	2.8	2.6
System interface						
Database link	3.5	4.3	3.9	4.0	4.0	4.0
Software link	2.5	4.3	3.8	3.6	3.2	3.1
Portability	3.5	4.1	3.7	3.8	3.9	3.9
Embeddability	3.8	4.1	3.9	4.0	4.3	3.6
Support						
Documentation	3.8	4.0	4.0	3.7	4.1	4.1
Example programs	3.0	3.5	3.2	3.5	3.3	3.5
Help desk	2.8	3.7	3.4	3.5	3.5	4.0

to consider a specific problem-solving paradigm for which they have expert system design experience when evaluating shell features. Table 2 shows an adaption of part of the results from this survey. Several observations are notable.

Historically, most developed expert systems have been rule-based. According to the survey, rules continue to be the knowledge representation technique of choice. Though most shells offer a poor explanation facility, designers feel that this is an important feature to consider. Rule-tracing appears to be the most popular debugging tool. Being able to embed the developed system into an existing software environment and have the system exchange information with that software, particularly with a database, is favored.

5. THE TOOL MARKET

Up to the mid-1980s, sales of expert system development software were made primarily to universities, the U.S. military, and a few research groups within major companies. Users of this software

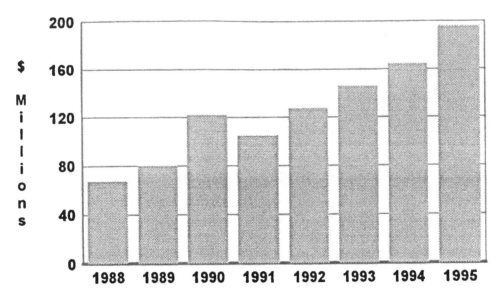

FIGURE 5   Sales of expert system development tools per year.

were principally researchers who were exploring the potential of the technology. Being used mainly for experimental reasons, rather than focused on solving practical commercial problems, the number of tool sales during this period was modest. This situation changed dramatically in the late 1980s as the commercial value of a deployed expert system was realized.

Figure 5 shows total sales figures for expert system tools during recent years, as reported in the monthly newsletter *Intelligent Software Strategies*, one of the best publications for monitoring the state of the field (Harmon, 1993; 1994; Hall, 1996). These sales figures include tool sales, upgrades, maintenance, and runtime licensing. All sales are for worldwide sales of commercial intelligent software development tools for North American vendors. The figure shows that total sales have grown at an average of approximately 17% per year since 1988. According to personal correspondence from Timothy Biebelhausen, associate vice president for investments at Kemper Securities, many economists argue that a healthy growth rate for any industry is around 10% per year. Clearly, the expert system tool vendors have had a good run.

One event worthy of note is the dip in sales between 1990 and 1991. It was during this period that many critics were pointing to the decline of tools sales as an indicator of a field that had fallen out of favor. Some concerned tool vendors even began to drop the AI label from their products, while maintaining the same product features. As Figure 5 shows, sales have rebounded quite well. Vendors now do not hesitate to advertise their products as containing AI capability. In fact, they often use it to their advantage to distinguish their product from competitors who market products without this capability.

Figure 6 shows total sales of LISP tools (Harmon, 1993; Hall, 1996). Sales of LISP tools had a dramatic drop in 1991 but have maintained a relatively constant level over the past several years. When compared with Figure 5, it is clear that the LISP market is relatively small. However, LISP offers symbolic processing capability that cannot be found in other languages. It should, therefore, continue to remain popular among many expert system developers, particularly in AI research activities.

Figure 7 shows sales of domain-specific tools, which shows a substantial growth in this tool category (Harmon, 1993; Hall, 1996). Representing only 4% of total tool sales in 1988, these tools rose to capture 39% of the market in 1995 — a tenfold increase. This is dramatic evidence of the evolution of the vendor market, with vendors moving from providing general-purpose tools to ones tailored to the specific needs of their customers. This trend is very likely to continue.

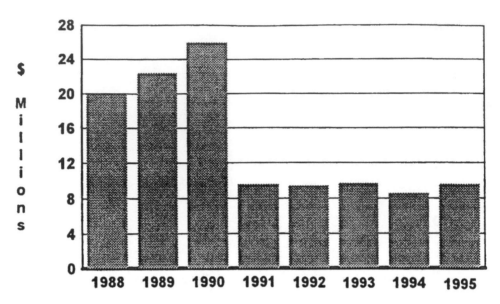

FIGURE 6   Sales of LISP tools per year.

Figures 8 through 10 show, respectively, tool sales for the PC and Mac, workstation, and mainframe. Recognize that, in general, the larger the platform the larger the tool cost. Therefore, these figures don't show how many tools are sold for each platform, only their total sales. Sales of PC and Mac tools showed a dramatic decrease coming out of the 1980s. Since then, sales have shown a small but steady increase. As these small platforms continue to become more powerful, this category of tool sales should show modest but sustained growth. Interesting, though, from a perspective of the technology, the decrease in small platform sales when entering the 1990s is a positive sign. Most organizations purchasing a small platform tool are looking to *test-the-water*, that is, can this technology help us? They will often take this initial step before committing to the purchase of a more costly tool that will run on a larger platform. Given the many success stories

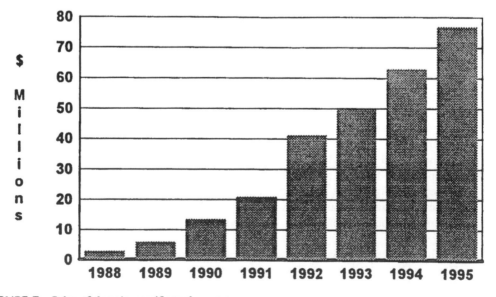

FIGURE 7   Sales of domain-specific tools per year.

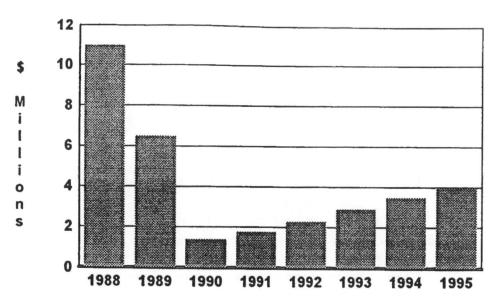

FIGURE 8   Sales of PC and Mac tools per year.

of expert system applications, many organizations are now confident in the technology and are shifting to larger platform tools.

Tools sold for workstations offer more features than ones that run on a smaller platform, such as a PC. They are designed to run in Unix, OS/2, or Windows NT environments. They are chosen for applications that require higher speed and integration needs, and are better suited for client-server development. As Figure 9 shows, sales of workstation tools have increased each year. This trend should continue.

Purchasers of mainframe tools are usually large organizations who presently have a large traditional application, such as a database management system found in a financial or insurance organization, who are looking to the technology for improving the use of the application. In general,

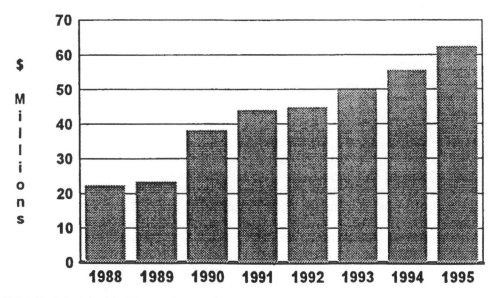

FIGURE 9   Sales of workstation tools per year.

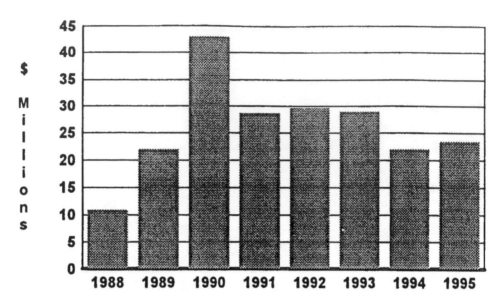

FIGURE 10   Sales of mainframe tools per year.

these types of organizations are conservative by nature and move slowly to adopt a new technology. As seen in Figure 10, there was a large decrease in mainframe sales between 1990 and 1991. This is the same period when it became popular to criticize the technology. Being conservative, these organizations began to back away. Recently, mainframe sales have increased and should continue as the commercial benefit of the technology is further realized.

Sales of CBR tools have shown a dramatic increase in recent years. From approximately $6 million in 1993, sales increased by a factor of over three to around $20 million in 1995 (Hall, 1996).

6.   THE FUTURE

During the past 2 decades, the field of expert systems has come far. From a technology confined to research circles in the early years, we find it today being used commercially to aid human decision making in a wide range of application areas. Supporting this transition has been the availability of expert system development tools that permitted a large audience to participate in this emerging field. The expert system tool market should continue to play a major role in future developments in the field. The following is a discussion on what might be expected in several areas.

6.1.   TOOL MARKET

The expert system tool market should show sustained growth in the future. Total sales have grown approximately 17% per year since 1988. This trend should continue. Vendors should continue their strategy to market tools that offer the ability of developing different types of expert systems, such as rule-based, frame-based, and fuzzy logic systems. Developers will then have in one package a set of AI tools to attack a given problem. New types of tools will also enter the market. Vendors in the past have been quick to react to promising new AI techniques. We have seen this recently, for example, with the introduction of CBR and data-mining tools. This is good business strategy. As new AI developments emerge from the laboratory demonstrating potential commercial value, we should see vendors marketing new tools wrapped around the new developments.

6.2. INTEGRATION

The early expert systems were stand-alone systems that were not linked to other conventional software programs or other computer systems. Some of the most valuable applications today are ones where an expert system works hand-in-hand with established software, such as a database management system (DBMS). Most tools today permit the development of an expert system that is relatively easy to integrate with conventional software environments. This trend will no doubt continue as the technology is no longer viewed as a research curiosity, but rather a powerful tool for solving practical real-world problems. The increased interest in the use of an expert system in a support role, such as *intelligent agent* in a large established software application, will also add to this trend.

6.3. DOMAIN-SPECIFIC TOOLS

Expert system tool vendors have been very responsive to the needs of the buyers of their tools. Early on, the typical buyer was looking to "test the water," exploring the potential of the technology. To accommodate this buyer, vendors offered general-purpose tools that could be used for a wide range of applications. Today, buyers are looking for tools that aid in the development of an expert system for a specific activity, such as process control, manufacturing scheduling, and so on. Responding to this need, vendors have begun to market domain-specific tools. Sales of these tools presently dominate the market and should show substantial growth in the future.

6.4. AUTOMATED KNOWLEDGE ACQUISITION

The majority of time spent when developing an expert system is with the knowledge acquisition task. Decreasing this time would significantly decrease development costs. One way to accomplish this is through software tools that would support knowledge acquisition activities. One promising area is self-learning systems. We have already discussed induction systems and their ability to uncover decision-making knowledge from a large set of examples. Another type of self-learning system would attempt to discover knowledge from database information (subject of Section XX). Because of the high costs of knowledge acquisition and the potential value offered by automated knowledge acquisition tools, we should see more of these types of tools available in the future.

6.5. KNOWLEDGE DISCOVERY IN DATABASES

One of the more exciting and potentially valuable AI applications on the horizon is knowledge discovery in databases (KDD). Given a database containing a large amount of data, KDD attempts to discover useful knowledge from the data. In the business arena, for example, the discovered knowledge could be potentially useful in such applications as assisting in financial investment advising, aiding fraud detection in financial transactions, and predicting marketing trends for a given product line. KDD is a multistep process, with *data mining* being one of the steps that extracts patterns from the data that are later used for knowledge discovery. Data mining tools have been a recent introduction into the market, and it shouldn't be long before vendors begin to offer KDD tools. For an excellent review of KDD, see Fayyad et al. (1996).

6.6. WORLD WIDE WEB

One very specialized area where we should see expert system applications in the future is in the areas of the internet and the World Wide Web (WWW). The WWW is growing exponentially, and so is the quantity of information that resides there. Even with the presently available search engines, intelligently navigating the WWW is a non-trivial task. Within seconds, these engines provide a list of sites where you can obtain information on the search subject. That's the good news. The bad news is that all too often there is either too much information to digest or irrelevant information. Infoseek's CEO Robin Johnson comments, "The best search engine is the one between your ears," — a target familiar to expert system developers.

The meteoric rise in the interest in the internet, coupled with the need for intelligent information retrieval, will serve as a magnet to expert system developers. Several expert system vendors, recognizing the potential of this emerging market, have already begun to offer internet-related products. Some of these have products that enable the WWW to serve as a front-end to server-based expert systems. They include Exsys, Neuron Data, Talarian, Inference, and Gensym. Level5 Research offers Level5 Quest, a fuzzy search and retrieval tool, which can be used for searching internet database applications by WWW browsers. We should see considerable AI activity in this area in the future, and tool vendors should be there quickly to support the effort.

REFERENCES

Aikens, J.S., J.C. Kunz, and E.H. Shortliffe, PUFF: an expert system for interpretation of pulmonary function data, *Computers and Biomedical Research*, Vol. 16, pp. 199–208, 1983.

Arentoft, M., et al., OPTIMUM-AIV: a planning and scheduling system for spacecraft AIV, 1991 Goddard Conference on Space Applications of Artificial Intelligence, NASA Publication 3110, pp. 3–13, May 13–15, 1991.

Arai, K., Y. Yamashita, and R. Mizoguchi, Shell for signal interpretation expert systems, *Expert Systems with Applications*, Vol. 5, No. 3–4, pp. 219–232, 1992.

Carnes, J. and D. Cutts, FMEAssist: a knowledge-based approach to failure modes and effects analysis, *Third Conference on Artificial Intelligence for Space Applications*, Part 1, NASA Conference Publication 2492, pp. 187–191, Nov. 2–3, 1987.

Chang, G., C. Chin, and N. Kartam, Selection of expert system shells for traffic signal design, *Journal of Advanced Transportation*, Vol. 26, No. 3, pp. 241–273, Winter 1992.

Citrenbaum, R., J.R. Geissman, and R. Schultz, Selecting a shell, *AI Expert*, pp. 30–39, Sept. 1987.

Cowles, S., L. Fesq, A. Stephan, and E. Wild, Expert systems: a new approach to spacecraft autonomy, *TRW Space & Defense Quest*, pp. 33–49, Summer 1990.

Daqing, H., M. McLeish, and A. Zhi, A decision support system for expert system shell evaluation and selection, *Proceedings of Moving Towards Expert Systems Globally in the 21st Century*, Lisbon/Estoril, Portugal, Publisher: Cognizant Commun. Corp., Elmsford, NY, pp. 768–74, Jan. 10–14, 1994.

Darwiche, A., R. Levitt, and B. Hayes-Roth, OARPLAN: generating project plans by reasoning about objects, actions and resources, *Artificial Intelligence for Engineering Design, Analysis and Manufacturing*, Vol. 2, No. 3, 1989.

Devedzic, V. and R. Krtolica, Development of an expert system shell for robotics and FMS applications, *Proceedings of the IASTED International Symposium. Expert Systems Theory and Applications*, Zurich, Switzerland, pp. 205–7, June 26–28, 1989.

Devedzic, V. and D. Velasevic, Implementing a real-time expert system shell, *ICARCV '92, Second International Conference on Automation, Robotics and Computer Vision*, Nanyang Technol. Univ., Singapore, IEE, Inst. Meas. & Control, Econom., Vol. 3, pp. 1–5, Sept. 16–18, 1992.

Doyle, R.J., A truth maintenance system, *Artificial Intelligence*, Vol. 12, 1979.

Doyle, R.J., S.M. Sellers, and D.J. Atkinson, Predictive monitoring based on causal simulation, *Proceedings of the Second Annual Research Forum*, Moffett Field, CA: NASA Ames Research Center, pp. 44–59, 1987.

Durkin, J., *Expert Systems: Catalog of Applications*, Intelligent Computer Systems, P.O. Box 4117, Akron, OH 44321-0117, 1993.

Erickson, W. and M. Rudokas, MTK: an AI tool for model-based reasoning, *Third Conference on Artificial Intelligence for Space Applications, Part 2*, NASA Conference Publication 2492, pp. 1–5, Nov. 2–3, 1987.

Evans, R.B. and R.D. Sanders, ORBIS-a tool for simulation development, *Proceedings of the 1994 Summer Computer Simulation Conference*, 26th Annual Summer Computer Simulation Conference, SCS, San Diego, CA, pp. 501–6, July 18–20, 1994.

Fayyad, U, G. Piatesky-Shapiro, and P. Smyth, From data mining to knowledge discovery in databases, *AI Magazine*, Vol. 17, No. 3, pp. 37–54, Fall, 1996.

Fohn, S.M., A.R. Greef, R.E. Young, and P.J. O'Grady, A constraint-system shell to support concurrent engineering approaches to design, *Artificial Intelligence in Engineering*, Vol. 9, Iss. 1, pp. 1–17, 1994.

Forgy, C., The OPS languages: an historical overview, *PC AI*, Vol. 9, No. 5, pp. 16–21, Sept./Oct., 1995.

Freedman, R., 27-product wrap-up: evaluating shells, *AI Expert*, pp. 69–74, Sept., 1987.

Fujita, S., M. Otsubo, and M. Watanabe, Intelligent control shell for CAD tools, *Proceedings of the 10th Conference on Artificial Intelligence for Applications*, San Antonio, TX, IEEE Technical Committee on Pattern Analysis and Machine Intelligence, pp. 16–22, 1994.

Gevarter, W.B., The nature and evaluation of commercial expert system building tools, *IEEE Computer*, pp. 24–41, May, 1987.

Gini, G. and P. Sassaroli, PRODE: a shell for industrial diagnosis, *Expert Systems with Applications*, Vol. 8, No. 1, pp. 67–76, Jan.–Mar., 1995.

Golden, C.J., Automating satellite control and telemetry networks, *Proc. Intern. Telemetering Conf.*, San Diego, CA, pp. 503–508, Oct. 26–29, 1987.

Hall, C., The intelligent software development tools market — part 1, *Intelligent Software Strategies*, Vol. 12, No. 2, pp. 1–12, 1996. Cutter Information Corp., 37 Broadway, Ste. 1, Arlington, MA 02174-5500.

Harmon, P. and B. Sawyer, *Creating Expert Systems for Business and Industry*, John Wiley, New York, NY, 1990.

Harmon, P., The market for expert systems building tools, *Intelligent Software Strategies*, Vol. 9, No. 2, pp. 3–13, 1993. See reference (Hall, 1996) for the publisher's address.

Harmon, P., The size of the commercial AI market, *Intelligent Software Strategies*, Vol. 10, No. 1, pp. 1–6, 1994. See reference (Hall 1996) for the publisher's address.

Hayes-Roth, F., D. Waterman, and D. Lenat, *Building Expert Systems*, Addison-Wesley, Reading, MA, 1984.

Hori, S., K. Ide, Y. Nakayama, and K. Otsubo, D-IAL: a diagnostic expert shell with plausible reasoning mechanism, *Systems and Computers in Japan*, Vol. 23, No. 11, pp. 1565–1573, 1992.

Ivashchenko, K.I., B.S. Kirsanov, and E.V. Popov, An expert domain-specific shell for the computer-aided evaluation of the state of hydraulic structures, *Journal of Computer and Systems Sciences International*, Vol. 32, Iss. 3, pp. 148–54, May–June, 1994,

Kartman, N. and R. Levitt, Intelligent planning of construction projects with repeated cycles of operation, *ASCE Jour. of Computing in Civil Engineering*, Vol. 4, 1990.

Kim, C.S. and Y. Yoon, Selection of a good expert system shell for instructional purposes in business, *Corrosion Science*, Vol. 33, No. 12, pp. 249, Dec., 1992.

Langley, W., M.B. Zaremba, and I. Popescu, Graphics-oriented expert shell for the design and configuration of distributed control systems, *Control Engineering Practice*, Vol. 3, Iss. 4, pp. 555–9, April, 1995.

Lipiatt, T.F. and D. Waterman, Potential applications of expert systems and operations research to space station logistics functions, NASA Report CR-180473, June, 1985.

MacCallum K.J., A knowledge base for engineering design relationships, in Proceedings of British Computer Society Expert Systems Group Technical Conference the Theory and Practice of Knowledge Based Systems, Brunel University, pp. 65–66, September, 1982.

Marshall, G., T. Barber, and J. Boardman, A methodology for modelling a project management control environment, *IEEE Proc.*, Vol. 134, 1987.

Martin, A. and R.K. Law, Expert system for selecting expert system shells, *Information and Software Technology*, Vol. 30, No. 10, pp. 579–586, Dec., 1988.

McLean, D., A. Tuchman, and W. Potter, Using C to build a satellite scheduling expert system: examples from the explorer platform planning system, *1991 Goddard Conference on Space Applications of Artificial Intelligence*, NASA Publication 3110, pp. 59–69, May 13–15, 1991.

Navinchandra, D., D. Sriram, and R. Logcher, GHOST: a project network generator, *ASCE Jour. of Computing in Civil Engineering*, Vol. 2, No. 3, 1988.

PC AI, *Product Update*, Vol. 4, No. 3, pp. 10, May/June, 1990.

Plant, R.T. and J.P. Salinas, Expert systems shell benchmarks: the missing comparison factor, *Information and Management*, (Netherlands), Vol. 27, Iss. 2, pp. 89–101, Aug., 1994.

Press, L., Expert system benchmarks, *IEEE Expert*, pp. 37–44, 1989.

Reichgelt, H. and F. van Harmelen, Criteria for choosing representation languages and control regimes for expert systems, *The Knowledge Engineering Review*, Vol. 1, No. 4, 1986.

Reinhardt, B. and S. Schewe, A shell for intelligent tutoring systems, Artificial Intelligence in Education, 1995, *Proceedings of AI-ED 95 — 7th World Conference on Artificial Intelligence in Education*, Assoc. Advancement of Comput. Edu., Washington, D.C., pp. 83–90, 1995.

Rushinek, A., Expert system shells (ES) case study: a product evaluation and selection system (PESS) for microcomputer users, vendors and consultants need assessment, *Economic Computation and Economic Cybernetics Studies and Research*, Vol. 28, Iss. 1–4, pp. 53–63, 1994.

Shortliffe, E.H., *Computer-Based Medical Consultation*, MYCIN, American Elsevier, New York, 1976.

Solotorevsky, G., E. Gudes, and A. Meisels, CSP and rule-based approaches for solving a real-life scheduling problem, *Proc. Moving Towards Expert Systems Globally in the 21st Century*, Lisbon/Estoril, Portugal, pp. 298–305, Jan. 10–14, 1994.

Stylianou, A.C., R.D. Smith, and G.R. Madey, An empirical model for the evaluation and selection of expert system shells, *Expert Systems With Applications*, Vol. 8, No. 1, pp. 143–155, 1995.

Thalman, N. and T. Sparn, SURE: A science planning scheduling assistant for a resource based environment, *Goddard Conference on Space Applications of Artificial Intelligence*, NASA Publication 3068, pp. 75–93, May 1–2, 1990.

Turksen, I.B., T. Yurtsever, and K. Demirli, Fuzzy expert system shell for scheduling, *Proceedings of the SPIE — The International Society for Optical Engineering*, Boston, MA, Vol. 2061, pp. 308–19, Sept. 8–10, 1993.

van Melle, W., A domain-independent production-rule system for consultation programs, *Proceedings IJCAI-79*, pp. 923–925, 1979.

Wakisaka, S., H. Nakashima, N. Sumida, and Y. Tetsu, Development of expert system building-tool for real-time control system — FAIN, Nippon Steel Technical Report No. 57, pp. 79–85, Apr., 1993.

Zozaya-Gorostiza, C., C. Hendrickson, and D. Rehak, *Knowledge-Based Process Planning for Construction and Manufacturing*, Academic Press, Boston, MA, 1989.

5 Foundation and Application of Expert System Verification and Validation

Anca I. Vermesan

CONTENTS

0-8493-3106-4/98/$0.00+$.50
© 1998 by CRC Press LLC

1.   INTRODUCTION

In the current practice of producing expert systems, much effort is expended in attempting to assure that the finished system does what it is supposed to do. The spectrum of effort is quite broad: debugging and testing, symbolic execution, proofs of specification's properties, as well as systematic techniques forming parts of well-defined methodologies for expert system construction. Recently, verification and validation (V&V) of expert systems has emerged as a distinct research field.

Many examples in the literature show the need for building reliable and dependable expert systems. As these systems become more and more complex, new and efficient techniques are needed to cope with their complexity.

The purpose of this chapter is to highlight the main issues associated with the V&V of expert systems and to describe practical solutions to the problems of expert system V & V. These issues first include discussion of the terminology used and a comparison between verification and validation as found in traditional software engineering and V&V of expert systems, pointing out what is special about the latter as compared with the former. The core of this chapter will then proceed as follows: we first define the theoretical foundation of expert system verification and validation, focusing on two principal methods for knowledge representation, i.e., production rules and object representation. Then, the characteristics of expert systems that pose special problems for V&V are discussed, along with techniques and methods currently used to overcome these problems. We proceed with descriptions of several verification and validation systems, followed by industrial requirements related to V&V. Finally, we point out some current and future research initiatives and provide a summary discussion.

1.1.   HISTORICAL OVERVIEW AND TERMINOLOGY

The rapid prototyping approach has been dominant in the area of expert systems for many years. Such systems employ "surface knowledge," consisting of "rules of thumb" that human experts commonly employ. The rules are highly specific to their particular domains, and are often expressed in the form of "if-then" production rules. As a consequence, the earliest techniques for V&V of expert systems were entirely empirical, i.e., adaptations of the Turing test.

A common characteristic of the early V&V methods is that they were mainly product oriented, i.e., the focus is the interface, or inference engine, or the knowledge base itself. When it comes to the V&V of knowledge bases, later work emphasized the verification of more formal properties, such as consistency and redundancy.

However, the systems constructed using the rapid prototyping approach have not in general had the expected success. This has led to more sophisticated methodologies for expert system construction. As a consequence, the focus of V&V has moved from the product to the validation of the process. In other words, the methods deal now with issues such as modeling and design.

An important step in the evolution of expert systems has been the identification of a level of discourse above the programming level, i.e., the "knowledge level," which is due to Newell. The adoption of a knowledge-level perspective focuses the analysis of expertise on issues such as identifying the abstract task features, what knowledge the task requires, and what kind of model the expert makes of the domain. The identification of the knowledge level in expert systems has facilitated the distinction between *deep* and *surface knowledge*. The distinction focuses not on the pattern of inference, but on the domain models which underly the expertise. Deep knowledge makes explicit the models of the domain and the inference calculus that operates on these models. Deep knowledge is that which includes a model of a particular world — principles, axioms, laws — that can be used to make inferences and deductions beyond those possible with rules. As a consequence, a large part of the work on V&V has been oriented toward the models underlying the domains and the transition between them.

The deep knowledge movement in knowledge engineering (KE) can be compared with a similar movement in software engineering (SE). In the early days of conventional software development, assembly or low-level languages were used in order to obtain efficient execution. Only later, were the advantages of high-level and both informal and formal languages taken into consideration. It is on the abstract representations that the arguments for correctness, completeness, and consistency are considered. A similar development in techniques has been observed in KE through the use of domain models. KE is more and more seen as the incremental discovery and creation of a model for the domain of interest.

The symbol/knowledge level distinction has been approached from the perspective of V&V by Vermesan and Bench-Capon, (1995). A further differentiation at the knowledge level is made, as the validity of a system depends on the validity of the underlying model, whether it is *incompletely* (or non-existent), *implicitly*, or *explicitly* defined. The three levels are defined as follows:

- *Symbol level*, which represents the executable representation of the knowledge
- *Knowledge level with implicit model*, often in the head of the expert
- *Knowledge level with explicit model*, initially independent of any implementation and not necessarily executable

This classification proved useful for surveying V&V of expert systems, as presented by Vermesan and Bench-Capon (1995), mainly because it answers the question: What is one verifying and validating against? At the symbol level, one mainly *checks* (i.e., one is not verifying and validating against something but rather is looking for internal coherence). At the knowledge level with implicit model, one mainly *validates* the system behavior against the human expert or/and other sources of knowledge. Finally, at the knowledge level with explicit model, one *verifies* the executable knowledge base against the model itself.

This raises the issue of defining the terminology in V & V; that is, what are the definitions for V&V? As verification and validation of expert systems is still a maturing field, a consensus among different definitions does not exist yet. SE defines validation as the process that ensures system compliance with software requirements, while verification ensures system compliance with the requirements established during the previous level of specification. Adopting these definitions to expert systems is not straightforward. Therefore, almost every application has developed and defined its own terminology, although to a great extent they converge toward a common meaning:

- *Verification* checks the well-defined properties of an expert system against its specification. Depending on the kind of properties, verification can focus on the knowledge base, the inference engine, or the user interface. Further distinctions can be made: verification of I/O behavior, verification of the path followed to achieve a given deduction, etc.
- *Validation* checks whether an expert system corresponds to the system it is supposed to represent. Like verification, validation can focus on the same particular system aspects.

Verification and validation terminology is extended with the terms *testing* and *evaluation:*

- *Testing* is the examination of the behavior of a program by executing the program on sample data sets.

- *Evaluation* focuses on the accuracy of the system's embedded knowledge and advice. It helps to determine the system's attributes, such as usefulness, intelligibility, credibility of results, etc.

Relevant material on testing can be found in (Miller, 1990), while for the evaluation aspect, a relevant discussion can be found in (Liebowitz, 1986).

1.2.   V&V in Conventional Software and V&V of Expert Systems

A major question within KE is how to benefit from a closer cooperation with SE. This problem is of particular interest in the area of V&V because notions such as dependability, reliability, and safety, as found in SE, are also relevant in KE.

Software engineering is an established discipline that has accumulated valuable experience over a long period of time. Verification and validation are terms that have been used for several years in SE. There are now many verification and validation techniques, plus considerable experience and expertise in using them. The potential usefulness of SE specification and V&V techniques has also been discussed in some studies, some going as far as to claim that expert systems are only computer programs and so conventional techniques can straightforwardly be applied to them. However, it is generally agreed that V&V techniques for conventional software can be directly applied to three of the four components of expert systems. Those three components are the inference engine, external interfaces, and tools or utilities. The fourth component is the knowledge base (KB), for which new V&V techniques must be developed. Indeed, it is on the V&V of the KB that work in V&V of expert systems has concentrated (Vermesan and Bench-Capon, 1995).

This section attempts to show what characteristics the AI software, i.e., expert systems have that create the need for extended or different V&V approaches. Most of these characteristics will relate to the KB component.

The crucial characteristic of KE which sets it apart from SE is related to the requirements specifications. According to traditional SE, a complete and possibly formalized specification given in advance is of vital importance for the development of reliable software. With KB software, the situation is different. In the first place, requirements specifications for expert systems are typically vague. This can make it difficult to tell if "the right system" has been built. Secondly, it is generally hard to specify in advance an expert system completely because of the incremental nature of the knowledge elicitation process. Third, even when requirements can be written down, they may not be amenable to formal analysis. All these characteristics come from the very nature of these systems, which solve those nonstructured, ill-defined problems that cannot be solved by conventional systems. Of course, similar criticisms have also been made with respect to some conventional systems, hence the growing popularity of the prototyping life cycle for conventional systems.

Moreover, in SE it is required that the specification is correct with respect to the real world. The software development process can then concentrate on producing efficient algorithms that implement the specification. No reference back to the real world is needed as long as it can be proved that they do indeed perform these transformations. In the case of expert systems, the output constantly needs to be referenced to the real world. Moreover, "correctness" of output can be a matter of opinion (or degree), and it is often difficult to get consensus among different human experts.

The functionality of a conventional system typically involves the transformation of some (well-defined) input into some (well-defined) output. In the expert system, what can serve as input is typically not well defined at the outset, and the relation of possible inputs to the output may not be clear either.

Other characteristics of expert systems which make it even more difficult to adapt the V & V techniques of conventional software are related to the problem-solving methods used by expert systems. Conventional problem solving deals with algorithmic software, while in expert systems solutions are found by search. While algorithms can be proved to be correct, the correctness of a collection of heuristics is quite a subjective matter, which can often only be determined by examing how they influence the behavior of the system, and is often further affected by their interaction with other heuristics in the system.

Another aspect is related to the declarativeness of knowledge bases. Expert systems are usually implemented using declarative programming languages, very often rule-based languages, while conventional software is typically implemented using procedural programming languages. The procedural and declarative styles lead to different types of errors and anomalies for which different V&V techniques must be employed. Rule bases, for instance, have offered scope for techniques to capture anomalies and errors such as redundancy, dead-end rules, missing rules, subsumption, auxiliary rules, and circular rules. While these have correspondences in conventional software (e.g., unreachable code), the effects and methods of detection are rather different.

Finally, there are, of course, open problems in verification and validation of conventional systems. Perhaps the biggest open problem in SE is to make verification a standard part of software production. There are numerous program design and construction methods in which verification takes place in parallel with program construction. But in the case of expert system construction, there is no generally accepted life cycle. Hence, V&V cannot be included in the life cycle a system does not have. While SE has consolidated a well-accepted life cycle, for the expert system life cycle a consensus is still missing, although it is no doubt fundamental for producing reliable systems.

All these essential differences suggest that applying V&V techniques from SE to expert systems is not straightforward. Although V&V techniques work very well for conventional systems, they must be extended and adapted to work also for expert systems. Moreover, the open problems in V&V of conventional systems should not be overlooked. This suggests that it is worthwhile to look for new V&V methods and techniques for expert systems. Unfortunately, many open problems that exist in SE, remain open in KE as well.

2. THEORETICAL FOUNDATION OF EXPERT SYSTEM VERIFICATION AND VALIDATION

In general, V & V of expert systems consists of identifying anomalies such as redundant, contradictory, or deficient knowledge. An anomaly is a difference between what is expected of KB structure and system performance, and what is actually observed. Anomalies are considered as potential errors since not all of them are errors. However, many common KB errors can be identified by identifying anomalies. Anomalies may also result in inefficiency in terms of performance, maintenance, etc.

Before commencing the discussion on the theoretical foundation of expert system V&V, a short note on representations is needed. Most of the work concerning the errors and anomalies that can occur in expert systems has been carried out on rule-based representations. Parallels do exist with frame- and object-based representations. In this section we concentrate on two principal methods of knowledge representation used in expert systems: production rules and object-based representations. Since both rule-based and structured object representational paradigms have their strengths, some efforts have been made to combine the two.

2.1. LOGICAL FOUNDATION OF RULE-BASED ANOMALIES

A variety of methods have been built for detecting the above-mentioned anomalies in rule bases. The early methods looked for anomalies between pairs of rules only, while the most sophisticated methods detect anomalies manifested over chains of inference.

Rule-based expert systems have foundation in formal logic. There is a relation between the production rules of such systems and the implication statements of logical theorems, and also between the facts of the knowledge base and the axioms of logic. This relationship has been the

TABLE 1
Consistency and Completeness in Logic and Rule Bases

	Logic	Rule bases
Consistency	A set of propositions is consistent if and only if there is some interpretation of the symbol in the set such that no contradictions are entailed.	A rule set is consistent if and only if there is no way the rules can assert a contradiction from valid input data. (the interpretation of the symbols is defined by the knowledge engineer).
Completeness	A set of propositions is complete if and only if all desired inferences can be derived from the set by a sound and complete inference engine.	A rule base is complete if and only if it can cope with all possible situations that can arise in its domain.

basis for systematic checking methods for rule bases. These methods can be used to determine the internal self-consistency and completeness of rule bases, by interpreting the rules as logical expression followed by syntactic inspection and manipulation. However, terms such as *consistency* and *completeness* have slightly different meanings, as shown in Table 1.

We choose to focus upon rule-based expert systems that are based on first-order logic because rule-based systems are the most widely used type of expert system and the semantics of rule-based systems based on logic are well known.

The theoretical framework in which anomaly detection systems for rule-based knowledge bases have been be analyzed is based on the first-order logic. The terminology and notation used to express the knowledge base is the following (Preece and Shinghal, 1994):

- A rule R_i is a formula of the form $l_1 \wedge \ldots \wedge l_n \to m$ where each l_i and m are first-order literals.
- For each rule R_i, we write $antec(R) = \{l_1, \ldots, l_n\}$ and $conseq(R) = m$.
- A rule set R is a set of rules
- The goal-literals is the set of all ground literals that could be output from the rule set.
- The input-literals is the set of all ground literals that constitute all possible inputs to the rule set.
- A semantic constraint is a set of literals $\{l_1, \ldots, l_n\}$ such that their conjunction is regarded as a semantic inconsistency. All semantic constraints for a rule set form the set of semantic constraints.
- An environment ε is a subset of the input literals that does not contain any semantic constraint. ε is the set of all possible such environments.

The anomalies of rule bases can be informally defined as follows:

- *Unsatisfiable rule*: A rule is unsatisfiable iff (iff = if and only if) there is no way of deducing the rule antecedent from any legal input.
- *Unusable rule*: A rule is unusable iff the consequent of the rule subsumes neither a goal literal nor any antecedent literal in the rule set.
- *Subsumed rule*: A rule is subsumed iff there exists a more general rule.
- *Redundant rule*: A rule is redundant in the rule set if the rule is not essential for the computation of any goal literal from any environment.
- *Inconsistent rule pair*: Two rules are an inconsistent pair iff both rules are applicable and derive a semantic constraint.
- *Inconsistent rule set*: A rule set is inconsistent iff from some legal input it is possible to derive a semantic constraint.

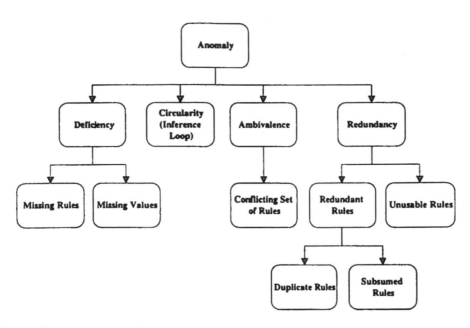

FIGURE 1 Four types of anomaly.

- *Circular rule set*: A rule set is circular iff the antecedents cannot be derived from any environment except by adding the rule set consequent.
- *Unused input*: An input literal is unused iff any result that can be computed from an environment can also be computed from that environment minus the literal input.
- *Incomplete rule set*: A rule set is incomplete iff there exists some output that cannot be computed from any environment.

The use of formal logic will enable us to detect each type of anomaly by considering only the syntactic form of expressions in the knowledge base. For example, consider the two rules $l_1 \wedge l_2 \to m$ and $l_1 \to m$. From an understanding of the semantics of the logical operators $\wedge$ ("and") and $\to$ ("implies"), the first rule is redundant, since it is just a specific version of the second one, which is more general. We can detect this by looking for that particular case of redundancy in which we have two rules with identical consequences, such that the literals in the antecedent of one rule are a subset of the literals in the antecedent of the other.

It is important to realize that such anomalies may not represent actual errors in a rule base, but rather symptoms of possible errors. For example, a redundant rule may occur because there is missing knowledge, the rule $l_1 \to m$ should have been $l_1 \wedge l_3 \to m$. It is up to the knowledge engineer together with the human expert to decide what actions to take when such anomalies are detected.

Based on the semantics of first-order logic, four basic types of anomaly have been identified by Preece et al. (1992), some of which have a number of special cases as shown in Figure 1.

2.1.1. Redundancy

A knowledge base contains redundancy if there are expressions within it that are not necessary to the inferring of any conclusion by the expert system. Four trivial cases of redundancy can be identified:

Unfireable rule. For example, a rule $l \to m$ would be unfireable if the system has no way of establishing l, because l is not an input of any rule of the form $\ldots \to l$. This anomaly would indicate the need of additional knowledge to obtain l. Another example of unfireable rule is $l \wedge \neg l \to m$.

Duplicate rules. An example of duplicate rules is the following: $l_1 \wedge l_2 \to m$ and $l_2 \wedge l_1 \to m$.

Subsumed rule. An example is the following: $l_1 \wedge l_2 \to m$ and $l_1 \to m$.

Redundant rule. An example of the general case of redundant rule is the following: $l \to m$, $m \to n$ and $l \to n$. The last rule is redundant, since it can be inferred from the first two rules.

Although redundancy does not indicate real error, it may affect the functioning of the expert system; for instance, if there are redundant rules and if modifications are made to one of the duplicate rules, the other will remain unchanged and thus incorrect. In other words, system builders need to be taken into consideration in redundancy.

2.1.2.   Ambivalence

A knowledge is ambivalent if it is possible to infer mutually incompatible conclusions from some set of inputs. Ambivalence anomalies often indicate potentially serious errors. Two cases of ambivalence can be identified:

1. *Conflicting rules.* For example, if the knowledge base contains the rules: $l_1 \wedge l_2 \to m$ and $l_1 \to \neg m$, then at least one of the rules must be incorrect in some way. Additional knowledge may be required to solve the conflicting situation.
2. *Ambivalent rules.* For example, if the knowledge base contains the rules: $l \to m$, $m \to n$, and $l \to \neg n$.

2.1.3.   Circularity

A knowledge base contains circularity if it is possible to enter an endless loop while following some chain of inference. This anomaly could be fatal at run-time if the inference engine does not check for circularity when it tries to fire rules, resulting in an endless loop. An example is the following: $l \to m$, $m \to n$ and $n \to l$. If the inference engine can detect and abort loops, then these kinds of anomalies do not have any ill effects.

2.1.4.   Deficiency

A knowledge base is deficient if there is some set of inputs for which it will infer no conclusion. Two cases can be identified:

- *Unused input.* For example, if l is declared to be an input but there is no rule of the form $\ldots \wedge l \wedge \ldots \to \ldots$, then l is an unused input.
- *Missing rule.* The example above suggests that the rule that is supposed to use the data item is missing.

The more general case of deficiency is where there is some logical combination of data items and their values, which, if fed to the knowledge base as input, will not result in any conclusion from the system. This case may suggest that additional knowledge is needed in order to correct the deficiency.

2.2.   FOUNDATION OF OBJECT-ORIENTED EXPERT SYSTEMS

In recent years, the AI community has shown increasing interest in object-oriented programming (OOP). For instance, a number of extensions have been made to conventional AI languages (PROLOG, LISP) to integrate object-oriented concepts. Such interest reflects a belief that the OOP can play an important role in the task of designing large expert systems.

Some expert system applications have dealt with hybrid representations, focusing on synergies and possible conflicts between OOP and traditional rule-based representation. Such hybrid representation systems can supplement the limited power of production rules with objects, which capture declarative knowledge in a hierarchy. Consequently, the V&V techniques that have been developed for rule bases have been adapted to deal with the kind of anomalies inherent in such hybrid systems.

In this section we provide a formulation of anomalies in hybrid systems that combine objects and rules. We define an *object-oriented expert system* (OOES) as a non-flat expert system that performs its reasoning (rules, pattern matching, making inferences) in a framework of structured classes of objects (the pattern matching is performed on objects). Such a formulation — not an easy task as the traditional formulation of the anomalies described in the previous section — specific to rule-based knowledge representation, which greatly restricts applicability. A better approach is to perform anomaly detection at the level of a conceptual model of the KB, rather than at the implementation level.

The conceptual model underlying our approach is derived from the KADS model of expertise (Wielinga et al., 1992) and has been described previously (Vermesan, 1996). Inferences are the principal building blocks of the model, as they are in general for KADS expertise models. The inference layer of the model describes the possible inferences that can be drawn on the basis of the domain knowledge. An *inference* is a declarative definition of the directional relationship between *input knowledge roles* and *output knowledge roles*. Knowledge roles are the knowledge elements on which inferences operate. In an OOES, knowledge roles are in fact objects, and in our graphical notation they are represented three-dimensionally. We have deliberately changed the graphical notation of the KADS knowledge roles to highlight the fact that knowledge roles are complex objects, embedding procedural knowledge, and among which there exist subtyping relationships. Some definitions are needed before proceeding further.

Terminological element A terminological element is a sort.

Terminology A terminology consists of terminological elements and a subtyping relation between them. The subtyping relation is denoted by $\prec$.

Knowledge role A *knowledge role* is a pair $(r : type)$ where r is a variable with the sort *type*. A sequence of roles is denoted $\vec{r}$. Input roles are denoted by $\vec{i}$, output roles by $\vec{o}$.

Inference step An *inference step* is a predicate having as arguments the variables corresponding to the connecting roles. The predicate specifies the input/output relation of the inference step:

$$s(\vec{i};\vec{o})$$

where $\vec{i}$ are the input roles and $\vec{o}$ are the output roles of the inference.

Inference structure An *inference structure* I is a set of inference steps:

$$I =_{def} \{s_1(\vec{i}_1;\vec{o}_1), \ldots, s_n(\vec{i}_n;\vec{o}_n)\}$$

where $\vec{i}_i, \vec{o}_i$, are the input and output roles, respectively, of inference $s_i(\vec{i}_i;\vec{o}_i)$. The roles in $\vec{i}_i, \vec{o}_i$ and $\vec{i}_j, \vec{o}_j$ may overlap for distinct i and j, in which case $s_i(\vec{i}_i;\vec{o}_i)$, and $s_j(\vec{i}_j;\vec{o}_j)$ are connected.

It is important to notice is that although inference steps are defined in terms of terminologies, they do not operate directly on sorts, but on instantiations of these sorts. An instance of an inference step is obtained by carrying a substitution of variables in the knowledge roles. An inference can be seen as a set of instances of inference steps. The definition of the inference structure is declarative and not procedural, as it expresses data dependencies among inference steps but does not specify any control flow.

Producers The *producers* P of a knowledge role r in an inference structure I, denoted by $P(r)$, are the inferences in I that have the role as an output.

Consumers The *consumers* C of a role r in an inference structure I, denoted by C (r), are the inferences in I that have the role as an input.

Initial roles The *initial roles* of an inference structure I are the input roles that are not produced by any inference step in I. We will use the notation $\bar{R}_s$ to denote the set of input roles of the inference step s. When no indices are given, $\bar{R}$ refers to the set of input roles of the whole inference structure.

Terminal roles The *terminal roles* of an inference structure I are the output roles that are not consumed by any inference step in I. We will use the notation $\bar{R}_s$ to denote the set of output roles of the inference step s.

Substitution to a knowledge role A substitution of a value a:*type* (where a is a ground term) to a knowledge role v:*type* is denoted by $\sigma = \{v/a\}$.

The instance of an inference step s obtained by carrying out substitution σ is denoted by $s\sigma$. For multiple substitution, σ is of the form $\sigma = \{(v_1/a_1), ..., (v_n/a_n)\}$. The instance of an inference structure I obtained by carrying out substitution σ to all its knowledge roles is denoted by $I\sigma$. We use the notation σ:*type*$(\bar{R})$ to denote that σ is a substitution for a set of variables of exactly the types of the initial roles. In this case $I\sigma$ denotes an instance of the inference structure I obtained by carrying out the substitution σ, i.e., substitutions of all its input roles. We use the notation $s\sigma$, where σ:*type*$(\bar{R}_s)$, to denote an instance of the inference step s obtained by substitution of its input roles. The same can be applied for terminal, internal, and external roles. When the type is not given, σ is a substitution for all knowledge roles in the inference step or inference structure.

Sequence of substitutions The sequence of two substitutions $\sigma = \{(v_1/a_1), ..., (v_n/a_n)\}$ and $v = \{(w_1/b_1), ..., (w_m/b_m)\}$ is denoted by $\sigma\vdash v = \{(v_1/a_1), ..., (v_n/a_n), (w_1/b_1), ..., (w_m/b_m)\}$.

The sequence operator has precedence over the application of the substitution to an inference step or structure. When two substitutions substitute different values to the same variable, the right-most substitution has precedence (i.e., overwrites the left-most substitution for that variable). Example: consider the following inference step $s(x_1, x_2; y)$, and two substitutions, σ:*type*$(\bar{R}_s)$ and v:*type*$(\bar{R}_s)$, where $\sigma = \{(x_1/5), (x_2/6)\}$ and $v = \{(y/5)\}$, $\sigma\vdash v = \{(x_1/5), (x_2/6), (y/5)\}$. $s\sigma\vdash v$ denotes an instance of s obtained by carrying out the substitution $\sigma\vdash v$.

Satisfying an inference structure Let σ be a substitution for all knowledge roles occurring in an inference structure I, and *DEF* the definitions of all inference steps occurring in I. σ satisfies I if and only if *DEF* | $= I\sigma$. To avoid writing *DEF* repetitively and to improve the readability, we will write *sat*$(I\sigma)$ to denote that the inference structure I is satisfied by a substitution σ, where σ corresponds to a valid execution of I. A valid execution of s means that the particular instance of s solves the problem-solving step for which it was designed. In the previous example, $s\sigma\vdash v$ is a valid instance of s if, for example, the inference step performs the minimum operation on its input knowledge roles. The same can be applied to inference structures. We use the notation *sat*$(s\sigma)$ to denote the satisfaction of the inference step s.

2.2.1. Subsumption

In hybrid systems, inheritance triggers subsumption among the objects and will lead to other types of anomalies unique to hybrid systems. A taxonomy of anomalies that can occur in such systems has been proposed by Lee and O'Keefe (1993):

- *Subsumed rules*: Subsumed rules arise due to the subsumption relationship between literals used in the rules.
- *Redundancy*: Redundancy arises as a direct consequence of subsumed rules.
- *Semantic conflict*: Semantic conflict occurs when any pair of rules that have the same conditions lead to semantically different actions, among which there exists a partial or complete subsumption relationship.
- *Structural conflict*: Structural conflict is identified by subsumption relationships in the condition and action parts of the rules.
- *Unnecessary conditions*: In hybrid systems, unnecessary conditions can occur when an action in a rule is propagated to another rule as a condition and results in at least one subsumption relationship between a pair of literals in the condition clause.
- *Unreachable goals*: Unreachable goals may arise due to mutual exclusivity among the objects used in the condition of the same rule.
- *Circular rules*: The definition of circular rules has been extended for hybrid systems.

Instead of addressing directly the different types of anomalies due to subsumption mentioned above, we define different types of subsumption, and identify the type of anomaly that may be caused by that specific type of subsumption. This approach abstracts from implementational details, by addressing these issues on a conceptual level. For each type of subsumption, we provide a counterpart example, where an object hierarchy of two levels is assumed: $S = a_1' \cup a_2' \cup \dots \cup a_n'$ being the first level and every $a_i' = \{a_{i1}, a_{i2}, \dots, a_{ij}\}$ being the second level, where the elements in the set are subclasses of a_i'.

A classification of the subsumption relation is given in Figure 2.

The *explicit subsumption* is the type of subsumption that has been considered in the traditional V&V activities in rule-bases. In rule base systems, subsumption occurs in the case that the more general rule can always be fired whenever the restrictive rule is fired. For example, whenever rule (1) succeeds, rule (2) will also succeed. Therefore, in what follows, rule (1) is subsumed by rule (2):

$$p(x) \land q(x) \rightarrow r(x) \tag{1}$$

$$p(x) \rightarrow r(x) \tag{2}$$

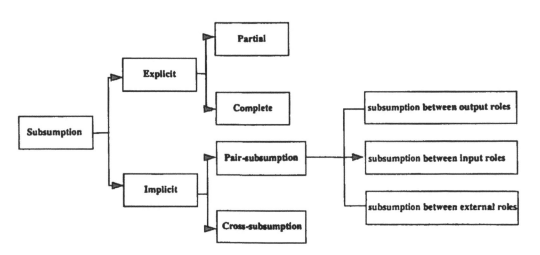

FIGURE 2   A classification of the subsumption relation.

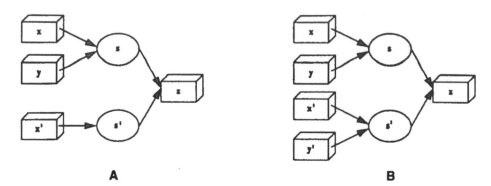

FIGURE 3 Partial (A) and complete (B) subsumption.

This kind of subsumption can be detected by comparing whether or not one rule has additional conditional statements to the other rule when the two rules have the same conclusion. However, such structural checking cannot cover the semantics of relationships in the rules of hybrid systems, which may include object hierarchies.

In order to cope with this problem, we introduce the notion of *implicit subsumption*. This type of subsumption[1] takes into consideration the semantic relationships that exists between the objects on which the rules operate.

Implicit subsumption Let $\sigma = \{(v_1/a_1), ..., (v_n/a_n)\}$ and $\sigma' = \{(v_1'/a_1'), ..., (v_m'/a_m')\}$ where $n \leq m$. σ is subsumed by σ', written as $\sigma \prec \sigma'$, iff

$$\forall(v_i / a_i) \in \sigma, \exists(v_j' / a_j') \subseteq \sigma' : (v_i : t_i, v_j' : t_j, t_i \prec t_j)$$

where a_i, a_j' may be sets of values.

We distinguish two types of implicit subsumption, depending on the relationship between knowledge roles: *partial* and *complete* subsumption. An example of partial subsumption is given in Figure 3A, where the graphical notation is equivalent to $s(x,y;z) \vee s'(x';z)$, using the notation provided in the previous section. An example of complete subsumption is given in Figure 3B, equivalent with $s(x,y;z) \vee s'(x',y';z)$.

In Figure 3, s is subsumed by s' as for any value of x, where x is a subtype of x', s' computes the same value for z as s does, regardless of y. We will use $\prec$ to denote partial or complete subsumption, and $\prec_c$ to denote complete subsumption.

In the following, we define the different types of subsumption. For each type, a brief analogy with the counterpart in rule bases is also given.

2.2.2.   Implicit Pair-Subsumption

Subtyping Between Output Roles of the Inference Steps. This type of implicit pair-subsumption occurs when any pair of inference steps which have the same input roles lead to different output roles, among which there exists partial or complete subtyping. The inference step s is subsumed by another inference step iff:

---

[1] We talk about subsumption between inference steps and subtyping between knowledge roles. In fact, subsumption between inference steps is caused by subtyping relationships between knowledge roles.

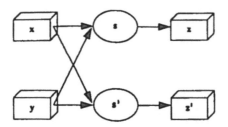

FIGURE 4 Implicit pair-subsumption arising from subtyping between output roles.

$$\exists s' \in I - \{s\}:$$

$$\forall \sigma : type(\bar{R}_s), \forall v : type(\bar{R}_s)$$

$$\text{if } sat(s\sigma \vdash v) \text{ then } \exists v' : type(\bar{R}_s'):$$

$$sat(s'\sigma \vdash v') \wedge v \prec v'$$

An example in given in Figure 4, where the same input roles lead to different output roles, among which there exists the relationship $z \prec z'$.

The counterpart anomaly in rule bases is called semantic conflict. An example is given below:

$$p(x) \wedge q(x) \rightarrow r(x, a_1')$$
$$p(y) \wedge q(y) \rightarrow r(y, a_{11}')$$

Although it is called a semantic conflict, there is not really a conflict. This case may be significant in some application domains, where the situation when an action is structurally subsumed may be sensible for the interpretation of the results. In decision-aid systems, for example, a general advise should not be given to the user when a more specific one can be suggested.

Subtyping Between Input Roles of the Inference Steps. This type of implicit pair-subsumption occurs when any pair of inference steps which have a complete subsumption relation between input roles, lead to different output roles among which there is no subsumption relationship. An inference step s is in conflict with another inference step iff:

$$\exists s' \in I - \{s\}:$$

$$\forall \sigma : type(\bar{R}_s), \forall v : type(\bar{R}_s)$$

$$\text{if } sat(s\sigma \vdash v) \text{ then } \exists \sigma' : type(\bar{R}_s'), \exists v' : type(\bar{R}_s'):$$

$$sat(s'\sigma \vdash v') \wedge \sigma' \wedge \neg (v \prec v' \vee (v' \prec v))$$

An example is given in Figure 5. Between s and s' there is a conflict relation rather than a subsumption relation. However, such a conflict may reveal incompleteness of specifications. A conflict situation may be the result of an attempt to prove some properties of the specification during the validation activities. Failure to prove a property may be caused by exactly the kind of situation described in Figure 5. The correction of such a conflict should be resolved by augmenting the specification with elements that allow the specific property to be proved. In this example, such an element would be either introducing an explicit subtyping relation between z and w if the situation requires so, or to relate z and w through an inference step (structure).

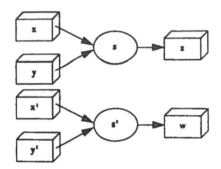

FIGURE 5   Implicit pair-subsumption based on subtyping between input roles.

The counterpart anomaly in rule bases also causes a conflict. An example is given below:

$$p(x, a_{11}) \land q(x, a_{21}) \rightarrow r(x, b_1)$$
$$p(x, a_{12}) \land q(x, a_{21}) \rightarrow r(x, b_1)$$

There is no conflict between these two rules, as a_{11} and a_{12} are children of a_1'. However, if we introduce the following rule

$$p(x, a_1') \land q(x, a_{21}) \rightarrow r(x, b_2)$$

a conflict occurs when substituting a_1' with any of its children.

Subtyping Between Output Roles of the Inference Steps. This type of implicit pair-subsumption occurs when any pair of inference steps that have a complete subsumption relation between input roles, lead to different output roles among which there exists partial or complete subsumption relationship.

Two situations can be identified. The first one where the input roles in the first inference of the pair are completely subsumed by the input roles in the second inference, and the output roles of the first inference is partially or completely subsumed by the output roles of the second one. An inference step s is subsumed by another inference step iff:

$$\exists s' \in I - \{s\}:$$

$$\forall \sigma : type(\bar{R}_s), \forall v : type(\bar{R}_s)$$

$$\text{if } sat(s\sigma \vdash v) \text{ then } \exists \sigma' : type(\bar{R}_s'), \exists v' : type(\bar{R}_s'):$$

$$sat(s'\sigma' \vdash v') \land \sigma \prec_c \sigma' \land v \prec v'$$

An example is given in Figure 6. The situation does not lead to any conflict anomaly, but rather is reduced to the case where the inference step s is redundant as is subsumed by s'.

FIGURE 6   Implicit pair-subsumption based on subtyping between external roles.

FIGURE 7   Implicit pair-subsumption based on (inverse) subtyping between external roles.

The second situation may occur where the input roles in the first inference of the pair are completely subsumed by the input roles in the second inference, and the output roles of the first inference partially or completely subsume the output roles of the second inference. This is expressed as follows:

$$\exists s' \in I - \{s\}:$$

$$\forall \sigma : type(\bar{R}_s), \forall v : type(\bar{R}_s)$$

$$\text{if } sat(s\sigma\vdash v)\text{ then}\exists\sigma' : type(\bar{R}_s'),\exists v' : type(\bar{R}_s'):$$

$$sat(s'\sigma'\vdash v')\wedge \sigma \prec_c \sigma' \wedge v' \prec v$$

An example is given in Figure 7.

This situation may lead to conflict, especially in situations where knowledge roles are not allowed to take multivalues.

2.2.3.   Implicit Cross-Subsumption

This type of subsumption can cause propagation anomalies, including unnecessary input role, unreachable goals, and circular inference structure. Such kinds of anomalies do not necessarily produce errors, but do affect the performance of the system.

Unnecessary Input Role. This type of cross-subsumption occurs when an inference step s produces an output role produced by no other inference step, and which is consumed by another inference step s'. In addition there is a subtyping relation between the input roles of the two inference steps. In such situation, the subsuming role becomes an unnecessary input role. An input role of the inference step s' becomes unnecessary iff

$$\exists s \in I - \{s'\}:$$

$$\forall \sigma : type(\bar{R}_s), \forall v : type(\bar{R}_s)$$

$$\exists\sigma' : type(\bar{R}_s'),\exists v' : type(\bar{R}_s'):$$

$$\text{if } sat(s'\sigma'\vdash v')\text{ then } sat(s'v\vdash\sigma'\vdash v')\wedge \sigma \prec \sigma'$$

An example is given in Figure 8, where the subsuming knowledge role y' is unnecessary input role for the inference step s', as there is the following subtyping relation: $y \prec y'$. In other words, any substitution for y that satisfies the inference step s, also satisfies s'.

The counterpart anomaly in rule bases can occur when an action in a rule is propagated to another rule as a condition and results in at least one subsumption relationship between a pair of literals in the condition clause. For example:

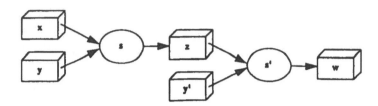

FIGURE 8   Unnecessary input role caused by implicit cross-subsumption.

$$p(x, a_{11}) \wedge q(x, a_{21}) \rightarrow r(x, b_1)$$
$$p(x, a_1') \wedge r(x, b_1) \rightarrow s(x)$$

After forward chaining, the condition in the second rule becomes:

$$p(x, a_{11}) \wedge q(x, a_{21}) \rightarrow p(x, a_1')$$

where the third subcondition subsumes the first one. Depending on the context, the two rules may be combined into one, or remove the unnecessary condition in the second rule.

Unreachable Goal. This type of cross-subsumption occurs when an inference step s produces an output role produced by no other inference step, and which is consumed by another inference step s'. In addition, the input roles of the two inference steps are subtypes of the same supertype. In such a situation, either of the two inference steps are unsatisfiable, and there the output goal becomes unreachable, unless the variables of supertypes are allowed to have multiple values. Mutual exclusiveness of objects instantiated makes a certain goal unreachable. The output role of an inference step s' is unreachable in the structure I iff

$$\forall s \in I - \{s'\}:$$

$$\forall \sigma : type(\bar{R}_s), \forall v : type(\bar{R}_s)$$

if $sat(s\sigma \vdash v)$ then $\forall \sigma' : type(\bar{R}_s'), \forall v' : type(\bar{R}_s'), \exists \sigma^s :$

$$\neg sat(s' v \vdash \sigma' \vdash v') \wedge \sigma \prec \sigma^s \wedge \sigma' \prec \sigma^s$$

An example is given in Figure 9. If there exists a supertype y^s, such $y' \prec y^s$ and $y'' \prec y^s$ does not allow multivalues, than the two inference steps are mutually exclusive. In any case, i.e., either the value is of type y' or y'', the goal w of the inference step s' is unreachable.

The counterpart anomaly in rule bases is shown in the following example:

$$p(x, a_{11}) \wedge q(x, a_{21}) \rightarrow r(x, b_1)$$
$$p(x, a_{12}) \wedge r(x, b_1) \rightarrow s(x)$$

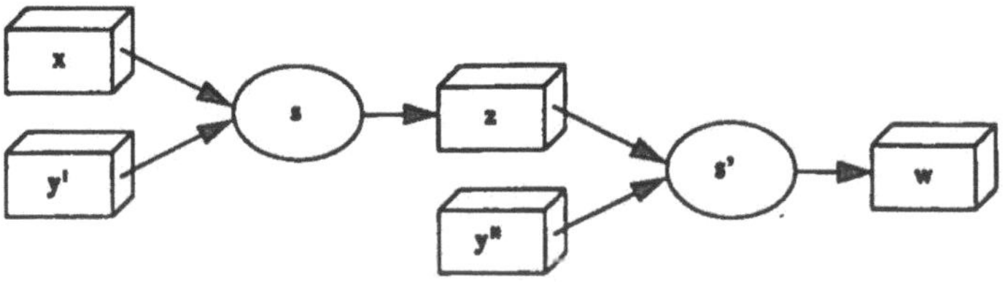

FIGURE 9   Unreachable goal role caused by implicit cross-subsumption.

As $p(x, a_{11})$ and $p(x, a_{12})$ cannot be satisfied simultaneously, $s(x)$ is unreachable goal.

2.2.4. Circular Inference Structure

In rule bases, a set of rules is circular if the chaining of those rules in the set forms a cycle. Circular rules causes that the system will enter an infinite chain at run time. The rules are connected so that at least one literal in action statements is syntactially matched with at least one literal in condition statements. However, syntactic match cannot cover the implicit relationships between literals. An example is the following:

$$p(x, a_1') \rightarrow q(x, a_{21})$$
$$q(x, a_2') \rightarrow r(x, a_{31})$$
$$r(x, a_3') \rightarrow p(x, a_{11})$$

In the case of inference structures, we say that an inference step s initiates a cycle iff

$$\exists s' \in I - \{s\}:$$

$$\forall \sigma : type(\bar{R}_s), \forall v : type(\bar{R}_s)$$

$$\text{if } sat(s\sigma \mid -v) \text{ then } \exists \sigma' : type(\bar{R}_s'), \exists v' : type(\bar{R}_s'):$$

$$\text{if } sat(s'\sigma' \mid -v') \text{ then } \exists \sigma'' : type(\bar{R}_s''), \exists v'' : type(\bar{R}_s''):$$

$$sat(s''\sigma'' \mid -v'') \wedge v \prec \sigma' \wedge v' \prec \sigma'' \wedge v'' \prec \sigma$$

An example is given in Figure 10.

2.2.5. Conclusions

Many vendors offer today software development tools that include both objects and rules and provide rapid development platforms for expert systems. However, most of these tools that are used for building hybrid systems do not provide support for analysis of subsumption relations that may cause anomalies. Consequently, the burden of maintaining the object structure and subsumption relations among literals in rules is left to developers. The perspective put forward in this section was that performing V&V activities might be easier at the level of conceptual model, rather than the level of implemented system. Good practices in software engineering, such as type checking, may help in automating the analysis of subsumption relations and detect anomalies.

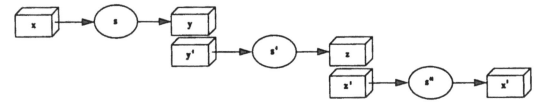

FIGURE 10 Circular inference structure caused by implicit cross-subsumption.

3.   APPLICATION OF EXPERT SYSTEM VERIFICATION AND VALIDATION

3.1.   COMPONENTS OF VERIFICATION AND VALIDATION

In the early days of expert systems, a lot of work emphasized the functional requirements of the system, or the specification of the expected behavior of the system. *Functional requirements* capture the nature of the interaction between the system and its environment — they specify what the system is *to do*. They can be expressed in two different ways. The *declarative* approach seeks to describe what the system must do without any indication of how it is to do it. The *procedural* approach, on the other hand, aims to describe what the system must do in terms of an outline design for accomplishing it.

However, good performance of the system may hide other faults that can create problems for the maintenance of the system or provision of explanations. *Nonfunctional requirements* (also called constraints) should also be taken into consideration, although they usually restrict the types of system solutions that should be considered. They often specify what the system should *not do*. Examples of nonfunctional requirements include safety, security, performance, operating constraints, and costs. These system level requirements are translated at the level of knowledge base in nonfunctional requirements, such as logical consistency of the knowledge, redundancy, efficiency, usefulness, etc.

Both functional and nonfunctional requirements should be considered in V&V activities. Some of the major V&V components are listed in Table 2. Although they reflect some of the well known features and characteristics of a software product as found in the ISO/IEC 9126 standard, the fundamental nature of expert system software requires slightly different components of the developing system to be considered.

3.2.   METHODS AND TECHNIQUES

The earliest validation technique on AI was Turing's proposal on how to decide if a program could be considered "intelligent"; the responses of the expert system, together with those from a human expert, are presented to an independent human expert. Although the techniques received some criticism, the idea of blind testing has remained central in validation of the earliest expert systems.

In addition to testing, other techniques have been used by expert system developers to analyze anomalies that are indicative of errors in the construction of such systems, and that can lead to faulty behavior at run-time. The most common anomalies included: inconsistency, redundancy, subsumption, circularity, unreachable goal, unfireable rule.

Currently, the dominant techniques for V&V activities cover a wide range. For the purpose of this chapter they are clustered into two main groups: non-method and method specific techniques, focusing on the latter.

3.2.1.   Nonmethod-Specific Techniques

These techniques usually involve human analysis of the product, relying on individuals to use their experience to find errors. Such analyses are error prone, as they do not rely on the semantics of the product, and in general are not automated. The most common non-method specific techniques are reviews, walkthroughs, and inspections. These actions are general examinations of programs and all seek to identify defects and discrepancies of the software against specifications, plans, and standards. At the *review*, the product is scrutinized in whatever way makes most sense: a piece of text can be taken page by page; a piece of code can be approached procedure by procedure; designs, diagram by diagram; diagrams, bloc by bloc. Informal reviews are conducted on an as-needed basis, while formal reviews are conducted at the end of each life cycle phase and the acquirer of the software is formally involved. *Inspections* attempt to detect and identify defects, while *walk-*

TABLE 2
Verification and Validation Components

Characteristic	Description
Competency	This deals with the quality of the knowledge in a system relative to human skills. It can be assessed by comparing the source with other sources of expertise.
Completeness	The completeness of a system with respect to the requirement specification is a measure of the portion of specification implemented in the system. Applied to an expert system, this involves ensuring that all the knowledge is referenced, and that there is no attempt to access non-existent knowledge .
Consistency	This means the requirement specification or expert system is free of internal contradiction. For example, a KB that contains two rules that specify opposite conclusions starting from same condition are not internally consistent.
Correctness	The knowledge within a knowledge base should be 100% correct. However, different human experts may have different opinions on the correctness of a knowledge base.
Testability	The system should be designed in such a way as to permit a testing plan to be carried out. For example, if the requirement specification for an expert system states that "the system should perform at the level of an expert," such a specification would be difficult to test. However, the same requirements could be stated in another way: "the system should arrive at the same conclusion as the human expert on 97% of a set of test cases" it is easier to test.
Relevance	This criteria determines if the system has extraneous information with respect to the requirement specification. For example, the relevance criteria is violated in the case where the expert system can solve problems or has features that are not specified in the requirement specification.
Usability	One can have a perfectly working system, but if it does not meet the demand of users, it will not be used.
Reliability	Reliability determines how often the system fails to arrive at the correct solution to a problem. An expert system has high reliability if it consistently arrives at the correct solution for a large proportion of problems that are given to it.

throughs in addition, consider possible solutions. Inspections and walkthroughs are performed by a group composed of peers from the software quality assurance, development, and test. Formal inspections are significantly more effective than walkthroughs as they are performed by teams led by a moderator who is formally trained in the inspection process.

Inspection of an expert system aims at detecting semantically incorrect knowledge in the KB. This activity is usually performed manually by a human expert who has expertise in the application domain. The expert can be the same expert who provided the knowledge for the KB, but could also be an expert independent of those involved in the ES development. There are a limited number of errors that human experts can detect "by eye," i.e., those errors that can be found within the same piece of knowledge. Errors that come from the interaction of several KB components are more difficult to detect.

Although important, nonmethod-specific techniques are generally not enough to assure that the software being developed will satisfy functional and other requirements and each step in the process of building the software will yield the right product.

3.2.2.   Method-Specific Techniques

Method-specific techniques are generally those that are more formal in nature. Formality means that the properties of the product or process are well defined and consequently easier to express in a structured and formal way. The method specific actions thus exploit the advantage of having the results of the software development amenable to such formal checks. These methods may offer from rigorous checks of the code functionality to mathematical proof of specification refinements. They are more focused on specific program features or problems than the non-method specific actions.

Empirical Methods. The literature on empirical testing of expert systems discusses a variety of methods. In general, empirical methods involve running a prototype system on a selection of test cases, and assessing the results.

Although many of the techniques used for testing conventional software can be used, expert systems pose a number of problems for validation. The number of paths through a large expert system makes exhaustive testing impossible. One solution to this problem has been to test specific aspects of the expert system such as the most frequently used paths, most critical elements in the knowledge base, the integration of the knowledge base with other parts of a more complex system.

The classical way is inspired by Turing's test: the responses of the expert system, together with those from a human expert, are presented to an independent human expert. Evaluation of the results from empirical methods can be done in an informal, qualitative manner, or by using quantitative methods.

These methods are in general "black-box validation techniques." As the name suggests, these techniques are used to determine the correctness of the system viewed as a "black box." Given some statements of user requirements, tests are applied to the system to establish whether or not it meets its requirements. The test cases are designed so as to exercise the system in a broad range of situations. Black-box tests are difficult to perform when there are many special-case situations that require special testing.

Logical Methods. These kind of methods are called "logical" due to the logical nature of the tests. Such methods are applied to detect anomalies such as inconsistency, redundancy, subsumption, circularity, unreachable goal, or unfireable rule.

These techniques are used to establish the internal correctness of the software, and therefore they are called "white-box" techniques. Glass-box techniques complement black-box techniques, revealing anomalies such as unreachable components, missing components, and incompatible or incorrect components. These techniques are difficult to apply when the expert system is internally very complex.

3.3.   EXPERT SYSTEM DEVELOPMENT METHODOLOGIES

Many of the methods and techniques mentioned in the previous sections are product oriented, in the sense that the V&V activities are oriented mainly toward the knowledge base, and to some extent to the inference engine and user interface. The process-oriented approach to V&V is connected with the more sophisticated methodologies and environments for the construction of expert systems. Central to these more principled methodologies has been one of the fundamental premises of SE, which distinguishes clearly the functional specification of a system from its design and implementation. Instead of directly encoding the knowledge gathered from the human expert, the aim is to build an equivalent of the functional specification, i.e., a knowledge level description or a conceptual model. Consequently, the focus of verification and validation has been concentrated on these models and their refinements rather than on the executable representation.

Some methodologies and environments, such as MEKAS, MAKE, and KADS, are described in Vermesan and Bench-Capon (1995) and Wielinga et al. (1992). They are concerned with developing a knowledge level model and transforming it to the symbol level. A major contribution of these approaches is that the V&V techniques are not isolated from the overall expert system development life cycle, but are part of safe and well-defined methodologies, which also provide techniques for moving to an executable representation.

The MAKE (Maintenance Assistance for Knowledge Engineers), for instance, addresses the latter stage in expert system development, which focuses on the actual construction of the KB. Its prime focus was the construction of maintainable systems, in domains based on regulations that are particularly vulnerable to change. It is argued that there is a strong relation between maintenance and V&V: maintenance involves the detection of flaws in the knowledge base, and any changes that are made must themselves be validated and verified. MAKE prescribes a development meth-

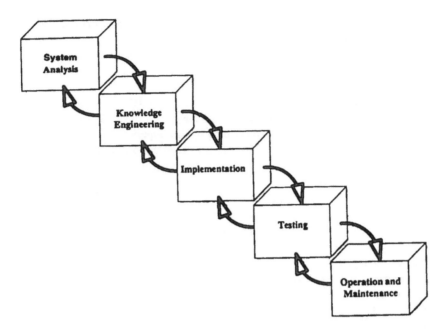

FIGURE 11 The waterfall expert system life-cycle paradigm.

odology that produces systems that are more capable of verification, validation, and maintenance. To be effective, these activities should not be considered only when the system has been produced, but must inform the whole development process. Central to this philosophy is that V&V should always be carried out at a higher level than the level of executable code. The primary focus of V&V must be on the models, and the transition between them, rather than simply on the executable representation.

There has been some research effort into and development of a number of techniques to support V&V of expert system, and in identifying the most appropriate phases in the development to which they may be applied. Thus, opportunities to perform verification and validation occur at various stages during the development of the expert system. In the waterfall approach to software development, V&V can be carried out at the end of each phase of development.

The equivalent waterfall model for expert systems (Figure 11) is similar in a way but presents a number of particularities (Coenen and Bench-Capon, 1993). These include:

- *System analysis*. Is not always clear that the same principles used in conventional software can be used for them too, since the estimates of costs, time, and benefits for an expert system are very unreliable.
- *Requirements analysis and definition*. It is difficult to provide clearly the requirements of the system and in many cases this stage is neglected because many expert system applications have used the prototyping life-cycle paradigm.
- *Software specification and design*. The notions of data structures and procedures are not relevant, and the KB is the focal point, with the design concentrating on the choice of representation for the knowledge and an inference engine to manipulate the knowledge.
- *Implementation*. The implementation is more complicated since the specification and the design are not so detailed as in the case of conventional software. The expert systems are normally implemented using languages such as PROLOG, LISP, or a shell and are generally application specific, which makes it difficult to apply standards in order to reuse the code or perform major changes to the KB software product.

- *Testing*. The testing stage is rather vague and in many cases is integrated into the stage of eliciting and refining knowledge from the expert.
- *Maintenance*. There are attempts to adapt Swanson's classification system for traditional software system maintenance.

More or less serious criticisms of the traditional waterfall model have led to alternative models such as *rapid prototyping* and *spiral modeling,* which have been developed to improve or replace the waterfall model. These models have been adopted by developers of expert systems as well. The software life cycle for spiral modeling is somewhat similar to the prototype model. In the analysis stage, the software development team specifies in the requirements documents of the software project the validation procedures, risk identification, a number of KB requirements, constraints on the computer memory required by the KB, schedule, resources, and an overall test strategy, including a verification and validation test plan.

The attempts to define life-cycle models for expert system construction has led to the possibility of coupling the V&V activities to the specific stages in the development. Thus, V&V techniques are not stand-alone, but part of this methodology. However, important to notice is that the focus of V&V is not the same at each stage since the objectives of each are stage different. An example of such a mapping between different development stages and the focus of V&V in each of them is summarized in Table 3.

Such a mapping gives guidance to *what* V&V can be done *when*. Essentially, V&V is spread over four stages: (1) *requirement analysis,* (2) *knowledge acquisition,* (3) *knowledge specification and refinement* and (4) *implementation.*

TABLE 3
Mapping Focus of V&V Methods to the Development Stages

Life cycle	Focus of V&V
Requirement analysis and initial knowledge acquisition	The focus is on achieving satisfactory requirements and consistent initial specifications. The use of traditional V&V techniques may not be applicable since an expert system is knowledge intensive rather than data intensive. The initial requirements are primarily related to questions about what kind of problems can be solved under which environments. Inconsistencies detected at this stage are resolved by supplying additional knowledge. The human expert is directly involved in the process of discarding or reflecting modifications in the initial knowledge specification.
Knowledge specification	V&V activities at this level exploit the structure of the conceptual model, focusing on validating the knowledge specification. During such activities, knowledge analysis can reveal potential errors. A failure to prove a desired property is a trigger to complete the knowledge specification. The human expert proposes a set of possible repairs.
Refinement of knowledge specification	The relation between knowledge analysis and refinement relies on the fact that the latter follows the former. The analysis of desired properties guides the refinement process. The V&V activities focus on performing correct refinements, thus ensuring consistency between two consecutive levels of specification.
Implementation	The focus is checking the implemented system for internal consistency, also demonstrating the compliance with the specification. Automated tools may greatly help in performing V&V activities.

3.4.   VERIFICATION AND VALIDATION SYSTEMS

To test for the anomalies and errors identified in previous chapters, many verification and validation systems have been built over the last decade. In the following, we will survey some of them, mentioning that the survey is necessarily incomplete, and it is based on depth rather than breadth. Our primary motivation in choosing these particular systems is that they provide a good cross-section of available verification and validation types of methods and tools. These systems along with others can be found in Vermesan and Bench-Capon (1995) and Preece et al. (1992), where pointers to the developers of the systems are also provided.

3.4.1.   KRUST

KRUST (Knowledge Refinement Using Semantic Trees) refines rule bases considering rule priority, taking into consideration the role of control. It is argued that refinement can enhance the functionality of validation systems. The goal is not only to simply identify possible faults, but to explore them further so that anomalies can be rectified.

In common with many other refinement tools, KRUST refines a rule-based expert system on evidence provided by examples that the KBS fails to solve correctly. In contrast with other systems, KRUST considers many possible refinements to cure a single failure. The architecture of KRUST is the following (Figure 12):

- A set of training examples that the expert system fails to solve is given to the input. Possible causes of failure are detected and rules are classified into different categories of interest.
- A set of possible refinements is generated, each consisting of a set of rule changes: rules can be strengthened (made more difficult to satisfy), weakened (made easier to satisfy), given an increased chance of firing, etc.
- The first filter discards those refinements that are poor (based on meta-knowledge). Those that remain are incorporated into the KB, creating a set of refined KBs.
- The KBs are run against the training examples and those that fail again are rejected.

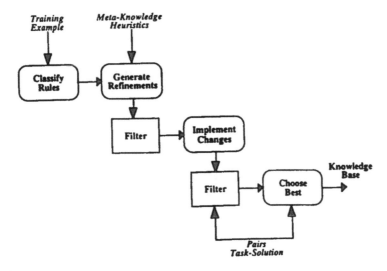

FIGURE 12   KRUST.

- The remaining KBs are suggested to the expert or ranked by a detailed judgment process. As a result, the most suitable KB is selected. Note that this last step requires an appeal to the implicit model in the mind of the expert.

KRUST reacts to the most common inconsistencies as follows:

- *Subsumed* rule: prevents the more general rule from firing by strengthening its condition in all possible ways to remove the redundancy with a more specialized rule
- *Unreachable* rule: weakens the rule's conditions so that it can be reached
- *Cycling* rule: breaks the cycle in all possible places by strengthening that rule
- *Attribute* with wrong arity: removes extra arguments, or adds suitable arguments, in all possible ways

The blame assignment algorithm allocates a measure of likelihood of error to individual rules, on the evidence of past cases. The statistics highlight those rules that commonly fail during routine testing. For each rule, the following occurrences are counted:

- True positive: cases where the rule fires correctly
- False positive: cases where the rule fired when it should not have fired
- True negative: cases where the rule did not fire and this was correct
- False negative: cases where the rule did not fire when it should have fired

False positive and false negative are the errors. A false positive indicates that the KB is too general and it should be specialized. Conversely, a false negative indicates that the KB is too specific, and it should be generalized.

3.4.2. COVADIS

The COVADIS system is an inconsistency checking system based on constraint propagation techniques designed to operate on expert systems developed using the MORSE shell. The shell uses forward chaining with attribute-value rules. It generates, from a rule base, the specifications of all fact bases from which absurdity can be deduced. These are then presented to a domain expert to determine whether they are meaningful or not. If a fact base is not considered meaningful, the expert is interactively asked to express why it is not meaningful, in the form of some integrity constraint. Again, this method requires a direct appeal to the expert's implicit model of the domain.

3.4.3. IMPROVER

Another approach to supporting the refinement of the knowledge base in expert system validation is IMPROVER, a knowledge-base refinement tool, guided by error importance. A classification of error importance is needed, based on the error type and on the elements involved in the error. In the medical diagnosis domain, a false negative (a diagnosis that does not appear in the ES output although it should) is a more serious error than a false positive (a diagnosis that appears in the ES but should not), since the consequences of this sort of error for the patient will be more serious.

The refinement is performed on the following expert system model: the KB consists of facts, rules, modules, and metarules. Rules may be concluding rules or up-down rules. Concerning uncertainty management, a Certainty Factor (CF) is assigned to each fact representing positive evidence. Uncertainty is propagated through rule firing. Two types of control are included. Implicit control is embedded into the conflict resolution strategy based on three criteria: most specific rule, highest CF, and the first rule. Explicit control is coded in metarules acting on modules or on the whole ES. The metarules can add or remove modules to/from a list of active modules. The expert system functions as follows: when it starts, a metarule builds a list of active modules. Then, the first module is selected as the current module. Its goals are pursued using the rules contained in it. As soon as new facts are deduced, metarules are tested for firing, and the list of active modules is eventually updated. When every goal in the current module has been tried, a new current module is selected. The same cycle restarts. The expert system stops when there are no modules in the list of active modules.

The task of the expert system is medical diagnosis, in particular to obtain the subset of microorganisms that have caused an infection. IMPROVER is based on the following assumptions:

- KB refinement is guided by importance of error, which is as follows:

  false negative > false positive > ordering mismatch.

- Any type of knowledge can be subject to refinement. Both domain and control knowledge may be responsible for the first two types of error, while only domain knowledge is responsible for the ordering mismatch error.
- The number of generated refinements is controlled by the following two choices: minimal changes are preferred and refinement cannot delete KB objects.

Based on these assumptions, the following refinement operators are legal:

- Generalize/specialize conditions in the left-hand side of rules and metarules
- Modify the CF of rules and metarules,
- Modify the CF in conclusions of up-down rules
- Modify the right hand side of metarules
- Add conditions to the left-hand side of rules and metarules
- Add new rules and metarules to the KB

IMPROVER goes through the following three stages in order: solving false negatives, solving false positives, and solving ordering mismatches. Each stage tries to solve the specific errors. IMPROVER has limited the generated refinements to one elementary change on a single KB object.

3.4.4. CONKRET

CONKRET (CONtrol Knowledge REfinement Tool) is a tool to refine control knowledge. It checks the functionality of metarules responsible for the dynamic generation of goals and strategies of an expert system. Implicit control is not treated. Explicit control is represented by metarules. It is assumed that the KB has already been checked and contains no structural anomalies, before executing CONKRET. The goal is to achieve a correct solution, and with CONKRET the user is trying to improve the way this solution is found. In other words, it improves the problem-solving strategies, so as to avoid exploring the whole search space.

The tool deals with expert systems represented in VETA, a metalanguage developed in VALID. A strategy in VETA is defined as a sequence of goals that the inference engine should pursue to reach a solution. A metarule has associated a CF used by the inference engine to select the metarule with the highest certainty when more than one is fireable. Every metarule belongs to a set of rules. The actions allowed as conclusions of metarules are the following:

- *Actions on rules*: inhibit a set of rules from firing
- *Actions on goals*: create, add, remove, or reorder goals from the current strategy
- *Problem-solving termination*

Metarules are responsible for the strategy generation during the problem-solving process. They may sometimes work improperly, making the problem-solving strategy deficient for a particular case. For example, when the metarule M is fired but the goals it provides are eventually found not to be relevant to the solution, it means that the firing of M wastes resources while trying to achieve the unnecessary goals. Another type of deficiency can be produced while solving a case when goals that should be considered are not. CONKRET does not automatically update the KB, it just suggests to the user which repairing actions better fit the given inputs. It works in the following way:

- Three types of deficiencies are detected: extra goal, omitted goal, and misplaced goal.
- The cause of every deficiency is identified by executing a particular algorithm for each type of deficiency.
- The most probable causes of the failure are selected.
- Suggestions are offered to the user to repair the deficiencies.

The deficiencies are detected by representing to the input of CONKRET the following information: a case (observable data of an expert system), a trace (information about the KBS execution of the case), and a goal standard (the correct sequence of goals that should follow the KBS inference mechanism to solve the case efficiently). Another tool has to be used to obtain the goal standard for a given case and produce a trace based on optimality criteria such as simplicity, path focus, etc.

3.4.5. IN-DEPTH

IN-DEPTH II is an incremental verifier that can perform the verification of a part of the KB or just consider some specific verification issues. The incremental verification process is formulated in the following way: let KB_0 be a verified knowledge base on which a change operator Θ is applied to an object *obj*, generating a new knowledge base KB_1, so that:

$$KB_1 = KB_0 + \Theta(obj)$$

where $\Theta \in \{ADD, MODIFY, REMOVE\}$ and $obj \in \{rule, module, metarule\}$.

As complexity is a fundamental problem, the question is what kind of test should be performed and on which elements of KB_1 to verify the new knowledge base with a minimum effort? The verification is composed of two steps:

1. If KB_1 contains new objects that do not appear in KB_0, these objects should be verified.
2. Changes in KB_1 can affect the verification results on objects in $KB_1 \cup KB_0$ (objects already verified at KB_0). Those verification tests and those objects for which verification results obtained in KB_0 do not hold in KB_1, should be repeated.

Consider the following example: $KB_1 = KB_0 + ADD(m)$ where m is a module; the first step consists of verifying the new module, i.e., testing that it does not contain inconsistencies. The second step consists of determining how m affects the results of verification tests performed on KB_0, and to what extent these results are maintained in KB_1. For example, if m contains a new way of deducing a fact f existing in KB_0, all verification tests involving f should be repeated since they are incomplete in KB_1.

The verification method is based on computing extended labels for KB objects and testing that some relations hold among these labels. In particular, KB_{inv} is the set of objects in $KB_1 \cap KB_0$ for which their extended labels do not change from KB_0 to KB_1, i.e., the results of verification tests in KB_0 are still valid in KB_1. It is shown that KB_{inv} does not depend on the changes performed in KB_1 by building a directed dependency graph G representing all dependencies on KB_{max}, where:

$$KB_{max} = KB_1, \text{ if } \Theta \in \{ADD, MODIFY\}$$
$$KB_{max} = KB_0, \text{ if } \Theta \in \{REMOVE\}$$

G is formed by (N,E) where N is a set of nodes and E is a set of directed edges. Each fact, rule, module, or metarule of KB_{max} is represented by a different node in N. Each node is labeled by the object it represents. There is an edge from n_i to n_j when the object labeling n_i depends on the object labeling n_j by three possible dependencies. The transitive closure is computed (C of G is a directed graph such that there is an edge v,w in C if there is a directed path from v to w in G). Those nodes that cannot be reached from the nodes corresponding to the modified objects, represent the objects forming the set KB_{inv}.

Using the method described above, IN-DEPTH II works in two steps:

1. It identifies the new objects added to the KB and verifies them
2. It verifies again the objects in KB that do not appear in the set KB_{inv}

3.4.6. Conclusions

In terms of current work, some of the verification systems are in use as research prototypes, while others come to supplement the existing commercial tools. Few of these tools include verification facilities, and those that do exist are largely restricted to simple checks. New and more sophisticated verification systems appear, although there is no getting away from the fact that full verification of anomalies in rule bases based on first-order logic is intractable. However, object orientation might solve some of the existing or potential problems inherent in the verification and validation of pure rule-based systems.

4. INDUSTRIAL REQUIREMENTS

4.1. ESTABLISHING A QUALITY CULTURE

The word "culture" does not have a precise definition, but its meaning in context is clear. There is no substitute for executive awarness of the importance of quality. Industry leaders care about quality and know how it might be achieved or assessed. This is not less true when applied to software, although many companies and organizations seem to be confused about the activities related to software quality.

In the software arena several activities related to software quality can be identified:

- *Software Quality Achievement:* Represents the process of obtaining methods about how to engineer quality into the software design, for example, during its development stages.
- *Software Quality Control:* Represents the process of checking at the end of some development stages (design stage, implementation stage) or at the end of some development process that has quality built in, that the quality required has been achieved using the specification, design, and implementation methods chosen during the software product life cycle.
- *Software Quality Assurance:* Represents that aspect of the overall management function that determines and implements the software quality policy that contains the overall quality intentions and objectives of an organization as formally expressed by senior management.
- *Software Quality Evaluation:* The process that involves measurements, tests static/dynamic analysis, and V&V techniques to determine the quality of the software (process/product).

- *Software Quality Assessment:* The process of comparing the actual tests and measurements of the characteristics of interest with the specifications of those characteristics.
- *Software Quality Certification:* The process by which a third independent party gives written assurance that a product, process, or service conforms to specified characteristics. In order to certificate, it is necessary to evaluate against a standard or some sort of requirement.

Within these activities, verification and validation plays an important role. V&V is one of the primary activities that requires addressing by software developers, independent V&V teams, and certification specialists. In this section we outline V&V as performed by indepenedent evaluation teams, and V&V in the view of certification. We conclude the section with some aspects related to the cost of V&V.

4.2.   INDEPENDENT VERIFICATION AND VALIDATION

Independent verification and validation (IV&V) is a process whereby the products of the software development life-cycle phases are independently reviewed, verified, and validated by an organization that is neither the provider nor the acquirer of the software. The IV&V activities duplicate the V&V activities step-by-step during the life cycle, with the exception that the testing performed is not "informal," but rather formal.

It is important to probe more closely into the relationship between verification, validation and testing, and IV&V. Testing and debugging refer to the analysis, exercise, and repair of software by the developers. IV&V is a process which is independent of normal development and testing activities. It is called IV&V to indicate that it is accomplished by parties who are not part of the immediate development team. The purpose of IV&V is not to directly assist in the development of reliable software, but to provide independent evidence that this is the case and that the system performs according to its requirements. Traditionally, V&V agents only discover problems, but they do not fix them. Correcting the problem is the task of the development team. However, the IV&V team is more likely to have a deeper understanding of testing methods, test-case construction, and a much better understanding of how to accomplish the complex task of repairing the detected problems completely, generally, and with fewer side effects.

There can easily be confusion regarding the relative roles of software quality assurance (SQA) and IV&V. Development management uses SQA to monitors its own organization and to ensure that established standards and procedures are followed. IV&V does essentially the same thing for the customer. The two types of activities need not overlap. In fact, an effective SQA program makes the IV&V process easier. IV&V cannot and should not replace SQA.

Expert systems are being increasingly applied to nontrivial problem domains, where erroneous advice may lead to loss of life, loss of considerable amounts of money, or loss of properties. There is an increased request for IV&V, especially from customers who want to make sure that the expert system they buy has the quality they need.

4.3.   V&V IN SUPPORT OF CERTIFICATION FOR CRITICAL SYSTEMS

Expert systems may be safety-critical where they must perform without failure. An inappropriately specified system may cause death, injury, or huge property losses. For example, many medical systems are safety-critical, meaning that errors in operation or use can lead to death or injury (and legal liability). Even where human safety is less of a consideration, a high degree of reliability is a requirement for an expert system. In the SE tradition, a safety-critical (computer) system is one whose malfunction could lead to "unacceptable consequences." This term has different meanings depending on the domain and tasks for which the systems are built: shipping, aerospace, process control, nuclear power plant, etc.

When safety issues are a primary consideration, a software-based system may be required to undergo certification corresponding to its application and criticality. Critical applications of software require rigorous attention to methods for reducing the probability of failure and ensuring the safety of those potentially affected by the failure of such software. This is not less true when applied to expert systems.

However, existing certification guidelines were not designed with AI or expert system software in mind. Although the major processes applied to conventional software are also applied to AI-based software, the unique characteristics associated with the development and testing of AI-based software are not covered in the standards existing in critical domains. Since AI is a relatively new technology, a lack of standardization exists. Standards relating to AI software are only beginning to emerge. Adherence to standards can have many benefits for developers, independent V&V teams, and certification specialists.

Key to the certification process for critical systems will be the faithful application of a thorough verification and validation process. Consequently, a new challenge in the field of V&V of expert systems is now to develop methods and techniques in support of certification.

4.4.   How Much V&V?

A general comment on V&V is that it is poorly understood and generally disliked. Adequate V&V is also expensive. This is not less true when applied to expert systems. Traditionally, it is one of the first activities to be cut when the project costs get tight. The need for V&V, especially for the benefits of reduced expert system maintenance, is seldom understood by management. Nevertheless, there is considerable agreement that V&V will always show a positive cost-avoidance benefit over the life of a system. Careful V&V will do so in some cases even when assessed just for the development stage.

How much V&V? is then a natural question within industrial applications. *Nonfunctional* features are relatively easy to define, and there are methods that can be applied straightforwardly to check them. However, conformity to the *functional* part of the specification is another matter. It is generally agreed that we cannot prove (guarantee) by testing that a program conforms to its specification. Therefore, it is important to define what level of checking will be sufficient for the specified purposes. However, there is no simple answer to the question "How much V&V should we do to ensure the quality of the system/subsystem/module/procedure?," as several factors should be taken into consideration.

Of particular concern from the point of view of V&V is the *system complexity.* The complexity of the system is defined by several characteristics which make the system harder to develop and analyze. Generally, the higher the complexity, the greater the opportunity for errors and the greater the need for V&V. However, there is another factor that needs to be considered in determining the extent of estimated V&V required: system integrity. *System integrity* refers to the joint capability of a system to operate for long periods without failures, to fail gracefully with reasonable warnings, to be able to recover rapidly without much difficulty, and to avoid causing expensive damage to property or harm to people or the environment. How much integrity is required of a system will be a function of several factors. Thus, a highly complex system with a low degree of required integrity should probably not need as much V&V as a highly complex system with a very high degree of required system integrity.

If we translate the system complexity and integrity requirements into quality requirements, then the above-mentioned question should be answered in connection with another one, i.e.: "How critical is the quality of the system/subsystem/ module/ procedure?"

5.   RESEARCH INITIATIVES

In Europe, many of the V&V projects have taken place under the European Strategic Programme for Research and Development in Information Technology. Some of the completed projects are KADS, VALID, VITAL, and VIVA. An ongoing project, demonstrating the feasibility of extending the expert system technology to safety critical systems, is Safe-KBS.

In U.S., the majority of research on V&V involves the development of tools to support automatic code-checking. NASA and its contractors have been involved in a number of verification and validation projects.

6.   FUTURE TRENDS AND SUMMARY

6.1.   HYBRID INTELLIGENT SYSTEMS

Hybrid intelligent systems are systems that combine the advantages offered by expert systems, neural networks, and fuzzy systems. The need for such systems has emerged due to the fact that we are at a stage of development in which further increase in performance of existing tools requires the use of intelligent tools offered by these systems. Until now, their use was limited to stand-alone architectures; today the intelligent hybrid systems are the emerging technology that could take advantage of the best of each technology's features. This synergistic approach recognizes both similarities and differences between these systems, and suggests that for many particular applications the resultant hybrid system could reflect the best aspects of each component of the system (Vermesan and Vermesan, 1996).

One landmark awaited in the maturing of hybrid system technology is verification and validation. Clearly, there is little benefit in employing such a complex system unless it can be trusted to perform its function. Verification and validation of expert systems is an established discipline that has accumulated valuable experience over recent years. There are now many verification and validation techniques, plus considerable experience and expertise in using them. The natural question is whether these techniques can be expanded and adapted to cope with hybrid systems, or new ones are needed.

In the case of rule-based systems, a difficult process is to guarantee that the addition, deletion, or modification of rules does not leave the system in a state of chaos. However, in the case of a hybrid system, e.g., neural network expert system, the process may not be that difficult due to the fact that automated tools can help. The most important automated tool is the learning algorithm itself. It can assure that by adding, deleting, or modifying training examples, the knowledge base remains consistent with the set of training examples. Two validation procedures with extracted rules and encoded rules are presented in Vermesan and Vermesan (1995).

Furthermore, one would expect to be able to use the good techniques from V&V of rule-based systems to fuzzy rules. It might appear that a fuzzy system can be verified and validated more easily than conventional rules, because a fuzzy system uses vague terms to explain the control actions, and would therefore be easier to understand and cope with. In reality, the verification and validation problems may be more difficult. As everything in fuzzy logic is a matter a degree, the consistency model valid for expert systems does not work in the case of fuzzy rules. The concept of consistency must be refined into a notion of degree of consistency. Moreover, verifying and validating a hybrid system is not simply a problem of verifying and validating each component separately. An integrated view is needed. Therefore, building models of the hybrid system and expressing them in a formal or less formal way may be a good practice. Such models can always provide an objective measure for the executable system.

6.2.   CONCLUSION: CURRENT STATE AND OPEN PROBLEMS

Research and development in expert system verification and validation has emerged as a distinct field only in the last decade, as expert systems have become more prevalent in real-world applications.

A lot of V&V work is found in the literature as structural verification. Extensive research has been oriented especially toward rule-based systems, i.e., detecting errors and anomalies such as redundancy, dead-end rules, subsumption, auxiliary rules, circular rules, etc. This has led to construction of tools for automatic detection of these errors and anomalies, some of which have been described as verification and validation systems. These anomaly detection techniques can be useful in highlighting areas of the knowledge base that require attention.

In real applications, many attempts have been made to formulate an underlying model. For various reasons many of these models are not explicitly defined. As a consequence, the validity of the knowledge base depends on the modeling process in ways that are difficult to check. The presence of explicit models of expertise have a higher impact on V&V, as it introduces new complexities to the V&V process compared to the other approaches and compared to conventional programs. Working from an explicit model gives a much higher degree of confidence concerning the quality of the expert systems.

It is fairly clear from the exposition of V&V methods, techniques, and systems that there is no one technique or approach that is appropriate for handling all V&V aspects of a complete expert system (another lesson from V&V of conventional software). Therefore, it would be worthwhile to inquire how these techniques can interact and communicate with each other in a useful manner. At the same time, further research is needed to compare and contrast specific alternative expert system verification and validation paradigms.

The many approaches reported by both research and industry suggest a coupling of V&V techniques to all stages of the expert system development. However, the question at what time should V&V of an expert system be considered — before it is constructed, while it is being constructed, or after it has been constructed — is still open. There are numerous, convincing arguments for various design and V&V methods, although V&V of expert systems is as fraught with problems and pitfalls as V&V of any software system. Fortunately, the existing knowledge and experience acquired through many years of software engineering can be utilized. In this way, repeating the same errors as in conventional software development can at least be avoided, and the attention can be focused on problems that are not common in conventional software, problems that are specific to expert systems and which add new difficulties to the V&V activities.

Another landmark awaited in the maturing of V&V technology is its active adoption by the industry. Although many good theoretical techniques and methods are published in the literature, one cannot go directly from the published examples to more complex examples. Nowadays, systems tend to become more and more complex and therefore the abstract models that have been used so far need to be reconsidered. The idealizing assumptions made for the development of an expert system must deal with the complexity of the environment in which the expert system runs. To develop operational, dependable, and reliable systems, developers need to work harder to define the scope of the application, the limitation of the domain, the requirements, and to verify and validate rigorously those aspects of the system. It is only in the context of practical applications that the various V&V methods will reveal their true worth.

Finally, this chapter has presented a view of the multifaceted work that is carried out in the area of verification and validation expert systems. Much ground has been covered, starting from theoretical foundation of V&V, continuing with V&V systems developed by research and industry, and finally approaching the industrial needs for V&V of expert systems. The perspective put forward in this chapter is that V&V is one of the primary activities that requires addressing by software developers, independent V&V teams, and certification specialists. The current research initiatives and industrial needs provide some evidence to suggest that more work is needed to make the existent V&V methods better understood and to answer the difficult questions of the open problems.

REFERENCES

Coenen, F. and Bench-Capon, T. (1993). *Maintenance of Knowledge-Based Systems*, Academic Press, London.

Lee, S. and O'Keefe, R.M. (1993). Subsumption anomalies in hybrid knowledge bases, *International Journal of Expert Systems: Research and Applications*, 6(3), pp. 299–318.

Liebowitz, J. (1986). Useful approach for evaluating expert systems, *Expert Systems*, 3(2), pp. 86–96.

Miller, L.A. (1990). Dynamic testing of knowledge bases using the heuristic testing approach, *Expert Systems With Applications*, Vol. 1, pp. 249–269.

Preece, A.D. and Shinghal, R. (1994). Foundation and application of knowledge base verification, *International Journal of Intelligent Systems*, Vol. 9, pp. 683–701.

Preece, A.D., Shinghal, R., and Batarekh, A. (1992). Principles and practice in verifying rule-based systems, *The Knowledge Engineering Review*, Vol. 7:2, 115–141.

Vermesan, A.I. (1996). A definition of subsumption anomalies in conceptual models of object-oriented KBSs. In *Proc. of AAAI96 Workshop on Verification and Validation of Knowledge-Based Systems and Subsystems*, Portland, OR.

Vermesan, A.I. and Bench-Capon, T. (1995). Techniques for the verification and validation of knowledge-based systems: A survey based on the symbol/knowledge level distinction, In *Software, Testing, Verification & Reliability*, John Wiley & Sons, pp. 233–271.

Vermesan, A.I. and Vermesan, O. (1996). An object-oriented framework for NN-ES hybrid systems, In Taylor, J.G. (Ed.), *Neural Networks and Their Applications*, John Wiley & Sons, chap. 15, pp. 205–227.

Vermesan, O. and Vermesan, A.I. (1995). The use of hybrid intelligent systems in telecommunications, In Liebowitz, J. and Prerau, D. (Eds.), *Worldwide Intelligent Systems*, IOS Press, chap. 10, pp. 186–226.

Wielinga, B.J., Schreiber, A.T., and Breuker, J.A. (1992). KADS: A modelling approach to knowledge engineering, *Knowledge Acquisition (Special issue: The KADS approach to knowledge engineering)*, March, 4(1), pp. 5–53.

Part II
Selected Important Elements of the
Expert System Development Process

6 Expert System Technology: Expert System Interface

Chaomei Chen and Roy Rada

CONTENTS

1. INTRODUCTION

An expert system is meant to embody the expertise of a human expert involved in a particular field, in such a way that non-expert users, looking for advice in that field, have the expert's knowledge at their disposal when questioning the system. An important feature of expert systems is that they are able to explain to the user the line of reasoning that led to the solution of a problem or the desired advice.

Expert systems have gone from academic laboratories, through industrial development, and have reached a substantial user population. One of the major concerns is whether these systems are hard to learn and difficult to use in practice. Real users of expert systems have a large body of knowledge about the problem in their specialized areas. They want to understand what is happening and be in control. They prefer to be in charge along the way, directing the machine and developing an effective cognitive model of the task domain that reduces their dependency on the expert system.

Human-Computer Interaction (HCI) addresses how a computer system can be made easy to learn and easy to use. A large number of methods have been developed for prototyping, inspecting, and evaluating the user interface of a system in particular and the overall system in general.

However, the existing literature of both HCI and AI (artificial intelligence) reveals relatively few studies that specifically focus on user interface design issues for expert systems. The link is weaker between the two fields than it ought to be. In this chapter, we aim identify reasons for the relative weakness of the link and clarify issues that will be essential to the strengthening of such a link and thereby increase the usability of expert systems as a whole.

First, we revisit the questions raised about a decade ago with emphasis on the needs of users. We refer the reader in particular to two edited collections of papers about expert systems and interfaces (Hendler, 1988; Berry and Hart, 1990). Second, we address issues that have the potential to help the design, implementation, and evaluation of user interfaces for expert systems.

1.1. Expert Systems

Expert systems are systems that are capable of offering solutions to specific problems in a given domain or that are able to give advice, both in a way and at a level comparable to that of experts in the field. Building expert systems for specific application domains is known as *knowledge engineering*.

The way that expert systems are built results in some unique advantages. Although expert systems are still expensive to build and maintain, they are inexpensive to operate. An expert system can be easily distributed in a number of copies, whereas training a new human expert is much more time-consuming and expensive. An expert system can reduce the information that human users need to process, reduce personnel costs, and increase throughput. Expert systems are likely to perform tasks more consistently than human experts. An expert system will handle similar situations in the same way and make comparable recommendations, whereas humans are influenced by various effects, such as recency and primacy effects. For example, most recent information has a disproportionate impact on one's judgment. On the other hand, primacy effects refer to the fact that early information dominates the judgment. An expert system can provide permanent documentation of the decision process.

The knowledge of several human experts can be combined to give a system more breadth than a single person is likely to achieve. Expert systems can help a firm create entry barriers for potential competitors. A central task underlying many of the activities of attorneys is inferring the legal consequences of a given set of facts. Some systems use a case-based reasoning approach in which new cases are compared with the smallest collections of precedent facts that justified an individual inference step in the explanation of a precedent case. This sets a precedent to be used in case comparison. Case comparison also is assisted by an expressive semantic network representation of case facts. Techniques are presented for retrieving and comparing cases represented in this formalism.

While expert systems have many advantages, they also have some weaknesses. For example, expert systems are not good at judgments that depend on meta-knowledge, i.e., knowledge about their own expertise. Expert systems are not good at recognizing when no answer exists or when the problem is outside their area of expertise. Human experts, in addition to technical knowledge, have common sense. Human experts automatically adapt to changing environments; expert systems must be explicitly updated. Human experts can respond creatively to unusual situations, while expert systems cannot. It is not yet known how to give expert systems common sense.

1.2.   The Acceptance and Success of an Expert System

Expert systems (ESs) are used in an increasingly wider range of application areas. Companies and businesses more and more rely on expert systems. Such widespread use raises issues concerning their value and factors that may affect the success of incorporating an expert system in practice. Are existing evaluation techniques from the HCI applicable for assessing expert systems?

It has been found that the success of ESs, in terms of user satisfaction, is directly related to the quality of developers and the ES shells used, end-user characteristics, and degree of user involvement in ES development. Several recommendations are proposed for ES project managers to enhance the likelihood of project success, including adding problem difficulty as a criterion for ES application selection; increasing ES developer training to improve people skills; having the ability to model and use a systems approach in solving business problems; sharpening end-user attitudes and expectations regarding ES; improving the selection of domain experts; more thoroughly understanding the ES impact on end-user jobs; restricting the acquisition of ES shells based on a set of criteria; and ensuring a proper match of ES development techniques and tools to the business problem at hand.

1.3.   The Role of Its User Interface

User interfaces need to deal with three fundamental problems: communication, control, and access. The first problem is about communication between users and the system. The second problem is about control and the issue of who does what when and task allocation in general. The third problem concerns making the full range of facilities and computational capabilities accessible and useful to users.

2.   BACKGROUND

The acceptance of an expert system by the end-user has been regarded as one of the major criteria for the success of an expert system. An expert system needs to be easy to learn and friendly to use. After all, it must fit into the existing work environment and be compatible with other computer systems in use. It is also known that user interface design is one of the main reasons that hindered expert systems transition from prototype into everyday use. The success of expert systems therefore depends upon the user interfaces as well as the efficiency of its knowledge encoding and reasoning.

2.1.   History

There are an ever-growing number of books and papers on expert systems. Several classic ones are discussed in Clancy and Shortliffe (1984). The first expert systems were developed as early as the late 1960s. The research in expert systems gained substantial growth in the 1970s. The early expert systems mostly concerned the field of medical diagnosis. The best-known expert system in medicine is MYCIN, developed in the 1970s at Standford University. The MYCIN system is able to assist internists in the diagnosis and treatment of a number of infectious diseases. This system has given an important impulse to the development of similar expert systems in fields other than medicine.

Another classic example is XCON, previously called R1, which can configure computer systems from Digital Equipment Corporation (DEC) such as VAX and PDP11. Configuring a computer system requires considerable skill and effort. In the late 1970s, DEC and Carnegie-Mellon University started the development of XCON. XCON has been fully operational since 1981.

2.2.   USABILITY ISSUES WITH EXPERT SYSTEMS

Expert systems raise new design issues concerning three separate but highly interacting aspects of a design process: knowledge capture, encoding the knowledge and expertise into the system, and ensuring that the system is accepted by an active user community. The designer of a user interface must consider many aspects of computer usage ranging from cognitive models of users to ergonomic issues. The designer must concentrate on many aspects of usability, including a focus on users and their tasks, getting empirical evidence about effectiveness, and stressing iteration between designers, implementers and users. It was sugggested in the introduction chapter of Hendler's book (1988) that these three aspects are special for user interfaces for expert systems:

- Providing tools for the different personnel involved in each of these stages. What are the particular needs by various users at each stage? How are these needs best addressed in the design of the system?
- The special needs of expert system users. The user community for expert systems is often different from those using traditional systems such as word-processors and operating systems. Although these users may be novices in computing, they are often experts in their own field.
- The efficacy of these interfaces. The design process requires getting empirical evidence about the effectiveness of the tools. The designer must therefore consider how to evaluate the interface designed for expert systems. How do we demonstrate that these systems are useful to the users? How do we present a rule base such that the eventual user is able to test it?

2.3.   SPECIAL NEEDS FOR EXPERT SYSTEM INTERFACES

Expert systems have some special interface needs. One of the most essential requirements is the need for explanation of the reasoning process. The requirement becomes crucial to the acceptance of the system by users.

An expert system is not just a tool that implements a process; rather, it is a representation of that process. Many of these processes correspond to judgments that can have critical consequences in the real world. The user interface must present not only final conclusions and recommendations, but an explication of the processes of how such conclusions are reached.

Expert systems are often used as a decision-making support tool. The interface designer must be able to provide support for a knowledge engineer who is trying to enter and encode the representation of the process as well as users who wish to see the process of decision-making per se.

2.4.   USER MODELING AND ADAPTIVE USER INTERFACES

User-centered system design in HCI emphasizes the importance of addressing users and their needs. On the other hand, researchers and practitioners have realized that the needs of users are not a constant, which implies that user interfaces must be adaptive so as to fit smoothly into the users' learning processes. Learner-centered design draws attention to the changing needs of users, both students and professionals, as they gain expertise and how these changes need to be reflected in the interface. Interface design must be tailored to support users as learners with case studies of their experiences in designing adaptive and adaptable interfaces for learners.

User modeling has made considerable progress, particularly in the last few years. The need has been recognized in many application areas for software systems to automatically adapt to their current users. As a result, research in user modeling has extended into many disciplines that are concerned with the development of interactive computer systems used by diverse groups of users. These fields include Intelligent Interfaces, Active and Passive Help Systems, Hypertext Systems,

Intelligent Information Retrieval, Natural-Language Systems, Intelligent Tutoring Systems, and Cooperative Expert Systems.

The following is a taxonomy that has been commonly used to organize a broad range of classification parameters for adaptive user interfaces, including tasks and agents, types, levels, scope, goals, methods, strategies, models and architectures of adaptation, and adaptation techniques. The taxonomy is presented as a classification tree.

- Aspects of Adaptivity in User Interfaces
- Stages and Agents in the Adaptation Process
- Type of Adaptation
- Level of Adaptation
- Scope of Adaptation
- Goal of Adaptation
- Methods of Adaptation
- Strategies of Adaptation

In addition, a number of formalisms and techniques are associated with user interface design, including user modelling, task modeling, dialog modeling, and plan recognition.

3. TECHNIQUES, PRACTICES, METHODOLOGIES, AND APPLICATIONS

Explanation is an important function in symbolic artificial intelligence. Explanation is used in machine learning, in case-based reasoning and, most importantly, in the explanation of the results of a reasoning process. Experience with expert systems has shown that the ability to generate explanations is important for the user acceptance of AI systems.

3.1. USER INTERFACE AND EXPLANATION

One of the main challenges in the development of user interfaces to expert systems is to provide both the end-user and the knowledge engineer with means for applying the knowledge in the system in different ways. For example, the same medical knowledge base may be consulted by a physician to solve a medical diagnostic problem, or it may be browsed to determine which findings are typical in a given disease, or it may even be used to instruct a medical student by explaining why the disease she or he suspects in a patient does or does not fit the patient data available. It is clear that such different ways of exploiting a knowledge base require different user interfaces.

Expert systems capable of adapting their behavior to the user are usually associated with a user model. The goals and roles of user behavior modeling are the major factors that determine how user behavior should be modeled, how the information is to be acquired and presented, and how the resultant model is to be used. The application of user models in expert systems is a subject of ongoing research. However, it seems evident that there is a substantial gap as well as conceptual discrepancies between HCI and AI in terms of user modeling (McTear, 1993).

There are various possible dialog forms for expert system users. A *user-initiated* dialog refers to the interaction that is always initiated on the side of the user, whereas a *computer-initiated* dialog refers to ones in which the computer asks users questions. Most current expert systems have a dialog form lying somewhere in between the two extremes, and the initiative of the dialog can be switched between the computer and the user. An expert system with such a dialog form is called a system supporting a *mixed-initiated* dialog. Expert systems primarily developed for the inexperienced user usually take the computer-initiated form. Systems for experienced users generally give the users more control to the discourse of dialog.

An important aspect of the interaction between user and expert systems is the explanation to a user of the line of reasoning undertaken by the system during a specific consultation. A clear and understandable explanation can be a valuable means for justifying the recommendations of the expert system, for indicating its limitations to the user, and for instructing users about the problem domain covered by the system.

Designing an expert system that is able to provide understandable and helpful explanations involves issues such as the level of detail of the information presented to the user, the structuring of the information presented, and the distinction between various types of knowledge. Explanation is a very complicated form of human communication that is not well understood. Most conventional expert systems provide a form of explanation limited to a description of the reasoning steps that were undertaken in confirming or rejecting a set of hypotheses. They usually are not able to adapt their behavior to the user's experience in the problem domain. Hendler (1988) remains a main source of information on the development of user interfaces for expert systems.

3.2. DIALOG MODELS

More directly related to user interface design for expert systems is to see explanations as communications or dialogs between users and expert systems. For example, human verbal explanations are essentially interactive. If someone is giving a complex explanation, the listener will be given the opportunity to indicate whether he/she is following as the explanation proceeds, and if necessary interrupt with clarification questions. These interactions allow the speaker to both clear up the listener's immediate difficulties as they arise, and to update assumptions about their level of understanding. Better models of the listener's level of understanding in turn allow the speaker to continue the explanation in a more appropriate manner, lessening the risk of continuing confusion. Despite its apparent importance, existing explanation and text generation systems fail to allow for this sort of interaction. Although some systems allow follow-up questions at the end of an explanation, they assume that a complete explanation has been planned and generated before such interactions are allowed. However, for complex explanations, interactions with the user should take place as the explanation progresses, and should influence how that explanation continues. Casey (1993) described the EDGE system, which is able to plan complex, extended explanations that allow such interactions with the user. The system can update assumptions about the user's knowledge on the basis of these interactions, and uses this information to influence the detailed further planning of the explanation. When the user appears confused, the system can attempt to fill in missing knowledge or to explain things another way.

In recent years the emphasis in natural language understanding research has shifted from studying mechanisms for understanding isolated utterances to developing strategies for interpreting sentences within the context of a discourse or an extended dialog. A very fruitful approach to this problem has derived from a view of human behavior as goal-directed and understanding as explanation-based. According to this view, people perform actions and communicate to advance their goals, and language understanding therefore involves recognizing and reasoning about the goals and plans of others.

3.3. THE ROLE OF A CONCEPTUAL MODEL

Several influential models in HCI emphasize that a high-level conceptual model of the interface is of major importance to the users' ability to learn an interface and to their comfort and efficiency in using it. When users approach a new system, they are trying to build a model of what the system does and how they will get it to do it. If the interface either encourages formation of a correct model, the users' ability to learn and use a system is enhanced.

The mental model is even more important for users of expert systems. It is crucial to a user, particularly an expert in a field, that a system is doing the reasoning correctly. If users find it difficult to understand the coverage of the system, the inference processes and the match to their own reasoning processes, their ability to use the system is undermined and acceptance becomes more problematic.

To enable a user to develop the conceptual model of the processes of the expert system, it is important that the system is able to explain both the reasoning process it uses and how that process is represented in the system. Explanation is also critical to the acceptance of systems by real users. Early medical expert systems based on Bayes Theorems, for example, often arrived at a correct conclusion. However, the users were unable to predict what questions the system would ask, were unable to follow the reasoning involved, and had no access to the knowledge base of the system. These systems were not accepted by the medical community because of such difficulties. In more recent knowledge-based systems, the trend is to open up the knowledge base for users to use the knowledge for inferencing and decision-making.

The level of conceptual level is usually built on top of the semantic level. At this level the designer is concerned with the meanings conveyed by the user's input and by the computer's output. Designing the semantic level of this type of interface is a prime concern of the designer of the expert systems shell. In the case of the interface design for an expert system, this level is complicated by the number of different types of users who may be involved. The designer, for example, must consider interfaces for different tasks, such as knowledge capture and end use of the expert system.

3.4. INTELLIGENT INTERFACE

Intelligent interfaces represent the latest development in human-computer interaction and interface design. The concept of an intelligent interface was introduced to offer innovative solutions to the problems encountered in human-computer interaction. An intelligent interface can be defined as an intelligent entity mediating between two or more interacting agents who possess an incomplete understanding of each others' knowledge and form of communication. A related concept is adaptive interfaces.

3.4.1. Models of the Intelligent Interface

The concept of an intelligent interface between humans and machines requires a notion of shared intelligence and cognition that creates technical challenges for interface designers. Much of the conceptual foundation for intelligent interfaces is being laid by research on human information processing. Previous literature on intelligent interfaces has been concerned principally with delineating functional attributes. For example, it has been suggested that interfaces should enhance human-computer interaction in terms of services, style, and clarity. Intelligent interfaces should provide services such as the automation of routine tasks, and provision of easy access to tools and to online assistance and documentation. These services should be provided so as to encourage experimentation, minimize errors and be non-intrusive. Furthermore, intelligent interfaces should present a smooth transition from novice to expert modes of operation.

3.4.2. Intelligent Interface and Machine Reasoning

An intelligent interface has also been seen as a machine reasoning system. In such cases, the key components are methods for representing task knowledge, user models, and inference tools for reasoning as the task progresses. Expert systems, on the other hand, typically do not incorporate extensive user models. Expert systems employ human knowledge to perform tasks that usually require human intelligence. Expert systems appear to provide the best means for implementing machine reasoning. Intelligent interfaces that are based on expert systems technology will either need enhancements to their user model or else the use input will be constrained to be rather specific to avoid the problems of ambiguity in language.

3.4.3.   Expert Systems As Intelligent Interfaces

Expert systems represent an alternative model of an intelligent interface where the interface plays a more active role in assisting the user with the performance of the task. Consider an advisory expert system where the user wants to make a decision with the assistance of an expert system. The machine reasoning capability of the intelligent interface is foremost, and the task is represented in the knowledge base and inference engine of the expert system. The discourse output machine will include the explanation facility along with the user interface tools that query the user and output the expert system's advice. The user interface will also implement the functions of the discourse input machine, structuring and parsing the user inputs into the form of facts and rules that can be recognized by the knowledge base and inference engine. Advisory expert systems represents only one type of expert system.

3.5.   DIRECT MANIPULATION

Ideally, the communication between the user and the system should be so natural that the user is not even aware that he is communicating through an interface. From this perspective, direct manipulation interfaces can be seen as types of intelligent interfaces. Major issues that have been addressed in the literature of interface design include memory load, visual representation, and transition between levels of abstraction. In spite of the influence of direct manipulation concepts, almost all interfaces involve a form of dialog between the human and the computer. Furnas, Landauer, Gomez, and Dumais (1987) show that there were very low rates of agreement in the words assigned by different users to the same function.

3.6.   USER INTERFACE MANAGEMENT SYSTEMS FOR EXPERT SYSTEMS

User Interface Management Systems (UIMS) is a method that helps interface designers to cope with the ever-increasing demands on their systems. UIMS systems provide various tools to facilitate interface design and evaluation, such as action logging mechanisms, automatic code generation, maintaining consistent interface design, and supporting the complete life cycle from prototype to final application. This is accomplished by maintaining consistency within and across applications and making it easier to rapidly iterate through the implement-and-test cycle.

For expert systems, an interface designer's productivity can be greatly increased by using UIMS systems in which interface design language closely matches the expert system languages used.

3.7.   WWW INTERFACES

The WWW has been a revolution on the computing scene since the early 1990s. Expert system developers realize the value to be gained by connecting their knowledge bases to the WWW interface. Such an interface improves the likelihood that the expert system can have wide accessibility.

At the simple end, an expert system simply uses text-based WWW interfaces to replace a text-based interface that would be delivered in some other more proprietary way. For instance, a lymph node expert system was developed in a class project and is accessible on the WWW (Cheng et al., 1996). At the other end, researchers are develoing virtual reality interfaces on top of the WWW that allow the user to be immersed in the environment about which the expert system is giving advice. For instance, in ship emergency handling with expert system support, a virtual reality interface supported on the WWW can be particularly valuable (Wilkins, 1996).

4.   RESEARCH ISSUES

The central issue of user interfaces to expert systems arises from the fact that an expert system may play a diverse range of roles in its practical use and maintenance. At present, expert systems technology is used opportunistically by organizations mainly on an individual application basis. As a result, assimilation of this technology can be slow as there is no proper coordination. With increasing awareness of its value and benefits, more organizations are venturing into this technology; but to maximize its potential, a systemic approach must be adopted. Research in expert systems reveals that besides technical issues, there are numerous human behavioral variables pertinent to the construction of the master plan. The culture of a corporation and its present level of computerization are significant factors related to the psychological readiness of its staff members to tap into expert system technology on a more massive scale.

4.1. ACCEPTANCE

One of the key issues an expert system designer must address is the ultimate acceptance of the system by intended users. The acceptance may be affected by many factors. One reason may be simply the natural scepticism about artificial intelligence that is still seen in many application domains. For some groups of users, such as doctors, lawyers, physicists, and managers, who are traditionally recognized as experts in their own field, it is essential for them to be convinced that the underlying reasoning is valid and the knowledge has been correctly encoded. An expert system therefore must be able to explain its behavior and show the reasoning process.

The designer must take ecological issues into account, including where and when users access an expert system and how the user interface of the expert system is compatible with other interfaces in the same working environment. These factors are often overlooked.

This need for pragmatic knowledge about the environment in which the expert system will be used is repeatedly emphasized by studies on the reasons for successes or failures of expert systems in practice. For instance, in one such recent study, the main conclusion was that management needs to be convinced that the expert system will affect company productivity and individual users need to see the benefits to their job performance (Duchessi and O'Keefe, 1995). These and other similar factors are most important in determining whether or not an expert system will be accepted in the work environment.

One popular new approach to expert systems development is to incorporate intelligent agents that support collaborative work. The expert system includes a model of the collaborative work situation of those who will use the system. Where the human activity can be performed by the computer, the agent detects the opportunity and assists the people (Bose, 1996).

4.2. EFFECTIVE MEANS OF EXPLANATION

Providing explanations for recommended actions is deemed one of the most important capabilities of expert systems. There is little empirical evidence, however, that explanation facilities indeed influence user confidence in, and acceptance of, decisions and recommendations made by expert systems. Some empirical studies recently investigated the impact of explanations provided by expert systems on changes in user beliefs toward conclusions generated by expert systems.

Based on a theoretical model of argument, three alternative types of explanations, (1) trace, (2) justification, and (3) strategy, were provided in a simulated diagnostic expert system performing auditing tasks. Twenty practicing auditors evaluated the outputs of the system in a laboratory setting. The results indicate that explanation facilities can make advice from expert systems more acceptable to users and that justification is the most effective type of explanation to bring about changes in user attitudes toward the system.

4.3. EMPIRICAL EXPLORATION

People have recognized that the ability to provide relevant and informative explanations regarding various machine reasoning processes is one of the most important features of an expert system. The "Wizard of Oz" technique has been used in the development of expert systems as well as in user interface design and evaluation. Using the "Wizard of Oz" technique where, unknown to the subject, a person provides a simulation of the system as an expert, an experiment was carried out that looked at the usefulness of various types of explanation.

Although explanation capability is one of the distinguishing characteristics of expert systems, the explanation facilities of most existing systems are quite primitive. The task of justifying expert decisions is an intelligence-requiring activity, and the appropriate model for machine-produced justifications should be explanations written by people. It is essential that an expert system is able to synthesize knowledge from a variety of sources and produce coherent, multisentential text similar to that produced by a domain expert.

Different types of explanations provided by an expert system may have significant impact on the usability, user satisfaction, and overall acceptance of the system. A number of studies addressed this issue. For example, three commonly used types of explanations are: (1) rule-based explanations, (2) condition-based explanations, and (3) rule-and-condition combined explanations. Available evidence indicates that the level of user satisfaction indeed depends on the type of explanation provided. In general, the rule-and-condition combined explanations tend to be the most satisfactory and useful.

Knowledge-based systems that interact with humans often need to define their terminology, elucidate their behavior, or support their recommendations or conclusions. In general, they need to explain themselves. Unfortunately, current computer systems often generate explanations that are unnatural, ill-connected, or simply incoherent. They typically have only one method of explanation that does not allow them to recover from failed communication. At a minimum, this can irritate an end-user and potentially decrease their productivity. More dangerous, poorly conveyed information may result in misconceptions on the part of the user that can lead to bad decisions or invalid conclusions, which may have costly or even dangerous implications. To address this problem, human-produced explanations have been studied with the aim of transferring explanation expertise to machines. It has been suggested that a domain-independent taxonomy of abstract explanatory utterances is needed to develop a taxonomy of multisentence explanations.

Explanatory utterances can be classified based on their content and communicative function. These utterance classes and additional text analysis can be used subsequently to construct a taxonomy of text types. This text taxonomy may characterize multisentence explanations according to the content they convey, the communicative acts they perform, and their intended effect on the addressee's knowledge, beliefs, goals, and plans. It is suggested that the act of explanation presentation is an action-based endeavor and introduces and defines an integrated theory of communicative acts (rhetorical, illocutionary, and locutionary acts).

To use this theory, one can formalize several of these communicative acts as plan operators and then show their use by a hierarchical text planner that composes natural language explanations. One can therefore classify a range of reactions that readers may have to explanations and illustrate how a system can respond to these given a plan-based approach.

In contrast to symbolic systems, neural networks have no explicit, declarative knowledge representation and therefore have considerable difficulties in generating explanation structures. In neural networks, knowledge is encoded in numeric parameters (weights) and distributed all over the system. It has been found that connectionist systems benefit from the explicit coding of relations and the use of highly structured networks in order to allow explanation and explanation components. Connectionist semantic networks, i.e., connectionist systems with an explicit conceptual hierarchy, belong to a class of artificial neural networks that can be extended by an explanation component which gives meaningful responses to a limited class of "How?" questions.

4.4. FITTING INTO THE USER ENVIRONMENT

Traditional wisdom has been that the design of an expert system requires iterative interaction with the knowledge engineer until the knowledge is satisfactorily encoded by the knowledge engineer into the system. To fit an expert system into a workflow, the interface designer must consider contextual issues associated with the acceptance of end-users. User-centered design, getting end-users involved early in the design process, has been recognized as a way to improve the situation. In this case, the interface designer needs to collaborate with end-users (who may not necessarily be domain experts themselves).

The ultimate criterion of success for interactive expert systems is that they will be used, and used to effect, by individuals other than the system developers. Many developers are still not involving users in an optimal way. New approaches have been suggested to better bring the user into the expert system development process, and these approaches incorporate both ethnographic analysis and formal user testing (Berry, 1994).

Expert systems have a range of use. For example, an expert system can be used to obtain "second opinion" in a much similar way to consulting a knowledgeable colleague; an expert system can be used as a "what if" system to predict and test various scenarios. The interface designer must be clear about the goals of the system and the user.

5. FUTURE TRENDS AND SUMMARY

Surveys of experts systems show that the majority of the expert system applications were in manufacturing, business, and medicine. In the late 1980s, there was a growth of expert system applications in the business and industrial areas, which increased from 10% of the market in 1986 to 60% in 1993.

The predominant type of expert systems (30%) is diagnosis systems, which help people to locate problems in a complex system. Interpretation and prescription systems are both more than 15%. The predominant role of expert systems has been diagnosis; in fact, that it the role most experts play in everyday life.

One reason for the large amount of diagnostic systems is because they are relatively easy to develop. Most diagnostic problems have a finite list of possible solutions and a manageable problem space. Another reason has to do with practical considerations. Most organizations prefer to take a low-risk solution when introducing new technology. Systems having the maximum chance of success at a low risk are easily accepted. Diagnostic systems are in this category.

Early expert systems took many experts and time to build. The MYCIN system was developed during the mid-1970s and took approximiately 20 person-years to complete. The major reason for the extended time was the lack of software development tools. The 1980s saw the proliferation of expert system shells. These software tools made expert systems development much easier and substantially reduced development life cycle. This is a trend that should continue in the future. In particular, there should be more UIMS tools for expert systems to simplify the design, implementation, and evaluation of expert system interfaces.

Surveys also predicted a shift from stand-alone expert systems to embedded intelligent agents. An embedded expert system builds on the existing functionality of existing software by performing some task in a more intelligent fashion. For example, with the exponential growth of the Internet and the World-Wide Web, future expert system applications would need to be integrated with various information management systems. Designers of expert system interfaces therefore will face a wider range of cognitive and social issues to increase the chance of success of an expert system in a larger context.

The number of expert system application domains are constantly increasing. Expert systems not only give advice and recommendations, but also provide a valuable source of knowledge and expertise for learning and training. Therefore, research in expert system user interface needs to focus on how to adapt an expert system user interface to a diverse group of users and adapt the system behavior to ever-changing requirements of users over an extended period of time.

REFERENCES

Berry, Dianne and Hart, Anna (Eds.). *Expert Systems: Human Issues*, Cambridge, MA: MIT Press, 1990.

Berry, Dianne (1994). Involving users in expert system development, *Expert Systems*, 11, 1, 23–28.

Bose, Ranjit (1996). Intelligent agents framework for developing knowledge-based decision support systems for collaborative organizational processes, *Expert Systems with Applications*, 11, 3, 247–261.

Casey, A. (1993). Planning interactive explanations, *International Journal of Man-Machine Studies*, 38(2), 169–199.

Cheng, Billy, Liao, Qun, Park, Nam-ki, Tubaishat, Mohammed, Yu Ching Sheng, and Yu, Jyh Hao (1996). Lymph Node Pathology Expert System, *http://www-scf.usc.edu/~bcheng/es/es.html*, University of Southern California, School of Business.

Clancey, B. C. and Shortliffe, E. H. (Eds.) (1984). *Readings in Medical Artificial Intelligence: The First Decade*, Reading, MA: Addison-Wesley.

Duchessi, Peter and O'Keefe, Robert (1995). Understanding expert systems success and failure, *Expert Systems with Applications*, 9, 2, 123–133.

Hendler, James (Ed.) (May 1988). *Expert Systems: The User Interface*, Norwood, NJ: Ablex Publishing Corp.

McTear, M. F. (1993). User modelling for adaptive computer-systems: a survey of recent developments, *Artificial Intelligence Review*, 7(3/4), 157–184.

Wilkins, David (1996). Knowledge based systems group, *http://www-kbs.ai.uiuc.edu*.

7 Design and Use of Explanation Facilities

Jasbir S. Dhaliwal

CONTENTS

1. INTRODUCTION

The ability to provide explanations that clarify its functioning and recommendations has long been recognized as being an integral component of an expert system (ES). For example, the MYCIN system incorporated a simple explanation facility providing justification and reasoning-trace explanations. There has also been evidence to suggest that ES explanations are highly utilized by users and that this has an impact on their performance (Ye and Johnson, 1995; Dhaliwal and Benbasat, 1996). The ability to provide explanations has also been rated as being the primary user requirement for an expert system (Teach and Shortliffe, 1981). Largely based on Clancey's (1983) characterization of the epistemological roles that knowledge can play in expert system explanations, it has generally come to be accepted that explanation facilities must provide three types of knowledge corresponding to the following explanation labels: Why, How, and Strategic explanations. *Why* explanations provide justification knowledge clarifying the underlying reasons and contextual underpinnings for an action or state based on causal models. *How* explanations provide reasoning trace knowledge that clarifies inference structure and describes contents. *Strategic* explanations provide meta-knowledge that clarifies problem-solving strategy and representational structure.

In the 1980s, early research into the design of explanation facilities focused on how the knowledge encased in the knowledge base of an ES could be represented in a manner that would facilitate both optimal ES operation as well as the provision of explanations to users. The focus was on machine learning algorithms and knowledge representational formalisms that could simultaneously achieve both objectives. In the 1990s, however, research into the design of ES explanation facilities has taken on an empirical interface design orientation that recognizes that not all the knowledge required for ES explanation purposes can be obtained from the knowledge base of an

ES. It is now viewed as a separate design problem that must be considered in isolation and that poses its own unique set of challenges.

This chapter focuses on development and design issues pertaining to the building of expert system explanation facilities. The next section discusses the relationship between the development life cycle of an expert system and that for building explanation facilities. It argues that special consideration must be given to the unique challenges pertaining to the development of explanation facilities. Section 3 focuses on the historical progression in the types of explanations that are incorporated in ES explanation facilities. These types of explanations are also linked to several generic strategies for providing explanations so as to foster user learning during the use of an ES and its explanations. Section 4 describes recent studies that have evaluated the provision of explanations to users as an interface design issue and summarizes their findings. Section 5 discusses various design considerations that have to be considered by designers of ES explanation facilities. Section 6 highlights various research areas that are currently being investigated by the ES explanations research community, and Section 7 presents the conclusion.

2.   STAGES IN THE DEVELOPMENT OF EXPLANATION FACILITIES

Knowledge acquisition (KA) represents the process of acquiring knowledge for the purpose of building an expert system. It is the first of three sequential stages — (1) knowledge acquisition, (2) knowledge validation, and (3) knowledge implementation — that have to be performed in building an expert system (ES). There exist various methods of knowledge acquisition, some of which are manual and others that are automated. There are also various tests and procedures that can be used to validate knowledge that is acquired prior to its implementation. As well, at the implementation level, there are a variety of knowledge representation formalisms as well as inference procedures available for selection by the knowledge engineer (KE).

While it is recognized that the explanation facility is but one critical aspect of the total set of capabilities that constitute an expert system, research into the design question of "how does one go about developing an explanation facility?" has not met with the same level of success as research into the question of "how does one go about developing an expert system?". Part of the reason is that the development process for explanation facilities has received comparatively less attention. Another reason becomes evident if one applies the three stages of developing expert systems to the process of developing an explanation facility, as in Table 1. While significant research has been devoted to all three stages of expert system development — knowledge acquisition, knowledge validation, and knowledge implementation — research into the development of explanation facilities has focused only on the *Explanation Implementation* stage. For example, see the *Proceedings of the AAAI Workshop on Explanation* (1988) and also Abu-Hakima and Oppacher (1990) for summaries. A review of the literature reveals that issues pertaining to the stages of *Explanation Acquisition and Explanation Validation* have not been studied to date.

TABLE 1
The Stages of Knowledge/Explanation Acquisition

Knowledge Acquisition (KA)
Knowledge Validation (KV)
Knowledge Implementation (KI)
Explanation Acquisition (EA)
Explanation Validation (EV)
Explanation Implementation (EI)

One reason why ES explanations research to date has focused mostly on Explanation Implementation as opposed to the two prior stages of Explanation Acquisition and Explanation Validation has been the belief that all the knowledge required for the purposes of providing explanations, i.e., the explanation base (EB), can be derived from the knowledge base (KB), which is the end-product of the three stages of expert system development, i.e., knowledge acquisition, knowledge validation, and knowledge validation, and represents the knowledge required for the purpose of ES operation. For example, early research into building explanation facilities focused on the manner in which the knowledge base could be represented and implemented to facilitate explanation (Swartout, 1983). Other work focused on the use of inference formalisms that facilitated the provision of explanations and the optimal derivation of an expert system conclusion. To fully understand this belief necessitates a comparison of the relationship between the explanation base (EB) and the knowledge base (KB).

The existing belief is that the EB is a subset of the KB, i.e., all the knowledge required for providing explanations can be derived from the total set of knowledge that has been captured and implemented as part of expert systems development. One manifestation of this belief becomes obvious if one considers the explanation facilities that are included in current expert system shells, e.g., VPExpert (Wordtech Systems, 1993). The REPORT command of this shell displays as an explanation the specific production rule in the KB that was last "instantiated" when either of the Why or How explanation options are accessed. These rules, while possibly being of use to knowledge engineers performing systems validation or debugging, as they are designed to facilitate KB functioning, are usually not very useful or comprehensible as explanations to users of expert systems. These explanations that present internal representations of knowledge in an expert system only partially meet the requirements of the How explanation but not those of the Why and Strategic explanations. Considering that these three kinds of explanations, comprising trace, justification, and strategic knowledge, together constitute an acceptable knowledge-based explanation facility, it follows that the KB, while being adequate for the purposes of expert systems problem-solving, is incomplete for the purpose of providing explanations. It is therefore necessary to consider newer models of the relationship between the EB and the KB.

This chapter proposes that it is only possible to derive some of the knowledge required for ES explanation from the knowledge base. Significant effort beyond those undertaken to build the knowledge base must also be exerted to complete the explanation base, especially for the justification and strategic knowledge required for providing Why and Strategic explanations. There are other reasons as well that support the argument that the EB should be regarded as a subset of the KB. For example, it is often difficult to predict beforehand the range of users who will ultimately be using an expert system. These users may differ in terms of purpose (problem solving vs. learning), experience (experts vs. novices), etc. It therefore makes sense to decouple the development of the knowledge base from the development of the explanation facility as design of the latter has to include critical user interface characteristics pertaining to whom explanations are to be provided.

There are several implications of adopting such models:

1. EA may require other tools and techniques, both automated and manual, beyond those that are currently available for KA.
2. EV may necessitate the use of other tests and procedures besides those that are currently used for KV.
3. There could be synergies in planning and coordinating KA and EA together.
4. It may be more efficient and effective to perform EA before KA.
5. EA may be of greater importance than KA for certain categories of users, e.g., novices who require more explanations providing justification and strategic knowledge.
6. EA may be of greater importance than KA for certain types of tasks, e.g., in the case of computer-aided teaching tasks that emphasize exploratory learning and tasks where multiple solutions are feasible. This is because the requirements for explanatory knowl-

edge will be greater than in the usual diagnostic problem-solving situations in which expert systems are used.

3. TYPES OF EXPERT SYSTEM EXPLANATIONS AND STRATEGIES FOR PROVIDING EXPLANATIONS

The Why and How explanations, which were first introduced in MYCIN (Shortliffe, 1976), remain the foundation of most explanation facilities found in current ES applications and development shells. Attempts have been made to incorporate other forms of explanations. These include the Strategic, What, and What-if explanations. The Strategic class of explanations provide insight into meta-knowledge, especially the control objectives and overall problem-solving strategies used by a system. For example, the NEOMYCIN system explicitly outlines problem-solving strategies in its own knowledge base and makes them available for explanation (Hasling, Clancey and Rennels, 1984). The What explanations are designed to give insight into object definitions or decision variables used by a system (Rubinoff, 1985). They serve as responses to queries such as: "What do you mean by *object or variable name?*" The What explanation is significantly different from the What-if query facilities commonly found in decision support systems. These refer to the ability to rerun a consultation with changed model parameters. While such What-if facilities can be provided as part of the ES interface, they are not viewed as being explanations per se, but rather as tools for sensitivity analysis. To be considered a distinct category of explanations, What-if has to be implemented as the direct and explicit provision of information about the sensitivity of decision variables to ES users, instead of being a facility for performing sensitivity analysis.

Various classifications of the many types of explanations that should be provided by ES have been suggested. These classifications can be condensed as subscribing to one of two possible criteria for distinguishing between the types of explanations. The first criteria is the nature of the explanation queries. For example, Wick and Slagle (1989) discuss explanations whose queries begin with What, Why, How, When, Where, etc. As well, Swartout (1983) considers the How, Why, When, and What range of queries, as part of XPLAIN's explanation facility. The second criteria is the nature of the explanation responses. Swartout and Smoliar (1987) distinguish between explanations that provide terminological knowledge, domain descriptive knowledge, and problem-solving knowledge. ES users require information about procedures, reasoning traces, action goals, control, and self-knowledge. There are two ways of distinguishing explanation responses. First, responses can provide case-specific knowledge, domain knowledge, or meta-knowledge. Second, they can provide taxonomic knowledge, formal knowledge, contingent knowledge, or control knowledge.

Irrespective of whether they are based on explanation queries or explanation responses, there is a major problem with all these classifications. Lacking a sound theoretical basis, the various types of explanations that comprise each of these classifications are neither consistently defined, nor is each classification comprehensive. However, largely based on Clancey's (1983) character-ization of the epistemological roles that knowledge can play in ES explanation, a consensus has emerged on the three primary types of explanations that ES ought to provide. Corresponding to the three epistemological roles of structure, support, and strategy, these three types of explanations are: (1) trace explanations that describe contents and reasoning (structure), (2) deep explanations that justify underlying reasons for a state or an action based on causal models (support), and (3) strategic explanations that clarify problem-solving strategy and meta-knowledge (strategy). This taxonomy of the three primary types of explanations has also led to a convergence of opinion on the matching of explanation queries with explanation responses. This is as follows: the How explanation queries are used to provide trace explanations; the Why explanation queries are used to provide causal justifications; and the Strategic explanation queries are used to provide clarifica-tions of control strategies and meta-knowledge.

Recent work has focused on the manner in which explanations should optimally be provided as part of the user-ES interaction. It has proposed that ES explanations can be presented to users in two distinct ways to facilitate user learning during the use of an expert system (Dhaliwal and Benbasat, 1996). These are termed feedforward and feedback explanation provision strategies and are relevant to all three of the Why, How, and Strategic explanations; that is, each of these types of explanations can be presented both as feedforward and feedback. Table 2 presents definitions for the three types of explanations when they are presented either as feedforward or feedback. The feedforward explanations differ from feedback explanations as follows: (1) the feedforward version is not case-specific, while the feedback version explains a particular case-specific outcome; (2) the feedforward version is presented prior to an assessment or diagnosis being performed, while the feedback version is presented subsequent to the assessment and after the presentation of the outcome of that assessment; and (3) the feedforward version focuses on the input cues while the feedback version focuses on the outcomes.

TABLE 2
Definitions of Explanations and Provision Strategies

Feedforward Why explanations justify the importance of, and the need for, input information to be used or a procedure that is to be performed.

Feedforward How explanations detail the manner in which input information is to be obtained for use and procedures that are to be performed.

Feedforward Strategic explanations clarify the overall manner in which input information to be used is organized or structured, and specify the manner in which each input cue to be used fits into the overall plan of assessment that is to be performed.

Feedback Why explanations justify the importance, and clarify the implications, of a particular conclusion that is reached by the system.

Feedback How explanations present a trace of the evaluations performed and intermediate inferences made in getting to a particular conclusion.

Feedback Strategic explanations clarify the overall goal structure used by a system to reach a particular conclusion, and specify the manner in which each particular assessment leading to the conclusion fits into the overall plan of assessments that were performed.

The idea that particular explanation provision strategies may be matched with the various types of explanations for optimizing value to ES users is an important one. It suggests that designers of ES explanation facilities must pay careful attention to the close relationship between the types of explanations and the feedforward and feedback explanation provision strategies.

4. RECENT STUDIES OF THE USE OF EXPERT SYSTEM EXPLANATIONS

Several recent studies have focused on the empirical evaluation of the use of explanations as part of the user-ES interface. As their findings hold significant implications for designers of explanation facilities, they are summarized in this section. They are primarily useful in the sense that they signal the situations in which the provision of ES explanations is potentially useful to users.

Lamberti and Wallace (1990) investigated interface requirements for knowledge presentation in knowledge-based systems. They examined interactions between user expertise, knowledge presentation format (procedural vs. declarative formats), question type (requiring abstract vs. concrete answers), and task uncertainty, in terms of the speed and accuracy of decision-making performance. They found that for highly uncertain tasks, response time and accuracy for questions with declaratively formatted explanations (as compared to procedural ones) were better for higher skill users. However, for low uncertainty tasks, the low-skilled subjects performed equally fast, but more accurately than high-skill users, when presented with declarative explanations to questions. Also, for explaining the procedures used in strategies of problem solving, both high- and low-skill users felt more confident with procedural explanations in contrast to declarative explanations. In relation to concrete vs. abstract knowledge organization, the study found that low-skill users performed significantly faster and more accurately when answering questions requiring concrete knowledge organization. High-skill users performed faster, although not necessarily more accurately, when responding to questions requiring abstract knowledge organization, in contrast to concrete knowledge organization.

Lerch et al., (1990) focused on some effects of the use of ES explanations. They measured user agreement with, and confidence in, conclusions presented by an ES. Subjects were told that these conclusions were obtained from one of three different sources of advice: novices, experts, or a knowledge-based system. As well, they used three different treatment conditions: no explanations provided, explanations provided in the form of English sentences, and explanations provided in production rule form. They found that while the use of explanations had an impact on the level of user agreement with the conclusions, it did not change users' confidence in the source of advice on which the conclusions was modeled. The different types of explanations were not considered in this study; rather, a generic category closely resembling the How explanation was used.

Ye and Johnson (1995) had subjects evaluate explanations presented in a fixed sequential order and compared user perceptions of usefulness and user preferences for the three different types of explanations. They found that the use of explanations had a positive effect on user agreement with ES conclusions, and that the Why explanation was the most preferred explanation across levels of user expertise and types of inference used for heuristic classification tasks. As well, experts and novices were found to have differing perceptions of usefulness for the various types of explanations presented. Experts perceived the How explanation as being most useful, and novices the Why explanation.

Dhaliwal (1993) studied the use of explanations in a judgmental decision-making situation involving the use of an ES that provided explanations. He found that users utilized ES explanations and that both experts and novices valued such explanations. While experts utilized the How explanations most extensively, novices used Why explanations most often. It was also found that feedback explanations were used more than feedforward explanations and that their use had a positive impact on the quality of decision-making. The study also found that users utilized explanations the least when their agreement with the ES was either very low or very high.

These studies have focused on various critical aspects of the ES explanation facility. They suggest that in designing an explanation facility, designers must pay careful attention to user perceptions for the three different types of explanations; the levels of source credibility; the content of explanations; as well as user agreement with the ES.

5. FACTORS INFLUENCING THE DESIGN OF EXPLANATION FACILITIES

Given the current state of ES explanations research, it is evident that designers of ES explanation facilities must pay careful attention to a host of factors that impact the design process. They can be classified into four distinct categories relating to the characteristics of: (1) the task setting in which explanations are used, (2) the nature of the explanations that are provided, (3) the interface design and explanation provision strategies used, and (4) the individual users of the ES.

5.1. TASK CHARACTERISTICS

The nature of the ES task and the context in which the ES is used is the first design factor that will influence the amount and the types of explanations that are used. The types of tasks that an ES performs can be categorized by various classifications, including analysis tasks vs. synthesis tasks, and heuristic classification tasks vs. heuristic configuration tasks. While these classifications overlap to some extent, each of them can be further decomposed into a larger hierarchy of many levels of tasks. For example, the heuristic classification task can be decomposed into the three inference processes (subtasks) of data abstraction, heuristic match, and solution refinement. Similarly, analysis tasks can be broken down into subcategories such as diagnosis, prediction, etc. The Ye and Johnson (1995) study directly investigated the influence of varying task types on the preference for the three types of explanations, by utilizing the data abstraction and heuristic match levels of heuristic classification as independent variables. However, it did not find significant differences in the preference for explanations between the two levels. The use of explanations that are provided by ES performing synthesis or heuristic configuration tasks, such as design or planning, has not been studied. Considering the critical differences between these tasks and the more common diagnostic tasks, it is reasonable to expect that they will result in different patterns of ES explanation use.

The context in which an ES is utilized will determine the purpose for which the explanation facility is used. Three contexts for the use of ES explanations can be identified: (1) by end-users in problem-solving contexts, (2) by knowledge engineers carrying out knowledge-base debugging activities, and (3) as part of ES validation activities carried out by domain experts and/or knowledge engineers. The distinctions between these three contexts are critical and stem from the fact that the use of ES explanations in systems development is motivated by a different set of objectives than when used as part of end-user applications. It can therefore reasonably be expected that end-users of ES applications will use explanations differently from when they are used during debugging, validation, or other ES development activities.

While explanations are commonly incorporated into most end-user applications of ES, they also play a significant role in the development of ES by offering enhanced debugging and validation abilities. Most current ES development shells and environments include tools that utilize explanations to aid efficient and effective system development, e.g., the Knowledge Engineering Environment (KEE) from Intellicorp. Another example is the REPORT command in the VPExpert shell. This command lists in sequential order all the explanations attached (using the BECAUSE clause) to rules that "fired" as part of a consultation. Such a listing assists in the debugging of processing logic by knowledge engineers. It also allows users and domain experts, who may not be familiar with representation schemes and inference engines, to participate in the validation of a knowledge base.

In contrast to debugging and validation, the use of explanations by end-users of ES applications is motivated by a different set of reasons. For example, it has been suggested that an explanation facility is used: (1) by decision makers because it aids them in formulating problems and models for analysis, (2) by sophisticated users because it assures them that the system's knowledge and reasoning process is appropriate, and (3) by novice users because it can instruct them about the knowledge in the system as it is applied to solve a particular problem. There are also a variety of contexts in which end-user applications of ES are used. For example, while some applications are used as tools for training novices in a domain, others are used by experts to support their own decision-making. The organizational context in which these end-user applications are used will also affect the use of the explanations. Some organizations institutionalize the use of such ES applications for making certain critical decisions. The use of explanations when end-users are compelled to use the ES will certainly be different from the situation when end-users utilize the ES as a decision aid by choice. In summary, many different contexts of the use of ES can be identified as potentially influencing the use of ES explanations.

5.2. CHARACTERISTICS OF THE EXPLANATIONS

The nature of the explanatory information provided by an ES to its users will certainly influence the explanations that are used. These can be divided into two major categories: explanation type and explanation content. While the types of explanations were discussed earlier, there is considerable overlap between these two categories. The three types of explanations are by definition different in content. For example, the Why explanations focus on providing declarative information about the task; the How explanations provide procedural task information; and the Strategic explanations present meta-knowledge of the task. Similarly, the various types of explanations will also differ in content in relation to whether they are provided as feedforward or feedback. For example, feedback explanations, being outcome specific, will by definition be more concrete and at a lower level of specificity than the more generalized feedforward explanations.

While the influence of the types of explanations is potentially more relevant, largely because both ES developers and users distinguish clearly between them, it is also important to consider the influence of various dimensions of content. Some relevant dimensions of explanation content include the following. The informational content of the explanations in terms of the number of signals that are incorporated represents the first dimension. The second dimension is the abstraction level of the explanations, i.e., how concrete or abstract they are from the perspective of users. The third dimension is the granularity and specificity of the explanations, e.g., the lowest level will have the most amount of detail and vice versa. Fourth, explanations can be focused toward particular user groups, such as knowledge engineers, domain experts, and end-users, or they can have a more general focus. Terminological differences in explanations can be expected depending on who are the target users of the explanations. Fifth, explanations can emphasize different aspects of that which is being explained, e.g., procedural aspects in contrast to declarative aspects.

5.3. INTERFACE DESIGN AND PROVISION STRATEGIES

The design features of the interface used to provide explanations, as well as the strategies used for providing explanations, will also influence the patterns of ES explanation use. Specific aspects of the interface design include the following. First, the amount of effort required for users to access the explanations, i.e., the accessibility of the explanations, will influence their use. Two possible classes of strategies for accessing explanations can be identified. These include an *active* strategy where the ES presents explanations without the user having to request them, and a range of *passive* strategies that require the user to make varying levels of explicit physical effort to access the explanations. Such effort can range from clicking on specialized explanation icons presented on the screen to hitting predesignated function keys for accessing and scanning the explanations. Generally, an active strategy has the system interrupt the dialog to provide explanations or makes them available continuously as part of every screen of the ES. In the design of ES explanation facilities, it is important that interface designers consider the amount of effort required for users to request and access the explanations. The results of studies on cost-benefit models of the effort involved in utilizing computerized decision aids suggest that the accessibility of explanations, i.e., the cost of accessing them, will exert a salient influence on the use of explanations. Second, the communication mode used for presenting the explanations, e.g., audio and/or visual modes, will also influence the use of explanations. Third, the presentation format utilized for the explanations is also a factor, e.g., text explanations in contrast to image-based explanations that use graphical, iconic, and animation formats.

Considering that the primary reason for the provision of ES explanations is to improve users' understanding of the ES and its domain, the feedforward and feedback explanation provision strategies presented earlier will also influence the use of explanations. The importance of these explanation provision strategies becomes obvious if one considers the analogy of a child engaged in a learning process to improve his or her understanding. While "an explanation machine," in the form of a child's parents, may be continuously available to provide explanations about some phenomenon that is the target of the learning, the child will only seek, attend to, and benefit from explanations provided at particular stages of the learning process. At different stages of the process, different types of explanations will be sought, and it can be expected that children at varying stages of cognitive development will seek different amounts and types of explanations. As well, it is also likely that explanations provided automatically without being requested, will at times impede rather than encourage the learning that takes place. This analogy therefore suggests that any evaluation of the influence of the explanation provision strategies must therefore take into consideration the other design factors.

5.4. USER CHARACTERISTICS

Three distinct categories of user characteristics that will impact the use of explanations can be identified: user expertise, individual differences, and the level of user agreement with the ES. Of these, user expertise is potentially the most significant to the design and use of ES explanations. Various theories of skill acquisition support this belief. As well, the empirical studies discussed in the last section, have also found significant effects for this factor. All these studies employed users' knowledge of the task domain to operationalize user expertise. The human-computer interface literature reveals another aspect of user expertise that can be considered as being just as relevant. This is the level of users' expertise or familiarity with expert systems themselves. This is termed *systems expertise.*

Various types of cognitive and personality-based individual differences can also be identified, primarily from the literature on decision support systems, as potentially influencing the use of ES explanations. However, while much is known of their influence on human cognitive functioning, they suffer from the lack of an adequate and coherent theoretical basis. Additionally, as is now recognized in the study of decision support systems, there is only a small likelihood that an individual differences approach to the design of decision aids will yield practical and cost-beneficial design requirements.

The final category of user characteristics that can be identified is the level of user agreement with the ES. Studies found that the use of explanations increased the level of user agreement with ES conclusions. Together with the finding that experts were more likely to agree with an ES's conclusions than novices, this suggests that there could potentially be a reverse effect as well. The level of initial user agreement with ES conclusions would influence, to some extent, the amount of explanations used. As the differences in the level of domain expertise can result in different levels of agreement with an ES's conclusions, this suggests that the level of user agreement potentially moderates the influence of user expertise on the use of explanations.

6. RESEARCH ISSUES AND FUTURE TRENDS

From an implementational perspective, it is accepted today that significant knowledge, beyond that which is required for purposes of ES operation, needs to be formalized for the purposes of ES explanation. An increasing amount of research is therefore being directed at what was earlier in this chapter termed as the explanation acquisition and explanation validation stages of the explanation facility development process. In commercial applications of ES as well, there is an increasing trend toward encapsulating explanatory information in the applications, often in the form of "canned" generic explanations that are relevant for multiple situations. This represents a suboptimal solution due to the difficulty of implementing fully contextual and relevant explanations that foster learning and problem-solving. A potentially useful approach to this situation is the development of computer-aided software engineering-type workbenches that facilitate the encoding of explanatory information during the knowledge acquisition phase of expert system development. Such tools may also be potentially useful for overcoming the "maintenance" problem that affects explanation facilities.

Learning theories are also becoming more prominent in the study of the design and use of ES explanations. This is because they provide a wider theoretical context and perspective to the role of explanations in expert systems. While we know much about how human experts explain to other humans for purposes of fostering learning, there is still much to be learned about how automated experts should explain in such situations. A related perspective here is that which is termed the "learning-working conflict," i.e., in many contexts, asking for and using ES explanations during a problem-solving process involves making a direct trade-off between long-term learning and immediate efficiency in problem-solving.

There are also efforts underway to extend our current understanding of ES explanations from the current largely diagnostic task environment to that of design or heuristic configuration tasks. Initial results suggest that the demand for explanations as well as the nature of explanation facilities for these tasks is significantly different from diagnostic settings. For example, explanations pertaining to "modelling notation," "sample applications," and "error-correction" have been found to be a necessary requisite for an expert system that supports object-oriented data modeling tasks. Such findings may well challenge and change our current conceptualizations of the types of explanations that expert systems ought to provide.

From an empirical perspective there is also a need for the development of a contingency theory for the use of expert system explanations. While it is recognized that ES explanations are not relevant for all applications of expert systems, our knowledge and understanding of which explanations are relevant to which situations is still not fully developed. However, the increasing number of studies that indicate that ES explanations are relevant to and of value to users certainly calls for more research attention to be directed to ES explanations technology and development methodologies.

7.   SUMMARY

This chapter has provided two vital perspectives pertaining to explanation facilities being viewed as part of the total expert systems functionality. First, it has considered the critical design issues pertaining to the development of such explanation technology as well as suggested a specific development process for it. Second, it has focused on the use of such explanation facilities as a means of understanding the interface design features for explanations. These have to be considered from the perspective that it may be prudent for the expert systems community to widen the definition of the "output" or value that such systems provide to their users. Given the "fragility" of expertise and the difficulty in modeling and maintaining knowledge, there may well be a need for us to view the explanations provided as the primary output, rather than focusing on specific optimal system recommendations. Human experts, after all, are not always correct but can consistently provide thoughtful, relevant, and contextual explanations that foster learning.

REFERENCES

Abu-Hakima, S. and F. Oppacher, Improving explanations in knowledge-based systems: RATIONALE, *Knowledge Acquisition*, Vol. 2, 1990, pp. 301–343.

American Association of Artificial Intelligence (AAAI), *Proceedings of the AAAI Workshop on Explanation*, St. Paul, MN, 1988.

Chandrasekaran, B., M. C. Tanner, and J.R. Josephson, Explanation: The role of control strategies and deep models, in J.A. Hendler, *Expert Systems: The User Interface*, Ablex, Norwood, NJ, 1988.

Clancey, W.J., The epistemology of a rule-based expert system — A framework for explanations, *Artificial Intelligence*, Vol. 20, 1983, pp. 215–231.

Dhaliwal, J.S. and I. Benbasat, The use and effects of knowledge-based system explanations: Theoretical foundations and a framework for empirical evaluation, *Information Systems Research*, Vol. 7, No. 3, September 1996, pp. 342–362.

Dhaliwal, J.S., An Experimental Investigation of the Use of Explanations Provided by Knowledge-Based Systems, Unpublished Doctoral Dissertation, University of British Columbia, Canada, 1993.

Lamberti, D.M. and W.A. Wallace, Intelligent interface design: An empirical assessment of knowledge presentation in expert systems, *MIS Quarterly*, Vol. 14, September 1990, pp. 279–311.

Lerch, F.J., M.J. Prietula, and C.T. Kulik, The Turing Effect: Discovering How We Trust Machine Advice, Unpublished Manuscript, Graduate School of Industrial Administration, Carnegie Mellon University, Pittsburgh, PA, 1990.

Swartout, W.R., XPLAIN: A system for creating and explaining expert consulting programs, *Artificial Intelligence*, Vol. 21, 1983, pp. 285–325.

Swartout, W.R. and S. W. Smoliar, On making expert systems more like experts, *Expert Systems*, Vol. 4, 1987, pp. 196–207.

Teach, R.L. and E.H. Shortliffe, An analysis of physicians' attitudes, *Computers In Biomedical Research*, 14, December, 1981, pp. 542–558.

Wexelblat, R.L., On interface requirements for expert systems, *AI Magazine*, Fall, 1989, pp. 66–78.

Wick, M.R. and J.R. Slagle, An explanation facility for today's expert systems," *IEEE Expert*, Spring, 1989, pp. 26–36.

Ye, R. and P.E. Johnson, The impact of explanation facilities on user acceptance of expert systems advice, *MIS Quarterly*, Vol. 19, No. 2, June 1995, pp. 157–172.

8 Expert Systems and Uncertainty

Patrick R. Harrison and Joseph G. Kovalchik

CONTENTS

1. INTRODUCTION

Artificial Intelligence (AI) has struggled to find ways to effectively use probabilistic reasoning to aid in solving problems where knowledge is incomplete, error-prone, or approximate. It has invented logics to deal with the problem symbolically. It has invented concepts to skirt the issue of conditional independence, prior probabilities, and the difficulties of conditional probabilities and causal inferences. A summary of the development of these ideas could be stated as, "We would use Bayesian models if only we could satisfy all the assumptions and were omniscient." We will focus on the dominant themes that have occupied most of the literature on uncertainty and expert systems. Those include the Bayesian approach, the certainty factor approach, the Dempster-Shafer approach, and the more advanced Bayesian belief networks approach. Fuzzy reasoning will not be discussed because it addresses the problem of vagueness rather than uncertainty. As Russell and Norvig (1995) point out, it is not a method for uncertain reasoning and is problematic in that it is inconsistent with the first-order predicate calculus.

2. DEFINITIONS

When we consider behavior and knowledge quantitatively, we are thinking in both numeric and empirical systems. If we make the statement $P(x) = 0.4$, we are making a statement in the numeric system. In that system, this is a probability statement based, for example, on frequency of occurrence (this is not the only way to frame this). If, on the other hand, we view the statement $P(x) = 0.4$ as stating a degree of belief that the event x will occur, we are making a statement in the empirical system. When we go on to manipulate this belief using the laws of mathematics, we are making strong assumptions about the isomorphism between the axioms in the numeric system and the corresponding axioms in the empirical system.

We are interested in certainty or degree of belief in something. The assumption is that probabilities as degrees of belief or certainty change as a function of what we know — as a function of evidence that supports or refutes the belief.

3.   WHERE DO WE START?

We start with a simple problem. Suppose that you get a new bread maker and when you make your first loaf of bread it does not rise. Your goal is to determine or diagnose this problem and to determine how to solve or fix it. The hypotheses you entertain are:

H1: The yeast used to make the bread was bad [Bad (Y)].
H2: The yeast was either omitted or mismeasured [OM (Y)].
H3: Ingredients omitted or mismeasured [OM (I)].
H4: Ingredients placed in bread maker incorrectly [P (I)].

We can assume that, based on our past experience making bread and whatever other knowledge or expertise we have concerning bread making, that each hypothesis has a prior probability of being the proper diagnosis for dough not rising during bread making. We will assume that each hypothesis is equally probable and assign each the certainty 0.25.

Consider also that we have the following rules that affect our belief in certain hypotheses (this set is not complete); we will for the sake of brevity omit the rules for H2 through H4:

R1: IF Old (Y) THEN Bad (Y) 0.6
R2: IF NotStoredProperly (Y) THEN Bad (Y) 0.3
R3: IF ContainerNotTight (Y) THEN NotStoredProperly (Y) 0.3
R4: IF MoistureInContainer (Y) THEN NotStoredProperly (Y) 0.6

Using R1 and H1, we can restate the rule as a conditional probability as follows:

$$P(H \, / \, E) = p(Bad(Y) \, / \, Old(Y))$$

where H is H1 and E is the left-hand side of R1.

If from R1, we know that the yeast is old, i.e., Old(Y), then our certainty in H1 changes to:

$$p(H \, / \, E) = \frac{p(E \, / \, H) \times p(H)}{p(E \, / \, H) \times p(H) + p(E \, / \, \sim H) \times p(\sim H)}$$

We know that:

$$p(H) = p(Bad(Y)) = 0.25$$
$$p(E \, / \, H) = p(Bad(Y) \, / \, Old(Y)) = 0.6$$
$$p(E \, / \, \sim H) = p(Bad(Y) \, / \, \sim Old(Y)) = 0.3$$
$$p(E) = p(E \, / \, H) \times p(H) + p(E \, / \, \sim H) = 0.6 \times 0.25 \times 0.3 \times 0.75 = 0.375$$

and

$$p(H / E) = \frac{0.6 \times 0.25}{0.375} = 0.4$$

That is, our belief in H1 has increased. We could go on to compute the probability of H1 given multiple pieces of evidence E1, E2, ... En. We must assume E1, E2, ..., En are independent events to do so. The basic form, which is discussed in Gonzalez and Dankel (1993), is:

$$p(H_i / E_1 E_2 ... E_n) = \frac{p(E_1 E_2 ... E_n / H_i) \times p(H_i)}{p(E_1 E_2 ... E_n)}$$

Stefik (1995) as well as Russell and Norvig (1995) provide excellent discussions of Bayesian probability models.

What we just did was to use a simple Bayesian approach. The problems with this approach are implicit in what we assumed. We assumed that the set of hypotheses were both inclusive and exhaustive. A Bayesian model must have this property. With expert systems, it will often be the case that such properties cannot be established. Secondly, we had to define prior probabilities. This is difficult and often impossible. Thirdly, if we combined evidence to compute the conditional probability for H given multiple pieces of evidence, we must assume that the evidences are independent with respect to each other.

4.   CERTAINTY FACTORS

The certainty factor (CF) approach has appeal because it is computationally simple, and therefore understandable, to a non-mathematician. It also provides a means of estimating belief that is more appealing and more natural to an expert. Probability statements that have varying boundaries are particularly nonintuitive. The certainty approach allows the expert to ignore prior probabilities that are decidedly difficult to estimate. They are essentially assumed away by observing that in the absence of knowledge in a large hypothesis space, they can be considered uniformly small (Buchanan and Shortliffe, 1984,p. 211).

The detailed motivation to consider uncertainty in expert- or knowledge-based systems is discussed in detail in Buchanan and Shortliffe (1984) and Shortliffe (1976). Buchanan and Shortliffe (1984) also discuss the uncertainty model in detail. This is an excellent starting place if you are interested in this approach. The most notable early use of certainty factors was in the MYCIN project.

5.   THE MYCIN APPROACH

A CF can vary in value from -1 to +1. A CF of 0 indicates no evidence for the hypothesis (H) in question. As the CF varies toward +1, evidence increasingly supports the hypothesis. As the CF moves toward -1, evidence increasingly disfavors the H.

CFs are associated with rules — rules in the usual expert system sense. The starting rules would be those whose left-hand side represent starting assumptions or premises. Associated with each rule is a CF indicating its contribution to the certainty of whatever hypothesis or subhypothesis is represented on the right-hand side of the rule. A simple abstract rule base modeled after Heckerman (1990, p. 171) illustrates the idea:

Rule 1: If A Then C 0.6
Rule 2: If B Then C 0.3
Rule 3: If C Then D 0.7

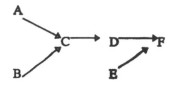

FIGURE 1   Inference chain for sample rule base.

Rule 4: IF D Then F 0.8
Rule 5: IF E Then F –0.1

The first rule says that if evidence A is a fact, then assert C but only with a certainty of +0.6. Notice that C is also used as evidence in Rule 3 for the hypothesis D which, in turn, is confirming evidence for hypothesis F. The rule base can be thought of as representing an inference chain with CF propagating down the inference chain with the degree of belief either increasing, remaining the same, or decreasing as the inference process continues. This is shown in Figure 1. Combination rules are needed for propagating the CF values when there are multiple sources of support. For example, both rules 1 and 2 support hypothesis C. The rules for parallel combination are:

$$\left\|\begin{cases} x+y-xy \Leftrightarrow x,y>0 \\ (x+y)/(1-\min(|x|,|y|)) \Leftrightarrow x<0 \vee y<0 \\ x+y+xy \Leftrightarrow x,y<0 \end{cases}\right\}$$

The parallel combination rules are based on the sign of the arguments. In our example, both A and B are positive so we would use the rule $x + y - xy \Leftrightarrow x, y > 0$ to update the CF at C. The new CF value is $0.6 + 0.3 - 0.6 \times 0.3 = 0.72$. If x and y are of opposite sign, we use the second equation. If both x and y are negative, we use the last equation.

The next question is: how do we propagate changes in belief? The rule for this is called the strength rule. It is as follows:

$$A - (x) \rightarrow B - (y) \rightarrow D, CF(D) = y\, Max(0, CF(B))$$

Since C has CF 0.72 and by Rule 3 C implies D, C $(x = 0.72)$ D $(y = 0.7)$, means that:

$$CF(D) = 0.7\, Max(0, 0.72) = 0.504$$

Finally, we note that the left-hand sides of rules can be complex with a variety of boolean combinations. We restrict ourselves to combinations using simple and/or Boolean combinations. The rules for Boolean combination are:

$$A(x) \wedge B(y), CF(A \wedge B) = Min(x, y)$$

$$A(x) \vee B(y), CF(A \vee B) = Max(x, y)$$

That is, if the LHS predicates are anded, propagate the lowest value. If the LHS predicates are ored, propagate the maximum value. The CF for each case would be:

$$A = 0.5, B = 0.7$$

$$CF(A \wedge B) = 0.5 \quad A = 0.5$$

$$CF(A \vee B) = 0.7$$

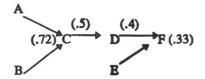

FIGURE 2   Inference chain for sample rule base with propagated values.

Figure 2 shows the rule base with propagated CF values.

As noted, CF has the advantage that estimating CFs is considerably less difficult than estimating prior and conditional probabilities. Further, CFs assume conditional independence and the combination methods insure locality, detachment, and modularity (Stefik, 1995, p. 474). What this means is that combinations can be computed whenever a rule's LHS is satisfied, and changed whenever a condition changes. The effects will propagate correctly. We can view the problem a rule at a time. This means that adding or deleting rules does not require rebuilding the entire certainty model. This is described in detail in Stefik (1995) and also in Heckerman (1990), and the reader is directed to these references for details.

This approach has proved useful in medical diagnosis. With tuning of CFs, it has performed in the MYCIN studies as well as expert physicians. It can be considered a practical and useful approach for diagnostic problems. It has the advantage that CFs are much easier for an expert to understand than prior and conditional probabilities.

It should be noted that this approach has limitations. First, there is a serious problem that is a function of the number of parallel rules supporting a hypothesis. It has been shown that as the number of parallel rules supporting a hypothesis increases, CF approaches 1 even for small values of CF. Also, there is no mechanism for adjusting CFs if evidence that has been used in a computation is later retracted. A conclusion once made, cannot be retracted. That is, the CF process is monotonic. Additional discussion of limitations and the relationship between certainty factors and probability models is discussed in Heckerman (1990). This is an excellent article that details the issues. If you are interested in how a MYCIN-like certainty factor approach is implemented, see Norvig (1992); Chapter 16 details the implementation of expert systems using certainty. The accompanying online code that implements a MYCIN-like system with CFs can be accessed from Norvig's Web page.

6.   DEMPSTER-SHAFER APPROACH

A key issue in using certainty factors is whether or not belief can be expressed in a single number. Dempster-Shafer (DS) can handle the narrowing of hypotheses by considering all combinations in the hypothesis set (the power set). The idea is that often the expert finds evidence that bears on a subset of hypotheses rather than just one. The evidence narrows down the likely set but does not bear on just one H. DS includes both Bayesian and CF functions as special cases (Gordon and Shortliffe, 1985a, p. 273). It is based on better mathematical foundations than the CF approach, but the computational requirements are more complex.

The frame of discernment Θ is the set of mutually exclusive and exhaustive hypotheses or ground propositions. So if we have the exclusive and exhaustive set {H1,H2,H3,H4} from the earlier bread baking example, then Θ = {H1,H2,H3,H4}. Figure 3 shows the powerset that includes the 2^Θ possible subsets of {H1,H2,H3,H4}.

DS uses a number between [0,1] to represent the degree of belief in a H, where H could represent any subset of the powerset. The impact of evidence on Θ is represented by what is called a basic probability assignment (bpa). Remember that a basic probability function would only assign probabilities to H1, H2, H3, and H4 singly. The bpa, on the other hand, assigns a probability m to every subset of Θ so that $\Sigma m(x) = 1$, $x \in 2^\Theta$. Every element in the powerset has a degree of belief

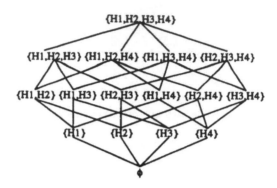

FIGURE 3   The powerset for the sample.

assigned to it. By convention, the null set has the bpa = 0. The value $m(\Theta)$ refers to that proportion of total belief that remains unassigned to any subset of Θ.

As an example, suppose that evidence supports the hypothesis that the bread did not rise because of a yeast problem (0.7) but does not discern between H1 and H2, bad or omitted/mismeasured yeast. Then $m(\{H1,H2\}) = 0.7$ and $m(\Theta) = 0.3$. Note that for this to be workable in an expert system context, we would have to have rules that correspond to this notion. For example: if A and B, then H1, H2 ($m = 0.7$).

The belief function *Bel* can be determined for any H in Θ. Suppose we want to compute *Bel* $(\{H1,H2\})$. *Bel* $(\{H1,H2\})$ in DS corresponds to the total belief in $\{H1,H2\}$ and all subsets of $\{H1,H2\}$. Thus, *Bel* $(\{H1,H2\}) = m(\{H1,H2\}) + m(\{H1\}) + m(\{H2\})$. It follows that the $Bel(\Theta)$ is always equal to 1.

Naturally, in order to use DS in an expert system context, it is also necessary to have a means of combining belief functions to derive a combined belief function when we have more than one observation within the same frame of discernment. Assume again that we have $m_1(\{H1,H2\}) = 0.8$, and we also have $m_2(\{H2,H3\}) = 0.6$. Table 1 shows what Gordon and Shortliffe (1985b) call an intersection tableau that provides a basis for computing the net belief denoted as $m_1 \otimes m_2$. So, the combined belief in $\{H1,H2\}$ designed $Bel_1 \otimes Bel_2$ is equal to:

$$Bel_1 \otimes Bel_2(\{H1, H2\}) = m_1 \otimes m_2(\{H1, H2\}) + m_1 \otimes m_2(\{H1\}) + m_1 \otimes m_2(\{H2\})$$

$$= 0.32 + 0 + 0.48 = 0.8$$

7.   BAYESIAN BELIEF NETWORKS

7.1.   WHAT IS A BELIEF NETWORK?

Concisely stated, a belief network is a graphical data structure that compactly represents the joint probability distribution (PD) of a problem domain by exploiting conditional dependencies. In what

---

TABLE 1
The Intersection Tableau for the
Bread Making Problem

M1/M2	{H2,H3} 0.6	Θ
{H1,H2} 0.8	{H2} 0.48	{H1,H2} 0.32
Θ	{H2,H3} 0.12	Θ 0.08

---

follows, the details involved in explicating the above definition will be expounded. It will also be evident that the belief network captures knowledge of a given problem domain in a natural and efficient way by using causal relationships. Several references provide a good introduction to belief networks (Charniak, 1991; Heckerman, 1995). Pearl (1988) is a comprehensive work on belief networks. The remainder of this section is organized as follows. First, the reasons for using the belief network model are given. Second, the structure of the model is highlighted. Third, the process of building a belief network is enumerated. Fourth, an example of an algorithm that calculates the probabilities desired is discussed. Last, a concrete example is given to illustrate the concepts explained herein.

7.2. Why Use a Belief Network?

Belief networks allow one to reason about uncertainty by exploiting conditional dependencies to compactly represent the joint probability distribution, thereby saving computational time and space. What kind of inferences can be made? There are at least four kinds of inferences. Diagnostic inference leads toward finding the probable cause of given evidence in the form of symptoms. Causal inference reasons toward the effect or symptom where the evidence is most likely the cause of the symptom. Intercausal inference reasons between causes of a common effect to find the most likely cause. Finally, mixed inference is a combination of two or more of the above. (Russell and Norvig, 1995).

7.3. Structure of a Belief Network

Before discussing the structure of the belief network, an example will be given in order to illustrate the concepts discussed herein. Suppose we are in the process of modeling the probability of the dough rising when making bread. The storage of the yeast is proper with a prior probability of 0.8. The yeast is within the expiration date with a prior probability of 0.9. The other ingredients are added correctly with a prior probability of 0.8. The storage and age of the yeast directly influence the condition of the yeast. The condition of the yeast and the proper addition of other ingredients directly affect the dough rising. Other probabilities will be given when needed. We now begin the discussion of the structure of the network using this example.

The components that make up a belief network as well as their relationships are presented. See Figure 4 for the complete belief network for the above problem statement. Components of the figure are explained below. As previously stated, the belief network is a graph structure. More precisely, the graph is a directed acyclic graph (DAG). Within any problem domain there are variables that are used to define the state of the domain. These variables are represented by the nodes of the belief network. Directed arcs from one node to another represent a causal relationship. For example, an arc from node A to node B means that the value of A has a direct effect on the probability of B. In graph terms, A is said to be a parent of B. Each root node (a node with no parents) has associated with it a prior probability. Each non-root node (a leaf node or interior node) of the has an associated conditional probability table (CPT) associated with it. CPTs provide a decomposed representation of the joint PD. The input to this truth table is each parent's state and the output is the belief that the node is in a certain state. Each row represents a possible combinations of states of the parents and each row adds up to 1.0. Since the rows of the CPTs add to 1.0, it is common to eliminate the last variable assignment probability from the table as shown above. Since the YeastOK is either true or false, only probabilities for true values are put in the table. An example of a belief network using the bread dough example is shown in Figure 4.

7.4. Knowledge Engineering

A method used to build the belief network for any given problem domain is given. This method guarantees that the belief network so constructed will be an acyclic network and will minimize

P(Storage = true) = 0.8
P(Ingred OK = true) = 0.8
P(Age = true) = 0.8

StorageOK	AgeOK	YeastOK
False	False	0.1
False	True	0.2
True	False	0.3
True	True	0.9

IngredOK	YeastOK	DoughRises
False	False	0.1
False	True	0.2
True	False	0.3
True	True	0.9

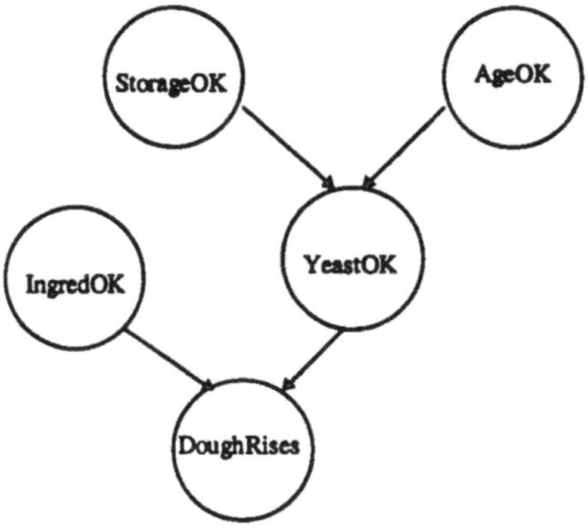

FIGURE 4   An example belief network.

redundant information. The process of building the network consists of the following steps: choose a set of domain variables, construct the topology of the belief network, and then specify the conditional probabilities. (Russell and Norvig, 1995).

In choosing a set of domain variables, decide what is relevant to the problem domain, that is, decide which factors/variables are of interest to track. In representing the problem, the degree of approximation can be improved if additional relevant information is provided, but at the expense of increased complexity. Once the variables have been identified, decide what to name the variables and determine their possible values. This last step may include discretizing a continuous variable. In the above example, each of the variables takes on only two possible values.

The next step is to construct the topology of the graph. The parents of a node should be only those nodes that DIRECTLY influence that node in order to capture the most gain in terms of simplicity of the derived network. Therefore, first decide what each node directly affects and what nodes directly affect it; then, choose a causal ordering for the variables. See Table 2 which contains the ordering for the example. The prerequisites for connecting the nodes have now been identified. The procedure begins by adding root variables first. Recall, these nodes have no parents in the causal ordering. Starting with the next node in the ordering, add it to the graph. Connect it to the minimal set of existing nodes in the network that directly influence the new node. Continue in this manner until all nodes are added. Figure 4 above displays the resultant topology.

TABLE 2
Variables, Values, and Orders

Variable	Values		Order
StorageOK	True	False	1
AgeOK	True	False	2
IngredOK	True	False	3
YeastOK	True	False	4
DoughRises	True	False	5

Once the relationships among the nodes are in place, the next step is to specify the conditional probabilities tables. Recall that CPTs express the probabilities of a node given the states of the parents. Values are obtained from expert subjective experience, measurement of frequencies, or a combination of the two. See Figure 4 for the CPTs that have been added for our example to the nodes YeastOK and DoughRises.

7.5. PROCESS OF USING A BELIEF NETWORK

All that is left to use the network is to encode an instance of a problem and pose queries to the inference engine. The task is to compute the probability for a single or set of query variables, Q, given exact values for some evidence variables P(Q|E). It should be noted that in the general case, the problem of updating the network is NP-Hard (Cooper, 1987). In fact, even approximations are NP-Hard (Dagum and Luby, 1993). A particular algorithm presented in Russell and Norvig (1995) uses backward chaining in a specific type of network with the topology of a singly connected network called a polytree. In a polytree there is at most one undirected path between any two nodes in the network. This routine has a linear time complexity and is used as the workhorse in more general networks. In multiply connected networks, the complexity is exponential in the worst case. The recursive procedure spreads out from the query variable Q along all paths. The basis cases occur on root nodes, evidence nodes, and leaf nodes. Recursive calls exclude the node from which they were called; thus, each node is covered only once. Those readers interested in the derivation of this algorithm are encouraged to see Russell and Norvig (1995). Pearl (1988) also presents an algorithm for polytrees. The values for evidence variable are obtained from sensors or other reasoning agents.

7.6. MULTIPLY CONNECTED BELIEF NETWORKS

More complex belief networks require other algorithms. Multiply connected networks contain more than one undirected path between two nodes. There are three basic algorithms for evaluating multiply connected networks. Clustering uses a merging of the offending nodes into an equivalent polytree. Conditioning transforms the network into several polytrees by instantiating variables to definite values and then evaluating each polytree. Finally, stochastic simulations use the network to generate a large number of concrete models of the domain that are consistent with the network distribution. Approximation by this method is the current method of choice.

7.7. EXAMPLE

To illustrate the fact that the belief network is a compact representation of the joint PD, we will calculate P(StorageOK = true, AgeOK = true, YeastOK = true, IngredOK = true, DoughRises = true). In order for the notation to be concise, let S = StorageOK, A = AgeOK, Y = YeastOK, I =

IngredOK, and D = DoughRises. Then, using the chain rule and the conditional independence shown in the belief network above, one obtains:

$$P(S, A, Y, I, D) = P(D \mid I, Y, A, S) * P(I \mid Y, A, S) * P(Y \mid A, S) * P(S \mid A) * P(A)$$

$$= P(D \mid I, Y) * P(I) * P(Y \mid A, S) * P(S) * P(A)$$

$$= (0.9)(0.8)(0.9)(0.8)(0.9)$$

$$= 0.46656$$

The following illustrates an example of a query given some evidence. Assume that we wish to calculate P(Y|S, I, ~D). We will first work out the details of the formulas starting with Bayes theorem and then add numbers from the belief network in Figure 4.

$$P(Y \mid S, I, \sim D) = P(Y, S, I, \sim D) / P(S, I, \sim D)$$

$$P(Y, S, I, \sim D) = P(Y, S, I, \sim D, A) + P(Y, S, I, \sim D, \sim A)$$
$$= P(Y \mid S, A) * P(\sim D \mid I, Y) * P(I) * P(S) * P(A)$$
$$+ P(Y \mid S, \sim A) * P(\sim D \mid I, Y) * P(I) * P(S) * P(\sim A)$$
$$= (0.9)(0.1)(0.8)(0.8)(0.8) + (0.3)(0.1)(0.8)(0.8)(0.2)$$
$$= (0.04608) + (0.00384)$$
$$= .04992$$

$$P(\sim D, I, S) = P(\sim D, I, S, Y, A) + P(\sim D, I, S, Y, \sim A)$$
$$+ P(\sim D, I, S, \sim Y, A) + P(\sim D, I, S, \sim Y, \sim A)$$
$$= 0.04992 + P(\sim D \mid I, \sim Y) * P(I) * P(S) * P(\sim Y \mid S, A) * P(A)$$
$$+ P(\sim D \mid I, \sim Y) * P(I) * P(S) * P(\sim Y \mid S, \sim A) * P(\sim A)$$
$$= 0.04992 + (0.7)(0.8)(0.8)(0.1)(0.8) + (0.7)(0.8)(0.8)(0.7)(0.2)$$
$$= 0.04992 + 0.03584 + 0.06272$$
$$= 0.14848$$

$$P(Y \mid S, I, \sim D) = P(Y, S, I, \sim D) / P(S, I \sim D)$$
$$= 0.04992 / 0.14848$$
$$= 0.03362$$

8.   FUTURE RESEARCH

We behave and problem-solve under uncertainty. Though there has been much discussion of how to think about uncertainty and a number of attempts to sidestep the problems with probabilistic reasoning have been made, Bayesian reasoning is theoretically anchored, the approach of choice, and the most important of the various approaches to the problem of uncertainty in reasoning systems. Some variant of Bayesian reasoning is desirable because it requires explicit detailing of the prior knowledge upon which a belief or decision is based. Decision-making under uncertainty is a difficult task. It requires lots of knowledge and a well-developed model. There is no way around this issue if one wants to build a refined and high-precision system. Bayesian belief networks are proving very valuable, for example, as a tool for implementing normative inferencing. They have been used for model-based diagnosis and in case-based reasoning systems to provide a way of organizing case bases and controlling problem-solving.

REFERENCES

Buchanan, B.G. and Shortliffe, E.H. (1985). *Rule-Based Expert Systems the MYCIN Experiments of the Stanford Heuristic Programming Project.* Reading, MA: Addison-Wesley.

Charniak, Eugene (1991). Bayesian networks without tears. *AI Magazine,* 12(2), 50–63.

Cooper, Gregory F. (1987). *Probabilistic Inference Using Belief Networks is NP-Hard* (Technical Report KSL-87-27). Medical Computer Science Group, Stanford University.

Dagum, Paul and Luby, Michael (1993). Approximating probabilistic inferences in Bayesian belief networks is NP-Hard. *Artificial Intelligence,* 60(1), 141–153.

Gonzalez, A.J. and Dankel, D. D. (1993). *The Engineering of Knowledge-Based Systems Theory and Practice.* Englewood Cliffs, NJ: Prentice-Hall.

Gordon, J. and Shortliffe, E.H. (1985a). The Dempster-Shafer theory of evidence. In Buchanan, B.G. and Shortliffe, E.H. (Eds.), *Rule-Based Expert Systems the MYCIN Experiments of the Stanford Heuristic Programming Project.* Reading, MA: Addison-Wesley.

Gordon, J. and Shortliffe, E.H. (1985b). Evidential reasoning in a hierarchy. *Artificial Intelligence,* 26(3), 323–357.

Heckerman, D. (1990). Probabilistic interpretations for MYCINS certainty factors. In Kanal, L.N. and Lemmer, J.F (Eds.), *Uncertainty in Artificial Intelligence.* New York: New-Holland.

Heckerman, D. (1995). *A Tutorial on Learning with Bayesian Networks* (Technical Report MSR-TR-95-06, Microsoft Research, 1995.

Kanal, L.N. and Lemmer, J.F. (Eds.). (1990) *Uncertainty in Artificial Intelligence.* New York: New-Holland.

Norvig, P. (1992). *Paradigms of Artificial Intelligence Programming.* Case Studies in Common Lisp. San Mateo, CA: Morgan Kaufmann.

Pearl, J. (1988). *Probabilistic Reasoning in Intelligent Systems: Networks of Plausible Reasoning.* San Mateo, CA: Morgan-Kaufmann.

Russell, S.J. and Norvig, P. (1995). *Artificial Intelligence: A Modern Approach.* Englewood Cliffs, NJ: Prentice-Hall.

Stefik, M. (1995). *Introduction to Knowledge Systems.* San Francisco: Morgan Kaufmann.

Shortliffe, E.H. (1976). *Computer-Based Medical Consultations: MYCIN.* New York: Elsevier.

9 Model-Based Reasoning

Roar Arne Fjellheim

CONTENTS

1. INTRODUCTION

Most early expert systems relied on a knowledge base acquired from domain experts through an elaborate knowledge acquisition process. This was a consequence of the insight that "knowledge is power," applied to artificial intelligence (AI) systems, and was a key factor in the rise and success of expert systems. However, the knowledge acquisition approach led to systems with inadequate behavior in situations not covered by the expert's experience. The knowledge bases developed in this manner were often difficult to maintain, and gradually became obsolete as the target domain inevitably changed. This partly explains the many cases of otherwise successful early expert systems that gradually fell out of use.

As demonstrated in other chapters of this book, many successful responses to the knowledge acquisition challenge have been developed, including improved knowledge acquisition methodologies and tools, machine learning, and so on. In this chapter, we are concerned with another response, the so-called *model-based reasoning* (MBR) approach. In this approach, the expert system is seen as composed of a *model* of the target domain, which is used by the MBR *engine* to solve problems of interest to the expert system's users. The key point is that the model does not just embody an expert's heuristic experience, but somehow is a more "first-principles" description of the target domain.

In subsequent sections of this chapter, we will further motivate the MBR approach by referring to its historical development as part of AI, followed by an overview of techniques and methodologies that are available for MBR systems. We will describe some categories and examples of applications of the MBR technology. Finally, we will offer some ideas on future trends and open issues.

2.   BACKGROUND AND HISTORY

A majority of early expert systems were *diagnostic* (or *classification*) systems, especially in the medical, electronic, and manufacturing domains (Buchanan and Shortliffe, 1984). We can better understand the reasons why model-based reasoning techniques were developed by briefly recapitulating the history of diagnostic systems. Early systems like MYCIN and INTERNIST relied on a knowledge base containing *diagnostic rules*:

IF *symptoms*$_1$ THEN *fault*$_1$
IF *symptoms*$_2$ THEN *fault*$_2$
Etc.

A rule is a direct link between an observed set of symptoms and the fault (or disease in the medical domain) that these symptoms indicate. Many extensions to this simple pattern were needed in practice, such as certainty factors, screening rules, etc. Each rule expresses a fragment of a domain expert's knowledge in a direct, compiled form. The advantages are easy comprehension and very efficient application (by a rule interpreter) of knowledge in this form. Indeed, many successful experts systems were, and still are, developed along those lines.

However, it soon became clear that the compiled diagnostic rule format for expressing diagnostic knowledge had distinct drawbacks:

- The system could not provide any conclusion if the expert had not entered a rule covering the exact symptoms that were observed.
- The expert reasoning behind the compiled form was lost, thereby impeding understanding and verification by other professionals.
- Unless carefully planned, the collection of diagnostic rules soon became unwieldy, and hard to maintain and improve upon.
- Building a new system often meant starting from scratch with a new expert, not being able to capitalize on knowledge already available in other rule systems.

In short, diagnostic systems developed according to the compiled rule paradigm tend to be lacking in coverage, clarity, flexibility, and cost-effective extendability. The model-based reasoning paradigm was developed, first in the diagnostic domain, in order to answer these deficiencies. In an MBR-based diagnostic system, the set of diagnostic rules is replaced by a *model* of the target system (patient, device), defining its *structure* and *behavior* (Davis, 1984):

- *Structural model*: What are the constituent parts of the target system, and how are the parts related (in a topological, spatial, and/or temporal sense)?
- *Behavioral model*: Given a set of "input" stimuli, what are the "output" responses of the target system? The *causality* of the target is often modeled.

Later, we will categorize and see specific examples of structural/behavioral models. Using a model of this kind, an *MBR diagnostic engine* is able to:

- Use the behavioral model to detect discrepancies between the faulty and normal behavior of the target system, thereby indicating symptoms.
- Use the behavioral and structural models to trace back from observed discrepancies to the underlying root causes, thereby indicating a diagnosis.

This approach has a number of advantages over the compiled rule approach, including:

- The diagnostic system is able to diagnose "new" faults, faults that could not be acquired by just formalizing empirical knowledge.
- Engineering or scientific knowledge, available in textbooks and other sources, can be applied in building the models, thereby avoiding personal biases.
- The models are compositional, thereby allowing the gradual accumulation of model component libraries and easing model construction.
- The MBR approach lends itself to better explanation of conclusions and improved verification of diagnostic capabilities.

The MBR approach is not without problems, including:

- It often involves reasoning algorithms with combinatorial complexity, leading to excessive or unacceptable computation time.
- Creating the required model may include insight and effort that is not available, or the model may in fact be unknown (e.g., certain physiological processes).

The distinction between expert systems built using the compiled rule paradigm and systems using models were recognized during the 1980s. The two types of systems were given different labels, such as "shallow" (compiled rules) and "deep" (model-based) systems. Model-based systems were also called "second-generation expert systems." Many researchers and practitioners saw the advantages of both approaches, and proposed *hybrid* solutions. In the diagnostic domain, these hybrids generally work along the following principles:

- The knowledge base contains both a set of diagnostic rules and a model, and the system has appropriate inference engines for both types of knowledge.
- Confronted with a diagnostic case, the rules are first applied. If they yield a solution, the search is over.
- If the rules fail, the MBR machinery is invoked. It will hopefully produce a solution, possibly after spending considerable time on this.
- If successful, the MBR solution is formulated as a rule and added to the rule base for efficient solution of similar cases in the future.

The MBR paradigm is not restricted to the diagnostic domain, even if most results have been reported for diagnostic applications. Other types of problems that have been attacked with this approach include design/configuration problems, and monitoring and control problems (the latter two often in combination with diagnostic systems). A recent survey of methods and applications of MBR can be found in Dague (1995). In a later section, some examples of application in these various domains will be described briefly.

3.   TECHNIQUES AND METHODOLOGIES

3.1.   INTRODUCTION

The central concept of model-based reasoning is of course the concept of a *model*. We therefore start this section by a discussion of model categories and their properties. Selecting a model and a reasoning algorithm for a given purpose are not independent choices, but we treat the latter in a separate subsection.

The term *model* is generally overused, and AI and the expert system field are no exceptions. In this chapter we link it to an "engineering" notion of a *system* as an entity that we wish to consider as a unity, whose *structure* can be decomposed into subsystems and components, and which exhibits certain *behavior*, i.e., given some input stimuli, it will respond with certain outputs. Based on this notion of a system, a *model* is a description of a system, using an appropriate modeling language, that makes explicit the structure and behavior of the system for purposes of analysis, prediction, diagnosis, etc.

Some researchers include the *function* (or purpose) of the system (Chandrasekaran, 1994), in addition to structure and behavior, in their system model. This allows certain types of reasoning that depend on the purpose of the system being studied. For example, in diagnosis, understanding the functional role of a system may help ascertain the impact of a fault and thereby help prioritize and direct the diagnostic search process. In this chapter, we will not include the functional model aspect further.

3.2. MODEL CATEGORIES

Our definition of what a model is, does not prescribe a specific modeling language or representation. Choices of model representation will depend on the purpose of the model, and on available knowledge, resources, tools, and reasoning engines. In defining the space of model categories, we use the distinctions given by Leitch (1992):

- *Declarative vs. Procedural.* Declarative representations describe relationships between phenomena in the real world, without implying a directionality of the relationship. An example is Ohm's law, $V = I * R$, which can be used to calculate any of the variables V, I, or R, given values of the other two variables. The lack of directionality makes a declarative representation very general, but can lead to combinatorial complex and inefficient reasoning algorithms. If the available knowledge contains a strong element of directionality, then a procedural representation may be more appropriate. A procedure will efficiently derive the output, given an input. The directionality may however be specific to a certain task or situation, and procedural models therefore tend to be highly specialized. The trend has been to make representation more and more declarative/general, at the expense of applying more computation power (for which the cost is steadily decreasing).
- *Quantitative vs. Qualitative.* In traditional engineering disciplines, all models are numerical, such as algebraic- or differential equation-based models. Very sophisticated methods for developing and applying such models are available. In AI, researchers have been interested in how models can be used in situations where available knowledge or resources do not enable or justify full quantification, but where qualitative models may suffice (Weld and de Kleer, 1990). In a qualitative model, model variables take on values like "low," "normal," and "high" instead of precise numerical values. Novel representation techniques, including approximate reasoning, fuzzy sets, and order of magnitude, have been developed in this strand of research. In addition to being better tuneable to real availability of domain knowledge, a qualitative model may better reflect a "human" point of view. Humans are good at making rough estimates and predictions of (everyday) physical phenomena based on nonnumerical reasoning.
- *Certain vs. Uncertain.* The distinction between certain and uncertain knowledge should not be confused with the quantitative vs. qualitative distinction; a mode can well be quantitative and uncertain, or qualitative and certain. However, if the knowledge is uncertain, this fact should somehow be represented in the model. Two main forms of uncertainty have been recognized. The first, probability theory, concerns the situation when exact knowledge is not available, and estimates based on frequency of occurrence are used. The second approach is to represent imprecision directly, for example, as a graded membership of a fuzzy set, a real number between 0 and 1.

- *Static vs. Dynamic.* Static models only represent steady-state, or equilibrium, behavior of systems. Dynamic models are in addition able to represent model behavior in transient states, as an evolution of state values over time. Until recently, most AI-based representations were based on static models. Such models can be useful, for example, in steady-state diagnosis. However, a dynamic model is essential for proper handling of, for example, control or diagnosis problems when the system is undergoing transient behavior. Dynamic models require the representation of state and storage of matter and energy, and hence delay, that occurs in the physical world. The choice of static or dynamic models fundamentally affects the representation language. In the former, algebraic equations will suffice, whereas in the latter, differential primitives are required.
- *Continuous vs. Discontinuous.* This final distinction records the fact that in some systems, behavior trajectories can only evolve smoothly through "adjacent" states. This is a characteristic of most systems in nature. However, manmade systems often display discrete state transitions, "jumping" from one state to another state with completely different properties. The latter type of behavior can, for example, be represented by finite-state automata.

The characteristics listed above define a space of possible models for use in model-based reasoning systems. Some of the positions in this space are densely populated, while others have not yet been explored. For example, procedural, quantitative, certain, dynamic, and continuous models represent well-established engineering practise (differential equation-based models), while declarative, qualitative, uncertain, dynamic, and continuous models are intensely investigated in AI. Since the latter category is of particular importance in expert system applications of MBR, we now give a brief overview of the most important developments.

3.3. Qualitative Models

Qualitative reasoning in AI covers a wide range of approaches that use qualitative models of physical systems to perform various reasoning tasks (Weld and de Kleer, 1990). Common to all approaches is a set of basic notions:

- *Quantity space*: The state of a physical system may be characterized by a number of variables. The range of symbols that are legal values of these variables, and an ordering between the values, constitute the quantity space. Since we deal with quantitative models, the space contains values like "high," "low," etc., or "decreasing," "stable," or "increasing" for change (differential) variables.
- *Qualitative state*: The qualitative state of a system (at a given instant in time) is the combination of states of all qualitative variables describing the system, each with assigned value from the quantity space. Simulating the qualitative behavior of the system means describing how the qualitative state changes over time.

There are three dominant approaches to building qualitative reasoning models.

Constraint-based approach. This approach was developed by Benjamin Kuipers (Kuipers, 1986) and is embodied in a family of programs called QSIM. A physical system is modeled by a set of qualitative *constraints* between the variables that comprise the model. The constraints can be seen as qualitative abstraction of the quantitative differential equations that would be used in ordinary mathematical models of the system. Kuipers introduces six constraints:

ADD — Qualitative addition
MULT — Qualitative multiplication
MINUS — Change of sign

DERIV — A variable is the derivative of another
M⁺ — A variable increases as another variable increases
M⁻ — A variable decreases as another variable increases

Using these constraints, QSIM is able to model a physical system and to predict its qualitative behavior (see next subsection).

Component-based approach. In QSIM, the system is defined by a set of mathematical constraints, where the physical properties of the system is abstracted away. In the component approach, pioneered by de Kleer and Brown (de Kleer and Brown, 1984), the topological structure of the target system is preserved in the model. A model consists of components, connections, and material that flow through connections. "Material" may be physical material, or more abstract entities like electrical current, or even information. The behavior of each component is described by a set of local *confluences*, i.e., relationships between inputs, internal states, and outputs. A component model is independent of how it is hooked up to the rest of the model (the "no function in structure" principle). In the ENVISION program that embodies this approach, all variables and their derivatives have the same simple quantity space: $\{-, 0, +\}$.

Process-based approach. Similar to the previous approach, this one (Forbus, 1984) is also based on component models and system topology. But unlike the component-based approach, the process-based approach allows conceptualizations of physical interactions, called *processes*. This concept is used to define the dynamic characteristics of the system. The approach is embodied in a system called QPT (Qualitative Process Theory). More details can be found in Forbus (1984).

After this brief foray into the "pure AI"-based approaches to qualitative modeling, we return to the general overview of MBR. Unfortunately, there is no unifying "theory" for models used in MBR, nor any agreed-upon set of guidelines for when to apply a certain type of model. There is a true plethora of model formalisms available, but selecting and modifying a technique for a given task or application is still an art, more than an engineering discipline. We will return briefly to this issue in a later section, but first we will survey some available MBR reasoning techniques.

3.4. QUALITATIVE SIMULATION

In building expert system applications, we will be interested in using a model of a particular target system to support the reasoning behavior of the application. We therefore need effective *reasoning techniques* that can utilize the model. Here, we concentrate on the two types of techniques that are used: applications (viz. qualitative simulation) and model-based diagnosis.

Of course, *simulation* as understood in engineering or computer science presupposes a model, most often of the purely procedural, quantitative variety. This type of simulation has a role to play in expert system building, but most frequently in the form of components of *hybrid* systems, where for example an expert system helps to formulate the simulation model, or to interpret the simulation output. The model itself is usually not accessible to the expert system, due to its nondeclarative and closed representation. We will not delve into this type of architecture here, since it falls outside of what is normally called "model-based reasoning."

If the model belongs to the family of qualitative models described in the previous section, the situation is different. In this case, the model is declarative and can be reasoned about. Prominent among the reasoning requirements, is the ability to simulate and predict behavior. Using qualitative models for this capability means that we obtain less precision than we would have obtained if we had used a more accurate quantitative model. Why would one be willing to give up precision in simulation? Some possible reasons are:

- The full quantitative model may be prohibitively computationally expensive to run, and the less precise results from the quantitative model may still be satisfactory for their intended use.

- To develop the full quantitative model may be either impossible, due lack of knowledge, or unrealistic, due to the scope of the problem (e.g., a large-scale chemical plant). Again, a qualitative model may be viable and sufficient.
- Especially in knowledge-based systems, we may wish to have models that correspond to common sense, rather than more abstract mathematical models. For example, this will facilitate explanation of simulation results to end-users.
- Finally, qualitative models may produce simulation results that "collapse" related behaviors into principally different classes, while quantitative models always produce an exact "point" solution.

The actual algorithm used to perform qualitative simulation depends of course on the particular model formalism. In general, these algorithms perform some sort of iterative *propagation* of values, using the elements of the model (e.g., constraints) to direct the propagation. Each propagation step takes one qualitative state as input and produces its successor state (S). We will use QSIM (Kuipers, 1984) as an example. The main steps of the QSIM algorithm are repeated execution of the following steps (details in the reference):

1. Select a qualitative state from among the active set of states for which successors need to be determined.
2. Determine the set of transitions that are possible from the current state.
3. For each constraint, generate the set of tuples of transitions of its arguments. Filter for consistency with the constraint.
4. Perform pairwise consistency filtering of the sets of tuples associated with the constraints, making sure that adjacent constraints must agree on transitions involving a shared variable.
5. Generate all possible global interpretations from the remaining tuples. If none is left, the behavior is inconsistent. Create new qualitative states resulting from each interpretation, and make them successors to the current state.
6. Apply global filtering rules to the new qualitative states, and place any remaining states in the active set of states for which successors need to be determined.

QSIM has the property that it produces *all possible behaviors*, a very strong and useful property for gaining an understanding of a system's behavior. Unfortunately, QSIM may also produce *additional spurious behaviors* that are not consistent with any real possible behavior. This is due to a combination of locality of computation with qualitative model descriptions. Finally, QSIM is not guaranteed to halt, since it may create new successor states ad infinitum.

QSIM is perhaps the best developed of the qualitative simulation algorithms, and the one that is closest to practical application. It is fair to state, though, that the use of qualitative models for simulation has remained a somewhat academic discipline, with relatively few and still experimental real-word applications (but see Section 4 of this chapter).

3.5. MODEL-BASED DIAGNOSIS

The requirements from diagnostic tasks have been a major driving force in developing MBR technology. The original motivation was presented in Section 2, and consisted of the dissatisfaction with purely heuristic diagnostic systems. Much of the early work on model-based diagnosis (MBD) was in the area of faultfinding of electronic circuitry. We can use an example from that domain to illustrate the reasoning strategies adopted in MBD (Faltings, 1996).

Consider a simple digital circuit, shown in Figure 1, comprising three multipliers and two adders. Values of measurements taken at various ports are shown.

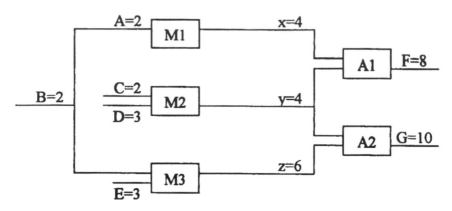

FIGURE 1   Example circuit and measurements.

In a *heuristic* expert system for finding faults in the circuit, one would have rules like:

IF incorrect(F) AND incorrect(G) THEN faulty(M2) CF = 0.5

where CF is a *certainty factor* meaning that the rule is valid with 50% certainty. The rule will have been obtained from an expert who "guesses" that M2 is the culprit if both F and G outputs are faulty, since M2 is a common input point to both A1 and A2.

In an MBD approach, knowledge about the circuit would be expressed by *models*, for example:

IF multiplier(m, x, y, z) AND NOT faulty(m) THEN equal(x $*$ y, z)

stating that if a multiplier has inputs x and y, output z, and is not faulty, then z = x $*$ y. This is a universally true statement about the device. The diagnostic problem can now be stated as follows: find the set of faulty components (each such set is a *candidate*) such that the relations implied by the model are consistent with the observations. Usually, the initial observations are not sufficient to allow only a single solution to the diagnostic problem. For the device shown, the measurements

Inputs: A = B = C = 2, D = E = 3
Outputs: F = 8, G = 10

allow many different diagnostic candidates. Since F depends on A, B, C, and D through components M1, M2, and A1, and the result does not agree with the model, at least one component in the set {M1, M2, A1} must be faulty. Similarly, since G is also incorrect, at least one of {M2, M3, A2} must also be faulty. A diagnostic candidate is a combination of components that contains at least one element from the first set and one from the second. For example, all the following are candidates:

{M2}, {M1, M3}, ..., {M1, M2, M3, A1, A2}

In order to narrow down this set of candidates, an MBD system requires additional machinery to rank diagnostic candidates, and to decide on a strategy for taking measurements. For example, an initial ranking might select {M2} since a single fault is more likely than a multiple fault. The optimal next measurement is y. Since this again turns out to be false, we now know that M2 must be faulty, which also explains both other faults.

The example illustrates that reasoning capabilities required in MBD include:

- Simulate or predict which observations are implied by the normal behavior of the target system. The qualitative simulation techniques described earlier have been used for this, as have other simulation techniques.
- Record dependencies between internal model variables and predicted observations. In some implemented systems, assumption-based truth maintenance systems (de Kleer, 1986) have been used for this and the next reasoning capability.
- Upon detection of unexpected actual observations, use the dependencies to identify (minimal combinations of) model assumptions that conflict with the observations.
- In the presence of multiple candidates, propose a measurement strategy that will reduce the number of candidates as cost effectively as possible.

A typical representative for the dependency-recording approach to MBD is the GDE (General Diagnosis Engine) (de Kleer and Williams, 1987).

4. APPLICATIONS OF MBR

4.1. INTRODUCTION

In Section 2 on the history and background of MBR, we motivated model-based reasoning techniques by certain deficiencies in the "expert mining" approach to building expert systems, such as inability to reason about situations not covered by the expert's knowledge, lack of transparency, and difficult maintenance. Consequently, many examples exist for applying MBR techniques to real-world problems.

However, it must be admitted that MBR techniques are not as widespread and in general use as some would have expected 10 years ago. In particular, the applications seem to be in a limited number of problem domains. We therefore start this section by a brief overview of expert system application areas, and point to those where MBR seems to be most successful. Then we present some examples of applications in these areas: *monitoring, control,* and *diagnosis.*

4.2. WHERE IS MBR USED?

It is common to categorize expert system applications according to the *tasks* the perform. One such task list is:

- *Design*: Create a new structure according to goals and constraints
- *Configuration*: Combine elements according to goals and constraints
- *Prediction*: Infer consequences of a situation
- *Planning*: Create a sequence of actions from an initial state to a goal state
- *Monitoring**: Track and compare observations to expectations
- *Control**: Govern system behavior to meet goals
- *Diagnosis**: Infer system malfunctions from observations

Of the task categories on this list, by far the most examples of MBR techniques can be found in those that are marked by an asterisk. Before going into details of those application areas, a few remarks on the other areas are in order.

Using models in design is of course nothing new. Most engineering design of artifacts involves building and experimenting with a model (or models) of the artifact. Models are useful both in *synthesis* of new designs, and in *analysis* of existing or redesigned ones. Very sophisticated methods and tools exist for supporting the use of numerical and other "classical" models. So ingrained are these methods and tools that MBR (as we understand it here) may have problems of being recognized as adding new value. We think this is an explanation of the relative paucity of reported design applications of MBR, in spite of the plausibility of, e.g., using qualitative simulation to check out the behavior of a proposed new mechanism.

For the configuration and planning tasks, the situation is that AI has produced some very efficient methods, including constraint-based reasoning and partial-order planning. One could argue that these are model-based, in that they rely upon an explicit domain model. However, they are usually not categorized as MBR, and are therefore not included here.

4.3. MONITORING

Earlier, we defined *monitoring* as the activity of tracking and comparing observations to expectations. Many examples of monitoring expert systems, using the MBR approach, can be found in the manufacturing and process industries. These industries already use monitoring systems based on conventional techniques. For example, this may mean tracking the value of a particular measurement over time, and warn the operator if the value exceeds a particular fixed alarm threshold. The resulting monitoring performance is often very crude, and may lead to excessive alarming (too narrow alarm limits), or under-reporting (too permissive limits). The trouble is that the monitoring limits are fixed and not related to the actual running conditions of the plant (device).

This is in contrast to the MBR approach, where monitoring is done by running a model of the physical system in parallel the system itself, producing expected values for different observations (measurements), comparing the actual observations of the system with those that the model predicts (dynamically), and reporting significant deviation. Dvorak and Kuipers (1991) presented an MBR monitoring application, called MIMIC. It exploits three different techniques:

- *Semiquantitative simulation.* In Section 3 we described qualitative simulation as a reasoning technique with a number of desirable properties for inferring behavior when a purely qualitative model exists. In MIMIC, additional numerical information that is always available in real plants, is used to improve the precision of the predictions. In particular, it removes inconsistent solution and permits direct comparison of measurements with numerical predictions.
- *Tracking (measurement interpretation).* MIMIC tries to maintain a set of models ("the tracking set") that is consistent with the measurements, and which represents a possible state of the target system. During diagnosis (see below), MIMIC adds interpretations to the tracking set that represent hypothesized faults. During tracking, it deletes models from the set when predictions fail to match observations.
- *Model-based diagnosis.* MIMIC also performs diagnosis as part of an integrated problem-solving architecture. Its role is to update the model (tracking set). We will return to model-based diagnosis in a subsequent section.

The MIMIC architecture was applied to a water heating system on an experimental basis. Among the advantages quoted by the authors of their approach are:

- More "intelligent" alarms limits
- Early detection of undesired behavior
- Availability of predicted values for non-observed variables
- Ability to predict effect of control actions ("what-if")

Several other MBR monitoring systems have been reported in the literature, often (as for MIMIC) as part of an overall monitoring-diagnosis application. Some examples are:

- BIOTECH (Bousson et al., 1993): Provides monitoring of key variables and diagnosis in a biological fermentation process.
- DIAPASON (Penalva et al., 1993): A system for supervision and operator support in a continuous process in the area of nuclear fuel reprocessing.

4.4. Control

Control means governing the behavior of the target system to meet stated goals. In the AI/expert system area in general, and in MBR-based systems in particular, there are not many real-world applications of *closed-loop* control systems, i.e., systems that directly control the target system without human intervention. On the other hand, there are numerous examples of *open-loop* systems, where the human is an essential link between observations and control actions. In manufacturing and process industries, one often refers to such systems as *operator support systems*. Their role is to provide the operator with insight into the status of the target system, and to suggest corrective or optimizing control action that the operator may implement. Such systems generally exist as an add-on to an underlying closed-loop control system that carries out low-level control in real time.

More systematically, we may distinguish between the following different ways in which expert system technology (and MBR) are being applied to control problems:

- *Expert control.* This term is often used to denote systems where an expert system is used to configure and tune conventional low-level controllers. MBR is not widely used.
- *Qualitative/fuzzy control.* In this case, closed-loop control is performed by AI/expert system techniques. Fuzzy logic has been widely deployed in this capacity. It can be argued that fuzzy logic is an MBR technique, but this is a matter of classification.
- *Qualitative model predictive control.* In model predictive control (MPC), a model is used online to predict the consequences of various control actions. Combined with an optimizing search engine, such a model may support very sophisticated control regimes. MBR is an ideal candidate for the model part of MPC, and may be combined with numerical techniques.

In this list, the last type most directly applies MBR in practice. As explained above, most existing systems of this type are open-loop operator support systems.

4.5. Diagnosis

Model-based diagnosis (MBD) has received more widespread practical application than any other application of MBR techniques. It appears that this is a particularly fertile ground for using these techniques. Diagnosis is a task of high practical and direct economic significance. Improving availability of, e.g., a manufacturing plant by as little as a few tenths of a percent can yield enormous benefits. A survey of techniques and applications of diagnostic advisory systems, including systems using MBR techniques, can be found in Kramer and Fjellheim (1995).

One can generalize the flow of activities in the *diagnostic process* to the following steps:

1. *Fault detection*: The fault manifests itself by some observable symptom. In the MBD approach, detection will be done by comparing actual with model-predicted values of one or several variables.
2. *Fault isolation*: Based on the detected symptom(s), one will try to trace back to the location of the underlying cause, e.g., which component in the circuit causes the faulty output. Again, a model may support this tracing.

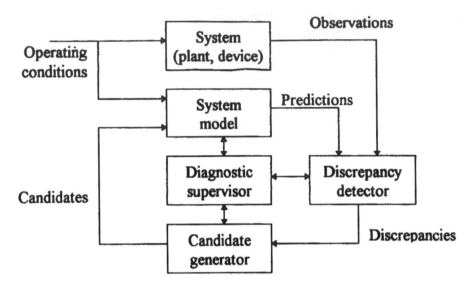

FIGURE 2   Generic MBD system architecture.

3. *Fault identification*: It may be desirable to go one step further after isolation, namely to identify the precise nature of the localized fault (e.g., short circuit). In MBD, this ability assumes *fault models* in addition to the nominal model.
4. *Fault correction*: Finally, a complete troubleshooting session should conclude with a recommended action, such as to repair or replace a component. This falls outside the scope of MBD, but may be an essential part of a deployed system.

A generic system architecture that supports this diagnostic process, using the model-based approach, is shown on Figure 2 (Leitch et al., 1992). The architecture is representative of a large number of MBD applications, even though details may differ significantly from system to system.

In this architecture, a *system model* is run in parallel with the *system* itself, producing *predictions* of what the *observations* "ought to be." A *discrepancy detector* module tracks observations and predictions, and triggers on significant deviations (note that this may in itself be a nontrivial operation, perhaps involving data validation and statistical processing). The *discrepancies* are fed into a *candidate generator* module, which proposes one or more fault *candidates*. These are used to modify the behavior of the system model according to the hypothesized fault. If the predictions now match the observations, we know that the fault has been identified. The whole diagnostic process is steered by a *diagnostic supervisor* module, which may range in complexity from a simple invocation interface to a sophisticated strategy reasoner.

A recent and very substantial MBD application is the TIGER system (Travé-Massuyés and Milne, 1996). The application domain of TIGER is monitoring and diagnosis of gas turbines, an area of large industrial interest. The TIGER system has been deployed at a large petroleum company. Some technical features characterizing this application are:

- It uses a qualitative model of the turbine and a qualitative simulation algorithm to predict normal turbine behavior.
- Fault detection is done by matching the actual measurements with the simulated normal behavior (just as in the reference architecture).
- The diagnosis algorithm is patterned after the framework of Reiter (1987): it collects conflict sets, i.e., sets of components that cannot behave normally according to the observations.

- Augmenting the MBD algorithm, TIGER also has a real-time expert system capable of monitoring alarms quickly and with guaranteed response time.
- Finally, the system has a temporal reasoning module for expressing and monitoring temporal dependencies in the turbine.

Other successful expert systems that use an MBD approach are (many other systems could have been listed):

- DCP (Fjalestad et al., 1994). Uses a mixed topological/numerical model to support pollution monitoring and diagnosis at a fertilizer plant.
- GIOTTO (Cermignani and Tornielli, 1993). A generic tool for building MBD systems for continuous and static processes.
- KARDIO (Bratko et al., 1989). Uses a qualitative model of the human heart to generate a diagnostic system for heart diseases.

5.   TRENDS AND OPEN ISSUES

As we have seen in previous sections of this chapter, the field of model-based reasoning (MBR) is very diverse and has similarly diverse applications. This diversity is at the same time a strength and a weakness. The diversity is unfortunately not supported by a set of clear taxonomies and methods for choosing an MBD technique for a certain purpose. The field does not present itself as a unified body of knowledge, apart from a common core where the abstract idea of a model occupies a central position. The MBD field is a collection of loosely connected techniques of variable degree of maturity. In this sense, the diversity is a weakness. Some attempts have been made to present a systematic methodology for subdomains, e.g., (Leitch et al., 1992) for model-based diagnosis, but these attempts have by no means been universally accepted.

On the other hand, the diversity is a sign of a field in progress, where new ideas are still being created. The diversity can therefore be seen as a sign of dynamism. According to a more pessimistic view (Dague, 1995), no real intellectual advance has been made in the area of qualitative reasoning since 1984, when de Kleer and Brown (1984) and Forbus (1984) were published, and the same could be said for the more general area of MBR. According to this view, progress has not been in major principles or insights, but rather in smaller improvements in theory, and verification in gradually more ambitious applications. A general problem of MBD systems is high computational complexity and unpredictable computation time.

If it is true that the main ideas behind MBD are understood, and the advantages of the MBD approach are equally accepted, what is keeping users from developing such systems *en masse*? One obvious obstacle is the effort and expertise required to build good models of new domains. It is maybe ironic that a technique that at the outset was supposed to alleviate the knowledge acquisition bottleneck, itself becomes victim of a similar "model acquisition bottleneck." The problem is being attacked along several dimensions:

- *Improved tools for modeling*. For example, general tools for building knowledge-based systems (Gensym, 1997) offer visual creation, debugging and deployment of complex model-based systems, and thereby improve the productivity of model building efforts.
- *Model libraries and reuse*. As users learn to develop models that separate the generic from specific information, they will be able to build libraries of component models that can be assembled in new models. Computer science ideas like object orientation, as well as model standardization efforts, facilitate this development.
- *Automatic acquisition of models*. Work is in progress to have systems automatically generate models for an application, based on available information and the needs of the

application (Xia and Smith, 1996). While still in its infancy, such work may have dramatic impact on the applicability of MBR.

We have briefly described a number of applications of MBR (and MBD). While a number of impressive applications have been built, their absolute number is still small. The "killer MBR application" that will lead to massive deployment is still missing. It is possible that no such application is imminent, and that MBR will remain a technology reserved for a small number of sophisticated applications. Another view, which is plausible, is that with the emergence of improved modeling support (see above), the cost of applying MBR will be lowered to a point where MBR becomes much more practicable. In the short run, better tools is a key success factor for this scenario to unfold. For example, the PRIDE project is developing a toolkit for easy deployment of MBD systems in the process industry (PRIDE, 1996).

In the longer run, it appears that intelligent systems of the future must be model-based in one sense or other, whether we call it AI or not. Modern interconnected society will require highly sophisticated computer systems, for example, in massive industrial plant supervision, coordination of large transportation systems, monitoring of ecosystems on a regional and global scale, autonomous control of deep-space missions, etc. We must expect that systems with the level of intelligence, flexibility, and robustness that will be required for such applications will need internal models of their domains, and the ability to reason about such models (Williams and Nayak, 1996).

6.   SUMMARY

We have presented model-based reasoning (MBR) as a field of AI, centered around the concept of representing the external domain in an internal model, and being able to reason about this model in order to solve problems. We have seen that apart from this central idea, the field contains a very diverse set of approaches. No unifying theory or (small) set of techniques can at the moment be presented as *the* MBR approach. In order to get a detailed understanding of the various approaches, one has to go to the sources. There is a need to provide better guidance to someone interested in applying MBR, maybe on a per-domain or per-task basis.

In spite of the lack of a unified theory, MBR has been put to practical use in many impressive real-world applications. The major category of application is model-based diagnosis. The benefits of such applications over more traditional rule-based expert systems, are the ability to reason about novel situations, less dependence upon expert opinion and experience, and higher flexibility and scope for expansion. If such systems have not yet reached their full potential, one reason is the cost and complexity of building models. Once this difficulty has been overcome, through better tools, model reuse, and automatic model building, there is every reason to expect that MBD will be a key technology in intelligent systems of the future.

REFERENCES

Bousson, K. et al., Qualitative prediction and interpretation for bioprocess supervision, *Proc. Int. Conf. on Fault Diagnosis Tooldiag '93*, 1044-1053, Toulouse, 1993.

Bratko, I. et al., *KARDIO: A Study in Deep and Qualitative Knowledge for Expert Systems*, MIT Press, MA, 1989.

Buchanan, B.G. and E.H. Shortliffe (Eds.), *Rule-Based Expert Systems*, Addison Wesley, MA, 1984.

Cermignani, S. and G. Tornielli Giotto, A diagnostic system for continuous static processes, *Proc. Int. Conf. Automation '93*, Milan, November 1993.

Chandrasekaran, B., Functional representation: A brief historical perspective, *Applied Artificial Intelligence*, 8:173–197, 1994.

Dague, P. (Ed.), Qualitative reasoning: A survey of techniques and applications, *AI Communications*, 8(3/4):119–192, Sept./Dec. 1995.

Davis, R., Diagnostic reasoning based on structure and behaviour, *Artificial Intelligence*, 24:347–410, 1984.

de Kleer, J. and J. Seely Brown, A qualitative physics based on confluences, *Artificial Intelligence*, 24:7–83, 1984, reproduced in (Weld and de Kleer, 1990).

de Kleer, J., An assumption-based truth maintenance system, *Artificial Intelligence*, 28:127–162, 1986.

de Kleer, J. and B.C. Williams, Diagnosing multiple faults, *Artificial Intelligence*, 32:97–130, 1987.

Dvorak, D. and B. Kuipers, Process monitoring and diagnosis — Model-based approach, *IEEE Expert*, 6(3):67–74, June 1991.

Faltings, B., Working group in model-based design and reasoning, *AI Communications*, 9:59–64, 1996.

Fjalestad, K. et al., A total quality management system for reduction of industrial pollution discharge, *Computers Chem. Engng.*, 18 (Suppl.):S369–S373, 1994.

Forbus, K.D, Qualitatative Process Theory, *Artificial Intelligence*, 24:85–168, 1984, reproduced in Weld and de Kleer, 1990.

Gensym Corp., G2 Programmer's Manual, Version 5.0, Cambridge, MA, 1997.

Kramer, M. and R. Fjellheim, Fault diagnosis and computer-aided diagnostic advisors, *Proc. IPSE '95 — Intelligent Systems in Process Engineering*, Snowmass, CO, July 1995.

Kuipers, B., Qualitative simulation, *Artificial Intelligence*, 29:289–388, 1986, reproduced in Weld and de Kleer, 1990.

Leitch, R., Artificial intelligence in control, *Computing & Control Engineering Journal*, U.K., July 1992.

Leitch, R. et al., ARTIST: A methodological approach to specifying model-based diagnostic systems, in Guida and Stefanini (Eds.), *Industrial Applications of Knowledge-Based Diagnosis*, 1992.

Penalva, J.M. et al., A supervision support system for industrial processes, *IEEE Expert*, 8(5):57–65, October 1993.

PRIDE, The PRIDE Consortium, Process Industry Diagnostic Environment, Esprit IV Project No. 20498, 1996.

Reiter, R., A theory of diagnosis from first principles, *Artificial Intelligence*, 32(1):57–96, 1987.

Travé-Massuyés, L. and R. Milne, Diagnosis of dynamic systems based on explicit and implicit behavioural models: An application to gas turbines in esprit project TIGER, *Applied Artificial Intelligence*, 10:257–277, 1966.

Weld, D.S. and J. de Kleer (Eds.), *Readings in Qualitative Reasoning about Physical Systems*, Morgan Kaufmann, California, 1990.

Williams, B.C. and P.P. Nayak, Immobile robots — AI in the new millennium, *AI Magazine*, 17(3):17–35, Fall 1996.

Xia, S. and N. Smith, Automated modelling: A discussion and review, *The Knowledge Engineering Review*, 11(2):137–160, 1996.

10 Knowledge Sharing and Reuse

Asunción Gómez-Pérez

CONTENTS

0-8493-3106-4/98/$0.00+$.50
© 1998 by CRC Press LLC

1.   INTRODUCTION

In 1991, the ARPA Knowledge Sharing Effort (Neches et al., 1991) revolutionized the way in which intelligent systems were built. They proposed the following:

> "Building knowledge-based systems today usually entails constructing new knowledge bases from scratch. It could instead be done by assembling reusable components. System developers would then only need to worry about creating the specialized knowledge and reasoners new to the specific task of their system. This new system would interoperate with existing systems, using them to perform some of its reasoning. In this way, declarative knowledge, problem-solving techniques and reasoning services would all be shared among systems. This approach would facilitate building bigger and better systems cheaply... ."

Since then, there have been workshops on ontologies in SSS-97 in Stanford, on ontological engineering; ECAI-96 in Budapest (August 1996), on the practical aspects of ontology development; IJCAI (August 1995), on basic ontological issues in knowledge sharing; La Jolla (November 1994); ECAI-94 in Amsterdam (August 1994) on implemented ontologies; IJCAI-93 in Chambery (August 1993), on knowledge sharing and information interchange; and the workshop on formal ontology in Padova, Italy (March 1993). Ideas from many papers included in the proceedings of recent conferences and ontologies workshops are collected here.

On examining the literature, it could be said that many ontologies have been developed by different groups, adopting different approaches and using different methods and techniques. However, few papers have been published about how to proceed, showing the practices, design criteria, activities, methodologies, and tools used to build ontologies. The implication is clear: the absence of standardized activities, life cycles, and systematic methodologies, as well as a set of well-defined design criteria, techniques, and tools make ontologies development a craft rather than an engineering activity. So, the art will become engineering when there is a definition and standardization of a life cycle that goes from requirements definition to maintenance of the finished product, as well as methodologies and techniques that drive development.

This chapter does not seek to transform the ontological art into engineering. It only presents a view of how the knowledge-sharing industry is evolving, its terminology, the infrastructure, technology, and methodologies that make it possible, its main developments, as well as the principal research issues and future trends. The chapter is organized into three main parts. The first part is an introduction to this field. The goal of the second part is to explain the activities that readers interested in building ontologies from scratch should perform and in which order, as well as the set of techniques to be used in each phase of the building process. Finally, the third part presents the most well-known ontologies and systems that use ontologies.

2.   PROBLEMS WITH REUSE SOFTWARE OR SHARE KNOWLEDGE

Suppose you are commissioned by an aircraft company to build an intelligent system for aircraft design, diagnosis, prediction, repair, and maintenance. The system must be ready in a short period of time and at minimum cost. Then, instead of starting from scratch, you raise if it is possible to adapt knowledge from existing knowledge bases (KBs) into your new system. You have two options: reuse software and share knowledge.

If you select the option of **reusing software already built**, after carefully investigating applications produced by others, you decide which modules are potentially useful and usable in your system.

1. The chosen modules satisfy 100% of your requirements. Then you can integrate them with your system, using a translator that umpires between existing programs and mod-

erates the communication between them, or a capsule or container that covers the programs to be reused, or you have to completely rewrite the original program.

2. The modules partially satisfy your requirements. Then you need to study carefully what portion (knowledge and software) is reusable for your objectives. Software Engineering provides guidelines, methods and techniques to reuse software made by others. Note that if the system you are trying to reuse is a KBS (knowledge-based system), together with the software reuse you are also reusing knowledge. In this case, after investigating which kind of knowledge and inference engines are reusable for your goals and which are not, you will probably find some of the following problems:

   a. *The heterogeneity of knowledge representation formalisms* (Neches et al., 1991). That is, each intelligent system has its own formalism to represent knowledge (rules, frames, logic, etc.) and its own techniques to perform inferences. The formalism and inference engine of the new system may, or may not, be coincident with those used in the systems you try to reuse.

   b. Supposing that the knowledge representation formalism and the inference engines of the two systems used to build the new system are the same, i.e., frames, then each system could have been implemented in a different language or shell from the target language in which the new system will be implemented. So, *the heterogeneity of the implementation languages and shells* could also be a problem when you try to reuse implemented knowledge.

   c. Even if the knowledge representation formalism and the computational environment of the source systems and of the new system are the same, additional problems emerge due to *lexical problems*. For example, the assertion that "person X is poor" could be represented in two knowledge bases as: "poor(x)" or "¬ rich(x)". If we mix these two expressions into one KB, it would be impossible to establish an inference sequence in which both sentences were involved simultaneously since the lexis used is not uniform.

   d. Even if the two KBs employ the same lexis, reusing their knowledge might be difficult due to *semantic problems*. This occurs when the new system and the source system use the same term with different meanings, that is, in different contexts. For example, the term "analysis" could refer to a blood analysis in medicine or to the activity to be performed during the life cycle of a software product.

   e. Additionally, *synonyms* may appear. In this case, different terms refer to the same concept. For example, "to pass" or "to be qualified" after doing an exam. A synonym problem always causes a lexical problem, but the reverse is not true. Note that the terms "poor" and "rich" are not synonyms.

   f. The *hidden assumptions* (Lenat, 1995) under which each system is built are important barriers if you try to reuse knowledge (e.g., assumptions about time, space, etc.). For example, the factor time in a medical system used in nonemergency situations (consultations) is usually treated implicitly in a discrete manner. Then if you try to reuse knowledge from this system to be processed in an intensive care unit, you may come up against serious problems since time is continuous there.

   g. Finally, loss of common sense knowledge; that is, it is always possible to forget something important, assuming something that everyone knows.

There are many strategies to solve these problems, including:

1. Translators between formalisms and languages and tools could be developed to solve problems caused by the heterogeneity of the knowledge representation formalisms,

languages, and tools. Since each language has its own expressiveness, much of knowledge is lost when the source is more expressive than the target.

2. Ontologies constitute a warehouse of vocabulary to solve lexical, semantic, and synonym problems, as well as assumptions.

3. Finally, machine learning, natural language understanding, and ontologies could be used to prevent loss of common sense knowledge. Machine learning and natural language are not appropriate since they need a broad KB underneath them, both to learn new knowledge and to do semantic disambiguation of terms (Lenat, 1995).

The second option is to **share knowledge** with other applications already built. In this approach, agents are distributed in agents networks. Agents ask other agents to solve problems according to a specific communication protocol. Independent systems carry out complementary tasks. One of the main problems of communication is the absence of a shared vocabulary pool. For example, if inside an American aircraft design system, distances are represented in "miles" and in a European aircraft diagnosis system distances are represented in "kilometers", and the European system requires information from the American system, someone must tell them that "a mile is about 1.6 kilometers." To share knowledge, you need to share the vocabulary and its meaning, a communication protocol between agents, and an interlingua.

3.   WHAT IS AN ONTOLOGY?

The word ontology has been taken from Philosophy, where it is a systematic explanation of Existence. Note that in the real world, anything known has a name, for example, a book, a car, a city, etc. In Artificial Intelligence, an intelligent system only knows what can be represented formally in a target language. So, it makes sense to use this word in our domain to mean: what the system knows. As a person does not only know what (s)he already has in her mind, but (s)he can consult other sources (experts, books, etc.) in order to solve a problem, the same can be said for an intelligent system. Ontologies play the role of unifying the vocabulary of different systems, enabling communication between them.

First, Neches and colleagues (Neches et al., 1991) defined an ontology as follows: "An ontology defines the basic terms and relations comprising the vocabulary of a topic area as well as the rules for combining terms and relations to define extensions to the vocabulary." We can say that this definition tells us how to proceed to build an ontology, giving us vague guidelines: identify basic terms, identify relations between terms, identify rules to combine them, provide definitions of such terms and relations. Note that according to this definition, an ontology includes not only the terms that are explicitly defined in it, but terms that can be inferred using rules. Later, in 1993, Gruber's definition (Gruber, 1993a) became famous, and is the most referenced in the literature: "An ontology is an explicit specification of a conceptualization." Since then, many declarative and procedural definitions of what an ontology is have been proposed in the literature. Guarino and Giaretta (Guarino and Giaretta, 1995) collect seven definitions and provide syntactic and semantic interpretations of them.

The question is not whether or not definitions are correct or wrong, but that definitions provide different and complementary points of view of the same reality. It is similar to the definition of continuity in Mathematics. There are many definitions; some are general, others specific, depending on different approaches, but all of them fit perfectly and none contradict the others.

4.   ONTOLOGIES AND KNOWLEDGE BASES

Sometimes people from the Knowledge Engineering community use the word ontology to refer to the KB or a part of the KB of their systems. But an ontology is not a KB. Of course, they do have

Knowledge Base

PART-OF (cylinder, engine)
PART-OF (battery, engine)

(a) Definitions in a knowledge base

Physical Devices

Concept: *Component*
Relation: *Part of*
Number of arguments: *2*
Type of Argument #1: *Component*
Type of Argument #2: *Component*

Mechanical Devices

Concept: *Cylinder*	
Subclass of: *Component*	
Part of: *Engine*	
	Concept: *Engine*
Concept: *Battery*	Subclass of: *Component*
Subclass of: *Component*	
Part of: *Engine*	

(b) Definitions in ontologies

FIGURE 1   Nature of definitions in KBs and ontologies.

in common that they both contain knowledge, but there are several differences between them. The most representative are:

1. *Features of the language used to codify the knowledge.* Ontologies should be written in an expressive, declarative, portable, domain-independent, and semantically well-defined, machine-readable language, which should be independent of any particular choice of target machine-readable language of the application that reuses and shares its definitions. Actually, many languages are used to implement ontologies: LOOM (MacGregor, 1991), CycL (Lenat and Guha, 1990), and Ontolingua (Gruber, 1993a). You cannot guarantee these properties when you codify a KB.

2. *Goal of the knowledge codification.* Ontologies are designed for knowledge sharing and reuse purposes and KBs are not. As a result, their definitions should be conceptualized with enough abstraction and generality. These two features guarantee that ontology definitions are independent of their final uses. The example given in Figure 1 shows knowledge in a KB that cannot be reused/shared and what type of knowledge should be in the ontology in order to be reused/shared. Note that the terms: "cylinder", "battery" and "engine" will be part of an ontology in a domain of "mechanical devices", while the concept "component" and the relation "part-of" will be in a meta-ontology to build any kind of physical devices.

3. *Requirements specification.* One of the main problems that KEs have when building KBSs is the difficulty of getting a set of requirements for the system. Requirements specify what is expected from the system. Since experts are not usually able to describe how they behave in the application domain in a concrete and complete manner, it is hard for KEs to specify the future behavior of KBSs. So, KBSs are usually built incrementally using evolving prototypes in which the deficiencies of the final product of each cycle can be used to get the specification of the next prototype. This is not the case with ontologies. Ontologies are built to be reused or shared anytime, anywhere, and independently of the behavior and domain of the application that uses them. So, ontologists are able to specify, at least partially, what is expected from the ontology, that is, most of the

vocabulary to be covered by the ontology for a given domain. This is the main difference between ontologies development process and KBSs development processes.

However, ontologies and KBs have a common foundational problem. They are incomplete, as it is impossible to capture everything known about the real world in a finite structure. As with KBs, one of the most important problems is to guarantee complete, consistent, and concise knowledge from the beginning, during each stage, and between stages of its development process.

5.   ONTOLOGICAL COMMITMENTS

A pipe is a long, round, hollow object, usually made of metal or plastic, through which a liquid or gas flows. But, in a smoker context, a pipe is an object used for smoking tobacco. When two plumbers who are also smokers talk and say "give me the pipe," they need to commit to which context they talking and, assuming a plumbing context, they need to know if they are talking about metal or plastic pipes. The same occurs when the plumber attends a course about new kinds of pipes; instructors and plumbers need to commit most of vocabulary and most of the meanings of those terms.

Certainly, when intelligent systems reuse or share knowledge of others, they need also to know and to commit to such terms and their meanings; these terminological agreements are called ontological commitments. Using Gruber and Olsen's definition (Gruber and Olsen, 1994), "Ontological commitments are agreement to use the shared vocabulary in a coherent and consistent manner." They guarantee consistency, but not completeness.

Ontological agreements are useful not only in distributed systems that share vocabularies, but also inside each system (Mark, Dukes-Schlossberg, and Kerber, 1995). In other words, any system needs to be coherent and consistent with itself throughout its entire life cycle. So, any knowledge added or modified in the KB needs to be coherent with the previous agreements established during its development. To follow on with the plumber example, if a new pipe is introduced into a KB, it must fit the ontological agreements about pipes.

Is sum, we can say that any source of knowledge (KB or ontology) codified in a formal language has, explicitly or implicitly, its own commitments. Any extension to the ontology must satisfy these ontological commitments.

6.   TYPES OF ONTOLOGIES

This section does not seek to give an exhaustive typology of ontologies as presented in (Mizoguchi, Vanwelkenhuysen, and Ikeda, 1995). But it is interesting to show the most commonly used types of ontologies so that the reader can get an idea of the knowledge to be included in each type of ontology. Basically, there are four kind of ontologies: domain ontologies, task ontologies, common sense ontologies, meta-ontologies, and knowledge representation ontologies.

Domain ontologies provide a vocabulary for describing a given domain. They include terms related to:

- Objects in the domain and its components; for example, in a medical domain, "scalpel," "scanner," "operating theater,"etc.
- A set of verbs and paraphrases that name activities and processes that take place in the domain; examples in a medical domain are: "anesthetize," "give birth," etc.
- Primitive concepts appearing in theories, relations, and formulas that govern the domain; for example, "after giving birth, the optimum APGAR test of the baby is 10."

Sometimes, if the domain ontology covers a large extension of objects, verbs, and primitive concepts, it is recommended to split the domain ontology into three categories of ontologies: *object ontologies*, *activities ontologies*, and *field ontologies* that cover, objects, activities, and primitive concepts respectively.

Task ontologies provide a vocabulary for describing terms involved in problem-solving processes, which could be attached to similar tasks that may, or may not, be in the same domain. They include nouns, verbs, paraphrases, and adjectives related to the task. For example, the terms "goal," "schedule," "to assign," "to classify," "to plan," "assigned" and so on will be in a planning ontology. We recommend that nouns be bunched together in a *generic nouns ontology*, verbs in a *generic verbs ontology*, and adjectives in a *generic adjectives ontology* if the task ontology is wide-ranging.

As mentioned above, ontologies are used to represent common sense knowledge such as time, space, causality, events, etc. These ontologies are called common sense **ontologies** and they include a wide-ranging amount of foundational knowledge. Prototypes of common sense ontologies are Cyc ontologies (Lenat and Guha, 1990).

Meta-ontologies provide the basic terms used to codify either a domain ontology, a task ontology, or a common-sense ontology in a formal language. Finally, **knowledge representation ontologies** captures the representation primitives used in knowledge representation languages. For example, in *Ontolingua* (Gruber, 1993a), the knowledge representation ontology is the frame ontology. A meta-ontology could also provide the basic core of concepts upon which other ontologies are built.

7.   HOW TO USE ONTOLOGIES?

Based on the nature of the software, who are its intended users, and how general the domain is, Uschold and Grüninger have identified three main categories of uses of ontologies (Uschold and Grüninger, 1996). They single out the following roles:

1. *Communication* between people and organizations, to unify different research fields.
2. *Interoperability* among software systems, using the ontology as interlingua to unify different languages and software tools.
3. *Systems Engineering Benefits*, when ontologies assist in building classic or knowledge-based software as follows:
   a. Reusability, the ontology is reused in another software component
   b. Reliability, for automatic consistency checking of software applications
   c. Specification, if ontologies are used to specify other systems

These three roles could be grouped depending on *when* ontologies are used: at (1) design time in systems engineering and at (2) run-time to allow communication and interoperability.

Ontologies at design time. Ontologies are useful for building KBSs because they allow the KE to use knowledge already acquired, conceptualized, and implemented in a formal language, reducing considerably the knowledge acquisition bottleneck and the conceptualization phase of the new system. As you can imagine, the KBS development process varies when you use ontologies to build it. Figure 2 summarizes graphically the sequence of activities performed by a KE when modeling the domain of vehicles reusing definitions from a library of ontologies. Once the KE has a clear idea of the knowledge to be modeled, the first thing to do is to select those ontologies that are potentially useful for its system. In the example, three ontologies from the library of ontologies are depicted: an ontology of numbers, which contains a taxonomy and relationships between concepts; an ontology of units of measures with a set of instances; and, the ontology of vehicles with concepts structured taxonomically. Note that not all the definitions in the ontology of vehicles are useful for this application. In fact, the KE looks for the definitions required (in this case, "vehicle," "car," "truck," "family car," and "sports car," and translates them into the target language

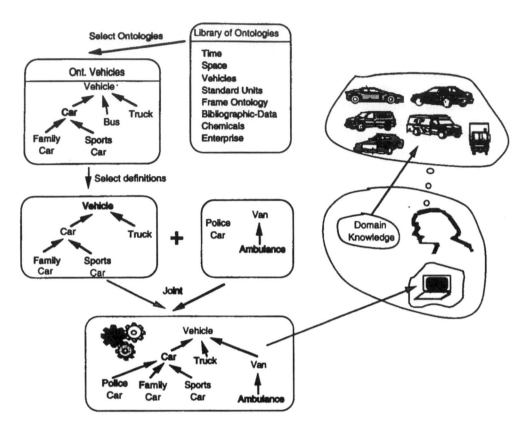

FIGURE 2   Ontologies used at design time.

used to formally express the KB). The other vehicles ("police car," "van," and "ambulance") that the KE has already identified in the application domain and do not appear in the ontology will be conceptualized, formalized, and implemented. Finally, both implemented parts are assembled in the new KB of the KBS. Note that in using ontologies, you only need to implement the definitions that the ontology does not provide.

Ontologies at run-time. Ontologies are also used at run-time by independent, heterogeneous and cooperative systems that share knowledge and inferences in agents networks. In this manner, when a given system does not have a given knowledge, it queries another system that makes inferences and gives the answer. So, a system temporally uses knowledge and reasonings of other systems. The ARPA Knowledge Sharing Effort (Neches et al., 1991) has identified the following three levels of an agent communication language (ACL), as graphically is shown in Figure 3.

1. The ACL vocabulary is the ontology. Each and every word in the dictionary has a natural language description and a formal description. Definitions of terms under different perspectives might coexist coherently in the dictionary. The ontology provides a common shared interpretation of the terms and indexes information resources distributed among agents, which are used when agents look for the source of knowledge needed to pursue a given task.
2. The ACL internal language is KIF (Knowledge Interchange Format) (Genesereth and Fikes, 1992). This language is used to provide formal definitions of the vocabulary. As Section 12.1 describes, KIF is a prefix version of first-order predicate calculus with extensions to improve its expressiveness.
3. The ACL external language is KQML (Knowledge Query Manipulation Language) (Finin, 1992), a communication protocol for orderly agents dialog.

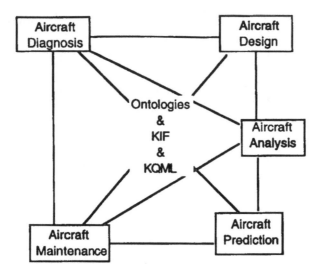

FIGURE 3   Ontologies used at run-time.

To write an expression in ACL, one should codify a KQML expression in which its arguments are KIF sentences built using words of the ontology.

8.   DESIGN CRITERIA

Here we summarize some design criteria and a set of principles that have proved useful in the development of ontologies.

- *Clarity* and *objectivity* (Gruber, 1993b). The ontology should provide the meaning of defined terms by providing objective definitions and also natural language documentation of all terms.
- *Completeness* (Gruber, 1993b). A definition expressed by a necessary and sufficient condition is preferred over a partial definition (defined only by a necessary or sufficient condition).
- *Coherence* (Gruber, 1993b). It should permit inferences that are consistent with the definitions.
- *Maximize monotonic extendibility* (Gruber, 1993b). It means that new general or specialized terms should be included in the ontology in a such way as does not require the revision of existing definitions.
- *Minimal ontological commitments* (Gruber, 1993b). It means making as few claims as possible about the world being modeled. In other words, the ontology should specify as little as possible about the meaning of its terms, giving the parties commited to the ontology freedom to specialize and instantiate the ontology as required. This openly contradicts Gruber's completeness criterion, which states that the semantics of the terms should be specified in as much detail as possible.
- *Ontological Distinction Principle* (Borgo, Guarino, and Masolo, 1996). It means that classes in an ontology should be disjoint. The criterion used to isolate the core of properties considered to be invariant for an instance of a class is called the Identity Criterion.

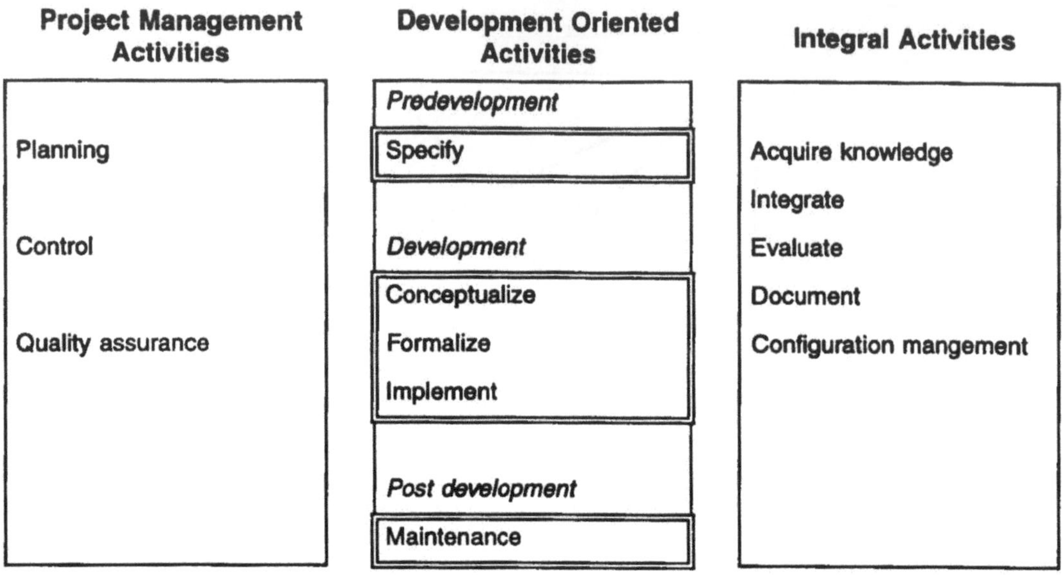

Project Management Activities	Development Oriented Activities	Integral Activities
Planning	*Predevelopment*	Acquire knowledge
	Specify	Integrate
Control	*Development*	Evaluate
	Conceptualize	Document
Quality assurance	Formalize	Configuration mangement
	Implement	
	Post development	
	Maintenance	

FIGURE 4   Ontology development process.

9.   ONTOLOGY DEVELOPMENT PROCESS

The ontology development process refers to *which* tasks you carry out when building ontologies. Verbs are used to refer to such tasks since they denote activities. Adapting the IEEE (IEEE, 1991) software process representation to the ontology development process, the tasks identified are classified in three categories as shown in Figure 4. Note that the development process *does not imply an order* of the execution of such tasks. Its goal is *only to identify* the list of activities to be completed.

If the ontologies are built on a small scale, some ontology tasks can be skipped. But, if you mean to build large ontologies on a large scale and with some guarantee of correctness and completeness, you should complete the three categories of activities presented below and steer clear of anarchic constructions.

9.1.   PROJECT MANAGEMENT ACTIVITIES

Unless you are making a toy ontology, you need to perform management activities. Their main aim is to assure a well-running ontology. The tasks included in this category are:

- *Planning*. Before building your ontology, you should decide what will be the main tasks of your ontology development process, how they will be arranged, and how much time you need to perform them and with which resources (people, software, and hardware). The chosen life cycle helps to order the set of activities that comprise the plan. This task produces a plan with detailed drawings that show a series of tasks to be done. This activity is done before starting development-oriented and integral activities.
- *Control*. Its goal is to guarantee that planned tasks are done in the way that they were intended to be performed. In other words, to control is to make all the important decisions about the way that your ontology is running. This activity should be completed as part of each and every task and between tasks in order to prevent delays, errors, omissions, etc. that could be propagated.
- *Quality Assurance*. The aim is to assure that each and every product obtained reaches the appropriate level of quality. As will be shown in later sections, the ontology codified

in a formal language is not the only product you get when you construct your ontology. Documentation, requirements specification documents, conceptual models, etc. are all products also produced by the ontology development process. Evaluation and quality assurance are different tasks. Evaluation is a technical activity that improves products by testing their correctness and validity. Once you have evaluated the product technically, the quality manager reviews the product and approves it.

9.2. DEVELOPMENT-ORIENTED ACTIVITIES

The following tasks describe the practical skills, techniques and methods used to develop an ontology.

- *Specify.* You should not start the development of your ontology without knowing why this ontology is being built and what are its intended uses and end-users. As an example of an informal and formal specification of two independent ontologies in the domain of enterprise modeling, we cite the Enterprise ontology (by Uschold) and TOVE ontology (by Grüninger) (Uschold and Grüninger, 1996). Although their outputs are almost the same (a set of terms), the degree of formality in writing their requirements specification documents are different. The Enterprise ontology has been specified in natural language and the TOVE ontology using a set of competence questions (Grüninger and Fox, 1995).
- *Conceptualize.* The goal is to build a conceptual model that describes the problem and its solution. A set of intermediate representations[1] for conceptualizing a domain ontology of objects were presented in Gómez-Pérez, Fernández, and de Vicente (1996).
- *Formalize.* This activity transforms the conceptual model into a formal model that is semicomputable. Frame-oriented or description logic representations systems could be used to formalize the ontology.
  - *Implement.* To make your ontology computable, you need to codify it in a formal language. As a reference framework for selecting target languages, we would cite the comparative study completed by Speel et al. (1995) as part of the Plinius project (Vet, Speel, and Mars, 1995).
- *Maintain.* Someone could ask for definitions to be included or modified in the ontology at anytime and anywhere. Guidelines for maintaining ontologies are also needed.

9.3. INTEGRAL ACTIVITIES

These activities back up development-oriented activities, giving them the support they need to succeed. The interaction between development-oriented and integral activities will be shown when the life cycle of the ontology is described. They include:

- *Acquire knowledge.* Unless you wish to build a toy ontology or you are an expert in the domain, you will elicit knowledge using KBS knowledge elicitation techniques. As a result, you should be able to list the sources of knowledge and give a rough description of how you carried out the processes and of the techniques you used. The most extensive work on capturing knowledge was reported by Uschold and Grüninger (1996).
- *Integrate.* Ontologies are built to be reused. Accordingly, duplication of work in building ontologies has even less sense than its duplication when you build traditional software. So, you should reuse existing ontologies as much as possible in your ontology. A method to integrate ontologically heterogeneous taxonomic knowledge and its application to the medical domain was presented in Gangemi, Steve, and Giacomelli (1996). However, no work has been done on selecting ontologies to be reused in other ontologies, although

---

[1] These intermediate representations have their roots in those presented in Pazos (1995).

four kinds of relationships between ontologies that have been integrated (inclusion, polymorphic refinement, circular dependencies, and restrictions) are identified in (Farquhar et al., 1995).

- *Evaluate.* Before making your ontology available to others, make a technical judgment with respect to a framework of reference. A framework for evaluating ontologies is given by Gómez-Pérez (1994) and Gómez-Pérez, Juristo, and Pazos (1995).
- *Document.* The absence of a sound documentation is also an important obstacle when you reuse/share built ontologies. So, if you wish your ontology to be reused/shared by others, try to document it as best you can. Skuce briefly analyzes how different ontologies are documented (Skuce, 1995).
- *Configuration management.* This activity involves records of each and every release. Software Engineering sets out how to perform this activity.

10.   ONTOLOGY LIFE CYCLE

"Don't build your house starting by the roof," says a Spanish proverb, pointing out that activities have an order and that they should be carried out step by step, in a planned manner, in order to achieve success. In the previous section, we divided the ontology development process into three categories of activities. Each one includes a set of tasks or subactivities. However, we did not indicate the *order* and *depth* in which such activities and tasks should be performed.

First, the ontology life cycle answers the previous questions by identifying the *set of stage* through which the ontology moves during its lifetime. Actually, only development-oriented activities are part of the transformations that conform the life cycle. Project management and integral activities interact with development-oriented activities during the ontology life cycle in order to make the development a success. Making an analogy, we could say that the development-oriented activities used to build ontologies are similar to the activities in a production line in a manufacturing domain. Project management activities (planning and control of the production line, stock control, etc.) and integral activities (raw material buying, inputs to the production line, final product packaging, quality control, and distribution) in a manufacturing domain correspond with their homonyms in the ontology domain. Therefore, the codified ontology and the final product that comes off the production line are the results of the technical activities in both domains.

Just as the life cycle of human beings moves forward sequentially and irreversibly through the following states — childhood, adolescence, youth, maturity, and old age — the ontology life cycle moves forward through the following states: specification, conceptualization, formalization, implementation, and maintenance. So, the technical activities transform the raw material (the need you have to build the ontology) into a final product (the evaluated and documented ontology, codified in a formal language). The states through which the ontology passes conform its life cycle, as shown in Figure 5.

Project management tasks and integral tasks interact with the life cycle as shown in Figure 5. Indeed, planning should be completed before starting to build the ontology, and control and quality assurance conducted during the entire building process. As regards integral activities, unless the ontologist is an expert in the application domain, most of the acquisition is done simultaneously with the requirements specification phase and decreases as the ontology development process moves forward. Integration tasks are done during the whole lifetime of the ontology — most at the conceptualization and less at the implementation. In order to prevent error propagation, most of the evaluation should also be done during the earliest stages of the ontology development process. Finally, you should be drawing a detailed documentation and carefully carry out configuration management at each stage.

Second, the ontology life cycle shows *when* you should perform the activities to move from a given state to the next and in how much *depth*. Some life-cycle models have been described in

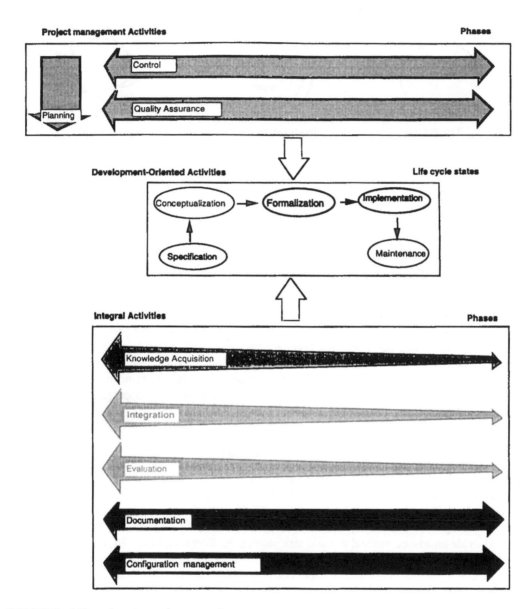

FIGURE 5   Life cycle states and process phases.

Software Engineering and transferred to Knowledge Engineering (Alonso et al., 1996). As stated before, the main problem facing a KE when (s)he begins a new KBS is to draw up a requirements specification document. On the other hand, an ontologist must be able to partially specify a set of requirements before building an ontology, which will constitute the initial core of the ontology. So, the ontology life cycle is closer to a classic software life cycle than it is to a KBS life cycle.

The waterfall life cycle (Royce, 1987) is the traditional life-cycle model. In this model, activities are *sequential* in the sense that you cannot move onto the next activity until you have completely finished the previous one. This model forces the ontologist to identify *all* the terms at the beginning, and the implementation must be a mirror of the specification, that is, it must satisfy the complete requirements specification document. The main drawback is that the ontology is static; you cannot include, remove, or modify terms in it during the development of the ontology. You only can modify definitions in the maintenance phase. The main inconvenience is that requirements are static once

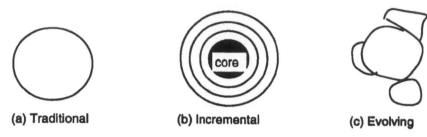

FIGURE 6   How the ontology grows.

the project has started. Thus, your frame of reference are the requirements you did. You cannot refer to the real world and implement new definitions until the maintenance starts. Obviously, the use of a waterfall life-cycle model is not adequate due to the absence of a complete requirements specification at the earliest stages of the development process and due to the evolution of the ontology definitions over time. Figure 6a shows how the system grows using this approach.

The incremental life cycle (McCracken, 1982) solves some problems, allowing the partial specification of requirements. According to this approach, the ontology would grow by layers, allowing the inclusion of new definitions *only* when a new *version* is planned. In other words, this model prevents the inclusion of new definitions if they are not planned, but it permits an incremental development. Figure 6b shows how the ontology grows according to this approach. Finally, the evolving prototype life cycle in Figure 6c solves the previous problems since the ontology grows depending on the needs. Indeed, this model lets you modify, add, and remove definitions in the ontology at any time. So, we propose the *evolving prototype* as the most appropriate life cycle for building ontologies.

11.   METHODOLOGY TO BUILD ONTOLOGIES

In general, methodologies give you a set of guidelines of *how* you should carry out the activities identified in the development process, what kinds of techniques are the most appropriate in each activity, and what products each one produces. Until now, few methodological approaches to building ontologies have been reported. In Mizoguchi, Vanwelkenhuysen, and Ikeda (1995), the authors provide an ad-hoc method to build task ontologies. Bernaras, Laregoiti, and Corera (1996) present the ontology building process carried out for the applications of disturbance diagnosis and service recovery planning in electrical networks, and identify the phases of ontology specification, ontology design, ontology use, and ontology reuse. However, Uschold and Grüninger (1996) and Gómez-Pérez, Fernández, and de Vicente (1996) propose a method with phases that are independent of the domain of the ontology. Figure 7 summarizes the phases proposed and their equivalence.

Obviously, it is almost impossible to take the above contributions to propose a general method for building any kind of ontology or meta-ontology. However, it is important to make an effort to define a methodology that guides the building of ontologies and that helps novice developers. Here, METHONTOLOGY is presented as a structured method to build ontologies. The phases of this methodology are presented as part of the ontology development process. METHONTOLOGY extends that section, showing how to carry out each of these phases.

11.1.   SPECIFICATION

The goal of the specification phase is to produce either an informal, semiformal, or formal ontology specification document written in natural language, using a set of intermediate representations or using competency questions, respectively. METHONTOLOGY proposes that at least the following information be included:

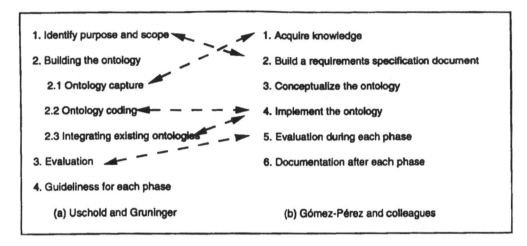

1. Identify purpose and scope   1. Acquire knowledge

2. Building the ontology   2. Build a requirements specification document

   2.1 Ontology capture   3. Conceptualize the ontology

   2.2 Ontology coding   4. Implement the ontology

   2.3 Integrating existing ontologies 5. Evaluation during each phase

3. Evaluation   6. Documentation after each phase

4. Guideliness for each phase

   (a) Uschold and Gruninger   (b) Gómez-Pérez and colleagues

FIGURE 7   Relationship between phases of two methodologies.

1. The purpose of the ontology, including its intended uses (for teaching, manufacturing, etc.), scenarios of use (from the student or teacher point of view), end-users (primary school or university teachers), etc.
2. Level of formality of the implemented ontology, depending on the formality that will be used to codify the terms and their meanings. Uschold and Grüninger (1996) classify the degree or level of formality of an ontology in a range of highly informal, semiinformal, semiformal, or rigorously formal ontologies, depending on whether terms and their meanings are codified in a language between natural language and a rigorous formal language.
3. Scope of the ontology, which includes the set of terms to be represented, its characteristics, and granularity.

The formality of the ontology specification document varies depending on whether you use natural language, competency questions (Grüninger and Fox, 1994), or a middle-out approach. For example, in a middle-out approach, you can use a glossary of terms to define an initial set of primitive concepts and use these concepts to define new ones. It is also advisable to group concepts in concepts classifications trees. The use of these intermediate representations will allow you not only to verify, at the earliest stage, relevant terms missed and include them in the specification document, but also to remove terms that are synonyms and no longer relevant in your ontology. The goal of these checks is to guarantee the conciseness and completeness of the ontology specification document. Figure 8 shows a short example of an ontology requirements specification document in the domain of chemicals.

An excellent argument on the use of a middle-out approach, as opposed to the classic bottom-up and top-down approaches, in identifying the main terms of your glossary is given by Uschold and Grüninger (1996). The middle-out approach allows you to identify the primary concepts of the ontology you are starting on. After reaching agreement on such terms and their definitions, you can move on to specialize or generalize them, only if this is necessary. As a result, the terms that you use are more stable, and less re-work and overall effort are required.

Grüninger and Fox (1994) propose the use of motivating scenarios that present the problem as a story of problems or examples and a set of intuitive solutions to the scenario problem. A set of informal competency questions includes the questions that an ontology must be able to answer in natural language. Then, the set of informal competency questions are translated into a formal set of competency questions using first-order logic (or possibly second-order logic). This formal set is also used to evaluate extensions of the ontology.

Ontology Requirement Specification Document

Domain: Chemicals
Date: May 15, 1996
Conceptualized by: Asunción Gómez-Pérez y Mariano Fernández-López
Implemented by: Mariano Fernández-López

Purpose: Ontology about chemical substances to be used when information about chemical elements is required in teaching, manufacturing, analysis, etc. This ontology could be used to ascertain, e.g., the atomic weight of the element Sodium.

Level of formality: Semiformal

Scope: List of 103 elements of substances: *Lithium, Sodium, Chlorine ...*
List of concepts: *Halogens, noble gases, semimetal, metal ...*
At least information about the following properties: *atomic number, atomic weight, atomic volume at 20°C, boiling point, density at 20°C,, electronegativity, electron affinity, and symbol.*

Sources of knowledge: *Handbook of Chemistry and Physis,* 65th edition, CRC Press, Inc., Boca Raton, FL, 1984–1985.

FIGURE 8   Ontology requirements specification.

As an ontology specification document cannot be tested for overall completeness, someone may find a new relevant term to be included at any time and anywhere. A good ontology specification document must have the following properties:

- Concision, that is, each and every term is relevant and there are no duplicated or irrelevant terms.
- Partial completeness, which is related to the coverage of the terms, the stopover solution (what decision has been taken with respect to the stopover problem), and level of granularity of each and every term.
- Consistency, which refers to all terms and their meanings making sense in the domain.

11.2.   KNOWLEDGE ACQUISITION

It is important to bear in mind that knowledge acquisition is an independent phase in the ontology development process. However, it is coincident with other phases. As stated previously, most of the acquisition is done simultaneously with the requirements specification phase, and decreases as the ontology development process moves forward.

Experts, books, handbooks, figures, tables, and even other ontologies are sources of knowledge from which the knowledge can be elicited, and acquired, and used in conjunction with techniques such as: brainstorming, interviews, questionnaires, formal and informal texts analysis, knowledge acquisition tools, etc. For example, if you have no clear idea of the purpose of your ontology, the brainstorming technique, informal interviews with experts, and examination of similar ontologies will allow you to elaborate a preliminary glossary with terms that are potentially relevant. To refine the list of terms and their meanings, formal and informal texts, analysis techniques in books and handbooks, combined with structured and nonstructured interviews with experts might be used to include or remove terms in the glossary. Interviews with experts might help you build concepts classification trees and compare them with figures given in books.

11.3. CONCEPTUALIZATION

In this phase, METHONTOLOGY proposes to structure the domain knowledge in a conceptual model (a noncomputable representation of the world) that describes the domain in terms of the domain vocabulary identified in the ontology specification phase. The first thing to do is to build a complete Glossary of Terms (GT) as shown in Table 1. Terms include concepts, instances, verbs, and properties. So, the GT identifies and gathers *all* the useful and potentially usable domain knowledge and its meanings. Note that you do not start from scratch when you develop your GT. If you have drawn up a good requirements specification document, many terms will have been identified in that document. Others will be identified as the ontology construction process advances. Then, these new terms must be included in the GT.

Once you have almost completed the GT, you need to group terms as concepts and verbs. Each set of concepts/verbs would include concepts/verbs that are closely related to other concepts/verbs inside the same group as opposed to other groups. Indeed, for each set of related concepts and related verbs, a **concepts classification tree** and a **verbs diagram** is built. Figures 9 and 10 show a concepts classification tree and a verbs diagram, respectively, in the domain of chemicals. After they have been built, you can split your ontology development process into different, but related, development teams. Figure 11 graphically summarizes the intermediate representations used in the conceptualization phase.

TABLE 1
Glossary of Terms

Name	Description
Alkali	Their valence layer electron structure is ns^1. The alkalis are soft; when they are cut, they have a silvery-white color. When they are exposed to air, they cloud because of oxidation. Therefore, they are kept in an inert atmosphere or submerged in mineral oil. The melting point, the boiling point, and the specific heat decrease as the atomic number increases. They react with the hydrogen.
Halogens	They have seven electrons at the valence layer, two of which are in an *s* orbit and other in a *p* orbit. They easily react because they only need one electron to obtain eight in their valence layer. Their melting point, boiling point, and density increase with the atomic number.
Element	It is a substance that is made up only of atoms with the same number of protons.
Atomic-Volume-At-20-Celsius-Degrees	It is the volume occupied by 1 Gram-Atom of a element at 20°C. The gram atom is the mass equal to atomic weight expressed in grams.
Atomic-Weight	The atomic weight is the relative mass of an atom of an element on a scale in the which is taken as a unit the twelfth part of the carbon 12 isotope.
Density-At-20-Celsius-Degrees	Density of a substance is the mass of a volume unit.
Chlorine	It is member of the halogen (salt-forming) group of elements; it is a greenish-yellow gas, combining with nearly all elements. Chlorine is widely used in making many everyday products. It is used for producing safe drinking water the world over. Even the smallest water supplies are now usually chlorinated. It is also extensively used in the production of paper products, dyestuffs, textiles, petroleum products, medicines, antiseptics, insecticides, foodstuffs, solvents, paints, plastics, and many other consumer goods. Most of the chlorine produced is used in the manufacture of chlorinated compounds, etc.

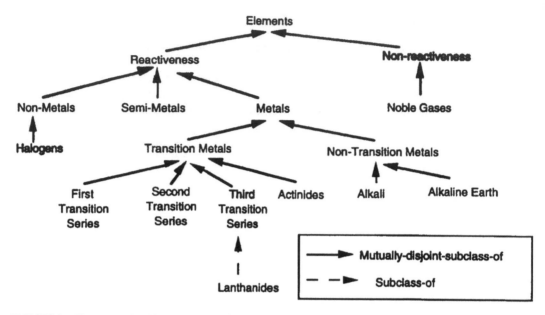

FIGURE 9   Concepts classification tree in the domain of chemicals.

11.3.1. Conceptualization of Concepts

For each concepts classification tree generated, you build a **Data Dictionary** (DD). Each DD identifies and includes *all* the useful and potentially usable domain concepts, their meanings, attributes, instances, etc. The ontologist should fill in the following fields: *Concept Name*; *Synonyms* and *Acronyms* of the concept name; *Instances*, which include the instances of the concept; *Class Attributes*, or relevant properties of the concept that describe the concept itself; *Instance Attributes* or relevant properties that describe the instances of a concept. Table 2 summarizes some concepts (Alkali, halogens, elements) identified in the domain of chemicals, as well as information about their attributes, instances, etc. To be sure that the DD is good, you should check that: (1) the concept description is concise; (2) all the relevant instance attributes, class attributes and instances in the application domain have been identified; and (3) the instance attributes and class attributes are consistent, that is, they make sense for the concept.

A **table of an instance attribute** provides information about the attribute and about its values at the instance. Indeed for each instance attribute included in the DD *Instance attribute* field, a table must be created. Each table includes the following fields: *Instance attribute name*; *Value type*, referring the class of values with which the attribute could be filled in; *Unit of measure*, for numerical values; *Precision* of the numerical value; *Range of values*, which specifies a list or set of possible

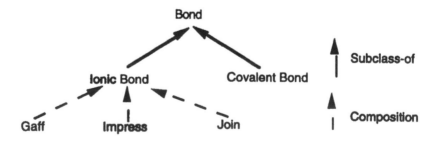

FIGURE 10   Verbs diagram in the domain of chemicals.

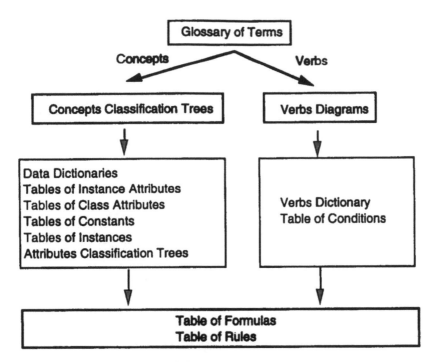

FIGURE 11 Set of intermediate representations in the conceptualization phase.

values of the attribute; *Default value*, if they are known and if they make sense for the attribute at the instance; *Cardinality*, which specifies the number of values of the attribute; *Inferred from instance attributes*, *inferred from class attributes*, and *Inferred from constants*, which include the name of those instance attributes, class attributes, and constants that enable inference of the value of this attribute; *Formula*, which includes cross-references to the tables of formulas that enable calculation of the numerical value of the attribute (there might be more than one formula); *To infer*, which contains the name of those instance attributes whose values could be inferred using the instance attribute; and *References*. Tables 3, 4, and 5 show definitions of the instance attributes: "Atomic-Volume-At-20-Celsius-Degrees," "Atomic-Weight," and "Density-At-20-Celsius-Degrees."

Tables of class attributes describe the concept itself, not its instances. For each concept included at the field, a table of class attributes must be created that specify the following fields: *Class attribute name*; *Relation attribute name*, which is the name of the attribute that participates in the relationship; *Logical relationship*, attaches two concepts across logic operators; *Value* of the class attribute; *Unit of measure* for numerical values; *To infer*, which contains the name of those instance attributes whose values could be inferred using the value of the class attributes; and *References*. Table 6 shows the definitions of the class attributes attached to the concept Halogens.

Constants are used to specify information related to the domain of knowledge that always take the same value. They are usually used in formulas: for example, gravitational acceleration is 9.8. Some constants in the domain of chemicals appear in Table 7. For each concepts classification tree, the ontologist should identify a set of constants in a **table of constants** and describe them as follows: *Constant name*; *Description*, which contains the meaning of the constant name; *Value* of the constant; *Unit of measure* for numerical values; *To infer*, with the name of the instance attributes whose values could be inferred using the value of the constant; and *References*.

If the ontologist is sure that all the instances mentioned at the *Instance* field of the DD exist in the domain, the next step is to create a **table of instances** for each instance identified in the DD. The fields to fill in are: *Instance name*; *Attributes* to be filled in the instance; and Values of these

TABLE 2
Data Dictionary in the Domain of Chemicals

Concept name	Synon.	Acron.	Instances	Class attributes	Instance attributes
Alkali	Group Ia	AlK.	Lithium. Sodium. Potassium. Rubidium. Cesium. Francium.	Group-Of-Alkali Metals Low-Electronegativity-Of- Alkali Metals Oxidation-States-Of-Alkali Metals Minimum-Electron-Affinity- Of-Alkali Metals Maximum-Electron-Affinity- Of-Alkali Metals	List-Of-Bases
Halogens	VIIa Group Halogenous	Hlg.	Fluorine. Chlorine. Bromine. Iodine. Astatine.	Group-Of-Halogens Minimum-Electron-Affinity- Of-Halogens Maximum-Of-Electron- Affinity-Of-Halogens Minimum-Melting-Point-Of- Halogens Maximum-Melting-Point-Of- Halogens	List-Of-Salts
Element		Elmts.			Atomic-Number. Atomic-Volume-At-20- Degrees-Celsius. Atomic-Weight. Boiling-Point. Crystalline-Structure. Density-At-20-Degrees- Celsius Electronegativity Electronic-Affinity Electronic-Structure Group Half-life Hardness-Scale Ionization-Energy Melting-Point Oxidation-States Period Radioactivity-Constant Resistivity-At-20-Degrees- Celsius Semi-disintegration-Period Specific-Heat-At- Standard-Temperature Symbol

TABLE 3
Table of Instance Attribute: *Atomic-Volume-At-20-Celsius-Degrees*

Instance attribute name	Atomic-Volume-At-20-Celsius-Degrees
Value type	Volume quantity
Unit of measure	pot(Centimeter, 3)/Gram-Atom
Precision	—
Range of values	(0, 100)
Default value	—
Cardinality	1
Inferred from instance attribute	Unknown
Inferred from class attribute	Unknown
Inferred from Constants	Unknown
Formula	Unknown
To infer	Density-at-20-degrees-Celsius

attributes. Check for consistency between attributes and their values. Table 8 is an example of a table of instances.

Attributes Classification Trees graphically show attributes and constants related in the inference sequence of the root attributes, as well as the sequence of formulas and rules to be executed to infer the root attributes. Using the fields *Inferred from instance attributes, Inferred from class attributes, Inferred from constants, To infer* and *Formula* defined in each table of instance attributes. The result will be several attributes classification trees. Figure 12 shows one of these trees and the formula that makes it possible.

11.3.2. Conceptualization of Verbs

Verbs represent actions in the domain. The verbs **dictionary** expresses declaratively the meaning of each verb declaratively by identifying the following fields: *Verb name*; *Attributes involved*, used

TABLE 4
Table of Instance Attribute: *Atomic-Weight*

Instance attribute name	Atomic-Weight
Value type	Mass quantity
Unit of measure	AMU[a]
Precision	—
Range of values	(1, 257)
Default value	—
Cardinality	1
Inferred from instance attribute	Unknown
Inferred from class attribute	Unknown
Inferred from constants	Unknown
Formula	Unknown
To infer	Density-at-20-degrees-Celsius

[a] It is the weight of a proton. A gram-atom of an element is the weight of 1/Avogadro's Number of atoms of this element.

TABLE 5
Table of Instance Attribute: *Density-At-20-Celsius-Degrees*

Instance attribute name	Density-At-20-Celsius-Degrees
Value type	Density quantity
Unit of measure	Gram/pot(Centimeter, 3)
Precision	—
Range of values	(0, 25)
Default value	—
Cardinality	1
Inferred from instance attribute	*Atomic-Weight* and *Atomic-Volume-At-20-Celsius-Degrees*
Inferred from class attributes	Unknown
Inferred from constants	Unknown
Formula	DENSITY = ATOMIC-WEIGHT /ATOMIC-VOLUME-AT-20-CELSIUS-DEGREES
To infer	Unknown

TABLE 6
Table of Class Attributes of the Concept Halogens

Class attribute name	Relation-attribute-name	Logical relationship	Value	Unit of measure	To infer	References
Minimum-Electron-Affinity-Of-Halogens	Electron-Affinity	>	2.5	Electronvolt	—	—
Maximum-Electron-Affinity-Of-Halogens	Electron-Affinity	<	4	Electronvolt	—	—
Minimum-Melting-Point-Of-Halogens	Electron-Affinity	≥	−219.62	Degree-Celsius	—	—
Maximums-Melting-Point-Of-Halogens	Electron-Affinity	£	302	Degree-Celsius	—	—

TABLE 7
Table of Constants in the Domain of Chemicals

Constant name	Description	Value	Unit of measure	To Infer
Standard-Temperature	It is the temperature at which many processes are observed and many measures are taken.	25	Celsius-Degree	—
Standard-Pressure	It is the pressure at which many processes are observed and many measures are taken.	1	Atmosphere	—

TABLE 8
Table of Instances: *Chlorine*

Instance name	Attributes	Values
Chlorine	Atomic-Number.	17
	Atomic-Volume-At-20-Degrees-Celsius.	Unknown
	Atomic-Weight.	35.453
	Boiling-Point.	−34.6
	Crystalline-Structure.	—
	Density-At-20-Degrees-Celsius.	Unknown
	Electronegativity.	3.0
	Electron-Affinity.	3.614
	Electron-Structure.	$3s^2 3p^5$
	Group.	VIIa
	Half-life.	—
	Hardness-Scale.	—
	Ionization-Energy.	12.967
	Melting-Point.	−100.98
	Oxidation-States.	[1, 3, 5, 7]
	Period.	3
	Radioactivity-Constant.	0
	Resistivity-At-20-Degrees-Celsius.	Unknown
	Resistivity-Temperature-Coefficient-per-Degree-Celsius.	Unknown
	Semidisintegration-Period.	—
	Specific-Heat-At-Standard.	Unknown
	Symbol.	Cl
	Thermal-Conductivity-At-Standard-Temperature.	Unknown
	List-Of-Salts	["Common-salt, "Carnallite", "Sylvite"]

to refer to the set of attributes which act or suffer the verb action; *Preconditions names*, which include the list of names of conditions that constrain the action represented by the verb; *Postcondition names*, with the list of names of conditions that are true when the verb has already acted; *Split verbs*, used to enumerate and order the verbs in to which the current verb is split of; *Rules name* and *Fomula* are the names of the rules and formula used to carry out actions. Table 9 summarizes a verbs dictionary in the chemicals domain.

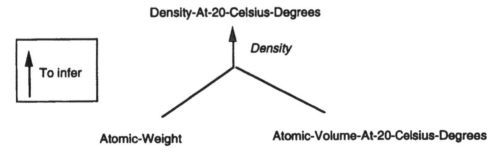

FIGURE 12   Attributes classification tree in the domain of chemicals.

TABLE 9
Verbs Dictionary in the Chemicals Domain

Verb name	Attributes involved	Precondition name	Postcondition name	Split verb	Rule	Formula
To bond	Electronegativity Electron-Affinity Electron-Structure	Ion-needed	Bond-performed	1. To impress 2. To gaff 3. To join	—	—
To gaff	Electron	Atomic-Distance	Bond-performed	—	—	—

Given a set of verbs, you can build a verbs diagram to graphically represent how a given verb is split. Basically, there are two kinds of relations: *Composition,* which refers to the fact that you need to carry out the actions into which the verb is split to complete a given action; and *Subclass-of,* which represents verbs hierarchies. Figure 12 graphically summarized a verbs diagram related to types of chemical bonds.

The conditions tables specify a set of conditions to be satisfied before executing an action or a set of conditions to be guaranteed after the execution of an action. For each identified condition, you should specify: *Condition name*; *Description* in natural language of the meaning of the constraint; *Attributes* that participate in the condition, and *Formal expression* of the condition.

11.3.3. Conceptualization of Rules and Formulas

In many domains, numerical values of instance attributes might be derived from numerical values of other attributes and constants by using formulas. A formula is conceptualized using a **Table of Formulas**. The standard definition of formulas includes: *Formula name*; *Inferred attribute*, which identifies the instance attribute that is calculated with the formula; *Formula, which* includes the mathematical formula to be used to calculate the inferred attribute; *Description*, which includes the theoretical foundations of the formula; *Basic instance attributes*, which refers to the list of instance attributes used by the formula to calculate the inferred attribute; *Basic class attributes,* containing the list of class attributes used to calculate the inferred attribute; *Constants*, which include the list of constants used by the formula to get the inferred attribute; *Precision* with which the number should be calculated (i.e., to two decimal places); *Constraint*, if the formula is appropriate for specific values of basic instance attributes, it is necessary to specify some conditions (i.e., the formula must no be used if the value of a basic instance attribute used as the divisor is zero); and *References*. Table 10 shows the definitions of the formula that calculates a value of the attribute "Density-At-20-Celsius-Degrees." Note that to infer its value, only values of instance attributes ("Atomic-Volume-At-20-Celsius-Degrees" and "Atomic-Weight") are used.

In sum, METHONTOLOGY produces a conceptual model expressed as a set of well-defined intermediate representations that allow one to: (1) to ascertain whether an ontology is useful and usable for a given application without examining its source code; and (2) compare the scope and completeness of several ontologies, their reusability, and sharability by analyzing the knowledge expressed in each IR.

11.4. FORMALIZATION

In this phase, you will transform the conceptual model into a formal model, that is, a semicomputable representation of the external world. Actually, the main task you perform in this phase is to select the knowledge representation system, such as: frame-oriented, conceptual graphs, relational representations, or description logic.

TABLE 10
Table of a Formula Density-At-20-Celsius-Degrees

Formula name	Density
Inferred Attribute	Density-At-20-Celsius-Degrees
Formula	Density-At-20-Celsius-Degrees -Atomic-Weight / Atomic-Volume-At-20-Degrees-Celsius
Description	It should be noted that the Atomic-Weight is given in AMUS, and the Atomic-Volume in cm³/gram-atom. There is no problem, 1 gram-atom of an element maps with the Atomic-Weight in grams; for instance, 1 gram-atom of oxygen is 15.999 grams. Therefore, when the units have bees transformad things are as they were.
Basic Instance Attributes	Atomic-Weight Atomic-Volume-At-20-Degrees-Celsius
Basic Class Attributes	—
Constants	—
Precision	—
Constraints	Atomic-Volume-At-20-Degrees-Celsius > 0

11.5. INTEGRATION

In order to speed up the construction of your ontology, you should consider reuse of definitions already built into other ontologies instead of starting the conceptualization and implementation from scratch. This is why integration is done during the whole life cycle of the ontology. In this activity, we propose the following:

1. Examine knowledge representation ontologies and meta-ontologies (i.e., in Cyc, in Onto-lingua, etc.) to select those that better fit your formalization. If existing meta-ontologies are not appropriate for your ontology, you should start the definition and implementation of a new meta-ontology in a formal language.
2. Whether or not you reuse existing knowledge representation ontologies and meta-ontol-ogies, the next step is to find which libraries of ontologies provide adequate definitions of terms whose conceptualization is coherent with the terms identified in your concep-tualization, foreseeing misinterpretation when they are reused in other ontologies.
3. Once you have chosen the most appropriate terms, you should check the existence of translators to transform definitions into your target language with as little loss of knowl-edge as possible.

Sometimes a term in your conceptualization (e.g., centimeter) that should be included in a given ontology (e.g., Standard units) is not provided by the ontology. In this case, you should justify the need to include the missed definitions, as well as the benefits of such inclusion, to the ontology maintainer.

As a result of this phase, METHONTOLOGY proposes the development of an integration document. Summarizing, the meta-ontology you will use and, for each and every term whose definition is going to be used, the name of the term in the conceptual model, the name of the ontology from which you will take its definition, the name of the definition, and its arguments in the ontology, as shown in Table 11.

When we developed the Chemical ontology, we used public Ontolingua ontologies like: KIF-numbers, Standard-Units, Physical-Quantities and EngMath (see http://www-ksl.stanford.edu). For example, the atomic volume units could be defined using the definition of "mole" given by the Standard Unit ontology, and "expt" defined in KIF-numbers.

TABLE 11
An Example of An Integration Document

Meta-ontology	The frame-ontology in Ontolingua	
Term in your conceptualization	Ontology to be reused	Name of the term in the ontology
Mole	Standard-Unit in Ontolingua	Mole
Centimeter	Standard-Unit in Ontolingua	Undefined
Exponent	KIF-Number in Ontolingua	Expt

11.6. IMPLEMENTATION

Ontology implementation requires the use of an environment that supports the knowledge representation ontology, the meta-ontology, and ontologies selected at the integration phase. The result of this phase is the ontology codified in a formal language. Description logic-based languages have their roots in the KL-ONE family: LOOM (MacGregor, 1991) and CLASSIC are the most commonly used. We cite Ontolingua (Farquhar et al., 1995) as the most representative frame-based representation language for building ontologies.

Any ontology development environment should provide, at least: a lexical and syntactic analyzer to ensure the absence of lexical and syntactic errors; translators, to guarantee the portability of the definitions into other target languages; an editor, to add, remove, or modify definitions; a browser, to inspect the library of ontologies and their definitions; a searcher, to look for the most appropriate definitions; evaluators, to detect incompleteness, inconsistencies, and redundant knowledge; an automatic maintainer, to manage the inclusion, removal, or modification of existing definitions, and so on. Below, some of the definitions previously conceptualized above have been codified in *Ontonlingua*.

Define-Class Alkali (?Alkali)
"Their valence layer electron-structure is ns^1. The Alkali are soft; when they are cut, they have a silvery-white color. When they are exposed to air, they cloud because of oxidation. Therefore, they are kept in an inert atmosphere or submerged in mineral oil. The melting point, the boiling point, and the specific heat decrease as the atomic number increases. They react with the hydrogen."
 :def
 (and
  (Non-Transition-Metals ?Alkali)
  (Has-Instance ?Alkali Lithium Sodium Potassium Rubidium Cesium Francium)))

(Define-Class Elements (?Elements)
"It is a substance that is made up only of atoms with the same number of protons."
 :def
 (and
  (Has-One ?Elements Atomic-Number)
  (Has-One ?Elements Atomic-Volume-At-20-Celsius-Degrees)
  (Has-One ?Elements Atomic-Weight)
  (Has-Some ?Elements Boiling-Point)
  (Has-Some ?Elements Crystalline-Structure)
  (Has-One ?Elements Density-At-20-Celsius-Degrees)
  (Has-One ?Elements Electronegativity)
  (Has-One ?Elements Electronic-Affinity)
  (Has-One ?Elements Electronic-Structure)
  (Has-One ?Elements Group)
  (Has-One ?Elements Half-Life)
  (Has-One ?Elements Hardness-Scale)

```
(Has-One ?Elements Ionization-Energies)
(Has-Some ?Elements Melting-Point)
(Has-One ?Elements Oxidation-State)
(Has-One ?Elements Period)
(Has-One ?Elements Radioactivity-Constant)
(Has-One ?Elements Resistivity-At-20-Celsius-Degrees)
(Has-One ?Elements Semi-disintegration-Period)
(Has-One ?Elements Specific-Heat-At-Std-Temperature)
(Has-One ?Elements Symbol)
:axiom-def
 (Exhaustive-Subclass-Partition Elements
  (Setof Reactiveless
  Reactiveness))

(Define-Class Metals (?Metals)
"They conduct electricity and the heat. They are solids that form very regular and wide nets. They
have a low electronegativity."
 :def
 (and
  (Reactiveness ?Metals))
:axiom-def
 (Exhaustive-Subclass-Partition Metals
  (Setof Non-Transition-Metals Transition-Metals))

(Define-Relation Density-At-20-Celsius-Degrees (?Elements ?Density-Quantity)
"Density of a substance is the mass of a volume unit."
 :def
 (and
  (Elements ?Elements)
  (Density-Quantity ?Density-Quantity)
  (>= ?Density-Quantity (/ (* 0 Gram) (expt Centimeter 3)))
  (=< ?Density-Quantity (/ (* 25 Gram) (expt Centimeter 3))))
 :Axiom-Def
  (and
  (Minimum-Slot-Cardinality Density-At-20-Celsius-Degrees 1)
  (Maximum-Slot-Cardinality Density-At-20-Celsius-Degrees 1)))
```

11.7. EVALUATION

A framework for evaluating knowledge-sharing technology (software, ontologies, and documentation) has been presented by Gómez-Pérez (1994). *Evaluation* means to carry out a technical judgment of the ontologies, their software environment, and documentation with respect to a frame of reference (in our case, the requirements specification document) during each phase and between phases of their life cycle. Evaluation subsumes the terms Verification and Validation. *Verification* refers to the technical process that guarantees the *correctness* of an ontology, its associated software environments, and documentation with respect to a frame of reference during each phase and between phases of their life cycle. *Validation* guarantees that the ontologies, the software environment, and documentation correspond to the system that they are supposed to represent. Based on the experience of verifying Ontolingua ontologies, a set of guidelines and methods of how to look for incompleteness, inconsistencies, and redundancies have been also presented (Gómez-Pérez, 1996).

The output proposed by METHONTOLOGY for this phase is an evaluation document, in which the ontologist will describe how the ontology has been evaluated, the techniques used, the kind of errors found in each phase, and the sources of knowledge used in the evaluation.

11.8. DOCUMENTATION

There are not widely accepted guidelines on how to document ontologies. In many cases, the only documentation available is in the code of the ontology, the natural language text attached to formal definitions, and papers published in conference proceedings and journals setting out important questions of the ontology already built. This problem is the result of a vicious circle: almost anyone documents ontologies, as there are no guidelines on documentation, there are no guidelines on how to document ontologies because of the absence of methodologies to build ontologies, and there are no standard methodologies to build ontologies because ontologists do not write the steps they take to build ontologies during the entire ontology development process.

METHONTOLOGY seeks to break this circle by including the documentation phase as an activity to be carried out throughout the entire ontology development process. Indeed, after the specification phase, you get a *requirements specification document*; after the knowledge acquisition phase, a *knowledge acquisition document*; after conceptualization, a *conceptual model document* that includes a set of intermediate representations that describe the application domain; after integration, an *integration document*; after implementation, the *implementation document*; and during evaluation, an *evaluation document*.

12. INTERLINGUAS

This section presents two interlinguas (KIF and PIF) used to interchange knowledge and processes between heterogeneous and independent applications.

12.1. KIF

One of the work groups created by the ARPA Knowledge-Sharing Effort (Neches et al., 1991) was the Interlingua Working Group at Stanford, led by Fikes and Genesereth. Their goal was to solve the problem of the heterogeneity of knowledge representation languages. In order to interchange knowledge between heterogeneous programs, they realized that a formal language was needed, which, like an interlingua, allowed knowledge in a given representation language to be expressed in another. The interlingua had to:

1. Be a language with declarative semantics and independent of any interpreter.
2. Be a language with sufficient expressive power to represent the declarative knowledge contained in typical applications system knowledge bases.
3. Have a structure that enabled semiautomatic translations into and out of typical representation languages.

The result was KIF (Genesereth and Fikes, 1992), a prefix version of first-order predicate calculus, with extensions to improve its expressiveness, such as: definition of terms, representation of knowledge about knowledge, reifying functions and relations, specifying sets, and nonmonotonic reasoning.

The basis for KIF semantics is a correlation between the terms and sentences of the language and a conceptualization of the world. Every term denotes an object in the universe of discourse associated with the conceptualization, and every sentence is either true or false. The semantics of KIF tell us the meaning of its complex expressions. We can unambiguously determine the referent of any term and the truth or falsity of any sentence.

The world is conceptualized in KIF in different universes of discourse. In fact, different users have different universes of discourse. Each universe of discourse is the set of all objects presumed or hypothesized to exist in the world. Objects can be concrete or abstract, primitive or composite, real or fictional. Relationships between objects are conceptualized by functions and relations of variable arity. Conceptually, relations and functions are sets of finite lists of objects. The difference between them is that the function associates a unique object (called value) for each combination of possible arguments, and the relation does not.

KIF also provides a standard vocabulary for dealing with: lists (listof, single, first, rest, last, etc.); sets (set, individual, union, intersection, etc.); numerical calculus and properties of numbers (cos, expt, log, integer, >, etc.); logical operations (negation, conjunction, disjunction, equation, inequality, etc.), rules, constraints, quantified expressions, metarules, programs, etc. More information about KIF can be found at *http://logic.stanford.edu/kif.html*.

12.2. PIF

As KIF is used to facilitate knowledge sharing, PIF (Process Interchange Format) is used to facilitate software process sharing (Lee et al., 1996). The PIF project started in October 1993 for a few groups at MIT, Stanford, the University of Toronto, and Digital Equipment Corporation to share heterogeneous software process descriptions. The goal is to develop an interlingua to automatically support exchange of heterogeneous business process descriptions within and among organizations.

The PIF-CORE provides the basic terminology for describing the simplest entities that can be used to describe the basic elements of any software process. Instead of having to write "ad hoc" translators for each pair of such systems, translators might translate any PIF-CORE description into and out of any target language with the minimum loss of information. Groups of users might extend the PIF-CORE descriptions using Partially Shared Views (PSV) to maximize information sharing among groups. A PSV module is built by specialization of the PIF-CORE or other PSV modules. In this case, translators only translate the additional PSV elements if they know about them. Since PIF is very expressive, translators do not always translate the whole PIF process into the chosen target language. The untranslatable parts are conserved and added when the process is translated back into PIF.

The PIF syntax is based on KIF syntax since: it allows the specification of classes, instances, values, and value restrictions in a structured way; the semantics of KIF reduces the ambiguity in the translation process between PIF and the target languages; it is possible to reuse some works already done in KIF; and Ontolingua translates standard KIF into other knowledge representation languages. More information about PIF requirements, PIF-CORE specification, the PSV mechanism for supporting multiple and partially overlapping class hierarchies, and translators can be found at *http://soa.cba.hawaii.edu/pif/*.

13. THE MOST WELL-KNOWN ONTOLOGIES

This section gives a brief overview of the most well-known ontologies. Many ontologies, like Ontolingua ontologies at Stanford (*http://www-ksl.stanford.edu:5915*) and WordNet at Princeton, are freely available over the Internet. A few, like some Cyc ontologies, are, in part, freely available. Others have been developed by companies for their own use and are not available over the Internet. The Ontology Page (*http://www.medg.lcs.mit.edu/doyle/top/*), also named TOP, identifies worldwide activity aimed at developing formalized ontologies.

This section seeks to summarize the most well-known ontologies, classifying them depending on the area of knowledge included. We will present: knowledge representation ontologies, like the Frame-Ontology in Ontolingua; linguistic ontologies, like GUM and EDR; engineering ontologies, like EngMath and PhysSys; and planning ontologies, like Multis.

13.1. Cyc

The Cyc project was started at the Microelectronics and Computer Technology Corporation (MCC) in 1984. Cyc goals (Lenat and Guha, 1990) were to undo the software bottleneck by constructing a foundation of basic common-sense knowledge that would enable a variety of knowledge-intensive products and services. In January 1995, Cycorp (*http://www.cyc.com/*) improved and commercialized Cyc technology.

Although Cyc goals have remained unchanged over the years, Cyc technology has evolved substantially since then[2]. Actually, Cyc is a very large, multicontextual knowledge base with inference engines upon which different applications are built. Cyc technology consists of three main parts: the Cyc Knowledge Base (that is, the Cyc ontology), the CycL representation language and inference engines, and the knowledge server utility. The Cyc system is available in Common Lisp and C.

Cyc ontology provides a vast amount of fundamental human knowledge. The ontology consists of a set of terms and assertions that relate those terms. The Cyc ontology is divided into many microtheories. Each microtheory only captures a consistent point of view of a given domain of knowledge. Some areas can handle several different microtheories, representing different perspectives and assumptions, levels of granularity, and distinctions.

CycL is Cyc's knowledge representation language. CycL is a declarative and expressive language, similar to first-order predicate calculus with extensions to handle equality, default reasoning, skolemization, and some second-order features. CycL uses a form of circumscription, includes the unique names assumption, and can make use of the closed-world assumption where appropriate. The Cyc inference engine performs general logical deduction, best-first-search using a set of proprietary heuristics, uses microtheories to optimize inferences in restricting domains, and includes several special-purpose inferencing modules for handling specific classes of inferences.

The knowledge server utility allows multiple people to work together simultaneously on building up the KB; and provides a methodology and several user interfaces to browse, edit, and extend the Cyc KB, put queries to the inference engine, and interact with natural-language and database integration modules.

The applications areas currently available or under development are: natural language processing, integration of heterogeneous databases and data mining, knowledge-enhanced retrieval of captioned information, distributed AI, WWW information retrieval, smart interfaces, and more.

The most representative Cyc application is the Cyc-NL system. Given a query in English, the Cyc-NL system converts it into a CycL expression with free variables. Using CycL inference engines, Cyc gets a CycL answer and answers generating English from CycL statements. So, communication between Cyc and its users might be performed in English instead of by the Application Program Interface used in the 1990s. The Cyc-NL system is used for user-friendly interfaces to database tools and retrieval of information applications.

In data mining and integration of heterogeneous databases applications, Cyc incorporates the semantic-level knowledge. Cyc's database tool handles an NL or CycL query in three phases: the interface phase, which transforms NL queries into CycL expressions; the planner phase, which converts CycL expressions into an intermediate database representation format called CSQL, used to represent high-level logical database queries; and the executor phase, which converts the logical CSQL queries into physical SQL queries. After, the SQL answer is converted into CycL. This application was developed in 1995 to integrate data from tables at pharmaceutical companies.

With regard to knowledge-enhanced searching of captioned information, an image retrieval application and a text retrieval application were developed in 1994 and 1995 to optimize the search in extensive libraries of captioned images and in text documents. As before, once the target images or text documents have been described using Cyc, both systems, integrated with the Cyc-NL system, accept NL queries and make inferences with the image or text descriptions and other knowledge gathered in the Cyc KB.

13.2. EXAMPLE OF A KNOWLEDGE REPRESENTATION ONTOLOGY: THE FRAME-ONTOLOGY

This ontology (Gruber, 1993a) plays an important role since:

---

[2] Cyc's evolution is presented in Enabling agents to work together, in *Communications of the ACM*, 37(7), 127–142, 1994.

1. It is an ontology that captures the representation primitives most commonly used in frame-based representation languages. However, it does not seek to completely capture the semantics of existing knowledge representation languages. Examples of terms included in this ontology are: "Subclass-of," "Instance-of," "Minimum-Slot-Cardinality," etc.

2. It is a knowledge representation ontology. It gives a set of second-order relations (relations that can take other relations as arguments) that allows ontologies to be codified using frame-based conventions. All Ontolingua ontologies use definitions from this ontology.

3. It is the basis upon which Ontolingua translators are built, enabling people that use different knowledge representation languages to share ontologies.

The ontology (*http://www-ksl.stanford.edu:5915*) has been specified using KIF 3.0, and the entire ontology can be translated into pure KIF without information loss. The basic ontological commitments are that relations are tuples, functions are special cases of a relation in which the last term is unique for the previous terms, and classes are unary relations.

13.3. LINGUISTIC ONTOLOGIES

The **Generalized Upper Model (GUM)** is a general task and domain-independent linguistic ontology, developed by Bateman and colleagues at GMD/IPSI, Germany (Bateman, Magnini, and Fabris, 1995). To make it portable across different languages, the GUM ontology only includes the main linguistic concepts and how they are organized across languages, and omits details that differentiate languages. This philosophy allowed the use of GUM to create ontologies about specific languages, like Italian, German, and English, by entering the semantic distinctions of each language. Further extensions include languages closely related with the above (French and Spanish) and totally different languages (Chinese and Japanese).

The GUM ontology uses two hierarchies to model the domain. A conceptual taxonomy for concepts and a relational taxonomy for relations between concepts. The ontology provides detailed information about different kind of relations, processes, objects, etc. The ontology has been implemented in LOOM. A full description of both hierarchies can be found at *http://www.darmstadt.gmd.de/publish/komet/gen-um/newUM.html*. Actually, GUM is being used in different natural language processing applications (Penman, Komet, TechDoc, Alfresco, GIST, etc.), which demonstrates the high level of portability of this ontology.

The **EDR Electronic Dictionary** (Yokoi, 1995) is a very large KB of world knowledge, built upon the generalized electronic dictionary. The generalized electronic dictionary is an integrated collection of data and knowledge about the language to be used for natural language processing. It structures linguistic information along three axes: the description unit that includes superficial, conceptual, and deep knowledge; the descriptive unit that includes words, sentences, text, and documents; and the type of language unit, like Japanese, French, and English.

WordNet is a general-purpose concept lexicon that was developed at Princeton University. It can be used both as an online dictionary or thesaurus for reference purposes, and as a taxonomic lexical database.

13.4. ENGINEERING ONTOLOGIES

EngMath (Gruber and Olsen, 1994) is an Ontolingua ontology (*http://www-ksl.stanford.edu:5915*), developed for mathematical modeling in engineering. The ontology includes conceptual foundations for scalar, vector, and tensor quantities, physical dimensions, units of measure, functions of quantities, and dimensionless quantities. This ontology provides:

1. Engineering models and domain theories represented in machine and human notation.

2. A formal specification of a shared conceptualization and vocabulary for software agents in engineering domains. The EngMath ontology enables unambiguous communication between software agents in the SHADE project.

3. A set of definitions to be reused for other engineering ontologies, for example, in the PhysSys ontology.

PhysSys ontology authors (Borst et al., 1996) propose incremental construction of ontologies in engineering domains by isolating types of knowledge in different ontologies, which are then used to build new ontologies by means of mapping ontologies. Mapping ontologies define interrelationships between ontologies.

PhysSys is a mapping ontology for modeling, simulating, and designing physical systems. The authors present three conceptual viewpoints of a physical system: system layout, physical processes underlying behavior, and descriptive mathematical relations. Three engineering ontologies formalize each of these viewpoints: a component ontology, a process ontology, and the EngMath (Gruber and Olsen, 1994) ontology.

There are two kinds of interrelationships between these three ontologies in PhysSys: interrelationships between the component and process ontologies, and interrelationships between the process ontology and the EngMath ontology. So, PhysSys proposes a new form of building and reusing ontologies.

13.5. Planning Ontologies

Multis (Mizoguchi, Vanwelkenhuysen, and Ikeda, 1995) is a task ontology consisting of generic nouns, generic verbs, generic adjectives, and other task-specific concepts. This ontology is used for scheduling tasks and developing a task analysis interview system that enables domain experts to build executable task models. It has been implemented in Ontolingua.

14. TOOLS: ONTOLOGY SERVER

The ontology server (Farquhar et al., 1995) is a set of tools and services that support the building of shared ontologies between geographically distributed groups. It was developed in the context of the ARPA Knowledge Sharing Effort by the Knowledge Systems Laboratory at Stanford University. This server is an extension of Ontolingua. Initially, the term Ontolingua was used to refer to both the language in which ontologies are expressed formally and the tool used to build such ontologies. Actually, when the community uses this term, it refers to the language provided by the ontology server.

Initially, the world was conceptualized in Ontolingua using relations, functions, classes, individuals, and axioms (Gruber, 1993a). Relations are defined as a set of tuples, where each tuple is a list of objects. Functions are a special case of relation, in which the last object in each tuple is unique, given the preceding objects. Classes are unary relations of one argument. Individuals are instances. Basically, all definitions in Ontolingua present the same pattern: an informal definition in natural language and a formal definition using KIF statements. Before each KIF sentence, a keyword appears: *:def*, to express necessary conditions; *:iff-def*, to express necessary and sufficient conditions; *:lambda-body*, to express the value of a function in terms of its arguments; and, *:axiom-def*, to constrain the object constant.

With the aim was to move from a relational representation toward a frame-based or object-oriented representation, the *Frame-Ontology* was built. Ontolingua allows the use of both languages simultaneously. However, their syntaxes are quite different. For example, the statement "dogs are mammals" in KIF is codified as *:def (... (mammal ?dog) ...)* and, using the frame ontology, as *(subclass-of dog mammal)*. As stated by Gruber (1993a), Ontolingua is inherently incomplete with respect to the KIF language since not all knowledge codified in KIF can be codified using the frame ontology. To solve this problem, Ontolingua allows the inclusion of KIF expressions in definitions made using the frame ontology. However, the translation programs do not support these statements.

Ontolingua is also a domain-independent tool (Gruber, 1993a). The portability of Ontolingua ontologies is in its translation architecture, which translates any ontology into different representation languages (e.g., prolog, loom, Epikit, KL-ONE style system, pure-kif), but not back again. Indeed, Ontolingua was accepted by the knowledge-sharing community as the main tool to implement ontologies due to this set of translators.

Ontolingua evolved toward the Ontology Server. The ontology server architecture provides access to a library of ontologies, translators to languages (LOOM, IDL, CLIPS, etc.), and an editor to create and browse ontologies. There are three modes of interaction: remote collaborators that are able to write and inspect ontologies; remote applications that may query and modify ontologies stored at the server over the Internet; and stand-alone applications. Browsing, creating, editing, maintaining, using, and sharing ontologies, as well as collaborative development by different groups are the most representative facilities provided by this Ontology Server. The ontology server may be accessed through the URL: *http://www-ksl-svc.stanford.edu:5915/.*

15.   SYSTEMS THAT USE ONTOLOGIES

This section briefly summarizes a few examples of how to use ontologies in real applications, like software systems design, engineering negotiation, unification of database schemata, etc.

Comet and **Cosmos** were developed by Mark, Dukes-Schlossberg, and Kerber (1995). Comet supports the design of software systems, and Cosmos supports engineering negotiation. Both systems give design feedback to their users. When a Comet user modifies a software module, Comet provides feedback on which other modules are affected and will require modifications. Cosmos provides hardware designers with analyses that indicate the impact of a proposed design change. In both systems, when a new software module is created and when new design changes are supplied, the changes create new LOOM concepts that are added to their knowledge bases. In both systems, it is essential that the commitments to be satisfied by an additional be encoded in the original core of the KB in order for it to be consistent and for the system's reasoning methods to act properly.

The goal of the **TOVE** (TOronto Virtual Enterprise) Enterprise Modeling project (Grüninger and Fox, 1995) is to create enterprise models that not only answer queries using what is explicitly represented, but is also able to deduce answers to queries.

The goal of the **Enterprise Project** (Uschold and Grüninger, 1996), developed by Uschold at AIAI in Edinburgh, is to improve and where necessary replace existing modeling methods with a framework for integrating methods and tools appropriate to enterprise modeling and the management of change. The Enterprise ontology plays an important role in this project. This ontology includes: a meta-ontology and ontologies related to activities and processes, strategies, organizations, and marketing.

KACTUS (Schreiber, Wielinga, and Jansweijer, 1995) is an ESPRIT project on modeling knowledge about complex technical systems for multiple use and the role of ontologies to support it. Ontologies in the domain of electrical networks, offshore oil production, and ship design and assessment have been already built.

Plinius (Vet, Speel, and Mars, 1995) is a semi-automatic knowledge acquisition system from natural language text in the domain of ceramic materials, their properties, and their production processes. The Plinius ontology is one of the cores of the Plinius system, because there exist many other things that make the system work. The Plinius ontology provides the semantics of the terms used by the Plinius system lexicon. This ontology might be classified as a domain ontology.

Top-down and bottom-up methods have been merged to build the ontology. One of the features of the Plinius ontology is that is stable and fixed, so that it can serve as an anchor point for the processes. Top-down methodologies are quite useful to provide the core of such concepts. In systems like Plinius, it is quite difficult to exhaustively predict in advance which concepts you are going to need. So, one of the main requirements was to be able to specify beforehand each and every possible substance. As the list of possible substances is infinitely large, this can only be done implicitly using bottom-up methods.

The design criteria followed in developing the Plinius ontology are: parsimony, faithfulness (i.e., domain experts would have to recognize the ontology as a correct rendering of the way their domain is organized); easy extendibility; limitableness; and relevance of the formal definitions and informal explications.

The Plinius ontology was conceptualized on the principle of a conceptual construction kit. According to this principle, an ontology consists of atomic concepts and a set of construction rules (also called transformation rules) that define other concepts. Nonatomic concepts are implicitly defined in the ontology. The ontology can be seen as a calculus. The deductive closure of this calculus produces the explicit list of concepts. In Plinius, atomic concepts are: *chemical elements*, which are defined by their atomic number, and *natural numbers*, defined in a number theory.

The Plinius ontology has been implemented in a wide range of representation languages and systems, such as: Ontolingua, CLASSIC, and Prolog (the Prolog implementation is the most satisfactory). This work is a framework of reference about advantages and disadvantages of choosing representation languages for ontologies. According to Plinius conceptualization, not all the conceptualized knowledge is easily implementable in the chosen target language since each language has its own expressiveness. Since large parts of the ontology are bottom-up, it is difficult to codify it in target languages that assume top-down ontologies like Ontolingua. In this case, most of the definitions in Ontolingua had to be written in pure KIF. As a result, the ontology cannot be translated into target languages like LOOM and EPIKIT because the automatic translation only works for pure Ontolingua. More detailed information of this system, including the Ontolingua ontology, can be examined at the following URL: *http://wwwis.cs.utwente.nl:8080/kbs/ontology/homepage.html.*

Dowell, Stephens, and Bonnell (1995) present an ontology of domain knowledge that can be used as a semantic gateway between different database schemata. The ontology allows the user to query and get information from nonlocal databases They first map each database schema to an extended conceptual model and link each part of the extended conceptual model with its corresponding items in the domain ontology. The domain ontology consists of two hierarchies: a hierarchy of types that correspond with entities in the database, and a hierarchy of links that represent relations and properties in the database.

16. CONCLUSION

This chapter presented an overview of the knowledge sharing and reuse technology, as well as METHONTOLOGY, a set of guideliness that allow to build an ontology since an engineering point of view, reducing the existing gap between the ontological art and ontological engineering. The main future trends include:

- With regard to the integration of ontologies, there is a need for criteria to select ontologies and definitions, as well as methods to carry out the integration in a consistent manner. Ontology brokers are required to help in the reuse of ontologies to build new ontologies.
- We need to investigate how to automatically merge two or more ontologies in the same domain into one large ontology in a complete and consistent manner.
- There is a need for a set of tools that helps ontologists build ontologies from scratch that covers the entire ontology life cycle, provides evaluation techniques during the entire life cycle, and includes knowledge acquisition techniques to speed up the knowledge acquisition phase.
- There is a need for some recomendations about how to use and advantages of having them as a basis for KR systems.

ACKNOWLEDGMENTS

The author takes this opportunity to thank to Juan Pazos and Natalia Juristo, who helped me in the discussions and implementations of the ideas presented in this chapter. Also, I´m grateful to Mariano Fernández for his contribution to Ontolingua Implementation of the CHEMICALS ontology.

REFERENCES

Alonso, F.; Juristo, N.; Maté, J.L.; Pazos, J. *Software Engineering and Knowledge Engineering: Towards a Common Life-Cycle.* Journal of Systems and Software. N° 33. 1996. p. 65–79.

Bateman, J.; Magnini, B.; Fabris, G. *The Generalized Upper Model Knowledge Base: Organization and Use.* Towards Very Large Knowledge Bases. Ed. by N. Mars. IOS Press, Amsterdam. 1995. p. 60–72.

Bernaras, A.; Laresgoiti, I.; Corera, J. *Building and Reusing Ontologies for Electrical Network Applications.* Proceedings of the ECAI'96. p. 298–302.

Borgo, S.; Guarino, N.; Masolo, C. *Stratified Ontologies: The Case of Physical Objects.* Workshop on Ontological Engineering. ECAI'96. Budapest, Hungary. p. 5–16.

Borst, P.; Benjamin, J.; Wielinga, B.; Akkermans, H. *An Application of Ontology Construction.* Workshop on Ontological Engineering. ECAI'96. Budapest, Hungary. p. 17–28.

Dowell, M.; Stephens, L.; Bonnell, R. *Using a Domain Knowledge Ontology As a Semantic Gateway among Databases.* IJCAI Workshop on Basic Ontological Issues in Knowledge Sharing. Montreal, Quebec, Canada. 1995.

Farquhar, A.; Fikes, R.; Pratt, W.; Rice, J. *Collaborative Ontology Construction for Information Integration.* Technical Report KSL-95-10. Knowledge Systems Laboratory. Stanford University, CA. 1995.

Finin, T. *An Overview of KQML: A Knowledge Query and Manipulation Language.* 1992.

Gangemi, A.; Steve, G.; Giacomelli, F. *ONIONS: An Ontological Methodology for Taxonomic Knowledge Integration.* Workshop on Ontological Engineering. ECAI'96. Budapest, Hungary. p. 29–40.

Genesereth, M.; Fikes, R. *Knowledge Interchange Format.* Version 3.0. Reference Manual. Report Logic-92-1. Computer Science Department. Stanford University, CA. 1992.

Gómez-Pérez, A. *A Framework to Verify Knowledge Sharing Technology.* Expert Systems with Application. Vol. 11, N° 4. 1996. p. 519–529.

Gómez-Pérez, A. *From Knowledge Based Systems to Knowledge Sharing Technology: Evaluation and Assessment.* Technical Report KSL-94-73. Knowledge Systems Laboratory. Stanford University, CA. 1994.

Gómez-Pérez, A.; Fernández, M.; de Vicente, A. *Towards a Method to Conceptualize Domain Ontologies.* Workshop on Ontological Engineering. ECAI'96. Budapest, Hungary. p. 41–52.

Gómez-Pérez, A.; Juristo, N.; Pazos, J. *Evaluation and Assessment of Knowledge Sharing Technology.* Towards Very Large Knowledge Bases. Ed. by N. Mars. IOS Press, Amsterdam. 1995. p. 289–296.

Gruber, T. *A translation Approach to Portable Ontology Specifications.* Knowledge Acquisition. Vol. 5. 1993. p. 199–220.

Gruber, T. *Toward Principles for the Design of Ontologies Used for Knowledge Sharing.* Technical Report KSL-93-04. Knowledge Systems Laboratory. Stanford University, CA. 1993.

Gruber, T.; Olsen, G. *An Ontology for Engineering Mathematics.* Fourth International Conference on Principles of Knowledge Representation and Reasoning. Ed. by Doyle and Torasso. Morgan Kaufmann, 1994. Also as KSL-94-18.

Grüninger, M.; Fox, M.S. *Methodology for the Design and Evaluation of Ontologies.* IJCAI Workshop on Basic Ontological Issues in Knowledge Sharing. Montreal, Quebec, Canada. 1995.

Grüninger, M.; Fox, M.S. *The Role of Competency Questions in Enterprise Engineering.* IFIP WG 5.7. Workshop on Benchmarking. Theory and Practice. Trondheim, Norway. 1994.

Guarino, N.; Giaretta, P. *Ontologies and Knowledge Bases: Towards a Terminological Clarification.* Towards Very Large Knowledge Bases: Knowledge Building & Knowledge Sharing. IOS Press, Amsterdam. 1995. p. 25–32.

IEEE Std. 1074-1991. IEEE Standard for Developing Software Life Cycle Processes.

Lee, J.; Grüninger, M. Jin, Y.; Malone, T.; Tate, A.; Yost, G. *Process Interchange Format (PIF).* Workshop on Ontological Engineering. ECAI'96. Budapest, Hungary. p. 65–76.

Lenat, D.B. *Steps to Sharing Knowledge.* Towards Very Large Knowledge Bases. Ed. by N. Mars. IOS Press, Amsterdam. 1995. p. 3–6.

Lenat, D.B., Guha, R.V. Building Large Knowledge-Based Systems: Representation and Inference in the Cyc Project. Addison-Wesley, CA. 1990.

MacGregor, R. *The Evolving Technology of Classification-Based Knowledge Representation Systems.* In J. Sowa, Ed. Principles of Semantic Networks: Explorations in the Representation of Knowledge. Morgan Kaufmann, San Mateo, CA. 1991.

Mark, W.; Dukes-Schlossberg, J.; Kerber, R. *Ontological Commitment and Domain-Specific Architectures: Experience with Comet and Cosmos.* Towards Very Large Knowledge Bases. Ed. by N. Mars. IOS Press, Amsterdam. 1995. p. 33–45.

McCracken; M. A. Jackson. *Life Cycle Concept Considered Harmful.* ACM Software Engineering Notes. April 1982. p. 29–32.

Mizoguchi, R., Vanwelkenhuysen, J.; Ikeda, M. *Task Ontology for Reuse of Problem Solving Knowledge.* Towards Very Large Knowledge Bases: Knowledge Building & Knowledge Sharing. IOS Press, Amsterdam. 1995. p. 46–59.

Neches, R.; Fikes, R.; Finin, T.; Gruber, T.; Patil, R.; Senator, T., Swartout, W.R. *Enabling Technology for Knowledge Sharing.* AI Magazine. Winter 1991. p. 36–56.

Pazos J. Conceptualización. Master en Ingeniería del Conocimiento. Facultad de Informática de Madrid. Universidad Politécnica de Madrid. Spain. 1995.

Royce W. M. *Managing the Development of Large Software Systems.* Proceedings of the 9th International Conference Software Engineering. IEEE Computer Society. 1987. p. 328–338.

Schreiber, G.; Wielinga, B.; Jansweijer, W. *The KACTUS View on the 'O' Word.* In Proceedings of the National Dutch AI Conference, NAIC'95.

Skuce, D. *Viewing Ontologies as Vocabulary: Merging and Documenting the Logical and Linguistic Views.* IJCAI Workshop on Basic Ontological Issues in Knowledge Sharing. Montreal, Quebec, Canada. 1995.

Speel, H.; Raalte, F; Vet, P.; Mars, N. *Scalability of the Performance of Knowledge Representation Systems.* Towards Very Large Knowledge Bases. Ed. by N. Mars. IOS Press, Amsterdam. 1995. p. 173–184.

Uschold, M.; Grüninger, M. *ONTOLOGIES: Principles, Methods and Applications.* Knowledge Engineering Review. Vol. 11; N. 2; June 1996.

Vet, P.; Speel, P.; Mars, N. *Ontologies for Very Large Knowledge Bases in Material Science: A Case Study.* Towards Very Large Knowledge Bases. Ed. by N. Mars. IOS Press, Amsterdam. 1995. p. 73–83.

Yokoy, T. *The Impact of EDR Electronic Dictionary on Very Large Knowledge Bases.* Towards Very Large Knowledge Bases. Ed. by N. Mars. IOS Press, Amsterdam. 1995. p. 13–22.

Part III
Critical Technologies Associated with Expert Systems

11 Case-Based Reasoning

Lean Suan Ong and Arcot Desai Narasimhalu

CONTENTS

1. INTRODUCTION

No matter what type of problem-solving task it is, people usually have more confidence in you when you say that you have done that particular task many times before, i.e., you have the *experience*. Why? Because by having done that task before, it means that you are able to do another similar task, better and faster, with less potential for failure; you are an "expert" in that problem-solving task. It is also a well-known fact that human experts solve problems by relying on their past experiences in solving similar problems. This is especially true in areas such as law and medicine, for example. Lawyers rely on previous cases to argue for or against a new case, just as doctors rely on previous patient cases that they have seen for diagnosis and treatment of a new patient. It was from this idea of reusing past experiences to solve new or current problems that an Artificial Intelligence (AI) approach called Case-Based Reasoning (CBR) was born. CBR is sometimes classified under Machine Learning, and supports knowledge acquisition and problem-solving. It is also sometimes associated with other technologies such as analogy, cognitive psychology modeling, machine learning, and information retrieval, for example.

2. HISTORY OF CBR

CBR by itself is not new technology; it has its origins in the work of Roger Shank on *Dynamic Memory* (Schank, 1982), which described a memory-based approach to reasoning. His ideas were further expanded by graduate students at Yale University and Janet Kolodner of Georgia Tech, who developed the CYRUS System (Kolodner, 1983). A series of annual workshops have been held since 1987, and it is workshops such as the CBR workshop sponsored by DARPA (Defense Advanced Research Project Agency) at Florida in 1989 that brought together the CBR researchers and spurred interest in this technology. Interest and participation in CBR has grown over the recent years, and there are conferences and workshops held regularly (such as the European Workshop on CBR (EWCBR)) that are very well received.

Early CBR systems developed include CHEF (Hammond, 1986) a meal planning system; PROTOS (Bareiss, 1988) for classifying and thus diagnosing hearing disorders; MEDIATOR (Simpson, 1985) in the domain of dispute mediation; and HYPO (Ashley and Rissland, 1988), which provides arguments for and against parties in U.S. nondisclosure litigation, behaving very much like a lawyer would. However, it is the availability of commercial CBR tools and success of help-desk applications such as the SMART (Acorn et al., 1992) system for Compaq computers that have given the impetus to this technology.

3. CBR CONCEPTS

The reasoning paradigm behind CBR is very simple: "past" cases closest (in characteristics) to the current problem situation are retrieved or recalled, and the best matching case's corresponding solution is transformed to solve the new one. The advantage here is that much effort is saved since one can re-derive lessons, explanations, plans, or solutions (e.g., treatment regimen for a new patient) by simply reusing the results from previous (patient) cases, which is close enough to how a human expert might carry out problem-solving. Of course, the catch to using CBR is that there must be a sufficiently large "database of cases" from which to draw from, but for practical and ethical reasons (say, in medicine), sometimes such a database may be hard to come by. The domain must also be well understood, i.e., not new medical areas where there is incomplete information or incorrect or controversial knowledge.

The traditional AI approach builds a system from scratch; attempting to solve problems by constructing solutions based on general principles (or rules) and substantial in-depth problem-solving knowledge. The pitfalls of acquiring knowledge from a human expert through interviews, for example, have been well documented, and have led to the term "knowledge acquisition bottle-neck" being coined by Feigenbaum. In contrast, CBR recalls "past" cases similar to the current problem situation and transforms the corresponding solution to solve the new one. Just as a doctor treats a new patient by recalling his experiences in diagnosing and treating previous patients, a CBR system retrieves from its library of cases, the most "similar" (in characteristics, problem description, etc.) old case, adapts the results to the new case, and hence proposes a solution to the new problem. In this way, the effort involved in solving a new problem is substantially reduced simply by reusing previous results, instead of from scratch.

The major steps in case-based reasoning are as in Figure 1.

1. A new problem or case is analyzed and represented in a form such that the CBR system can retrieve relevant past cases ("remembering" or case retrieval). The goal is to retrieve useful cases; that is, those that have the potential to provide a solution to the new problem at hand.
2. Once relevant cases are retrieved, they are ranked (based on some knowledge of similarity) and the best subset, or most promising case(s), is returned to the user for browsing.

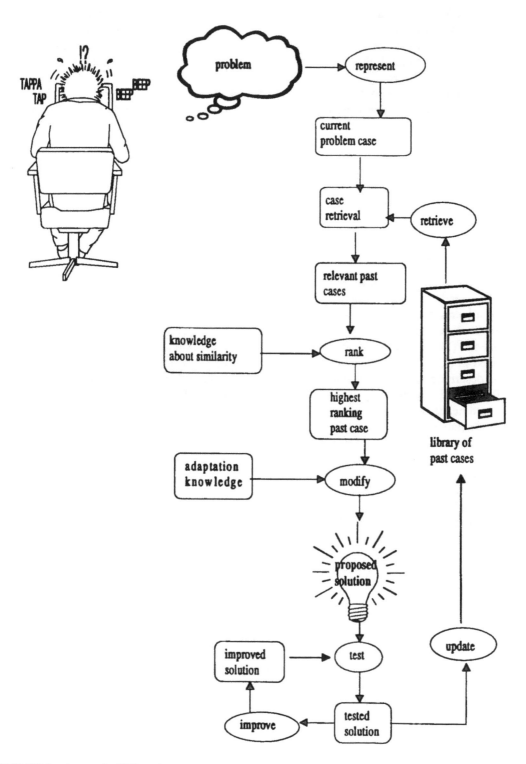

FIGURE 1 A generic CBR architecture.

3. Very often, an old case does not fit the new one exactly; hence, it is necessary to modify or make changes to an old solution to fit the new problem situation. The process of making these changes (known as adaptation) may range from a minor substitution of values, to structural changes. What adaptation, and how it is to be done, depends on domain knowledge.

4. The initial solution to the new case is then proposed to the user.

5. The proposed solution is tested or evaluated, and improvements made on it. Feedback is obtained and analyzed. If it does not perform as expected, an explanation of the anomalous results is given. Follow-up procedures include explaining failures and attempts to repair them are stored, so that future failures can be predicted and avoided.

6. The new case is updated into the case library for future use. By adding new situations/cases into the case library, the system is actually carrying out an incremental learning process. This is especially useful for dynamic domains that need to "keep up with the times."

3.1. REPRESENTING A CASE

A case could resemble a database entry, with a list of characteristics or features describing a particular situation. A case is usually complete by itself, or may be connected to a set of subcases, forming a hierarchical structure of the problem-solving task. Cases are usually represented in the form of predicates, frames, or even database-like records. A case is usually made up of three components: (1) the description of the problem, (2) the description of the solution to the problem mentioned in (1), and (3) the outcome as a result of applying the solution.

The description in (1) would contain all descriptive information needed to achieve the goal of the CBR system. For example, if the goal of the system is to diagnose the cause of the patient's illness, and hence provide the appropriate treatment, then the descriptive information in (1) would contain the patient's symptoms, laboratory test results, etc. for diagnosis of the disease; and the patient's medical history, drug allergies, etc. for the treatment. It is essential that as much relevant information as possible to the problem-solving goal is captured since a case is only as useful as the information it holds.

The description of the solution to the problem essentially allows the user, once a similar case has been retrieved, to reuse a previous solution without starting from scratch. Hence, if a match on the patient's problem has been found (i.e., diagnosed the disease-causing agent of the patient), then whatever treatment that worked before would have been stored in the solution description. Obviously, a patient that died as a result of a particular treatment would not be stored, but it may be stored with a different objective, i.e., to avoid such failures in the future. Hence, an explanation of why a particular failure occurred, and the remedy, may be stored and used as a guide to avoid or anticipate such a failure in future. Some CBR systems may also store the reasoning steps used to solve the problem, justifications for decisions made, and acceptable or alternative solutions as part of the description of the solution.

The outcome as the result of applying the solution refers to the results derived from feedback after the solution has been carried out. The outcome description may contain explanations of what was carried out, whether the outcome was a success or failure, the repair strategy (in the case of failure) and what could have been done to avoid the failure, and the results after applying the repair. The outcome component of a case is useful for predicting potential failures and how to avoid them.

3.2. INDEXING CASES

In order for the case-based reasoner to retrieve "similar" cases, labels (known as indexes) must be assigned to a case to "identify" it as an appropriate case to be retrieved, given a particular situation. Hence, indexes signify which cases are relevant (hence useful) and are potentially able to provide a solution to a problem. Deciding on a good index requires a good understanding of the problem domain and the problem-solving goal. Since indexes represent an interpretation of a situation, a good index (appropriate for the problem-solving situation) would allow relevant cases (with potential solutions) to be retrieved quickly and accurately. However, choosing a good index may not be as simple as it sounds since there are no guidelines or established methods that exist for choosing good indexes. As a guide, however, there are four qualities of good indexes (Kolodner, 1993):

1. *Predictive features:* Indexes should address the problem-solving goal of the cases.
2. *Abstractness of indexes:* Indexes should be abstract enough so that a case can be used in a variety of future situations.
3. *Concreteness of indexes:* Indexes should be obvious and recognizable in future situations, without further interpretation.
4. *Usefulness of indexes*: Indexes should be able to differentiate cases from each other in useful ways, and able to give guidance about the decisions that the case-based reasoner deals with.

In summary, the indexing problem is "the problem of retrieving applicable cases at appropriate times — problem of assigning labels (called indexes) to cases that designate under what conditions each case can be used to make useful inferences" (Kolodner, 1993).

3.3. SIMILARITY MATCHING

Given the particulars of a new case, the case-based reasoner looks at all the existing cases and retrieves those "most similar." "Most similar" is determined by matching each individual feature of the new case with all the existing cases. One such matching process is known as *nearest-neighbor matching*, where given a new case and a retrieved case, for each feature, the case-based reasoner computes their degree of match by looking first at each field type (whether text, numeric, Boolean, etc.) to define how the scoring is to be handled, and then comparing the values. A similarity score is then assigned to the feature. This is repeated for all features that have been defined by the user (i.e., features that contribute to the reasoning goal). Each feature is also given a weightage to reflect their relative importance. The overall similarity score for the case is computed by using a formula such as:

$$\frac{\sum_{i=1}^{n} w_i * sim(f_i I, f_i R)}{\sum_{i=1}^{n} w_i}$$

where w_i is the importance of the feature i, *sim* is the similarity function for primitives, and $f_i I$ and $f_i R$ are the values of feature f_i in the input and retrieved cases, respectively. After computing the extent of the match, and based on a weighted sum of all features, the case-based reasoner retrieves the highest-ranking or best-matching cases. These cases are then displayed to the user for browsing.

3.4. ADAPTATION

Adaptation means modifying the solution as suggested by the retrieved case, to suit and meet the requirements of the new case. The modification process may involve a series of steps covering simple substitutions (replacing values), to a more substantial structure modification. There are two general kinds of adaptation: (1) structural adaptation, where adaptation rules are applied directly to the solution retrieved from the most similar case; and (2) derivational adaptation, where rules that generated the original solution are rerun to generate a new solution appropriate to the new case. This means that parts of the retrieved solution are re-executed, rather than modified directly.

Adaptation rules are easiest to define for simple substitutions of values, or adjusting or interpolating numerical parameters. Adaptation rules are most difficult to define for structural modifications which may involve deletions or insertions of features, and such adaptation rules are usually guided by a causal model or model-based repair strategies. Retrieved cases may even be used to suggest suitable adaptations. An adaptation process can be quite complex since much domain knowledge is required to determine what adaptation should be done, and how to do it.

All of the above CBR concepts will be re-visited under the paragraph on 'Research Challenges' to discuss some of the existing problems and difficulties facing CBR.

4.   CBR APPLICATIONS

CBR has been applied to a variety of applications including diagnosis, classification, story understanding, interpretation, tutoring, planning, scheduling, design, and forecasting/prediction. In solving planning and design problems, for example, CBR has proven useful in that plans and designs that have been used successfully in the past are re-used, instead of having to start from scratch. CBR is able to suggest solutions to complex planning problems through previously used plans indexed by the conjunction of goals they satisfy. Hence, in complex real-world problems with many competing and interacting goals and exponentially increasing numbers of constraints to satisfy, a case-based planner can reduce this complexity by doing a "pattern match" on achieving several goals simultaneously or in conjunction with each other, without really "understanding" the individual goals themselves. Similarly, previous failure allows the anticipation of problems before execution time, thus avoiding it (as in CHEF).

For complex design problems, there are many constraints that must be satisfied. However, which are the important ones to focus on first, and how can a solution be constructed? Most design problems are specified in the form of constraints, without any guidance on how the solution is to be derived. CBR's solution to design problems is to re-use an old design case as the starting point, thus providing a partial solution or framework that can be adapted to fit the new problem requirements by filling in the relevant details.

For applications such as legal reasoning, CBR systems have been built that are able to argue for or against a case (very much like how a lawyer would operate) by retrieving past cases whose interpretation or classification is known. By evaluating, comparing, and contrasting a new case with past cases, the system is able to give reasons on how a situation should be interpreted. Similarly, CBR systems are able to "understand stories" by asking questions and making assumptions when information is incomplete.

Since it is not possible to describe all possible applications of CBR, two systems, very different in nature, are described here to illustrate the versatility of this technology and how it has been applied.

4.1.   SMART System

CBR has been most successful in the area of help desks, the most notable being SMART (Support Management Automated Reasoning Technology) (Acorn, 1992) for Compaq Computer Corporation. Compaq manufactures personal computer systems and one of its strategic business objectives is to provide quality customer support. Its Customer Support Center provides technical support, ranging from product information requests to problem resolution, on its wide variety of products. The workflow for the SMART System is shown in Figure 2.

When a customer calls in with a problem (e.g., printouts from the printer are faded), the details are gathered and entered into the SMART system. An initial search is then performed on the case

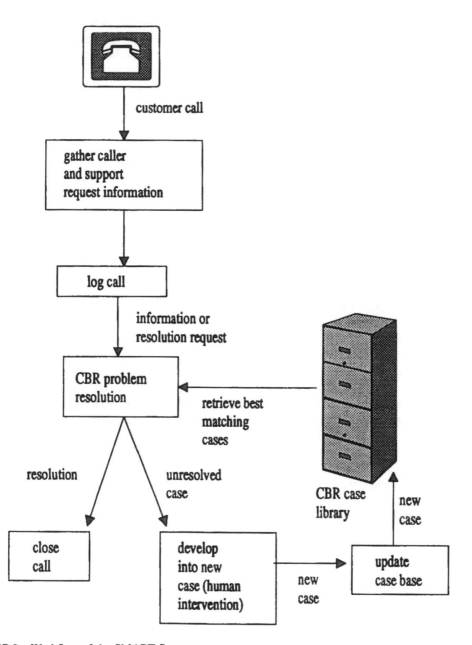

FIGURE 2   Workflow of the SMART System.

library to locate previous cases with similar problem characteristics. Where information is incomplete, the system suggests further questions to be asked from the caller in order to determine more precisely, the category of the problem. Once a predefined threshold for matching is reached (i.e., the retrieved cases matches the new case by a certain percentage, say, 80%), the resolution from the retrieved case is then recommended to the caller. Hence, the SMART system makes use of previous cases to resolve new ones, instead of trying to diagnose a new problem from scratch. This has greatly enhanced the customer service and efficiency of the Customer Support Center by providing timely and accurate information to Compaq's customers within minimal response time. In addition, the system may be used as a training tool, while empowering the Support Center employees with more in-depth technical knowledge, thus increasing productivity.

Compaq has since extended the SMART system one step further by delivering intelligence and human expertise directly to the customers to help them solve their own problems, through the system known as QUICKSOURCE (Nguyen,1993). QUICKSOURCE is an example of knowledge publishing, in that the customer support function is put directly in the hands of the consumers. The system is sufficiently friendly to allow the customers to troubleshoot and solve their own problems, calling the Customer Support Center only as a last resort.

4.2.   THE CARES SYSTEM

The Institute of Systems Science at the National University of Singapore is currently working on a research project with the Department of Colorectal Surgery at the Singapore General Hospital (SGH) to develop a system named Cancer Recurrence Support (CARES) system (Ong, 1997) that will predict the recurrence of colorectal cancer, using CBR as the primary technology. The CARES system employs CBR to compare and contrast between the new and past colorectal cancer patient cases, and makes inferences based on those comparisons to determine the high-risk patient groups.

The primary modality of treatment for colorectal cancer is surgery. However, although over two thirds of patients with primary disease undergo potentially curative surgery where all gross tumor is removed, up to 50% of these will eventually die in the ensuing 5 years, the majority from local, regional, or distant tumor recurrence. Adding to the problem is the difficulty in predicting the site of recurrence. This is, at the moment, difficult to do since primary colorectal cancers at different locations in the bowel may have different recurrence patterns.

The key to a successful follow-up program lies in the selective application of intensive follow-up and appropriate diagnostic tests and intensive chemotherapy for patients at high risk of cancer recurrence. Early identification of recurrence increases the effectiveness of therapy and survival of patients. Although the value of early detection of recurrence is recognized, the means by which this can be achieved is still controversial. It is argued that some form of follow-up is indicated for the remainder of the patient's life but the exact protocol to attain maximum benefit is debatable. In addition, many investigative tools, such as tumor markers, colonoscopy, imaging studies, and even exploratory surgery have added to the sensitivity of detection of recurrences, but if these were indiscriminately applied, it could lead to additional costs and patient morbidity without eventual survival benefit. Various statistical techniques have been proposed to identify high-risk patients; for example, a multivariate analysis of survival time using Cox's proportional hazard model to identify important prognostic factors. The CARES project, however, utilizes CBR to predict colorectal cancer recurrence by matching against past cases.

SGH currently has a clinical database (maintained on the hospital's mainframe computer) of more than 10,000 medical records of patients seen by the Department of Colorectal Surgery. The data acquired for each patient includes all relevant clinical and pathological information at the time of diagnosis and surgery as well as follow-up information that is collected according to a strict protocol. The historical data stored in this database is an invaluable resource that may contain unknown patterns, trends, or hidden meanings that can allow one to make predictions or forecasts. This hidden knowledge is not easily uncovered through conventional database queries. CBR is used in this application to match and retrieve past (i.e., existing) cases by recognizing their similarity to a new case. It makes assumptions about the present by looking at the past: "What was true yesterday is likely to be true today" (Kolodner, 1993). CBR is used to tap into the colorectal database to predict the risk of recurrence for a particular patient, based on matching his "profile" with the database records of previous patients who have known outcome (recurrence or no recurrence).

Most current medical Expert Systems are based upon expert knowledge and heuristics encoded directly as rules of the form:

"IF patient age > 60 yrs and has low fiber diet, THEN recurrence is likely"

For this application, namely the prediction of colorectal cancer recurrence, there is no clear body of heuristic knowledge available from which to build a rule set. Consequently, the use of CBR, which does not require knowledge to be made explicit in the form of rules, has clear advantages. The CARES system employs CBR to compare and contrast new and past colorectal cancer patient cases, and it then makes inferences based on those comparisons to determine high-risk groups.

The objective of the CARES system is to predict the length of disease-free period (number of months of no recurrence) after the first operation. In addition, the system is to suggest a follow-up regimen (tests) most appropriate for a particular patient. The objective here is to minimize the number of costly follow-up tests performed on a patient by customizing the test selection for that patient. To do this, the system will attempt to categorize the existing patients into groups according to which follow-up tests are most useful for recurrence prediction. A new patient can then be matched against these groups to recommend tests most appropriate or, alternatively, most inappropriate. The computation to support the recommendation will be done external to the CBR component. It should be noted that this functionality is highly dependent on the quality of data available; that is, there must be enough information already captured in the colorectal database such that the "categorization" of patients is possible. This project is currently on-going, and the estimated date of the implementation is October 1997.

5.   CBR TOOLS

CBR technology gained prominence with the emergence of commercial software tools, some of which are listed in Table 1.

Table 2 shows some general categories of applications, and the suitablility of some of the tools mentioned earlier, based on the report by Althoff, K.D et. al in 1996. A black bullet • indicates that the tool is likely to be suited to the domain. A ♦ indicates that the tool's features can be extended in order to cope with the domain. The symbol ♣, given to CBR Express for help-desk applications, reflects the fact that this tool has been specially designed to cope with this particular domain. A review of the commercial tools can be found in Althoff et al. (1996).

However, at this point in time, these tools are not sufficiently powerful to meet all the requirements normally posed by real-world applications. While CBR2 from Inference Corporation can be considered sufficiently mature for the help-desk/customer-support applications; for other types of applications (such as planning, forecasting, design, etc.), the commercial tools need more powerful and flexible functionalities such as communication and integration with other applications (for embedded systems) and databases (for import and export of records from existing databases). A development environment that provides better support for building case libraries, and algorithms for more effective search and retrieval of cases, are needed to improve the performance of case-based systems. To overcome these shortcomings, tool developers need to consider combining CBR with other problem-solving mechanisms (mixed paradigm reasoning) to produce integrated architectures for hybrid systems (see later paragraph on hybrid systems).

6.   RESEARCH CHALLENGES

While CBR sounds simple enough, there are still unresolved weaknesses at this point in time. There are three main issues:

- Case representation
- Case indexing
- Case adaptation and learning

TABLE 1
CBR Tools

Tool name	Vendor
CBR 2 version 2.0 (incorporating CBR-Express and CasePoint)	Inference Corporation 101 Rowland Way, Suite 310 Nocato, California 94945
ReMind version 1.3	Cognitive System Inc. 220-230 Commercial Street Boston, MA 02109
CASECRAFT, the KATE tools (KATE-INDUCTION, KATE-CBR, KATE-EDITOR, KATE-RUNTIME) version 4.0	AcknoSoft 58a, Rue du Dessous des Berger, 75013 Paris, France and 396 Shasta Drive Palo Alto CA 94306-4541
ESTEEM version 1.4	Esteem Software Inc. 302E Main Street Cambridge City, IN 47327
ReCall version 1.2	Isoft Chemin de Moulon F-91190 Gif sur Yvette France
S³-CASE version 1.0	tecInno GmbH Sauerwiesen 2 67661 KAISERSLAUTERN Germany
MEM-1 version 1.0	CECASE 2291 Irving Hill Road Lawrence, KS 66045-2969
CasePower	Inductive Solution Inc. 380 Rector Place, Suit 4A New York, NY 10280
Eclipse	The Haley Enterprise Inc. 413 Orchard Street Sewickley, PA 15143
CASE-1	Astea International 55 Middlesex Turnpike Dedford, MA 01730

6.1. CASE REPRESENTATION

How are cases defined and represented? There are many ways of representing a case, including predicate representations, frames, or even entries resembling database records. In general, there are three features that need to be captured: the problem-situation description, the solution, and the outcome. The problem-situation is essentially a description of the characteristics of the problem, the context, or situation in which it occurs. The representation must match the reasoning goals of the system. However, it is not always obvious what a case should be. A problem description may need to include features that are intermediary, or solution-in-progress. A description, after some reasoning, may need to be redescribed to reflect the situation more accurately (for example, the condition of a patient as the disease progresses). Most of the difficulty comes when information is time-based, or which changes over time. Current methods of representing cases are mostly static;

TABLE 2
Suitability of Tools for Different Categories of Applications

	CBR express	ESTEEM	KATE 3.0	ReMind	S³-CASE
Classification					
Prediction		♦	•	♦	
Assessment	♦	•	•	•	•
Help Desk	♦	♦	•	•	•
Diagnosis	•	♦	•	♦	•
Data Mining			♦	♦	
In-process control			♦	♦	
Off-line Control		•	•	•	♦
Synthesis					
Design			♦		
Planning					
Configuration			♦		♦

From Althoff, K.D., Auriol, E., Barletta, R., and Manago, M. (1996). A Review of Industrial Case-based Reasoning Tools. An AI Perspectives Report. Series Editor: Alex Goodall. With permission.

how should the case representation be made dynamic in order to reflect changes? Should a situation be represented as one large monolithic case or distributed cases with portions related to each other? How can such distributed cases be retrieved and judged similar?

An important problem to be addressed is the question of when to admit a new case as a new case and not as an adaptation of an existing case. In other words, what should be the extent of dissimilarity between two cases before they are considered to be two separate cases? Is it when they differ in sufficient number of features, or is it when they differ in significant features but differ significantly, or is it some combination of the two? Should there be a "metric of goodness" developed to decide whether a case is sufficiently different for being treated as a new case?

With the introduction of video clips as evidence in a court of law, it may also be time to start addressing the challenges of managing cases that are multimedia in nature. Questions such as "What aspects of a video?" are important to a case. Is there a significant segment in the video that alone is sufficient to be captured? When can one say that two video clips represent the same content or different content? Research in this direction may not yield immediate results since it touches upon the territory of making computers understand in a human manner, a problem that has not been successfully addressed even in a context-sensitive situation.

Another issue worth addressing is to understand whether it is important to know that a case was derived from another case. If such knowledge is important, then should such derived cases be handled as versions of the initial case? Also, should comparisons always be made with the original cases only, or should similarities tested against the derived ones as well? One may argue that it may be sufficient to test similarities against the most recent cases, as is normal in the fields of medicine and law. If such is a position, then one needs to address the potential pitfall of reaching the old case by modifying the most recent ones. In other words, how much of past cases need to be considered without worrying about reinventing some *really old* cases?

Although a number of CBR applications tend to represent and treat the structured information, it may be worthwhile to establish the goodness of the model chosen for representation of the features? Will the unstructured information left out from consideration for the purposes of either similarity calculation or indexing contribute to some false negatives and, if so, what impact is it likely to have on the application?

Another research issue might be to examine how the different clustering techniques would help in deciding which problem cases should become the new cases.

6.2.   CASE INDEXING

Indexing allows the cases to be retrieved selectively, quickly, and accurately. Identifying the relevant features to be indexed is not trivial, especially for indexes that are not just surface or shallow features. Retrieving the correct or relevant case is crucial to the success of CBR to solve new problems. Once cases are represented and indexed, they need to be stored and organized in an efficient structure for fast and accurate retrieval. Memory may be organized as a simple list, or a discrimination or dependency graph in order to reduce the search effort, and the most efficient retrieval algorithm determined. Another problem is the uncontrolled growth of the case base. How do we determine which cases to store, and which are to be weeded out? Essentially, what makes a "good" case? Currently, maintaining the case library is carried out manually, with a case-base administrator browsing through each case and deciding whether to keep it or remove it. While there are simple procedures (such as time-stamping) to assist the administrator, it is still a time-consuming process, especially with thousands of cases in the library.

6.3.   CASE ADAPTATION AND LEARNING

A CBR system learns through adaptation, i.e., modifying a retrieved case (that partially matches the current problem) to solve the new problem. This means that over time, new cases are acquired, and the system's problem-solving performance should improve as it "learns." Learning may be from positive examples given by the domain expert, or from its own success (or even from its failure) in achieving the problem-solving goal. However, adaptation formulas are not always easy to define, even by a domain expert. How does the case-based reasoner know what to adapt, and when? Can adaptation rules that are sufficiently generic (for all situations) be built such that the case-based reasoner is able to detect the differences between the new and retrieved case, decide what needs to be adapted, and determine which adaptation strategy to choose (from several appropriate strategies) and project the likelihood of succeeding?

In summary, some of the open issues and research challenges are in the areas of case representation, similarity matching, selecting indices and generating new indices dynamically, case library organization (as new cases are encountered and entered into the library), as well as mixing CBR with other paradigms to build hybrid systems (see Section 7).

7.   EMERGING HYBRID SYSTEMS

CBR hybrid systems capitalize on the inherent strengths of the other reasoning paradigms to counter the weaknesses in CBR, and complement its strengths. The most common combination attempted at this point in time is combining rule-based reasoning (RBR) with CBR, and model-based reasoning with CBR.

7.1.   CBR AND RULE-BASED REASONING (RBR)

Rules of the form IF-THEN-ELSE cover a single aspect of knowledge, whereas a case covers a particular problem-solving situation. It is sometimes difficult for a domain expert to come up with rules to problem-solving, whereas cases are actually examples of a particular situation. Hence, in general, acquiring cases are easier than rules.

RBR has some inherent weaknesses:

- Past experiences are not "learned"
- New, novel problems that deviate from the norm cannot be solved (because no rules are applicable)
- Maintaining a large rule base is difficult and time-consuming

Wrong information in rules must be individually edited, and every time a new rule is added, there is the risk of redundancy or contradiction. Deleting a rule may interrupt the reasoning process, whereas removing an individual case does not have the same extent of consequence. Hence, RBR systems are more difficult to maintain, and more difficult to update to keep up with rapidly changing domains.

Thus, most hybrid systems have a combination of rules and cases, and may be according to whether rules and cases are independent, or whether one was derived from the other (i.e., derive cases from rules, or rules from a set of sample cases). Rules may be used to capture broad trends in the domain, while cases are used to support exceptions to the rules or violations to rules. Cases may be kept as positive examples to support, explain, or justify rules; or as counter-examples to rules; or when rules fail because they are ill-defined. However, there are problems integrating cases and rules, and these have to do with control — which mode of reasoning to use, and when. As yet, there is still a lack of cognitive models of how human experts integrate rules and cases.

7.2. CBR AND INFORMATION RETRIEVAL

An AAAI symposium was organized in the spring of 1993 at Stanford University to see how CBR can benefit from the experiences of the Information Retrieval (IR) community. While there were interesting discussions on what may be useful for CBR to adapt from the IR research, no conclusions were reached.

IR researchers have development indexing mechanisms that can successfully manage the storage and retrieval of a large number of documents, where the documents can be of any size and are normally considered to be unstructured data. They have considerable experience in defining similarity measures across several features and have also been good at identifying relevance feedback methods for modifying search results. These are areas that CBR can adopt from IR and adapt to fit its own requirements. What CBR needs in addition is the need to store structured data, methods for modifying a retrieved case, and the need to know when a new problem case should be documented as a new case and not as a minor adaptation of an old case. These are areas where the research results and the application development experience from the IR community cannot help the CBR application.

7.3. CBR IN THE CASE OF MULTIPLE MEDIA

An interesting application development framework that CBR might consider for adoption is the one used in the treatment of multimedia (image + text + structured data) applications such as CAFIIR (Wu, 1997). The concept of iconic indexing used in the development of CAFIIR resembles very closely to the needs of the CBR for maintaining cases and subcases. CAFIIR stands for Computer Assisted Face Identification and Information Retrieval system. It is primarily a mug-shot system that is used to retrieve from a composite of a suspect's face and then search a database using the composed face and other descriptions of the suspect and crime. The system has several features for input. Some of the features are derived from the image input and take on continuous values. Some other features are structured data about the suspect (such as height, weight, color of the eyes, hairstyle, etc.) and/or information from the scene of the crime, such as the type of tool used in the assault, etc. Other features are unstructured description about the scene of the crime and witness descriptions.

Iconic indexing uses the concept of subgroupings at different levels where each level corresponds to a feature. Subgroups in each level store pointers to the cases (or objects) that have similar values for that feature. There is also a candidate chosen to represent that group and such a prototypical candidate would have its feature value equicentric to all other cases in that subgroup.

Iconic indexing uses an icon to visually represent the prototypical candidate for each subgroup. The index tree starts with the most important feature and unfolds into successive layers of less important features. The index is built to handle very large collections and the scheme allows navigation from the root of the index tree to the different features, one feature at a time, as well as across different subgroups corresponding to a feature. See Figure 3, an iconic index in CAFIIR.

Where possible, the subgroups can be organized according to semantics. In other cases, it is possible to organize the subgroups according to some arbitrary criteria such as balanced distribution of cases across the subgroups or organizing the subgroups around the modes in the distribution of values for that feature.

Unstructured information is dealt with using traditional IR techniques. The results from these two are combined to present a consolidated rank list of cases in response to search for cases similar to the problem case.

7.4. CBR AND MODEL-BASED REASONING

Model-based reasoning emphasizes the use of large chunks of general knowledge, based on models that cover the normative situations. Model-based reasoning is usually used for well-understood domains that can be accurately represented in a formal language, and which tends to be static. Hence, building a model is time-consuming, and so is maintaining it. In combining model-based reasoning with CBR, the model-based reasoning handles the well-understood components, while the CBR component covers aspects of the domain that are "weak theory." In addition, by incorporating domain knowledge into the CBR system, it may also address the research challenges of case library organization (for more efficient search and retrieval) and case adaptation.

8. CONCLUSION

Case-Based Reasoning (CBR) has come a long way from a laboratory model to a methodology supported by commercial products. There is no doubt that CBR is becoming increasingly important, judging from the number of conferences and workshops focusing on CBR, CBR research papers being published in Europe and the U.S., the number of World Wide Web pages on CBR, and the CBR mailing lists (e.g., CBR-Newsletter, AI-CBR and CBR-MED).

One future challenge lies in the realm of CBR tools, which are currently inadequate for real-world applications. Better tools are needed for representing cases, indexing, designing and building case-based systems, adaptation, and integration with other reasoning paradigms and technologies (such as multimedia, information retrieval, databases, etc.). Methodologies for building and validating case-based systems, maintaining the case library, and for collecting cases are needed as currently, CBR systems are built in an ad-hoc manner, which is very much dependent on the application domain and the common-sense experience of the knowledge engineer. As CBR systems become part of an organization's information and decision-support system, the case libraries will becoming the "organizational memories" of the organization, capturing the experiences of its human resource. "It is the sum of everything everybody in your organization knows that gives you the competitive edge" (Fortune Magazine, July 1992). Protocols are then needed for organizational and control issues in a distributed system, such as, who can update the case library and how is it to be managed?

The case studies presented in this section highlight the exploitation of CBR in real situations and the resulting benefits. Widespread use of CBR will take place when CBR is able to leverage concepts and technologies from related disciplines. Database technologies can help in building

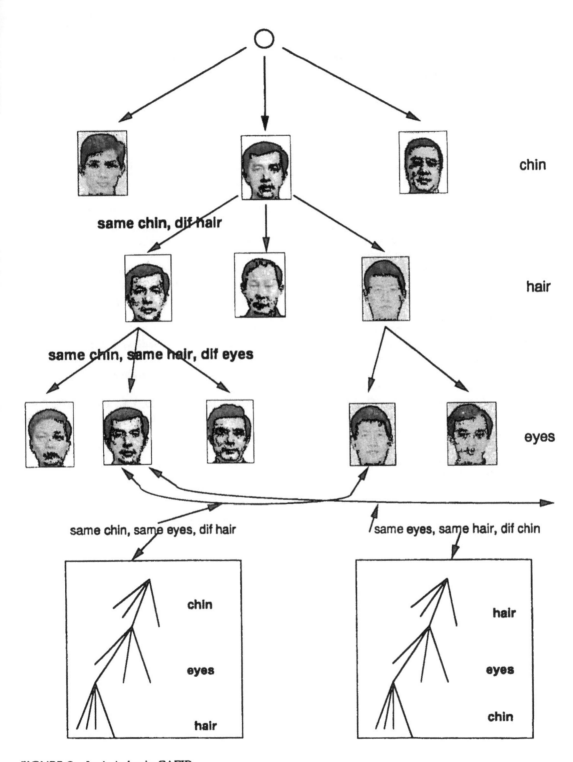

FIGURE 3 Ionic index in CAFIR.

larger case bases. Information retrieval technologies can help in the handling of unstructured information in the cases. Content-based retrieval can help broaden CBR's deployment to include multimedia applications. We have outlined several interesting research directions that are worth pursuing. We do hope that these suggestions will spur further research and development activities in making CBR a multimodal, robust, and scalable technology.

REFERENCES

Acorn, T. and Walden, S. (1992). SMART: Support management cultivated reasoning technology for Compaq customer service. In *Proceedings of AAAI92*. Cambridge, MA: AAAI Press/MIT Press.

Althoff, K.D., Auriol, E., Barletta, R., and Manago, M. (1996). A Review of Industrial Case-based Reasoning Tools. An AI Perspectives Report. Series Editor: Alex Goodall.

Ashley, K.D. and Rissland, E.L. (1988). Waiting on Weighting: A Symbolic Least Committment Approach". In *Proceedings of the Seventh National Conference on Artificial Intelligence*, pp. 239–244.

Bareiss, E., Porter, B., and Wier, C. (1988). PROTOS: An Exemplar-based Learning Apprentice. *International Journal of Man-Machine Studies*, 29: 549–561.

Hammond, K. (1986). A model of case-based planning. In *Proceedings of the Fifth National Conference on Artificial Intelligence*, 65–95. Menlo Park, Calif.: American Associan for Artificial Intelligence.

Kolodner, J.L. (1983). Maintaining Organization in a Dynamic Long-term memory. *Cognitive Science*, 7(4): 243–280.

Kolodner, J.L. (1993). *Case-based Reasoning*. San Mateo, CA: Morgan Kaufmann (1993).

Koton, P. (1988). Reasoning about Evidence in Causal Explanantions. In *Proceedings of the National Conference on Artificial Intelligence*, pp. 256–261.

Nguyen, T., Czerwinski, M., and Lee, D. (1993). Compaq QUICKSOURCE: Providing the Consumer with the power of AI. *AI Magazine*, Fall 1993, pp. 50–60.

Ong, L.S., Shepherd, S., Tong, L.C., Seow-Choen, F., Ho, Y. H., Tang, C.L., Ho, Y.S., and Tan, K. (1997). The Colorectal Cancer Recurrence Support (CARES) System, *Artificial Intelligence in Medicine Journal*, Elsevier, April 1997.

Schank, R. (Ed.) (1982). *Dynamic Memory: A Theory of Learning in Computers and People*. New York: Cambridge University Press.

Simpson, R.L. (1985). A computer model of case-based reasoning in problem solving: An investigation in the domain of dispute mediation. Ph.D. thesis, School of Information and Computer Science, Georgia Institute of Technology.

Wu, J.K. (1997) Content-based Indexing of Multimedia Databases, *IEEE Trans. Knowledge and Data Engineering*. (to be published).

12 Genetic Algorithms

George Hluck

CONTENTS

1. INTRODUCTION

Genetic algorithms solve problems using the Darwinian concept of evolution. They were first described by John Holland in the 1970s (Holland, 1975). We can apply genetic algorithms, or GAs, when we are not quite sure how to solve a problem that has a very large search space. GAs are best used to find nonlinear solutions where there does not exist any previously developed mathematical or heuristic approach.

In many fields, and especially in artificial intelligence, practitioners often combine various techniques in order to take advantage of the best characteristics of each technique. Most of these systems are known as hybrid systems. There are many examples of hybrid systems. Typically, you can find implementations that combine techniques. These implementations include:

- Using neural networks to adjust the parameters in a fuzzy expert system.
- Extracting symbolic information from a neural network to use in a rule-based system.
- Using genetic algorithms to create more efficient and compact neural networks. A popular approach is for a genetic algorithm to prepare a problem for genotype by a neural network. There are also implementations that use a neural network to support a genetic algorithm.
- Using genetic algorithms to tune the parameters of a fuzzy control system.
- Using case-based reasoning to supplement the problem-solving capabilities of an expert system.

The artificial intelligence field is not replete with examples that use genetic algorithms combined with expert system technology. In this chapter several applications that successfully combined the two approaches, and also discuss in general how someone can use the two technologies to create a successful system.

GAs have been used in a variety of real-world applications. They have been implemented in the areas of:

- Design
- Scheduling
- Configuration
- Financial portfolio management
- Adaptive control systems
- Noisy data interpretation

2.   BACKGROUND

There exist various approaches to problem-solving that follow some type of biological paradigm. In computer science, and especially artificial intelligence, a family of problem-solving techniques has grown and become popular. These techniques emulate Darwinian evolution by following the *only the strongest survive strategy*. Genetic algorithms, along with several other strategies, fall into this category. The following tree in Figure 1 illustrates the relationships (Schwefel, 1994).

Although the terminology is similar, the evolutionary computational techniques differ in unique ways. Evolutionary Computing, also known as Evolutionary Algorithms, is a term that encompasses the entire range of problem-solving systems which use evolution as the key implementation mechanism. GAs use chromosomes, or genotypes, of fixed length that encode the genetic constitution of an organism. Another term frequently encountered when discussing GAs is phenotype, which is used to refer to the physical appearance of an organism. Each chromosome represents a solution that is tested for fitness, with better solutions passing their genes to subsequent generations. Genetic programming is similar to GAs, but differs in the fact that the genotypes are executable code. Genetic programming is normally done in LISP to take advantage of its symbolic nature, but there are implementations that use pointers in C/C++. Evolutionary Strategies (ES) and Evolutionary Programming (EP) are very similar. ES depend on mutation and recombination and use real valued parameters. EP uses only mutation to evolve a population; it emphasizes the link between parent and offspring. EP also follows a top-down approach, as opposed to the bottom-up approach of GAs. Successful evolution using EP depends on the expressed behavior of an object, while in GAs it depends on the individual genes. Classifier systems generally start with no prior knowledge and learn a program by induction from a randomly generated population.

GAs, along with other aforementioned paradigms, solve problems by emulating evolutionary concepts. A population of possible genotypes (genetic constitution of an organism) is created,

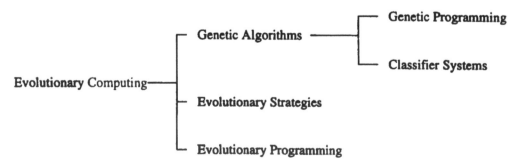

FIGURE 1   Evolutionary computing.

evaluated, recombined, and mutated to generate more and different genotypes. The best are kept as a basis for evolving better genotypes. The general steps to applying GAs are as follows:

1. Start creating an initial population of possible genotypes.
2. Evaluate each genotype by applying a fitness function.
3. Select the more promising genotypes.
4. Search for new genotypes by exchanging genetic material.
5. Check for a terminating condition. If the terminating condition has not been reached, return to step 2.

We can solve a problem using genetic algorithms by first generating a population of possible genotypes. We then apply a fitness function that assigns a fitness value to each genotype. Computing fitness is usually the most time-consuming portion of the algorithm, since the fitness is calculated for each individual in the population. The population is then recombined, with the number of each genotype increasing proportionally to its fitness. In other words, if a genotype is twice as good as another genotype, then there now would be approximately twice as many good genotypes as these other genotypes now in the population. Next, the best genotypes, paired off like parents, are combined in a manner that hopefully passes along the best genes of each genotype to the new child genotype. The fitness function is again applied and the cycle continues until a certain number of trials have been reached or a measured fitness equals some goal. The biological parallel is obvious. Parent genotypes combine to pass their best genes to their children, which hopefully have retained the best characteristics of their parents. Mutation, where a small percentage of genes are switched to help generate different genotypes, also can be used. The following sections describe these steps in detail.

2.1. INITIALIZATION

First, one must decide on the best way to encode possible solutions. Each encoding is known as a chromosome or genotype, which consists of a number of genes. Typically, a binary coding is used to create a genotype, with 1 indicating the presence of an gene and 0 indicating absence. These genes are then concatenated to form a chromosome of fixed length n, where n is the number of genes. Binary encoding is normally used; however, there are cases where a real number may be appropriate. For an example, refer to Table 1.

In Table 1, each car has certain genes. In the transmission column, 0 indicates a manual transmission, while 1 indicates an automatic transmission. In the drive column, 0 indicates 2-wheel drive, while 1 indicates 4-wheel drive. In the passenger column, 0 indicates two passengers, and 1 indicates four passengers. So, the *Car 1* chromosome would be encoded as *010*, while the *Car 2* chromosome would be encoded as *101*. Thus, a population of two has just been generated. GAs are not limited to binary encoding. Real numbers or string values can also be used, as well as variable-length chromosomes. However, GAs traditionally use fixed-length encodings. The population size should be relatively small while in testing phases (<500 genotypes). Once the system

TABLE 1
Encoding Example

Car	Transmission	Drive	Passengers
Car 1	0	1	0
Car 2	1	0	1

matures, the population should expand as much as possible, constrained by computer resources and time. The bigger the population, the better chance that the GA will find a close-to-optimal solution.

The initial population should be diverse, since these genotypes will be combined to create new solutions that did not previously exist in the population. One of the advantages of GAs is that they can investigate new solutions that humans don't have the time to think about or generate. The initial population can be generated randomly. A better starting point for GAs, though, would be to heuristically generate an initial population. The better the starting point, the more quickly GAs can converge or find a good solution. The remaining steps attempt to improve on the overall quality of the population.

2.2.   EVALUATION

The purpose of this step is to evaluate the fitness of all the genotypes in the population. This step is typically the most difficult and computationally costly, since the fitness function must be applied to each member of the population. Depending on the domain, it is also sometimes difficult to create an effective fitness function. One alternative is to partially compute the fitness, and require the user to finish evaluating potentially promising genotypes. This might prove useful for those situations where the fitness function cannot be explicitly encoded, and requires human input for accurate evaluation.

Fitness functions should be able to evaluate both the valid and invalid genotypes in the population. An invalid genotype is a solution that is not feasible or applicable for the problem. The fitness function should evaluate these invalid genotypes since they may still contain good genetic material. If your fitness function automatically discards those genotypes, then that combination of genes will be lost.

Plotting all possible genotypes and their evaluated fitness produces a fitness landscape, an n-dimensional region that contains all possible solutions. The peaks and valleys of this landscape indicate the maxima or minima that the GA is searching for.

In the car example, an example fitness function could be the decimal equivalent of the chromosome, i.e., the genotype encoded as *101* would be evaluated to have a fitness of *5*. This is a trivial fitness function, and an actual implementation of a GA would certainly use a more realistic function. The result of this step is a population ordered by fitness. The determination can then be made on which genotypes will survive to the next generation, simulating the evolutionary paradigm.

2.3.   SELECTION

In this step, selected members in the population reproduce and exchange genetic material. Generally, the low fitness genotypes are culled and the best are rewarded. The genotypes with better fitness can expand to take up a larger percentage of the population, while those genotypes with poor fitness will decrease in numbers. There are a variety of selection operators that can be applied:

1. Tournament selection. This is one of the more popular selection operators. In tournament selection, genotypes are randomly paired. The individual with the higher fitness "wins" and survives to the next generation. The lower fitness individual is discarded. Variations of tournament selection include grouping n-number of genotypes to compete for survival.
2. Roulette wheel selection. In roulette wheel selection, genotypes can expand proportionately into the next generation according to their fitness. Those with a higher fitness take up a proportionately larger section of the next generation's population.
3. Elite selection. In elite selection, the genotypes are rank ordered according to their fitness. The bottom half of the ranking is culled, and the remaining doubled, leaving the best for the next generation.

The selection operators are not limited to those explained, as there are many variations that can exist for particular domains.

2.4. SEARCH

Now that the population has adjusted itself to take advantage of the higher fitness genotypes, search operators are used to recombine or create new genotypes. The two most popular are crossover and mutation. Crossover exchanges genetic material between genotypes, and mutation injects random changes to selected genes.

2.4.1. Crossover

The crossover operation allows genotypes to exchange genes. Crossover is not essential for success, but it does allow genotypes to essentially exchange genetic information. Figure 2 illustrates a crossover operation of length 2 acting on two genotypes of length 5. In this case, the two genotypes exchange their tails (the last two positions, hence a crossover of 2), resulting in two new and different genotypes. Crossover will not always create a new genotype that was not present in the current population, but it does allow the exchange of genes.

The crossover operation is not limited to the one explained here. Different types of problem-specific crossover operations have been implemented.

2.4.2. Mutation

Mutation is used to inject an element of diversity into the population of genotypes. A GA that uses mutation will randomly select a genotype, and, within that genotype, randomly select a gene to mutate. If the genotype is using binary encoding, then the selected gene is complemented. If real numbers are used, then a number is selected at random within the range used to replace the mutated gene. This operation is done probabilistically at a very low rate. Typical mutation rates are low, in the range of less than 6%. This element of randomness will hopefully create new genotypes that may prove to be of better fitness than what is currently in the population. A good strategy to follow is to keep the mutation rate low in the earlier trials. As the GA settles in a particular region and does not seem to progress, the mutation rate can be increased to perhaps enable the GA to jump out of the local minima. Mutation is not necessary for a GA; however, it may prove to be of value if the GA is trapped in a local maxima.

Referring to Figure 3, one could inject mutation by taking one of the genotypes in the population, such as *11010*, and mutate it to *11110*. Now a new genotype is added to the population that may prove to be of better fitness. Be careful with increasing the mutation rate. Too high an increase will create genotypes that jump all around the fitness landscape and the GA will not converge.

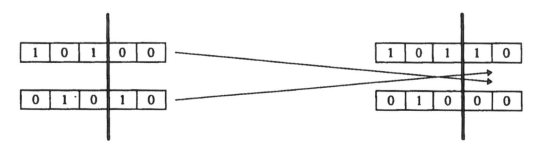

FIGURE 2   Crossover operation.

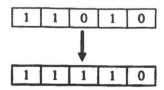

FIGURE 3   Mutation.

Typically, binary encoding is used for genotype creation. An alternate method is to use Gray Codes, an encoding scheme that differs from binary encoding in that only one position is changed when enumerating. Some GAs use Gray Codes because only one position is switched when moving from one number to the next to lessen the effect of mutation. Table 2 illustrates the differences between the two encoding schemes. This is not always the case for binary encoding (e.g., moving from 1 to 2 entails changing two positions). The effects of mutation can be multiplied depending on which gene is complemented. For example, moving from decimal *3* (binary *011*) to decimal *4* (binary *100*) requires complementing every bit position. This can make it more difficult for mutation to help move a near optimal solution to the optimal solution. There is a trade-off, though. In Gray Codes, fewer mutations lead to much larger jumps. For example, changing the left-most bit in decimal *7* (Gray *100*) results in decimal *0* (Gray *000*). Some might see this as an advantage, since most mutations will cause small changes, and some mutations will induce larger changes or jumps to explore new regions.

A GA's performance can be highly domain specific. Do not be afraid to try different combinations of the selection operators described here. Many times, experience will be the best guide for a successful implementation.

2.5.   TERMINATION

GAs will continually evolve until some terminating condition is reached. Some typical terminating conditions include:

- Temporal. Run the GA for a certain amount of time.
- Objective. Run the GA until some fitness value is reached.
- Delta. Run the GA until no difference is detected between the best evaluated fitness of each generation.

TABLE 2
Gray Codes

Decimal	Binary code	Gray code
0	000	000
1	001	001
2	010	011
3	011	010
4	100	110
5	101	111
6	110	101
7	111	100

If using the delta terminating condition, a good strategy is to increase the mutation rate once the GA stops. Hopefully this will move some genotypes into previously unexplored regions of the problem space.

2.6. VARIATIONS

GAs usually converge to a single genotype, or solution. There are times when it might be necessary to find either several or all the optimal solutions for a problem. Methods that prevent a GA from converging to a single solution are known as niching methods. Niching methods reduce competition between genotypes where there is sufficient difference, thus allowing subpopulations to exist. Each of these subpopulations occupy one section of the entire search space. Within each subpopulation, the genotypes would hopefully evolve to the local maximum. If each subpopulation successfully evolved, then multiple maximums could be found, as opposed to one single optimal solution. Niching can also be used to prevent premature convergence even when a single solution is desired.

There are two classes of niching methods: crowding and sharing. Crowding methods restrict individual replacement to reduce competition between genotypes that greatly differ within a niche. When a new genotype is introduced into the population, it replaces an individual who most resembles it. Sharing methods reduce a genotype's fitness when similar genotypes exist within a particular niche. Using the sharing method incurs an additional computational cost, since genotypes must be compared to each other.

There exist iterative techniques where the same population is run several times, or subpopulations run with communication between them, in the hope that different solutions could be discovered. This usually does not happen. Beasley addressed this problem by using derating functions. Derating functions vary the fitness function between runs so that the same search space is not explored. The difficulty lies in knowing when all the solutions have been found so that the runs may be terminated.

Another variation of GAs is to implement them in parallel. Large and complex problems usually require bigger populations and costly fitness evaluations. Partitioning the computational load across n-number of processors would reduce overall processing time. Typically, each subpopulation or each individual genotype can be separately processed in parallel. Parallel GAs can be classified into four categories: global parallelization, coarse- and fine-grained algorithms, and hybrid approaches (Cantu-Paz, 1995). Global parallelized GAs are relatively easy to implement. In global parallelization, genotype evaluation and selection operator application are accomplished in parallel. Coarse-grained parallel GAs divide the population into isolated subpopulations and use a migration operator to exchange individuals between subpopulations. Fine-grained parallel GAs divide the populations even smaller, using a large parallel system to process each tiny population. Finally, the hybrid approach uses a combination of the first three. It seems that parallelization is not a difficult task; however, studies are needed to focus on the particular aspects of these systems (Cantu-Paz, 1995).

Genetic algorithms are described as weak methods. These algorithms do not need to know anything about the problem domain to generate solutions. They can easily be applied to a variety of problems. Weak methods, though, rarely find the optimal solution to a problem. GAs are not guaranteed to find the optimal solution in a given problem. They do, however, find a good solution in the time allotted. Given enough time, they could find an optimal solution, but then so could more traditional methods. And, we rarely have that much time to allocate for problem-solving.

3. TECHNIQUES AND APPLICATIONS

GAs can be used in unison with expert systems. Most hybrid systems combine other AI techniques. Two basic ways to use GAs and expert systems together is to either:

- Use the expert system to generate a number of coarse solutions for the GA to use as an initial population, or
- Use the GA to generate the parameters that could be used as confidence factors or to fine-tune the rules in an expert system.

Attitude Determination. Recent work has been done in the area of attitude determination using the global positioning system (GPS). This approach uses an adaptive scheme that employs a fuzzy expert system to improve a Kalman filter's performance (Ghisleni and Marradi, 1996). GAs are used in this approach to design the membership functions of the fuzzy rules. So far, this system has provided good results in comparison to traditional approaches.

Production Planning. Researchers have applied GAs and expert systems using the first approach (Hamada, Baba, Sato, and Yufu, 1995). Their problem involved creating the best schedule for steelmaking processes. They created a system that greatly reduced the workload of the human operators and produced efficient schedules. Their approach was to divide the problem into sub-problems, and developed optimization software that consists of:

- A procedural approach
- An object-oriented, rule-based system
- A GA developer's kit

The scheduling problem consisted of how to create the most efficient charge (pot of molten steel) groups. There are numerous constraints that the scheduler must follow to use the furnaces most efficiently. For example, some charges could not follow others due to temperature changes. The group used a procedural method to create the charge groups, an expert system to generate coarse schedules, and a GA to optimize the coarse solutions into the best solution (Hamada et al., 1995, p. 65). They compared their schedules with manmade schedules, and found that the GA generated schedules were superior in quality and took less time to prepare.

A schedule is created by first using the procedural approach to form charge groups, taking into account constraints and costs. The expert system then orders the charge groups as best as possible to meet production constraints. The researchers could not extract enough knowledge from the human operators to create rules that could generate a good schedule (Hamada et al., 1995, p. 65).

The GA in this case uses chromosomes (genotypes) that consist of three blocks, with each block representing a category. Each block is a sequence of charge groups belonging to one of these categories. Decoding the chromosome results in a schedule. Both crossover and mutation operators are used here. The roulette-wheel selection operator is used to perform crossover, and is implemented in such a way so that invalid schedules are avoided. The mutation operator uses two operations: the first switches two genes at random, and the second selects a random gene and inserts it into another position (Hamada et al., 1995, p. 65).

Controller Design. GAs have also been used to find the optimal design for a fuzzy logic controller (Kim and Zeigler, 1996). In this case, the fuzzy logic controller is a working prototype of a plant for producing oxygen from a Martian atmosphere. They developed Hierarchical Distributed Genetic Algorithms (HDGA), which supports a multiresolutional search paradigm that finds a design that can satisfy stringent operational specifications. HDGA can dynamically create clusters that are used for problem-solving. In this case, HDGA optimizes the fuzzy rules used by the controller by manipulating their membership functions. Optimization resulted in a fuzzy controller design that maintained an error rate of ±2%, comfortably under the maximum tolerance of ±5% (Kim et al., 1996).

HDGA consists of multilevel clusters; each cluster consists of a controller and agents that solve an abstracted version of the given problem (Kim et al., 1996, p. 77). The controller, not to be confused with the fuzzy logic controller, is a small expert system that controls execution of the agent GAs. This expert system makes decisions based on the information gathered by the agent GAs. HDGA uses a binary encoding scheme for the chromosomes, and has the ability to vary search resolutions.

Rule Induction. Another use of GAs that is somewhat related to rule-based systems is applying GAs to extract or symbolically learn rules or patterns from data. Symbolic learning is a supervised learning paradigm that can derive rules from data. Unfortunately, experience has shown that even to extract a small number of rules without applying any other heuristic strategies results in lengthy evolution times. The evolution times required to derive a small number of rules (less than six) from even small data sets (several hundred records) can typically be hours (Al-Attar, 1994).

Symbolic learning extracts rules from data in the form of a classification tree. The nodes of the tree consist of attributes extracted from the data set. The leaves of the tree nodes are the possible outcomes. The basic concept behind the GA approach is to evolve these trees, with each gene representing a node in a classification tree. This approach was applied to loan data obtained from a bank (Al-Attar, 1994, p. 37), 430 data records were available. Both the traditional algorithm, known as ID3, and the GA hybrid were run on the same data. ID3-type algorithms build classification trees from data using entropy as a heuristic measure and use heuristic tree-pruning to prevent the tree from growing too large. Table 3 summarizes the results.

The GA hybrid approach for extracting rules from data shows some improvement over the traditional approach.

It was mentioned in the beginning of this section that there are basically two ways to combine GAs and expert systems into one system. The first approach uses the expert system to create or generate initial solutions, taking advantage of any domain knowledge. Remember that GAs are weak methods; no knowledge of the problem is required. You can increase the chances of success of finding a satisfactory solution by using what domain knowledge you have to generate the initial population of genotypes for the GA. Typically, a starting point is created by random population generation. A much better starting point is a population where some domain knowledge was used to create at least some feasible solutions. Unless you check, generating a random population of solutions does not guarantee that any of the starting points are good or even valid. It is also important to ensure that the fitness function used by the GA agrees with the derived initial population. In other words, you do not want to take the time to create an initial population that the fitness function evaluates as poor. For example, if I were trying to schedule a list of classes for students, and I was concerned about student satisfaction, then I could obtain knowledge about their class preferences (times preferred, etc.). I could then encode this knowledge into an expert system, and use the results as starting points for the GA to optimize. This can only be taken so far, since too many constraints could be generated when collecting this knowledge (e.g., nobody wants to take a morning class). Note that you are not constraining the solution space with the derived initial population. There is nothing to stop the GA from exploring the entire search space, especially if the fitness function evaluates other solutions as much better. With the derived initial population, you are hopefully providing a good starting point.

TABLE 3
ID3 and GA Comparison

Approach	# of rules extracted	# of attributes extracted	Classification accuracy
ID3	5	3	73%
GA hybrid	11	6	78%

Another approach to combining the two technologies is to use GAs and expert systems to refine parameters such as certainty factors for rules or membership functions for fuzzy expert systems. This approach was used in one of the previously mentioned applications (Ghisleni et al., 1996). The greatest concern here is one of time. A basic approach is to set up the GA to generate a population of solutions, with each solution containing a set of parameters. These parameters are then tested by inserting them into the expert system, running the expert system, and checking the expert system's output. In this approach, the expert system is acting as a fitness function, since to find the best solution you must evaluate each one using the expert system. This, of course, can take much time and also leads to other considerations such as how many test cases do you use with the expert system. A similar approach can be used for fuzzy expert systems. With fuzzy systems, though, it is the membership functions that are being refined and not certainty factors. The fuzzy expert system is still being used as a fitness function. After evaluating the population, you then continue with the evolutionary procedure with selection, search, and eventual termination.

4. RESEARCH ISSUES

Using GAs and expert systems by themselves are well-established AI problem-solving techniques. Using them together, however, is not. GAs are computationally oriented, weak methods that do not need to know anything about the problem. Expert systems, on the other hand, are symbolically based with a structure that primarily depends on domain knowledge. Since expert system understanding is assumed of the reader, this section will primarily discuss GA research issues.

The section explained that GAs use an evolutionary approach for generating new solutions. All of us understand the basic Darwinian concept; however, there are variations in the biological world that can be simulated using GAs for possible improvements. Bacterial genetics provides one such world. Bacteria can transfer DNA to recipient cells through mating. The female recipient cells can then change to male cells, thus facilitating the transfer of the acquired DNA to the entire bacteria population. This approach has been implemented to find fuzzy rules for a semi-active suspension controller (Hashiyama, Furuhashi, and Uchikawa, 1995). There are possibly other variations in the biological world that can be mimicked in order to improve the effectiveness of GAs.

The knowledge representation issue is an important consideration in any type of AI implementation. In GAs, the traditional binary encoding can be replaced by other encodings depending on the problem domain. Gray codes were mentioned as one alternative. There presently exists numerous variations that were developed for a particular problem. Take, for example, the traditional traveling salesman problem. This problem can be solved using GAs. However, since each genotype in this case would represent a route between cities, it would be inefficient to have genotypes consisting of a sequence of numbered cities, since the crossover operation could create many invalid routes (duplication of cities, etc.). There are numerous ways to solve this representation problem. One generic implementation is to use random-key encoding. Each genotype would consist of a sequence of random numbers. To decode the genotype, the positioning of the genes would be decoded as the city number. For example, the genotype *6-1-4* would decode into the route *city 2* → *city 3* → *city 1*. It is up to the user's creativity to implement an encoding that would work best for their problem domain.

GAs are concerned with adaptive behavior of populations of genotypes. Taking that concept to the next level results in a GA whose overall structure can adapt to the problem. Not only are the genotypes evolving, but also the structural components of the GA: fitness function, selection operators, and the search operators. As the GA works through many generations, information could be gathered about the problem which can be used to focus the GA toward better solutions. This can be called co-evolution or multilevel evolution, and research has been done on such systems (Wang, Goodman, and Punch, 1995). This type of GA model holds many promises and requires more research to fully explore its potential.

5. FUTURE TRENDS AND SUMMARY

One of the major trends is the subject of this article: hybrid systems. Researchers are constantly exploring different methods of combining AI tools to solve problems. These efforts attempt to combine different systems to take advantage of the strengths of different tools. Ideally, the strengths of one of the combined tools makes up for the weaknesses of the other.

Exploring very large search spaces with GAs can be computationally taxing. The continual developments in computers and processing power allows researchers to tackle larger problems. Work is being done in the field of distributed or parallel GAs, which would take advantage of multiple platforms. Other research trends include explorations into multilevel evolution and finding the optimum parameter values for a given problem. Another theme that has been arising with increasing frequency is the inclusion of self-adapting mechanisms with GAs to control parameters involving the internal representation, mutation, recombination, and population size (DeJong, 1994).

There has been much work since John Holland's initial research of genetic algorithms. Twenty years of additional research have led to various ideas and implementations in an effort to take advantage of the concept of evolution in the computer science field. The next 20 years should be just as interesting, as greater numbers of researchers work in this field and the tools available to them increase in speed and efficiency.

REFERENCES

Al-Attar, A. (1994, September). A hybrid GA-heuristic search strategy. *AI Expert*.

Cantu-Paz, E. (1995, July). A Summary of Research on Parallel Genetic Algorithms. The Illinois Genetic Algorithms Laboratory (IlliGAL).

DeJong, K.A. (1994). Genetic algorithms: A 25 year perspective. In J.M. Zurada, R.J. Marks II and C.J. Robinson (Eds.), *Computational Intelligence Imitating Life*. IEEE Press.

Ghisleni, C. and Marradi, L. (1996, 2 December). Attitude Determination Using Global Positioning System (LABEN) [*Http://www.dcs.napier.ac.uk/evonet/news2/news2214.htm*]. EvoNet (10 February).

Hamada, K., Baba, T., Sato, K., and Yufu, M. (1995, October). Hybridizing a genetic algorithm with rule-based reasoning for production planning. *IEEE Expert*, 10(5).

Hashiyama, T., Furuhashi, T., and Uchikawa, Y. (1995). A study on finding rules for semi-active suspension controllers with genetic algorithm [*Http://www.bioele.nuee.nagoya-u.ac.jp/member/tom/papers/icec/*]. First Online Workshop on Evolutionary Computing (27 Aug).

Holland, J.H. (1975). *Adaptation in Natural and Artificial Systems*. University of Michigan Press.

Kim, J. and Zeigler, B.P. (1996, June). Hierarchical distributed genetic algorithms: A fuzzy logic controller design application. *IEEE Expert*.

Schwefel, H. (1994). On the evolution of evolutionary computation. In J.M. Zurada, R.J. Marks II and C.J. Robinson (Eds.), *Computational Intelligence Imitating Life*. IEEE Press.

Wang, G., Goodman, E.D., and Punch, I., William F. (1995). Simultaneous Multi-Level Evolution [WWW]. Genetic Algorithm Research and Applications Group (GARAGe), Department of Computer Science and Case Center for Computer-Aided Engineering & Manufacturing, Michigan State University.

13 Hybrid Systems: Fuzzy Neural Integration

I. Burhan Türkşen

CONTENTS

1. INTRODUCTION

In this chapter, hybrid system model developments are discussed with a perspective of fuzzy neural integration. In particular, a fuzzy system is a set of rules that maps inputs to outputs. The set of rules defines a many-to-many map $F: X \rightarrow Y$. The set consists of linguistic "IF ... THEN" rules in the form of "IF X isr A THEN Y isr B," where X and Y are input and output base variables, respectively, of a system, and A and B are corresponding fuzzy sets that contain the elements $x \in X$ and $y \in Y$ to some degree (Zadeh, 1965); that is:

$$A = \{(x, \mu_A(x)) \mid x \in X, \mu_A(x) \in [0,1]\} \text{ and } B = \{(y, \mu_B(y)) \mid y \in Y, \mu_B(y) \in [0,1]\}$$

and "isr" is a shorthand notation that may stand for "is contained in," "is a member of," "is compatible with," "belongs to," "is a possible member of ," etc., depending on the context (Zadeh, 1996).

Fuzzy rules represent our approximate knowledge extracted from a systems input-output analysis and identified by combinations of membership functions in the input-output space of XxY. They define information granules (Zadeh, 1996) or subsets of the state space. Less certain, more imprecise rules specify large information granules. More certain and more precise rules define smaller information granules. In practice, however, we do not know the exact shape of the information granules, i.e., the membership functions or the structure of the rules that connect the inputs to outputs of a system. Hence, we ask an expert or implement supervised or unsupervised learning techniques to find and/or modify fuzzy information granules as close as we can for a given system with the available expertise and/or sample data. In this context, supervised means that we have a target membership functions, whereas unsupervised means we do not have a target membership function. In the supervised learning, the aim is to minimize the error between the target and the initial membership functions. In the unsupervised learning, the aim is to determine the initial membership function that can be obtained from a given raw data set. The best learning schemes ideally provide a good coverage of the optimal information granules of a given system's hidden-inherent rules. In current literature it is found that most adaptive fuzzy system models are built without an adequate knowledge of the systems goals. Hence, these are unsupervised learning schemes. This often creates the exponential complexity associated with many learning schemes.

Learning schemes may be either unsupervised clustering techniques (Bazdek, 1981; Sugeno and Yasukawa, 1993; Nakanishi, Türkşen and Sugeno, 1993; Emani, Türkşen, and Goldenberg, 1996) or supervised gradient decent methods (Ishibuchi, Morioka, and Türkşen, 1995). Unsupervised learning is faster but it produces a first level of approximation in knowledge representation. Usually, a good sample data set is satisfactory for this purpose. Supervised learning requires more knowledge of a system and/or a large sample data set in order to compute a more accurate representation and often requires orders of magnitude more training cycles. Learning schemes utilized in most neural network investigations are generally supervised schemes. Hence, we have to deal with computational complexity and/or various approximation heuristics.

Fuzzy rule bases have a natural explanatory power embeded within their structure and semantics, i.e., in their meaning representation via fuzzy set membership functions; whereas, neural networks are black-box approximators and have all the advantages or disadvantages that come from them. Both fuzzy systems and neural networks do not admit proof of concepts in traditional senses. The feedforward version of neural networks provides more control but less power than their feedback versions. However, we cannot be sure of functions and patterns that were learned and represented by them until a large number of input-output test cases have been tried and they have been verified and validated. On the other hand, fuzzy rules are linguistic representations that can be tuned and modified more readily.

Neural networks provide a distributed connectionist structure and hence cannot be easily decoded, but they are useful to tune membership functions of fuzzy sets or provide distributed computational speed after appropriate learning. However, most neural nets forget part of their learning each time they learn new patterns. In general, patterns are usually modified and changed after learning. Fuzzy neural systems usually learn with the same laws that a neural network learns. Such systems are usually called "fuzzy-neural" systems. In this sense, "fuzzy-neural" system models are fuzzy system models that have been subject to some supervised learning in their development.

Let us next review briefly two essential components of a fuzzy expert system: (1) a knowledge base consisting of a set of linguistic rules, and (2) an inference engine that executes an approximate reasoning algorithm.

1.1.   KNOWLEDGE BASE

A linguistic rule "IF X isr A THEN Y isr B" of a fuzzy knowledge base may be interpreted as an information granule, depending on our knowledge of a system characteristics in at least three different ways as follows:

1. Interpolative Reasoning Perspective: It defines a Cartesian product A × B. This is a standard interpolation model (Zadeh, 1973; 1975; 1996) that is used most often in fuzzy control systems. At times, this is known as Mamdani's (1974) heuristic.
2. Generalized Modus Ponens Perspective: It defines an implication between A and B, i.e., A → B, depending on whether it is a strong implication S or a residual implication R (Zadeh, 1973; Demirli and Türkşen, 1994).

    The interpretations (1) and (2) are a "myopic" view of fuzzy theory known as Type I fuzzy theory. It is based on the reductionist view that the combination of two first-order fuzzy sets produces a fuzzy set of the first order; i.e., $\mu_A: X \to [0,1]$, $\mu_B: Y \to [0,1]$ such that for each interpretation stated above we have:

$\mu_{A \times B}: X \times Y \to [0,1]$ for case (1) above and, and $\mu_{A \to B}: X \times Y \to [0,1]$ for case (2) above

3. Type II Fuzzy Set Perspective: It is based on the realization that the combination of two first-order, i.e., Type I fuzzy sets, produce a fuzzy set of the second order, known as Type II (Türkşen, 1986; 1995; 1996) fuzzy sets; i.e., $\mu_A: X \to [0,1]$, $\mu_B: Y \to [0,1]$ such that $\mu_{A \to B}: X \times Y \to P[0,1]$ where $P[0,1]$ is the power set of $[0,1]$.

1.2   INFERENCE ENGINE

Now, from the perspective of approximate reasoning, each of the three interpretations stated above provides a different solution when faced with a new system observation A'(x). When a new sytem state is observed, say A'(x), with these three interpretations of knowledge representation, three different consequences may be obtained when we are interested in providing a decision support for system diagnosis or prediction or control. These are:

1. $\mu_B^*(y) = \bigvee_{x \in X} \mu_A'(x) T \mu_A(x) T \mu_B(y), \quad y \in Y;$

2. $\mu_B^*(y) = \bigvee_{x \in X} \mu_A'(x) T[\mu_{CNF(A \to B)}(x,y)], \quad y \in Y;$

3. $\mu_B^*(y) \in \left[\bigvee_{x \in X} \mu_A'(x) T[\mu_{PDNF(A \to B)}(x,y)], \bigvee_{x \in X} \mu_A'(x) T[\mu_{FCNF(A \to B)}(x,y)] \right], \quad y \in Y,$

where, $\mu_B^*(y)$, $\forall y \in Y$ is a consequence of an inference result that may be obtained for each of the three cases of approximate reasoning for a given rule: "IF $x \in X$ isr A, THEN $y \in Y$ isr B" and a given observation A'(x). The rule is interpreted in accordance with one of the three perspectives stated above. In the three inference schemes stated above, V is the maximum operator and T is a t-norm to be selected from an infinitely many possibilities of t-norms introduced by Schweitzer and Sklar (1983) where $\mu_A'(x)$, $x \in X$, is the observed membership value $\mu_A(x)$, $\mu_B(y) \in [0,1]$, $x \in X$, $y \in Y$ are membership values of input, and output variables, respectively. In addition, $\mu_A(x) T \mu_B(y)$ is the interpolation heuristic-based approximate knowledge representation, whereas $\mu_{CNF(A \to B)}(x,y)$ is the membership value of A → B, which is a direct and common use of the Boolean Conjunctive normal form, CNF, of implication. Hence, approximate reasoning with cases (1) and

(2) are dependent on the myopic view of knowledge representation in fuzzy set and logic theory. (Türkşen, 1986; 1995).

But, approximate reasoning with case (3) is based on nonreductionist interpretation, as stated above. It is worthwhile to emphasize that $\mu_{FDNF(A \to B)}(x,y)$ and $\mu_{FCNF(A \to B)}(x,y)$ are the boundaries of Type II "Interval-Valued" fuzzy set representation of our knowledge. It should be recalled that Fuzzy Disjunctive Normal Form, FDNF, of A → B and Fuzzy Conjunctive Normal Form, FCNF, of A → B represent bounds on the representation of membership values of A → B. This is because FDNF(•) ≠ FCNF(•) for all the combined concepts in fuzzy theory, whereas DNF(•) = CNF(•) in two-valued theory (Türkşen, 1986; 1995).

Since most of the current fuzzy expert systems are constructed either with case (1) or (2) representation and inference, in Section 3 of this chapter, we will present a unique knowledge representation and inference approach that unifies (1) and (2) interpretations of fuzzy knowledge representation and inference. Type II fuzzy knowledge representation and inference is not discussed in this chapter.

2. MEMBERSHIP FUNCTIONS

Since Zadeh (1965) introduced fuzzy sets, the main difficulties have been with the meaning and measurement of membership functions as well as their extraction, modification, and adaptation to dynamically changing conditions.

2.1. MEANING OF MEMBERSHIP

In particular, lack of a consensus on the meaning of membership functions has created some confusion. This confusion is neither bizarre nor unsound. However, this cloud of confusion has already been diffused with rigorous semantics and practical elicitation methods for membership functions (Bilgic and Türkoşen, 1996).

In general, there are various interpretations as to where fuzziness might arise from. Depending on the interpretation of fuzziness one subscribes to, the meaning attached to the membership function changes. It is the objective of this subsection to review very briefly the various interpretations of membership functions.

We first start with the formal (i.e., mathematical) definition of a membership function. A fuzzy (sub)set, say F, has a membership function μ_F, defined as a function from a well-defined universe (the referential set), X, into the unit interval as: $\mu_F: X \to [0,1]$ (Zadeh, 1965).

Thus, the vague predicate "temperature (x = 35°C) is high (H)" for a summer day is represented by a number in the unit interval, $\mu_H(x) \in [0,1]$. There are several possible answers to the question, "What does it mean to say $\mu_H(x) = 0.7$?":

Likelihood view: 70% of a given population declares that the temperature value of 35°C is high.

Random set view: 70% of a given population describes "high" to be in an interval containing the given temperture value, 35°C.

Similarity view: the given temperature value, 35°C, is away from the prototypical temperature value, say 45°C, which is considered truly "high" to the degree 0.3 (a normalized distance).

Utility view: 0.7 is the utility of asserting that the given temperature value, 35°C, is high.

Measurement view: When compared to other temperatures, the given temperature value, 35°C, is higher than some and this fact can be encoded as 0.7 on some scale.

It is important to realize that each of these interpretations is a hypotheses about where fuzziness arises from and each interpretation suggests a calculus for manipulating membership functions. The calculus of fuzzy sets as described by Zadeh (1965; 1973) and his followers is sometimes appropriate as the calculus of fuzziness but sometimes inappropriate, depending on the interpretation.

2.2. GRADE OF MEMBERSHIP

When someone is introduced to the fuzzy set theory, the concept of the grade of membership sounds fairly intuitive since this is just an extension of a well-known concept. That is, one extends the notion of membership in a set to "a grade of membership" in a set. However, this extension is quite a bit more demanding: "How can a grade of membership be measured?" This question has been considered in the context of many-valued sets by many people from different disciplines.

Although more than 2000 years ago, Aristotle commented on an "indeterminate membership value," the interest in formal aspects of many-valued sets started in early 1900s (McCall and Ajdukiewicz, 1967; Rosser and Turquette, 1977). But the meaning of multiple membership values has not been explained satisfactorily. For some, this is sufficient to discard many-valued sets altogether (Kneale, 1962; French, 1984). On the other hand, the intellectual curiosity never lets go of the subject (Scott, 1976).

Part of the confusion arises from the fact that in two-valued theory, both the membership assignments, i.e., {0,1}, to a set and the truth value assignments {F,T} to a proposition are taken to be the same without a loss of generality. But this creates a problem in infinite-valued theory. As explained recently (Türkşen, 1966), the graded membership assignments in a fuzzy set must be separated and distinguished from the truthood assignments given to a fuzzy proposition.

In general and in particular, anyone who is to use fuzzy sets must answer the following three questions:

1. What does graded membership mean?
2. How is it measured?
3. What operations are meaningful to perform on it?

To answer the first question, one has to subscribe to a certain view of fuzziness. Basically, there has been two trends in the interpretations of fuzziness: those who think that fuzziness is subjective as opposed to objective, and those who think that fuzziness stems from an individual's use of words in a language as opposed to a group of people's use of words (or individual sensor readings versus a group of sensor readings, etc.).

Both the likelihood and the random set views of the membership function implicitly assume that there is more than one evaluator or experiments are repeated. Therefore, if one thinks of membership functions as "meaning representation," one comes close to the claim that "meaning is essentially objective" and fuzziness arises from inconsistency or errors in measurement. On the other hand, during the initial phases of the development of fuzzy sets, it has been widely accepted that membership functions are subjective and context dependent (Zadeh, 1965; 1975). The similarity and utility views of the membership function differ from the others in their espousing a subjective interpretation. The measurement view is applicable to both the subjective and objective views in the sense that the problem can be defined in both ways, depending on the observer(s) who is (are) making the comparison. The comparisons can be results of subjective evaluations or results of "precise" (or idealized) measurements (Bilgic and Türkşen, 1996).

2.3. FUZZY CLUSTERING

An intuitive approach to objective rule generation is based upon fuzzy clustering of input-output data. One simple and applicable idea, especially for systems with large numbers of input variables, was suggested by Sugeno and Yasukawa (1993). In this approach, one first clusters only the output space, which can be always considered as a single-dimensional space in fuzzy models. The fuzzy partition of the input space is specified at the next step by generating the projection of the output clusters into each input variable space separately. Using this method, the rule generation step could be separated from the input selection step, as will be discussed later.

The idea of fuzzy clustering is to divide the output data into fuzzy clusters that overlap each other. Therefore, the assignment of each data point to each cluster is defined by a membership grade in [0,1]. Formally, clustering unlabeled data $X = \{x_1, x_2, ..., x_N\} \subset R^h$, where N is the number of data vectors and h is the dimension of each data vector, is the assignment of c number of cluster labels to the vectors in X. c-Clusters of X are sets with (c,N) membership values $\{u_{ik}\}$ that can be conveniently arranged as a (cxN) matrix $U = [u_{ik}]$. The problem of fuzzy clustering is to find the optimum membership matrix U for fuzzy clustering in X. The most widely used objective function is the weighted within-groups sum of squared errors function J_m, which is defined as the constrained optimization problem (Bezdek, 1981):

$$\min_{(u, v)} \left\{ J_m(U, V; X) = \sum_{k=1}^{N} \sum_{i=1}^{c} (u_{ik})^m \| x_k - v_i \|_A \right\}$$

where $0 \le u_{ik} \le 1, \ \forall i, k; \ \forall k, \exists i,$ such that $u_{ik} > 0; 0 < \sum_{k=1}^{N} u_{ik} < N, \forall i; \sum_{i=1}^{N} u_{ik} = 1, \forall k; \ V = \{v_1,$

$v_2, ..., v_c\}$ is the vector of (unknown) cluster centers, and $\| x \|_A = \sqrt{x^T A x}$ is any inner product norm.

A is a positive definite matrix that specifies the shape of the cluster. The common selection for the matrix A is the identity matrix, leading to the definition of Euclidean distance, and consequently to spherical clusters. There are, however, investigations where the matrix A is taken as the covariance matrix that generates models with elliptic clusters (Kosko, 1996).

In current literature, most fuzzy clustering studies are carried out by the Fuzzy C-Means (FCM) algorithm through an iterative optimization. However, there are three major difficulties with FCM clustering algorithm:

1. Number of clusters (c) should be assigned *a priori.*
2. No theoretical basis has been established for an optimal choice of weighting exponent "m."
3. Conditions of the FCM algorithm are only necessary conditions for local extrema of J_m.

That is, different choices of initial V_0 might lead to different local extrema. Therefore, it is desirable to modify the FCM algorithm.

2.4.   MODIFICATION OF FCM ALGORITHM

In order to complete the systematic methodology of fuzzy system identification and modeling, it is necessary to find generic solutions to the above problems. For this purpose, it is proposed that a theoretical basis be found for the first two problems. The proposed approach produces a more efficient strategy than the other solutions, as explained next.

First, in an attempt to derive a generic criterion for assignment of number of clusters from a theoretical point of view, it is proposed (Emami, Türkşen, and Goldenberg, 1996) that one perform a proper generalization of scatter criteria that are mainly applied as suitable tools for expressing the compactness and separation of the hard clusters (Duda and Hart, 1973). It should be noted that the total mean vector is not weighted in the Sugeno and Yasukawa (1993) index. We propose that the total mean vector, $\bar{v}$, be weighted with the membership values, u_{ik}. It turns out that the difference so generated is significant for large values of weighting exponent (m) in the FCM algorithm.

Secondly, weighting exponent controls the extent of membership sharing between fuzzy clusters in the data set. Therefore, for "m" in the range of $(1, \infty)$, the larger "m" generates large overlaps among fuzzy sets. To date, no theoretical basis for an optimal choice of "m" has been suggested. In order to identify the guideline for selection of "m," one should consider the behavior of cluster validity criterion, S, as m varies.

In principle, for a "reliable" performance of the cluster validity criterion, S, the weighting exponent m should be far from both of its limits, i.e., one and infinity (Emami, Türkşen, and Goldenberg, 1996).

Now, in order to satisfy this principle, the extremes of "m" should be clearly identified. The limit "one" is well defined, but the limit "infinity" for "m" depends on the data at hand. Let us define S_T, called fuzzy total scatter matrix, to be the index to indicate the behaviour of "m" as it varies from "one" to "infinity":

$$S_T = S_W + S_B = \sum_{k=1}^{N}\left[\sum_{i=1}^{c}(u_{ik})^m\right](x_k - \bar{v})(x_k - \bar{v})^T$$

It is observed (Emami, Türkşen, and Goldenberg, 1996) that the trace of S_T decreases monotionically from a constant value K to zero, as "m" varies from one to infinity, where K depends only on the data set:

$$K = \text{trace}\left(\sum_{k=1}^{N}\left[\left(x_k - \frac{1}{N}\sum_{k=1}^{N}x_k\right)\left(x_k - \frac{1}{N}\sum_{k=1}^{N}x_k\right)^T\right]\right)$$

Therefore, for a data set to be clustered in an "efficient" manner, a suitable value of "m" is that which gives a value of S_T in a region around K/2. A suitable value of "m" should be determined experimentally in this region around K/2 for different values of "c" that minimize S_T.

Third, FCM algorithm generally produce only local minima, as indicated above. Therefore, different initial guesses for cluster centers may lead to different optimum results. This fact affects the cluster validity as well as cluster analysis.

In order to efficiently obtain a preference for initial locations of cluster prototypes, one should start with an Agglomerative Hierarchical Clustering (AHC) algorithm as an introductory procedure to find a suitable guess for the initial locations of cluster prototypes for the FCM algorithm. Among the various AHC algorithms, a specific method to be suggested is Ward's method (1963).

The result of AHC is "c" hard clusters for the data, which is a good start for the fuzzy clustering procedure. By this method, one can choose the initial prototypes without any knowledge of the data *a priori*. This approach is much more efficient than random searches among different initial guesses.

Finally with the values of "m" and "c" that would be determined with the proposed developments discussed above, one would apply the well-known FCM algorithm in order to find the fuzzy clusters. This will be called the ETG, i.e., Emami, Türkşen, and Goldenberg, method of clustering.

It should be pointed out that in fuzzy modeling activities in general, the output sample data are assigned into several fuzzy clusters. In order to extend the assigned fuzzy clusters to the entire output space, one more step is required, known as the classification process. In most investigations, this step has not been addressed properly. In the clustering process, we make a suitable clustering for a sample data set $X \subset R^h$, whereas in the classification procedure, every data point in the entire space R^h is labeled. Therefore, the problem of membership function formation for the entire output space is a classification problem. Since classifier design is usually performed using labeled data, clustering the output sample data is a good tool to design the appropriate classifiers for the entire output space. A fuzzy version of the probabilistic classification method called K-nearest neighbor has been introduced by Keller et al. (1985).

In order to obtain simple membership functions, after the assignment of the data of the entire space to the fuzzy partition, one needs to approximate the classified data by trapezodial functions in such a way that, for each fuzzy cluster, convex points are picked up and a trapezoid is fitted to them (Sugeno and Yasukawa, 1993; Nakanishi, Türkşen, and Sugeno, 1993).

2.5.   INPUT SELECTION

The phase of input selection in fuzzy system identification is to find the most dominant input variables among a finite number of input candidates. A combinatorial approach is proposed by Sugeno and Yasukawa (1993) and implemented by Nakanishi, Türkşen, and Sugeno (1993), in which all combinations of input candidates are considered and the combinations of input variables that minimize a specific regularity criterion are selected. The main drawback of this approach is that for a system with a large number of input candidates, a large number of combinations must be considered.

This problem of the input selection may be resolved in a simpler and more efficient fashion. It is proposed that the input selection be directly related to the procedure of input membership functions construction. In the proposed approach, those input points that have membership grades close or equal to "one" in each cluster are assigned the same input membership grades, i.e., membership of "one."

Consequently, those input variables that do not have a dominant effect on the output, will have membership grades equal to "one" all across their domain. This is the result of the antecedent aggregation of the fuzzy rules that is performed by t-norm operators. Since "one" is the neutral element for these operators, the ineffective input candidates with membership grades of "one" in their entire range can be canceled from the fuzzy rules. Thus, the remaining variables become selected as input variables.

2.6.   FUZZIFIED NEURAL NETWORK

Fuzzy sets that are obtained with the fuzzy cluster analysis method discussed in the above sections can be modified and/or adapted to newer circumstances with a fuzzified neural network training. For this purpose, fuzzified neural networks are reviewed here briefly (Ishibuchi, Morioka, and Türkşen, 1995).

The inputs, weights, and biases of the standard feedforward neural network can be extended to fuzzy sets in a natural manner. In this chapter, the fuzzification of neural networks means just this extension. Therefore, the fuzzification does not change the neural network architecture. That is, the fuzzified neural network has the same network architecture as the standard neural network.

Let us denote fuzzy sets by uppercase letters, e.g., A, B, ..., and real numbers by lowercase letters, e.g., a, b, ..., respectively. Then the input-output relation of the fuzzified neural network can be written for a fuzzy input vector $F_p = (F_{p1}, F_{p2}, ..., F_{pn_1})$ as follows:

$$
\begin{array}{lll}
\text{Input units:} & O_{pi} = F_{pi}, & i = 1, 2, \ldots, n_I, \\[2mm]
\text{Hidden units:} & O_{pj} = f(\Gamma_{pj}), & j = 1, 2, \ldots, n_H, \\[2mm]
& \Gamma_{pj} = \sum_{i=1}^{n_I} W_{ji} \cdot O_{pi} + \Theta_j, & j = 1, 2, \ldots, n_H, \\[2mm]
\text{Output units:} & O_{pk} = f(\Gamma_{pk}), & k = 1, 2, \ldots, n_O, \\[2mm]
& \Gamma_{pk} = \sum_{j=1}^{n_H} W_{kj} \cdot O_{pj} + \Theta_k, & k = 1, 2, \ldots, n_O
\end{array}
$$

where W_{ji} and W_{kj} are fuzzy weights, and Θ_j and Θ_k are fuzzy biases.

2.6.1. Input-Output Relation

The input-output operations are defined by the extension principle of Zadeh (1975). This means that the fuzzy arithmetic (Kaufmann and Gupta, 1985) is employed for calculating the input-output relation of the fuzzified neural network. The following addition, multiplication, and nonlinear mapping of fuzzy numbers are used for defining our fuzzified neural network:

$$
\mu_{A+B}(x) = \max\{\mu_A(x) \wedge \mu_B(y) \mid z = x + y\} \tag{a}
$$

$$
\mu_{AB}(z) = \max\{\mu_A(x) \wedge \mu_B(y) \mid z = xy\} \tag{b}
$$

$$
\mu_{f(\Gamma)}(z) = \max\{\mu_\Gamma(x) \mid z = f(x)\} \tag{c}
$$

where A, B, and Γ are fuzzy sets, $\mu_\bullet(\cdot)$ denotes the membership function of each fuzzy set, and $\wedge$ is the minimum operator.

The above operations of fuzzy sets are numerically performed on level sets, i.e., α-cuts. The α-level set of a fuzzy set F is defined as:

$$
F_\alpha = \{x \mid \mu_F(x) \geq \alpha, x \in R\}, \quad \text{for } 0 < \alpha \leq 1 \tag{d}
$$

where $\mu_F(x)$ is the membership function of F, and R is the set of real numbers. Because level sets of fuzzy sets are closed intervals (Kaufmann and Gupta, 1985), we can denote F_α as:

$$
F_\alpha = [F_\alpha^L, F_\alpha^U] \tag{e}
$$

where F_α^L and F_α^U are the lower and the upper limits of the α-level set, F_α, respectively.

From interval arithmetic (Alefeld and Herzberger, 1983), the above operations of fuzzy numbers in (a)–(c) can be rewritten for α-level sets as follows:

$$
A_\alpha + B_\alpha = [A_\alpha^L, A_\alpha^U] + [B_\alpha^L, B_\alpha^U] = [A_\alpha^L + B_\alpha^L, A_\alpha^U + B_\alpha^U] \tag{a'}
$$

$$A_\alpha \cdot B_\alpha = [A_\alpha^L, A_\alpha^U] \cdot [B_\alpha^L, B_\alpha^U]$$

$$= [\min\{A_\alpha^L \cdot B_\alpha^L, A_\alpha^L \cdot B_\alpha^U, A_\alpha^U \cdot B_\alpha^L, A_\mu^U \cdot B_\alpha^U\} \tag{b'}$$

$$\max\{A_\alpha^L \cdot B_\alpha^L, A_\alpha^L \cdot B_\alpha^U, A_\alpha^U \cdot B_\alpha^L, A_\alpha^U \cdot B_\alpha^U\}]$$

$$f(_\alpha^\Gamma) = f([\Gamma_\alpha^L, \Gamma_\alpha^U]) = [f(\Gamma_\alpha^L), f(\Gamma_\alpha^U)] \tag{c'}$$

If the α-level sets of B are nonnegative, i.e., if $0 \leq B_\alpha^L \leq B_\alpha^U$, the multiplication in (b') can be simplified as:

$$A_\alpha \cdot B_\alpha = [\min\{A_\alpha^L \cdot B_\alpha^L, A_\alpha^L \cdot B_\alpha^U\}, \max\{A_\alpha^U \cdot B_\alpha^L, A_\alpha^U \cdot B_\alpha^U\}] \tag{b''}$$

The input-output relation of our fuzzified neural network is numerically calculated for the α-level sets of fuzzy inputs, fuzzy weights, and fuzzy biases. The input-output relation for the α-level sets can be written as

Input units : $\quad O_{pi\alpha} = F_{pi\alpha}, \qquad\qquad i = 1, 2, \ldots, n_I$

Hidden units : $\quad O_{pj\alpha} = f(\Gamma_{pj\alpha}), \qquad\qquad j = 1, 2, \ldots, n_H$

$$\Gamma_{pj\alpha} = \sum_{i=1}^{n_I} W_{ji\alpha} \cdot O_{pi\alpha} + \Theta_{j\alpha}, \quad j = 1, 2, \ldots, n_H$$

Output units : $\quad O_{pk\alpha} = f(\Gamma_{pk\alpha}), \qquad\qquad k = 1, 2, \ldots, n_O$

$$\Gamma_{pk\alpha} = \sum_{j=1}^{n_I} W_{kj\alpha} \cdot O_{pj\alpha} + \Theta_{k\alpha} \quad k = 1, 2, \ldots, n_O$$

We can see that the α-level sets of the fuzzy inputs F_{pi} are mapped to the α-level sets of the fuzzy outputs O_{pk}. This means that the α-level sets of the fuzzy outputs O_{pk} can be calculated by interval arithmetic on the α-level sets of the fuzzy inputs, fuzzy weights, and fuzzy biases. These calculations are performed based on the relations in (a')–(b') (b'').

2.6.2. An Example

As an example of the fuzzified neural network, let us consider a three-layer network with two input units, two hidden units, and a single output unit. Using this simple example, we illustrate the input-output relations of the fuzzified neural network defined above.

The fuzzy outputs from the input units are the same as the fuzzy inputs F_{p1} and F_{p2}. Therefore, the total fuzzy inputs Γ_{p1} and Γ_{p2} to the hidden units are calculated as follows:

$$\Gamma_{p1} = F_{p1} \cdot W_{11} + F_{p2} \cdot W_{12} + \Theta_1$$

$$\Gamma_{p2} = F_{p1} \cdot W_{21} + F_{p2} \cdot W_{22} + \Theta_2$$

Then, the fuzzy outputs O_{p1} and O_{p2} from the hidden units are obtained as

$$O_{p1} = f(\Gamma_{p1})$$

$$O_{p2} = f(\Gamma_{p2})$$

These two fuzzy outputs are then fed to the output unit. The total fuzzy input Γ_p to the output unit is:

$$\Gamma_p = O_{p1} \cdot W_1 + O_{p2} \cdot W_2 + \Theta$$

Finally, the fuzzy output from the output unit (i.e., the fuzzy output from the fuzzified neural network) is calculated as:

$$O_p = f(\Gamma_p)$$

These formulations of the input-output relations of each unit are almost the same as the standard feedforward neural network. The only difference is that fuzzy arithmetic is used with fuzzy sets in the fuzzified neural network, while real number arithmetic is used in the standard neural network.

The numerical calculations in the formula above are performed for the α-level sets of fuzzy sets using interval arithmetic. It is suggested that the results of the interval arithmetic be computed with 100 level sets, i.e., $\alpha = 0.01, 0.02, \ldots, 1.00$.

2.6.3.   Learning Algorithm

In this section, we describe a general learning algorithm for the fuzzified neural network. This learning algorithm can be applied to the adjustment of the fuzzy weights of various shapes.

When the fuzzy input vector $F_p = (F_{p1}, F_{p2}, \ldots, F_{pn_l})$ is presented to the fuzzified neural network as defined above, the actual output vector is obtained as the fuzzy vector $O_p = (O_{p1}, O_{p2}, \ldots, O_{pn_p})$. Let us assume that a fuzzy vector $T_p = (T_{p1}, T_{p2}, \ldots, T_{pn_o})$ is given as the target vector corresponding to the fuzzy input vector F_p. That is, we assume that the input-output pair (F_p, T_p) is given for the supervised learning of the fuzzified neural network.

The aim of the learning of the fuzzified neural network is to decrease the difference between O_p and T_p. That is, it is desired that the following equality holds approximately:

$$T_{pk} \cong O_{pk} \quad \text{for } k = 1, 3, \ldots, n_O$$

A cost function to be minimized in the learning of the fuzzified neural network should measure the difference between the fuzzy target vector T_p and the fuzzy output vector O_p. First, we define a cost function

$$e_{pk\alpha} = e_{pk\alpha}^L + e_{pk\alpha}^U$$

where

$$e_{pk\alpha}^L = \frac{\alpha}{2}(T_{pk\alpha}^L - O_{pk\alpha}^L)^2$$

$$e_{pk\alpha}^U = \frac{\alpha}{2}(T_{pk\alpha}^U - O_{pk\alpha}^U)^2$$

In the cost functions $e_{pk\alpha}$, $e_{pk\alpha}^L$, and $e_{pk\alpha}^U$ are the squared errors for the lower and the upper limits of the α-level sets, respectively. Those squared errors are weighted by the value of α. Therefore, the squared errors for a large value of α have a large effect on the learning of the fuzzified neural network.

The cost functions $e_{pk\alpha}$'s for the α-level set can be summed up over the n_O output units of the fuzzified neural network as:

$$e_{p\alpha} = \sum_{k=1}^{n_O} e_{pk\alpha}$$

Therefore, the cost function $e_{p\alpha}$ is the squared error between the α-level set of the fuzzy target vector T_p and the fuzzy output vector O_p.

The cost functions e_p that measure the difference T_p and O_p can be defined by summing over all values of α as follows:

$$e_p = \sum_{\alpha} e_{p\alpha}$$

In computer simulations, one could use five or ten values of α.

When N input-output pairs, (F_p, T_p), $p = 1, 2, ..., N$, are given as training data, we have the following cost function for these training data:

$$e = \sum_{p=1}^{N} e_p$$

3.   UNIFIED FUZZY MODEL

Zadeh's proposal (1975) of a linguistic approach as the model of human thinking introduced the "fuzziness" into systems theory. Fuzzy systems are the outcome of such a linguistic approach in our attempt to obtain more flexibility and better capability of handling and processing uncertainties of complicated and ill-defined systems. This idea was further developed by Tong (1979), Pedrycz (1984), Sugeno and Yasukawa (1993), and Yager and Filev (1994).

In the most general form, the encoded knowledge of a Multi-Input Multi-Output (MIMO) system can be interpreted by fuzzy models consisting of IF-THEN rules with multi-antecedent and multiconsequent variables. However, conceptually, a system with multiple independent outputs can be presented as a collection of Multi-Input Single-Output (MISO) fuzzy systems such that for a system with s outputs, each multiconsequent rule is broken into s single-consequent rule. Modeling and inference is more straightforward for MISO fuzzy systems. That is the reason why the literature concentrates on multi-input, single-output rules as a generic presentation of fuzzy systems.

For these reasons, we will consider in this section a fuzzy rule base that may be obtained with methods described in Section 2 as follows:

$$R_1 : \text{IF } X_1 \text{ isr } A_{11} \text{ AND } X_2 \text{ isr } A_{12} \text{ AND} ... \text{AND } X_r \text{ isr } A_{1r}, \text{ THEN Y isr } B_1$$
$$R_2 : \text{IF } X_1 \text{ isr } A_{21} \text{ AND } X_2 \text{ isr } A_{22} \text{ AND} ... \text{AND } X_r \text{ isr } A_{2r}, \text{ THEN Y isr } B_2$$
$$\vdots \qquad\qquad\qquad\qquad\qquad\qquad\qquad \vdots$$
$$R_n : \text{IF } X_1 \text{ isr } A_{n1} \text{ AND } X_2 \text{ isr } A_{n2} \text{ AND} ... \text{AND } X_r \text{ isr } A_{1r}, \text{ THEN Y isr } B_n$$

where $X_1, ..., X_r$ are input variables, and Y is the output variable, A_{ij}, $i = 1, ..., n$, $j = 1, ..., r$, and B_j, $i = 1, ..., n$ are fuzzy sets of the universes of discourse $X_1, X_2, ..., X_r$ and Y, respectively. It is clear that a fuzzy rule base is the first essential component of fuzzy system models.

The second essential component of fuzzy system models is the reasoning mechanism, i.e., the manner in which the information is processed in a fuzzy model. In current methods of fuzzy system models, the connectives of the inference mechanism are selected *a priori* before the identification procedure without any theoretical basis. In order to improve the objectivity of the fuzzy modeling, one needs to introduce a unified parameterized formulation to the reasoning process in fuzzy systems. For this purpose, four reasoning parameters, p, q, α, and β, are introduced the values of which will cause a continuous range of variation in the reasoning mechanism. Therefore, we are no longer restricted to stay at the extremes in any step of the reasoning process. Consequently, rather than selecting the connectives *a priori* for fuzzy system models, it is desirable to have the reasoning process adjust the above parameters with supervised training using system input-output data, such that the objective would be to minimize performance index errors. Hence, the selection of the connectives would be in agreement with system behavior patterns. In order to reduce the computational effort, a fast computational algorithm is introduced for the calculation of the parameterized family of triangular functions (Emami, Türkşen, and Goldenberg, 1996).

3.1. APPROXIMATE REASONING

In approximate reasoning, we have essentially two methods:

1. First Infer Then Aggregate, FITA
2. First Aggregate Then Infer, FATI (Türkşen and Tian, 1993)

In FITA method, we need to:

1. Determine fuzzy aggregation of antecedents in each rule (AND connective)
2. Determine implication relation for each individual rule (IF-THEN connective)
3. Make inference with each rule of the set of rules, using the observed input
4. Aggregate the fuzzy outputs obtained in (3) above to get the final fuzzy output (ALSO connective)
5. Defuzzify the final fuzzy output

Whereas in FATI method, steps (3) and (4) are modified as follows:

6. Aggregate all the rules of the rule base to determine the overall rule (ALSO connective)
7. Make inference with the overall rule using the observed input

It can be shown that the two methods of inference with a rule set, i.e., FATI and FITA, always give the same fuzzy output for a singleton input (Emami, Türkşen, and Goldenberg, 1996). Moreover, we propose a reasoning formulation that combines Mamdani's and formal logical approximate reasonings, i.e., two mypoic reasoning approaches. This then forms the foundation of a unified parameterized fuzzy reasoning formulation. It should be recalled that in the introduction section, we have identified Mamdani's reasoning as the case (1) and formal logical reasoning as the case (2). Both of these are in Type I theory and hence are myopic.

3.2.   CRISP CONNECTIVES OF FUZZY THEORY

In order to cover various types of set operators used in fuzzy set theory, a parameterized family of t-norms (T) and t-conorms (S) is chosen among the parametric Schweizer and Skalar's operators (1983):

$$T(a,b) = 1 - [(1-a)^p + (1-b)^p - (1-a)^p(1-b)^p]^{1/p}$$

$$S(a,b) = [a^p + b^p - a^p b^p]^{1/p}, \quad p > 0$$

The main features of this parameterized family of t-norms and co-norms are that they are analytically simple and symmetric, which are basic advantages in implementations. Furthermore, when p changes continuously as a positive real number, this parametric form covers all t-norms and t-conorms.

Analogous to the classical set theory, De Morgan laws establish a link between union and intersection via complementation. The conjoint t-norms and t-conorms introduced above are De Morgan duals when considered with the standard negation $c(a) = 1-a$ (Ruan and Kerre, 1993).

Although t-norm and t-conorm functions are defined as binary operators on [0,1], their associativity property allows them to be extended to n-ary operations as :

$$T_n : [0,1]^n \rightarrow [0,1] \text{ and } S_n : [0,1]^n \rightarrow [0,1],$$

$$(a_1, a_2, ..., a_n) \rightarrow \begin{cases} T(T_{n-1}(a_1, a_2, ..., a_{n-1}), a_n) \\ S(S_{n-1}(a_1, a_2, ..., a_{n-1}), a_n) \end{cases}$$

where, $T(...)$ and $S(...)$ are the binary operators. It is proved that the n-ary operators T_n and S_n satisfy similar properties as the original binary T and S (Ruan and Kerre, 1993; Emami, Türkşen, and Goldenberg, 1996).

The extension of these t-conorm operators to n arguments can be computed with a fast algorithm (Emami, Türkşen, and Goldenberg, 1996). That is, the original formula:

$$S(a_1, a_2, ..., a_n) = \left[\sum_{i=1}^{n} a_i^p - \sum_{i=1}^{n} \sum_{\substack{j=1 \\ j \neq i}}^{n} a_i^p a_j^p + \sum_{\substack{j=1}}^{n} \sum_{\substack{j=1 \\ j \neq i}}^{n} \sum_{\substack{k=1 \\ k \neq j \\ k \neq i}}^{n} a_i^p a_j^p a_k^p \pm ... \pm \prod_{i=1}^{n} a_i^p \right]^{1/p}$$

can be transformed into:

$$S(a_1, a_2, ..., a_n) = [a_1^p + (1 - a_1^p)[a_2^p + (1 - a_2^p)[...[a_{n-2}^p + (1 - a_{n-2}^p)[a_{n-1}^p + (1 - a_{n-1}^p)a_n^p]]...]]]^{1/p}$$

where for both $T(\cdot)$ formula is computed as:

$$T(a_1, a_2, ..., a_n) = 1 - S((1 - a_1), (1 - a_2), ..., (1 - a_n))$$

It should be noted that the computational complexity of the original formula is $O(2^n)$, whereas for the transformed formula, it is $O(n)$.

3.3. IMPLICATION AND AGGREGATION

Within the theory of approximate reasoning (Zadeh, 1973), each fuzzy rule is specified as:

$$R_i - IF\ X_1\ isr\ A_{i1}\ AND\ ...\ AND\ X_r\ isr\ A_{ir}\ THEN\ Y\ isr\ B_i$$

where R is a fuzzy relation defined on the Cartesian product universe of $X_1 \times X_2 \times ... \times X_r \times Y$.

In agreement with the discussion presented above, t-norm operators are used to define conjunctions in the antecedent of the multi-input rule. Furthermore, modeling of implication relations is not unique in fuzzy logics. Two extreme paradigms for forming the implication relation are the conjunctive and disjunctive methods, which are identified as cases (1) and (2) in the introduction section. Under the conjunctive method, the fuzzy relation R is simply the conjunction of antecedent and consequent spaces. Therefore:

$$R_{ci}(x_1, x_2, ..., x_r, y) = T(T'(A_{i1}(x_1), A_{i2}(x_2), ..., A_{ir}(x_r)), B_i(y))$$

where $A_{ij}(x_j)$ and $B_i(y)$ are the membership grades used in the computations of R_{ci}, T is t-norm operator (with parameter p) for the rule implication, and T' is t-norm operator (with parameter q) for the antecedent aggregation. On the other hand, the disjunctive method is obtained directly by generalizing the material implication defined in classical set theory as $A \rightarrow B \equiv \overline{A} \cup B$, where $\overline{A}$ is the standard negation of A. Therefore, we have:

$$R_{di}(x_1, x_2, ..., x_r, y) = S(c(T'(A_{i1}(x_1), A_{i2}(x_2), ..., A_{ir}(x_r)), B_i(y))$$
$$= S(S'((1 - A_{i1}(x_1)), (1 - A_{i2}(x_2)), ..., (1 - A_{ir}(x_r))), B_i(y))$$

in which, S and S' are t-conorm operators with parameters p and q, respectively.

Selection of the rule aggregation function depends on the selection of implication function for individual rules (Türkşen and Tian, 1993). For the conjunctive method, the aggretation of the rules should be with a disjunction (union) operator. In other words, the ALSO connective should be an OR operator, i.e., a t-conorm, in particular, it is the Max operator.

$$R_c(x_1, x_2, ..., x_r, y) = \underset{i}{V}(R_{ci}(x_1, x_2, ..., x_r, y))$$

Let $x = (x_1, x_2, ..., x_r)$, then more compactly, we have: $R_c(x, y) = \underset{i}{V} R_{ci}(x, y)$.

This method of aggregation was introduced originally by Zadeh (1993) as the interpolative reasoning, and at times, it is known as the Mamdani (1974) method, which is a myopic inference method.

On the other hand, if each basic proposition is regarded as "[X isr $\overline{A}_{ij}$] $\cup$ [Y isr B_i]," which is the disjunctive method, then the knowledge "$(X_1, X_2, ..., X_r, Y)$ isr F' should be aggregated with the conjunction (intersection) of the rules. In other words, the ALSO connective is an AND opeartor; i.e., t-norm, in particular with Min operator.

$$R_d(x_1, x_2, ..., x_r, y) = \underset{i}{\wedge}(R_{di}(x_1, x_2, ..., x_r, y))$$

More compactly, we have: $R_d(x, y) = \underset{i}{\wedge} R_{di}(x, y)$.

This method is the formal logical myopic approximate reasoning, as explained in the introduction.

3.4.   INFERENCE WITH A RULE SET

Considering a Single-Input Single-Outout (SISO) system, given the relationship "$(X \rightarrow Y)$ isr R'''" and the information that X belongs to a fuzzy set $A'(x)$ is observed, then the problem of inference is finding the fuzzy value for Y. According to Zadeh's Compositional Rule of Inference (CRI) (1973), the membership function of the output is defined as:

$$F(y) = \vee_x [T''(A'(x), R(x,y))]$$

where $\vee_x$ means the maximum for all values of $x \in X$ and T'' is a t-norm.

It is known that generally two different methods of computing, i.e., FITA or FATI with a rule base, R, lead to two different reasoning results (Türkşen and Lucas, 1991). Whether it is executed with Mamdani's Reasoning, or with Formal Logical Myopic Reasoning, i.e.:

$$F_C(y) = \vee_x[T''[A'(x), R_c(x,y)]], F_D(y) = \vee_x[T''[A(x), R_d(x,y)]], \text{ respectively.}$$

The reason for this is that triangular norm and co-norm operators are not distributive. Hence, it is necessary first to combine all the rules to get the overall relation R of the set of rules and then compose it with the fuzzy input $A'(x)$. This method, called First-Aggregate-Then-Infer (FATI), is quite inefficient in terms of computational time and memory (Türkşen and Tian, 1993).

However, in most applications of fuzzy modeling and control, the input x^* is crisp and therefore, the input fuzzy set $A'(x^*)$ is a fuzzy singleton. In this case, it can be shown that the distributivity property holds for any type of t-norm and t-conrom family. Hence, it is possible to fire each single rule first and calculate individual fuzzy reasoning output F_i and finally aggregate fuzzy outputs of all the rules to obtain the inferred fuzzy output $F(y)$. This method, called First-Infer-Then-Aggregate (FITA), is computationally more efficient than FATI but equivalent to it.

For multi-input single-output systems, the antecedent of each rule i is a conjunction of r fuzzy sets $A_{i1}, A_{i2}, ..., A_{ir}$. For crisp input $x^* = (x_1^*, x_2^*, ..., x_r^*)$, given a rule i:

$$R_i - IF \ X_1 \ isr \ A_{i1} \ AND \ ... \ AND \ X_r \ isr \ A_{ir} \ THEN \ Y \ isr \ B_i$$

we need to compute:

$$\tau_i(x^*) = T'(A_{i1}(x_1^*), A_{i2}(x_2^*), ..., A_{ir}(x_r^*))$$

where τ_i is called the Degree Of Firing (DOF) of the rule i. By using the arguments presented above, it is clear that the fuzzy output membership function may be computed either by FITA or by FATI, producing the same result for both of the reasoning mechanisms as:

$$F_C(y) = \bigvee_i \bigvee_x R_{ic}(x^*,y) = \bigvee_x \bigvee_i R_{ic}(x^*,y) = \bigvee_i R_{ic}(x^*,y)$$
$$F_D(y) = \bigwedge_i \bigvee_x R_{id}(x^*,y) = \bigvee_x \bigwedge_i R_{id}(x^*,y) = \bigwedge_i R_{id}(x^*,y)$$

Note that there is no need to aggregate over all x, since $x = x^*$ is a singleton, i.e., $A'(x^*) = 1$. Therefore, it is computationally more efficient to do the execution by the FITA method.

With these preliminaries, the unified reasoning mechanism is introduced as a linear combination of the two extremes, i.e., the myopic approaches of Mamdani's reasoning and formal logical reasoning:

$$E(y) = \beta F_D(y) + (1 - \beta)F_C(y), \quad 0 \le \beta \le 1$$

3.4.1. Defuzzification

Yager and Filev (1994) suggest a general defuzzification method, based on the probabilistic nature of the selection process among the values of a fuzzy set, called Basic Defuzzification Distribution (BADD) method:

$$y_B^* = \frac{\int_{y_0}^{y_1} yE^{\alpha}(y)dy}{\int_{y_0}^{y_1} E^{\alpha}(y)dy}$$

As we can see, BADD method is essentially a family of defuzzification methods parameterized by parameter α. By varying α continuously in the real interval, it is possible to have more appropriate mappings from the fuzzy set to the crisp value, depending on the system behavior.

It should be clear that the unified reasoning mechanism that is combined with BADD method of defuzzification, allows us to train the parameters p, q, α, and β of this model with a given set of data in order to minimize the error between the model output results and the actual system outputs; and hence this approach provides us with a better fiting of the system model.

4. CASE STUDY

In this section, two textbook case study results are presented first; then a real-life industrial process model is discussed.

4.1. A NONLINEAR SYSTEM

In this example, we re-analyze the fuzzy modeling process of the nonlinear system discussed in Sugeno and Yasukawa (1993) and Nakanishi, Türkşen, and Sugeno (1993). After deriving the output fuzzy clusters and performing the classification for the entire output space, significant input variables are identified as the first two input variables,i.e., x_1 and x_2; the dummy input variables were discarded as expected. The fuzzy system identification is based on 50 input-output data. Two dummy input variables x_3 and x_4 have been added to check the input selection strategy. Instead of Sugeno-Yasukawas's approach, which divides the data into two sets and uses a time-demanding combinatorial strategy, we apply the straightforward strategy described in the sequel where input membership functions are assigned through fuzzy line clustering. After approximating the input and output fuzzy clusters by suitable trapezoidal functions, the first-step forms the fuzzy model of the system. Note that no inference mechanism is required up to this point. The next step is to select and tune the set of parameters of the fuzzy model, which consists of the inference parameters (p, q, α, β), and the input and output membership function parameters. At this step of parameter identification, the optimum inference paramters are identified as:

$$p = 19.9959; \quad q = 0.4536; \quad \alpha = 5.3715; \quad \beta = 0.0255.$$

By optimizing the inference paramters, the fuzzy model performance index, PI, is determined to be PI = 0.171. The second step of parameter identification is to adjust the input and output membership parameters with supervised training. After five iterations, the error is reduced to PI = 0.0106 and after five more iterations, the performance index becomes PI = 0.0040. The performance index of Sugeno-Yasukawa's fuzzy model of the same type (position type) starts from PI = 0.318, and after 20 iterations, it reaches to PI = 0.079.

4.2.   GAS FURNACE MODEL

The proposed algorithm was applied to a famous example of the system identification given by Box and Jenkins (Box, 1970). The process is a gas furnace with single input u(t) (gas flow rate) and single output y(t) (CO_2 concentration). For this dynamic system, 10 input candidates y(t − 1), ..., y(t − 4), u(t − 1), ..., u(t − 6) are considered. We use the same 296 data as in the Sugeno and Yasukawa (1993) analysis. With the ETG (i.e., Emami, Türkşen, Goldenberg) method, it is found that m = 2.5 and c = 6 are suitable for the system. The significant input variables are determined as y(t − 1), u(t − 2), and u(t − 3). The optimum inference parameters for the gas furnace system are derived as:

$$p = 102.0147; \quad q = 8.5918; \quad \alpha = 27.9338; \quad \beta = 0.3782$$

After 10 iterations, the performance index reduces to a value of PI = 0.1584, which is less than both the identified linear model (PI = 0.193) and the Sugeno-Yasukawa position-gradient fuzzy model (PI = 0.190).

4.3.   INDUSTRIAL PROCESS MODEL

A recent case study is briefly discussed in this section to demonstrate the effectiveness of the integrated knowledge representation and inference model presented in the previous sections of this chapter.

Real-life process data was provided by an industrial company. It consists of 93 input-output data vectors. Each data vector has 46 input variables and 1 output variable.

First, the improved clustering method discussed in Section 2.4 and identified as ETG method is applied with the data. In Figure 1, the trace of Fuzzy Total Scatter Matrix is shown as a function of "m" for various "c" values. After proper analyses of the cluster validity index as a function of c within the reliable domain, it is found that m = 2.5 with c = 7 are suitable values for this industrial process.

Next, the most important input variables that affect the output significantly are determined among all of the 46 input variables. It is found that only 13 variables, i.e., x_4, x_9, x_{10}, x_{11}, x_{12}, x_{17}, x_{18}, x_{20}, x_{21}, x_{28}, x_{34}, x_{44}, and x_{45}, have a significant effect on the output variable, which is the throughput efficiency measure of the process. The fuzzy rule base for this industrial process is shown in Figure 2. It is observed that there are seven effective rules, rule 0 to rule 6, that control the hidden behavior of this industrial process.

In Figure 2, it should be noted that the four numbers shown on the right-hand side of each trapezoid are the four values that define the trapezoid, e.g., in rule 3, variable x_4 has a trapezoid membership function defined by ⟨218.95, 229.00, 310.72, 997.95⟩, etc.

The integrated fuzzy inference model of this industrial system is developed next. The combined Mamdani and Logical myopic model with parameters p = 1.6190, q = 0.8438, α = 8.2935, and β = 0.001 produces the best fit for this industrial process with PI = 0.0886 for the test data. The comparison of the combined model output and the actual system output are shown in Figure 3.

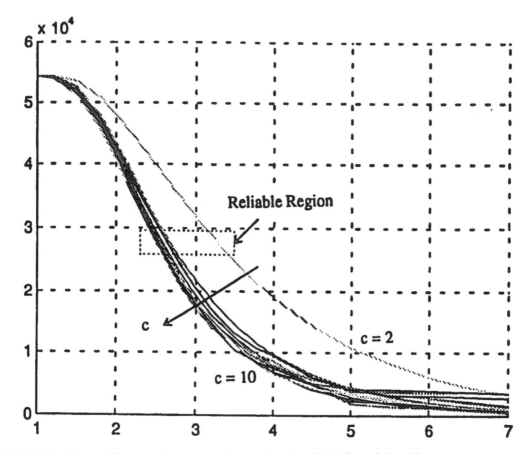

FIGURE 1   Trace of fuzzy total scatter matrix as a function of "m" for an industrial process.

5.   RESEARCH ISSUES

In this chapter, we have proposed and discussed a fuzzy-neural system development schema. For this purpose, we have identified three knowledge representation and approximate reasoning approaches. For the Type I fuzzy theory, we have described the extraction of fuzzy sets and fuzzy rules with the application of an improved fuzzy clustering technique called the ETG method, which is essentially an unsupervised learning of the fuzzy sets and rules from a given input-output data set. Next we have described how this set of rules and its fuzzy sets may be adapted and/or modified for known target sets with supervised learning within a fuzzified neural network architecture. Finally, we have introduced a unified (fuzzy) approximate reasoning formulation for fuzzy modeling and control. For this purpose, approximate reasoning parameters are introduced as p, q, α, and β. In particular, we have unified two common but myopic knowledge representation and approximate reasoning methods in our proposed schema.

Unification of myopic reasoning methods still leave a lot to be desired from a theoretical point of view. It is left for future research to develop a unified knowledge representation and reasoning method with the developments of Type II fuzzy set theory. It is conjectured that with developments in Type II fuzzy theory, fuzzy-neural system models will provide much more powerful results for real-life applications. In such a future development, FDNF($\cdot$) and FCNF($\cdot$) limits of the Type II fuzzy sets will have to be integrated for a unified optimal system modeling and reasoning with it.

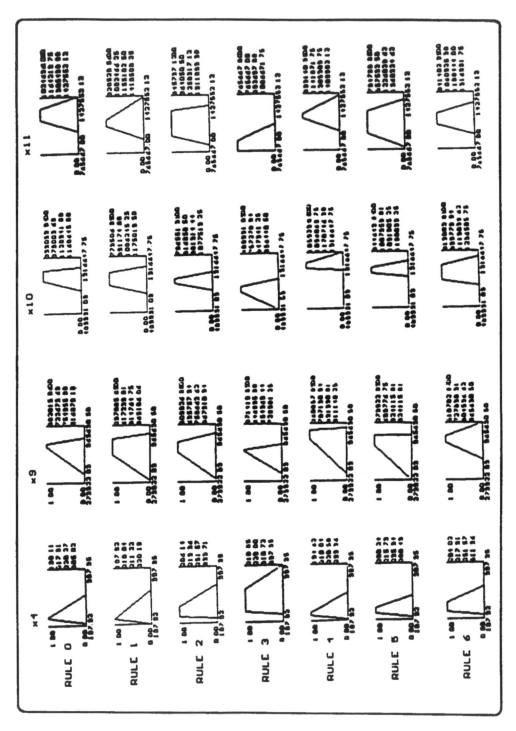

FIGURE 2a Fuzzy logic model for an industrial process.

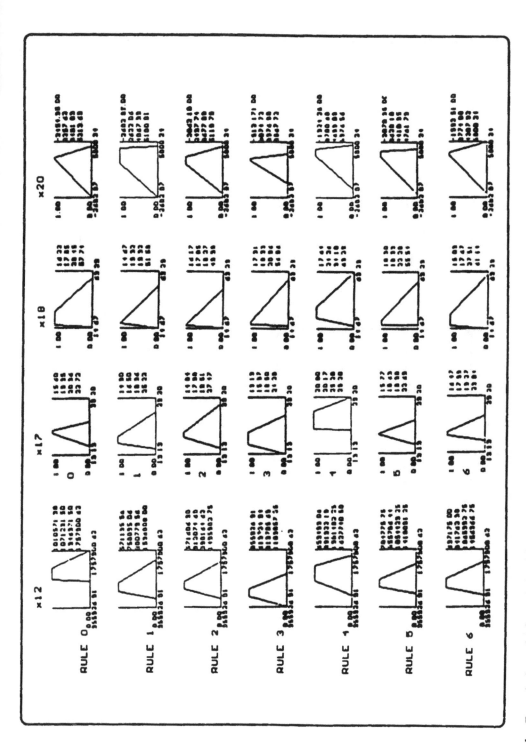

FIGURE 2b Fuzzy logic model for an industrial process.

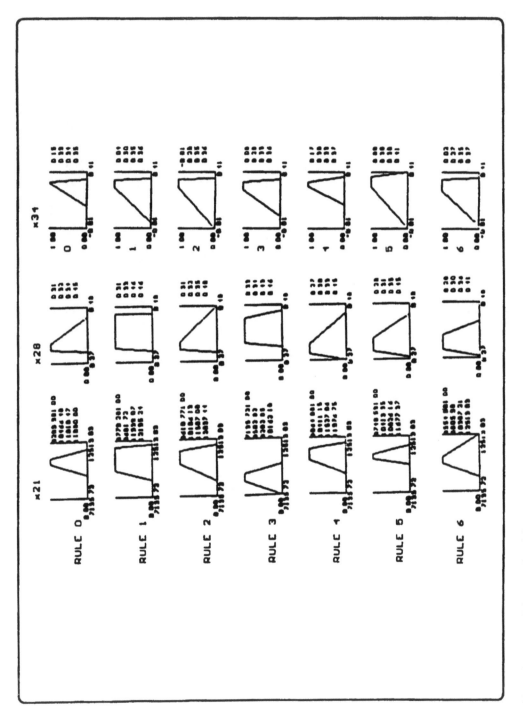

FIGURE 2c   Fuzzy logic model for an industrial process.

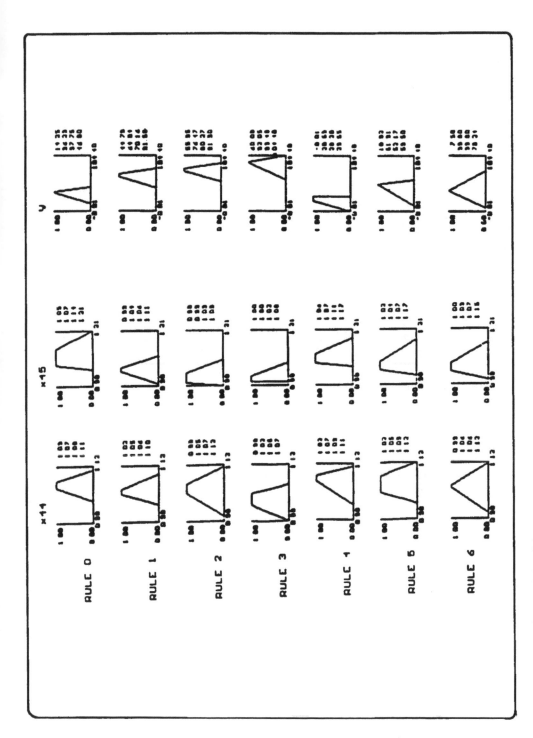

FIGURE 2d Fuzzy logic model for an industrial process.

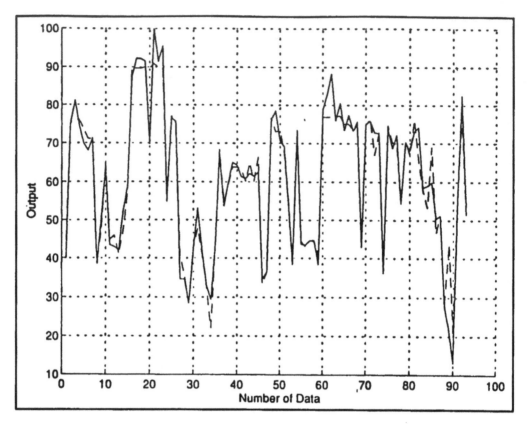

FIGURE 3 Comparison of the combined Mamdani and logical fuzzy model (- - -) and real data (——) of an industrial process.

REFERENCES

Alefeld, G. and Herzberger, J. (1983). *Introduction of Interval Computations*, New York, Academic Press.

Bezdek, J.C. (1981). *Pattern Recognition with Fuzzy Objective Function Algorithms*, New York, Plenum Press.

Bilgic, T. and Türkoşen, I.B. (1996). Measurement of membership function theoretical and empirical work, *Handbook of Fuzzy Systems*, Vol. 1, Foundations, (to be published).

Box, G.E.P. and Jenkins, G.M. (1970). Time Series Analyses, Forecasting and Control, Holden Day, San Francisco.

Demirli, K. and Türkoşen, I.B. (1994). A review of implication and generalized modus ponens, *Proceedings of IEEE Fuzzy Systems Conference*, June 26–29, 1994, Vol. II, 1440–1445.

Duda, R.O. and Hart, P.E. (1973). *Pattern Classification and Scene Analysis*, John Wiley & Sons.

Emami, M.R., Türkoşen, I.B., and Goldenberg, A.A. (1996). An improved fuzzy modeling algorithm Part I: Inference mechanism, *Proceedings of NAFIPS 96*, Berkeley, CA, 289–293.

Emami, M.R., Türkoşen, I.B., and Goldenberg, A.A. (1996). An improved fuzzy modeling, Part II: Systems identification, *Proceedings of NAFIPS 96*, Berkeley, CA, 294–298.

French, S. (1984). Fuzzy decision analysis: some criticisms, in: H.J. Zimmerman, L.A. Zadeh and B. Gaines (Eds.) *Fuzzy Sets and Decision Analysis*, North Holland, 29–44.

Ishibuchi, H., Morioka, K., and Türkoşen, I.B. (1995). Learning by fuzzified neural networks, *Int. J. of Approximate Reasoning*, 13, 4, 327–358.

Kaufmann, A. and Gupta, M.M. (1985). *Introduction to Fuzzy Arithmetic*, Van Nostrand Reinhold.

Keller, J.M., Gray, M.R., and Givens, J.A. (1985). A fuzzy k-nearest algorithm, *IEEE Trans. Systems, Man, and Cybernetics*, Vol. SMC-15, No. 4, 580–585.

Kneale, W.C. (1962). *The Development of Logic*, Oxford, Clarendon Press.

Kosko, B. (1997). *Fuzzy Engineering*, Prentice Hall.

Mamdani, E. H. (1974). Application of fuzzy algorithms for control of simple dynamic plant, *Proc. IEEE*, 121, 1585–1588.

McCall, S. and Aydukiewica, K. (1967). *Polish Logic: Papers by Ajdukiewicz et. al.* 1920–1939 Oxford, Clarendon Press.

Nakanishi, H., Türkoşen, I.B., and Sugeno, M. (1993). A review of six reasoning methods, *Fuzzy Sets and Systems*, 57, 3, 257–294.

Pedrycz, W. (1984). Identification in fuzzy systems, *IEEE Trans. on Systems, Man, and Cybernetics*, No. 14, 361–366.

Rosser, T.B. and Turquette, A.R. (1977). *Many Valued Logics*, Westport, Connecticut, Greenwood Press.

Ruan, D. and Kerre, E.E. (1993). On the extension of the compositional rule of inference, *International Journal of Intelligent Systems*, 8, 807–817.

Schweizer, B. and Sklar, A. (1983). *Probabilistic Metric Spaces*, North-Holland, Amsterdam.

Scott, D. (1976). Does many-valued logics have any use? in: S. Korner (Ed.), *Philosophy of Logic*, Southampton, Camelot Press, Great Britian, Chapter 2, 64–95.

Sugeno, M. and Yasukawa, T. (1993). A fuzzy-logic-based approach to qualitative modeling, *IEEE Trans. Fuzzy Systems*, Vol. 1; No. 1, 7–31.

Tong, R.M. (1979). The construction and evaluation of fuzzy models; in Gupta M.M., Regade, R.K., Yager, R.R., (Eds.), *Advances in Fuzzy Set Theory and Application*, North-Holland, Amsterdam.

Türkşen, I.B. (1986). Interval-valued fuzzy sets based on normal forms, *Fuzzy Sets and Systems*, 20, 2, 191–210.

Türkşen, I.B. and Tian Y. (1993). Combination of rules and their consequences in fuzzy expert systems, *Fuzzy Sets and Systems*, No. 58, 3–40.

Türkşen, I.B. and Lucas, C. (1991). A pattern matching inference method and its comparison with known inference methods, *Proceedings of IFSA'91*, July 7–12, Brussels, 231–234.

Türkşen, I.B. (1995). Type I and Interval-valued Type II fuzzy sets and logics, in: P.P. Wang (Ed.), *Advances in Fuzzy Theory and Technology*, Vol. 3, 31–82, Bookright Press, Raleigh, NC.

Türkşen, I.B. (1996). Fuzzy truth tables and normal forms, *Proceedings of BOFL'96*, December 15–18, 1996, TIT, Nagatsuta, Yokohama, Japan, 7–12.

Ward, J.H. (1963). Hierarchical grouping to optimize an objective function, *J. American Statistics Association*, No. 58, 236–244.

Yager, R.R. and Filev, D.P. (1994). *Essentials of Fuzzy Modeling and Control*, John Wiley & Sons.

Zadeh, L.A. (1965). Fuzzy sets, *Information and Control*, 8, 338–353.

Zadeh, L. (1973). Outline of a new approach to the analysis of complex systems and decision processes, *IEEE Trans. Systems, Man, and Cybernetics*, SMC-3, 28–44.

Zadeh, L.A. (1975). The concept of a linguistic vairable and its application to approximate reasoning I, II and III, *Information Science.* 8, 199–249, 301–357, and 9, 43–80.

Zadeh, L.A. (1996). Fuzzy Logic=Computing with Words, *IEEE Transaction on Fuzzy Systems*, 4, 2, 103–111.

14 Multimedia Expert Systems

James M. Ragusa

CONTENTS

1. INTRODUCTION

"Information overload," predicted by Toffer (1970) over 2 decades ago in *Future Shock*, has become a reality; and many of us seem to be drowning in a sea of multiple-media information. There is no reason to believe that the future will be any better. In fact, numerous surveys and predictions indicate that there will be a significant expansion in the volume and type of information we constantly receive in print, during broadcasts, and on our computer screens via programs and the Internet.

This explosion has stimulated the need for more object-oriented systems, paradigms, and databases for information storage and the use of hypertext, hypermedia, and intelligent (and personal) agents for improved information location, filtering, and retrieval. Through the use of software agents, real-world applications are occurring in human resource management, banking, retail sales, manufacturing, transportation, and telecommunications (Blanchard, 1996).

The future holds even more information challenges and opportunities as we move from two-dimensional to more virtual technologies and immersion environments using virtual reality and other 3-D views (Chinnock, 1996; Machover, 1996). According to Hayashi and Varney (1996), information technology advances in the areas of holographic data storage, terabit-per-second fiber optic communications, and other focused research will radically change our lives in the 21st century.

Many of our present and future applications will necessitate technology integration because of the various information forms that users will require in their work, recreation, and entertainment worlds. Within the domain of microcomputer technology (the focus of this chapter), information media exist in various multimedia (MM) forms, including text, data, graphics, still images, animation, motion video, and audio. Various MM integrated platforms, which make microcomputer-based MM information presentations possible, include various media hardware and software systems. Because of the volume and diversity of these media and platforms, a number of information management problems are now coming to light. They include issues of (1) classification and storage of the complex myriad of available information; (2) interactive access, retrieval, and display of what is needed; and (3) assimilation and learning from this profusion of information and accumulated knowledge. While these issues are being investigated by a variety of specialists, more needs to be done.

Increasingly, information in various forms is being stored electronically, optically, and digitally. Magnetic and laser-mediated optical devices have the potential to help solve the MM storage problem. These MM devices include laserdiscs, Compact Disc-Read Only Memory (CD-ROM), rewritable magneto-optical (MO), erasable re-writable optical discs (EROD), write-once-read-many times (WORM), and, more recently, recordable CD-ROM, and photo compact disc (Photo CD) systems. Network-connected computers and digital online information systems (which will dominate future data storage) greatly facilitate access and display needs.

It is the opinion of the author and others that integrated expert systems (ES) and MM have the potential to address many unresolved issues by providing new synergies, "intelligent" user interfaces, additional informational dimensions, and interesting, beneficial application solutions. These applications are made intelligent by the embedding of reasoning capabilities provided by an ES through knowledge-based representation and inferencing features. As a result, intelligent MM systems enable a wide range of users to interact in a nonlinear, seamless, context-sensitive manner with varying types of complex applications, including information classification, retrieval, assimilation, and learning.

With the issues of intelligent information management in mind, this chapter explores models and applications of interactive ES and MM, hypermedia (HM), and intellimedia (IM) — the latter being an advanced intelligent media concept identified by the author. A background of media technologies and integration advantages is first presented, followed by a description of software architectures, integration orientations, and an evolving framework of system integration models. Representative application domains and 30 integrated applications are identified to provide examples for future application developers. Finally, some research issues are identified and discussed, followed by a projection of future trends and a chapter summary.

2.   BACKGROUND

2.1.   MEDIA TECHNOLOGIES OVERVIEW

Integration possibilities other than ES/MM are also the subject of this overview. Additional media technologies to be combined with ES include hypermedia (HM) and intellimedia (IM), the latter

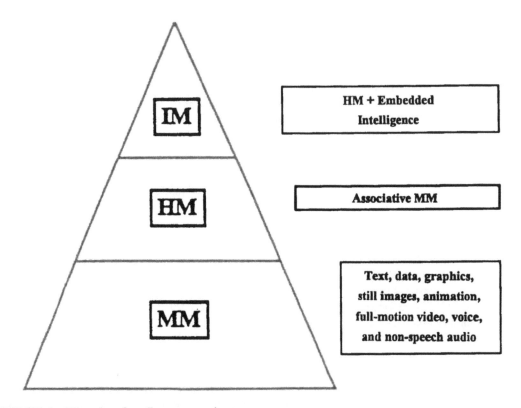

FIGURE 1 Hierarchy of media systems robustness.

being a new concept of intelligent MM. Figure 1 depicts a hierarchy and evolution of MM, HM, and IM. The area allocated to each represents the approximate extent of general research interest indicated in the popular press, research reports, and journal articles. As will be briefly discussed later, IM is a form of the emerging technology of dynamic intelligent agents.

2.1.1.   Multimedia

An earlier study of MM (Lougheed and Ragusa, 1992) found that there is no universally accepted definition of MM. Fermoyle (1990) best explained the difficulties in defining MM with the following statement:

> MM denotes different thing to different people, depending on their backgrounds, viewpoints, and sometimes their own self-interests. Just a few years ago, a multimedia presentation consisted of multiple slide projectors, screens and a soundtrack with maybe some film, video, or fireworks thrown in (p. 32).

In addition to presentation systems, definitions included orientations toward hardware, software, integrated platforms, standards, and user interaction. In an article describing MM as the next frontier for business, Raskin (1990) states, "MM is not a product, nor even a technology. It's better seen as a platform — a combination of hardware and software elements that together support a multi-sensory information environment" (p. 152).

Adding to this confusion has been a lack of standards, which initially delayed the full adoption of MM devices, software, and platforms. The situation has improved with the acceptance of industry standards, which is important for product and media consistency and user acceptance. Presently, industry standards exist for multimedia PC (MPC) hardware and software products and have been developed by the Joint Photographic Experts Group (JPEG) for the compression and decompression of color still images. Standards also exist for full-motion video and audio, which were developed by the international Motion Picture Experts Group (MPEG).

For the purpose of this chapter, MM is defined as the computer-facilitated integration of multiple information formats. As such, MM includes the use of two or more media forms, including (1) static media: text, data, graphics, still images; and (2) dynamic or time-varying media: animation, full-motion video, speech, and nonspeech audio (Ragusa, 1994).

MM application systems strive to take advantage of human senses in order to facilitate communication and have become an important method of effective and expressive communications. Contrary to earlier forms of audio-visual technology, computer-based MM is a powerful technology that (1) allows the presentation of several media formats separately or simultaneously, and (2) has the functionality to provide nonlinear links within and between these media formats. This latter feature relates to the more advanced media technology form of HM.

2.1.2. Hypermedia

HM has evolved from an earlier concept of hypertext (HT), which was first defined by Nelson in the early 1960s to mean "nonsequential writing, text that branches and allows choices to the reader, best read at an interactive screen" (Paske, 1990, p. 54). Like MM, HT can be defined from various perspectives. HT can be viewed in the context of a new model for textbook material. It can also be thought of as a computerized network of nodes or database objects and links to traverse between nodes to create and browse through complex networks of linked text and documents. More recently, HT has been widely used and accepted as a context linking methodology. However, because HT is primarily a single media form (text), it is not included further in the discussion in this chapter.

Nelson later coined the term "hypermedia" to describe a higher bandwidth technology (and extension of HT) that combines various media forms (including text) in a unified information delivery system centered around the personal computer (Paske, 1990). Thus, HM represents the marriage of HT and MM. Included in this union are MM components such as two- and three-dimensional structured graphics, spreadsheets, video, sound, and animation.

Frequently, the terms MM and HM are used interchangeably; however, HM is defined as a kind of MM information management and delivery system that links two or more media in an associative, nonlinear (nonserial) way, usually through a software application program. Currently, associative links are established by the system developer. More on this subject later.

HM has also been characterized as (1) having several information structures where links are explicit; (2) being a form of MM (e.g., text, presentation, graphics, animations, voice); and (3) allowing information to be linked by association. The latter is consistent with the belief that HM should be able to reflect the ever-changing connections inherent in all information. A true HM system, however, (1) allows the connection of any piece of information (often called a node) with any other piece in a logical and coherent way; (2) allows users to attach annotations to any piece of information; and (3) provides maps and other navigational aids so users do not become lost in its information space.

Ideally, users are able to interactively navigate through an MM information base by using their intuition, memory, and interests as a guide while always maintaining control. If carefully developed, HM makes information from multiple perspectives more meaningful. In effect, the user becomes the "interactor." In this way, HM can be used for a fast search of specific information because it has an open architecture and can be used with relative ease by non-programmers. This is distinctly different from ES "navigation" where the system provides control through user prompts and the rule inferencing process.

2.1.3. Intellimedia

For discussion purposes, intellimedia (IM) is defined as a fully integrated knowledge and HM-based development and delivery system containing embedded intelligence for static and dynamic multimodal (textual, visual, and auditory) information and knowledge management, sharing, and display (Ragusa, 1994). In effect, IM represents the convergence of nonlinear MM, associative HM links, MM data management methods, a knowledge representation scheme, and a human interface modality. As Figure 1 indicates, IM is an extension of HM enhanced by the inclusion of embedded intelligence, which offers richer and more robust applications than presently provided by ES and HM systems.

In addition to captured knowledge and associative links within IM systems, intelligent interfaces and other enhancements are essential to overcome the limitations of HM. According to Halasz (1988, p. 839) "the simple node and link model is just not rich and complete enough to support the information representation, management, and presentation tasks required by many applications." According to Maybury (1992, p. 75), the key to overcoming this limitation is the notion that intelligent interfaces "go beyond traditional hypermedia or hypertext environments in that they process input and generate output in an 'intelligent' or knowledge-based manner."

Other researchers offer IM-related observations concerned with object association enhancements and their importance. Coyne (1990, p. 207) believes that

> ... the associations that one user brings to a set of data objects may be different than the associations another user may bring to the *same* set of objects. Such software would permit the same objects to be linked differently by different users.

Short (1992, p. 12) indicates that "when applied to non-text media as well as text, the use of hyper links between media 'objects' offers limitless potential for information technology." Not only can a variety of media types be accessed at electronic speed, but MM computers enable nonsequential access to non-print media that previously was available only in a linear manner. With an IM system, intelligent interfaces and customized user associative links to a variety of media become functional realities.

In effect, the described IM implementation is being accomplished by "intelligent agent" technology. These agents serve users to filter, identify, and display user-specific data, information, or knowledge. The topic of intelligent agents is beyond the scope of this chapter and is omitted from further discussion.

2.2.   INTEGRATION ADVANTAGES

The emerging fields of independent, computerized ES and MM exist in various stages of commercial application viability, with a growing number of interesting applications in each field since the mid-1980s. Although these technologies have developed separately, they are related conceptually. Both involve the transfer of knowledge and learning, but they do so from two different perspectives. A primary application of ES provides users with advice based on accumulated knowledge; MM provides an improved presentation of information. Thus, these two technologies have the potential to complement each other and, when combined in the same application, to overcome inherent individual system limitations.

The merger of ES and MM provides an unparalleled impact on the presentation of advisory or training expertise. As is now generally acknowledged, interest, attention, and the retention rate of the audience grows as the number of media forms presented increases. In general, adding MM to the development and use of ES brings many benefits, ranging from the increase of productivity during system development to a better acceptance of the system by the user. More specifically, according to Minsky (1986), at least two media forms are needed for learning to take place.

While HM creates a different kind of open, interactive experience for users, it also presents new problems for system designers who have been burdened by the need for better tools and increased capabilities. Developers have an overriding need for an effective and efficient means of linking information in the MM database. Some investigators believe that the solution to this problem and the ultimate success of HM systems will be dependent on ES technology; for example, the labor-intensive linking, association, and integration required by active HM could be performed by an ES tailored to a specific application domain. By adding knowledge-based control structures to HM systems, not only are designer problems reduced but more robust computer-aided instruction, CAD, CASE, cooperative authoring, and groupware systems are possible.

The author supports the view that greatly improved MM information management is needed and possible. Several investigators with a dominant ES orientation believe that as the two technologies are integrated, there is a greatly expanded potential for interactive MM application. Others who are more MM oriented have addressed the need for more intelligent integrated MM systems. Various ES and MM orientations and system integration models are suggested, depending on user needs. Such integrations have the potential to create new and innovative applications. They may also increase the effectiveness and efficiency of existing applications.

Another way of understanding integration advantages is to consider the pairwise synergy possible between ES and various media forms. An analysis is identified in Table 1, and as indicated, synergistic combinations exist that offer interesting and enhancing possibilities. Of course, combinations of three or more variables are possible and likely when integrated systems are used to their full potential.

This background section has provided an overview of media technologies, definitions of terms, and an identification of integration advantages. Throughout the remainder of this chapter, MM is used in its generic form to identify the use of multiple static and dynamic media forms; however, the terms HM and IM are used for specific discussion where appropriate. The following section provides identification and discussion of integration models, including software architectures and integration orientations, and describes an evolution of system integration models.

3. INTEGRATION MODELS

3.1. SOFTWARE ARCHITECTURES

Synergistic integration of ES and MM technologies requires architectural designs that offer advantages over conventional systems. Figure 2 illustrates a continuum of software architecture possibilities. They are (1) stand-alone, (2) translational, (3) loose coupling, (4) tight coupling, and (5) full integration. Table 2 identifies the level of integration and predominant features, and it summarizes advantages and disadvantages of these software design integration variations. The following discussion briefly describes the predominant features of these software architectures.

3.1.1. Stand-Alone

Much interest has been shown in stand-alone and independent use of ES shells and MM technologies for application development. Large numbers of successful applications of both types are now operational. Numerous ES-oriented references that report successful applications do exist. Similar references exist for MM-based systems. As Table 2 indicates, advantages of stand-alone architectures include availability of commercial tools, ease and speed of development, and independent maintenance. However, disadvantages include total lack of integration, double maintenance, and a lack of synergy. In the context of this chapter, these forms of system development represent a zero level of ES/MM integration.

3.1.2. Translational

The translational form is a variation of separate system development and use. Using this model (Figure 2), an application is developed with one tool (e.g., the ES) and, after translation, migrated to the other (e.g., the MM system). The order of development is driven by user needs and the desired or required form of the final system. Advantages of this Level 1 integration architecture

TABLE 1
Examples of Pairwise Synergy

In using	Rule mgmt.	Text	Graphics	Still	Motion	Sound
Rule mgmt.	Embed consultation requests in rule conclusions	Incorporate inference results in text (immediate or delayed)	Generate graphs using inferenced variables as data source	Display still images based on inferred variables	Display motion based on inferred variables	Activate sound based on rule conclusions
Text	Enable rules to manipulate text content; textual specification of rule set	Incorporate one piece of text into another	Integrate graphical screen with textual display	Integrate still screen with textual display	Integrate motion with textual displays	Integrate sound with textural display
Graphics	Specify graphic operations in rule conclusions	Incorporate graphics into text (immediate or delayed)	Superimpose one graph on another graph	Incorporate graphics into still image	Superimpose graphics onto motion images	Integrate graphics and sound
Still	Specific still identified in rule conclusion	Incorporate still images into text	Superimpose graph on/with still image	Superimpose still image on or/with another	Superimpose motion on still image	Display still image with sound
Sound	Specify sound operation in rule conclusions	Attach sound to text	Attach sound to graphics	Attach sound to still image	Attach sound to motion	Integrate sound on sound

Adapted from Watabe, K., Holsapple, C.W., and Whinston, A.B. (1991). *Journal of Computer Information Systems*, 31(3), 2–8.

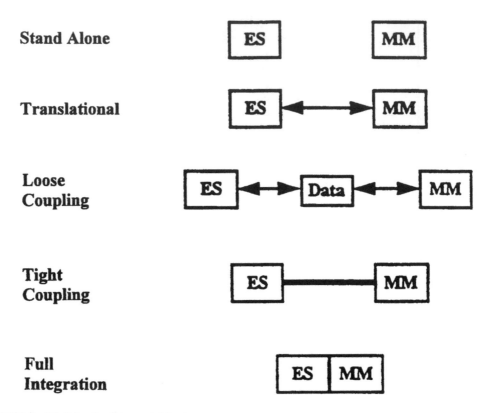

FIGURE 2   Models of software architectures.

(Table 2), like the stand-alone form discussed earlier, include availability of commercial tools, ease and speed of development and maintenance (after selection of the best system), and speed of delivery. Disadvantages include redundant development and the possibility that complete and accurate translation may not be possible, thus requiring retranslation. Also, there is limited synergy in this model, with the exception of the insights provided by the initial development.

3.1.3.   Loose Coupling

Software coupling is the measure of module interdependency. For example, in a conventional CAD/CAM application, application attribute data from a drawing management system would be exported to an independent data file. These data would then be imported from the file by a supportive database management system. Thus, for a change in one system to be reflected in the other, the process of data exportation and importation would have to be invoked.

The loose coupling architecture illustrated in Figure 2, represents an application that has been decomposed into separate ES and MM modules. Intermodular communication occurs via a linked data file. In operation, the ES would use a data-passing capability (inherent in most ES shells) to export system-acquired user data to an external database file for storage and use by the MM system; or, it would import MM acquired user data for knowledge-based manipulation. As Table 2 indicates for this Level 2 integration, advantages include improved synergy and ease of systems development because of available commercial tools, simplicity of design, and reduced data maintenance. Disadvantages include reduction in speed of operations because of communications overhead and overlap in data input and processing, poor overall system maintainability, and the ripple effect caused by an input error.

TABLE 2
Software Architectures and Their Properties

Architecture	Integ. level	Features	Advantages	Disadvantages
Stand-alone	0	Independent modules Independent construction No interaction	Commercial tools available Ease of development Speed of development Independent systems maintenance	No integration Double maintenance No synergy

Translation	1	Independent development
		Development and delivery
		  emphasis
		Begin with either system
			Commercial tools available
			Deliver best system
			Independent systems
			  maintenance
			Speed of delivery
				Redundancy in development
				Accurate translation may be
				  difficult
				Retranslation may be
				  required
				Limited synergy

Loose coupling	2	Application decomposition
		Inter-module
		  communication via data
		Many variations
			Commercial tools available
			Ease of development
			Synergy possible
			Simplicity of design
			Reduced data maintenance
				Overlap in inputs and
				  processing
				High communications
				  overhead
				Speed of operations
				Poor maintainability
				Ripple effect of error

Tight coupling	3	Application decomposition
		  into separate independent
		  modules
		Inter-modular
		  communication via
		  parameter or data passing
			Reduced communications
			  overhead
			Improved run-time
			  performance
			Retention of modularity
			Flexibility in design
			Improved robustness
				Lack of commercial tools
				Increased development and
				  maintenance complexity
				Redundant parameters and
				  data processing
				Validation and verification
				  issues

Full integration	4	ES and MM share data and
		  knowledge representation
		Communications via dual
		  nature of structures
		Cooperative reasoning
			Robustness
			Runtime performance and
			  resource utility
			No redundancy in parameter
			  and data processing
			Potential for improved
			  problem solving
				Specification and design
				  issues
				Development time
				No commercial tools
				Validation and verification
				Maintenance compatibility

3.1.4. Tight Coupling

As Figure 2 illustrates, a tight coupling software architecture consists of linked, separate modules. In this Level 3 integration, the application is decomposed into *independent* modules. Modular decomposition eliminates interdependency on intermediate files and provides virtual seamless integration. Intermodular communication is accomplished by direct parameter or data passing. An example of a tightly integrated system is an application that takes advantage of the capability of many ES shells to call executable programs directly and then return control to the ES when the called program is finished. In a more advanced variation, the ES directly controls the output of the MM system; for example, to display still or motion images in support of ES user needs.

Tight coupling has been found to be especially practical when a small subset of ES techniques is needed, or vice versa, so the designer can focus on one environment in order to provide a better user interface and less system maintenance. As Table 2 indicates, advantages of this architecture include improved run-time operation because of reduced interprogram communications, retention of modularity and flexibility in design, and improved robustness. Disadvantages include a lack of integrated commercial tools, increased development and maintenance complexity, redundant parameter and data processing, and issues of system validation and verification.

3.1.5.   Full Integration

In a full integration software architecture, as indicated in Figure 2, both systems are integrally linked. The ES and MM elements act in virtual unison, share data and knowledge representations, offer communication via their dual structure, and allow cooperative reasoning. An example is an interactive intelligent tutoring system in which various media forms, including test questions, are presented to a student by the MM system, while an embedded ES system continually monitors progress and performance and prescribes remediation. With this architecture, interactive exchange between system elements is done in real time and in a seamless way without user interaction. As indicated in Table 2, this architecture represents the highest integration possible (Level 4). Advantages include robustness, excellent runtime performance and resource utility, no redundancy in parameter or data processing, and improved problem-solving potential. From a design perspective at this level of integration, the designer is concerned with only one virtual environment — better design and implementation of the overall application is possible. Also, a more uniform user interface and reduced system maintenance can be achieved with better design and implementation of the overall application.

This architecture is not without some disadvantages. Experienced and proficient developers and programmers are needed to create and implement such a high-level and interactive architecture. Other disadvantages include specification and design issues, increased development time, lack of existing commercially available tools, validation and verification issues, and maintenance compatibility.

3.2.   Integration Orientations

The benefits of integration depend on specific system design orientations and their functionalities. From a user perspective, Figure 3 illustrates three integration orientations: (1) ES supported by MM, (2) MM supported by ES, and (3) complementary (joint venture) systems. In the first two orientations, one technology is dominant over the other. Both share equal status in the last orientation, with each technology executing different tasks to support the other.

3.2.1.   ES Supported by MM

Figure 4 illustrates the support MM can provide to ES. For discussion purposes, the structure of an ES is divided by a dashed line between the development and consultation environments. A series of numbered MM symbols shows the points of MM support during these ES phases.

3.2.1.1.   Support to the Development Environment

Providing knowledge. Knowledge for ES is acquired from two major sources: undocumented (experts) and documentation (e.g., manuals, procedures, databases, video/films, and textbooks). In many ES developments, multiple sources of undocumented and documented knowledge are used in the same application. Undocumented knowledge may be in various MM forms such as taped interviews (audio), interview transcripts (text), and knowledge structures and mental models (diagrams). Documented knowledge sources include an even larger variety of MM forms, including text, illustrations, still pictures, motion film, video, and audio recordings. It is becoming common for these analog and digital forms of knowledge to be stored magnetically and optically (MM 1 in Figure 4). If documentation knowledge is represented in one of these media forms and storage formats, it is easier to use than if it is resident in people who may not be available when needed or at all.

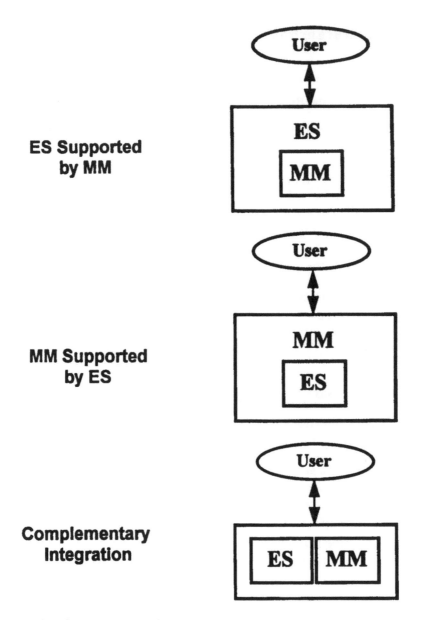

FIGURE 3 Models of integration orientation.

Acquisition of knowledge. One of the most difficult tasks in building ES is to acquire knowledge from human experts. Knowledge acquisition is a discovery activity that has been widely used to transfer knowledge from a source of expertise to a representational form. MM technologies have the potential to support this process (MM 2 in Figure 4) and include:

- Knowledge diagramming, a top-down graphical description of domain knowledge. This method uses graphic techniques to define scope, enhance understanding, and define modules of knowledge.
- Knowledge acquisition student training. An example would be the educational MM tool called KARTT (see Liebowitz and Bland, 1992), which is used to teach the knowledge acquisition process with the use of HT and video clips related to knowledge elicitation.
- General MM support during the knowledge acquisition process.

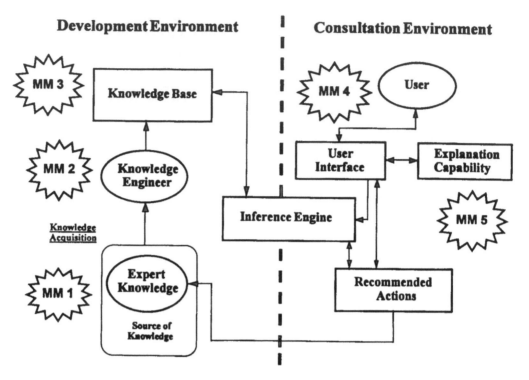

FIGURE 4   Support multimedia can provide to an expert system.

Representing the knowledge base. While traditional ES mainly use rules in their knowledge base, newer systems are venturing into the use of MM devices for knowledge-base rules and media storage and retrieval (e.g., CD-ROM, EROD, and WORM drives [MM 3 in Figure 4]). An example is the knowledge-based system described by Dean (1992) that writes specifications for building construction. The system stores rules and current specifications on a CD-ROM disk. Other knowledge representation such as frames and semantic networks may be stored as MM schema and object-oriented programming formats (e.g., icons [MM 3 in Figure 4]).

3.2.1.2.   Support to the Consultation Environment

Improving user dialogue. In most ES, the dialogue between the system and the user is done via the keyboard with the system asking questions (frequently by showing menus and prompting questions) and the user providing answers. MM enhances this dialogue (MM 4 in Figure 4), for example, by asking questions while the person who answers appears on the computer screen. User replies are currently entered via the keyboard; however, as speaker-independent voice recognition systems become more effective and economical, verbal system inputs will become feasible. Users can then ask for and receive verbal or other appropriate MM explanations.

Displaying results. ES primarily provide advice to users. This includes diagnoses and suggestions on ways to correct an equipment problem; for example, appropriate repair procedures are identified, retrieved, and displayed during a troubleshooting dialogue. When complex equipment is involved, the advice will be supported either individually or in combination with schematics, drawings, still and full-motion pictures and audio instructions (MM 4 in Figure 4). Another way to display results is by developing special interface designs that are enhanced by MM; this will provide effective means of accessing MM database information. These types of support are also very important for intelligent computer-based training instruction and remediation.

Providing explanations. While displaying results and providing recommendations are essential features of ES, MM supplements explanations of "why?" "why not?" and "what if?" user questions

(MM 5 in Figure 4). Examples include supporting graphs (e.g., trend lines), display of pictures (still and motion), or graphical comparisons of alternatives. This functionality provides HM explanations for knowledge-based equipment diagnosis applications. The HM user interface includes template-based text, graphics, and icons that represent linked objects. These objects communicate by messages and use a standard, object-oriented programming approach. Another advantage of MM-enhanced explanation capabilities is the potential to increase user system acceptance.

3.2.2. MM Supported by ES

The idea of making MM more intelligent has been pursued for several years in commercial and university research laboratories. In recognition of this important topic, the American Association for Artificial Intelligence (AAAI) organized a special (and pioneering) "Intelligent Multimedia Interfaces" workshop at their Ninth National Conference (*AAAI Proceedings*, 1991). Various research topics and applications were identified and discussed during this workshop. In the following situations, MM presentation is the primary objective of the integrated system with intelligent support provided by an ES component.

3.2.2.1. Support to the Mix of Media Tools and/or Their Output

ES technology can assist users in selecting, retrieving, and manipulating MM information. For example, a system that reasons in detail about user needs or about the meaning of viewer questions and is then able to choose intelligently among media alternatives available to the user for improved presentations and response. Once this type of system becomes economically feasible, it could be added, for example, to executive information systems (EIS) for the purpose of providing a personal touch, which is considered important to some executives.

3.2.2.2. Design of Appropriate Mix of Text and Graphics

An ES combined with a natural language processor to support a mix of text and graphics development, layout, and presentation was developed by Wahlster, Andre', Graf, and Rist (1991). The result is a variety of customized MM documents for the intended audience and situation. The system is composed of a presentation planner and text generator and a layout manager and graphics generator. All components are guided by an embedded ES knowledge base.

3.2.2.3. Using an ES as a Guide for HM

HM may contain highly sophisticated textual, graphic, image, or motion forms of knowledge. While the user of an HM system has complete freedom of navigation, a systematic procedure to navigate through the accumulated knowledge does not exist. The objective of the system determines the quality of navigation requirements. If the goal is learning or exploration, the results can be excellent. If specific knowledge is the objective, the user may inadvertently navigate around (and therefore miss) important points of information.

ES can be used to explore knowledge by presenting the user with options or by evaluating user inputs. The system then branches to an appropriate portion of the knowledge base and presents other options to the user. This process continues until a conclusion is reached or a recommended option list is presented. In this way, all the critical knowledge components are touched with predefined, mapped, or guided navigation. By merging ES and HM, the user is guided so that a complete use of the HM system is achieved.

3.2.3. Complementary Integration (Joint-Venture)

In the previous configurations, either the ES played the major role and MM supported it, or vice versa. However, the two technologies can be used *independently* to perform different tasks of the same job. Thus, instead of supporting each other as in previous software architectures, they complement each other.

Such a combination is likely to occur in complex systems where the ES itself is integrated with other computer-based information systems (e.g., databases or complex applications). In these systems, the MM can be part of the application itself (e.g., displaying MM educational material) while the ES performs some advisory or monitoring task (e.g., determining student learning style preference and identifying the best type of presentation material or providing remediation guidance). In this complementary manner, ES/MM integration will be expanded to include other computer-based and database-oriented information systems.

3.3.   An Evolution of System Integration Models

Software architectures and integration orientations have been identified in previous discussions. Figure 5 integrates these design considerations and illustrates a spectrum of system integration models: past, present, near-term, and future. This phased evolution of system synergy serves as a framework for subsequent analysis and discussion. While Figure 5 may not include all possible combinations of the focus technologies (ES, MM, HM, and IM), it does provide a perspective of the breadth and scope of major design considerations and integration possibilities. Other model variations will, of course, evolve in the future.

3.3.1.   Separate Systems (Phase 1)

Figure 5 identifies various models of separate ES and MM systems. Forms 1a and 1b illustrate the stand-alone and independent use of ES shells and MM systems that were dominant in the past. There are now thousands of Form 1a operational ES and a growing number of Form 1b MM systems that use authoring systems for program development and control. Form 1c is translational in nature; i.e., an application is initially developed with one tool and, after content and structure translation, migrated to another. With Form 1c, the order of system development may not be important unless requirements call for a specific final user system design, early application viability, or functionality testing. If functional testing is important, the ES should be developed first in order to take advantage of the rapid prototyping and validation/verification methodologies customarily used in the ES development process. For obvious reasons, and those discussed earlier, separate system models lack real integration synergy even though certain development advantages exist. Separate system models do, however, represent embryonic development stages of integrated systems.

3.3.2.   MM Integration (Phase 2)

MM integration shown in Figure 5 is the present state of the technology marriage. Form 2a uses the functionality built into most ES development tools to call external executable programs. As Bielawski and Lewand (1991, p. 95) note, "It is this feature that enables developers to transcend the constraints of a rigid expert system paradigm and to create systems that are more intelligent." In this manner, access to formatted alphanumeric data and unformatted text is retrieved and updated. Usually, this form of integration allows access to only one media type at a time. However, calls to executable programs allow access to various static and dynamic media (still images, drawings, animation, full-motion, and audio) stored on laserdiscs, and WORM devices. These program "hooks" allow more robust program functionality and provide a synergy not previously possible without time-consuming and costly raw code or symbolic program development.

Loosely coupled models, Forms 2b and 2c, allow dominance by either technology. In these designs, the external call concept is expanded to take advantage of ES hooks to databases and spreadsheets. The database context allows the passage of bi-directional data to one or more shared database file(s), which can be resident on either PC or mainframe systems. An example of the Form 2b integration model is the development of a PC-based intelligent visual database management systems (IVDBMS) that uses ES to classify and retrieve still pictures and alphanumeric data from a shared database.

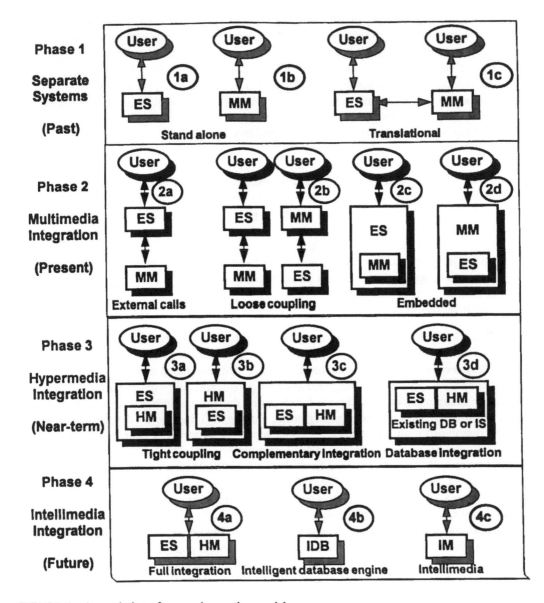

FIGURE 5   An evolution of system integration models.

Forms 2d and 2e represent embedded designs that result in a more seamless integration of MM and ES than external calls and loose coupling can accommodate. The essence of these embedded designs, which is important to both developers and users, is that the interface is transparent with control maintained by the dominant system and supported by the other. An example of an embedded system would be one in which either the ES or the MM system contained an embedded database or subprogram that was of only secondary importance to the other.

3.3.3.   HM Integration (Phase 3)

Near-term HM integration models that link two or more media in an associative way are shown in Figure 5. Forms 3a and 3b represent tight coupling paradigms of virtual seamless integration. Similar to previously discussed embedded systems, direct data and parameter passing are used between systems. However, unlike embedded design Forms 2d and 2e, these models take advantage of the associative links inherent in HM systems. The specific form used is determined by the dominant application methodology. For example, knowledge-intensive applications would use Form 3a where the ES is supported by HM. Conversely, media-dominated applications (for example, one which is text or data intensive) would use Form 3b where ES support the HM system.

Form 3c represents complementary integration where one system supports the other in a joint-venture manner. In these systems, MM is part of the application itself (e.g., animation of the simulation process), while the ES performs some advisory task (e.g., dealing with selection of models or giving advice about the length of the simulation).

Form 3d, another near-term design possibility, is a hybrid that combines the features of complementary integration (Form 3c), embedded designs (Forms 2d and 2e), and tightly coupled features (Forms 3a and 3b) in an HM context. For this database supporting design, a complementary ES and HM system is used to interface in a seamless way to existing "legacy" corporate databases and information systems, primarily through the use of 4th-generation structured query language (SQL). In this model, the ES provides procedural control of the system and access to the corporate database. HM elements support a flexible user interface and provide access to online help. While many ES tools support SQL query and database access, none presently possess complementary HM functionality. As a result, applications of Form 3d are limited.

3.3.4.   IM Integration (Phase 4)

Figure 5 illustrates three forms of future integration design. These models are not defined as well as those previously discussed and, in effect, represent a future enabling technology. By design and definition, they are a robust implementation of Phase 3, HM integration concepts and models.

As defined earlier, IM is a fully integrated knowledge- and HM-based development and delivery system that contains embedded intelligence for static and dynamic multimodal (textual, visual, and auditory) information and knowledge management, sharing, and display. By definition, these systems allow distributed multiple user, bidirectional access to all forms of MM and possess unrestricted, intelligent association-linking between elements.

These futuristic IM integration forms have several functional features in common. They allow system developers and users to share ES/MM information and knowledge representations, offer communication via the dual nature of their structures and networks, and fully support cooperative reasoning. They also possess "interoperability," which implies the seamless connection of distributed, heterogeneous information and knowledge resources. The term "interoperability" designates a need; however, it is a capability associated with very few real application solutions. While IM systems share common functionality, several models and implementations are possible.

Form 4a in Figure 5, a full integration model, allows total integration in an autonomous, stand-alone manner. Full and seamless integration is achieved through a shared data and knowledge representation structure and inherent linked communications. Among design goals of this model are easier system design, "seamless modularity," and autonomous, unrestricted user control.

This design is best illustrated by the object-oriented hypermedia support systems (HSS) conceptual model developed by Garrity and Volonino (1993). HSS is a hybrid system that provides user access to MM information and knowledge through the integration of three software technologies: hyper-navigational user control, MM, and object-orientated programming. Hyper-navigation, which allows branching to any MM information and knowledge node in an HM network, provides users with intuitive and flexible access. MM of various types exist at various nodes within the system. An object-oriented methodology using software topics is the integrating mechanism for this virtual information system. These software topics include program code, window or screen objects, production rules, MM objects, database information, and meta-knowledge and meta-information (Garrity and Volonino, 1993).

Another IM integration model, Form 4b, supports direct user interfacing to an intelligent database engine. This engine would need to have the capability to implement the features of a deductive, object-oriented intelligent database model. For those working on intelligent database engines, HM has important object-oriented database implications. For example, current relational databases cannot directly support natural representations of graph-structured object spaces. As a result, complex relationships between MM products and objects cannot be expressed directly.

Object-oriented databases form an important and necessary phase in the evolution of databases and data models. Integration will be required in such diverse fields as object-oriented concepts, ES, HM, and information retrieval. The future of these systems lies in intelligent databases that provide new technologies for information management presently and into the 21st Century.

Form 4c is a full IM model not yet modeled which cannot be fully defined or described. Basically, it is an ideal system that provides system developers and users with a full range of functionalities. This hypothetical system includes user independent, bidirectional natural language (or virtual reality interfaces) and full-bandwidth network access.

Various concepts of future intelligent computer systems will require features for such systems. They include MM database capabilities that create, import, store, retrieve, edit, and delete a full range of MM information. Virtual reality features are included; these transform the user into a simulated world. Intelligent agent enhancements that mimic intelligence and provide personalized services tailored to specific user needs.

As with other models in this category, the system possesses intelligent inferencing capabilities to represent specific and general knowledge and a full range of rich capabilities to accommodate multiple user attributes, preferences, capabilities, goals, and objectives. The systems's information annotation and navigational utilities will prevent users from becoming lost in "virtual hyperspace."

As requisite individual and integrated capabilities become a practical reality, these advanced Phase 4 IM models will provide users with multisensory, nonlinear, highly interactive, edit-oriented, multi-user capabilities. Virtual reality and other 3-D perspective systems that are presently evolving, display objects in ways that take advantage of our natural binocular vision (i.e., stereopsis) to create an illusion of depth. In the future, the expanded depth provided by 3-D will provide a much richer dimension to science, industry, and medical applications. Until then, other contemporary integration models must suffice.

The software architectures, orientations, and system integration models presented in this section provided a framework for descriptive analysis and feature definition. The following section briefly identifies application domains and some representative integrated ES/MM examples.

4.   APPLICATION DOMAINS AND EMERGING INTEGRATED APPLICATIONS

4.1.   APPLICATION DOMAINS

As previously discussed, several investigators have recognized the promise and advantage of ES/MM integration synergy. Many have concluded that these integrated technologies provide opportunities for solution of specific domain problems that presently cannot be solved or are more productively resolved in this manner. As a result, a wider interest beyond laboratory research and technical reports is being shown for integrated applications.

Interactive MM systems are primarily used for diagnostic applications that were formerly the mainstay of ES. Future, not yet fully explored, possibilities include (1) intelligent computer aided tutoring, (2) simulation and training, (3) human resources development, and (4) performance measurement. Additional opportunities within the productions operations domain include (1) inventory management, (2) planning and control, (3) operations management, (4) purchasing, (5) quality control, and (6) logistics. Upon reflection, other domain-specific applications can be identified.

Table 3 identifies a spectrum of business, science and engineering, education, and entertainment domains where integrated ES/MM solutions are appropriate; undoubtedly, others exist. Also indicated are representative application examples of each, including diagnostic, information preparation

TABLE 3
Examples of ES/MM Integration Synergy

Domains	Representative application examples
Executive information	Capture, store, distribute, present, and manage internal corporate asset knowledge and experience between top managers with the ES used to correlate MM information (Karr, 1992).
Distributed MM information systems	Facilitate the storage, retrieval, integration, and transmission of formatted data (database management systems), unformatted text (document retrieval systems), pictures/diagrams/schematics (image management systems), audio (message systems), and expertise (knowledge-based systems) (Coyne, 1990).
Diagnostics	Use captured expert knowledge to guide and provide explanations (and training support) for troubleshooting with the support of MM repair procedures, graphics, schematics, still images, and full-motion video where appropriate.
Intelligent educational/training	Construct intelligent computer-aided instructional systems that model the student and/or the instructional domain to support interactive learning and remediation based on competency level, learning preference, progress, and needs of the student (or teacher). Use MM for learning and comprehension enhancement.
Interactive presentations	Create and synthesize from a MM database, interactive MM presentations based on audience attributes, needs, and desired level of participation; and presenter objectives and available resources.
Scientific/engineering	Use graphics and animation to visualize data, experimental results, layouts, and designs; and provide capabilities for assisted interactive analysis and revision.
Technical documentation	Use the power of an integrated system to select and combine various static media (text, graphics, and still images) into compound documents.
Multimedia documents	Create compound MM documents that contain static and time-varying media for user-interactive exploration and manipulation, publication, or transmission to colleagues, customers, or suppliers.
Home entertainment	Use personal preference and mood knowledge/information to create real-time entertainment presentations and interactive games.
Video productions	Use an integrated system to intelligently select, locate, and combine stored full-motion veideo and audio segments for review, edit, and presentation.
Consumer sales/service	Provide selective MM product and service information to consumers based on needs, preferences, cost limitations, and product/service availability.
Simulation and modeling	Use knowledge-based expertise to advise on the best simulation model to use and the length of the simulation, and MM to animate the simulation itself.
MM networking	Support resource setup, operation, and management for MM conferencing, videoconferencing, collaborative systems, E-mail, and broadband and wide/local-area networks.

and presentation, sales and services, and communications. While this list may not be exhaustive, it shows a depth and breadth of user and application possibilities. Various architectures, orientations, models, and media forms will be required because of the diversity of these domain and application possibilities.

4.2. A SURVEY OF EMERGING INTEGRATED APPLICATIONS

The author's review of research and development reports, journal articles, conference proceedings, workshops, and other sources identifies a number of instances in which ES, MM, and HM have been successfully integrated in one application. Table 4 lists 30 integrated ES/MM applications that have been categorized and identified by model form number (Figure 5), application acronym or name, user/developer/sponsor, function, media used, and reference source. Because of the dynamic nature of these applications, their status (prototype, under development, or operational) has not been identified.

Table 4 applications were limited to PC and rule-based systems where enough information existed to identify model forms and system descriptions. In some cases, developers were contacted to corroborate information. Excluded from this survey were (1) systems based primarily on semantic networks, frames, natural language, or virtual reality and (3-D) designs (few of which exist), (2) Phase 1 — Separate Systems (e.g., individual ES and MM system) that are abundant, and (3) Phase 4 — IM integrated systems that are yet to be fully developed.

Even with these exclusions, the number and variety of identified systems demonstrate the interest in integrated ES/MM systems. The review revealed that system developers and users reported numerous instances where integration provided benefits greater than those possible with separate, independent systems. Also noted was the fact that synergy and potential benefits of such systems are just now being realized. In some cases (for example, operational systems), quantitative cost/benefit data are being collected and analyzed. Table 4 lists a variety of public and private sector applications and users. However, help desk and other forms of equipment diagnostics appear to be the dominant application, consistent with the findings of Szuprowicz (1991). Text, data, and graphics are the predominant media forms; not unexpectedly so since these media forms are used by most computer users accustomed to word processors, spreadsheets, and database applications. Still images and motion are growing in use, while animation and audio are not as widely used.

The integration of ES or knowledge-based systems in the form of intelligent agents and MM (including virtual reality) presently remains virtually unexplored. Numerous application categories and visual perspectives exist. They include: MM information access and management, collaboration in which users work together on shared media forms using personal video-conferencing, Internet electronic commerce to match buyer needs and provider goods and services, and more adaptive user interfaces. Requirements for such virtual systems are beginning to evolve (see Stuart, 1996; Machover, 1996). Numerous other possibilities are yet to be identified and developed.

5. RESEARCH ISSUES

This chapter discussion and applications survey indicate that ES/MM integration offers opportunities to produce innovative applications that should appeal to a large number of users. However, various research issues must be addressed if ES/MM integration is to be accepted more readily by system developers and application users. Design/development and implementation issues and tasks include the following.

Design/development

- Developing more robust integration tools for applications design, development, and use.
- Identifying criteria for the use of alternative knowledge representation (frames, semantic nets, etc.) and user interface systems (e.g., natural language, virtual reality).

TABLE 4
Integrated Expert System/Multimedia Applications

Form	Name	User	Function	Media	Reference
2a	The Chateau Connoisseur	Univ. of Cent. FL–Institute for Simulation and Training	Demonstration of interactive interfacing between an ES shell and laserdisc for MM information presentation	Text, graphics, still images, motion, and sound	Ragusa and Orwig (1991)
2a	General Dynamics–Expert System Prototype (GD-ESP)	General Dynamics Space Systems Division	MM diagnostics for an Atlas-Centaur commercial launch vehicle subsystem	Text, data, still images, motion, and sound	Acuna, Crossley, and Gay (1990)
2a	Intelligent Study Individualized Instruction System (ISIIS)	Florida School Board of Education	Demonstration of intelligent computer-based instruction	Text, data, still images, motion, and sound	Kraus and Rogers (1991)
2a	The Environmental Learning Multimedia Application (THELMA)	Florida School Board of Eduation/EPA	Intelligent computer-based tutoring elementary school students in environmental education	Text, data, still images, motion, and sound	Eglin, Dietzel, Gilliam, and Padden (1991)
2a	Physics Expert Recertification Multimedia Inservice Training System (PERMITS)	Florida School Board of Education	Intelligent computer-based recertification and inservice training for middle school physics teachers	Text, data, still images, motion, and sound	Gamble, Lelewellyn, and Weeks (1991)
2a	Marketing Expert System (M.E.S.)	Orange County Convention/Civic Center	Orlando Florida Convention Center marketing sales and booking assistance	Still images and text	Ragusa and Turban (1992)
2a	Sea World Intelligent Multi Media Expert (SWIMMER)	Sea World of Orlando	Interactive curator of marine life for visitors	Text and still images	Jones, Scholer, Cardinal, and Frulio (1991)
2a	Total Organization Productivity Support (TOPS-1)	U.S. Post Office	Operation and maintenance for electromechanical letter scanning and sorting equipment	Text, graphics, still images, motion, and sound	Schmuller (1992)
2a	Crop Rotation Planning System (CROPS)	Various agricultural groups	Virginia and N. Carolina crop planning, scheduling, and management advisement	Text, data, and graphics	Stone (1992)

	System	Organization	Application	Media	Reference
2a	Advanced Cooling Cart Expert System (ACES)	Department of Defense	Technician advisor to locate and repair faults in electromechanical military equipment	Text, data, still images, and motion graphics	Ford (1990)
2b	SA*VANT	Electric Power Research Institute	Troubleshooting and rapid diagnosis advice and repair suggestions for power systems	Voice, text, video, and graphics	Turban (1992)
2b	CSI	Competitive Solutions, Inc.	Home buyer visual inspection and mortgage analysis	Images, data, and voice	Turban (1992)
2b	TI	Texas Instruments	Hand-held mainframe information delivery for tourist guidance or commodity trading	Voice, text, and graphics	Turban (1992)
2b	Automated Work-Station Expert System of Maintained Equipment (AWESOME)	City of Los Angeles	Help desk support for city-wide computer systems	Text, data, and still images	Clarke, Turban, and Wang (1993)
2b	Photo REtrieval Search System (PRESS)	NASA-Public Affairs	Intelligent photo classification and retrieval system for NASA Public Affairs press site	Text, data, and still images	Ptacek, Pepe, Rogers, and Kraus (1990)
2c	Intelligent Visual DBMS	NASA-Lockheed	Intelligent visual database management for space shuttle processing image classification, storage, transmission, and retrieval	Text, data, and still images	Leigh, Ragusa, and Gilliam (1993); Ragusa, Dologite, Orwig, and Mockler (in press)
2d	Help desk	Color Tile, Inc.	Help desk assistance for company hardware, software, data communications, financial, and sales support	Text, data, and graphics	Kulik (1992)
2d	Consumer Appliance Diagnostic System (CADS)	Whirlpool Corp.	Diagnostics and service advice to Whirlpool appliance help desk representatives	Text and graphics	Danilewitz and Freiheit (1992)
2d	Weapon Control Consol	U.S. Navy	Technician adviser for submarine Weapon Control Console electronic fault logic diagnoses	Text and graphics	Bielawski and Lewand (1991), 128–136
2d	SPECSystem	The American Institute of Architects	Specification preparation assistance for building construction	Text and graphics (drawings)	Dean (1992)

TABLE 4
Integrated Expert System/Multimedia Applications *(continued)*

Form	Name	User	Function	Media	Reference
2e	InfoXpert	Zenith Data Systems	Company microcomputer product information and customer assistance	Text, graphics, and animation	Bielawski and Lewand (1991), 151–156
3a	ACE 196	Intel Corp.	Customer product information and programming help	Text, graphics, and data (computer code)	Bielawski and Lewand (1991), 121–128
3b	Executive Information Application (EIA)	Digital Equipment Corporation	Quality improvement of executive interactions and information sharing	Text, data, graphics, and video	Karr (1992)
3c	Integrated Maintenance ADvisor (IMAD)	Carnegie Group, Inc.	Diagnostics and problem-solving assistance for information management of large, complex online textual databases	Text and graphics	Bielawski and Lewand (1991), 51–55; Hayes and Pepper (1989)
3c	The Benefits Administration Consultant (BAC)	Westinghouse Electric Corp.	Employee health-care benefits planning and administration	Text and data	Bielawski and Lewand (1991), 168–175
3d	Key indicator tracking systems	RWD Technologies Inc.	Internal customer dissatisfaction tracking, and market potential and new product release advice	Text, graphics, and data	Bielawski and Lewand (1991), 175–189
3d	REGional Information System (REGIS)	United Nations/U.S. Government	Presentation of organizational and general information about African aquaculture	Text, data, and graphics	Bielawski and Lewand (1991), 145–151
3a	Fire control system Maintenance Advisor	Naval Postgraduate School	Diagnostics advisor for MK 92 Mod 2 fire control systems	Graphics, video, sound and text	Meisch (1994)
3a	Operator training and diagnostics system	IBM	CMOS fabricator computer-aided training certification and diagnostics system	Text, graphics, still images, sound, motion, and animation	IBM (1993)
3a	Help desk advisor	Software Artistry	Help desk problem solver and call/problem tracker	Graphics, animation, and text	Frances (1993)

- Developing a more formalized method for matching software architectures, orientations, and integration models (loose, embedded, tight, complementary, and full integration) to application domains and types.
- Investigating improved methods of multiple media dynamic coordination, coherent textural and graphical generation, and automatic design of graphic systems.
- Developing the means to extend hyperlinks to virtually unlimited and varied MM information and knowledge sources.
- Continuing to investigate the concepts and various forms of IM.
- Determining through empirical means what resolution and color pixel depth combinations are best suited to various applications and user needs. Considerations for visual display systems in virtual environments includes spatial resolution, depth resolution, system responsiveness, field of view, storage and refresh rate, and color (Stuart, 1996)

Implementation

- Determining how best to use existing and near-term information networks and client servers for applications requiring high-quality color still images, full motion, and digital audio.
- Determining empirically if MM-based ES are more acceptable and functional to users than stand alone ES.
- Investigating the relationship between creativity and interactive MM.
- Evaluating the impact of intelligent MM systems on people and organizations (for example: Is retention rate really improved when more media are added? Does individual and organizational productivity improve?).
- Developing adoption strategies for integrated systems.
- Investigating the use of integrated ES/MM to support group work in general and group decision support systems (DSS) in particular.
- Developing an appropriate cost-benefit framework for the justification of such systems.

When answers to these and related issues are known, many existing integrated system design and development problems will be solved and implementation opportunities expanded. The problem is not a lack of challenges but, rather, the priority of the issues to be resolved.

6. FUTURE TRENDS AND SUMMARY

Increased information in a variety of static and dynamic media forms (text, data, graphics, still images, animation, full-motion video, speech, and nonspeech audio) is creating information management problems for a variety of users and application domains. As a result, a need exists to design and construct improved and more sophisticated information management, sharing, and display systems. A case has been made to show that integrated ES/MM systems containing embedded intelligence are being used to solve a diversity of media format problems and user information processing needs. Past, present, near-term, and future synergistic models and orientations of MM, HM, and IM integration with ES were identified and described.

Because of projected increased computer and network system capabilities and reduced hardware and software costs, it is reasonable to assume that integrated systems will be found in a greater number of applications in the future. An identification of application domains and a survey emerging applications indicated that diverse and varied needs exist. This technology marriage offers possibilities for an even wider range of applications, limited only by the imagination of developers and users.

Continued analysis and further applications research are necessary. These activities will explore the full range of possibilities for interactive integrated MM and ES technologies and make these synergistic integrations more widespread and infused into daily work, training, educational, and recreational activities. Hopefully, this chapter will stimulate discussion, causing others to further identify issues and priorities, expand fundamental research, increase the realization of integrated system potential, and identify and build additional integrated applications.

ACKNOWLEDGMENTS

Research on this topic was sponsored under a University of Central Florida/NASA-Kennedy Space Center (NASA-KSC) Cooperative Agreement (NAG-10-0058). Appreciation is expressed to members of NASA-KSC's Advanced Projects Office for their vision and support during this project; and to Dr. Efraim Turban of California State–Long Beach and Dr. Jay Liebowitz of The George Washington University for their guidance and encouragement.

GENERAL REFERENCES

AAAI Proceedings of the 1991 Workshop on Intelligent Multimedia Interfaces, (1991, July). Anaheim, CA: AAAI Publications.

Bielawski, L. and Lewand, R. (1991). *Intelligent Systems Design: Integrating Expert Systems, Hypermedia, and Database Technologies.* New York, NY: Wiley.

Blanchard, D.(1996). Agents infiltrate the business world, *PCAI,* 10(4), 39–42.

Chinnock, C. (1996). Virtual reality goes to work. *Byte,* 21(3), 26–28.

Coyne, J. (1990). The importance of expert systems in a hypermedia environment. *Proceedings of the IEEE Conference on Managing Expert System Programs and Projects* (pp. 205–208), Bethesda, MD: IEEE.

Fermoyle, K. (1990, November). The magic of multimedia. *Presentation Products Magazine,* pp. 32–36.

Garrity, E.J. and Volonino, L. (1993). Object-oriented hypermedia support systems. *Proceedings of the 26th Annual Hawaii International Conference on System Sciences* (pp. 311–319). Kauai, Hawaii: HICSS.

Halasz, F.G. (1988). Reflections on NoteCards: Seven issues for the next generation of hypermedia systems. *Communications of the ACM,* 31(7), 836–852.

Hayashi, A.M. and Varney, S.E. (1996). Six hot technologies for the 21st century. *Datamation,* 42(14), 68–73.

Liebowitz, J. and Bland, K. (1992). KARTT: A multimedia tool that builds knowledge acquisition skills. *PC AI,* 6(6), 28–30.

Lougheed, K. and Ragusa, J.M. (1992). *Multimedia for Business: A Survey of Definition, Categories, and Applications* (Research Report #4). Orlando: University of Central Florida, Intelligent Multimedia Applications Laboratory.

Machover, C. (1996, June). What virtual reality needs. *Information Display,* 32–34.

Maybury, M. (1992). Intelligent multimedia interfaces. *IEEE Expert,* 7(1), 75–77.

Minsky, M. (1986). *The Society of Mind,* New York, NY: Simon and Schuster.

Paske, R. (1990). Hypermedia: A brief history and progress report. *T.H.E. Journal,* 18(1), 53–56.

Ragusa, J.M. (1994). Models and applications of multimedia, hypermedia, and intellimedia integration with expert systems. *Expert Systems with Applications,* 7(3) 407–426.

Raskin, R. (1990). Multimedia: The next frontier for business? *PC Magazine,* 9(13), 151–192.

Short, D.D. (1992). Instruction in a postliterate culture: Multimedia in higher education. *Journal of Information Systems Education,* 4(3), 11–21.

Stuart, R. (1996). *The Design of Virtual Environments.* New York, NY: McGraw Hill.

Szuprowicz, B.O. (1991). The multimedia connection. *Expert Systems: Planning/Implementation/Integration,* 2(4), 59–63.

Toffer, A. (1970). *Future Shock.* New York, NY: Random House.

Wahlster, W., Andre, E., Graf, W., and Rist, T. (1991). Designing illustrated texts: How language production is influenced by graphics generation. *Proceedings of the Ninth National Conference on Artificial Intelligence (AAAI-91): Workshop Notes on Intelligent Multimedia Interfaces,* Anaheim, CA, 9–20.

Watabe, K., Holsapple, C.W., and Whinston, A.B. (1991). Solving complex problems via software integration. *Journal of Computer Information Systems,* 31(3), 2–8.

APPLICATION REFERENCES

Acuna, A., Crossley, B., and Gay, K. (1990). General Dynamics-expert system prototype (GD-ESP). Unpublished manuscript, University of Central Florida, Intelligent Multimedia Applications Laboratory, Orlando.

Bielawski, L. and Lewand, R. (1991). *Intelligent Systems Design: Integrating Expert Systems, Hypermedia, and Database Technologies.* New York, NY: Wiley.

Clark, D.E., Turban, E., and Wang, P. (1993). An integrated expert system/multimedia for troubleshooting of computer hardware at the city of Los Angeles. *Expert Systems with Applications,* 7(3), 441–449.

Danilewitz, D.B. and Freiheit, F.E. (1992). A knowledge-based system within a cooperative processing environment. In A.C. Scott and P. Klahr (Eds.), *Proceedings of the IAAI-92 Conference* (pp. 19–36). Anaheim, CA: AAAI Press.

Dean, R.P. (1992). SPECSystem: A knowledge-based system on CD-ROM. *PC AI,* 6(6), 36–38.

Eglin, R., Dietzel, R.A., Gilliam, M.C., and Padden, C. (1991). The environmental learning multimedia application (THELMA). Unpublished manuscript, University of Central Florida, Intelligent Multimedia Applications Laboratory, Orlando.

Ford, B. (1990). An Expert Diagnostic System Using Multimedia. *Expert Systems: Planning, Implementation, Integration,* 2(3), 19–24.

Frances, R. (1993). Help for the help desk. *Datamation,* 39, 59–60.

Gamble, D. Llewellyn, M., and Weeks, D. (1991). Physics expert recertification multimedia inservice training system (PERMITS). Unpublished manuscript, University of Central Florida, Intelligent Multimedia Applications Laboratory, Orlando.

Hayes, J. and Pepper, J. (1989). Toward an integrated maintenance advisor. *Proceedings of Hypertext '89,* (pp. 119–127). New York, NY: ACM.

Hofferd, T., Roulston, M., McGuire, B., and Shoemaker, K. (1991). Orange county convention/civic center marketing expert system (M.E.S.). Unpublished manuscript, University of Central Florida, Intelligent Multimedia Applications Laboratory, Orlando.

International Business Machines Corp. (1993). FTDD973: A multimedia knowledge-based system and methodology for operator training and diagnostics, *Proceeding of the 1993 Conference on Intelligent Computer-Aided Training and Virtual Environment Technology,* (pp. 161–170), Houston, TX: NASA: Johnson Space Center.

Jones, A.C., Scholer, A., Cardinal, A.L., and Frulio, F.P. (1991). Sea World intelligent multi media expert (SWIMMER). Unpublished manuscript, University of Central Florida, Intelligent Multimedia Applications Laboratory, Orlando.

Karr, R.A. (1992). Intermedia for Executives. *PC AI,* 6(6), 34–35.

Kraus, R. and Rogers, R. (1991). Intelligent student individualized instruction system (ISIIS). Unpublished manuscript, University of Central Florida, Intelligent Multimedia Applications Laboratory, Orlando.

Kulik, P. (1992). Automating a help desk. *PC AI,* 6(6), 26–27.

Leigh, W., Ragusa, J.M., and Gilliam, M. (1993). An architecture for a heterogeneous information environment. *The Journal of Computer Information Systems,* 34, 42–49.

Meisch, P.J. (1994). Applying multimedia to the MK 92 Mod 2 maintenance advisor expert. Master's thesis, Naval Postgraduate School, Monterey, CA.

Ptacek, M.E., Pepe, M., Rogers, R.T., and Kraus, R. (1990). Photo retrieval search system (PRESS). Unpublished manuscript, University of Central Florida, Intelligent Multimedia Applications Laboratory, Orlando.

Ragusa, J.M., Dologite, D.G., Orwig, G.W., and Mockler, R.J. (1993). Adding knowledge-assistance to PC-based photographic image database management systems. *Information Resources Management Journal,* 6(2), 27–36.

Ragusa, J.M. and Orwig, G.W. (1991). Integrating expert systems to multimedia: The reality and promise. In J. Liebowitz (Ed.), *World Congress on Expert Systems Proceedings* (pp. 2919–2930). Orlando, FL: Pergamon Press.

Schmuller, J. (1992). [Interview with Dustin Huntington, founder and president of EXSYS, Inc.]. *PC AI,* 6(4), 54–55, 64.

Shaw, J.(1993). Help desk helper. *PC AI,* 7(6), 56.

Stone, N.D. (1992) AI and the environment. *PC AI.* 6(6), 21–25, 39.

Turban, E. (1992). Intelligent computerized multimedia (Parts 1 and 2). *Decision Line: The Newsletter of the Decision Science Institute*, 23(1) 5–6 ; 23(2), 6.

Utilities test SA*VANT for turbine troubleshooting. (1992). *EPRI Journal*, 17(2), 26–27.

15 Unification of Artificial Intelligence with Optimization

Jae Kyu Lee

CONTENTS

ABSTRACT

This chapter reviews the UNIK project, which unifies the Artificial Intelligence (AI) with optimization models for decision support. Our goal is to unify the specification of problems, to encompass as many hybrid types of problems as possible, from both AI and optimization. Currently, the types of problems selected from the AI side are the rules, compatibility constraints, and neural network, while linear programming and integer programming models are selected from the optimization side. A key issue to be resolved for the unification is the unified representation of the optimization model and rules so that they can understand each other. The next issue is designing the unified architecture and devising the solution method. This chapter reviews the above issues one by one, with illustrative applications.

1.   INTRODUCTION

Artificial Intelligence (AI) and optimization are two of the most popular paradigms for decision aid. Since a large group of problems requires adopting both paradigms in a unified manner, we need to develop methods of formulating and solving such problems, which might be named *Unified Programming*. The basic components from the optimization side of Unified Programming are Linear Programming, Integer Programming, and Nonlinear Programming; while Rule-based Reasoning, Neural Network, Constraint Satisfaction Problems, and Case-Based Reasoning, and Search techniques come from the AI side.

Linear Programming is a basic decision modeling technique that optimizes a linear objective function subject to the linear constraints as illustrated in (1)–(4) in Section 2.1. The decision variables in the linear programming models are continuous real numbers. If the decision variables are restricted to integer numbers, the model becomes Integer Programming. If any functions in the linear programming becomes nonlinear, the model becomes a Nonlinear Programming model (Murty, 1995). A typical Constraint Satisfaction Problem is a decision model that seeks consistent solutions that satisfy the multiple compatibility constraints (Kuman, 1992). Case Based Reasoning is a paradigm that searches for solutions used in the most similar case to the newly faced problem, and adjusts the difference, if there exists discrepancy, between the new problem and the prior similar problem.

To achieve the framework of Unified Programming, the mutually interpretable representation of problems is an essential foundation. For a literature review on unification of AI with optimization, readers may refer to the two special issues: "Integration and Competition of AI with Quantitative Methods for Decision Support" in *Expert Systems with Applications* (Vol. 1, 1990) and "Unified Programming" in *Decision Support Systems* (Vol. 18, No. 3, 1996). As a book, refer to Holsapple et al. (1995).

In Section 2, we represent linear programming models in objects at a semantic level, which is understandable not only by the optimization solver, but also by the rules. UNIK-OPT is a knowledge-assisted optimization modeling system that can easily produce such a semantic optimization formulation. Since the initial scope of UNIK-OPT is Linear Programming (LP), the system for LP is named UNIK-LP (Lee and Kim, 1995). In Section 3, the independently prepared rule-based systems and optimization models are integrated via the shared decision variables. The trade-offs among the goals in the rule-based system and the optimization model are supported by using the Post-Model Analysis approach (Lee and Song, 1995). This approach makes integrated modeling possible for a class of Multiple Criteria Decision-Making problems that include both quantitative and qualitative factors. Several illustrative cases are discussed along with a tool UNIK-PMA (Lee and Song, 1996). This approach can be extended to the group decision aid (Lee and Jeong, 1995).

In Section 4, UNIK-LP, which initially started with the linear programming, is now extended to cover the high-level representation of integer programming models (UNIK-IP) (Yeom and Lee, 1996) and Lagrangian relaxation models (UNIK-RELAX) (Kim and Lee, 1996). In Section 5, the neural network is applied to the adaptive control on the optimization model and a tool UNIK-LP/NN is developed for this purpose. An application is demonstrated with refinery (Lee and Kim, 1996). In Section 6, a hybrid representation and reasoning that satisfies both constraints and rules are presented. The framework can be applied to many planning and design problems because it allows for trade-offs among conflicting goals. We illustrate the system UNIK-CRSP with examples for planning and configuration (Lee, Shim, and Kwon, 1996).

2.   REPRESENTATION OF LINEAR PROGRAMMING MODELS: UNIK-LP

2.1.   OBJECT-ORIENTED REPRESENTATION OF LINEAR PROGRAMMING MODELS

A specific Linear Programming model should be represented in such a way as to be understood by rule-based systems. To accomplish this, the LP model needs to be represented in objects, which

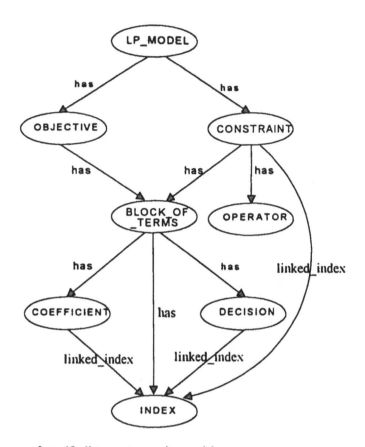

FIGURE 1 Structure of specific linear programming model.

is named as semantic form. The object-oriented LP model (named a semantic form) can be transformed to the notational form, modeling language form, and tabular form, as depicted in Figure 1. A specific semantic model is composed of constraints, blocks of terms (BOT), attributes, and indices, as depicted in Figure 1. This idea is implemented in UNIK-LP (Lee and Kim, 1995).

For instance, consider the monthly product mix planning model, which decides the production and inventory levels.

$$\min \sum_{ijt} C_i X_{ijt} \tag{1}$$

subject to

$$\sum_i a_{ij} X_{ijt} \le b_{jt} \qquad j \in J,\ t \in T \tag{2}$$

$$\sum_j X_{ijt} + I_{i,t-1} - I_{it} = s_{it} \qquad i \in I,\ t \in T \tag{3}$$

$$X_{ijt},\ I_{it} \ge 0 \qquad \text{for all } i,\ j,\ t \tag{4}$$

The attributes imply:

X: production amount
I: inventory
a: unit processing time
b: capacity
c: unit cost
s: sales quantity

and the indices imply:

i: product
j: facility
t: month.

The LP model (1)–(4) is a mathematical notational form. However, this form is not compatible with the rule-based systems. So, the model may be represented in an object as follows.

```
{{monthly_product_mix_a
        IS_A: LP_MODEL
        DIRECTION: MIN
        OBJ_FN: (+ production_cost_BOT)
        CONSTRAINTS: production_capacity_constraint
                        production_sales_balance_constraint
        CONTEXT: (TIME_UNIT month)
                    (PERIOD multiple) }}
```

The production_capacity_constraint can also be represented in an object.

```
{{production_capacity_constraint
        IS_A: constraint
        OPERATOR: LE
        LHS: (+ processing_time_BOT)
        RHS: (+ facility_capacity_BOT)
        INDEX: facility time
        DOMAIN: (f1,...,fN) (t1,...,tT) }}.
```

In this manner, the variables, constants, and indices can be represented in a top-down manner.

```
{{production_amount
        IS_A: attribute
        SYMBOL: X
        ROLE: variable
        LINKED_INDEX: product facility time }}
{{unit_processing_time
        IS_A: attribute
        SYMBOL: a
        ROLE: constant
        LINKED INDEX: product facility }}
```

```
{{product
       IS_A: index
       DESCRIPTION:
       SYMBOL: i
       LINKED_ATTRIBUTES:   production_amount
                            inventory
                            unit_cost
                            unit_processing_time
                            sales_quantity }}
```

Since the semantic form possess more information than the mathematical notational form, we can transform the semantic form to notational form as depicted in Figure 2. The semantic form can be transformed to the aggregated notational form (Figure 3) and individual notational form (Figure 4). Since these models usually have thousands of variables and constraints, the maintenance of the models can be made much easier by using a tool like UNIK-LP.

2.2.   KNOWLEDGE ASSISTED MODEL FORMULATION

Since the formulation of the semantic LP model is not an easy task for novice model builders, the function of knowledge-assisted LP model formulation is developed for UNIK-LP. For this purpose,

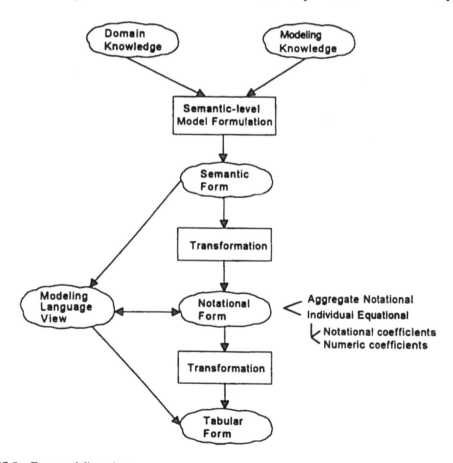

FIGURE 2   Four modeling views.

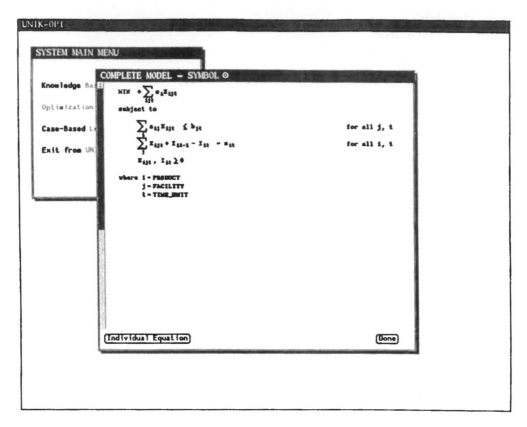

FIGURE 3   An Illustrative aggregte notational model.

the knowledge base needs to retain the LP model's structure knowledge and domain-specific knowledge (such as information about products and facilities). Using this knowledge, the LP model can be generated simply by identifying the relevant indices, decision variables, and constraints from the menu in a guided manner. For a detailed step-by-step explanation, readers may refer to Lee and Kim (1995).

3.   UNIFICATION OF LP MODEL WITH RULE-BASED SYSTEM: UNIK-PMA

To unify an LP model with a rule base, the two should share some of the decision variables. The unified model is thus virtually a multiobjective decision-making problem that considers both the numeric objective in the linear programming model and the symbolic objectives in the rule base. To solve the unified model, the Post-Model Analysis procedure is adopted as depicted in Figure 5 (Lee and Hurst, 1988; Lee and Song, 1996; Lee and Song, 1995). In this figure, note that the LP model and rule base are independently prepared. But since the LP model is formulated in semantic form, the LP model can communicate with the rule base at the semantic level.

3.1.   POST-MODEL ANALYSIS PROCEDURE

The Post-Model Analysis procedure starts by finding the optimal solution of an LP model. The optimal solution is then inputted into the fact base of the rule-based system for evaluation. If the goals in the rule base are satisfied with the current optimal solution, the current solution can be selected as a satisfactory nondominated solution both for the optimization and rule-based system.

```
shelltool - /bin/csh

LP MODEL : MPSX_MONTHLY_PRODUCT_MIX

MIN
    5 XP1F1MAR + 5 XP1F1APR + 5 XP1F1MAY + 5 XP1F1JUN + 5 XP1F1JUL + 5 XP1F1AUG
  + 5 XP1F1SEP + 5 XP1F1OCT + 4 XP2F1JAN + 4 XP2F1FEB + 4 XP2F1MAR + 4 XP2F1APR
  + 4 XP2F1MAY + 4 XP2F1JUN + 4 XP2F1JUL + 4 XP2F1AUG + 4 XP2F1SEP + 4 XP2F1OCT
  + 4 XP2F1NOV + 4 XP2F1DEC + 4 XP2F2JAN + 4 XP2F2FEB + 4 XP2F2MAR + 4 XP2F2APR
  + 4 XP2F2MAY + 4 XP2F2JUN + 4 XP2F2JUL + 4 XP2F2AUG + 4 XP2F2SEP + 4 XP2F2OCT
  + 4 XP2F2NOV + 4 XP2F2DEC + 7 XP3F2JAN + 7 XP3F2FEB + 7 XP3F2MAR + 7 XP3F2APR
  + 7 XP3F2MAY + 7 XP3F2JUN + 7 XP3F2SEP + 7 XP3F2OCT + 7 XP3F2NOV + 7 XP3F2DEC

ST
    8.5 XP2F1JAN <=  95
    8.5 XP2F1FEB <=  95
   10.5 XP1F1MAR + 8.5 XP2F1MAR <= 100
   10.5 XP1F1APR + 8.5 XP2F1APR <= 100
   10.5 XP1F1MAY + 8.5 XP2F1MAY <= 100
   10.5 XP1F1JUN + 8.5 XP2F1JUN <= 100
   10.5 XP1F1JUL + 8.5 XP2F1JUL <= 100
   10.5 XP1F1AUG + 8.5 XP2F1AUG <= 100
   10.5 XP1F1SEP + 8.5 XP2F1SEP <= 100
   10.5 XP1F1OCT + 8.5 XP2F1OCT <= 100
    8.5 XP2F1NOV <= 100
    8.5 XP2F1DEC <=  95
    8 XP2F2JAN + 7.5 XP3F2JAN  <= 150
    8 XP2F2FEB + 7.5 XP3F2FEB  <= 125
    8 XP2F2MAR + 7.5 XP3F2MAR  <= 150
    8 XP2F2APR + 7.5 XP3F2APR  <= 150
    8 XP2F2MAY + 7.5 XP3F2MAY  <= 150
    8 XP2F2JUN + 7.5 XP3F2JUN  <= 150
    8 XP2F2JUL <= 150
    8 XP2F2AUG <= 150
    8 XP2F2SEP + 7.5 XP3F2SEP  <= 150
    8 XP2F2OCT + 7.5 XP3F2OCT  <= 150
    8 XP2F2NOV + 7.50 XP3F2NOV <= 150
    8 XP2F2DEC + 7.50 XP3F2DEC <= 145
    1 XP1F1MAR + 1 IP1FEB - 1 IP1MAR = 65
    1 XP1F1APR + 1 IP1MAR - 1 IP1APR = 65
    1 XP1F1MAY + 1 IP1APR - 1 IP1MAY = 65
    1 XP1F1JUN + 1 IP1MAY - 1 IP1JUN = 65
    1 XP1F1JUL + 1 IP1JUN - 1 IP1JUL = 65
    1 XP1F1AUG + 1 IP1JUL - 1 IP1AUG = 65
    1 XP1F1SEP + 1 IP1AUG - 1 IP1SEP = 65
    1 XP1F1OCT + 1 IP1SEP - 1 IP1OCT = 65
    1 XP2F1JAN + 1 XP2F2JAN + 1 IP2DEC - 1 IP2JAN = 50
    1 XP2F1FEB + 1 XP2F2FEB + 1 IP2JAN - 1 IP2FEB = 50
```

FIGURE 4   An illustrative individual notational model.

However, if the current solution is not satisfactory, the adjusted goal in the rule base should be interpreted as the additional constraints to the LP model. Transforming the rules associated with the adjusted goal to the objects of semantic LP model is the key technological function in this process. For the details, readers may refer to Lee and Song (1996). Finally, the LP model with the additional constraints should be re-solved to assure the adjusted goals.

3.2.   TRADE-OFFS BETWEEN GOALS IN THE OPTIMIZATION MODEL AND RULE-BASED SYSTEM

The major advantage of the PMA procedure is that it can support the trade-offs between the goals regardless of their association with the optimization model or rule base. Three types of trade-offs can be supported systematically (Lee and Song, 1995):

1. Ask the impact of changed goals in the rule base in terms of the objective function in the LP model.
2. Ask the impact of changed goals in the rule base on the other goals in the rule base while sustaining the current objective function value of LP model.
3. Ask the impact of changed objective function value in an LP model on the designated goals in the rule base.

If such trade-offs happen in the organization in which one department uses a rule-based model, while the other department uses an optimization model, the PMA procedure can be used for negotiating support procedures between different departments. An experimental application devel-

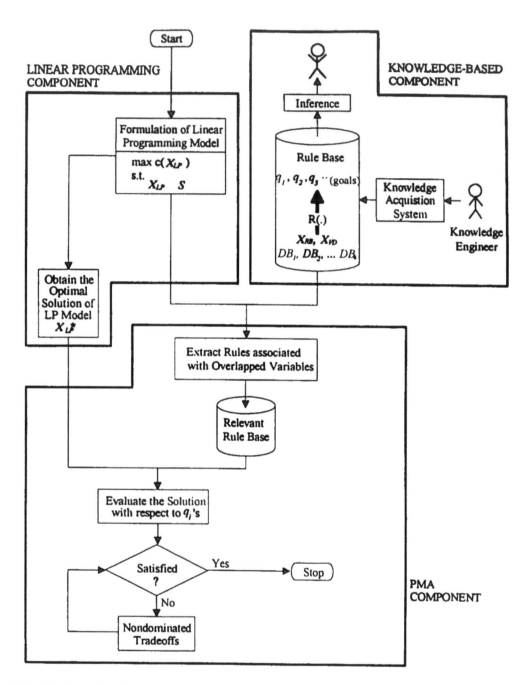

FIGURE 5 Procedure of post-model analysis using rule base.

oped in this line is the negotiation of work schedule between the auditing firm and multiple individual auditors. The auditing firm seeks the firm's profit, while each auditor seeks an individually preferred schedule (Lee and Jeong, 1995). To help with communication among the agents, we need to employ the agents' communication language. This application can also be extended for use in negotiations between hostile agents.

4.   REPRESENTATION OF INTEGER PROGRAMMING: UNIK-IP

The next step of UNIK-LP is the extention of the LP to integer programming (IP). The IP model can be easily represented on the linear programming model simply by additionally identifying whether the variables are integer, 0 or 1. This level of representation is called a *base level*. However, it will be much easier if the models can be represented using the high-level logical operators such as IF-THEN and EITHER-OR. So, UNIK-IP is designed to allow such logical operators; automatically transforming the high-level representation to the base-level representation. The logical operators necessary for IP models formulation are: *AND, k-fold, at_least, at_most, NOT, Binary, XOR, OR, EITHER-OR, IF-THEN*, and *FIXED-CHARGE*. So, all these operators are adopted in UNIK-IP (Yeom and Lee, 1996).

For instance, the operator that needs to satisfy at least k out of m constraints — *At_Least_<k>_Constraint_<m>*$(f_1(X) \leq 0, ..., f_m(X) \leq 0)$ — implies the addition of the technical constraints in Equations 5 and 7 to the original model. Note that the constraints in the list should have the canonical form of $f_i(X) \leq 0$.

$$f_i(X) \leq M \ Y_i \qquad i = 1, \ ..., \ m \tag{5}$$

$$\sum_{i=1} Y_i \leq m - k \tag{6}$$

$$Y_i \in \{0, \ 1\} \qquad i = 1, \ ..., \ m \tag{7}$$

If the model builder is required to identify *At_Least_<k>_Constraint_<m>(...)*, this will be much easier than formulating the model (5)–(7) at base level.

4.1.   AN ILLUSTRATIVE INTEGER PROGRAMMING MODEL FOR OPTIMAL SAVINGS PLAN

UNIK-IP is applied to the formulation of optimal savings plan. In this example, there are six groups of complex constraints. Among the constraints, the minimum balance restriction of an account requires the saving balance EITHER to exceed the minimum amount to open the account OR to stay unopened. This means that the EITHER-OR operator is adequate in expressing the situation.

As another example, some savings products are not allowed to be possessed together. Such mutually exclusive relationships can be effectively represented by using the IF-THEN expression. IF the balance of a product, which has a mutually exclusive relationship, is non-zero, THEN the balance of other products in the mutually exclusive group should be kept zero (Lee and Nam, 1996). In this manner, UNIK-IP can effectively support the formulation of complex IP model.

4.2.   KNOWLEDGE-BASED RELAXATION

Usually, a large-scale IP model is not easy to solve. So, finding a series of solution algorithm is an important issue in solving the IP problem. One of the most popular approaches to solving IP models is Lagrangian Relaxation (Fisher, 1981). Lagrangian relaxation is a scheme of relaxing the portion of constraints that makes the model too complex to solve, and finding a tight bound with the relaxed problem to evaluate the performance of some heuristic algorithms. UNIK-RELAX identifies the structural characteristics of the IP model to determine which constraints should be relaxed to generate the Lagrangian model. For the identification of the structure, the relationship among the embedded structures, constraints, and blocks of terms are identified as depicted in Figure 6 (Kim and Lee, 1996).

For instance, the embedded structure of 0_1_knapsack subproblem can be identified by the following rule:

IF	($\exists$ CONSTRAINT(Capacity))
AND	XOR(Max, Min)
THEN	STRUCTURE = 0_1_Knapsack.

This means that if there exists a *capacity* constraint in the IP model, with either maximizing or minimizing objective function, the model includes the 0_1_knapsack subproblem. The capacity constraint can be identified by the following condition:

ALL BOT

	(AT_LHS(Volume_Sum_0_1)
AND	AT_RHS(Nonnegative_Real_Coefficient)
AND	OPERATOR = LE

This means that if a constraint represented in the object has the *Volume_Sum_0_1* blocks of terms (BOT) in the left-hand side and the *Nonnegative_Real_Coefficient* BOT in the right-hand side, this constraint is a *capacity constraint*.

The distinctiveness of Volume_Sum_0_1 BOT can be identified by Volume_Sum_0_1 = AND(Nonnegative_Real_Coefficient 0_1_Integer_Variable). Note that those distinctions can be identified owing to the object-oriented representation of the integer programming model. For the identification of Lagrangian Relaxation, we need 15 elementary distinctive BOTs, 6 composite distinctive BOTs, 10 distinctive constraints, and 7 embedded subproblem structures. Although the current study has identified only 7 embedded structures in the IP model, the beauty of this approach is its expandability by adding more rules. This is extremely important because we have opened the way of automatically identifying the characteristics of problems. Clearly, this implies that an appropriate solution method can also be automatically identified.

5. NEURAL NETWORK BASED ADAPTIVE OPTIMAL CONTROL: UNIK-LP/NN

5.1. NEURAL NETWORK MODEL FOR THE CONTROL OF OPTIMIZATION MODEL

When the future information for an LP model is not complete, the model tends to incorporate uncertainties as some assumptions for the coefficients. As time passes and more precise information is accumulated, the initial LP model may no longer correctly represent the problem. For instance, the daily demand cannot be reliably estimated at the crude purchase point, which is usually 3 months ahead. So the daily demands, which should appear as coefficients, are estimated by the average of monthly demands. As time passes, we become able to identify which day tankers will arrive to pick up the final products. Then we have to adjust the coefficients concerning daily demands, while maintaining the initial optimal solution as much as possible.

So we have developed a tool — UNIK-LP/NN — that can support the construction and recall of the neural network model on top of the semantic optimization model UNIK-LP, and the semantic neural network building aid UNIK-NEURO. Basically, the semantic neural network means that the architecture and details about the model is represented by objects, so that the neural network model can communicate with the semantic optimization model. In this manner, UNIK-LP/NN can effectively automate most of the neural network construction and recall procedure for optimal control (Lee and Kim, 1996).

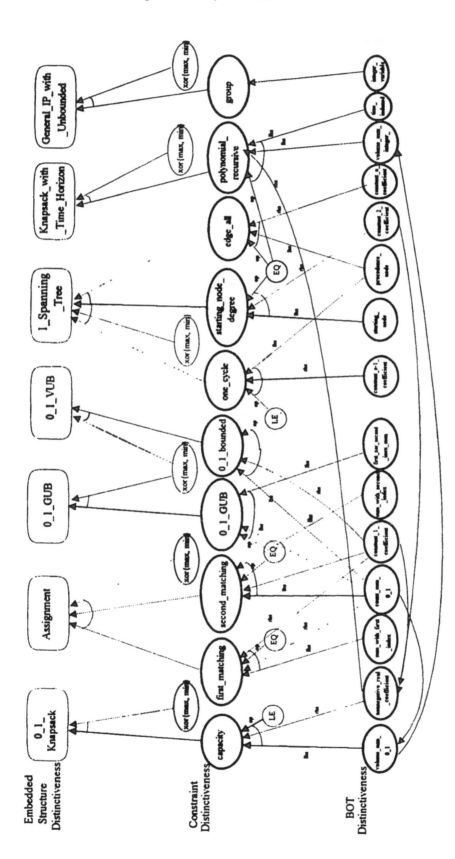

FIGURE 6 AND/OR graphical relationships among embedded structures, constraints, and BOT distinctivenesses.

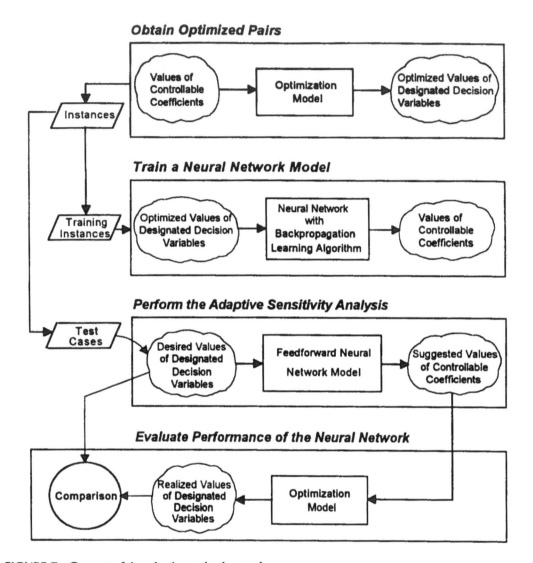

FIGURE 7   Concept of the adaptive optimal control.

The process of adaptive optimal control on an LP model is diagrammatically shown in Figure 7. The process of performing the adaptive optimal control using the neural network can be summarized as follows.

1. Generate instances of paired values of controllable coefficients and optimized values of designated decision variables from the optimization model.
2. Using the instances, train a neural network model that has the designated decision variables as input nodes and the controllable coefficients as output nodes.
3. Input the desired values of designated decision variables into the neural network to obtain the suggested values of controllable coefficients.
4. To evaluate the performance of neural network based control, the optimization model is modified with the suggested coefficients from the neural network, and the optimal solution is obtained accordingly. By comparing the desired decision values and the realized ones from the optimization model with the modified coefficients, the error of

the neural network model can be computed. This process is graphically depicted in Figure 7. The validity of the neural network approach is proven with real-world problems found in the refinery plant.

5.2. ARCHITECTURE OF UNIK-LP/NN

The architecture of UNIK-LP/NN is depicted in Figure 8. UNIK-LP/NN has two major parts: *adaptive optimal control model constructor* and *adaptive optimal controller.* The constructor supports users in choosing a target optimization model and in defining a specific neural network model for adaptive optimal control. From the adaptive optimal control model definition, the constructor automatically develops a neural network model via the interaction with UNIK-LP and UNIK-NEURO. The adaptive optimal controller computes the values of adjusted controllable coefficients along with the corresponding feasible decision variables.

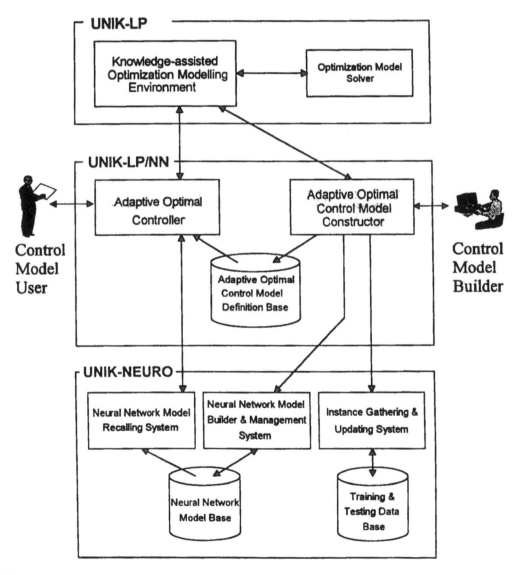

FIGURE 8   Architecture of UNIK-LP/NN environment.

6.   INTEGRATION OF RULES WITH CONSTRAINT SATISFACTION PROBLEM: UNIK-CRSP

Constraint and Rule Satisfaction Problem (CRSP) is a hybrid representation and reasoning method encompassing both Constraint Satisfaction Problems (CSP) and rule-based systems. CSP is a kind of problem in Artificial Intelligence that requires the assignment of values to variables that are subject to a set of compatibility constraints (Kumay, 1992; Macworth, 1986). Much research has improved the applicability of CSP methodology to practical field problems (Bowen and Bahler, 1991; Davis and Rosenfield, 1981; Detcher and Pearl, 1988; Montanari and Rossi, 1991). To enhance the representational power of CSP, the integration of constraints and rules in a unified framework is attempted (Lee and Kwon, 1995).

6.1.   CONSTRAINT AND RULE SATISFACTION PROBLEMS

To understand CRSP, consider the differences between CSP and the rule-based model. Typical constraints in CSP represent compatibility between variables, thus they have no directionality, and all relationships between constraints are conjunctive. The disjunctive relationship can be implicitly represented within a constraint by arranging disjunctive values to a variable. The rule, on the other hand, can effectively represent causality and subsumption relationships, so rules have directionality. A rule may have multiple conjunctive conditional variables, while the relationship between rules that directs the same consequent variables is regarded as disjunctive. Considering the contrast between CSP and rule-based systems, CRSP can be formally defined as follows.

"For the given variables associated with a set of constraints and rules, solving CRSP is the assignment of values to variables so as to satisfy the concerned goals without violating the set of constraints and rules."

6.2.   UNIFIED REASONING FOR CRSP

Unified reasoning is a process of assigning consistent values to each variable so as to satisfy the concerned goals without violating constraints and rules. Unified reasoning involves the following three features:

1. The decision maker should be able to interactively input his/her intention about the problematic situation and control the negotiation process among multiple conflicting objectives.
2. CRSP should be able to be decomposed into multiple subproblems so that concurrent reasoning would be possible, starting from the multiple most critical variables. The possible conflicts at the boundary of subproblems becomes the point of negotiation between conflicting associated objectives.
3. The forward and backward reasoning methods usually used in rule-based systems are integrated with constraint propagation methods developed for CSP.

6.3.   ILLUSTRATIONS

The CRSP approach is applied to configuration and planning. For the configuration of personal computers, 69 decision variables (like processor, main memory, and price) are associated with 34 constraints categorized in four types (value compatibility, algebraic inequality, identity, and functional assignment) and 21 rules (Lee, Shim, and Kwon, 1996). For the planning of expert system development, 55 variables (like user hardware, software tool, budget, and target problems) are associated with 38 constraints and 13 rules (Lee and Kwon, 1995). These applications show the validity of UNIK-CRSP for interactive configuration and planning with conflicting goals.

7. CONCLUSION

We have shown that linear programming and integer programming can be integrated with rule-based systems and neural networks; solution methods can be identified based on the structure of problem; and rules can be integrated with constraint satisfaction problems. These integrations are implemented in the tool named UNIK (UNIfied Knowledge) and a series of applications for each type of integration has shown the validity of integrations.

Currently, the concept of expert system is extended to agent for the electronic commerce by additionally including the capability of a problem-solving method selector and a communication controller (Lee and Lee, 1995; Lee and Lee, 1997). Two other ongoing research topics address the integration of CSP with an optimization model and the description formalism of problem-solving procedures, which is composed of a set of linear programming models and arbitrary heuristic algorithm modules.

REFERENCES

Bowen, J. and D. Bahler, "Conditional Existence of Variables in Generalized Constraint Network," *Proceedings of AAAI-91*, pp. 215–220.

Davis, L.S. and A.R. Rosenfeld, "Cooperating Process for Low-level Vision: A Survey," *Artificial Intelligence*, Vol. 17, 1981, pp. 245–263.

Detcher, R. and J. Pearl, "Network-Based Heuristics for Constraint-Satisfaction Problem," *Artificial Intelligence*, Vol. 34, 1988, pp. 1–38.

Fisher, M. L., "The Lagrangian Relaxation method for solving Integer Programming Problems, *Management Science*, Vol. 27, No. 1, 1981.

Holsapple, C. W., V. S. Jacob, and A. B. Whinston, *Operations Research and Artificial Intelligence*, Ablex Publishing Corp., 1994.

Kim, W. "Connection of Neural Network with Expert System," *Intelligent Information System* (in Korean), Vol. 2, No. 3, 1993, pp. 102–110.

Kim, C. and Jae K. Lee, "Automatic Structural Identification and Relaxation for Integer Programming," *Decision Support Systems*, Vol. 18, pp. 253–271, 1996.

Kumar, V., "Algorithm for Constraint-Satisfaction Problems: A Survey," *AI Magazine*, Vol. 13, No. 1, Spr., 1992, pp. 32–44.

Lee, Jae K. and E. Gerald Hurst, Jr., "Multiple-Criteria Decision Making including Qualitative Factors: The Post-Model Analysis Approach," *Decision Sciences*, Vol. 19, No. 2, 1988, pp. 334–352.

Lee, Jae K. and H.G. Lee, "Integration of Strategic Planning and Short-Term Planning: An Intelligent DSS Approach by the Post-Model Analysis Approach," *Decision Support Systems*, Vol. 3, No. 2, 1987, pp. 141–154.

Lee, Jae K. and M.W. Jeong, "Intelligent Audit Planning System for Multiple Auditors: IAPS," *Expert Systems with Applications*, Vol. 9, No. 4, 1995, pp. 579–589.

Lee, Jae K. and M.Y. Kim, "Knowledge-assisted Optimization Model Formulation: UNIK-OPT," *Decision Support Systems*, Vol. 13, 1995, pp. 111–132.

Lee, Jae K. and S.B. Kwon, "ES*: An Expert System Developemnt Planner using A Constraint and Rule-based Approach," *Expert Systems with Applications*, Vol. 9, No. 1, 1995, pp. 3–14.

Lee, Jae K. and S. Nam, "Object-Oriented Optimal Savings System: Hyper-Savings," *International Journal of Intelligent Systems for Accounting, Finance and Management*, 1996, to be published.

Lee, Jae K. and W. Kim, "UNIK-OPT/NN: Neural Network based Adaptive Optimal Controller on the Optimization Models," *Decision Support Systems*, Vol. 18, 1996, pp. 43–62

Lee, Jae K. and W. Lee, "Intelligent Agent Based Electronic Marketing: UNIK-AGENT," *Pacific-Asian Conference on Expert Systems*, Huangsan, China, May, 1995.

Lee, Jae K. and W. Lee, "Intelligent Agent Based Contract Process in Electronic Commerce: UNIK-AGENT Approach," *Proceedings of Hawaii International Conference on Systems Sciences*, 1997.

Lee, Jae K., S.H. Shim, and S.B. Kwon, "Configuration of Personal Computer by Constraint and Rule Satisfaction Problem Approach," *First Asian Pacific DSI Conference*, Hongkong, June 21–22, 1996.

Lee, Jae K. and Y.U. Song, "UNIK-PMA: A Unifiner of Optimization Model with Rule-Based Systems by Post-Model Analysis," *Annals of Operations Research*, Vol. 65, pp. 157–179, 1996.

Lee, Jae K. and Y.U. Song, "Unification of Linear Programming with a Rule-based System by the Post-Model Analysis Approach," *Management Science*, Vol. 41, No. 5, 1995, pp. 111–132.

Macworth, A.K., "Constraint Satisfaction," *Encyclopedia of AI*, S.C. Shapiro, Ed. pp. 205–211, 1986.

Montanari U. and F. Rossi, "Constraint Relaxation May Be Perfect," *Artificial Intelligence*, Vol. 48, 1991, pp. 143–170.

Murty, Katta G., *Operations Research: Deterministic Optimization Models,* Prentice Hall, 1995.

Yeom, K. and Jae K. Lee, "Higer Level Representation Aid for Integer Programming," *Decision Support Systems*, Vol. 18, pp. 227–251, 1996.

16 Intelligent Agent Technology

*David Prerau, Mark Adler, Dhiraj K. Pathak,
and Alan Gunderson*

CONTENTS

1. INTRODUCTION

An *agent* is an application that acts on a user's behalf as an intelligent software assistant, simplifying or completely automating a task for the user.

An agent is delegated to perform some task for the user and is given constraints under which it can operate. The agent's processing is attributable to knowledge of the task and the domain in which the task is situated.

Some agent applications use machine learning to improve their performance over time. There are two general types of learning by agents. Some agents adapt to a user's preferences, as given explicitly or implicitly. For example, an agent can learn a user's preference for information on certain topics and then retrieve related items. In this way, the agent becomes customized to a user's preferences over time.

An agent can also learn to perform a given task better. For example, an agent that uses some software tool to perform tasks could learn properties of the tool that would enable it to use the tool more effectively over time. Similarly, an agent that performs in some domain can learn properties of the domain that enable it to perform tasks more effectively over time.

In this chapter, we will describe and discuss the types of agents in use or under research today and the technologies that are being developed to support the use of agents.

The primary types of agents currently deployed include Internet agents, electronic commerce agents, business application agents (including customer service), interface agents, and data mining agents. Intelligent agents to enhance entertainment software are also an active area of advanced development. The supporting technologies for agent applications include knowledge-based systems, machine learning, distributed computing, agent communication languages, and representations of intentional and emotional states.

2.   HISTORICAL ACCOUNT/BACKGROUND

The agent metaphor came to the fore in the early 1990s. In Artificial Intelligence there was a recognition that an alternative to working on complex problems such as factory scheduling and medical diagnosis was to focus on simpler tasks such as personal calendar management and automatic filtering of electronic mail and online information sources. These simpler tasks were typically those that a user would consider delegating to a personal assistant. Since these tasks were intrinsically simpler, they were more tractable to design and implement. These applications were termed "agents" because they undertook to perform routine tasks for users.

The origins of intelligent agents come primarily from artificial intelligence research work done in the 1970s and 1980s in areas such as planning, robotics, knowledge-based systems, and learning techniques. The significant applied R&D work done on autonomous vehicle navigation for the DoD in the 1980s also explored many of the concepts now appearing in intelligent agents. Probably the key transition from the AI research mentioned above and intelligent agents involved the concept of a softbot, i.e., a transition to the concept of autonomously functioning software robots rather than physical industrial robots or robot vehicles that could roam a battlefield.

Gradually, the agent metaphor has extended to applications outside Artificial Intelligence. Today, the concept of an agent has become somewhat independent of its roots in Artificial Intelligence. If an application performs an intelligent task automatically that is of the sort that one could imagine a person performing manually, then the application can be called an agent. So, an agent is now a label for an application belonging to a certain class — the class of applications that automate intelligent tasks people could perform manually.

There is no one way to build agents. A multitude of technologies are employed. There is no one domain where agents are deployed. Agents can be found in virtually all domains. The exact nature of the computation performed by an agent application is determined by the task the agent is meant to perform. The task specification also determines what underlying technology is emphasized in the design of an agent application for that task.

The pervasive nature of the Internet has helped fuel the growth of agent applications. Vast amounts of information were becoming available online, and users could simply not keep up with the information explosion. Therefore, Internet agents were devised to help users to benefit from the available information. Now that the Internet is moving into the realm of electronic commerce, agents to automatically negotiate and obtain services from electronic storefronts are being developed.

The success of database technology has led to explosive growth in the number of databases deployed to support businesses, and huge quantities of data are accumulating in these databases. It is impossible to analyze manually such large quantities of data. Therefore, data mining agents are emerging to automatically examine large data sets to derive value for businesses.

The entertainment software industry is one of the fastest growing segments of the commercial software industry, with revenues in excess of $1 billion annually. One way to design more engaging games is to inject intelligent decision-making into the software. This gives rise to agents embedded in software games. These agents exhibit interesting behaviors and sometimes adapt in response to interactions with users.

Business process automation is proving to be a profitable focus for agent technology. Many steps in a business process can be automated by using agents. For example, consider an order filling process whose goal is to order replenishments for a certain product at the best possible price. The first step is to monitor the inventory level for the product and generate a reordering signal when appropriate. Then, all the possible sourcing alternatives need to be queried to determine the best pricing and availability for the product. An agent can be set up for each of the steps of the order filling process. This way, an entire business process can be automated. Such process automation is a powerful means to reduce the operating cost structure of a business. In addition to reducing cost, automation increases process efficiency.

It is well known that maintenance costs constitute the bulk of the expenditure incurred on computer systems. Intelligent agent technology has provided a means to reduce these costs.

Two types of agents have been deployed in the customer support area. First, self-help agents have been deployed that carry out an intelligent dialog with users to provide solutions to support problems with computer hardware and software systems. Second, self-repair agents have been packaged with computer systems to identify various types of equipment failures and either rectify the errors through software actions or log calls for onsite service or remote diagnosis.

In the next section, we discuss each of the primary types of agent applications that have been successfully deployed.

3. TECHNIQUES, PRACTICES, AND APPLICATIONS

In this section we will investigate each of primary areas in which intelligent agents are currently deployed.

3.1. INTERNET AGENTS

The use of intelligent agent technology on the Internet is growing rapidly. The explosive expansion of information on the Internet, particularly on the World Wide Web, and the lack of organization and quality control of that information has led to the urgent need for an intelligent and personalized way to find and use only the specific Internet information in which one is interested. Intelligent agents provide possibly the best solution for this growing problem.

There are several ways in which intelligent agents are being utilized on the Internet. These include:

- Searching the Internet for information pertinent to the user
- Retrieving information in a desired frequency and manner
- Filtering information, selecting only the appropriate items of interest
- Present information in a desired form
- Alerting the user when information of interest is available
- Alerting the user when specific events occur or when a parameter reaches a particular value
- Speeding use of the Internet for the user
- Aiding in the management of World Wide Web sites

Many additional types of agent applications are being developed and deployed as well, including applications in electronic commerce and business, which we discuss in later sections.

Personal information agents provide users a way to customize an Internet work search engine to search through large quantities of information that the users would not have time search through themselves. Documents are compared intelligently against user requirements to select only the most pertinent.

Users can create personalized search profiles. The desired information is described via keyword lists, menu selections, responses to simple queries, or natural language. Intelligent search engines can utilize such techniques as advanced search operators, concept search, fuzzy logic, proximity methods, and statistical methods.

Information can be retrieved in a manner and frequency suitable to the user, determined either by direct user specification or intelligent analysis of user actions. The information sources to be used might be user-specified or all available sources might be used, but a more intelligent agent could determine the best available information sources from an analysis of the content desired.

Retrieved information can be tightly filtered to present only the most relevant, or a broad amount of information can be presented. Documents can be analyzed and then prioritized for delivery based upon a ranking of their pertinence to the user's objectives. The intelligent agent can tailor the quantity of information and the level of detail presented.

The information can be presented to the user using various mechanisms, such as on a Web page, via e-mail, by Fax, in printed form, or using a paging device. The information can be delivered as soon as available or on a scheduled basis, or the agent can base delivery times upon an analysis of the quantity and importance of the information retrieved.

In addition to gathering information on a regular basis, intelligent Internet agents are also used to monitor information on the Internet and then to alert a user when a certain situation occurs or a certain condition is met. For example, a user might want to read only those articles in the *Wall Street Journal* that refer to his or her company, and an agent can monitor each issue of the *Journal* for this. Also, a user might want to know when a particular stock reaches a certain price or volume. An intelligent agent can be set up to monitor stock price information and alert the user when the desired price point or volume level is met or exceeded. Intelligent agent systems are being developed to use the many available financial information resources on the Internet (e.g., market data, financial reports, analysts' reports, etc.) to monitor and manage a user's financial portfolio taking into account such factors as uncertainty, timeliness of data, deadlines, etc.

In addition to aiding users in finding and using information on the Internet, intelligent agents are also being used to aid in the use and management of the Internet itself. While an Internet-surfing user is reading one Web page, intelligent agent software anticipates the next request by loading linked pages into the browser. Then, when the user selects a link, the new page loads as if it were already in cache. Furthermore, the intelligent agent can learn the user's favorite sites and pre-load these as well. Agents are also being used to aid in managing World Wide Web sites. For example, agents are being used to manage massive multiple-server Web sites — collecting data, monitoring the site, ensuring standards, identifying problems (such as finding all broken hyperlinks), reporting why the problems occurred, and suggesting how to fix them.

3.2. Electronic Commerce Agents

Intelligent agents enable new and improved approaches to electronic commerce. Agents can aid a user in searching for a product or service of interest. For example, agents search online bookstores to find information and prices for a particular book, or to find a list of books on a particular topic. Also, agent systems have been developed to aid a user in the selection of recorded music. By explicit input from the user and by monitoring the user's selections over time, they learn the user's music preferences and then suggest for purchase CDs that likely would be of most interest to the user.

Agent systems can provide personalized shopping, aiding both the shopper and the vendor. Agent-enabled electronic shopping services have been developed to learn an Internet shopper's browsing and shopping habits. Then they can assist the user by allowing each vendor's display to be customized in a way that is most convenient to the shopper, while also aiding the vendor by allowing the vendor to individualize the marketing of its products.

3.3. Business Application Agents

Intelligent agent technology is being used in a wide variety of applications related to business operations. Agent-based systems are in use in customer service, human resources, manufacturing, sales, and several other areas. Business application of data-mining agents is discussed in Section 3.5.

Intelligent agents are being used as automated customer service agents, providing information to customers without the need for human intervention. For example, intelligent agents are used in

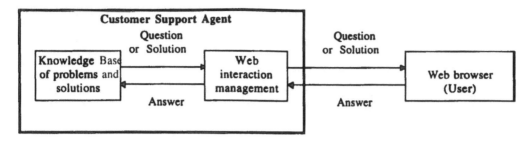

FIGURE 1   Customer support agent.

systems to provide banking information to bank customers and information on the status of shipments to customers of shipping companies. Customer service systems such as these are less expensive than human customer service personnel. They are often faster in providing standard requested information, and they allow the human customer service personnel to be used to provide answers to more difficult or unusual requests. Another major advantage of the agent systems is that they can offer some degree of intelligent service to customers 24 hours a day, 7 days a week.

Figure 1 illustrates a customer support agent that carries out a dialog with users on the Web to solve routine hardware and software problems. For example, a user may be having trouble with a printer or a word-processing application. Instead of calling a help desk about the problem, the user could have a dialog with the support agent on the Web. The support agent becomes the first line of response to customer problems. The agent is meant to only address relatively simple problems that are easy for the user to specify and can be resolved without complex steps.

The agent starts the dialog by asking the user a question. The set of possible answers to the question are also provided. Since the goal is to keep the dialog simple, questions have three to four possible answers. For example, the question may ask the type of printer being used. The user selects one response from the available choices. The user's response tells the agent a single fact about the problem. The user can also indicate that the question is irrelevant to the problem.

The response to each question is added to the representation of the user's problem being assembled by the agent. The agent's knowledge base contains additional knowledge about the class of problems it can resolve. This domain knowledge allows the agent to infer additional knowledge about the user's problem. For example, knowing what printer the user has, the agent could infer that this type of printer has been having ribbon problems. Then, the agent could ask the user to check if the ribbon is properly installed on the printer.

The agent's representation of problems consists of a set of problem attributes with specified values. The solution to a problem is represented as a text file describing the solution. Essentially, the purpose of the dialog is to enable the agent to understand the user's problem. This understanding is represented as the values of attributes that underlie the questions the user is asked. When the user's problem matches the stored representation of a problem in the knowledge base, the agent retrieves the corresponding solution file and provides the contents of the file to the user.

Agents are also being used to provide systems for business operations, such as human resources departments. For example, agents are an important enabler of a paperless wage review system for a division of Hewlett-Packard. Each of over 10,000 employees is reviewed quarterly. Intelligent agents in this review system insure that the wage review process for all of these employees is performed in a timely manner. The agents automatically initiate the wage review process on the appropriate date for each employee, sending the wage review forms to the manager. Then, they monitor the progress of the process and insure timeliness.

Employee benefits systems have been developed to automate other human resources tasks. For example, such systems provide benefits information to employees, or make available an employment verification service to banks and other external companies that need to verify employee status and title.

Agents are in use in manufacturing applications. They are being used for several different purposes, for example, to plan, verify, or optimize production schedules, as well as to gather and integrate manufacturing data.

In sales, agent-enabled sales systems have been developed to link a company's sales force with its manufacturing and distribution systems. When such a system receives a request for delivery of a certain quantity of a particular product, it can check the availability of the product or its raw materials, the availability of delivery capacity, etc., and give a real-time response. Some systems utilize constraint-based reasoning to allocate or suggest allocation of company manufacturing and distribution resources to optimize delivery schedules and costs.

A key term being used in the business application domain is online analytic processing (OLAP). Comshare has a program called *Robot for OLAP* that searches OLAP databases for trends and patterns using multidimensional views of the data. This system is used by the Hertz car rental company to analyze pricing moves by other car rental companies. Allied Signal is also using the Comshare OLAP software to provide sector level business information. Previously, they only had business unit level information and did not have rework costs available for cost of quality computations.

Comshare also has robots to monitor news feeds, stock quotes, and for internal Lotus Notes databases. This capability illustrates the evolution of executive business information needs to encompass external information and data stored in in-house intranets.

3.4.   INTERFACE AGENTS

There are two general types of interface agents. One class of interface agents helps users by filtering various data sources. For example, consider an interface agent that intelligently filters a user's electronic mail. If the mail agent is any good, it weeds out messages that the user is unlikely to find useful. The main benefit provided by this type of an interface agent is a reduction of the amount of data that users need to process.

The second class of interface agents mediates between users and applications. As an example, consider a software agent for heterogeneous access to military command and control (C2) databases to support joint armed services contingency planning (Gunderson, 1994). The agent mediates between the user and various C2 databases. Within the framework of a fault-tolerant multidatabase transaction model, the agent software formulates applicable cross-database joins and unions for the user based upon high-level information entered into a graphical user interface. Another good example of a mediating agent is the GeneQuiz application that automatically analyzes a genome sequence using a variety of applications. As a third example, consider an interface agent that automatically uses a computer algebra system, such as Mathematica, to perform an engineering design task, such as the sensitivity analysis of a dynamic system. This agent mediates between the user and the computer algebra system. The main benefit provided by mediating interface agents is the hiding of the complexity of the underlying application from users.

Interface agents for data reduction generally are built as rule-based programs that apply a profile to the items in the data sources. The profile is a specification of the attributes of desirable items in the data source. For example, a mail agent can use a set of rules that is applied to an incoming message to determine its usefulness for a user.

A key property of data reduction interface agents is their customization to specific users. For example, a mail agent is specific to a particular user. One user's mail agent will not be useful for another user. While a rule-based approach to the design of a data reduction agent has been successful for certain applications, the need for a set of rules specific to individual users is a stumbling block. Many users are averse to devoting significant effort to specifying rules for their preference for items from a given data source. In many cases, even if users are inclined to specify rules, the nature of the data reduction task makes it hard to explicate such rules. For example, consider a database of music titles. Suppose a user wants an interface agent to automatically select titles that interest the user. The user may find it hard to articulate a set of rules for the agent that enable effective selection by the agent. An alternative approach is to have the agent learn a set of selection rules based on selections made by the user over time. Essentially, the learning task is the induction of a classifier that classifies new items as being interesting to a user based on the user's previous selection of items.

A recent approach to improve the performance of data reduction agents is to combine the individual experiences of a group of users through collaboration among the agents serving these users. For example, consider an interface agent for the task of selecting good movies to watch. The user's agent interacts with similar agents for other users to find out about a much larger set of good movies to suggest to its user.

Interface agents for mediating in the use of applications are usually built as knowledge-based systems. A mediating agent has knowledge of the application that it uses and knowledge of the tasks that it solves using the application. The agent reduces the input task into a set of actions that can be performed using the application. The essential idea is to have the mediating agent automate the activity of manually using an application to perform a task. In the general case, a mediating agent constructs two different types of plans. One plan corresponds to the set of operations required to achieve the task. The second plan corresponds to the actions performed using the application. Some of the operations in the task plan correspond to actions performed by the application. This is how the agent uses the application to help in performing the input task. The agent also requires interpretation knowledge to interpret the data obtained by the execution of an action by the application.

An important characteristic of application mediating interface agents is the amount of effort required to develop computing infrastructure to allow the agent software to function. An Application Execution Environment (AEE) will be needed to provide an Application Programmer Interface (API) to the application. The AEE will need to process results from the application and may need to process operations in a distributed environment, possibly to the level of a fault-tolerant transaction model.

In the software agent for access to heterogeneous military C2 databases, the AEE provides an API to access the Purdue University InterBase system. The AEE provides the capability to process an InterBase Parallel Language (IPL) program generated by the user front end, called the Intelligent Database Kernel (IDK). The AEE parses the IPL program, checks its syntax, and breaks it down into the task tree necessary to produce results. The tasks and their execution instructions are then routed to the appropriate Remote System Interfaces (RSIs) using the InterBase fault-tolerant transaction environment. Then, the data returned from the RSIs are processed and presented to the user. The RSIs provide a uniform interface to the heterogeneous database systems. Figure 2 illustrates the structure of the C2 software agent.

As well as the infrastructure described above, the IDK in the C2 software agent is also a major infrastructure component. The IDK utilizes several AI techniques: semantic transition-net grammars, a frame-based knowledge representation, and extensive symbolic processing for various query language transformations, including a cross-database join determination algorithm, which determines the join declarations that could occur across heterogeneous databases.

Mediating agents make the most sense for complex tasks performed with complex applications. The reason is that the cost of building these agents is substantial. Some of this cost is due to the need to develop infrastructure software in support of the intelligent agent, as illustrated in the C2 software agent. The development of frameworks for the development of multiagent architectures, such as the Brown University CAF/Dispel/Coracle (Lejter, 1996) software system, may reduce some of this cost.

3.5. DATA MINING AGENTS

Data mining agents process large datasets to extract useful information. There are two classes of data mining agents. One class uses deductive techniques to mine databases. For example, consider

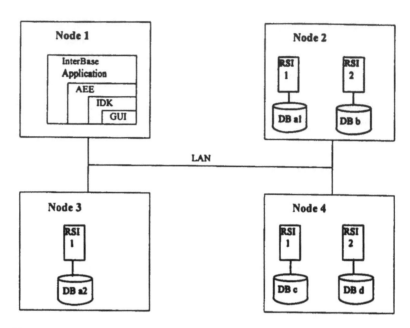

FIGURE 2   C2 software agent structure.

a data warehouse containing performance data on multiple product lines in a manufacturing company. A deductive data mining agent can be built to monitor specified quality metrics, such as the number of product defects. When the agent detects a defect rate higher than a set limit, it performs additional analysis to determine possible causes for the high defect rate. Therefore, the agent automates the deductive reasoning of business analysts responsible for manufacturing quality. The power of such an agent is that it exhaustively analyzes manufacturing quality on a continuous basis and alerts supervisory management of slippage in quality in real-time.

The second class of data mining agents applies inductive classification techniques such as neural networks and decision trees to large data sets to automatically recognize significant patterns. For example, consider a telecommunications network consisting of thousands of devices carrying huge volumes of voice and data traffic. A device failure can cost the company dearly, not to speak of the inconvenience to customers. By building classifiers based on historical network data at the time of a device failure, data mining agents are built to predict failure ahead of time.

4.   SUPPORTING TECHNOLOGIES AND RESEARCH ISSUES

Technologies and research areas supporting agent applications include agent communication languages, mobile and autonomous agent technologies, and work in cooperation and coordination and in learning.

4.1.   AGENT COMMUNICATION LANGUAGES

When agents interact with each other, how do they communicate? The essential motivation is to develop standard language definitions for inter-agent communication in order to enable agents developed in a decentralized fashion to collaborate. For example, an agent shopping for the best interest rates on a housing loan should be able to communicate with the online loan agents from different banks. Clearly, such interaction requires a standard language that all these agents understand.

KQML is currently the best-known agent communication language and has been used in prototype applications requiring agents to communicate with each other. KQML highlights several key requirements of a successful agent communication language. It separates the communication language, meant to express communication requests, from the content language, meant to represent domain knowledge. This separation is achieved by a three-layer language model. The message layer and the communication layer are responsible for performing communicative acts, while the content layer carries the domain-specific representations. KQML leaves open the specification of the content language. Therefore, applications are free to select any content language to use with KQML. The set of communication primitives provided by KQML is quite comprehensive and meets the requirements of a variety of application scenarios. KQML can be used easily with common transport mechanisms such as TCP/IP, SMTP, HTTP, and CORBA.

The infrastructure for agent communications is evolving rapidly. Object Request Brokers (ORBs) allow object interoperability. ORBs based around the Object Management Group's (OMG) CORBA 2.0 support the Internet Inter-ORB Protocol (IIOP). IIOP is a distributed object inter-process communication (IPC) protocol. IIOP will allow seamless object method access across heterogeneous ORBs, operating systems, and hardware. Three examples of this infrastructure evolution will be described to illustrate what is becoming available to support intelligent agent communication.

APM Ltd., of Cambridge, U.K., is pursuing a collaborative program called the Advanced Network System Architecture (ANSA) that uses IIOP. They are working on an IIOP-to-HTTP gateway that allows CORBA clients to access Web resources. Their infrastructure also contains an HTTP to IIOP gateway that will allow Web clients to access CORBA resources. Figure 3 from APM illustrates this infrastructure.

Clients will be able to invoke CORBA services, and the ORB (Object Request Broker) will locate and invoke the right service. If the service is outside CORBA, access takes place via the IIOP-to-HTTP gateway (which also converts from IIOP to other protocols such as FTP). The remote object looks like a CORBA object to the CORBA client (URLs look like CORBA objects). Clients outside the CORBA world see CORBA objects as Web objects and will be able to direct HTTP requests to these objects through the HTTP-to-IIOP gateway.

Lotus' Domino Web server allows Lotus Notes applications to be viewable as HTML. The server has a CORBA ORB with IIOP. With this server, the gateway between Web resources and CORBA objects is similar to the APM infrastructure.

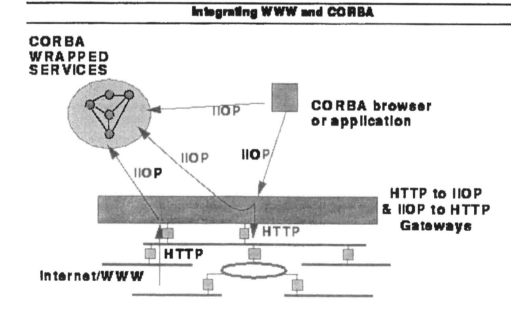

FIGURE 3   The Internet and CORBA.

Netscape Communications Corporation has licensed an IIOP-compliant ORB from Visigenic Software, Inc. for their browser and server software. The Netscape IIOP infrastructure can support distribute method invocation for Java classes, simplifying the development of Web-based distributed applications.

Another aspect of agent communications is the need to interface with existing legacy systems and databases. As discussed in Section 3.4 for the C2 software agent, this infrastructure programming can consume a large portion of the software development process when building intelligent agents. Fortunately, the existence of *de facto* standards, such as ODBC (Open DataBase Connectivity), have simplified some of this interfacing. The effort involved in this aspect of agent communications should not be underestimated, though, especially if high transaction performance is required. One of the lessons learned from the development and deployment of expert systems in the 1980s was the need to build systems on conventional hardware platforms with robust interfaces to existing data and legacy systems.

4.2.   MOBILE AGENTS

Mobile agents travel on the computer network to go to the site of a server they need to use. The interaction with the server occurs at the server site, and then agents travel back to their origin to provide users the results. Essentially, mobile agents are a solution to the limited bandwidth of the network. By sending an agent to the server site, the amount of network traffic generated is minimized. For example, consider a library catalog server on the network. A nonmobile interface agent queries the server for certain items. The results of the query are returned to the agent. Suppose the desired item is not available at this server and the agent must query another server. In this case, the network transmission from the first server can be avoided if the agent were to visit the server site. Then, upon finding that the server does not have the desired item, the agent could travel to the second server site, and so on.

Mobile agents are particularly attractive for mobile workers. Typically, the network bandwidth available from an offsite location is quite limited. In this case, agents that travel on the network and return with results are an answer to the limited bandwidth.

One of the difficult issues with mobile agents is security. Methods to verify the trustworthiness of arriving agents at a server are needed prior to allowing them access to data and computing resources. With regard to computing resource consumption, mobile agents should be self-aware of their resource consumption relative to the server load to avoid overwhelming the server. A mobile agent must also provide a means to securely carry gathered data back to the user.

4.3.   AUTONOMOUS AGENTS

Autonomous agents are computational systems designed to operate in a changing, unpredictable universe. Within their universe these systems sense their environment through sensory inputs, and they may explore their surroundings through the execution of commands that effect change either literally for robotic systems, or figuratively for those systems that wander through cyberspace.

The problem of autonomous systems is to understand how they develop and modify the principles by which they control their behavior while becoming and remaining effective as systems achieving their goals in complex dynamic environments.

Autonomous systems are those that develop, for themselves, the laws and strategies according to which they regulate their behavior. Once started, they determine their actions on their own. The term "autonomous agents" can refer to either to roving robotic systems of various forms, or to purely software robots or softbots that have no physical form, and explore the universe of computer memory and computer networks.

These agents may perform a variety of tasks in their environments. For example, some robots may work in hazardous physical environments, interacting primarily with other robots and physical objects. On the other hand, softbots may act as personal assistants to office workers by running on a single PC or workstation, or may serve a wider set of users by running on a network. Such agents use knowledge about the interests and priorities of people to perform routine organizational tasks such as automatically screening, directing, revising, and responding to information.

With the explosion of interest in the Internet, there are a number of software agents currently available or under development to aid in the search, filtering, and organization of information on the World Wide Web. Such systems are often called searchbots.

Agents that modify their behavior over time to adapt to their environment are viewed as intelligent autonomous agents. Research in this area is concerned with developing autonomous agents that can improve their performance over time, or "learn" to adapt to their changing environment.

4.4. COOPERATION AND COORDINATION

As autonomous agents are developed to take over a variety of tasks for people, there is a need for developing agents that can cooperate and coordinate with other agents operating in the same environment. (Have your agent get in touch with my agent to arrange a meeting.)

Developing systems so that agents can communicate among themselves as well as sensing and operating within their environment is the focus of research in Distributed Artificial Intelligence. Such systems may either consist of multiple agents working together to solve a single problem; or multiple agents, each working to solve their own problem, that occasionally need to interact with other agents to achieve their goals.

Research under the direction of Professor Victor R. Lesser at the University of Massachusetts at Amherst focuses on how to achieve effective cooperation among agents, balancing several interdependent criteria including efficient use of processor and communication resources, responsiveness to unexpected situations and real-time deadlines, and reliability. Three conceptual ideas motivate Lesser's approach to achieving effective coordination: satisficing versus optimality, tolerance of inconsistency, and control intelligence.

Agents solving independent goals may exploit each other's different sets of world knowledge. Instead of each agent relearning what other agents have already learned through experience, agents can simply ask each other for help. This gives each agent access to the experience that other agents already possess. This is the focus of the work of Pattie Maes et al. at the MIT Media Laboratory.

For agents to communicate and collaborate, they must speak a common language as well as follow a common protocol, as discussed in Section 4.1.

4.5. LEARNING

To be truly successful, autonomous agents must adapt to their changing environments. A number of different techniques are being incorporated into autonomous agent systems to allow improvements to behavior.

In multi-agent systems, various agents can communicate with each other. An agent may learn simply by interrogating another agent for information that it has gathered. This new information and meta-information, such as the availability and reliability of the information received, is one example of agent learning.

Machine Learning techniques can also be used to help filter and find information. Agents are able to learn from the experience, using Machine Learning methods. For instance, softbot agents can analyze past user's queries to understand where and how interesting information can be retrieved. Inductive Logic Programming can be used to learn rules able to help the agents during the searching phase.

The use of Genetic Algorithms to aid in the development of better Information Filtering techniques is another approach explored by the MIT Media Lab. The information filtering agent is modeled as a population of profiles. Each profile searches for documents that match itself and recommends them to the user. User feedback can change the fitness of the profiles. If the user provides positive (negative) feedback for a document, the fitness of the profile that retrieved that document is increased (decreased). In addition, the profile can be modified in response to user feedback. The population as a whole continually adapts to the dynamic needs of the user.

5.   FUTURE TRENDS AND SUMMARY

The use of intelligent agents is growing very rapidly. As this occurs, there are several issues and several technical areas that are becoming of increasing interest.

Among the issues that will become increasingly important as the use of intelligent agents becomes more widespread are the issues of privacy and security of derived agent information, and the impartiality of the agent system. An intelligent agent is given and infers information about the likes and preferences of a user in professional and personal areas. This information can be of great interest to marketers, business competitors, personal acquaintances, and many others. Many users will not want this information to be available to such people, and intelligent agent systems must insure that promised privacy is maintained.

In addition, there is the possibility of an agent being "influenced" without the user's knowledge — either intentionally by the agent provider or by external means through a security breach — to weigh decisions in a certain directions, e.g., to favor a particular brand or get information from a particular source. Users must be able to trust that the agent represents them with no bias put in by the agent provider, and that the agent is secure from subversion by external sources.

For truly flexible behavior, an agent application requires a very large common-sense knowledge base. Over the next several years we will see increasing emphasis on technology to build very large knowledge bases and to maintain them automatically. Many technical hurdles will have to be overcome, including automatic resolution of inconsistencies in knowledge from diverse sources, knowledge acquisition from text, and automatic refinement of knowledge bases with problem-solving experience.

Much progress is required on improving the interaction between agents and users. Agent interfaces will have to be multimodal, including speech, image, and language understanding capabilities, in order to have flexible dialogues with people (Reddy, 1996).

The construction of intelligent agent software should become less complex as intelligent agent object-oriented frameworks and applets appear. The availability of frameworks should also encourage developers to incorporate agent communication capabilities into their intelligent agents. As agent communications become more of an issue, the activity in this area should grow, with real-world development shaking out the most appropriate and robust agent communication mechanisms. The widespread availability of *de facto* standards such as Open Database Connectivity (ODBC) should greatly simplify linking intelligent agents to legacy data sources. New standards such as CORBA should also provide nice infrastructure bases to facilitate intelligent agent construction.

As the uses and benefits of intelligent agents grow, the agent development community should be careful to not oversell the technology and engender unrealistic expectations. It is incumbent upon technical practitioners to insure that they, their management, and related agencies realistically describe the potential of the technology, and refrain from promoting the technology as the new software panacea. Also, (adapting Marvin Minsky's advice to the AI community), it is important for agent practitioners not to so focus on a certain agent technologies that they neglect the wealth of available techniques. The best systems of the future will likely be the ones that are hybrids of many powerful agent and non-agent techniques.

REFERENCES

Adler, 1995. Learning Agents for Telecommunications, M. Adler, W. Frawley, in J. Liebowitz and D. Prerau (Ed.), *Worldwide Intelligent Systems*, IOS Press, Amsterdam, and Ohmsha, Tokyo, 1995.

Casari, 1996. GeneQuizII: Automatic Function Assignment for Genome Sequence Analysis, G. Casari, C. Ouzounis, A. Valencia, C. Sander, *Proceedings of the First Annual Pacific Symposium on Biocomputing, Hawaii, World Scientific*, 1996, pp. 707–709.

FTP, 1996. Introduction to Intelligent Agents and FTP Software CyberAgent Technology, White Paper, FTP Software, September, 1996.

Finin, 1992. A Language and Protocol to Support Intelligent Agent Interoperability, T. Finin, R. Fritzson, D. McKay, *Proceedings of the CE & CALS Washington '92 Conference*, June 1992.

Finin, 1994. KQML: An Information and Knowledge Exchange Protocol, T. Finin, D. McKay, R. Fritzson, R. McEntire, in K. Fuchi, T. Yokoi (Ed.), *Knowledge Building and Knowledge Sharing*, Ohmsha and IOS Press, 1994.

Gunderson, 1994. *An Intelligent Software Agent for Heterogeneous Database Access* by A. Gunderson, R. Renner, and LTC S. Butler, The Sixth International Conference on Artificial Intelligence and Expert Systems Applications (EXPERSYS-94), Houston, TX, December 1994, pp. 9–16.

IBM, 1996. 1) *IBM Aglets Workbench*, White Paper, IBM Corporation, September, 1996.

IBM, 1996. 2) *IBM Intelligent Agents*, by Don Gilbert with Peter Janca, IBM Corporation, Research Triangle Park, NC USA, December 1996.

Keller, 1994. *Three Neural Network Based Sensor Systems for Environmental Monitoring*, P. E. Keller, R. T. Kouzes, L. J. Kangas, IEEE Electro94 Conference, Boston, MA, May 1994.

Lejter, 1996. A Framework for Development of Multiagent Architectures by Moises Lejter and Thomas Dean, *IEEE Expert*, Volume 11, Number 6, December 1996, pp. 47–59.

Maes, 1994. *Agents that Reduce Work and Information Overload*, P. Maes, Communications of the ACM, July, 1994, pp. 30.

Maltz, 1995. *Pointing the Way: Active Collaborative Filtering*, D. Maltz, K. Ehrlich, CHI95 Proceedings, ACM Press, 1995.

Oracle, 1994. *Oracle Mobile Agents*, White Paper, Oracle Corporation, January, 1996.

Pathak, 1993. Automatic Use of Software Systems, D. K. Pathak, Ph.D. Dissertation, Carnegie Mellon University, 1993.

Reddy, 1996. Turing Award Lecture: To dream the possible dream, R. Reddy, CACM 39, 5 (May 1996), 105–112.

Sasisekharan, 1996. Data Mining and Forecasting in Large-Scale Telecommunication Networks, R. Sasisekharan, V. Seshadri, S. M. Weiss, *IEEE Expert*, February, 1996, pp. 37–43.

Weiss, 1992. *Building Expert Systems for Controlling Complex Programs*, S. Weiss, C. Kulikowski, C. Apte, M. Uschold, J. Patchett, R. Brighman, B. Spitzer, Proceedings of AAAI, 1992, pp. 322–326.

17 Constraint Programming

Mark Wallace

CONTENTS

1.   INTRODUCTION

Constraint programming is a paradigm that is tailored to hard search problems. To date the main application areas are those of planning, scheduling, timetabling, routing, placement, investment, configuration, design, and insurance. Constraint programming incorporates techniques from mathematics, artificial intelligence, and operations research, and it offers significant advantages in these areas since it supports fast program development, economic program maintenance, and efficient runtime performance. The direct representation of the problem, in terms of constraints, results in short, simple programs that can be easily adapted to changing requirements. The integration of these techniques into a coherent high-level language enables the programmer to concentrate on choosing the best combination for the problem at hand. Because programs are quick to develop and to modify, it is possible to experiment with ways of solving a problem until the best and fastest program has been found. Moreover, more complex problems can be tackled without the programming task becoming unmanageable. A tutorial introduction to constraint logic programming can be found in Frühwirth et al. (1992).

Constraint logic programming (CLP) combines logic, which is used to specify a set of possibilities explored via a very simple inbuilt search method, with constraints, which are used to minimize the search by eliminating impossible alternatives in advance. The programmer can state the factors that must be taken into account in any solution — the constraints, state the possibilities — the logic program, and use the system to combine reasoning and search. The constraints are used to restrict and guide search.

The whole field of software research and development has one aim, viz. to optimize the task of specifying and writing and maintaining correct, functioning programs. Three important factors to be optimized are:

- Correctness of programs
- Clarity and brevity of programs
- Efficiency of programs

Constraint programming is, perhaps, unique in making a direct contribution in all three areas. This is why it is such an exciting paradigm.

2.   HISTORY

In 1963, Sutherland introduced the Sketchpad system, a constraint language for graphical interaction. Other early constraint programming languages were Fikes' Ref-Arf, Lauriere's Alice, Sussmann's CONSTRAINTS, and Borning's ThingLab. These languages already offered the most important features of constraint programming: declarative problem modeling and efficient constraint enforcement; propagation of the effects of decisions; flexible and intelligent search for feasible solutions. Each of these three features has been the study of extensive research over a long period.

The current flowering of constraint programming owes itself to a generation of languages in which declarative modeling, constraint propagation, and explicit search control are supported in a coherent architecture that makes them easy to understand, combine, and apply.

2.1.   DECLARATIVE MODELING AND EFFICIENT ENFORCEMENT

2.1.1.   Algorithm = Logic + Control

Declarative programming has a long history yielding languages such as LISP, Prolog, and other purer functional and logic programming languages, and of course it underpinned the introduction of relational databases and produced SQL which, for all its faults, is today's most commercially successful declarative programming language.

There has been a recognition that declarative programming has problems with performance and scaleability. One consequence has been a swing back to traditional procedural programming. However, constraint programming, while recognizing that efficiency is an important issue, retains the underlying declarative approach. The idea is not to abandon declarative programming (that would amount to throwing away the baby with the bathwater), but to augment it with explicit facilities to control evaluation. Hence, Kowalski's maxim that *Algorithm = Logic + Control.*

When constraints are used in an application, both the issues of modeling and performance are considered. An early use of constraints was in the modeling of electrical circuits. Such circuits involve a variety of constraints — from simple equations (the current at any two points in a sequential circuit is the same), to linear equations (when a circuit divides, the current flowing in is the sum of the currents flowing out), to quadratic equations (voltage equals current multiplied by resistance), and so on. A constraint solver that can handle all the constraints on a circuit would be prohibitively inefficient. Consequently, Sussmann sought to model circuits using only a simple class of constraints. He showed that the lack of expressive power of simple constraints can be compensated for by using multiple orthogonal models of the circuit. The different constraints of the different models interact to produce more information than could be extracted from the models independently.

2.1.2. Constraints for Multidirectional Programming

In many early constraint systems, constraints were little more than functions that were evaluated in a data-driven way. The logic programming paradigm, however, suggested that programs should be runnable "in both directions'.' In addition to evaluating a function $f(\overline{X})$ yielding the result Y, it must be possible to solve the equation $f(\overline{X}) = Y$ for a given value Y but unknown arguments $\overline{X}$.

Naturally, when a function is evaluated "backwards" — i.e., from its result producing its input — it is no longer a function! Attempts to integrate functional and logic programming motivated much research on equation-solving systems, and in the end spawned constraint logic programming.

It was recognized that constraint solving lies at the heart of logic programming, in its built-in unification. Researchers began to replace (syntactic) unification with other equation solvers. An important example of this was Boolean unification: this is a solver for equations between Boolean expressions, whose possible values are only *true* or *false*. This development has now found a commercially successful application for design and verification of digital circuits. Moreover, Boolean unification is also being applied to the design and verification of real-time control software.

2.1.3. Constraint Logic Programming

Soon an even more radical step was taken when it was recognized that unification could be replaced by any constraint system and solver, provided certain conditions were satisfied. There was no need for a unification algorithm (which reduces an equation between expressions to an equivalent set of variable assignments). Indeed, the constraints need not be equations at all.

The resulting scheme (Jaffar and Lassez, 1987) called the Constraint Logic Programming Scheme, and written CLP(X), was illustrated by choosing mathematical equations and inequations as the constraint system, and the Simplex algorithm as the solver. This instance of CLP(X) is called CLP($\mathcal{R}$), and is described in a later section.

It has inspired a whole research area, exploring the interface between logic and mathematical programming. One resulting constraint programming language is 2LP (Linear Programming and Logic Programming), which embeds mixed integer programming in a constraint programming system. Another is Newton, which uses interval constraints to do solve hard mathematical problems involving polynomials.

While constraint logic programming offers a powerful modeling language, new constraint propagation algorithms and a clean execution model, mathematical programming offers some sophisticated algorithms, highly optimized implementations, and a wealth of industrial application know-how.

The next step beyond the standard constraint logic programming scheme was to include more than one constraint system and solver in a single system. Even CLP($\Re$) was, in fact, such a combination including syntactic unification, Gaussian elimination, and the Simplex. CLP systems nowadays include a variety of solvers that exchange information through shared variables. For numeric variables, in addition to the above solvers, there may also be a Groebner base rewriting system for handling polynomial equations, a very powerful CAD solver, and a weaker but very useful constraint handler for reasoning on numeric intervals. The latter three systems are typically useful for nonlinear constraints, containing expressions in which variables are multiplied together.

2.2. PROPAGATION

2.2.1. Early Applications

Constraint propagation was used in 1972 for scene labeling applications, and has produced a long line of local consistency algorithms, recently surveyed by Tsang (1993).

Constraint propagation offers a natural way for a system to spontaneously produce the consequences of a decision. (*Propagation* is defined in the dictionary as "dissemination, or diffusion of statements, beliefs, practices".) Propagation is the most important form of immediate feedback for a decision-maker.

Propagation works very effectively in interactive decision support tools. In many applications, constraint programming is used in conjunction with other software tools, taking their results as input, performing propagation, and outputting the consequences. Typically, feedback from the propagation tool is given in the form of a spreadsheet interface.

Many early applications of constraint programming were related to graphics: geometric layout, user interface toolkits, graphical simulations, and graphical editors. Constraint propagation has played a key role in all these applications, with the result that control over the propagation has been thoroughly investigated: leading to a current generation of very high-performance constraint-based graphics application.

2.2.2. Constraint Satisfaction Problems

On the other hand, constraint propagation has been the core algorithm used in solving a large class of problems termed constraint satisfaction problems (CSPs). Standard CSPs have a fixed finite number of problem variables, and each variable has a finite set of possible values it can take (called its domain). The constraints between the variables can always be expressed as a set of admissible combinations of values. These constraints can be directly represented as relations in a relational database, in which case each admissible combination is a tuple of the relation. CSPs have inspired a fascinating variety of research because despite their simplicity they can be used to express, in a very natural way, real, difficult problems.[1]

One line of research has focused on constraint propagation, showing how to propagate more and more information (forward checking, arc-consistency, path-consistency, k-consistency, relational consistency, and so on). For example, arc-consistency is achieved by reducing the domains of the problem variables until the remaining values are all supported; a value is supported if every constraint on the variable includes a tuple in which the variable takes this value and the other variables all take supported values.

Even if none of the arc-consistent domains are empty, this does not imply the CSP has a solution! To find a solution it is still necessary to try out specific values for the problem variables. Only if all the variables can be assigned a specific value, such that they all support each other, has

---

[1] The class of CSP problems is NP complete.

a solution been found. One algorithm for solving CSPs, which has proved useful in practice, is to select a value for each variable in turn, but, after making each selection, to re-establish arc-consistency. Thus, search is interleaved with constraint propagation. In this way, the domains of the remaining values are reduced further and further until either one becomes empty, in which case some previous choice must be changed, or else the remaining domains contain only one value, in which case the problem is solved.

Another line of research has investigated the global shape of the problem. This shape can be viewed as a graph, where each variable is a node and each constraint an edge (or hyper-edge) in the graph. Tree-structured problems are relatively easy to solve, but research has also revealed a variety of ways of dealing with more awkward structures, by breaking down a problem into easier subproblems, whose results can be combined into a solution of the original problem. Picturesque names have been invented for these techniques such as "perfect relaxation" and "hinge decomposition."

More recently, researchers have begun to explore the structure of the individual constraints. If the constraints belong to certain classes, propagation can be much more efficient — or it can even be used to find globally consistent solutions in polynomial time. Indeed, there are quite nice sufficient conditions to distinguish between NP-complete problem classes and problem classes solvable with known polynomial algorithms.

2.2.3. Constraint Propagation in Logic Programming

The practical benefits of constraint propagation really began to emerge when it was embedded in a programming language (Van Hentenryck, 1989). Again it was logic programming that was first used as a host language, producing impressive results first on some difficult puzzles and then on industrial problems such as scheduling, warehouse location, cutting stock, and so on (Dincbas et al., 1988). The embedding suggested new kinds of propagation, new ways of interleaving propagation and search, and new ways of varying the propagation according to the particular features of the problem at hand.

These advantages were very clearly illustrated when, using lessons learned from the Operations Research community, constraint logic programming began to outperform specialized algorithms on a variety of benchmark problems. However, the main advantage of constraint programming is not the good performance that can be obtained on benchmarks, but its flexibility in modeling and efficiently solving complex problems.

A constraint program for an application such as Vehicle Scheduling, or Bin Packing, not only admits the standard constraints typically associated with that class of problems, but it also admits other side-constraints that cause severe headaches for Operations Research approaches.

Currently, several companies are offering constraint programming tools and constraint programming solutions for complex industrial applications. As host programming language, not only logic programming but also LISP and C++ are offered.

2.3. SEARCH

The topic of search has been at the heart of AI since GPS. Some fundamental search algorithms were generate-and-test, branch and bound, the A* algorithm, iterative deepening, and tree search guided by the global problem structure, or by information elicited during search, or by intelligent backtracking.

The contribution of constraint programming is to allow the end-user to control the search, combining generic techniques and problem-specific heuristics. A nice illustration of this is the n-queens problems: how to place n queens on an nXn chess board, so that no queens can take each other. For $n = 8$, depth-first generate-and-test with backtracking is quite sufficient, finding a solution in a few seconds. However, when $n = 16$, it is necessary to interleave constraint propagation with the search so as to obtain a solution quickly. However, when $n = 32$, it is necessary to add more intelligence to the search algorithm. A very general technique is to choose as the next variable to label the one with the smallest domain, i.e., the smallest number of possible values. This is called *first-fail*. It is particularly effective in conjunction with constraint propagation, which reduces the size of the domains of the unlabeled variables (as described for arc-consistency above), For n queens, the first-fail technique works very well, yielding a solution within a second. Unfortunately, even first-fail doesn't scale up beyond $n = 70$. However, there is a problem-specific heuristic that starts by placing queens in the middle of the board, and then moving outward. With the combination of depth-first search, interleaved with constraint propagation, using the first-fail ordering for choosing which queen to place next, and placing queens in the center of the board first, the 70-queens problem is solved within a second, and the algorithm scales up easily to 200 queens.[2]

3. PROGRAMMING WITH A CONSTRAINT STORE

3.1. PRIMITIVE CONSTRAINTS

The traditional model of a computer store admits only two possible states for a variable: assigned or unassigned. Constraint programming uses a generalization of this model. A so-called *constraint store* can hold partial information about a variable, expressed as constraints on the variable. In this model, an unassigned variable is an unconstrained variable. An assigned variable is maximally constrained: no further nonredundant constraints can be imposed on the variable, without introducing an inconsistency.

Primitive constraints are the constraints that can be held in the constraint store. The simplest constraint store is the ordinary single-assignment store used in functional programming. In our terms, it is a constraint store in which all constraints have the form *Variable = Value*.

The first generalization is the introduction of the logical variable. This allows information of the form *Variable = Term* to be stored, where *Term* is any term in first-order logic. For example it is possible to store $X = f(Y)$. The same representation can be used to store partial information about X. Thus, if nothing is known about the argument of f, we can store $X = f(\_)$. This is the model used in logic programming, and in particular by Prolog.

The storage model used by logic programming has a weakness, however. This is best illustrated by a simple example. The equation $X - 3 = Y + 5$ is rejected because logic programming does not associate any meaning with $-$ or $+$ in such an equation.

The extension of logic programming to store equations involving mathematical functions was an important breakthrough. Equations involving mathematical functions are passed to the constraint store, and checked by a specialized solver. In fact, not only (linear) equations but also inequations can be checked for consistency by standard mathematical techniques. It is necessary, each time a new equation or inequation is encountered, to check it against the complete set of equations encountered so far.

Linear equations and inequations are examples of primitive constraints. Thus, we have an example of a *constraint store*. Further constraint stores can be built for different classes of primitive constraints, by designing constraint solvers specifically for those classes of constraints.

We use the term storage model, rather than data model, because the facility to store constraints is independent of the choice of data model — object-oriented, temporal, etc. On the other hand, the term storage model as used here does not refer to any physical representation of the stored information.

Definition: *A constraint store is a storage model that admits primitive constraints of a specific class. Each new primitive constraint that is added to the store is automatically checked for consistency with the currently stored constraints.*

---

[2] Solutions for n queens can be generated by a deterministic algorithm; however, this problem is useful for providing a simple and illuminating example of techniques that also pay off where there are no such alternative algorithms!

This definition of a constraint store specifies an equivalent operation to writing to a traditional store. However, no equivalent to the read statement is specified. There are two important faciltes useful for extracting information from a constraint store.

First, it is useful to retrieve all those constraints that involve a given variable, or set of variables. For example, if the constraint store held three constraints $X \geq Z$, $Y \geq X$, $W \geq Z$, the constraints involving X would be $Y \geq X$ and $X \geq Z$. However, retrieving only constraints explicitly involving a variable may not give a full picture of the entailed constraints on the variable. For example, the store $X \geq Y$, $Y \geq Z$ entails $X \geq Z$. The mechanism necessary to return all the constraints and entailed constraints on a given variable or set of variables is termed *projection*. A very useful property of a class of primitive constraints is the property that the projection of a set of primitive constraints on a given variable, or set of variables, is also expressible as a set of primitive constraints. If the primitive constraints have this property, it is possible, for example, to drop a variable from the constraint store when it is no longer relevant. This is the equivalent to reclaiming the store associated with a variable in a traditional programming language when the variable passes out of scope.

Second, it is useful to retrieve particular kinds of entailed constraints from a constraint store. For example, it is very useful to know when a constraint store entails that a particular variable has a fixed value. For example, the constraint store $\$X \geq Y$, $Y \geq 3$, $3 \geq X$, entails that both X and Y have the value 3.

3.2. CLP($\Re$)

The constraint logic programming scheme, written CLP(X), is a generic extension of logic programming to compute over any given constraint store. Logic programming over a constraint store has all the advantages of traditional logic programming, plus many further advantages for high-level modeling and efficient evaluation. If the constraint store holds primitive constraints from the class X, logic programming over this constraint store is termed *CLP(X)*. In this section, we shall use a particular class of primitive constraints, linear equations, and inequations, termed $\Re$, to illustrate the scheme. We shall use an example from Colmerauer (1990) to illustrate how it works.

Given the definition of a meal as consisting of an appetizer, a main meal, and a dessert, and given a database of foods and their calorific values, we wish to construct light meals, i.e., meals whose total calorific value does not exceed 10.

A *CLP($\Re$)* program for solving this problem is shown in Figure 1.

```
lightmeal(A,M,D) :-              appetizer(radishes,1).
  I>0, J>0, K>0,                 appetizer(pasta,6).
  I+J+K <= 10,
  appetizer(A,I),                meat(beef,5).
  main(M,J),                     meat(pork,7).
  dessert(D,K).
                                 fish(sole,2).
                                 fish(tuna,4).
  main(M,I) :-
    meat(M,I).
  main(M,I) :-                   dessert(fruit,2).
    fish(M,I).                   dessert(icecream,6).
```

FIGURE 1   The Lightmeal Program in *CLP($\Re$)*.

A *CLP(ℜ)* program is syntactically a collection of *clauses* that are either *rules* or *facts*. Rules are as in logic programming, with the addition that they can include constraints, such as $I + J + K \leq 10$, in their bodies.

The intermediate results of the execution of this program will be descibed as computation states. Each such state comprises two components, the constraint store, and the remaining goals to be solved. We shall represent such a state as `Store @ Goals`. *CLP(ℜ)* programs are executed by reducing the goals using the program clauses. Consider the query `lightmeal(X,Y,Z)`, which asks for any way of putting together a light meal. The initial state has an empty constraint store and one goal: `lightmeal(X,Y,Z)`.

This goal is reduced using the clause whose head matches the goal. The goal is then replaced by the body of the clause, adding any constraints to the constraint store[3]:

```
X=A,Y=M,Z=D,  I+J+K =< 10,  I>=0,  J>=0,  K>=0 @
appetiser(A,I),  main(M,J),  dessert(D,K)
```

The execution continues, choosing a matching clause for each goal and using it to reduce the goal. Variables that neither appear in the original goal, nor any of the currently remaining goals are projected out, as described above. A successful derivation is a sequence of such steps that reduces all the goals without ever meeting an inconsistency on adding constraints to the store. An example is:

```
X=radishes,  Y=M,  Z=D,  1+J+K=<10,  J>=0,  K>=0 @
main(M,J),  dessert(D,K)
```

```
X=radishes,  Y=M,  Z=D,  1+J+K=<10,  J>=0,  K>=0 @
meat(M,J),  dessert(D,K)
```

```
X=radishes,  Y=beef,  Z=D,  1+5+K=<10,  K>=0 @
dessert(D,K)
```

```
X=radishes,  Y=beef,  Z=fruit @
```

Note that at the last step, the constraint $1 + 5 + 2 = {<}10$ is added to the store, but it is immediately projected out.

Next we give an example of a failed derivation. The initial goal is the same as before, but this time `pasta` is chosen as an appetizer instead of `radishes`:

```
X=A,Y=M,Z=D,  I+J+K =< 10,  I>=0,  J>=0,  K>=0 @
appetiser(A,I),  main(M,J),  dessert(D,K)
```

```
X=pasta,  Y=M,  Z=D,  6+J+K=<10,  J>=0,  K>=0 @
main(M,J),  dessert(D,K)
```

```
X=pasta,  Y=M,  Z=D,  6+J+K=<10,  J>=0,  K>=0 @
meat(M,J),  dessert(D,K)
```

At the next step, whichever clause is used to reduce the goal `meat(M,J)`, an inconsistent constraint is encountered. For example, choosing beef requires the constraint $J = 5$ to be added to the store, but this is inconsistent with the two constraints $6 + J + K \geq 10$ and $K \geq 0$.

---

[3] Strictly, all variables in the clause are renamed, but we omit this detail for simplicity.

When the attempt to add a constraint to the store fails, due to inconsistency, a *CLP(X)* program abandons the current branch of the search tree and tries another choice. In sequential implementations, this is usually achieved by backtracking to some previous choice of clause to match with a goal. However, there are or-parallel implementations where several branches are explored at the same time, and a failing branch is simply given up, allowing the newly available processor to be assigned to another branch.

4. CONSTRAINT PROPAGATION

4.1. PROPAGATING CHANGES

A key innovation behind constraint programming is constraint propagation. Propagation is a generalization of data-driven computation. Consider the constraint $x = y + 1$, where x and y are variables. In a constraint program, any assignment to the variable y (e.g., $y = 5$) causes an assignment to x ($x = 6$). Moreover, the very same constraint also works in the other direction: any assignment to x (e.g., $x = 3$) causes an assignment to y ($y = 2$).

In a graphical application, constraint propagation can be used to maintain constraints between graphical objects when they are moved. For example, if one object is constrained to appear on top of another object, and the end-user then moves one of the objects sideways, the other object will move with it as a result of constraint propagation.

In general, each object may be involved in many constraints. Consequently, the assignment of a new position to a given object as a result of propagation, may propagate further new assignments to other objects, which may cause further propagation in turn. If each constraint between two objects is represented as an edge in a graph, the propagation spreads through the connected components of the graph.

When a particular object is assigned a new position, and the change is propagated from the object to other objects, there is a causal direction. In this case, we can assign a direction with each edge of the (connected component of) the graph. As long as the graph is free of cycles, the propagation behavior is guaranteed to terminate, and produce the same final state irrespective of the order in which constraints are propagated. Efficient algorithms, such as the *DeltaBlue* algorithm, have been developed for propagation of graphical constraints. They work by firstly generating the directed graph whenever an object is moved, and then compiling this directed graph into highly efficient event-driven code.

However, if the graph contains cycles, both these issues arise. Consider, as a simple example, the three constraints C1, C2, and C3 specified thus — C1: $x = y + 1$, C2: $y = z + 1$ and C3: $z = x + 1$ (see Figure 2).

Assigning $y = 3$ may start a nonterminating sequence of propagations cycling through the constraints C1 (which yields $x = 4$), then C3 (which yields $z = 5$), then C2 (which yields $y = 6$), and then C1 again and so on. Alternatively, the same assignment $y = 3$ could propagate through C2 yielding $z = 2$, thence $x = 1$ and $y = 0$ via C3 and C1. In this case, the propagation also goes on for ever, but this time the values of the variables decrease on each cycle! Third, the same assignment $y = 3$ could yield $z = 5$ via C1 and C3, and $z = 2$ via C2!

In this example, the original constraints are, logically, inconsistent. However, similar behavior can occur when the constraints are consistent. In the following example there are constraints on three variables. C4: $x + y = z$, C5: $x - y = z$. Suppose the initial (consistent) assignments are $x = 2$, $y = 0$, $z = 2$. Now a new assignment is made to z: $z = 3$. If constraint propagation on C4 yields $y = 1$, then propagation on C5 yields $x = 4$. Now propagation on C4 and C5 can continue forever, alternately updating y and x.

Propagation algorithms have been developed that can deal with cycles, but if the class of admissible constraints is too general, it is not possible to guarantee that the propagation is confluent and terminating.

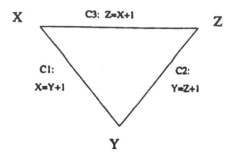

An Example Constraint Graph

FIGURE 2   An example constraint graph.

4.2.   ACTIVE CONSTRAINTS

4.2.1.   Propagating New Information

The changes propagated by label propagation, as discussed in the previous section, are variable assignments as held in a traditional program store. However, in this section we explore the application of constraint propagation to constraint stores, which maintain partial information about the program variables expressed as primitive constraints. Using a constraint store, it is possible to develop a quite different model of computation in which the store is never destructively changed by propagation, but only augmented. One great advantage of this combination is that confluence properties are easy to establish, and consequently there is little need for the programmer or applications designer to know in what order the propagation steps take place.

4.2.2.   Constraint Agents

We have encountered two very different kinds of constraints. Primitive constraints are held in a constraint store, and tested for consistency by a constraint solver. On the other hand, propagation constraints actively propagate new information, and they operate independently of each other. Propagation constraints are more commonly called *constraint agents*. The behavior of a constraint agent is to propagate information to the underlying store. In case the underlying store is a constraint store, the information propagated is expressed as primitive constraints.

Constraint agents are processes that involve a fixed set of variables. During their lifetime they alternate between suspended and waking states. They are woken from suspension when an extra primitive constraint on one or more of their variables is recorded. Sometimes, after checking certain conditions, the woken agent simply suspends again. Otherwise, the agent exhibits some active behavior that may result in new agents being spawned, new primitive constraints being added to the store, or an inconsistency being detected (which is equivalent to an inconsistent constraint being added to the store). Subsequently, the agent either suspends again, or exits, according to its specification.

4.2.3.   Some Built-In Constraint Agents

The simplest constraint agent is one which adds a primitive constraint to the constraint store and then exits. The most fundamental example is assigning a value to a variable, e.g., $X = 3$. This agent adds $X = 3$ to the constraint store and exits.

The next two examples are disequality constraints, which will be illustrated in the next section. The first disequality constraint is invoked by the syntax $X \neq Y$. This agent does not do anything until both X and Y have a fixed value. Only when the primitive constraints in the store entail $X =$

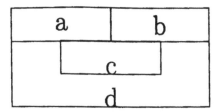

FIGURE 3   A simple map to color.

val_x and $Y = val_y$ for some unique values val_x and val_y does the agent wake up. Then its behavior is to check that val_x is different from val_y. In case they are the same, an inconsistency has been detected.

If the constraint store holds finite domain constraints, then the more powerful constraint agent invoked by the syntax X ## Y can be used. This agent wakes up as soon as either X or Y has a fixed value. It then removes this value from the finite domain of the other variable and exits.

4.3.   MAP COLORING

4.3.1.   The Map Coloring Program

As a toy example, let us write a program to color a map so that no two neighboring countries have the same color (Figure 3). In constraint logic programs, variables start with a capital letter (e.g., A), and constants with a small letter (e.g., red).

A generic logic program, in Prolog syntax, that tries to find possible ways of coloring this map with only three colors (red, green, and blue) is given in Figure 4.

In this program, the (as yet undefined) predicate *ne* constrains its arguments to take different values. We will show how different definitions of *ne* cause the program to behave in different ways.

The predicate *chosen* can be satisfied in three ways. At runtime the system tries each alternative in turn. If a failure occurs later in the computation, then the alternatives are tried in a last-in, first-out basis.

The first definition of *ne* uses the original disequality of Prolog:

```
ne(X,Y)  :- X\=Y
```

If invoked when either of its arguments are uninstantiated variables, X\=Y simply fails. To avoid this incorrect behavior, it is possible to place the constraints after all the choices. In this case, the program correctly detects that there is no possible coloring after checking all 81 alternatives.

A more efficient Prolog program can be written by interleaving choices and constraints, but this requires the programmer to think in terms of the operational behaviour of the program on this particular map. The same effect can be achieved much more cleanly by using the program of Figure 4 with a new definition:

```
colored(A,B,C,D)  :-
  ne(A,B), ne(A,C), ne(A,D), ne(B,C), ne(B,D), ne(C,D),
  chosen(A), chosen(B), chosen(C), chosen(D).

chosen(red).
chosen(green).
chosen (blue).
```

FIGURE 4   A generic logic program for map coloring.

```
colored(A,B,C,D) :-
  [A,B,C,D]::[red,green,blue],
  ne(A,B), ne(A,C), ne(A,D), ne(B,C), ne(B,D), ne(C,D),
  chosen(A), chosen(B), chosen(C), chosen(D).

ne(X,Y) :- X##Y.

chosen(red). chosen(green). chosen(blue).
```

FIGURE 5   A finite domain CLP program for map coloring.

```
ne(X,Y) :- X~=Y
```

This disequality predicate *delays* until both arguments have a fixed value. It then immediately wakes up and fails if both values are the same. If the values are different, it succeeds. This program detects that our map cannot be colored with three colors after trying only 33 alternatives.

Another disequality constraint is available in CLP, which assumes its arguments have a finite set of possible values. We can use it by defining

```
ne(X,Y) :- X##Y
```

This disequality delays until one of its arguments has a fixed value. This value is then removed from the set of possible values for the other. To obtain the advantage of X##Y, it is necessary to declare the set of possible values for each variable, by writing [A,B,C,D]::[red,green,blue] (Figure 5).

This program detects that the map cannot be colored after trying only 6 alternatives.

Although this example is so trivial that it is quite simple to solve it in Prolog, the CLP program scales up to complex maps and graphs in a way that is impossible using a programming language without constraints.

4.4.   BUILDING CONSTRAINT AGENTS

4.4.1.Guards

Constraint agents can be built by directly defining their waking behavior using the notion of a "guard." As an example, we take a resource constraint on two tasks, $t1$ with duration $d1$ and $t2$ with duration $d2$ forcing them not to overlap. The variable ST_1 denotes the start time of $t1$, and ST_2 denotes the start time of $t2$. Suppose we wish to define the agent constraint $agent(ST_1,ST_2)$ thus: if the domain constraints on the start time of $t1$ and $t2$ prevent $t1$ from starting after $t2$ has finished, constrain it to finish before $t2$ has started.

This behavior can be expressed as follows:

```
agent(ST_1,ST_2)<==>           % agent name and parameters
      ST_1 #< ST_2+d2 |        % guard
          ST_1+d1 #<= ST_2     % body
```

The guard will keep the agent suspended until the domains of ST_1 and ST_2 are reduced to the point that the inequation $ST_1 \leq ST_2 + d2$ holds for every possible value of ST_1 and ST_2. When this is true, it wakes up and executes the body, invoking a new agent ST_1+d1 #<= ST_2. Of course, this guard may never become true, in case task $t2$ runs before task $t1$. To cope with this alternative, we add another guard and body, yielding the final definition:

```
agent(ST_1,ST_2)  <==>              % agent  name  and  parameters
        ST_1 #< ST_2+d2 |           % guard1
            ST_1+d1 #<= ST_2 ;      % body1
        ST_2 #< ST_1+d2 |           % guard 2
            ST_2+d2 #<= ST_1        % body2
```

This agent wakes up as soon as either of the guards are satisfied, and executes the relevant body. As soon as one guard is satisfied, the other guard and body are discarded.

4.4.2.   Agents Defined by Specific Codes

Constraint programming systems implement their built-in agents using specific codes that wake up, for example, whenever the upper or lower bound of the domain constraint on a given variable is altered.

Using specific codes, it is also possible to build complex constraints and constraint behaviors to obtain good performance on large complex problems. Indeed, this is the approach that has been very successfully applied on job-shop scheduling benchmarks and incorporated into commercial constraint programming tools such as CHIP and ILOG SCHEDULE.

5.   IMPLEMENTATION AND APPLICATIONS

5.1.   CONSTRAINTS EMBEDDED IN A HOST PROGRAMMING LANGUAGE

5.1.1.   Control

A constraint programming language is the result of embedding constraints into a host programming language. The host program sends new constraints to the constraint handler, under program control. The information that can be returned to the host program depends on how tightly the constraints are embedded in the host language. Most basically, the constraint handler can report consistency or inconsistency. Given a closer embedding, it can also return variable bindings. Most closely it might allow the host programming language to be extended with guards and other annotations, so as to allow host program statements to be suspended and woken up like other constraint agents.

We can diagram the behavior of a constraint program as in Figure 6.

The diagram shows three successive phases occurring during program execution.

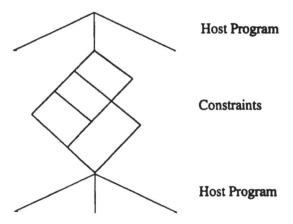

Host Program

Constraints

Host Program

FIGURE 6   Control in constraint programming.

In the first phase, the host program is executing under explicit program control. The host program performs such tasks as input/output, event handling, and search. It may execute for some time before finally sending a constraint to the handler. The diagram illustrates the host program performing search over three branches. For the purposes of the diagram, it does not matter how these branches are explored (sequentially, or in parallel) and how they are expressed (by recursion over a set of alternatives, or by nondeterministic choice and backtracking). The succeeding phases of the execution are only shown for the second branch.

In the second phase, the constraint handler is executing, and its control is constraint-driven. The constraint handler only becomes active when it receives a new constraint from the host program. The behavior of the constraint handler (represented in Figure 6 as a network of thick lines) is defined by a set of atomic behaviors (each of which is represented by a single arc in the network). An atomic behavior is the posting of a new constraint to the store, or a single propagation step performed by a constraint agent, or the invocation of the body in a guarded constraint. When no more constraint propagation is possible, the constraint handler returns to the host program with success, and the host program resumes control, as illustrated in the third phase of Figure 6.

5.1.2. Concurrency

The challenge for embedding constraint handling in a host programming language is to deal with constraint agents acting concurrently. Assuming the programmer has little or no control over the waking and resuspending of constraint agents, the constraint programming framework must ensure that the final result of constraint propagation, before the host program resumes control, is independent of the order in which the agents wake up and post new basic constraints to the constraint store. The concurrent constraints framework (Saraswat, 1993) enables this condition to be met for large classes of practically useful constraint agents.

5.1.3. Logic Programming as a Host Language

Constraints fit hand in glove with declarative host programming languages. Three of the most influential constraint programming languages were embedded in Prolog, Prolog III, CLP($\Re$) and CHIP. While all three system are still developing further, there are many new constraint programming systems emerging, including ECLiPSe, Oz, 2LP, and Newton.

From a theoretical point of view, the extension of logic programming to *Constraint Logic Programming* (CLP) has been very fruitful. A good survey is given by Jaffar and Maher (1994). For example, ALPS — a form of logic programming with guards — was an extremely influential language, becoming the forerunner of the *Concurrent Constraints* paradigm (Saraswat, 1993). Concurrent constraint programming has in turn provided a very clean model of concurrent and multi-agent computing. Constraints can also be modeled in terms of information systems, which allow us to reason about the behavior of constraint programs at an abstract level.

5.1.4. Libraries for Embedded Constraint Programming

The constraint programming technology has matured to the point where it is possible to isolate some essential features and offer them as libraries or embedded cleanly in general-purpose host programming languages.

For example, isolating constraints as libraries has made possible the development of sophisticated constraint-based scheduling systems (see Zweben and Fox, 1994). More generally, there are commercially available libraries supporting constraint handling such as the CHIP and ILOG {C++} constraint libraries.

5.2. APPLICATIONS OF CONSTRAINT PROGRAMMING

Based on a few constraint programming languages that support the storage of basic constraints and the waking and resuspension of constraint agents, the technology has achieved a number of remarkable successes on benchmarks and, more importantly, real industrial applications. A recent survey of practical applications of constraint programming (Wallace, 1996) estimated the annual revenue from constraint technology at around $100 million per annum.

One early application, developed in 1990, was in container port planning in Hong Kong. The application was built by ICL, using finite domain constraints. Another early user was Siemens, who have applied Boolean constraints to problems of circuit design and integration. Both Siemens and Xerox are now applying constraints to real-time control problems.

Constraints are used for graphical interface design and implementation at Object Technology International. Constraint-based scheduling has made a big impact in the U.S., with applications in heavy industry, NASA, and the Army. The application developers are typically small companies such as Recom, Red Pepper, and the Kestrel Institute.

One company, ILOG, has sold constraint technology both in the U.S. and Europe. ILOG also has applications in Southeast Asia. Its French rival, Cosytec, is perhaps the only company to make all its business from constraint technology and applications. Cras (1993) gives a survey of industrial constraint-solving tools.

Areas where constraint programming has proven very successful include scheduling, rostering, and transportation. Constraints are used for production scheduling in the chemical industry, oil refinery scheduling, factory scheduling in the aviation industry, mine planning and scheduling, steel plant scheduling, log cutting and transportation, vehicle packaging and loading, food transportation scheduling, nuclear fuel transportation planning and scheduling, platform scheduling, airport gate allocation and stand planning, aircraft rescheduling, crew rostering and scheduling, nurse scheduling, personnel rostering, shift planning, maintenance planning, timetabling, and even financial planning and investment management.

There is a regular conference on the Practical Applications of Constraint Technology, presented on http://www.demon.co.uk/ar/PACT.

6. CURRENT DEVELOPMENTS

6.1. CONSTRAINTS IN THE COMPUTING ENVIRONMENT

Naturally, there is a great deal of useful research exploring ways of using constraints in an object oriented programming environment, in databases, and on the Internet. The field of constraint databases, in particular, has developed into a growing community of researchers who are exploring the theoretical and practical possibilities of storing constraints in databases, imposing constraints on databases, and retrieving constraints from databases. This work is starting to be noticed in the field of geographical information systems. There is a growing need for databases to handle space, in two and three dimensions, and time. Examples are environmental monitoring and protection, air traffic control, and reasoning about motion in three dimensions. The constraint database technology appears to address these requirements.

6.2. MIXED INITIATIVE PROGRAMMING

One of the great bugbears of constraint programming is how to deal with overconstrained problems. As Jean-Francois Puget put it, "What solution do you return when there are no solutions?" The traditional approach in mathematical programming is to associate a penalty with each violated constraint, and seek the solution that minimizes the total penalties.

A related approach is to decide between the different constraints which ones are more important than which others. The constraint program then only enforces a constraint if this does not cause a more important constraint to be violated.

The drawback is that it is not easy for the user to estimate the importance of a constraint, and the solution produced by the software may well not be the best solution in the opinion of the end-users of the system. Moreover, this approach is a black box, and the end-users receive no feedback about "nearby" solutions, which might prove better on the ground.

Accordingly, one current area of research is how to help the end-user solve overconstrained problems, and multicriteria optimization problems that have different, and possibly conflicting, optimization criteria. The challenge is to allow the end-user to explore the solution space interactively, eliciting information about solutions, and potential solutions, which then enable the user to choose the very best solution for his or her purposes. This is called mixed initiative programming.

6.3.   INTERVAL REASONING

Intelligent software systems have often been highly specialized for symbolic computation, but weaker on numeric computation. This is one reason why the combination of symbolic constraint solving and mathematical programming are proving to be so interesting both in theory and practice.

One recalcitrant problem for numeric computation is the problem of numeric instability. Under certain, unlikely, circumstances, tiny rounding errors in the basic mathematical routines can unexpectedly cause serious errors in the final result. The difficulty is that these errors are hard to predict, and no practical way has been found to predict them.

A way to contain this instability is to reason on numeric intervals, instead of numbers, ensuring that at each calculation the interval is rounded out so as to ensure the actual solution lies inside it. Unfortunately, these intervals tend to grow too wide to be useful. Recently, however, the use of intervals as primitive constraints in a constraint programming framework has produced some excellent results for well-known mathematical benchmarks. These results compete with the best mathematical programming approaches, in particular when the input intervals are quite wide.

Intervals appear in a multitude of different contexts as a way of approximating values. In particular, they are used in database indexing, in constraint propagation, and for specifying uncertainty.

The author predicts that interval constraints will play a crucial role in spatial and temporal databases and in the handling of uncertainty.

6.4.   STOCHASTIC TECHNIQUES

Organizations are increasingly able to capture an up-to-date picture of their global resources, and they are seeking to optimize their use of these resources. However, for large organizations, this optimization problem is unmanageable: no algorithm could ever find the guaranteed best solution for the whole organization.

Stochastic techniques are a way of exploring very large solution spaces and finding good solutions even when it is only possible to visit a (vanishingly!) small proportion of the solutions. Well-known techniques include simulated annealing, genetic algorithms, and tabu search. A drawback is that for structured problems, where constraints impose complex dependencies between different parts of the solution, stochastic techniques are not able to enforce these constraints.

Recently, researchers have begun to explore ways of embedding constraint propagation in stochastic algorithms, thus ensuring that the solutions visited by the algorithm satisfy the problem constraints. To date, such hybrid algorithms have been rather loosely coupled. For example, the stochastic technique only works on a small subset of the problem variables, producing skeleton solutions. These are then fleshed out using constraint handling techniques, and the cost of the resulting full solution is calculated, and fed back to the stochastic algorithm which generates another skeleton solution.

Tightly integrated algorithms combining techniques from mathematical programming, constraint programming, and stochastic algorithms are now the vision of a growing research community. These algorithms may still not be the "golden bullet" that cuts through all forms of complexity, but they would certainly represent an important step in the right direction!

REFERENCES

A. Colmerauer. An introduction to Prolog III. *Communications of the ACM*, 33(7):69–90, July 1990.

J.-Y. Cras. A Review of Industrial Constraint Solving Tools ISBN 1-898804-001, AI Intelligence, 1993.

M. Dincbas, H. Simonis, and P. Van Hentenryck. Solving large scheduling problems in logic programming. In *EURO-TIMS Joint Internation Conference on Operations Research and Management Science*, Paris, July 1988.

T. Frühwirth, A. Herold, V. Küchenhoff, T. Le Provost, P. Lim, E. Monfroy, and M. Wallace. Constraint logic programming: An informal introduction. Technical Report ECRC-93-5, ECRC, 1993.

J. Jaffar and J.-L. Lassez. Constraint logic programming. In *POPL'87: Proceedings 14th ACM Symposium on Principles of programming Languages*, pages 111–119, Munich, January 1987. ACM.

V. A. Saraswat. *Concurrent Constraint Programming*. MIT Press, 1993.

E. Tsang. *Foundations of Constraint Satisfaction*. Academic Press, 1993.

P. Van Hentenryck. *Constraint Satisfaction in Logic Programming*. Logic Programming Series. MIT Press, Cambridge, MA, 1989.

M. G. Wallace. Practical applications of constraint programming. *Constraints*, 1(1), 1996.

M. Zweben and M. S. Fox, editors. *Intelligent Scheduling*. Morgan Kaufmann, 1994.

18 Logic

R.G. (Randy) Goebel and Francisco J. Cantu-Ortiz

CONTENTS

1. INTRODUCTION

Logic has had great influence on the development of expert systems, but its role has often been implicit rather than explicit, and that influence has not always been clearly described or understood. One reason is that the concept of logic is quite broad, and it is sometimes difficult to keep all of its important aspects in mind when considering the role and use of logic in knowledge-based systems applications. Another reason is that logic was originally developed as an abstract description of reasoning, and has only recently been widely adapted for use as a computational system.

As stated by a pioneer of using logic for computation, Alan Robinson has described logic as "the science of what follows from what." In other words, logic is about what kinds of conclusions can be reasonably drawn from what one already knows.

Even on the basis of that informal (but concise!) definition, the relationship to expert systems is clear. Logic provides a tool for both the analysis of expert reasoning, and for the articulation and use of what is known about a problem for which expertise is required: logic is about the relationship between what is known, and how what is known can be deployed to reason about problems and situations.

To understand logic and its role in expert systems is to first dispel some of the many misconceptions about logic. One is that logic is only about reasoning. The fault behind that misconception is that one cannot practically reason without knowing about something. Even the simplest syllogisms are little more than syntactically obvious without interpretation: "All men are mortal; Socrates is a man, therefore Socrates is mortal," is much more instructive than the relatively sterile "A implies B; A, therefore B."

Similarly, logic is not preoccupied with syntax, or the form in which what one knows is expressed. This misconception arises only when one misconstrues the particular *form* of knowledge with the reasoning itself. For example, it has been typical to misconstrue the conclusion that A is above B in the simple diagram

A

B

as a kind of reasoning distinct from that within the purview of logic. This is a misconception that arises from confusing the immediately apparent form of the information, in this case as encoded in two dimensions. However, the essence of logic is independent of the form in which information to be reasoned about is represented. Logic requires only that there is some more-or-less conventional way of representing information, and that there is some conventional way of using it.

2.   HISTORICAL BACKGROUND

The deep history of logic is typically associated with ancient Greek thinkers like Aristotle, and their pursuit of rules of reasoning. These historical roots continue to flow through the development of modern mathematics, for example, with the Leibniz goal of reducing thought to calculation. The modern application of logic to computation could be attributed to the formalization of logical reasoning first proposed by the German mathematician Gottlob Frege, and subsequently, to the formalization of the interpretation or semantics of logic by Alfred Tarski (see van Heijenoort and Tarski). Their combined insight into the relationship among the three essential ingredients of logic— syntax, semantics, and proof (or reasoning) rules — has laid the foundation for the modern application of logic within the field of computation.

The general impetus for the use of logic within artificial intelligence (AI) first arose with McCarthy's proposal for an advice taking program (McCarthy). The thesis is that no program or system is intelligent unless it can accept some form of input that is interpreted as advice about how to improve performance in some task. Expert systems can be considered a subclass of intelligent systems that attempt to capture and deploy the advice of an expert or collection of experts.

Some of the confusion about the role of logic with respect to expert systems arises within this longstanding framework first proposed by McCarthy, and with the difficult challenges it entails. Developments in the principled implementation of logic systems in the support of building advice takers has taken a lot longer than alternatives based on more expedient approaches.

The major development in understanding the application of logic as a practical computational tool lies with the development of programs to automate logical reasoning, including the early work of Prawitz, Davis, and Putnam, and Gilmore (Prawitz, Davisputnam, and Gilmore).

These first demonstrations on the programmability of logical reasoning revealed the essential programmability of logic, but didn't provide any clear indication that such an endeavor was practical. Robinson's (Robinson) proposal for a machine-oriented logic modestly revolutionized the use of logic as a method of machine reasoning, by demonstrating that a very simple system of inference focusing on only one inference rule could be deployed in a kind of naive or mechanical way — instead of perpetuating the idea that reasoning consisted of the rather clever choice from a large repertoire of complex reasoning rules.

The development of logic-based artificial intelligence in the 1960s was paralleled by a kind of alternative development of heuristic methods, including a lot of work on knowledge structures for general problem-solving and the development of meaning representation systems largely motivated by natural language processing. The mere existence of an informal logic and nonlogical research style helped develop a myth that the two styles of artificial intelligence development were somehow fundamentally different (cf. McDermott, Levesque, and Goebel).

The momentum of this distinction between the so-called "logicists" and non-logicists is at least partly the reason that the logical framework embedded within the first expert systems was overshadowed by the excitement of their performance in complex tasks.

One of the earliest systems to establish a recognized framework for the idea of an expert system was the Dendral system of Feigenbaum, Buchanan, and Lederberg (Feigen and Baumbuchanan). The problem was to interpret mass spectrographs using rules about the relationship between segments of spectrograms and their corresponding molecular structure, in order to infer the structure of a complete molecular compound. Unlike previously successful performance systems, for example Gerlenter's geometry reasoning system (Gerlenter), the appeal of Dendral was not just its human-level performance of interpreting spectrograms, but the intuitive appeal of its reasoning framework. Specifically, it was the notion of modular, self-contained rules that had a reasonable clear meaning both as statements about the relationship between spectrogram segments and molecular structure, and as procedurally interpreted "antecedent-consequent" relations of "if-then-else" rules.

The early adoption of these rules as a representation of expertise, combined with the important promotion of a rule-level debugging ("explanation" supporting user queries like "why" or "how" a certain result was obtained) sealed the popular appeal of the expert system idea and provides the departure point for many of the other expositions in this volume.

However, the point here with respect to logic and its relation to expert systems lies with the conception of the ways in which rules in Dendral were conceived, and what the logic of their use was intended to be.

In the example of Figure 1, the rule antecedent expresses properties of a spectrogram that suggest the rule consequent as conclusion. Contrary to its role within a logical reasoning system; such rules have attracted the misnomer "inference rule," assuming they encode some rule of logical inference instead of a fact about the application domain. To see the difference, consider the most common of inference rules, modus ponens: "From a fact A, and a fact A implies B, then one can infer B."

Again, there is a logic underlying the rule structure of Dendral (and all of its rule-based descendants), but to uncover the logic first requires an analysis of the intended meaning of the Dendral rules. The required analysis is clear in hindsight (especially based on recent work by Konolige, Poole, and others (Poole, Konolige, and Poole): in all rules of the form "A if B" one can make one of two analyses: one is that situation A being true *causes* situation B. Such is the case in causal models of diagnosis, where a certain disease is the cause of certain symptoms. Within

> IF the spectrum of the molecule has two peaks
> at masses x1 and x2 such that
> a) $x1 + x2 = M + 28$ AND
> b) $x1 - 28$ is a high peak AND
> c) $x2 - 28$ is a high peak AND
> d) at least one of x1 or x2 is high
> THEN the molecule contains a ketone group

FIGURE 1   An example rule from the Dendral Expert System.

the details of Figure 1, this kind of causal analysis might misleadingly suggest that the antecedent regarding the two mass peaks at $X1$ and $X2$ somehow cause the consequence that the molecule contains a ketone group. However, this is obviously false, as the antecedent lists properties that are causal consequences of the ketone property, not vice versa.

Alternatively, and like the intended interpretation of Dendral rules, the antecedent A is taken as evidence suggesting or supporting the tentative conclusion that situation B holds. Thus, the Dendral rule structure encodes the causal relationship in an operational form: to hypothesize a ketone first requires one to establish certain properties about mass peaks of components.

This relationship between a reasoning strategy and causal knowledge is implicit in the use of all such rule-based systems, and is a part of the reason for their popularity. The challenge of building knowledge-based systems based on such rules can focus on the articulation of more-or-less independent rules that can be used to articulate such relationships in an incremental fashion.

The key to understanding the role of logic in this earliest of expert systems and its rule-based successors is to first understand that the knowledge or axioms encoded as the system's expert knowledge are statements about evidential reasoning. In fact, it has been shown that program transformation methods can take a formal specification of the reasoning strategy of such rules together with the causal form of axioms, and automatically produce the equivalent rule-based form (e.g., [Goebel]). The idea is to view the schema of the Dendral rules as an abductive rule (see below) of the form

given A causes B, to determine the cause of B, assume A

and combine that generic reasoning strategy with causal knowledge, e.g., "colds cause runny noses." The combination provides an instance of a combined reasoning strategy and causal relation rendered as an evidential rule: "if you have a runny nose, assume it is caused by a cold."

It is somewhat ironic that some of the earliest work on expert systems including that of Buchanan et al. (Churchman and Buchanan) was based on this kind of abductive reasoning, but it took several more years to re-extract the ideas (e.g., Poole, Poole, and Konolige). From the viewpoint of logic's impact on expert systems, the newer analysis explicitly acknowledges the important role of a clearly defined method for using logic for knowledge-based systems (e.g., PMG97).

3.   LOGIC AND REASONING

Logic studies the principles of reasoning. As a scientific discipline, logic has found a wide range of applications in many disciplines, which include computer science and artificial intelligence (gen_and_nil). In the design of AI systems, logic has often been regarded as one of several knowledge tools. While some important aspects of logic have been criticized (e.g., see Minsky and Minsky), the best of those criticisms have typically resulted in strengthening the role of logic within AI by using the simplest of logics — deductive logic — as a basis for important extensions.

3.1.   DEDUCTION

Logical inference or deduction is the classical approach to reasoning. We have a knowledge base that is a set of logic formulae and one or more sound inference rules from which we can derive new knowledge that we add to the knowledge base. As a transformation of a given knowledge base, deduction (or deductive rules of inference that define a deductive proof procedure) has the property of preserving truth: sound rules of inference will preserve the truth of original information in deduced information. From another view, deduction forms the basis upon which AI-motivated extensions can be constructed.

As a mathematical structure, logic is characterized by the following three components: a formal language in which knowledge can be expressed, a semantics to give meaning to the sentences of the language, and proof procedures to infer knowledge. A formal language is defined by a syntax that uses an alphabet of symbols and defines rules to combine the elements of the alphabet to form sentences called well-formed formulae. Symbols of the alphabet include constants, variables, functions, predicates, and connectives.

The semantics of classical logic assigns meaning to the formulae by defining a mapping between the symbols of the formula and the objects and relationships of the world. This mapping is called an interpretation. An interpretation consists of a domain and a mapping from elements, functions, and relations of the domain to constant, variables, function, and predicate symbols in the formula. Constants, variables, and terms denote elements of the domain. A formula can take the values *true* or *false*. A model $\mathcal{M}$ is an interpretation that makes a formula α true and is denoted: $\mathcal{M} \vDash \alpha$, which is read "$\mathcal{M}$ satisfies α." A formula α is valid if it is true for every interpretation, and denoted by $\vDash \alpha$. A formula is satisfiable if it has a model, and is a contradiction if it is false for every interpretation. A set of formulae Γ is satisfiable if there is an interpretation that satisfies every formula in Γ. The fact that every interpretation that satisfies a set of formulae Γ also satisfies a formula α, is denoted by $\Gamma \vDash \alpha$ and read "Γ logically implies α." A proof procedure (or calculus) consists of a set of axioms, and a set of rules of inference for deductive reasoning. A formula α which is derived from the axioms by a sequence of inference rules applications is called a theorem and is denoted by: $\vdash \alpha$. If α is derived from a set of formulae Γ, we write $\Gamma \vdash \alpha$, which is read α is deduced from Γ. Soundness and completeness are two attributes of a proof procedure with respect to semantics. Soundness means that any theorem deduced by the proof procedure is valid. Completeness means that any valid formula can be proved by the proof procedure. The completeness theorem establishes the relationship between deduction and logical implication:

$$\Gamma \vDash \alpha \leftrightarrow \Gamma \vdash \alpha$$

which establishes the equivalence between logical consequence and deduction.

In the following section we characterize deductive reasoning for various types of logics, and then we study variations to the deductive approach, which include nonmonotonic reasoning, induction, abduction, and probabilistic reasoning.

Many types of logics can and have been derived, depending upon the constraints imposed on the syntax and semantics of the logic. Without being exhaustive, we survey some of the main logics: propositional logic, first-order logic, and higher-order logic.

Logic can be studied with respect to ontological and epistemological commitments. Ontological commitments have to do with what is assumed to exist in the world; thus, propositional logic assumes that the world consists of facts that are either true or false. First-order logic assumes that the world consists of objects with relationships among them that either hold or do not hold; quantification is made only on objects. Higher-order logic assumes that the world is made of objects, categories of objects, and relationships among them; quantification is made over objects, predicates, and functions. Epistemological commitments have to do with the possible states of knowledge owned by an intelligent system. A system that represents knowledge using propositional, first-order, or higher-order logic believes a formula that represents a fact about the world to be true, to be false, or it could be unable to conclude either way. Systems that represent uncertain knowledge using probability theory, on the other hand, can have any degree of belief, typcially rendered as numbers in the range 0 (e.g., "total disbelief") to 1 (e.g., "total belief"). Systems that represent uncertain knowledge using fuzzy logic can have degrees of belief in a sentence like probabilistic systems, but their ontological commitment assumes that what exists does so with associated degrees of truth.

3.1.1.   Propositional Logic

Propositional logic was first proposed by the English mathematician George Boole to specify a way in which elementary sentences called *propositions* can be combined using connecting words like *and*, *or*, *not*, etc. Boole's logic was the first departure from the Aristotelian tradition, which considered syllogisms as the only valid forms of correct arguments. But the 19 syllogisms discovered by Aristotle describe only a small subset of correct arguments. For instance, we cannot connect together several sentences to form a hypothesis as we can in propositional logic, in which we can construct hypotheses and conclusions of arbitrary complexity. However, in propositional logic, we cannot analyze the structure of the proposition as we can in a syllogism. Thus, Boole's propositional logic and Aristotle's syllogisms describe two disjoint families of correct reasoning forms, but they do not exhaust all the correct forms.

To construct sentences, propositional logic uses an alphabet of logical symbols with a fixed meaning (connectives, parentheses), and a set of non-logical symbols with variable meaning (propositions), with which sentences (well-formed formulae) can be constructed. A truth assignment (or interpretation) assigns formulae one of the values, true or false. A formula that is valid under every interpretation is called *valid*. Valid formulae are called tautologies. Propositional logic is decidable and there are procedures for establishing the validity of a formula (e.g., truth tables). However, the problem of satisfiability for propositional logic is known to be *NP*-complete. Finding a model that satisfies a formula is known as the *SAT* problem (Gallier).

3.1.2.   First-Order Logic

First-order logic (FOL), which was first formalized by the German mathematician Gottlob Frege in 1879, has played an important role in the development of mathematics, computer science, and artificial intelligence. FOL extends the correct forms of reasoning of syllogisms and propositional logic by defining a more general ontological view of the world in which the building blocks are objects and relations (predicates) among objects. First-order logic was introduced to AI by John McCarthy in 1958 (McCarthy). First-order logic assumes that the world consists of objects with their own properties that distinguish them from other objects, and relationships among the objects. Some of these relationships are functions that identify objects and some are relations that characterize a subset of objects. The domain can be any set. Universal and existential quantification is used to define relations over elements of potentially infinite domains. A term denotes an element of the domain; predicates can take one of the values *true* or *false*. First-order logic is more expressive than propositional logic and we can express facts about the world that cannot be expressed with propositional logic. Proof procedures for first-order logic have been developed that are sound and complete, although when one introduces particular theories (e.g., lists, arithmetic), they may become incomplete. Proof procedures in general are semi-decidable, which means that if a formula is valid there are proof methods that will establish this fact, but if the formula is not valid, these same methods may run forever without detecting this fact. Two of these procedures are resolution and mathematical induction.

The resolution procedure was first proposed by Robinson (Robinson). It is a simple yet extremely powerful rule of inference that has been shown sound and complete, and the associated proof procedure is very amenable to machine implementation. Resolution stimulated research and development in automatic theorem proving and found many applications in natural language understanding, planning, database systems, and logic programming, among other areas.

Resolution is a refutation system, that is, to prove that a formula ϕ follows from a set of formulae Δ, we negate ϕ, add the negation of ϕ to Δ, and try to derive a contradiction. Resolution requires ϕ and the formulae in Δ to be in a normal form called clausal form, in which each formula is expressed as a disjunction of literals. A procedure exists to convert any set of formulae into clausal form. Resolution also requires a unification procedure that collapses two predicates $P(t_1,$

..., t_n) and $P(t'_1,...,t'_n)$ into a predicate $P(t''_1,...,t''_n)$ by finding a most general unifier γ, which is obtained by performing substitutions among the terms t_i and t'_i to yield t''_i; that is:

$$P(t_1,...,t_n)_\gamma = P(t'_1,...,t'_n)_\gamma = P(t''_1,...,t''_n)$$

The resolution rule is given as follows: Suppose that α and β are two clauses, if there is a literal ϕ in α and a literal ω in β such that ϕ and ω have a most general unifier γ, then we can infer the clause obtained by applying the substitution γ to the union of α and β minus the complementary literals ϕ and ω:

$$\frac{\alpha, \beta}{((\alpha - \{\phi\}) \cup (\beta - \{-\omega\}))}$$

Looking for a contradiction requires search. Many search techniques as well as constraints on the form of the clauses have been proposed to make the search efficient, such as linear resolution, ordered resolution, SL resolution, and SLD resolution, which, with a depth-first search strategy, is used in the PROLOG programming language as well as in numerous expert system shells.

Mathematical induction is a family of inference rules that is required for reasoning about object and events containing repetition. Since repetition is ubiquitous in many application areas and inductive reasoning is very difficult to automate, research has focused on the automation of proof for mathematical induction. Inductive proofs are characterized by the application of inference rules for mathematical induction such as Peano induction and structural induction on lists and other data structures. All these forms of induction are subsumed by a single, general schema of well-founded induction:

$$\frac{\forall x : \tau \cdot (\forall y : \tau \cdot x \succ y \rightarrow P(y)) \rightarrow P(x)}{\forall x : \tau \cdot P(x)}$$

where $\succ$ is some well-founded relation of the type τ, i.e., there is no infinite descending sequence: $a_1 \succ a_2 \succ a_3 \succ \dots$. The data structure, control flow, time step, etc., over which induction is to be applied, is represented by the type τ. The inductive proof is formalized in a many-sorted or typed logical system. Success in proving a conjecture, P, by well-founded induction is highly dependent on the choice of x, τ, and $\succ$. For many types, τ, there is an infinite variety of possible well-orderings, $\succ$. Thus, choosing an appropriate induction rule to prove a conjecture is one of the most challenging search problems to be solved in automating mathematical induction.

Resolution and mathematical induction are being used in the design of many types of intelligent systems applications, which include natural language interfaces, verification and synthesis of programs and circuits, and programming languages.

3.1.3.   Higher-Order Logic

Higher-order logic extends the ontological commitment of first-order logic by assuming the the world consists of objects, subsets of objects, and relationships between them, in such a way that it is possible to reason about not just the objects but about the properties and subsets of objects specified by functions and predicates. Thus, in higher-order logic, variables range over predicates and functions as well as over individuals of the domain. This means that predicates and functions can be quantified, given as arguments of other predicates or functions, and be outputs of other predicates and functions as well. This makes higher-order logic very expressive, mathematically elegant, and permits a concise description of complex problems. But this increased complexity makes reasoning more difficult as the logic becomes undecidable, inconsistencies can be introduced, and proof systems also become incomplete. To alleviate these problems, the domain is usually constrained to have decidable or semi-decidable subclasses, a type discipline is used to avoid inconsistencies (e.g., Russell's paradox) by introducing hierarchies among the elements of the domain, and heuristics are developed to cope with incompleteness. With these amendments that retain its expressive advantages, higher-order logic has become very popular for reasoning about many types of problems and designing intelligent systems in areas such as hardware, software, protocols, and safety-critical systems (Gordon).

3.2. NONCLASSICAL LOGICS

Classical deductive logic has several important limitations, among which are: (1) classical logic cannot express everything we want to say about the world, (2) there may be facts that have to be retracted when when new facts are derived, and (3) the typical language of logic cannot express uncertain knowledge. Nonmonotonic reasoning, probabilistic reasoning, induction, and abduction represent styles of logic that attempt to alleviate some of these limitations.

3.2.1. Nonmonotonic Reasoning

A characteristic of classical logic is the monotonicity of the derived inferences. This means that deduced facts never contradict the premises nor previously derived facts. However, in many real-world situations this is not necessarily the case. Nonmonotonic reasoning is a logic-based formalism that sanctions inferences that do not deductively follow from a set of sentences stored in a knowledge base Δ. For instance, we may have inference techniques, the application of which depends on certain sentences not being in Δ. With such inference rules, if a new sentence is added to Δ, a previous inference may have to be retracted.

There are many cases in which it is appropriate for an intelligent system to augment its knowledge base with new facts that do not deductively follow from the facts in the knowledge base. For example, circumstances may force immediate action from the system before acquiring all the required facts. Several techniques have been developed for nonmonotonic reasoning. Among these are the *closed-world assumption*, which allows us to infer the negation of an unprovable ground predicate (Reiter); *predicate completion*, in which a formula is computed and added to Δ to restrict the domain of a selected predicate to just those that Δ must satisfy the predicate (Clark); *default reasoning*, where typical properties of objects are described and then rules of inference called defaults are added to perform default inferences (Reiter); and *circumscription*, which is based on the idea of identifying minimal models of a knowledge base with respect to a selected predicate (McCarthy).

Given a new sentence to be added to Δ, the number of sentences in Δ that have to be retracted may be very big, if not infinite. This problem is called the *qualification problem* and is often cited as one of the reasons that a strict logic approach to AI will not work and has motivated much of the work in nonmonotonic reasoning.

3.3. PROBABILISTIC REASONING

Uncertainty, manifested as partial or incomplete knowledge about the world is another problem with the classical logic approach to intelligent system design. We associate with the sentences stored in the knowledge base their evidence, which is the degree of belief that the system has about facts of the world described by those sentences. The main tool for dealing with degrees of beliefs is probability theory, which typically assigns to sentences numbers between 0 and 1, interpreted to represent the degree of belief that the system has over that sentence. Probability theory only recently has been adopted in AI as a principled method of representing uncertainty, largely because of the intractability of the most general techniques that existed in computing conditional probabilities. An important key to recent improvements has been the exploitation of explicit dependence and independence assumptions, largely established with research started in the middle 1980s, which led to the development of *belief networks*, a technique for efficiently computing conditional and joint probabilities distributions (Pearl). A belief network is a directed acyclic graph in which: (1) the nodes represent random variables, (2) an arrow between two nodes represents the influence of one node over the other, and (3) each node has a conditional probability table that measures the effects that the parents have over that node. The joint probability distribution can be calculated from the information in the network. Algorithms have been developed to incrementally build a belief network corresponding to n random variables $x_1, ..., x_n$ from which the joint probability distribution $P(x_1, ..., x_n)$ can be computed. This kind of computation requires one to select an ordering of the random variables that guarantees the conditional independence property between a given node and its parents and furthermore, requires that the construction of the network is such that the axioms of probability are not violated. Once a network has been constructed, then it can be used to make inferences of various types, for example, those found in diagnostic and model-based systems and many other intelligent systems applications.

The Dempster-Shafer theory was designed to deal with the distinction between uncertainty and ignorance (Dempster; Shafer). In this approach, formulae are assigned an interval [*Belief, Plausibility*] in which the degree of certainty must lie. *Belief* measures the strength of the evidence in favor of a set of formulae. *Plausibility* measures the extent to which evidence in favor of a formula leaves room for belief in the negation of the formula. Thus, the believe-plausibility interval measures not only our level of belief in a formula, but also the amount of information we have.

Fuzzy set theory was developed to determine how well an object satisfies a vague description by allowing degrees of set membership (Zadeh). Fuzzy logic determines the degree of truth of a sentence as a function of the degree of truth of its components. It has the problem that it is inconsistent when rendered as propositional or first-order logic as the truth of $P \vee \neg P$ does not necessarily evaluate to 1. However, fuzzy logic has been very successful in commercial applications, particularly in control systems of home electronic appliances. There are arguments that the success of these applications has to do with the fact that the knowledge bases are small, inferences are simple, tunable parameters exist to improve system performance, and that the fuzzy logic implementation is independent of their success. Scaling fuzzy logic to more complex problems will result in the same problems faced by probabilistic techniques and certainty factors (Elk).

Certainty factors was a popular technique for uncertain reasoning in expert systems during the 1970s and 1980s. It was invented for use in the medical expert system MYCIN. Numeric values between $-a$ and a were assigned to rules and input data and ad-hoc heuristics were used to calculate the certainty factor of the output of a fact, which was inferred by one or more rules. It was assumed that the rules had little interaction between them so that an independence assumption between them could be made. But as rule interaction increased, incorrect degrees of belief were computed that overcounted evidence. Certainty factors have been shown to be more or less equivalent to a kind of probabilistic reasoning, which has largely been supplanted in modern knowledge-based systems development by belief networks, Dempster-Shafer theory, and fuzzy logic.

3.4.   INDUCTION

Induction is used to generalize knowledge from particular observations. We start with a set of formulae representing facts about the world. We distinguish a subset of these facts as knowledge to be generalized and treat the rest as background theory. We require that the background theory Γ does not imply the knowledge base Δ.

$$\neg(\Gamma \vDash \Delta)$$

We define a formula ϕ to be an inductive conclusion if and only if the following conditions hold:

1. The conclusion is consistent with the background theory and knowledge base:

$$\neg(\Gamma \cup \Delta \models \neg\phi)$$

2. The conclusion explains the data:

$$\neg(\Gamma \cup \{\Delta\} \models \Delta)$$

Inductive reasoning is not necessarily sound. Although an inductive conclusion must be consistent with the formulae in the background theory and knowledge base, it need not be a logical consequence of these formulae, although not every induction conclusion is unsound. Thus, inductive inference is a type of nonmonotonic reasoning.

Concept formation is a common type of inductive inference. The knowledge base asserts a common property of some observations and denies that property to others, and the inductive conclusion is a universally quantified formula that summarizes the conditions under which an observation has that property. The work of Winston (Winston), Mitchell (Mitchell), Michalski (Michalski), Buchanan (Buchanan), and Lenat (Lenat) have contributed to the development of concept-formation as a type of knowledge acquisition and machine learning for expert systems.

3.5.   ABDUCTION

Abduction is used for finding plausible explanations for some observed events, in contrast to deduction, which is normally used for deriving facts from premises. Reasoning by abduction can be described by the following inference rule:

$$\frac{\alpha \rightarrow \beta, \beta}{\alpha}$$

Contrary to this abductive rule, deductive inference is typically based on modus ponens: α is a premise and β is a derived fact. Another difference concerns the nature of the implication. Modus ponens assumes material implication as defined in classical logic, whereas abuction characterizes the relationship between α and β with more freedom. Material implication says that α is a reason for β to be true, establishing in this way, a causal relationship between α and β. However, not all abduction is concerned with cause and effect. Levesque suggests the extension of the notion of explanation in order to include the case that α is sufficient and not just necessary to explain why β must be true.

The concept of abduction was first presented by the philosopher Peirce (Peirce) and introduced to AI by Pople (Pople) and by Charniak and McDermott (Charniak). Peirce sees abduction as a reasoning process from effect to cause that yields explanations. Induction and abduction can be utilized together: abduction is used to synthesize an explanation, which is then generalized by induction.

The most important part of an abductive procedure is the formation of a new theory that explains the observed data. Among the methods used to generate hypotheses are a type of linear resolution and an assumption-based truth maintenance system (Merziger; Kakaskowalskitoni). In general, there are several possible abductive hypotheses to choose from. Criteria that a good explanation should meet include: a hypothesis that should account for the facts and should be the simplest hypothesis available.

Abduction is a type of nonmonotonic reasoning because as a system becomes more experienced by knowing more observations, it is possible that previous explanations have to be rejected. Default logic is a nonmonotonic formalism that can be adapted to find explanations (Poole).

4. LOGICAL REASONING SYSTEMS

During the 1960s, research efforts in AI concentrated on finding problem representation formalism for general problem-solving. The General Problem Solver (GPS) of Newell and Simon is the best known example of this work (Newell-Simon). A fundamental contribution of the research around the paradigmatic expert systems DENDRAL an MYCIN was the idea that key to effective problem-solving was the emphasis on knowledge required to solve the problem, thus changing the focus of research efforts from problem representation to knowledge representation. Another important contribution was the distinction between domain knowledge and control knowledge. The former is specific to the domain in which the problem is being solved; the latter is about how to conduct the search for a desired solution in a search space and is independent of the problem domain. This idea led to the concept of *shells*, which included control, inference, and knowledge acquisition mechanisms that could be used throughout domains and started the establishments of AI companies that commercialized expert system development tools. In this section we describe the main systems that use logic as the underlying mechanism for accomplishing reasoning and intelligent behavior. This include rule-based systems, logic programming systems, theorem provers, semantic networks and frame systems, description logics, and truth-maintenance systems.

4.1. RULE-BASED SYSTEMS

Production rules were first proposed by Emil Post in 1943 (Post), to characterize a general method of computation. They were subsequently used by Chomsky as rewrite rules in the context of language processing in 1957, and used by Newell and Simon for modeling human problem-solving in 1972 (Newell-Simon). This technique was adopted in the DENDRAL and MYCIN projects to represent knowledge and became a popular technique in developing expert systems applications during the 1970s. As introduced above, rules are implications of the form *if P then Q*. The consequent of a rule can be interpreted as a new knowledge or as an action to be taken. In the former, we have a *deduction rule-based system*; and in the latter, we have a *reactive rule-based system*. In a rule-based system, if we move in the direction of the antecedents to the consequents of the rules, we do *forward-chaining*, and if we move in the direction of the consequents to the antecedents, we do *backward-chaining*.

Forward-chaining rule-based systems, which reason from input facts to conclusions, are more appropriate for modeling intelligent systems that interact with an environment and respond to stimuli in many possible ways. Backward-chaining rule-based systems, which hypothesize a certain goal and reason backwards to justify the hypothesis with input facts, are more appropriate in designing diagnostic systems or types of goal-directed reasoning systems such as theorem provers and logic programming languages. We notice that the reasoning conducted in backward-chaining rule-based systems is simply a form of abductive reasoning.

A typical rule-based system works as follows:

- The system keeps a *rule base* with rules of the form $x_1 \wedge \ldots x_n \rightarrow y_1 \wedge \ldots y_m$ where the x_i represent facts and the y_i represent actions to be performed.
- The system also keeps a *working memory* to store facts obtained from the environment or inferred by the system.
- In each cycle, the system computes a subset of rules whose left-hand side matches the facts stored in the working memory. This is called the *match phase*.
- A rule from the computed subset of matching rules is selected for execution. This is called the *conflict resolution phase*.
- The selected rule is then executed by performing the action specified by the right-hand side of the rule. This is called the *act phase*.

The XCON expert system, built for the configuration of computer systems for the customers of Digital Equipment Corporation, is the best known forward-chaining rule-based system. Forward-chaining rule-based systems are also used for cognitive modeling where the working memory models the short-term memory and the rule-base models the long-term memory. The SOAR expert system is the best representative of this type of system (Laird-Soar).

4.2. Logic Programming Systems and Theorem Provers

Logic has also been used as the basis for the development of programming languages. A programming language based in logic typically restricts the logic for computational efficiency, avoiding the full treatment of features like negation, disjunction, and equality. The most popular family of logic programming languages use backward-chaining, depth-first search, backtracking, resolution inference, and add nonlogical features for input-output. The best-known example of logic programming languages is PROLOG. The relationship between logic and algorithm has been popularized by Robert Kowalski in his equation:

$$Algorithm = Logic + Control$$

which suggests that an algorithm results from appropriately augmenting a knowledge base of formulae with information to control the inference process that uses that knowledge (Kowalski). PROLOG has been widely used as a rapid prototyping language and in the implementation of many expert system applications in most domains.

Theorem provers use a proof procedure such as resolution, sequent, calculus, tableaux, mathematical induction, etc. to prove that a formula can be deduced from a knowledge base using some type of logic. Typically, they use backward-chaining reasoning, search control methods, and heuristics to prune the search space generated by the potential application of inference rules. OTTER and NQTHM are two of the best-known theorem provers. OTTER is based on resolution and NQTHM is based on mathematical induction. Both have been used extensibly in the construction of intelligent development environments for the design of software and hardware systems.

4.3. Semantic Networks and Frame Systems

Semantic networks and frame systems use a network structure to represent knowledge and reasoning techniques. The nodes of the graph represent objects that may have a hierarchical structure, and the arcs represent binary relations between the nodes. Thus, conceptually both systems use the same representation formalism, although the implementation is different. In a frame system, the arcs are regarded as slots of one frame that are filled by another frame, whereas in a semantic network the arcs are regarded as mathematical relations. Frame representations are represented by nested boxes and semantic networks are represented by graphs. Semantic networks emerged right after Peano formalized the notation of FOL around 1886 and were first proposed by Charles Peirce. Frame systems were proposed by Marvin Minsky who used them as a knowledge representation formalism in the area of computer vision (Minsky). Now, we know that any semantic network or frame representation can be translated into a logic representation, where the important aspects are the semantics and the proof procedures defined, rather that the notation features of the formalism. Both formalisms define nonmonotonic inference to reason about properties inherited by a class of objects to subclasses and objects in the hierarchy. Semantic networks and frame systems tools are also widely used in many expert and intelligent systems. CYCL, which is the representation language used in the CYC project, represents most of the features of a frame-based system (Lenat).

Description logics have evolved from semantic networks to facilitate the definition of categories of objects; thus, they are a type of higher-order logic. The ability to describe and reason about categories increases the expressibility of the logic. The main inference rules are subsumption to determine category membership and classification to determine object membership. The problem with this formalism is that inference can become intractable and incomplete, so the language is often restricted, and operations like negation and disjunction are either not allowed or limited in their form. The CLASSIC system is an example of a language of description logics (Borgida). This formalism has had application in domains like finance, information systems, and system interfaces.

Truth maintenance systems define mechanisms for the update of the knowledge base in non-monotonic reasoning, where previously derived knowledge may have to be retracted in the presence of new knowledge. A truth-maintenance system keeps track of dependencies among elements of a knowledge base to efficiently update the knowledge base and keep it consistent. Truth-maintenance operations easily become intractable and are difficult to implement in complex applications (Doyle).

4.4.   CASE-BASED SYSTEMS

Deductive reasoning is a type of reasoning from first principles (axioms and inference rules). However, human experts often solve problems by recalling past experiences and situations where similar problems have been found and solved, remembering the result, and possibly, the reasoning used to obtain that result. The problem at hand is then solved by adapting past solutions to similar problems by a kind of analogical reasoning. The systems that adopt this paradigm are called case-based reasoning (Schank). The main problem here is the storage and retrieval of the relevant cases for the current case. Indexing techniques have been developed to establish navigation paths among cases by different attributes and classes of attributes. CBR tools exist (i.e., CBR Express) and are being used to develop expert systems in diverse areas of application.

4.5.   META-LEVEL REASONING

Meta-level reasoning is concerned with inferences using meta-knowledge, which is the knowledge about the knowledge owned by an intelligent system. A type of meta-knowledge is control knowledge, defined as rules that specify which rules to fire in a given situation or the order in which to solve subgoals. Control knowledge can also be represented as frames as implemented in the CYC project. Another type of meta-knowledge is the knowledge used to disambiguate sentences in natural language processing as implemented in CYC as well. CYC maintains two levels of representation: the epistemological level and the heuristic level. The former represents knowledge in a logic language, which is the language known to the user; the latter represents the same knowledge in computational structures for efficient processing. This distinction represents a way of combining the elegance of logic with the computational efficiency of frames (Lenat). Meta-level inference started with the work of Hayes in 1973 (Hayes) and continued with the work of several researchers who developed systems, including AMORD (deKleer), TEIRESIAS (Davis), MRS (Genesereth), METALOG (Dincbas), PRESS (Silver), and CLAM (Bundy).

5.   RESEARCH ISSUES

Most of the current research issues related to logic and its use in expert and knowledge-based systems focus on either methodologies for using logic methods for induction (learning) of relevant rules (e.g., Muggleton), or on the development of logical reasoning methods that incorporate probability (e.g., Poole, Bacchus, BGHK:AIJ).

Regarding the role of logic in learning, the relevant issue is the long-standing concern with what has been labeled the "knowledge acquisition bottleneck" (Feigenbaum and Buchanan). The capture of expert knowledge has always been resource intensive, and learning technology (e.g., Quinlan) has similarly held the promise for easing the bottleneck. The relatively recent development of logic-based inductive techniques (e.g., Muggletonderaedt) has begun to provide results (e.g., Muggleton).

The work on the application of logic to learning has been accelerated by simple, robust, and relatively efficient methods of induction. As the acquisition of knowledge has always been a challenge, the rewards for improved automatic acquisition will be significant.

Similarly, the role of uncertainty in expert systems has been a fundamental issue at least since the development of MYCIN (Buchanan and Shortliffe). While there have been significant developments in the theory and practice of applied probability in artificial intelligence (e.g., Pearl), more recently the role of probability within a logical framework has provided new promise for exploiting that combination for applications like expert systems (e.g., Poole).

Regarding the cominbation of logic and probability, these two previously separate areas now hold promise for providing a foundation for a new generation of knowledge-based systems, where the principled use of statistics and probability is possible within the more abstract reasoning framework of logic.

6. FUTURE TRENDS AND SUMMARY

The future role of logic in expert systems is really a subset of the general role of logic within computing science. Perhaps the simplest analysis is that, despite the relative success of nonlogical methods like neural networks and genetic programming, logic provides the advantage of relatively transparent semantic analysis of knowledge. As the technological basis for the development of complex knowledge-based systems evolves, the importance of verification and validation will grow, and therefore the need for strong tools for formal analysis based on semantics. The general picture of logic portrayed here is a significant component of that future.

ACKNOWLEDGMENTS

Bruce Buchanan graciously provided guidance on the initial threads seeking to connect research in philosophy of science and applied reasoning with the fundamental reasoning structures of expert systems. In this regard, his early work on fundamentals is sometimes forgotten amid the excitement of expert and knowledge-based system performance.

REFERENCES

Fahiem Bacchus. *Representing and Reasoning with Probabilistic Knowledge: A Logical Approach to Probabilities*. MIT Press, Cambridge, 1993.

A. Borgida, R.J. Brachman, D.L. McGuinness, and L. Asperin Resnick. Classic: a structural data model for objects. *SIGMOD Record*. 18(2):58–67, 1989.

F. Bacchus, A. J. Grove, J. Y. Halpern, and D. Killer. From statistical knowledge bases to degrees of belief. *Artificial Intelligence*, 87:75–143, 1996.

B.G. Buchanan and T.M. Mitchell. Model-directed learning of production rules. In D.A. Waterman and F. Hayes-Roth, Eds., *Pattern-Directed Inference Systems*, p. 297–312. Academic Press, New York, 1978.

B.G. Buchanan and E.H. Shortliffe, Eds. *Rule-Based Expert Systems: The MYCIN Experiments of the Stanford Heuristic Programming Project*. Addison-Wesley, Reading, MA, 1984.

Alan Bundy, F. van Harmelen, C. Horn, and A. Smaill. The Oyster-Clam system. In M.E. Stickel, Ed., *10th International Conference on Automated Deduction*, p. 647–648. Springer-Verlag, 1990. Lecture Notes in Artificial Intelligence No. 449. Also available from Edinburgh as DAI Research Paper 507.

C.W. Churchman and B.G. Buchanan. On the design of inductive systems: some philosophical problems. *Journal for the Philosophy of Science*, 20(211): 1969.

K.L. Clark. Negation as failure. In H. Galliere and J. Minker, Eds., *Logica and Data Bases*, p. 293–322. Plenum Press, New York, 1978.

E. Charniak and D. McDermott. *Introduction to Artificial Intelligence*. Addison Wesley, Reading, MA, 1985.

R. Davis and B.G. Buchanan. Meta-level knowledge: overview and applications. In R. Reddy, Ed., *Proceedings of IJCAI-77*, p. 920–927. IJCAI, 1977.

A.P. Dempster. A generalization of bayesian inference. *Royal Statistical Society*, 30:205–247, 1968.

J. De Kleer. Qualitative and quantitative knowledge in classical mechanics. Ai-tr-352, MIT AI Laboratory, 1975.

M. Dincbas and J. LePape. Metacontrol of logic programs in metalog. In Elsevier-North Holland, editor, *Proceedings of Fifth-Generation Computer Systems*, 1984.

J. Doyle. A truth maintenance system. *Artificial Intelligence*, 12(3):231–272, 1979.

M. Davis and H. Putnam. A computing procedure for quantification theory. *Journal of the ACM*, 7(3):201–215, 1960.

C. Elkan. The paradoxical success of fuzzy logic. In *Proceedings of the 11th National Conference of AI*, p. 698–703. AAAI Press, 1993.

Edward A. Feigenbaum and Bruce G. Buchanan. Dendral and meta-dendral: roots of knowledge systems and expert systems applications. *Artificial Intelligence*, 59:233–240, 1993.

Jean H. Gallier. *Logic for Computer Science*. John Wiley, 1988.

H. Gerlenter. Realization of a geometry-theorem proving machine. In E.A. Feigenbaum and J. Feldman, Eds., *Computers and Thought*, p. 134–152. McGraw-Hill, New York, 1963. (Reprinted from *Proceedings of an International Conference on Information Processing*, Paris, 1959, UNESCOHouse, 273–282.)

R. Goebel, K. Furukawa, and D.L. Poole. Using definite clauses and integrity constraints as the basis for a theory formation approach to diagnostic reasoning. In *Third International Conference on Logic Programming*, p. 211–222, London, England, July 14–18 1986. Imperial College of Science and Technology. *Lecture Notes in Computer Science* No. , Springer-Verlag.

P. Gilmore. A proof method for quantification theory: its justification and realization. *IBM Journal of Research and Development*, 7(3):201–215, 1960.

M.R. Genesereth and N.J. Nilsson. *Logical Foundations of Artificial Intelligence*. Morgan Kaufmann, Palo Alto, CA, 1987.

R. Goebel. Exhuming the criticism of the logicist. *Computational Intelligence*, 4(4):401–404, 1988.

M. Gordon. HOL: A proof generating system for higher-order logic. In G. Birtwistle and P.A. Subrahmanyam, Eds., *VLSI Specification, Verification and Synthesis*. Kluwer, 1988.

M.R. Genesereth and D. Smith. Meta-level architecture. memo hpp-81-6, Department of Computer Science Stanford University, CA, 1981.

P. Hayes. Computation and deduction. In *Proceedings of the Second Symposium on Mathematical Foundations of Computer Science*. Czech. Academy of Sciences, 1973.

A.C. Kakas, R.A. Kowalski, and F. Toni. Abductive logic programming. *Journal of Logica and Computation*, 2(6):719–770, 1993.

K. Konolige. Abduction versus closure in causal theories. *Artificial Intelligence*, 27:97–109, 1992.

R. Kowalski. Algorithm = logic + control. *Communications of the ACM*, 22:424–436, 1979.

R.K. Lindsay, B.G. Buchanan, E.A. Feigenbaum, and J. Lederberg. *Applications of Artificial Intelligence for Chemical Inference: The DENDRAL Project*. McGraw-Hill, New York, 1980.

H. Levesque, Ed., Taking issue: Mcdermott's a critique of pure reason. *Computational Intelligence*, 3(3), 1987.

D.B. Lenat. AM: an artificial intelligence approach to discovery in mathematics as heuristic search. In *Knowledge-Based Systems in Artificial Intelligence*. McGraw Hill, 1982. Also available from Stanford as TechReport AIM 286.

D.B. Lenat and R.V. Guha. *Building Large Knowledge-Based Systems: Representation and Inference in the CYC Project*. Addison Wesley, MA, 1990.

J.E. Laird, A. Newell, and P.S. Rosenbloom. Soar: an architecture for general intelligence. *Artificial Intelligence*, 33(1):1–64, 1987.

J. McCarthy. Programs with common sense. In *Mechanisation of Thought Processes* (Proceedings of a symposium held at the National Physics Laboratory, London, Nov. 1959), p. 77–84, London, 1959. HMSO.

J. McCarthy. Circumscription: a form of non-monotonic reasoning. *Artificial Intelligence*, 13:27–39, 1980. Also in *Readings in Nonmonotonic Reasoning*, Ginsberg, M.L., Ed., Morgan Kaufmann, San Mateo, CA, 1987.

D.V. McDermott. A critique of pure reason. *Computational Intelligence*, 3(3):151–160, 1987.

G. Merziger. Approaches to abductive reasoning — an overview. Technical Report RR-92-08, German Research Center for Artificial Intelligence, 1992.

R.S. Michalski. Pattern recognition as rule-guided inductive inference. *Transactions on Pattern Analysis and Machine Intelligence,* 2(2–4):349–361, 1980.

Marvin Minsky. Steps towards artificial intelligence. *Proceedings of the IRE,* 49(1):8–30, 1961.

Marvin Minsky. A framework for representing knowledge. In P.H. Winston, Ed., *The Psychology of Computer Vision,* p. 211–277. McGraw Hill, New York, 1975.

T.M. Mitchell. Version Spaces: An Approach to Concept Learning. Ph.D. thesis, Stanford University, CA, 1978.

S. Muggleton and L. De Raedt. Inductive logic programming: theory and methods. *Journal of Logic Programming,* 19&20:629–679, 1994.

S. Muggleton. *Inductive Logic Programming.* Academic Press, New York, 1992.

S. Muggleton. Learning from positive data. In *Proceedings of the Sixth Inductive Logic Programming Workshop,* p. 225–244, July 14–18 1996. *Lecture Notes in Computer Science* No. , Springer-Verlag.

A Newell and H. Simon. GPS, a program that simulates human thought. In E. Feigenbaum and J. Feldman, Eds., *Computer and Thought,* p. 279–296. McGraw Hill, New York, 1963.

A. Newell and H. Simon. *Human Problem Solvings.* Prentice hall, New York, 1972.

J. Pearl. *Probabilistic Reasoning in Intelligent Systems: Networks of Plausible Inference.* Morgan Kaufmann, San Mateo, CA, 1988.

C.S. Peirce. *Collected Papers of Charles Sanders Peirce,* Vol. 2. Harvard University Press, 1959. Edited by Harston, C. and Weiss, P.

D.L. Poole, Alan K. Mackworth, and Randy Goebel. *Computational Intelligence: A Logical Approach.* Oxford University Press, New York, 1997.

D. Poole. A logical framework for default reasoning. *Artificial Intelligence,* 36:27–47, 1988.

D. Poole. Representing knowledge for logic-based diagnosis. In *International Conference on Fifth Generation Computing Systems,* p. 1282–1290, Tokyo, Japan, November 1988.

D.L. Poole. Explanation and prediction. *Computational Intelligence,* 5(2):97–110, 1989.

D. Poole. Logic programming, abduction and probability: a top-down anytime algorithm for computing prior and posterior probabilities. *New Generation Computing,* 11(3–4):377–400, 1993.

D.L. Poole. Probabilistic Horn abduction and Bayesian networks. *Artificial Intelligence,* 64(1):81–129, 1993.

D.L. Poole. Representing diagnosis knowledge. *Annals of Mathematics and Artificial Intelligence,* 11:33–50, 1994.

H.E. Pople. On the mechanization of abductive logic. In *Proceedings of the 3rd International Joint Conference on Artificial Intelligence,* p. 147–151, 1973.

E.L. Post. Introduction to a general theory of elementary propositions. *American Journal of Mathematics,* 43:163–185, 1921.

D. Prawitz, H. Prawitz, and N. Vogera. A mechanical proof procedure and its realization in an electronic computer. *Journal of the ACM,* 7(1&2):102–128, 1960.

J.R. Quinlan. *C4.5: Programs for Machine Learning.* Morgan Kaufmann, San Mateo, CA, 1993.

Ray Reiter. A logic for default reasoning. *Arcial Intelligence,* 13(1–2):81–132, 1980.

J.A. Robinson. A machine-oriented logic based on the resolution principle. *Journal of the ACM,* 12(1):23–41, 1965.

R. Schank and R.P. Abelson. *Scripts, Plans, Goals, and Understanding.* Lawrence Elbaum Associates, Potomac, MD, 1977.

G. Shafer. *A Mathematical Theory of Evidence.* Princeton University Press, Princeton, NJ, 1959.

B. Silver. *Meta-Level Inference: Representing and Learning Control Information in Artificial Intelligence.* North Holland, 1985.

Alfred Tarski. *Logic, Semantics, and Metamathematics.* Oxford University Press, 1956.

Jean van Heijenoort. *From Frege to Gödel: a Source Book in Mathematical Logice, 1879–1931.* Harvard University Press, 1967.

P. Winston. Learning structural descriptions from examples. In P.H. Winston, Ed., *The Psychology of Computer Vision.* McGraw Hill, 1975.

Lotfi Zadeh. Fuzzy sets. *Information and Control,* 8:338–353, 1965.

19 Natural Language Processing Associated with Expert Systems

Gian Piero Zarri

CONTENTS

1. INTRODUCTION

Natural language processing (NLP) can be defined, in a very general way, as the discipline having as its ultimate, very ambitious goal that of enabling people to interact with machines using their "natural" faculties and skills. This means, in practice, that machines should be able to understand spoken or written sentences constructed according to the rules of some natural language (NL), and should be capable of generating in reply meaningful sentences in this language. Computers able to fully decipher NL would, *inter alia*, remove the need to become computer literate, given that it would be possible to give the machine instructions directly in some natural, native language.

0-8493-3106-4/98/$0.00+$.50
© 1998 by CRC Press LLC

In its most ambitious form, this sort of endeavor is an extremely difficult one — a full, fluent, and totally automated man/machine interaction is surely beyond the possibilities of the current technology. Nevertheless, in these last 20 years, some successes in dealing in an (at least partial) automatic way with NL have been achieved in several specific fields, and NLP techniques have gained considerably in popularity, attracting an increasing number of researchers and practitioners. Consequently, the NLP domain is now split into a multitude of lively subfields — from speech recognition to handwriting analysis, from parsing to written and spoken language generation, from discourse and dialog modeling to document retrieval and mechanical translation, to mathematical methods, etc. — which ask, in turn, for the intervention of several disciplines like linguistics, of course, but also psychology (see, e.g., the "user models"), mathematics, logics, physics, engineering, computer science, etc.

In this Chapter, we will focus on the NLP subfields that are of specific interest for ESs (and, more in general, for knowledge-based systems, KBSs). After having presented, in Section 2, a (short) historical account of the development of the NLP field, and in Section 3 the challenges proper to the NLP endeavor and the standard technical solutions adopted in this domain, we will describe briefly, in Section 4, the "state of the art" and the future trends of the domain. Section 5 concerns the summary and the conclusion, and is followed by References.

2. HISTORY

2.1. THE ORIGINS

We can trace NLP's appearance to the Second World War and to the extensive utilization of statistical techniques for (automatically) breaking enemy codes: they made use, in fact, of "linguistic" (lexicographic) tools consisting of tables of letter frequencies, word frequencies, transition frequencies between successive letters, etc. After the War, this aptitude of the machine for manipulating symbols and helping in the lexicographer's work was soon applied to literary studies. Starting in the late 1950s and the early 1960s, there has been, in fact, a huge, computer-based production of lexicographic tools — as word indexes (lists of word occurrences) and concordances (indexes where each word is accompanied by a line of context) — intended to assist in the apprehension of the style and of the thoughts of authors like Livy, Thomas Aquinas, Dante, or Shakespeare.

The sentiment that the use of NLP techniques could go beyond the simple counting and rearranging of words did not take long to appear. In 1946, Warren Weaver and A. Donald Booth began working on the idea that computers could be used to implement solutions to the worldwide problems concerning translation from a natural language into another. They were both familiar with the work on code breaking, and were convinced that translation could also be tackled as a decoding problem: the only real difficulty was, for them, that of incorporating in the decoding system a full, automated dictionary of the two languages. In the 1949 "Weaver Memorandum" — which Weaver distributed to about 200 of his acquaintances and which marks the official beginning of the machine translation (MT) subfield — he writes: "... when I look at an article written in Russian, I say, 'This is really written in English, but it has been coded in some strange symbols. I will now proceed to decode'." This (evidently erroneous) idea that the source and the target texts say exactly the same thing influenced strongly early work on MT. The systems produced until 1954 followed a very simple paradigm based, essentially, on a word-for-word translation technique supported by a dictionary-lookup program. Words in the target language were arranged in the same order as in the source text and, when a source word happened to have two or more target equivalents, all the alternatives were registered.

In 1954, a research group from IBM and Georgetown University set up a public demonstration of a system translating from Russian to English; the system had no particular scientific value, but it encouraged the belief that MT was feasible and within easy reach. This system was representative of the "direct translation" approach, a slight improvement on the early word-for-word techniques.

The "direct" systems were monolithic pieces of software specifically designed, in all details, for a particular pair of languages. Linguistic analysis was very elementary: for example, syntactic analysis was normally reduced to do little more than recognition of word classes (noun, verbs, adjectives, etc.) to alleviate ambiguity problems like that, e.g., of "claim" as verb or noun. We must, however, mention here the fact that the popularity of MT in the 1950s and early 1960s was not without influencing favorably the development of other disciplines. For example, the necessity of systematically rearranging the sequence of words produced by the early word-for-word MT systems had made it apparent that some sort of "real" syntactic analysis was urgently needed. This period is then remembered as the golden age of syntax, characterized by the publication of important work by Y. Bar Hillel, Zellig Harris and, mainly, Noam Chomsky — even if, as already shown, this wave of interest for syntactic theory had little impact on the design of MT systems. Chomsky's "Syntactic Structures," where "transformational grammars" were introduced (see subsection 3.4.1) was published in 1957. In parallel, the need for programming languages well-suited for the manipulation of linguistic structures led to the creation of the first languages, COMIT and SNOBOL, geared more toward symbolic calculus than toward "number crunching" — this was not without influencing the creation, in 1960, of both ALGOL and LISP, characterized by the presence of new features such as lists and recursion.

2.2.   The ALPAC Report and the First AI Programs

Semantics, however, was lagging behind. In 1960, Bar-Hillel published a survey of MT where he expressed the opinion that the syntactic aspects of current MT systems could, in effect, be greatly improved through the incorporation of theoretical research, but that semantic problems could never be completely solved because of the huge quantity of implicit "world knowledge" necessary to translate correctly from one language into another. His famous example concerns the two sentences "The pen is in the box" and "The box is in the pen," and the impossibility for a machine to determine that the word "pen" in the second sentence means "an enclosure where small children can play" without having at its disposal some sort of universal encyclopedia. Therefore, high-quality MT was simply impossible. Not all researchers agreed with Bar-Hillel's conclusions; however, they were officially endorsed by the publication, in 1966, of the so-called ALPAC (Automatic Language Processing Advisory Committee) report. In this document, it was stated that MT was slower, less accurate, and much more expensive than human translation; no machine translation of general scientific texts was demonstrable, and none was foreseeable in the immediate prospect. A severe reduction of public investment in MT was recommended, and immediately put into effect.

The ALPAC report could have sounded the knell of any hope to see NLP techniques go beyond the simple production of indexes and concordances. Fortunately, Artificial Intelligence (AI) was, at that moment, already established as an autonomous discipline — the official start of AI corresponds with the Dartmouth Summer School of 1956 — and AI researchers were already working on NLP programs that tried to go beyond syntactical analysis, searching for key words or statistical techniques, for dealing instead with the "meaning" hidden behind words and sentences.

The early 1960s saw the burgeoning of a series of AI programs that can be considered, in a sense, as the first examples of NL interfaces to databases and KBSs. We can mention here SAD-SAM (Syntactic Appraiser and Diagrammer–Semantic Analyzing Machine), BASEBALL, SIR (Semantic Information Retrieval), STUDENT, and mainly ELIZA, perhaps the most famous among these early AI programs, written by Joseph Weizenbaum in 1966 and programmed in the SLIP language (Symmetric List Processor) developed by the same Weizenbaum. All these programs dealt only with very restricted domains — e.g., kinship relationships in SAD-SAM, or the American League games during 1 year in BASEBALL. Their dialog capabilities were very limited (with input sentences reduced to simple declarative and interrogative forms) and, mainly, their syntactic and semantic capabilities were particularly meagre. No real syntactic analysis of the queries was in fact performed; they were simply scanned to find keywords or patterns related to the chosen domain (and representing, therefore, the only semantic knowledge of the system), used then in a pattern-matching mode to retrieve information inside some sort of fact database. Heuristic rules were often used to augment the possibility of recognizing useful keywords and patterns: for example, two simple heuristics used in STUDENT are "one half always means .5" and "distance equals speed times time."

The amazing results obtained by ELIZA in simulating the interaction between a (nondirective) psychiatrist and his patient were largely due to some enhancements of this sort of heuristics, that allowed the program to produce dialogs which appear to be surprisingly realistic. For example, assuming that the retrieved keyword is "me," this will trigger a set of associated patterns to look for in the patient's input: one of these will correspond, e.g., to "0 you 0 me" (0 in the pattern can match any string of words). Patterns like this are linked in turn with a set of "transformation rules," as "what makes you think I 3 you," where 3 indicates here the third element matched, i.e., everything in the input between "you" and "me." A user's utterance like "you bother me" will then produce an ELIZA's answer like "WHAT MAKES YOU THINK I BOTHER YOU." Weizenbaum himself argued later (1976) that, to the extent the ELIZA's results were particularly impressive, they were also particularly misleading. Another, later dialog system (early 1970s) in the same vein was PARRY, by C. Colby, where the basic technique consisted again in matching a sequence of keywords extracted from the user's input against a long list of predefined patterns (about 1700).

We must wait until early 1970s to see the coming of two NL question-answering systems, William Woods' LUNAR and Terry Winograd's SHRDLU, attempting to deal in a comprehensive way with both syntax and semantics, and trying to do some real "reasoning," at least to some limited extent. Both LUNAR and SHRDLU are representative of the "procedural" approach to knowledge representation: knowledge about the world is represented as procedures (programs) within the system, and reasoning about this knowledge corresponds to executing the related programs. The dispute about the relative merits of "declarative" (semantic nets, logic formulae, frames, etc.) versus procedural representations was an important, historical issue in Artificial Intelligence, superseded today. In the declarative approach, some general knowledge representation structures are manipulated by a general deductive process.

LUNAR was an NL interface to a database provided by NASA that concerned chemical analysis data on the samples of rock brought back from the moon by the Apollo 11 mission. LUNAR handled NL queries in the style of: "What is the average concentration of aluminium in high alkali rocks?" in three steps:

1. Syntactic analysis of the query. This was executed making use of (a) an ATN (Augmented Transition Network) grammar, and (b) heuristic information to prune the results, in order to produce the most likely "derivation tree" corresponding to the query. A derivation tree is a hierarchical structure indicating the syntactic functions (e.g., surface subject) of the words of the analyzed expression, and the relationships (e.g., adjective/noun) between them. ATN is a formalism for describing and applying NL grammars, developed by William Wood himself, which was considered a sort of standard for syntactical analysis until at least the mid-1980s — see subsection 3.4.3 for some additional information on ATNs

2. Semantic interpretation of the results of (1) in order to produce a representation of the "meaning" of the query; in practice, the query was translated into a formal language in the predicate calculus style. The language included essentially "propositions," formed by "predicates" having as arguments "object designators," and "commands," which started actions. An example is: "(TEST (CONTAIN 810046 OLIV))," where TEST is a command concerning the evaluation of a truth-test, CONTAIN is a predicate, 810046 is the designator of a particular sample, and OLIV the designator of the olivine mineral.

3. Execution on the database of the program represented by the formal query to produce an answer ("procedural semantics").

Even if the type of internal representation adopted in LUNAR was supposed to favor the independence between the database and the query modules, the design of the last one was, to some extent, specific to the project's needs, and portability was not assured.

SHRDLU was a computer program that carried on a dialog via teletype with a user: in this dialog, the system simulated the behaviour of a robot's arm in a tabletop world of toy objects (blocks, pyramids, spheres, etc.). SHRDLU could answer questions about the state of the world ("Is the red block clear?"), carry out commands ("Put the red pyramid on the red block."), and add new facts about the world ("The pyramid is on the table."). The simulated world was displayed on a CRT, and it was possible, therefore, to follow the activities carried out by SHRDLU when moving the objects around. The system was composed, basically, of three modules: for syntax, semantics (to convert a sentence into a sequence of commands for the arm or into a query of the system's database), and problem-solving. The modules were physically separated, but they were able to interact all the time: this was particularly new for that period, when all the systems were fundamentally sequential systems. Thanks to the naturalness of the dialog, and to its apparent reasoning ability, SHRDLU has been one of the most popular AI programs ever built up, and it is still one of the most frequently mentioned, especially in introductory texts on AI.

We can mention here briefly some important technical features of SHRDLU:

1. In this system, the procedural approach was systematically followed, and realized by using the deductive properties of the MICRO-PLANNER programming language. For example, instead of representing a linguistic notion saying that a sentence is composed of a noun phrase and a verb phrase under the form of a rule in a grammar, "S → NP VP," see subsection 3.4.1, this notion was directly represented as a MICRO-PLANNER procedure that called other procedures under the form of (PARSE NP) and (PARSE VP).

2. Coherently with the above, SHRDLU was characterized by an "imperative" conception of NL, derived from the "speech act" theories. According to this, the meaning of an utterance is not represented declaratively as a fact about the world, but as a command addressed to the system in order to do something. For example, a simple assertion like "the pyramid is on the table," is translated as a command (a program) for adding information to the database.

3. The problem-solver component of the system (i.e., the modules that know about how to accomplish tasks in the block world) contained some form of explicit representation of the cognitive context. For example, SHRDLU has embedded the notion of "focus" (see, below, Section 3.4.4.2) that, in front of an assertion relating to "the red block," is able to link this assertion with one of all the possible red blocks of the world, the block which is more in focus of the others because of having been mentioned or acted upon recently.

SHRDLU represents a significant step forward in NLP research because of its successful attempt to implement both a "serious" linguistic analysis and some "realistic" reasoning methods. The system had, of course, many limitations, mainly due to the fact of dealing with a simple, logical, and closed domain: this allowed one, e.g., to avoid handling many of the more complex features of English.

Thanks to the successes, real or (at least partly) emphasized, of these first AI query-answering systems, the domain of NL interfaces to database became very popular from the late 1970s onward. A complete overview of the domain is beyond, of course, the possibilities of this section, and we will limit ourselves to indicate here some systems that have been mentioned intensively in the literature; see Androutsopoulos et al. (1995) for an exhaustive bibliography.

In the late 1970s LADDER, by Hendrix and colleagues, and PLANES, by Waltz, are examples of systems based on the "semantic grammars" approach, see subsection 3.5.2.1: semantic grammars are linguistic tools, very effective from an engineering point of view, where the domain knowledge is hard-wired into the grammar. In the early 1980s, some systems were developed that, in the absence of the required data, tried to avoid the ambiguous "silence" of traditional databases by informing the user that his assumptions about the contents and the structure of the base might be wrong. The most well-known example of this type of systems is CO-OP, by Kaplan. CHAT-80, by Pereira and Warren, is an example of the PROLOG system, where the English questions were translated into PROLOG expressions, and then evaluated against a PROLOG database. In the mid-1980s, TEAM, by Grosz and colleagues, was designed with the aim of being easily configurable by database administrators with no knowledge of NLP. ASK, by Thomson and Thomson, and, in the late-1980s, JANUS, by Bobrow, Resnick, and Weischedel, were characterized, *inter alia*, by the presence of an NL interface capable of interacting with multiple external databases, electronic mail programs, and other computer applications. Examples of contemporary, commercial NL interface systems are INTELLECT (Trinzic), Q&A (Symantec), and NATURAL LANGUAGE (Natural Language Inc.). We can remark here that, as it was already the case with SHRLDU, etc., current interfaces to databases can only cope with limited subsets of NL, and this can explain why they have not reached wide acceptance on the commercial market, where other alternatives (e.g., graphical and form-based interfaces) are still preferred.

2.3.   THE "CONCEPTUAL" APPROACH

The real appearance of a "semantic" approach to NLP — i.e., the awareness that the most complex types of utilization of computers in the natural language field, like, e.g., mechanical translation, could not be satisfactorily executed without some sort of "understanding" of the meaning of the original documents — must be associated mainly with the elaboration by Roger Schank, in the late 1960s, of the theory of Conceptual Dependency (CD). This last was based on the thought that the "meaning" of a given sentence could be represented as a formal sentence or group of sentences written according to the syntax of a particular conceptual language — two sentences identical in meaning, and independently from the particular language in which they were originally written or uttered, should have necessarily the same conceptual representation.

Conceptual dependency representations were organized around a small number of semantic primitives, which included primitive acts (11 in the 1977 formulation) and primitive states. An example of a primitive act is ATRANS, representing the transfer of an abstract relationship: "to give" corresponds to ATRANS the relationship of possession. Other examples of primitive acts are PTRANS, the transfer of an object to a new physical location, like "putting" an object somewhere; MTRANS, the transfer of a mental information between people, like in "telling;" MBUILD, used to represent the construction of new information from old, like in "imagining" or "inferring;" or PROPEL, the application of a physical force to an object. Primitive states consisted of predicates with associated numerical values in the range $-10/+10$: e.g., HEALTH(-10) means that a particular individual is dead; the number of primitive states is much larger than that of primitive acts.

The association of primitive acts, primitive states, and "concepts" through a small set of dependency links in the form of "case grammar" labels gives rise to "conceptualizations" which, in the original Schank's notation, are represented in a particular semantic network style, including several sorts of arrow. For example, the "conceptualization" translating the "deep meaning" of the sentence, "John gives Mary a book" will then be centered around the ATRANS deep predicate; the concept corresponding to "book" will be introduced through the "objective dependency," labeled with "o," and the recipient-donor dependency between Mary and John, on one hand, and the book, on the other, through the recipient-donor dependency "R." An example of conceptualization including a primitive state could correspond to the NL sentence, "Mary tells John that Bill is dead;" in this case, the primitive act used is MTRANS, and the argument introduced through the objective dependency is, in a simplified form, "(Bill BE HEALTH(-10))." The important point about conceptualizations is that they no more represent, as the structures built up in many of the preceding systems, some sort of surface analysis of a given sentence through the representation of the syntactic relationships among its components, but a representation of the semantic links that link together the (language independent) elements of meaning corresponding to this sentence.

Schank's theories have been severely criticized: by the linguists, because the Conceptual Dependency Theory is not a theory of the language; by the psychologists, because conceptualizations have no real correspondence with the mechanisms of human thought; by the logicians, because CD is not sufficiently formalized and it does not include the existential and universal quantifiers; by the computer scientists, because CD is too vague and, for this reason, difficult to translate into computer algorithms. It had, however (and it continues to have), a strong influence on all the work intended to deal with the "deep meaning" corresponding to surface, NL utterances [see, in the late 1970s, Sowa's Conceptual Graphs and, more recently, Zarri's NKRL (Narrative Knowledge Representation Language); see also subsection 3.5.3].

Schank's disciples (and, more in general, members of the so-called "Yale school;" Schank was for many years Professor of Computer Science at Yale) have developed, during the 1970s and at the beginning of the 1980s, several NLP systems based on CD. MARGIE (Riesbeck, Rieger, and Goldberg), e.g., was a very complex system: in a first phase, a "conceptual parser" translated from NL into a CD-like sort of representation using a specific sort of rules ("expectations") that tested first if some particular, surface linguistic clues (normally, words) were present in the original text, and then executed an action concerning how to convert the input just found into CD terms, what to look for next in the NL input, etc. The middle part of the system was an inference engine capable of deducing facts from the information coming from the original texts and translating into CD format. For example, from the CD equivalent of "John hit Mary," the system was able to deduce that "John was angry with Mary" or that "Mary might get hurt." The last part of the system was a generation module, able to convert back into English the result, in CD format, produced by the inference engine. SAM (Schank and Riesbeck; this system made use, as a front end, of ELI, a strengthened conceptual parser developed by Riesbeck from that of MARGIE) and PAM (Wilensky) worked in the context of the hypotheses on the activity of human story-understanding developed by Schank in collaboration with Abelson. For them, this activity consists in a mixture of applying known "scripts" (a script is a standardized sequence of events, represented in CD format, that describe some sort of stereotyped human activity, like going to the restaurant or visiting a doctor) and of inferring goals when an appropriate script does not exist. PHRAN (Wilensky and Arens) developed further the "conceptual parsing" techniques of MARGIE by including complex "patterns" (standard semantic structures) in the test parts of the rules; FRUMP (de Jong), a "text skimmer," used "sketchy scripts" to produce a surface analysis of stories coming off the AP news wire. We can also mention here another "conceptual" system: Wilks' MT system from English to French, making use of no syntactic analysis and based on the instantiation of templates having a basic agent-action-object structure, like "<MAN GET THING>".

All these systems were flawed in at least two respects. The first one concerns a very general problem, that of the huge quantity of "common sense knowledge" necessary for activating correctly the different inference mechanisms that are proper to any conceptual approach; no global solution has been found, until now, for this sort of problem. The second one concerns the absence, for all of the above systems, of a syntactic analysis component, considered as heterogeneous with respect to a semantic/conceptual approach. This lack implied the introduction into these systems of very *ad hoc* tools — like the "recency rule," introduced to partially obviate the absence of simple syntactic relations such as "subject" or "direct object." Modern systems that follow, at least partly, the conceptual approach, like KERNEL, by Palmer et al., or SCISOR, by Jacobs and Rau, all make use now of syntactic tools (see Pereira and Grosz, 1994).

2.4. MODERN TIMES

To conclude this short picture of the developments of NLP techniques in the 1960s and the 1970s, we will mention here the beginnings of a field that is particularly important for setting up more comfortable, natural, and efficient interfaces between people and computer systems, i.e., the field of the "speech understanding systems." First work in this area, in the 1960s, concerned some successes in the set up of isolated-word recognition systems, using the technique of (1) comparing the incoming speech signal with the internal representation of the acoustical pattern of each word pertaining to a relatively small vocabulary, and (2), selecting the best match by using some sort of distance metrics. Systems like these could not, however, deal with the problem of connected speech signals, where the utterances contain whole phrases or sentences: these signals have, in fact, very few characteristics in common with the simple concatenation of the signals of the single words. This is due mainly to the fact that the pronunciation of the different words changes when these words are associated to form a sentence. Final syllables are often altered in the junction, and sometimes dropped; finding the boundaries between words in connected speech is, in reality, one of the most difficult aspects of the whole problem.

Confronted with this situation, the Advanced Research Projects Agency of the U.S. Department of Defense (ARPA) promoted, starting in 1971, a 5-year program in speech understanding research. Several projects were therefore financed within this framework: at Bolt, Beranek, and Newman, Inc. (BBN), SRI International, etc. At Carnegie-Mellon University, the systems developed within the ARPA framework were HEARSAY-I and DRAGON in the first phase of the program (1971–1973), HARPY, and HEARSAY-II by 1976. The HEARSAY systems are particularly well known, given that they were the first AI systems using the "blackboard" architecture. This last one is based on the idea of making use of independent knowledge sources that cooperatively solve a problem by posting hypotheses on a global data structure (blackboard) — in the HEARSAY projects, the knowledge sources concerned acoustics, phonetics, syntax, and semantics. This architecture has been applied in several domains besides speech, and still constitutes one of the most powerful tools used by the AI community to set up complex, interconnected systems. The ARPA program ended in September 1976; the best performances (an error rate of 5% for connected speech, taking into account a limited vocabulary of 1000 words) were attained by the HARPY program, very efficient thanks to the large utilization of precompiled knowledge, but very difficult to modify.

In the 1980s, there were no real novelties to mention in our field, excepting the rise of a new wave of pessimism about the future of (industrial) NLP. This was produced by many concomitant factors, e.g., the difficulties of transforming the Schankian prototypes into industrial products (see, however, the relative success of ATRANS, a system capable of dealing correctly with bank telex in natural language), the disappointments with the expectations arising from the NL interfaces to DBs (the 1985 OVUM report on NLP spoke of an "exponential growth" of the sales of industrial products in this field for the beginning of the 1990s, a largely unrealized prevision), more in general, the morose climate generated by the "AI Winter," etc. In 1989, the Financial Times spoke about the NLP commercial systems as "not yet robust enough," characterized by a modest coverage, etc. NLP people were invited to abandon the idea of building up big, complex systems, and to concentrate instead on linguistic theory and on the theoretical and formal study of accurately stripped-down, toy problems.

Fortunately enough, a mini-revolution took place at the end of the 1980s. This event had been prepared by the considerable publicity stirred up about some successful programs for extracting information from NL texts created in an industrial environment — see the GE's SCISOR system already mentioned in the previous subsection. SCISOR — in some sort, an outgrowth of De Jong's FRUMP, see before — was characterized by the presence of a linguistic analysis that (1) was, in some way, inspired by the AI techniques for text understanding promoted by the Yale school, but that (2) included a real syntactic phase, and, mainly, (3) was "shallow," i.e., it performed only a surface analysis of the texts without trying to attain a "deep understanding" of these texts. SCISOR is, therefore, one of the first examples of a trend that is now particularly popular in the NLP domain, i.e., that of building up systems that combine the use of AI techniques with that of robust but shallow methods of textual analysis. This trend — leading to systems that, like SCISOR, do not really try to understand the "meaning" of the texts analyzed — combines well with the resurgence of the interest for the statistical methods, triggered in this case mainly by the recent success of the modern methods for speech understanding, based only on pure stochastic techniques (see also subsection 3.3 and Section 4).

The success of this new type of NLP philosophy is also deeply indebted to some recent, ARPA-sponsored initiatives, such as the MUC (Message Understanding) and TREC (Text Retrieval) Conferences, or the Tipster Text Program, which have powerfully contributed to the popularity of above "shallow but robust" approach. We will conclude this (biased and incomplete) history of NLP saying few words about such initiatives — please note that, even if they address mainly the problem of the extraction of information from texts, their impact on the aspect of the whole field has been considerable; moreover, these sorts of techniques can also be useful in a strict expert systems context, e.g., to help to set up large knowledge bases.

The MUC conferences (see also Cowie and Lehnert, 1996) are, in reality, competitions. Very succinctly, the contestant systems — previously developed and tested on training data — must read news agency-like messages and then perform an information extraction task. This task consists of automatically filling predefined, object-oriented data structures called "templates" with information extracted from the news stories; templates correspond to a fixed-format formulation of the canonical *who, what, where, when,* and *why* questions about the characteristics of a specific event in a particular domain. The templates and their slots are then scored by using an automatic scoring program with analyst-produced templates as the "keys." The Fifth Message Understanding Conference (MUC-5), in August 1993, focused, e.g., on information extraction from news stories concerning two different domains, joint ventures (JV) and microelectronics (ME). For each application, the extraction task could be performed in either English and/or Japanese, giving rise, therefore, to four combinations: English Joint Ventures, Japanese Joint Ventures, English Microelectronics, and Japanese Microelectronics. Some very general, interesting conclusions that proceed from the global, semi-automatic scoring of the results are: (1) the most frequent type of error committed by the MUC-5 systems was to miss pertinent information; (2) summary scores for error per response fill indicate a better performance in Japanese than in English for both domains (this may be explained by a linguistic structure that is less varied in the Japanese than in the English documents, and by the fact that domain concepts are expressed, in the Japanese texts, in a more standardized way); (3) summary scores indicate a slightly better performance in the microelectronics domain than in the joint ventures domain for both languages, English and Japanese; (4) a study conducted on the English microelectronics task indicates that the best machine system performs with an error rate of about 62%, a little less than twice the error rate of a highly skilled human analyst (33%). However, very good performances (34%) have been attained by the "best" system (the SHOGUN system, jointly developed by General Electric and Carnegie Mellon University) on some limited tasks, such as, e.g., extracting information in the joint ventures domains with only the core portion of the templates being scored. These results, even if they certainly show that machine performance is at least comparable with human performance, should however tone down any over-enthusiastic prediction about their appearance on the market as commercial products.

3. CHALLENGES AND SOLUTIONS

3.1. INTRODUCTION

The task of NLP is that of accepting inputs in a human, natural language (NL), and to transform the inputs into some sort of formal statements that are to be "meaningful" for a computer. The computer will be, therefore, able to react correctly to the given input; sometimes, the reaction will take the form of a NL "answer," i.e., the computer will use the formal representation corresponding to the analysis of the input to generate, in turn, statements in natural language.

If we follow the above approach, this means that, for us, NLP is characterized by the presence of some, very primitive and idiosyncratic indeed, form of "understanding" of the "meaning" of a given statement. As a consequence, we will exclude from the description of the NLP domain some trivial and purely passive forms of processing of NL inputs. Examples are the simple transfer on magnetic support of a spoken input through the use of a voice recorder, or the handling of inputs formed by single words, e.g., all sort of commands, entered by a keyboard or spoken through a voice recognition system. We consider, in fact, that a real problem of "meaning" begins only when several words combine together inside a written string or an utterance.

We can also remark that, in the sentences above, we have formulated no hypothesis about the nature of the input, written or typed string of words, or utterances spoken into a microphone. Likewise, no hypothesis has been formulated on the eventual function of the formal "meaning" to be extracted from the input: it can be used directly to feed a knowledge base, be transformed into a SQL query for a relational database, be entered into a transfer structure to produce an output in a language different from that of the input, etc. In all these cases, in fact, the sequence of operations to be executed on the input is virtually the same, from the segmentation into words and the recognition of their grammatical category (morphological analysis), the organization of the words in a structure reflecting their functional (syntactic analysis) and semantic (semantic analysis) relationships, the resolution of the ambiguities and the grouping in wider structures (discourse analysis), the use of the final, formal representation to perform a particular task (pragmatic analysis), etc.

In reality, this sort of "classical" paradigm has been set up mainly for the needs of the analysis, offline, of written texts of a certain length; it must be inflected in a certain number of cases, for Spoken Language Understanding (SLU) for example, or for interactive systems, and especially for dialog systems with spoken input. Whereas interactive systems in general are characterized, e.g., by sentences that are shorter than those normally encountered in written texts ("Who is the manager of the R&D department?"), and by the strong presence of incompleteness phenomena, mainly pronominal anaphora ("What is his salary?") and ellipsis ("His phone number?"), the spoken dialog systems present an additional number of deviations from the standard patterns. Acoustic ambiguities can affect the recognition of input words; in spoken dialogs, we do not deal with "sentences" according to the ordinary meaning of this word, but with fragmentary utterances deprived of the ordinary punctuation marks that allow us to delimit sentences and clauses; there is a considerable noise due to hesitations, repetitions, false starts, spurious words; etc. This means that, in this sort of system, the classical sequence of steps is reduced and the analysis simplified. Moreover, of course, specific procedures must be introduced to deal with the spoken input, etc.

Our analysis of the technical issues, in the following, will be based mainly on the standard approach — which, anyway, still represents the main paradigm for NLP — its goals, its problems, and the solutions found. In subsection 3.8 and Section 4, we will supply, however, some information on Spoken Language Understanding systems and an example — please note that SLU could become particularly important in an expert systems framework, where the expectations for effective NL interfaces are very high.

3.2.   THE STANDARD PARADIGM FOR NLP

We can decompose this paradigm according to the sequence:

- Morphological analysis
- Syntactic analysis
- Semantic analysis
- Discourse and pragmatic analysis

We will now examine each of these steps; moreover, we will add a specific subsection (3.7) to describe briefly the generation procedures. Please note that, of course, this sort of division is more a didactic artifice than a description of the actual organization of some concrete systems. In fact, several systems combine at least two of these phases into a single step, e.g., syntactic and semantic analysis — when, as in the conceptual analysers of Schankian inspiration, the analysis is, mainly, semantically driven — or the semantic and the discourse/pragmatic phases. Some authors prefer to split the morphological phase into a morphological phase proper and a phase of lexicon's inspection, etc. A well-known description of the "classical" paradigm can be found in Allen (1987).

3.3. MORPHOLOGICAL ANALYSIS

For simplicity's sake, we collect under this label a series of operations that consist of (at least) (1) segmenting an input sequence into words (lexical analysis); (2) executing, in case, some normalization operations on the segmented words; (3) executing the morphological analysis proper; (4) producing, as final result, a sequence of words where each of them is associated, minimally, with the corresponding part(s) of speech.

Given the limits of this chapter, we cannot deal here in detail with the segmentation problems proper to the lexical analysis. In the case of written language, automatic recognition — i.e., the task of automatically transforming a sequence of spatial-organized graphical marks into characters and words — is satisfactorily dealt with by using off-the-shelf OCR (Optical Character Recognition) software for neatly printed texts. There are also some successes in the field of handwriting recognition, particularly for isolated hand-printed characters and words and in constrained domains like postal addresses and bank checks. With respect to speech recognition, i.e., the conversion of an acoustic signal captured, e.g., by a microphone, into a stream of words, we have already mentioned in
subsection 3.1 some well-known problems that make this task so difficult. In spite of these problems, dramatic improvements in speech recognition technology have been accomplished in the last decade, and applications based on speech input capabilities are now commercially available (voice dialling, e.g., *call home*, call routing, e.g., "I would like to make a collect call," simple data entry like entering a credit card number, etc.). The actual technologies for passing from an acoustic signal to a sequence of word hypothesis are all based on statistical methods. For example, the most well-known technique used to recognize the different speech sounds is the so-called "Hidden Markov Model" (HMM); an HMM is a composition of two stochastic processes, a hidden Markov chain that takes into account temporal variability, and an observable process that describes spectral variability. After a "speech recognizer" has converted the observed acoustic signal into the corresponding orthographic representation, a "recognizer" makes its estimations about the identity of the words in the spoken sequence by choosing from a finite vocabulary of words that can be recognized. A statistical model used for these tasks is based on the joint distribution $p(W,O)$ of the sequence of spoken words W and the corresponding observed sequence of acoustic information O.

Having isolated the words in the input sequence, the first step of the analysis concerns the computation of their grammatical category (part of speech, "tag"), i.e., the association with information like "noun," "verb," "adjective," etc.; this particular information will then be used in all the subsequent phases of the procedure. If the analysis system could be permanently associated with a list (a "lexicon") including all the words of a given language the system is capable to deal with at a given moment, associated with their proper category (plus, in case, additional information concerning, e.g., the semantic category, like "animate" vs. "inanimate"), the problem should be reduced to a search of the word under examination among the words of the lexicon. Please note that, in practice, this last can be structured in a very sophisticated way for efficiency's sake. In reality, the determination of the grammatical category can be more or less difficult according to the type of word we are dealing with: a "grammatical" word or a "lexical" word.

Grammatical words include the adjectives, excepting the qualitative adjectives, the articles, the predeterminers ("such," "half," "both," etc.), the prepositions, and the pronouns. Generally, they have a very precise grammatical function; their (reduced) number is stable, i.e., they are not normally interested in the evolutionary phenomena that modify the language. Therefore, they do not present any particular difficulty with respect to the computation of their grammatical category, given that the hypothesis of inserting in the lexicon, *a priori*, a list of all the grammatical words of a particular language accompanied by their category is not particularly odd.

The problem is neatly more difficult for the lexical words: this category includes the adverbs, the qualitative adjectives, the nouns, and the verbs. They account for the large majority of terms of the given language, and they are largely affected by the evolutionary phenomena proper to the language. We are now faced with two types of problems:

- The first is mainly an optimization problem. Even if we decide to renounce to insert in the lexicon all the vocabulary proper to a given NL, and we specialize the lexicon according to a particular application, or class of applications, there is still the problem of how to build up this tool without being obliged to list all the possible "regular forms" (lexemes) that can still appear in the input sequence — we do not take here into consideration all the phenomena of "ill-formedness" like misspelling, ungrammaticality, syntactic and semantic constraint violations, etc. Please note that forms like "say" and "says," or "rose" and "roses," are all different lexemes that can be found in the input, and that will be associated with different categories: infinitive verb, third person verb, singular noun (but "rose" can also be an adjective, or the past tense of "rise"), or plural nouns. Verbal forms are much more abundant in the Latin languages than in English; moreover, case phenomena multiply the noun forms in German or in the Slavonic languages, etc.
- The second, a more important problem, is a "knowledge acquisition" problem. Given that, in reality, it is practically impossible to circumscribe the vocabulary of an application or class of applications and that, moreover, new lexical words can always be created, how to face the problem that consists of finding in the input a word that cannot be reduced to one of the forms listed in the lexicon, i.e., a word that cannot be "recognized" with respect to its proper part of speech.

The first problem — which concerns, in short, finding a way of reducing the size of the lexicon — is classically dealt with having recourse to a branch of linguistics, i.e., "morphological analysis." This consists of examining how words are built up of more basic meaning units called "morphemes" ("root forms"), where a word may consist of a root form plus additional affixes. We have already mentioned phenomena like the formation of plural forms from the singular ones. In more general terms, a word like, e.g., "familiar" can be considered as a "root form": from this adjective, we can derive another adjective, "unfamiliar," by adding the prefix "-un"; by adding the suffixes "-ity" and "-ly" we can derive, respectively, the uncount name "familiarity" and the adverb "familiarly"; a more complex derivation rule could also allow us to establish a link with the verb "familiarize," etc. We will now, therefore, store in the lexicon only the root forms (infinitive for the verbs, singular for the nouns, singular masculine for the adjectives, etc.), and supply the analysis system with a morphological analyzer that make use of a list of affixes (suffixes and prefixes) and a set of rules that describes, for a given language, how pieces are combined. Please note that the algorithms implementing the morphological analysis are far from being trivial, giving the presence, in all the languages, of several exceptions with respect to the standard rules of formation: to give a very simple example, in English "go" plus the suffix "-ed" for the past tense becomes "went." The computational techniques used for implementing the morphological analysis algorithms are usually based on some form of finite-state technology as, e.g., in the Koskenniemi's "two-level model" (1983), which makes use of a set of parallel finite-state transducers. Please note that, after the morphological analysis, the result can consist of the production of several grammatical hypotheses, see the example of "rose" before (singular noun, past tense verb, adjective). These ambiguities are normally solved during the syntactical analysis phase (e.g., the presence of an article at the beginning of a sentence normally requires the set up of a noun group, and the rejection of a verbal form as

---

TABLE 1
Tagging Rules for String of Capitalized Words

1. If a word is a known acronym (e.g., DRAM) or an abbreviation that is normally capitalized (e.g., "Mbit"), then just pass the word as a regular lexeme.
2. If the string ends in a word like "Corp" or "Co," tag the string as a company name.
3. If a string is followed by a word like "President" or "Spokesman," and then another string, make the first part a company name and the rest a person name.
4. If a string is followed by a comma and then a state name, tag it as a city/state pair.

---

the immediate, following item). Their settlement in the semantic phase is more unusual; it may also be the case that the sentence is inherently ambiguous.

The second problem can be reduced to what is now called "full automated tagging," i.e., to the problem of finding a set of procedures that, given an input sequence (normally, a sentence), are able to automatically determining the correct part(s) of speech for each word of the sequence also in the presence of "unknown words." Historically, two main approaches have been used, a "rule-based" approach and a "probabilistic" approach; more recently, some work has been proposed making use of connectionist models.

The rule-based approach covers, in reality, a broad spectrum of techniques. They range from the use of very simple, empirical and *ad-hoc* sets of rules, often suitable only for particular categories of texts, to complex systems that try to induce not only the morphological characteristics of an unknown word, but also its syntactic and semantic properties. As an example of the first category, we have collected in Table 1 some rules used, for MUC-5 (see subsection 2.4), in the LINK system built up at the Artificial Intelligence Laboratory of the University of Michigan (Ann Arbor, MI) by Steven Lytinen and colleagues — in MUC-5 (1993), LINK was used to analyze articles concerning the microelectronics domain (more exactly, four types of chip fabrication technologies). The rules of Table 1 are relative to the tagging of strings of capitalized words that have been pre-isolated, within the input text, by a preprocessor called "Tokenizer."

As an example of a more complex approach, we can mention here some work done at the GE Research and Development Center (Schenectady, NY) by Paul Jacobs and Uri Zernik in the late 1980s. In this approach, a variety of linguistic and conceptual clues are used to "guess" the general category of a new word. For example, faced with an input from the domain of corporate takeovers like: "Warnaco received another merger offer ...," where all the words in the input string are known excepting "merger," an initial analysis making use of morphological and syntactic clues produces an "analysis chart" where "merger" is analyzed as (1) a possible comparative adjective meaning more "merge," (2) a noun derived from the nominalization of a verb, or (3) a single adjective. Introducing now the three possibilities in the syntactic analysis for the whole sentence, it is possible to construct a "hypothesis chart" where the noun phrase "another merger offer" is interpreted as (1) a determiner, "another," associated with a "modified noun phrase" (comparative adjective "merger" + noun "offer"); (2) "another" associated with a "compound noun phrase" (noun "merger" + noun "offer"); (3) "another" associated with a "modified noun phrase" (adjective "merger" + noun "offer"). From this, three conceptual structures can be deduced: (1) an offer that is "merger" (perhaps larger) than a previous known offer; (2) an offer for a "merger" that is now some unknown type of transaction; (3) an offer having as a property the quality of being a "merger." Making use of other conceptual operations, like the utilization of the previous context of the sentence where an offer of acquiring Warnaco is mentioned, the hypothesis "merger" is a noun, corresponding to a concept in the style "company-acquisition" is privileged; this last hypothesis is confirmed by a second encounter with "merger" under the form: "The merger was completed last week," which allows, e.g., one to rule out the hypothesis of a new offer that is "merger" than the preceding one.

Given however the general renewal of interest in the use of statistical methods in NLP, provoked mainly by the successes obtained through the use of these models in speech processing, the probabilistic approach to the "tagging" problem in general is now widely used.

A well-known, general module in this style is POST (Part-Of-Speech Tagger), developed at BBN Systems and Technologies (Cambridge, MA) and used in their PLUM data extraction from texts system, one of the best MUC systems (see subsection 2.4). The problem to be solved consists, given a particular word sequence $W = (w_1, w_2 \ldots w_n)$ where we suppose, at the moment, that all the words w_i are known, of finding the corresponding, most likely tag sequence $T = (t_1, t_2 \ldots t_n)$. According to the Bayes' rule, the conditional probability of a given tag sequence T given the word sequence W, $p(T|W)$, depends on the product of $p(T)$, a priori probability of the tag sequence T, and $p(W|T)$, conditional probability of the occurrence of the word sequence W given that the sequence T of tags occurred. The solution of the above problem requires then (1) the evaluation of all the possible tag sequences in order to calculate $p(T|W)$ for each of them, and (2) the choice as the most likely tag sequence T of the sequence that maximize $p(T|W)$. Given that the resolution formula for $p(T|W)$ can be rewritten as the product Π of n terms, where each term is the product of the conditional probability of the tag t_i given all the previous tags and the conditional probability of the word w_i given also all the previous tags, it is evident that the computation of $p(T|W)$ can be particularly complex.

In order to reduce the complexity of the problem, POST makes two simplifying assumptions. The first consists of assuming that each word w_i in the sequence W depends only on t_i; this allows us to make use in the previous product Π, instead of the conditional probability of the word w_i given all the previous tags, only of $p(w_i|t_i)$, i.e., the probability of each word given a tag (lexical probabilities). The second consists of the adoption of some sort of "n-Gram model" which, for the problem at hand, is reduced to evaluating the conditional probability of the tag t_i taking into account, instead of the whole sequence of previous tags, (1) only the tag t_{i-1} assigned to the word w_{i-1} (bi-tag models), or (2) this last tag plus the tag t_{i-2} (three-tag models). While the bi-tag model is faster at processing time, the tri-tag model has a lower error rate. To make use of this approach, a system like POST must obviously be "trained," i.e., it must have at its disposal a (relatively large) corpus where all the tags have already been manually assigned. In this case, and adopting a three-tag model, the probability $p(t'|t_2, t_1)$ that a tag t' occurs after tags t_1 and t_2 can be estimated by computing the number of times t' occurs after tags t_1 and t_2 divided by the number of times t_1 and t_2 are followed by any third tag. A training set is also necessary for estimating $p(w_i|t_i)$ for an observed word w_i. Please take into consideration the fact that, no matter how large the training corpus, it is not possible to observe all the possible pairs or triples of tags; if a particular triple $t_1\ t_2\ t_3$ is not present in the corpus, it is still possible to estimate $p(t_3|t_2,t_1)$ making use of techniques called "padding," based on the number of times m we can observe triples beginning with $t_1\ t_2$ and on the number j of possible distinct tags. Having now obtained all the required conditional probabilities, it is now possible, for a sequence of known words W, to determine the sequence T of tags for which $p(T|W)$ is maximized. Using the approach summarized above, POST is able to calculate sequences of tags with an error rate that fluctuates between 3.30 and 3.87% according to the size of the training corpus.

In the presence now of "unknown words" — i.e., words that a system like POST has never seen before — the values $p(w_i|t_i)$ computed for a known word w_i thanks to the use of a training set cannot be utilized. Given the poor results obtained under these conditions through the use of "blind" statistical methods, POST has included in its strategy the usual morphological clues exploited by the "symbolic" approaches. POST takes into account, in particular, four categories of morphological features: inflectional endings (-ed, -s, -ing), derivational endings (including -ion, -al, -ive, -ly), hyphenation, and capitalization. The probability that a particular word w_i will occur given a particular tag depends now on the probability that the previous features will appear given this particular tag; it now becomes:

$$p(w_i|t_i) = p(\text{unknown-word}|t_i) * p(\text{Capital-feature}|t_i) * p(\text{endings, hyph}|t_i)$$

Making use of this modified statistical model, the error rate for the unknown words decreases to 15/18%. We will end this short description of POST by mentioning the possibility of running this module according to an alternative modality, in which POST return the *set* of most likely tags for each word rather than a single tag.

We can conclude this subsection about "morphology" and "lexicon" by mentioning a recent trend in these fields; it consists of the construction of very large, semantically structured lexical databases including rich information intended to support not only grammatical analysis, but also large sections of syntactic and (mainly) semantic analysis. Two well-known projects in this field are Miller's WordNet and Yokoi's Electronic Dictionary (EDR). In the first system, English nouns, verbs, adjectives, and adverbs are organized into sets of synonyms ("synsets"); the synsets, and the single word forms, can then be linked by simple sorts of semantic relations like antonymy, hyponymy, meronymy, etc. The Electronic Dictionary is organized around several interrelated dictionaries. For example, The Word Dictionary includes (1) the tools (morphological and syntactic information) necessary for determining the syntactic structure of each sentence, and (2) the tools (semantic information) that, for each word in a given sentence, identify all the possible concepts that correspond to that word. The Concept Dictionary contains information on the 400,000 concepts listed in the Word Dictionary; one of its main functions is supplying the tools needed to produce a semantic (conceptual) representation of a given sentence. The Co-occurrence Dictionary describes collocational information in the form of binary relations, and it is used mainly to select words in the target language when executing mechanical translation operations, etc.

3.4. Syntactic Analysis

Even if the words of the input are now endowed with a "tag" (part of speech category), they still represent no more than a simple, flat string of words. To begin understanding the "meaning" carried on by the statement, it is necessary to make clear first its "structure," i.e., to determine, e.g., the subject and the object of each verb, to understand what modifying words modify what other words, what words are of primary importance, etc. Assigning such structure to an input statement is called "syntactic analysis" or "parsing"; a computer procedure that executes this sort of task is called a "parser." A parser is then a sort of transducer that takes as input a flat string of words (already linked with their part of speech tags) and produces as output a structure (e.g., a "syntactic tree") where the mutual relationships of the words in the statement are indicated.

3.4.1. Formal Grammars

In the usual approach to parsing, each parser is based, implicitly or explicitly, on a "grammar," i.e., on a set of rules that, at least in principle, describe or predict all and only the possible sentences in a given NL; this implies that, being in possession of the ideal, perfect grammar for a given language, we can classify all the statements presented as input for the corresponding parser into the legal ones (the "grammatical" ones), for which the parse is successful and a complete structure can be determined, and the illegal, ungrammatical ones for which the parser is unable to find a complete structure. Examples of rules ("productions") that can be found in a grammar for English are the classical "S → NP VP," stating that "a sentence consists of a noun phrase followed by a verb phrase," or "NP → ADJ+N," stating that "a noun phrase may contain a sequence of adjectives followed by a noun." We can remark here, however, that a new approach to parsing is beginning to appear in the research literature, where it is sometimes called "data-oriented processing" (DOP) parsing. According to the DOP approach, parsing (and NLP in general) must not be based on a nonredundant set of formal rules, but on a probabilistic process that parses new inputs by analogy,

TABLE 2
Definition of Phrase-Structure Grammar

A phrase-structure grammar G is a quadruple $<V_N, V_T, P, S>$ where:

V_N is a finite set of *nonterminal symbols* that correspond to syntactic and grammatical categories like "noun phrase" or "adjective"

V_T is a finite set of *terminal symbols* that coincide, in practice, with the words of a given NL

P is a finite set of rules, called "production," that are of the form "$\alpha \rightarrow \beta$" (α rewrites as β), where both α and β stand for strings of elements of V_N and V_T

S is the "starting symbol" or "root of the grammar" (sentence). It pertains to V_N and must appear at least once on the left-hand side of the rewrite arrow (i.e., in the place of α) in the set of productions

---

making use of a corpus of representations of past language experiences. These are represented as strings of words associated with their syntactic structures, their contexts, and their meanings.

In spite of the considerations of the last paragraph, "formal grammars" are an still a very active domain of investigation in linguistics; a first example of formal grammar — in this case, a "phrase-structure grammar" — can be defined as in Table 2. Phrase-structure grammars have been classified by Chomsky into four different types (four levels) that depend on the form of the strings α and β, i.e., on what elements of V_N and V_T can appear in α and β. Levels go from level 0, where no constraints are imposed on the form of α and β, to level 3, where productions are severely constrained and, as a consequence, the descriptive power of the corresponding grammars is very poor. The two productions for English shown in the previous paragraph are part of a possible "context-free grammar"; this type of grammar pertains to level 2. In context-free grammars, productions are of the form "$A \rightarrow \alpha$," where A is a (unique) symbol pertaining to V_N, and α is a string of terminals and/or nonterminals. No constraint is, therefore, imposed on the form of the right side of the production. The name "context-free" takes origin from the fact that no sequence of surrounding symbols, equivalent then to the presence of a required "context," is associated with A in the left side of the production; the simple appearance of A is sufficient to trigger the production. "Context-sensitive grammars" pertain to level 1.

The phrase-structure model of formal grammars is only partly well-suited to the description of English. For example, a "distributive" structure like that introduced by the adverb "respectively," "Mary, Jane, and Elaine are the wives of Tom, Arthur, and Charles, respectively" cannot be dealt with properly (cannot be generated) by level 3 and 2 grammars; on the other hand, context-sensitive grammars (level 1) do not represent, in practice, a better solution given that they give rise, among other things, to descriptions of English that are unnecessarily awkward and complex. This sort of reasoning led Chomsky to propose, in 1957 and 1965, a new formal model called "transformational grammars." This model consists, in short, of a "base component" and a "transformational component." The base component consists of a context-free grammar, see before, that produces a set of "deep structure" trees. The transformational component is a set of tree-rewriting rules that, when applied to a particular deep structure tree, gives rise to one or more possible "surface structure" trees. The sequences of terminal nodes (words) of the surface structure trees are the sentences of the language; their common "meaning" is represented by the deep structure tree. The theory postulates, then, that the application of transformational rules to deep structures must preserve meaning, as in the case of simple alternation of active and passive constructions.

Other formal models of grammars that have a more "semantic" flavor than those discussed previously, are, e.g., "systemic grammars," developed by Michael Halliday and colleagues at the University of London in the early 1960s, and "case grammars," proposed by Fillmore in 1968 and particularly popular in an Artificial Intelligence context — Schankian conceptual dependency representation can be considered as variants of case grammar representations, etc.

3.4.2.   Unification Grammars

Today, the predominant, formal models of grammar pertain to a class of linguistic formalisms that can be grouped under the name of "constraint-based grammars" or "unification grammars" [see Shieber (1992)]. More productive and flexible than Chomsky's models, they are characterized by the adoption of a very clean sort of denotational semantics, which allows the encoding of grammatical knowledge independently from the use of any particular processing algorithm ("declarative approach").

Within this general framework, a number of different formalisms exist: we can mention here Functional Unification Grammars (FUG), Head-Driven Phrase-Structure Grammars (HPSG), Lexical Functional Grammars (LFG), Categorial Unification Grammars (CUG), and Tree Adjunction Grammars (TAG). All these formalisms share two essential characteristics:

1. All the grammatical units (words, phrases, sentences) are described by means of uniform formalisms based on the use of sets of attribute-value pairs, which are called "feature structures" (f-structures).
2. The formal characteristics of f-structures are exploited through the use of a basic mechanism for merging and checking the grammatical information, which is called "unification."

For comprehensibility's sake, f-structures can be introduced — independently from any strict grammatical and syntactic consideration — simply as an extension of the usual Artificial Intelligence, first-order terms formed by a predicate and its arguments. Each f-structure consists then, see the generic example of Figure 1, of two columns of entries enclosed in large square brackets. The elements a_i of the left-hand column are the "attributes"; attributes are always atomic symbols, syntactic like "NP," "VP," or "object," but also semantic like "name" or "age," logic-oriented like "quantifier" or "logical-connective," discourse-oriented, etc. The elements v_i of the right-hand column are the "values." Values can be atomic symbols or subordinate f-structures, as in the case of the value assumed by the attribute a_{14} in the example of Figure 1; i.e., f-structures can be nested. Values can be replaced by variables. Constraints under the form of "equality statements," see also Figure 5, can be expressed by associating with some variables the same numerical "coreference marker"; this means that the values assumed by those variables must be the same. Attributes and values are, obviously, paired, and the members of a pair are written on the same line; the order in which lines occur in an f-structure has no significance.

We can now transform the abstract framework of Figure 1 into a concrete example, see Figure 2; we will then assume that the above structure represents, in a "nested relations" style, something like: "There is a person whose name is Tom, who is 27 years old, and who is married to a girl

$$
\begin{bmatrix}
a_{11} & v_{11} \\
a_{12} & v_{12} \\
a_{13} & v_{13} \\
a_{14} & \begin{bmatrix} a_{21} & v_{21} \\ a_{22} & v_{22} \end{bmatrix}
\end{bmatrix}
$$

FIGURE 1   Nested f-structures.

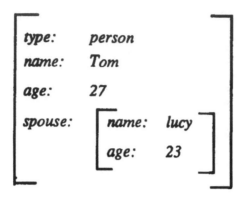

FIGURE 2   A concrete example of nested f-structures.

named Lucy who is 23 years old." If we want now to introduce a simple constraint in the formulation of Figure 2, imposing, e.g., that "Tom can be married with any girl, but she must be exactly as old as he is," we will insert a free variable, [ ], as value of the attribute "name" in the enclosed f-structure, and another variable, labeled with the coreference marker "1," [1], as value of the attribute "age" in both the external and the internal f-structures.

Let now examine briefly how this type of mechanism can be used for syntactic analysis. The main principle is that of utilizing the f-structure formalism to represent, at the same time, (1) the lexical entries; (2) the grammar rules; and (3) the analysis of the sentences. In particular, grammar rules specify how the words, represented by the lexical entries, can be combined with one another to give rise to the different elements of the analysis: these last f-structures are called "constituents." Examples of constituents are the classical "noun phrase" (NP) and "verb phrase" (VP) groups. In all the f-structures that represent lexical entries, grammar rules, or constituents, a particular attribute, "category," must always be present: its value indicates the (general) grammatical or syntactic category of that particular f-structure. We will make use here of a simple example, adapted from Knight (1989).

Suppose we want to analyze the sentence "the boy eats noodles." The lexical entry for "boy" is given in Figure 3.

To analyze this sentence according to the unification grammars approach, we will make use of "augmented rules" that correspond to a sort of "augmented context-free grammar" (see the previous subsection and, also, the ATN techniques in the next subsection). Accordingly, some classical rules in the S → NP VP style will be "augmented" with constraints to be used both (1) to block the spurious developments of the analysis, and (2) to specify the details of the construction of the constituents. Using for the moment only context-free rules, we can now analyze the two symmetrical

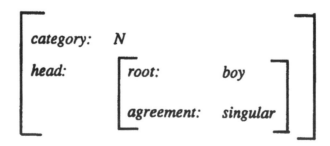

FIGURE 3   An example of lexical entry represented as f-structure.

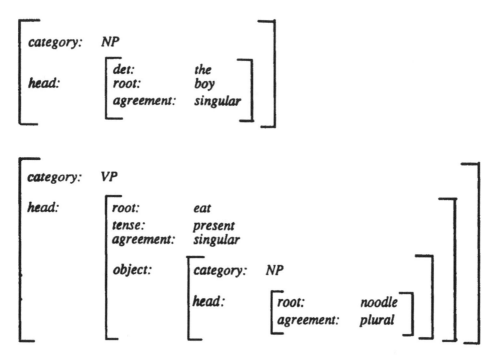

FIGURE 4   f-structure representation of NP and VP constituents.

halves of the example, building up from the lexical entries associated with its words the NP and VP constituents represented, in a "unification" style, in Figure 4.

Turning now to the augmented part of the grammar, the augmented S → NP VP rule is represented in Figure 5, both under the form of a (declarative) rule with constraints and of the corresponding f-structure. The rule and the first three constraints say that the final analysis will give rise to a structure f_0 having the category of S (sentence); the analysis will succeed only if the constituents of $f_0, f_1,$ and $f_2,$ are characterized by the categories NP and VP, respectively. The fourth constraint states that the number feature, *agreement*, of the head of f_1 (NP) must be the same as the number feature of the head of f_2 (VP). This constraint will therefore rule out a sentence like "The boy eat." The fifth constraint says that the feature *object* of the head of f_0 (S) must be equal to the head of f_1 (NP); this means that, after application of the grammar, the head of f_0 will be an f-structure with at least one feature, called *subject* and having as its value the head of f_1. The sixth constraint states that the head of f_0 (S) must contain all the features included in the head of f_2 (VP), i.e., the global sentence will inherit all the features of the verbal constituent. Finally, a *mood* (modality) feature with value *declarative* must be inserted in the head of f_0. In the f-structure part of Figure 5, the equalities imposed by the constraints are expressed by making use, as usual, of numerical coreference markers.

If we now assign the symbolic labels f_1 and f_2 to, respectively, the f-structures representing the constituents NP and VP in Figure 4 above, we will obtain the global analysis of our example sentence by "unifying" these last f-structures with the f-structure of Figure 5. In the context of constraint-based grammars, "unification" must be understood mainly as "superposition." In a well-known paper on the subject, Martin Kay tried to visualize this particular type of unification by evoking the possibility of reconstructing some photographic transparencies that have been partially damaged using the technique of comparing homogeneous "...sets of pictures by *superposing* them and holding them up to the light." When unifying (superposing) two f-structures, we will check, first of all, that no contradictions exist (e.g., the presence of two identical attributes associated with

$$f_0 \rightarrow f_1 f_2$$
$$(f_0 \, category) = S$$
$$(f_1 \, category) = NP$$
$$(f_2 \, category) = VP$$
$$(f_1 \, head \, agreement) = (f_2 \, head \, agreement)$$
$$(f_0 \, head \, subject) = (f_1 \, head)$$
$$(f_0 \, head) = (f_2 \, head)$$
$$(f_0 \, head \, mood) = declarative$$

$$
\begin{bmatrix}
f_0: & \begin{bmatrix} category: & S \\ head: & [1] \end{bmatrix} \\[2em]
f_1: & \begin{bmatrix} category: & NP \\ head: & [3] \end{bmatrix} \begin{bmatrix} agreement: & [2] \end{bmatrix} \\[2em]
f_2: & \begin{bmatrix} category: & VP \\ head: & [1] \end{bmatrix} \begin{bmatrix} agreement: & [2] \, [] \\ subject: & [3] \\ mood: & declarative \end{bmatrix}
\end{bmatrix}
$$

FIGURE 5   Augmented context-free grammar rule under the form of f-structure.

contradictory values, as in the features *"agreement: singular"* and *"agreement: plural"*). If this check has been passed, the final f-structure is then built up by (1) introducing in it all the features (attribute + value) present in the original f-structures; (2) by assigning the most specific values to the common attributes; and (3) by taking into account the equalities imposed by the coreference markers.

In our case, the unification of the f-structures of the constituents with that of the rule $f_0 \rightarrow f_1 f_2$ will lead to the f-structure of Figure 6. The final result, Figure 7, i.e., the syntactical analysis of the example, will be obtained by retrieving from Figure 6 the specific f_0 structure (the "sentence").

Within the general class of constraint-based grammars, Lexical Functional Grammars (LFG) are particularly popular. Even if they have been created by John Bresnan and Ron Kaplan, at the end of the 1970s, essentially for theoretical reasons (as a reaction against the supposed "lack of psychological reality" of Chomsky's Transformational Grammar), they are of a strong practical interest, essentially for two reasons:

1. Concrete, useful NLP systems are necessarily characterized by the presence of large-scale dictionaries online. LFG is particularly useful in this context, given the importance it attributes to the lexical entries and the conspicuous guidance it offers for the structuring of these entries.
2. LFG has been developed from the beginning with a particular concern for computational tractability and efficiency.

According to LFG, the construction of the internal structure of a sentence (syntactic analysis) begins with the construction of a "classical" syntactic tree (constituent structure tree, or C-structure), which indicates the hierarchical structure of the phrasal constituents (NP, VP, etc.) of the original sentence. C-structures are produced making use of context-free grammars characterized by the presence of particular "annotations," or "functional schemata," on the rules; e.g., the standard S → NP VP rule will be written as:

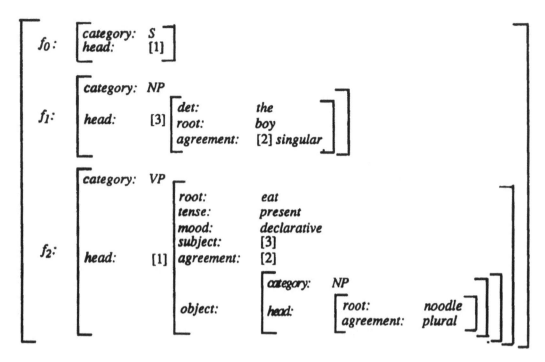

FIGURE 6 Unifying the constituents and the rule structure.

$$S \rightarrow \quad \underset{(\uparrow \text{subject})=\downarrow}{\text{NP}} \quad \underset{\uparrow=\downarrow}{\text{VP}}$$

When constructing the tree, the annotations are transferred onto the corresponding nodes of the tree, and the arrows take on the meaning of "pointers," where $\uparrow$ points toward the father-node, and $\downarrow$ toward the offspring-node. Taking also into account the fact that the notation $(a\, p_1 \ldots p_n)$ represents something in the style of "$p_1 \ldots p_n$ are the attributes (properties) of the element a," and remembering that the S node is the father-node for both NP and VP, the elementary tree corresponding to the above equation means, eventually, that the subject of the final S will be the first NP, and that the

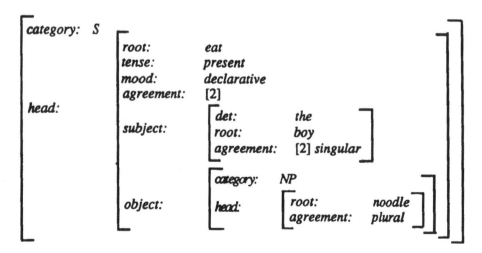

FIGURE 7 Final syntactic analysis of the example.

lexical entry	syntactic category	functional schemata
loves	V	$(\uparrow predicate) = $ 'love $<(\uparrow subject)\ (\uparrow object)>$'
		$(\uparrow subj\ agreement) = singular$
		$(\uparrow subj\ person) = 3$

FIGURE 8 An example of lexical entry in LFG.

structure of this final S will be the same as the structure of the VP. In the case of the analysis of a concrete sentence, like "John loves Mary," the C-structure will be completed by introducing on the tree, information found in the lexical entries of the words of the sentence. As already stated, lexical entries in LFG are particularly structured, and they contain not only the usual information about the form of word and its grammatical category, but also a description, using the mechanism of functional schemata, of the syntactic functions of the word according to its meaning. For example, the lexical entry for "loves" will be as in Figure 8.

When the final, annotated C-structure has been built up, the next phase of the analysis is the "instantiation," which consists in (1) introducing a correspondence between each node of the C-structure tree and a variable f_n; (2) using the structure of the tree to find the referents, under f_n form, of all the $\uparrow$ and $\downarrow$ symbols found on the tree. After this, the set of functional schemata that appeared on the tree, where they had been introduced by the rules of the grammar, and the lexical entries, are now reduced to a set of constraints on the variables f_n having the same form of the set reproduced above in Figure 5. This set of constraints is called a "functional description" (f-description). If we introduce now a correspondence between each f_n variable and one of the f-structures proper to constraint-based grammars, we are reduced to the usual f-structure scenario, similar to that examined above for the "the boy eats noodles" example. The C-structure (the tree) is abandoned, and it will be no longer utilized in the final phases of the syntactic analysis.

3.4.3.   Technical Issues

Independently now from the model of formal grammar used, there are some general, technical issues that concern the optimal way of making use of this grammar, i.e., of matching the input strings of words against the patterns of the grammar. For example, some typical choices that the designer of a parser must face are (1) top-down versus bottom-up processing, (2) backtracking versus parallel parsing (or the use of a deterministic parser, see below), (3) unidirectional processing or island driving processing, etc.

In (1), top-down processing means looking first for the rules that can produce a certain type of top-level structure (e.g., a certain type of sentence), then looking for the rules that can give rise to the second-level constituents of these top-level structures, and then proceeding in this way until a complete structure for the sentence has been built up. If this is not possible, the top-down parser normally backtracks, generating another type of top-level structure. In the bottom-up strategy, parsing starts from the words of the input sentence, trying to apply first the rules that can combine these words into larger constituents, and then combining in turn these constituents to show how all the words of the sentence can be inserted into a general, top-level sentence of the grammar. Independently from the strategy chosen, a common problem encountered concerns the fact that the elements of natural language do not always have unique meanings; see the example already mentioned of "rose" that can be a noun, a verb, or an adjective: this can introduce an alternative between the instantiation of a noun phrase or a verb phrase, or an ambiguity in the structure of the noun phrase, etc. These sorts of ambiguities compel the parser to choose among multiple options when proceeding through a sentence; the strategies mentioned in (2) concern dealing with all the alternatives at the same time (parallel processing), or dealing with one alternative at the time using, in case of failure, a form of "backtracking" to come back to the choice point and choosing another option. Both of these methods require a considerable amount of bookkeeping to deal with the multiple choices problem: in the parallel case, to take account of all the possibilities being tried; in the backtracking case, to take account of all the possibilities not yet tried. Please note that, in the case of backtracking, the number of alternatives that must effectively be considered can be considerably reduced by making use of "heuristic knowledge" about their likelihood in a given situation. Finally, the design option mentioned in (3) concerns the possibility of proceeding systematically in one direction with the parsing, normally from left to right, or to start anywhere and looking first at the neighboring words in order to build up structured constituents of increasing size (island driving). This second approach has been used often in the speech understanding system as a means to deal with input uncertainty.

A way to escape from the necessity of choosing, see (2), between parallel parsing and backtracking is given by the so-called "deterministic parsers" — popularized by the work of Mitchell Marcus at Bell Laboratories in New Jersey, and having a wide popularity in the 1980s. The basic principles of a deterministic parse are that of (1) trying to build up syntactic structures only when they are presumably correct; (2) never building up syntactic structures that are not used in the complete parse; and (3) never destroying any structure that has already been built. From a concrete point of view, Marcus' parser is structured around a three-cell buffer in which are stored three consecutive "constituents" of the syntactic structure that is being built up; the constituents can range from words to complete clauses. In each phase of the procedure, only these three constituents are taken into account. Parsing proceeds by matching, making use of a rule-based grammar, the constituents found in the buffer to the requirements of the syntactic structure already set up and stored in a "parse stack"; the parse stack evidences then the current state of the parse operations.

Let us consider, for example, the sentence "the boy eats the apple," and let us suppose that the first NP ("the boy") has already been parsed. We are now in a situation where (1) the parse stack contains only, at the top level, a "S(entence)" syntactic structure having this last NP as its SUBJ(ect); and (2) the three cells of the buffer contain, respectively, the words "eats," "the," and "apple." The state of the stack, and the grammar rules, requires the attachment of the main verb to the S structure; the lexical entry for "eats" is then removed from the buffer and inserted in S as the main verb. At the same time, the grammar requires the creation of a second, empty NP (which will be used to parse "the apple") that is pushed onto the stack. This second NP will be then constructed by making use of the words "the" and "apple" of the buffer. After this sequence of operations, the buffer will then be empty and the parse buffer will contain two structures, the S structure corresponding to "the boy eats" and, on top of this, the NP structure for "the apple." This last structure is now popped and pushed back onto the buffer, leaving again S as the top-level structure of the parse stack. The state of the parse stack, and the grammar rules, now require one to build the final structure by taking the NP for "the apple" from the buffer and inserting it as an OBJ(ect) in the S structure.

Deterministic parsers, where backtracking or parallel processing are eliminated, are evidently computationally very efficient; from a linguistic point of view, they cannot however provide a syntactically correct parse when the parse depends on looking ahead for more than three constituents. A situation like this is encountered, e.g., in parsing the so-called "garden-path" sentences, where we are led first toward a given interpretation by the first words in the sentence, but we discover in the following that this interpretation is a dead end, and we are obliged to retrace our steps to find a new one. A well-known example of garden-path sentence is "The horse raced past the barn fell." Marcus' deterministic theory has then evolved into the so-called "D-theory" (Description theory). According to this theory, a deterministic parser that looks ahead for three elements in the sentence must be used not to set up a complete tree structure as the result of the parse, but rather to construct a simplified "description" of the syntactic structure of the sentence. In this way, e.g., syntagmes introduced by a preposition like "from" or "by" (prepositional phrases, PPs) will not be attached precisely into the parse tree, but only simply described as "dominated" by a verb phrase node (see also the next subsection).

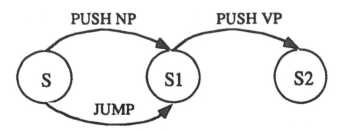

FIGURE 9A A simple RTN.

Marcus' work was inspired by the desire of freeing NLP from the need of executing the laborious backtracking operations characteristic of the ATN parsers, like the parser used by William Wood in his famous LUNAR system. The ATN approach has formed the bulk of the operational syntactic parser all over the world for a long period, until at least the end of the 1980s. Even if they are now supplanted by the more fashionable unification parsers, they deserve at least a short mention here.

ATN (Augmented Transition Networks) evolved from simpler, Recursive Transition Networks (RTN). An RTN, see Figure 9, is a network of nodes, called "states," which are connected by arcs; one node is identified as the "initial state," and one or more nodes as the "final state." Some arcs, called CAT arcs, are labeled with lexical categories, like N (noun), V (verb), DET (determiner), ADJ (adjective), or ADV (adverb).

An RTN works according to the following principles. When presented with an input sentence, and starting at the initial state node of the RTN with the initial word of the sentence, it is possible to traverse an arc if the current word is in the category shown on the arc. If this arc can be followed, the current word is "consumed," and the input is updated to the next word. If the RTN comes to the final state and the entire sentence has been consumed — possibly after one or more "backtrack" operations (the RTN returns to the last choice point) if there is an incompatibility between the arc the RTN would follow and the category of the word under examination — then the sentence is accepted as "grammatical" with respect to the grammar that the RTN implicitly represents. Particular types of arcs are the PUSH and POP arcs; see again Figure 9. PUSH arcs, labeled with constituents like NP (noun phrase) and VP (verb phrase), are used to transfer the control to a subnetwork that is in charge of analyzing, e.g., a noun group or a verb group; a POP arc is used then to come back to the main network. JUMP arcs are also allowed; these arcs transfer the control to a new state without consuming any input word.

For example, when analyzing the noun phrase "the boy," see Figure 9B, and starting with the initial state node NP, it will be possible to pass to the node NP1 by following the arc labeled DET, given that the first word is "the." A JUMP arc will allow to direct passage to NP1 in the absence

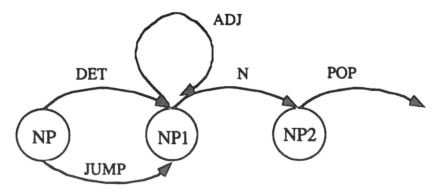

FIGURE 9B The NP subnetwork included in the previous RTN.

of the article, like in "John" in place of "the boy"; the ADJ arc accounts for the presence of one or more optional adjectives ("the big boy") in the NP group. Control is then transferred to the node NP2 following the arc N and using the noun "boy." At this point, we have reached a POP arc, and this means that "the boy" is a legal noun phrase. As a second example of the utility of a JUMP arc, please consider the main, simple RTN of Figure 9A: this network can account for an imperative sentence (without initial NP), like "Eat quickly!," where the node S1 must be reached directly without consuming any word of the input sentence.

This type of tool is affected by two major problems. The first concerns the fact that the grammars implemented by the RTNs are equivalent to context-free grammars, which are notoriously insufficient, as we have already seen, for an accurate analysis of NL. Moreover, a parser that tells simply if a sentence is or is not a grammatical one, without showing the analysis of the sentence, is not really interesting. The two problems have been solved by Wood by "augmenting" the RTN arcs with actions, giving rise to "Augmented Transition Networks," ATNs. Actions are fundamentally of two types, in order to reply to the two sorts of objections arising against RTNs. To go beyond the strict context-free framework, ATN allows one to implement complex "tests" on any arc. Tests are arbitrary pieces of code that act as predicates, and allows one to perform checks that would be unmanageable to implement using only the lexical category mechanism. For example, a CAT arc that accounts for the main verb of a sentence may be "augmented" with a test that checks if the verbs agrees in person and number with the subject of the sentence. Second, in order to document the progression of the parse operations, each ATN is supplied with a set of registers, like DET, ADJS, HEAD, and NUM, for an NP subnetwork; actions, in this case, consist typically of setting a register to a certain value or getting a value from a register. Registers are reset to their original values upon backtracking; moreover, when a PUSH occurs, the current contents of the registers are saved and the called subnetworks get a fresh set of empty registers. When a POP arc is followed, all the registers that have been set in the current network are compiled in a structure formed by the name of the network, followed by a list of the registers with their values: the parsing operations executed in the network are now documented.

Compiling ATN into LISP code is very easy, and the ATN mechanism can be represented in its totality by making use of very few instructions: using in fact the normal function-calling mechanism of LISP to represent state transitions, backtracking is obtained practically for free. This is probably the main reason for the popularity of this tool, for so many years, in the NLP community (e.g., the well-known INTELLECT system, one of the first commercially available NL interface for DBMSs, and which is still in use, was ATN-based). There are, however, objective reasons for the decline in popularity of ATNs. They are related mainly to (1) their inflexibility, which obliges an ATN parser to arrive at an end-state in order to make clear the structure of a sentence, and (2) the threat of combinatorial explosion linked with the number of possible backtracking operations, which grows exponentially with the complexity of the network — even if it is possible to make use of heuristic rules to determine the order of priority given to the different arcs that proceed from a particular node.

3.4.4. Linguistic Problems That Affect the Parse Operations

Independent of the grammar and from the type of tool used, all the parsers have to face some well-known linguistic problems, those which hinder a fully unambiguous syntactic analysis and, eventually, render NLP so difficult. We will examine here quickly some of these problems and the proposed solutions.

3.4.4.1. *Prepositional Phrases Attachment*

A problem similar to that of the "garden-path" sentences evoked in Section 3.4.3, and that is, unfortunately, really ubiquitous, is that of the "prepositional phrases attachment" (PP-attachment problem). This concerns the problem of identifying the constituent in the syntactic analysis to which a modifying phrase (or "adjunct") introduced by a preposition like "of, with, by, in ..." must be attached. We can illustrate the problem by using a famous example like: "I saw the man in the park with a telescope." In this sentence, it is not clear whether the adjunct "with a telescope" modifies "park" (the man has been seen in a particular park that is characterized by the presence of a telescope, may be as a facility for the tourists), "man" (the man had a telescope with him), or "saw" (I made use of a telescope to localize the man); moreover, "in the park" may modify "man" or "saw."

In principle, the best way of dealing with this sort of problem would be that of tackling it at the semantic or pragmatic level, making use of our "context knowledge" about the particularities of the man, the park, etc. in a specific situation. Given, however, the intrinsic uncertainty about the best way of executing semantic analysis, and the difficulties of using semantic criteria on a large scale, the problem is often dealt with at the syntactic parser level, by way of "heuristics" based only on the results of the morphological/syntactic analysis. For example, the "most right association principle" can be used to solve relative clause attachment: this means that these clauses are assumed to modify the rightmost available constituent. In the example: "I know a lady who was attacked by a woman whose husband had deserted her," the relative clause "whose husband had deserted her" is assumed to modify "a woman" and not "a lady." Another popular heuristic rule is the "attach low and parallel" principle, which suggests to attach constituents as low as possible and, if possible, in parallel with other constituents. A specialization of this rule proposes to favor the attachment of postmodifiers to the closest possible site, skipping over proper nouns; a particular case of this rule is used to settle the problems linked with the attachment of prepositional phrases introduced by "of." As J.R. Hobbs remarks, every noun can be subcategorised for "of"; using the postmodifiers rule, "of" prepositional phrases are nearly always attached to the immediate preceding word. According to Hobbs, more than 98% of the ambiguities linked with the presence of "of" can be solved using this very simple heuristic.

3.4.4.2.   Anaphora and Ellipsis

One of the hardiest problems in Computational Linguistic and NLP processing concerns finding algorithmic procedures for solving anaphora. Anaphora is a linguistic problem concerning the fact that pronouns (like "he," "himself," or "they"), possessive determiners (like "her" or "their") and full noun phrases (like "the patient," see below), can be used to denote implicitly entities already mentioned in the discourse; by "discourse" we mean here a coherent segment of text, either written or spoken. Examples can be, respectively, "John went to the party and he got drunk," "this girl is very nice, and her brother is charming," "Jack was admitted to the hospital early this morning. The patient complained of chest pain." Solving anaphors implies then the following two steps:

1. Realising that the pronoun, the possessive determiner, or the noun phrase (NP) represents an implicit reference (normally, an abbreviated reference) to some other entities — this first step is not so trivial, especially when the anaphora is constructed through an NP; not all the personal pronouns are necessarily anaphoric, etc.
2. Disambiguating the reference, by substituting to this last one the entity (the "antecedent) that represents its real identity.

A detailed analysis of all the techniques that have been proposed for solving the anaphora problem is, of course, beside the limits of this chapter (see Carter, 1987). We can also say here that these methods can be roughly classed into two categories, syntactic and semantic methods.

The first are based only on the results of the morphosyntactic analysis. In some cases, especially when the implicit reference is created by making use of pronouns (pronominal anaphora), the syntactic procedures for resolution can be very simple. In such cases, a list is kept of all the entities mentioned in the discourse. When a pronoun is encountered, the list is examined starting from the more recent entries, and each pronoun is associated with the most recently mentioned entity that satisfies grammatical and semantic constraints. For example, in the previous sentence: "John went to the party and he got drunk," we can stick to the fact that "he" must refer to a previous, animate NP; we look for such an NP and we find "John," so we can now proceed to disambiguate the reference by substituting "John" for "he." Of course, this very simple method of resolution cannot be generalized, even in the case of pronominal anaphora, given that, *inter alia*, it is very difficult to conjecture with some precision, as we have done in the previous example, the semantic type and the syntactic structure of the antecedent. We can mention, in this context, the following example where the antecedent ("to buy a new dress") is not a simple NP, but a structured verbal phrase: "I have to buy a new dress. I prefer to do it before holidays."

Some reliable syntactic procedures exist in very limited domain; for pronominal anaphora, they are linked with the concepts of "dominating node" and "command." In a syntactic tree, a node A dominates a node B if B is included in the syntactic sub-tree stemming from A. A node A commands now a node B if (1) neither A nor B dominates the other; (2) the S(entence) or NP node that *most immediately* dominates A (i.e., the lowest S or NP node dominating A) also dominates B. For pronominal anaphora, a first rule then says that a pronoun cannot both precede and command its antecedent. Let us consider, as an example, the two sentences: "John left the room after he shot the girl" and "He left the room after John shot the girl." In the two, the node corresponding to the subject of the main clause (... left the room) commands the node corresponding to the subject of the subordinate clause (... shot the girl). Then in the second sentence, according to the previous rule, "he," which precedes "John," cannot have this last noun as its antecedent. Please note that a rule like this is mainly a "negative" one, allowing us to exclude some NPs as possible antecedents of a pronoun, but without allowing a precise identification of this antecedent. A more precise rule exists for anaphoric situations created by the use of reflexive and reciprocal pronouns like "each other," "herself," or "himself." It says that (1) the antecedent of a reflexive pronoun must be dominated by the same, lowest S or NP node that dominates the pronoun; (2) a nonreflexive pronoun may not have an antecedent dominated by this node. Looking now to the following David Carter example: "I took my dog to the vet on Friday. He bit him at the hand," we can say, using simple morphosyntactic criteria like that of the "list" expounded before, that "he" is either "dog" or "vet"; applying semantic information for "hand," i.e., "only people have hands," we can add that "him" is the "vet." The second part of the previous rule tells us that the predictions "he = vet" and "him = vet" are inconsistent, since both pronouns are dominated by the same S node and are not reflexive. The prediction "he = vet" is then rejected because the pronoun "he" has another alternative, i.e., he = dog.

Syntactic methods for anaphora resolution exist also for anaphoric noun phrases; they are often based, as in the previous example, on the search of conflicts between information in the anaphoric noun phrase and information in the candidate antecedents.

With respect now to the semantic methods, we will limit ourselves to mention briefly here the resolution methods based on "focusing mechanisms" that have been popularized by Candice Sidner. This mechanism is based on the fact that, in a discourse, speakers always center their attention on a particular discourse element: this element is the "discourse focus." The speaker uses several linguistic artifices, that the hearer tries to interpret, to evidence the element on which he is focusing his attention; as the discourse progresses, the speaker may maintain the same discourse focus or may focus on another entity. A change in discourse focus, or the lack of a change, are signaled by the linguistic choices the speaker makes, particularly by his use of various anaphoric expressions: the hearer must then solve these expressions to be able to follow the changes in discourse focus.

Very roughly (see Carter's book for more details), a resolution process based on focusing mechanism consists of the following phases:

1. Finding the discourse focus. The focus recognition algorithm begins with the selection, in the first sentence of a text, of an initial focus (the "expected focus"), which may or may not be confirmed in the subsequent sentences of the text. The validation procedure

is based on syntactic or semantic rules. In the most general case, the decision implies a "case grammar" analysis of the input sentences: the most reliable focus default then fills the "object case of a verb" where, e.g., the "agent" position has the weakest capacity to determine the focus.

2. Setting a set of six "registers" that represents the state of the focus at a given point in the text. The registers are: (1) the "discourse focus" (DF), which is set initially to the value of the expected focus; (2) the "actor focus" (AF) that is a parallel structure to the discourse focus, but concerning an animated entity, i.e., an entity characterized by the semantic feature [+animate]; (3) the "potential discourse focus" (PDF); (4) the "potential actor focus" (PAF); (5) the "discourse focus stack" (DFS); (6) the "actor focus stack" (AFS). Each of these registers contain a list of zero or more entities.

3. Anaphora resolution, based on the semantic representations (case grammar representation) of the input sentences, and taking into account the state of the focus. The expected focus algorithm, applied to the first sentence of the text and making use of syntactic and semantic criteria, allows us to set the DF register. In the following sentences, an "interpreter" is made up of a set of algorithms to try to identify and to resolve the anaphoric ambiguities. Each algorithm applies to a given type of anaphoric situation; depending on this type and on the content of the focus registers, the interpreter predicts the registers as to where to find one or more antecedents for a given anaphora. The suggestions are evaluated by an inference mechanism based on the detection of contradictions, e.g., the violation of semantic constraints on the arguments of the verb.

4. Updating the focus registers. A "focusing algorithm" refreshes the focus registers using the (validated) anaphoric interpretation chosen by the interpreter. This algorithm is also in charge to confirm or to reject the predicted focus; in case of rejection, it suggests a new focus.

Another frequent source of ambiguities typical of NL dialog systems and sharing some similarities with the anaphoric phenomena concerns the presence of elliptical sentences, i.e., sentences that appear ill-formed because they do not form complete sentences. This phenomenon is illustrated by this simple dialog: "Who is the director of the computer science department? Professor Smith. Of the nuclear physics department?"; "of the nuclear physics department" is an elliptical sentence. The resolution methods for dealing with ellipsis try typically to extract the missing parts, "Who is the director" in our example, from the previous, complete sentences. This can be accomplished by making use, e.g., of "context registers" in which to store the most significant, recent items found in the complete sentences, to be paired with the fragments according to their semantic category.

3.4.4.3.   Other Types of Ambiguities

Even if "PP-attachment," "anaphora," and "ellipsis" constitute probably the most pervasive classes of linguistic problems that can affect the parse operations, they (unfortunately) do not exhaust the catalog of possible sources of ambiguities; see Androutsopoulos et al. (1995). The "quantifier scope" problem concerns the difficulty, in sentences with many words, in determining which quantifier, like "a," "each," "all," "there exists," should receive the wider scope. A classical example of this ambiguity is given by the two sentences, where the second is simply the passive of the first: "Everyone in the room speaks two languages" and "Two languages are spoken by everyone in the room." In interpreting them, people normally attribute wider scope to the quantifier "all in the room" in the first sentence (therefore, the two languages may be different for different people); while in the second sentence, they attribute wider scope to the quantifier "there exist two languages" (therefore, the languages are the same for everybody). This example also shows that if two interpretations are equally plausible, the preferred one is that where the quantifier ordering corresponds to the surface ordering of the noun phrases. Other ambiguity phenomena concern, e.g., the possibility that the word "and" denotes disjunction rather than conjunction ("How many people live in Boston and New York?"), the nominal compound problem (e.g., "computer science" has a totally different functional role in "a computer science department" and "a computer science device"), etc.

3.5. SEMANTIC ANALYSIS

Having determined the structural properties of an NL statement, sentence, or utterance, thanks to the use of the morphological and syntactic tools, we should now utilize the final syntactic structure and the semantic categories associated with the individual words to construct the overall "meaning" of the sentence. It is more or less admitted that, in its more general form, this meaning should consist of a formal statement expressed by making use of some "knowledge representation language" in the Artificial Intelligence acceptation of this term.

In reality, both the aims and the proper methods of the semantic phase are not very well defined, and this phase is much more fuzzy and problematic than the previous syntactic phase. The central problem concerns, of course, the fact that it is very difficult to find agreement on what the "meaning" of a statement can be — and this, of course, has an heavy influence on the choice of the final representation and on its degree of "deepness." In this context, the traditional assumption of theoretical computational semantics consists of assuming that the determination of the meaning of a sentence can be equated with the elucidation if its "truth conditions," i.e., determining what the world would be like if the sentence were true. Apart from the problems that can rise when we try to adapt this sort of definition to questions and imperatives, it is evident that, when the aim is that of building up practical NLP components of KBSs, the main interest is certainly not in the problematics concerning true or false sentences. Intuitively, what we would like to obtain is a sort of standardised representation, independent from the different natural languages, unambiguous, and characterized by a well-defined set of basic inferences, that could be easily interfaced with, e.g., a DB language like SQL, the formal language of a robot command system, etc. Unfortunately, theoretical semantics is of little help here.

Moreover, apart from this type of epistemological consideration, there are all sorts of practical problems that make semantic analysis so difficult. For example, even if an agreement could be reached about the formal representation of the meaning, it must be considered that the meaning of a written or spoken statement is always sensitive to the context of the discourse: the context can be used to determine the proper signification of a word, the signification of the overall statement, or to determine how the statement can be used. Formalization of the context is a very advanced research topic where few concrete results have been already obtained — even if we can admit that, e.g., dealing automatically with the anaphora problems according to the modalities mentioned, before, in Section 3.4.4.2, is already a first way of dealing automatically with the context problems. This is why the meaning representations concretely used are still, in practice, largely independent from the context, and based on the implicit assumption that the context-independent part of this meaning is, nevertheless, worthwhile to be represented, and sufficient for allowing a variety of useful applications. Of course, this is only an approximation.

The reasons expounded before are only a part of those that can be used to explain why: (1) whereas there are now a significant number of systems that display a (relatively) wide syntactic coverage, there are still few that can provide a corresponding degree of semantic coverage; (2) for the last, the label "semantic analysis" is used to identify procedures that have very few characteristics in common. Very roughly, we can distinguish three classes of procedures making use of some sort of "semantics": (1) procedures that are still, basically, of a syntactic nature, and where the semantic component is used, e.g., to solve some of the parsing ambiguities examined (see Section 3.4.4); (2) procedures characterized by some form of shallow semantic analysis; (3) procedures aiming to produce a sort of (quite) complete, formal representation of the "meaning" of the original statement. We shall now examine these three classes in turn.

3.5.1.   Use of Semantic Procedures to Supplement the Syntactic Analysis

Several NLP tasks of practical relevance (e.g., message routing, information retrieval, categorization of textual documents) can be executed, at least to some extent, using techniques like statistical analysis, keywords or pattern matching, that do not imply any reference to the "meaning" of the textual matter with which they are dealing. This is not true for many other applications, even if they do not attempt to produce any sort of deep semantic content analysis. It is evident, e.g., that NL interfaces to DBs must be able to tackle at least some limited form of ellipsis: this cannot be done without inspecting, in some way, the semantic class to which the elliptical fragment pertain, and its congruence with the semantic class of the most significant elements of the previous, complete sentences (see subsection 3.4.4.2).

An important class of application of semantic methods concerns, therefore, supplementing the traditional morphosyntactic analysis in order to obtain more reliable and complete results. It is now impossible to give a full description of all the possible applications of semantic techniques in a syntactic context (which, very often, are very limited and *ad hoc*). We give here only an example, a (relatively general) strategy for making use of semantic rules in a context of PP-attachment resolution (see subsection 3.4.4.1). This semantic application has been realized in the context of a project, COBALT, partially financed by the European Community. COBALT has, in reality, very ambitious objectives with respect to the representation of the "meaning" of its basic linguistic material, Reuter's news in the financial domain, that it encodes according to the format of a high-level representation language, NKRL (see subsection 3.5.3.3). However, the basic PP-attachment strategy of COBALT can be very well described independently from the main semantic procedures; moreover, this example will allow us to introduce a very actual concept in the NLP practice, that of "underspecified representation."

An underspecified, syntactic representation is a type of representation where, in the presence of potential ambiguities, no effort is put forth in order to represent all the possible solutions that could be proposed to solve these ambiguities. We can then avoid any danger of combinatorial explosion, which is particularly likely when the number of words in a statement exceeds 25. The typical example of underspecified representation is given by the so-called "quasilogical form" (QLF form), a sort of formal representation allowing the reduction of logical formulas of higher order to a conjunction of first-order terms formed by a predicate and its arguments. This is possible thanks to the introduction of "event predicates," see below, or "event variables": these last, e.g., act as indexes that allow us to identify, for each predicate, the event to which this predicate refers. To give a first, very simple example, the sentence "Mary writes the paper quickly," which we could represent in a traditional way such as: "quickly(writes(Mary, paper))," is now coded as: "writes(w) & agent (w, m) & object(w, a) & paper (a) & quickly (w)," where w is the event variable and "m, a" are constants. We can paraphrase this expression as: there exists an event w, such as w concerns a writing event, and the agent of this event is "m" (Mary), and the object of this event is "a," and "a" is an article, and the event is progressing quickly. This type of representation presents all sorts of logical and computational advantages; we will mention here the fact that, using this sort of analysis, it is possible to build up very robust syntactic parsers producing always a *single* QLF analysis of an input sentence, thanks to a technique that consists of: (1) avoiding having to choose in the presence of syntactic ambiguities like the prepositional groups attachment; (2) accepting as final syntactic analysis a set of nonoverlapping QLF parse fragments that span the input sentence. The global coherence must then be reconstructed later, at the semantic level.

For example, we reproduce in Figure 10 the QLF image produced by the COBALT's parser for a fragment like: "Sharp Corporation said it has shifted production of low value personal computers from Japan to companies in Taiwan and Korea." No effort has been made, at this level, to solve the PP-attachment ambiguities linked with the presence of "of," "from," "to," and "in." In Figure 10, _e1 and _e2 are "event predicates"; their arguments (arg0, arg1, etc.) are in turn two-

```
say (_e1), arg0 (_e1, _sh), arg1(_e1, _e2),
sharp_corp (_sh),
shift (_e2), arg0 (_e2, _it), arg1 (_e2, _p), it (_it), production (_p),
of (_of, _, _nn), nn (_nn, _v, _c),
low (_l, _v), value (_v), personal (_p, _c), computer (_c),
from (_fr, _, _j), japan (_j),
to (_to, _, _co), company (_co),
in (_in, _, _and1), and (_and1, _t, _k), taiwan (_t), korea (_k)
```

FIGURE 10   QLF representation of the "Sharp Corporation" fragment.

place predicates where the first argument refers to the event whose argument they are, and the second argument refers to the participant itself. All the prepositions are translated into three-place predicates. The first argument is the preposition relation, and the other arguments are the indices of the entities for which the relation is valid. Ambiguity in the PP-attachment is expressed in QLF by leaving the second argument of the predicate unspecified (see again Figure 10).

The COBALT parser then converts the QLF representation into some sort of "standard" tree representation; in our case, given the presence of the unspecified arguments, we obtain the four syntactic subtrees of Figure 11, i.e., a "forest" instead of a complete tree structure. The four subtrees correspond to the presence of the four prepositions in the original fragment; the first ambiguity, which concerns "of," can be solved making use of the "postmodifiers rule" mentioned in subsection 3.4.4.1; its use results in the reattachment of the PP subtree introduced by "of," see Figure 11, to the tree corresponding to the beginning of the sentence. The residual ambiguities cannot be solved by using tools based only on syntactic factors, and require the use of the semantic disambiguation module of COBALT.

We will only say here that the "attachment algorithm" proper to this module makes use of a strategy based on two main principles:

- The use of a "generate and test" procedure, allowing us to construct all the possible semantic interpretations ("readings") of the textual fragment examined; more specifically, a reading is a set of output structures, expressed in the conceptual language (NKRL) used in COBALT, that corresponds to an identical semantic interpretation of the fragment.
- The use, for each possible ambiguous preposition, of a set of "attachment rules" having the format: "syntactic condition (antecedent) — operations concerning the final, NKRL representation (consequent)," which are used to reduce to a minimum the number of readings. In each rule, the consequent specifies the mandatory conditions under which the term(s) corresponding to the head noun of an ambiguous PP (prepositional phrase) can fill a particular position in one or more of the conceptual (NKRL) structures produced by the general semantic analyzer of COBALT.

We reproduce in Table 3 a simplified version of some of the "attachment rules" associated with three of the propositions of the "Sharp Corporation" fragment: "from" ("from Japan"), "to" ("to companies"), and "in" ("in Taiwan and Korea"). The antecedent parts refer to the results of the syntactic analysis, i.e., to the forest produced by the parser. SUBJ(ect), OBJ(ect), SOURCE, and DEST(ination) are conceptual roles proper to the NKRL language (see subsection 3.5.3.3). The SOURCE role refers to the animate entity (group of entities) that is responsible for the particular behavior of the SUBJ(ect) mentioned in an NKRL output structure; the DEST(ination) role — sometimes called "benefactive" in other knowledge representation systems — refers to the "addressee" of the activity of the SUBJ(ect). Please note the lack of precision of rule c), owing to the very ambiguous character of the preposition "in."

```
(s
 (np sharp_corp)
 (vp
  (vtrans said)
  (s
   (np it)
   (vp
    (vtrans shifted)
    (np production_1)))))

(pp
 (prep of)
 (np low_value_added_pc_1))

(pp
 (prep from)
 (np japan_))

(pp
 (prep to)
 (np company_1))

(pp
 (prep in)
 (np
  (conj and)
  (taiwan_ korea_))))
```

FIGURE 11   A "forest" corresponding to the QLF analysis of the "Sharp Corporation" fragment.

3.5.2.   Shallow Semantic Representations

We will first examine a very well-known semantic tool, i.e., the "semantic grammars," and we will then look briefly at some of the semantic techniques used in the context of the MUC conferences (see subsection 2.4).

3.5.2.1.   Semantic Grammars

The basic idea behind the use of semantic grammars is that of unifying the two phases of syntactic and semantic analysis. This is obtained through the use of production (rewriting) rules characterized

---

TABLE 3
Attachment Rules

a) "from" followed by a generic term pertaining to the conceptual class *<location_>* ("from" + *<xl – location_>*) → make use of the value bound to the variable *xl* to fill the "initial location" position of the "location attribute" linked with the OBJ(ect) argument of a MOVE3.2 ("move a method or process") NKRL structure ("template," see subsection 3.5.3.3).

b) 1) "to" + *<xl – human_being_or_social_body>* → make use of the value bound to the *xl* variable to fill the DEST slot of a MOVE3.2 structure;

   2) "to" + *<xl – location_>* → use the value bound to the *xl* variable to fill the "final location" position of the "location attribute" linked with the OBJ of a MOVE3.2 structure

c) "in" + *<xl – location_>* → use the value bound to the *xl* variable to fill any generic "location attribute" linked with any possible SUBJ, OBJ, SOURCE, or DEST argument

```
S  →  QUERY SHIP-PROPERTY of SHIP
QUERY  →  what is | tell me
SHIP-PROPERTY  →  the SHIP-PROP | SHIP-PROP
SHIP-PROP  →  speed | length | type
SHIP  →  the SHIP-NAME | the fastest SHIP2
SHIP-NAME  →  Kennedy | Kitty Hawk | Constellation | …
SHIP2  →  COUNTRYS SHIP3 | SHIP3
SHIP3  →  SHIPTYPE LOCATION | SHIPTYPE
SHYPTYPE  →  carrier | submarine | …
COUNTRYS  →  American | British | Russian | …
LOCATION  →  …
```

FIGURE 12 An example of semantic grammar.

by the two following, main properties: (1) they produce parse trees where the categories of the grammar (i.e., the non-leaf nodes that appear in the tree, like NP or VP in the traditional syntactic analysis) do not coincide necessarily with the traditional syntactic categories; (2) these categories have been chosen to correspond as closely as possible to the desired inputs of the target program (e.g., a DB query program) and to the set of actions this last program must execute. In other words, the rules of a semantic grammar contain, hard-wired, the semantic information about the particular domain they are dealing with.

Figure 12 shows a (simplified) subset of the rules contained in one of the semantic grammars developed in the LADDER's context: LADDER was a famous NL interface to DBs developed in the late 1970s by G. Hendrix and colleagues, see, e.g., Androutsopoulos et al., 1995. It is very evident that, making use of this sort of grammars, we will produce — when parsing, e.g., a query like "What is the speed of the Kennedy?" — a parse tree having as intermediate nodes, in-between S and the actual words, very *ad-hoc* categories like QUERY, SHIP-PROPERTY, or SHIP.

The main computational advantage of this type of tool is the possibility of avoiding the need of a special apparatus — e.g., a system of variables and constraints on the variables — in order to enforce the semantic constraints. The disadvantages are self-evident: since semantic grammars contain, hard-wired, the knowledge proper to a specific application domain, a new semantic grammar must be developed whenever the system must be ported to another domain. This is why this sort of tool has been progressively abandoned, even for applications, like the NL interfaces for DBs, where the semantic grammar approach was (formerly) particularly cherished. However, semantic grammars are still mentioned in a recent survey (Androutsopoulos et al., 1995); moreover, a revival of this sort of tools can now be detected in the Spoken Language Understanding systems domain (see Section 4).

3.5.2.2.   Shallow Semantic Techniques Used in the MUC-Like Systems

In subsection 3.3 above, we mentioned the "semantic" rules used by an MUC-5 system, LINK, to execute the tagging of strings of capitalized words. These rules are a good example of the special-purpose rules used by almost all the MUC systems to recognize quickly, without any in-depth syntactic or semantic analysis but by utilizing, e.g., local pattern matching, the semantic category of particular phrasal units, like company names, places, people's names, dates, acronyms, currencies, and equipment names.

However, the use of "shallow" (and, consequently, ad least partially *ad-hoc*) semantic techniques is really pervasive in the MUC systems. When dealing, as it is normal in the knowledge extraction domain, with considerable amounts of linguistic data, an important problem concerns that of reducing as much as possible the amount of the "knowledge engineering" effort, i.e., the effort necessary to build up the knowledge sources (mainly, dictionaries and rules) necessary to process correctly the texts. In order to be economically convenient, many MUC systems have then chosen to make use in general of "shallow knowledge" (i.e., knowledge very domain-specific, and so difficult to generalize and to reuse in other applications) (see also Cowie and Lehnert, 1996). The "shallow knowledge hypothesis" can be formulated in this way: (1) it should be possible to acquire automatically, at very low cost, this type of shallow, *ad-hoc* knowledge; (2) if the above is correct (i.e., if the automatic acquisition of shallow knowledge is really cost-effective), it may be interesting to make use of this sort of knowledge even if it should prove to be adequate only for the application at hand, in a single domain, and for the utilization of a single system.

An example of a system that adheres completely to the shallow knowledge hypothesis is given by CIRCUS, a (relatively) successful MUC-5 system developed jointly by the Department of Computer Science of the University of Massachusetts (UMass) and by Hughes Research Laboratories. The general approach of CIRCUS to the knowledge extraction problem consists, in fact, of automating as much as possible the construction of domain-specific dictionaries and other language-related resources, so that information extraction can be customized for specific applications with a minimal amount of human assistance. CIRCUS is then organized around seven trainable language components, which can be developed in few hours by domain experts who have no background in natural language or machine learning, and are intended to handle (1) lexical recognition and part-of-speech tagging; (2) dictionary generation (using the AutoSlog system); (3) semantic features tagging; (4) noun phrase analysis; (5) limited coreference resolution; (6) domain object recognition, and (7) relational link recognition.

Of all these components, the most well-known is AutoSlog, a tool for the automatic construction of dictionaries of "concept nodes" (CN), developed at UMass and used, in CIRCUS, in conjunction with the sentence analyzer — AutoSlog makes use of predefined "key templates" to analyze a training corpus and construct then the CN structures. To give only a very simplified example of the use of the AutoSlog results, let us consider the following CN generated, in a MUC-5 context, after examination of a training corpus concerning the microelectronics domain (ME):

(CN %ME-ENTITY-NAME-SUBJECT-VERB-AND-INFINITIVE-PLANS-TO-MARKET%)

When dealing with a fragment of "real" microelectronics text like: "...Nikon Corp. plans to market the NSR-1755EX8A, a new stepper intended for use in the production of 64-Mbit DRAMs ..." — already processed by previous trainable modules that have tagged, e.g., the sequence "plans to market" as "plans (verb) to (infinitive) market (verb)" — the previous CN is triggered by the presence of "plans to market" and validated by the concordance between the tags and the constraints inserted in the CN. "Nikon Corp." is then picked up by the CN, and categorized as "me-entity." This example is sufficient to show that, in this type of approach, there is little of really general and transferable to other domains. The procedure is, however, very cost-effective: the CIRCUS dictionary used in MUC-5 was based exclusively on the CN definitions obtained from AutoSlog (3017 CN definitions for the "joint venture," and 4220 for the "microelectronics" dictionary). No hand-coded or manually altered definitions were added to these results.

3.5.3.   High-Level Languages for Meaning Representation

As already stated, the final aim of an in-depth semantic analysis is that of producing an image of the "meaning" of a particular statement making use of some advanced representation languages. This image should consist in some form of a combination of high-level world concepts, pertaining to a type of "interlingua" independent from the particular type of application (NL interfaces to DBs, populating the knowledge base of an ES, case-based reasoning, intelligent information retrieval, etc.) and, to some extent, from the particular knowledge proper to a specific application domain. Until now, no agreement exists about the characteristics of this representation language, that should be particularly well adapted to the representation of linguistic knowledge; after having mentioned, first, the predicate logic tradition, we will describe briefly two languages, Conceptual Graphs (CGs) and NKRL, that have been often used to represent this particular type of knowledge and that can be considered, at least partly, as a distant progeny of the Schankian Conceptual Dependency approach (see subsection 2.3).

3.5.3.1.   Logical Approaches

Logic-based approaches to knowledge representation emphasize particularly the role of "inference" (deductive inference). They consist mainly, in fact, of (1) a knowledge base of axioms written in some variant of the First-Order Predicate Calculus (FOPC), that makes up the proper knowledge representation component of a logic-based system; and (2) a collection of theorem-proving strategies that represent the deductive component.

In FOPC, we deal with "terms" and "predicates." A term corresponds to some "object" in the universe; predicates are functions that map their arguments (i.e., the terms) into the logic values "true" and "false." If we consider this example built up on the model of the famous "all men are mortal": "All the Artificial Intelligence professors are mad. X is an AI professor. X is mad," we can now say that, if M represents the predicate "mad," $M(X)$ represents the sentence "X is mad." An expression like $M(X)$ is an "atom," and corresponds to a proposition in propositional logic. As is well known, FOPC adds to the usual logical operators used in propositional logic, "and $= \wedge$," "or $= \vee$," "not $= \neg$," "implication $= \rightarrow$," two new operators corresponding to the "universal" ("for all, $\forall$") and existential ("there is one, $\exists$") quantification. Making use of them, we can now represent the sentence "all the AI professors are mad" as "$(\forall x) A(x) \rightarrow M(x)$," i.e., "for all x, if x is an AI professor, then x is mad"; using simple logical artifices like the "universal instantiation" and the "modus ponens," we can deduce from $x = X$ that $M(X)$.

It should be noticed that, under the influence of the programming language PROLOG, several modern FOPC-based representation systems are, in reality, "Horn clauses systems." These systems are characterized by two important properties. The first is that, in these systems, all logical formulas are converted to a normal form, called "clause form." Horn clauses are disjunctive logic formulas with at most one positive (unnegated) "literal"; a literal is an atomic formula P (term$_1$, ..., term$_n$) for some predicate P, where "term..." are, as usual, the arguments. Restriction to Horn clauses is conceptually equivalent to disallowing implications of the type "A $\rightarrow$ B $\vee$ C," i.e., giving rise to disjunctions within the body of the clause. The second property consists of the fact that Horn clauses systems make use of a single deductive mechanism based on Robinson's "resolution principle." The resolution principle tries to prove that a "theorem," i.e., a clause whose truth value is as yet unknown, can be derived from a set of "axioms," i.e., clauses that are assumed to be true. This principle is based on the notion of contradiction, i.e., a clause and its negation cannot both be true.

Having chosen some form of FOPC for semantic representation, the automatic or semi-automatic translation from NL into this form is normally a two-step procedure. In the first one, a syntactic parse of the input is accomplished. The second translates this parse into a FOPC expression by establishing a correspondence between the types of syntactic constructs found in the input and the FOPC types to be inserted in the output. For example, and sticking to the most general from of FOPC representation, the root of the syntactic tree, S(entence), will give rise to the overall FOPC formula according to a "compositional principle" stating that we can compute the logical form associated with each nonterminal node of the parse tree as a function of the logical form of its immediate constituents. Within the general formula, proper names are translated straightway into terms, with the verb giving rise to the predicate. NPs other than proper names usually introduce variables and set theoretic denotations, as in the example "every professor" which can be translated as "$(\forall p \in professors)$": the NP is represented here as a quantifier over a set, where the set corresponds to the noun, and the quantifier is obtained from the determiner, etc.

From a knowledge representation point of view, pure predicate calculus is constrained by all sorts of limitations, where the main ones concern the impossibility of representing modality (possible, necessary etc.), time, and belief. Even in the quantifier domain, FOPC presents some important limitations: for example, quantifying expressions like "most" or "more than half" cannot be fully rendered within FOPC. Following Montague and his disciples, several extensions to FOPC have been proposed, trying to capture additional linguistic phenomena when conserving the very precise, formal semantics of FOPC. Montague himself has proposed an "intensional logic" for the representation of the semantics of natural language, giving very accurate rules for a limited subset of English where he emphasizes the quantification problems. We can mention here Kamp's "Discourse Representation Theory," see also subsection 3.6. Another well-known, formal semantic theory is Barwise and Perry's "Situation Semantics," which reformulates the logical foundations of FOPC and other formal semantic theories in order to produce a sound formulation of the notion of "partial state of the world" or "situation." Other formal semantic theories are the "Dynamic Predicate Logic," the "Property Theory," etc. We must emphasize here that all these formal semantic theories, which try to extend the conceptual framework of FOPC while conserving its rigid formal properties, had been until now a very limited impact on the production of practical NLP systems, even if they are sometimes invoked *a posteriori* to give a theoretical justification to some successful prototype.

3.5.3.2.   Conceptual Approaches: The Conceptual Graphs

"Conceptual Graphs" (CGs) is a knowledge representation system that makes use of a graph based notation and is specially devoted to the representation of NL semantics. This particular type of notation has been developed by John Sowa [see Sowa (1991)], originally for incrementing the expressive power of the database languages, and made known to the general public in 1984.

The basic representational primitives used in CGs are (1) the classes of concepts ("concept-types," organized into a type-hierarchy), (2) the "concepts" and the corresponding "referents," and (3) the "conceptual relations." Concept-types represent general classes of entities, attributes, states and events; in NL terms, they correspond not only to nouns, but also to other categories of "lexical words" like verbs, qualitative adjectives, and adverbs. We can, therefore, meet CGs concept-types like CAT, SIT, DANCE, GRACEFUL (corresponding to both the adjective and the adverb "gracefully"), TIME, PERSON, SITUATION, PROPOSITION, etc.; it is assumed that, for any conceptual graphs system, there exists a predefined set of such types, which is different according to the domain to formalize. As already stated, concept-types are inserted into a type-hierarchy; this is, in fact, a lattice defined by a partial ordering relation, "<," which means that some concepts are totally subsumed in others. Therefore, if ANIMAL, CAT, MAMMAL and PHYS-ICAL-OBJECT are concept-types, they are linked, within the type-hierarchy, by the relationship: CAT < MAMMAL < ANIMAL < PHYSICAL-OBJECT, i.e., MAMMAL is, at the same time, a "super-type" of CAT and a "subtype" of ANIMAL. Like the set inclusion, the relation "<" is transitive and antisymmetric. The type-hierarchy has the appearance of a lattice given that, e.g., a concept like ELEPHANT may be, at the same type, a subtype of both MAMMAL and WILD-ANIMAL. In technical terms, a lattice of types is characterized by the fact that every two types must have at most one maximal common subtype and one minimal common supertype; this condition is not always easy to respect without being obliged to introduce artificial types in the lattice, in the style of a possible WILD-MAMMAL.

A "concept" is an incarnation of a concept-type: a concept like [CAT] represents an (unnamed) entity of type CAT (with the meaning "there exists a cat"), and can be considered as the simplest form of a conceptual graph. Adding a "referent field" to a concept allows one to designate specific individuals. If we know that, e.g., the current cat is named "Yojo," this situation is represented as: [CAT: Yojo], with the meaning "the entity Yojo is a cat." Therefore, a concept "box" is normally divided into two parts: the "type field" on the left side of the colon, and the "referent field" on the right side. In general, an "indexical referent" — i.e., a definite reference to an entity that is known contextually, but that is not precisely named, as when we make use of the definite article "the" — is represented making use of the symbol "#" in the referent field. In this way, "the cat" is represented as [CAT: #]. When the referent is identified with one of the entities already known in the system, the serial number of this entity is appended to the # symbol: therefore, [CAT: #123] means

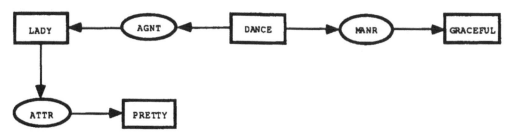

FIGURE 13A A simple example of conceptual graph.

that "the entity #123 is a cat." This particular way of indicating the relationship between a concept-type and a referent can be further specialized. For example, plural situations require the use of a new symbol, "*," to indicate a plural referent. The expression "three cats" is then represented as [CAT: {*}@3]. The plural referent {*} indicates here some unspecified entities of the type CAT, and the "qualifier" @3 indicates that there are 3 of them. The same type of solution is adopted in the presence of "quantifiers," as "many" or "all"; the symbolism [CAT: {*}@many] corresponds then to "many cats"; etc.

Finally, "conceptual relations" indicate the roles that the concepts play with respect to each other. They are similar to the "cases" used in the different AI interpretations of the case grammar theory and to the Jackendoff's "thematic roles." Some of the most common CGs conceptual relations are, e.g., AGNT in "LADY is an *agent* of DANCE," ATTR in "PRETTY is an *attribute* of LADY," MANR in "GRACEFUL is a *manner* of DANCE," DEST in "CITY is a *destination* of GO," etc.

From a semantic point of view, a conceptual graph corresponds to an assertion about some individuals that exists in the particular application domain to be considered. Accordingly, the graphical representation of Figure 13A corresponds to the assertion: "A (generic) pretty lady is dancing gracefully." The arrows on the arcs are used to distinguish the first and the second arguments of the predicate ("dancing"). Very often, conceptual graphs are expressed in a sort of "linear" representation; the representation in linear form of the assertion: "The (specific) pretty lady iden-tified as the entity #1520 of the system is dancing gracefully" is then given in Fig. 13b.

An important formal property of conceptual graphs concerns the possibility of their exact mapping into FOPC formulas thanks to the operator ϕ. The mapping produces a conjunction of predicates, one corresponding to each node of the graph; generic concepts map to variables, individual concepts map to constants. Therefore, if u is the graph represented in Figure 13B, its translation in predicate calculus gives:

$$\phi u = \exists x \, \exists y \, \exists z \, (\text{Lady}(\#1520) \wedge \text{Attr}(\#1520, x) \wedge \text{Pretty}(x) \wedge \text{Agent}(y, \#1520) \wedge \text{Dance}(y) \wedge \text{Manner}(y, z) \wedge \text{Graceful}(z))$$

To give, however, to conceptual graphs the full power of first-order logic, it is necessary to introduce some "second-order" extensions of the notions above. These extensions make use mainly of two particular concept-types, PROPOSITION — concepts of the type PROPOSITION are used to represent contexts: PROPOSITION can take, in fact, one or more conceptual graphs as referent — and SITUATION. The difference between the two is explained in this way by Sowa: "When a conceptual graph is the referent of a concept of type PROPOSITION, it represents the proposition stated by the graph. When it is the referent of a concept of the type SITUATION, it represents the situation described by the proposition stated by the graph." Combinations of the two are then used to represent second-order structures like those corresponding to the "subordinate" or "completive"

[PRETTY] ← (ATTR) ←[LADY: #1520] ←(AGNT) ← [DANCE] → (MANR)
                                                        → [GRACEFUL]

FIGURE 13B Conceptual graph in linear form.

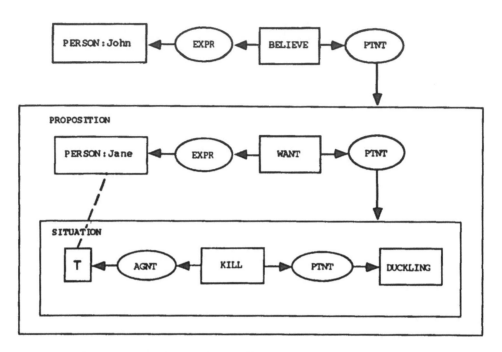

FIGURE 14 Graphical representation of second-order constructions.

constructions of natural language. We reproduce here, Figure 14. In the figure 14, John believes a proposition: Jane, on the contrary, wants a situation; we can note that the "subjects" of the "states" represented by BELIEVE and WANT are represented by "experiencers" (EXPR) rather than "agents" (AGNT). As Sowa states, in general, negation, modalities, and the "patients" (objects), PTNT, of verbs like "think" and "know" are linked with contexts of the type PROPOSITION; times, locations, and the patients of verbs like "want" and "fear" are linked with SITUATION contexts. The way contexts are nested determines the scope of the quantifiers. In Figure 14, DUCKLING is existentially quantified inside the situation that Jane wants, which is in turn existentially quantified inside John's belief. Figure 15 is the linear form of Figure 14: as we can see, the graphical form is surely more legible in order to show the nesting of contexts.

We can conclude these few notes about conceptual graphs by giving some information about an important CG construction, the "lambda abstraction." λ-abstraction can be defined as a conceptual graph with one or more generic concepts identified as formal parameters (variables); the relationship with the analogous LISP construction is evident. As in LISP, the main function of λ-abstraction is that of allowing new definitions: monadic abstractions are used to define "concept" types, and n-adic abstractions are used to define n-adic "relation" types. Moreover, an important, specific function of λ-abstraction is that of allowing the definition of "single-use" types: instead of inserting in the type field of a concept a label corresponding to a concept-type defined in a permanent way, this type field can contain a λ-abstraction that is expressly created for a single use. This possibility is typically used to represent restrictive relative clauses (see below). Other possible

```
[PERSON: John]  ← (EXPR)  ← [BELIEVE]  → (PTNT)  → [PROPOSITION:
  [PERSON: Jane*x]  ← (EXPR)  ← [WANT]  → (PTNT)  → [SITUATION:
      [*x]  ← (AGNT)  ← [MARRY]  → (PTNT)  → [SAILOR]]]
```

FIGURE 15 Linear representation of second-order constructions.

```
PET-CAT = (λx) [CAT: *x] ← (PTNT) ← [OWN] ← (STAT) ← [PERSON]
```

FIGURE 16 Defining a new concept using the λ-abstraction.

utilizations of λ-abstraction concern the possibility of defining schemata used to represent defaults and expectations, of defining new individuals as aggregations of parts, and of defining typical individuals as prototypes. We give now, in Figure 16, a simple example of use of λ-abstraction to define `PET-CAT` as a type of `CAT` owned by some person — `CAT` is then a supertype of the newly defined concept `PET-CAT`. The equals sign that appears in the definition means that the type label (PET-CAT) is a synonym for the λ-expression that defines the type, i.e., any occurrence of the type label `PET-CAT` could be replaced by the λ-expression.

As a second example of use of the λ-abstraction, we give in Figure 17 the representation of the sentence "some elephants that perform in a circus earn money." A λ-expression is used here to define the "single-use" concept "elephants that perform in a circus"; the BENF relation indicates that the elephants are the beneficiaries of the earning. In this conceptual graph, the (global) single-use concept has a "generic plural referent" represented by the symbol "{*}" that, in this case, indicates some unspecified elements of the type "elephants that perform in a circus." In CGs theory, plurals are regarded as generalized quantifiers, and represented in the same way as other quantifiers. For example, the representation of the sentences "every elephant that performs in a circus earns money" and "many elephants that perform in a circus earn money" is still that of Figure 17, with the symbols "∀" and "{*}@many" in place of the generic plural referent "{*}"; "@" is a "qualifier," and the expression "@many" indicates "many of them."

3.5.3.3. Conceptual Approaches: The Narrative Knowledge Representation Language

While the Conceptual Graphs theory is presented by Sowa as a tool for representing, in general, the semantics of natural languages, Zarri's NKRL (Narrative Knowledge Representation Language) has a less ambitious goal. NKRL is aimed, in fact, at proposing some possible, pragmatic solutions for the set-up of a standardized description of the semantic contents (the "meaning") of a specific class of NL texts, the "narrative documents." With the term "narrative documents," NKRL denotes NL texts of a particular industrial and economic interest corresponding, e.g., to news stories, corporate documents, normative texts, intelligence messages, etc.

NKRL is a two-layer language. The lower layer consists of a set of general tools that are structured into several integrated components, four in this case.

The descriptive component concerns the tools used to produce the formal representations (called predicative templates) of general classes of narrative events, like "moving a generic object," "formulate a need," "be present somewhere." Predicative templates are characterized by a threefold format, where the central piece is a semantic predicate (a primitive, like BEHAVE, EXPERIENCE, MOVE, PRODUCE, etc.) whose arguments (role fillers) are introduced by such roles as SUBJ(ect), OBJ(ect), SOURCE, DEST(ination), etc.; the data structures proper to the descriptive component are then similar to the case-grammar structures. Templates are structured into a hierarchy, H_TEMP(lates), corresponding, therefore, to a "taxonomy of events."

Templates' instances (predicative occurrences), i.e., the NKRL representation of single, specific events, like "Tomorrow, I will move the wardrobe," "Lucy was looking for a taxi," "Peter lives in Paris," are in the domain of the factual component. The definitional component supplies the NKRL representations, called concepts, of all the general notions, like *physical_entity*, *human_being*, *taxi_*, *city_*, etc., that can play the role of arguments within the data structures of the two components

```
[(λx) [ELEPHANT: *x] ← (AGNT) ← [PERFORM] → (IN) → [CIRCUS]: {*}]
          - (BENF) ← [EARN] → (PTNT) → [MONEY].
```

FIGURE 17 A λ-expression used to define a "single-use" concept.

above. The concepts correspond to sets or collections, organized according to a generalization/specialization (tangled) hierarchy which, for historical reasons, is called H_CLASS(es). The data structures used for the concepts are, substantially, frame-like structures; H_CLASS corresponds relatively well, therefore, to the usual ontologies of terms.

The enumerative component of NKRL concerns the formal representation of the instances (concrete, countable examples, see lucy_, wardrobe_1, taxi_53) of the concepts of H_CLASS; their formal representations take the name of individuals. In the following, we will use the italic type style to represent a "*concept_*" and the roman style to represent an "individual_."

The upper layer of NKRL consists of two parts. The first is a "catalog," giving a complete description of the formal characteristics and the modalities of use of the well-formed, "basic templates" (like "moving a generic object" mentioned above) associated with the language — presently, about 150, pertaining mainly to a (very general) socio-economico-political context where the main characters are human beings or social bodies. By means of proper specialization operations, it is then possible to obtain, from the basic templates, the (specific) "derived" templates that could be concretely needed to implement a particular, practical application — e.g., "move an industrial process" — and the corresponding occurrences. In NKRL, the set of legal, basic templates can be considered, at least in a first approach, as fixed. Analogously, the general concepts that pertain to the upper levels of H_CLASS — such as *human_being, physical_entity, modality_*, etc. — form a type of upper-level, invariable ontology.

Figure 18 supplies a simple example of NKRL code. It translates a small fragment of news story: "Milan, October 15, 1993. The financial daily Il Sole 24 Ore reported Mediobanca had called a special board meeting concerning plans for capital increase."

In this figure, c1 and c2 are symbolic labels of occurrences; MOVE and PRODUCE are predicates; SUBJ, OBJ, TOPIC ("à propos of...") are roles. With respect to the arguments, sole_24_ore, milan_, mediobanca_ (an Italian merchant bank), summoning_1, etc. are individuals; *financial_daily, special_, cardinality_,* and *several_* (this last belonging, like *some_, all_* etc., to the *logical_quantifier* intensional subtree of H_CLASS) are concepts. The attributive operator, SPECIF(ication), with syntax (SPECIF e_1 p_1 ... p_n), is used to represent some of the properties that can be asserted about the first element e_1, concept or individual, of a SPECIF list; *several_* is used within a SPECIF list having *cardinality_* as first element as a standard way of representing the plural number mark (see c2). The arguments, and the templates/occurrences as a whole, may be characterized by the presence of particular codes, the determiners: e.g., the location determiners, represented as lists, are associated with the arguments (role fillers) by using the colon, ":," operator (see c1). For some information on the determiners date-1 and date-2, see Zarri (1995).

A MOVE construction like that of occurrence c1 (completive construction) is necessarily used to translate any event concerning the transmission of information ("... Il Sole 24 Ore reported ...").

```
c1)     MOVE SUBJ (SPECIF sole_24_ore financial_daily): (milan_)
             OBJ   #c2
             date-1: 15_october_93
             date-2:
c2)     PRODUCE SUBJ   mediobanca_
             OBJ     (SPECIF summoning_1 (SPECIF board_meeting_1
                             mediobanca_ special_))
             TOPIC   (SPECIF plan_1 (SPECIF cardinality_ several_)
                             capital_increase_1)
             date-1:   circa_15_october_93
             date-2:
```

FIGURE 18   An example of NKRL coding.

```
c3)   MOVE         SUBJ  human_being_or_social_body
                   OBJ   #c4

c4)   EXPERIENCE   SUBJ  peter_
                   OBJ   fevered_state_1

c5)   EXPERIENCE   SUBJ  peter_
                   OBJ   flushing_state_1
                   [obs]

c6)   (CAUSE c3 c5)
```

FIGURE 19 An implicit enunciative situation.

Accordingly, the filler of the OBJ(ect) slot in the occurrences (here, c1) that instantiates the MOVE transmission template is always a symbolic label (c2) which refers to another predicative occurrence, i.e., that bearing the informational content to be spread out ("... Mediobanca had called a meeting ..."). We can note that the enunciative situation can be both explicit or implicit. For example, the completive construction can be used to deal with the problem of the correct rendering of causal situations where the general framework of the antecedent consists of an (implicit) speech situation. Let us examine briefly the following example: "Peter has a fever since he is flushed," where "being flushed" is not the "cause" of "having a fever," but that of an implicit enunciative situation where we claim (affirm, assert, etc.) that someone has a fever. Using the completive construction, this example is easily translated using the four occurrences of Figure 19.

We can remark that, in Figure 19, c6 is a binding occurrence. Binding structures — i.e., lists where the elements are conceptual labels, c3 and c5 in Figure 19 — are second-order structures used to represent the logico–semantic links that can exist between predicative templates or occurrences. The binding occurrence c6 — meaning that c3, the main event, has been caused by c5 — is labeled using one (CAUSE) of the four operators that define together the taxonomy of causality of NKRL. The presence in c5 of a specific determiner — a temporal modulator, "obs(erve)" — leads to an interpretation of this occurrence as the description of a situation that, at that very moment, is observed to exist.

We give now, Figure 20, a (slightly simplified) NKRL representation of the narrative sentence: "We have to make orange juice": this example, introduced by Hwang and Schubert in a paper for the 13th Joint Conference on Artificial Itelligence (1993), illustrates, in fact, several interesting semantic phenomena.

Figure 20 describes the standard NKRL way of representing the "wishes, desires, intention" domain. To translate the idea of "acting in order to obtain a given result," NKRL makes use of:

```
c7)   BEHAVE    SUBJ  (COORD informant_1 (SPECIF human_being (SPECIF
                             cardinality_ several_)))
                [oblig, ment]
                date1:  observed date
                date2:

c8)   *PRODUCE  SUBJ  (COORD informant_1 (SPECIF human_being (SPECIF
                             cardinality_ several_)))
                OBJ   (SPECIF orange_juice (SPECIF amount_ ()))
                date1:  observed date + i
                date2:

c9)   (GOAL c7 c8)
```

FIGURE 20 Wishes and intentions in NKRL.

1. An occurrence (here c7), instance of a basic template pertaining to the BEHAVE branch of the H_TEMP hierarchy, and corresponding to the general meaning of focusing on a result. This occurrence is used to express the "acting" component — i.e., it identifies the SUBJ(ect) of the action, the temporal coordinates, etc.
2. A second predicative occurrence, here c8, an instance of a template structured around a different predicate (e.g., PRODUCE in Figure 20) and used to express the "intended result" component.
3. A binding occurrence, c9, which links together the previous predicative occurrences and which is labeled by means of GOAL, another operator included in the taxonomy of causality of NKRL.

Please note that "oblig" and "ment" in Figure 20 are, like "obs" in Figure 19, "modulators," i.e., particular determiners used to refine or modify the primary interpretation of a template or occurrence as given by the basic "predicate — roles — argument" association. "ment(al)" pertains to the modality modulators. "oblig(atory)" suggests that "someone is obliged to do or to endure something, e.g., by authority," and pertains to the deontic modulators series. Other modulators are the temporal modulators, "begin," "end," "obs(erve)," see also Figure 19. Modulators work as global operators that take as their argument the whole (predicative) template or occurrence. When a list of modulators is present, as in the occurrence c7 of Figure 20, they apply successively to the template/occurrence in a Polish notation style to avoid any possibility of scope ambiguity. In the standard constructions for expressing wishes, desires, and intentions, the absence of the "ment(al)" modulator in the BEHAVE occurrence means that the SUBJ(ect) of BEHAVE takes some concrete initiative (acts explicitly) in order to fulfil the result; if "ment" is present, as in Figure 20, no concrete action is undertaken, and the "result" reflects only the wishes and desires of the SUBJ(ect).

3.5.3.4.   "Translating" from NL into Conceptual Format

We will only mention here, very briefly, the NL/NKRL "translation" procedures. The equivalent procedures used in a CGs context are not fundamentally different, in essence, from those that will be expounded here.

The NL/NKRL (and NL/CGs) translation procedures are based on the well-known principle of locating, within the original texts, the syntactic and semantic indexes that can evoke the conceptual structures used to represent these texts. The specific NKRL contribution has consisted, in particular, in the set-up of a rigorous algorithmic procedure, centered around the two following conceptual tools:

• The use of rules — evoked by particular lexical items in the text examined and stored in proper conceptual dictionaries — that take the form of generalized production rules. The left-hand side (antecedent part) is always a syntactic condition, expressed as a fragment of tree-like structure, which must be unified with the results of the general parse tree produced by the syntactic specialist of the translation system (see also the rules in Table 3 above). If the unification succeeds, the right hand sides (consequent parts) are used, e.g., to generate well-formed templates ("triggering rules").

• The use, within the rules, of advanced mechanisms to deal with the variables. For example, in the specific "triggering" family of NKRL rules, the antecedent variables (a-variables) are first declared in the syntactic (antecedent) part of the rules, and then "echoed" in the consequent parts, where they appear under the form of arguments and constraints associated with the roles of the activated templates. Their function is that of "capturing" — during the match between the antecedents and the results of the syntactic specialist — NL or H_CLASS terms to be then used as specialisation terms for filling up the activated templates and building the final NKRL structures.

trigger: "call"

syntactic condition:

```
(s (subj (np (noun x1)))
  (vcl (voice active) (t = x2 = call))
  (dir-obj
    (np (modifiers (adjs x31))
      (noun x3)
      (modifiers (pp (prep about I concerning I ... )
        (np (noun x4)
        (modifiers (pp (prep of I for ...)
          (np (noun x5)))))))))))
```

parameters for the template:

(PRODUCE4.12 (roles subj *x1* obj (SPECIF *x2* (SPECIF *x3 x31*)) +topic (specif *x4 x5*))
(constr *x3 assembly_ x31 quality_ x5 modification_procedures*))

FIGURE 21   An example of NKRL triggering rule.

A detailed description of these tools can be found, e.g., in (Zarri, 1995). We reproduce now, Figure 21, one of the several triggering rules to which the lexical entry "call" — pertaining to the fragment of news story, "the financial daily Il Sole 24 Ore reported ...," examined in the previous subsection — contains a pointer, i.e., one of the rules corresponding to the meaning "to issue a call to convene." This rule allows the activation of a basic template (PRODUCE4.12) giving rise, at a later stage, to the occurrence c2 of Figure 18 before; the *x* symbols in Figure 21 correspond to *a*-variables.

We can remark that all the details of the full template are not actually stored in the consequent, given that the H_TEMP hierarchy is part of the "common shared data structures" used by the translator. Only the parameters relating to the specific triggering rule are, therefore, really stored. For example, in Figure 21, the list "constr" specializes the constraints on some of the variables, while others — e.g., the constraints on the variables *x1* (*human_being/social_body*) and *x4* (*planning_activity*) — are unchanged with respect to the constraints permanently associated with the variables of template PRODUCE4.12.

Please note that techniques like these, even when they can be associated with large knowledge bases of rules in the style of that shown in Figure 21, cannot guarantee that they will allow the translation into conceptual format to be carried out in a completely automated (and correct) way. This sort of procedures require then, always, some sort of human intervention — excepting in all those cases (categorization, abstracting, etc.) where some sort of rough (and also partially erroneous) analysis can be tolerated.

3.6.   DISCOURSE AND PRAGMATIC ANALYSIS

Up to now, we have dealt mainly with the analysis of single statements, written sentences, or utterances — even if, in the previous sections, we have seen how advanced knowledge representation systems like Conceptual Graphs or NKRL allow one to perform a sort of "clustering" of the "meaning" of several statements making use of second order mechanisms like PROPOSITIONs and SITUATIONs in Conceptual Graphs, or binding structures in NKRL. There exists, however, a specific branch of Linguistics that deals, in a systematic way, with the problem of studying the logical and semantic connections that normally exist, in a text or a dialog, among the different statements: this is the "discourse analysis." Discourse analysis deals, in general, with the two following problems: (1) determining the nature of the information that, in a sequence of statements, goes beyond the simple addition of the information conveyed by the single sentences or utterances; and (2) determining the influence of the context in which a statement is used on the meaning of the individual statement, or part of it.

Especially when the generic "statements" become, more precisely, spoken utterances, "pragmatic analysis" — i.e., how to use the global, final analysis of a linguistic sequence to perform a particular task — interacts strongly with discourse analysis. To determine, in fact, the pragmatic properties of a sequence of utterances — i.e., what kinds of "speech acts" the speakers are performing (are they asking a question, answering a previous question, making a proposal, etc.) — it is often necessary to have a global representation of their meaning. Conversely, in order to identify this global meaning it is often necessary to determine exactly the pragmatic role the sequence of utterances is meant to play.

The difficulty in obtaining, in these fields, results of a general import is well evident, and the availability of concrete tools is still scarce. With respect to the discourse analysis of written texts, early work was accomplished in the 1970s in the context of the so-called "text grammars," intended to define the conditions that must be satisfied for a text to be coherent — for example, the "condition of introduction" requires that an entity must be introduced, e.g., by an existential quantifier, before it can used as a discourse referent, e.g., in a definite noun phrase. Other work that dates back to the 1970s is the work originated by the introduction of the notion of "script" by Schank and Abelson (see subsection 2.3), and the introduction, by Schank and disciples, of tools like MOPs ("Memory Organization Packets") or TAUs ("Thematic Affect Units"). Unlike scripts, which only consider the actions performed by some characters within a given setting, MOPs include goals and intentions; TAUs have, among other things, a strong "affective" component, i.e., they can account for the different feelings of the characters.

More recent work in the area of discourse analysis of written texts includes that of Hahn, Hobbs, and Schubert. In the TOPIC system, Hahn deals with the detection of the "thematic progression patterns" that represent the global structure of the input texts: this is mainly performed by analyzing the semantic links between the concepts represented by nominal expressions in the texts. TOPIC is then able to detect various "coherence phenomena" that bring about some congruent aspects of the different "chunks of knowledge" isolated inside an NL text, like the "constant theme," i.e., the possibility to show that a variety of facts are, in reality, related to the same topic. Hobbs' work on "interpretation as abduction" is based on the theoretical assumption that the coherence of discourse follows from semantic relationships between the information conveyed by the successive statements — abductive reasoning is based on inferences of the type: "if A implies B and B has been observed, hypothesize A," and consists in computationally intensive inference techniques in a backward chaining style. After having executed the parse of a given statement into quasilogical form (see subsection 3.5.1), Hobbs' TACITUS system tries to prove, allowing a minimal set of assumptions to be made, that this logical form stems from the preceding statements and from the adherence to some form of general explanatory schema for the global text. The optimum (most complete) set of assumptions bringing out the proof can then be regarded as the best "explanation" of this text. Schubert's "Episodic Logic" (EL) is based on a Montague style of representation coupling syntactic forms and logical forms, while incorporating from situation semantics the idea that sentences describe situations (events, states, narrative episodes, eventualities, etc.). From the point of view of the text's coherence, EL makes use, among other things, of "episodic variables," which are used to make implicit temporal and causal relationships between situations fully explicit.

With respect to the discourse analysis of dialogs, we can mention here a theoretical work, Kamp's "Discourse Representation Theory" (DRT), a complex sort of "intermediate conceptual representation" devoted to the formalization of the connectivity phenomena, that has been expressly developed for the purpose of representing and computing trans-sentential anaphora, contexts, and other forms of discourse cohesion. In spite of his very general, theoretical framework, DRT has also been used for the design of some concrete prototypes, in particular for the design of advanced experimental question-answering systems. In a recent (1993) project like VERBMOBIL, e.g., DRT is used as unifying semantic representation formalism for developing a machine translation system taking into account face-to-face spoken dialogs.

3.7. LANGUAGE GENERATION

The Natural Language Generation (NLG) domain concerns the construction of computer programs able to produce a (high-quality) NL text from the computer-internal representation of given information. Motivations for working in this domain range from strongly theoretical reasons, which concern mainly research in the linguistic and psycholinguistic domains, to very practical ones that relate to the concrete production of understandable outputs for all sorts of computer programs. In this last context, we can mention here the following, practical applications of NLG techniques: display of database content, expert system explanation, speech generation, generator systems for producing standardized multiparagraph texts like business letters or monthly reports, multimedia presentation, automated production of summaries, etc.

In spite of these very exciting, practical and theoretical opportunities, NLG has received, until recently, substantially less attention from computational linguists and computer scientists than the "classical" problems concerning NL analysis. For example, most expert systems are equipped, still, with very simple generation modules in the "canned texts" or "template" style (see below). This situation is now changing, and the international NLG community is rapidly growing, even if generation is still perceived as a quite marginal domain in the global NLP enterprise.

It is normally assumed that every NLG system can always be decomposed into two main components:

- A "planning component," which selects and organizes the information to be included in the output, and produces accordingly, in some internal format, an expression representing the content of the proposed statement(s)
- A "realization component," which converts sentence-sized fragments pertaining to the previous expression into grammatically correct sentences

In the real system, this type of decomposition is, sometimes, really difficult to operate. For example, in the "canned text systems," the less sophisticated type of NLG systems, "planning" and "realization" practically coincide, given that these systems simply print out predefined strings of words without any change. The canned text systems are commonly used, e.g., for producing the error messages in all sorts of software components; they can also be used to produce warnings, letters, etc. Slightly more sophisticated techniques in the same style are those used, e.g., in the ELIZA system evoked, before, in subsection 2.2. In ELIZA, in fact, an at least embryonic form of planning component exists, given that the user's input was reused for constructing parts of the output. The systems in the next level of sophistication, the "template systems" — where the basic technique consists in filling predetermined patterns with the results of a given computer run — are used whenever a general type of message must be reproduced several times with some slight modifications. When the type of texts to be generated are fairly regular in structure, like some types of business reports, it is possible to use the template technique for the generation of paragraphs including multiple sentences. Given the predefined format of the texts to be output, in the template system the planning component is a very rudimentary one.

A first, concrete differentiation between "planning" and "realization" can be found in the most advanced realizations of the template technique, like McKeown's TEXT (1985), where it was possible to dynamically combine instances of four standard paragraph models, called "schemas," to create multisentence texts. The technique that is still the most widely used when the (mono- or multisentence) text to be generated must be a "flexible" and "well-written" one is the "phrase-based" approach, that can be seen as a generalization of the template approach. In the phrase-based technique, a phrasal pattern is associated with each main "type" that characterizes the internal representation to be converted into NL. For example, phrasal patterns can be associated with conceptual elements like "predicate" and "slots fillers" in a semantic network (or conceptual graph, NKRL etc.) type of representation, or with syntactic categories in a syntactic tree. Starting then from the phrasal pattern that matches the top level of internal representation — e.g., <SUBJ VERB OBJ> in the case of a syntactic-tree — each part of the pattern is expanded in turn into more specific phrasal patterns, like <DET ADJ NOUN MODIF>, that match particular subparts of the internal representation. This splitting process continues until all the phrasal patterns have been replaced by one or more words. For example, for a semantic network or frame representation having BUY has the top predicate, the first phrasal pattern selected, associated with BUY, can ask to search for the AGENT, the TENSE, the OBJECT, and the FROM-POSS(essor) cases; a pattern associated with AGENT will then ask to find the NL equivalent, e.g., "Bill," of the symbolic filler BILL; the phrasal pattern associated with TENSE will use the filler of this slot, e.g., PRESENT, to generate "buys" and, therefore, "Bill buys," etc. Used first for the generation of single sentences, the phrase-based systems were adapted in the late 1980s to the generation of multisentences texts. In this last case, they are often called "text planners," where each "plan" is a sort of phrasal pattern that specifies the structure of a portion of the whole discourse, and which is successively split in more specific plans until the level of the single clause is attained.

From the point of view of the concrete realizations, the advantages of text generation over text analysis are linked with the fact that, for the former, it is normally always possible to select *a priori* the minimal level of complexity of the NL output to be generated that can guarantee a correct understanding of the internal information. This, obviously, is not possible when analyzing a text, whose level of complexity is, at least in principle, totally unknown at the start. However, when the option of attaining a high level of linguistic refinement of the output is chosen, the NLG problem becomes at least as difficult as the corresponding analysis problem. Among these difficulties, we can mention: (1) those linked with the lexical selection, as soon as the internal representation approaches a realistic level of complexity, and the lexicon of the generation module is large enough to permit alternative locutions — an (apparently simple) problem of this type, which involves both the "planning" and "realization" components, concerns the use of pronouns and possessive adjectives and pronouns, see, e.g., "John's car" vs. "his car"; (2) in general, the difficulties linked with the selection of the appropriate granularity for the presentation of the internal information — this last can be, in fact, packaged into different units depending on several contingencies like the structure of the original information, the purpose of the output text, the expected audience, the stylistic biases, etc.; (3) the mismatch between some rudimentary forms of knowledge representation used in the original information — e.g., the tabular model of relational databases — and the (sometimes really advanced) linguistic features required in the output; and (4) the difficulties in designing realistic text planners, capable of generating texts with several paragraphs.

If we should want to condense into a few words the actual "state of the art" in the NLG field, we could say that it is now possible to produce commercially effective, general-purpose NL generators for single sentences. Partial and limited solutions exist at the moment, on the contrary, for the generation of well-formed, multisentence texts and paragraphs.

3.8. Interactive Systems and Spoken Language Understanding (SLU)

"Spoken Language Understanding" is a subdomain of NLP that only recently has acquired a particular importance, both from an academic and an industrial point of view. It is based on the association of two technologies: speech recognition and natural language understanding.

I SpeechActs, for example, is a prototype testbed for building up spoken NL applications, developed at the Sun Microsystems Laboratories, Chelmsford, MA, see the paper by Paul Martin and colleagues in *Special Section* ... (1996) — a continuous speech recognizer (i.e., a recognizer that accepts normally spoken speech with no artificial pauses between words) is coupled with a "traditional" NLP system, Swiftus, with a discourse manager, a text-to-speech manager, building tools, and third-party components relative to the particular application at hand (see Figure 22). This figure is a simplified version of the figure on page 35 of *Special Section ...* (1996). SpeechActs is independent of a particular speech technology, in that it can support several types of speech recognizers. Typical applications that can be developed using the SpeechActs tools are telephone-based applications where a business traveller dialogs in natural language with the system asking, after having entered his name and a password, for a series of services. He can ask the system, e.g., to read his e-mail making use of the text-to-speech facilities of SpeechActs (System: "Message 2 is from Mr. Brown"; User: "Let me hear it"), to consult his calendar (User: "What do I have the Friday after New Year's?"; System: "On Friday, January 3rd, you have no appointments"), hear weather forecasts, convert currency amounts, etc. To support a more natural dialog, SpeechActs also performs an, even though elementary, "discourse analysis" activity (see subsection 3.6). A system like this is, as already stated, a *prototype*; at the moment, there does not seem to exist an interactive SLU system really working in a field application, with the exception of the Philips train timetable system developed for Swiss Rail.

We will now examine briefly some of the blocks of Figure 22, trying to emphasize some particularities that the presence of speech and an interactive environment can introduce with respect to the "standard" paradigm for NLP (see subsection 3.1).

The flow of information is as follows. The speech recognizer analyzes the digitized audio data received from, e.g., the telephone via an audio server; when he considers that the user has completed an utterance, it sends a list of recognized words to the Swiftus module. The speech recognizer can only identify the words that appear in its lexicon, a specialized database containing all the words, with all their forms, that are needed for a given application. The speech recognition grammar is an artificial grammar used to reduce the word choice by imposing constraints on the permissible combinations of words. This grammar is then used to reduce "perplexity," a popular measure in

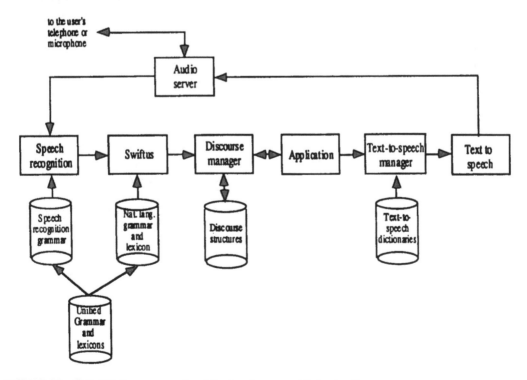

FIGURE 22   SpeechActs, an example of Spoken Language Understanding.

the speech recognition domain, loosely defined as a measure of the size of the set of words from which the next word can be chosen. Perplexity depends on the domain of discourse: for example, it is divided by ten when we pass from general English to a very specific and relatively delimited domain such as, e.g., radiology. Swiftus parses the word list received by the speech recognition module using a sort of semantic grammar (see subsection 3.5.2.1). The semantic analysis performed by Swiftus is then, as the builders of the system say, "medium-grained," somewhere between coarse keyword matching and full, in-depth semantic analysis. The grammar is, of course, relative to a particular application of SpeechActs, and must be changed, as the relevant lexicon, when another application is activated — an advantage of this approach is that the grammar can be exactly tuned to a specific application domain, and it is then possible to build up Swiftus grammars that are particularly robust.

The output of the parser is in the form of "feature-value pairs": for example, for the "business traveller" application mentioned before, the management of the calendar implies the production of pairs like: "USERID=jsmith," "DATE=3 January 1997," and "ACTION=appointment-lookup." However, the application module can work only if all the elements in the user's utterance, translated into Swiftus' pairs, are fully specified. If this is not the case, the application module can rely on the discourse module in order to obtain the missing information. Discourse management is performed making use of a stack where appropriate "discourse structures" are pushed, i.e., data structures specialized for dealing with particular situations, including functions capable of reacting to particular user inputs. For example, in the context of a dialog about conversion rates, the user can ask the system, "What's the rate for the franc." Given that the application does not have enough information to reply directly to this query, the corresponding Swiftus pair activates the discourse manager that pushes an appropriate discourse structure onto the stack. This then asks in turn the user for the type of franc (Belgian, French or Swiss) that must be considered: the answer "French" pushes a new discourse structure onto the stack that resolves "French" into "France." The application is now in possession of all the necessary information, and the disambiguation structures are popped.

An interesting feature of the system concerns the organization of the lexica and of the grammars. There is only a permanent lexicon, which is used by both Swiftus and the speech recognition module. Given that the speech module requires an explicit list of all the possible forms required by an application, the lexicon loader produces automatically all the forms like "shows," "showed," and "shown" from the permanent lexical entry concerning "show" *before* a concrete application really starts, i.e., morphological analysis is performed *a priori* and not on the fly. Analogously, a "Unified Grammar" is used for both recognition and parsing. The rules of the Unified Grammar consist, fundamentally, of a "pattern" (series of words) to be matched against the user's entry, and an "augmentation" component composed of "tests" that compare the features of particular pattern elements to one other or to constant elements, and of "actions" (e.g., lookup in the calendar) to be taken iff the pattern is matched. From this grammar, the Unified Grammar compiler produces both a grammar for a specific speech recognizer and a grammar for Swiftus. This last is a simple rearrangement of the rules of the Unified Grammar; the former requires a set of rewriting activities in order to reduce the original rules, which are relatively general in their expression, to sequences of terminal forms that, as already stated, are only used to constrain the word sequences produced by the speech recognizer in order to reduce the "perplexity."

4.   STATE OF THE ART AND FUTURE TRENDS IN THE NLP DOMAIN

We will mention here some recent developments in the NLP domain that are, or could be, of a particular importance for applications in the ES or KBS style.

The speech recognition area has experienced significant progress in the past decade: for speaker-independent systems, performances vary now from an error rate of 0.3% in the recognition of digits to about 7% in dictation applications, and word error rates continue to be reduced by a factor of two every 2 years. This success is largely due to the resolute adoption of pure statistical methods, see the so-called Hidden Markov Modeling (HMM), for generating a sequence of word hypotheses from an acoustic signal. A model like HMM is particularly powerful given that, in the presence of training data, the parameters of the model can be adjusted automatically to produce optimal performance. Other factors that have contributed to the outstanding achievements obtained in this field are, e.g., the development of large speech corpora (up to tens of thousands of sentences) for system development, training and testing, the establishment of sound standards for performance evaluation, etc. There is room, however, for many other sorts of improvements. They concern robustness, portability (at present, speech recognition systems tend to experiment significant degradation when they are moved to a news task, which implies that they must be trained again), progress in the modeling of language by incorporation syntactic and semantic constraints in the pure statistical models, the possibility of handling out-of-vocabulary words (presently, the systems are designed for being used with a particular set of words that can include, however, more than 20,000 words), etc.

From an ES/KBS point of view, Spoken Language Understanding (SLU) systems — where (as we have seen in the previous subsection) speech recognition techniques are associated with natural language comprehension — should normally be more interesting than simple speech recognition systems. SLU technology constitutes, in fact, the only way of building up ES/KBS (not only database systems) where the access can be realized in spoken natural language. Nevertheless, there are, many problems to solve before being able to achieve really integrated systems. To the contrary (at least partially), of the SpeechActs system examined in the previous subsection, many SLU systems still adhere to a very elementary architectural model that consists simply of the concatenation of an existing speech recognition system with an existing NL understanding system. This sort of concatenation, however, does not tend to work very well, mainly because existing NL understanding systems have been normally built up for dealing with written texts, i.e., according to modalities very different from those occurring in a spoken language environment. Moreover, the two components cannot really collaborate, etc.

To surmount this sort of difficulties, two tendencies have recently appeared. The first consists, as in SpeechActs, of a revitalization of the semantic grammars (task-oriented grammars) role: because semantic grammars focus on finding an interpretation of the input that is based only on the semantic properties of the domain, without requiring a very precise "grammaticality" (syntactic correctness) of this input, they can be more robust in face of the grammatical deviations that are typical in a spoken language context. The second option, which is now becoming popular, consists of the adoption of the so-called "n-best" approach. In this case, the effects of a strictly serial connection of two existing systems are mitigated by the fact that the speech recognition system sends to the NL component not just the best word hypothesis obtained from the acoustic signal, but the n-best, where n may be between 10 and 100. The NL component makes use of its syntactic and semantic tools to narrow progressively the search space to determine the best-scoring hypothesis.

In general, even if SLU technology has progressed notably in recent years, a considerable amount of work is still necessary in order to obtain systems that, at the difference of the actual ones, could be portable and not limited to specific application domains. For example, two problems that are still waiting for effective, industrial solutions are those (1) of the concrete utilization of the "prosodic" information, and (2) of the handling of the "disfluencies" (typical phenomena of the spontaneous speech like interjections, repeated words, repairs, false starts, etc.). Prosody refers to acoustic phenomena like stress, intonation, and rhythm (phrase breaks), that all convey important information about syntactic structures, discourse, and word recognition; prosody can also provide information about emotion and attitude through the user's intonation (e.g., sarcasm, anger).

Passing now to the traditional written input, we can note immediately that, in spite of more than 3 decades of research effort, we still cannot name a commercially usable parser that is, actually, both domain-independent and capable of dealing with unrestricted texts. The main technical problems concern (1) the correct segmentation of the input text into syntactically parsable inputs (this problem is particularly evident when the text sentences contain "text adjuncts" delimited by dashes, brackets or commas); (2) the resolution of the syntactic ambiguities (see subsection 3.4.4); (3) the cases where the input is outside the lexical and/or syntactic coverage of the system (see the problem of the "unknown words" in subsection 3.3).

Faced with this situation, and confronted with the exigency of having at its disposal "robust" tools to meet the increasing need for NLP applications, the NLP community is making use more and more of "shallow parsing" techniques; we have already encountered, in subsection 3.5.1, a first form of shallow parsing, consisting of the use of an underspecified form of representation for the output of the syntactic analyzers. This form of parsing is normally used when the application requires the analysis of large text corpora: in this case, in fact, because of the problems outlined in the previous paragraph, the use of the traditional, "deep" syntactic parsers can be both arduous and cumbersome. In general, shallow parsing is characterized by the fact that its output is not the usual phrase-structure tree, but a (much) less detailed form of syntactic analysis where, normally, only some phrasal constituents are recognized. These can consist, e.g., of noun phrases — without, however, the indication of their internal structure and of their function in the sentence — or of the main verb accompanied by its direct arguments. Inspired by the success of stochastic methods like HMM in the field of speech understanding, the builders of modern shallow parsers often make use of probabilistic methods that are tested and refined, e.g., on the basis of reference corpora composed of sets of manually bracketed sentences.

With respect now to the application side of NLP techniques, we will limit ourselves to mentioning two classes of applications that are becoming increasingly popular. A domain particularly important in the context of the present "full text revolution" — and which is also important for the development of efficient ESs/KBSs, for the same reasons we have already examined when speaking about the extraction of information from NL texts (see subsection 3.5.2.2) — is that of "summarization" (automatic abstracting). In the past, summarisation has been executed mainly by selecting "relevant" sentences in the input text through the use of statistical cues or of keywords. Today, under the influence of the MUC results, there is a tendency toward coupling pure statistical methods with more analytical techniques, like those used in the past in systems such as FRUMP and SCISOR (see Section 2.3). A second, "new" NLP domain that is gaining every day in importance, and that is at least partly related to domains like information extraction and summarization, is that of the so-called "controlled languages." These languages have been developed in an industrial framework to counter the tendencies of technical writers to freely make use of special vocabularies (jargons), of proper styles, and of unusual grammatical constructions. A controlled language (CL) is then a subset of a particular NL where some restrictions have been imposed on the use of the lexicon (only the authorized words can be used), of the grammar/syntax (e.g., the number of words that can be inserted in a NP group is limited, and the active voice is privileged with respect to the passive voice), of the semantics (by normalizing the expression of the agent, the action, the goal, the instrument, etc.), and of the style (e.g., the length of the sentences can be limited to no more than 20 words). The best known example of CL is the AECMA Simplified English, which has been adopted by the entire aerospace industry to write aircraft maintenance documentation. From an NLP point of view, the interest of CLs resides, evidently, in the conspicuous reduction of the difficulties proper to the syntactic/semantic analysis, which renders computationally conceivable particularly complex applications like mechanical translation and summarization .

6.   SUMMARY AND CONCLUSION

In this chapter, we have examined the Natural Language Processing (NLP) techniques that can be of some utility in an expert system (and, more generally, knowledge-based system) context. After a short historical introduction, we recalled the traditional differentiation of the NLP domain into morphological analysis, syntactic analysis, semantic analysis, discourse, and pragmatic analysis — even if this sort of distinction becomes sometimes blurred in modern systems (see, e.g., the dialog, and the Spoken Language Understanding systems), it is still particularly effective from a didactic point of view. For each of these subfields, we have analyzed quickly the most important techniques used, devoting some additional space to particularly "hot" topics like unification grammars in syntax and conceptual representation in semantics. A section mentioning some of the most promising trends in the NLP domain concludes the chapter.

The NLP domain has changed dramatically over recent years. Some, not necessarily trivial, commercial NLP products are now on the market, and it is easy to anticipate the fact that future ESs and KBSs will increasingly integrate components produced by the NLP technology. The success of pragmatically based applications such as extraction of information from texts or speech recognition systems has moved the focus from pure theoretical research, oriented toward the production of toy systems in very limited domains, to applied research largely motivated by industrial considerations, and oriented toward the construction of larger-scale NLP systems. Even if NLP still constitutes one of the more complex and difficult endeavors in computer science, the domain seems now sufficiently ripe to contribute to the establishment and to the consolidation of a concrete, sound, and human-friendly computer technology for the next millennium.

REFERENCES

Allen, J. (1987) *Natural Language Understanding*. Menlo Park (CA): Benjamin/Cummings.

Androutsopoulos, I., Ritchie, G.D., and Thanisch, P. (1995) "Natural Language Interfaces to Databases — An Introduction," *Natural Language Engineering*, 1, 29–81.

Carter, D. (1987) *Interpreting Anaphors in Natural Language Texts*. Chichester: Ellis Horwood.

Cowie, J., and Lehnert, W. (1996) "Information Extraction," *Communications of the ACM*, 39(1), 80-91.

Knight, K. (1989) "Unification: A Multidisciplinary Survey," *ACM Computing Surveys*, 21, 93–124.

Pereira, F.C.N., and Grosz, B.J., Eds. (1994) *Natural Language Processing*. Cambridge (MA): The MIT Press.

Shieber, S.M. (1992) *Constraint-Based Grammar Formalisms*. Cambridge (MA): The MIT Press.

Sowa, J.F. (1991) "Toward the Expressive Power of Natural Language," in *Principles of Semantic Networks*, Sowa, J.F., Ed. San Mateo (CA): Morgan Kaufmann.

Special Section on Interactive Natural Language Processing, 1996, Manaris, B.Z., and Slator, B.M., Eds., *IEEE Computer*, 29(7), 28–86.

Zarri, G.P. (1995) "Knowledge Acquisition from Complex Narrative Texts Using the NKRL Technology," in *Proceedings of the 9th Banff Knowledge Acquisition for Knowledge-Based Systems Workshop*, Vol. 1. Calgary: Department of Computer Science of the University.

Section B
Selected Expert Systems Applications

Part I
Engineering-Related Expert Systems

20 Power Industry

Odin Taylor, Peter Smith, John MacIntyre, and John Tait

CONTENTS

1. INTRODUCTION

The power industry has undergone continuous change ever since its beginnings in the late 19th century. From the early days when the industry consisted of numerous small companies, largely meeting local needs for lighting, industrial power, and public transport, the industry has evolved to become one of major importance to the world's economy.

Power generation is a large industry, with over 100,000 employees working at 20 different companies in the United Kingdom (U.K.) alone. The approximate turnover of the U.K. power generation sector is around £28 billion per year. Indeed, until recently, the industry accounted for some three quarters of the U.K. coal market, and about a third of the country's primary fuel consumption. Revenues from the industry amount to almost 2% of the national income. The price and security of the power supply is a key factor in the competitiveness of U.K. industry.

In recent times, the power industry has had to face the harsh competitive realities of a new marketplace, and look to all avenues for competitive advantage. Power generation companies are continually searching for means by which they can improve performance and cut costs, through efficiency, productivity, and plant availability. New and advanced technologies are playing an increasing role in the quest for continuous improvement and, among these technologies, the use of expert systems is rapidly growing in terms of research, development, and application.

This chapter will examine some applications of expert system technology within the power industry, the benefits offered by these systems, the problems encountered in development, and future trends for expert systems in the power generation field.

2. HISTORY OF EXPERT SYSTEMS WITHIN THE POWER INDUSTRY

One of the first areas where expert systems were utilized in the power industry was in the field of complex machine diagnostics. An early example was developed by Sakaguchi and Matsumo in 1983 (Sakaguchi and Matsumo, 1983). One of the next substantial systems was VIAD (Scheibel et al., 1986) which was later released commercially as EXPLORE-EX (a vibration advisor expert system) in 1990 by Entek Corporation. Later in 1990, AMETHYST appeared on the market and was, at the time, one of the most widely used expert systems for diagnosing problems with rotating machinery (Milne, 1990). Also in 1990, VARMINT (a vibration advisor for complex machinery) came onto the market. This was one of the first condition monitoring expert system to utilize the Microsoft Windows 3.0 interface (VARMINT, 1991). Table 1 gives a list of the major systems described in this chapter, with the year and continent in which they were developed.

The power industry has been, in general, slow to embrace Artificial Intelligence (AI). Expert systems have to some extent been investigated, and their use is growing; the U.K. Institute of

TABLE 1
Sample List of Systems

Authors	Year	Continent	Purpose
Sakaguchi and Matsumo	1983	Asia	Knowledge-based system for power system restoration
EPRI	1984	U.S.	SA-VANT: Start-up advisor for gas turbines
Scheibel et al.	1986	U.S.	VIAD: Vibration advisor expert system
Hajek et al.	1989	U.S.	Operator advisor for nuclear power plants
Entek Corporation	1990	U.S.	EXPLORE-EX: Rotating equipment vibration advisor
Goto et al.	1990	Asia	Expert system for operation and guidance systems
Milne	1990	Europe	AMETHYST: Rotating machinery condition monitoring
Milne	1991	Europe	VARMINT: Vibration analysis for rotating machinery internals
Siemens	1993	Europe	KNOBOS: Monitors the entire generation process
Jeong et al.	1994	U.S.	OASYS: Online operator aid system
Varga et al.	1994	Europe	CIDIM: Distributed AI system developed using ARCHON
Milne	1995	Europe	TIGER: Expert system for condition monitoring of gas turbines
MacIntyre et al.	1995	Europe	Neural system for condition monitoring of off-line plant
Bruel and Kjaer	1996	Europe	ADVISOR: Expert system to diagnose machinery problems
Leonard et al.	1996	Europe	Expert system for forecasting short term gas demand

Mechanical Engineers organized a seminar on this specific issue in November 1993; this seminar contained a number of presentations on the application of expert systems within the industry.

Most of these systems relate to the provision of diagnostic information to power plant control room operators, to assist them in the decision-making process. For example, Gemmell et al. (1993) discuss an expert system that provides diagnostic information on the cause of faults observed from plant data on turbine generators; Lausterer et al. (1993) discuss another expert system for provision of information to operators, and particularly the practical difficulties experienced in deploying the expert system in a power plant environment. A slightly different application, being used by Scottish Power, is the system used for cost and performance modeling in power generation, which uses a rule-based approach to plant simulation (Adams and MacDonald, 1993).

The level of use of AI techniques in the U.K. contrasts sharply with the power industry in the U.S., which is much more diverse, with many small private generating companies. There, the Electrical Power Research Institute (EPRI) has developed (and is continuing to develop) numerous advisory systems using expert system methods, and is actively investigating emerging AI techniques.

Clearly, the uptake of expert systems/knowledge based systems (KBS) in the power industry has increased considerably in recent years. Also, the use of other AI techniques, such as neural networks and hybrid systems, is becoming popular.

3. APPLICATIONS

Expert systems have been applied to various aspects of the power generation process, from diagnosing problems on steam turbines to monitoring and diagnosing problems in the entire generation process.

Many of the systems described in this chapter involve a form of machine condition monitoring. Condition monitoring is not a single technique, but in fact is an "umbrella" term used to describe a wide variety of different but complimentary techniques that can be used to determine machinery condition. Other terms such as "predictive maintenance," "condition-based maintenance," and "reliability-centered maintenance" have been used to describe the same principles. The purpose of implementing condition monitoring within an industrial plant is to move away from the maintenance strategies of breakdown maintenance (where machinery is repaired or replaced after breakdown) or planned maintenance (where maintenance work is carried out at regular intervals, whether or not it is actually required).

Condition monitoring, in simple terms, involves the capture of data that describes various parameters of machinery, and the analysis of these data to determine the condition of a given machine at a given point in time. Data analysis can be a complex process, often involving qualitative judgments made by experienced engineers who cannot always express fully the reasons for their interpretations; this presents a difficulty in the application of condition monitoring and an opportunity for the application of expert system technology.

Examples of systems are given in the sections that follow. The systems are categorized into their relevant areas of operation within the power generation process.

3.1. THE ENTIRE GENERATION PROCESS

3.1.1. KNOBOS

One real-time, predictive online expert system, developed in 1993 by Siemens of Germany to monitor and diagnose the overall power generation process was the Knowledge-Based Operator System (KNOBOS) (Lausterer et al., 1993). KNOBOS uses monitoring and diagnosis subsystems to examine instrumentation signals from machinery and uses these to determine if a deviation from a predetermined reference pattern is present. If a deviation does occur, the system will examine a set of predetermined variables and, if these exceed a certain threshold, it will then swap into a diagnostic state. If faults are identified, the system selectively informs the system operator of problems. This is done intelligently by the expert system so that false alarms are not triggered by small deviations from the norm.

When a problem is identified, KNOBOS informs the machine operator by displaying a message on the message board and highlighting the plant diagram, with the problem area shown in red. The system also provides suggestions about identified problems such as how to rectify it or prevent it from escalating into a critical problem. Along with the identified problems, and suggestions, KNOBOS also gives a detailed explanation of how it reached its conclusions.

KNOBOS was developed by knowledge engineers working with domain experts. After each knowledge acquisition session, the notes were transcribed and given to the domain expert for verification. This method proved to be time-consuming and error-prone, as errors and ambiguities were found within the knowledge. The KNOBOS system provides a built-in graphical knowledge acquisition tool that enables plant operators to update or change the system's knowledge base and plant structure models as time goes by.

KNOBOS represents knowledge by describing the entire plant process as a hierarchy with faults assigned to specific components. A structural model is used to model the plant, process components, and process media with a fault model representing the world of faults and symptoms.

3.1.2.   VIAD

VIAD is a VIbration ADvisor expert system developed by Scheibel et al. in 1989. Initial versions of VIAD worked offline, with later versions being fully automatic. VIAD's knowledge base consists of over 300 rules, 50% of which are generic. The system can use over 200 symptoms to identify over 50 possible causes of vibration problems and give a conclusion along with a confidence factor. The VIAD system can be used with various plant equipment, including centrifugal pumps, fans, steam turbines, centrifugal compressors, electric motors, and gearboxes.

The initial industry response to VIAD was favorable, as the system knowledge was good for examining vibration data. However, some users felt that VIAD might exceed the data analysis limitations of the average user. The developers decided to re-implement VIAD as a multilevel expert system, where the first level would examine an initial set of data for possible faults and the next two levels (level two and level three) would be used to give a more detailed diagnosis. The first level, level 1, is completely automatic with level 2 and level 3 requiring user interaction (see Figure 1).

LEVEL	FUNCTION
LEVEL 1	Requires information about the type of machine it is monitoring and the spectral data associated with that machine. From this information, it attempts to reach conclusions about possible causes of vibration problems.
LEVEL 2	Requires a dialog with the operator. Asks questions about recent maintenance work and current performance. New data are used to reinforce conclusions reached in level 1 or to redirect the user to other possible equipment faults.
LEVEL 3	Interactively recommends and considers additional information, such as types of measurements, that are not normally taken during the usual monitoring process.

FIGURE 1   The VIAD system.

A later version of VIAD was released by Entek Corporation as EXPLORE-EX and is still an important expert system application (Entek, 1992).

3.1.3.   ADVISOR

The ADVISOR system (Bruel and Kjaer, 1996) also uses expert system technology to perform automatic machine diagnosis. ADVISOR is an add-on package for COMPASS (COMputerized Prediction Analysis and Safety System). COMPASS is designed to monitor any process-related parameters and display an alarm if the signal exceeds a given threshold. However, this is only part of the automation process, as COMPASS does not identify what the problem is. ADVISOR runs in the background and performs a diagnosis with the available data, with a list of possible faults displayed on-screen, ranked in order by a weighting or likelihood value. The system also supplies a list of explanations that go with the identified faults. This also helps novice engineers gain more experience, thus acting as an intelligent tutor.

ADVISOR's knowledge base started out as general rules for vibration analysis, supplied by Bruel and Kjaer's own team of expert machine analysts. The knowledge base, when implemented at a site, can be tailored for a specific machine by taking into account the operator's knowledge of the machine and his/her experiences with any special cases. The system's basic rules can also be modified by the machine operator if they are insufficient or over-reactive in certain situations.

The effectiveness of ADVISOR was shown in a case study (Bruel and Kjaer, 1996):

"After an overhaul of a single stage turbine with a centrifugal compressor and inward-flow turbine, previously absent vibration levels became apparent at 128Hz and 192Hz."

The ADVISOR system examined the vibration data, looking at the vibration component of the middle shaft output gearwheel. This component showed an increase relative to the reference, thus indicating a misalignment of the middle shaft of the gearbox. Trending of the vibration data before and after the overhaul of the turbine showed that the increase in vibration started immediately after the start-up of the turbine. The tooth-meshing vibration frequency on the output shaft gearwheel also showed a slight increase in amplitude. This aided in confirming the fault to be a misalignment between the output and middle shaft, which caused a sliding toothmesh instead of a rolling toothmesh (Bruel and Kjaer, 1996).

3.1.4.   Forecasting Gas Demand

British Gas plc. buys gas from 40 different suppliers, with distribution controlled by various control centers around the different regions. Gas is acquired at a steady rate in order to avoid large fluctuations at the wellheads. However, customers do not use gas at a steady rate and a varying consumption can mean a fivefold increase in demand between the morning and the evening. This variation is controlled by the use of regional gas storage.

The gas company has to estimate how much gas is needed for the next day of service, and this estimation is used to order the gas before the next day (see Figure 2). One principal factor affecting the state of the demand for gas is the weather, as demand is high during the winter, especially if the winter is severe. In order to produce a good estimate, a good forecast for the future weather is needed. To aid in this task, the local Meteorological Offices for the regions send forecast data to the control centers in a standard format, which are used in the predictions. Inaccurate predictions will either produce a lower amount of gas than the demand, resulting in a shortage, or a higher amount than the demand, which will result in a waste of fuel.

Current forecasting systems vary from region to region. At the time of the study (Leonard et al., 1996), the northern region used a Box-Jenkins approach employing PASCAL software and

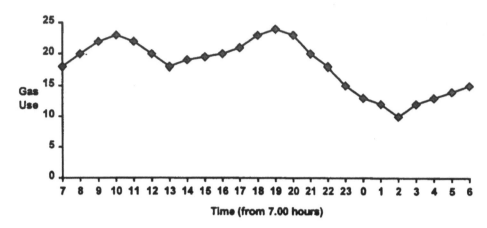

FIGURE 2 Weekday gas usage.

Lotus 1-2-3 spreadsheets, whereas other areas used databases to predict the next day's gas demand from historical data. Regression analysis methods were available in stand-alone software packages and macros within spreadsheets. However, no method was proven to be significantly better than the prediction obtained from an experienced Shift Control Officer (the domain expert).

At the time of the expert system development project, there were 72 expert forecasters spread geographically around the country in various regions. The experts worked different shift patterns and so could never be gathered in one place, even within a single region.

Knowledge acquisition was used in two stages: first to get an overall picture of the national problem of forecasting gas demand, and second, to improve the forecasting within the northern region. Knowledge acquisition for the national picture consisted of the use of structured interviews and questionnaires. Four regional grid control centers were visited, and the knowledge acquisition sessions used a questionnaire as the basis of the interview. Questions were asked in order but interviewees were allowed to digress from the question. Questionnaires were also sent to all of the regions, and the replies were used to establish what methods and data each region used in their forecasting procedures.

Knowledge acquisition for the northern region involved structured interviews, the card-sorting method, and the use of retrospective case descriptions. Structured interviews had two purposes; first, to explain the objectives of the expert system and, second, to discover each expert's individual technique in estimating the demand for gas. From the interviews it was established that all of the experts followed the same basic method in arriving at a forecast estimate.

From the knowledge acquisition sessions, a model was derived to estimate the gas delivery for the next day's demand. The actual expert system was built using the Crystal expert system shell with the aim of making it generic for use by each region and also giving it the ability to interface with other prediction tools.

The finished system was evaluated by a Shift Control Officer; after he had manually predicted the next day's gas forecast in his usual manner, he would then use the expert system to see what forecast it gave. The results showed that the expert system was more accurate in forecasting than the Shift Control Officer and also more accurate than any of the other forecasting tools (Leonard et al., 1996).

3.2. GAS TURBINE DIAGNOSTICS

Advanced gas turbines have offered substantial gains in firing temperatures, thermal efficiency, and electrical output. However, problems resulting in the shutdown of a gas turbine can be very serious, with disastrous safety, energy, and production cost implications. Gas turbines also have the feature of being able to start quickly, which makes them important for peak duty, i.e., to provide short-term power when there is a high demand. Failure to start on these turbines must be diagnosed quickly and efficiently (Milne, 1992; Armor et al., 1993).

Expert systems have been developed to monitor gas turbine performance and condition, and to determine when a fault is occurring in its early stages before an alarm or trip (an emergency shutdown of the turbine) is triggered. Alarms themselves do not provide any in-depth information about a problem, which means that engineers must diagnose the problem manually in detail to determine what caused the alarm.

3.2.1.   TIGER

Milne (1992) developed an online monitoring expert system for use with gas turbines that sample data every second. The initial system has two modes of operation, the first being online and the second a post-crash analysis.

The system provides the user with various information displays showing the current state of the turbine, including a turbine overview, real-time exhaust spread, a summary of current faults, a summary of current alarms, a history of past faults, trend displays, and displays showing data input in real-time. The system also provides facilities for the historical logging of data to disk for trending purposes.

The system is comprised of various subsystems: an interface to the turbine's instrumentation hardware, signal decoders for analog and digital signals, a 4-minute buffer of recent data (in case a crash occurs), a trending mechanism, and the interface to the expert system itself. The interface between the instrumentation hardware and the expert system is achieved by Intelligent Application's ANNIE package.

Diagnosis is broken up into three subareas:

- Alarm diagnostics
- Analog-related alarms
- Trip log and analysis

Alarm diagnostics consists of two major groups of alarms that can be diagnosed: normal operation and start-up alarms. The normal operation alarms are of primary importance as the system will be able to give a more precise diagnosis of why an alarm has triggered as (Milne, 1992):

"One of the common problems of alarm messages on gas turbines is that many possible things can go wrong all leading to the same alarm."

Analog-related diagnostics are used as a predictive maintenance strategy to detect a developing fault before it triggers an alarm or trip situation. This diagnostic method uses relatively simple comparisons of analog values to detect significant changes in the data.

Trip log and analysis are used when an alarm or trip situation occurs. Data in the system's 4-minute buffer are stored onto disk for later examination. These data samples can then be used to identify faults. Fault logs are also stored to disk in order to provide a history of problems that have occurred with the turbine.

At the time of its implementation in 1992, TIGER was the largest online expert system in regular use with a gas turbine. The system was developed for and used by Exxon Chemicals and was found to be very effective. By 1995, the system was being expanded as part of a European project: TIGER (ESPRIT 6862) (Milne, 1995). The developed application is still considered to be the most advanced software tool available for condition monitoring of gas turbines. The system runs constantly, sampling key operational parameters every second, and uses these data samples to perform a wide variety of examinations, including limit checking, dynamic response, and consistency checks using model-based predictions. The system also provides an extensive graphical user interface to relay information to the system operator, including extensive data trending facilities, which are user configurable, to allow the user to specify what data to sample and when.

The application has been in constant use by Exxon chemicals for over 2 years and has been instrumental in identifying many problems with the gas turbine that it was monitoring. Turbine sensor data are constantly sampled, via a link to instrumentation systems, and evaluated every second. The package can also be configured to connect to any serial link equipment or any real-time database over a network.

The latest version of the TIGER system consists of three individual diagnostic tools:

- KHEOPS
- IxTeT
- CA-EN

KHEOPS is a full-power, high-speed, rule-based system whose primary purpose is the limit checking of data. IxTeT is a powerful tool that has the capability to monitor the dynamic reaction of a gas turbine. This feature is unique to TIGER, in that no other condition monitoring system has this facility. The CA-EN tool is a model-based prediction and diagnosis system used for fault detection and the isolation of faulty components (Milne, 1995).

3.2.2. SA-VANT

In 1984, EPRI (the U.S. Electric Power Research Institute) started the SA-VANT project with the aim of initially studying the viability of expert system job aids for field use by maintenance engineers (Armor et al., 1993). First development models using expert system technology showed good results, with the system diagnosing problems in 25 minutes that normally took an hour for an expert technician. There were some problems that novice technicians could not solve without help, which only took them 26 minutes when they were aided by the system.

Due to the promising experiences with the early system, EPRI chose to use SA-VANT to aid technicians in diagnosing *failure to start-up* problems on large gas turbines. The initial reliability of the turbines was at a level of 85% or lower. Industry, however, set the required reliability to at least 95%. EPRI believed that, using its expert system, the 95% reliability level could be reached by avoiding aborted start-ups, which could possibly damage the engine and inflict costly delays at a critical time.

The knowledge base for SA-VANT was developed by gathering experts with knowledge on various different models of gas turbines, including utility "trouble shooters." The knowledge acquisition was done using a round-table format with leading technicians carefully going step-by-step through symptom-to-cause scenarios. EPRI also decided to include several multimedia concepts in the system, such as diagrams, video clips, and audio.

After development, the system was tested in the field to determine its effectiveness by a broad range of technicians ranging in experience from 6 months to 16 years. The use of SA-VANT resulted in a 25% decrease in time to diagnose a problem, with an 81% decrease in calls for assistance, and an 89% decrease in the number of aborted re-start attempts.

In the period from 1992 to 1995, the SA-VANT system was in use by Jersey Central Power & Light and has produced a savings of approximately $50,000, with a predicted 15-year (from 1992) savings of $235,361 (EPRI, 1996).

3.3. STEAM TURBINE DIAGNOSTICS

3.3.1. STES

The Steam Turbine Expert System (STES) (Armor, 1993) uses all available turbine monitoring information such as phase angle, temperature, shaft position, and vibration readings from various machine running states. Data samples are captured at a specific time interval and stored in a database that is then examined automatically by the expert system. The system extracts features from the data that might indicate a major flaw in the condition of a turbine and then examines these features in more detail for specific flaws as well as the associated cause. The system provides an in-depth diagnosis of any faults that it finds. Faults that can be examined include:

- Bowing
- Rubbing
- Misalignments
- Instabilities
- Mounting problems
- Oil whirl
- Rotor cracks

The system also has the facility to automatically schedule for repair after a diagnosis has been made.

The system was built with the GEN-X software package, with the knowledge base consisting of a collection of production rules and the inference mechanism using both forward and backward chaining. Probability values were assigned to a conclusion when a diagnosis was made. A separate subsystem was developed for the conversion of numerical readings into a symbolic form with which the expert system could manipulate and reason. The system also has a database that enables the operator to plot historical data, and an easy-to-use interface facilitates interaction between the expert system and the operator.

A large version of STES (called LSTES, Large Steam Turbine Expert System) was released; it had the capability to interface to a turbine's instrumentation and take readings online. The LSTES system also facilitates the use of a modem for remote access purposes, so that the system could be used off-site.

3.4. GENERATORS

3.4.1. GEMS

A system developed by EPRI for use with generators was GEMS (Generator Expert Monitoring System). Failures on generators are rare, but a severe failure of a major insulation or core can force an extended plant outage.

An effective monitoring system would provide the operator with early warning of developing generator faults, which would reduce the duration and frequency of generator down-time. The GEMS system interfaces with existing generator sensor equipment and provides operators with warnings of developing problems and recommends corrective action (Armor et al., 1993).

The knowledge base for GEMS consists of an extensive set of files put together by experts aimed at covering every possible occurrence of trouble within a generator. GEMS was originally developed as a rule-based system; however, subsequent application of causal networks revealed a number of advantages over the original confidence calculations. The causal networks also made the knowledge acquisition from domain experts easier as (Armor et al., 1993):

"The knowledge was easy to specify and modify for different generator designs and the resultant advice was sharper and more accurate in the simulated test cases."

GEMS works in four operation modes, with different data interpretation for each mode. The four operating modes are for different operational states of the turbines:

- Turning
- Run-up and coast-down
- Field applied
- Synchronized and loaded

The system can diagnose problems with stator winding, stator core and frame, rotor winding and body, bearings and lubrication oil, excitation, hydrogen cooling, stator cooling, and oil seals. The system also has an installation advisor that allows the machine operator to configure the expert system to a specific generator by including details of the generator, sensors, and the particular operating policies of the power generation company.

For field testing, prototype versions of GEMS were installed on a 500-MW Parsons generator at Ontario Hydro's Nanticoke station and on a 700-MW Westinghouse generator at Nigra Mohawk's Oswego station. During the testing phase, no major problems occurred on any of the machines; however, GEMS did manage to correctly diagnose minor problems at both locations.

3.4.2.   MICCA

Another EPRI developed expert system is MICCA (Machine Insulation Condition Assessment Advisor) which was designed for use with motor and generator insulation systems. The cost of critical failure of such a system is estimated to be in the region of $250,000. A survey of approximately 7,500 large motors in power generation facilities revealed that 37% of failures were due to stator winding problems and that an additional 10% of failures were due to rotor winding problems.

The MICCA system relies heavily on user interaction, with a menu-based interface and an extensive context sensitive help that describes technical terms and explains about 50 tests and inspections.

The knowledge base contains over 50 separate databases, including information on each major motor and generator insulation system, the most probable aging mechanism of these systems, and diagnostic and inspection tests for confirming or rejecting the operation of a particular aging mechanism. MICCA uses information from these databases to deduce the most likely aging process occurring within the stator and rotor windings and recommends diagnostic tests to indicate what the operator or engineer should look for in a visual inspection and how to interpret the results of these inspections.

The results from the visual inspections are inputted into the MICCA system by the use of multiple choice questions. Results from the visual inspection are used to reinforce conclusions or re-direct diagnostics to another area.

3.5.   THE NUCLEAR POWER INDUSTRY

Perhaps one of the most critical processes in the entire field of power generation is that of generating electricity with nuclear reactors. Although human operators are well trusted and are well-trained to cope with an emergency, they are not infallible, and the possible outcome of a human error could be very costly, as was demonstrated in Russia on the night of 26th April 1986. Chernobyl was the worst nuclear accident of all time, with low safety standards, ill-designed safety tests and poor construction standards all contributing to the disaster. Read (1993) in his book, describes the courage, panic and terror of the fateful night:

> "Scientists and technicians — who thought at first the war had broken out — streamed along corridors in the dark as their instruments failed. They heaved at twisted metal doors to reach the control rods and put their hands into radioactive pools to turn safety valves. They slung injured colleagues over their shoulders as they fled for the exits, even though the radioactivity from their contaminated clothing burned deep sores into their flesh. Thirty-one people died immediately or within days. They watched their own bodies rot, their intestines dissolve and the skin on their legs fall down like loose socks."

The disaster left severe contamination to thousands of acres of farmland in Belarus, the Ukraine, and Russia as well as thousands of people being exposed to extremely high levels of radiation. Europe was also affected; for instance in Britain 400,000 acres of land and millions of sheep were contaminated by the radiation cloud that passed over on 3rd May and 4th May 1986. As a result 4.2 million sheep were slaughtered and to this day there are still restrictions on the use of some farm land.

The after effects of Chernobyl overshadow the rest of the world's nuclear power industries, with heightened public concern about safety of these power stations. Could the use of expert system and artificial intelligence products help relieve some of the public worries and prevent another Chernobyl from happening?

Their are two main types of reactor within the industry namely: Boiling Water Reactors (BWR) and Pressurised Water Reactors (PWR). A boiling water reactor works by boiling its cooling water to produce steam, which is then used to drive a turbo-generator unit. However, since the water has been in close proximity to the reactor, it will be itself radioactive, which in turn means that the turbo-generator must now be classified as a radioactive piece of machinery and the required safety or emergency procedures must be applied to it. It should also be noted that different sensors and wiring setups will be needed to connect monitoring equipment to the radioactive piece of machinery.

A pressurized water reactor works on the same principal as the boiling water reactor, only this time the cooling water is not allowed to boil. The cooling water gets extremely hot, and is used to heat water in pipes, which is allowed to boil, produce steam and drive a turbo-generator. The steam driving the turbo-generator on this type of reactor is not radioactive and can be handled as such. It should also be noted that there are also many different variations of both the boiling and pressurised water reactors.

Beck et al. (1992) note some points that future expert system or any other software developers should note when attempting to develop systems for the nuclear power industry. Most components within a nuclear power plant are Safety Rated (SR); this means that the component designer must have considered the major "what-if" scenarios to ensure that the component is safe from Design-Based Accidents (DBA) or Design-Based Events (DBE). An expert system which monitors (or even controls) a safety rated component should itself be safety rated.

Control rooms of nuclear facilities present their operators with thousands of switches, lights, meters, recorders and alarm windows, and most of this data must be presented to an expert system in some way. This is no trivial task when you consider the sheer number of sensors, the difference in signal types (which may also need converting into a symbolic form) and that interference may occur between Safety Rated and Non Safety Rated Equipment.

Beck et al. (1992) also notes that nuclear facilities hold a wealth of information in the form of diagrams, procedures and plans, but the greatest wealth of information comes from the expertise of engineers, technicians and operators who work there. Sun et al. (1989) tell us that:

> "Expertise is a kind of intellectual capital which represents a substantial portion of the electric industry's worth."

Other points raised by Beck are:

- Expert systems should be able to cope with the prospect of multiple failures occurring
- Expert systems should be able to model reactor physics
- Expert systems should contain knowledge about site operating licenses and regulations
- Contradictory sensor readings should be identified in order to prevent errors from occurring

3.5.1. Systems Developed by EPRI

Nuclear facilities face the same competitive problems as other types of generating facilities and must also enhance power generation and increase productivity while also increasing the safety of the plant. To help accomplish these goals, EPRI have been using expert system technology for many years within the power generation field and believe that this technology can be safely put to use in their nuclear facilities (Sun et al., 1989).

One system developed using the commercial toolkit, Knowledge Engineering Environment (KEE) was PLEXSYS (PLant EXpert SYStem) which allows the facility operator to represent a plant schematically in the form of CAD drawings. Knowledge bases can be associated with the drawings, so that the expert system can automate the problem solving tasks associated with modifications to the plant.

The Emergency Operating Procedures Tracking System (EOPTS) is another EPRI development using a custom made inference engine and knowledge representation schema to interpret and compile Emergency Operating Procedure logic. The result is a fast running software module that interfaces to and is co-resident with the nuclear plant's Safety Parameter Display System.

A planning application that EPRI have implemented is the Refueling Insert Shuffle Planner (RISP) which determines an efficient crane moving pattern for the fuel insert shuffle of nuclear reactors. The application, based on KEE, does not find the optimal solution as this would be far too time consuming, but instead uses heuristics to find a number of efficient solutions.

3.5.2. OASYS (On-Line Operator Aid System)

OASYS was developed as an on-line advisory system to nuclear plant operators (Jeong et al., 1994). OASYS is an integrated system with four modules (see Figure 3):

- When the nuclear power plant is in a normal condition state, it maintains the system condition to prevent an abnormal state from occurring
- If the nuclear power plant is in an abnormal state, it prevents the reactor from tripping by using alarm processing and failure diagnosis
- If the reactor is tripped, it achieves early and safe plant shut-down by employing the emergency operating procedures

3.5.3. Modular Real-Time Operator Advisor Expert System

Another expert system developed by Hajek et al. (1989) was the Operator Advisor Expert System. The knowledge engineers working on the project identified four tasks that nuclear power plant operators carry out:

- Monitor and comprehend the state of the plant
- Identify normal and abnormal plant conditions
- Diagnose abnormal conditions
- Predict plant response to specific control actions they plan to take in response to diagnosed abnormal condition

Module	Function
Signal validation	Ensures that the readings from the nuclear plant are correct
Alarm processing	Grades alarms into a hierarchy
Diagnosis	Determines problems before a reactor trip occurs
Dynamic emergency procedure tracking	Manages emergency response guidelines, including optimal recovery guidelines and function restoration guidelines

FIGURE 3   Modules in OASYS.

If a fault is detected the system evaluates the fault as either a Emergency Operating Procedure (EOP), Abnormal Operating Procedure (AOP) or an Alarm Response procedure (ARP). The system then gives the steps that are needed to rectify the fault in accordance to the industry accepted Emergency Procedure Guidelines (EPGs). The systems monitors the operators' progress as the emergency procedures are executed and provides backup steps should an emergency step fail.

3.5.4.   Plant Operation and Guidance System

Plant automation is widely used in Japan with nearly all of the generating components such as turbines, feedwater pumps, and generators being controlled by computer. As a result of the large level of automation it is important that the nuclear plant operator receives direct and unambiguous messages about the state of the components.

Expert systems are used to ensure that plant functions are performed in a safe and reliable manner. Incorporation of expert systems into the nuclear plant's operation and guidance systems is difficult to accomplish with a traditional shell. To accomplish this task Goto et al. (1990) developed a domain-specific expert system shell with the specific aims of enhancing plant safety, increasing plant reliability, enhancement of operational flexibility and efficiency, and reduced operator workload.

The system uses a knowledge representation structure that was specifically designed for this problem, called Plant Tables (PT). A PT consists of a section describing plant conditions with multiple inputs and one output, and a large number of operation inputs for several plant conditions; divided into timing conditions, pre-conditions and completion conditions.

Using their new expert system shell Goto et al. developed a nuclear power plant operation and guidance system. The knowledge base was constructed by using the knowledge from multiple domain experts, including nuclear plant operators, startup test engineers, automatic control design engineers and plant characteristic analysis engineers. Knowledge was also gained from analysing plant manuals, operational data, design specifications, design drawings and plant dynamic characteristics.

The inference engine uses both forward and backward chaining, and checks alarms and control limits against a Monitoring Control Table. The system provides various outputs to the operator including screen, voice announcement, warning lights and graphical displays. The system has already been supplied to five Japanese boiling water reactor type plants and automates the following systems: reactor pressure control, main turbo-generator control, reactor feedwater transfer control and reactor power control.

3.5.5.   The French Experience — Expert Training System (SEPIA)

Expert systems have also proved to be useful for training; particularly when incorporated within a fully functional simulator. In 1987 the French built a combined expert system and simulator (International Power Generation, 1991), for training operators to react to plant malfunctions or breakdowns and deal with them quickly before a major catastrophe occurred. One of the first problems to be modeled with the simulator was steam generator tube failure. The simulator mimics

Message	
Error 1	Action forbidden by the procedure
Error 2	Action required by the procedure has been omitted
Error 3	Action was carried out too late or too early
Error 4	Action was too strong or too weak

FIGURE 4   Output of sepia.

the actions and responses of the nuclear plant's main components and variations in parameters can be simulated very realistically. The results from the simulator have been checked against Electiricité De France (EDF) reference codes.

Normal staff training is a two stage process. The first stage involves the operator using the simulator and experiencing various different accident scenarios, with all data from the simulator, including the operator's responses being recorded. The second stage involves a highly skilled technician manually going through the simulation replay step by step and commenting on the operator's performance.

The expert system, which is called SEPIA (a French acronym for Training system using Artificial Intelligence), and the simulator run on SUN workstations. SEPIA uses artificial intelligence, an investigation model and a model of the instructions and how they should be applied. All of these systems are controlled by an expert system with a knowledge base containing over 1,000 rules and over 2,000 objects. The SEPIA systems offers a range of powerful functions:

- It analyzes event sequences, whether automatic or triggered by operators, and checks that the appropriate procedure is applied
- It displays curves of variations over time
- It explains complex thermohydraulic phenomena
- It provides theoretical lessons illustrated by examples drawn from the simulation exercise

SEPIA takes the place of a highly skilled technician instructor, and exhaustively analyses an operator's performance during a simulated exercise. SEPIA goes through the simulation step by step and generates error messages, as shown in Figure 4.

4.   RESEARCH ISSUES AND FUTURE TRENDS

Expert systems have made some important advances in the area of complex machine diagnostics. However, large complex machines each have their own individuality and conventional expert system technology may not be flexible enough to model the entire problem. For this reason, researchers have in recent years been experimenting with other AI technologies. The most important of these are discussed in this section.

4.1.   NEURAL NETWORKS

Neural networks are being used in the field of complex machine diagnostics as they have the ability to learn a machine's operating characteristics. Bruel and Kjaer (1996) believe that neural technology must be used as it has the ability to "learn by input of data about its surrounding environment". One European EUREKA project, NEURAL-MAINE (EUREKA project 1250), (Harris et al., 1995)

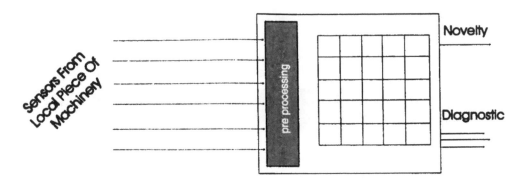

FIGURE 5   Local fusion system.

aims to advance the technology available for complex machine diagnostics by the use of multiple sensor technology, data fusion and neural networks.

The NEURAL-MAINE system is currently under development by the project consortium. It will compromise a number of neural network based 'local fusion systems' and an 'overseer' system. The local fusion systems will 'represent' one part of a complex machine, for example a bearing. Each part of a machine will have its own local fusion system. Thus a turbine with twelve bearings will have twelve local fusion systems. The local fusion system will be responsible for taking all of the sensor data (of varying types) and fusing it into one model, which represents the piece of machinery for that specific time slice, as shown in Figure 5. The fused data model will be then passed to the neural network which will evaluate it as being normal or unique (novelty). If the data are different then the local fusion system will flag that a 'novelty' situation has occurred, and allow a more complex diagnosis to continue at the local level.

The overseer system will sit above the local fusion systems, and take as input the output from the local fusion systems and also other machinery operating parameters, as shown in Figure 6. The NEURAL-MAINE consortium identify the following objectives for the overseer system:

- It should alert plant operators to any problem well in advance of any failure event.
- It should continually monitor the outputs of the local fusion systems, and perform higher level data fusion with running parameters and other data.
- It should perform whole plant diagnostics, based on a more complex version of the local fusion system.

To accomplish this, the overseer will work in two modes - firstly as a novelty detection system and secondly as a diagnostic aid.

4.2.   DISTRIBUTED ARTIFICIAL INTELLIGENCE

Another new field that is starting to take shape is that of Distributed Artificial Intelligence systems (DAI). DAI uses the approach that a large problem can be separated up into specific areas where "agents" can perform specific intelligence-related tasks. The agents have the ability to control their own problem solving and communicate with each other. Interactions between agents usually involve cooperation and communication with each other with the aim of "enhancing their individual problem solving and to better solve the overall application problem" (Jennings, 1994).

ARCHON (ARchitecture for Cooperative Heterogeneous ON-line systems) was Europe's largest project in the area of Distributed Artificial Intelligence (DAI) (Huhns, 1994). The project resulted in the development of a general-purpose architecture, software framework and methodology which

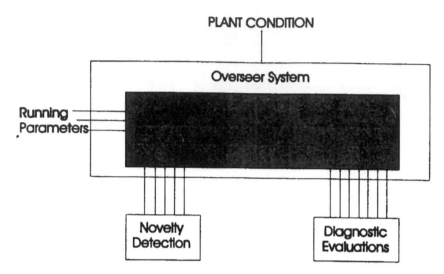

FIGURE 6   Overseer system.

has been used to support the development of a number of DAI systems in a number of real world industrial environments including the power generation industry, control of a cement kiln, control of a particle accelerator and control of robotic equipment.

ARCHON provides a decentralised software framework for creating Distributed AI (DAI) systems for industrial applications and provides a methodology which can offer guidance on how to decompose an application to best fit with the ARCHON approach.

One application that was created using the ARCHON architecture is CIDIM (Huhns, 1994). CIDIM provides an intelligent aid to Control Engineers (CE) whose task is to ensure that there is a constant electric supply to customers (Varga et al., 1994). The control engineer's main tasks are to carry out maintenance work safely with the cooperation of field engineers, to identify faults on the power network and to carry out restoration to provide continuous electricity supply.

The control engineer uses an electric network control system which allows remote operation of circuit breakers across the network and reports any automatic switch operation that occurs in response to a fault. The system also displays alarms and provides the engineer with various other pieces of information such as load readings. The system covers the High-Voltage Network (HVN) and has partial coverage of the Low-Voltage Network (LVN). The rest of the switching operations for the LVN are done manually by the field engineer who is in contact with the control engineer.

CIDIM provides fault diagnosis, lightning detection, user-driven restoration planning and automatic re-checking of restoration plans. The main advantage of CIDIM is that it automatically collates the information which previously the control engineer had to manually acquire and integrate from several separate stand-alone systems.

The CIDIM systems consists of seven agents, with the ARCHON architecture helping to share information between agents which results in a greater consistency across the application (see Figure 7).

4.3.   HYBRID SYSTEMS

One example of a hybrid system is that developed by MacIntyre et al. for National Power's Blyth Power Station, U.K. (MacIntyre et al., 1995). As part of an ongoing project at Blyth, several software systems have been developed for the analysis of vibration spectra from the Primary Air Fan bearings. However, the most successful application has been a hybrid system which uses an expert system

No.	Agent	Function
1	Telemetry agent	Receives telemetry and converts it into a standard format
2	Information agent (IA)	Contains information about the physical network
3	Weather watcher agent	Knows about the time and location of lightning strikes
4	High voltage diagnosis agent	Uses telemetry to diagnose the location, time and type of fault
5	Low voltage diagnosis	Takes into account customer information, lightning information and telemetry to diagnose faults
6	Switch planning agent	Allows the user to plan maintenance work
7	Advisor agent	Acts as the interface between the system and the user

FIGURE 7 The seven agents in CIDIM.

rule base, along with numerical techniques, to pre-process vibration data in order to produce a reduced input vector for presentation to a neural network.

The neural networks used within the hybrid system are based on the Multi-Layer Perceptron (MLP) architecture, using the back propagation training algorithm. The use of back propagation allows the adjustment of weights in the neural connections in multiple layers; this is critical if a network is to solve non-linearly separable problems. The MLP architecture using back propagation relies on a technique referred to as "supervised training," in which an input vector (that is, a numerical representation of the input pattern, in vector form) is presented to the neural network along with a target output vector (a numerical representation of the desired output for the given input, again in vector form). The importance of producing the best input vector is paramount; it is for this reason that expert systems are used along with numerical techniques to ensure that this occurs. Similarly, expert systems are used to interpret the output of the system.

The actual output is compared to the target output for each input vector, and the root mean squared (RMS) error is calculated. This error is then propagated backwards through the neural connections, and the process is repeated until the RMS error is within an acceptable threshold.

The heart of the system is the Neural Bearing Analyzer (NBA) model. This model was developed initially taking only certain areas of the vibration spectrum as the input vector, selected by the use of an expert system. The network had a relatively large output set, with separate classes for each of the bearing components, and different levels of defect severity. This version of the network demonstrated the difficulties of back propagation in achieving convergence to within an acceptable RMS error level. To achieve convergence it was necessary to alter the learning parameters in order to avoid the algorithm sticking in local minima. Convergence was eventually achieved, and in testing the network produced 93% agreement with a consultant diagnostic engineer's classifications.

A different approach involved presentation of the full vibration spectrum (400 datu points) to the network, and a simplified output set, with condition estimates for the bearing as a whole. In both cases, training data sets were constructed from real data collected from Station machinery, where the target output could be confidently generated as a result of known bearing condition due to inspection or replacement of bearings. Testing of the models was performed both with real data acquired from the Primary Air Fans, some of which had known conditions from inspection, and

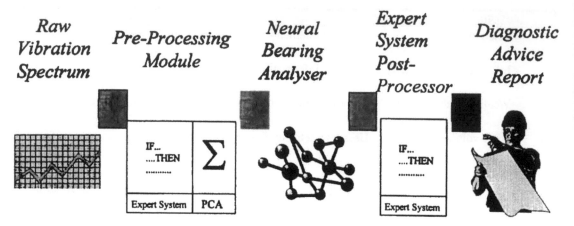

FIGURE 8   The hybrid system.

also with artificially-generated data to examine the network's performance in identifying particular defect types. The network's classifications were compared with known condition data, and also with the classifications of the consultant engineer. This model proved much more difficult to train effectively. Convergence was only achieved after raising the RMS threshold to 0.01, and much "tweaking" of the learning parameters. Running on a 33Mhz 486 PC, the network took almost 1.5 hours to train, using over 100,000 training iterations. In training, this version of the network performed less well than the first, with only 81% agreement in classifications.

These models have been further developed and refined, in the areas of selection of the input parameters, and the formulation of the output classes. The use of all 400 points in a vibration spectrum presents difficulties due to file sizes and can be slow; furthermore, it is apparent that a substantial part of this information is redundant in terms of performing the classification task. In order to reduce the dimensionality of the problem, the numerical technique of Principal Components Analysis (PCA) has been used to determine which, if any, variables should be added to those selected by the expert system approach as the necessary inputs to the network. A diagram of the system is shown in Figure 8.

5.   SUMMARY

This chapter has presented an overview of the applications of expert systems and related technology in the power industry. There is clearly a lot of activity in this area. The authors believe that this work will continue, and that, in particular, the field of hybrid systems will receive increased attention in the future.

The major research issues to be addressed in the future will focus around how hybrid technology can best be utilized to more closely model power systems. The systems in use in power generation are extremely complex, so any improvement in modeling capability will represent a great advance. Future hybrid systems will integrate AI, neural, and simulation technology. It is also vital to find a way to fully validate the complex software systems that will result.

REFERENCES

Adams, D. and MacDonald, D., "A cost and performance modelling system for power generators," *Proceedings of Seminar on Applications of Expert Systems in the Power Industry,* Institute of Mechanical Engineers Headquarters, London, November, 1993.

Armor A.F., Divakaruni S.M., and Pflasterer G.R., "Computerized knowledge-based systems for fossil plant productivity," *The Application of Expert Systems in the Power Generation Industry,* pp. 1–16, 1993.

Beck C.E., Behera A.K. and Reed M.L., "Expert system applications in nuclear plants: discussion of the key issues," *IEEE Transactions on Nuclear Science,* Vol. 39, No. 5, October 1992.

Bruel and Kjaer, "ADVISOR," Euromaintenance 1996, *The 13th European Maintenance Conference and Fair,* May 21–23, pp. 401–410, 1996.

Entek, "EXPLORE-EX rotating equipment vibration advisory software," Product Information, 1992.

EPRI, "Gas Turbine Startup Advisor helps JCP&L avoid costly failures," EPRI Electronic Editions, 1996.

Gemmell et al., "A Consultative Expert System for Fault Diagnosis of Turbine-Generator Plant," *Proceedings of Seminar on Applications of Expert Systems in the Power Industry,* Institute of Mechanical Engineers Headquarters, London, November, 1993.

Goto M. and Takada Y., "Application of expert system to nuclear power plant operation and guidance system," *Artificial Intelligence in Nuclear Power Plants, UTT Symposium 109–110,* pg. 185–196, 1990.

Hajek B.K., Miller D.W., Bhatnagar R., and Maresh J.L., "A modular real time operator advisor expert system for installation on a full function nuclear power plant simulator," *Proceedings of the 7th Power Plant Dynamics Control & Testings Symposium,* Vol. 1, 1989.

Harris, T. et al., "Neural-Maine': intelligent on-line multiple sensor diagnostics for complex machinery," *8th International Congress on Condition Monitoring and Diagnostic Engineering Management (COMADEM 95),* Kingston, Ontario, Canada, 1995.

Huhns M.N., "A DAI perspective on cooperating knowledge-based systems," *Proceedings of Second International Working Conference on Cooperating Knowledge Based Systems,* University of Keele, June, 1994.

International Power Generation, "The French experience," *International Power Generation,* September, Vol. 14, pg. 72–75, 1991.

Jennings, A., *International Conference on Co-operating Knowledge Based Systems,* Dean, S.M. (Ed.), 1994.

Jeong H.K., Yi C.U., Kang K.S., Choi S.S., Kim H.G., and Chang S.H., "Artificial intelligence in nuclear science engineering," *Transactions of the American Nuclear Society,* ISSN 0003018X, 1994.

Lausterer G.K., Klinger-Reinhold R. and Seibert E., "A knowledge based operator system — concepts, knowledge acquisition, and practical experience," *The Application of Expert Systems in the Power Generation Industry,* 1993.

Leonard D.T., Smith P. and Husein S., "Forecasting short term regional gas demand using an expert system," *Expert Systems with Applications,* Vol. 10, No. 2, pp. 265–273, 1996

MacIntyre J. et al., "Application of hybrid systems in the power industry," in *Intelligent Hybrid Systems,* Larry Medsker (Ed.), Kluwer Academic, 1995.

Milne R., "AMETHYST: Rotating Machinery Condition Monitoring," *Proceedings of AAAI 90,* Washington, D.C., 1990.

Milne R., "On-Line Diagnostic Expert System for Gas Turbines," *12th Annual Conference of the British Computer Society Specialist Group on Expert Systems, Proceedings of the Applications Track,* 1992.

Milne R., "TIGER: knowledge based gas turbine condition monitoring", Applications and Innovations in Expert Systems, *Proceedings of the Expert Systems'95 Conference,* Ed. Macintosh A. and Cooper C., Published by SGES Publications, pp. 23-43, 1995.

Moyes A., Burt G.M., McDonald J.R., Capener J.R., Dray J. and Goodfellow R., "An intelligent system for fault diagnosis of generator support systems," COMADEM 95, *Proceedings of the 8th International Congress on Condition Monitoring and Diagnostic Engineering,* Vol. 2, 1995.

Read P.P., *The Story Of Chernobyl,* Secker & Warburg, 1993.

Sakaguchi T. and Matsumo K., "Development of a knowledge based system for power system restoration," *IEEE Trans.* PAS-201 (2), pp. 320–326, 1983.

Schiebel J.R. et al., "VIAD Expert System for Vibration Monitoring," American Power Conference, 1989.

Sun B.K., Naser J.A., and Sudduth A., "Applications of expert systems technology in nuclear power plants — an industry perspective," *Proceedings of the American Power Conference,* 1989.

Varga L., Jennings N.R., and Cockburn D., "Integrating Intelligent Systems into a Cooperating Community for Electricity Distribution Management," *Expert Systems with Application,* No. 7, 1994.

VARMINT, "VARMINT: Vibration Analysis for Rotating Machinery Internals," Product information, June, 1991.

21 Configuration Design: An Overview

Timothy P. Darr and Clive L. Dym

CONTENTS

1. INTRODUCTION

In addition to being the central activity of engineering, design is also a central issue in artificial intelligence research. Indeed, recent advances in the field of artificial intelligence (AI), particularly symbolic representation and related problem-solving methods, including knowledge-based (expert) systems, have provided significant opportunities to clarify and articulate concepts of design so as to lay a better framework for design research and design education (Dym and Levitt, 1991; Dym, 1994). Inasmuch as there is within AI a substantial body of material concerned with understanding and modeling cognitive processes, and since the level of articulation in this work transcends in many ways the common vocabulary of engineering design, we here adapt and appropriate some of the vocabulary and paradigms of AI to enhance our understanding of configuration design.

Designs can be characterized as falling into one of three broad classes: *creative*, the rarest, in which case completely new products are found; *variant*, wherein we understand the sources of design knowledge quite well, but we are not entirely sure how that design knowledge should be applied; and *routine*, for which we know exactly how to complete a design. *Configuration selection* refers to the task of assembling or organizing a known set of parts into a specified architecture, and it would be considered as routine. However, configuration selection problems may present significant challenges because the search space can be quite large if there are many feasible combinations of large numbers of parts. The pioneering R1/XCON system for configuring VAX computer systems for assembly incorporated just such a configuration selection task (McDermott, 1981).

The completion of *configuration design* tasks requires that a known set of parts be fit within an architecture that has not been specified in advance. As a result, the architecture and some parts have to be designed as part of the organization process. There may be a large number of design parameters, and there may be significant spatial reasoning issues that need to be addressed during the configuration of the architecture. The PRIDE system for the design of paper paths in copier systems is considered the pioneering complex configuration design system (Mittal, Dym, et al., 1986).

Many configuration selection and design systems have been built and described in the last 15 years because the tasks they encapsulate are important in both engineering design and manufacturing. Reviews of such systems can be found in Dym and Levitt, 1991; Dym, 1994; and Darr, 1996.

2.   BACKGROUND

Configuration design problems are generally *exponentially complex*, that is, they suffer from a combinatorial explosion of parts and their possible interactions. Parts have *ports* that limit the ways they can be connected or interact, which reduces the problem combinatorics. In addition, *functional decompositions* are used to identify one-to-one mappings from parts to the functions they perform in the design. Functional decompositions reduce the combinatorics by limiting candidate parts to those that implement low-level functions, thus reducing the allowable combinations of parts. The sum total of the individual low-level functions implemented by the parts in the configuration is the functionality desired of the complete designed artifact by the user.

A variety of techniques have been developed to manage the complexity of configuration design. In early work, the problem was viewed as the selection of given parts from parts libraries that would be properly combined to obtain the functionality specified by their use, satisfy constraints, and achieve optimality goals (Mittal and Frayman, 1989).

Early design applications include: paper-handling system design (Mittal, Dym, et al., 1986), elevator design (Marcus, Stout, et al., 1988), and computer design (Birmingham, Gupta, et al., 1992). The most common technique utilized in these early systems was a *centralized system* that maps functions into parts that perform those functions. Configurations are then formed by selecting parts to implement functions, and the design is then extended by eliminating the remaining choices according to: (1) the functions that have already been implemented, (2) the allowed connectivity of the configuration, (3) design constraints, and (4) optimality criteria.

Now, when parts implement more than one function, termed the *multifunction part problem*, configuration design is further complicated. Similarly, when parts require additional functions for their correct operation — the *support-function problem* — additional complications ensue. In both cases, the increased complexity results from the need to consider the topology of the selected parts in solving the problem. In multifunction part problems, parts can implement more than one function (Mittal and Frayman, 1989; Haworth, Birmingham et al., 1993), so a designer must take into account two major issues when selecting a set of parts to achieve the functionality desired by the user: minimizing the number of extraneous or redundant functions implemented by the selected parts, and minimizing the number of selected parts. Minimizing the number of extraneous or redundant functions eliminates waste, since all the functions implemented by a part are used. Minimizing the number of selected parts tends to minimize performance attributes of the final solution (e.g., cost, power consumption, area, weight) because multifunction parts tend to behave better than a set of single-function parts that implement the same functions (e.g., cost less, consume less power, etc.). The *GOPS algorithm* solves the multifunction part problem optimally in a centralized, *nondistributed* way (Haworth, Birmingham, et al., 1993).

Support functions are functions that are required for the correct operation of a part (Mittal and Frayman, 1989; Gupta, Birmingham, et al., 1993; Haworth, Birmingham, et al., 1993). These functions are needed in addition to the original functions specified by the designer. With support

TABLE 1
Multifunction Part/Support Parts

Name of part	Cost ($)	Power (W)	Function(s)
80186	20.0	3.0	CPU, timer, address-decoder, interrupt-controller
8086	10.0	2.5	CPU
8259A	3.0	0.425	Interrupt-controller
PAL18P8L	3.0	0.05	Address-decoder
PAL18P8B	3.12	0.05	Address-decoder
PAL18P8A	3.02	0.05	Address-decoder
8254A5	4.95	1.0	Timer

functions, a designer must keep track of which functions are needed at any point in the design process, based on the current set of selected parts.

Table 1 illustrates the multifunction part problem. In this table, each part has a cost, consumes a certain amount of power, and implements one or more functions. Suppose that parts must be selected to implement the functions CPU, Timer, Address-decoder, and Interrupt-controller, and that the designer wants to minimize cost and power consumption. In this case, the part 80186 is preferred since it implements all the desired functions, costs less ($20), and consumes less power (3.0 W) than any other selection of parts that implement the desired functions. For example, the set {8086, 8259A, PAL18P8L, 8254A5}, which costs $20.95 and consumes 3.975 W.

This example also illustrates the support-function problem. The part 8086 that implements the CPU function cannot be selected by itself since it requires the support function Timer, among others, to operate correctly. Thus, when the 8086 is selected a number of other parts must be selected, as well, which tends to increase the cost and power consumed by the final design.

The availability of computer networks has resulted in a number of systems for solving design problems in a *distributed* or *collaborative* way. We divide these systems into two categories:

- *Shared-memory systems* use a shared, global representation of the design. Access to the design is strictly controlled, with *design agents* using their knowledge to modify the design when given access.
- *Non-shared memory systems* do not use a shared, global representation of the design, but sequentially pass portions of the design from agent to agent, with each agent modifying it and passing it to the next agent.

Shared-memory systems offer varying levels of automation, often depending on whether human agents (i.e., users) participate in the design. They also differ in the degree of support for notifying other agents of design conflicts such as constraint violations, and in the amount of support provided for resolving such conflicts. Those shared-memory systems that are the least automated and provide the least computational support tend to give designers access to design information through *electronic notebooks* that contain records of previous and current designs.

By far, the most common shared-memory system is based on the *blackboard paradigm* in which the evolving design is stored in a shared, global blackboard. Access to the blackboard is controlled by an *agenda* that allows agents to opportunistically modify, extend, or critique a design, as their particular knowledge is relevant to the evolving design.

Figure 1 shows an example shared-memory/blackboard system. In this example, there are three *partial designs* (P-D$_1$, P-D$_2$, P-D$_3$) and four agents (A$_1$, A$_2$, A$_3$, A$_4$). Each agent can act on any of

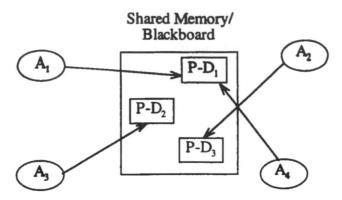

FIGURE 1   Shared-memory system.

the partial designs at a given time by evaluating the design, adding to it, extending it, or creating a new design. If a design is generated that all agents find acceptable, then that design is stored as *a complete design*. After a certain amount of time, the design process stops and one of the complete designs is selected as the final product.

Inasmuch as constraints often drive unfolding designs, work has focused on developing constraint-based languages that facilitate access to a shared design by allowing designers to define their perspectives in terms of *design constraints* and *design attributes*. Galileo is such a constraint-based language (Bowen and Bahler, 1992). Constraint-based perspectives define communication links among design-team members who are interested in the same set of attributes. Thus, when one design-team member changes the value of an attribute, all team members who expressed an interest in that that attribute are notified of the change. If a conflict results, the interested team members are notified so that they can resolve the conflict.

Nonshared memory systems have no shared memory that agents access. Rather, complete designs or portions of a complete design are passed from agent to agent, using some agreed-upon communication protocol. One example of this class of system is the ParMan parametric-design assistant (Kuokka and Livezey, 1994), in which users define constraints over shared attributes and the system manages the notification and resolution of conflicts among members of the design team. ParMan also includes facilities for registering and identifying agents with specific capabilities using a shared *communication language*. That is, unlike the Galileo systems that have a shared language for the actual design, ParMan uses a shared language only for communication.

Figure 2 shows an example nonshared memory system with *one* partial or complete design (P-D) and *four* agents (A_1, A_2, A_3, A_4). In this example, A_1 receives the design, evaluates it, extends it, or adds to it, then passes it to A_2. A_2 does the same and passes it to A_3, and so on, until all agents find the design acceptable.

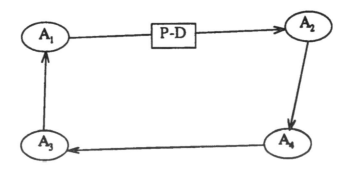

FIGURE 2   Nonshared memory system.

3.   TECHNIQUES I: PROBLEM DEFINITION

Broadly speaking, the *configuration-design* problem is defined as that of selecting parts to obtain some specified functionality subject to: (1) constraints that restrict the allowable combinations and topologies of the parts, and (2) optimality criteria. A solution is a set of parts that exhibit the required functions, meet the constraints, and is optimal in some sense, even though that might not necessarily be globally optimal. In this section, we define the building blocks of configuration design, including what we mean by functions exhibited by parts, design attributes, design constraints, and design specifications.

3.1.   FUNCTIONS

The distinguishing characteristic of the configuration-design problem is that it is solved by selecting predefined parts that can be connected only in certain ways to perform some high-level *functionality* (Mittal and Frayman, 1989). Functions have been variously defined as "what a device is for" or "a description of behavior abstracted by humans through recognition of the behavior in order to utilize it." For our purposes, a function is a property of a part that, alone or in combination with other parts, achieves a high-level, user-defined functionality. The *design* is that collection of parts that exhibits the high-level functionality. In other words, new parts cannot be created at will, constraints restrict the ways that parts can be connected, and parts exhibit low-level functions whose combination results in the desired high-level functionality.

One way design complexity is managed is through *functional decomposition*, the process in which the high-level functionality expected of the entire design is decomposed into functions exhibited by individual parts. For example, in the automotive domain (Figure 3) the high-level function of "power generation" is decomposed into the functions "engine" and "transmission." The "engine" function is further decomposed into the functions "pistons," "cylinders," "fuel injection," etc. The decomposition halts when the functions can be exhibited or implemented by individual parts. Viewed in this way, the *part* is the fundamental entity for describing a design. Then we construct a design by first selecting and connecting parts, and then by verifying that the design satisfies all constraints. The primary criteria for selecting a part are, in decreasing order of application, the function the part implements; the ability to *physically* connect to other parts; and the satisfaction of the constraints. If a part does not implement the desired function, or cannot connect to the existing design, or violates the constraints, we select another part.

The drawback of viewing the part as the central entity is that it fails to take advantage of the possibility of using constraints to direct the search for a solution. However, we can choose an alternate representation in which *attributes* are the fundamental entities for describing parts, functions, and designs. This is consistent with our definitions (above) and with using parts as the basic

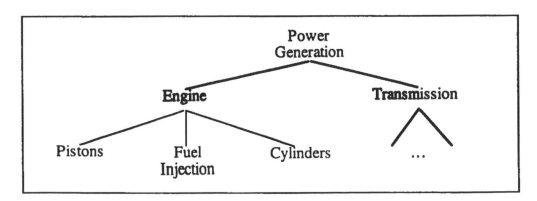

FIGURE 3   Functional decomposition.

element to describe a design, as well as with optimization techniques that use state and decision variables. Using attributes to define the problem also allows us to use constraints to define properties of a design that can be used to eliminate parts that ordinarily might be chosen to implement some function, even if that part violates a constraint or set of constraints. Once all constraints are satisfied, parts are selected to implement the desired functionality.

3.2.   ATTRIBUTES, PARTS, AND CATALOGS

An *attribute* is a *two-tuple* that consists of a name and a domain. The domain is the set of values that can be assigned to the attribute. For example, an attribute of "engine" might be <cylinders, 6>. Here, the number of cylinders, six, is typical of the most common type of domain: a number that is usually an integer or a real number, although a domain can be a string, as in, say <fuel-type, diesel>. Numeric-valued domains are generally *ordered*, that is, the domain elements can be ordered by the $\leq$ or $\geq$ relation.

Parts are sets of attributes. A special subset of attributes is the *part-function multiplicity*, which is the set of functions implemented by the part.

A *catalog* is a collection of parts, generally organized by vendor-product line. The *catalog attributes* are the set of attributes that define the parts in the catalog. The domain of each catalog attribute is the union of the domains of *all* parts in the catalog that have that domain attribute. The *catalog-function* multiplicity consists of the set of functions and the number of instances implemented by all parts in the catalog.

The set of parts we had shown in Table 1 is an example of a catalog that we will call IC. This catalog contains five types of parts: parts that implement the {CPU, Address-Decoder, Interrupt-controller, Timer} functions, parts that implement the {CPU} function, parts that implement the {Address-Decoder} function, parts that implement the {Interrupt-controller} function, and parts that implement the {Timer} function. The part 80186 is defined by the set {<part-name, 80186>, <cost, 20.0>, <power, 3.0>}. The set of catalog attributes is IC^{attr} = {<cost, {10, 15, 20, 25, 30, 40}>, <power, {150, 250, 260, 340, 440, 530}>}. The catalog-function multiplicity is the set IC^{pfm} = {{CPU, Address-decoder, Interrupt-controller, Timer}, {CPU}, {Address-decoder}, {Interrupt-controller}, {Timer}}. In Table 2 we show two catalogs from the elevator-configuration domain

---

TABLE 2
Example of Motor and Machine-Unit Catalogs

(a) machine-unit catalog

part_name	min_hp	max_hp	weight
model18	10	15	1100
model28	15	20	1700
model38	20	40	2400
model58	40	40	2750

(b) motor catalog

part_name	hp	weight
10HP	10	374
15HP	15	473
20HP	20	534
25HP	25	680
30HP	30	715

---

that we will use as an example for the remainder of the chapter. The catalogs represent sets of motors and machine units. The machine-unit is an assembly that houses the motor that drives the elevator cab up and down the elevator shaft.

The *design* is an artifact that is the object of some design process. In configuration design, the design is a collection of parts that is evaluated with respect to constraints and preferences (defined below). A design defines when all the parts have been selected and whether or not the design process is complete. Formally, a *design* is an assignment of attribute values from their domains. The *design space* is the set of *all* possible assignments of values to attributes in the design, or the cross-product of all attribute domains. In other words, the design space is the set of all possible designs.

In Table 2, we assume that the design is described by the set of attributes {motor part_name, motor hp, machine-unit part_name, total-weight}, where total-weight = motor.weight + machine-unit.weight. One possible design is given by {motor part_name = 10HP, motor hp = 10, machine-unit part_name = model18, total-weight = 1474}. The design space is the set of *all* possible motor and machine-unit selections: {{motor part_name = 10HP, motor hp = 10, machine-unit part_name = model18, total-weight = 1474}, {motor part_name = 15HP, motor hp = 15, machine-unit part_name = model18, total-weight = 1573}, ..., {motor part_name = 30HP, motor hp = 30, machine-unit part_name = model58, total-weight = 3465}}.

3.3. CONSTRAINTS

Constraints are fundamental to the design problem since they restrict the allowed part combinations to what is allowed by the laws of physics. (Note that we are expressing a somewhat controversial view here that constraints are physically-based and "hard," while traditionally "soft" constraints such as cost are *preferences* that are subsumed into and expressed in value functions.) Constraints define a network that describe relationships among all the parts in the design and they can be used for two purposes: *evaluation* and *propagation*. In evaluation, constraints determine whether or not the current assignment of values to design attributes is physically allowed, or *feasible*. In propagation, constraints *infer* the values of unassigned design attributes, given the values of assigned design attributes, potentially restricting future assignments. Constraint propagation is very useful in design because it can detect the infeasibility of an assignment before all design attributes are assigned values. This reduces *thrashing*, or pursuing an assignment that will eventually be found to be infeasible (Mackworth, 1977).

In Figure 4 we display an illustrative constraint between the horsepower of the selected motor (motor.hp) and the minimum horsepower required by the selected machine unit (machine-unit.min_hp).

We show the constraint network for our example in Figure 5. The constraints represent feasibility constraints between the motor horsepower and machine-unit allowed horsepower, and a feasibility constraint specifying the maximum total weight. A solution to the problem is a selection of a motor and machine-unit satisfying the constraints that the horsepower value of the selected motor lies between the minimum and maximum allowed horsepower values of the selected machine-unit, and that the total weight be no more than 2760 lb. These constraints are represented by the expressions:

- machine-unit.min_hp $\leq$ motor.hp
- motor.hp $\leq$ machine-unit.max_hp
- machine-unit.weight + motor.weight $\leq$ 2760

One difficulty that arises in configuration-design problems is that the set of constraints necessary to evaluate the evolving design *changes* as parts are selected to implement functions. Some knowledge-based design systems address this problem by allowing human designers to add or retract constraints as the design progresses. Our definition of constraints includes a precise specification of when the constraint is to be evaluated in the form of a predicate *precondition*.

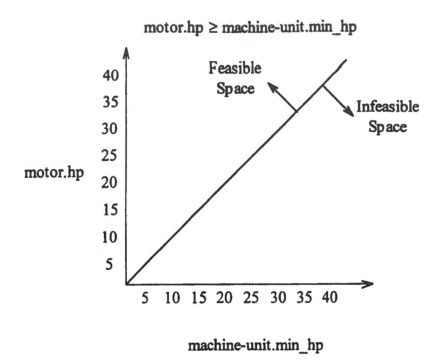

FIGURE 4 Example of constraint.

Constraints are used in a variety of ways to propagate the effects of an assignment to a design attribute in order to evaluate specific design decisions. In configuration design, parts are selected to implement functions; the constraints are then used to propagate the effects of how that decision affects other design attributes. If constraint violations result, a previous part selection is retracted and another selection is made. Such a *backtracking* process can be minimized by providing a definition of propagation functions and then using the constraints themselves to guide the selection of parts to implement functions.

Formally, a *constraint* is a relation defined over a subset of the attributes that restrict the attribute domains. The set of attributes over which the constraint is defined is the set of the constraint's arguments. There are two functions associated with a constraint. A *constraint-evaluation function* maps from an attribute assignment to the Boolean values T or F. If the assignment maps to T, then the assignment satisfies the constraint (the assignment is *feasible*); if the assignment maps to F, then the assignment violates the constraint (the assignment is *infeasible*). The *constraint-propagation function* maps from an assignment of domain values for all but one of the constraint's arguments to the domain of the remaining argument. This function restricts the domain of the remaining argument, given the assignment of domain values to all other attributes.

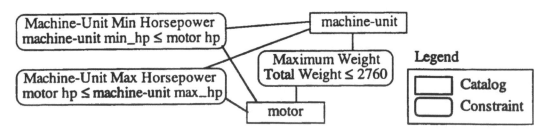

FIGURE 5 Example of a constraint network.

In many configuration-design problems, constraints are defined over attributes that are not catalog attributes. For example, a designer is often interested in the total weight of a design, that is, the sum of the weights of individual parts. We represent these attributes as *state variables* that are defined as functions over some set of catalog attributes and other state variables. The state-variable function determines the value of the state variable for given values of a set of attributes.

A *precondition* is a relation defined over a subset of the attributes that define the conditions under which a constraint is active. The set of attributes over which the precondition is defined forms the precondition's arguments. The *precondition-evaluation function* maps from an attribute assignment to the Boolean values T or F. If the assignment maps to T, then the assignment satisfies the precondition and the constraint is *active*; if the assignment maps to F, then the assignment violates the precondition and the constraint is *inactive*.

3.4.   PROPERTIES OF A DESIGN

We now define two important properties of a design, each expressed in terms of properties of constraints and parts, i.e., *consistency* and *decomposability*, that are derived from the constraint-satisfaction problem (CSP) literature (van Beek, 1992; Mackworth, 1977). Such problems are described by a set of variables, a set of domain values for each variable, and a set of constraints, and their solutions are an assignment of values to variables that satisfies the constraints. Clearly, consistency and decomposability are implicit in any design system that uses propagation to rule out assignments to unassigned variables (consistency) in order to find a solution to the problem (decomposability).

A constraint is *consistent* if for each attribute in the constraint's argument and every assignment to that attribute, there exist values for all the other attributes that satisfy the constraints (Mackworth, 1977). If a constraint is consistent, then each of the constraint's arguments is *consistent with respect to the constraint*, and each argument domain value is a consistent value. The consistency propagation function is defined such that it generates a consistent set of values for some constraint argument with respect to the constraint.

Consistency also applies to catalogs and design spaces. A catalog is a *consistent catalog* if each catalog attribute is consistent with respect to each constraint in which it appears in the constraint's arguments. If a catalog is a consistent catalog, then each part in the catalog is a *consistent part*. A design space is a *consistent design space* if each constraint is consistent.

To illustrate the consistency property, we return to the example introduced earlier. Consider the total-weight constraint. Solving for each term yields the propagation functions:

- machine-unit.weight $\leq$ 2760 – motor.weight
- motor.weight $\leq$ 2760 — machine-unit.weight

These propagation functions restrict the allowed assignments to machine-unit weight and motor weight, respectively, given the assignment to the other attribute. The first function is interpreted as follows for the consistency property: for each possible machine-unit weight, there exists a motor such that the constraint is satisfied. If no such motor exists for a given machine-unit, then that machine-unit is not consistent and should be removed.

For example, the parts model38 and model58 can be eliminated from consideration without losing any solutions, since if either model38 or model58 is selected, there is no motor light enough to satisfy the total-weight constraint. Removing inconsistent parts reduces the search space and eliminates the dead-ends that would result if these parts were selected. Table 3 shows the catalogs with all inconsistent parts removed.

Decomposability is a stronger property than consistency. Decomposability means that all designs in the design space satisfy all the constraints (van Beek, 1992). In other words, all designs

TABLE 3
The Catalog of Table 2 Modified to
Show Only Consistent Parts

(a) machine-unit catalog

part_name	min_hp	max_hp	weight
model18	10	15	1100
model28	15	20	1700

(b) motor catalog

part_name	hp	weight
10HP	10	374
15HP	15	473
20HP	20	534

are guaranteed to satisfy all constraints. If a constraint is decomposable, then each of the constraint's arguments is *decomposable with respect to the constraint.*

Decomposability also applies to catalogs and design spaces. A catalog is a *decomposable catalog* if each catalog attribute is decomposable with respect to each constraint in which it appears in the constraint's arguments. If a catalog is a decomposable catalog, then each part in the catalog is a decomposable part. A design space is a *decomposable design space* if each constraint is decomposable.

To illustrate the decomposability property, consider the constraints between the machine-unit minimum and maximum horsepower and the motor horsepower shown below:

- machine-unit.min_hp ≤ motor.hp
- motor.hp ≤ machine-unit.max_hp

The first function is interpreted as follows for the decomposability property: for each possible pair of machine-units and motors, the constraint is satisfied. By examination, the constraint is not decomposable, since there exists an assignment that violates the constraint, namely, machine-unit.min_hp = 15 and motor.hp = 10. Thus, to satisfy this constraint, an effective heuristic for monotonic constraints such as these removes the machine-unit with value min_hp = 15 and the motor with value hp = 10. Removing infeasible designs using this heuristic moves the constraint toward decomposability. This heuristic does not guarantee that only infeasible designs are removed, however. For example, there may be a feasible design that contains a 10-horsepower motor. If necessary in a case such as this, backtracking is initiated to re-introduce removed parts.

Finally, the time it takes to confirm consistency and to explore decomposability are central to practical configuration-design systems. While consistency is achieved in linear time, decomposability is achieved in worst-case exponential time. There is a class of CSPs where the constraints are monotonic and the variable domain values are single-valued, in which case decomposability can be achieved in linear time (Deville and Van Hentenryck, 1991). This is a very fortunate result since a large number of the constraints in configuration-design problems are monotonic.

3.5. Specifying a Design Problem

What do we mean by a problem? Or, more formally, how do we specify a design problem?

A design problem specifies the: functions that must be exhibited, constraints that must be satisfied, set of catalogs of available parts, and a set of the designer's preferences represented as a linear, weighted *value function*. Formally, the *design problem* is a tuple *<required-functions, constraints, catalogs, v()>* that describes the desired design in terms of a set of specifications:

- *required-functions* is the set of functions desired by the designer
- *constraints* is the set of feasibility constraints, with preconditions (and a subset of the constraints define support-function relationships)
- *catalogs* is a set of part catalogs
- *v()* is a linear, weighted value function that: assigns a real number to a design or part, defines a partial order on the designs or parts, and represents the *desirability* of the part or design from the designer's perspective

Support-function constraints represent support-function relationships. By definition, support functions are functions that are *not* included in the list of required functions specified by the designer. These constraints have a precondition that defines when the support functions are required. The support functions, which are not in the list of required functions defined in the problem definition, are contained in the constraint expression.

A solution to the design problem is a set of parts S with the following properties:

- For each required or support function, there exists a part in S such that the part implements the required or support function
- The set of parts S is decomposable
- For each required or support function and each part in S, there is no other decomposable part that has a higher value, i.e., the set of parts S is optimal.

4.   TECHNIQUES II: CURRENT METHODS

We now outline two approaches to solving configuration-design problems. One is based on constraint-satisfaction problems, and as such it represents a centralized, nondistributive approach. The second method is a distributed approach in which independent agents solve parts of the design problem, typically in an opportunistic fashion, with guidance provided through a variety of architectures.

4.1.   CSP-BASED METHODS

A constraint-satisfaction problem (CSP) is formally defined as a set of variables V with domains D and a set of constraints C defined over the variables that restrict the assignment of values to variables. A solution to a CSP is an assignment of values to variables such that all constraints are satisfied. CSP variables and constraints can have preconditions that define when a variable needs to be assigned or when a constraint needs to be evaluated. We now apply CSPs to configuration-design problems.

The configuration-design problem defined above maps naturally to a CSP. This mapping thus provides a strong theoretical framework for analyzing configuration-design problems and applying results from research in CSPs to solve configuration-design problems, including techniques for achieving consistency and decomposability of a constraint network. To apply the CSP model to configuration-design problems, required- and support-functions map to CSP variables, and feasibility constraints map to CSP constraints. We show an example design network in Figure 6, where $V = \{f_{1,1}, f_{1,2}, f_{2,2}, f_{3,1}, f_{3,2}, f_{4,1}\}$ and $C = \{c_1, c_2, c_3, c_4\}$. The variable domains are parts from possibly distributed part catalogs that implement the functions corresponding to the variables. For example, the domain of variable $f_{1,1}$ is taken from catalog$_1$ and catalog$_3$.

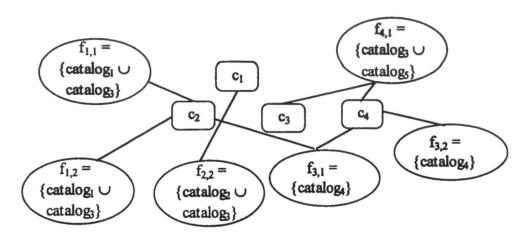

FIGURE 6 Example design network.

The existence of preconditions on the constraint and variables allows the inclusion of support-function relationships and dynamic constraints that are found in configuration-design problems. Given this mapping, a solution to the CSP corresponds to a selection of parts that implements all the required- and support-functions and meets all the constraints.

4.2. DISTRIBUTED AGENT METHODS

Most configuration-design systems solve the general configuration-design problem, including some that solve the multifunction part and support-function problems, but they do not acknowledge the naturally distributed nature of large-scale configuration-design problems. As a result, they do not take advantage of networks to solve the problem in a distributed way. Each requires a central repository of all design knowledge.

In *distributed* configuration design, the knowledge necessary to solve the problem is distributed among a set of decision-making *agents* that communicate to achieve *shared* design goals. These agents are computational processes with:

- Knowledge about portions of the design problem
- Individual and shared goals
- Operations to achieve their goals
- Communication protocols that allow them to interact with other agents in well-defined ways to achieve their goals

It is assumed that these agents use their own internal representations and problem-solving methods to contribute to the shared goals.

In addition to assuming that design knowledge is distributed, we also assume that the *representation* of the design is shared among the agents. Thus, there is no shared, global memory, such as a blackboard, that agents read to and write from, and the agents do not send a complete or partial design from agent to agent in some prescribed order. All communication is done by sending messages from one agent to another agent.

To solve a configuration-design problem, agents organize themselves into an *agent network*. Agents are *autonomous* to the extent that they can reason about their own resources and goals to make a decision whether or not to participate in a design, and they have implicit goal structures. While agents may represent any portion of the design problem, particular kinds of agents are most natural and correspond best to the knowledge in actual design settings. Each type of agent is a decision maker that communicates with other agents.

We now identify three classes of agents that solve distributed configuration-design problems (i.e., catalog agents, constraint agents, and system agents) in terms of the features of the design problem they represent, the capabilities they have, and the decisions that they are allowed to make. The *design network* is a set of agents {catalog-agents, constraint-agents, system-agent} organized to solve distributed configuration-design problems.

Catalog agents represent part catalogs. They have the capability to transform their parts into an appropriate representation and to communicate elements of the representation to other agents. Catalog agents make decisions about how to modify attribute domains to achieve design properties defined above, and about which parts to select from a decomposable set to submit as a solution. Thus, the representation of the design is distributed among the catalog agents — who are the only agents with the authority to modify attribute assignments.

Constraint agents represent constraints. Constraint agents have the capability to evaluate an attribute assignment for consistency and decomposability, and to communicate the result of this evaluation to other agents. Constraint agents decide if the assignment is consistent or decomposable, use the constraint-propagation functions to achieve a consistent space, and suggest ways to modify a nondecomposable space, respectively.

The *system agent* represents the *required-functions* and $v()$ elements of the design problem. A single system agent exists for each instance of a design problem. The system agent has the capability to: (1) create a design network by identifying catalog and constraint agents necessary to solve a configuration-design problem; (2) communicate with other agents; (3) broadcast the problem specifications to the agents in the network; and (4) verify that all functions are implemented by the parts submitted by the catalog agents.

The properties defined earlier, that is, consistency and decomposability, apply straightforwardly to catalog and constraint agents. A catalog agent is *consistent* if and only if (iff) the catalog that it represents is a consistent catalog. A constraint agent is *consistent* iff the constraint that it represents is consistent. A catalog agent is *decomposable* iff the catalog that it represents is a decomposable catalog. A constraint agent is *decomposable* iff the constraint that it represents is *decomposable*.

Properties of the design network follow from the properties of the agents in the network. The design network is a *consistent network* iff all catalog- and constraint-agents are consistent. The design network is a *decomposable network* iff catalog and constraint agents are decomposable.

A *distributed design problem* is a tuple <design problem, design network> organized to solve the design problem:

- For each catalog in the design problem, there is a catalog agent that represents the catalog in the design network. Each catalog agent has the capabilities defined above.
- For each constraint in the design problem, there is a constraint agent that represents the constraint in the design network. Each constraint agent has the capabilities defined above.

A solution to the distributed design problem is a set of parts S, selected by the catalog agents, with the following properties:

- For each required and support function, there exists a part in S that implements it. The system agent verifies this property.
- The design network is decomposable. Catalog and constraint agents collaborate to achieve this property.
- For each required- and support-function, and each part in S, such that the part implements the required- or support-function, there is no other decomposable part that has higher value. The system agent verifies this property.

5. RESEARCH ISSUES

The basic premise for the need to distribute a design task is that for any reasonably sized problem, the knowledge required to solve the problem is distributed among several designers: design agents do not bring the same knowledge to bear on the design problem. In addition, there exist *practical* barriers that prevent a single agent from solving the problem. These barriers include *geographic* ones, where agents do not reside in the same physical location; and *corporate* ones, where agents do not reside in the same corporation. The geographic and corporate barriers result from the trend toward integrating suppliers, and even customers, into the design of large-scale products. This trend is accelerated by the availability and use of computer networks, and the popularity of the World-Wide Web. This suggests several avenues for future research.

In many cases, it is impractical, indeed impossible for many applications, to assume shared memory or data structures, such as blackboards, as a communication medium. Thus, minimal shared representations are needed to facilitate compact communication among design agents of potentially large design spaces.

The complexity of the configuration-design problems requires that effective heuristics be developed to manage the problem complexity. This chapter has proposed a CSP computational model to facilitate analysis of such heuristics, and suggested one such decomposability heuristic for constraints with certain properties (monotonicity).

Existing distributed systems focus on techniques for inter-agent negotiation and collaboration within a specific domain, or providing the infrastructure to facilitate agent interaction (Pan and Tenenbaum, 1991). More work needs to be done in this area to create *generalized* mechanisms for the configuration-design domain that can be applied to a wide range of problems.

6. TRENDS AND SUMMARY

With the rising popularity of the World-Wide Web and the increasing use of the Internet, the trend in design research is clearly toward facilitating interaction among teams of human designers or computer agents, or both. In this chapter, we have defined the configuration-design problem in such a way as to provide the framework for using computational design agents to solve the problem in a distributed way. We have proposed a set of specific agents for solving the problem that correspond to part catalogs and design constraints, and have identified a related set of research issues. Finally, we also show in Table 4 list of some of the more notable configuration design systems.

TABLE 4
A List of Some Notable Configuration Design Systems

Name	Function/task domain	Reference
MICON	Single-board computer systems	(Birmingham, Gupta, and Siewiorek, 1992; Gupta, Birmingham, and Siewiorek, 1993)
ACDS	Distributed part selection	(Darr 1997)
GOPS	Optimal part selection with multi-function parts	(Haworth, Birmingham, and Haworth, 1993)
ParMan	Agent-based parametric design	(Kuokka and Livezey, 1994)
VT	Elevator systems	(Marcus, Stout and McDermott, 1988)
R1/XCON	Computer systems	(McDermott, 1981)
PRIDE	Paper-handling systems	(Mittal, Dym, and Morjaria, 1986)
COSSACK	Computer systems	(Mittal and Frayman, 1987)
Trilogy Development Group[1]	Sales-force configuration	(McHugh, 1996)

[1] Used with permission.

ACKNOWLEDGMENTS

The authors are especially grateful to Professor William P. Birmingham of the Department of Electrical Engineering and Computer Science at the University of Michigan for forging our collaborative effort and commenting on our manuscript.

REFERENCES

Birmingham, W. P., A. P. Gupta, et al. (1992). *Automating the Design of Computer Systems*, Jones and Bartlett Publishers.

Bowen, J. and D. Bahler (1992). "Supporting multiple perspectives: a constraint-based approach to concurrent engineering," in *Artificial Intelligence in Design '92*, Kluwer Academic Publishers, Dordrecht, The Netherlands. pp. 85–96.

Darr, T. P. (1997). A Constraint-Satisfaction Problem Computational Model forDistributed Part Selection, Doctoral Dissertation, Department of Electrical Engineering and Computer Science, The University of Michigan, Ann Arbor, MI.

Deville, Y. and P. Van Hentenryck (1991). "An efficient arc consistency algorithm for a class of CSP problems," *Twelfth International Joint Conference on Artificial Intelligence*, Sydney, Australia, Morgan Kaufmann Publishers, San Mateo, CA. pp. 325–330.

Dym, C. L. (1994). *Engineering Design: A Synthesis of Views*, Cambridge University Press, New York.

Dym, C. L. and R. E. Levitt (1991). *Knowledge-Based Systems in Engineering*, McGraw-Hill, New York.

Gupta, A. P., W. P. Birmingham and D. P. Siewiorek (1993). "Automating the design of computer systems." *IEEE Transactions on Computer-Aided Design of Integrated Circuits and Systems*, Vol. 12, No. 4. pp. 473–487.

Haworth, M. S., W. P. Birmingham and D. E. Haworth (1993). "Optimal part selection." *IEEE Transactions on Computer-Aided Design of Integrated Circuits and Systems*, Vol. 12, No. 10. pp. 1611–1617.

Kuokka, D. and B. Livezey (1994). "A collaborative parametric design agent," *Twelfth National Conference on Artificial Intelligence*, Seattle, WA. pp. 387–393.

Mackworth, A. K. (1977). "Consistency in networks of relations," *Artificial Intelligence*, Vol. 8, No. 1. pp. 99–118.

Marcus, S., J. Stout and J. McDermott (1988). "VT: an expert elevator designer that uses knowledge-based backtracking," *AI Magazine*, Vol. 9, No. 1. 95–112.

McDermott, J. (1981). "R1: the formative years," *AI Magazine*, Vol. 2, No. 2. pp. 21–29.

McHugh, J. (1996). "Holy Cow, No One's Done This!," *Forbes*, June 3, 1996, Vol. 157, No. 11. pp. 122-128.

Mittal, S., C. L. Dym, and M. Morjaria, (1986). "PRIDE: an expert system for the design of paper handling systems," *IEEE Computer*, Vol. 19, No. 7. pp. 102–114.

Mittal, S. and F. Frayman (1987). "COSSACK: a constraints-based expert system for configuration tasks," *Proceedings of the 2nd International Conference on Applications of AI to Engineering*, Boston, MA.

Mittal, S. and F. Frayman (1989). "Toward a generic model of configuration tasks," *Eleventh International Joint Conference on Artificial Intelligence (IJCAI-89)*, Morgan Kaufmann, Detroit, MI. pp. 1395–1401.

Pan, J. Y. C. and J. M. Tenenbaum (1991). "An intelligent agent framework for enterprise integration," *IEEE Transactions on Systems, Man, and Cybernetics*, Vol. 21, No. 6. pp. 1391–1408.

van Beek, P. (1992). "On the minimality and decomposability of constraint networks," *Tenth National Conference on Artificial Intelligence (AAAI-92)*. pp. 447–452.

22 Intelligent Manufacturing and Engineering

Gen'ichi Yasuda

CONTENTS

1. INTRODUCTION

The purpose of this chapter is to illustrate and discuss some uses of expert system techniques in manufacturing and engineering fields. The fields include integrated computer-aided manufacturing with real-time adaptive control in the metal fabrication industry, where machining and welding are the two major categories, although many expert systems have also been developed in such manufacturing fields as grinding, injection molding, electrical discharge machining, assembly, etc. Owing to rapid progress in microelectronics, computer science, and control theory over the past 30 years, there has been a very significant development of automation techniques aiming at unattended manufacturing. Today's industrial robots have efficient and reliable abilities for simple material handling or welding tasks in regulated and fixed environments of factories. In engineering fields, integration of CAD with artificial intelligence techniques has surprisingly progressed to develop design-with-feature systems and image understanding systems based on human mental processes.

However, it is observed that the actual implementation of computer control systems for manufacturing control often incorporates a substantial amount of human operators' knowledge or skills and heuristic control logic. This is true for simple feedback control laws as well as for more sophisticated multivariable control loops with many interacting process variables, as required in most of manufacturing processes. Consequently, well-functioning control systems should be provided with a more considerable amount of heuristic logic for selection and supervision of operating conditions carried out by lower level controls. Human operators' knowledge and skills concerning equipment operations are often more efficient than present automated systems, but not easily encoded by numerically based algorithms for optimization and control. Thus, development of intelligent control schemes that can learn and synthesize knowledge effectively in automated manufacturing is urgently required because of the serious shortage of experienced operators in industry.

Basically, the expert system paradigm enables the separation of the inference mechanism and the domain knowledge. The inference mechanism is domain independent. This separation allows the user to deal easily with the knowledge base and the inference structure, and provides a systematic approach for applying heuristic logic using human operators' knowledge or skills in manufacturing and engineering.

In this chapter, first, the historical background of the needs of expert systems in manufacturing and engineering is discussed with the nature of multilayered manufacturing processes. Welding is taken as a representative example because it is considered to be one of the most difficult fields for automation. Methodologies, techniques, and practices in existing expert system applications, especially intelligent process control, adaptive machining control, selection of optimum machining parameters, process monitoring, and failure diagnosis, are critically reviewed. Then, an expert system that integrates welding procedure selection and welding process control is briefly described as a whole. Finally, research issues with respect to methodologies, especially concerning the implementation of integrated and real-time expert systems, and advanced knowledge representation with inductive learning abilities, are briefly discussed.

2.   HISTORICAL BACKGROUND

An extensive survey on most of the aspects of manufacturing automation, taking into account different levels of automation, reveals the hierarchical or multilayered architecture of expert systems applying various types of information and intelligent components at different levels. Some information is about the structure of the system and other parts are more connected to the lower level of signals and their interpretation. Each type of information has its own appropriate knowledge representation.

Figure 1 shows the hierarchical feedback control diagram for submerged arc welding as an example. Generally, welding is considered to be one of the most difficult fields for automation. Welding processes involve many physical factors, such as geometrical, thermohydrodynamical, mechanical, and metallurgical. Furthermore, very diverse welding methods and equipment types must be taken into account. On the other hand, many pieces of knowledge concerning the determination of welding conditions and welding process control are very difficult to quantify.

Since welding is situated downstream in the whole flow of manufacturing, more restrictions due to accumulated variability of the factors are imposed. The existing standards cannot correspond to these changes (Fukuda, 1988). Furthermore, different kinds of welding for different kinds of metal or nonmetal, and welding for rehabilitation that differs from case to case, are also considered. Thus, the great complexity of the weld planning task requires computer-aided or automated welding procedure selection and online process control techniques for reducing the burden of welding engineers.

In real-time control applications, an intelligent method can be used to generate a control action directly or adapt a conventional control scheme by tuning its parameters according to the performance of the system. At the lowest control level, a variety of intelligent control schemes have been used in place of conventional control algorithms. For batch weighing control of powdery or granular materials, for example, time parameters of feeding rate are searched and learned from experience of previous batches to improve the weighing performance. The initial feeding pattern

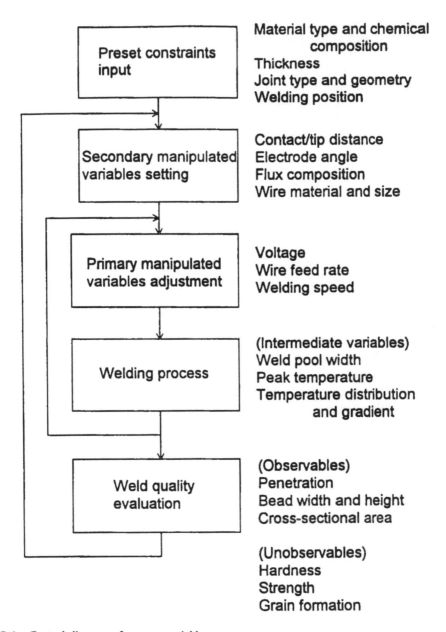

FIGURE 1   Control diagram of process variables.

is determined based on the approximately optimum control strategy using an empirical process model (Yasuda and Tachibana, 1988). Such intelligent control schemes are called *learning control* or *optimizing control.*

However, control using only a single input variable may not yield optimum conditions for most of manufacturing applications. For example, in robotic welding, arc length and weld shape should be kept constant during welding to obtain a good quality weld. The mass balance and the heat balance are simultaneously controlled. Since the state equations of the wire feed system and welding phenomena are complicated, feedback control algorithms based on modern control theory are nearly inapplicable. Therefore, an intelligent control method such as fuzzy logic control, which is suitable for cooperative control of several process variables, should be developed.

In machining, conventional computer control schemes suffer from the drawback that their operating parameters, such as feed rate, depth of cut, and cutting velocity, are programmed offline. If perfect and fixed mathematical models of the manufacturing process were available, it would be possible to select optimum operating conditions prior to the process. However, no reliable models are available due to the complexity of the process, inherent variations in tool and workpiece properties, and other varying environmental conditions. User-chosen constraints also are variable according to different manufacturing conditions.

Formerly, theoretical relationships expressing each of output variables in terms of the input variables have been modeled empirically, but are not very useful in practical situations because of various differences in workpiece and tool properties and machine conditions. A large number of empirical data have to be generated and processed offline to develop the suitable model. So, there is a strong motivation for developing schemes that are able to learn appropriate input-output mappings based solely on online sensor measurements. The success of unattended manufacturing depends, to a great extent, on the development of appropriate sensors and computer-based learning strategies.

Furthermore, adaptive machining control must be achieved in the presence of more crucial constraints, such as tool wear, tool deflection, and chatter vibration. These phenomena are difficult to measure directly and must be inferred from process variables that can be monitored. The knowledge-based system could incorporate these constraints easily as compared to conventional control systems.

Up to the present, many expert systems have been developed and implemented in the welding and machining industries. However, many problems exist in practical use to utilize the outcome provided by such expert systems, because they are mainly confined to the selection of plausible and conservative procedures and their conditions from those available in a database based on industrial handbooks or textbooks. From the experience of expert system development for the determination of welding conditions, it was considered that pieces of knowledge represented as production rules in a knowledge base would serve nothing to welding engineers, so it should be necessary to allow the user to process the pieces of knowledge in the knowledge base according to his own way, which is based on his experience (Fukuda, 1988). Ultimately, domain experts should be able to develop, modify, and integrate their rule bases and resolution strategies easily without intervention by computer engineers.

From these facts, hierarchical integrated expert systems are required which support knowledge representation, including inference mechanism. At the higher levels, explicitly described knowledge with advanced reasoning strategies for problem-solving plays an important role. At the lower levels, normal signal processing for in-process monitoring and control plays an important role, as used in conventional mathematical methods. To sum up, generally, effectively integrated expert systems are not found, or under development, corresponding to multilayered control structures from problem-solving or task planning to real-time adaptive control.

3.   METHODOLOGIES, TECHNIQUES, AND PRACTICES

In building an expert system, knowledge acquisition or elicitation and knowledge representation are key issues. In knowledge acquisition, conventionally, the knowledge engineer interviews a domain expert and asks him to talk through a number of examples of problems and their solution. Knowledge representation is to develop computer-based models of those aspects of a problem that are not naturally amenable to numerical representation or that can be more efficiently represented by the knowledge and procedures used by a human expert. Many different approaches, such as first-order predicate calculus, semantic networks, production systems, and frames, have been attempted in the manufacturing and engineering fields. The knowledge acquisition, representation, and inference or decision-making in a "design"-type expert system are more complex and difficult than a "diagnostic"-type expert system.

Although expert systems have been applied in many fields, the acquisition of knowledge is a time-consuming task and may be a bottleneck due to the gap between experts in a field and expert system builders. Furthermore, even the experts themselves may find it difficult to formalize their expertise. The advent of neural networks has made it possible to acquire knowledge from a sort of data rather than from human experts. Expert systems with neural networks are called *neural expert systems*. The application areas of neural networks are divided into two main categories: general information processing and processing of sensory information (Monostori and Barschdorff, 1992). The former category concerns the "design"-type expert systems, and the latter concerns the "diagnostic" type. In the "design"-type expert systems, neural networks with learning abilities substitute for time-consuming simulation of real industrial processes. In this section, such knowledge-based systems in manufacturing and engineering fields are briefly illustrated.

3.1. INTELLIGENT PROCESS CONTROL

Expert systems in intelligent process control include the computer-aided design and online adaptive adjustment of parameters of conventional feedback control algorithms such as PID control and optimum control. In a typical prototype with a self-tuning regulator (Astrom, Anton, and Arzen, 1986), the expert system was composed of several software parts. The expert system part was implemented using a production system framework, OPS4, and other parts such as user interface part, real-time control part, and action parts in rule expressions were written in Lisp. The rule base contains the production rules, which are typically described as: *if <situation> then <action>*. The data base in the knowledge base is the repository of facts, evidence, hypotheses, and goals. The facts would include static data concerning sensor measurement tolerances, operating thresholds, constraints on operational sequencing, etc., and parameter and state estimates based on noisy observations are included in the database as evidence and hypothesis.

The inference engine repeatedly finds all the rules that are matched. It selects one of them and performs its actions. When no more rules are found, the system waits for incoming messages from the user interface part or the low-level control part. A message is either a new element to be entered into working memory or a Lisp function that should be evaluated. New memory elements may cause new rules to match and thus start the rule execution again. The total expert system can be efficiently executed under a real-time multitask operating system with mailboxes for message passing between parallel processes. Since there is no difference between data and program in Lisp programs, it is simply implemented for the user to do with the expert system and to add, delete, and edit rules online by a message of an arbitrary Lisp expression.

Experience from building expert systems for real applications has shown that their power is most apparent when the problem considered is sufficiently complex. Process control problems with multiple loops under unpredictable material variations are admittedly complex. In the area of online real-time process control, use of an expert system development tool, such as G2 by Gensym Corp., where the domain knowledge can be embedded in the knowledge base, reduces the burden of plant engineers.

Currently, many intelligent process control systems are being developed, utilizing neural network modeling, to monitor process outputs, to correct the control inputs, and to keep the process output within the desired range in the real process. Neural networks model the process output from the real input data by the feedforward error back propagation algorithm for learning. To search for the appropriate choice of control input, which makes the model output closer to the target output, the neural network model can be employed with an optimization technique such as the genetic algorithm. Using the neural network-based statistical process control method, the process shift due to abnormal cause can be detected. To compensate the process shift by abnormality, model modification and selection of the new control input are performed to recover the process output to the target output.

3.2.   KNOWLEDGE-BASED ADAPTIVE CONTROL IN MACHINING

To enhance the effective range of present adaptive control strategies in machining, a knowledge-based adaptive control system was developed (Lingarkar, Liu, Elbestawi, and Sinha, 1990). The system can regulate the cutting force by adjusting the feed rate against unpredictable changes in the cutting process dynamics during a milling operation. The knowledge-based system is a part of the primary feedback loop, and the supervision level to monitor range violations is efficiently built into a frame-based knowledge representation scheme. A frame is composed of slots, and predicates attached to slots are used to encode the heuristics for adaptive control. These predicates behave as demons for proper functioning and maintaining the integrity of the controller. Hierarchical representation of frames allows sharing of information among frames by inheritance. Symbolic processing in Prolog and numeric algorithms written in C are combined by interface clauses within a rule written in Prolog.

Although knowledge in a knowledge-based controller is application dependent, the fundamental structure of the controller can be easily applied to other manufacturing fields such as grinding, injection molding, and electrical discharge machining. For more complex controllers, where the sampling period is very small, use of parallel processors (such as INMOS transputers) or dedicated hardware to do symbolic processing is recommended, since chronological backtracking by Prolog is exponential in time.

3.3.   MACHINE LEARNING USING NEURAL NETWORKS

In order to code operational knowledge and use this knowledge for determining optimum strategies for machining operations, a feedforward neural network was studied. Based on the trained network, an optimization technique predicts the input conditions to be used by the machine tool to maximize a performance index under the appropriate operating constraints. The constraints are considered on the input variables due to machine limitations and upper bounds of some output variables in order to protect against factors such as excessive tool wear and tool breakage (Rangwala and Dornfeld, 1989). It was reported that for a turning operation, the neural network with 3 input, 4 hidden, and 4 output nodes can learn the mappings between input and output variables by observing the training samples. The input variables are the feed rate, depth of cut, and cutting velocity. The output variables predict the sensor outputs, such as cutting force, temperature, power, and surface finish.

The performance index is defined taking into account both goodness and efficiency. The former is reflected by some output variables kept sufficiently close to a desired value to ensure a good quality of cutting. The latter is represented using the material removal rate, which is simply the product of the three input variables. An optimization method using local computations based on the back propagation or an augmented Lagrangian method was proposed, although it gives a locally optimum set of input variables. The learning scheme can allow the partially trained network to predict an optimum set of input variables with the current state of knowledge, which is a crucial property required for real-time adaptive control. Usually, the training samples for neural networks, which are preset by the user, span the allowable range of the input variables. In the scheme that learns and synthesizes simultaneously, fewer samples need to be learned for only local knowledge in the vicinity of an optimum. In such cases, it is needed to guarantee the learning and synthesizing abilities using noisy sensor data in real manufacturing environments. In addition, it is required to assure the obtained result to be the global optimum when the synthesis algorithm adopts a gradient-based optimization.

3.4.   GENETIC ALGORITHMS IN MANUFACTURING AND ENGINEERING

Traditional operations research approaches cannot resolve the long computation time needed for optimization with combinatorial complexity, so new techniques that assure the attainment of the global optimum with an allowable convergence speed have been investigated. Recently, genetic algorithms have been applied to optimization problems in a variety of manufacturing and engineering fields, such as the determination of optimum cutting conditions, tool selection scheduling, assembly process planning, and routing in traffic control of automated guided vehicles. At present, efficient codification methods to reduce the large search space of the genetic algorithm and implementation methods on parallel processing architectures for computational speed up are required.

3.5. PROCESS DIAGNOSIS USING PROBABILISTIC INFERENCE

The knowledge representation and reasoning with uncertainty is a critical issue for expert system development in manufacturing and process control. Production rules based on predicate calculus and classical binary logic have trouble taking into account competing or nondeterministic rules and imperfections in the measuring instruments. Several techniques have been proposed, such as Bayesian probabilities, fuzzy probabilities, Dempster-Shafer theory, etc. Influence diagrams provide an intuitive graphical framework for representing and combining evidence and can integrate dynamic sensor readings, statistical data, and subjective expertise in symbolic and numerical data structures. Probabilistic dependence between process variables in machining was represented using topological diagrams, and a polynomial-time symbolic-level algorithm for probabilistic inference and decision-making was applied to diagnostic reasoning, monitoring, and supervising control (Agogino, Srinivas, and Schneider, 1988). The system can determine the most likely process state from the observable sensor readings. Dynamic programming is used to optimize a parameterized utility function taking into account the cost trade-offs and assessed uncertainty of the possible failure states.

A machine troubleshooting expert system is being developed that determines the most efficient reasoning sequence in the diagnostic tree by a fuzzy multiattribute decision-making method. An inference engine controls the diagnosis process, considering the uncertainty with regard to the validity of a knowledge base rule and a user's response. A learning module trains the knowledge base by the failure-driven learning method from the past cases (Liu and Chen, 1995).

3.6. FAILURE DIAGNOSIS USING CASE-BASED REASONING

Case-based decision support systems can deal with ill-structured problems, for which mathematical models or formalized rules are nonexistent at present. An example in engineering fields is failure diagnosis of fractured parts in a factory, where due to the complexity of the metallographic features of the failed parts, there are no explicit rules or models to determine their failure mechanisms. A neural network with the back propagation algorithm is employed to learn the mapping between the cause sets and the result sets of verified cases based on metallographic features associated with the failure analysis problem to be solved (Gan and Yang, 1994).

3.7. EXPERT SYSTEMS FOR WELDING

Up to the present, many expert systems have been developed and implemented in the welding industry, especially for welding procedure selection and weld defect diagnosis. This section briefly discusses the features of expert systems for welding. These include online and offline expert system techniques to help the user to analyze weld tasks in the preweld, weld, and postweld phases.

In the preweld phase, expert systems emulate weld tasks such as joint design, including edge preparation, welding procedure selection, and material selection. It is also recommended to perform welding procedure selection based on preweld inspection. Expert systems produce procedures that achieve acceptable weld bead geometries and avoid hydrogen cracking, solidification cracking, and fracture toughness impairment.

During the weld phase, sensors to detect process features are used, and based on this information along with the preweld information, conditions varying from the present welding procedure are identified, analyzed, and modified accordingly.

Knowledge base

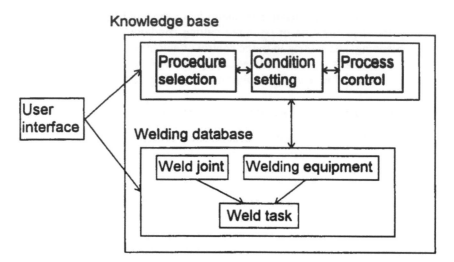

FIGURE 2   Example of software organization of expert system for welding.

Postweld expert systems conduct fault diagnosis and weld inspection interpretation. For weld defect diagnosis, the user is asked for information about welding process variables and the welding methods used, and then the system lists its conclusions about the most probable causes of the defect.

Figure 2 shows the software structure of an integrated expert system for welding procedure selection and process control (Yasuda and Tachibana, 1996). To clarify the practices of expert systems in welding, the expert system is described briefly in the following:

For welding automation, the expert system and a welding process controller are combined with a welding robot, various sensors, and/or a CAD system. The procedure selection software is part of the weld task planner that contains all the necessary knowledge to supervise the weld task planning. The user defines the preset variables such as base material composition, plate thickness, joint type, and welding position. The user also defines acceptable limits on parameters such as weld beat geometry, penetration, and cooling rate. Data such as electrode material and size, and desired type of metal transfer are optionally required. The system then can generate values for voltage, current, wire feed rate, and welding speed. Conventional reasoning methods, such as forward reasoning and backward reasoning are contained in the expert system to support different and bidirectional reasoning according to the user's needs at arbitrary stages.

The secondary manipulated variables are selected using a set of production rules that control the access to the weld joint and welding equipment databases. The hierarchical class structure indicating inheritance relations between objects in the weld joint database is shown in Figure 3.

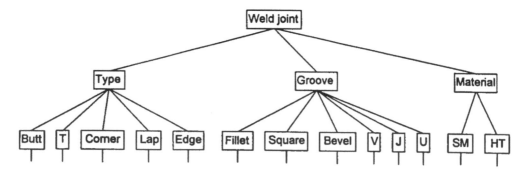

FIGURE 3   Hierarchical class structure of weld joint data.

```
Kb::
[Thickness, 'mm', positive,[ ], [1, 100]],

[Welding position, '', atom, [ ], ['flat', 'horizontal', 'vertical', 'overhead']],

[Groove, '', atom, [Thickness, Welding position], ['V', 'J', 'X', 'K', 'L', 'U']]

Rule1:: Welding position == 'flat',
        Thickness >= 6,
        Thickness <= 30

        ==> Groove = 'V'
```

FIGURE 4 Example of knowledge and rule representation for welding procedure selection.

For example, the type of weld groove is selected based on the plate thickness and the welding position using a production rule as shown in Figure 4, where the associated knowledge and the rule are written in a conventional expert system shell language.

Forward reasoning by data-driven or bottom-up inference is used for adjustment of parameters to satisfy specified constraints in the welding condition setting as shown in Figure 5. The system can schedule preheating temperature, and postweld heat treatment temperature and time. All feasible solutions to meet specified constraints are graphically visualized for the user to select the most allowable candidate on the screen.

Object-oriented approaches have been used for building databases in welding engineering. In the developed example, data of weld joint, weld equipment, and weld task are represented as frames into the respective class hierarchy. The static data of an object is expressed by "attribute" slots of the frame. Numerical calculating procedures and heuristic logic concerning the object are expressed by "method" slots and "rule" slots, respectively.

Figure 6 shows a neural expert system for the determination of submerged arc welding conditions. The input nodes of the neural network represent the preset, fixed variables or the secondary manupulated variables which include base material type, plate thickness, joint type, welding position, electrode material type, groove type, etc. The output nodes represent primary manipulated

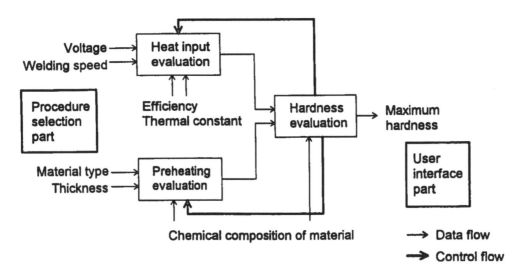

FIGURE 5 Data and control flow diagram in welding condition adjustment.

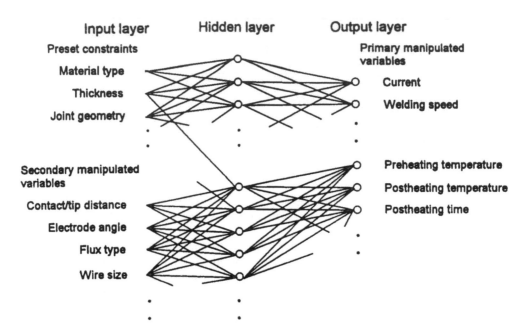

FIGURE 6 Neural network for the determination of welding conditions.

variables, which include welding current, welding speed, preheating temperature, and postheating temperature and time. The prototype can learn a provisional set of samples from industrial standards by the back propagation algorithm with inertia terms, and can be embedded in the developed knowledge-based expert system (Yasuda and Tachibana, 1996).

In the neural expert system, the user can change the number of the hidden layer and the steepness of the sigmoid function of the neuron model so that the performance of learning is satisfactory to determine the welding conditions in the allowable range of process variables.

The realized hardware architecture is composed of an engineering workstation and a network of transputers (IMS T805). The former, including the neural expert system, deals with the expert welding procedure selection, while the latter implements the real-time expert welding control. Owing to the distributed properties of the expert system, some wide area network such as Internet and ISDN systems can be utilized for communication and cooperative reasoning between the global expert system on the host workstation and local expert control systems at remote sites. At remote sites, only knowledge concerned with the specified items such as plate thickness, joint type, welding method, and equipment, can be loaded into the knowledge base when the expert system is executed.

3.8. Neural and Fuzzy Rule-Based Expert Systems for Automated Welding

Neural networks are also being used to acoustically determine if a weld is good or bad for Navy ships. The welding arc sound emits a unique frequency spectrum according to the welding conditions such as electrode extension, and unstable arc largely changes the pattern of the spectrum, providing the useful information about the phenomena of the molten pool and the transfer of droplets. Similar pattern recognition techniques using neural networks are adopted in grinding such that the change of grinding state can be detected before the occurrence of the grinding burn or the chatter.

A fuzzy rule-based expert system was developed for modification of welding conditions by applying fuzzy rules (Fukuda and Kamio, 1990). IF parts define the fuzziness of unacceptable defects of the weld that is produced under the previously determined conditions, and THEN parts define the degree of modification of an input variable. The expert system is not a fully fuzzy system, because knowledge is not enough to develop the membership functions in the THEN parts. However, it provides a fundamental basis for constructing a truly adaptive and automated control loop using appropriate sensors for robotic welding.

3.9. EXPERT SYSTEM DEVELOPMENT TOOLS

Because of a shell's ease of use and availability for commercial personal computers, it is quickly becoming the realistic means of creating an expert system. When creating an expert system with a shell, only the knowledge base needs to be created. However, there is a limit to what existing shells can do in manufacturing and engineering applications; expert systems made with a shell might run slower and have limited I/O capabilities.

The knowledge base and inference engine can be created with code in AI programming languages, such as Prolog and Lisp, according to the user's needs. However, it takes much time and needs extensive programming skills, especially for manufacturing engineers. Furthermore, there are some problems for utilizing these AI programming languages in manufacturing and engineering applications, for example, welding:

1. In the determination of optimum welding conditions, numerical computations are largely required, such as FEM simulation of welding heat conduction and parameter estimation of empirical formulas using statistical analysis.
2. Data and control flows for welding condition setting and real-time control imply some concurrency, as shown in Figure 5.

By using a programming tool for knowledge representation, such as OPS83, the user can also construct his own inference mechanism and link it with programs written in C. Thus, welding engineers' experience could be also reflected in meta-knowledge rather than the knowledge itself.

For conventional process control applications, the expert system is regarded as a separate knowledge module and combined with the control part in a distributed control system. To fully bring out latent potentialities of the expert system, hierarchical integration between the expert system part and the control part is a possible solution, since many real systems are represented as an inherently hierarchical structure. An object-oriented programming methodology integrates heuristic knowledge and model-based knowledge for complex, ill-structured problems into the class hierarchy formality.

The frame language integrates static attributes and dynamic operations as a whole. Each frame is viewed as a basic knowledge block and can be used in the different parts of the knowledge base. The static knowledge of objects is expressed by "attribute" slots of the frame. Numerical calculating procedures and heuristic logic are expressed by "method" slots and "rule" slots, respectively. The expert system part and the process control part are tightly coupled at all levels of class hierarchy. Some object-oriented expert system development shells on workstations or personal computers are available, for example, Ext Kernel with ESP (Extended Self-contained Prolog) on MELCOM PSI workstation in Japan.

3.10. KNOWLEDGE REPRESENTATION USING HIGH-LEVEL PETRI NETS

To realize expert control systems that require real-time processing, it is necessary to model the necessary knowledge clearly and simply, and implement it on a parallel and distributed processing architecture. High-level colored Petri nets have been used as a knowledge representation tool for image understanding, where output tokens represent extracted features at various decision levels, and directly applied to vision-based real-time mobile robot navigation. The similar approaches were applied to the determination and adjustment of welding conditions (Yasuda and Tachibana, 1996).

Use of Petri nets insures some important properties for expert systems, such as boundedness or safeness, liveness or freedom from deadlock, and reversibility.

4.   RESEARCH ISSUES

4.1.   HIERARCHICAL INTEGRATION OF INTELLIGENT STRATEGIES

An intelligent manufacturing system can be seen as the basic multilayered structure of intelligent machines, in which the layers are composed according to the principle of increasing precision with decreasing intelligence. This principle can be generalized for the development of expert systems with a low-level intelligent controller that consists of several parts, each with its own type of intelligence.

At the lower levels of automation, normal signal processing plays an important role, as used in neural networks and conventional mathematical methods. The knowledge available may be structured or not, and symbolic or numeric. Symbolic knowledge represents global features, while numeric knowledge represents specific or individual features. At the lower levels, before the pieces of symbolic knowledge are applied, they should resort to conventional numerical procedures. At the lowest level, user-written routines and simple logic are very well suited.

At the higher levels of automation, explicitly described knowledge with advanced reasoning strategies plays an important role. The corresponding knowledge representation can be found in high-level object-oriented descriptions, such as in sophisticated expert system shells. An integration of various AI-based strategies in an intelligent manufacturing scheme requires an integration of various methods of information processing, involving both typical symbolic processing and connectionist methods such as neural networks.

4.2.   REAL-TIME ISSUES

In manufacturing fields such as robotic welding and computer control machining, recent research interests mainly tend to develop real-time expert systems for adaptive parameter adjustment. In the higher levels of plant automation, knowledge-based problem-solving techniques have been applied in domains with static data. No time-critical responses were required. In a real-time control environment, it is important to meet the strict requirements concerning the response time. It is necessary to have much smaller cycle times for real-time performance when implementing the expert system in multiple feedback control loops to munufacturing equipment. Several hardware options are implementing part of the system on a microchip, using add-on boards for signal processing in hardware and array processing for the numerical computation (Agogino, Srinivas, and Schneider, 1988).

For online control, various knowledge-based systems are embedded in a real-time environment, and therefore special attention must be paid to the time handling. Semantic networks and production rules become unmanageable as the size of the knowledge base increases, which is a very serious problem for the performance of real-time control. So, a good allocation of tasks between the expert system and the real-time control environment is necessary.

For efficient diagnosis of complex system failures in real-time environments, multiple diagnostic expert systems that cooperate with one another to solve problems beyond an individual domain of expertise are being implemented on a hierarchically distributed and cooperative processing architecture (Schwuttke, Veregge, and Quan, 1996).

A real-time control system must be composed of asynchronous concurrent processes, capable of being interrupted to accept input from unscheduled or asynchronous events. A blackboard architecture can implement a system with a multiple number of expert system kernels running in parallel, each of which can be used to solve a subproblem. Several knowledge sources can access the blackboard, like a short-term memory, and share information through the blackboard control mechanism. In progressive reasoning, the problem-solving procedure is split up into more detailed procedures, which are evaluated according to the time available. Advanced techniques for real-time requirements, such as temporal reasoning and switching of attention in reasoning, are also applicable to intelligent process control and manufacturing systems.

4.3. ADVANCED KNOWLEDGE REPRESENTATION WITH LEARNING ABILITIES

The limitation of current expert system technology is that expert systems can only use deductive inference and not inductive inference; therefore, a known starting point must be present in order to make a conclusion. In addition, expert systems have the ability to represent a human's factual knowledge, but not conceptual knowledge, and neural networks have the ability to do empirical learning, but not analytical learning. In these respects, the following target issues are important to the realization of intelligent manufacturing and engineering systems:

1. Integration of an operational knowledge base, such as an influence diagram and a Petri net, with the neural network based learning scheme
2. Automatic generation of the knowledge base by inductive learning from a given set of training sample operations

5. FUTURE TRENDS AND SUMMARY

Expert systems and other intelligent techniques have been widely applied to many fields in manufacturing and engineering. The current review of expert system applications has revealed the substantial effectiveness of the approaches. Developed learning and synthesizing schemes using neural networks and fuzzy logic are fairly general and could be applied to other advanced manufacturing processes such as laser or electron beam materials processing and microfabrication. In the future, unsupervised online learning and self-organizing techniques (Burke, 1992) are crucial to the development of unattended manufacturing systems to emulate a human expert fully, which obviate the need for detailed controller design or knowledge base development by hard-to-find experts and knowledge engineers.

Three difficulties, namely, hierarchical integration of various intelligent strategies, real-time performance, and knowledge representation with inductive learning abilities, have prevented conventional expert systems from producing the most efficient solutions for some problems in manufacturing and engineering. Furthermore, global optimization techniques including evaluation criteria are also practically important in optimum design and learning.

The vigorous theoretical development of artificial intelligence and control theory over the past 10 years has thus far only had a modest impact on the practice of unattended manufacturing processes, because of real-time issues and expensiveness in hardware and software realization. However, owing to the recent advances in this field and other related information technologies such as networked distributed architecures, multimedia, and human interfaces, many more expert systems that enable domain experts to develop their knowledge bases easily should be developed in order to overcome many of the weakness of conventional expert systems.

REFERENCES

Agogino, A.M., Srinivas, S., and Schneider, K.M. (1988). Multiple sensor expert system for diagnostic reasoning, monitoring and control of mechanical systems, *Mechanical Systems and Signal Processing*, 2(2), 165–185.

Astrom, K.J., Anton, J.J., and Arzen, K.E. (1986). Expert control, *Automatica*, 22(3), 277–286.

Burke, L.I. (1992). Competitive learning based approaches to tool-wear identification, *IEEE Transactions on Systems, Man, and Cybernetics*, 22(3), 559–563.

Fukuda, S. (1988). Welding expert system: from the Welsys experience, in *Weld Quality The Role of Computers (Proceedings of the International Conference on Improved Weldment Control with Special Reference to Computer Technology)*, Pergamon Press, Oxvord, UK, pp. 181–188.

Fukuda, S., and Kamio, Y. (1990). A fuzzy expert system for adaptive robotic welding, *Proceedings of 1990 Japan–U.S.A. Symposium on Flexible Automation*, 775–780.

Gan, R. and Yang, D. (1994). Case-based decision support system with artificial neural network, *Proceedings of the 16th International Conference on Computers & Industrial Engineering*, 233–236.

Lingarkar, R., Liu, L., Elbestawi, M.A., and Sinha, N.K. (1990). Knowledge-based adaptive computer control in manufacturing systems: a case study, *IEEE Transactions on Systems, Man, and Cybernetics*, 20 (3), 606–618.

Liu, S. and Chen, J. (1995). Development of a machine troubleshooting expert system via fuzzy multiattribute decision-making approach, *Expert Systems with Applications*, 8 (1), 187–201.

Monostori, L. and Barschdorff, D. (1992). Artificial neural networks in intelligent manufacturing, *Robotics and Computer-Integrated Manufacturing*, 9(6), 421–437.

Rangwala, S.R. and Dornfeld, D.A. (1989). Learning and optimization of machining operations using computing abilities of neural networks, *IEEE Transactions on Systems, Man, and Cybernetics*, 19(2), 299–314.

Schwuttke, U.M., Veregge, J.R., and Quan, A.G. (1996). Cooperating expert systems for the next generation of real-time monitoring applications, *Proceedings of the Third World Congress on Expert Systems*, 521–528.

Yasuda, G. and Tachibana, K. (1988). An intelligent control scheme for weighing systems, *ACTA IMEKO 88*, Vol. I, 361–367.

Yasuda, G. and Tachibana, K. (1996). An integrated object-oriented expert system for welding procedure selection and process control, *Proceedings of the Third World Congress on Expert Systems*, 186–193.

23 Scheduling

Jay Liebowitz, Vijaya Krishnamurthy, Ira Rodens,
and William Potter

CONTENTS

1. GENERAL BACKGROUND ON INTELLIGENT SCHEDULING ISSUES, TRENDS, AND RESEARCH DIRECTIONS

Scheduling is a popular topic for intelligent systems. In a survey of operational expert system applications in business from 1980 to 1993 (Eom, 1995), the largest percentage (48%) of operational expert systems was in productions and operations management and expert scheduling systems were a dominant percentage of these.

Scheduling involves accomplishing a number of things that tie up various resources for periods of time. It is constraint-driven, meaning that a scheduling problem can be defined as a set of constraints to satisfy. A solution to the scheduling problem is a set of compatible scheduling decisions that guarantee the satisfaction of the constraints (Noronha and Sarma, 1991). Guaranteeing the compatibility of the decisions made is the role of constraint propagation. The order in which decisions must be made needs to be determined.

Most schedules need to be redone. In manufacturing, for example, reports from shop personnel in industries as diverse as semiconductor fabrication and automobile manufacturing estimate that the effective useful life of a daily schedule is an hour or less (Fox and Zweben, 1994). Thus, the 8-hour or 16-hour production schedules need to be reworked. A critical element of scheduling, therefore, is the effective ability to reschedule.

In identifying expert scheduling system approaches used, Liebowitz (1993) did a literature review of 250 references, over 2 years, dealing with expert scheduling systems. Liebowitz found that 137 used a heuristic scheduling approach, 16 used an optimization/algorithmic scheduling approach, 42 used a hybrid scheduling approach (heuristic and optimization), and 55 were unknown (no scheduling approach was mentioned). In all, there were 24 major scheduling approaches used in these expert scheduling systems. Three classes of expert scheduling system approaches emerged.

The first class deals with optimization scheduling methods. These include enumerative algorithms and mathematical programming methods. Enumerative algorithms search for an optimal solution by enumerating and comparing all possible solutions. Branch and bound and dynamic programming are examples of such. Mathematical programming methods formulate the problem as a mathematical model, like integer and mixed-integer programming. The problem with optimality in scheduling is that optimality is hard, if not impossible, to define in a realistic scheduling environment. The number of possible solutions increases so fast that there are no practical results, and it may be too time consuming to determine the optimum solution. This is because scheduling deals with NP-complete problems where no method can be discovered that doesn't grow exponentially in problem size.

The second class of scheduling approaches in intelligent systems is the use of heuristic approaches. There are several heuristic algorithms that have been used in scheduling, including neural network algorithms, greedy algorithms, intelligent pertubation algorithms, simulated annealing algorithms, and genetic algorithms. Other heuristic scheduling methods have also been used extensively, for example, conflict resolution strategies, resource-based scheduling, order-based scheduling, blackboard-based scheduling, lookahead scheduling, and the like. The heuristic approach for scheduling produces and maintains "satisficing" schedules over time; that is, schedules that are good, workable solutions derived quickly, but may not necessarily be the optimum schedule.

The third class of intelligent scheduling approaches is hybrid methods. These include artificial intelligence (AI) plus simulation-based scheduling, optimization/operations research plus AI scheduling, and hybrid systems combining the strengths of the other approaches.

In looking at the NASA mission planning environment, Liebowitz (1993) identified 63 major requirements for a mission planning expert scheduling system. These requirements fit under the classes of: general requirements, resources/constraints requirements, activity requirements, scheduling capability requirements, rescheduling capability requirements, output requirements, user interface and control requirements, and system interface requirements. The recurring themes in studying the expert scheduling system literature are the need for a hierarchical architecture for scheduling, the ability to quickly and effectively perform rescheduling automatically, the need for good user and system interface design, and the need to have various techniques accessible for use in scheduling (a toolkit approach).

In the NASA environment, scheduling is a critically important area. According to the Engineering Services Group of McDonnell Douglas, projecting out to the space station of the next decade, scheduling will be required for 365 days of the year and could take 2000 to 3000 people working continuously. NASA Headquarters officials have mentioned that two of the most pressing tasks that NASA will have to deal with in the future are data analysis and scheduling. With the scheduling domain, people have learned two things: (1) scheduling is a difficult area, and (2) nothing goes according to schedule (Brown and Scherer, 1995). In the ATDRSS (Advanced Tracking Data and Relay Satellite System) at NASA, ATDRSS era service requests will increase 3- to 10-fold in number from today's TDRS requests for using the satellites. Human aids, like expert scheduling systems, are needed to assist the human schedulers. Within NASA, intelligent scheduling systems are already being used for such tasks as scheduling Shuttle and payload launches, scheduling satellite experimenter use of the satellite, and a number of other scheduling applications (Liebowitz, Lightfoot, and Dent, 1991; Liebowitz and Lightfoot, 1993).

Outside of NASA, many of the major airlines like Singapore Air, Japan Air, United, TWA, Iberia, and others are using expert scheduling systems for aircraft gate assignment. A number of international applications of intelligent scheduling systems are being used for daily, medium-term production scheduling, aircraft maintenance, scheduling power generating units, job shop scheduling, semiconductor wafer production, newspaper printing runs, paper production, real-time factory

TABLE 1
Sample List of International Intelligent Scheduling Systems (Liebowitz, 1994)

Singapore	Changi Airport Resource Allocation System: schedules ramp handling services to the airlines
Korea	DAS (Daewoo Shipbuilding Scheduling) project for scheduling ship repair and shipbuilding tasks
	UNIK-PCS (Yukong Ltd.) — schedules daily purchase and deliveries of oil
	Pohang Iron and Steel Co. — expert scheduling systems for steel manufacturing
Norway	SINTEF SI (Oslo) — developing expert scheduling systems for improving logistics performance in industry and civil services (oil well activity scheduling)
	TRUTH (Esprit 6463) — developed generic software for reactive scheduling
Australia	SACSS (Steel making and casting scheduling system) at BHP
France	ILOG SOLVER/SCHEDULE (Ilog, Inc.) — an object-oriented, constraint-based satisfaction tool
Mexico	An intelligent scheduling system at HYLSA to assign steel rolls to electric furnaces for reheating
Japan	Expert scheduling systems in steel and metal industry (NKK)

scheduling in a VLSI development line, flight crew scheduling, and airport staff rostering. A sample of intelligent scheduling systems being used worldwide is shown in Table 1.

As the maturity of the intelligent scheduling system field has grown, a number of tools (like in the constraint-solving area) have been developed to help in the development process of intelligent scheduling systems. Examples of worldwide constraint solving tools include:

- CHARME (Bull)
- CHIP (Cosytec)
- CHLEO and CHLARE (Axia Recherche)
- DECISION POWER (ICL)
- ORION (Interactive Engineering/Machine Reasoning)
- ILOG SOLVER/SCHEDULE (Ilog, Inc.)
- PROLOG III (Prologia)
- SNI PROLOG (Siemens)
- APSHELL/SCHEDES (Fujitsu)
- ES/PROMOTE/PLAN (Hitachi)

Another emerging development in the intelligent scheduling system field has been on generic scheduling and building tools to facilitate generic scheduling. Examples of such generic expert scheduling or planning system tools are: O-Plan2 and TOSCA at the University of Edinburgh, PARR (Bendix/Allied Signal), ROSE (Loral), AMP (Stottler-Henke Associates), and UNIK (KAIST, Korea).

Most of the intelligent scheduling systems use either a constructive scheduling method or a repair-based method. The constructive method grew out of the ISIS work at CMU, and incrementally extends a partial schedule until it is complete. The repair method, developed from NASA Ames' work, iteratively modifies a complete schedule to remove conflicts or to further optimize the schedule.

Looking to the near term, what are some research areas that need to be addressed in the intelligent scheduling area? Some of the research needed includes:

- Benchmarking intelligent scheduling systems and doing performance analysis (see the Special Issue on "Expert Scheduling Systems and Their Performances," *Expert Systems With Applications Journal*, Vol. 6, No. 3, Elsevier, Oxford, 1993).
- Establishing a methodology for building intelligent scheduling systems that clarifies the scope of their applicability.

- Developing general or generic intelligent scheduling systems/tools.
- Developing problem description vocabulary, classification scheme, and map of the problem space (Karl Kempf at Intel has echoed this point).
- Constructing a mapping between problem leaf nodes and solutions leaf nodes (mapping problem requirements to scheduling approaches for use in expert systems).
- Realizing that the AI part of the scheduling system may be very little in terms of the overall scheduling system development — integration issues, user interface design issues, and other non-AI issues may consume much of the development time.
- Researching the relationship between, and integration of, planning and scheduling techniques (unified framework).
- Applying machine learning techniques in scheduling (see Aytug et al., "Review of Machine Learning in Scheduling," *IEEE Transactions on Engineering Management*, IEEE, May 1994).
- Improving management awareness/technology transfer/implementation methods.

Another important research area is "cooperative scheduling." This involves keeping the human in the loop. Under cooperative scheduling, procedures, rules, and the user cooperate to make a schedule. This doesn't replace the user and automatically produce an optimal solution to a problem that the user has formulated, but rather collaborates with the user in designing a feasible solution. This is regarded as a decision-making rather than a constraint-satisfaction problem. Scheplan, of IBM Tokyo and NKK, Japan, uses this approach for steel-making production scheduling.

Most intelligent scheduling systems today have the inability to adapt and learn. Future research issues for learning methods in AI scheduling systems are:

- Continue to explore ways and paradigms for learning (rote learning, inductive learning, neural network learning, case-based learning, classifier systems, etc.).
- Provide means to learn how to trade off management goals, which are often inconsistent and time-varying.
- Learn about the uncertainties that exist in a given production environment.
- Validate the results that machine learning has produced.
- Examine a richer representation for handling the complexities and nuances of scheduling environments.
- Need better methods for inherently dynamic learning techniques and for real-time learning.

Aside from these technical issues, management issues are just as, and perhaps even more, important than the technical ones. The technology may not be the limiting factor, but the "management" of the technology may curtail a project or technology. One may have a technical success but a technology transfer failure. According to Gill (1995) and Yoon et al. (1995), the downfall of expert systems has been primarily due to organizational/management-related issues. Thus, future research should concentrate on improving technology transfer, institutionalization, and organizational factors.

Overall, the major trends in intelligent scheduling systems are:

- The majority of the AI approaches to scheduling have been constraint-based; the last 7 to 8 years have seen the emergence of constraint-based programming languages [e.g., CC(FD)].
- Movement toward expert scheduling system shells/generic constraint-based satisfaction problem-solvers.
- Interest in object-oriented programming paradigms and hierarchical architectures used in intelligent scheduling systems.

- Continued use of hybrid intelligent systems for scheduling (knowledge-based, neural networks, fuzzy logic, genetic algorithms, optimization/operations research, etc.).

2. GUESS (GENERICALLY USED EXPERT SCHEDULING SYSTEM)

As stated previously in the research directions for intelligent scheduling, there is great need to develop a generic scheduling toolkit in order to minimize the "reinventing the wheel" phenomenon. Toward this goal, GUESS (Generically Used Expert Scheduling System) has been developed as a generic expert scheduling system architecture and toolkit.

GUESS is designed to aid the human scheduler and to keep him/her in the loop. GUESS is a decision support aid as opposed to an automated replacement for the human scheduler. GUESS is programmed in C++ and runs on an IBM-PC Windows environment. GUESS has been designed to take advantage of an object-oriented, hierarchical architecture. GUESS contains two major levels of schedulers. The low-level schedulers are composed of different scheduling methods, mainly heuristic-based and optimization/algorithmic-based. The high-level scheduler, called the metascheduler, coordinates the activation of the low-level schedulers and injects any new information that is pertinent to the scheduling problem.

An object-oriented approach has been used for GUESS in order to maximize the reusability and corresponding generality of GUESS. As an example, GUESS can schedule 2551 events and over 14,000 constraints in under 45 seconds on a Dell 486 computer.

The next sections will discuss the design and development of GUESS.

3. THE OBJECT-ORIENTED STRUCTURE OF GUESS

A schedule has an events list and the resource list. A resource list is made up of resources of different types that directly or indirectly have an impact on the schedule. The events list is made up of different kinds of events. Most of the events have to be scheduled, while some act more like markers in the schedule to support the resource modeling.

The primary organizing construct is a class that describes an object. GUESS is a generic scheduling system. It can schedule different kinds of things. The OOPS feature of GUESS is that classes represent various abstractions of scheduling objects, such as events, constraints, resources, etc. An event in the schedule is implemented as a class that has members and functions acting on it. An event has its priority, start time, end time, a constraint list acting on it, an effects list, and finally a text-based name for human benefit to improve the readability and maintenance.

All events are inputted with a start and stop time. If an event has time conflicts, the event will be rescheduled. Technically, this qualifies GUESS as a repair-based scheduling system. Always having start and stop times avoids the concept of having to track an event's status as scheduled versus unscheduled. Also, the many objects in the system that deal with events don't have to know about scheduled/unscheduled status as an event is always considered scheduled.

The constraint list in an event has different kinds of constraints acting on the event. A constraint class has the weight of the constraint and the constraining resource or event. A constraint can indicate its satisfaction level. An event's satisfaction level is computed as a weighted average of its constraints satisfaction. An event's satisfaction is a measure of how well scheduled it is. In addition to after-the-fact measuring, constraints are also used to generate start and stop times for events.

A constraint by an event is a relational constraint. Relational constraints have the following subclasses: Before, After, During, NotDuring, StartsWith, EndsWith. A relational constraint is time based and can be between any two events. Suppose event E1 has to come before event E2. Event E1 would then have a Before constraint to E2. The other relational constraints operate as expected. Note, the previous case of E1 having a Before constraint does not imply that E2 has an After constraint. If desired, the After constraint would have to be separately created for event E2.

Event classes, constraint classes, and resource classes all have names for user readability and inputting. With inheritance, they can all use the same name handling code by inheriting from a common parent class. The subclasses of events, constraints, and resources get the same name handling code by default. Also by inheritance, the list handling code is used by many classes.

Objects in lists are accessed by the cached reference system. A cached reference to an object has both the name of the object in question and a pointer to the object. The pointer is found once by searching the list. By caching the pointer, the cached reference needs only to look up an object in a list once, saving time. A more important feature of cached references is the ability to refer to an object that hasn't been created yet. Interdependent object systems can have the problem of needing to reference an object before it exists. We don't look up the reference until it is needed, thus allowing a legal reference to an object before it exists.

3.1. Major Scheduling Approaches Used in GUESS

GUESS currently uses three major techniques for scheduling. The first scheduling method uses the Suggestion Tabulator, which is a heuristic approach where GUESS uses information derived from the constraints. The second method is a hill-climbing algorithm. The last scheduling method used in GUESS is a genetic algorithm approach, which is novel in that few scheduling systems have tried using such an approach. The first two techniques will be briefly discussed since they are more commonly used in intelligent scheduling systems. The genetic algorithm approach will be described more fully as it has rarely been used in intelligent scheduling applications.

3.1.1. Suggestion Tabulator (Sugtab)

The input file is read first. Depending on the technique chosen, the scheduling of the events takes place and the overall schedule is generated as output. Events are scheduled one at a time, starting with an event of highest priority. To start, an event is scheduled by asking all of its constraints for their suggestions. A suggestion tabulator is given to an event, and the event passes it to each of the event's constraints. Each constraint can make zero or more suggestions to the suggestion tabulator, after which it can deduce the best beginning and ending times for the event based on the accumulated suggestions. The sugtab for an event is of four types: beginning range, ending range, beginning and ending equal suggestions. The range is controlled by greater and less than suggestions. Some constraints suggest a specific time for the beginning or end. An equal tabulator tabulates the equal condition suggestions and returns the value. The range tabulator tabulates the range by keeping a low and high limit.

3.1.2. Hill Climbing

This is another technique available for scheduling events in GUESS. The initial beginning time and satisfaction of the event is assumed to be the best, and a nonlinear search for better values is done on both sides of the initial value of time to search for better time and satisfaction. As the search transverses through either sides of the hill, the exponential increment for the time change can be adjusted for speed improvement. Similar to other techniques, the satisfaction of a particular event is calculated based on the satisfaction level of all its corresponding constraints. The higher the satisfaction level of an event, the happier it is in the schedule.

3.1.3. Genetic Algorithm Approach

Implementation of a genetic algorithm (GA) approach for GUESS is done using the Evolutionary Object System (EOS) developed by Man Machine Interfaces, Inc. EOS is a C++ class library for creating genetic algorithms. The first decision that must be made is how to encode the schedule information as a chromosome. The standard encoding used in most classical genetic algorithm work is binary encoding. Each gene with the chromosome is a series of bits. The genes are linked together to build a long chromosome. EOS supports a variety of other possible encodings; however, the binary encoding is the most generic and was also recommended by the EOS vendor; so the decision was made to use the binary encoding in the implementation of a genetic algorithm within GUESS.

The only significant variable information associated with the schedule is the time at which each event is scheduled to occur. GUESS assumes that the duration of an event is fixed and determined by the user at the time the event is entered; therefore, the only significant information that must be associated with the event is the starting time of the event. Each event has a specific gene within the chromosome. The gene occupies a series of bits of size Time that are sufficient to record the starting time of an event.

The calculation of fitness comprises the core of the genetic algorithm. The basis of calculating the fitness was chosen to be the schedule satisfaction normalized to a positive number. Division by the number of events that cannot be scheduled (due to resource conflicts) is done to impose a stiff penalty to resource constraint violations. Without the penalty, the genetic algorithm tends to produce solutions with unschedulable events in alarming frequency.

After experimentation, it was decided that an elitist replacement strategy with a uniform crossover breeding approach would be used. The elitist replacement strategy replaces the worst individuals in the next generation with the best individuals from the current generation. This strategy was used because it appeared during preliminary analysis that some of the good solutions were being lost in the reproduction process.

Uniform crossover mates two chromosomes by introducing a randomly generated crossover mask. Genes represented by bits set in the mask are taken from the mother; genes represented by cleared bits in the mask are taken from the father. This appeared to give the best results in the trials. A population size of 10 and allowing the algorithm to continue for 10 generations before stopping gives excellent results.

The genetic algorithm yields very tight compact schedules with events scheduled in the minimum time span required. By contrast, while satisfying the schedule constraints, the traditional methods, namely suggestion tabulator and hill climbing, tend to do so by spreading out the schedule and increasing the schedule makespan. The length of time that the genetic algorithm takes is due mainly to the need to calculate schedule satisfaction for multiple schedules each generation. Compounding this is the requirement to process many generations before arriving at the solution. By contrast, the hill climbing and suggestion tabulator deal with the schedule in a much more localized manner. Each event has its satisfaction calculated individually and is then moved accordingly, resulting in fewer satisfaction calculations in arriving at a final solution.

3.2.   RESOURCE MODELING IN GUESS

Another major component of GUESS deserves attention. This is the resource modeling capability. Almost all scheduling problems depend in part on the availability of the necessary resources being present at the time of execution of a scheduled event. Some problems are primarily resource constrained, while in other problems there are a sufficient abundance of resources such that resources do not seriously constrain the scheduling. For GUESS, it was deemed necessary to add a generic resource model, capable of handling most resources that could conceivably be used in scheduling situations.

For purposes of scheduling there appear to be two generic types of resources that could be used to model most resources used within a scheduling scenario. These are termed "binary" and "depletable" resources, respectively. A binary resource is a resource in which a fixed amount is available at any given time; the resource is not depleted or consumed by the events utilizing it. An example of a binary resource might be the crew members on a space shuttle mission. Crew members may be utilized on a specific task but are not depleted or destroyed by the event. They are immediately available to tackle another task on completion of the present task. The function of the scheduling algorithm is to make sure that these binary resources are not overcommitted at any given point in time.

Depletable resources, on the other hand, are in fact consumed by tasks using them. As different events occur, these events utilize a portion of the resource until the resource is completely consumed and there is nothing left to consume. As well as consuming the resource, it is possible for certain events to replenish the resource. Typical systems that might be modeled by this approach include the consumption of propellant by a spacecraft as a result of various maneuvering events or the drain on the spacecraft battery caused by the operation of electrical equipment. In the case of the propellant, it is unlikely that events would occur to replenish the resource — in the case of the battery, recharging could occur by orienting the solar panels toward the sun.

The function of the resource scheduler is to schedule the activities to prevent depletion of the resource before all of the required activities are complete. In the case of resources that may be recharged, the scheduling algorithm must schedule sufficient recharging events between uses to keep adequate resources in hand to perform the necessary consuming activities. This involves alternating recharging and consuming activities in some pattern to sustain the resource.

These two types of resources are the most generic resources that can be used within a scheduling context; however, it was also deemed necessary to allow the addition of custom resource models that could be user-designed yet easily integrated within the GUESS scheduling engine. These custom models could be integrated as Dynamic Link Libraries (DLLs) and attached on the fly to the GUESS executable. This would allow unlimited flexibility for GUESS and would relieve the designers of having to anticipate unusual resource models or bloating the code in trying to incorporate every conceivable resource model within GUESS.

This choice of models provided a suitable methodology for the modeling of resources within GUESS while providing plenty of room for future expansion. The next decision was the scheduling algorithms to be used in satisfying the resource constraints and their relationship to the algorithms already being used to schedule other constraints within the schedule. Rather than attempting to build an external resource model, it was felt beneficial to integrate the resource constraint satisfaction mechanism within the existing constraint satisfaction methods.

There are in fact two reasons for deciding upon this approach:

- Resource constraints are in fact just another form of constraint, and it is beneficial to treat them in the same manner as other constraints from both a computational efficiency standpoint, as well as eliminating the need for doing several iterative calculations going from resources to constraints, in a back and forth motion, until the optimal solution to both problems is found.
- Having a single algorithmic model makes for a very elegant solution. In fact, the same optimization techniques can be used — the difference between the two types of constraints lies in the computation of its satisfaction score. The optimization algorithm need not be different. The "satisfaction criteria" is the only difference between the two.

The main emphasis in implementing a resource model for GUESS becomes a matter of determining the appropriate functions to use in computing resource satisfaction. The resource satisfaction should be a low value, indicating a lack of satisfaction and forcing the offending event to be rescheduled if the event makes the resource usage exceed the total allowed. The resource usage, if below the maximum allowed, is an acceptable state of affairs and should give a satisfaction rating consistent with this. For a binary resource, maximum resource usage should be encouraged (as long as the maximum limit is not exceeded), since this will tend to decrease the schedule span and make use of the resource.

For a depletable resource, the situation is not quite so clear-cut, since once a resource is gone, it must be either recharged (if it can be) or the resource is unusable for future activities. Therefore, the same positive satisfaction value is returned for all depletable resources whose usage is below the limit. A further simplifying assumption was made that resource usage is constant throughout the duration of the event. To get a profile of resource usage, resource usage is sampled throughout the duration of each event. A resource constraint satisfaction is obtained for each resource utilized by an event. A binary resource constraint will compute usage by integrating the resource usage over the time period of the event.

The algorithm first discards all events that do not overlap with the time period of interest. Then an adjustment is performed to obtain an adjusted average over the period of time for which the event overlaps. The implicit assumption is made that resource usage is linear over the event duration and multiple parallel events affect depletion in a linear additive fashion.

Usage for a depletable resource is calculated in a similar manner as that for a binary resource, with the principal difference being that all events scheduled prior to the beginning of the time period of interest must also be summed. In this instance, an overlapping event is defined as an event whose start time is less than the end of the interval of interest.

To allow the resource model in GUESS to be readily extensible, a feature for allowing the addition of custom resources is incorporated. The most flexible approach to doing this is to allow the user to add a custom dynamic link library that can be linked on the fly to the GUESS application. Doing so requires the development of a standard application programming interface (API) to allow communication between the DLL and the GUESS engine. This requires a definition of entry points and types to be utilized within the DLL. The GUESS executable loads the DLL using the standard Windows function LoadLibrary function and then attempts to load each of the exported entry points by name. GUESS loads each of the entry points by name rather than the number, even though loading by number is slightly more efficient — loading by name is easier to use and manage. As GUESS looks up the function pointers when the DLL is initially loaded, this causes an imperceptible performance penalty. If GUESS either cannot load the library or cannot find one of the required functions, then an error message is reported.

The scheduling engine in GUESS uses the suggestion tabulator. When a resource is over-committed and needs to be rescheduled, the suggestion preferred is to reschedule the current event to occur just after the last event using the resource. Since events are processed in priority order, this forces lower priority items to be scheduled later than high-priority events. A more sophisticated means of producing suggestions could be included as a later enhancement; however, for the test cases considered, the suggestion strategy yielded acceptable results.

4. TESTING AND PERFORMANCE OF GUESS

Scheduling problems are often complicated by large numbers of constraints relating activities to each other, resources to activities and to each other, and either resources or activities to events external to the system (Morton and Pentico, 1993). For example, there may be "precedence constraints" connecting activities that specify which activities must precede other activities, and by how much of a delay, or by how much allowed overlap. Or two particular activities may interfere with each other and be unable to use the same required resource simultaneously. Or it may not be possible to use two resources simultaneously during certain parts of the day or on the same activity. Or a resource may be unavailable during specified intervals due to planned maintenance or planned use outside the system. Since these complex interrelationships can make exact or even approximate solutions of large scheduling problems very difficult, it is natural to attempt to solve simpler versions of a problem first in order to gain insight. Then one can test how sensitive the solution is to this complexity and find approximate solutions to difficult problems where the complexity proves central (Morton and Pentico, 1993). This is the approach that the GUESS team followed in testing GUESS for proper verification and validation, as well as for its generic capabilities.

Morton and Pentico (1993) point out that a major need exists for the development of generic heuristic scheduling shells that would allow software houses or even sophisticated users to craft a scheduling system by inputting a description of the system structure and general parameters. Pinedo (1995) also suggests the need for a generic scheduling system. He indicates the following typical features of a generic scheduler (1995):

- Most generic scheduling systems have automatic scheduling routines to generate a "first" schedule for the user.
- Almost all generic scheduling systems have user interfaces that include Gantt charts and enable the human scheduler to manipulate schedules manually.
- Generic scheduling systems usually have report generators.
- Generic scheduling systems have a number of advantages over application-specific systems, including if the scheduling problem is a fairly standard problem and only a minor customization of a generic system suffices, then such an option is usually less expensive than developing an application-specific system from scratch.

GUESS is currently being tested in a number of applications. For NASA applications, such as scheduling satellite experimenter requests to use the NASA supported satellites, GUESS can schedule 2551 events and over 14,000 constraints in 45 seconds on a Dell 486 computer. This performance corresponds well with other NASA expert scheduling systems that can schedule up to 6000 events in 2.5 to 3 minutes.

We are also currently testing GUESS in other scheduling domains. These include: (1) scheduling for an Army strategic decision support application (i.e., force mobilization in a deployed theater); (2) scheduling Department of Computer Science courses and corresponding sections for a local college; (3) scheduling the baseball games; and (4) scheduling Army battalion training exercies. From preliminary results, we are optimistic that GUESS is generic enough to be easily used in these different scheduling applications.

5.   SUMMARY

In the coming years, the major trends in intelligent scheduling systems will be:

- The majority of the AI approaches to scheduling will continue to be constraint-based.
- Movement will continue toward expert scheduling system shells/generic constraint-based satisfaction problem-solvers.
- Interest will expand in object-oriented/agent-based programming paradigms and hierarchical architectures used in intelligent scheduling systems.
- Increased use will occur of hybrid intelligent systems for scheduling (knowledge-based, neural networks, fuzzy logic, genetic algorithms, optimization/operations research, etc.).

We feel that GUESS is an effort that supplements well these future directions in intelligent scheduling. More testing for the generic qualities of GUESS will be conducted in the near term, as will the expansion of the number of scheduling techniques in the GUESS toolkit.

ACKNOWLEDGMENTS

The authors appreciate the support from Colonel Wilkes and Professor Campbell at the Center for Strategic Leadership at the U.S. Army War College, George Washington University, and support from NASA Goddard Space Flight Center.

REFERENCES

Brown, D. And W. Scherer (Eds.) (1995), *Intelligent Scheduling Systems*, Kluwer Publishers, MA.

Eom, S. (1995), "Survey of operational expert system applications in business and management," *Interfaces*, TIMS.

Fox, M. and M. Zweben (Eds.) (1994), *Intelligent Scheduling*, AAAI Press/MIT Press, Menlo Park, CA.

Gill, T.G. (1995), "Early expert systems: where are they now?" *MIS Quarterly*, SIM, Minnesota, Vol. 19, No. 1, March.

Lee, J.K., M. Fox, and P. Watkins, Special issue on "Scheduling Expert Systems and Their Performances," *Expert Systems with Applications: An International Journal* (J. Liebowitz, Ed.), Elsevier/Pergamon Press, New York, Vol. 6, No. 3, 1993.

Liebowitz, J. (1993), Mapping Problem Requirements to Solution Scheduling Approaches in Expert Scheduling Systems for Mission Planning, Phase I Report, American Minority Engineering Corporation, NTIS, Arlington, VA.

Liebowitz, J. (Ed.) (1994), *Worldwide Expert System Activities and Trends*, Cognizant Communication Corp., New York.

Liebowitz, J. and P. Lightfoot (1993), "Scheduling approaches in expert systems: a study of their applicability," *Expert Systems with Applications Journal*, Elsevier, Oxford, Vol. 6, No. 3, July–September.

Liebowitz, J., P. Lightfoot, and P. Dent (1991), "Conflict resolution strategies in expert scheduling systems: survey and case study," *The Knowledge Engineering Review*, Cambridge University Press, England, Vol. 6, No. 4.

Morton, T. And J. Pentico (1993), *Heuristic Scheduling Systems*, John Wiley & Sons, New York.

NASA Goddard Space Flight Center, *Proceedings of the 1995 Goddard Conference on Space Applications of Artificial Intelligence*, Greenbelt, MD, May, 1995.

Noronha, S.J. and V.V.V. Sarma (1991), "Knowledge-based approaches for scheduling problems: a survey," *IEEE Transactions on Knowledge and Data Engineering*, IEEE, Vol. 3, No. 2, June.

Pinedo, M. (1995), *Scheduling Theory, Algorithms, and Systems*, Prentice Hall, Englewood Cliffs, NJ.

Stolte, A., An object-oriented approach to scheduling, *AI Expert*, Miller Freeman Publications, San Francisco, CA, 1994.

Wentworth, J.A. and R. Knaus (1994), "Highway Applications of Expert Systems: Guide for Test and Evaluation," White Paper, U.S. Federal Highway Administration Research Center, Washington, D.C.

Yoon, Y., T. Guimaraes, and Q. O'Neal (1995), "Exploring the factors associated with expert systems success," *MIS Quarterly*, SIM, Minnesota, Vol. 19, No. 1, March.

Zweben, M. And M. Fox (Eds.) (1994), *Intelligent Scheduling*, AAAI/MIT Press, Cambridge, MA.

24 Telecommunications

Ming Tan

CONTENTS

1. INTRODUCTION

Telecommunications is one of the most rapidly growing industries worldwide. In developing countries, there is a huge market to offer both wireline and wireless telephone services. The majority of people there simply do not have the basic telephone service. Many of these countries have started to privatize their telephone industry. In the developed countries such as the U.S., the explosion of Internet usage and the growth of personal computers are forcing telecommunications companies to expand the facility to offer both data and voice services. As the deregulation of the telephone industry gradually opens up the U.S. market for competition, telecommunications companies here will rely on advanced technologies for competitive leverage.

One such technology is the expert system technology that enables telecommunications companies to offer improved products and services at low cost. Expert systems in this context are computer programs that emulate the behavior of telecommunications experts and automate the operation of telecommunications systems using artificial intelligence techniques. Telecommunications expertise is a critical corporate asset, especially when companies are losing experts due to fierce competition and early retirement. New telecommunications technologies in the area of wireless and digital data services require skilled technicians to operate. Expert systems can help capture the knowledge and heuristics acquired by the experts over many years of experience and train a young generation of technicians to use and maintain advanced telecommunications systems.

Since the first bloom of expert systems in the early 1980s, the telecommunications industry has been in the forefront of applying expert system technology (Liebowitz, 1988; Liebowitz, 1995). Various expert systems have been developed for network diagnosis, repair, and maintenance. Yet, there is still room for expert system applications to meet the demand. The goal of this chapter is to bridge the gap between expert systems and telecommunications domains, and to make artificial intelligence techniques commonly accessible tools to accomplish some of important telecommunications tasks.

This chapter starts with some background information on telecommunications management and the application history of expert systems in this field. It then characterizes telecommunications domains and corresponding tasks, and describes common artificial intelligence techniques. This is followed by presenting some fielded applications that use these techniques. Finally, it draws some lessons and outlines future research and development directions.

2.   BACKGROUND

A telecommunications network is a complex aggregate of switches and a transmission medium, which together provide a multiplicity of channels over which many customers' messages and associated control signals can be transmitted. The telecommunications network provides access to different types of circuits and services that use them. Network switch software is one of the most complex software systems in the world. These networks must be managed carefully for efficient and reliable operation.

According to the Telecommunications Management Network (TMN) framework, there are four layers of functionalities in a telecommunications management model: element management layer that manages network elements, network management layer that manages telecommunications networks, service management layer that deals with customers, and business management layer that handles business decisions (see Figure 1). The information required to make a decision is passed upward toward the higher layers, whereas control messages are always directed downward the lower layers.

Specifically, in the bottom element management layer, one deals with network elements such as switches, cell sites, transmission medium, signaling system components (e.g., SS7), or customer

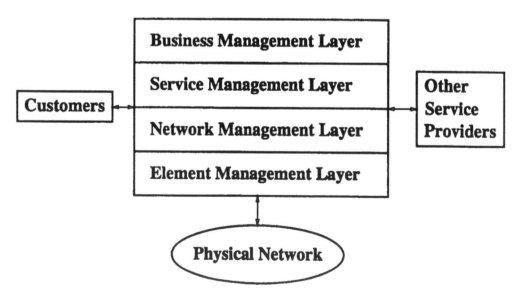

FIGURE 1   The TMN framework.

access facilities (e.g., PBX). Each element generates alarms that need to be monitored and filtered. Hardware problems must be corrected on the spot quickly. In the next network management layer, there are (1) fault management that is concerned with the detection, isolation, and correction of anomalous network conditions, (2) performance management that evaluates the quality of network services and determines the effectiveness of communication processes, (3) configuration management that allows technicians to view and modify the network configuration, (4) security management that authorizes use of system resources and protects network management data, and (5) accounting management that addresses costs associated with the use of network resources and allocates charges for the usage. Above that, the service management layer deals with customers including service setup, quality control and response, and billing. It often needs information retrieval. Finally, at the top layer, the business management makes decisions about network planning, market analysis, finance and budget, and resource allocation. Not all telecommunications companies follow the exact same management model, but TMN does summarize telecommunications management tasks.

Historically, expert system applications mainly focused on the network management layer (Liebowitz, 1988). Due to the complexity and diversity of telecommunications systems, telephone companies started to invest resource on artificial intelligence (AI) technology in the early 1980s to automate some of the operations. As a result, various rule-based expert systems were prototyped and fielded, especially in the areas of network repair and maintenance requiring monitoring and diagnosis. Some of them saved companies millions of dollars. Based on these initial successes, other AI techniques were also explored, including case-based reasoning, distributed AI, data mining, and machine learning. Cooperation between industries and universities on AI technology in that period was frequent. People had high expectation for AI in general.

Around the late 1980s and early 1990s, the hype of AI technology hit the wall. Meanwhile, the telecommunications industry also began to experience downsizing and focus on the bottom line. It was needed then to reaccess AI technology based on its value. Rule-based expert systems continued to serve important roles, either as independent systems or embedded within other systems. Yet, many other AI-based systems often stopped at the prototype level and did not become products. There was a gap between good concepts and hard reality. This, in some way, demonstrated the difficulty of telecommunications domains and the lack of understanding them when applying new AI techniques.

With continuing downsizing and early retirement of domain experts, AI technology was once again pushed to front in the mid 1990s. This time, deregulation spurred competition, automation is needed in all four management layers to cut cost and becomes critical to the lifehood of a company. New growth opportunities in wireless and digital services and international markets demand every company to do more with the same or less resources. In addition, many telecommunications software systems have been developed over the years. They input and output tremendous amounts of data that need to be interpreted and analyzed. This is similar to the "data overflow" of the information highway. Expert systems based on AI techniques can help to analyze this information, alleviate technicians from many routine tasks, and train them to be the experts of new technologies. More importantly, AI practitioners have learned from past lessons, and understood the potentials as well as the limitations of AI technology and what it take to develop AI-based products. Consequently, various types of expert systems have been fielded (see Section 5) and more are coming.

3.   TELECOMMUNICATIONS DOMAINS AND POTENTIAL TASKS

The telecommunications domains are very diverse, ranging from wireline telephone service, wireless communication, and satellite communication, to Internet service. Each domain has its own requirements. However, they all share the following characteristics, which makes them quite different from other application domains. These characteristics present challenges and opportunities for expert system applications:

1. *Large amount of data* — A typical network switch generates alarms on the order of a million per week and can handle millions of calls per day. Large databases are needed to store various types of data.
2. *Real time* — Many network operations must be carried out online in real-time. Delayed reactions can result in loss of revenue and customer confidence.
3. *Mission critical* — Hardware equipment and software systems often have redundancy built-in and expert systems must be equally reliable. Sometimes, misdiagnosis of a key transmission trunk can have a catastrophic result.
4. *Dealing with legacy systems* — Some switch technologies have existed for decades and it is expensive to replace them right now. Communicating and integrating with them is essential for many expert systems.
5. *Embedded AI* — Expert systems are often just a portion of a large system that uses AI techniques to accomplish special subtasks. The success of an expert system also depends on the rest of the system.
6. *Different user skills* — Some operation support personnel are highly trained and others are not computer literate. Knowledge acquisition must be specialized accordingly.
7. *Adaptive* — Switch version, usage pattern, telecommunications technology, and policy change frequently. Any expert systems should be adaptive to changes.

With these characteristics in mind, the following are some potential AI application tasks in each of four management layers:

1. *Element management layer* — Alarm filtering, monitoring and correlation, and admission control.
2. *Network management layer* — Alarm correlation, fault isolation and diagnosis; repair and maintenance; performance monitoring and tuning; traffic control and routing; configuration management and dynamic channel allocation; and workflow management that coordinates task assignments.
3. *Service management layer* — Service order, customer helpdesk, fraud detection, churning management, Internet service offering, billing automation, international market customization, and language translation and speech recognition.
4. *Business management layer* — Growth planning, facility design, resource scheduling, finance and contract management, and workforce training.

Some tasks are across the layers. They include data classification and interpretation, cooperation and negotiation among different systems, and data mining and trending analysis. In the next section, we discuss which AI techniques can be used for these tasks in telecommunications domains.

4.   AI TECHNIQUES

Expert systems use AI techniques to emulate the behavior of experts and automate the operation of systems. Determining a right technique for a specific application is crucial for any AI-based product. There are many AI techniques that have been and can be applied to telecommunications domains. The following AI techniques have been reported extensively. The detail of each technique can be found in many AI textbooks.

4.1.   RULE-BASED SYSTEMS

Rule-based systems emphasize declarative knowledge rather than search in the problem space. Knowledge is organized in IF-THEN-style rules. Rules are fired in sequence by an inference engine built in a rule-based shell. This kind of forward/backward chaining of fired rules captures a problem-solving strategy that is highly data driven. One quality of rule-based systems is that individual rules can be added, deleted, or changed independently. On the other hand, rule acquisition is a challenging aspect in the construction of rule-based systems.

Rule-based systems have been widely used in telecommunication domains where a "rule-of-thumb" or data-driven method is suitable. Their tasks include alarm correlation, fault isolation and diagnosis, repair and maintenance, traffic control and routing, service order, customer helpdesk, and resource allocation.

4.2.   SEARCH

Search is a generic problem-solving technique. A typical problem space consists of a number of decisions and each decision has a range of possible choice. A search technique allows one to systematically examine each choice at each decision until one finds a satisfactory solution. To speed up the search, one can use problem-specific heuristics to reduce the number of decisions or choices and prune the problem space. Another strategy is to modify the representation of the problem space to simplify the search. The search technique can also be used in different forms, e.g., by genetic algorithm and simulated annealing.

The search technique has been employed for a class of constraint satisfaction problems encountered in dynamic channel allocation, reconfiguring capacity, growth planning, and resource scheduling.

4.3.   NEURAL NETWORKS

Typical neural networks consist of several layers of nodes and links that connect the nodes between adjacent layers. They must be trained first before they can classify a pattern. Using an architecture loosely analogous to how neurons are organized in a brain, a neural network learns patterns by strengthening and weakening the weights of link connections between nodes when given a sufficient number of training patterns. Neural networks are suitable for knowledge-poor and data-rich domains. They are adaptive and noise tolerant. Training a large-size neural network is time consuming. This limits the scope of neural network applications.

Neural networks have been applied to the task of classification and interpretation, including admission control, performance tuning, data mining, traffic control and routing, dynamic channel allocation, fraud detection, network reconfiguration, and speech recognition.

4.4.   DECISION TREES AND CASE-BASED REASONING

Both machine learning techniques take a set of training examples/cases as input. Each training example/case consists of a set of decision choices and a corresponding class. The decision tree approach constructs a decision tree that has internal nodes labeled as decisions and the leaves labeled as classes. At run time, a classification is done by following a path from the root node to a leaf, given only a set of decision choices. In contrast, the case-based reasoning approach just stores training cases in a memory. It classifies a new case by comparing it with stored cases at run time using a variety of indexing and matching strategies. The class of the most similar case is determined as the classification. These two machine learning techniques can be used to acquire domain knowledge through collecting training examples, and complement the direct approach of rule acquisition. Unlike neural networks, their reasoning processes can be analyzed symbolically. Note that each technique has its own specific classification bias (e.g., the decision tree approach is sensitive to the order of decision choices).

Decision tree and case-based reasoning have been utilized to analyze data and construct domain expertise incrementally in telecommunications domains. Their tasks include alarm diagnosis, traffic control, workflow management, customer helpdesk, churning management, and data mining.

4.5. MODEL-BASED REASONING

Model-based reasoning is often used in the telecommunications domains where the dynamics or behavior can be modeled. Inference based on a correct model can be deep, direct, and efficient. The representation of such a model can be tables, finite machines, semantic networks, logic formulas, or Hidden Markov models. Typically, given the observed input, model-based systems use a model to predict the expected behavior, compare it with actual behavior, and then proceed to the next step in the model or stop to draw some conclusion. If a model is available, the correctness and completeness of the model determines the quality of model-based reasoning.

Model-based reasoning has been traditionally used for well-defined physical systems, yet it has also found its place in alarm correlation, network monitoring, configuration management, language translation, and speech recognition.

4.6. DISTRIBUTED ARTIFICIAL INTELLIGENCE

Distributed Artificial Intelligence (DAI) addresses cooperative and distributed problem-solving. Its paradigms include contracting, blackboard systems, distributed search, speech-act communication, and agent-based belief systems. DAI's goal is to find a globally acceptable solution from distributed and often limited local systems through their communication and coordination. Research in DAI involves studying the emerging behavior and convergence property of distributed agents. It also investigates the trade-off between problem solving and communication. DAI adds distribution to the complexity of AI technology.

Telecommunications domains are often distributed along spatial, functional, and organizational dimensions. In the past, special-purpose expert systems were developed independently. Recently, there is a trend to push toward the convergence and integration of these systems. For example, cooperation of management tasks is needed not only within the same management layer but also across all four layers. Public and private networks should be managed from both a logical network perspective and a physical network perspective. DAI techniques can be used to glue different expert systems (Velthuijsen, 1996). They have been tried in fault isolation, network design and management, dynamic channel allocation, resource scheduling, traffic control and routing, service order, and workflow management.

4.7. APPROXIMATE REASONING

Approximate reasoning deals with reasoning under uncertainty. This class of techniques is based on statistics, probability theory, fuzzy logic, or decision theory. They conduct reasoning processes using numbers rather than symbols, and their reasoning relies on a large amount of data, known prior beliefs, or some likelihood distribution. Their approaches range from combining rules using likelihoods or fuzzy logic to using utility-based decisions or Bayesian networks. They are often used to enhance the robustness of logic-based techniques and their conclusions, by nature, include uncertainty.

Due to the imprecise nature of many telecommunications domains and poor quality of information in databases, approximate reasoning has been found useful for fault isolation, trending analysis, data mining, billing, and growth planning.

4.8. HYBRID SYSTEMS

Each of above AI techniques has certain strengths and weaknesses. In practice, two or more of them are often used together to complement each other. Examples include combining rule-based systems and neural networks (Tan, 1996), rule-based and model-based systems (Worrest, 1996), search and DAI (Low, 1995), model-based systems and approximate reasoning (Chen, 1996), and case-based reasoning and decision trees (Masand, 1996). They can be loosely coupled (e.g., one's output is other's input), tightly coupled (e.g., blackboard paradigm allows different AI techniques to communicate with each other during problem-solving), or fully integrated (e.g., fuzzy rule-based systems). Keep in mind that no one AI technique is effective in all domains. Every AI technique has its respective domains where it is effective. Again, the key is to find a good match between AI techniques and a specific domain.

5. APPLICATIONS

Today, telecommunications networks are highly advanced, rapidly evolving systems of complex, interdependent technologies. As telecommunications networks fuse with the Internet, and as the underlying technologies continue their rapid evolution, these networks will become increasingly difficult to manage. AI is playing a large and growing role in various telecommunications management tasks. This section describes some of fielded AI applications in wireline and wireless communications.

5.1. WIRELINE COMMUNICATION

There are many existing automated network management systems containing AI modules for diagnosis, repair, and service dispatching. AT&T's ACE maintenance expert system was developed in the early 1980s (Liebowitz, 1988). Today, ACE has been sold and installed in more than 100 sites. ACE is a rule-based system that assists telephone engineers in maintaining the local loop. The local loop is the part of the telephone network that connects residential or business telephones with a local switching center. ACE is a background data analyzer that does its analysis by querying the database of daily test results stored in the Cable Repair Administration System (CRAS) and looks for patterns in the data that indicate where trouble may exist in the local loop. Each output of ACE is a classification or diagnosis of the problem, along with detailed support evidence from the CRAS system. ACE uses a forward-chaining rules strategy that breaks the overall problem into independent subproblems. Each subproblem can therefore be solved independently and the results assembled into a complete solution.

In contrast, NYNEX's MAX, developed in the late 1980s, is a telephone trouble screening expert that takes customer reports as input to initiate a local loop diagnosis (Rabinowitz, 1991). MAX works on one trouble at a time and communicates with the Loop Maintenance Operation System (LMOS), just like a human user sitting at an LMOS terminal. It uses forward-chaining rules to perform its diagnosis based on electrical measurements, customer's service class, weather, and network topology information, and enters the recommended dispatch instructions on the original LMOS screen. A goal of MAX is to reduce the number of double and false dispatches. MAX's rules can be customized to local conditions by a set of parameters. MAX is running in every residence-oriented maintenance center of NYNEX.

An even more proactive approach was used by TCAF (Silver, 1995), a rule-based expert system that performs 24-hour monitoring and surveillance of the local loop in GTE's telephone network. The aim of TCAF is to identify and fix developing faults before the customer detects any problem. At the same time, TCAF is designed to be quickly reactive to such problems that cannot be foreseen. Like MAX, TCAF diagnoses faults using several sources of information, including electrical measurements, customer's service class, and network topology (no weather information). Unlike MAX relying on customer reports, TCAF combines interrupt-driven events (switch alarms) that trigger measurements, and an intelligent polling algorithm (based on prior test results, customer fault history, and loop topology) to schedule measurements, for fault discovery. There is no human input to the whole process of trouble detection. TCAF can correctly detect cable cuts and coin faults over 90% of time. It is monitoring over 8 million GTE telephone lines (out of total 18 million).

Recently, Pacific Bell adopted a different approach for the same local loop problem. The Trouble Localization (TL) system (Chen, 1996) utilizes probabilistic reasoning techniques and logical operators to determine which component has the highest failure probability. This is achieved by building a topology of the local cable network and constructing a causal (Bayesian) network model. The model contains belief of failure for each component, given their current status, history data, cable pair distribution, and connectivity to other components. The resulting system can handle the poor quality of information in databases, perform nonmonotonic reasoning, and generate a ranked list of faulty components. The TL system is a crucial part of Outside Plant Analysis System that has been deployed statewide in California.

SSCFI (Special Service Circuit Fault Isolation) is a rule-based expert system that is in operation at all GTE's U.S. sites (Worrest, 1996). Special circuits are the telephone circuits other than the regular ones in the local loop (e.g., bank ATM, or any high-capacity, hard-wired, customized circuits). They are considered more complex than regular circuits. SSCFI diagnoses problems by recursively partitioning the circuit until the responsible fault is isolated. SSCFI reads and interprets trouble reports based on the design of special service circuits, conducts analog and digital tests via remotely activated test equipment, and routes the report to the appropriate repair group with the results of its analysis. This rule-based system also has a model-based component. SSCFI reads the target circuit's design to generate an internal circuit model to select tests that maximize diagnosis quality and minimize test time.

A telecommunications network can also be thought of as having two parts: the local loop and the interoffice facilities (IOF) network. The IOF network connects the local switching centers to one another. NYNEX has developed an expert system called Arachne for planning the IOF network (Alesi, 1996). Arachne's task is to ensure that NYNEX's investment in the IOF portion of its network satisfies the forecasted demand between switching centers, while achieving the maximum benefit per dollar invested. Arachne views the IOF network in terms of four layers of multiplexed signals: DS0, DS1, DS3, and Optical. It decomposes the planning task into two types of subtasks: (1) subtasks (in DS0 and DS1 levels) in which the size of the data is large, the variation in planning styles is great, and the equipment cost of decisions is small, and (2) subtasks (in DS3 and Optical levels) in which the data size is small and the equipment cost of decisions is high. Efficient heuristics are used to make the routing decisions in the former, while optimization techniques (dynamic programming) are used to optimize the routing decisions over the entire network for the latter. This cost-effective approach of combining heuristics and optimization techniques saves the company millions of dollars in IOF planning.

Telephone companies deal with customers on a daily basis. SAR, developed by Telesoft, is an expert system that supports salespeople in selling Intelligent Network services (Liebowitz, 1995). Intelligent Network services are a class of complex and flexible telecommunication services, whose configuration can be significantly personalized by salespeople in order to fit customer needs (using special circuits). Salespeople use SAR while they interact with customers to define all the information needed to set up a service configuration. SAR is a helpdesk application that provides congruency check, completeness check, cost estimation, and checking available resources for each service order. SAR uses forward-chaining rules and interacts with databases based on standard SQL queries. SAR has been fielded since 1993.

Telecommunications databases contain hundreds of millions of customer records. Controlling uncollectables falls into the larger risk management process. Predicting or modeling uncollectables is inherently probabilistic. Therefore, AT&T's APRI system (Ezawa, 1996) uses a special type of Bayesian network model for classifying uncollectible calls, which can be constructed efficiently from extremely large databases (reading a database just five times). APRI automatically constructs graphical probability models using the entropy-based concept of mutual information to select nodes and links of the Baysian networks. Given 800 million bytes of test data, the resulting models correctly classified 37% of the uncollectable calls, compared with only 10% by other approaches.

5.2. WIRELESS OR SATELLITE COMMUNICATION

A cellular network is a telecommunications network with some distinct features. It consists of a mobile switch center and a number of radio base stations, each responsible for covering a geographical service area called a cell. A mobile unit (portable or handheld) communicates with the base station via a voice channel. All base stations are linked by some transmission facilities to the switch center, which coordinates the operation for the entire system and serves as a connection point to the public switched telephone network. For satellite communication, each satellite can be treated as a big cell in this context. The cellular industry has been experiencing tremendous growth in recent years and needs AI technology to assist the operation and management of cellular networks.

AutoCell is a distributed client/server expert system operated by Singapore Telecom (Low, 1995). AutoCell periodically acquires cellular network status and traffic data. Based on these, it generates traffic forecasts for all cells, and performs automatic frequency reassignments to make more channels available at cells that are congested due to unexpected high demands or faulty channels. AutoCell also provides a performance reporting facility. AutoCell is implemented based on a multi-agent architecture where each agent is assigned a specific function, and agents communicate via the exchange of messages. It uses a heuristic search approach that combines hill climbing and branch-and-bound pruning to perform dynamic channel assignment. The revenue generated by improved traffic capacity due to AutoCell is estimated at over 1 million Singapore dollars in the first year (1994) alone.

PERFEX is a performance analysis and tuning expert system for cellular networks developed at GTE (Tan, 1996). Like AutoCell, it collects and displays the network status and traffic data. Based on performance and configuration data, PERFEX uses a neural network to discover generic performance problems in the network, and then uses rules to generate expert advice on how to fine-tune the system parameters to improve performance before resorting to adding or reassigning channels. These parameters include handoff thresholds, reassignment of handoff neighbors, configuration errors, and dynamic power control parameters. PERFEX provides a set of cellular tools to examine the network in finer detail and tightly integrates its different information presentation forms such as the map, tools, graphs, reports, and templates. PERFEX is in daily use at most GTE mobile switch centers.

InCharge is a system developed by SMARTS for real-time isolation and handling of network system problems (Kliger, 1996). InCharge employs a coding approach that reduces the event correlation time significantly by replacing a causal graph with simple codebooks. In a codebook, each problem is associated with a collapsed set of symptoms. At runtime, the actual symptoms are compared with the ones in the codebook by calculating the Hamming distance. The stored problem with the smallest Hamming distance is selected as the actual problem. InCharge has been adopted by Motorola Satellite Communications, which is using InCharge's codebook event correlation for their IRIDIUM project. The IRIDIUM project is a worldwide satellite-based communications system that will receive thousands of problems or symptoms at very high rate in real-time.

CHAMP is a churn analysis, modeling, and prediction system developed for GTE Mobilnet (Masand, 1996). Churn, a term for customer disconnecting the cellular service, is a very serious problem for the cellular industry, with churn rates ranging between 20 and 30% a year in most markets. CHAMP tries to identify those customers most likely to churn, which can be contacted for proactive churn prevention. CHAMP analyzes billing data using neural networks, decision trees, case-based reasoning, or a combination of the three methods. Its training and test data are preprocessed by eliminating irrelevant data fields, pruning unrelated subscribers, merging data from different months, sampling data, and selecting best fields using decision trees. The CHAMP system is able to identify a large part of predictable churn, with prediction rates (lift) usually 5 to 6 times better than random.

6. LESSONS AND RESEARCH ISSUES

Developing an expert system for telecommunications domains typically involves the following stages and each of them has a certain focus:

1. *Selection of an appropriate domain.* A successful expert system should tackle the bottleneck of an operation process and have a high impact. Listening to direct user feedback and conducting data analysis are needed to confirm the selection.
2. *Knowledge engineering.* Study the domain, collect information, and learn domain-specific knowledge from the experts. Is this a knowledge-rich or data-rich domain? What are the special requirements of this domain? What databases or legacy systems does it need to communicate with?
3. *Selection of AI techniques.* Appropriate AI techniques should be able to meet the requirements, and their potential weaknesses have little impact on the specific task. Different techniques can be compared or integrated. Their development and software cost should be taken into account.
4. *Prototype development.* A proof-of-concept system should be quickly developed and tried out by users. The preliminary result can be used to refine the prototype. Sometimes, a system can be developed in well-defined phases.
5. *Field trial.* A production system must be verified through several field trials. Is its speed efficient? Is its interface user-friendly? Is its operation reliable? At this stage, users do not care which techniques have been used as long as the system does the job.
6. *System transfer and maintenance.* An expert system that cannot be maintained or upgraded easily will not live very long because telecommunications technologies and their domain knowledge change constantly. An organization should be identified for the maintenance. A user manual is needed for interactive systems.

During more than a decade of developing expert systems for telecommunications domains, some valuable lessons on using AI techniques have been learned. First, an AI module is often embedded in a large system. It is the core component of the system, but is not everything. Typical telecommunications systems often require database accesses and good graphical user interface. Resource is needed to build these basic modules. Their roles are equivalent important. Second, there are many existing (or legacy) systems that a telecommunications company heavily depends on; an expert system often cannot operate alone. It must talk to these systems. In many situations, one must recognize the fact that an expert system is just a front or rear end of an existing system. Understanding these systems is necessary. Third, not every expert system needs to use the most advanced AI techniques. Simple AI techniques are often sufficient in practice. This reduces the complexity of an expert system. Fourth, expert systems are not a solution for all problems. An expert system approach is needed when it offers the best value among all other alternatives for a specific task. Fifth, to the end-users, an expert system should appear as a useful tool to increase their productivity rather than as a threat to their job security. Expert systems and human operators can often complement each other in terms of their capabilities. Finally, expert systems often need to communicate with each other (within a management layer or across management layers) or with other systems. A common platform and message interface for expert systems is essential for distributed application and system maintenance.

Today's telecommunications domains need AI techniques more than ever. They present a realistic but challenging testbed for AI techniques moving toward real-time, distributed, reliable, and adaptive.

For example, no existing alarm correlation system has the capability to correlate switching alarms, transmission alarms, Signaling System Number 7 alarms, and customer access facility alarms at the same time. The problem could be that there are just too many alarms to correlate in one central deposit. However, if one can limit and customize each monitoring agent to a focused area of problems, it becomes manageable. This requires distributed, personalized monitoring agents.

As another example, telecommunications fraud becomes a major issue in both wireline communication due to wire-tapping or unauthorized use and wireless communication due to customer ID cloning. Detecting fraudulent usage patterns is a nontrivial task because of the vast quantity of data that varies with time and location. This requires real-time data-mining techniques and both short- and long-term trending analyses.

The Internet presents a new opportunity and also poses a threat for the telecommunications industry. It could redefine telecommunications companies as only sellers of big pipes if they do not get into Internet connection and content services. The Internet offers the platform for electronic commerce, voice/data/audio/video communication, and even personal communication by shared virtual reality. Internet content applications include search tools, analysis tools, and personal-filtering tools. For example, GTE provides national electronic yellow pages (http://super-pages.gte.net). These tools need AI technology to make them smart, efficient, and adaptive.

Telecommunications tasks are often mission-critical. So far, there is little research on the reliability of AI techniques. When one copy of an expert system dies, how can another copy residing on a different machine recover the inference process and start from a clean state? Some Distributed AI techniques can be useful, but they have not been tried in practice. These are some of the critical tasks that need to be addressed now.

7. CONCLUSIONS

Artificial Intelligence (AI) technology is filling an essential need in telecommunications management tasks as networks grow in size, complexity, and importance. When conventional software approaches become severely stressed in certain areas, expert systems using AI technology have been demonstrated as viable alternative solutions. This chapter first lays out the overall picture of telecommunications management tasks, and then identifies those tasks where expert systems have made significant contributions. To benefit future expert system developers, it characterizes telecommunications domains and provides a list of commonly used AI techniques, where each of the techniques is described in terms of its main strength and weakness, plus its possible application tasks. In addition, this chapter describes some recent fielded expert systems in both wireline and wireless communication domains and sheds some light on the current state-of-the-art. Finally, it discusses development methodology, lists common development pitfalls found in telecommunications domains, and addresses research issues by challenging AI techniques for some currently needed tasks.

In the future, intelligent networks will self-diagnose, engage in distributed cooperative problem-solving, and perform proactive network management. People will have instant access to the information highway through intelligent agents that can navigate heterogeneous data sources, finding and presenting the information they need. Office and home computers will behave as smart telephones loaded with capabilities such as speech recognition, natural language translators and schedulers, and handle voice, fax, data, and video seamlessly. Clearly, AI will play an important enabling role in the communications network of the future.

REFERENCES

Alesi, C. Barnea, T. Benanav, D. Lee, E. Martin, J. Peterson, J., and Pope, R. Arachne: planning the telephone network at NYNEX. *Proceedings of the 3rd World Congress on Expert Systems.* (pp. 397–404) Seoul, Korea, 1996.

Chen, C. Hollidge, T., and Sharma, D.D. Localization of troubles in telephone cable networks. *Proceedings of AAAI96/IAA896*, (pp. 1461–1470). Portland, Oregon. 1996.

Ezawa, K. and Norton, S. Constructing Bayesian networks to predict uncollectible telecommunications accounts. *Journal of IEEE Expert*, Vol. 11, No. 5. (pp. 45–51). 1996.

Kliger, S. et al. High speed and robust event correlation. *IEEE Communications Magazine*, May 1996.

Liebowitz, J. (Eds.) *Expert System Applications to Telecommunications*. John Wiley & Sons, Inc. New York. 1988.

Liebowitz, J., and Prerau, D. (Eds.) *Worldwide Intelligent Systems: Approaches to Telecommunications & Network Management*. IOS Press, Inc. Amsterdam. 1995.

Low, C. Tan, Y. Choo, S. Lau, S., and Tay, S. AutoCell — An intelligent cellular mobile network management system. *Proceedings of IAAI95*, (pp. 114–124). Montreal, Quebec. 1995.

Masand, B. and Piatetsky-Shapiro, G. A comparison of approaches for maximizing business payoff of prediction models, *Proceedings of KDD-96*, Ed. J. Han, E. Simoudis, AAAI Press, 1996.

Rabinowitz, H. Flamholz, J. Wolin, E., and Eucher, J. NYNEX MAX: a telephone trouble screening expert. *PROCEEDINGS OF IAAI91*, (pp. 217–230). Anaheim, California. 1991.

Silver, B. Moghe, M. Eichen, E., Doleac, J. Bhatnagar, R. Qian, Z. Wan, H., and Brooks, D. Preemptive detection of failures in telephone networks. *Proceedings of GLOBECOM '95*, (pp. 1840–1844). Singapore. 1995.

Tan, M. Lafond, C. Jakobson, G., and Young, G. Supporting performance and configuration management of GTE cellular networks. *Proceedings of AAAI96/IAAI96*, (pp. 1556–1563). Portland, Oregon. 1996.

Velthuijsen, H. and Albayrak, S. *Intelligent Agents in Telecommunications Applications*. IOS Press, Amsterdam, 1996.

Worrest, R. Zito-Wolf, R. Wang, H., and Goyal, S. SSCFI: autonomous fault isolation in communications circuits. *Proceedings of AAAI96/IAAI96*, (pp. 1579–1587). Portland, Oregon. 1996.

25 Software Engineering for Expert Systems

Peter Grogono

CONTENTS

1. INTRODUCTION

In conventional programming, facts and reasoning are inextricably entwined. The earliest expert systems exploited LISP's symbolic processing capabilities to separate a set of rules, the *knowledge base*, from a procedure that derived inferences from the rules, the *inference engine*. The separation of facts from reasoning was then, and is now, the most important single factor that distinguishes expert systems from conventional software.

As a consequence of this separation, expert system development was at first quite different from software development. An expert and a researcher — who would later be known as a *knowledge engineer* — invented rules, added them to the knowledge base, and periodically checked the expert system for appropriate responses.

As expert systems grew larger and more complex, and as they moved from the laboratory into the commercial world, the similarities between the development of an expert system and the development of software became more important than their differences. Activities such as requirements analysis, specification, design, and maintenance have common features that transcend differences of architecture and implementation. In fact, some or all of these activities underlie the construction of any complex system, whether it is a building, a software system, or an expert system.

The evolution of expert systems that occurred during the 1970s and 1980s paralleled the evolution of software development in the 1950s and 1960s. Early computers were too small to support complex systems. As speed and capacity increased, so did the complexity of software. Researchers and practitioners turned for guidance to engineering, perceiving that engineers had established techniques for understanding and developing large systems. The term "software engineering" was coined at a NATO workshop in 1967 and was the theme of a NATO conference in 1968 (Naur, Randell, and Buxton, 1976).

As expert systems grew in size and complexity, developers adopted the same strategy as software developers: they borrowed and adapted techniques from a related area in which the problems had apparently been solved.

In this chapter, we assume familiarity with the basic principles and concepts of expert systems. We review software engineering principles, and we discuss ways in which software engineering techniques can be applied to expert system development. In the final section, we briefly discuss the application of expert systems to software engineering.

2. EXPERT SYSTEMS: THE BACKGROUND

The first expert systems were developed by researchers in both academic and industrial milieus. Although there were not many expert systems, the best of them clearly demonstrated the potential of the new technology. MYCIN, Prospector, and Xcon are well-known examples. The accomplishments of these expert systems attracted widespread interest and resulted in hundreds of companies applying expert system techniques to a large variety of problems. There were many early successes but, with hindsight, it became apparent that most of the successful expert systems were solving relatively simple problems (Durkin, 1996).

By the mid-1980s, expert systems were being built to solve new kinds of problems, many of which were extremely complex. Many of these systems failed to meet expectations, and there was a period of disillusionment. There were several reasons for failure: designers, impressed by the promises of "thinking machines" attempted to solve problems that were beyond the reach even of human experts; other designers took on projects so large that they could not be completed within a reasonable time frame; and yet other designers developed impressive systems that were never used because they failed to meet the requirements of the client (Durkin, 1996).

During the late 1980s, confidence returned and the popularity of expert systems began to rise again. The resurgence is probably due to two factors: first, there was a return to straightforward, well-defined applications and consequently projects were completed successfully; second, techniques from disciplines outside the mainstream of artificial intelligence — software engineering in particular — enabled the development of larger and more complex expert systems.

Another important development that occurred during the 1980s was the emergence of software tools for expert system development. Rather than offering complete expert systems, vendors began to provide expert system shells. A *shell* is a set of tools that simplify the development of an expert system. A company in need of an expert system no longer had to go through the time-consuming and expensive process of procuring a custom-built expert system; instead, they could acquire a shell and use it to create as many expert systems as they needed. Sales of software tools for expert system development increased from $60 million in 1988 to $140 million in 1993 (Durkin, 1996).

Meyer and Curley (1991) provide a two-dimensional classification scheme for knowledge-based systems; see Figure 1. The vertical dimension is the level of knowledge complexity embodied in

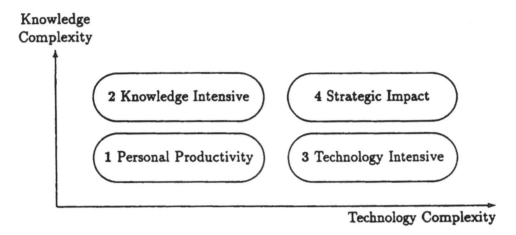

FIGURE 1   Classification of expert systems.

the system; this includes the depth and specialization of the encoded knowledge, the scope of the decisions made by the system, and the level of expertise needed to solve problems in the domain of the system. The horizontal dimension is the level of technological complexity used to build the system; this includes the nature of the hardware and software used in the construction of the system, the complexity of the user interface, and the use of database, network, user interface, and other specialized technologies.

Bradley and Hauser (1995) identify four categories of expert system within this classification. In Figure 1, expert systems in category 1 are the result of "personal productivity": they embody a relatively small amount of knowledge and little technology. Expert systems in category 2 incorporate extensive knowledge provided by one or more experts. Category 3 systems are like category 1 systems in that they capture only a modest body of knowledge, but they are enriched by advanced computing technology. Finally, expert systems in category 4 combine extensive knowledge and advanced technology. Although a particular expert system does not necessarily fall precisely into one of these categories, the categories provide reference points for many kinds of expert system.

Expert systems with high technology content — categories 3 and 4 in Figure 1 — are likely to require software engineering techniques in their development. It is expert systems of this kind that are the concern of this chapter.

3.   SOFTWARE ENGINEERING: AN OVERVIEW

The primary contribution of software engineering is to identify and describe the various activities involved in the development of a complex software artifact. Figure 2 shows some of these activities. For a small system, activities may be merged, performed implicitly, or even omitted entirely. The development of a large system may require repetition of the activities, and perhaps additional activities.

The second contribution of software engineering is to identify various ways of ordering the activities into a *life cycle*. The first life cycle proposed was the *waterfall* (Royce, 1970), which required the activities to be performed sequentially in the order listed above but provided for some feedback between consecutive activities. For example, a specification could be changed during the design phase but not during the implementation phase.

The waterfall is adequate when the people who will eventually use the system (the *clients*) have a clear idea of their requirements. If the proposed system incorporates novel ideas or techniques, the clients will probably not know what they want until they have gained experience with the system, by which time it may be too late to reconsider early design decisions and rebuild the

Requirements analysis

Specification

Design

Implementation

Testing

Maintenance

Documentation

FIGURE 2   Activities in software development.

system. For this reason, the waterfall life cycle is not usually considered to be suitable for expert system development.

The *spiral* life cycle (Boehm, 1986) avoids some of the problems of the waterfall. Development is a sequence of tasks that leads toward the final product. Each task is preceded by a *risk analysis* and followed by *verification.* The risk analysis identifies the things most likely to go wrong during the current cycle; if the problems appear to be insoluble, the project may be abandoned. Verification ensures that the chosen task has been completed successfully. Each cycle — analyze risk, perform task, verify — yields a partial product that can be demonstrated to the user. A task in the spiral approach may correspond to a phase of the waterfall, but it is more likely to be the complete development of a component of the system.

For each phase in the development of software, there is a corresponding activity in the development of an expert system. The details of the phase may be different, but the underlying principles and purposes are the same.

In software development, the *requirements analysis* phase determines the needs of the client. Requirements are often divided into *functional* and *nonfunctional* requirements. The functional requirements of an expert system include aspects such as the breadth and depth of the knowledge base, facilities for maintaining and updating the knowledge base, and the form of the user interface. Nonfunctional requirements would include the number of users supported, response times, and the ability to cooperate with other software components.

After obtaining requirements, the supplier develops a *specification.* The specification plays a dual role, acting as a *contract* and a *blueprint* (Batarekh, Preece, Bennett, and Grogono, 1991). As a contract, the specification provides a detailed description of what the system must do and, perhaps, what it must not do. If possible, the specification should include a set of *acceptance tests:* the client and the supplier agree that the contract has been honored when the expert system has passed all — or perhaps a specified percentage — of the acceptance tests.

In software development, it is usually considered undesirable to include implementation information in the specification. Inevitably, however, specifications do contain explicit and implicit hints of possible implementations; if this were not the case, the world would be full of unimplementable specifications. It is particularly difficult to keep implementation information out of an expert system specification. The specification should describe the accessibility of the knowledge in the knowledge base, and this accessibility influences the structure of the knowledge base. In this sense, the specification is a blueprint as well as a contract: it provides the developers with a ground plan for the next phase, design.

A software *design* is a description of the proposed systems at a level of detail that enables programmers to code the parts for which they are responsible without necessarily understanding the system as a whole. A design typically has at least three components: the *architecture* shows the modules that constitute the system and the connections between them; the *module interface specifications* define the external behavior of each module; and the *internal module descriptions* describe the implementation details of each module.

An expert system design is similar in form but is usually less detailed. The architecture identifies the major components of the expert system; these may include user interfaces, report generators, databases, and other software components, as well as the knowledge base. The knowledge base itself may be divided into modules to simplify its development and maintenance. As in a software design, the module interface specifications define the responsibilities of each module. But the internal module descriptions may be simpler, or even nonexistent, for modules that will be implemented simply as sets of rules.

Building of the system takes place during the implementation phase. (In a business context, "implementation" is often used to mean the installation of existing software within the company (Bradley and Hauser, 1995). In this chapter, "implementation" denotes the construction of a system from its design.) Programmers write code for the software components and knowledge engineers perform knowledge acquisition and then translate declarative statements into rules for knowledge base components.

Testing may be postponed until implementation is complete, but it is usually preferable to start testing as soon as there are individual components to test. When *unit tests* have demonstrated that all components are functioning correctly, *integration tests* are run to check the performance of the complete system. Testing a knowledge base is quite different from testing code, and Section 4.1 provides a detailed discussion of this aspect of expert system development.

When the expert system has passed a sufficient number of acceptance tests, it is delivered to the client. The developer does not stop working on the project, however, because all large systems require *maintenance*. Software maintenance is commonly divided into three categories. *Corrective maintenance* consists of finding and fixing faults in the system. Even after thorough testing, a complex system will usually still have faults, and they must be corrected as soon as possible after the client has discovered them. *Perfective maintenance* consists of improving the usefulness or performance of the system, usually in response to requests from the client or users. For an expert system, perfective maintenance might include adding or modifying rules, shortening response times for common requests, or improving the user interface. Finally, *adaptive maintenance* may be necessary to enable the system to operate in a modified environment: the client may have obtained more user terminals, larger and sharper screens, or have upgraded the hardware or operating system. In each case, the system must be adapted to the new conditions.

If the costs associated with a large system are measured over its entire lifespan, from inception to obsolescence, maintenance costs dominate, often accounting for 80% or more of the total cost. It follows that developers should expend effort during the early phases to simplify maintenance.

4. CONTRIBUTIONS OF SOFTWARE ENGINEERING TO EXPERT SYSTEM DEVELOPMENT

Software engineering has made a number of significant contributions to expert system development. We review these in this section.

4.1. EVALUATION

There are two ways of ensuring the correctness of a system. One is to prevent errors from occurring during construction; the other is to check for errors after construction is completed. Since error-free construction is generally considered to be infeasible, construction is almost always followed by evaluation. We have referred to the evaluation phase informally above as "testing." In software engineering, evaluation is more formally considered as having two components: verification and validation.

We make a distinction between verification and validation that is widely but not universally accepted. Indeed, some authors use the abbreviation "V&V" as if it was a single noun. Following Boehm (1979), we define *verification* to denote the process of checking that the system is internally consistent, and we define validation to denote the process of checking that the system performs according to the client's requirements. Informally, we can say that verification answers the question "Have we built the system right?" and validation answers the question "Have we built the right system?"

Evaluation of early expert systems was straightforward: if the expert system gave the same answers as the expert, it was assumed to be correct. As expert systems have increased in complexity, the importance of evaluating them has increased, and evaluation techniques have been borrowed from software engineering (Grogono, Batarekh, Preece, Shinghal, and Suen, 1990).

4.1.1.   Verification

Geldof et al. (1996) distinguish two forms of verification: *macroverification* takes place early in the development cycle and identifies structural and conceptual problems; *microverification* takes place later in development and provides a detailed analysis of the components of the system.

Software verification is very difficult; even after 20 years or more of research, only a very small proportion of software is formally verified. (Compilers check the syntax and "static semantics" of programs, but this is not usually considered to constitute verification.) The situation for expert systems is somewhat different: since rule bases have a simple and logical structure, verification is straightforward and can even be automated.

An expert system that fails verification is internally inconsistent or has *structural defects*. The possible defects of a rule base fall into four main categories: ambivalence, circularity, deficiency, and redundancy.

Ambivalence. A rule base is ambivalent if it can derive contradictory or inconsistent results from a single set of input data. A rule base containing the rules

$$A \wedge B \to R$$

$$B \wedge A \to \neg R$$

is ambivalent because, given the set $\{A,B\}$ as input facts, the rule base can use either the first rule to infer that R is true or the second rule to infer that R is false. (The first rule is read "From A and B, infer R." The second rule is read "From B and A, infer not-R.")

Circularity. A rule base is circular if there are infinite chains of rules. For example, a rule base containing the rules

$$A \to B$$

$$B \to C$$

$$C \to A$$

is circular. Even if the inference engine is clever enough to avoid getting stuck in a loop, circularity strongly suggests an error in the formulation of the rules.

Deficiency. A rule base is deficient if it contains incomplete rule chains. For example, if we assume that the set of possible input facts is $\{A,B\}$ and the set of possible conclusions is $\{C,D\}$, then the rule base

$$A \to X$$

$$B \rightarrow Y$$

$$X \rightarrow C$$

$$Z \rightarrow D$$

is doubly deficient because input B cannot be used to infer any conclusions and conclusion D can never be derived from the input data.

Redundancy. A rule base is redundant if rules can be deleted from it without changing the set of possible inferences. The rule base

$$A \rightarrow B$$

$$B \rightarrow C$$

$$A \rightarrow C$$

is redundant because the first two rules are sufficient to infer C from A, by transitivity. Redundancy is harmless — although it may affect the response time of the expert system — but its presence suggests errors in the formulation of the rules.

Structural errors in a rule base are not necessarily due to mistakes in formalizing the expert's knowledge. They are usually present for more mundane reasons. The deficiency in the example above is due to the rules $B \rightarrow Y$ and $Z \rightarrow D$. In an actual rule base, these rules might be

large-flat-base $\rightarrow$ box-is-stable

and

box-stable $\rightarrow$ can-take-load

In this case, the deficiency is caused by inconsistent naming rather than a logical error.

Verification treats the rule base as a formal system; consequently, verification can be automated, at least in principle. In practice, full verification of a large rule base may be infeasible. Suppose that the rule base contains N rules. Processing each individual rule requires time time proportional to N. Processing all pairs of rules (perhaps for a partial ambivalence check) requires time time proportional to N^2. Processing all chains of k rules requires time time proportional to N^k. It follows that full verification of a rule base in which inferences may involve k steps will also require time time proportional to N^k. Since N may be in the thousands, full verification is infeasible even for moderate values of k. The time complexity may be reduced by modularizing the rule base, a possibility discussed further in Section 4.2.

In the above discussion, we have assumed that there are no certainty factors associated with rules and that verification can be based on classical logic. If rules are associated with certainty factors, verification is possible but the results may not be so clear-cut. For example, an apparently redundant rule may not be redundant if its presence increases the certainty of a conclusion.

4.1.2. Validation

Validation is the process of ensuring that an expert system satisfies the requirements of the clients. Since the requirements of the expert system are expressed informally, it is not possible to automate validation completely. However, software tools can be used to facilitate some phases of the validation process.

Practical validation usually consists of constructing a set of test problems, obtaining the responses of the expert system to these problems, and comparing the results with expected responses. Although the idea is simple, validating a large expert system can be a formidable task.

The expectations for early expert systems were straightforward: users thought that the expert system should behave like a human expert. For example, the performance of an expert system designed to diagnose disease should be comparable to that of an experienced doctor performing diagnosis. But even this simple criterion is fraught with difficulties. Should the expert system behave like a particular doctor or like a panel of doctors? Doctors occasionally make mistakes and are sometimes subjected to malpractice suits; if an expert system makes a mistake, who is liable? These issues, however, are outside the scope of this chapter. For the purpose of validation, we need to know two things: how the problem set is designed, and how the results provided by the expert system in response to the problems are evaluated.

The easiest approach to validation is to ask the expert or experts whose knowledge is embodied in the expert system. The disadvantage of this approach is that the experts will tend to test for exactly the cases that they put into the expert system initially and they will not adequately test scenarios that did not occur to them.

A more difficult and expensive approach to validation is to recruit an independent group of experts to design tests and specify acceptable responses. This approach is not always feasible: in some areas of expertise, there may be different "schools" who disagree about the test results. If the expert system is proprietary, the clients may not want to reveal its capabilities to experts who are not employed by the company.

It is sometimes possible to derive test problems from previous experience. Consider, for example, an expert system used by a bank to assess loan requests. The bank could use data obtained from previous loans and repayment records to construct the test cases for the expert system and then compare the predictions of the expert system to what actually happened.

4.2. MODULARIZATION

As mentioned in Section 1, the development of expert system technology has followed the development of software engineering technology. During the 1970s, for example, software engineers recognized the importance of modular program structure and added features to programming languages to support modularity. They introduced the principle of "high cohesion and low coupling" as an aid to module design: an individual module is "cohesive" if it performs a simple, well-defined task; a complete system is "weakly coupled" if the connections between modules are minimized. During the 1980s, expert system designers followed the lead of software engineers and began to build modular expert systems.

There are several reasons for preferring a modular system to a monolithic system. A modular system is easier to understand because modules can be understood individually. A modular system is easier to test because modules can be tested independently. Module testing reduces the time complexity of testing, mentioned in Section 4.1.1. Correction and maintenance are both simplified if the expert system is modularized because the scope of many changes is restricted to a small number of modules or even to a single module.

A module in an expert system is a group of rules (Philip, 1993). Since a rule has several "inputs" (facts that must be asserted in order for the rule to fire) and a single "output" (the rule fires, asserting its conclusion), a rule is analogous to a function or procedure rather than to a single statement in a software system. Thus, the number of rules in a module is arbitrary: even a single rule may constitute a module.

An expert system module is cohesive if it is responsible for a well-defined subdomain of the knowledge embodied in the expert system. An individual rule is cohesive if each of its clauses are part of a single piece of knowledge.

Attempts to simplify a modular rule base can lead to loss of cohesion. Suppose that the rule base contains two rules, R_1 and R_2, that are cohesive but contain a number of clauses in common. Creating a third rule, R_3, containing the common rules may reduce the total size of the rule base. But the new rule base may be harder to understand, test, and maintain if the new rule R_3 is not cohesive (Philip, 1993). Consequently, the designer of a modular rule base should focus on high cohesion and low coupling rather than on the number and complexity of individual rules.

4.3.   LIFE CYCLE MODELS

In Section 3, we identified the waterfall and the spiral as the principal life cycle models in software engineering. This is a simplification, of course: many life cycles have been proposed for both software development and expert system development. In this section, we comment briefly on aspects of the life cycle that relate specifically to expert systems.

From the early days of expert systems, it has been recognized that incremental development is better than monolithic development (Lyons, 1992). For example, O'Keefe (1990) shows how the spiral model can be adapted to expert system development.

Figure 3 shows the life cycle proposed by Gonzalez and Dankel (1993) for the development of knowledge-based systems. The purpose of the *analysis* phase is to evaluate the problem and the available resources. The *specification* phase is a formal presentation of the results of analysis; since knowledge-based systems are heuristic, a specification is essential. The *preliminary design* phase includes enough high-level design decisions to enable the construction of a prototype. The *initial prototyping* phase is a key step in the life cycle because the prototype justifies the design decisions. The prototype should be similar to the proposed system but may lack breadth; it does not need to be robust. During the *evaluation* phase, all of the previous steps are reviewed and a decision is made as to whether to complete the project. The *final design* phase involves completing the initial design and choosing resources for the system to be delivered.

Incremental development is used to implement the system. The *implementation* phase consists of acquiring all of the required knowledge and encoding it in the rule base. At various stages,

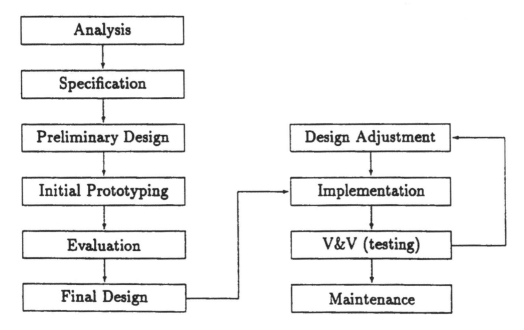

FIGURE 3   Knowledge-based system life cycle.

testing is performed to evaluate the encoded knowledge. If necessary, *design adjustment* is performed between testing and the next implementation step. Finally, when the complete system has been tested, the *maintenance* phase begins.

4.4.   METHODS OF KNOWLEDGE REPRESENTATION

We have assumed above that knowledge in the expert system is represented as rules. This is not always the case. Several other methods for representing knowledge are available. We discuss only software engineering aspects of knowledge representation here: other aspects may be found elsewhere (Gonzalez and Dankel, 1993; Chapter 6).

Frames. It has long been recognized that rule collections have significant limitations. They do not provide easy methods for grouping facts into convenient clusters or for associating procedural knowledge with factual knowledge. A *frame* encapsulates a collection of related facts and procedures. A frame has a number of *slots*, each of which can hold data or, exploiting LISP's capabilities, code. Frames are used in expert systems that employ *model-based* or *case-based* reasoning. Some expert systems, called *hybrid* systems, use both rules and frames.

Associative networks. An associative (or *semantic*) network is a labeled, directed graph in which nodes represent concepts and edges represent associations between concepts. Networks tend to be more explicit and succinct, and may be more efficient to process, than rules. But they have severe disadvantages: there is no accepted standard for interpretation; care must be taken to avoid invalid inferences; and combinatorial explosion may occur.

From the point of view of software engineering, there is little difference between rules, frames, and associative networks. In each case, there is a knowledge base and an inference engine, and similar development techniques are applicable. The importance of these alternative representations is that they were eventually combined with a new development in software engineering: object-oriented programming.

Objects. An *object* is a collection of data and a description, in the form of procedures and functions, of how the data can be manipulated. The object-oriented programming paradigm has become popular for a number of reasons, not the least of which is the fact that people find modeling with objects more natural than modeling with functions. Since programming with objects is quite different from programming with functions, new programming languages, such as Smalltalk, Eiffel, and C++, and new development paradigms have been introduced.

Object technology has been applied successfully to the engineering of expert systems. An object is in many respects similar to a frame. Objects, however, have a number of advantages over frames, including: encapsulation, or the ability of objects to hide information; inheritance, or describing properties of specific objects in terms of more general objects; and polymorphism, which enables objects of different kinds to recognize the same protocol, facilitating reuse. There is also evidence that object-oriented techniques "scale up" well, allowing the development of larger systems than other techniques from a given set of resources.

4.5.   WALKTHROUGHS

Software developers use walkthroughs and inspections to check the quality of code. During a walkthrough, a group of people examine source code line by line, "walking through" it and looking for logical errors, omissions, and inconsistencies. The group is small: four members are typical, although there can be as many as eight. The author of the code is usually present. Although walkthroughs involve several people and proceed slowly — a few hundred lines of code per hour at most — they are more cost effective than individual debugging efforts (Russell, 1991). Inspections are similar in principle to walkthroughs but different in detail. A design inspection, for example, might be used to check that the design fulfills the requirements of a specification.

Walkthroughs are also effective for expert system development (Lyons, 1992). Experts and users can collaborate in a careful reading of the rules that is often more productive than simply running the expert system and looking at its answers.

4.6. METRICS

Effective project management requires estimation and prediction. Quantitative measurements can be used to predict the amount of effort required to complete a project, to estimate completion dates, to monitor progress, and to assess quality. Unfortunately, simple metrics, such as lines of code written, are not particularly useful. Creating better measurement tools is an active area of research.

Metrication is another area in which expert system research appears to be following the lead established by software engineering. Quantitative analysis of expert systems will enable developers to improve their estimates of the cost of constructing and maintaining particular systems (Chen, Grogono, and Suen, 1994).

4.7. REUSE

A major goal of software engineering during the last decade has been "software reusability." The term refers to the fact that programmers tend to spend most of their time writing code that is very similar to code that already exists. Although this is clearly wasteful, the structured programming techniques introduced in the 1970s make it hard to avoid. The more recent paradigm, object-oriented programming, mentioned in Section 4.4, promises to simplify the task of reusing existing software.

Among expert systems, the number and size of existing rule bases is already more than sufficient to warrant interest in the reuse of rules. Modularity is a factor in the design of expert systems because a rule module is more likely to be reusable than an unstructured collection of rules. If the analogy with object-oriented programming holds, it is possible that frame-based expert systems will provide more opportunities for reuse than rule-based expert systems.

4.8. INVOLVING THE CLIENTS

In some kinds of business, the client and the supplier write a contract and then do not meet again until the product is delivered. Software engineers know that this scenario will not succeed for a product of any complexity. It is important to keep the client involved during the development of the product. This can be accomplished by incremental development, in which a series of deliverables are delivered to and accepted by the client.

The obvious advantage of client involvement is that problems that may lead to the client failing to accept the product can be recognized and corrected during development. A more subtle advantage is that the client's employees will become familiar with the expert system during development and will be less likely to reject it when the final version is delivered (Bradley and Hauser, 1995).

4.9. TRAINING THE CLIENTS

The supplier may provide the client with a "user manual" for the expert system or, if the expert system is supposed to be "user friendly," may deliver it with minimal documentation. For systems with any degree of complexity, both of these approaches are unlikely to succeed. The client may refuse delivery, or accept the system but fail to use it.

To avoid rejection of the system, client training should be included in the development of any complex expert system. Good training significantly increases the probability that the expert system will be accepted and used by the client (Liebowitz, 1991, p. 51).

5. APPLYING EXPERT SYSTEMS TO SOFTWARE ENGINEERING

The main focus of this chapter is the application of software engineering principles to expert system development. There is another side to the coin: the application of expert systems to software development. From the earliest days, programmers have enjoyed automated assistance from assemblers, compilers, debuggers, and other tools. As artificial intelligence matured, it was natural to look for intelligent assistance (Winograd, 1973). There have indeed been a number of fruitful collaborations between artificial intelligence and software engineering (Partridge, 1991). In this section, we focus specifically on the use of expert and rule-based systems in software engineering. Two issues of *IEEE Expert* have been devoted to the use of knowledge-based and expert systems in software engineering (Sriram and Rychener, 1986; Tanik and Yeh, 1988).

Tools that embody knowledge are ubiquitous in software engineering. For example, smart editors incorporate knowledge about the syntax of the programming language in use, and compilers embody knowledge of its semantics. These, however, are passive tools: their functions are disjoint from the activities of the programmer. The novelty introduced by artificial intelligence techniques is the *interactiveness* of the tools.

5.1. PECOS

PECOS represents one of the earliest attempts to apply rule-based reasoning to program development (Barstow, 1979). It uses about 400 rules, of which roughly three quarters are independent of the target language (INTERLISP). The programming methodology is similar to stepwise refinement: PECOS starts with a high-level, but formal, representation of a problem; as rules are applied, the abstract concepts of the problem statement are mapped onto lower level implementation structures; implementations are mapped onto code segments; and, eventually, the entire problem statement has been translated into code.

It is sometimes possible to apply more than one rule to a given configuration. It is therefore possible for PECOS to generate several implementations from a single problem statement, a capability that could be exploited by downstream tools to select a solution that matches particular criteria. For example, PECOS generated about a dozen different programs from a problem statement that specified a test for membership of a collection: the solutions depend on properties of the collection, such as how it is represented and whether items are ordered.

5.2. THE PROGRAMMER'S APPRENTICE

One of the best known applications of artificial intelligence to program development is the Programmer's Apprentice (PA) (Rich and Waters, 1990), a system that depends upon knowledge that is *shared* between the programmer and the programming environment. PA is implemented as KBEmacs — the Knowledge-Based Editor in Emacs.

PA has a library of *clichés* that codify programming concepts over a wide spectrum, ranging from high-level designs such as *command processor* to low-level implementations such as *binary search*. PA uses the knowledge embodied in a cliché in several different ways: to refine the program's outline into detailed code; to detect inconsistencies between the cliché and the program's purported use of it; and to explain its (PS's) actions and decisions.

Clichés are represented in Plan Calculus. A plan is a directed graph that describes both control flow and data flow. The graphical representation avoids dependence on a particular programming language: PA has been used to assist programmers writing in LISP, Ada, and other languages. The formal meaning of a plan is the set of computations that the plan describes. Formalization allows PA to reason about plans.

PA is a knowledge-based system but not, in the strict sense, an expert system. It uses a hybrid reasoning system, called Cake, with four layers. The top layer is the Plan Calculus, and it rests on a frames layer, an algebraic reasoning layer, and a propositional logic layer. The propositional logic layer supports nonmonotonic reasoning so that facts may be retracted when they cease being true.

The Programmer's Apprentice addresses the implementation phase of software engineering. Rich and Waters have proposed apprentices for earlier phases of development: the Designer's Apprentice and the Requirements Apprentice (Rich, Waters, and Reubenstein, 1987).

5.3. PROFESSOR MARVEL

Professor Marvel is a programming assistant that provides insights about the system under development (Kaiser, Feler, and Popovich, 1988). Marvel also automates some of the purely routine activities of software development, such as recompiling after source code changes and recording errors found by the compiler.

Marvel uses rules that are slightly more complicated than conventional IF-THEN rules. A Marvel rule has three components: a precondition, an activity, and a postcondition. The precondition must be true before the activity can be performed, and performing the activity ensures that the postcondition is true. For example, a rule for compiling the module M has: precondition *not-compiled* (M); activity *compile* (M); and postcondition *compiled* $(M) \vee$ *errors* (M). (The actual rule used in Marvel is more complex than this, but has the same structure.) Marvel uses both forward and backward chaining. For example, if the programmer tries to execute a program P, and Marvel does not have *compiled* (P) asserted, it will apply the rule above to compile P.

Obtrusive automation can be annoying to users. Marvel uses hints (rules without postconditions) to avoid unnecessary tasks, such as recompiling while the programmer is still browsing (and perhaps considering changing) the source code. Marvel also has programmer-selectable strategies, which are collections of rules and hints. For example, a programmer can choose between "minor revision" and "major revision" strategies.

5.4. THE SPECIFICATION-TRANSFORMATION EXPERT SYSTEM

The Specification-Transformation Expert System (STES) translates requirements specifications into design specifications (Tsai and Ridge, 1988). STES, which is based on structured design methodology (Yourdon and Constantine, 1979), transforms dataflow diagrams into structure charts. The transformation is a natural application of expert system techniques because it requires both algorithmic and heuristic tasks. For example, the classification of the components of a dataflow diagram can be performed more or less mechanically, but heuristics are required to obtain a design that has desirable coupling and cohesion characteristics. STES is implemented in OPS5.

Other software development environments that use expert system techniques include Micro-Scope and ADS. MicroScope is a system for program modification and, as such, uses rules that are based on the practice of software maintenance experts (Ambras and O'Day, 1988). ADS, or Automatic Design Synthesizer, uses a three-level decision process to select a suitable algorithm for an optimization problem (Rogers and Barthelemy, 1986).

6. CONCLUSION

The principles developed within the discipline of software engineering can be applied to many kinds of system, including expert systems. The goal of any engineering discipline is to provide technologies for ensuring that products meet the requirements of their users, are robust and reliable, and that they are delivered on time and within cost estimates. Expert system developers can use software engineering techniques to achieve this goal.

ACKNOWLEDGMENTS

Many of the ideas in this chapter began life in discussions with Aïda Batarekh, Alun Preece, Rajjan Shinghal, Ching Suen, and Neli Zlatareva of the expert systems group at the Centre for Pattern Analysis and Machine Intelligence (CENPARMI) at Concordia University.

REFERENCES

Ambras, J. and V. O'Day (1988, May). MicroScope: a knowledge-based programming environment. *IEEE Software* 5 (3), 50–58.

Barstow, D. (1979). An experiment in knowledge-based programming. *Artificial Intelligence* 12 (2), 73–119.

Batarekh, A., A. Preece, A. Bennett, and P. Grogono (1991). Specifying an expert system. *Expert Systems with Applications (U.S.)* 2 (4), 285–303.

Boehm, B. W. (1979). Software engineering: R & D trends and defense needs. In P. Wegner (Ed.), *Research Directions in Software Technology.* MIT Press.

Boehm, B. W. (1986, March). A spiral model of software development and enhancement. In *Proc. International Workshop on the Software Process and Software Environments,* pp. 21–42. Reprinted in *ACM Software Engineering Notes,* 11:4 (August 1986) and in IEEE Computer, 21(5), 61–72 (May 1988).

Bradley, J. H. and R. D. Hauser, Jr. (1995). A framework for expert system implementation. *Expert Systems with Applications (U.S.)* 8 (1), 157–167.

Chen, Z., P. Grogono, and C. Y. Suen (1994, October). Quantitative evaluation of expert systems. In *Proc. of the IEEE Conference on Systems, Man, and Cybernetics,* pp. 2195–2200.

Durkin, J. (1996, April). Expert systems: a view of the field. *IEEE Expert,* 56–63.

Geldof, S., A. Slodzian, and V. de Velde (1996, April). From verification to life cycle support. *IEEE Expert,* 67–73.

Gonzalez, A. J. and D. D. Dankel (1993). *The Engineering of Knowledge-Based Systems.* An Alan R. Apt Book. Prentice Hall.

Grogono, P., A. Batarekh, A. Preece, R. Shinghal, and C. Y. Suen (1991, November). Expert system evaluation techniques: a selected bibliography. *Expert Systems (U.K.)* 8 (4), 227–239.

Kaiser, G. E., P. H. Feler, and S. S. Popovich (1988, May). Intelligent assistance for software development and maintenance. *IEEE Software* 5 (3), 40–49.

Liebowitz, J. (1991). *Institutional Expert Systems: A Handbook for Managers.* Prentice Hall.

Lyons, P. J. (1992). Designing knowledge-based systems for incrmental development. *Expert Systems with Applications (U.S.)* 4, 87–97.

Meyer, M. and K. Curley (1991). An applied framework for classifying the complexity of knowledge-based systems. *MIS Quarterly* 15, 455–472.

Naur, P., B. Randell, and J. Buxton (Eds.) (1976). *Software Engineering: Concepts and Techniques (Proceedings of the NATO Conferences).* New York: Petrocelli-Charter.

O'Keefe, R. (1990). An integrative model of expert system verification and validation. *Expert Systems with Applications (U.S.)* 1 (3), 231–236.

Partridge, D. (Ed.) (1991). *Artificial Intelligence and Software Engineering.* Ablex.

Philip, G. C. (1993). Guidelines on improving the maintainability and consultation of rule-based expert systems. *Expert Systems with Applications (U.S.)* 6, 169–179.

Rich, C., R. Waters, and H. Reubenstein (1987, April). Towards a requirements apprentice. In *Proc. 4th Int. Workshop on Software Specification and Design,* pp. 79–86.

Rich, C. and R. C. Waters (1990). *The Programmer's Apprentice.* Addison-Wesley.

Rogers, J. and J. Barthelemy (1986, March). An expert system for choosing options in program for design. *IEEE Software* 3 (2), 51–52.

Royce, W. W. (1970). Managing the development of large software systems: Concept and techniques. In *1970 WESCON Technical Papers, Western Electric Show and Convention,* pp. A/1.1–A/1.9. Reprinted in *Proceedings of the 11th International Conference on Software Engineering,* Pittsburgh, May 1989, pp. 328–338.

Russell, G. (1991, January). Inspection in ultralarge-scale development. *IEEE Software* 8 (1), 25–31.

Sriram, D. and M. D. Rychener (Eds.) (1986, March). *IEEE Software*. Special issue on knowledge-based systems for engineering.

Tanik, M. M. and R. T. Yeh (Eds.) (1988, March). *IEEE Software*. Special issue on expert systems.

Tsai, J. J.-P. and J. C. Ridge (1988, November). Intelligent support for specifications transformation. *IEEE Software* 5 (6), 28–35.

Winograd, T. (1973). Breaking the complexity barrier (again). In *Proc. ACM SIGPLAN-SIGIR Interface Meeting on Programming Languages — Information Retrieval*, pp. 11–30. ACM. Reprinted in *Interactive Programming Environments*, D.R. Barstow, H.E. Shrobe, and E. Sandewall, Editors, McGraw-Hill, 1984.

Yourdon, E. and L. Constantine (1979). *Structured Design: Fundamentals of a Discipline of Computer Program and System Design*. Prentice-Hall.

Part II
Business- and Management-Related Expert Systems

26 Finance and Investments

Barbro Back, Jefferson Davis, and Alan Sangster

CONTENTS

1. INTRODUCTION

The world of finance includes the very challenging problem of relating past information to what the future will bring. Decisions in the financial markets of bonds, stocks, currency, commodities, real estate, and decisions relating to capital budgeting, financial distress, etc. provide a steady diet of complex prediction and classification tasks that require the experience and expertise of the decision-maker. Consistently making efficient and reliable decisions is not easily achieved. The size, complexity and, in some cases, less frequent repetition of these financial judgment tasks also hinders development of expertise by an individual. One important tool used in financial judgement tasks is expert systems — computer-based systems intended to provide intelligent judgments similar to those of human experts.

Expert system business applications started to emerge in the late 1970s, with the major growth occurring in the mid-1980s. In their review of business applications of expert systems, Wong and Monaco (1995a, b) found 214 articles that they classified as describing business expert systems. Finance was identified as the second largest application area, after Production/Operations. Their search involved the ABI/INFORM database and, in the Business Periodical Index (BPI) for the period January 1980 through December 1992, 24 textbooks on expert systems and related topics, and five journals that were not included in the ABI/INFORM database or the BPI, but were known to publish expert system articles.

In another review, Hayes-Roth and Jacobstein (1994) found that the area of Finance dominated the 87 systems described in the first four volumes of the *Innovative Applications of Artificial Intelligence* series during the period 1990 to 1992.

Eom (1996) compiled a bibliography of 291 papers that describes 440 operational ES applications. Similar to Wong and Monaco, he found that the largest number of operational expert systems are in production and operations management (47%), followed by finance (17%). Eom applied the criteria that the expert system be in actual use. He excluded prototype systems, systems being tested, expert systems that have fallen into disuse, and systems in non-business areas such as chemistry, physics, government, and medicine.

Coakes and Merchant (1996) surveyed 1000 companies across the U.K. in the Spring of 1994 to find out the use of information systems in general and expert systems in particular. A response rate of 22.5% showed that 50 out of 214 organizations use expert systems for a variety of applications, ranging from strategic to operational. About 24% of the respondents that claimed to use expert systems were in the financial service sector. The financial services companies used their systems primarily for routine activities and decision support. Interestingly, the study showed that it is not only large organizations that use expert systems — 28% of the respondents using them had less than 200 employees.

This chapter describes a sample of finance expert systems that are either in use or have given very promising results in the prototype stage and can therefore be predicted to proceed to implementation. The specific aspects of finance covered in the chapter are stock options pricing, commercial loan analysis (or credit granting or financial risk assessment), capital budgeting (investments), and stock market prediction, along with finance-related applications of neural networks-based systems.

2. BACKGROUND

There are several reasons why the area of finance has become such a popular a domain for expert system applications. Finance deals, to a large extent, with uncertain data, but most problems in finance can be decomposed into quantitative parts and qualitative parts and, to some extent, formulated as rules and facts, cases, or as frames, or semantic networks. The finance domain can, therefore, clearly benefit from the application of expert system technology.

Hayes-Roth and Jacobstein (1994, p .31) list the following benefits for building expert systems, all of which hold for finance applications, some examples of which are in italics:

- Order-of magnitude increases in speed of complex task accomplishment
  XSEL reduced a 3-hour system configuration task to 15 minutes

- Increased quality
- Reduced errors
- Decreased personnel required
  Canons Optex camera lens design system has made scarce highly skilled lens design-ers 12 times more productive
- Reduced cost
- Reduced training time
- Improved decisions
  American Express claims its Authorizer's Assistant system that evaluates whether to grant or deny credit to its customers has reduced decisions to deny credit by one third, which the company estimates is worth over $27 million per year
- Retention of volatile or portable knowledge
- Improved customer service
  The British Government's DHSS PC-based Performance Analyst System reduced the time required for an evaluation task from 2 hours to 9 minutes — a factor of 80 productivity gain

As a specific subdomain example, credit granting assessment systems lend themselves very well to the adoption of expert system technology, decision-making problems in the area often being too complex for handling with conventional methods. The judgment procedures are often inherently nondeterministic, and assessment also involves making judgments based on uncertain data. More-over, the reasoning often takes place on several levels and has therefore to be decomposed. The process then leads to separate judgments for each level. For the final assessment, the subassessments have to be weighted according to some defined heuristic or rules.

3.   APPLICATIONS

3.1.   STOCK OPTIONS PRICING — AESOP

The AESOP system is an attempt to apply expert system methodology to the domain of stock options pricing to be used at the American Stock Exchange. At the time when AESOP was developed, many of the options specialists at the American Stock Exchange Market (AMEX) used a classical model for valuing options developed by Black and Scholes. The Black-Scholes model arrives at a theoretical options price based on a number of assumptions (Clifford et al., 1992):

1. A known and constant interest rate
2. A stock price following a random walk with a variance proportional to the square of the price
3. The stock pays no dividend
4. The option is exercised only at expiration
5. There are no transaction costs
6. One can borrow to purchase or hold at the interest rate (see 1 above)
7. There are no penalties to selling short, i.e., selling without owning the security

AESOP integrates the Black-Scholes mathematical model with a symbolic model in the form of an expert system. It provides recommendation quotations for the specialists that are closer to what they can post than the theoretical prices produced by the mathematical model alone. AESOP is an example of an expert system that has to operate close to "real-time" as the market changes.

3.1.1.   The Symbolic Model

The symbolic part of AESOP represents the pricing strategy of a specialist on the AMEX, a domain that may not be receptive to mathematical modeling. The symbolic model always considers the specialist's desired spreads (the difference between bid and ask price) and always applies the specialist's rounding rules. It takes the output of the mathematical Black-Scholes model and adjusts it to incorporate the pricing strategies, with the goal of recommending bid and ask prices for each put and call for particular option series assigned to the specialist.

If the specialist's position in any series exceeds a threshold level, the symbolic model adjusts the price of that option to encourage (specialist is long) or discourage (specialist is short) trading. The symbolic model also looks for limit orders and adjusts the bid/ask prices based on the presence of these orders. Limit order adjustments are the most complicated and, potentially, the most valuable feature of the symbolic model.

The symbolic model always checks the AMEX rules to be sure that exchange regulations are not violated, and also scans for arbitrage possibilities. In almost all cases, arbitrage arises because bid/ask prices have been adjusted away from the theoretical price for some reason, most often because of the presence of a limit order.

3.1.2.   Knowledge Representation

AESOP uses rules to represent the knowledge of a senior specialist at the AMEX. The developers considered this a natural approach to knowledge representation given that the American Stock Exchange has a series of rules that apply to option prices. They also observed that the heuristics used by the expert specialist seemed to follow an *if-then* structure, for example, "*if* I am long on contracts, *then* reduce the asking price by one increment."

3.1.3.   Rules

The symbolic model of AESOP is represented using over 3000 lines of Prolog with nearly 200 rules (predicates) consisting of 400 clauses and nearly 1500 terms. Some of these predicates capture the pricing rules used by the specialist and constitute the knowledge base of AESOP, while other predicates are used to control the overall execution of AESOP, in particular the priority of various rules in the overall pricing strategy. The rules comprise Limit Order Rules, AMEX Rules, and Arbitrage Rules.

3.1.4.   System Validation

The system was validated by testing the relationship between the decisions developed by the system and the decisions developed by human experts. Recommended prices were compared with the prices posted by the expert specialist on various days when the system was in use at the exchange. The designers logged all user input for a sample of different days over a 1-month period.

AESOP presents the recommended quotations of the symbolic model along with the theoretical prices generated by the mathematical model. The user can override any recommendations, ask for an explanation or trace of the symbolic model, and/or change parameters and rerun the entire system. The results indicated that AESOP tended to recommend a call price that was too high and a put price that was too low. However, it was clear that AESOP represented an improvement over the regular Black-Scholes model for this application.

3.1.5.   System Performance

The user interacts with the system through the menu-driven user interface, which is managed by AESOP's control module and activated by function keys. AESOP provides the following functions:

1. Entering and processing limit orders
2. Invoking the OVS system for updating contracts, positions, etc.
3. Changing parameters in the Black-Scholes model or bid/ask spreads
4. Explaining the reasoning behind each price quotation
5. Alerting the user to arbitrage possibilities
6. Manually overriding any recommended price
7. Simulating the of prices to the current 'board'
8. Displaying the position or changing the threshold position for position rules to apply
9. Logging the interaction with the system
10. Running the Black-Scholes model

3.1.6.   Summary

The AESOP experiment provides evidence that the integration of symbolic and mathematical models offer great promise for matching models to specific problem domains. AESOP was used on an experimental basis successfully for 2 months by a specialist on the exchange market.

Reference: Condensed from Clifford, J., Lucas, H.C. Jr., and Srikanth, R.: Integrating mathematical and symbolic models through AESOP: an expert for stock options pricing. *Information Systems Research*, Vol. 3 No. 4, Dec. 1992, pp. 359–378.

3.2.   COMMERCIAL LOAN ANALYSIS

Loan approval systems have become very popular expert system applications. Typically these are cumulative hurdle decision-making systems. This is where a number of decisions are made linearly, but the problem may be solvable without overcoming every decision hurdle. An expert system can handle the first hurdle — logical consistency of the loan application, basic credit worthiness, etc. When a reject decision or perhaps an obvious grant decision cannot be made, the application can be passed over to an expert for further review. This separation of routine and more complex decision-making can be very beneficial when the number of routine problems is a large proportion of the volume and the cost of the complex decision making is large (O'Keefe and Preece, 1996).

3.2.1.   D&B Expert System

The Dun & Bradstreet (D&B) credit clearing house provides risk analysis to manufacturers, wholesalers, jobbers, and marketers in the apparel industry. It maintains and updates a database of credit rating on approximately 200,000 businesses in the U.S., which it then uses in order to recommend specific credit amounts to its clients.

Difficulties in the updating of data and inconsistencies in recommendations led to the development of their expert system for credit analysis. The system can handle more than 90% of all requests and it was developed using ART-IM. It consists of a knowledge base with more than 1000 rules and accompanying databases. D&B has benefited from the system being able to reduce the response times from 3 days to less than a minute and a high level of consistency in the recommendations generated.

References: This condensed version is from Turban, E., McLean, E., and Wetherbe, J. (1996) It is based on Neuquist, H. P. III, No summer returns, *AI Expert*, October 1990.

3.2.2.   CREDEX

CREDEX helps in the assessment of the risk involved in granting a loan. Its purpose is to help the analysts responsible for bank loans to judge the quality of a company seeking funds. It makes a match between the level of risk and the loan request, together with an explanation. It uses economic, financial, and social data on the company and its sector of activity, and also on the bank's lending policy. It provides a diagnosis of each of the firm's functions in terms of weaknesses and strengths, and it states the degree of partial risk inherent in each function. Moreover, it states the degree of overall risk associated with the granting of the loan and provides suggestions regarding loan acceptance.

3.2.2.1.   Model

The CREDEX system consists of a *meta-expert, experiential experts,* and *judgmental experts.* The meta-expert distributes control among the different experts and manages the problem-solving process. It determines which expert should be activated. The experiential experts are activated in order of importance. When one of the experiential experts has finished its task, the meta-model selects one of the judgmental experts to handle the task in question.

The experiential experts consist of a *commercial expert,* a *financial expert,* a *production and operations expert,* and a *management expert.* These experts deduce the importance of their respective subdomain characteristics and make an initial assessment in terms of strong and weak points and elementary associated risks. The *commercial expert* analyzes the quality of the commercial function. The *financial expert* assesses financial and accounting data. The *production and operations expert* handles production, research, and development data, and the *management expert* assesses the managing team and capital structure.

The *judgmental experts* consists of a *compensatory expert,* a *lexicographic expert,* a *disjunctive expert,* and a *conjunctive expert.* They contain general cognitive models of information processing and carry out deeper analysis. They examine the elementary risks and their importance, and combine them into a partial risk through a set of general lexiographical, compensatory, or conjunctive decision rules.

3.2.2.2.   Knowledge Representation and Reasoning Mechanism

CREDEX is built on the SNARK inference engine and formalism. The knowledge is represented in first- and, in some cases, second-order logic. The system has about 300 rules, of which over half are for the *experiential experts.* Reasoning heuristics are formalized in classic fashion through production rules. Variables are instantiable by the objects of the memory and propagated in the rule conclusion.

In the working memory, the properties of the objects, the associations between them, and statements are represented by associative triplets in the form <object relation value>, where relation and value can also be structured objects.

The CREDEX control strategy is mixed: it is both goal- and data-driven.

3.2.2.3.   System Performance

The system operates on two modes: Diagnosis (D) mode, which gives a final report after each function of the company has been diagnosed; and Assessment (A) mode, which, using specific heuristics, can skip certain functions and therefore draw quicker conclusions. The system starts by asking the user questions about:

1. The operating mode: diagnosis or assessment
2. The entity to be assessed: name, type, sector
3. The assessment period: initial or ultimate yearly result
4. The ponderation method for the company's functions: ponderation by default or explicit ponderation by the user

The reasoning process then starts and the system guides the user through a logical sequence of questions on the company, provides an elementary diagnosis on each company function, prints out a quality judgment on the function, and recommends actions to be taken to improve this quality if possible in the case of this analysis. It ends by printing out a global qualitative judgment of the company in terms of corporate risk.

The system is very fast. A session in A mode takes 1.3 seconds, and a session in D mode takes 6 to 8 seconds on an IBM 3090 computer under MVS.

Reference: Condensed from Pinson, S. A multi-expert architecture for credit risk assessment. The Credex system, in *Expert Systems in Finance*, edited by D.E. O'Leary and P.R. Watkins, 1992.

3.2.3.   COMPASS

COMPASS was developed for the Bank of Scotland over a 7-year period, coming online in 1994. It was initially applied to all commercial loan applications in excess of $375,000. The development costs were recouped during the validation phase and, since its introduction, the bank has suffered no losses on new loans of that magnitude.

COMPASS was written in C++ and runs on both Windows and OS/2 platforms. Its modular design means that the data and information specific to the Bank of Scotland can be removed, leaving a generic shell that can be adopted by any bank in any market to perform similar assessments on their loan portfolios and loan applications. By mid-1995, COMPASS was being used or tested by banks in the U.K., Ireland, Europe, and a number of other locations worldwide.

3.2.3.1.   Model

COMPASS is a rule-based system. Its knowledge base contains the encapsulated expertise of a loan officer that seeks the relevant knowledge from the loan officer conducting the assessment, applies it to the financial ratios calculated by COMPASS and other relevant information held, and makes recommendations concerning the lending proposal. The bank's loan officers are required to use the system, though they are not required to adhere to its recommendations.

During a consultation, COMPASS accesses centrally stored information on the customer and on existing agreements with the customer, and utilizes accounting data for the customer spreading over 7 years: three historic, the present year, and three future periods.

Through the inclusion of three key modules — VIABILITY (the potential of the customer to attain and support the proposed activity), SAFETY (the assessment of the means by which the loan facility may be recouped), and CREDENTIALS (how well the customer is known to the bank, including qualitative factors such as its management style) — quantitative and qualitative customer-specific information is filtered by COMPASS in the context of the environment in which the customer operates, accounting values are adjusted accordingly, and the resulting recommendations are presented to the loan officer in context so that he or she may explain the recommendations to the customer in a relevant and informative way. To assist this process, at the end of each COMPASS consultation, a natural language report is produced containing recommendations to the bank loan officer on the customer's request for lending. The entire consultation process takes between 5 and 30 minutes, compared with up to a week under the system in use prior to COMPASS being introduced.

3.2.3.2.   Validation

The first prototype was completed in 1988 and the first fully working system started testing in 1992. Testing was initially by the bank's staff. In 1993, they were augmented by a team of chartered accountants from one of the largest international accountancy firms.

3.2.3.3.   Implementation

By mid-1994, COMPASS was installed in 20% of the bank's corporate branches throughout the U.K., covering, as a result, 80% of the bank's corporate lending portfolio. Within 1 year, it was installed throughout the bank and it had been extended for use in respect of all loans in excess of

$15,000. Steps were then taken to redefine the terms of all existing loans that it assessed as being at risk, thus minimizing the risk they held for the bank.

Reference: Condensed from Sangster, A. The Bank of Scotland's COMPASS — the future of bank lending?, *Expert Systems with Applications*, Vol 9, 1995, 457–468.

3.2.4. CUBUS

CUBUS provides an evaluation of a commercial customer's annual accounts. Testing of over 1000 cases has shown it to be as good as an experienced expert at indicating the financial strength or the default probability of a company. It is written in ART-IM and takes about 3 minutes to complete a full analysis of a customer's annual accounts.

Reference: Condensed from Wolf, M.F. New technologies for customer rating: Integration of knowledge-based systems and human judgement. *Intelligent Systems in Accounting, Finance and Management*, Vol. 2, 1995, 289–301.

3.2.5. PARMENIDE

PARMENIDE was developed for the Italian Banco di Napoli. It reviews loan applications on the basis of its prediction of the future position of the company applying for the loan facility. In order to assess the working conditions, assets, etc., the customer is visited during the assessment. The management, background of the company, and its market are incorporated into the analysis. Information from external agencies is used in order to incorporate market data. While it is an example of a move toward the use of qualitative data and related heuristics, much of the analysis requires expertise on the part of the loan officer and the assessment is, to some extent, made in the absence of detailed quantitative knowledge of the sector in which the company operates. It guides the loan officer through the entire process, but requires input of generic risk-related expertise, part of which is provided centrally by the Bank's lending expert, not the loan officer dealing with the application, during the second phase of the assessment.

Reference: Condensed from Butera, G., Frascari, E., and Iacona, G. (1990). Parmenide: an expert system for assessing the credit of industrial clients. *International Journal of Expert Systems*. Vol. 3, 1990, 73–85.

3.2.6. KABAL

KABAL is a bank loan authorization expert system developed with the Norwegian Tromsø Spare-bank. It performs analysis of financial statements. It also considers guarantees, market, and company management/organization. The user is guided through the appraisal but there are many points where the loan officer is required to have relatively deep expertise.

Reference: Condensed from Hartvigsen, G. KABAL: a knowledge-based system for financial analysis in banking. *Expert Systems for Information Management*. Vol. 3, 1990, 213–31.

3.2.7. EVENT

Money lending is one of the main acitivities of all banks. A bank must decide whether or not to grant a loan by judging the customer's ability to repay the loan according to lending guidelines established by the bank. This task may be repeated often for different customers, requiring select bank personnel who must repeat the same routine steps when processing the loans. Evalog, a French bank, faced the situation when processing large loans to companies and decided to investigate the application of expert systems to ease the workload. The system they developed, EvEnt, judges a company's overall credibility and performance when making its recommendation. It considers such factors as the company's financial structure, size, and management performance to evaluate the risk in lending the company funds. EvEnt decreased the cost of processing loans tenfold, helped Evalog process more loan applications, and helped minimize the bank's exposure to risk.

Reference: Durkin, J.: Expert systems: a view of the field. *IEEE Expert,* Vol. 11 (2), 1996, 56–63.

3.3. CAPITAL INVESTMENT

3.3.1. Management Advisor

Management Advisor is used for decisions involving financial investment in new business opportunities. It is intended for use by executives and managers. It considers financial issues, risk, timing, competition, and the organizational impact. Among the financial factors considered during a consultation are prices, market share, costs, depreciation, and taxes. Users can customize the expert system to match their own terminology, financial assumptions, and preferences. The system comprises around 200,000 lines of code and is written in PSL, a LISP-based language.

Reference: Condensed from Reitman, W. and Shim, S.J. Expert systems for evaluating business opportunities: implementing the management advisor at Krypton Chemical, *Intelligent Systems in Accounting, Finance and Management.* Vol. 2, 1993, 191–204.

3.3.2. AFFIN

AFFIN is used by bank managers for the evaluation of industrial investment projects. It determines the feasibility and economic convenience of a proposed project. Included in the analysis are consideration of productive, plant location, and technology aspects, along with company capability (managerial and employee) and company financial factors. AFFIN performs a market analysis considering product description, market size and segmentation, and forecasted sales. It was developed in C and is backward-chaining, using both rules and semantic nets.

Reference: Condensed from Durkin, J. *Expert Systems Catalog of Applications.* Intelligent Computer Systems Inc: Akron, OH, 1993, 16.

3.3.3. Cash Flow Profiler

The system was written using the Leonardo Level III expert system shell. It is rule-based and includes links from the shell to external packages — a DBMS and a spreadsheet. The system produces an estimate of the cash flow profile of capital projects, thereby enabling decisions on, for example, whether to proceed or not to be taken. The estimates are at three levels: best guess, lower limit, and upper limit. Data input is via a macro-driven spreadsheet. Forward-chaining is employed. The knowledge base was built using the cash flow profiles of 76 projects along with semistructured interviews with four domain experts. As more projects are assessed using the system, the actual outcomes are added to the database and the paramenters adjusted accordingly.

Reference: Condensed from Lowe, J.G., Moussa, N., and Lowe, H. Cash flow management: an expert system for the construction client, *International Journal of Applied Expert Systems.* Vol. 1, 1993, 134–152.

3.3.4. PROJECT

PROJECT is used by local authorities in France to test the financial impacts of a portfolio of projects. Its knowledge base includes information on the legal aspects of local taxation, and on operating costs associated with generic investments, such as schools.

Reference: Condensed from Klein, M. and Methlie, L.B. *Expert Systems: a decision support approach.* Addison Wesley: Wokingham, 1990, 465–6.

3.4.   PREDICTING STOCK MARKET BEHAVIOR

The stock market behavior prototype system developed by Braun and Chandler (1987) using a rule-induction approach is an attempt to provide stock market analysts with a tool that combines both quantitative and categorical measures. Statistical techniques, such as discriminant analysis and regression analysis, are suitable when analyzing the quantitative measures, while techniques such as logit and probit analysis can address the categorial measures to some extent.

3.4.1.1.   Model

The rule-induction method is based on the learning-from-example approach. The rule induction system is presented with examples of a decision (its inputs and outcomes) and attempts to induce a decision model. A software system called ACLS (Analog Concept Learning System) was used to analyze past examples and formulate decision rules. Rules were generated to predict both an expert market analyst's prediction of the market and the actual market's movement. A single expert with 12 years of experience as stock market analyzer was used as the source of expertise. The expert also had experience in giving verbal advice to a large audience — he was writing a newsletter in which he gave biweekly recommendations on the stock market. These recommendations provided the basis for the model. The Dow Jones industrial average (DJI) was used as reference point for the system.

3.4.1.2.   Knowledge Representation

The knowledge was represented in the form of induced rules. The expert identified the 20 cues that he found most relevant from a list of 20. The cues and outcomes set up the structure of the example database. Three types of outcomes were used to categorize the weekly recommendations: bullish (forecasting an upward trend), bearish (forecasting a downward trend), and neutral (indicating that either call was too risky). The example database consisted of data at closing time on a certain time on a weekday for each of a number of weeks. For the prototype, it was data at closing time on Friday for each of 108 weeks during the period of 20 March 1981 to 9 April 1983. Most of the data was collected from the *Wall Street Journal.*

3.4.1.3.   Validation

The validation was performed in two steps. In the first, an initial database of 80 examples of the expert's predictions from a 1.5-year period was validated. The first test split the examples into two groups of 40 on a random basis. One group was used to induce a rule using ACLS; the other was used to test the induced rule. The degree of consensus between rule-generated predictions and the expert was 57.5%. The hit rate was improved to 65% when the number of examples was increased to 60 for rule inducing, leaving 20 examples for testing.

In step 2, each of the example databases was expanded to 108 examples. Two situations were replicated: one predicting the expert's predictions and one predicting actual market movements. The average hit rate predicting the actual market's movement was 64.4. The expert was correct only 60.2% of the time.

Reference: Condensed from Braun, H. and Chandler, J.: Predicting stock market behavior through rule induction: an application of the learning/from/example approach. *Decision Sciences,* Vol. 18, 1987, pp. 415–429.

3.5.   NEURAL NETWORK APPLICATIONS

There have been many attempts to apply neural network technology to the finance domain. One such system is in use in a major financial institution in the U.K. where it is used to predict the type of customers who may go into arrears on their house financing loans. The neural network was built using 150,000 past loan records and is used in order to assess whether or not to proceed with a loan application. In testing, it was found to correctly predict the risk in 91.8% of 160,000 loans.

Reference: Torsun, I.S. A neural network for a loan application scoring system, *The New Review of Applied Expert Systems.* Vol. 2, 1996, 47–62.

3.6. HYBRID SYSTEMS

This class of product has yet to make a major impact in this domain. However, such systems are being developed and put to use. *IEEE Expert,* for example, carried a description of an intelligent software system, called ProfitMax, in its "new product" section in February 1996. ProfitMax provides transaction-based, real-time authorization action decisions for managing the profitability of credit card portfolios. It uses neural networks, expert rule bases, and cardholder behavior profiling technology to analyze each cardholder account and predict its profit. Historical data and three neural network-based models — credit risk, revenue, and attrition risk — are used to predict profitability. The profit evaluation is customized to the using issuer's definition of financial profit. ProfitMax updates the profitability prediction whenever a new transaction or event takes place. Transaction-based scoring enables online, real-time decision-making, even during authorization.

The system also offers profitability-based decision-making. Business strategies and account management tactics can be entered into the system's rule base to automatically apply actions (for example, to extend a credit line) based on each account's expected behavior and profit. ProfitMax implements the actions and monitors to measure their impact. Portfolio managers can use simulation to perform decision-making in a test mode before implementing the actions in the live cardholder base.

ProfitMax interfaces with the issuer's authorization system, whether installed on a mainframe or a UNIX platform. Client PCs handle management and reporting functions.

Source: IEEE Expert, Vol. 11 (1), 1996, 87.

4. RESEARCH ISSUES

The research issues can generally be classified into in three main groups. The first includes statistical, model development, and validations issues; the second deals with cognitive issues, including understanding cognitive tasks; and the third is directed at explanation and user acceptance issues.

4.1. STATISTICAL, MODEL DEVELOPMENT, AND VALIDATION ISSUES

For the most part, statistical, model development, and validation issues are not just issues related to expert systems, but to any statistical procedure. To be useful in a real application, a trading system, for example, should be validated using an objective function that is very specific to the trading strategy and objective (e.g., profit maximization). Fitting systems into trading strategies and market mechanisms may require use of a hybrid system.

Another validation issue relates to the comparison of expert system results with neural networks, traditional statistical models, and human experts. Different systems cannot always be evaluated in the same way or through use of the same measurement metrics. However, in the end, the comparison of one system to another, or to a human expert, must be a comparison of how well the clearly defined objectives are met.

4.2. COGNITIVE ISSUES

One view of developing intelligent systems is to obtain a system that does a good job of solving problems regardless of whether the system mimics human intelligence or not. However, understanding the ability of people to solve problems and perform complex judgement tasks will still be beneficial to designing systems because much can be learned from how people solve problems and perform judgment tasks. An important issue for developing systems is understanding the characteristics of different tasks, characteristics of human expertise, and appropriately matching different types of intelligent systems that have the knowledge acquisition, knowledge representation, and judgment processing characteristics best suited for the task. For example, a general theory for matching the appropriate intelligent system type with characteristics of semistructured judgment tasks, such as financial prediction and classification, can be developed and refined. A related issue concerns how to integrate different types of systems from a system design perspective.

4.3. USER ACCEPTANCE

Development of a dependable and accurate system does not amount to very much if the system is not seen as a useful tool by the intended users. Ease of use and ability of the system to provide explanation of its prediction or "decision" are key ingredients for successful deployment of an intelligent system.

5.   FUTURE TRENDS

Financial judgment tasks may exhibit both analytical reasoning and pattern recognition characteristics. Judgment tasks can be viewed as a continuum between pattern recognition tasks and analytical reasoning tasks. Or an overall task may be broken down into pattern recognition and analytical reasoning components. For example, one discrete, definitive rule may be that a buy order is triggered when a certain event in the market occurs. Although such definitive rules are often used, financial judgments require recognition of patterns in the whole set of interdependent financial data. The key to automating analytical reasoning tasks versus pattern recognition tasks is choosing the intelligent system tool with characteristics suited to performing such tasks.

Artificial neural networks (ANNs) are essentially statistical devices with the capability to inductively (from experience with the data) infer complex, nonlinear relationships or patterns within the provided data. This capability provides a strength for ANNs to perform prediction and classification using the complex, nonlinear, interdependent relationships inherent in financial data. Using a neural network for financial prediction and classification still requires substantial expertise in both the ANN development and the financial domain. Choice of variables, data significance, correlation, normalization, etc. are part of preprocessing the data prior to ANN development. During ANN development and validation, experimentation with network parameters is usually extensive and time consuming. Finally, the inductive inference capabilities come with a drawback — explicit explanation of how the ANN made the judgement is very difficult to obtain from the complex mathematical equations inductively derived from the data (Refenes, 1995). However, ANNs have shown some promise in recognizing trends in the chaotic data of the financial world such that some additional profits may be made due to the use of this technology.

Medsker and Turban (1994) state that integrating expert systems and neural computing has the potential to provide solutions that neither system alone can deliver, or to lead to good solutions with less system complexity. Each technology has deficiencies that can be overcome by the other. For example, an ANN cannot provide explanation, while an expert system can. Expert systems cannot recognize patterns in historical data, whereas ANNs can. The different characteristics of the technologies suggest that they can enhance each other. Typically, a loan assessment system, such as COMPASS, could include an ANN module that would take care of the prediction part and an expert system module that could take care of the rest. By integrating the technologies, we pursue a synergism based on their respective strengths.

ANN can be used in conjunction with a KBS in a hybrid system where, for example, certain data used as input to the KBS are preclassified by a front-end ANN — for example, for predicting bankruptcies as part of a loan assessment hybrid system.

Brown et al. (1995) state that the financial services industry with its large databases has already fielded several successful neural network applications, and that neural networks based on information about customers or potential customers have proved effective. In fraud detection, they are integrated effectively into expert systems. If large databases exist with which to train a neural network, then use of that technology should be considered. For a neural network, the large database can be used as the equivalent of the human expert. Each type of reasoning can be matched to tasks that require its specific reasoning strengths.

A major barrier to identifying where applications are being used in finance, particularly for capital markets work, is the proprietary nature of the models developed. Due to the potential profitability of any ANN model that does well as a tool for making a profit in the financial markets, many ANN models are kept secret, particularly concerning the details of what variables are used and what parameters are used in the ANN. Occasionally, an article in application journals and newspapers tells of a company using ANNs for financial market transactions, such as Fidelity Investments (see the *Wall Street Journal,* Oct. 27, 1992) and LBS Capital Management, (see *Futures,* August 1992, p. 34).

There is still much research to be done into gaining an insight into how to approach different finance problems with intelligent systems. Refenes (1995) and Trippi and Turban (1996) each provide a compilation of papers using neural networks applied to equity applications; including picking stocks, forecasting trading indices, predicting options volatility, pricing, and hedging derivative securities. Debt applications, such as mortgage risk assessment, bond rating, and credit scoring, are also included. Other finance applications presented include commodities trading, exchange rate prediction (see also Episcopos and Davis, 1996), and business failure prediction. These paper collations provide insight into what type of ANN and what variables were used, and what other established types of models the ANN results were compared to, such as linear regression, multiple discriminant, autoregressive (time series) models, etc.

The future will bring more integration of different types of intelligent systems to complement the strengths and mitigate the weaknesses of different intelligent systems. Particularly, the lack of explanation ability of ANNs will be overcome by using other intelligent systems to interpret the ANN. Future research should also include much more empirical documentation concerning the acceptance of intelligent systems as a viable decision aid tool for finance and other professional users.

REFERENCES

Braun, H. and Chandler, J. (1987) Predicting stock market behavior through rule induction: an application of the learning/from/example approach. *Decision Sciences*, 18, 415–429.

Brown, C. Coakley, J. and Phillips, M. (1995) Neural networks enter the world of management accounting. *Management Accounting*, May, 51–57.

Clifford, J. Lucas, H.C. Jr. Srikanth, R. (1992) Integrating mathematical and symbolic models through AESOP: an expert for stock options pricing. *Information Systems Research*, 3, 359–378.

Coakes, E. and Merchant, K. (1996) Expert systems: a survey of their use in U.K. business. *Information and Management*, 30, 223–230.

Eom, S.B. (1996) A Survey of Operational ES in Business (1980–1993). *Interfaces*, 26(5), 50–70.

Episcopos, A. and Davis, J. (1996) Predicting returns on major canadian Exchange rates with artificial neural networks and EGARCH-M models. *Neural Computing and Applications*.

Hayes-Roth, F. and Jacobstein, N. (1994) The state of knowledge-based systems. *Communications of the ACM*, 37(3), 27–39.

Medsker, L. and Turban E. (1994) Integrating expert systems and neural computing for decision support. *Expert Systems with Applications*, 7(4), 553–562.

O'Keefe, R.M. and Preece, A.D. (1996) The development, validation and implementation of knowledge -based systems. *European Journal of Operational Research*, (92), 458–73.

Refenes, A. (Ed.) (1995) *Neural Networks in the Capital Markets.* New York: John Wiley & Sons.

Trippi R. and Turban, E. (Eds.) (1996) *Neural Networks in Finance and Investing.* Chicago: Irwin.

Turban, E., McLean, E., and Wetherbe, J. (1996) *Information Technology for Management. Improving Quality and Productivity.* John Wiley & Sons, New York.

Wong, B.K. and Monaco, J.A. (1995a) Expert system applications in business: a review and analysis of the literature (1977–1993). *Information & Management*, 29, 141–152.
Wong, B.K. and Monaco, J.A. (1995b) A bibliography of expert system applications for business (1984–1992). *European Journal of Operational Research*, 85, 416–432.

SUGGESTED NEURAL NETWORK
AND FINANCE INTERNET ADDRESS

Sarle, W. Frequently Asked Questions (AI-FAQ/neural-nets). ftp://ftp.sas.com/pub/neural/FAQ.html

27 Accounting and Auditing

Carol E. Brown, Amelia A. Baldwin, and Alan Sangster

CONTENTS

1. INTRODUCTION

In a rapidly changing and highly competitive business environment, professionals in accounting struggle with managing information, integrating research, and applying technologies to practical accounting situations. Since the mid-1980s, the use of expert systems to solve practical accounting problems and to assist with financial decision-making has spread throughout business, industry, and government.

With the continued growth of expert systems use, substantial benefits have been reported. In the mid-1980s, accounting and auditing firms put their first expert systems into field use. By the late 1980s, accounting expert systems were already providing substantial payoffs for leading U.S. companies. For example, Texas Instruments' capital-budgeting proposal package increases the speed of processing time for requisition goods by 20 times, reduces cost overruns, and saves $2 million in preparation expenses.

Financial applications are by far the most frequent users of expert system technology. Companies in a variety of industries are using expert systems to prepare complex entries for their accounting records, analyze division performance, assist with capital budgeting decisions, analyze variances, prepare audit plans, assist with tax planning, and perform many other accounting-related tasks. Companies must now decide if expert system technology is suitable and cost effective for their accounting tasks.

The background section of this chapter (Section 2) describes why both accounting firms and companies for which accounting is a staff function develop expert systems for accounting tasks. The historical account section describes the beginnings of expert system research and use in accounting, and how accounting expert systems became a field of study and application. Sections then follow on current applications and areas of study related to accounting expert systems.

2.   BACKGROUND

Organizations develop accounting expert systems because they are *discovery* systems that can affect *competition, productivity,* and *task process.* Expert systems are a part of the organizational strategy of many accounting organizations.

Discovery. Expert systems development is a discovery process. The development of an expert system requires a deep understanding of the domain and task; thus, organizations acquire information during development. Accounting expert systems can, therefore, impact the organization's knowledge level.

Competition. Another motivation for accounting expert systems development is to affect or influence competitive forces. Within the auditing industry, expert systems development grew rapidly as competition and litigation increased and clients began to shop around for lower audit fees.

Productivity. Accounting expert systems can provide measurable improvements in individual and organizational productivity. Expert systems may increase personnel productivity, increase task efficiency, improve quality control, or result in other productivity impacts. In fact, a number of expert systems for audit tasks have resulted in both improvements in efficiency and effectiveness overall, and particularly, in faster expertise development for novice auditors.

Task process. Accounting expert systems have also changed task processes. The development process provides a deeper understanding of the task and therefore the process can be improved. The task process may also be changed as a result of the expert system enabling tasks to be done by users with less experience. In addition, the system may allow for more inputs and outputs than the task could incorporate prior to the creation of the expert system. This is particularly true for tasks whose complexity is often largely the result of the amount of inputs that must be processed, as in some audit, tax, and financial planning tasks.

Organizational strategy. These impacts and motivations highlight the sometimes mysterious relationship between expert systems and organizational strategy. The interaction between organizational strategy and expert systems is a continuous process that can be described as having six steps.

1. The state of the accounting organization is gauged in light of the organization's strategy, i.e., its broad plan for the future and its goals. The state of the organization includes both macro (e.g., industry position) and micro (e.g., task efficiency) measurements.
2. The current state of the organization is compared to the strategically desirable state, and a need for improvement is indicated.
3. Expert systems are developed.
4. They are used as a part of the organization's strategy for changing itself. For example, Coopers & Lybrand's **ExperTax**, which supports both tax accrual and tax planning tasks, became part of a strategy that linked audit and tax services.
5. The state of the organization impacts the development and use of expert systems. Clearly, corporations and accounting firms with a previous history of using technology strategically, have been the most likely to utilize expert systems. IBM, for example, successfully developed and uses CONSULTANT, an expert system that helps field representatives in the bidding process. On the contrary, an organization that has been historically very slow to change is more likely to have an unsuccessful development and implementation. For example, a bank that historically discouraged the use of computers by loan officers failed to take advantage of an expert system for commercial loan analysis, even though the system helped loan officers avoid bad loans.

6. The development and use of expert systems impact the state of the organization. The development of an expert system may result in a better understanding of the task process, improvement in efficiency and effectiveness of organizational members, or even a change in competitive position. It is for these reasons that expert systems are developed for accounting applications.

3. HISTORICAL ACCOUNT

Although development of accounting expert systems started in the early 1970s, published research on the topic only started to appear in 1977: TAXMAN in the tax domain and TICOM in the financial reporting/audit domain. The few papers that appeared before 1982 were mostly related to those two early development efforts. From 1982, the number of published papers approximately doubled each year until beginning to level off around 1987–1988 (Brown 1989).

3.1. THE ERA OF THE RESEARCH PROTOTYPES

Publications during the first decade included a few survey papers that were mostly tutorials, because there was such a small base of work to survey, and a few papers that outlined accounting areas appropriate for expert system development. By far the greatest number of publications during this early period described research prototypes developed in the financial reporting/auditing, tax, and managerial accounting domains, many being funded by the large accounting firms and forming the foundation upon which some of the later deployed applications were built. Prototype development is often an attempt to understand how decisions are made, in this domain, by expert accountants; and research prototypes continue to be developed in an on-going effort to achieve a better understanding of how judgment-based accounting decisions are made.

3.1.1. Financial Reporting/Auditing

The early development efforts in the financial reporting/auditing domain address basic financial reporting issues from an auditing perspective. These systems focused on the areas of accounting that were clearly judgment based, including evaluating internal controls, assessing inherent risk, going-concern judgments, and materiality judgments. Later systems included all these areas in comprehensive audit planning systems. The *discovery* nature of expert system development is clearly demonstrated in these early systems, as they achieved a deeper understanding of how decisions traditionally based on judgment were actually being made. In some cases, what was learned has led to better, more-consistent decision processes.

Internal control related systems include: TICOM (The Internal Control Model), developed by Bailey, Duke, Gerlach, Ko, Meservy, and Whinston, for modeling internal controls and querying the model to evaluate their adequacy; ARISC (Auditor Response to Identified Systems Controls) developed by Meservy, Bailey, and Johnson, which models internal control evaluation in the purchasing cycle; EDP-Expert, developed by Hansen and Messier, to assist computer audit specialists make judgments on the reliability of controls in advanced computer environments; ICE (Internal Control Evaluation), developed by Kelly, to model auditor judgment in internal control evaluation; ICES (Internal Control Expert System) developed by Grudnitski, focusing on sales and accounts receivable transactions; Internal-Control-Analyzer, developed by Gal, examines the evaluation of revenue cycle controls using data in the firm's physical database and determines the adequacy of the allowance for bad debts; AUDITOR, developed by Chandler, Dungan, and Braun, assists in assessing the appropriateness of the allowance for doubtful accounts provision; and Auditing Internal Controls makes qualitative judgments similar to the ways in which an expert auditor performs the judgment.

Systems focusing on the going-concern judgment include: GC-X (Going Concern Expert), developed by Biggs and Selfridge, to investigate the diagnostic reasoning processes used by auditors to make a prediction and take action regarding a firm's ability to continue to operate as a going concern; AOD (Audit Opinion Decision), developed by Dillard and Muchler, to assess solvency in the context of the going concern judgment of auditors; and FCEX, developed by Boritz to support the auditor's evaluation of financial condition, risk of business failure, and the validity of the going-concern assumption for an audit client.

Audit planning systems were developed for all stages of the audit planning process. Three systems, IRE (Inherent Risk Expert) by Dhar and Peters; APE (Audit Planning Expert), by Denna; and Inherent Risk Assessment, by Boritz, Kielstra, and Albuquerque, were developed to explore inherent audit risk assessment as part of audit planning; AuditPlanner, developed by Steinbart, related to the materiality judgment made by auditors; CAPEX (Canadian Audit Planning Expert), was developed by Boritz and Wensley for creating comprehensive audit program plans for banking, retailing and manufacturing firms; APX (Audit Planning Expert), outlined and partially implemented by Bharadwai, Mahapatra, Karan, and Murthy, was also concerned with comprehensive audit planning; and AUDPLAN, developed by Killingsworth, was designed to plan the compliance audit of a firm's sales transaction cycle.

Expert system development for accounting is not limited to English-speaking countries. A number of German researchers have developed expert systems for financial statement analysis (Back, 1991).

The major accounting firms were working on their own prototypes during this same period. CFILE was developed by the Audit Research Group of Peat Marwick for bank audits; and CHECK-GAAP was developed by Deloitte, Haskins, and Sells as an automated checklist to assist auditors in determining that the company complied with the U.K. Companies Act.

Many of the auditing expert systems are discussed by O'Leary and Watkins (1989), Edwards and Connell (1989), and by Boritz and Wensley (1996). These research prototype systems were used as models for commercial systems developed later. For example, Inherent Risk Assessment was used as the basis for the Price Waterhouse PLANET system, and CAPEX was used as the basis for Grant Thornton's ADAPT system (Boritz and Wensley, 1996).

3.1.2. Tax

Like auditing, taxation was an early entrant into expert systems development (Michaelsen and Messier, 1987). Its plethora of rules and regulations make it an intuitively obvious and appropriate domain for expert systems development, particularly rule-based systems.

The earliest development effort in tax was TAXMAN, a system primarily developed to investigate legal reasoning rather than accounting reasoning. TAXMAN-I, developed by McCarty, could represent the statutory requirements, but not the additional substantive requirements identified by the Supreme Court. TAXMAN-II, developed by McCarty and Sridharan, used a prototype and deformation model to represent the concepts involving substance over form.

Systems that followed relating to U.S. tax law were BLAH, developed by Weiner, a system based on a subset of U.S. Income Tax Law that structured explanations so they did not appear complex and thus were easy to understand; TAXADVISOR, developed by Michaelsen, determined if the client met the profile for which the system was designed and, if so, provided recommendations regarding: potential insurance purchases, retirement investments, trust and tax shelter actions, transfers of wealth, and modifications to gift and will provisions; TA (Tax Advisor) developed by Schlobohm, COTES (Constructive Ownership Tax Expert System), and TaXpert developed by Black deal with the constructive ownership of stock for income tax purposes; INVESTOR, developed by Michaelsen, assists in the selection of real estate or oil and gas tax shelters.

As the result of an environmental scan of artificial intelligence in 1983, the U.S. Internal Revenue Service decided to begin training employees in the emerging technology. By 1986 they had at least eight systems in progress (Needham, 1986). IRS systems addressed such diverse topics as identifying audit issues on tax returns, perfecting estate tax returns, assessing pension plans, processing tentative carryback claims, and allocation of income and expenses by multinationals.

Systems relating to U.K. tax law included: CORPTAX, developed by Hellawell, models the tax law relating to Section 302b of the IR Code that deals with tax treatment for stock redemption; ACCI, developed by Roycroft, addresses the apportionment of close companies' income in the U.K. (Close companies are similar to closely held companies in the U.S.) The intended users were tax inspectors. PAYE was written in Prolog and its domain knowledge is U.K. employee income tax, National Insurance Contributions, and Statutory Sick Pay.

A very interesting system related to Finnish tax law is FINSTEX (Financial Statements Expert), developed by Back (1991). It does the very complex task of financial statement planning that seeks to achieve high, stable earnings on financial statements while minimizing taxes. The system was demonstrated to both achieve high-quality results and improve learning by novices.

3.1.3.   Management Accounting

As would be expected for a staff rather than line function, the early work in management accounting was sparse. Early prototype systems include: PREFACE-EXPERT, reported by Senicourt, a rule-based expert system that identified financial problems with new projects and suggested ways in which to increase profitability while decreasing risk; FINEX, an expert support system for financial analysis based upon ratio analysis, used an "intelligent spreadsheet" approach to ascertain a company's well-being; Variance Analysis, a rule-based approach to variance analysis; Standard Cost Variances, which considered whether a particular variance merited further investigation; Sales Analysis produced a list of the items or salespersons that required attention because of possible problems with sales (Böer, 1989).

3.2.   MOVING INTO PRACTICE

In 1986, with much fanfare, the major accounting firms began to publish articles about their development efforts. The large CPA firms have literally hundreds of relatively small semi-independent offices scattered around the U.S. and the world. Thus, systems for these organizations at that time had to run on relatively low-power personal computers to be used effectively in the field by their auditors. This requirement set severe restrictions on what could be deployed. The most prominent early commercial systems for use by a single audit firm were ExperTAX and Loan Probe. The primary motivation for development of commercial systems has been to automate processes that nonartificial intelligence techniques have not been able to automate. The desire to automate can come from a desire for higher-quality, more-consistent performance and from a desire to make the process more efficient. The earliest commercial entrants into the marketplace were motivated by a desire for better, more consistent performance.

ExperTAX: assists auditors with assessing the adequacy of the deferred tax accrual and with tax planning. ExperTAX was developed by Coopers & Lybrand and was in field use by 1986. With over 2000 rules, ExperTAX incorporated both tax planning and auditing of the deferred tax accrual for corporations; thus, it related both to auditing and to tax. One of the goals of ExperTAX was to set a minimum standard of excellence for tax planning in all their U.S. offices. Later, modules for the insurance industry (1988) and the oil and gas industry (1989) were added.

Loan Probe: assists auditors in assessing the adequacy of the loan loss reserve for commercial loans. Loan Probe was in field use by 1987. The system ran on a Macintosh and contained in excess of 7000 rules. Early papers refer to the system as CFILE — it was called Loan Probe when used commercially by KPMG Peat Marwick. The system was deployed during the time when the savings and loan industry collapsed. While Peat Marwick had originally planned to market their system to others, they scrapped the idea because, given the climate, the risk was simply unacceptable. Use of the Loan Probe was discontinued primarily due to work flow issues. A stand-alone system with a relatively narrow task domain simply did not fit well in the audit practice environment.

Another interesting early system is VATIA. Ernst and Whinney had 600 copies in use by May 1988, assisting with ensuring their clients' compliance with U.K. Value Added Tax. By 1991, all the Big 6 accounting firms had expert systems in use and under development. Brown (1991) lists well over 50 such systems.

During the same time period, expert systems were developed and marketed for use by smaller public accounting firms, businesses, and the general public. ANSWERS assists auditors in audit risk assessment and audit planning. Other companies use ANSWERS for financial analysis tasks. Development of ANSWERS by Blocher began in 1984 and the product was formally introduced in January 1986 by Financial Audit Systems.

Financial Advisor (renamed **Management Advisor**): developed by Palladian for advising managers in Fortune 1000 companies on products, projects, mergers, and acquisitions, including both tax and non-tax considerations. The system had an impressive list of experts (eight faculty members from the Sloan School of Management and MIT and ten senior financial officers from major corporations).

With the introduction of commercial accounting expert systems, the nature of research and publications in the area began to change. In the period between 1987 and 1992, several conferences, journals, and books began publication that focused on accounting expert systems.

3.3.   A FIELD IS BORN

Daniel E. O'Leary, Paul Watkins, and the Advanced Technologies in Information Systems Program (ATISP) in the School of Accounting at the University of Southern California (USC) played a key role in bringing these separate streams of research into a cohesive and well-focused research area. In 1987, the ATISP began publication of *Expert Systems Review for Business and Accounting* (O'Leary, 1987–1990), the first expert systems journal including an accounting focus with Daniel O'Leary as Editor. The publication continued for 4 years until the end of 1990.

During that period it evolved from a quasi-newsletter format to being a respected journal. Though relatively short-lived, it played a key role in bringing the field together. Articles in *Expert Systems Review* included survey papers with extensive bibliographies: one on auditing expert systems by O'Leary and Watkins (1989), and two on tax expert systems by Carol Brown et al. Carol Brown's (1989) annotated bibliography, which contained bibliographic references and abstracts to 478 papers related to accounting expert systems, has been widely cited as evidence that a body of research on accounting expert systems exists. *Expert Systems Review* also attracted excellent papers on topics ranging from "Using Rules to Model Variance Analysis" by Anita Hollander, to "The Architecture of Expertise: The Auditor's Going-Concern Judgment" by Mallory Selfridge and Stanley F. Biggs.

In 1988, the first in a series of five International Conferences on *Expert Systems in Business, Finance, and Accounting* (Watkins, 1988–1993) drew together researchers from all over the world. The conference series was sponsored by The Peat, Marwick, Main Foundation and the Advanced Technologies in Information Systems Program at USC. Papers on cutting-edge research were presented by authors from academic, government, and industry backgrounds. This series of conferences provided a forum where researchers could exchange ideas and find out about each other's most recent work.

In 1989, the first in a series of collections of papers published as books under the running title *Artificial Intelligence in Accounting and Auditing* appeared (Vasarhelyi, 1989; 1995; 1995). That same year, a book entitled *Expert Systems in Accounting* by Edwards and Connell (1989) was published under the auspices of the Institute of Chartered Accountants in England and Wales. It included the preliminary results of a survey indicating that as many as 29% of U.S. companies and

22% of U.K. companies asserted that they had a major department dedicated to the exploitation of expert systems.

In 1990 and 1991, Ed Blocher spearheaded efforts to establish a new special interest section of the American Accounting Association to bring together researchers interested in accounting expert systems. The Artificial Intelligence/Expert Systems Section of the American Accounting Association was established as a provisional section in 1991, held its first of a continuing series of workshops in 1992 (AI/ES, 1992–continuing), and achieved permanent section status in 1994.

In 1991, *Expert Systems with Applications*, a well-regarded international journal, published a special issue (Brown, 1991), on Expert Systems for Accounting, Auditing, and Tax. A second special issue on the same theme appeared in 1995 (Brown and Wensley, 1995).

In 1992, the *International Journal of Intelligent Systems in Accounting, Finance & Management* (O'Leary 1992–1997; continuing) was launched as the successor *to Expert Systems Review for Business and Accounting*. The third issue of each volume is dedicated to accounting research and applications. The third issue of each year has been adopted as a member benefit for the AI/ES Section of the American Accounting Association.

In 1995, the First International Meeting on Artificial Intelligence in Accounting, Finance, and Tax was held in Huelva, Spain (Sierra and Bonsón, 1995). The meeting has become an annual event.

4. APPLICATIONS AND IMPACTS OF ACCOUNTING EXPERT SYSTEMS

Today, the research domain of expert systems for accounting tasks is a rich body of literature that ranges from descriptions of expert systems development using neural networks (authors include Boritz, Kennedy, Coakley, Hoyt and Lay, Hansen, Messier, and others) or case-based reasoning (authors include Morris, Denna, Hansen, Meservy, Wood, O'leary, Mott, Stottler, Bryant and others) to studies of the impacts on organizations of using such systems (authors include Baldwin, Trewin, and others). Expert systems encompassing financial accounting and taxation rules and regulations are in widespread use across the profession, particularly in the larger accounting firms. Audit firms have expert support systems in place for many of their tasks (Brown, 1991). Taxation has seen a large growth in development, as has management accounting. Taxation expert systems include both systems to assist the taxpayer, whether individual or corporation, and systems used by government tax agencies in the collection and audit process.

While much effort still revolves around audit and tax, the literature has moved to encompass other accounting tasks. Brown and Philips (1995) chronicled the entire body of application-oriented research relating to a broad range of management accounting tasks, an area in which literally hundreds of expert systems have been developed. However, despite the many systems that have been developed and are in use, there is still only scattered adoption of expert systems technology across the thousands of companies that practice management accounting.

The continuing development of expert systems for accounting tasks has sparked growth in studies of the impacts of using those systems. Organizations develop expert systems because they believe the systems will provide more knowledge about the task, improve effectiveness and efficiency, and provide a comparative advantage. A number of studies of accounting expert systems have attempted to identify the existence of those and other expected impacts. A future forecasting Delphi study attempted to predict the impact of expert systems on auditing firms in the year 2000. Expertise, effectiveness, and education impacts were identified as most likely (Baldwin-Morgan and Stone, 1995). Others have projected other social and organizational impacts.

Impacts on novices. Most studies that have investigated the impact of expert system use on novice auditors have reported better accuracy and efficiency for expert system users. Even when little impact is reported for more knowledgeable users, an effect is noticed for novices. This has also been the case with novice financial analysts.

Experienced decision-makers. Impacts on more experienced decision-makers are less clear. Some systems tend to have little effect on experienced auditors, for example, while others show differential impact associated with different attributes of the system. For example, a system utilizing negative explanations may generate more user reliance.

Workflow and task impacts. Impacts have also been observed on task and task processes. Expert system use has resulted in less need for supervision, broader problem handling by users, improved quality, shorter task time, improvements in decision consistency, and changes in task process.

Organizational effects. Accounting expert systems also affect organizations at the macro level. Organizations may encounter changes in technology orientation, organizational structure, and organizational culture.

5.   THE STATE OF THE ART

Expert systems for accounting tasks are now in use throughout all parts of the accounting profession. However, individual firm or company use is still very spotty. Intelligent questionnaires that were once developed as stand-alone expert system applications are now integrated into standard auditing and tax software. Personal financial planning services once affordable by only the very well off are now being marketed to families with moderate incomes at a price they can afford. Expert system applications, including neural networks and case-based reasoning, are in use. Following are some interesting examples of expert systems at work in accounting practice today.

PaperLess Management (Brown and Phillips, 1995) is seven clusters of 25 computer programs, designed to provide individual stores, corporate headquarters, and field operations with the information necessary to manage a multilocation retail business efficiently. Many of the modules are rule-based and two, Operations Expert System and General Ledger Expert System, incorporate an inference engine. The payoff from PaperLess Management takes many forms, including the following reported by one user: reduction of management training time and the time managers spend in the hiring process, saved about 4% of the company's labor costs by reducing overtime, better production planning saved an amount equal to 6% of daily sales. PaperLess Management's systems reduce stress, thereby reducing turnover. At corporate level, the systems are used to reduce the number of people necessary to run the business.

FALCON (Brown and Phillips, 1995) is a credit card fraud prevention system used by several of the largest credit card companies. FALCON incorporates neural network, database, rule-based, and statistical modeling capabilities. It creates an individual user behavior file for each account using pools of fraud data. FALCON examines each transaction, looking for patterns that may be fraudulent. If FALCON decides that fraud is likely, it provides strategies for follow-up. According to FALCON's developer, HNC, Inc., the system has been saving clients from 20 to 50% over what their previous fraud detection systems could deliver.

Retail Sales Prediction (Brown and Phillips, 1995) is a commercially used expert system that incorporates case-based reasoning to predict daily sales volume for each individual store. Predictions are made 2 weeks in advance so they can be used by store managers to determine the number of sales people to schedule on a daily basis. The system uses similar days, including the closest same day of the week (e.g., Tuesday) and days from a holiday (e.g., Christmas eve) for a baseline. The baseline sales are then adjusted for differences in the year, special events, school holidays, etc. The system makes predictions with only about 8% variability from actual.

Planet is used by Price Waterhouse audit professionals for expert planning assistance. Planet's expert knowledge is derived from the expertise of Price Waterhouse audit partners and managers worldwide. Planet identifies risks based on auditors' responses to a series of questions and creates an audit plan that addresses those risks. With Planet's assistance, an efficient and focused audit plan can be produced in significantly less time. The audit engagement teams in several countries who first used Planet following its preliminary release in October of 1994 were so happy with it that they used it to produce their audit plans even after the test period was over. The full release of Planet began in September of 1995.

Comet, also developed by Price Waterhouse, provides support for evaluating internal controls based on modeling and analyzing business processes. Comet assists users in building a hierarchical, structured, annotated flowchart describing a business process and associated internal controls. Comet uses a proprietary approach to analyze potential errors, the relative effectiveness of compensating controls, and control weaknesses. Comet is designed for financial service clients and multinational firms, where auditors expect that high audit reliance can be placed on system controls. In addition, Comet is considered particularly useful for new clients or when a client is changing computerized information systems. Comet won a 1996 AAAI Innovative Applications of Artificial Intelligence award. Additional information on Planet, Comet, and other Price Waterhouse expert systems may be obtained on their web site, [http://www.pw.com/].

MomsExperten uses basic expert system technology to support the activities of Swedish VAT offices by dealing with the large volume of simple questions and the training of new, inexperienced staff [http://www.attar.com/pages/case_vat.htm]. With rising costs of experienced staff and increased pressure to keep costs down, even systems that use only very basic expert systems technology are likely to increase.

A very good glimpse of current research efforts in accounting expert systems can be found by looking at recent special issues on accounting applications of two journals, *Expert Systems With Applications* 9(4), 1995 and the *International Journal of Intelligent Systems in Accounting, Finance and Management* 3(3), 1994; 4(3), 1995; and 5(3), 1996. Research topics represented in these special issues include:

- Selecting suitable accounting tasks for expert system development (1)
- Knowledge elicitation for financial expert systems (3)
- Cooperating expert systems (1)
- Prototype development (3)
- Decision bias with implications for expert systems (1)
- Issues related to concurrent use by multiple users of the same expert system (1)
- Integrating expert systems and other accounting modeling methods (e.g., database or REA) (2)
- Neural networks applied to accounting tasks (3)
- Case-based reasoning applied to accounting tasks (1)
- Belief functions and belief networks (2)
- Genetic algorithms (1)
- The value and effects of explanation in accounting expert systems (2)
- Validation of accounting expert systems (1)
- Impacts of accounting expert systems (2)
- Legal liability related to the use of accounting expert systems (1)
- Diffusion of accounting expert systems (1)
- Citation analysis (1)

Examining current research leads to the following observations on open research issues in accounting expert systems.

6.   RESEARCH ISSUES

What are the impacts of accounting expert systems on tasks, users, and organizations?

Additional impact studies are needed, particularly in accounting subdomains in which expert system use has rapidly advanced in the last 5 years, such as taxation and management accounting.

Such research is important to accounting organizations, developers, and users. *Organizations* need to know whether the strategic decision to implement expert systems actually produced the desired results. *Developers* need to know what impacts a system has caused so that information can be used to alter or improve future development projects. Users are traditionally uncomfortable with technological change. Therefore, a better understanding of how expert systems impact users will provide reassurance to users about the realities of expert systems and may indeed dispel potential anxiety and future dissatisfaction.

What explanation facilities are needed to maximize the usefulness of a particular expert system?

The explanation element of expert systems is particularly important when use of the expert system is expected to have an impact on the development of expertise by users. Studies of various types of explanation will not only help identify the optimal explanation interface for a particular type of system, but will also illustrate how alternative explanation facilities may impact user performance and perceptions. Few studies exist of explanation of accounting knowledge. Accounting tasks, including financial accounting, taxation, and auditing, are highly complex tasks that require deep knowledge of principles, regulations, and laws for which explanation is problematic.

What is the role of expert systems in reengineering accounting tasks?

Business process reengineering involves the use of modern information technologies to overhaul business processes for significant improvements in performance. Radical redesign of some processes is needed, particularly, for example, in the volatile legal environment of auditing. A reengineering of the audit process is needed to keep up with the legally and technologically transforming audit environment. The concepts of expert systems and business process reengineering are not new. However, the assertion that expert systems can be, in fact, have been used to transform audit processes as part of an overall audit process engineering activity, should be investigated. Rich case studies of such development could also provide useful insights for other accounting subdomains.

How can conflict and ambiguity of accounting knowledge be resolved?

Some relevant research issues are particularly difficult, particularly in taxation and other areas that not only have complex and sometimes ambiguous elements, but also may frequently change. Research must address methods for resolving conflicts and ambiguity in tax laws and regulations for inclusion in a knowledge base. In addition, maintenance of such systems must necessarily include plans for frequent updates to the knowledge base, which may be characterized by a high level of complexity.

Obstacles?

One of the obstacles to research on expert systems in accounting is the proprietary nature of many expert systems, particularly those used by public accounting firms. Gaining complete information about such projects is unlikely.

7.   FUTURE TRENDS AND SUMMARY

In the future, expert systems will tend to be more integrated with traditional information systems and technologies and less likely to be stand-alone systems. Accordingly, expert systems in accounting will slowly gain a more important, but less obvious role. An expert auditing planning system will become just another element of a broader audit support system that has both expert elements and traditional audit task elements, such as modules for statistical sampling and other common audit tests. In taxation, this integration will result in fewer isolated expert systems that address very specific tax issues, and broader intelligent tax information systems that perform a broader, well-rounded tax planning task.

Accounting expert systems will become more modular as they become more integrated in order to facilitate maintenance and update of knowledge bases. Particularly in taxation, such integration must be coupled with modularity, because of the rate of change in the laws, knowledge and facts that are needed to solve particular tax problems.

Another important trend involves the legal standing given to accounting expert systems. In auditing, for example, litigation has skyrocketed. As more audit firms utilize expert systems, legal issues will move to the forefront. The future will show us whether organizations will be able to use their expert systems as part of the documentation in defense of audit opinions.

Furthermore, increasing pressures on accounting firms and corporate accounting departments to show improved cost-benefit ratios for their services will perpetuate the need for on-going expert systems development. Accounting and auditing information-centered services will be expected to be delivered with increasingly more effectiveness and decreased costs, which can be facilitated through the strategic use of advanced technologies.

REFERENCES

AI/ES — Artificial Intelligence/Expert Systems Section of the American Accounting Association, (1992–1996 continuing) *Collected Working Papers presented at the Annual Research Workshop on AI/ES in Accounting, Auditing and Tax*, First: O'Leary, D.E. chair, August 9, 1992, Washington, D.C.; Brown, C.E. chair, August 7, 1993, San Francisco, CA; Srivastava, R.P. and Gillett, P.R. co-chairs, August 9, 1994, New York, N.Y.; Watkins, P.R. August 2, 1995, Orlando, FL; Vasaherlyi, M. chair, August 18, 1996, Chicago, IL.

Back, B. (1991) *An Expert System for Financial Statements Planning*. ABO Academy Press: Finland.

Baldwin-Morgan, A. A. and Stone, M. F. (1995) A matrix model of expert systems impacts, *Expert Systems with Applications: An International Journal*, 9(4), 599–608.

Boritz, J.E. and Wensley, A.K.P. (1996) *CAPEX: A Knowledge-Based Expert System for Substantive Audit Planning*, Princeton, NJ: Markus Wiener Publishers, 1–308.

Böer, G. (1989) *Use of Expert Systems in Management Accounting*. NAA: NJ.

Brown, C. E. (1989) Accounting expert systems: a comprehensive, annotated bibliography, *Expert Systems Review for Business and Accounting*, 2(1&2), 34–129.

Brown, C. E., Guest Editor. (1991) Special issue: expert systems for accounting, auditing, and tax, *Expert Systems with Applications*, 3(1), 1–169.

Brown, C. E. (1991) Expert systems in public accounting: current practice and future directions, *Expert Systems with Applications*, 3(1), 3–18.

Brown, C.E. and Gupta, U.G. (1994) Applying case-based reasoning to the accounting domain, *International Journal of Intelligent Systems in Accounting, Finance and Management*, 3(3), 205–221.

Brown, C.E. and Phillips, M.E. (1995) *Expert Systems for Management Accounting Tasks*, Montvale, NJ: The Institute of Management Accountants Foundation for Applied Research, Inc.

Brown C.E. and Wensley, A.K.P., Guest Editors. (1995) Special issue: expert systems in accounting auditing, and finance. *Expert Systems with Applications*, 9(4) 433–608.

Connell, N.A.D. (1987) Expert systems in accountancy: a review of some recent applications. *Accounting and Business Research*, 17(3), 221–233.

Durkin, J. (1993) *Expert Systems: Catalog of Applications*. Akron, OH: University of Akron Printing.

Edwards, Alex and Connell, N.A.D. (1989) *Expert Systems in Accounting*, U.K.: Prentice Hall International Ltd.

Grady, G.J. and Schreiber, R.K. (1989) Expert systems applications in the IRS, *Journal of Policy Analysis and Management*, 8(2) 193–199.

King, M. and McAulay, L. (1995) A review of expert systems in management accountancy. *The New Review of Applied Expert Systems*, 1, 3–17.

McCarthy, W.E., Denna, E., Gal, G., and Rockwell, S.R. (1992) Expert systems and AI-based decision support in auditing: progress and perspectives, *International Journal of Intelligent Systems in Accounting, Finance & Management*, 1(1), 53–63.

Michaelsen, R.H. and Messier, W.F. Jr. (1987) Expert systems in taxation. *The Journal of the American Taxation Association*, 8(2), 7–21.

Needham, J. T. (Research Division, Artificial Intelligence Laboratory, IRS). *Trends In Artificial Intelligence. Trend Analysis and Related Statistics*. Washington, D.C.: IRS Publications, 1986, Doc 6011, 39–45.

O'Leary, D.E., Editor (1987–1990) *Expert Systems Review for Business & Accounting*, 1(1)–2(3).

O'Leary, D.E., Editor (1992–1997 continuing) *International Journal of Intelligent Systems in Accounting, Finance & Management*, 1(1)–6(1) continuing.

O'Leary, D.E. and Watkins, P.R. (1989) Review of expert systems in auditing, *Expert Systems Review for Business and Accounting*, 2(1&2), 3–22.

O'Leary, D.E. and Watkins, P.R., Editors. (1992) Part 2: Accounting, *Expert Systems in Finance*, Amsterdam, The Netherlands: North-Holland, 127–267.

O'Leary, D.E. and Watkins, P.R. (1995) *Expert Systems and Artificial Intelligence in Internal Auditing*, Princeton, NJ: Markus Wiener Publishers.

Reitman, W. and Shim, S.J. (1992) Expert systems for evaluating business opportunities: implementing the management advisor at Krypton Chemical, *International Journal of Intelligent Systems in Accounting, Finance and Management*, 2(3), 191–204.

Sangster, A. (1996) Expert systems diffusion among management accountants, *Journal of Management Accounting Research*, 8, 171–182.

Sierra, G.J. and Bonsón E., Editors. (1996) *Intelligent Systems in Accounting and Finance*, Universidad de Huelva, Spain. *Second International Meeting on Artificial Intelligence in Accounting, Finance, and Tax*, Punta Umbría, Huelva (Spain). 27–28 September 1996

Sierra, G.J. and Bonsón, E., Editors. (1995) *Artificial Intelligence in Accounting, Finance, and Tax*, Universidad de Huelva, Spain. *Proceedings of the First International Meeting on Artificial Intelligence in Accounting, Finance, and Tax*, Matalascañas (Huelva) Spain. October 4–6 1995.

Thierauf, R.J. (1990) *Expert Systems in Finance and Accounting*, Westport, Connecticut: Greenwood Press, Inc.

van Dijk, J.C. and Williams, P. (1990) *Expert Systems in Auditing*, UK: MacMillan Publishers Ltd.

Vasarhelyi, M.A., Editor. (1989) *Artificial Intelligence in Accounting and Auditing: The Use of Expert Systems*, New York, N.Y.: Markus Wiener Publishing, Inc.

Vasarhelyi, M.A., Editor. (1995) *Artificial Intelligence in Accounting and Auditing: Using Expert Systems:* Vol. 2, Princeton, NJ: Markus Wiener Publishing, Inc.

Vasarhelyi, M.A., Editor. (1995) *Artificial Intelligence in Accounting and Auditing: Knowledge Representation, Accounting Applications and the Future:* Vol. 3, Princeton, NJ: Markus Wiener Publishing, Inc.

Watkins, P.R., Chairman (1988–1993) *Collected papers of the First — Fifth International Symposia on Expert Systems in Accounting Finance and Management.* September–October, 1988; Newport Beach, CA; October 29–November 1, 1989, Newport Beach, CA; September 26–28, 1990, Laguna Niguel, CA; October 31–November 1, 1991, Pasadena California; November 11–13, 1993, Stanford University, CA..

Watkins, P.R. and Eliot, L.B. (1992) *Expert Systems in Business and Finance*, Chichester, U.K.: John Wiley & Sons.

28 Designing Innovative Business Systems through Reengineering

Tom Beckman

CONTENTS

0-8493-3106-4/98/$0.00+$.50
© 1998 by CRC Press LLC

1.   INTRODUCTION

The potential today for applying ES in business settings is unparalleled. This author believes that promising ES applications for business can now be systematically and comprehensively uncovered. By integrating the perspectives and strengths from three disciplines — business reengineering, design, and expert systems — a particularly fertile environment and framework can be created for designing innovative business systems.

In business reengineering, an entire business system, or large segment, is radically redesigned. Many of the best opportunities for making dramatic improvements in organizational performance come from applying information technology (IT), often in the form of ES. Conversely, by adding reengineering and design techniques to their arsenal, IT and ES developers can solve one of their most vexing problems: how to determine design specifications that are stable, comprehensive, and satisfy their customers. By focusing on customer and organizational needs, complexes of ES with strategic value can be developed, some of which may provide lasting competitive advantage.

Unfortunately, these potential gains from applying ES have been overlooked by many in the business and consulting communities. There are a number of reasons for this:

- Lack of knowledge
- Fear of the technology
- Distrust and disbelief in the benefits of ES
- Inability to identify promising ES applications
- Inability to define business, IT, and ES requirements and constraints
- Inability to design the business and IT systems

As a result, the use of ES to achieve dramatic performance improvements, increases in customer value, and sustainable competitive advantage has been bypassed.

More specifically, this chapter addresses the following areas:

- Business reengineering concepts that encompass the business system and methodology
- Design concepts and reengineering methods that produce requirements and constraints
- Expert system concepts that help define the problem and select the best application type
- Approaches to identifying promising ES applications
- Examples of ES applications that help create innovative business systems
- Achieving the ideal enterprise through a long-term transition process

2.   BUSINESS REENGINEERING

Business reengineering is a very young discipline compared with ES; it was formally christened by Michael Hammer in 1990, whereas ES have been around for almost 30 years. Reengineering grew out of the quality movement, but it also has roots in work systems design, process innovation, and leading practices from management consulting firms. According to Hammer (Hammer and Champy, 1993), "Reengineering is the fundamental rethinking and radical redesign of business processes to achieve dramatic improvements in critical measures of performance."

An alternate definition proposed here is: "Reengineering is the **fundamental rethinking** and **radical redesign** of an **entire business system** to achieve **dramatic improvements** in customer value and organizational performance."

- Fundamental rethinking starts fresh by examining the mission and strategy, scanning the environment, as well as surfacing and challenging existing assumptions and policies — not just accepting the existing situation.
- Radical redesign starts with best practices and then applies innovative information technology (IT) — not just improving incrementally.
- Redesigning an entire business system includes products, services, management, IT, and motivation — not just reworking the process.
- Dramatic improvements are gains of at least 50% in measures such as functionality, cost, quality, and time — not just 10 to 20% gains in internal measures of performance.

The primary focus of reengineering should be external — on customer value expressed through products and services. The secondary emphasis should be internal — on organizational performance organized around the work processes.

2.1. REENGINEERING METHODOLOGY

A methodology is a body of methods, rules, and postulates employed by a discipline. Most methodologies consist of three parts:

- Purpose or goal state
- Model or system with components, features, or dimensions
- Process that achieves the purpose

Reengineering methodologies are basically formal design processes. For reengineering, the goal is creating a highly desirable or ideal business system that delivers greatly improved organizational performance and/or customer value. The design artifact is the business system that is divided into components, each one representing a different aspect or functionality. Finally, the design process is the reengineering life cycle, beginning with project definition and scoping, and ending with implementation.

A good methodology provides guidance and structure without being overly restrictive. It should also strike a balance between theory and practice. Methodologies should be thorough and disciplined without being too detailed and inflexible. Methodologies should occupy a middle ground between intuition and a cookbook. Some ideas are to provide principles, guidelines, and assessment tools, as well as examples, tips, and pitfalls.

2.2. BUSINESS SYSTEM

The business system is defined in terms of its constituent components or dimensions, and their linkages, interactions, and feedback. In this model, processes enabled by infrastructure components create desirable products and services that meet customer needs. This business system has two complementary perspectives: the internal organization and the external environment. The internal perspective is concerned with redesigning the process and enabling infrastructure components in order to achieve superior organizational performance. The external perspective, on the other hand, is focused on redesigning the products and services, as well as redefining and influencing the other environmental components in order to achieve greatly improved customer value and marketplace success. The business system is composed of the following components:

- Customer:
    — Customer profile, market segment
    — Customer needs, values, perceptions, and expectations
    — Competition, market, and industry
    — External environment: demographics, social, political, regulatory
- Product:
    — Product and service features: functionality, quality, time, and cost
    — Service process: product information, transaction, delivery, use, and repair
    — Cost, pricing, marketing, and sales
- Process:
    — Workflow decomposition, mapping, measures, simulation
    — Activity triggers, suppliers and inputs, outcomes and interfaces
    — Policy, practices, procedures, methods
    — Workflow analysis and simulation: capacity, bottlenecks, constraints
- Infrastructure:
    — Management
    — Expertise
    — Technology
    — Workforce
- Environment:
    — Market
    — Competition
    — Government

2.3. INFRASTRUCTURE ELEMENTS

Organizational performance is largely dependent on processes, which in turn are dependent on the infrastructure. Jointly, the infrastructure elements and the processes determine the level and sustainability of organizational performance in the face of trends in customer needs, the marketplace, competition, and government regulation. The internal infrastructure is composed of the following elements:

- Management:
    — Strategic planning: mission, vision, goals, objectives, and strategies
    — Performance management and workflow optimization: scheduling, assigning, structuring, monitoring, and controlling
    — Resource: planning, budgeting, logistics, optimization, and sourcing
    — Structure: organizational, team, job, role
    — Reward: measurement, appraisal, and compensation
    — Improvement: continuous, incremental, reengineering, change
- Expertise:
    — Data, information, knowledge, expertise, organizational competence
    — Knowledge acquisition and management
    — Exploring, experimenting, learning, innovation, teaching
    — Centers of expertise
- Technology:
    — IT platform and client/server architecture
    — ES: Knowledge repositories, performance support systems, personal assistants
    — Communications and groupware software
- Workforce:
    — Motivation, development, empowerment

Business Model

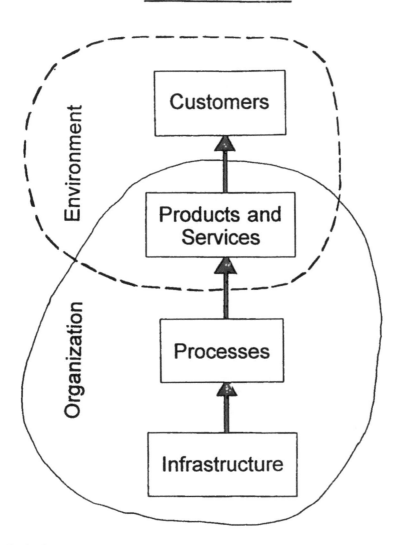

FIGURE 1 The business system.

— Staffing and career paths
— Culture: values, beliefs, norms, symbols

2.4. REENGINEERING LIFE CYCLE

The *reengineering life cycle* is the content and sequence of the methodology. The life cycle describes in detail how the future business system will be defined, developed, and implemented. The methodology spans business activities from strategic planning, through product development and process redesign, to operations. The author's version of the methodology has five phases (Beckman, 1996):

Phase 1: Determine strategy
Phase 2: Assess current state
Phase 3: Develop conceptual design

Organization Model

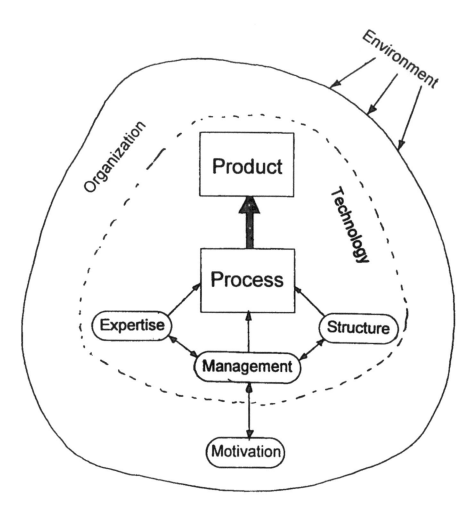

FIGURE 2   Infrastructure elements.

Phase 4: Build and test detailed design
Phase 5: Implement design

   The *determine strategy* phase focuses on setting and/or validating the strategic direction through analysis of industry, market segments, customer needs, competition, core competencies, and external trends and forces. Mission, vision, improvement initiatives, and plans are melded into a business strategy. Then, strategic initiatives, primarily reengineering projects, are scoped and aligned to ensure commitment of executive leadership. Outcomes from phase 1 are the business strategy, targeted market segments, and approved project charter.

   The *assess current state* phase assesses the current state of each of the components in the business system. Needs, values, and expectations of current customers, targeted market segments, including the interests and issues of key stakeholders, are determined, clustered, and prioritized. Next, constraints such as project funding, political sacred cows, technology feasibility, market dynamics, resources, and workforce expertise are determined. Conflicting needs and unnecessary constraints are negotiated and resolved. The resultant customer needs are then transformed into high-level business requirements and constraints. Further, problems and defects in the current system are identified and also converted into requirements. The outcomes from phase 2 are the case for action that documents the current state, defined value and performance gaps, and a set of high-level business requirements and constraints.

The *develop conceptual design* phase starts with the high-level business requirements and tries to design an ideal system by decomposing the design into work system components. Design enablers such as customer needs, value gaps, performance gaps, best practices, innovative IT, and creative thinking are used to improve and enhance the design. Next, design functionality/features are prioritized by the stakeholders, clustered into releases, and assessed for costs, benefits, risks, and dependencies. Outcomes are the conceptual design and high-level business case.

The *build and test detailed design* phase takes the conceptual design and decomposes each component into its detailed attributes. An operational prototype of each component is developed and tested for feasibility and effectiveness. After component testing, an integrated test is conducted of the overall design that is evaluated by the various customers and stakeholders. Design modifications are made and tested until the customers are satisfied. Outcomes are the detailed design, release strategy, and business case.

The *implement* phase first conducts a release pilot at an operational site to field test the design. Once proven, releases are rolled out across all sites. The final activity, *transition to operate*, includes measurement, problem-solving, and learning.

At the end of each phase, a decision point with three options — go, no go, or wait — is used to determine whether staffing and funding resources for the next phase will be approved and committed. Thus, resources are both managed efficiently, and more promising or urgent initiatives may displace or delay, but not kill, an existing one.

3.   DESIGN CONCEPTS

Advice on design is both scarce and often difficult to generalize across domains. Design is a creative, problem-solving process that attempts to produce an artifact with functionality that meets specified needs or goals. Design goals and needs must be translated and articulated into a measureable set of specifications. These specifications are in turn decomposed into requirements and constraints. Requirements describe the desired functionality; constraints place limitations on the design. Design components are then created or selected with features that satisfy various requirements and constraints. Finally, the overall design is assembled, integrated, and optimized.

According to Darr and Dym (1997), designs can be categorized into three classes:

- Creative: entirely new design artifact created to meet new purpose
- Variant: creation of new components and improvements to an existing artifact, resulting in significant new functionality
- Routine: assembly and configuration of existing components to meet expected or customized needs

Creative designs are required to meet ill-structured problems; variant designs are needed to solve semistructured problems; and routine designs can be used to optimize well-structured problems.

One goal of designers is to convert difficult ill-structured design problems into easier routine design problems by accumulating knowledge in the artifact's domain. Knowledge of prior successful designs can often be used as the basis for modified new designs. Case-based reasoning (Kolodner, 1993) can be applied to find the closest matching design solution in the case base, and modify it using rules to fit the current problem situation. Routine design problems can also be termed *configuration problems*. Configuration design tasks often require that a known set of parts be assembled into an artifact framework that has not been specified in advance (Ruby and Kibler, 1993).

3.1.   DESIGN PROCESS

According to Asimow (in Coyne et al., 1990), a generic design process has three steps:

1. Analysis
2. Synthesis
3. Evaluation

The *analysis* step assesses customer needs and determines the requirements and constraints. The *synthesis* step builds, configures, assembles, and integrates components that should satisfy or optimize the requirements and constraints. The *evaluation* step verifies and validates the design artifact. This process may be repeated many times as complex design problems are decomposed in greater detail, with the evaluation leading to a new understanding and revised analysis of the problem.

Design for ill- or semi-structured problems is usually best accomplished as a process of iterative deepening, recursively applying Asimow's design process. Later in this section the author will propose a more comprehensive design model. In the IS domain, for example, two Systems Development Life Cycle (SDLC) methodologies are dominant. Barry Boehm's Spiral Model is now favored for ill- and semi-structured problems, such as ES development. In this approach, designs are selected from the most closely matching prototypes, and then are iteratively refined. Unlike the linear Waterfall Model, the Spiral Model allows for more customer participation throughout the design, development, testing, and implementation processes. In addition, there is fast and frequent feedback to earlier phases of development. Also, prototypes are used to quickly create a design artifact to which the client can respond.

3.2.   REQUIREMENTS

Reengineering provides powerful techniques to transform needs into requirements. Differing groups, including customers, users, domain experts, designers, and owners, may have convergent or competing interests. These varying interests are expressed in terms of needs, preferences, and expectations. Requirements and constraints are then articulated from needs, preferences, and expectations that have been filtered through values and perceptions. Requirements are often expressed in terms of functionality, quality, service, and adaptability. Constraints are often expressed in terms of available resources and external limitations. Next, the resulting specifications are then assessed, prioritized, and negotiated across interest groups based on importance, need, resources, and constraints.

3.3.   CONSTRAINTS

Constraints are limitations imposed on the design description. Resource availability is the most common constraint in developing and implementing designs. This includes financial, raw material, intellectual, computing, and human resources. Other limitations may include physical, temporal, logical, technical, social, political, legal, regulatory, and cultural constraints.

Design limitations can be viewed as either hard or soft constraints (Ruby and Kibler, 1993). Hard constraints are Boolean-valued parameters that satisfy important design goals. Soft constraints are real-valued variables that measure the quality of a solution. Hard constraints must be met, while soft constraints are optimized.

Kolodner (1993) has pointed out that design problems can be over-constrained, as well as under-constrained. JULIA is a case-based reasoner (CBR) program that designs (plans) meals for parties. In a well-known case, some guests have preferences and many guests have constraints — types of food they will not eat. JULIA recalls prior meals or dishes from its case base that most closely match the preferences and constraints of its guests. It then adapts the best partial meal designs and creates dishes that will satisfy all the guests.

3.4.   DESIGN REALIZATION AND OPTIMIZATION

Once conceptual design specifications have been defined, designers begin the process of optimizing and negotiating between design requirements and those design constraints that limit the realization of the ideal or optimal design. Some requirements are desireable, but not essential, and can be reduced or eliminated; some constraints are artificial or cultural, and can be altered or minimized. If requirements are highly valued, resource constraints can sometimes be lifted. However, resource estimates are only meaningful once a conceptual design has been developed into a prototype and tested. Requirements, by themselves, often give little guidance on how to generate designs (Kolodner, 1993). Often, resource constraints can be overcome by lengthening the project development time frame, or breaking the project into smaller releases.

When problems are ill-structured and therefore under-constrained, a very large number of solutions may be possible, and often must be assessed in order to find the best one. For example, "Architect, design me a house; make a statement; cost is not a problem." In this case, the only limits are those set by the architect and the local building and zoning codes. Creative thinking that begins with the conceptual requirements and constraints as an anchor may be quite useful in exploring and defining the design problem, as well as generating ideas to reach design solutions. Texts by Couger (1996) and Van Grundy (1992) provide excellent advice on available techniques and when to apply them.

However, when design problems are over-constrained, often no solution is possible. Either the problem definition of the design artifact must be altered, or some of the constraints must be removed. For example, "Fifty thousand dollars is the most I can afford to spend on this house." Either the definition of a house must be loosened or broadened to be a "shelter" or at least one constraint must be lifted. Redefinition would mean that a house trailer, recreational vehicle, mobile housing, or owner-built housing might be solutions. Another solution would be to allocate more funds to the house-building budget. A third alternative might be to develop the dream house in stages over several years. Of course, in the case of designing a house, there might be more than 50 significant variables, and as many constraints.

3.5.   DESIGN GUIDELINES

The author believes that some design guidelines exist:

- Spend more up-front effort defining and exploring the problem space: determine its scope, requirements, constraints, and resources
- Identify customer groups and their needs, values, and resources
- Define the artifact in terms of functionality, service, quality, materials, and cost
- Apply domain knowledge in the form of models and components, as well as best practice design prototypes and expertise
- Apply domain knowledge to transform design problems into configuration problems
- First design the ideal artifact, then apply constraints
- If problem is under-specified, apply more domain knowledge or gather more detailed requirements and constraints
- If problem is over-specified, redefine the problem or delete requirements or constraints

Initially, designers must strive to create the most desireable, optimal, ideal artifact possible, without considering constraints. Later, constraints can be identified and applied, and compromises can and will be made. By establishing the vision of the ideal design, developers can often develop a multiple-release, long-range plan to reach the ultimate goal.

Another design tenet is to try to convert ill-structured design problems into structured configuration problems with standardized components. By creating domain models and applying knowledge from reengineering, design, and the domain, very difficult design problems can be reduced

Generic Design Process

Procedure	Elements	Players

1 Define Problem   Goals   Customers

Procedure	Elements	Players
1 Define Problem	**Goals**	**Customers**
Define Customers	Needs	Market Segments
Identify Needs/Values	Values	Stakeholders
Prioritize Needs	Budget	Funders
Determine Budget		Strategists
2 Analyze Problem	**Specifications**	**Analysts**
Decompose Needs	Requirements	Product/Service
Determine Reqts.	Constraints	Process
Determine Constraints	Resources	Technology
Tradeoff Reqts.		Financial
3 Develop Design	**Design Description**	**Designers**
Select Prototypes	Features	Product/Service
Generate Features	Components	Process
Describe Design Alts.	Prototype	Technology
Negotiate Reqts.		Integration
4 Build Artifact	**Design Artifact**	**Builders**
Build/Test Compnts.	Product	Developers
Build/Test Artifact	Service	Testers
Optimize Design	Process	Implementers
Tradeoff Reqts. & Constraints	Infrastructure	Assessors

FIGURE 3   A generic design model.

to manageable problems in component configuration. Knowledge can consist of component descriptions of functionality and constraints, as well as libraries of successful design cases.

3.6.   GENERIC DESIGN MODEL

A generic design model is proposed that describes the procedural steps, the design elements, and the participants that influence and enable the resulting design artifact. Although shown as a linear process, in practice this model would really look more like a spiral process, with feedback between process steps, and iteratively deepening and repeating the cycle until an optimal or acceptable design artifact was built.

4.   REENGINEERING DESIGN

One of the most significant aspect of reengineering, the design, is too often given little thought and is performed quite poorly due to a lack of design knowledge. In good reengineering design practice, the same design principles apply — imagine an ideal future state for the redesigned business system components and elements that best meets the needs and purposes of the defined customers. Customer and organizational needs are then translated into requirements and constraints. Next, design alternatives are created that best satisfy the requirements and constraints.

4.1. REENGINEERING DESIGN PROCESS

A reengineering design process can be described that closely follows the generic design model presented above. A design order exists among components that follows the business system flow in reverse. First, based on the strategy, the business should attempt to redefine, reshape, and/or influence its environment in terms of markets, customer needs, industry standards and certification, government regulation, and other sociopolitical forces. For example, customers often are willing to perform services in exchange for convenience or cost savings. Second, products and services are redesigned in accordance with prioritized customer and organizational needs. Next, processes are designed that produce products and services. Finally, the various elements of the infrastructure that enable the processes are reengineered.

The enhanced goal of reengineering is to radically redesign entire business systems in order to create value-added products and services that delight the customer, as well as to ensure the success and growth of the enterprise and personal careers. During the *assess current state* phase, value gaps from inferior products and services are determined from market and product analyses, sales data, and customer feedback. Performance gaps from poor process execution are identified from internal measures of cost, quality, and cycle time, as well as industry best practices. Finally, customer and organizational needs are identified and prioritized from the gap analyses.

Next, a feasibility study for each business system component is performed to determine the difficulty of reaching the ideal future state. Components are analyzed and ranked by the size of their gaps and the feasibility of reaching the future state. Designers should prioritize for immediate redesign those components with large gaps in which it is also relatively easy to reach the future state. This approach ensures the greatest results for the resources expended.

4.2. REENGINEERING DESIGN LEVELS

In reengineering, design occurs at three levels: enterprise, project, and component. Design at the enterprise level is abstract and broad-scoped, focusing on determining the core businesses/industries and markets and customers to be served. Outcomes are the enterprise mission, vision, objectives, programs, and strategies that are described in terms of markets, customers, and products. The outcomes from the enterprise level are used to guide the decomposition and scoping at the conceptual, project level in identifying customer needs, determining business requirements and constraints, and creating a conceptual design that describes the major aspects of each component in the future business system. The outcomes from the project level are used at the detailed, component level to drive the construction of an implementable, testable detailed design. Given this reengineering methodology, design artifacts at each level can be tested for correctness and completeness, as well as repeating and deepening the design process at each level until the outcomes are satisfactory.

There is a design focus and outcome at each level of decomposition from the broad and abstract to the specific and operationalizable:

Focus	Outcomes
Enterprise level:	
1. Core business or industry	Mission and vision
2. Markets and customers	Business objectives, strategy, mkt. segments
Project level:	
3. Customer needs	Requirements and constraints
4. Product/service specifications	Product/service functionality and value
Component level:	
5. Process design	Products and services
6. Support Components	Process performance, innovation, flexibility

Establishing and/or validating the business strategy is a necessary first step; otherwise, the wrong customers, their needs, and related products and services may be selected for redesign. Part of the business strategy consists of identifying promising future markets, customer groups, and their needs that the enterprise can meet. The selection of market segments and the determination of current and future customer needs will determine what components of the business system need to be redesigned. Different customer groups will have differing needs, values, perceptions, and expectations. These varied and sometimes conflicting interests must be balanced, weighed, and negotiated. Once resolved, the bundle of needs can be translated into a set of consistent requirements and constraints.

As indicated in the business system schematic, products and services exist to meet customer needs. In turn, processes are the primary mechanism for producing and delivering products and services. Therefore, initial redesign efforts should focus on the product, service, and process. However, choices for component redesign should be dependent on the relative size of gaps between current and ideal future states, and their ease of realization, specified in terms of business requirements. Reengineering projects typically redesign of all three of these components — a new product may also require customization and superior service, and both of these redesigns will require large changes in how the process is designed. In turn, large changes in the process will necessitate changes to most or all of the infrastructure elements.

4.3.   SOURCES OF DESIGN IDEAS

External sources of design ideas include:

- Customer needs, values, expectations, and perceptions
- Customer complaints, solicited feedback, market intelligence
- Competition and market products and services: functionality and features
- Industry best practices and environmental scan
- Domain literature and research
- Lead customers: innovative and demanding
- Industry user groups, seminars, conferences

Internal sources of design ideas include:

- Strategic direction: mission, vision, concept of operations
- Operational problems: poor quality, cost overruns, schedule and time delays
- Formal assessments, lessons learned, process feedback
- Performance measurements: process, results, customer, employee, supplier
- Domain experts
- Workforce complaints and quality of work life issues
- Reengineering component best practice
- Creative thinking
- Innovative IT

4.4.   CUSTOMER ANALYSIS PROCESS

The author has defined a customer analysis process that begins with identification of customers and ends with the translation of customer needs into business requirements and constraints:

1. Define the customer groups with an interest in the reengineering project
2. Determine needs, values, expectations, and perceptions separately for each customer group

3. Organize customer needs around product, service, and process
4. Prioritize customer needs
5. Identify, negotiate, and resolve customer need conflicts
6. Transform customer needs into business requirements and constraints

4.5. TYPES OF CUSTOMERS

- User/beneficiary:
    - — Primary customer that receives and uses product
    - — External focus: cares only about value package attributes
    - — Consumer also directly selects and funds product
- Owner/Funder:
    - — Entity that pays for development/delivery of product
    - — Responsible for funding processes and organization
    - — Balanced focus: internal on profits and costs; external perceptions
- Regulator:
    - — Entity that influences and controls profits, product features, HR practices
    - — Responsible to beneficiary and workforce
    - — Balanced focus: fairness to and safety of users and workforce
- Management:
    - — Controls and manages Business Systems that produce value
    - — Responsible for delivering value to beneficiary and oversight
    - — Balanced focus: value-added, profits, safety, compensation
- Workforce:
    - — Responsible for performing processes and producing products
    - — Internal focus: Career, compensation, and work environment

4.6. TRANSFORMING CUSTOMER NEEDS INTO BUSINESS REQUIREMENTS

Customer needs are often initially expressed as awareness in relatively general and ill-formed terms. These needs, values, expectations, and perceptions can be categorized by customer type and are usually in response to one of the following situations:

Customer Type	Situation	Business system components
User/Beneficiary	Unfulfilled need	Product functionality and service features
	Criticism	Product/service features, quality, timeliness
	Poor sales	Competition on product/service pricing, quality
Owner/funder	Poor performance	Process and infrastructure components
Regulator	Illegal acts	Service and management components
Management	Poor performance	Process and infrastructure components
	Low profits	Product/service and competition components
Workforce	Poor performance	Development, empowerment, reward elements
	Unsafe workplace	Management and environmental components

Customer needs must be articulated in more detail into business requirements and constraints. The quality and value to customers of the resulting products and services depends heavily on the business requirements being correct, complete, and robust — easy to modify in order to meet future customer needs. In order to ensure completeness and robustness, customer needs are transformed and articulated in requirements for each business system component in sequence, working from outcome backward to provider:

1. Product
2. Service
3. Process
4. Management
5. Workforce
6. Expertise   Components 4–7 can be designed in parallel
7. Infrastructure

Users and regulators specify external business requirements in terms of *value components:*

- Specify product attributes:
    — Functionality and features
    — Customization and personalization
    — Reliability and durability
    — Ease of use, learning, and repair
    — Aesthetics
    — Innovation and extendability
- Specify customer service attributes:
    — Pre-sale: product information and marketing
    — Transaction: features bundling, pricing, and payment
    — Post-sale: delivery, repairs, and advice
- Specify pricing and cost attributes:
    — Monetary costs and pricing: purchase, maintenance, and upgrades
    — Time costs: learning, setup, ease of use, availability
    — Stress: convenience and hassle
- Customer satisfaction index

Owners and funders requirements often reflect problems internally or externally:

- Business direction and strategy
- Profit margin:
    — Examine product lines and competition's products and services
    — Operational efficiencies start with the process, but usually involve the infrastructure components
- The management component is assessed by owners in terms of planning, budgeting, scheduling, monitoring, and evaluating
- Environmental issues in terms of political, social, demographic, and regulatory influences often involve customer, product, management, and workforce components

Management requirements are internal and specify desired operational performance:

- Business objectives: key performance indicators
- Quality: process, product, service
- Cost: process, infrastructure, and workforce
- Timeliness: process cycle time, responsiveness
- Flexibility and modularity: process, product design, expertise
- Capacity and idle resources: process, infrastructure

Workforce requirements are internally focused on the *support components:*

- Empowerment: management component
- Development: expertise component
- Compensation: measures, appraisal, and rewards — management component
- Work environment: infrastructure and management
- Security: management

5.   EXPERT SYSTEM CONCEPTS

ES are computer programs created to apply domain knowledge to specific problem and decision situations. In this chapter, we will focus our attention on identifying and applying ES in situations where expertise and knowledge are required during the reengineering process. Before this, however, we must define what we mean by expertise. The characteristics of expertise include fast and accurate performance, usually in a narrow domain of knowledge. In addition, an expert can explain and justify the recommendation or result, as well as explain the reasoning process leading to the result. Further, experts quickly learn from experience, resulting in improved performance. Expertise implies the ability to solve unique and unusual cases — often reasoning from basic principles or a model, or from a body of experience structured into cases or rules. Finally, experts often must reason under uncertainty and apply common-sense and general world knowledge to the situation.

In order to identify potential ES applications, it is useful to distinguish between the types of ES. Very often, one type of ES may be a much better choice depending on several factors —the situation particulars, degree of structure in the domain knowledge, the knowledge representation schema, and user characteristics. There are three general types of ES:

- Case-based
- Rule-based
- Model-based

5.1.   CASE-BASED REASONING (CBR)

CBR relies on expertise in the form of worked cases. CBR works by measuring how similar a new situation is to an existing case in the case base, and retrieving the most similar (most relevant) case. A case consists of the attributes and values of a problem situation, as well as its solution. CBR does not require much of a domain theory — it requires nothing more than a representative sample of stereotypical worked cases. Knowledge discovery and database mining techniques can often generalize, induce, and transform cases, or portions of cases, into useful rules.

Case-based reasoning should be used when:

- The solution alternatives can be explictly enumerated
- Numerous examples of worked cases exist that cover domain knowledge
- No domain model or theory exists
- Experts represent domain in terms of cases
- Human experts or expertise are not available
- Situational information is conflicting, uncertain, or missing
- Knowledge is volatile and dynamic
- Domain knowledge and expertise already captured by past cases
- Workforce experience and performance are low
- Need a fast way to acquire domain knowledge
- Want to illustrate an outcome or explanation with an example

- Want to contrast and compare potential solutions
- Want to assess pros and cons of a situation
- Want to test a theory or solution with cases

5.2. RULE-BASED SYSTEMS (RBS)

RBS use many small slivers of knowledge organized into conditional If-Then rules. Inference engines for RBS are either goal-driven, backward-chaining, or data-driven, forward-chaining, depending on the type of application or generic task. Rules often represent heuristics —shortcuts or rules-of-thumb for solving problems. Regarding the amount of structure, RBS fall in between CBR and MBR — rules of thumb are abstracted and generalized from experience into small chunks of knowledge. Both CBR and RBS can be developed incrementally and can provide some value in an unfinished state. RBS can also be transformed into objects or frames using knowledge discovery and database mining techniques.

Rule-based systems should be used when:

- Human experts think in terms of rules and heuristics
- Task involves decision-making, problem-solving, heuristics, or judgment
- Domain is complex and substantial expertise exists
- Knowledge is stable and is well- or semi-structured
- Expertise is primarily symbolic, not numeric
- Human experts are willing and available for knowledge elicitation
- Work performance and product quality are poor
- Employee turnover is high and training is expensive
- Impending loss of domain experts

5.3. MODEL-BASED REASONING (MBR)

MBR provides a representational and conceptual framework for knowledge that defines both knowledge structures and inferencing methods. MBR defines and structures relevant domain objects/concepts, their attributes, and their behaviors in order to organize work in complex domains and perform simulations. MBR also defines the relationships between the objects in terms of class hierarchies, composition, and causation. The most basic knowledge structure, governing all types of knowledge, is the <Object Attribute Value> triple.

MBR encompasses, represents, and organizes all types of knowledge, including CBR and RBS, as well as databases, text, images, and other media. Types of MBR are object-based, frame-based, and domain-specific; MBR models can also be categorized as quantitative or qualitative. MBR requires a well-structured, well-understood domain theory. In simulation, MBR components are often so tightly linked together that MBR has limited value without a completed model. MBR is also very useful for organizing and structuring complex domains and work processes.

Model-based reasoning should be used when:

- A consensus framework of concepts and domain theory exists
- Business processes, methods, and events need to be represented and modeled
- Want to represent and organize large-scale, complex systems
- Want to simulate performance and side-effects from future work system design
- Want to control, monitor, and measure information workflows
- Want to represent, organize, and integrate elements of knowledge repositories and related performance support systems
- System navigation and presentation are important
- Environment and data are relatively dynamic

- IT infrastructure uses a client/server architecture
- Results from knowledge elicitation and acquisition need to be organized

6. APPROACHES TO IDENTIFYING EXPERT SYSTEM APPLICATIONS

Following is a list of approaches in which potential ES applications have been found:

- Knowledge-Intensive Areas:
  — Industries
  — Organizational functions
  — Work activities
- Business system components
- ES generic task
- ES typology: when to use which type of ES (covered in Section 5)

6.1. KNOWLEDGE-INTENSIVE ORGANIZATIONAL FUNCTIONS APPROACH

One key to finding promising ES applications is to locate industries, organizational functions, business activities, and work system components where work is information- and knowledge-intensive.

The following organizational functions are information- and knowledge-intensive:

- Research and Development
- Engineering
- Marketing
- Sales
- Customer Service
- Management
- Contracting
- Legal
- Human Resources/Administration
- Training
- Information Systems

6.2. KNOWLEDGE-INTENSIVE WORK ACTIVITIES APPROACH

On a finer-grained level within an organization, activities within functions can also be classified as information- and knowledge-intensive. These following business activities that are knowledge-intensive can occur within any of the organizational functions:

- Communicating
- Facilitating, coordinating, negotiating
- Managing
  — Planning
  — Budgeting
  — Organizing
  — Controlling
  — Evaluating
- Creating/retrieving/updating/distributing information

- Decision-making
- Problem-solving
- Researching
- Designing
- Teaching, coaching, tutoring, training
- Learning
- Diagnosing, repairing
- Computing
- Perceiving, sensing

6.3. BUSINESS SYSTEM COMPONENTS APPROACH

Another approach is to examine the Business System components, elements, and cross-components for aspects that are knowledge-intensive:

- Customer:
    - Market and competitive intelligence and analysis
    - Customer needs and profiling
    - Cross-product marketing
- Product:
    - Information product functionality
    - Matching customer needs to available products: assisting customers in optimizing product functionality, quality, and cost tradeoffs
    - Product configuration, customization, and pricing
    - Product performance monitoring
    - Helpdesk: product use, problem diagnosis, repair procedures
    - Optimize delivery and repair scheduling and logistics
- Process:
    - Quality assurance for information products
    - Measurement system analyses and forecasts
    - Process modeling and simulation
    - Workflow management, control, and monitoring
- Management:
    - Environmental scanning with intelligent assistants
    - Workflow optimization: time, quality, cost
    - Best practice application
- Workforce:
    - Decision support
    - Work assignment: matching skills, performance, availability, preference
    - Structuring problem-solving
    - Automated appraisals
    - Personal assistant
    - Integrated performance support system: help, training, testing, examples
- Expertise:
    - Knowledge representation and structuring
    - Knowledge repository
    - Knowledge acquisition/elicitation
    - Knowledge discovery and data mining
    - Intelligent tutoring systems
    - Advisory expert systems

        — Selection of creative thinking method
- Infrastructure:
    - Logical knowledge representation of financial and physical infrastructures
    - Logical knowledge representation of IT infrastructure/architecture
    - Inventory management: minimize inventory and shortages
    - Logistics management: optimize the flow of material by time and cost

6.4. ES GENERIC TASK APPROACH

ES applications are plentiful in industries and companies where work is management-critical — that is, management excellence is critical to success. In addition to identifying management tasks (such as planning, scheduling, monitoring, regulating, and controlling), the *generic task approach* to identifying promising ES also identifies certain types of work tasks that are highly amenable to ES. Waterman (1983) proposed a list of ten tasks that were natural ES applications, and Beckman (1996) has added several additional task types:

- Interpreting
- Predicting
- Diagnosing
- Designing/configuring
- Planning
- Monitoring
- Debugging
- Repairing
- Instructing
- Controlling

- Classifying
- Evaluating
- Filtering
- Regulating
- Scheduling
- Matching/Assigning
- Organizing
- Optimizing

7. BUSINESS APPLICATIONS OF EXPERT SYSTEMS

In this section, numerous examples of prototypical business applications of expert systems will be described. In no sense is this list exhaustive, and it is hoped that these applications may spur additional ideas from the reader. The section is organized around the business system components.

7.1. PRODUCT APPLICATIONS OF EXPERT SYSTEMS

Many types of products can have expert systems embedded in them. For example, ES can be used to monitor the performance or health of engines, appliances, and computer systems, reporting problems to the owner or the manufacturer. In addition to monitoring, ES can make diagnoses and suggest repairs. In another type of application, ES are used to control and optimize the performance of many products. For example, ES controllers are used to minimize energy usage in air conditioners and clothes dryers. In control tasks, ES using fuzzy logic are most often employed.

Software products offer many opportunities to employ ES. E-mail and voice-mail can be screened using evaluating and filtering generic tasks so that the most important and urgent messages are presented first. In addition, the system might signal the user as to the sender and message topic on important messages. Many messages approximating junk mail can be automatically deleted. Some message categories, such as confirmation, may receive automated replies.

Intelligent meeting schedulers could be especially valuable. An electronic scheduler could determine likely participants from the topic and prior meetings. It would poll the electronic calendars of potential participants looking for the optimal time and place, taking into account prior commitments, interests, roles, and work relationships. The scheduler could also do some limited negotiation and rescheduling of subordinate calendars.

7.2.   CUSTOMER SERVICE APPLICATIONS OF EXPERT SYSTEMS

The *customer service process* is highly informational and thus affords numerous opportunities for applying ES. This process involves three stages: pre-sale, transaction, and post-sale. In the pre-sale stage, the customer collects product information, compares products, selects features, and makes the purchase decision. During the transaction stage, customers input their orders and select payment, warranty, delivery, and installation options. During the post-sale stage, customers receive product training and advice, use the product, and request repairs. A toll-free or Internet customer service helpdesk can be used to integrate these various applications, as well as provide more personalized service by accessing customer profiles.

Product comparison and selection: During the pre-sale stage, a CBR application could assist customers in selecting the product and features that would best meet their needs. The CBR application would find the best match between customer needs, requirements, and constraints such as cost and time; and available options in the company's product line, including product and service features and options.

Electronic salesman: Given an extensive customer knowledge repository, an RBS could send out customized advertisements targeted to known customer needs and values. These marketing proposals could recommend follow-on and augmented products and services based on prior purchase history. Another option would be to use the Electronic Salesman as an assistant during telemarketing. For example, Sang Kee Lee (1996) suggests a salesman expert system for the customized purchasing support of men's wear using an integrated approach of RBS and constraint satisfaction methods.

Delivery and repair routing schedulers: In many retail and service industries, deliveries and repairs must be made at the customer's site. Knowledge of best traffic routes and times during rush-hour and off-peak traffic hours is essential. For deliveries, average installation times should be well-known; and for repairs, rough estimates can be made based on the diagnosis from the symptoms. Incidentally, the diagnosis also includes the parts that will likely be needed, so that return repair trips can be minimized. RBS, CBR, or specialized GIS MBR can be used to not only optimize the routing, but also to give customers much more precise time windows for meeting the service personnel.

Product diagnosis and repair: RBS and CBR applications exist in many domains that perform the generic ES tasks of diagnosis and repair. Automobile, mainframe computer, and elevator repair ES are typical examples. CBR can be especially useful because new worked cases can be added by the users.

Product advice and assistance: Customers very often need help with installing, assembling, configuring, using, and trouble-shooting complex products. Advice could be accessed through toll-free phone numbers in which customer service representatives serve as intermediaries between the ES and the customer. Examples of this approach are IRS' Taxpayer Service Assistant (Beckman, 1990) and American Express' Credit Analyzer Assistant. The Internet and kiosks at retail outlets could be used to deliver advice directly — ranging from interactive tutorials to more specific job aids. For extensive tutorials, MBR and RBS are both usually needed. For more focused advice and assistance, either CBR or RBS can be used.

7.3. PROCESS APPLICATIONS OF EXPERT SYSTEMS

All internal aspects of a reengineered enterprise are organized around the process component. Decomposition of the process structures and organizes the supporting business system components. MBR, and in particular, object technology, can be used to represent the process workflows, as well as simulating the performance of future designs and experimenting with various design alternatives. As the causal relationships between the business system components are better understood, better models can be built to forecast and plan future organizational performance.

Once work is assigned to an individual employee or work group, work can be structured and controlled using integrated MBR workflow management software that guides employees through the required or suggested best practice-procedure. If completion dates are in jeopardy, then a reminder will be sent to the employee and his/her manager so that work can be reassigned or rescheduled if necessary. The MIS module will capture data on all work in progress and all completed work.

7.4. MANAGEMENT APPLICATIONS OF EXPERT SYSTEMS

Many aspects of management can be automated, resulting in a higher level of performance than is possible from any human manager or management team. The management tasks with the largest potential gains include dynamic workflow modeling and simulation for process improvement; automated workload management for allocating, scheduling, and assigning cases; automated case management for work requiring multiple specialists; automated quality assurance; and analyzing and forecasting trends in measurement data.

Dynamic workflow modeling and simulation: All business concepts, practices, and processes can be documented and available online as text, process maps, supporting work system elements, and process simulation models. In addition, all relevant measurement data, as well as performance standards and employee compensation criteria, will also be available online, and will be integrated with the process models. The Management Information System (MIS) will be integrated with the related process models. Thus, all employees will be able to access, design, and test new process models through simulation by modifying the input variables. Modeling and simulation software will assist in improving the work processes.

Automated workload management: Work that is informational in nature can usually be performed independent of location simply by transferring caseloads electronically between sites. To accomplish this, an enterprise-wide *object-oriented* MBR is used to structure, organize, and sequence the work. Then, specialized algorithms can be selected by RBS and applied to level workloads dynamically enterprise-wide. When corporate workload leveling is combined with sophisticated workload allocation, scheduling, and assignment algorithms, large gains in productivity and staff utilization are possible.

Automated case management: Cases can be structured using MBR to represent several important variables in allocating and scheduling work: the amount, type, location dependence, and timing of receipt of the work; the quantity, skills, prior performance, and availability of staff; and the required completion date and accuracy. CBR and/or RBS can be used to optimize work assignments as well as workforce development. When workloads are high and inventories are backing up, the scheduler module will assign new work to the highest performing specialists available at the lowest appropriate skill and experience levels. When workloads are low, the module will assign or suggest to managers that they assign developmental tasks to employees that stretch their abilities. The module can also be used to plan future workloads and resource needs.

Complex work requests may require processing from a variety of specialists, sometimes in a certain sequence. This system serves as the case manager, creating a virtual single point of contact for the client. For example, hiring an employee might include tasks such as ordering furniture and computers, getting security clearances and ID badges, performing orientation and initiation, and establishing payroll and benefits.

This system also allows customers to request a completion date that can be negotiated by a RBS module based on user priorities if the requested date cannot be met. The system can reschedule other work assignments and renegotiate related completion dates to meet a truly urgent request. The system also sends notifications to customers when it forecasts that agreed-to completion dates will not be met.

Automated quality assurance (QA): All work performed electronically can be automatically sampled and compared for quality. CBR software allows for the comparison of stereotypical cases against newly worked cases. Sampled cases that are very similar to stereotypical cases are assumed to be correct. Cases that are dissimilar are referred to managers and/or appropriate QA employees. New cases are reviewed for accuracy and method of solution. There are three possibilities: the new case is either incorrectly worked, represents a new type of work, or has a different valid or better solution method than exists in the case base.

In addition to online QA, the evaluation module can also generate simulated test cases in certain situations. In real time, the evaluation module generates test cases or selects them from a case base in response to recent errors in certain types of cases, or when analysis of performance measures indicates a problem. Test cases are sent to employees when QA or the manager detects errors. Test cases can also be sent to employees to evaluate recent training or the need for remedial training.

Analysis and forecasting of trends in measurement data: Standardized Management Information System (MIS) reports will provide raw and percentage change comparisons to the immediate prior period as well as the same period for the prior year for all requested levels. Exception reporting with user-set default settings or highlighted variances of specified sizes can be selected. Users will be able to customize the reports to suit their own preferences by changing a few parameters. Sophisticated user interface design will allow users to more easily browse, explore, or produce desired ad hoc requests.

A variety of techniques are available for analyzing the MIS results. RBS can detect significant variances in historical measurement data, and MBR can forecast future trends and problems based on causal or empirical relationships between measures. Text generation AI software can explain the variances in English prose. Process simulation MBR models can be used to predict the down-stream consequences of the variances. Time-series trend analysis software also will be used to forecast future performance. Information access and presentation will have functionality similar to that described for external environmental scanning.

7.5.   WORKFORCE APPLICATIONS OF EXPERT SYSTEMS

There are many workforce applications that are better performed by computer or that provide intelligent support to the workforce. Many routine operational tasks of an informational nature can be partially or totally automated. More important are the uses of ES to empower front-line employees to make decisions once reserved for management. To ensure accountability and security, electronic audit trails and ES monitoring are used. Using CBR and RBS, job announcements and assignments can be made automatically, with management providing criteria for content and selection. Employees indicate interest in and availability for positions and assignments, and the system evaluates applicant performance and capabilities to find the best matches to the needed requirements and skills. Automated employee appraisals already exist in some companies using agreed-to standards and measurement criteria, as well as customer and peer evaluations.

Automation of routine work: Routine, simple, boring tasks will be automated to the extent possible. Examples will be data entry, form correctness and completeness checks, and simple approvals. Employees will no longer process and control paper, but rather will provide value-added advice and services that require knowledge and judgment. Electronic templates, supplanted by RBS, will be provided to capture data from paper forms, immediately applying entity, validity, consistency, and reality checks to the data entered. The information captured will be stored in knowledge repositories for later use.

Empowering employees: Front-line employees will have immediate access to needed information sources on-line. They also will have expanded decision-making authority and responsibility for results. RBS and CBR can push decision-making down to the working level in many instances. ES can automate some decisions, as well as support most other decisions while leaving the human in control. An electronic audit trail can be kept of all personnel actions, purchases, and consequential decisions.

Automated job announcements and assignments: A job announcements database will list the skills, assignment duration, and project leader for specific projects. Employees will be able to proactively apply for assignments individually online or can request receipt of all announcements of a certain type by location and duration. Employees can use CBR to select the best match between their skills, experience, interest, and availability, and the characteristics of available positions. Project offices can also assign project development work automatically through use of RBS and CBR by determining the skills needed for the job, evaluating the applications submitted, and searching the skills inventory, employee leave, and employee career development data stores for available employees with the needed skills and performance. This approach will eliminate favoritism and promote true merit selection.

Automated employee appraisal: A multiple perspective approach to appraisal, such as the balanced scorecard (Kaplan and Norton, 1992), is recommended. An automated employee appraisal system using this approach can be used to align enterprise-wide strategies with the compensation system. Performance metrics will be cascaded down from the enterprise-wide level into clusters of relevant supporting measures for each individual employee. Performance measures and quality assurance samplings will provide most information on employee performance. Information on training and education received by employees will also be online. Structured appraisal templates will be issued automatically by the system to peers, project managers, and functional experts. Responses, including free text, will be received, scored, and analyzed. Text generation AI software can convert numeric scores, text, and other inputs into a written appraisal that the manager can use or modify, according to need.

Automation of administrative tasks: Many personnel and administrative tasks will be automated, eliminating the need for most administrative managers and personnel. CBR software can be used by employees to select the most appropriate health benefits plan. Employees enter their requirements and preferences and the CBR returns the plans with the closest match on the features. An RBS module can be added to assist in choosing the features, as well as compute the likely plan cost of a number of desired features.

Personal assistants: Personal Assistants (PAs) can assist employees in a variety of tasks. PAs using RBS and CBR can screen and prioritize E-mail and voice-mail messages, including the deletion of duplicate messages. Voice-mail can be first transformed into text using speech recognition software. Particular topics and individuals can be selected for priority sorting. Users will be able to create PAs to perform complex procedural tasks, information retrieval tasks, or monitor-and-search tasks that humans are not good at. PAs can continually roam the intranet and/or Internet searching for and retrieving topics of interest.

Intelligent servers will schedule meetings automatically by cooperatively working with other servers to arrange and rearrange individual schedules according to user preferences and manager requests. When there are scheduling conflicts, the RBS mediates between participants depending on the reporting relationships, urgency, and existing assigned work. Intelligent meeting schedulers can also suggest potential participants and meeting roles, as well as compose meeting agendas, depending on the topic, type of meeting, and prior meeting action items.

7.6.   EXPERTISE APPLICATIONS OF EXPERT SYSTEMS

Knowledge repository: A *knowledge repository* (Beckman, 1996) is an online, computer-based storehouse of expertise, knowledge, experience, and documentation about a particular domain of expertise. In creating a knowledge repository, knowledge is collected, summarized, and integrated across information sources. *Knowledge acquisition*, a discipline related to expert systems, consists of a collection of techniques that are used to elicit implicit knowledge from a domain expert. In conjunction with *knowledge representation*, these concepts can be used to collect, organize, integrate, and summarize knowledge about a particular speciality/domain.

A knowledge repository consists of many different kinds of knowledge and information:

- Directory of knowledge sources and skill sets
- Plans and schedules
- Procedures
- Principles, guidelines
- Standards, policies
- Causal models (MBR)
- Process maps and workflows (MBR)
- Information/data stores
- Decision rules (RBS)
- Performance measures and other data
- Worked cases (CBR)
- Designs of business system components
- Stakeholder and customer profiles: needs, values, expectations, perceptions
- Products and services: features, functionality, pricing, sales, repair
- Domain workforce profiles: knowledge, experience, preferences, interests
- Domain best practices
- Current state assessments and learnings

Integrated performance support systems: We have been discussing the application of ES at the microlevel in an organization. It is also possible to consider the totality of workforce needs by designing Integrated Performance Support Systems (IPSS) that make use of various AI disciplines (Winslow and Bramer, 1994). IPSS can be categorized into the following services (after Winslow and Bramer):

- Infrastructure: organizing and structuring the work environment (MBR and knowledge repositories)
- Controller: monitoring, coordinating, and controlling IPSS services (RBS)
- Navigation: human-computer interaction (MBR)
- Presentation: users can tailor and customize data and other service aspects (MBR)
- Acquisition: capturing knowledge, cases, opinions, learnings, and sensory data in various media forms and transforming them to an internal form (smart templates)
- Advisory: provides advice, reminders, assistance (RBS and CBR)
- Instruction: help, job aids, tutoring, training (MBR, RBS, and CBR)

- Evaluation: assessing and certifying based on performance measures, automated QA, and administered tests (CBR and RBS)
- Reference: source of workforce and organizational knowledge and expertise, as well as source of intranet, Internet, and other databases and information (CBR and AI search engines)

In addition to ES, other AI disciplines involved in providing IPSS include intelligent tutoring, knowledge discovery and learning, intelligent information retrieval, smart form templates, uncertainty, as well as speech recognition, intelligent OCR, natural language understanding through conceptual dependencies, and text generation.

8. THE FUTURE OF EXPERT SYSTEMS IN BUSINESS — ACHIEVING THE IDEAL ENTERPRISE

The future of ES in business reengineering is bright. The convergence of ES and reengineering in the redesign of an enterprise provide powerful sustainable competitive advantages. By applying the ideas and methods in this chapter, leading-edge organizations can achieve market leadership, customer intimacy, superior operational performance, as well as higher profit margins. The transition to an ideal future capability can evolve through four sequential, but overlapping stages:

Stage 1: Establish an installed networked IT infrastructure for all employees
Stage 2: Create enterprise-wide data, object, and knowledge repositories
Stage 3: Automate and enable operations, management, and support activities
Stage 4: Develop integrated performance support systems and knowledge discovery and data mining applications

8.1. STAGE 1: IS AND IT INFRASTRUCTURE

It is not enough to identify and develop isolated ES applications for reengineering. The prerequisite is that there must be a networked IT platform installed across the organization to support the ES applications. Every employee is equipped with a workstation that supports complex computational, informational, and communication needs. Every employee can communicate electronically with all other employees, both as individuals and collaboratively in groups.

Powerful system navigation and information exploration tools are available that use flexible keyword search, hypermedia, dynamic visual querying, and tree maps (Shneiderman, 1992). Every employee is provided with a suite of standard office automation software, including text processing, presentation graphics, spreadsheets, relational DBMS, calendaring, meeting schedulers, Web browsers, E-mail, voice-mail, and fax-mail. This standard software should be integrated with the custom IS.

8.2. STAGE 2: KNOWLEDGE REPOSITORIES

In stage 2, enterprise-wide relational and object models are created, populated, and regulated. Consistent corporate-wide data or object dictionaries are created. Existing online data are transformed and reformatted onto relational databases, or wrapped for object models. Because most data were previously kept on paper, a massive data entry effort may be required to populate the databases. Smart data-entry templates are available to ensure quality by checking for entity, validity, consistency, and reality.

Later, multimedia object repositories that hold data, text, graphics, images, full-motion video, audio, objects, cases, and rules have replaced relational data models. Knowledge repositories are built for special-purpose, functional, corporate, and external uses. ES and other AI software exist to translate from most media into text and to understand what the text means using intelligent OCR for document images, voice recognition for audio, vision understanding into textual features, and from text into meaning using natural language understanding.

8.3. STAGE 3: AUTOMATED AND SUPPORT ES APPLICATIONS

Stage 3 is completed through use of ES applications in the sections described above. Coupled with electronic audit trails, many routine decisions and tasks are automated within the organization, and many others are supported by ES. In marketing and sales, ES help the organization establish better relationships and partnerships with their customers, better match products to customer needs, and to increase profit margins through improved pricing. Outside the organization, customers have direct access to powerful ES tools provided by the organization to help them understand and purchase products, as well as maintain and repair products. Many products also have embedded ES for improved performance and service.

8.4. STAGE 4: IPSS AND KNOWLEDGE DISCOVERY

In Stage 4, Centers of Expertise (COE) are formed that are responsible for the collecting, learning, organizing, and distributing of knowledge for core competencies and other domain specialities of importance to the organization. COE educate and certify workers in their specialities, provide qualified workers and consulting services both online and in person to clients, and set and enforce standards for their specialities. COE also create, maintain, and enhance knowledge repositories and IPSS through internal and external research, as well as employee and organizational feedback.

Other artificial intelligence disciplines are also applied to solve business problems. In particular, machine learning techniques are applied for dynamic optimization of resource allocation and workload scheduling applications, resulting in dramatic gains in performance. Machine learning is also used for knowledge discovery and data mining (Fayyad et. al., 1996), as well as to detect trends in data, such as MIS data. Intelligent Assistants, combined with natural language understanding and text generation, are used to search for, select, and summarize news stories on certain topics.

The most dramatic performance gains will come from the deployment of Integrated Performance Support Systems (IPSS) that provide employees with coordinated services for task information, advice, training, job aids, reference, and administrative and personal resources to meet organizational and individual needs. These services might include sophisticated automation of and/or support for task processing and structuring; tutoring; problem-solving; decision-making; and information analysis through knowledge discovery and data mining techniques.

Creating the *knowledge organization* could be the next great challenge for the application of ES in business. If, as some authors on strategic management have claimed, knowledge is the only real source of competitive advantage, then knowledge organizations may be the primary competitive weapon of the future. And if this is so, then knowledge engineers and business applications of ES have a very bright future indeed.

REFERENCES

Beckman, T. "An expert system in taxation: the taxpayer service assistant." Chapter in *Managing and Developing Expert Systems*. J. Liebowitz, Ed. Yourdan. 1990.

Beckman, T. Applying AI to Business Reengineering Tutorial. 146 pages. Presented at the World Congress on Expert Systems III. Seoul, Korea. February, 1996.

Couger, D. *Creativity and Innovation in Information System Organizations*. Course Technology. 1996.

Coyne, R., Rosenman, M., Radford, A., Balachandran, M., and Gero, J. *Knowledge-Based Design Systems*. Addison-Wesley. 1990.

Darr, T. and Dym, C. "Configuration Design: An Overview." In this volume.

Fayyad, U., Piatetsky-Shapiro, G., Smyth, P., Uthurusamy, R., Eds. *Advances in Knowledge Discovery and Data Mining*. MIT Press. 1996.

Hammer, M. and Champy, J. *Reengineering the Corporation: A Manifesto for Business Revolution*. Harper-Collins. 1993.

Kaplan R. and Norton, D. "The balanced scorecard — measures that drive performance," *Harvard Business Review*. Jan–Feb 1992.

Kolodner, J. *Case-Based Reasoning*. Morgan Kaufmann. 1993.

Lee, S.K. "Salesman expert system for customized purchasing support," In *Critical Technology: Proceedings of The Third World Congress on Expert Systems*. Cognizant Communication Corp. 1996.

Ruby, D. and Kibler, D. "Learning recurring subplans," in *Machine Learning Methods for Planning*. Minton, S., Ed. Morgan Kaufmann. 1993.

Shneiderman, B. *Designing the User Interface: Strategies for Effective Human-Computer Interface*, 2nd ed. Addison-Wesley. 1992.

VanGundy, A. *Idea Power: Techniques and Resources to Unleash the Creativity in Your Organization*. AMA-COM. 1992.

Waterman, D. in Hayes-Roth, F., Waterman, D., and Lenat, D., Ed. *Building Expert Systems*. Addison-Wesley. 1983.

Winslow, C. and Bramer, W. *Future Work: Putting Knowledge to Work in the Knowledge Economy*. Free Press. 1994.

29 Expert Systems for Marketing: From Decision Aid to Interactive Marketing

Sang-Kee Lee and Jae Kyu Lee

CONTENTS

1. APPLICATION AREAS OF MARKETING EXPERT SYSTEMS

Marketing has been one of the most active areas of expert system research and applications (Murdoch, 1990). The functional areas of marketing to which an expert systems approach has been applied include:

- Advertising design (RAD: McCann, Tadlaoui, and Gallagher, 1990; ADCAD: Burke, Rangaswamy, Wind and Eliashberg, 1990)
- Advertising response prediction (ADDUCE: Burke, 1991)
- Brand management (BMA: McCann, Lahti, and Hill, 1991)

- Deal design (DEALMAKER: McCann and Gallagher, 1990)
- Financial marketing (FAME: Apte et al., 1992)
- Marketing negotiation (NEGOTEX: Rangaswamy, Eliasberg, Burke, and Wind, 1989)
- Market share analysis (SHANEX: Alpar, 1991)
- Media planning (Mitchell, 1987)
- New product pricing (Casey and Murphy, 1994) and transfer pricing (TRANSFER: Kirsh et al., 1991)
- News search using scanner data (INFER: Rangaswamy, Harlam, and Lodish, 1991; CoverStory: Schmitz, Armstrong, and Little, 1990; SalesPartner: Schmitz, 1994; SCAN*EXPERT: Bayer and Harter, 1991)
- Product configuration (UNIK-SES: Lee, Lee, and Lee, 1996)
- Promotion evaluation (Poh and Jasic, 1995; PROMOTIONSCAN: Abraham and Lodish, 1993)
- Retail sales forecasting (Mcintyre, Achabal, and Miller, 1993)
- Retail space allocation (Resource-opt: Singh, Cook, and Corstjens, 1988)

2. PROBLEM TYPES AND AI TECHNIQUES OF MARKETING EXPERT SYSTEMS

The research can be classified according to problem type as follows:

- Consulting (McCann, Tadlaoui, and Gallagher, 1990; Casey and Murphy, 1994; Burke, Rangaswamy, Wind, and Eliashberg, 1990; Burke, 1991; Rangaswamy, Eliasberg, Burke, and Wind, 1989)
- Data analysis and mining (Alpar, 1991; Bayer and Harter, 1991; Rangaswamy, Harlam, and Lodish, 1991; Abraham and Lodish, 1993; Poh and Jasic, 1995, Schmitz, Armstrong, and Little, 1990; Schmitz, 1994; Rangaswamy, Harlam, and Lodish, 1991)
- Forecasting (Mcintyre, Achabal, and Miller, 1993)
- Planning and control (McCann, Lathi, and Hill, 1991; Apte et al., 1992)
- Configuration (Lee, Lee, and Lee, 1996)
- Resource allocation (Singh, Cook, and Corstjens, 1988)

As we can see from the above, two major problem types are consulting and data analysis and mining. This reflects the need of many marketing activities to be supported by consulting activities, and the motivation that the existence of enormous amounts of scanner data provided to research and development of expert systems that analyze and mine them for marketing success. For marketing research, expert system concepts, paradigms, techniques, and tools provide new ways to build models that apply marketing knowledge. Besides the rule-based approach, which is the most popular, case-based approaches (Mcintyre, Achabal, and Miller, 1993; Burke, 1991), model-based approaches (McCann and Gallagher, 1990; McCann, Lahti, and Hill, 1991), and neural networks (Poh and Jasic, 1995) have also been used as AI techniques for marketing decision-making.

Mitchell et al. (Mitchell, Russo, and Wittink, 1991) compared the use of human judgment, expert systems, and statistical/optimization models for marketing decisions and claimed that the construction of expert systems in marketing poses problems that are either quantitatively or qualitatively more difficult than those faced by expert systems builders in non-human domains. Some systems, for instance, had to use hybrid techniques such as knowledge-based techniques with algorithmic techniques (Singh, Cook, and Corstjens, 1988), knowledge-based techniques with statistical methods (Abraham and Lodish, 1993; Rangaswamy, Harlam, and Lodish, 1991), and constraint-and rule-based techniques (Lee, Lee, and Lee, 1996).

3.   FROM DECISION AID TO TRUE MARKETING

In a most recent and comprehensive survey (Burke, 1994) of expert systems for marketing, the systems were classified into two categories: ones for everyday decisions and ones for strategic decisions. Previously, AI techniques were used only for marketing decisions rather than for marketing itself. In other words, the users of the intelligent marketing systems were not customers, but rather marketing managers, marketing analysts, advertising agents, and salesmen. While marketing managers were focusing on their own users, a new highway to customers was growing, and now, with the advent of the World Wide Web, marketers must be ready to utilize this revolutionary new medium (Hoffman and Novak, 1996; Quelch and Klein, 1996). An early response in expert system research to this new opportunity was UNIK-SES (Lee, Lee, and Lee, 1996), which will be described in this chapter. Lee, Lee, and Lee described an expert system with customized purchasing support; the intended user was not marketers, but the end-customers. This is an effort to integrate interactive marketing (Blattberg and Deighton, 1991) with database marketing (Cespedes and Smith, 1993) in the World Wide Web environment.

4.   EXPERT SYSTEM FOR CUSTOMIZED PURCHASING SUPPORT

The existing two-way home shopping systems have so far been predominantly hypertext and database oriented. Thus, their major role is providing interactive retrieval of text and data (including figures) about product items. Since neither the hypertext and database approach nor the current expert systems can effectively support the selection of the customer's personalized preference, we propose to develop an expert system named UNIK-SES (Salesman Expert System) that can support the generation of a custom-tailored product configuration. To allow the natural interactive setting of the customer's preference and constraints, the Constraint and Rule Satisfaction Problems (CRSP) approach is adopted (Lee and Kwon, 1995). A particular domain that we have attempted to study is the process of purchasing menswear through an electronic market.

CRSP consists of a set of variables, an associated domain for each variable, and a set of constraints and rules to serve as relationships among the variables. The first advantage of adopting the CRSP is its representational richness. In UNIK-CRSP, four types of constraints are allowed: value compatibility (and incompatibility), algebraic inequality, mandatory equality, and functional assignment (Lee and Kwon, 1995).

The distinctive characteristics of the reasoning in UNIK-CRSP can be identified by three features: concurrent, integrated, and interactive reasoning. What we mean by *concurrent* reasoning is that a user can select the variables that he or she is most concerned about (goal variables or tightly constrained variables, so called "seed variables") as the starting point of the reasoning. Then each seed variable with a target value initiates the propagation concurrently until it reaches a variable(s) from different directions of propagation that has conflicting value requirements. For each individual propagation, the satisfaction of both the constraints and rules is pursued. This is why this reasoning process is called *integrated reasoning*. If a variable cannot simultaneously meet the requirements of both directional propagations, the customer is called on to decide which goal should be treated with a higher priority. Then the reasoning mechanism traces back to find out how much the level of lower prioritized goal must be degraded from the initial target. Thus, *interactive reasoning* is necessary to help in the tradeoff process, and the overall reasoning process devised for UNIK-CRSP matches very well with the human's natural decision-making process.

5.   ARCHITECTURE OF SALESMAN EXPERT SYSTEM

The architecture of UNIK-SES is depicted in Figure 1. It is equipped with five types of knowledge: product database, customer database, constraints about customers and products, rules about cus-

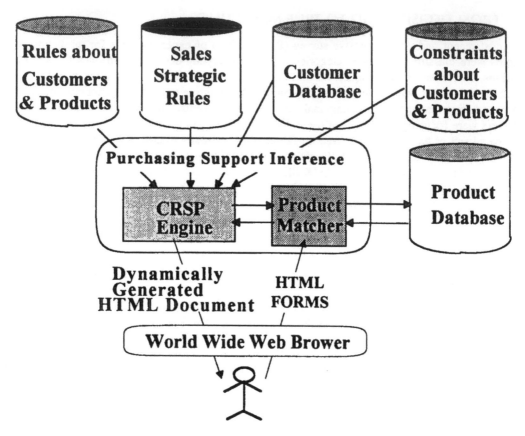

FIGURE 1   Architecture of the UNIK-SES.

tomers and products, and sales strategic rules. UNIK-SES consists of two reasoning capabilities:
a *CRSP Engine* that configures the specification of the products, and a *Product Matcher* that retrieves
the product component instances that meet a given requirement. The product database matcher
must first initialize the domain of values for each decision variable. Since the values should be
updated whenever there is any change in the product database (e.g., introduction of new products,
price change, and stock out), a data-driven, forward-chaining capability is called for. So, a forward-
chaining subsystem UNIK-FWD is employed along with UNIK-CRSP.

The product configuration process requires two classes of constraints among variables. One is
an ordinary constraint between product types. For instance, the suitable color-matching between
jacket and slacks belongs to this category. The other is a constraint within a product type. The latter
constraint implies that the existence of such a product instance should be confirmed. Since imposing
the within-product-type constraints for each product instance is very burdensome, it is better to
store the instance items in an object-oriented database and go to confirm its existence. To operate
in this manner, the domain of values should be dynamically arranged by retrieving the existing
products that meet the user's requirement. For this reason, the product database matching capability
should be closely embedded in the CRSP reasoning process for product specification.

The following steps summarize the CRSP reasoning process for the Salesman Expert System
incorporating the product database matching routine.

> **Step 1. Goal setting.** A customer selects the goal variables that he or she is interested in
> (e.g., types of products) and sets the desired target levels (e.g., available budget).

Step 2. Variable ordering. UNIK-SES computes the tightness of variables, and orders the variables according to the tightness measure and customer-dependent variable ordering rules.

Step 3. Seed variable selection. Customer selects seed variables from which the concurrent reasoning starts. The seed variables may be determined either by customer's choice or by selecting the variables whose tightness is above a threshold. Set the currency to each of the seed variables.

Step 4. Rule and constraint propagation. For each seed, propagate rules and constraints as described in steps 4a through 4d.

 Step 4.1. Rule inference. Perform the backward-chaining inference taking the current variable (Xc) as a root node.

 Step 4.2. Functional assignment. If there exists a functional assignment constraint that has Xc as a dependent variable, compute the value of Xc by asking the customer the values of independent variables, or by deriving the values of independent variables from the associated constraints and rules. Assign the computed value to Xc.

 Step 4.3. Value ordering. To propagate the associated compatibility constraints with Xc, order the values of Xc by the least constraining order criterion and customer-dependent value ordering rules. Select a value of Xc to propagate with.

 Step 4.4. Compatibility constraint propagation and product matching. With the selected value, propagate the associated compatibility constraints with Xc one by one, following to the constraint ordering criteria and considering importance of constraints.

Match the current requirement specification derived from the constraint propagation with the product database to retrieve the products that satisfy the requirements.

IF the propagation succeeds AND products satisfying the specification exist

 IF the active values of the variables are changed by the current propagation,

 THEN perform truth-maintenance for consistency among multiple paths of constraint propagation.

 ELSE move the currency to one of propagated variables and go to step 4a.

ELSE

 IF there exists a chance of backtracking,

 THEN backtrack the variable by moving the currency via the traced path. Go to step 4a.

 ELSE go to Step 5.

Step 5. Inconsistency elimination and goal tradeoffs.

Identify the reason of backtracking failure.

IF the failure is associated with a goal variable,

AND adjustment of the current goal is possible,

THEN relax the goal to resolve the backtracking failure.

IF the failure is caused by an inherent inconsistency between multiple goal variables,

THEN resolve the inconsistency by negotiating between associated goal variables.

6. MENSWEAR CASE: VARIABLES

The decision variables for the configuration of the menswear case are listed in Figure 2. In this study, we consider five product types (suit, shirt, slacks, necktie, and jacket). Each product attribute corresponds to a variable. For the product-related variables, when the values that meet the customer's requirement for a certain criteria are identified, the Product Matcher should dynamically retrieve the items that meet the requirement from the product database, as illustrated in Figure 2. For each access of a given customer, the customer information is initialized by retrieving the data from the customer database as revealed in the example in Figure 3. For an advanced system, we may wish

Suit	Shirt	Slacks	Necktie	Jacket	Customer	Buying-plan
model-name	model-name	model-name	model-name	occupation	budget-upper-bound	budget-lower-bound
price	price	price	price	price	sex	total-amount
size	size	size	material	size	income-level	purpose
material	material	material	brand	material	age	decision
brand	brand	brand	color	brand	face-color	
color	color	color	pattern	color	body-type	
pattern	pattern	pattern	inventory	pattern	height	
style	brightness	style		material-thickness		
brightness	collar	brightness		inventory		
breasted	inventory	material-thickness				
inventory		inventory				

FIGURE 2   Variables in menswear case.

to store the history of purchase and learn to guess what each particular customer will need, but this is beyond the scope of the current version.

7. MENSWEAR CASE: CONSTRAINTS

The constraints can be classified by structural characteristics. Note that the constraints have an importance indicator to set their priorities relative to each other.

7.1. IMPORTANCE OF CONSTRAINTS

The importance of each constraint is marked in the importance slot ranging between 0 and 1. The measurement of "1" implies "must," and "0" implies "not necessary." The following constraint implies that the compatibility between customer's face color and shirt color must be met.

{{ Constraint-C9
Importance: 1
Associated-variables: customer.face-color shirt.color
Compatible-value-set: (pale (pink light-blue)) }}

{{ ODNAB-101

is-a: suit
model-name: 101
price: $500
size: medium
material: wool
brand: ODNAB
color: gray
pattern: none
style: American silhouette
brightness: bright
breasted: double-breasted
inventory: 50 }}

FIGURE 3   Representation of a product.

```
{{ Lee-J-H

is-a: customer
occupation: businessman
sex: male
income-level: high
age: 45
face-color: yellow
body-type: thin
height: 178}}
```

FIGURE 4   Representation of a customer.

7.2.   TYPES OF CONSTRAINTS

From a structural perspective, the constraints in UNIK-SES can be classified into four types: value compatibility, value incompatibility, algebraic inequality, and functional assignment.

7.2.1.   Value Compatibility Constraints

The value compatibility constraints are the what-matches-what relationships between products. The following example shows a constraint, which means the "wide-spread" collar of a shirt goes well with the "double-breasted" suit.

```
{{ Constraint-C1
Importance: 1
Associated-variables: shirt.collar suit.breasted
Compatible-value-set: (wide-spread double-breasted) }}
```

Another type of value compatibility constraint would be general tendencies for matching of customers and products based on the salesman's experience. For instance, the occupation may influence the style of a shirt as the following example shows, but the importance level of this kind of constraint should be weaker.

```
{{ Constraint-C6
Importance: 0.5
Associated-variables: customer.occupation shirt.collar buying-plan.purchasing-purpose
Compatible-value-set: (salary-man regular office-work-use) }}
```

7.2.2.   Value Incompatibility Constraints

On the other hand, there are also many constraints that prohibit the what-does-not-match-what incompatible relationships in the configuration domain. The following example shows an incompatibility constraint: a heavy man does not look well when he wears a suit with horizontal stripes.

```
{{ Constraint-I1
Importance: 1
Associated-variables: customer.body-type suit.pattern
Incompatible-value-set: (heavy horizontal-stripe) }}
```

7.2.3.   Functional Assignment Constraints

Functional assignment constraints represent the assignment relationships between independent variables and a dependent variable. For instance, the total amount of a sale is computed by summing five price components. The reverse directional inference cannot be applied.

```
{{ Constraint-F1
Dependent-variable: buying-plan.total-amount
Independent-variable: suit.price shirt.price slacks.price neck-tie.price jacket.price
Relation: buying-plan.total-amount = suit.price + shirt.price + slacks.price + neck-tie.price
   + jacket.price }}
```

7.2.4.   Algebraic Inequality Constraints

The budget constraint of a customer, for instance, can be represented using algebraic inequality constraints.

```
{{ Constraint-A1
Importance: 0.3
Associated-variables: buying-plan.total-amount buying-plan.total-amount-upper-limit
Relation: buying-plan.total-amount >= buying-plan.total-amount-upper-limit}}
```

8.   RULES IN MENSWEAR CASE

The purpose of rules used in Salesman Expert System can be classified into customer-product rules and sales strategic rules.

8.1.   CUSTOMER-PRODUCT RULES

While a constraint handles the what-does-not-match-what kinds of relationships without any directional nature, a rule has a directionality such as "if a jacket is going to have patterns, the slacks should not have any." The reverse relationship in general does not hold.

```
{{ Rule-1
IF (jacket.pattern IS checkered) THEN (slacks.pattern IS no-pattern) Importance: 1 }}
```

The role of the importance slot in the rules is the same as in the constraints.

8.2.   SALES STRATEGIC RULES FOR VARIABLE AND VALUE ORDERING

Sales strategies are represented as variable and value ordering rules that play the role of meta-rules in CRSP reasoning.

8.2.1.   Variable Ordering Rules

An experienced salesman may ask a student customer the affordable price range first, but may ask a 40-year-old lady customer whether she wants a one-piece or two-piece first. Being able to ask quesions in the right sequence is a skill that is essential for business success. In CRSP terms, the sequencing of questions is the variable ordering. An example is :

```
{{ Variable-ordering-rule-1
IF (income-level IS high)) THEN (seed.variable IS brand) Importance: 0.5 }}
```

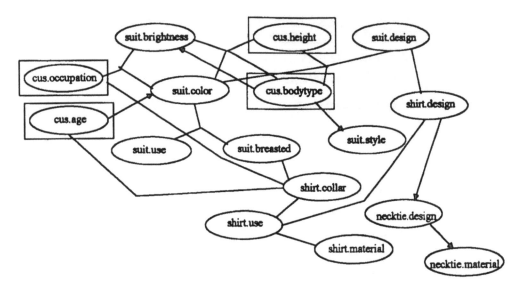

FIGURE 5 A constraint and rule graph for menswear case.

8.2.2. Value Ordering Rules

The value ordering means which value the salesman is going to suggest first out of many alternative values for a certain variable. For instance, in the case of a businessman, the suit color is given by the following sequence: navy-blue, gray, and brown.

```
{{ Value-ordering-rule-1
IF (customer.occupation IS business) THEN (suit.color IS (ORDER navy-blue gray brown))
    Importance: 0.7 }}
```

The relationships between variables and the associated constraints and rules can be depicted in the constraint and rule graph of Figure 5. The oval bubbles mean variables, and the ones enclosed in rectangles denote the seed variables. The directed arcs show the rules, while the undirected arcs indicate constraints.

9. REASONING PROCEDURE IN SALESMAN EXPERT SYSTEM

In this section, we illustrate an example of reasoning with UNIK-SES. Although the dialog is assisted by menu-driven windows, we illustrate the reasoning process with rules and constraints to show the logic behind the screen. Let us suppose the customer is a young teacher, who is tall and heavy with a pale-looking face. He is going to buy a shirt, suit, and necktie. Figure 6 shows the customer's input screen in the browser, which will be saved in the objects as follows.

```
{{Customer (occupation: teacher) (face-color: pale) (age: 20-29) (height: 180-190)
    (body-type: heavy)}}
{{(buying-plan (purpose: teaching) (budget-upper-bound: 700)}
{{ goal (target-variables: suit shirt neck-tie) }}
```

Let us assume the customer does not set any values for the seed variables. The system UNIK-SES begins reasoning with its knowledge and default strategy to generate values from steps 1 to 5.

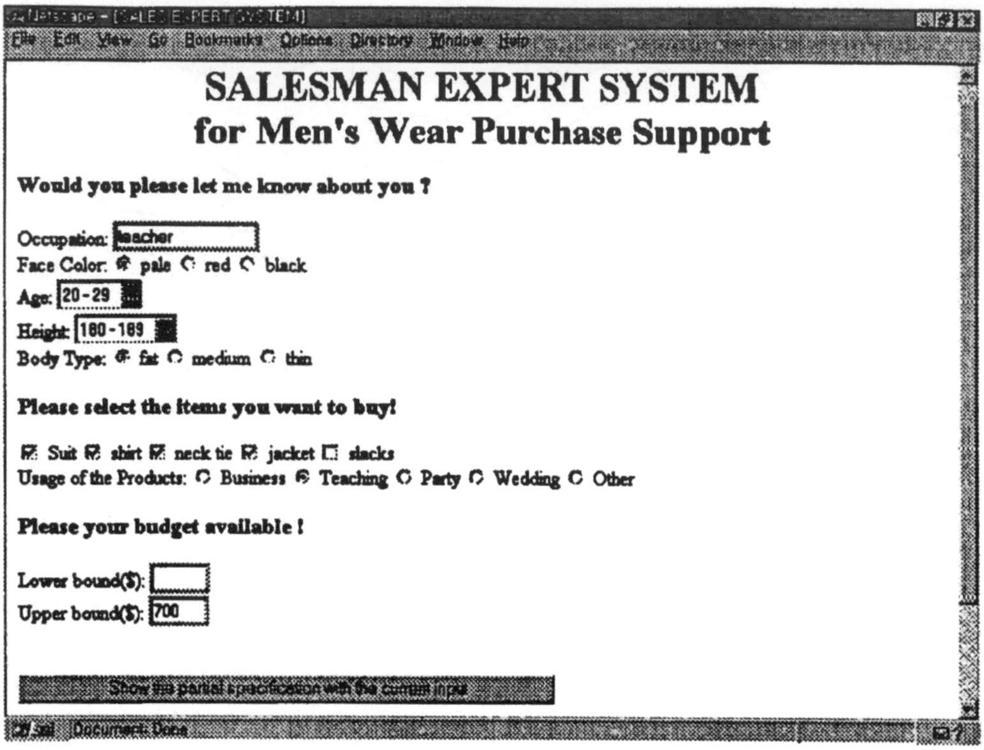

FIGURE 6   Customer input screen using HTML forms.

> Step 1.   {{ Rule-1 IF (customer.height tall) (customer.body-type heavy)
                          THEN (suit.brightness dark) }}
                          → (suit (brightness dark))

> Step 2.   {{ Rule-9 IF (customer.body-type heavy) THEN (suit.style American-silhouette) }}
                          → (suit (style American-silhouette) (brightness dark))

> Step 3.   {{ Rule-C8 IF (customer.occupation (teacher public-officer))
                          (buying-plan.purpose teaching)
                          THEN (suit.color (brown blue)) }}
                  → (suit (style American-silhouette) (color (brown blue)) (brightness dark))

> Step 4.   {{ Rule-C9 IF (customer.face-color pale) THEN (shirt.color pink) }}
                  → (suit (style American-silhouette) (color (brown blue)) (brightness dark))
                          → (shirt (color pink))

> Step 5.   {{ Rule-C12 IF: (customer.age young) THEN: (shirt.collar button-down) }}
                  → (suit (style American-silhouette) (color (brown blue)) (brightness dark))
                          → (shirt (collar button-down) (color pink))

Up to now, UNIK-SES has automatically generated the specification for the customer using rules. In step 6, the system finds that there are no applicable rules although there are variables still left to be determined, such as design of shirt, design and material of necktie, etc. In this case, there are two options that can be pursued. One is constraint propagation by ordering the undetermined

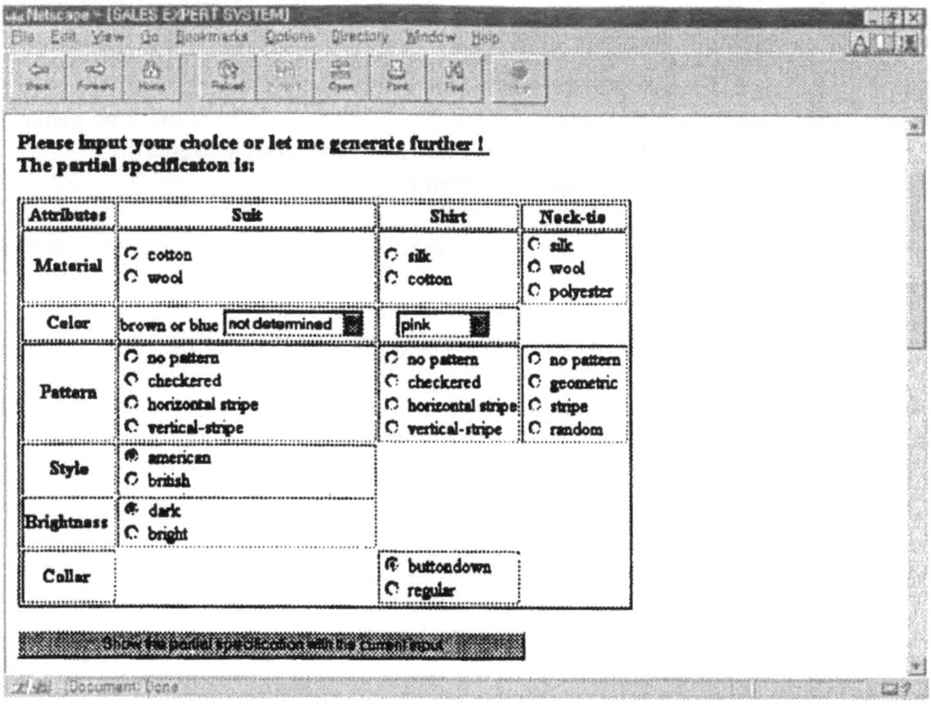

FIGURE 7   Intermediate specification.

variables and assigning their values according to the value ordering strategy. The other is an interactive reasoning with the customer by requesting the customer to select values of the variables he wants. In this example, suppose that the customer selects "horizontal-stripe" for the design of his suit, "checkered" for the design of his shirt, and "brown" for the color of his suit. Then, the system begins reasoning with these values.

> Step 6.   "There are no applicable rules."
                          (User-input: 'suit 'design 'horizontal-stripe)
                              (User-input: 'suit 'color 'brown)
                              (User-Input: 'shirt 'pattern 'checkered)
        → (suit (style American-silhouette) (color brown) (brightness dark)
                                  (pattern horizontal-stripe))
            → (shirt (collar button-down) (color pink) (pattern checkered))

Figure 7 is a suggested specification waiting for customer's interaction.

However, the value that the customer input violates the incompatibility constraint-I1: the horizontal stripe does not suit a heavy person. In such a case, the system shows the incompatibility constraint and recommends other possible values on the design of his suit. Of course, the customer can adhere to his previous decision. In this example, suppose the customer selects "no-pattern" for his suit and the system resumes reasoning with the changed value.

> Step 7.   "Cpnstraint-I1 is violated"
    {{ Constraint-I1 Associated-variables: customer.height customer.body-type suit.pattern
                        Incompatible-value-set: (heavy horizontal-stripe) }}
                          (User-input 'suit 'pattern 'no-pattern)

→ (suit (style American-silhouette) (color brown) (brightness dark) (pattern no-pattern))
    (shirt (collar button-sown) (color pink) (pattern checkered))

> Step 8.   {{ Rule-6 IF: (shirt.pattern checkered) THEN: (neck-tie.pattern no-pattern) }}
    → (suit (style American-silhouette) (color brown) (brightness dark) (pattern no-pattern))
        → (shirt (collar button-down) (color pink) (pattern checkered))
            → (neck-tie (pattern no-pattern))

> Step 9.   {{ Rule-7 IF: (neck-tie.pattern no-pattern) THEN: (neck-tie.material (silk wool)) }}
    → (suit (style American-silhouette) (color brown) (brightness dark) (pattern no-pattern))
        → (shirt (collar button-down) (color pink) (pattern checkered))
            → (neck-tie (pattern no-pattern) (material (silk wool)))

At any step, the customer may stop the reasoning and accept the currently suggested items. Then the system stops reasoning and displays the resulting specification of the customer's choice. Figure 8 shows the final specification.

> Step 10   (User-input: 'buying-plan 'decision 'yes)
        (suit (style American-silhouette) (color brown) (brightness dark) (pattern no-pattern))
            (shirt (collar button-down) (color pink) (pattern checkered))
                (neck-tie (pattern no-pattern) (material (silk wool)))

For every step of the process, a user-friendly interface is neccessary because the system has to be directly accessible to the customers. Thus, a graphical user interface is under development using HTML (HyperText Mark-up Language), CGI (Common Gateway Interface) programming (NCSA, 1995), and JavaScript. For the given specification, UNIK-SES can display the combination of suit,

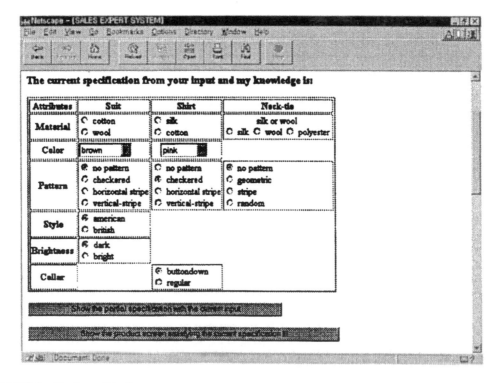

FIGURE 8   Final specification.

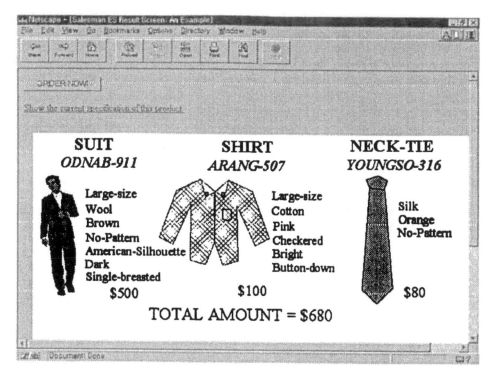

FIGURE 9   Display screen showing selected items.

shirt, and necktie in a multimedia-based screen as, illustrated in Figure 9. Upon reviewing the display, the customer may select the combination as a final decision or may request UNIK-SES to resume the reasoning process and modify the current specification.

10.   TRENDS OF AI RESEARCH FOR MARKETING

To make the Salesman Expert System more intelligent, the purchase history of individual customers could be maintained as user models. From this history, it would be possible to observe the purchasing patterns of each customer, and suitable combinations could then be suggested in light of the customer's current possessions. In addition, it is important to understand the customer behavior in electronic shopping malls. Thus, consumer research on the electronic market is considered to be an important new area of marketing research (Richmond, 1996; Burke, 1996).

Some of the most active research related to marketing expert system research is being done on *electronic agents* in the electronic market (Crowston, 1996; Lee and Lee, 1997; Chavez and Maes, 1996; Doorenbos, Etzioni, and Weld, 1996; Kohda and Endo, 1996). Kasbah (Chavez and Maes, 1996) is a virtual marketplace on the Web where users create autonomous agents to buy and sell goods on their behalf. ShopBot (Doorenbos, Etzioni, and Weld, 1996) is a comparison shopping agent that autonomously learns how to shop at vendor home pages, extracts product information such as availability and price, and summarizes the results for the user. UNIK-AGENT (Lee and Lee, 1997) presents an architecture of intelligent agents for electronic commerce, which is an extension of an expert system with the additional capabilities of communication control and metaproblem solving. Kohda and Endo (1996) propose an advertising agent placed between advertisers and users. These agents aim to give benefits like favorable price, more availability, and reduced search cost to economic market entities such as buyers, advertisers, and sellers, etc. Since the agents can become both the opportunity and the threat to marketing managers, it will be critical for a marketing manager to have the capability of understanding and predicting the marketing situations resulting from the interactions among electronic market agents. Crowston (1996) presented a model of the competitive effects of purchasing agents and discussed the possible resistance and benefit when an agent appears in an electronic market. The role of intermediate agents in electronic markets also has important implications to marketing managers (Bailey, 1996; Sarkar, Butler, and Steinfield, 1995). Inventing favorable agents and competing with hostile agents will be an important issue for successful marketing in the electronic commerce environment of the future.

ACKNOWLEDGMENTS

A part of this chapter has been adopted from the paper, "Customized purchase supporting expert system: UNIK-SES," published in *Expert Systems with Applications: An International Journal*, Volume 11, No. 4, 1996. At the request of the editor, the authors have tried to reduce the references and apologize for missing the important works of others.

REFERENCES

Abraham, M. and Lodish, L., "An implemented system for improving promotion productivity using store scanner data," *Marketing Science*, 12(3), 248–269, Summer, 1993.

Alpar, P., "Knowledge-based modelling of marketing manager's problem solving behavior," *International Journal of Research in Marketing*, 8, 5–16, 1991.

Apte, C., Dionne, R., Griesmer, J., Karnaugh, M., Kastner, J., Laker, M., and Mays, E., "An experiment in constructing an open expert system using a knowledge substrate," *IBM Journal of Research and Development*, 36(3), 409–434, May, 1992.

Bailey, J., "The emergence of electronic market intermediaries," *Proceedings of the Seventeenth International Conference on Information Systems*, pp. 391–399, 1996.

Bayer, J. and Harter, R., "Miner, manager, and researcher: three models of analysis of scanner data," *International Journal of Research in Marketing*, 8, 17–27, 1991.

Blattberg, R. and Deighton, J., "Interactive marketing: exploiting the age of addressability," *Sloan Management Review*, pp. 5–14, Fall, 1991.

Burke, R, Rangaswamy, A., Wind, J., and Eliashberg, J., "A knowledge-based system for advertising design," *Marketing Science*, 9(3), 212–229, 1990.

Burke, R., "Artificial intelligence for designing marketing decision-making tools," *The Marketing Information Revolution* (Blattberg, R., Glazer, R. and Little, J., Eds.), pp. 204–227, Harvard Business School Press, 1994.

Burke, R., "Virtual shopping: breakthrough in marketing research," *Harvard Business Review*, pp. 120–131, March/April, 1996.

Burke, R., "Reasoning with empirical marketing knowledge," *International Journal of Research in Marketing*, 8, 75–90, 1991.

Casey, C. and Murphy, C., "Expert systems in marketing: an application for pricing new products," 7(4), 545–552, 1994.

Cespedes, F. and Smith, H., "Database marketing: new rules for policy and practice," *Sloan Management Review*, pp. 7–22, Summer, 1993.

Chavez, A. and Maes, P., "Kasbah: an agent marketplace for buying and selling goods," *Proceedings of the First International Conference on the Practical Application of Intelligent Agents and Multi-Agent Technology*, London, U.K., April 1996.

Crowston, K., "Market-enabling internet agents," *Proceedings of the Seventeenth International Conference on Information Systems*, pp. 381–390, 1996.

Doorenbos, R., Etzioni, O., and Weld, D., "A Scalabale Comparison-Shopping Agent for the World Wide Web," Technical Report, UW-CSE-96-01-03, Department of Computer Science and Engineering, University of Washington, 1996.

Hoffman, D. and Novak, T., "Marketing in hypermedia computer mediated environments: conceptual foundations," *Journal of Marketing*, 60, 50–68, 1996.

Kirsh, R., Strouble, D., Johnson, W., and August, S., "Transfer: an expert system approach to transfer pricing," *Expert Systems with Applications*, 3(4), 481–487.

Kohda, Y. and Endo, S., "Ubiquitous advertising on the WWW: merging advertisement on the browser," *Computer Networks and ISDN Systems*, 28(711), 1493–1500, 1996.

Lee, J. and Kwon, S., "ES*: an expert systems development planner using a constraint and rule-based approach," *Expert Systems with Applications*, 9(1), 1995.

Lee, J. and Lee, W., "Intelligent agent based contract process in electronic commerce: UNIK-AGENT approach," *Proceedings of Hawaiian International Conference on System Science*, 1997.

Lee, S., Lee, J., and Lee, K., "Customized purchase supporting expert system: UNIK-SES," *Expert Systems with Applications*, 11(4), 431–441, 1996.

McCann, J. and Gallagher, J., *Expert Systems for Scanner Data Environments*, Kluwer Academic Publishers, 1990.

McCann, J., Tadlaoui, A., and Gallagher, J., "Knowledge systems in merchandising: advertising design," *Journal of Retailing*, 66(3), 256–276, 1990.

McCann, J., Lahti, W., and Hill, J., "The Brand Manager's Assistant: a knowledge-based system approach to brand management," *International Journal of Research in Marketing*, 8, 51–73, 1991.

Mcintyre, S., Achabal, D., and Miller, C., "Applying case-based reasoning to forecasting retail sales," *Journal of Retailing*, 69(4), 372–398, 1993.

Mitchell, A., Russo, E., and Wittink, D., "Issues in the development and use of expert systems for marketing decisions," *International Journal of Research in Marketing*, 8, 41–50, 1991.

Mitchell, A., "The use of alternative knowledge acquisition procedures in the development of a knowledge based media planning problem," *International Journal of Man-Machine Studies*, 26, 399–411, 1987.

Poh, H. and Jasic, T., "Forecasting and analysis of marketing data using neural networks: a case of advertising and promotion impact," *IEEE Proceedings of Conference on Artificial Intelligence Application*, pp. 224–230, 1995.

Quelch, J. and Klein, L., "The Internet and international marketing," *Sloan Management Review*, pp. 60–75, Spring, 1996.

Rangaswamy, A., Eliasberg, J., Burke, R., and Wind, J., "Developing marketing expert systems: an application in international negotiations," *Journal of Marketing*, pp. 24–39, 1989.

Rangaswamy, A., Harlam, B., and Lodish, L., "INFER: an expert system for automatic analysis of scanner data," *International Journal of Research in Marketing*, 8, 29–40, 1991.

Richmond, A., "Enticing online shoppers to buy — a human behavior study," *Computer Networks and ISDN Systems*, 28(711), 1469–1480, 1996.

Sarkar, M., Butler, B., and Steinfield, C., "Intermediaries and cybermediaries: a continuing role for mediating players in the electronic marketplace," *Journal of Computer Mediated Communications*, 3(1), 1995.

Schmits, J., Armstrong, G., and Little, J., "Coverstory — automated news finding in marketing," *Interfaces*, 20(6), 29–38, November–December, 1990.

Schmitz, J., "Expert systems for scanner data in practice," *The Marketing Information Revolution* (Blattberg, R., Glazer, R., and Little, J., Eds.), pp. 102–119, Harvard Business School Press, 1994.

Singh, M., Cook, R., and Corstjens, M., "A hybrid knowledge-based system for allocating retail space and for other allocation problems," *Interfaces*, 18(5), 1988.

30 Expert Systems for Management of Natural Resources

Bernt A. Bremdal

CONTENTS

0-8493-3106-4/98/$0.00+$.50
© 1998 by CRC Press LLC

1.   INTRODUCTION

1.1.   MANAGEMENT OF NATURAL RESOURCES

Management of natural resources embraces a whole range of subjects pertaining to both the concept of good management as well as to "natural resources." The management part suggests elements of control, decision-making, execution of actions including both intervention and monitoring, as well as elements such as guidance and protection. Resolute and efficient decision-making is often associated with good management. This in turn is dependent on both knowledge and data related to aspects that influence what is to be managed.

Much of our life is dependent on our ability to enjoy and harvest from what the earth can supply. Fish, game, minerals, water, sunlight, wood, and a diversity of herbs and plants provide us with food, drink, shelter and protection, heat and chill, light and shade. They appeal to our esthetic and emotional senses. Most of them constitute elements in an ecological balance that we are both directly and indirectly dependent on. Man has since his first day used his wit to develop skills for exploiting these resources for his own benefit. At the beginning there were simple ways and tools of bone and rock for fishing, hunting, and gathering. Tools for making fire came next. Eventually, bronze replaced stone and bone and weapons became more sophisticated. As Man learned to mine and create new aids for living, he paid increasing attention to the resource issue. His extended intellect gave rise to new ideas about what to use, how to build, and where to explore. All his new needs and sophisticated manners imposed a greater demand for control of the resources. Mineral resources implied wealth and power. Today the world's nations maintain policies that are modern versions of the survival doctrine practiced by the first Man. They will go to extremes in order to secure known resources of oil. They are painfully aware of their vulnerability with respect to the scarcity of hydrocarbons. This scramble for control has often tipped management into mismanagement. Over the past few decades, Man has learned a new lesson. Natural resources are finite. Extensive exploitation might lead to severe ecological imbalance and ruin the foundation for not only Man, but all life. His modern lifestyle encourages activities that hurt the earth and ruin vulnerable resources such as water, wildlife, fish, etc. through pollution and contamination. Management of resources no longer involves purely selfish goals. Nature and the needs of the whole environment require attention. Good management implies fulfilling a conjunction of many apparently contradictory goals. In order to meet these ends, management of our natural resources has become one of the most critical issues that Man has ever been challenged with. The question is no longer only "how to find and how to get?", but just as much as "how to dispose and how to replace?" In his usual way, Man is looking for new aids in order to help him cope with the challenge. Expert systems (ES) are one of them. ES were invented to assist human decision-making. They are meant for knowledge intensive tasks that require expertise.

1.2. Expert Systems

Expert systems for management of natural resources date back to the origin of the expert system era itself. When reading the history of expert systems, it is hard to miss references to work like Prospector (Duda 78) applied for mineral exploration. Many early students of LISP studied the examples printed in Winston's book (Winston 81) on the programming language. Through this they were also introduced to ideas on how to build rule-based systems directed toward wildlife taxonomy.

According to a recent estimate reported by Durkin (Durkin 96), approximately 12,500 systems have been built over the years. Most of these systems are assumed to have been developed for business, medicine, and manufacturing. Less than 10% is assumed to serve purposes with the heading "Management of mineral resources." Yet, works on many of these systems stand out as pioneering efforts within the field of expert systems, and AI in general. According to Durkin, approximately 50% of the systems surveyed were built between 1990 and 1992. There was a predominance of systems treating diagnosis-type of problems. Durkin explains this observation with the fact that diagnosis is an activity that most experts deal with. Diagnostic systems are relatively easy to develop and pose less risk to an organization wishing to pioneer the ES potential. Looking at expert systems for management of natural resources alone, we will find contours of the same pattern. During the early years the problems addressed were limited to interpretation and diagnosis kinds of tasks. The scope was highly constrained and focused on a single mineral or an isolated subject. Later, focus was extended to handle more of the management issues. The latest efforts address the whole planet and its diversity in terms of resources. They include several problem-solving strategies beyond diagnosis and seek to fuse input from different types of expertise. At the start, the oil industry became a driving force. The main concern was how to find more oil. Systems for log analysis and geological interpretation were the first to receive operational status. For a decade, the work in R&D departments at Schlumberger, Elf, Arco, and Exxon dominated the scene. Later, significant results related to resources such as forestry and ecology were published. Today, the variety in initiatives is very broad, both in terms of the technology applied and the domain of concern.

1.3. Technological Development

The narrow scope of the early systems did not call upon very sophisticated techniques. Most expert system developments followed the overall pattern using rapid prototyping and expert system shells. During the first years, expert systems became strongly associated with backward-chaining, rule-based programs founded on the MYCIN tradition (Shortliffe 76). This conception tends to linger in spite of new and powerful techniques that many of today's efforts capitalize on. This was also the situation for the system developments of the type discussed here. The development pattern reflected by the history of geological systems is typical for the whole field of expert systems.

Over the years, knowledge representation has developed and many new representational schemes have been explored. Standard inferences have been augmented by several new control paradigms, many of which use knowledge about the problem-solving process itself to govern the execution of the system. The use of a single knowledge base was the most common when interest in expert systems took off. At the end of the 1980s, systems using multiple knowledge bases were explored. Multi-agent systems and cooperating expert systems were frequently reported. Model-based versus purely heuristically based systems proved useful. Systems using a hybrid set of techniques were common at the start of the 1990s.

The first expert systems for management of natural resources were simple single-user, stand-alone programs. The focus of the development effort was the knowledge base, the inference engine, and the knowledge acquisition effort. User-friendliness was not a significant issue and integration into a wider computing environment was not addressed. Systems seeking operational status soon found themselves placed in a network or in a setting where they exchanged data with both databases, ordinary number crunching programs, simulators, and geographical information systems (GIS).

For many, the embodiment of knowledge in an expert system must be explicit. However, the expertise that can be implicitly captured in a neural network might well outperform human experts for both recognition tasks and interpretation. Developers within the oil domain became aware early on of the benefits posed by soft computing techniques related to neural networks, fuzzy systems, and genetic algorithms. Hence, they adopted these problem-solving techniques for purposes that traditional rule-based systems had failed or proven costly to develop. Today, many systems incorporate expertise dedicated for tasks that are especially suited for soft computing. This trend has manifested itself over the past 5 years. Soft computing techniques must therefore be considered part of the toolbox of the expert system developer.

Object-oriented systems development has had a significant effect on expert systems trends. Many of the systems presented here apply variants of object-oriented software techniques. The object-oriented paradigm promises very good models of the real world. It lends itself very well to explicit knowledge modeling and incorporates representational power shared by both semantic networks and frames. Other cherished features include the reusability of code and thus knowledge. In addition, the flexibility of message passing has made it easy to build separate knowledge agents capable of self-organizing and cooperative problem-solving.

Of particular interest are those new systems that apply old ways in new settings. The advent of the Internet and the WorldWideWeb has opened a new world for expert systems. Some development efforts demonstrate both existing capabilities as well as future potentials that will be highlighted here.

1.4.   Scope

Our discourse covers a broad range of systems. But it is admittedly colored by the dominance of geology-related systems in the 1980s and early 1990s. This is due both to their abundance at the start and their significance in terms of technology development. Expert systems builders seeking new solutions for persistent problems related to exploration, oil well logging, and seismic interpretation worked shoulder-to-shoulder with computer scientists concerned with the fundamental aspects of artificial intelligence. Real-world tasks replaced the toy problems nursed and cherished in the university labs. This shift and the funds invested to tackle the new problems became a driving force for both practical and theoretical conquests. So, looking at the developments within the mineral domain is like looking at the general evolution of expert systems itself.

At the turn of the decade, the picture became less crisp. Many more initiatives surfaced. For management of natural resources, incipient work in areas such as forestry left significant traces. This can be seen in conjunction with the efforts initiated around agricultural problems. Problems related to farming received a boost in interest at the end of the 1980s and have contributed to a number of expert systems. Systems dealing with forestry, water, and the like tend to blend into purely agricultural problems. Crop cultivation and forestry share some of the same problems. Pest management is an example of this. When delimiting the scope of this discourse, we have tried to keep out expert systems that are predominantly agriculture oriented. These types of systems deserve to be addressed separately. Yet it is often hard to draw a borderline between the domains.

Ecological systems have emerged as archetypes of complex knowledge-based systems. Often dealing with difficult data fusion supported by remote sensing, they cover aspects of both local and global value. The recognition that many ecosystems are fragile and vulnerable to unexpected influences has set forth activities aimed a wildlife preservation and habitat conservation. Vegetation and atmospheric condition monitoring are also important. The domain of ecosystem management is rich in different types of expertise and demands. The common focus for most of them are the state and health of the environment. Other ES types to be concerned with are those dealing with pollution and accidental releases from chemical plants and similar. However, the objective of most of these is the optimal safety and reliability of the plant. Other systems are more medically inclined and focus mostly on human health.

The selection of systems presented here reflects the general development of applications within the field of management of natural resources. The novel features that each system pioneered or emphasized are highlighted. The novelties of the early systems often became the "bread and butter" of many of those that came later. Understanding how the early, simple ones work will help us comprehend the fundamental structure of the more complex systems.

Diversity in terms of technology is a key word. Systems representing different approaches have been deliberately focused on. This enables both comparison and a better overview. Both prototypes and commercial successes have been addressed. Accounts on prototypes tend to focus on technical aspects only, while reports on deployed systems and systems for sale address usability features. Both are relevant and interesting. The blend presented here is meant to expose elements of importance to both system development, system deployment, and commercialization.

2.   GEOLOGICAL EXPLORATION AND MINERAL ANALYSIS

2.1.   Scope and Historical Development

The pioneering effort behind MYCIN and PROSPECTOR (Gaschnig 81) encouraged similar work in many areas. Several laboratories replicated the PROSPECTOR effort. These early systems also spurred the interests of the oil industry. This development had significant effects on both R&D funding as well as on commercialization. The oil industry was a wealthy and technology-oriented industry, well prepared to recognize the potentials of expert systems. In particular, exploration departments and exploration contractors embraced the advent of this technology. Despite a long tradition with logging and seismic shooting that yielded hard facts about a geological area, exploration still relied on expert judgment, intelligent guessing, and many qualitative elements in the decision process. It took a long time for a person to learn. Expert system technology promised a formalization of the heuristics that resided with very experienced geologists. It pledged a future of effective knowledge sharing and improved data analysis, blending many types of data with apt knowledge of a particular geological field. Slight improvements could yield potential rewards in the multibillion dollar range.

Almost as important as PROSPECTOR was the DIPMETER ADVISOR (Davis 81). This was a system initiated by Schlumberger-Doll Research Centre (SDRC) and developed in part together with MIT and Fairchild Lab for AI Research. DIPMETER-ADVISOR proved to be an efficient aid in interpreting log data produced by dipmeter sensors dropped into bore holes. Data of this kind indicate how different types of energy interact with a geological formation. In this way, subsurface geological structures can be inferred. The interpretation of well logs can be very difficult. One of the reasons was (and still is) the rapid development of the well logging discipline and technology itself. In 1984, Schlumberger-Doll commercialized the system.

Due to the success of the system and because Schlumberger-Doll was a significant operator in the exploration business, DIPMETER ADVISOR drew a lot of attention from the industry. Many companies initiated their own R&D activities, both on their own as well as together with laboratories with a standing record of expert systems development. In Europe, Elf Aquitaine became a driving force. Amoco and Schlumberger-Doll locomoted the developments in the U.S. The work on MUD (Kahn 84) carried out at Carnegie-Mellon University was also significant. By the end of the 1980s, the petroleum industry became a major R&D partner not only in terms of expert systems, but also within AI in general. AI-related research and system development covered many disciplines and eventually many types of knowledge-oriented approaches. The petroleum domain became a test bench for all kinds of systems. Because of its early initiatives and great spending the petroleum related work was significant in the development of the whole field of AI and thus also enabling developments in other areas of natural resources. At the World Conference on Expert Systems in

Portugal in 1994, a panel session was held that addressed the history and standings of petroleum-related AI. The projection of the work within the petroleum industry could well be a mirror of AI itself. In particular, the exploration and resource management efforts reverberate the change in technology emphasis from a simple rule-based system (RBS) to a blend of case-based reasoning (CBR), fuzzy retrieval, and neural networks. The exploration-oriented work gave important incentives to other types of mineral exploration and in turn to other types of resource management. Today the resource oriented systems within the petroleum industry represent only a fraction of the total. The expansion in this particular area has been less than in other areas. This could be related to the fact that RBS for interpretation and analysis have reached a certain maturity, making it less interesting for further publication. Another reason is of course the fact that many petroleum companies invested heavily very early on and evaluated their returns prematurely. Many disappointments accompanied the real successes. This led to budget cuts and a redirection of attention on the account of the R&D departments.

If we look at the records of exploration systems that pertain to the group of systems that we discuss in this discourse, we have the following list:

- Source rock evaluation
- Fossil identification
- Mineral identification
- Mineral prospecting
- Well log analysis
    - Quality control of well logs
    - Well log interpretation
    - Well log correlation
- Dipmetering
- Sedimentary environment
- Classification
- Basin analysis
- Play analysis
- Structural style identification
- Gridding advice
- Risk analysis
- Overall resource assessment
- Seismics
    - Geophone array design
    - Vibrosis parameter
    - Selection
    - VSP advice
    - Tape format identification
    - Velocity analysis
    - Processing sequence
    - Design
    - Interpretation
- Remote sensing
    - Sedimentary environment
    - Image processing

Much of the work published on AI applications within the petroleum field has been channeled through the CAIPEP conference organized in Texas and later the EUROCAIPEP conferences in Europe. In 1995, these conferences were merged to form AI Petro. A fair cross-section of both

R&D and commercialization can be found in the work of Braunschweig et al. (Braunschweig 95; Braunschweig 96).

The early systems like PROSPECTOR and DIPMETER ADVISOR were true representatives of the rule-based paradigm within the field. Many new systems followed these. Development trends are roughly depicted in Table 1.

The systems discussed represents a selection of systems reported over past years. Log and mineral analysis are recurrent subjects for several initiatives. Proper log analysis is still an issue more than 15 years after the first work on the DIPMETER ADVISOR to the system that Baldwin and colleagues built at the turn of the decade (Baldwin 90)

The continued interest can be explained in two different ways. The first work based on rule-based systems produced grossly inadequate results, so that new techniques had to be tried out. The debut based on rule-based systems was so encouraging that it gave rise to greater ambitions and thus the need to investigate new techniques. The truth probably lies somewhere between. The first RBS was a significant leap forward. Yet, it became clear that it had shortcomings. This gave rise to new AI-related initiatives. With renewed interests in neural networks at the end of the 1980s, this paradigm also became a research candidate for the log analyst and other geologists. In fact, today we see a tendency toward using a hybrid set of techniques to capture and represent different types of knowledge.

In the following paragraphs, we will discuss some of these systems in more detail.

2.2.   PROSPECTOR

Duda et al. 1978
SRI International

The work behind PROSPECTOR was very much inspired by the encouraging results reported from the MYCIN effort (Shortliffe 76). The medical type of diagnosis that MYCIN was able to demonstrate lent itself very well to that of analyzing rocks and minerals. PROSPECTOR was patterned according to this type of schemata, but pioneered some important new aspects on its own.

PROSPECTOR was built to help geologists in exploring for hard-rock mineral deposits (Duda 78; Gaschnig 81; Duda 81). To achieve that, the developers created a knowledge model along the same lines as that of MYCIN. With the aid of this model, the system should be able to emulate the reasoning process of an experienced exploration geologist in asserting the likelihood that a given prospect area could contain the type of mineral that the geologist would desire. The user of PROSPECTOR would obtain some promising field data and then consult the system for assessing these data. Based on the input given, the system would infer the presence of minerals such as sulfides, uranium, lead, zinc, copper, nickel, and others.

A novel feature of PROSPECTOR at the time was its ability to accept rock data and information on minerals found together with other observations that the user volunteered. In fact, part of the input came from a digitized map. After the first match on this input, the system would possibly request additional information in a standard question-driven manner.

Part of the output could be given in the form of color-coded graphical displays that showed the favorbility of each cell with respect to prospect drilling.

PROSPECTOR also demonstrated capabilities of explaining its conclusions and actions. When prompted for data, the user could enter WHY, thus initiating a process whereby the system produced a simple geological rationale for its query. In order to achieve this, the system would trace its rule network and produce an answer. In this way it reflected the causal structure between the rules themselves.

The system was built up around the backward driven rule schemata that became very popular during the early 1980s (Duda 81). An example rule would typically be of the form:

TABLE 1
A List of Principal Systems on Geology and Mineralogy

Year reported	Name of system	Domain knowledge	Technology applied	Reference
1978	PROSPECTOR	Minerals, prospecting	Production rules, Bayesian inferencing	(Gaschnig 81)
1981	DIPMETER ADVISOR	Log interpretation	Production rules, goal-directed programming, and more	(Davis 81)
1982	ELAS	Log interpretation	Production rules	
1982	LITHO	Interpretation of oil-well drilling logs	Production rules/EMYCIN	(Bonnet 83)
1982	PHOENIX	Oil well log interpretation/knowledge engineering	Models and production rules	(Barstow 82)
1982	Amoco/X-ray	Mineralogy	Production rules, various inferencing techniques	(Ennis 82)
1983	ANALOG	Petroleum geology	Production rules	(Hawkins 83)
1984	IKBM	Evaluate petrophysical formations	Production rules, explicit geological models	(ES 84)
1987	MuPETROL	Basin classification	Production rules, explicit geological models	
1987	SPECTRUM	Remote sensing/geology	Mixed-initiative, agents	(Borchardt 87)
1987	META/LOG	Log interpretation and resource estimation	Hybrid approach, production rules, blackboard	(SPECTRUM 87)
1988	EXPERTEST	Reservoir and formation modeling	Production-rules	
1988	XX	Identification, modeling, analysis of hydrocarbon plays and prospects	Suite of many knowledge modules, production rules, approximate reasoning	(Kendall 88)
1990	Contouring Assistant	Intelligent front-end and advisor to a complex contouring and gridding system for geological data	Object-oriented technology, production rules, hybrid system, interface to numerical models	(Sines 96)
1990	Baldwin et al.	Log interpretation/dentificatio n of minerals and lithofacies	Neural networks/Hyper Cube	(Baldwin 90)
1991	GeoX	Analysis of hydrocarbon plays, resource estimation	Decision support, object-oriented technology, production rules, structured justification	(Stabell 90)
1992	I2SAdvisor	Remote sensing for geological exploration	Planning, decision-support, case-based planning	(Bremdal 95)
1992	PLAYMAKER	Characterization of hydrocarbon plays	Production rules, knowledge discovery techniques	

TABLE 1 *(continued)*
A List of Principal Systems on Geology and Mineralogy

Year reported	Name of system	Domain knowledge	Technology applied	Reference
1993	Sismonaute	Detecting and interpreting wave fronts in seismic simulations	Model-based reasoning	(Junker 95)
1993	GeCoS 3D	Building 3D models from geoloogical cross-sections	Assumption-based truth maintenance, model-based reasoning, constraints	(Hamburger 95)
1993	Kemme's E&P	Subsurface modelling	Business models, object-oriented methods, constraints	(Kemme 95)
1993	Urwongse	Prediciting hydrocarbon potential	DBMS, fuzzy analogs, neural networks	(Urwongse 95)
1993	MatchMod	Interpretation of X-ray diffraction patterns	Genetic algorithms	(Schuette 95)
1993	Maceral analysis	Automatic analysis of coal macerals	Production rules, hybdrids, image analysis	(Catalina 94)
1995	Baygun et al.	Geological modeling of a mature hydrocarbon reservoir	Neural networks, fuzzy classification	(Baygun 96)
1995	Hatton et al.	Crude oil fingerprinting	Self-organizing neural networks	(Hatton 96)
1995	Abel et al.	Petrographic analysis	Case-based reasoning	(Abel 96)

IF: There is hornblende pervasively altered to biolite
THEN: There is strong evidence (320,0.001) for potassic zone alteration

All rules were kept in a separate rule base. The inference engine would load rules into a rule-interpreter that would determine a match between the existing input data or intermediate conclusion and the clauses of the rules. Given a match, the rule would "fire," producing a new conclusion with a particular uncertainty.

PROSPECTOR explored plausible reasoning to a much greater extent than its successors. It introduced odds as the basic element. Odds can be expressed by means of Bayesian statistics:

$$O(H|E) = LS * O(H), \text{ where } O(H) = P(H)/(1 - P(H))$$

with the nomenclature given as follows:

O = odds
H = a given hypothesis
E = a given evidence
LS = measure of sufficiency
P(H) = probability that a hypothesis is true

The numbers given in the hypothesis part of the rule above represent the measures of sufficiency and measures of necessity, respectively. Both of them are likelihood expressions.

LS = P(E|H)/P(E|~H) prescribes a numerical value for updating the probability and thus odds on the hypothesis H given that the evidence is observed or present. If LS is large for a particular rule, it means that the observation of E is encouraging for H. If LS is low, the observation of E is discouraging for the hypothesis.

LN = P(~E|H)/P(~E|~H) expresses the measure of necessity. A very low value for LN means that the absence of the prescribed evidence encourages the hypothesis, while the opposite implies that a hypothesis is weakened if that particular evidence is missing.

The measures given provide some metric on the necessary availibility and importance of a set of evidence in order to reach a particular conclusion. One rule may challenge a settlement despite a vast amount of evidence in favor if, among the existing data, there exists a single evidence that greatly opposes it. The different rules were organized in an inference network.

The developers behind PROSPECTOR pioneered the use of fuzzy inferencing by applying fuzzy logical relations to the suite of clauses supporting a hypothesis. The propagated evidential strength for a set of conjunctive clauses would be the minimum. For a set of disjunctive clauses, the propagated value would be the maximum value among them.

The major architectural features characterizing the system can be summarized as follows:

1. Rule networks for expressing judgmental knowledge
2. Semantic networks for expressing the meaning of the propositions employed in the rules
3. Taxonomic networks for representing static knowledge about the relations among the terms in the domain

These features were exploited when Reboh built and added the knowledge acquisition system KAS (Reboh 79) to PROSPECTOR to reduce the burden on the knowledge engineers. KAS is a network editor that allows the user to add nodes to expand and modify the knowledge structures in PROS-PECTOR in a fairly straight forward manner. A network of rules is illustrated in Figure 1.

2.3.   DIPMETER ADVISOR

Davis et al.
MIT/Schlumberger-Doll Research Centre/Fairchild Labs for AI Research, 1981

A detailed description of DIPMETER ADVISOR can be found in the account of Davis et al. (Davis 81) and that of Baker a few years later (Baker 84). Patterned according to the first expert systems like MYCIN and PROSPECTOR, the most interesting thing beyond the technical issues addressed was the fact that DIPMETER ADVISOR was brought to full commercialization. In 1984, it had established its position in the Schlumberger organization on a basis similar to that of other

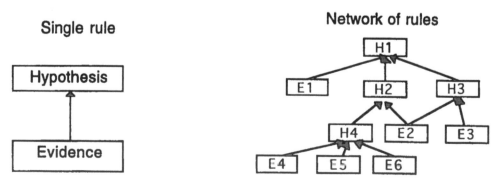

FIGURE 1   Combining rules into networks.

computer programs in routine use. Not many expert systems had managed to reach acknowledgment at that level before 1985.

DIPMETER ADVISOR takes data from dipmeters that are lowered into bore holes. The data are plotted on logs. These are long sheets of paper with records of how different kinds of energy such as sonic, nuclear, and electrical energy interact with the geological formation surrounding the bore hole. The expert system attempts to emulate a special type of interpretation knowledge used to determine the nature of the formation.

The original version of the system was purely rule based, like MYCIN and PROSPECTOR. However, it underwent significant developments. Many of the changes were imposed due to new understanding of the knowledge engineering work. But it was also influenced by the rapid changes in the log domain itself. This called for greater flexibility and posed problems that remain partly unresolved today, namely, how to cope with a knowledge engineering effort where the domain knowledge undergoes continued evolution.

Eventually, the DIPMETER ADVISOR came out as a hybrid system. Knowledge of the qualitative aspects of the log interpretation task, an interacting set of different knowledge bodies, including expertise on mineralogy, petrophysics, geology, the physics of the behavior of the individual logging and drilling tools themselves, were *incorporated.* This was again coupled with numerical approximation techniques, algebra, and calculus.

In order to handle the diversity of this knowledge, several means of knowledge representation were called upon. One paramount aspect that DIPMETER ADVISOR pioneered was the use of "deeper" knowledge to augment the heuristics emphasized in the beginning. Deep knowledge was represented in terms of causal and aggregate structures. As static knowledge, this was supported by frame structures.

The control of the system was flexible. Meta-programming was introduced in the form of a goal-directed module. This module incorporated a model of the problem-solving process itself, making it possible for DIPMETER ADVISOR to reason about its own actions and pursue and shift objectives in accordance with the state of the problem-solving process itself. This contrasted with the early initiative that looked much the same as that of PROSPECTOR where the goals are fixed and blended with the core knowledge. The meta-module would rationalize the endeavors of DIP-METER ADVISOR and reduce the chance of pursuing "dead" leads. A simple illustration of this concept is given in Figure 2.

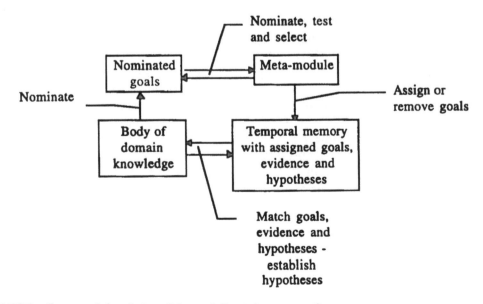

FIGURE 2   Conceptual description of the goal-directed meta-operation.

2.4.   LITHO

Bonnet et al.
Schlumberger/LRI/University Paris-Sud, 1982

The purpose of LITHO was to interpret oil-well measurements (Bonnet 83). Inherent in this is the need to elucidate curves measuring physical properties of rocks. Apart from this, the interesting thing about LITHO was the fact that it was built by means of the first expert system shell created, EMYCIN. As such, it was based on the original MYCIN concept using rules. LITHO contained several hundred production rules that contained knowledge of both petrography and paleontology.

The EMYCIN shell created a structure for the final system together with a fixed type of rule schemata like that used in MYCIN. A well-defined interface enabled the knowledge engineer to concentrate on the knowledge issues rather than on software engineering. For a suitable type of problem, this could be very efficient. However, a shell like this often proved too narrow for many problems and the knowledge engineer could often find himself fighting the limits of the shell rather than concentrating on the cognitive issues. But LITHO proved that it was possible to build a substantial system using a standard off-the-shelf shell, although problems like the one indicated were encountered during the building process.

2.5.   META/LOG: A KNOWLEDGE-BASED EXPERT SYSTEM FOR LOG ANALYSIS

SPECTRUM 2000 Mindware
Denver, Colorado, 1987

Throughout the era of expert systems, two application ideas have prevailed. One is the benefits of efficient knowledge sharing; the other is that of separating a body of knowledge from a single person and make it available independently of the human. The latter can be perceived as a manager's dream. Seen from the point of view of an oil company, it can be difficult to accept the fact that their primary source of income and asset making and the employment of as many as 60,000 to 70,000 employees are dependent on a few hundred explorationists. A top score explorationist may take 15 to 20 years to develop his skills and expertise. Still his services and advice are unreliable and expensive.

DIPMETER ADVISOR had succeeded in isolating a type of exploration knowledge and made it available to a broader audience. SPECTRUM 2000 Mindware sought to exploit commercial benefits through its endeavors with the META/LOG system, which they claimed incorporated more than 25 years of log analysis experience. SPECTRUM 2000 Mindware was basically a consulting firm that was one of the first within the geological domain and possibly within the whole world of expert system development to seek commercial opportunities through sales of computer-based knowledge. Instead of relying on sales of knowledge at an hourly rate and databased computer systems, SPECTRUM 2000 Mindware pursued repetitive sales of their log analysis knowledge through the building and marketing of the META/LOG system.

In this discourse, we will use SPECTRUM 2000 Mindware mainly as a case of commercialization of expert systems, although the developers of META/LOG were bold enough to apply some very novel techniques that are interesting in their own right.

META/LOG was launched as a knowledge-based expert system for log analysis (SPECTRUM 87), although its scope was much broader than many of its successors. It contained economical implications of the log interpretations that had not been part of comparable knowledge bases at the time. It produced conclusions on such things as reservoirs, recoverable reserves, productivity, and potential cash flow.

When it was launched in 1987, META/LOG was part of a suite of programs including databases on well history, traditional log and core analysis processors, graphics, and a system for oil exploration economics. The system itself featured a set of modules:

- A database containing raw log data, default analysis parameters and a mathematical model for analyzing the data
- A knowledge acquisition module for determining the local geologic setting and preferences for the user
- A rule base for determining the best log analysis method, based on the available data, borehole conditions, and the expected rock and fluid type
- A knowledge base containing rock, fluid, and reservoir properties for the most common reservoir types
- A rule base for determining the appropriate parameters for the selected method and the expected rock and fluid type

In order for all these components to work together, the developers applied a novel architecture at the time called the "blackboard." Each module would communicate through the blackboard, posting its hypotheses and facts there. The blackboard would thus hold the current status of the shared problem-solving effort. A meta-module would assess the posted goals and determine any changes in the problem-solving strategy. The blackboard paradigm originated with the Hearsay programs at Carnegie-Mellon University (Lesser 77) and was a way of making individual knowledge bases communicate and cooperate to reach a solution that they could not produce on their own.

The basic control paradigm applied beyond this was secured by the use of an inference engine applying the various contributions in a forward-type of manner. In addition, an audit trailer was included in order to monitor the problem-solving process. The developers realized the need for allowing the user stay in control. Users of the traditional expert system approach could not control the problem-solving process. The system itself made the initiatives. It prompted and expected an answer. Once finished, it would launch a nonnegotiable answer. META/LOG included a manual override mode that could fine-tune the results produced by the system or bypass them. An important aspect, considering that this was a purely commercial initiative, was the fact that META/LOG did not require sophisticated hardware nor any particular software considerations. It was meant for the IBM-PC or compatibles and came in two versions, implemented on top of Lotus 1-2-3 or Symphony. The entire suite of programs was marketed at a price of $950.

2.6. SPECTRUM: A KBS for Interpretation of Imaging Spectrometer Data

Borchardt et al.
California Institute of Technology, 1987

As can be judged from the paragraphs above, many of the principal geological expert systems built during the 1980s were focused on the complex and highly qualitiative log analysis task. The system developed by Borchardt et al. (Borchardt 87) addresses another type of problem that has become more and more important to both geology and to the whole domain of natural resource management over the years. Remote sensing by means of aircraft- and satellite-mounted instruments has become an increasingly important means for both exploration as well as for monitoring the earth's surface. If mineralogy and log analysis can be considered analysis of our resources at the microlevel, remote sensing by means of satellites and the subsequent image analysis must be considered a macrolevel approach.

As will be pointed out in later, remote sensing has been addressed for many different purposes. SPECTRUM, built by Borchardt et al., appears to be the first of its kind. The aim of the system was to analyze so called airborne imaging spectrometer (AIS) data. The AIS instrument carried aboard an aircraft would record data over 128 bands in the near-infrared portion of the spectrum for a geographical region of interest. The purpose behind the use of AIS was to manage the remote identification of surface minerals. Various minerals exhibit identifiable characteristics in the spectral range covered by AIS. The recorded image produced by the AIS contains pixels and classes of pixels that can be matched with spectral signatures for tested samples of minerals. However, the richness of the data recorded adds a degree of complexity in the data analysis that is not easily coped with. An AIS data set would typically measure 32 pixels in width, several hundred pixels in length, and 128 levels in depth along the spectral dimension, making a set of more than 2 million individual 8-bit data values. Ordinary pattern recognition techniques are used in order to process the raw image and make it ready for comparison with existing signatures. However, such techniques require substantial expert judgment in order to be applied, due to subtle influences on the recordings caused by atmospheric conditions, calibration of the instruments, and situations where two or more minerals in combination become indistinguishable from a third mineral appearing alone.

The SPECTRUM work aimed at building an intelligent support system for both ground-based as well as on-board operation. Its knowledge included pertinent geology, including descriptions of various minerals, concepts of the relative abundance of minerals, stability under general weather conditions, and interassociations among minerals. It would address materials such as hornblende, albite, anatase, bauxite, epidote, and many more. In addition, it contained a substantial knowledge base about analytic procedures.

Its main representation objects included materials, bands, maps, plots, goals, and plans. In order to achieve its purpose, the developers pursued an architectural approach similar to that used in META/LOG. The system was organized around several knowledge sources called intelligent agents that cooperated in order to reach a common conclusion. The contributing agents were both symbolically as well as numerically based. Another significant aspect of this system was its use of the "mixed-initiative" approach. Both will be explained briefly.

Like many other systems, SPECTRUM included a meta-reasoning unit that could manage different goals according to the development of the problem-solving process. But in addition, it could assign whole plans to achieve these. Goals and plans were applied to direct the ASI data analysis process. Individual goals are appointed and suitable plans that fulfill such a goal are asserted. SPECTRUM carried two plans for each goal. One such plan would be the "combined identification plan." When asserted, it would direct the analysis in the identification of one or more plots, considering both spectral characteristics of plots and the qualitative information describing materials associated with the various plots. Each part of the plan would be associated with one or more agents that would be called upon when that part of the plan was executed.

Like MINDWARE, the group behind SPECTRUM realized the necessity for building a system for practical operations. Among other things, this required the user to stay in control of the analysis if he wanted. The standard rule-based systems up to then had provided little latitude for the user. The "mixed initiative" introduced with SPECTRUM enabled the user not only to override the contributions of the system, but to make it a subordinate partner in terms of control too. As such, SPECTRUM was among the first approaches that combined the standard rule-based approach with a more decision support-like method. One important effect of this was the need for proper truth maintenance. Whenever the user would try to overrule some contribution from a system agent, the chain of dependent assertions would have to be redone to avoid inconsistencies.

The ideas found in SPECTRUM were later adopted independently in other areas such as forestry and ecology. They will be discussed later.

2.7.   XX/MAGIC: A Workstation Toolbox for the Explorationist

Kendall et al.
Departments of Geology and Computer Science,
University of South Carolina, 1987

One of the most pronounced features of this ambitious effort (Kendall 88; Morgan 87) was the fact that it was marketed as an expert database system and a decision support tool. At this point, an expert system was often associated with a single, straightforward rule base of the MYCIN type. Lessons over the past years had taught that knowledge modules of that kind had to be delivered together with other software modules, typically databases and numerical calculation modules in order to provide sufficient benefits for the user. Moreover, the traditional expert system was not associated with the mixed initiative effort. Hence, the decision support label was applied to highlight this and to emphasize the fact that the user would not necessarily have to rely solely on the conclusions made by the program. Another important factor in the commercial world was the term "expert system" itself, which tended to challenge the competence of the user. In other words, using an expert system could diminish the role of the user, something that was unheard of in many situations.

XX was the acronym for eXpert eXplorer. It had an extended scope in terms of exploration compared to that of log analysis systems. It supported the identification, modeling, analysis and presentation of potential hydrocarbon plays and prospects. A prospect in terms of exploration is a potential enclosure of hydrocarbons set in a reservoir rock. A play is a geological model at a higher level that includes a number of prospects as well as source rock considerations. The time aspects involving temporal considerations related to maturation and expulsion of hydrocarbons are also significant at this level. A play model also includes migration aspects involving the transportation of the hydrocarbons from the source to the reservoir.

In its first version, the XX system included seven main components:

1. A module containing representation of the essential characteristics of fields and plays used as exploration keys.
2. A knowledge-based system that elicites field attributes from the user. This unit enables users to build partial representations of the target play from whatever sources are at their disposal.
3. Database of field data such as maps, charts, notes, well logs, and seismics.
4. A suite of programs that provide users with the ability to interactively build simulations of sedimentary depositions in the host basin.
5. A set of pattern recognition algorithms that enable the user to retrieve field analogs to the target play. Similarities can be based on combinations of field attributes.
6. A report generator.
7. A control unit that controls the functions of the various modules.

Based on historical data, input from the users, simulations, and its own decisions, XX would produce risk assessments, drilling recommendations, engineering considerations, and various types of graphics: maps, cluster dendograms, charts, etc.

The architecture of XX was organized around the cooperation of several knowledge sources similar to that of a blackboard. But in contrast to the standard blackboard, there was no persistent use of a common data exchange area. The control enforced on the different parts of the system was more passive and in the hands of the user. Still, the use of a common database and a central database manager that monitor the functions of the various modules makes XX comparable to that of the META/LOG. Indeed, the communication with the GIS facility, a database, and a knowledge base has emerged as a standard architecture for many systems.

Two of the most interesting aspects of XX were the casebook approach and its solution to approximate reasoning. As a case-oriented system, it pioneered in a simple way a paradigm that became extremely popular at a later point in time. The case-based reasoning (CBR) method proved very efficient with the XX system. Surprisingly few records of CBR related to management of natural resources are recorded. Within the domain of geological exploration, the remote sensing application of Bremdal (Bremdal 95) and the petrographic system by Abel (Abel 96), which will be discussed later, are known. In XX, the known characteristics of some predefined plays were matched against the description of the target play. Based on a similarity analysis, a geologic structure was deduced and the hydrocarbon potentials determined.

Most of the knowledge captured in XX was in the form of rules like "IF mostly a THEN mostly b." Inexact reasoning involving belief values were successfully applied using the Dempster-Shafer technique. In contrast to PROSPECTOR-type systems, the clause part of a rule is considered a pattern, of which the conclusion part is dependent. There may be several conclusions associated with a pattern, each with a belief factor projecting the expert's degree of belief that the conclusion is related to the pattern on the left-hand side. In the Dempster-Shafer framework, a piece of evidence may support a single hypothesis as a conclusion. It may also support a set of hypotheses as a conclusion. The rule-based modules in XX applying this kind of inexact reasoning were built using a shell called MIDST, Mixed Inferencing Dempster Shafer Tool.

2.8.   Contouring Assistant

Sines et al.
Landmark/Zycor, 1991

Contouring Assistant began as a research project at Landmark/Zycor in 1990 (Sines 96). Despite hardships and trial and error, the system was successfully fielded as a product in December 1994.

Geoscientists build contour maps of geologic surfaces. These are often referred to as "horizons." Similar maps can be produced for thicknesses and other rock attributes to help scientists understand hydrocrabon deposition and reservoir environments. In the past, much of this work has been performed manually. Geologists have hand-drawn contours after posting values from seismic and well data on a map. According to Sines et al., this operation requires both dense and accurate data in order to provide useful results. The manual operation is very time consuming and places great burdens on the person performing the work. Because of this, computer-based tools have been launched in order to alleviate the burden. Increased speed, ease of update, repeatability, and objectivity can be achieved. However, a computer approach is susceptible to both data volume and data quality. In contrast to the computer, a person is able to apply his expertise and intuition to compensate for lack of data. When ZYCOR launched its surface modeling toolkit called Z-MapPlus, they became aware of the fact that its use was complex. In some aspects, it in fact increased manual labor. This gave rise to the development of a support tool, an intelligent front-end that later became known as the Contouring Assistant. Once built and interacting with the modeling software, Contouring Assistant builds a map that would take hundreds of button clicks and a lot of insight using a more conventional modeling package.

The Contouring Assistant knowledge base embodies years of gridding and mapping experience. As an expert system, it incorporates many of the standard features. The project was initiated along the same lines as a standard expert system effort at the time. What makes Contouring Assistant different from the other systems presented thus far is the fact that it successfully applied an object-oriented technique and blended it with the use of standard production rules. The documentation by Sines et al. provides a sincere description of the process from the proof of concept to the commercial system, including descriptions of both setbacks and progress.

Classes and objects were used for organizing static knowledge. Class hierarchies represent the Contouring Assistant's understanding of the problem specification. This includes data and default files, area of interest, data and fault spatial characteristics, smoothing, and mapping preferences for the contours. Hierarchies were also built to accommodate objects containing solutions, i.e., gridding algorithms, grid and data operations, and key control parameters. Rules are accommodated within this framework. They create recommended surface modeling procedures based on the input specification. These procedures are constructed as dynamic object hierarchies. They are translated into the syntax compatible with the associated gridding and contouring software. The inference strategy is basically of the backward type.

An important retrospective observation that Sines et al. made in their final publication (Sines 96) is the fact that expert systems development suffers from the same pains and challenges as ordinary software development. It appears that the Contouring Assistant project suffered more from these types of problems rather than particulars of the expert system concept itself. The need for good project management with clear-cut goals is especially emphasized. It shines through from this experience that expertise-oriented software projects like the Contouring Assistant are more susceptible to management weaknesses than ordinary software work.

Contouring Assistant was developed with Nexpert Object and runs on a SUN platform. By 1996, ZYCOR had sold more than 125 copies of the system.

2.9.   BALDWIN's SNN FOR MINERAL IDENTIFICATION FROM WELL LOGS

Baldwin et al.
Halliburton Logging Services, 1990.

One of the first efforts that attempted to use simulated neural networks (SNN) in the field of mineral identification and geology is the system that Baldwin et al. built (Baldwin 90) at the end of the 1980s. Once again, well logs and the knowledge-intensive effort of interpretation were the subjects for a pioneering effort. In terms of Baldwin's system, the problem of mineral and lithofacie interpretation from well log data is treated in two steps:

1. Identification of log patterns representing minerals and lithofacies for a selected log interval
2. Recognition level-by-level of the identified patterns

Unlike the original approaches used to tackle the mineral interpretation task, Baldwin's system treats it as a direct vision interpretation task.

The effort undertaken to perform the first step was based on the concept of a self-organized network (SON) (Kohonen 88). Self-organizing implies adjusting the network structure as new data becomes available. Hence, self-organization is essentially a self-learning-process. The network that was applied in this case was a fairly sophisticated version assumed to be well suited for vision-oriented recognition tasks.

According to Baldwin, visual images can provide information in two ways. The brain and mind can impose a structure on the visual images. If a person thinks about curve shapes or expects a certain shape to be present, he claims information by means of conscious or subconscious willpower. A log analyst that studies different plots might use his interpretation experience and recognition capability to decide that a single, noisy, irregular-shaped data cloud represents two distinct geological features. Later, once this is established, he may view the plots over again and then see the original cloud consisting of two groups of data.

In order to handle the pattern identification part of the interpretation task, Baldwin's system applied another type of processing using a different principle that precludes the type of high-level, logic-based operations typical for the other systems presented above.

The basic neuron architecture applied for the first step of the procedure was a 2-D self-organizing activation (SOA) concept arranged in an 8D hypercube making room for 8^8 neurons. Neurons and synapses were represented as elements in an array. Each neuron in one dimension can be characterized by its inhibition and excitation proxies. These are radial limits with respect to deactivation and activation of other neurons. The degree of inhibition and excitation is specific for each neuron and can be described by a mathematical function. The excitation and inhibition qualities of a neuron define the neuron's influence and relative magnitudes. The excitation and inhibition influence changes with time. In order to avoid problems related to available computer power, the resolution of the cube was limited to eight segments per log range. The model ran successfully on an IBM 3090. Once the hypercube organized itself, a final process terminated the first step. This process is called "on-center-off-surrounding" competitive activation. This implies that a set of neurons in a representational group compete among themselves until the strongest neuron eventually surpresses the rest. This allowed a pattern to be determined and consequently decide how many minerals or lithofacies were present.

The identified patterns were thus presented before a different network. Because petrophysicists usually recognize log data patterns by deciding among parameter models and, due to the presence of noise and inconsistencies in logs, the so called "Competetive-Activiation Pattern Classification" (CAPC) was applied. This paradigm is described by McClelland (McClelleand 88). The constructed CAPC network consisted of pools of input log neurons and one pool of mineral or lithofacie output neurons. The number of input pools was equal to the number of input logs (see Figure 3). The number of neurons per input log pool equaled the number of segments applied for the log measurements in the previous step (which was 8). Segmentation can be conceived as the resolution along the bore hole axis, as in a geologic column. The discovered number of minerals and lithofacies that the hypercube determined the number of neurons in the output pool. Every neuron in the input pool was connected to every neuron in the output pool. The connections were made bidirectional. The two networks communicate by means of a Hebbian learning rule. This implicates that the neurons in the output pool of the second network were manipulated by means of a training operation.

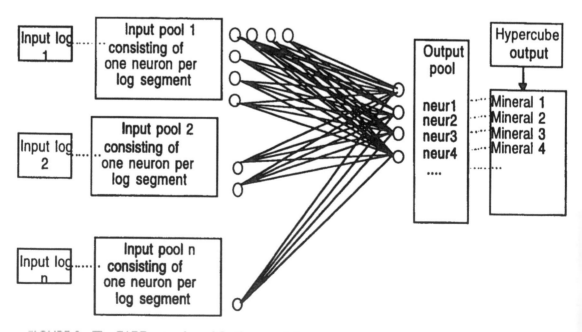

FIGURE 3   The CAPC network used for the second step.

Baldwin demonstrated that his system was able to apply the hypercube for viewing a complete log interval and discover mineral and lithofacies such as limestone, siltstone, and soft shale. The CAPC network finally generated activations that pinpointed the various discoveries and projected them in the fashion of an ordinary geologic column. An ordinary multivariate, statistically based program was compared to the SNN constructed. Both could identify the prominent lithofacies and minerals. Yet the SNN was able to recognize transient zones between facies and mineralogical units that the other could not. As such, a biologically inspired way of emulating human expertise in a computer environment produced output of value that few humans can match.

2.10. GeoX: A Knowledge-Based Decision Support System for Mineral Exploration

Stabell et al.
GeoKnowledge a.s, Norway, 1990.

GeoX shares some of the same technical features as the SPECTRUM, META/LOG, and Contouring Assistant. It is a commercial system that has generated significant sales during the 1990s. GeoX is another case of a commercial success that is built on a hybrid approach, object-oriented technology, and multiple knowledge sources set in a blackboard type of fashion. In addition to this, it contains some characteristics that are particular to that system. GeoX was built to support the exploration process, primarily at the play level, but later versions address prospect-specific issues. Recent extensions also include economic aspects. The decision process thus supported is often referred to as "full cycle." The key features of the original GeoX (Stabell 90; Mikkelsen 92) can be listed as follows:

- Supports the whole decision-making process in exploration at play level
- Supports planning and management of an exploration process
- Aids the assembly and structure of information
- Makes explorationists conscious of every choice and data provided
- Secures effective documentation of results
- Makes the final report consistent with the information established
- Allows and encourages customized, knowledge-based workbench solutions

Acknowledging the fact that decision-making addresses a vast amount of issues and data GeoX aims at supporting the explorationist through advice and critique rather than pursuing the exploration objectives on its own. In fact, the GeoX project recognized the fact that real value lies in harmonizing the contributions of many decision-makers. With a hit rate of approximately 10% in areas such as the North Sea, human geologists are performing at a level that oil company management and government authorities deem grossly unsatisfactory. The philosophy behind GeoX thus became two-folded: to organize the decision-making process in a structured manner so that work going on in different areas could be compared; and to concentrate not so much on the result of the decision-making like ordinary expert systems in the domain, but toward its rationale. By mobilizing expertise to standardize and structure the argumentation process of individuals, the work performance could be enhanced. Hence, a structured and knowledge-based justification tool was added to GeoX. This tool determines suitable justification templates for the type of arguments that the user applies. Increased transparency of the decision-making, comparison of argumentation, and biases as well as impoved sharing and re-use of decision strategies could be achieved.

GeoKnowledge later published the first initiative results from an empirical study (Mikkelsen 96) where the GeoX's approach was extensively tested. Six explorationists were given a modified

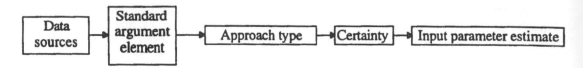

FIGURE 4   Standard justification template in GeoX.

Southeast Asian play. They had 2 hours of clock time for understanding the goal of the system and the purpose of the evaluation, and for producing an interpretation by interacting with GeoX. The increased conformation of the decision process introduced by the structured justifications imposed by GeoX did not reduce the effectiveness of the explorationists. The benefits of making it possible to compare each person's approach to the qualitative aspects of the play analysis are obvious. It enables the management of an efficient group process involving multiple experts and a vast amount of experience.

The structured justification approach resides on a model-based description of the play implemented by means of objects (see Figure 4). This defines a context for the user in which he enters facts and hypotheses about the play. Given the basic input quantities and contextual descriptions entered by the user, the system uses an estimation tool that produces a report that links calculated output like recoverable reserves to risk probabilities and the qualitative rationale produced together with the explorationist.

GeoX was implemented by means of an in-house tool called K2. K2 is a knowledge representation environment for Smalltalk-80. The most recent version runs under VisualWorks 2.5.1.

2.11.   MACERAL ANALYSIS

Catalina et al.
AITEMIN/INCAR
Spain, 1993

This expert system built in Spain is particularly interesting in this discourse for two reasons. First of all, it focuses on a different mineral than most other systems within this category. Next, it combines image analysis with traditional expert systems techniques.

In contrast to most people's beliefs, coal is not a homogeneous substance. It contains several constituents analogous to the minerals of inorganic rocks. These are called macerals, and are the fossilized remains of plant tissues. According to Catalina et al. (Catalina 94), macerals are recognized by their reflectance as well as by their morphology, which can be only recognized using a microscope.

Several components and features can be recognized when coal is analyzed in this way. In addition to more than 20 maceral types, other minerals such as pyrite and quartz may be identified. Furthermore, defects in coal preparation and empty spaces in the coal can be present.

Understanding the maceral composition is very important in determining the best use of each type of coal found. Coal that is going to be traded or applied must also be classified according to the United Nations standard "International Codification System for Medium and High Rank Coals."

Reflectance of light is an important factor when analyzing coal samples. The proportion of direct incident light reflected from a plane-polished surface is the dominating parameter in determining the constituency, since reflectance bands for some components overlap other parameters, which must also be considered. Assessment of morphology can support the analysis in order to distinguish between macerals. Maceral analysis requires both experience and time.

The knowledge-based system created supports the maceral analysis in three ways. It provides a component for image processing and a rule base built up around the actual maceral analysis. In addition, it contains a third component that manages the whole analytic process, thus alleviating the human from a lengthy and tedious task of both observing, analyzing, and concluding.

The activation of the image processing system and the rule-based part is controlled entirely by the management component. It controls the dialog between the user and the system, and it manages the microscope controller. The image processing system is fairly independent, but provides the basis for the expert system rules.

Originally, only the rule base was created. It was patterned according to most of the traditional backward-chaining systems. The goal was to imitate the reasoning of a coal petrography expert when undertaking a maceral analysis without being personally able to see the sample. Queries were also produced to guide the observation that the user makes when using the microscope.

In the latest version, a direct link between the rule-based part and the image processing system was established. In this way, a complete system for automatic maceral analysis was put to test.

According to Catalina et al., the coal maceral analysis system is able to successfully work through the following steps:

- Selection of the area of the sample to be analyzed
- Coal sample scanning, field by field, following a square grid
- Microscope focusing, average image acquisition, and lighting nonuniformity correction
- The ES determines the component occupying the center of each image, posing questions to the specialized image processing system
- Presentation of results

The original system was developed under UNIX using an in-house built shell that was programmed in C++ for the work on the knowledge base. The rules have a LISP-type format and there is a set of specialized functions to support the project-specific requirements. The graphical interface was written for X Window and Motif.

2.12. MatchMod

Schuette and Pevear
Exxon, 1993

MatchMod departs from both the neural network approach and the symbolic tradition cut-out by PROSPECTOR in mineral analysis. Schuette and Pevear (Schuette 95) pioneered evolutionary computing in interpretation of X-ray diffraction patterns. Their research effort was essentially motivated by the need to develop diagnostic systems that could handle uncertainty and nonlinearity differently from the more established approaches.

The application developed estimates of the composition and structure of a clay sample given its X-ray diffraction (XRD) pattern. This pattern is produced through a process where a clay sample is rotated in front of an X-ray source. The plot creates a pattern along in a two-dimensional system. The x-axis represents the rotational angle. The range is given along the y-axis. This defines interference from various atomic planes in the mineral crystal structure. The XRD pattern is a function of the combination of mineral present in the clay as well as the relative proportions of minerals. The peaks and valleys of the plot is the subject for interpretation. The interpreted result is used for Illite Age Analysis (IAA). This is a sample dating technique that distinguishes between illite of different ages. However, the classification process poses a challenge and is not very well taken care of by traditional means.

There are two common ways to interpret the structure of minerals using XRD patterns. The so called "Rietveld" method and a manual expertise guided trial-and-error search. The former is a deterministic least-squares method that is useful for compositional judgment. The latter is a heuristic-driven method where the user is trying to minimize error. MatchMod is a new approach that applies a stochastic optimization technique based on ideas from biology.

Genetic algorithms (GA) are optimization techniques inspired by our understanding of how nature deals with the issue of staying alive: survival of the fittest, genetic recombination, and mutation. In a GA, new possibilities are explored by letting genetic operators modify known elements to produce new ones. The process is guided by fitness measures related to population of possibilities. In contrast to other stochastic methods, GA use the fitness criteria as the engine rather than a random generator. Its ability to do radical non-local leaps in the search space distinguishes it from the more traditional approaches. Moreover, it pursues the objective function along a wide front. For more information on GA, see Goldberg (89).

Schuette and Pevear exploit the strengths of GAs in MatchMod. The system is a forward-driven process where known references are established and instantiated in order to produce new tentative patterns. These areas are crossed and the results tested against the existing log pattern, which serves as the objective function. MatchMod consists of six components:

- 1 genetic algorithm
- 4 clay mineral models
- 1 XRD pattern combiner

The four models represent MatchMod's knowledge about X-ray crystallography and clay mineralogy. All four models use information about the chemical composition of clays and their crystal structures to estimate the XRD pattern produced by a sample of that clay. They encompass parameters such as the number of iron atoms added to the crystal structure, the sequence of mixed-phase layering, the characteristics of the crystals, and more. Some of them are specific to the laboratory used; others are more general. In MatchMod, 15 parameters are manipulated by the genetic algorithm. The combiner creates new patterns based on the instantiated models given as input. The weighted output XRD pattern is matched against the original pattern. The relative goodness of the new patterns produced is highlighted before the user, who may intervene in several ways.

Parameters such as "degree of preferred crystal organization" and "percentage of illite in illite/smectite component" are represented by a bit vector representing its range of values. Hence, a paramater can be expressed as #(0 1 0 1 1 0 0 1 1 1 0 0). Contribution from two parent vector elements are concatenated and a so called "crossover point" selected. Thus, for each parameter, MatchMod swaps the bits after the crossover point in a parent, element with the corresponding bits in the other parent, as:

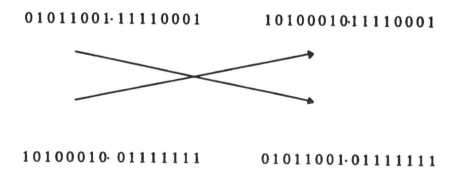

In this manner, a new generation of patterns is produced. MatchMod applies multiple crossover points. This increases the diversity from one generation to the next. The fitness function applied is a standard error minimizing model:

$$F = 1/(1 + crr)$$

where err is the sum of squares error measured at each calculated angle in the XRD pattern, and F is at its maximum when err is at its minimum.

MatchMod has been used to match several hundred patterns of many types. Compared to the manual expert method, MatchMod produced equal or better quality results. In one example, illite, known to be 400 to 500 million years old, was estimated to be 218 million years old in the best manual try. MatchMod came out with a result of 439 million years. In addition to precision MatchMod computes its result in a fraction of time compared to that of a person. Due to its independence from its user, a person can be relieved of as much as a full day's work using MatchMod.

3.   FORESTRY

3.1.   INTRODUCTION

Brack (Brack 91) put expert system use in forestry and forest planning on the agenda in his degree work. Though few systems were started during the first half of the 1980s a number of systems have been subjected to both testing and use at the end of the decade. Those and their successors have addressed several aspects of the management issue.

Forests are managed for multiple purposes; timber production, recreation, fish and wildlife, hydrology, and grazing are a few to mention. Forests are also a kind of resource in constant demand. Pulp, building materials, and firewood are all appreciated. However, over the years, people have learned that forests play an important regulating role both locally and globally; they influence climate, binds the soil, and give rise to nitrogen recirculation. The management of forests includes cultivation, protection, and careful harvesting. Forestry shares important issues with crop management for large farmlands. Agroforestry is a term that addresses both the farming aspect as well as forestry.

TABLE 2
Forestry Systems

Year reported	Name of system	Domain knowledge	Technology applied	Reference
1989	PHOENIX	Management of forest fires	Real-time planning, intelligent agents	(Cohen 89)
1989	GYPSEX	Aerial application of pesticides against gypsy moth	Frames and objects, C	(Foster 89)
1990	ISPBEX	Pest management	Hybrid system, production rules	(Flamm 91)
1993	SEIDAM	Data management in forestry	Machine-learning, planning, co-operative expert systems, hybrid units, agents	(Matwin 95; Bhogal 96)
1994	Kendon et al.	Agroforestry in developing countries	Task language, decision support, small systems	(Kendon 95)
1995	Alwast and Miliszewska	Integration of management facilities	Hybrid system, intelligent cooperative agents, decision support	(Alwast 95)
1995	UNU-AES	Land-use, fuel wood supplies	Production rules, expert system shell, objects	(Warkentin 96)
1996	University of Georgia	Forest inventory	Production rules, expert system shell	(EXSYS 96)

A forest may represent tremendous commercial value. Threats, such as fire and pests must be dealt with in a systematic manner. Fighting pests will often involve harmful secondary effects on people and the environment if not carried out in a careful manner. Pest fighting is a field of expertise that has evolved rapidly over the last decade; many aspects are still qualitative and include a good deal of heuristics. The field lends itself to expert system building and early systems like GYPSEX (Foster 89) demonstrate both purpose and benefit. Firefighting is an obvious expertise area where expert system development may produce significant rewards.

Another aspect of the management task is to determine where to harvest and how to do it. This requires a good overview of the various resources. The use of remote sensing has become popular in order to provide a foundation for decision-making pertinent to large areas. A large amount of data, difficult processing, and the need for in-depth knowledge in several related domains make the management job on this scale a very challenging job. In the 1990s, sophisticated knowledge-based paradigms have made the problem mature for expert system modeling. Several attempts have also been tried to get on top of it. Sophisticated data fusion, scheduling, and planning of forest operations are typical for these initiatives.

Other applications have been created that border on the agriculture domain; tree planting is one of them. This deals with applying woods for shelter and regulating devices to avoid erosion and improper taxation of the land. Again, the field is expertise demanding. However, the problem is often treated as a diagnostic one, lending itself to standard rule-based treatment. In Table 2, a list of forestry systems are compiled; it covers a broad field of application and spans several years. Next to mineral exploration and analysis, forestry seems to be the most active area in terms of expert system development.

3.2.   PHOENIX: A REAL-TIME, ADAPTIVE PLANNER THAT MANAGES FOREST FIRES IN A SIMULATED ENVIRONMENT

Cohen et al.
University of Massachusetts, Amherst, 1989

PHOENIX represents the traditional line of expert systems in the sense that it came out of university labs as a typical R&D system. But like its academic predecessors, it broke new ground, both as a planning system and as a forest management system. It departs from the major line, first of all for being a simulator that advises by showing and demonstrating rather than concluding and explaining.

The PHOENIX project (Cohen 89) was directed toward three main goals, each addressing ground-breaking aspects of both AI planning, knowledge engineering, and system architecture. Its scope included:

1. To pursue research on planning in a complex environment
   a. To build a real-time adaptive planner for controlling simulated forest fires
   b. To develop approximate scheduling algorithms for coordinating multiple planning activities
   c. To define knowledge representations for plans and measuring progress toward goals as well as for accommodating distributed planning algorithms
2. To understand how complex environments constrain on the design of intelligent agents
   a. To seek general rules that justify and explain why an agent should be designed one way rather than another
3. To place AI beyond trivial environments and to study the impacts of complex environment on system design

Given the last goal, PHOENIX is a tribute from the R&D community to those struggling with the issues of building intelligent systems for practical, real-world operations.

PHOENIX was an investigation into management problems typically related to that of administering natural resources. Its task was to control simulated forest fires by deploying simulated bulldozers, crews, airplanes, and other objects. The target area was the Yellowstone National Park. Fires can spread in irregular manners, in various shapes, and at variable rates. This is governed by the state of the environment in which the blaze takes place. Ground cover and elevations, moisture content, wind speed and direction, as well as natural boundaries, are among the most important factors determining the behavior of forest fires. According to Cohen et al., PHOENIX simulates forest fires with accuracy. The system is also capable of simulating firefighting objects such as people and bulldozers in a close to real-life manner. Forest fires are fought by removing one or more of the elements that keep them burning. This can be fuel, heat, and/or air. Cutting a fire line through the forest removes fuel. Water dropped on the fire removes heat. Air can be expelled by means of a fire retardant. Fires of some scale are fought by setting off backfires that are meant to intercept wild fires and denying them fuel. All of this has to be coordinated. For major fires, there can be several geographically dispersed fire bosses and hundreds of firefighters.

PHOENIX is not capable of handling a full-scale fire. It restricts itself to fires that can be handled with one fire boss and a few firefighting objects. But its capabilities include abilities to exploit natural firebreaks such as rivers, to initiate backfires, to apply common firefighting plans using bulldozers to isolate fires, and to adjust to new and changing information about weather and fire development.

PHOENIX was built using a set of specialized, semiautonomous agents such as bulldozers that carry a distinct purpose, its own knowledge base, an acting script, and protocols for communication and response.

Agent design in PHOENIX was circumscribed by what the authors called the "Behavioral Ecology Triangle." The triangle addresses the relationships between environmental characteristics and necessary agent behavior. The connections are obviously given by the design of the agent. As such, PHOENIX touches upon some fundamental epistemologic of knowledge-based design systems. In terms of the forest fire, the agents are subjected to a dynamic, ongoing, and changing world that is both unpredictable and varied. This can be illustrated with changing winds, humidity, and fuel type. It represents a continuous flow of problems, not merely a single challenge (like many expert systems have traditionally focused on) that can be dealt with once and then abandoned. The fire will pose the problems in real-time and in an ever-changing manner that can be truly unexpected.

Agents have to cope with multiple scales of time and spatial distribution. The agents involved must be able to prognosticate actions over time and make attempts to foresee developments. Bulldozers do not have unlimited amounts of gasoline and will thus have to determine actions in accordance with the available resources. Uncertainty is a major factor for all agents and can be illustrated by the decision situations to be faced. It is impossible to gain a perfect overview. Information can be scarce. All this requires acute resource management, control of uncertainty, cooperative capabilities, and the ability to plan.

PHOENIX is part of an experimental bench that has four layers. It consists of a coordinator, the environment, the agents, and the organization of agents. The coordinator takes care of the actual simulation, maintaining the temporal records of fire development and the movements of the different agents involved. The environment layer handles the factual representation of the fire settings, including maps of Yellowstone National Park. The agents layer contains the agent design. Compared to a traditional expert system using rules, these agents can be conceived as the embodiment of firefighting knowledge. But in addition to specialized domain knowledge, each agent is equipped with a meta-knowledge protocol that evaluates its own problem-solving strategy in terms of overall firefighting objectives. This protocol also includes a communication capability, an ability to replace goals issued by superior agents, and knowledge to coordinate its own actions with others. Like SPECTRUM, agents carry stored, skeletal plans that are stored in a library. When an agent is faced with a particular objective, a matching plan is retrieved, instantiated, and placed on the timeline.

The organizing layer defines the operating structure among agents. Agents are specialized, but a force of agents can be organized in different ways and along a scale of different authority and capability. An organizing layer represents a particular knowledge profile capable of doing something better than can be achieved with other configurations. The fire boss can be made the principal agent for many configurations. In the most centralized version, no lateral communication is allowed; everything goes through the boss.

The system was built using a Texas Explorer Lisp Machine. Implementation employed object-oriented techniques.

3.3.   GYPSEX: A KNOWLEDGE-BASED SYSTEM FOR AERIAL APPLICATION
OF PESTICIDES AGAINST GYPSY MOTH

Foster et al.
U.S. Forest Service, Penn State University, Forest Pest Management, USDA Forest Service, 1989

GYPSEX was reported in 1989 (Foster 89) after field verification. This expert system provides knowledge-based decision support for two aspects of aerial application of insecticides against gypsy moth: calibration and characterization. According to the makers of the system, the successful aerial application of pesticides against gypsy moth requires information about gypsy moth population dynamics, insect sampling techniques, potential gypsy moth impact on trees, weather, pesticide effectiveness, and aircraft spraying systems. Problems of particular difficulty are spray system configuration for the desired flow rate (calibration) and for adequate, evenly distributed pesticide deposition (characterization). The system includes so called Desk Calculations and Field Tests for calibration. Desk Calculation supports the user with advice on the configuration of spray systems. The Field Test section provides troubleshooting advice when initial tests on flow rate is not in accord with expectations.

In terms of characterization, the principal purpose is to assure appropriate pesticide deposition. The Characterization module first provides the user with a pairwise juxtaposition of the test spray pattern. Next, the user will select one of the spray patterns suggested. Finally, the system will provide heuristic advice on the spray nozzle numbers and positions.

A third module was ready for field test at the turn of the decade. This has been called Spray Timing. Its purpose is to advise on the optimal date for aerial application of *Bacillus thuringiensis* against gypsy moth based on weather forecasts and insect and host tree phenology.

At the time of verification, the system was supported by Macintosh SE and IBM PC platforms. It was written in C by means of a frame-based, object-oriented toolkit. Heuristic rules were accommodated in frame structures. The heuristic modules were built to cooperate with both simulation models and calculation-based system components.

3.4.   ISPBEX: THE INTEGRATED SOUTHERN PINE BEETLE EXPERT SYSTEM

Flamm et al.
Texas A&M University, USDA Forest Service, Texas Forest Service, 1991

The ISPBEX system is similar to GYPSEX in objective and approach. It was developed at the same time, and it is interesting to note how the builders move toward interconnected systems applying a register of databases, different platforms, and different tools.

The ISPBEX system addresses pest management in forestry (Flamm 91). Its focus is the southern pine beetle, *Dendroctonus frontalis*, found in the U.S. The effort behind the system was driven by the wish to define the problem of southern pine beetle management and to develop a knowledge-based system to both promote and demonstrate the capabilities of an expert system within the field of pest management in forestry. The pine beetle is a pest insect that infests and kills yellow pines throughout the southern U.S. It can severely disrupt forest management goals, plans, and practices.

Managing damage caused by the southern pine beetle is difficult for two reasons. The first reason centers on the process of decision-making by the forest manager, and the second deals with efficient use of information derived from research.

Before the system research on the southern pine beetle pest was initiated, few immediate results on the forest management practice were experienced. One paramount cause for this was the fact that newly acquired knowledge could not be readily delivered to the forest managers. It was found necessary to find ways to facilitate integration, interpretation, and use of the different types of information needed. Another principal requirement was the need to blend the qualitative knowledge of the manager with the quantitative results derived from the R&D programs.

The ISPBEX initiative was antedated by the SPDSS (Southern Pine Beetle Decision Support System). This was the first concerted effort to use computer technology to accommodate the R&D results generated. The principal task of this system was to present information to the user and not directly solve problems. Since the system never came into practical use, a formal examination was triggered. Investigation of the unsuccessful effort revealed lack of user involvement and user-specific needs. The lack of heuristic knowledge in the system disfavored its use. This gave lead to the ISPBEX system.

The ISPBEX system is built around three functional objectives:

- To incorporate qualitative domain-specific information into the insect pest management (IPM) process
- To accommodate problems that do not respond to algorithmic solutions
- To use meta-level knowledge (knowledge about the problem-solving process itself) to effect more sophisticated control of problem-solving strategies
- To integrate the different representations of knowledge for IPM problem-solving and decision-making

As a task-oriented system, ISPBEX considers three aspects of IPM: suppression, prevention, and utilization. Suppression deals with actions that enable regulation and modification of the insect population. Prevention deals with actions taken to minimize risks of adverse impacts of the insect on resource management goals. Utilization deals with actions taken to make use of resources damaged by the activities of the insect. The ISPBEX systems has three modules that are built around each of these tasks (see Figure 5). The knowledge bases are built around rules that are very much fact driven. Yet, typically for the second-generation expert system, ISPBEX is much more than an accumulation of rules.

The system accesses several databases on a central mainframe computer. These include bases like the GIS forest stand maps, SPB historical data, and the SPBIS (Southern Beetle Information System). The databases fuel the system with data required to support the various tasks.

In order not to compromise early user-specific lessons, the development team made serious efforts in order to suit the system to the target user group. As an example of this, they structured menus to resemble Forest Service data forms and reports. The number of keystrokes were minimized. In addition, extensive help menus were included.

In addition to the important database connections, the system includes a geographical information system (GIS). Simulation models were also added to the system along with a significant amount of heuristics. Simulation models of both southern pine beetle population dynamics and

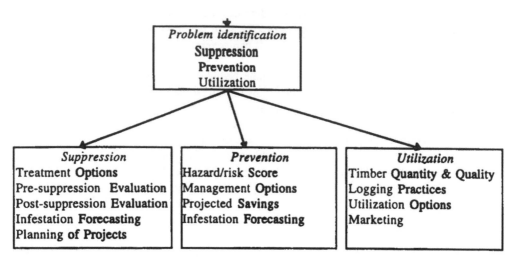

FIGURE 5   The task structure of ISPBEX.

infestation geometry were included when management decisions affect infestation located in wilderness areas and within close proximity of other special use forest.

Several tools were used to implement the system. The most important being CLIPS, FIFTH, and KERMIT. CLIPS is a forward-chaining expert system shell that was developed by NASA. FIFTH is a programming environment for FORTH that was used to develop the user interface. It compiles menus defined in a textual format into binary code. KERMIT is a widely used communication protocol for transferring files between computers. It was especially popular during the 1980s. ISPBEX is based on hybrid code written in many languages ranging from C and FORTRAN to Assembler.

ISPBEX is run on PCs and interacts with the Forest Service Data General mainframe computer. Version 1.0 of ISPBEX was released for Beta testing in May 1989. It has been subjected to continued development. In the early 1990s, the developers initiated work around the same domain, pursuing the knowledge system environment approach.

3.5.   UNU-AES

Warkentin et al.
George Mason University/UN
Virginia, 1995

UNU-AES is a good example of how expert systems can be applied for transfer and deployment of expertise that can have profound effects on human living, practices, and use of natural resources. Like Kendon's system (Kendon 95), UNU-AES addresses a particular difficult domain of application, namely agroforestry systems in developing countries. The system represents the link between established knowledge centers in the Western world and areas in the Third World that are faced with severe problems land mismanagement.

The goal of the United Nations University Agroforestry Expert System (UNU-AES) was to assist land-use officials, research scientists, farmers, and others in maximizing the benefits gained from applying agroforestry approaches to land management (Warketin 96). Although important to the industrialized world, these issues are paramount for agricultural and forestry management in South America, parts of Asia, and in Africa.

Agroforestry studies encompass issues in which woods are deliberately grown on the same piece of land as agricultural crops. Woods of this kind, arranged in different ways, provide lasting shields and ecological support to their proximity. In agroforestry systems, the woods cultivated interact ecologically and economically with other components in the system, being food crops or animals. This can be illustrated by an example. Alley cropping is a type of agroforestry in which leguminous trees are planted in rows with food crops cultivated between them. Pruning minimizes the shade and provides nitrogen-rich foliage. In addition, these trees contribute to the recycling of nutrients and eventually yield both food for organisms and firewood for people.

UNU-AES was aimed at supporting agroforestry practices and thinking in developing countries. It addresses the problems of land management and forests as a benefit to agricultural and ecological production. The knowledge-base has qualifying knowledge pertaining to a number of things, including: annual rainfall in an area, number of rainy seasons per year, landscape, soil texture, soil fertility, and soil recreation data. Its conclusions give advice on how to utilize the land and in particular how to explore the benefits of woods in this context.

The system consists of a rule base supported by frame-like structures. The EXSYS Professional expert system shell was selected for this work. The system can be interfaced with other programs through custom commands and linkable objects.

It runs under MS-DOS and operates successfully on a portable computer. The latter is important because it simplifies demonstration and use in developing countries.

3.6.   SEIDAM FOR FORESTRY

Bhogal, Matwin et al.
Pacific Forestry Centre, University of Ottawa
Canada, 1995

Remote sensing has manfiested itself as an important means to manage natural resources. But remote sensing is complicated and involves a diverse set of knowledge pertaining both to the target area, the technology applied, the general environment, and image processing.

In a previous paragraph we discussed the SPECTRUM system developed by Borchardt et al. (Borchardt 87) that was put into use for mineral exploration. I2SAdvisor (Bremdal 95) is a case-based variant from the same geology domain. Both emphasized the usefulness of an appropriate remote sensing operation in mineral exploration and management. In a later paragraph, remote sensing was revisited in the context of more general ecological management.

Matwin's (Matwin 95) and Bhogal's (Bhogal 96) accounts of the SEIDAM (System of Experts for Intelligent Data Management) system describe a sophisticated support system for remote sensing, developed over several years that addresses the same important issues in forestry.

According to Matwin et al. (Matwin 95), management of forests in British Columbia is becoming increasingly complex. In recent years large repositories of data have been established. This data help to understand the state of the biosphere and changes in vegetation over large areas. This understanding and the underlying data can lead to improved management of resources. The largest vegetative component on the earth's surface is forestry. Management of this is important for several reasons, the most important being the fact that the current rate of harvesting to meet commercial demands is higher than actual growth. In sum, the combined yield of plantation forest and available natural resources cannot meet the demand. A prime issue emerging from this is how to supply the market while maintaining ecological goals. This requires highly sophisticated, timely, and focused forest-management practices. The issue becomes even more pronounced when constraints imposed by the variability in terrain, climate, forest conditions, and Canada's new Forest Practices Code are taken into account. A lot of data is necessary to cope with the issue both nationwide and locally. The problem with the access, use, and analysis of forest data is its diversity and complexity. According to Matwin et al., this diversity is reflected in a variety of formats, media, and data granularities. Complexity is due to the heterogeneity of available computing facilities and software. Advanced information systems for forestry integrate forest-cover descriptions, topographic maps, remote-sensing data, and application knowledge. Matwin et al. claim that the rate of data acquisition for the whole of Canada will reach 1 terrabyte per day by the year 2000.

The SEIDAM project was initiated in 1991 to develop a system of expertise for intelligent data management for forest and environmental monitoring. It is a hybrid system (see Figure 6) built around a knowledge-based core called Palermo (Planning and Learning for Resource Management and Organization). It is a complex system that relies on extesnive cooperation between different expert systems and processing agents. Most processing agents are third-party software packages

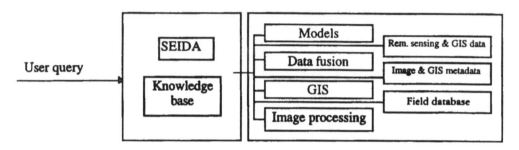

FIGURE 6   A conceptual view of SEIDAM.

providing database management (Ingres), geographical information systems such as ARC/Ingres, image analysis programs like Ldias, and visualization tools such as AVS.

Decision-makers need fast access to the most recent information about forests. A typical query produced in the context of forest management can be illustrated by an example given by Matwin et al. (Matwin 95): "What is the spatial distribution of Douglas fir in the Greater Victoria Watershed area?" The Greater Victora Watershed covers six 1:20000 maps. There are GIS files covering topographic information, forest cover, soils, hydrology, geographic names, and transportation. In order to navigate through the data and software repositories, a good aid is needed. This is a knowledge-based problem-solving effort. Matwin et al. sees the answer to the query as synthesis from many parts. Pertinent to the given example, both expertise on forestry, topographic mapping, remote sensing analysis, GIS operation, database design, and visual representations are called upon.

Palermo handles this as a planning process like the I2SAdvisor system (Bremdal 95). Given a set of desired properties, it tries to construct a plan that produces a state with desired properties. In order to handle this, it applies a mixed planning paradigm:

- Case-based reasoning (CBR)
- Derivational analogy
- Goal regression

The CBR part contains a case base of plans. Historic plans can be recognized and retrieved and applied as a prototype for the new problem. The derivational analogy part is a searched-based problem-solving unit that operates on a case base of derivations. Derivations suggest what planning operator to choose at a given step in the planning, if a similar result in the past resulted in the derivation of a successful plan. The goal regression part is constituted by a more search-based, problem-solving approach in the STRIPS tradition. It posts goals and works at them one at a time. When sub-goal interactions are discovered, it backtracks and reorders the sub-goals. Palermo handles a conjunction of goals. Each query is treated as a kind of goal conjunction. Each conjunct is attacked independently. The end results from each are combined. When the plan is constructed, a controller assigns tasks to specific processing agents and coordinates their execution. The agents are together responsible for achieving the goals that the plan pursues. SEIDAM and the agents communicate using sockets and the planning operators that send commands to the third-party software and await responses. The choice of operators is based on training observed when a human domain expert has performed similar interactions with the third-party software. For each step of the solution, the agents report on the state of the processing. These reports let SEIDAM learn about its successes and failures. In this manner it can refine its case base and its knowledge of the processing agents.

SEIDAM runs on a SUN Sparcstation using the Solaris 2.3 version of UNIX.

4. WILDLIFE TAXONOMY

4.1. INTRODUCTION

When Winston introduced his book on LISP, he also initiated a rule-based system on animal taxonomy (Winston 81). Although meant as an illustration on how to create a rule-based system in LISP, the accompanied example served as a fine depiction on how to do capture taxonomic knowledge in a rule-based model. A rule would typically read:

IF	animal has pointed teeth
AND	animal has claws
AND	animal has forward eyes
THEN	animal is a carnivore

The simplicity of the approach inspired many people and students of expert systems at the time. Over the years we must assume that multiple prototypes of the kind were made, yet few seem to have become more than that. The initiatives that Jeffers (Jeffers 85) reports are, however, typical. Correct identification of species of plants and animals is necessary for ecological management. But the taxonomic systems with a professional inclination tend to be of value for purely biological purposes. Over the years neural networks have augmented the traditional rule-based approach. Neural networks applications tend to bring the support aspect much further. Instead of expecting structured information from an intelligent user, neural networks applications try to interpret much more unrefined data. In 1994, Boddy (Boddy 94) wrote about two systems that had successfully applied neural networks technology. One system was able to identify and classify 40 species of phytoplankton and fungal species from flow cytometry data. Another system was used for distinguishing between European and Africanized bees based on training on morphometric data. These type of applications, although addressing a complicated field, are pursuing the technology application aspect in much the same manner as the mineral analytic systems. Several varieties of neural networks have been tried with much the same conclusions as that for other types of applications. The training and vectorization problems are the hardest to resolve. Since the knowledge lies implicit in the network, their inherent knowledge structures are indistinguishable from those in geology that we have previously discussed.

We will report on an expert system that builds directly on the PROSPECTOR tradition. It is unique in its simplicity, yet has a very profound and powerful use potential. It is particularly relevant to the field we are discussing here, where large and complex systems dominate. The Whale Watcher Expert System should serve as an instance of the saying "keep it simple and beautiful." The Acquire expert system for whale identification is a system that addresses a problem that concerns many professionals within animal taxation and wildlife management. The approach that Acquire uses may well be as important to the field as the use of numbered identification rings and tags to mark species of birds, fish, and animals.

4.2.   WHALE WATCHER EXPERT SYSTEM

Acquired Intelligence, Ministry of Fisheries and Oceans Canada
Canada, 1995

The Whale Watcher Expert System contains a simple taxonomic knowledge base on whales. The primary resource for this knowledge was a booklet that was produced by Fisheries and Oceans Canada. The system will prompt the user for observations it believes are pertinent. Queries are produced in a rule-driven, backward-chaining manner and presented as selection menus on the screen. Hence, the dialog is very simple. Questions of the kind: "Did the whale have a hump on its back?" are characteristic for the type of interaction that it pursues. You are expected to select either "yes," "no," or "unknown" from the accompanying menu. After a series of questions, the system reaches a conclusion and presents it to the user. Obviously, the knowledge base that it possesses is not a big step from the rule-based taxonomy system that Winston first built. What makes it powerful is the combination with multimedia and the fact that it is available to the public on the Internet. In spite of the original intention of making the system a demo to illustrate the capabilities of an expert system shell, the system illustrates very well its application to natural resource management. The early expert systems operated in a way that could be defined as telephone support systems. This is much like the one described for the maceral analysis above. Interaction depends on a form of communication that is typical for people that try to solve problems in a remote fashion, unable to observe the things that the problem owner can see. The Whale Watcher Expert System produces pictures, movies, and sounds to support its communication with the user. Hence, the users become more aware of the context that the query assumes.

The fact that this simple system is publicly available illustrates an important issue on its own. Biologists and others concerned with the state of our wildlife resources depend on the interest and commitment of the public. A person cannot be everywhere to observe and to determine. For years the professionals have been dependent on the often informal reports and observations called in by amateurs. Though having value as a first-line detection system, the inputs received vary in quality. The Whale Watcher Expert System shows that it is possible to efficiently deploy and distribute a simple knowledge-based system that can support amateurs at the time when they report (provided that they apply E-mail for this purpose). The effect should be obvious. More reliable reports that improve the conveyance of a particular impression.

The system uses simple rules accompanied by an object-oriented approach. The interface is accommodated in HTML so that it can be browsed and viewed by tools such as the Netscape version 2.0 or higher. CGI constructions support the menus used for questioning. The Whale Watcher Expert System was created by means of the Acquire shell that is customized for Web interaction.

5.   MANAGEMENT OF WATER RESOURCES

5.1.   INTRODUCTION

Water is the most important natural resource on earth. The "blue planet" is distinguished from the other orbs in our solar system by the fact that much of the surface is covered with water. Water is the essence for all life and the constant subject of concern both in political debates as well as in science. Its scarcity in one region and its abundance in others have challenged Man since his origin. Contamination of drinking water has been a major issue for both health organizations and community planners. The increasing pollution from growing industry and modern farming has added to the concern for our water resources, both locally and globally. Indeed, the management of these resources has become extremely difficult. Great difficulties arise from the diverse and often conflicting use of the same water resources for purposes such as irrigation, drinking, fishing, bird and animal habitat preservation, power production, waste permission, and floating traffic. The knowledge required to understand and manage all aspects of our water resources is both diverse and vast. The need for more acute decision support, advise, as well as efficient knowledge sharing has inspired both researchers and domain professionals to exploit the use of expert systems for this purpose. Since the late 1980s an increasing activity is seen in this field. Yet most tangible results appear to have surfaced after the turn of the decade. Development trends have followed the same pattern as that illustrated for mineral exploration. However, the core is constituted by the traditional rule-based approach using a backward-chaining inference strategy. As in other domains, this has been augmented by multiple interfaces. Databases, GIS, simulation models, multi-media, and the WWW are typical companions to the rule-based knowledge base. In terms of application, many of the expert

TABLE 3
Systems Dealing with Management of Water Resources

Year reported	Name of system	Domain knowledge	Technology applied	Reference
1990	Li et al.	Weed control in Florida waters using herbicide	Intelligent databases, production rules	(Li 90)
1992	Rhykerd et al.	Lead contamination detection in drinking water	Production rules, frames	(Rhykerd 92)
1993	Booty et al.	Point source water quality modeling	Production rules	(Booty 94)
1994	Expert GIS	Water resource planning	GIS, rule-based system, network model	(McKinney 94)
1994	Lam et al	Watershed management and planning; Information retrieval	Intelligent database, production rules	(Lam 95)
1996	STEWARD	Water quality control	Production rules, hypertext, WorldWideWeb	(PennState 96)
1996	CORMIX	Analysis of discharge and water mixing conditions	Production rules, quantitative models	(Doneker 96)
1997	COLOSS	Support for management of Columbia River resources	Decision-support, production rules	(Doneker 96)

systems directed toward water resource management tend to blend resource issues with an agricultural inclination. Since farming is a major beneficiary, this is not surprising. In Table 3 we have included a list of some representative systems. A selection of these will be discussed in more detail.

5.2.   EXPERT GIS FOR WATER RESOURCE PLANNING

McKinney et al.
Texas University at Austin/ Texas Water Resources Institute, 1994

The Texas Water Development Board (TWDB) is a state agency responsible for long-term water supply planning. One of its major tasks is to assure water resources for a wide region through good planning and sound water management. TWDB has long practiced a standard for planning that, according to McKinney et al. (McKinney 94), includes the following steps:

1. Water demands are estimated for a base planning year and 10-year intervals for periods up to 50 years. Available water supplies are estimated for reservoirs, rivers, and aquifers.
2. Supplies and demands are reconciled on a county-by-county basis and deficits are noted.

3. When deficits occur, a search is conducted for nearby supply sources that could be allocated and potential new projects that could be developed to meet these shortfalls.

Once a plan is developed, comments are requested from both regional and statewide interests.

The manual planning process is very tedious and difficult. Originally it was heavily dependent upon the expertise and judgment of a few professional staff members. Moreover, results developed in the manual way cannot be rigorously documented or replicated. Because of this, it was decided at the beginning of the 1990s to have this planning process automated.

An expert geographic information system (expert GIS) for long-term regional water supply planning was completed in 1994 by a team at the Texas Water Resources Institute. The planning system comprises the following:

- An expert rule system
- A geographic information system (GIS)
- A network flow solver

The rule-based system contains expertise acquired from water resources planning experts. The GIS systems stores and analyzes spatially distributed water supply and demand data. It also produces geographic displays of alternative water allocation plans. The task of the the network flow solver is to balance the flows in networks developed by the expert GIS with input from a water resource analyst. The objective for this part is to find the least costly resource allocation solution.

The model incorporates source units such as reservoirs and aquifers. Demand areas include counties and cities. Planning problems are represented by a series of points, lines, nodes, and arcs. Line coverage or potential arcs (PARCs) describe ways in which water can be transmitted from supplies to users. Abstractions were developed so that problems could be represented geographically, functionally, and in a planning mode. Given annual yields for reservoirs, water demand forecasts, and institutional requirements, the expert GIS is able to calculate potential water supply deficits or excesses. In case of a deficit, it is able to suggest alternative supplies that are both efficient and cost effective.

The rule base includes several categories of rules with more or less specific application. State-wide rules correct obvious problems. Regional rules incorporate specific water supply and demand conditions that apply to that particular area. Generic categories of rules for regional water planning appear to be one of the more powerful aspects of the system. The basic system model is object based.

The model was initially tested using a hypothetical example developed by the TWDB. The system was later tested using a case study of the Corpus Christi region for a 50-year planning horizon involving 19 counties. Groundwater costs were developed based on information on well depths and drilling costs supplied by TWDB staff. Surface water costs were estimated for each reservoir based on construction and operations and maintenance costs and firm yields. Demands were estimated for Corpus Christi and other municipalities in the region, as well as for agricultural and industrial use. The system has also been successfully applied to the Coastal Bend planning region of the TWDB.

The expert GIS system has been developed so that it can be expanded to include additional constraints and handle large water resources planning regions. According to the development team, the system will be capable of analyzing entire river basins, given appropriate information concerning the supply and demand for water.

5.3.   CORMIX Mixing Zone Model

Doneker et al.
USEPA NPDS, 1996

CORMIX is a rule-based expert system for analysis and modeling of discharge and water mixing conditions (Doneker 96). As a system, it illustrates well how expertise about a very complex problem can be captured and incorporated in a knowledge base on a computer using simple techniques. The lesson is fairly straightforward: the sophistication of the system is primarily a function of the expertise incorporated rather than the way it is captured and delivered.

The system is based on knowledge on turbulent buoyant jet mixing applied to discharge problems and water condition evaluation.

According to Doneker (Doneker 96), the Cornell Mixing Zone Expert System (CORMIX) consists of a series of software subsystems for the analysis, prediction, and design of aqueous discharges into watercourses, with emphasis on the geometry and dilution characteristics of the initial mixing zone, including the evaluation of regulatory requirements.

On an overall level, CORMIX can be described as an analysis and prediction system. It can estimate the mixing behavior from a diverse menu of discharge types. Such discharge types encompass power plant cooling waters, brines from desalinization facilities, drilling rig-produced waters, municipal effluents, or thermal atmospheric plumes. CORMIX can also be applied across a broad range of discharge conditions ranging from estuaries, deep oceans, and swift shallow rivers, to stratified reservoirs. CORMIX will aid its users in determining the effects of both planned and nonintentional releases into a river or water area. Contamination, thermodynamic-related issues, and depositional problems can be addressed by means of the system.

Doneker highlights the system features as follows:

- Near-field and far-field plume trajectory; definition including geometric shape, concentration, and dilution predictions
- Applications to unsteady ambient currents, tides, or stagnant conditions
- Graphical display of plume and concentration
- Prediction of plume boundary attachments/interactions

CORMIX has three subsystems:

1. *CORMIX1-Single-Port Submerged Outfalls.* CORMIX1 deals with buoyant, submerged single-port discharges into flowing unstratified or stratified water environments, such as rivers, lake, estuaries, and coastal waters. It includes a knowledge body pertinent to both nonbuoyant and negatively buoyant discharges and stagnant ambient conditions. It also deals with tidal reversing flow conditions.
2. *CORMIX2-Multiport Submerged Outfalls.* Subsystem CORMIX2 will handle similar problems, but given multiple flow discharges.
3. *CORMIX3-Surface Buoyant Discharge.* Subsystem CORMIX3 deals with only positively buoyant surface discharges released into environments similar to the ones decribed above.

CORMIX runs on a DOS-based IBM-PC. It carries 2000 mixing rules. The rule-based part of the system is linked to a hydrodynamic simulation model.

The CD-CORMIX is a recent extension to the CORMIX expert system. Like the former version, CD-CORMIX is a rule-based program containing rules for turbulent buoyant jet mixing behavior. The extension addresses in particular problems related to continuous dredge disposal and its associated water quality impacts. Both particle settling and plume behavior can be subjected to analysis by the system. CD-CORMIX takes into considerations five particle size fractions of discharge material and is able to predict the water quality, including the concentration and dimensions of the resultant disposal plume. Added up, the new extension will handle the following:

- Discharge conditions above the surface
- Negatively buoyant surface discharges
- Bottom density currents with particle settling

- Effect of bottom slope on plume behavior
- Particle deposition rates

The CD-CORMIX is still under development at the time of writing.

5.4.   STEWARD

Lehning et al.
Center for Artificial Intelligence Applications in Water Quality
Penn State University, 1996.

STEWARD (Support Technology for Environmental, Water and Agricultural Resource Decisions) is basically a hypertext system carrying a large body of textual knowledge related to multiple aspects of water resource management. It is available on the Internet (PennState 96). It is supported by a few active knowledge bases (Foster 94).

The development of STEWARD was driven by the center's wish to develop software applications that solve water contamination problems and efficient water quality tests. Another aspect was the need to centralize written information, databases, and computer-based applications in water quality control processes in an electronic format and make them available to the public in an efficient manner.

STEWARD incorporates several knowledge elements. These address issues such as general monitoring of water quality, water transport, contamination testing, treatment of contamination, environmental fate, health effects, and site management. This extensive expertise is controlled by the use of HTML-based hyper links on the WWW. Using an ordinary Web browser, STEWARD is accessed by means of "point-and-click" operations. The interaction with the knowledge units is not as simple as with the Whale Watcher Expert System described earlier. In contrast, the expertise that it contains seems overwhelming. Much of the information that the system can deliver is supported by multimedia such as images, sound, and animation. The active knowledge body follows the traditional rule-based IF-THEN schemata. They encompass both quantitative and qualitative problem-solving abilities. The rule base is linked to a set of databases.

An example using the Control Systems Module highlights the scope of the system. Once selected, the module prompts you with the type of contaminant to be controlled. The user may select from a list of 20 alternatives, including ammonia, dissolved oxygen, dissolved nitrogen, organic matter, pesticide, sediment, etc. It will let the user put forward queries like "What is the leaching potential of the soil?", "What is the soil hydrologic group?", and "What is the nutrient application rate?" Each query is accompanied by a set of standard answers, which provide a state description of the site selected for control.

5.5.   COLOSS

Doneker et al.
U.S. Army Corps Of Engineers, 1997

Columbia River Decision Support System (COLOSS) is a simple, but representative expert advisor currently under development for U.S. Army Corps of Engineers. Its objective is to provide support for decision-makers that anticipate a competing set of use for the water resources of the Columbia River.

The system Like CORMIX it is being built by Doneker (Doneker 96) using production rules as the dominant representation schema. COLOSS will provide decision support for management of the competing water resource requirements of the lower Columbia River system. The rule base will include the physical and regulatory constraints for river and reservoir operation. COLOSS will aid in reservoir operation for water supply, navigation, hydropower production, recreation, flood control, and fishery needs. The intent of the project is to demonstrate the capability of a rule-based system for decision support of river operations. In general, the knowledge base that COLOSS will operate is to include aspects of use, timing, depositions, mixing, and other elements related to the varied use of the water resources in the area.

The software will be linked to the Columbia River Operation Hydromet Management System (CROHMS). Results will be conveyed via tables, messages, and graphics on a window-based system.

6.   ECOSYSTEM MANAGEMENT

6.1.   INTRODUCTION

Ecosystem management clinches nearly every aspect of natural resource management. Even topics addressed by the systems within the mineral, water, and forestry domain are encompassed by this type of administration. Its scope is tremendous, which is well illustrated by Short et al. (Short 95) in their report on Earth System Science (ESS). Although ecosystem management may impose a regional locus of interest, it is becoming more evident that its character is truly global. Rainforest management in Brazil can no longer be considered a national issue as long as these forests influence the global climate. When the Tchernobyl disaster in 1986 threatens the wildlife habitat of the Laps in the northern regions 10 years later, nuclear power for regional supply is no longer an issue only for Russians. Moreover, if the herring in the North Atlantic are over-taxed by Spanish, Portuguese, Scottish, Norwegian, and Russian trawlers, it is not solely a case for the EU fishing interests. It will ruin the balance in the ocean, threatening for instance the subsistence of cod, seal, and birds, and the livelihood of coastal communities in Greenland, Iceland, and northern Norway. True ecosystem management must be supernational and keep a sustained focus on nature's genuine diversity.

Fundamental to all kinds of modern ecosystem management are monitoring and control. This calls for a tremendous amount of data about almost every aspect of our planet. In a more limited sense, it addresses monitoring and control of pollution. Environmental impact assessment (EIA) and environmental protection are both essential. The former deals with how our resources are maintained and exploited. Environmental protection issues embrace both pollution restriction, contamination from hazardous materials, and habitat shielding.

Due to its increased importance and expanding complexity and scope, there is an increased need for more tools to aid the management task. Expert systems that assist in determining the effects on the environment due to various industrial, agricultural, or municipal initiatives have arisen. The work of Hushon (Hushon 91) is an early example of that. The system made by Sturrock et al. (Sturrock 94) shares some of the same intention, but sees the issue from the point of the industry. In other words, mismanagement of production plants may lead to pollution and thus create problems for the industry. That type of system is not discussed here.

"Think globally, act locally" is a slogan that can be applied in conjunction with ecosystem management. In undeveloped countries, fire is often used as a farming tool to clear new areas and fertilize new crops. Applied on a large scale, this practice can have devastating effects on both farmland and the surrounding wildlife. One major implication is soil erosion and dehydration of the soil, which paves the way for exhaustion and desert-like conditions. Although harmful to a large area, management practices must be distributed to local areas. Knowledge sharing is a key word in this context, and the early work on a system for vegetation succession advice by Dr. Noble (Jeffers 85) stands out as a very good example.

Global or large area monitoring today implies some kind of remote sensing. Some of the expert systems in the geological domain have been built to support remote sensing for mineral exploration. We have also seen an example of this in forestry. Its application is general and paves the way for a complete overview of the whole earth and multiple aspects of an ecological system. The work undertaken by NASA (Short 95) is clearly the most ambitious of all the initiatives reported in this direction. Remote sensing inevitably calls for advanced image processing. Every expert system dealing with this addresses the image processing task to create meaningful representations. However, in terms of ecosystem management, intelligent data fusion is perhaps an equally important issue.

The nature of the management task discussed here is complex and calls for many types of support. Hence, most systems within this genre are hybrid systems applying a wide variety of computing resources. GIS is central, advanced database technology; simulation in addition to a diverse set of knowledge bases are common elements. Neural networks have moved into application (Wong 93; Boddy 94). Web technology and multimedia often support the delivery of expertise.

An extreme version of a hybrid approach is documented in the description of the underwater robot system documented by Stoker et al. (Stoker 95). Here, artificial intelligence supports the use of virtual reality and telepresence technology to explore and monitor an underwater habitat in Antarctica.

TABLE 4
Systems for Ecosystem Management and Pollution Control

Year reported	Name of system	Domain knowledge	Technology applied	Reference
1985	Noble et al.	Advisory system on vegetation succession		(Jeffers 85)
1987	TSDSYS	Identification of appropriate waste treatment services	Client-server, rule-based system	(Hushon 91)
1993	Wong and Lam	Prediction of missing environmental data	Neural networks	(Wong 93)
1994	SIRENAS	Hazardous pollution	Hybrid system, production rules and objects	(Murcia 94)
1995	SEA	Nuclear ban treaty control	Decision support, semantic network, assumption-based reasoning, hybrid	(Mason 95)
1995	TROV Antarctica	Telepresence and VR support for ROV operations	Spatial models, intelligent control	(Stoker 95)
1995	CERES	Facilitates data and decision support for improved environmental planning	Intelligent database, GIS, hybrid system, multimedia, WWW	(CRA 96)
1995	ESS/IIFS	Data fusion of remotely sensed data	Large hybrid, neural networks, rule base, decision trees, object-oriented	(Short 95)

In Table 4 we have included a list of systems that address ecosystem management at different levels. The 10 years between Noble's system and the IIFS represents a leap in technology. However, both systems serve a good purpose within their own scope. The comparison acts to emphasize that expert system technology must be suited for its use — namely, to deliver expertise in a situation or place where it is otherwise not immediately available.

6.2.   VEGETATION SUCCESSION

Dr. Ian Noble
Australian National University
Australia, 1985

This system is among the first ecological-oriented advisors reported to be in operation. It is considered a pioneer system in its field and has been field tested and deployed with some measurable success. This expert system on vegetation succession demonstrates capabilities of predicting the alternating changes in ecosystems. The system includes knowledge of the species known to exist in the communities of the various successional states of vegetation. The purpose of the system is to provide advice regarding vegetation dynamics and succession. This advice is pertinent in situations to determine the effects on a particular ecological system if it is subjected to man-controlled manipulation in some way. Such situations could be related to the management and protection of vegetation against fires. Sometimes, small bush fires are beneficial and may prevent the occurrence of a large and hot fire that can have devastating effects. It can also be applied in management of shifting cultivation in Third World countries.

The system uses predicate logic to operate its rule base. According to Jeffers (Jeffers 85), the system was successfully tested on community problems in Australia and China.

6.3.   TSDSYS: Treatment Storage and Disposal System

Hushon
ERM-Program Management Company
Virginia, 1987

Judith Hushon (Hushon 91) reports on a number of systems in a 1991 paper. All of them deal with so-called First Emergency Response systems that treat aspects of accidental releases of chemicals and waste. Some of the systems reported blend into what can be termed the "health-oriented universe." Yet, at the heart of most of these system are the issues of pollution control and environmental protection.

One of these early initiatives was the TSDSYS program. The purpose of the system was to meet the need for some kind of assistance for early responders to emergency situations. They need help to identify appropriate contractors for treating, storing, and disposal of chemicals and waste that pose a threat to the environment. This recognition process is complicated because of time constraints and the fact that the government requires three bids, thus imposing the need for multiple contacts.

The system is fed with input like the type of waste and the potential pollutant chemicals involved. The geographic location may also be important. The system will in return provide a short summary of information on each vendor that meets the search criteria. This output is sufficient for making telephone contact with the service contractor. If desired, a more extensive output can be produced. This will include elaboration on the types of chemicals confronted with and the type of process that the service company is likely to undertake. With this, there are implications for a first response on site.

The system consists of a rule-driven interface and a database. The data was gathered from in-house reports, practical experience, and service directories. TSDSYS was originally designed for the KES expert system shell for operation on a PC/AT-type machine. Its intended users were scientists and technical personnel. Due to the fact that the database required revision three times a year, it became evident that it would be too costly to do maintenance on many stand-alone versions. The application was then reprogrammed in DM and implemented on a VAX 8350. Once having established the rule concepts with KES, the transition to DM worked well. A rule-based, forward-chaining system exploits the database. The assistance teams that were supposed to use this system were equipped with Crosstalk script files to accomplish dial-up and login to the central system. The interaction was patterned after the one originally designed for the PC.

The system was deployed in 1987 and has been commercially available since then.

6.4.   SIRENAS

Murcia et al.
CIEMAT, Spain, 1993

SIRENAS is a decision support system for management of release emergencies. Its purpose is to yield interpretations of accidental situations as quickly as possible, despite lack of data (Murcia

94). The system supports the task of determining what kind of release of hazardous material accompanies a given accident. This is done by providing the system with the physical characteristics of the situation. The system simulates a contamination scenario. It applies knowledge about surface dispersion, groundwater dispersion, or atmospheric dispersion to do this. The results of a working session is a graphic output that represents the evolution of the pollution from the beginning of the accident to the moment the concentration is not yet dangerous. At the end, the system provides an overview about the effect of the toxic substances on both human health and the environment.

The knowledge base built is a synthesis of expertise from many individuals. The application was developed partly in C/C++ and the MFC-SDK programming language. NEXPERT OBJECT, the expert system development tool was applied for the knowledge engineering task. Physical data and material specifications, including their toxity, is maintained by an ORACLE RDBMS.

6.5.   CERES: California Environmental Resource Evaluation System

California Resource Agency (CRA), 1996

The purpose of CERES is to improve information services regarding California's rich and diverse environments. By combining databases and expert systems techniques and making them available on the Internet, a person can get access to a diverse set of electronic data on the natural resources of the state. The ultimate purpose of the CRA is to improve environmental analysis and planning. This is sought and achieved by integrating natural and cultural resources information from multiple contributors and made available and useful to a wide variety of users. In this sense, it matches much of the same idea as the Whale Watcher Expert System introduced previously.

The system is able to help the public with problems such as how to obtain a hunting or fishing licence. It can also respond to queries related to the status of current water supplies in the state.

CERES can be characterized as an intelligent database that is accessible through the World Wide Web. The functions of the knowledge-base part in CERES can be compared to a librarian. The main body of CERES is a library with several departments. In addition, it includes GIS capabilities. The library consists of data like satellite imagery and photography, information on environmental impacts, reports, and vegetation and wildlife data. The system contains electronic data catalogs and advanced searching capabilities.

It is defined as a cooperative system using agents to provide the type of decision support specified. It applies several multimedia features that can be handled through the use of ordinary Web browsers.

6.6.   SEA

Mason
NASA Ames Research Center, 1995

TSDSYS and SIRENAS discussed above are systems intended to preserve the environment on a local level. The impact they address will have a serious effect on the environment and the life that this environment accommodates. Yet, on a global level, a single event causing a chemical release or waste disposal will usually be confined to a fairly limited region. Hence, local monitoring is sufficient. Both TSDSYS and SIRENAS address different views on this type of environmental threat. The scope of the NASA Ames system, SEA (Seismic Event Analyzer) is much wider. It applies to a global threat that may have devastating effects on the whole earth if not controlled properly.

SEA analyses data from the NORESS experimental seismic array station in Norway (Mason 95). The principal purpose of SEA is to monitor seismic reactions registered by NORESS and transmitted via satellite to the NASA Ames Research Center. Inherent in this is the need to monitor nuclear test activity and distinguish this from earthquakes. Different states have signed nuclear weapon test ban treaties that need to be enforced. Enforcement has an immediate political motivation, but its ultimate objective is to ensure that the global environment is preserved. Neither war acts nor gradual contamination through re-armament processes must be allowed. Obedience to both comprehensive test treaties as well as so called low-yield test ban treaties are required.

Seismic monitoring is the most reliable means available to verify compliance with treaties regulating underground nuclear weapons testing. However, it is a difficult task. Treaty violations can be disguised. Nuclear tests can be designed to produce weak seismic signals. Events of this type are characterized by a low signal-to-noise ratio often hidden in background noise or discharged concurrently with other seismic occurrences. According to Mason, up to 20,000 events need to be analyzed for potential ban treaty violations. Since few experts are available for this, an automated system was required to help interpret and classify seismic events.

SEA interprets data from multiple sensors. The data transmitted is stored onto an optical disk. An event-detection program analyzes the raw data for a possible seismic event. If a seismic event is registered, the data is stored in a unique file and passed on for further examination. SEA checks the wave pattern that represents the event. Different types of events produce different types of patterns. Such signatures are characterized by a distinct frequency, phases, and the paths followed through the earth. The latter determines the velocity of the propagating wavefront and therefore also the time before detection. The distinctions caused by this phenomenon enables a seismologist to estimate the distance of an event. The direction is determined by means of signal-processing tools to calculate phase characteristics. In this way, the location of the event can be determined. In real cases the signals detected may be of poor quality and wavefronts following certain paths may be totally missing. This makes the signatures blurred and complicates interpretation. In other situations, interference between two concurrent events may obscure impressions. In order to handle the challenging task of identifying ban violations, SEA applies a technique of partial interpretations (see Figure 7). This implies building a series of intermediate conclusions, each one an extension of the one before. Finally, each part is examined for inconsistencies; parts of that kind are rejected.

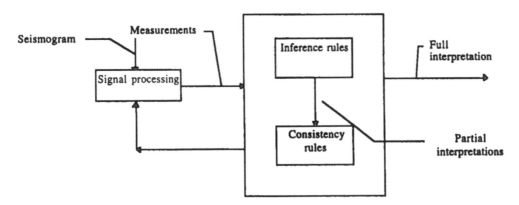

FIGURE 7   Interpretation strategy of SEA.

A belief-revision system is applied in the partial interpretation. If the belief in the validity of some step is contradicted, it is judged incorrect. The dependencies on the rejected part is kept track of so that these can also be revised. The type of truth maintenance used has been coined "multi-context truth maintenance." It is typically applied in situations where a number of solutions must be found. The use of this has been qualified by the fact that seismologists are seldom able to arrive at a single interpretation. This is due to lack of sufficient discriminating knowledge or data.

The principal knowledge representation scheme is semantic networks. The network includes concepts such as Event, Phase, Segment, etc. They are interlinked by relationships such as Number-Of-Phases, Has-Phase, Phase-Id, and Begin-Time. IF-THEN rules are used to encode the actual interpretation knowledge. The rule-inference is data driven, operating in a forward-chaining manner. The action part of a rule may call a function in C, Fortran, or LISP. The truth-maintenance element is supported by an assumption-based reasoning technique. The system tags each deduced fact with a justification indicating the rule and antecedent facts used to create it and the assumptions that supports the fact that is believed. SEA uses this both for producing explanations as well as for rule operation trace. It aids in determining the current set of beliefs and supports the required dependency-directed backtracking. The assumption-based reasoning part consists of both an assumption database and truth-maintenance rules.

SEA may operate on its own and as an interactive partner for a person. It was partially written in LISP, C, and Fortran. The interface is accommodated in the MIT X Window System. It is supported by a SUN3/160.

SEA has been field tested with fair success and development continues. In order to cope with the great amounts of data related to this kind of interpretation, a multi-agent kind of architecture is considered.

6.7.   ESS/IIFS

Short et al.
NASA/Goddard Space Flight Center, 1995

Earth System Science (ESS) is a new science promoted by the U.S. Government. In the programs Mission to Planet Earth and Global Change Research, this new science is manifested. ESS describes the earth as a dynamic system where parts interact in response to natural and other processes. The goal of ESS is to understand the earth as a holistic system. Both air, ocean, land, and living organisms constitute the focus. Central to all of this is the use of remote sensing. Like SEIDAM, I2Sadvisor and SPECTRUM presented before ESS will pursue research through object recognition using spectral characteristics. However, the scope is much wider.

NASA has involved itself in ESS. Together with its European counterpart ESA, and Japanese and Canadian interests, the agency has decided to pursue means that will enable integrated studies of the earth's geosphere, biosphere, atmosphere, and cryosphere. Observations needed for these studies will be supported using space-based platforms that will enable recordings of temperatures, ozone depletion, greenhouse effects, land vegetation, and ocean productivity. It will also focus on deserts, forests, and other types of vegetation patterns. Once this is enabled, the data recorded must be made accessible to people with different interests. The task is formidable. Within the 15-year time horizon anticipated, the information system required will produce somewhere around 11,000 terabytes of data. Some of the archive problems will be solved by new mass storage devices. However, the needed accessibility is not guaranteed by this. An Intelligent Information Fusion System (IIFS) is endeavored.

In remote sensing, spectral signatures in the electromagnetic spectrum of known objects are compared to unknown spectral identities. In this way different land forms, vegetation, atmospheric conditions, and artifacts can be recognized in a recorded spectral image. The raw data can cover several bands by means of satellite-mounted sensors. The image processing part involved applies different types of computer-based statistics and classification techniques in order to produce a suitable characterization. The classification effort is positively supported by external data in the form of ground observations, demographics, economics, industrial life, energy consumption, health situation, etc. All this data should be available in a database. GIS is needed in order to produce maps and photo interpretations. The essence of ESS is to produce predictive models about the earth. For this to be possible, the data sampling must cover the entire planet. Another aspect is the need to standardize and integrate recordings taken and produced over a wide time span. Until today, recordings produced by different satellite systems such as Landsat, NIMBUS, and GOES have not followed a common standard. The results from many different platforms and sensors must be coordinated and integrated. In addition to these, more platforms are needed. In order to achieve the holistic goals defined, the ESS initiative must be well managed and pursue the most unified approach possible. The IIFS system will be a critical factor in this. According to Short et al. (Short 95), the purpose of the system is to develop, incorporate, and evaluate state-of-the-art techniques for handling scientific data challenges related to the Earth Observing System required for ESS.

Apart from the satellite systems that produce the raw data, IIFS currently consists of:

- Mass storage
    - Many devices
    - Semantic modeling
    - Storage hierarchy
- Object database
    - Object-oriented DBMS
    - Catalog of earth and space meta-data
    - Distributed over many devices
- Planner/scheduler
    - Expected data rates
    - System and network load
    - Task constraints
- Meta-data extraction
    - Low-level signal/image processing
    - Neural networks/decision trees
    - Knowledge bases
    - High-performance computing
- Intelligent user interface
    - Graphical and English querying
    - User customization
    - Planner for analysis assistance

IIFS carries two data storing units. One is for the new data received from the satellite units. The other is an object-oriented database customized for fast retrieval of both simple and complex data such as bitmaps.

A meta-data unit is included in order to increase efficient retrieval of complex data. It contains structured key information about complex data stored. Moreover, it includes spatial data structures called "sphere quadtrees" (SQT). Data originating from particular parts of the earth's surface can be organized according to this structure. One effect is that linearization of the globe surface will be more accurate and thus reflect area projections more precisely. Most of us are familiar with the big, white blob in our school atlas called Greenland. The relative dominance of geographical objects due to 3-D projections onto 2-D maps have always been a source for concern. The SQT structures will minimize these problems.

The SQT can also be conceived as the global knowledge representation scheme in IIFS. It provides a uniform and recursive structure that is invariant to the size and location of the region represented. SQT can in turn provide a structure called the "hyper cylinder," which organizes all meta-data about satellite observations of the earth or space in the object-oriented database. Hence, a mosaic of results within a region can be efficiently built up. It will be produced by putting together several pieces of data recorded, processed, and stored independently of each other.

Apart from being able to store complex data structures such as geographic images, the object-oriented database is also more readily maintainable. When data types are known and data are available, the retrieve operation is fairly standard. If the query includes names of unknown concepts, these types can easily be incorporated. When data are not immediately available, the planner module is invoked. This implies that the data requested is not in store, but can be ordered. The planner posts the required result as a goal and tries to define a plan that will achieve this goal. The plan may involve several processing steps, as illustrated by the following:

- Identify an appropriate scene
- Identify and allocate machine resources for the given task
- Isolate the region of interest
- Compute the algorithms involved
- Place the resulting image file at an appropriate location
- Inform the object database of the status and availability of results

As a human warehouse manager, the object database will then relay the final result to the user. The planner distinguishes between different types of goals. A major distinction exists between hard goals and soft goals. When pursuing a conjunction of goals, as many as possible are attempted. However, if rewards are low, the system reduces its demand according to the status of its goals. Soft goals are first discarded.

One of the most challenging things addressed in this system is the automated characterization of image content. This is important because images can be indexed according to content rather than less specific keys such as time and geographic area. In IIFS, the substance of each image is defined and summarized. The features contained in an image are held in a characterization vector. Different sensors are assigned distinct recognition objectives. Each one will detect a finite set of objects. Image processing algorithms are specifically created for a sensor and the kind of objects that it will focus toward. All characterization algorithms use clustering techniques. Both supervised and nonsupervised classification can be undertaken. Approaches used include traditional Bayesian classifiers as well as neural networks. Backpropagation variants have been applied. These have produced the highest level of accuracy.

For more information on this extensive system and the ESS, we refer the reader to the comprehensive article by Short et al (Short 95).

REFERENCES

Alwast, T., Miliszewska, I. An Agent Based Architecture for Intelligent Decision Support Systems for Natural Resource Management, *New Review of Applied Expert Systems*, Vol. 1 1995.

Acquired Intelligence Inc.: Whale Watcher Expert System. http://vvv.com/ai/ demos/whale.html.

Baldwin, J.L., Bateman, R.M., and Wheatley, C.L.: Application of Neural Network to the Problem of Mineral Identification from Well Logs, *The Log Analyst*, Sept–Oct 1990.

Baldwin, J.L. and Malki, H.: Comparision of Neural Network Training and Processing of Two Service Company's Data in a Single Wellbore. *Artificial Intelligence in the Petroleum Industry: Symbolic and Computational Applications.* Vol. 1. (Ed. Braunschweig and Day). Éditions Technip, Paris 1995.

Baker, J.D. DIPMETER ADVISOR: An Expert Log Analysis System at Schlumberger. *The AI Business: The Commercial Uses of Artificial Intelligence.* (Ed: Winston and Prendergast). MIT press, 1984.

Barnwell, T.O., Brown, L.C., and Marek, W. Application of Expert Systems Technology in Water Quality Modeling. *14th Biennial Conference of the International Association on Water Pollution Research and Control*, Brighton, U.K., July 1988.

Barstow, D., Duffey, R., Smoliar, S., and Vestal, S.: An Overview of PHOENIX. *AAAI-82*, Pittsburgh 1982.

Bhogal, P., Goodenough, D.G., Charlebois, D., and Matwin, S. : SEIDAM for Forestry: Intelligent Fusion and Analysis of Multi-Temporal Imaging Spectrometer Data. http://www.csi.uottawa.ca/~daniel/abstract.irss-96.html.

Boddy, L. and Morris, C.W. : Harnessing Neural Networks to Environmental Research, *Expert Systems Applications*, Vol. 9 No. 10, 1994.

Bonnet, A. and Dahan, C.: Oil-Well Data Interpreation Using Expert System and Pattern Recognition Techniques. *IJCAI-83*, Karlsruhe, 1983.

Booty, W.G., Wong, I.W.S., Lam, D.C.L., Kerby, J.P, and Kay, D.F. Application of An Expert System for Point Source Water Quality Modelling. Computer Support for Environmental Assessment (Ed: Guariso and Page). *Proc. IFIP Conference on Computer Support for Environmental Impact Assessment,* Elsevier Science B.V. 1994.

Borchardt, G.C., Martin, M., Groom, S.L., Brady, R.B., and Solomon, J.E.: SPECTRUM User's Guide and Design Summary, Jet Propulsion Laboratory, California Institute of Technology, Pasadena, CA, August 1987.

Brack, L.: Knowledge-Based Approaches to Forest Operations Scheduling Problems. Ph.D. Thesis. University of British Columbia, Canada, November 1991.

Braunschweig, B. and Day, R. (Eds.): *Artificial Intelligence in the Petroleum Industry: Symbolic and Computational Applications,* Vol. 1. Édition Technip, Paris 1995.

Braunschweig, B. and Bremdal, B.A.. (Eds.): *Artificial Intelligence in the Petroleum Industry: Symbolic and Computational Applications,* Vol. 2. Édition Technip, Paris 1996.

Bremdal, B.A., Brenne, I., Sæther, B.M., and Rueslåtten, H.G.: Defining Analytic Strategies in Remote Sensing Using a Hybrid, Knowledge-Based Decision Support System. *Artificial Intelligence in the Petroleum Industry: Symbolic and Computational Applications,* Vol. 1. (Ed: Braunschweig and Day), Édition Technip, Paris 1995.

Catalina, J.G., Alarcon, D., and Prado, J.G.: Automatic Coal Maceral Analysis by Means of Expert System and Computer Vision. *Moving Toward Expert Systems Globally in the 21st Century,* Cognizant, Macmillan new Media, Cambridge, MA, 1994.

Cohen, P.R. , Greenberg, M.L., Hart D.M., and Howe, A.E.: Trial by Fire: Understanding the Design Requirement for Agents in Complex Environment. *AI Magazine,* Vol. 10, No.3, Fall 1989.

California Resource Agency: CERES: A Co-Operative Program for the Decision-Support on the Net for Resource Conservation. http://ceres.ca.gov. /help.desk/CERESHelp.html 1996.

Davis, R., Austin, H., Carlbom, I. Frawley, B. Pruchnik, P., Snederman, R., and Gilreath, J.A.: The DIPMETER ADVISOR: Interpretation of Geologic Signals. *IJCAI-81,* Vancouver 1981.

Doneker, R.L.: CORMIX Mixing Zone Model. http://www.up.edu/contrib/ doneker/cmxpg1.html.

Duda, R.O., Hart, P.E., Barrett, P., Gaschnig, J., Konolige, K., Reboh, R., and Slocum, J.: Development of the Prospector System for Mineral Exploration, Final Rep SRO Projects 5821 and 6415, SRI International, Menlo Park, CA, October 1978.

Duda, R.O. and Gaschnig, J.G.: Knowledge-Based Expert Systems Come of Age. *BYTE,* September 1981.

Durkin, J.: Expert Systems: A View of the Field. *IEEE Expert,* Vol. 11, No. 2 April 1996.

Ennis, S.P. Expert Systems: A User's Perspective of Some Current Tools. *AAAI-82,* Pittsburgh 1982.
Expert Systems: The International Journal of Knowledge Engineering. Vol. 1, No.1, 1984.

University of Georgia: A Forest Inventory Expert System. http://www.exsysinfo. com/Appnotes/forest.html.

Firschein, O.: Guest Editor's Introduction: The Image Understanding Program at ARPA, *IEEE Expert,* October 1995.

Flamm, R.O., Coulson, R.N., Jordan, J.A., Sterle, M.E., Brodale, Mayer, R.J., Oliveria, F.L., Drummond, D., Barry, P.J., and Swain, K.M.: The Integrated Southern Pine Beetle Expert System: ISPBEX. *Expert Systems with Aplications,* Vol. 2, pp. 97–105, 1991.

Foster, M.A., Saunders, M.C., Mierzejewski, K., and Twardus, D.: Gypsex: A Knowledge-Based System for Aerial Application of Pesticides against Gypsy Moth. *Expersys* (Ed: J. Liebowitz), IIIT, Paris 1989.

Foster, M.A., Zhao, R., and Robillard, P.D.: RCWP Expert: A Knowledge and GIS Based Software System for Site Specific Recommendation of Water Quality Control Practices. *Water Quality Evaluation Project Notes,* 66: 2–5. Penn State University 1994.

Gaschnig, J.G.: Prospector: An Expert System for Mineral Exploration. Technical Paper. AI Center, SRI International, Menlo Park, CA 1981.

Goldberg, D.E.: *Genetic Algorithms in Search, Optimization, and MachineLearning.* Addison-Wesley, Reading, MA 1989.

Hawkins, D.: An analysis of expert thinking. *International Journal of Man-Machine Studies,* No. 18, 1983.

Hushon, J.M.: Expert Systems to Assist First Responders to Chemical Emergencies. *Expert System with Applications,* Vol. 2, 1991.

Jeffers, J.N.R.: Ecological Advice Through Expert Systems, *First International Expert Systems Conference,* London, October 1–3, 1985

Kahn, G. and McDermott, J.: The MUD system. *Proc. First Conference on Artificial Intelligence Applications,* IEEE/AAI, Denver 1984.

Kendall C., Cannon, R.L., Biswas, G., and Bezdek, J.C.: XX Expert Explorer: A Workstation Toolbox for the Explorationist. Proposal for funding, Department of Geology, University of South Carolina, 1988.

Kendon, G., Walker, D.H., Robertson, D., Haggith, M., Sinclair, F.L., and Muetzelfeldt, R.I.: Supporting Customised Reasoning in the Agroforestry Domain. *New Review of Applied Expert Systems,* Vol. 1, 1995.

Kohonen, T.: The Neural Phonetic Typewriter. *Computer,* Vol. 21, No. 3.

Lam, D.C.L., Mayfield, C.I., Swayne, D.A., and Hopkins, K.: A Prototype Information System for Watershed Management and Planning. *Journal of Biological Systems,* Vol. 4, No. 2.

Lesser, V.R. and Erman, L.D.: A Retrospective View of the Hearsay II Architecture. *IJCAI-77,* Cambridge MA, 1977.

Li, L., Beck, H., and Peart, R.M.: A Knowledge-Based Information Retrieval System for Florida Aquatic Weed Control. AI Applications in Natural Resource Management, *AI Applications,* Vol. 4, No. 2, Moscow, Idaho 1990.

Malafeyev, O.A., Merkurijev, S. P., and Popov, V.V.: An Expert System for the Problem of Environment Pollution. *Moving Toward Expert Systems Globally in the 21st Century,* Cognizant, Macmillan new Media, Cambridge, MA, 1994.

Mason, C.L. An Intelligent Assistant for Nuclear Test Ban Treaty Verification. *IEEE Expert,* December 1995.

Matwin, S., Charlebois, D., Goodenough, D.G., and Bhogal, P.: Machine Learning and Planning for Data Management in Forestry. *IEEE Expert,* December 1995

McClelland, J.L. and Rumelhart, D.: *Explorations in Parallell Distributed Processing: A Handbook of Models, Programs and Exercises.* The MIT Press, Cambridge, MA 1988.

McKinney, D., Burgin, J., and Maidment, D.: Developing an Expert Geographic Information System for Water Supply Planning. http://twri.tamu.edu/~twri/ twripubs/NewWaves/v9n1/abstract-3.html.

Mikkelsen, J.O., Bremdal, B., and Hirdes, D.: A Computerised Environment for the Automation of Form-Based Procedures, *Expert Systems with Applications,* Vol. 5, 1992.

Mikkelsen, J.O., Stabell, C.B., and Sinding-Larsen, R.: Knowledge-Based Advice & Critique Support for Play and Prospect Evaluation. *Artificial Intelligence in the Petroleum Industry: Symbolic and Computational Applications,* Vol. 2. (Ed: Braunshweig and Bremdal), Édition Technip, Paris 1996.

Morgan, P., Bezdek, J.C., Biswas, G., and Kendall C.: MAGIK: A Knowledge Assistance Tool for Hydrocarbon Exploration. Technical Note. Departments of Geology and Computer Science, University of South Carolina, May 1987.

Murcia, C.G., de Lara, P.A., Garcia, E.S. Ferreras, A.B. Luque, A. R., and Giralda, C.G.: Decision Support System for Industrial Accidents on Environment: 'SIRENAS'. *Moving Toward Expert Systems Globally in the 21st Century,* Cognizant, MacMillan New Media, Cambridge, MA 1994.

Penn State University: STEWARD Support Technology for Environmental, Water, and Agricultural Resource Decisions. http://rcwpsun.cas.psu.edu/stewaes/index.html.

Reboh, R.: The Knowledge Acqusition System. Report on Project 6415, SRI International, Menlo Park, CA, October 1978.

Rhykerd, L.M., Engel, B.A., Urban, C., and Dalessandro, J.: A Knowledge-Base for the Detection of Lead Contamination in Drinking Water. *4th International Conference on Computers in Agricultural Extension Programs.* American Society of Agricultural Engineers. Orlando, FL 1992.

Schuette, J.F. and Pevear, D.R.: Matcmod: A Genetic Algorithm to Intepret X-Ray Diffraction Patterns. *Artificial Intelligence in the Petroleum Industry: Symbolic and Computational Applications,* Vol. 1. (Ed: Braunschweig and Day), Édition Technip, Paris 1995.

Short, N.M., Cromp, R.F., Campbell, W.J., Tilton, J.C., LeMoigne, J.J., Fekete, G., Netanyahu, N.S., Wickmann, K., and Ligon, W.B.: Mission to Planet Earth: AI Views the World. *IEEE Expert,* December 1995.

Shortliffe, E.H.: *Computer-Based Medical Consultations: MYCIN.* American-Elsevier Publications, New York 1976.

Sines, L.J., Shostak, M., and Zoraster, S.: Contouring Assistant Research Project to Released Success. *Artificial Intelligence in the Petroleum Industry: Symbolic and Computational Applications,* Vol. 2. (Ed: Braunschweig and Bremdal), Édition Technip, Paris 1996.

SPECTRUM 2000 Mindware: SPECTRUM's Users Guide and Design Summary. SPECTRUM 2000 Mindware, Denver, CO, 1987.

Stabell, C.B.: Decision project planning. GeoKnowledge Technical Note: 4/90, Sandvika, Norway 1990.

Stoker, C.R., Barch, D.R., Hine, B.P., and Barry, J.: Antarctic Undersea Exploration Using a Robotic Submarine with a Telepresence User Interface. IEEE Expert, December 1995.

Sturrock, C.P. and Mashayekhi, B.: The impact on environment due to hazards: Expert Systems for the Handling and Storage of Hazardous Chemicals, *Moving Toward Expert Systems Globally in the 21st Century*, Cognizant, MacMillan New Media, Cambridge, MA 1994.

Warkentin, M.E., Ruth, S., and Sprague, K.: A Knowledge-Based Expert System for Planning and Design of Agroforestry Systems. http://www.exsysinfo.com/Appnotes/ agroforestry.html.

Winston, P.H. and Horn, B.K.P.: *LISP*, Addison-Wesley, Readings, MA 1981.

Wong, I.W.S and Lam, D.C.L.: A Neural Network Approach to Predict Missing Environmental Data. NWRI Contribution 93-153.

Part III
Medical and Other Important
Expert Systems Applications

31 Diagnosis

Juan Pazos

CONTENTS

1. DIAGNOSTICS

Experts in a domain execute generic tasks that define how competent they are in their specialty. These tasks are cataloged either hierarchically, as shown in Figure 1 (Schreiber, 1993) or in a table (Maté, 1989; Liebowitz, 1989; Hayes-Roth, 1983).

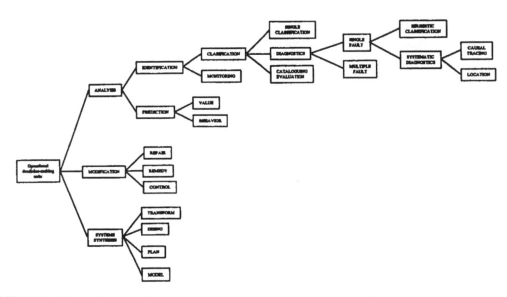

FIGURE 1 Hierarchical classification of known problems in knowledge engineering

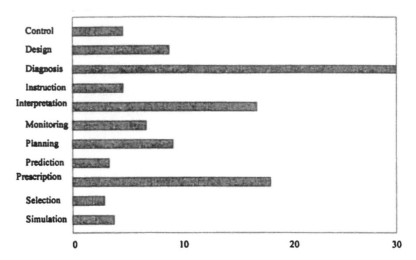

FIGURE 2   Percent application of expert systems by problem type.

An examination of these tasks provides an understanding of what makes expert problem-solving behavior difficult. Of these generic tasks, which identify a host of technical solutions to particular problems, the most universally applied is, as shown in Figure 2, unquestionably what is referred to as "diagnosis."

As if the mere extension of the diagnostic task were not enough to underline its importance, consider the possible consequences of not knowing the exact and precise cause of a malfunction in a nuclear power plant. The resulting disasters, Chernobyl is a paradigmatic example of this, are costly in terms of material (cost of the plant, patient treatment, etc.), human (immediate and later deaths from radioactivity), and ecological (destruction of the environment) losses. The above can be extended to domains as far apart as the explosion of Challenger in 1986, when Judith Resnik, the first American woman to go into space, died, together with her fellow astronauts, and its financial cost; or faults in aviation systems, causing planes to crash with a dismal sequel of deaths, etc.

Therefore, whatever the system, it is vitally important to be able to accurately determine the faulty subsystem or component. There are two main reasons for this. First, to take precautions against and, as far as possible, prevent disasters and accidents actually occurring. Second, today's systems are becoming more and more sophisticated and, taking into account the potentially devastating consequences of a system fault, correct and meticulous maintenance is a vital and extremely difficult exercise, making diagnosis a demanding task, relying heavily on expertise, as a large amount of knowledge has to be assimilated and rapidly and expediently accessed.

Although this maintenance and control work is carried out by expert operators, this is often insufficient, as human capabilities are overwhelmed by the requirements of these systems. Their operation usually requires enormous computing power and real-time performance, such as short response time and continual adaptation to changes in system variables.

We can conclude that human beings are incapable of efficiently controlling systems, such as those described above. Fortunately, human beings' limitations in the field of industrial and natural diagnosis can be overcome by developing computer technology. Computers can react faster than human beings, filter the information received, and show only the most important information or the information most relevant in a given situation. It is in these circumstances that a knowledge-based system, and particularly an expert system (ES), can be of great use, because it has the capability of rapidly and efficiently processing huge amounts of knowledge. Therefore, there is a tendency today to perform diagnostics with the aid of computer systems that enable the operator to perform his/her work safely, comfortably, rapidly, and reliably. Expert systems began to be used in diagnostics because human beings were found to be poor diagnosticians. The reasons (Krishna,

1991) for this are operator inexperience in complex environments; the stress to which the operator is subject because of the need to make quick decisions about systems, when a slow or mistaken action could lead to irreparable damage; slowness of reaction, which usually occurs precisely in events that require utmost expediency; information overload (human beings are only capable of assimilating a limited amount of input information and they can be clearly overwhelmed by the enormous amount of data produced by the system under control); limited processing capability (our calculation capability is insufficient to perform all the calculations required), and fatigue (human beings naturally get tired and bored, which leads to errors).

Though there are as many definitions of diagnosis as there are authors who address the question, all have a common denominator. Diagnosis, from the Greek δια, through, and γνωσιζ, knowledge, means the analysis of system malfunction from noisy information or observable or non-observable facts related to both its behavior or function and its structure. The information may be quantitative, and therefore objectifiable and measurable, what are referred to as signs, or qualitative, "detectable" or subjective, called symptoms. Faults may sometimes be masked by signs and/or symptoms of other faults or they may be intermittent, in which case a system has to be forced to reveal faults. The diagnostic equipment itself may even fail. This category of problems includes electronic, financial, industrial, medical, social, software diagnostics, etc.

2.   DIAGNOSTIC TECHNIQUES AND METHODS

It is advisable and, sometimes, essential to have a sound understanding of system organization, that is, its structure and the relations and interactions between subsystems and/or components, to make a correct diagnosis. Structure can be used in a top-down approach to determine function. For example, given a structural description of a cistern, physical principles can be used to simulate its behavior and infer its function, which requires descriptions of its components. Taking a bottom-up approach, the required function may suggest what structures could be used. For example, if we know that the ball of the cistern must float in water, we can conceive of replacing this structure with any other that behaves in the same way. Basically, understanding a mechanism requires an insight into how its structure implements its function. However, often, as is the case in anatomy or the structure of animal systems, this is not fully understood and several partial models have to be combined, which may give rise to inconsistencies.

As shown in Table 1, there are a series of techniques and method for conducting automated diagnostics. Each one has its advantages and drawbacks, but they all have one common characteristic: their limitation. Indeed, each individual technique resolves at best only one aspect of the diagnostic problem. So, they need to be integrated individually or collectively into a knowledge-based system for synergetic use.

3.   DIAGNOSTICS CONCEPTUALIZATION

As pointed out by Pepper (1990), "All human diagnosticians, whether they work in automotive repair or medicine, have certain characteristics in common. Both groups have an internal mental model of the task domain. This model is a body of knowledge about the parts of the mechanism or organism they are trying to fix and about how those parts fit together. This model is closely tied to two additional knowledge sources: the expert's formal understanding of the laws of the domain (such as electrical theory) and a large loosely structured body of knowledge consisting of common sense and experience gained simply by living in the world. Taken together, these three knowledge sources are very powerful and enable human beings to solve new problems by reasoning them through..."

So, regardless of the type of diagnostics performed, industrial or medical and so on, the same method can be used to conceptualize the diagnostician's internal mental model. Therefore, this

TABLE 1
Individual Techniques Most Commonly Used in Automated Diagnostics

Name	Approach	Knowledge used	Description
Fault dictionary (Hudlická, 1988)	None	Shallow	A fault dictionary is a collection of pairs (data, fault). If there are multiple potential causes for a datum (sign or symptom), a probability factor is associated with each possible cause. To use this technique, systems must be stable, with known fault modes, of unknown structure and with few data or faults.
Hierarchical Classification (Maté, 1988)	Structural/functional	Shallow	Association of the data output about the problem with a set of dysfunctions, organized hierarchically. The hierarchy reflects relations, considering the system as a combination of subsystems, subsubsystems, etc., or considering functions and subfunctions, etc.
Fault trees (Roberts, 1981)	Functional	Deep, based on first principles	Logical tree representing system fault modes and the logical relations between basic events that lead to a fault or the tree root, which generally represents a disastrous system fault. It is a qualitative model that creates a dual "success-failure space" that is evaluated quantitatively.
AQ11 (Michalski, 1980)	Functional	Shallow	Example-based rule learning schema.
Neural nets (Ríos, 1991)	Functional	Shallow	Training set-based fault learning method.

section first gives a declarative description of what conceptualization is and then how it is performed, showing the different stages, steps, and actions to be completed.

3.1. WHAT IS CONCEPTUALIZATION?

The importance of conceptualization in any problem-solving activity and particularly in diagnostics is never stressed enough. Indeed, an intelligent being's understanding of reality is determined by two systems, whose interaction is obvious and so requires no further explanation. The first is the sensory system and its amplifications, equipped with systems to collect, directly or indirectly, information from the environment. The second is the conceptual system, which extracts from all the above information the relevant concepts for solving the problem at hand, their internal relations, and necessary or sufficient reasoning to arrive at the right conclusions. So, conceptualization is modeling by the diagnostician. This means that there are many ways of conceptualizing and the items (concepts, relations, and functions) in the different conceptualizations are not necessarily related. For example, if we were to calculate the height of a building using a barometer, the problem could be conceptualized in many different ways, ranging from calculating the pressure on the ground floor and on the roof, through measuring it in barometric units, to dropping the barometer from the roof and measuring how long it takes the noise it makes when it hits the ground to reach the roof, etc., and they are all valid. Alternatively, a particular conceptualization of a problem may make it impossible to express given types of knowledge and, therefore, solve the problems thus conceptualized. This is precisely the case when light is conceptualized as waves to express reflection and as particles to describe refraction. Again, a conceptualization may not prevent given types of knowledge from being expressed, but it may make it more difficult, as is the case of the geocentric conceptualization of solar movement. This ontological *promiscuity*, making several conceptualizations apt for one and the same problem, means that being human inventions, only the alternative most useful for the purpose at hand is retained. That is, a conceptualization apt for diagnostics must both model the behavior of the diagnostician and meet previously established levels of performance and success.

Conceptualization in computer science generally and in knowledge engineering particularly is located in the problem domain tempered by the demands of the software design process. In this sense, apart from modeling diagnostician behavior, conceptualization provides an orientation on how the software should meet a need and is, therefore, a specification of what an ES is to do. So, conceptualization determines system validity; that is, whether the product is correct and meets user needs. It represents the diagnostician's view of the problem, and is, as a result, declarative or explanatory.

3.2. COMPONENTS OF CONCEPTUALIZATION

More formally, a conceptualization is composed of a threesome: concepts, relations, and functions.

The notion of *concept* is used in a fairly broad sense. It refers to both concrete (objects, persons, etc.) and abstract things (number 2, set of all integers), elemental concepts (electron) or compounds (atoms), and fictitious (unicorn) or real (detective) entities. In short, a concept is anything about which something is to be said and could, therefore, also be the description of a task, function, action, strategy, reasoning process, etc. When concepts are determined, there is little or no concern for classifications, relations, or details. An expert usually works with approximately 12 concepts. So, if more appear during conceptualization, their number has to be constrained to the above value. Two fairly well-known powerful techniques — generalization and abstraction — are used to reduce the number of concepts. Formally, generalization is the move from considering a concept to considering a set containing that concept, or the move from considering a small to a more comprehensive set of concepts containing the smaller one. And abstraction consists, at least theoretically, of removing irrelevant items, as discussed by Lwoff (Lwoff, 1975) and retaining only what is necessary.

A relation is a type of interaction between concepts in a universe of discourse. In a conceptualization of part of the world, some relations are stressed and others are ignored. The set of relations in a conceptualization are called the basic relational set.

A description and example of the most important relations used in knowledge engineering (KE) is given in Table 2. Obviously, not all of these relations have to be used for a particular problem, and there is always the possibility of other relations not contemplated in the table appearing.

Relations or links have the three properties discussed below.

1. **Valence,** which describes the quantitative manner in which the elements participate in the relation: one-to-one, many-to-one, etc.
   a. One-One, represented by: $A — B$
   b. Many-one, represented by: $A \vdash B$
   c. Injection, represented by: $A \succ\!\!— B$
   d. Surjection, represented by: $A \rightarrow B$
   e. O-implies, represented by: $A \overset{>}{\hookrightarrow} B$; that is, many-one and injective
   f. 1-implies, represented by: $A \rightarrow B$; that is, many-one and surjective
   g. Equivalence, represented by: $A \Leftrightarrow B$; that is, one-one and surjective
   h. Many-many, represented by: $A \dashv\!\!\vdash B$; without constraints
2. **Functionality,** which indicates how a relation is implemented: injective or monomorphic and surjective or epimorphic.
3. **Cardinality** or "arity," which determines the number of arguments participating in the relation: unary, when composed of a single argument; binary, when the number of

TABLE 2
Most Common Relations in ES

Relation type	Description	Example
Equivalence	Establishes the equality or equivalence between two apparently different expressions	Profit = Income − Expenses
Taxonomic	Classifies a specific concept as part of a general concept	A is B A can be classified as B, C, or D
Structural	Describes how a concept or a system of concepts can be decomposed into parts or subsystems	A is part of B A is composed of B and C A forms part of B A is disjunct of B A is not disjunct of B A are mutually B disjunct A and B are exhaustive partitions of C A and B are partitions of C
Dependence	Special type of relation ranging from an association, through responsibilities, parenthood, property, etc., to participation	A is part of B A and B are associated to build B A is responsible for B
Topological	Describes the spatial distribution of physical concepts and interconnections between these concepts	A is to the right of B A is above B A is below B A is inside B A contains B A intersects B A is connected to B A is in contact with B
Causal	Describes how given states or actions induce other states or actions	A is the cause of B A needs B A fires B
Functional	Describes the conditions for actions and reactions to take place and possible consequences of the actions	A enables B A needs B A fires B
Chronological	Describes the time sequence in which events occur	A occurs before B A occurs after B A and B occur simultaneously A occurs during B A starts before B ends
Similarity	Establishes which concepts are equal or analogous and to what extent	Valve A is open = admits petrol
Conditional	Defines the conditions in which given things take place	For highly accelerated small masses moving at low speed, use quantum hypotheses
Purpose	Establishes the whys and wherefores of concepts	Codes were created by human beings to transmit ideas

arguments is two; ternary, if composed of three, and so on, up to n-ary, when referring to n arguments.

Finally, there are *functions*. These are special cases of relations whose *prima facie* result is only a value, which, owing to their importance and specificity, should be considered separately. Examples of functions are:

Mother-of: Person → Woman
Squared: Number → Positive-Number
Car_Price: Model × Year × No. kilometers → Price

A function is, therefore, a second type of interrelation between concepts in a universe of discourse. Although many functions can be defined for a given set of concepts, usually, some functions are stressed and others ignored in order conceptualize part of the world. The set of stressed functions in a conceptualization is called a basic functional set.

By defining the concepts, relations, and functions, the conceptual model also shows the sequence of steps according to which the expert will execute his/her task, the inferences made, and the processing of data, news, and knowledge, that is, information, used. That is, this model represents how the expert, in this case the diagnostician, behaves when resolving the tasks at hand, describing what expert knowledge and where, how, when, why, and for what purpose it comes into play in performing the task.

Conceptualization presupposes the existence of information obtained by means of what is referred to in KE as knowledge acquisition (KA). These can be acquired from documents and recordings containing explicit information, a process known as knowledge extraction, or from the expert(s), a process called knowledge elicitation. Elicited knowledge is not explicit; it is what the expert has internalized and what makes up the expert's true expertise. Document analysis, classification, etc., are techniques used for extraction, whereas other techniques, including protocol analysis, repertory grid, etc., are used for elicitation.

When the knowledge has been acquired, it has to be analyzed, organized, classified, and, finally, structured to model diagnostician behavior. This consists of a two-stage process, as shown in Figure 3.

The first stage consists of an activity of analysis, whereas the second centers on synthesis. This section discusses how to detect strategic, tactical, and factual knowledge and meta-knowledge during the analysis stage and how, in the synthesis stage, the above knowledge will have a bigger or smaller part in the static and dynamic models integrated into the knowledge map and constituting the conceptual model of the system.

Pursuant to the above, the steps to be taken to produce an external conceptualization or representation of the knowledge, taking into account the items shown in Figure 3, are as follows:

- Analyze the acquired knowledge to identify strategic, tactical, and factual knowledge and meta-knowledge;
- Identify concepts and record their attributes and associated values in a **concept dictionary**; that is, build a static model. This is an extremely important, but difficult task, because, as Plato said, anyone capable of making good definitions and classifications should be considered a god.
- Establish the **dynamic process and control model**.
- Design the **knowledge map**.
- **Structure and model knowledge**, examining segmentation.
- Produce the **conceptual model** on the basis of all the above components. That is, the conceptual model is the structured integration of the static and dynamic models and the knowledge map of each problem segment, provided it can be segmented and decomposed.

3.3. IDENTIFICATION OF STRATEGIC, TACTICAL, AND FACTUAL KNOWLEDGE

As several authors, and Scott et al. (Scott et al., 1991) with whom we largely agree, rightly pointed out, the first thing to look for is strategic knowledge and meta-knowledge to produce a clear definition of the modular steps making up the expert's task. Modularity is important because it enables each module to be addressed separately, there being no collateral effects nor interrelations between each module, as they are disjunct. Second, it also defines the control flow that will take

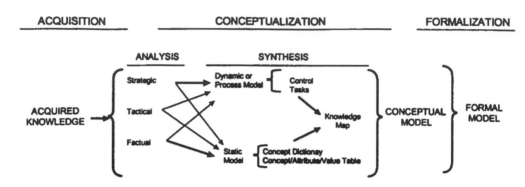

FIGURE 3   Analysis and synthesis for conceptualization.

place within the ES. This knowledge can then be synthesized, restructuring, where necessary, the different parts, modules, or subtasks making up the system.

So, it is important first of all to identify and establish a very detailed sequence of actions executed by the expert and to be executed by the ES. We can start by revising the low-level actions performed by the expert and try to describe them very generally. This description should include actions considered significant by the expert. Each action should be a functional unit that can be implemented and verified separately, hence the name of modular step. The actions in this description correspond with the high-level steps to be executed by the ES.

These steps have to be numbered and then organized, using one or more external or intermediate representation(s): organizational chart, heterarchical graphs, hierarchical trees, etc., illustrating the manner in which the ES should execute the above steps. If the current system development cycle does not cover the whole task, it is important to ensure that the representation also includes the omitted subtasks. That is, the following actions will be performed:

- Describe what the expert does and the ES should do in the step.
- Identify the substeps corresponding to the actions in the description.
- Number the substeps.
- Use an external representation to illustrate the manner in which the expert executes and the ES is to execute the substeps.

The above high-level steps then have to be decomposed recursively into as many substeps as necessary. This involves studying what the expert did and what the ES is to do until we fully understand the step. Then any step composed of more than a small number of input actions, reasoning modes, and output actions has to be subdivided. The preceding process has to be repeated to subdivide a step.

Then, each of those substeps are revised to see whether any or all can be further decomposed. If they can be decomposed, the process has to be repeated as many times as necessary. If a lot of substep decomposition levels are defined, we will need to draw a functional decomposition tree, if the structure is hierarchical, or a diagram or net, if it is heterarchical, to illustrate how the task executed by the expert and to be executed by the ES can be decomposed into smaller steps. The tree or net starts with the node corresponding to the complete expert/ES task.

Early ES sought to assist physicians in diagnosing and curing certain diseases. Therefore, an example from the medical field has been chosen to illustrate this part of conceptualization: diagnosis of malaria. In this case, the first thing the expert does is to study the patient's clinical record, then he/she tries to diagnose the disease and, finally, tries to cure the patient. So, as regards the definition of high-level steps, the expert's work is composed of four major steps: anamnesis, studies of signs and symptoms, diagnosis and treatment, which are then decomposed into the following substeps.

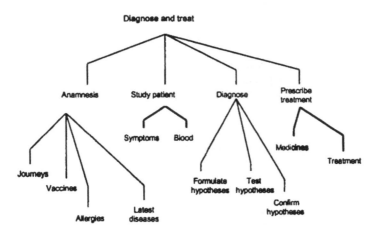

FIGURE 4 Functional decomposition tree.

1. Patient anamnesis; that is, consider latest trips, vaccines, allergies, diseases
2. Study the patient considering his/her case history; that is, establish the symptoms (appearance, pain, etc.), take a sample of blood and do a test
3. Diagnosis; that is, formulate, test and confirm hypotheses
4. Prescribe treatment; that is, select the medicines to cure the disease or relieve the symptoms, infer the treatment considering allergies and age (for dosage)

Figure 4 shows the functional decomposition tree for the diagnosis and treatment task.

Having identified the high-level steps and their decomposition into substeps, these have to be studied in depth to ensure that they are error free, that is, that the decomposition is consistent: nothing is missing (i.e., it is complete) and nothing is over (i.e., it is efficient).

Finally, the input sequence, the inference and/or reasoning mode, and the output sequences to be performed by the ES within each low-level substep have to be ascertained. That is, after having divided the task into modular steps, the steps contained in the leaves of the functional breakdown tree or net nodes have to be defined: the lowest level steps still not subdivided. The step definition should specify:

- The purpose of the step.
- The conditions in which the expert executes the step; in other words, state the information that must be available for use before the step is taken. Here, it is important to consider, for instance, whether another step has to have been executed beforehand or whether a given attribute must have a given value for the step at hand to be started. In the malaria example, a blood sample is only taken if it is likely to be necessary, specifying whether a full analysis is required or it is sufficient to measure the amount of particular chemical or biological components.
- The input actions and data and sequence, reasoning mode, and output actions to be executed in the step. Here, we have to describe how to start the step, whether information should be requested from the user and/or an attribute value located in the user file, etc., and the input source must also be identified.

Then, we have to describe the reasoning carried out in this step. This basically involves defining inferences made about or involving the step. If a particular attribute is to be inferred, the inference made and the inferred attribute must be defined for later consideration.

Finally, we have to establish what to do with the outputs obtained in each step. In this respect, the outputs may be merely informative or form part of another, higher level step, etc. In this case, it is important to check that their location and use is correct. For example, after having studied all the child nodes of a parent node in a functional decomposition tree, check that the necessary information, for instance, the child node information, will be available for use at the start of the parent step. This involves the following activities for each low-level substep:

- For each input action, determine its source. The most common are: users, experts, databases, operation results, and documents.
- For each output action, its use and destination, that is, specify whether it is part of a higher level step or whether it is terminal. In this case, its most common destinations are: printer, screen, memory, etc.
- Write the procedural step definition document. This document summarizes the above points, stating all the characteristics of each step from the lowest to the highest level.

Finally, we need to check that the collection of lowest level steps captures each expert action. Otherwise, the omitted steps have to be added.

It is important to think up a standard format for the ES step definitions. This should include additional information that will be useful in future activities: design, implementation, and checking. For example, leave a space in the definition for the names of the corresponding knowledge base inputs, for references to other sources of information, and for implementation and checking.

An example will clarify what was discussed above. Let us go back to the malaria case and consider the step: Treatment, a low level step appearing on the far right of the functional decomposition tree shown in Figure 4, whose purpose is to cure the patient, while inconveniencing him/her as little as possible. So, the first thing we need is the diagnosis of the disease. Then, we establish first the inputs, composed of (a) a list of medicines to treat the illness (output in a previous substep and retrieved from a database) and (b) patient allergies (specified by the user), and then the reasoning: (a) if the patient is not allergic to any of the proposed medicines, then the treatment will be composed of the proposed medicines (this involves tactical and strategic knowledge); (b) if the patient is allergic to one of the medicines, then infer the proposed medicines attribute (to search for other equivalent drugs), and finally, the output, that is, the treatment, the medicines to be taken by the patient (output on screen and to memory) to be able to use the determine_daily_amount attribute in the next step.

When these tasks have been identified, specifying whether external routines or database have to be accessed, whether the task is executed once or several times, and describing the inputs needed to achieve the goals, it is now possible to start the document containing strategic knowledge.

Having identified and structured the strategic knowledge, the acquired knowledge is analyzed to determine **tactical knowledge**, which basically consists of inferences and reasoning modes, and associated uncertainties concerning their implementation. The expert's tactical knowledge specifies how the ES can routinely use known facts and current hypotheses on the case to get new facts and hypotheses in both deterministic situations and conditions of uncertainty. So, the knowledge has to be analyzed within the context of the task to be executed by the system, and we need to understand how the ES will use this knowledge. This analysis should produce detailed definitions of each reasoning step to be executed by the ES. An inference step may indicate that the ES should infer a specific attribute or should use a specific attribute to infer new information. Then, we have to define the individual reasoning steps that should summarize the overall structure of the ES inferences that will be considered later. These steps are as follows: Obtaining conclusions, reactions to new information, description of inference structure, and checking.

1. **Obtaining conclusions**. At this point, we have to examine each reasoning step detected when identifying the expert strategic knowledge. If a reasoning step specifies that the system should infer a particular attribute, we need to define how the ES can infer this attribute in all the possible circumstances. So we need to (a), identify the attributes on which this type of inferences may be based; (b) examine whether the inferences of this type have a standard structure (are all these inferences based on the same attributes?); and (c) select an intermediate representation that illustrates how the expert makes and how the ES should make this type of inference.

2. **Reaction to new information**. Some ES have to react immediately, in real time, to the input data they receive or the conclusions reached. In these systems, some reasoning steps will specify that the system should infer the consequences of a new data item or recent conclusion. This knowledge is essential in industrial systems and very important in biological systems. For example, an ES that monitors sensors and is part of a diagnostic and repair/treatment system in a processing plant or in an intensive care unit will not infer a standard set of attributes each time it reads the data from the sensors; it will compare the sensor data with normal measures to detect unusual conditions. When an abnormal condition is detected, it will infer the plant attributes resulting from the abnormal condition, as shown in Figure 5, which represents an organizational chart for high-level control of a simple monitoring application. Note that step 3 is a reasoning step specifying an important basic attribute, but not a specific end attribute. Depending on the condition identified, the system may infer different end attributes. In a reasoning step, such as step 3 in Figure 5, information appears about some basic attributes that fire the inference process. This attribute is referred to as the **firing attribute**. When analyzing a reasoning step that specifies a firing attribute, it is important to describe how the system should infer the effects of this firing attribute in all possible circumstances. So, we have to (a) identify all the end attributes that can be inferred from the firing attribute; (b) examine which other basic attributes are required in conjunction with the firing attribute; (c) determine whether inferences used by the firing attribute have a standard structure; and (d) select the intermediate representations that illustrate how the ES should infer the effects of the firing attribute.

The intermediate representations described above are just as relevant for tactical knowledge fired when the ES receives information. However, instead of grouping the inferences by the end attribute, they should be grouped by the firing attribute. So, decision tables should be used if the firing attribute is used along with a small number of additional basic attributes to conclude a fixed set of end attributes. Pseudorules are preferable if the system is to make very different types of inferences in different circumstances. It is better to use a decision tree if given characteristics have to be considered in a specified order. Formula definitions should be employed to describe calculations if the attribute is used to calculate other attributes. Finally, a step definition should be created if a procedure to be followed by the ES to infer consequences from the firing attribute needs to be described.

3. **Inference structure description**. If the ES gets several intermediate levels of output conclusions, an **inference net** may be of assistance in understanding the interdependencies between the attributes of a case. An inference net is a directed graph that shows the overall structure of the inferences within an ES. The net illustrates how the different attributes are inferred and used during the system inference process. Each node in the graph represents an attribute, each arc connecting attributes indicates that the first attribute can be used as a basis for inferring the second. If the ES reasons about a large number of attributes, several inference nets may be needed to illustrate the total system inference structure.

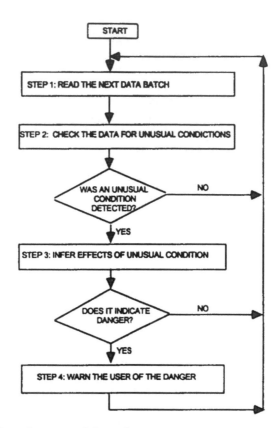

FIGURE 5   Diagram of reaction to new information.

As an inference net provides a perspective of the interdependencies in a conceptual model, this representation is a particularly useful tool during ES extension and refinement. When the definition of an attribute needs to be modified, the inference net shows what other attributes may be affected by the modification.

The analysis of acquired knowledge is concluded by determining **factual knowledge**. This knowledge contains information known *a priori* by the ES about the application area, and information that the system will gain about a specific case by executing the task. Here, first the information collected about each general attribute has to be organized within the written definition of the attribute; then the application-relevant attributes have to be classified and the facts about the application area, relating case-independent concepts, processes, or conceptual entities have to be organized. Finally, the interrelations between the concepts, processes, and other conceptual entities identified have to be defined. All these steps are discussed in further detail below.

1. **Creation of case attribute definitions.** General attributes are used by the ES as input data, conclusions, or output results. Once the information about an attribute has been collected, it has to be organized in a written definition. Table 3 describes the contents to be included in an attribute definition.

It is very important to develop a standard format for attribute definitions that shows what information has been obtained and what further information has to be obtained in future knowledge acquisition sessions. As shown in Table 3, different details about different attributes are required. For example, one definition of an input information may contain a question for the user, whereas the definition of another input information may contain a database query. There is sometimes a

TABLE 3
Attribute Definition Content

Information	Description
Name	The standard term naming the attribute.
Description	Brief explanation of a case particular represented by the attribute.
Value type	The value class, which may be a specific example of the attribute: numerical, logical, etc.
	The units for numerical values, e.g., centimeters, seconds, volts, red blood cells, etc.
	Numerical value accuracy, i.e., 4 decimals.
Value range	A list of possible descriptive values.
	A range of numerical values.
	A description of the syntax or admissible structure of a value.
Number of values per case	The number of values for the attribute: one or many.
Source	The method by which the case attribute is to be located, i.e., the sources from which an attribute value is to be obtained, the order in which each source is to be consulted, and the circumstances in which it should be consulted.
	The action to be taken by the system if it is unable to determine the case attribute, e.g., if unavailable, continue without information or end with an informative message.
Details on how to obtain information	For user inputs, the information-related text and diagrams to be displayed.
	For inputs from other sources, include details on the source and data format.
	For input data, a description of how to check input data validity, if necessary.
	For inferred attributes, cross-references for descriptions of relevant tactical knowledge.
	Default values, where applicable
Input data accounting	If the input is not always reliable, a description has to be given of how the system can deal with "unreliability."
Use	Notes that describe how the ES will use the attribute, what are the bases for inference to control the sequence of actions to be executed by the system, etc.
	Cross-references to other inputs in the design document that describe attribute use.
Output results format	If the output is shown to a user, the format of the text and diagrams to be used to report the attribute to the user.
	If the output is to be transmitted to a file or device, details on the destination and output format for numerical attributes, accuracy, and format with which the values are to be printed.
Support material	References to knowledge acquisition documents and sessions that supply information about the attribute.

tendency to pass over information that does not fit the standard format given in the table. This has to be avoided as far as possible. The definition of an attribute should include all the information obtained about the attribute. If details are found that do not fit the standard format, the format should be modified. When developing a standard format for definitions, it is important to try to foresee what information will be useful when we start to implement and verify the ES. For example, a space may be left in the definition for (1) the name used for the attribute in the knowledge base and (2) a list of cases in which the attribute is important, if the attribute does not figure in each case. Additionally, we have to specify whether the ES is capable of using the attribute routinely as planned.

A well-designed definition will be a useful guide both for design and implementation and for future knowledge acquisition sessions.

2. **Attribute classification.** Typically, each attribute refers to a specific item of information about a particular type of concept, process, or other conceptual entity. These standard objects can be used to organize attributes. Here, we have to (1) identify the type of concept described by each attribute; (2) group attributes that supply information about

a similar concept type; (3) name each concept type and add this name to the project concept dictionary, if not already defined; and (4) revise the attributes of each concept type, checking whether these attributes can be further classified and categorizing the concept types to identify as many classificational levels as required.

An intermediate representation has to be selected to illustrate how the attributes that will be used by the ES have been organized. If the organization is simple, a list of concept types will suffice. If the attributes have been organized in a multilevel classification, classificational hierarchies are a possible option. Additionally, it is important to define each identified concept type, specifying which attributes are relevant for this concept type. If the concept type is part of a multilevel classification, its definition should contain cross-references to both more general and more specific concept types.

3. **Organize case-independent facts.** So far, we have discussed that an ES reasons with facts and hypotheses about case attributes. However, most ES also use facts about application-dependent areas that are independent of any specific case. Just as a concept type serves to organize attributes, the concepts themselves may serve to organize the case-independent facts. This involves: (1) revising the notes on knowledge acquisition sessions and identifying the case-independent facts that specify the values of concept attributes, considering only the facts to be used by the ES when executing a task; (2) identifying the concept — process, object or entity, etc. — to which each fact belongs; (3) grouping the facts and groups of facts by the concepts to which they belong; (4) listing the attributes that specify the facts about each concept type; and (5) developing intermediate representations that summarize collections of related facts.
So, each case-independent fact specifies the value of an attribute of a particular concept. These facts take the form: "a general concept attribute is value," for example, the patient's temperature is 39°C.

4. **Identify case-independent relations.** Many ES use case-independent facts to express relations between different concepts. A relation may be expressed as "concept 1 relation concept 2"; for example, *cable x is connected to plug y*. Alternatively, a relation may take the form: "relation between concept 1 and concept 2 is value," for example, *the distance between the computer and the wall is 15 cm*. The notes on knowledge acquisition have to be revised to identify relations that are not facts and that will be used by the ES in the reasoning process. Here, we have to (1) identify the facts specifying relations between concepts, looking particularly for expert statements concerning taxonomies, structures and other types of relations; (2) group facts specifying the same type of relation; (3) check each relation against the strategic and tactical knowledge gathered, separating the relations used by the ES from additional relations providing an understanding of the basic reason for system actions and checking whether the relations have already been captured in the tactical knowledge representations; and (4) develop intermediate representations to illustrate the relations to be used by the ES that have yet to be captured in the intermediate representations of tactical knowledge.

The most useful representations for relations are graphs and trees, in which the nodes correspond to concepts and the arcs to relations. Generally, each graph would illustrate a simple relation type; for example, *part of* or *cause*. Arcs are used to indicate the direction of an asymmetric relation.

3.4. CONSTRUCTION OF THE STATIC SUBMODEL: CONCEPT DICTIONARY

Having identified the strategic, tactical, and factual knowledge during the analysis stage of the conceptualization phase, we move on to synthesis, which begins with the construction of the concept dictionary.

TABLE 4
Concept Dictionary for any Disease

Concept	Function	Synonyms/acronyms	Attributes	Inferred from
Clinical record	Record patient treatment and clinical record	Case history, CH	Name, age, sex, date of treatment, test, results, allergies, etc.	Tests and care
Medicines	Cure disease or relieve symptoms	Treatments, prescription, chemical formula	Chemical group, proprietary name, active ingredient, contraindications, dosage	Treatments, texts, vade mecum, etc.
Diagnosis	Treatment prescription	Examination, tests	Causal agent, side effects, differential diagnosis	Clinical symptoms, signs, test results
Treatment	Cure the patient	Patient management	System, mode of administration	Diagnosis, texts, physician experience

The identification of high-level concepts or functional subconcepts and key terminology is described in a **concept dictionary**. For each concept, the dictionary will specify its utility or function, synonyms and acronyms, defining attributes, values, data source, etc. It is important to mention that dictionary construction is not a quick job, and that it will not be amended later. Indeed, it is a *living list*, far from easy to construct, which synthesizes and summarizes everything obtained using the different knowledge acquisition methods. Table 4 shows part of the concept dictionary of a medical diagnostic and treatment system. Any other inputs deemed appropriate, such as cross-references, may be added. The important point about this simple example is that it identifies the components essential in any dictionary and how they should be specified.

The concept dictionary is useful because it isolates prominent particulars, that is, attributes, properties, or characteristics that distinguish the task concepts. Similarities and differences are explained and explicitly recorded. Questions, such as what makes A, B, and C similar?, what is the difference between A and B?, or is there any overlap or common point between A and B?, may be asked in order to identify these similarities and differences. When checking for similarities or differences, which may not always be immediately obvious, a possible technique is **concept classification**, whereby a list of concepts, taken of course from the concept dictionary, is given to the expert, and he/she is asked to order them in two sets. Each set is given a name or label that best describes why they were grouped in this manner. The process is repeated with three sets and so on. The concepts related with common properties or particulars are grouped and represent a concept classificational taxonomy or tree. The classificational and distinguishing properties are specified at the bottom of the tree as it is built. The classificational tree is one of the most natural means of representation and is also easy to understand, proving to be a very useful technique for using organizational knowledge and representing hierarchical classifications, where the lowest items in the hierarchy *inherit* the properties of their ancestors.

This concept identification and recording stage is a prerequisite for later conceptualization steps. It also enables the KE to understand and define the meaning of certain important words most commonly used by the expert. A possible method of identifying these concepts and building the associated **concept/attribute/value** table is given below.

1. Underline, for example in red, each name or noun mentioned by the expert.
2. List all the underlined names sequentially, as they appear in the working document, to form a *Glossary of Terms*.

3. Examine the full list and group as many names as possible on a new sheet to form classes of things, that is, concepts. In other words, a concept may be unique, a class, or a related group of concepts. Concepts may be, as discussed earlier, objects, items, or events with attributes and values. The concepts and their interrelations reflect how the expert views or interprets the problem domain. By comparing the names on the original list with the list of concepts, the grouping of many will be immediately obvious from the structure of the document or interview.

3.5. CREATION OF THE DYNAMIC SUBMODEL

An analysis of the tasks obtained in the analysis stage makes it possible to outline the expert's **dynamic or process model** and check that there are not too many errors or omissions. Here, it is important to recall each task studied during the strategic knowledge identification stage. Then, we have to define a hierarchy between the tasks. For example, if task 1 has to fire task 2 to get information, then task 1 must be a parent of task 2, as shown in Figure 6.

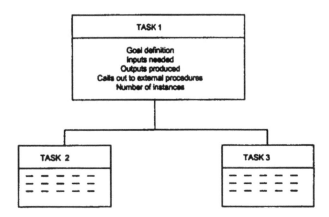

FIGURE 6   Task hierarchy.

Then, the formalisms needed to execute the task have to be established. For this purpose, it is important to note down the possible goal values M = m1, etc. These should normally have been ascertained in the first stage of tactical knowledge identification, but they should be discussed with the expert for confirmation. Then, they need to be represented, as shown in Figure 7, where M represents the goal defined in TASK 1 of Figure 6, and m_1, m_2, and m_3 are alternative subgoals characterizing the composition of goal M. Finally, A_1 and A_2 are the attributes concerning goal m_1, and are elemental either because they are easily obtained from an inference or because they are explicit. That is, these attributes and/or their values are obtained either from an external source, such as a text or database, or are requested from the expert and/or users who enter a value or use a default value.

Then, meta-knowledge has to be considered. The best means of doing this is to (1) add the information to be shown during the inference to Figure 7 (for example, if A1 = a1.val1, the system must show the user a text on laws) and (b) implement priorities. If an attribute has a particular value, the system must immediately switch the process to a given attribute or ignore another one (for example, when A1 = a1.val2, check whether M = m1 is true; if not, check whether M = m2 is true, as shown in Figure 8).

Having identified the subdecisions (i.e., the individual stages leading up to the decision), it is important to get the expert to confirm that they are correct. At the same time, the expert is asked to state which concepts and attributes are used in each stage. This knowledge has to be recorded by (1) adding new metarules; (2) applying the subdecisions in the model and cross-checking that

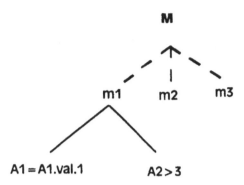

FIGURE 7   Assignation of values to task goals.

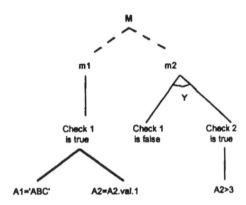

FIGURE 8   Priority implementation.

the model contains all the concepts required to carry out each stage; and (3) listing the order of the subdecisions in the process document.

Finally, the whole process should be completely and consistently established using a standard representation as shown in Table 5.

3.6.   KNOWLEDGE MAP GENERATION

Whereas the dynamic model is composed of strategies, priorities, etc., making up the process submodel, and the static submodel contains the concept dictionary and its associated Concept/Attribute/Value table, the knowledge map is the synthesis of these two submodels. Although it basically represents the static part of expert knowledge, it should really also show its dynamic part.

A knowledge map, hereafter referred to as KM, is similar to a *mental map*. It is a method of representing the connections made by the brain when it understands facts about something in 2-D on paper. This map is easily recalled by the designer when revised some time later. Therefore, a KM represents the process of inferring attribute values. Relations between attributes and inferred values constitute an important part of knowledge. Liebowitz (1989) points out that KMs have several notable features. First, when fully developed, they are considered a powerful means of showing how much and what type of expert knowledge has been gathered. Second, the KM's visual format helps the KE in preparing later knowledge acquisition sessions, as it guides KE planning and behavior in these sessions. Without this positive and efficient expert-driven control mechanism, knowledge acquisition sessions would become random circumlocutions around subjects, that is, the knowledge acquisition sessions would deteriorate, becoming costly and excessively time consuming. Third, subjects can be embedded in the KM, reflecting the layers of knowledge gathered

TABLE 5
Standard Description of Procedures

KNOWLEDGE BASE **NAME:**...
PURPOSES:...
INFORMATION REQUIRED: ....
ACTIONS: ....
BASIC REASON: ....
INTERVIEW **NOTES:**...
STATUS: ....

from the expert. This makes it possible to specify (using suitable signs, follow-on topics, following keywords) how to hierarchically order subjects to carry out a critical control function. Additionally, other references are permitted, for example, numbering knowledge acquisition sessions to allow direct backtracking of all the previous analytical steps until one can establish exactly where the knowledge was obtained and under what circumstances. Backtracking is required to keep adulteration of expert knowledge to a minimum. Finally, this notation can be transformed almost directly into a computer implementation. So, this approach allows complex elicited expert knowledge to be *applied* and implemented in a verifiable, documentable, and auditable manner.

Additionally, it is important to note that a KM is not a semantic net. So, each attribute appearing in the left-hand side of a rule, for example, must appear in the KM connected to an attribute inferred in the right-hand side of the rule. But each connected attribute does not necessarily appear in each rule used to infer the value of the attribute in the right-hand side of the rule. The rules containing heuristic knowledge or meta-knowledge often only contain one or two attributes in the left-hand side of the rule.

The signs found when the expert and the KE jointly review the KM have two purposes. First, when the sign is followed by a keyword, the expert is asked to explain it. If the response is "No further knowledge and/or data or news are required," this is stated in the KM, no further inquiries are made, and the issue is considered closed. If, on the other hand, the response is affirmative, the expert has to be asked punctually and rapidly for some keys on this issue in later knowledge acquisition sessions. Similar questions are raised in the lower layers of the KM. In this manner, it is the expert who has final control over the depth to be achieved in a given subject, rather than the KE deciding which subjects to pursue and which not to pursue. So, the expert always controls the relative importance of each subject and how much attention is paid to it.

The KM is built on the basis of the following actions.

1. *Identify the task decisions made by the ES.* The ES goal(s) should be already decided. Therefore, it is important to ensure that the goal(s) has/have been explicitly defined in such a manner as to be accepted by all parties.
2. *Design the goal decision block.* The purpose of the ES is to make a decision about a concept. Place the concept in the center of a piece of paper. The concept will be one of the identified attributes. Refer to this concept as the goal decision. Frame this name in a rectangle.
3. *Add attributes to infer the goal decision.* Place around the goal decision the attributes that will be used both in the formalisms (rules, frames, etc.) to infer the value of a goal decision and in the calculations to determine the goal decision.

   Each attribute around the goal decision must be involved in inferring or calculating the value of the goal decision, but this does not mean that all attributes are used in a single formalism. Usually, there will be between three and six different attributes used in a number of rules, frames, etc., to infer the values of the goal decision. Most human brains can only handle four attributes at the same time. If over four attributes are used to infer the value of the goal decision, the expert will probably calculate the value of some intermediate attributes in order to infer the value of the goal decision. Generally, the number of attributes immediately around the goal decision can be reduced by introducing intermediate attributes.

4. *Extend the KM.* Here, you need to add the attributes used to infer or calculate the values of each attribute employed to infer the goal decision. Continue extending the KM to include each attribute used to infer the value of another attribute. Gradually, a network of attributes can be built, resembling a "spider's web," though without interconnections between the edges.

   Rules, and of course any other formalisms, may contain uncertainty, either because we are not absolutely sure how the rule has been represented or because the knowledge expressed in the formalisms is itself uncertain. In both cases, the link or relation between attributes is represented in the KM in the same way as relations without uncertainty. Rule uncertainty is recorded in the leaves of the rules.

5. *Enter multiple attribute uses.* When many examples of an attribute are to be used in the left-hand side of a rule before the right-hand attribute is inferred, these examples are indicated with an M along the arrow connecting the two attributes. The expert may state when an example of a specific attribute value should be inferred in the decision-making process. When the links are not identified by M, they are assumed to be one-to-one, which is the most usual case. Apart from showing multiple examples of an attribute, the KM does not represent a data structure. In this sense, it is a representation of the process of inferring attribute values. If the KM is to be extended to include other attributes that can be used to infer the values of a multiple example of an attribute, this should be considered as a single example for purposes of KM extension. For example, whether other attributes can be used to infer the tool value required, rather than another that infers many values.

6. *Use the external states of the pseudoformalism, particularly pseudorules.* Now we have to match the names of the attributes defined to the names of the concepts in the formalisms. The words used by the expert in the pseudoformalisms will probably have to be changed, taking care not to lose the meaning. The values of the attributes may be numerical, strings of characters or words, or one or many values selected from a particular list. The names of the attributes should be the same as those given to the expert. It is important to match the names and admissible values to the words in the pseudoformalisms, ensuring that they resemble natural language expressions as far as possible.

7. *Use a special notation to prevent duplicated inferences* There may be hundreds of attributes in a large ES, many of which will be used in more than one place in the KM. Where the attribute value is inferred from one or more pseudoformalisms, it is not necessary to duplicate all the attributes used to infer the value. Instead, it is important to specify that the attribute has already been fully defined in another part of the KM. The KM box can be marked with an asterisk to identify duplicate attributes.

8. *Supplement the KM to include additional attributes and interrelations.* Attributes continue to be added and the KM modified to reflect new attributes, values, and formalisms identified in the working document.

An example will better explain the manner in which a KM is built. In this case, we are going to design a KM for psychological diagnosis, confining the field of diagnosis to the different types of neurosis: anxiety, phobia, hysteria, and obsessive behavior, using the concepts obtained in preceding knowledge acquisition sessions: illness, patient, background (aspect of psychological interest in the patient's past), disorder, behavior, attitude, appearance, thought, fear. in Figure 9.

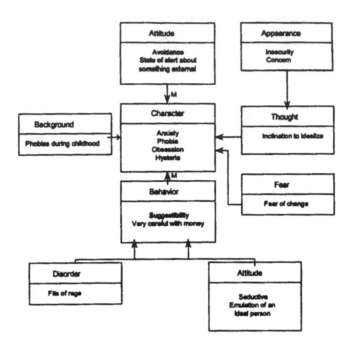

FIGURE 9   Knowledge map for the identification the type of neurosis.

The patient's attitudes, appearances, behavior, and background have to be analyzed to determine the type of illness. This is illustrated by the KM shown

The expert may possibly know nothing about the patient's background, because he/she is reluctant to speak about his/her childhood. So, the expert must supply a rule or a default value to handle the situation. He/she may question the patient or deduce that if he/she does not wish to relive the past, it is because he/she does not want to go through it again. Additionally, the thoughts of the patient are difficult to analyze. Often, there are uncertainties, but the system must not stop. It must reason with the uncertainties. Reasoning may take longer, but the system has to make certain inferences from uncertain information, introducing other tests; for example, by putting further questions to the patient and checking them later.

3.7.   VERIFICATIONS

Having designed the two submodels (static and dynamic) and integrated them into the KM in the synthesis stage to build the conceptual model, a series of checks have to be carried out to eliminate subjectivities, consider unknown conditions and/or address uncertainty, and verify the completeness and consistency of the whole model. All these questions will be considered in more detail below.

Verify responses to eliminate subjectivities. Having designed the preliminary KM, consider the peripheral attribute values. There are only three ways of establishing the values of the above attributes, namely: obtaining the value from an external source, i.e., a file; asking the user to enter the value; or using a default value if neither of the above methods can be used. As it is not possible to infer the values from an intermediate representation in the case of peripheral attributes, it is important to examine the possible values assigned to these attributes and identify the values that would force the user to make a subjective decision. Moreover, intermediate representations should ignore user subjectivity. Any subjectivity should be contained in the expert rules. The KE should not ask questions or raise issues that imply evaluations. All issues and questions should be related to the facts.

Examine unknown and default conditions. It is also important to ensure that the KM and the dynamic submodel, especially the pseudorules, contain links and values to handle unknown conditions. If there is a possibility of the user not knowing an attribute value, it is important to ensure that the expert supplies either a pseudorule or any other pseudoformalism to handle the situation or an acceptable default value. If no pseudorule or default value exists, unknown conditions may arise. This problem must be added to the list of questions in the next structured interview with the expert during the next knowledge acquisition session.

Verify negative conditions. The pseudoformalisms not only should state what to do when given conditions are met or arise, but also provide a means of expressing what to do when such conditions do not exist, the expert often knows what to do when the expected conditions do not occur or exist. Therefore, it is important to check with the expert during the knowledge acquisition whether the non-existent conditions are important and whether there are potential ways of covering such cases.

Address uncertainty. Any pseudoformalism or information may contain uncertainty. It is important to confront experts about what to do if a fact is uncertain. Additional pseudoformalisms that incorporate uncertainty may be needed to address these cases. There are few ES that use certainty factors in the formalism. Certainty factors are not the same as probabilities. If they are required, procedures must be defined to manage them.

Verify completeness and consistency. Check that each known attribute value is used in a knowledge representation pseudoformalism. All the values should be in the Concept/Attribute/Value table. Unless the attribute is in the periphery of the KM, the KE must ensure that each value can be inferred from a pseudoformalism or obtained from a default value. If the values are not used, ask the expert why. Also, it is important to verify that each attribute value, except the goal decision, is used in the left-hand side of a rule or appears in any other place in association with an attribute. Otherwise, ask the expert why it has been entered as a possible value and has not been used. Additionally, it is important to verify the KM to ensure that a value does not follow a recursive loop in which the attribute is inferred from the second value of a second attribute, which is, in turn, inferred from a value of the first attribute. Similarly, unnecessary IF conditions, subfunctions, etc., must also be verified.

3.8. SYSTEM DECOMPOSITION

When the static and dynamic models have been completed, it is often possible and desirable to decompose and segment the ES. Sometimes, segmentation is left until several ES development process cycles are completed and the KM illustrates system complexity. Segmentation is possible if users accept subsets of the ES until the full system is completed. It is important to underline that this segmentation is not incompatible with the decomposition of a task into subtasks. On the contrary, whereas the decomposition is carried out during knowledge analysis, segmentation is carried out when the conceptual model is almost finished. Additionally, while decomposition into subtasks strictly concerns the conceptualization phase, segmentation also involves the implementation phase.

Segmentation is desirable if it reduces development time and maintenance effort. Segmentation will only produce this reduction if there are many concepts, attributes, and values proper to each system subset. If a subset uses over 30 different attributes and over 100 different attribute values, times will be reduced significantly if the subset is developed separately.

Segmentation is carried out in the following stages.

1. *Examine the model and locate any concepts that have many parents and independent relations.* In particular, look for concepts involved in a large set of one-to-many relations. These concepts are ideal candidates for segmentation and will reduce the size and complexity of the KM more than any other concept.

2. *If the subset uses many attribute values, there are good reasons for segmenting the system around the concept to which that attribute belongs.* Go over these attributes together with the expert, examining the Concept/Attribute/Value table.

3. *To segment a concept, locate subsets acceptable to both the expert and the users.* Typical subsets are: (a) the instances of individual concepts identified by an attribute name or attribute number; (b) subclassifications of concepts that are well understood within the task (it must be possible to identify these subclassifications by one of the concept attributes); and (c) alternative parent concepts that have been identified as differing significantly from each other (some alternative parent entities will be the same, but others will be unique for a particular alternative parent concept).

4. *The decision to segment the system* will affect both the questions raised in future knowledge acquisition sessions, potential rules and other identified formalisms, and attributes and values recorded in the KM.

The KM can be used to identify the subsets of the segmentation. In this case, it is important to look for attributes that repeatedly appear in the KM.

4.   CONCLUSIONS

It goes without saying that a diagnostic system will be no good unless the problem, involving correct and timely diagnosis, has not been well conceptualized.

Additionally, conceptualization is only one stage of a global methodological process, in this case the IDEAL methodology (Gómez et al., 1997) and its associated life cycle.

Finally, it is important to note that this diagnostic methodology generally and the conceptualization phase particularly is backed by the construction of 20 general-purpose ES and 6 diagnostic ES in fields such as: medicine; aircraft; vehicle; and ship maintenance; and nuclear plants.

REFERENCES

GÓMEZ et. al. 1997
A. Gómez, N. Juristo, J. Pazos
Ingeniería del conocimiento. Construcción de sistemas expertos
Ceura. Madrid, 1997.

HAYES-ROTH et. al., 1983
F. Hayes-Roth; D. A. Waterman; D. B. Lenat
Building Expert Systems
Addison-Wesley Publishing Company, Inc. 1983

HUDLICKÁ 1988
Eva Hudlická
"Construction and Use of a Causal Model for Diagnosis"
International Journal of Intelligent Systems Vol. 3. 1988

KRISHNA et. al. 1991
C.M. Krishna, Y. H. Lee
"Real-Time Systems"
IEEE Transactions on Computer, May 1991

LIEBOWITZ, 1989
J. Liebowitz, D. A. De Salvo, Editors
Structuring Expert Systems. Domain, Design, and Development
Yourdon Press. Englewood Cliffs, NJ, 1989.

LWOFF, 1975
A. Lwoff
El Orden Biologico
Siglo XXI Editores, S.A. México, 1975.

MATÉ et al., 1988
J. L. Maté, J. Pazos
Ingeniería del conocimiento. Diseño y construcción de sistemas expertos
SEPA. Cordoba, Agentina, 1988

MICHALSKI et al. 1980
R. S. Michalski, R. L. Chilansky
"Learning by Being Told and Learning from Examples: An Experimental Comarison of the Two Methods of
    Knowledge Acquisition in the Context of Developing an ES for Soybean Disease Diagnosis"
International Journal of Policy Analysis and Information Systems 4
Vol IV, No. 2, June 1980

PEPPER, 1990
J. Pepper
"An Expert System for Automotive Diagnosis"
In R. Kuezweil *The Age of Intelligent Machines*
The MIT Press, Cambridge, MA, 1990.

RÍOS et al., 1991
J. Ríos, A. Pazos, N. R. Brisabaa, S. Caridad
Estructura, dinámica y aplicaciones de las redes de neuronas artificiales
Centro de Estudios Ramón Areces. Madrid. 1991.

ROBERTS, 1981
N.H. Roberts, W.E. Vesely, D.F. Haasl, F.F. Goldberg
Fault Tree Handbook
U.S. Nuclear Regulatory Commission, 1981

SCHREIBER, 1993
G. Schreiber, B. Wielinga, J. Breuker.
KADS, A Principled Approach to Knowledge-Based System Development
Academic Press, New York. 1993.

SCOTT, 1991
A. C. Scott, J. E. Clayton, E. L. Gibson
A Practical Guide to Knowledge Acquisition
Addison-Wesley Publishing Company 1991

32 Expert Systems in Medicine

Young Moon Chae

CONTENTS

I. INTRODUCTION

This chapter reviews the research on expert systems designed as aids to medical decision-making. Because complex medical decisions are often made when major uncertainties are present and when the stakes are extremely high, expert systems are ideally suited for decision analysis. Over the last 30 years, many medical expert systems have been developed. Motivations for the development of expert systems in medicine have been numerous. Assisting physicians in making diagnoses and treatment recommendations is the most commonly found application of expert systems in medicine. A physician may have knowledge of most diseases, but, due to the extensive number of diseases, a physician could benefit from the support provided by an expert system to quickly isolate the disease. Specifically, the goals of developing expert systems for medicine are as follows (Shortliffe et al., 1979):

1. To improve the *accuracy* of clinical diagnosis through approaches that are systematic, complete, and able to integrate data from diverse sources
2. To improve the *reliability* of clinical decisions by avoiding unwarranted influences of similar but not identical cases
3. To improve the *cost efficiency* of tests and therapies by balancing the expenses of time, inconvenience against benefits, and risks of definitive actions
4. To improve our *understanding of the structure of medical knowledge*, with the associated development of techniques for identifying inconsistencies and inadequacies in that knowledge
5. To improve our *understanding of clinical decision-making*, in order to improve medical teaching and to make the system more effective and easier to understand

In medical diagnosis, the exhaustive nature of problem-solving in expert systems to ensure that remote possibilities are not overlooked is important (Barr and Feigenbaum, 1982). Often, the very codification of expertise in suitable form for an expert systems is an illuminating and valuable part of the expert systems development. Furthermore, since the nature of the problem in medicine is not sufficiently understood, large amounts of domain-specific knowledge have to be represented and reasoned with.

Medical treatment decisions are another prime area for applying expert systems. This is so because such decisions must typically be made by patients and their physicians at a point in the diagnostic process that has produced a relatively stable determination of the patient's problem and where specific treatment or more invasive testing options are being considered.

An expert system should be used in medical practice only if it improves the quality of care at an acceptable cost in time or money, or if it maintains the existing standard of care at a reduced cost in time or money. Miller et al. (1985) defined improved quality of care by one or more of the following criteria: improved diagnositc accuracy; improved therapeutic results; an improved sense of the patients well-being; easier and more rapid access to patient information via better record-keeping systems; and a better representation of facts in medical records and better documentation of the reasons for the physicians' actions. These criteria may be used in evaluating medical expert systems when they are applied in a clinical setting.

The development of medical expert systems brings with it many formidable technical, behavioral, legal, and ethical problems that must be addressed by the researchers in this field. These include acquiring and representing medical knowledge, validating the systems, getting physicians and patients to accept them, and deciding the responsibility for clinical decisions made with the help of these systems. This chapter reviews historical accounts of expert systems in medicine, key techniques, applications, research issues, and future trends of medical expert systems.

2.   HISTORICAL ACCOUNT

The use of computers in medical decision-making began in the early 1960s with the implementation of programs that performed well-known statistical analysis. These programs focused on the diagnosis part of the consultation. They accepted a set of findings and selected one disease from a fixed set, using methods such as pattern recognition through discriminant functions, Bayesian decision theory, and decision-tree techniques.

In the 1970s, medical expert systems were primarily concerned with performing diagnoses and making therapy recommendations (e.g., PIP, CASNET, MYCIN, and INTERNIST, CADUCEUS, PUFF, etc.). As early efforts, they were prototypes directed at two questions (Barr and Feigenbaum, 1982): What would make such a system acceptable to physician users? How can factual and judgmental knowledge be integrated? Despite the extensive work that has been done, none of these systems was in routine clinical use because of limitation of knowledge representation techniques and physician resistance, which will be discussed later.

During the 1980s, we witnessed the proliferation of expert systems in medicine. They had a great impact on many areas of the medical field where knowledge provides the power for solving important medical problems. According to the survey conducted in 1992 (Durkin, 1994), the total number of expert systems uncovered in all fields was approximately 2500 in the 1980s. However, this number is estimated to represent only 20% of the total population — 12,500 developed systems. Of these, 12% of the applications were in the field of medicine. A 1986 survey conducted by Waterman (1986) showed that an even higher percentage of the applications (30%) was in the field of medicine. These surveys showed that this field was very attractive to expert system developers in the 1980s.

It is interesting to follow the growth rate of the expert systems in general. During the 1970s, when researchers were focusing on developing intelligent programming techniques, only a handful of systems were built. During the 1980s, the number of developed expert systems increased from 50 in 1985 to 2200 in 1988 (Harmon and Sawyer, 1990). The impressive growth rate of expert systems is an indicator of the acceptance of the technology by industry. These surveys also showed that expert systems are merging with the mainstream of information processing that was previously dominated by conventional data processors.

We can attribute the large growth rate in developed systems in part to the new hardware and software technologies. During the 1970s, most expert systems were developed on powerful workstations, using languages such as LISP, PROLOG, and OPS. This placed the challenge of developing systems in the hands of the select few who could afford the platforms and had the patience to learn the complexities of the available languages. During the 1980s, we witnessed the proliferation of personal computers, and the introduction of easy-to-use expert system software development tools called "shells." A shell is a programming environment that contains all of the necessary utilities for both developing and running an expert system. During the last decade, large numbers of shells were marketed for use on personal computers. The opportunity to develop an expert system was now in the hands of many individuals, including physicians. According to the survey conducted by Kraut and Mann (1996), well-known expert system "shells" applied were ProMD (31%), HUGIN (19%), NEXPERT (12%), KAPPA (8%), and ClassicaD3 (8%).

In 1990s, the complexity and volume of medical knowledge has increased continuously. As seen in the Appendix, a total of 233 medical expert systems were found from the following sources between 1992 and 1996: Medline database, Proceedings of the Medical Informatics Europe '96 (Brender et al., 1996), Proceedings of the 3rd World Congress on Expert Systems (Lee et al., 1996), and Proceedings of the 8th World Congress on Medical Informatics (Greenes et al., 1995). From the review of these articles, it appears that current medical knowledge at all levels of medical care was applied in developing these expert systems in order to achieve high-quality medical care as well as to reduce costs in medical care.

Furthermore, a major change can be seen in the last few years. In the process of developing an expert system, the basic methodological problems like knowledge representation and inference mechanisms are no longer holding the spotlight. Rather, problems of introducing the systems in the clinical environment and questions of the application-oriented research are receiving the attention. Adequate user interfaces, a satisfactory cost/benefit ratio, and the adaptation of system functions to the requests of the clinical environment have become important research issues.

3. METHODOLOGIES

Since the beginning of expert systems technology, knowledge acquisition and representation have long been considered the major constraint in the development of expert systems in the medical field. A majority of incidences of reported knowledge acquisition problems involved problems with the quality of knowledge elicited. Much of this was because doctors either tended to communicate shallow knowledge rather than the required deep knowledge structure, or they found it difficult to describe procedures and routines. In addition, knowledge acquisition from a standard clinical examination is also troublesome because patient's responses are very subjective, and they may contradict themselves, sometimes repeatedly, when describing symptoms (Mouradian, 1990).

Knowledge acquisition and representation is a kind of knowledge model that can be used to predict or explain behavior in the world. Thus, diagnosis is based on a causal explanation of what is happening to the patient, and therapy is based on predictions about how the disease process can be modified. Knowledge models in medicine are incomplete in that they are approximated and omit levels of detail (Clancey and Shortliff, 1984). One reason for this incompleteness is that there is no practical way to build systems that display more than a fraction of what any physician knows about the body and how it works. There is just too much knowledge, and we are still struggling to formalize even small portions of it. A second reason for leaving out levels of detail is that useful problem-solving performance can usually be produced even if we omit the pathophysiological knowledge about the disease. Among the knowledge models used in medicine are the following.

3.1. BAYESIAN STATISTICAL APPROACHES

The Bayesian approach is a mechanism to calculate the probability of a disease, in light of specified evidence, from the *a priori* probability of the disease and the conditional probabilities relating the observations to the diseases in which they may occur. A variety of additional assumptions must be made in this approach, such as: (1) the diseases under consideration are assumed to be mutually exclusive and exhaustive (i.e., the patient is assumed to have exactly one of n diseases); (2) the clinical observations are assumed to be conditionally independent over a given disease; and (3) the incidence of the symptoms of a disease are assumed to be stationary (i.e., the model generally does not allow for changes in disease patterns over time).

In several domains, the technique has been shown to be exceedingly accurate, but there are also several limitations to this approach that make a particular application unrealistic and hence unworkable (Shortliffe et al., 1979):

- The assumption of conditional independence of symptoms usually does not apply and can lead to substantial errors in certain settings.
- The assumption of mutual exclusiveness and exhaustion of disease categories is usually false. In actual practice, concurrent and overlapping disease categories are common.
- In many domains, it may be inaccurate to assume that relevant conditional probabilities are stable over time. Furthermore, diagnostic categories and definitions are constantly changing, as are physicians' observational techniques, thus invalidating data previously accumulated.

While much work has been done on Bayesian approaches to medical expert systems in the earlier studies, few applications were recently found, perhaps due to the above limitations.

3.2. RULE-BASED REASONING

Rule-based reasoning is the most general structure — it is also called a production system. It uses knowledge encoded in generation rule (IF ... THEN). Rules usually have a condition part (antecedent) and an action part (conclusion). Each rule represents one of the knowledge units related to an expert field. Many related rules may correspond to an inference chain, which deduces a useful conclusion from several facts known.

Rule-based reasoning has been the most popular choice of knowledge engineers for building an expert system in medicine. Through previous experience in developing rule-based systems (including MYCIN) came a better understanding for their development, bringing about an explosion of applications. Of 233 medical expert systems developed since 1992, as seen in the Appendix, 110 systems (47.2%) were developed by the rule-based reasoning. The survey conducted in Germany (Kraut and Mann, 1996) showed an even higher percentage (69%) for the rule-based reasoning approach.

There are several advantages of the rule-based reasoning approach (Durkin, 1994). First, it has a natural expression. For many problems, humans naturally express their problem-solving knowledge in IF ... THEN type statements. Second, since rules are independent pieces of knowledge, they can easily be reviewed and verified. Third, rules are transparent, and are certainly far more transparent than the modes of knowledge representation employed by neural networks, as discussed later. However, there are also several disadvantages. First, it requires exact matching. If we do not have an exact match, the rule will not work. Second, rules do not efficiently or naturally capture the representation of complex domain knowledge. Third, systems with a large set of rules can be slow.

3.3. NEURAL NETWORK

To solve some of these problems, there have been several attempts to acquire a knowledge base directly from the medical database. A neural network is one such attempt. A neural network is essentially a type of information processing technology inspired by studies of the designs in the brain and nervous system. Consequently, these systems operate in a fundamentally different manner from traditional computing systems. They are made up of many simple, highly interconnected processing elements that dynamically interact with each other to "learn" or "respond to" information rather than simply carry out algorithmic steps or programmed instructions. Information is represented in a neural network in that pattern of interconnection strengths among the processing elements. Information is processed by a changing pattern of activity distributed across many units. Learning occurs through an interactive adjustment of interconnection strengths based upon information within a learning sample. The neural network is considered to be a kind of nonlinear discriminant function.

A self-learning mechanism of the neural network has been applied to medical expert systems as an automatic knowledge acquisition and representation method. As seen in the Appendix, the neural network has been applied to the following medical domains for the last 5 years: analysis of protein structure, male infertility, trauma, neuroscience, nuclear medicine, lung scan, psychiatry, cardiac surgery, cervix cancer, stomach cancer, molecular biology, genetics, asymptomatic liver disease, hepatobiliary disease, epilepsy, pediatric, rheumatic disease, allergic rhinitis, asthma, orthodontia, acute abdominal pain, brain auditory evoked potentials, glaucoma, dentistry, and nurse scheduling. Of 233 expert systems listed in the Appendix, 54 systems (23.2%) were developed by neural network. The survey of expert systems developed in Germany (Kraut and Mann, 1996) also showed a similar percentage for neural networks.

Neural networks have various advantages and disadvantages compared with the rule-based system (Hillman, 1990). Rule-based systems tend to be domain specific and function extremely well when problems are well defined, but neural networks have a broad response capability based on their ability to provide a general classification of a set of inputs. Furthermore, the rule-based system implementation can be a lengthy process, depending on the size of the domain and the range of cases that must be realized; neural networks can analyze a large number of cases quickly to provide accurate responses. However, validation of the content of neural network (i.e., the determination of the completeness and consistency of the representation) is relatively more difficult than rule-based reasoning. Another problem in the use of neural networks in medical decision-making has been the evaluation of the reliability of the output of the networks. Moreover, the output of the neural network systems is difficult to interpret for most of clinical practitioners. There should be more studies on these problems to help the user of the system evaluate the confidence on the suggested diagnosis by neural network.

3.4.   CASE-BASED REASONING

While the neural network approach offers a useful tool for knowledge acquisition and representation, and is unlike human experts, this approach solves problems by reasoning from principles; that is, it explains the reasoning by reporting the string of deductions that lead from the input data to the conclusion. Medical doctors, however, solve new problems by analogy with old cases and explain reasons in terms of prior experience. Computer systems that solve by analogy with old ones are called case-based reasoning (CBR) systems (Rich et al., 1991). CBR systems solve problems by searching a collection of stored cases to find and retrieve the cases that most closely resemble (match) a newly presented case using match score. A CBR system draws its power from a large case library, rather than from a set of principles.

As seen in the Appendix, CBR has been applied to the following medical domains: analysis of skull structure, general surgery, radiation therapy, biochemistry, post-operative care, hemodynamics, nursing care, psychotherapy, heart disease, diagnostic imaging procedure, protein analysis, eating disorders, allergic rhinitis, jaundice, ICU care, HIV, radiology, kidney function, asthma, and leukemia. Of 233 expert systems listed in the Appendix, 30 systems (12.9%) were developed by CBR. The survey of expert systems developed in Germany (Kraut and Mann, 1996) also showed a similar percentage for CBR.

CBR enables the expert system to tap into a medical knowledge source (e.g., medical records and clinical case database) that is often more readily available in hospitals than outside practices. The neural network and CBR have complementary strengths. The neural network systems capture broad trends in the domain, while the CBR systems are good at filling in small pockets of exceptions.

3.5.   OBJECT-ORIENTED PROGRAMMING

Object-oriented programming refers to all of their data structures as objects. Each object contains two basic types of information: information that describes the object and information that specifies what the object can do. In the expert system, each object has a declarative and procedural knowledge (Durkin, 1994). It provides a natural way of representing real-world objects. According to the survey conducted by Kraut and Mann (1996) of Germany, object-oriented programming was the second most frequently used method (54%) in medicine, next to rule-based reasoning (69%).

4.   THE STATUS OF APPLICATIONS RESEARCH

This section reviews some of the well-known medical expert systems developed over the last 2 decades.

4.1.   INTERNIST/CADUCEUS: AN EXPERT SYSTEM IN INTERNAL MEDICINE

The INTERNIST project was started in the early 1970s, and continues today under the name CADUCEUS (People, 1984). The goal of INTERNIST is to perform a diagnosis of the majority of diseases associated with the field of internal medicine. This, in itself, is an ambitious endeavor as there are hundreds of such diseases. However, not only is INTERNIST/CADUCEUS intended to diagnose each disease, it is designed to consider all the possible combinations of diseases that might be present in the patient. It is estimated that the number of such combinations is of the order of 10 to the 40th power. Consequently, as in the case of DENDRAL, we are faced with a problem that exhibits combinatorial explosiveness, a problem for which the heuristic approach is most appropriate.

4.2.   MYCIN: AN EXPERT SYSTEM IN BLOOD INFECTIONS

MYCIN is, at this time, probably the most widely known of all expert systems thus far developed (Shortliffe, 1976), despite the fact that it has never been put into actual practice. Many early texts on expert systems have focused primarily on the MYCIN system and the project has served to substantially influence much of the subsequent work in the construction and implementation of expert systems. MYCIN was designed solely as a research effort to demonstrate how expert systems might actually be constructed for reasonably large and complex real-world problems. MYCIN is thus somewhat akin to INTERNIST/CADUCEUS in its purpose, except that it focuses on a far smaller number of diseases and thus requires a considerably smaller knowledge base.

The knowledge base of MYCIN contains the heuristic rules used by physicians in the identification of certain infections. EMYCIN (empty MYCIN)is the name given to MYCIN when this specific knowledge base is removed. In many cases, one may collect a knowledge base associated with a different domain and insert this into EMYCIN, where the result is a new, working expert system shell. The result of incorporating a knowledge base associated with pulmonary disorders into EMYCIN resulted in a new expert system known as PUFF.

4.3. PUFF: An Expert System in Pulmonary Disorders

PUFF was developed in 1979, using the EMYCIN shell (Aikens et al., 1984). The purpose of PUFF is to interpret measurements related to respiratory tests and to identify pulmonary disorders. PUFF interfaces directly with the pulmonary test instruments used in such measurements. At the conclusion of the testing, PUFF presents the physician with its interpretation of the measurements, a diagnosis of the illness, and a proposed treatment scheme. The first version of PUFF had 64 production rules; a more recent version (coded in BASIC) has about 400 rules.

The validation procedure for PUFF was conducted by comparing its diagnosis with that of two expert pulmonary physiologists. The conclusions of PUFF and that of the physiologists were consistent in more than 90% of test cases. As a result, PUFF is now used on a routine basis.

One particularly interesting feature of PUFF is that the physical appearance is indistinguishable from conventional laboratory tools. The acceptance of PUFF by the medical profession may be based, in large part, on this perception; that is, PUFF is viewed as an ordinary piece of laboratory equipment, rather than as an intelligent (and possibly superior) competitor.

4.4. QMR: A Medical Diagnostic Expert System

Using the massive knowledge base first developed for INTERNIST, QMR (Quick Medical Reference) assists physicians in the diagnosis of an illness based upon the patient's symptoms, examination findings, and laboratory tests (Kane and Rucker, 1988). QMR, utilized at the University of Pittsburgh, incorporates over 4000 possible manifestations of diseases and is said to perform at a level comparable to practicing physicians.

4.5. EEG Analysis System

This system was developed for the automated detection of spikes and sharp waves in the EEG for the detection of epileptiform activity (Davey et al., 1989). The system consists of two distinct stages. The first is a feature extractor, written in FORTRAN, which uses spike detection algorithms to produce a list of all spike-like occurrences in the EEG. The second stage, written in "shell," OPS5, reads the list and uses rules incorporating knowledge elicited from an EEGer to confirm or exclude each of the possible spikes. Information such as the time of occurrence, polarity, and channel relationship is used in this process.

4.6. Other Expert Systems Developed in the 1990s

Experts systems were applied to the following medical fields in the 1990s: surgery (acute abdominal pain), microbiology (borreliosis), radiology (thoracic diseases), pharmacology, neurosurgery (meningitis), anesthetics and intensive care, pediatrics (metabolic diseases), neurology (cerebrovascular diseases), laboratory medicine (diseases of the thyroid gland, borreliosis, nephrology), internal medicine (rheumatology, diabetes mellitus, nephrology, hepatology), opthomology, physiology, and dentistry. A list of the selected applications are included in the Appendix.

In a 1996 survey conducted by Kraut and Mann, goals for the purpose of patient care were pursued by 90% of the promoted projects, 8% attempted to improve patient care indirectly by supplying knowledge, and only 2% of all systems pursued goals exclusively associated with medical information; 85% of the developed systems include a component for decision support based on patient data, 65% include a knowledge-based encyclopedia, and 31% include a tutoring component. In addition, 54% of the projects provide "added values" (e.g., statistics about performance or reports) to improve the cost/benefit ratio.

5.   RESEARCH ISSUES

In assessing applications, it is pertinent to examine the following research issues that affect the success of expert systems in medicine.

- What is the appropriate domain in medicine?
- How is the clinical knowledge acquired and represented? How does it facilitate the performance goals of the system described?
- How accurate is the system?
- Are there any legal and ethical problems?
- Is the system accepted by the users for whom it is intended?
- Is the interface with the user adequate?
- Does the system function outside of a research setting?
- Is it suitable for dissemination?

5.1.   SELECTING A MEDICAL DOMAIN

The ingredient for a successful application in medicine appears to be a careful choice of the medical domain. In selecting a medical domain, one should take into account whether the system is indispensable to users, the complexity and uncertainty in domain, and the number of users.

The domain must be narrow and relatively self-contained. The system should provide substantive assistance to the physician, and the task should be one that the physician either cannot do without it or is willing to let a system do. As clinical domains become more complex, a number of difficult problems have tended to degrade the quality of performance of medical expert systems. Significant clinical problems require large knowledge bases that contain complex interrelationships, including time and functional dependencies.

A particularly important feature in selecting a medical domain for designing an expert system is the desire to increase the quality of decision-making on the part of patients, physicians, or both. In the general practice of medicine, the quality of decision-making is diminished by the inability of humans, and physicians in particular, to deal effectively with uncertainty. Among other consequences, this inability promotes the abuse of diagnostic procedures by encouraging physicians to search for causal relationships without regard to the cost of their search (Holtzman, 1989).

The attractiveness of a medical domain for an expert system is also affected by the routine usage and the use of major testing procedures. Examples of such procedures might include biopsies, endoscopies, amniocenteses, exploratory laparotomies, or any other diagnostic task having considerable financial cost, toxicity, invasiveness, and/or threat to life. These procedures increase the worth of a decision-analytic-based approach for selecting medical strategies because value-of-information calculations can be used very effectively to better make the selection.

Finally, the number of users is another important factor in the success of a medical expert system. Consider, for example, the case of heart and lung transplant patients. Although the stakes involved in deciding whether or not to undergo these treatments are very high, the affected patient population is probably too small to make it worthwhile to develop a full-scale expert system. In these cases, individual decision analyses are likely to be more economical.

5.2. KNOWLEDGE ACQUISITION AND REPRESENTATION

Central to ensuring a system's adequate performance is matching the most appropriate knowledge acquisition and representation methods with the problem domain. Good statistical data may support an effective Bayesian approach or other statistical method, such as discriminant analysis in settings where diagnostic categories are small in number, nonoverlapping, and well defined. But the inability to use qualitative medical knowledge limits the effectiveness of the statistical approach in more difficult patient management or diagnostic environments. On the other hand, neural network or CBR systems may support decision-making in complex and uncertain domains in which observations are typically quantified. Chae et al. (1996) compared three knowledge representation methods (namely, neural network, discriminant analysis, and CBR) for the diagnosis of asthma. The neural network had the best overall prediction rate (92%) and the best prediction rate for asthma (96%). The discriminant analysis had the best prediction rate for non-asthma (80%), and the CBR had the lowest prediction rates in all categories.

5.3. VALIDATION AND VERIFICATION

Just as the effectiveness of the various instruments and drugs used by physicians must be validated, the accuracy, utility, and dependability of medical expert systems must eventually be assessed. Validation and verification (V & V) issues are more important in the field of medicine than in other fields because of potential problems that may result from an incorrect system. For example, an incorrect diagnosis or prescription provided by the system could threaten the life of a patient.

Concepts of validation and verification are different, but often they are not clearly distinguished. They can be defined as follows (Ayel and Laurent, 1991):

- Verification: the process of determining whether or not the products of a given phase of system development meet all the requirements established during the previous phase.
- Validation: the process of evaluating a system at the end of the development process to ensure compliance with software requirements.

These definitions are well founded in classical software with a life cycle. The V & V process can be distinguished according to the persons who use them. The "customer," the person placing the order and/or the future user, is concerned with the validation process. The customer looks for usefulness, competencies, performances, and the reliability of the product. The validation process is directly concerned with the behavior of the expert system. Unlike the validation process, the verification process is based on the designer's knowledge through development. This knowledge is mainly concerned with technical details about the product and with its components.

The validation and verification of expert systems is different from that of other types of computer systems (O'Leary, 1991). These differences include: a focus on symbolic knowledge rather than numeric; an investigation of previously unstructured problems; inclusion of both symbolic and numerical information in the same program (e.g., rules of the form "IF ... THEN" and uncertainty factors on the weights); and the general lack of a means by which to determine the quality of a solution by means other than a human verification.

To date, most of the methods for V & V have been developed for business fields, and they are often not suitable for the medical field. Accordingly, a trends that we expect to see increase with regard to V & V are the clinical trial methods that have widely been used in validating new drugs. Just as the effectiveness of new drugs must be validated by clinical trials, the accuracy and dependability of expert systems must undergo extensive clinical trials and be rated in experimental evaluation performing at human-expert levels in their respective domains.

5.4.   ETHICAL AND LEGAL CONSIDERATIONS

As an increasing number of computer programs are being promoted for medical use, ethical and legal problems will also result from the application of such programs in clinical settings. While the legal problems associated with expert systems that provide medical advice have fyet to be addressed by the courts, there are several important ethical and legal questions related to the use of expert systems in clinical medicine. Who should be authorized to use such systems, and in what ways? How can doctors and patients evaluate whether an expert system is safe for use with humans?

The major factor in determining the liabilities of a medical expert system is the classification of the system. If classified as a product, strict product liability will be imposed. But, if classified as a service, professional misconduct or negligence will be imposed (Cook and Whittaker, 1989). Since the physicians' acts of making a diagnosis and providing therapy have traditionally been classified as services, it is likely that adverse outcomes resulting from the use of such systems will be governed by the legal principle of negligence liability. As an increasing number of such systems are expected to be promoted for mecial use in the future, there should be proper research on these legal issue to prevent adverse outcomes.

The issue of responsibility is closely tied to the assignment of liability when a poor decision is made. It should be apparent that liability be assigned to the designers of an expert system a well as to its users. This should be an important consideration for potential developers of expert systems.

Furthermore, potential dangers exist in allowing open access to an expert system because the user might not be sufficiently trained to operate the system properly. Unauthorized or improper use of the system can result in legal problems. Moreover, the user must provide medically reliable information as input and be able to override a system's advice if the advice is in error. Access to some systems might therefore be limited to licensed professionals of specific categories. To use a program properly, the user would need the requisite educational background.

Using expert systems for decision-making raises many important ethical ussues, especially in dealing with medical decisions. Current technological advances have further complicated the relationship between physician and patient, forcing medical professionals to review even the most basic concepts on which their discipline is based (Holtzman, 1989). Moreover, using expert systems implies that knowledge engineers and domain experts will indirectly participate in the medical decision process. This ultimately means that we must carefully consider the extent to which such participation is desirable.

This discussion shows that using medical expert systems requires careful attention to ethical matters. Although the potential benefits of these systems can be great, they are also potentially subject to major abuse. Placing these systems in perspective within their human context is an essential factor in our ability to use them wisely.

5.5.   ACCEPTABILITY ISSUES

Most systems have not been effectively utilized outside a research environment, even when their performance has been shown to be excellent. This suggests that it is an error to concentrate research primarily on methods for improving the system's decision-making performance when clinical impact depends on solving behavioral problems of acceptance as well.

There are some conditions which exist in clinical environment that are uniquely related to developing and using expert systems, which may result in "problems." In many instances, user expectations have been raised too far regarding what can be achieved from expert systems. Users are often expecting dramatic improvements in decision-making and innovative new ways of treating patients. One message is that users must have realistic expectations about what a system can do, how much it costs, and how long it will take to effectively use it. Furthermore, there are some who would say that the bias of medical doctors with respect to computers is so strong that systems will inevitably be rejected, regardless of performance (Startsman and Robinson, 1972). Training may be the best way to deal with these situations.

However, we are beginning to see examples of applications in which initial resistance to these systems has gradually been overcome through the incorporation of adequate system benefits. A heightened awareness of human engineering issues will also make systems more acceptable to physicians by making the system easier and more friendly to use. The issues range from the graphic user interfaces (GUI) capability of the system that tailors the style of the interaction to the needs and desires of individual physicians to the features of the system that make it appear as a helpful tool rather than a complicting burden. Introduction of the Intelligent Computer-Assisted Instruction (ICAI) feature to the medical expert system may be needed in designing the system because, according to the survey by Kraut and Mann in 1996, the most frequent users in the future are expected to be physicians with little computer knowledge.

6.   FUTURE TRENDS

The applications of expert systems in medicine appear to be increasing at an almost exponential rate. However, among the expert systems that have been implemented, there are questions concerning the actual success of at least some of these implementations. Most of the systems published in papers have not been successful in practice, especially in the clinical environment. In some cases, failures have definitely occurred, and many of these failures have been due to an improper selection of domains or a neglect of the critical factor of expert system maintenance. In others, failure may be traced to the choice of the wrong knowledge acquisition and representation methods. However, several studies have shown that most problems encountered in the implementation of expert systems have not been a fault of the methodology. Rather, the faults most often can be ascribed to ethical and legal problems, behavioral problems, and certain errors on the part of those who have attempted to implement the methodology. Current research suggests that the following areas require attention in the future.

6.1.   PROCESSING OF TEMPORAL KNOWLEDGE

Physicians faced with diagnostic and therapeutic decisions must reason about clinical features that change over time. In diagnostic, prognostic, and therapeutic problem-solving, the chronology of disease symptoms, cures, and failures gives the physician insight into what may lie ahead for their patient. Temporal reasoning involves using a theory of change to predict the future or an explanation of the pat or present. Most current expert systems lack the ability to represent or infer temporal events consistently. However, a system that provides advice regarding patients with chronic diseases must be able to handle temporal issues since they should be managed with repetitive trials of empirical therapy.

Despite the importance of temporal features in medical decision-making, representing and reasoning about temporal concepts have proven difficult for medical expert systems. Simply adding a time stamp to each patient observation is insufficient in many applications. The appropriate interpretation of medical data is complicated by the effect of the current and past clinical contexts on the usefulness and validity of a measurement.

Temporal reasoning has been applied to the following areas in recent years: management of cholesterol (Rucker et al., 1990), interpretation of ECG (Tong et al., 1993), and patient monitoring (Shahar et al., 1993). As the prevalence of chronic diseases increases in the future, there will be many studies on temperoal reasoning that perform well in working medical expert systems. According to the 1996 survey conducted by Kraut and Mann, the most important future interests of research in the field of medical expert systems are: processing of uncertain and temporal knowledge (54%), aspects of system integration (35%), and aspects of knowledge acquisition and maintenance (27%).

6.2.   SYSTEM INTEGRATION

Most of the expert systems that have been developed in the field of medicine are essentially stand-alone systems. However, in the very near future, it is likely that a large segment of the expert systems being developed in this field will be integrated with other information systems. Integration with a hospital information system permits the expert system to have direct access to the medical database. Such access is often of considerable value. Integrating a medical database with an expert system can greatly improve the knowledge base construction. This has been a major impediment to the development of expert systems, because such methods as neural network or case-based reasoning can acquire knowledge directly from the database through the interface mechanism.

As the technology of the electronic medical record (EMR) improves, such integration will solve many technical problems in knowledge acquisition. Integration EMR can also greatly improve an accuracy of Bayesian system. Among the most commonly recognized problems with the use of a Bayesian approach has been the large amount of data required to determine all the conditional probabilities needed in the rigorous application of the formula. Such integration with the large medical database allows most of the necessary conditional probabilities to be obtained.

Another form of integration is that of the interface between expert systems with medical instruments such as ECG, EEG, laboratory analyzers, CT scanner, and MRI. For example, while the EEG analysis system developed by Davey et al. (1989) can automatically detect spikes and sharp waves in the EEG for the detection of epileptiform activity, this system is stand-alone. On the other hand, a computerized ECG interpretation system capable of diagnosing complex cardiac arrhythmias (Tong et al., 1993) would be of great practical value in patient care by decreasing the time required from the ECG acquisition to physician interpretation because the expert system interfaces with the ECG online. The costs of health care would also decrease with such a system by reducing the need fro hujman expertise to interpret ECG recordings. In addition, the quality of patient care may increase as a result of the consistency of interpretations offered by the computerized analysis system.

Similarly, the interpretation of CT scans can be automated by interfacing the expert system with CT scan (Natarajan et al., 1991). Since most of these medical instruments have an internal computer, such integration can easily be accomplished with current interfacing technology. Moreover, integration of fmedical instruments can also solve the problem of selecting proper domains because medical instruments are indispensable to the practice of medicine and physicians cannot perform adequately without them.

6.3.   SYSTEM EVALUATION

While formal evaluation of medical expert system is acknowledged as an important requirement for acceptance of expert systems in clinical environment, the lack of appropriate evaluation studies contributes to clinicians' reluctance to medical expert systems. As a part of evaluation, the validation of the expert system performance encounters several major problems (O'Keefe et al., 1987). Decisions about what to validate, what to validate against, what to validate with, or when to validate find not ready-made guidelines to support them. Especially, validation of expert system become more problematic when no standards are available, as it is the case in a wide variety of clinical settings. The majority of validation studies solve such a situation by considering, in rather different ways, the opinion of several experts. A major criticism to this approach comes from the fact that different specialists do not always reach an agreement, and the opinion of several experts may not always be accurate. Martin-Baranera et al. (1996) suggested to introduce an external reference, through simulation of non-experts, in validating the expert system for assessing the etiology of community-acquired pheumonia in absence of standards.

Diagnostic systems have tended to be assessed on the basis of their decision-making accuracy. Yet there are several additional components to the evaluation process when it is performed optimally. In order to demonstrate the effectiveness of a medical expert system, Shortliffe and Davis (1975) have suggested that system evaluations should be undertaken in a series of steps as follows:

1. Demonstrate a need for the system.
2. Demonstrate that the system performs at the level of an expert.
3. Demonstrate the system's useability.
4. Demonstrate acceptance of the system by physicians.
5. Demonstrate an impact on the mangement of patients.
6. Demonstrate an impact on the well-being of patients.
7. Demonstrate cost-effectiveness of the system.

Even though nearly 2 decades have passed since these seven-step evaluation criteria were published, not many medical expert systems have shown to meet formal validation criteria at all seven steps. In fact, most systems still have been assessed only at step 2, and remarkably few have met even the criterion of the need specified in step 1. However, if the system is to be used in a clinical environment rather than a research environment, formal system evaluations should be undertaken in these steps.

REFERENCES

Aikens, J.S., Kung, J.C., Shortliffe, E.H., and Fallat, R.J., "PUFF: an expert system for interpretation of pulmonary function data," in *Readings in Medical Artificialf Intelligence: The First Decade,* Clancey, B.C. and Shortliffe, E.H., (Eds.). Addison-Wesley, Reading, MA, 1984.

Ayel, M. and Laurent, J.P., *Validation, Verification and Test of Knowledge-Based Systems.* John Wiley & Sons Ltd., 1991.

Brender, J., Christensen, J.P., Sherrer, J.R., and McNair, P., *Proceedings of the Medical Informatics Europe '96,* IOS Press, Amsterdam, Netherlands, 1996.

Barr, A. and Feigenbaum, E.A., *The Handbook of Artificial Intelligence.* Heur is Tech Press. Stanford, CA. 1982.

Chae, Y.M., Ho, S.H., Hong, C.S., and Kim, C.W., Comparison of alternative knowledge model for the diagnosis of asthma. *Expert Systems with Applications,* 1996: 11(4); 423–429.

Clancey, W.J. and Shortliffe, E.H., *Readings in Medical Artificial Intelligence: The First Decade.* Addison-Wesley, Reading, MA, 1984.

Cook, D.F. and Whittaker, A.D., Legal issues of expert system use. *Applied Artificial Intelligence,* 1989: 3; 69–81.

Davey, B., et al., Expert system approach to detection of epileptiform activity in the EEG. *Medical and Biological Engineering and Computing,* 1989: 27(4); 365–370.

Durkin, J., *Expert Systems: Design and Development.* Macmillan Publishing Co. 1994.

Greenes, R.A., Peterson, H.E., and Protti, D.J., *Proceedings of the 8th World Congress on Medical Informatics,* North-Holland, Amsterdam, Netherlands, 1995.

Hillman, D.V., Integrating neural nets and expert systems. *AI Expert.* 1990: 4; 54–59.

Holtzman, S., *Intelligent Decision Systems.* Addison-Wesley, Reading MA, 1989.

Kane, B. and Rucker, D.W., AI in medicine. *AI Expert.* November 1988: 48–55.

Kraut, U. and Mann, F., Current research on medical knowledge-based systems in Germany. *Proceeddings of Medical Informatics Europe '96,* 1996: 532–536.

Lee, J.K., Liebowitz, J., and Chae, Y.M., *Proceedings of the 3rd World Congress on Expert Systems.* Cognizant Communication Corp., New York, 1996.

Martin-Baranera, M., Sancho, J.J., and Sanz, F., Simulation applied to medical expert systems validation in a absence of gold standard. *Proceedings of Medical Informatics Europe '96,* 1996: 506–510.

Miller, R.A., Schaffner, K.F., and Meifsel, A., Ethical and legal issues related to the use of computer programs in clinical medicine. *Annals of Internal Medicine*, 1985: 102; 529–36.

Mouradian, W.H., Knowledge acquisition in a medical domain. *AI Expert*, 1990: 5(7); 34–38.

Natarajan, K., Cawkey, MG., and Newell, J.A., A knowledge-based system paradigm for automatic interpretation of CT scans. *Medical Informatics*, 1991: 16(2); 167–181.

O'Keefe, R.M., Balci, O., and Smith, E.P., Validating expert system performance. *IEEE Expert*, 1987: 2(4); 81–90.

Pople, H.E., "CADUCEUS: an experimental expert system for medical diagnosis," in *The AI Business*, Winston, P.H. and Prendergast, K.A. (Eds.). M.I.T., Cambridge, MA, 1984, pp. 67–80.

Rich, E. and Knight, K., *Artificial Intelligence*, 2nd ed. McGraw-Hill, 1991.

Rucker, D.W., Maron, D.J., and Shortliffe, E.H., Temporal representation of clinical algorithms using expert-system and database tool. *Computers and Biomedical Research*, 1990: 23; 222–239.

Shahar, Y. and Musen, M.A., RESUME: a temporal-abstraction system for patient monitoring. *Computers and Biomedical Research*, 1993: 26; 255–273.

Shortliffe, E. and Davis, R., Some consideration of knowledge-based expert systems. *SIGART Newsletter*, 55; 9–12.

Shortliffe, E.H., Buchanan, B.G., and Feigenbaum, E.A. Knowledge engineering for medical decision making: a review of computer-based clinical decision aids. *Proceedings of the IEEE*, 1979: 67; 1207–1224.

Startsman, T.S. and Robinson, R.E., The attitudes of medical and paramedical personnel towards computers. *Computers and Biomedical Research*, 1972: 5; 218–227.

Tong, D.A. and Widman, L.E., Model-based interpretation of the ECG: a methodology for temporal and spatial reasoning. *Computers and Biomedical Research*, 1993: 26; 206–219.

APPENDIX
Medical Expert Systems Developed from 1992 to 1996

Year	System	Domain	Knowledge representation
1992	Bernelot Moens H.J. (AI/RHEUM)	Rheumatology	Rule-based reasoning
	Satomura Y. et al.	Medical diagnosis	Rule-based reasoning
	A-Rassk M. et al. (QSAR)	Molecularity	Rule-based reasoning (tree-structured series of rules)
	Schecke T. et al.	Cardiology	Fuzzy
	Metz D.E. et al.	Acoustics	Neural networks
	Fischer F. et al.	Self-instruction	Rule-based reasoning
	Musen M.A. (PROTEGE-II)	Medicine	Rule-based reasoning
	Lanzola G. et al.	Medical diagnosis	Rule-based reasoning
	Lill W. et al.	Skull structure (maxillofacial area)	Case-based reasoning
	Karp P.D.	Metabolism	Rule-based reasoning
	Learning M.S. et al.	Oncology	Rule-based reasoning
	Heathfield H. et al.	Breast disease	Rule-based reasoning
	Macura (CBT-RAD)	Tutor for neuroradiology	Case-based reasoning
	Guigo R. et al.	Genetics	Rule-based reasoning
	Long W.J. et al.	Cardiology (Heart failure)	Rule-based reasoning
	Rapoport G.N. et al.	Bioscience	Rule-based reasoning
	Stoker N.G. et al.	General surgery	Case-based reasoning
	Niemierko A. (RONSC)	Radiation Therapy (Tumor control and normal tissue)	Case-based reasoning
	Sneiderman C.A. et al.	Medical Thesauruses	Rule-based reasoning
	Uckun S.	Biomedicine	Model-based reasoning
	Engle R.L.	Medical diagnosis	Rule-based reasoning
	Demiling L.	Medicine	Chaos research, fuzzy logic
	Xing Y. et al. (QUALICON)	Neurology	Rule-based reasoning
	Valdiguie P.M. et al.	Biochemistry	Case-based reasoning
	Bonadonna F. et al.	Radiology	Visual knowledge processing
	Heckerman D.E. et al. (Pathfinder-Part I)	Medical diagnosis (Lymph node disease)	Non-decision-theoretic
	Kotzke K.	Nuclear medicine	Rule-based reasoning
	Heckerman D.E. et al. (Part II)	Medical diagnosis	Decision theory Rule-based reasoning
	Ohmann C. et al.	Gastroenterology	Decision analysis
	Dupuits F.M.H.M. (HIOS[a])	Daily medical care	Rule-based reasoning
	Fuzzy decision making (Yoshida K.)	Uncertainty in medical decision-making	Fuzzy set theory
	Popper M. (OOP)	Medicine	Rule-based reasoning
	Sotiropouls M.Th.	Urology	Concepts structure
	Miller (Q M R)	Medicine	Case-based reasoning
	Amaral M.B. (DSM-IIIR)	Medicine	Rule-based reasoning
	Amaral M.B. (NLP, DSM-IIIR)	Medicine	Rule-based reasoning
	Karp V.P. (Consilium-1)	Medicine	Rule-based reasoning
	Zhong Lijie (CHDDT)	Congenital heart disease	Rule-based reasoning
	Sawar M.J. (POEMS)	Postoperative care	Case-based reasoning Rule-based reasoning
	Schwaiger J. et al. (NIMON)	Renal disease	Rule-based reasoning (Causal probabilistic networks)
	Ketikidis P.H. et al. (ARRES)	Adverse respiratory and circulatory conditions in post-anaesthesia	Rule-based reasoning

APPENDIX *(continued)*
Medical Expert Systems Developed from 1992 to 1996

Year	System	Domain	Knowledge representation
	Ferri F. et al. (VOQUEL)	Pancreatic disease	Rule-based reasoning
	Bonfa I. et al.	Chronic liver disease	Rule-based reasoning
	Ohayon M. et al. (Adinfer)	Psychiatry	Rule-based reasoning
	Ong L.S. et al.	Hospital bed	Rule-based reasoning
	Bayasitoglu A. et al.	Liver disease	Rule-based reasoning
	Johansson B.G. et al.	Medicine	Arden syntax, C++
	Leao B. de F. et al.	Congenital heart disease	Three-layer model
	Fuge C.F. et al.	Diabetic disease (Hyperglycemia)	Computer-assisted instruction
	Berger J. (ROENTGEN)	Radiation therapy	Case-based reasoning
	Wenkebach U. et al.	Critical care patients	Rule-based reasoning
	Shahar Y. et al.	Patient monitoring	Three temporal-abstraction mechanism
	Muggletion S. et al.	Biology	Rule-based reasoning
	Westenskow D.R. et al.	Anesthesiology (Misdiagnosis)	Neural networks
	King R.D. et al. (GOLEM)	Pharmacy	Rule-based reasoning
	Shoemaker W.C. et al.	Hemodynamic (oxygen transport)	Physiology model based
1993	Alnahi H. et al.	Molecular biology	Statistical inductive algorithm
	Cohen D. et al.	DNA crystallographic data	Rule-based reasoning
	Clark D.A. et al. (CBS1, CBS2)	Protein structure	Logic language
	Clerkauer K.J. et al.	Protein structure	Neural networks
	Aaronson J.S. et al.	Nucleic acid	Case-based reasoning
	Mephu Nguifo E. et al.	Genetics	Symbolic-numeric machine learning system
	Bahler D. et al.	Chemical carcinogen	Rule-based reasoning (Induction-based method)
	Leng B. et al.	Protein structure	Case-based reasoning
	Graves M. (WEAVE)	Genetics	Rule-based reasoning
	Ferran E.A. et al.	Protein structure	Neural networks
	Conkklin D. et al.	Protein structure	Rule-based reasoning
	Widman L.E. et al. (EINTHOVEN)	Cardiology	Model-based system Heuristic rules
	Brezillon P.J. et al. (SAIC)	DNA sequence	Rule-based reasoning
	Lamb D.J. et al.	Male infertility	Neural networks
	Chow J.L. et al. (NMRES)	Cardiology	Rule-based reasoning
	Cavallo V. et al.	Radiology	Computer-based simulation
	Coleman W.P. et al.	Physiologic	Computational logic
	Weiver A.	Decision-making of critical care (Life-support)	Rule-based reasoning
	Lau F. et al.	Hemodynamics	Case-based reasoning
	Shahar Y. et al. (RESUME)	Patient monitoring	CLIPS knowledge-representation shell
	Berman L. et al. (DBX)	Biomedicine	Rule-based reasoning
	Tong D.A. et al.	Cardiology (Electrocardiograph)	Rule-based reasoning
	Rozenbojn J. et al.	Clinical diagnosis	ESE IBM Expert system language
	McKenzie D.P. et al.	Diagnostic decision	Rules, Linear discriminant analysis
	Giuse N.B. et al.	Acute perinephric abscess	Rule-based reasoning
	Cimino J.J. et al.	Medicine	Rule-based reasoning
	McGonigal M.D. et al.	Trauma	Neural networks
	Bishop C.W. et al.	Medical records, drug and test ordering	Rule-based reasoning

APPENDIX *(continued)*
Medical Expert Systems Developed from 1992 to 1996

Year	System	Domain	Knowledge representation
	Barosi G. et al.	Medical diagnosis	Diagnostic reasoning
	Ohayon M.M.	Psychiatry	Rule-based reasoning
	Mastsuo Y. et al.	Protein structure	Rule-based reasoning
	van Daalen C. et al.	Neurology (Brachial plexus injuries)	Rule-based reasoning
	Reeke G.N. Jr. et al.	Neuroscience	Neural networks
	Aynsley M. et al.	Biotechnology	Neural networks
	Ebell M.H.	Cardiology (CPR)	Neural networks
	Scott R.	Nuclear medicine	Neural networks
	Scott J.A. et al.	Lung scan	Neural networks
	Klopman G. et al.	Mutagenicity	Case-based reasoning
	Mural R.J. et al.	Genetics (DNA sequence)	Rule-based reasoning
	Wildnar M. et al.	Waiting lists	Fuzzy logic
	Cibulskis R.E. et al.	Health service	Rule-based reasoning
	Howells, S.L. et al.	Tumor	Neural networks
	Cohen O. et al. (RCPc)	Genetics	Rule-based reasoning
	Stemberg M.J. et al. (GOLEM)	Protein structure	Rule-based reasoning
	Sumner W. et al.	Medical practice	Rule-based reasoning
	Dojat M. et al.	Ventilation of patients	Rule-based reasoning
	Tape T.G. et al.	Ambulatory care	Rule-based reasoning
	Poon A.D. et al.	Medical care	Rule-based reasoning
	Bradabwm (FLORENCE)	Nursing care	Case-based reasoning
	Smith (Psychotherapy)	Psychotherapy of addictive behavior and psychological trauma	Case-based reasoning
	Jang (HYDI)	Heart disease	Case-based reasoning
	Modai L. et al.	Psychiatry	Neural networks
	Nicolas S.T. et al.	Human sleep	Neural networks
	Jack V.T. et al.	Cardiac surgery	Neural networks
	James R.G.	Amnesia in diffuse cerebral atrophy	Neural networks
	Khan (ISIS)	diagnostic imaging procedure	Case-based reasoning
1994	Paoli G. et al.	Hematology	Rule-based reasoning
	Leng B. et al.	Protein analysis	Case-based reasoning
	Hafner C.D. et al.	Biology	Rule-based reasoning
	Bichindaritz (Psychiatry)	Eating disorder	Case-based reasoning
	Chae Y.M. et al.	Allergic rhinitis	Neural networks Case-based reasoning
	Kim J.A. et al.	Nursing scheduling	Neural networks
1995	Dojat M. et al.	Medicine	Object-oriented programming Rule-based reasoning
	Likothanasis S.D. et al.	Cervix cancer	Neural networks
	Karp P.D.	Molecular biology	Neural networks
	Prokosch H.U. et al.	Rheumatology	Semantic networks
	Van den Heuvel F. et al. (SmaCS)	Heart disease	Rule-based reasoning
	Boegl K. et al.	Rheumatologic disease	Fuzzy theory
	Learner B. et al.	Genetics	Neural networks
	Sukhaswami M.B. et al.	Telugu (Characters)	Neural networks
	Korning P.G.	Genetics	Neural networks
	Kischell E.R. et al.	Neuroradiology	Neural networks
	Safran C. et al.	Patient record	Rule-based reasoning

APPENDIX   *(continued)*
Medical Expert Systems Developed from 1992 to 1996

Year	System	Domain	Knowledge representation
	Babic A. et al.	Asymptomatic liver disease	Neural networks
	Doering A. et al.	Epilepsy	Neural networks
	Dumitra A. et al.	Psychiatric mood disorder	Neural networks
	Leao B. et al. (HYCON S II)	CHD and renal disease	Neural networks
	Ohno-Machado L. et al.	AIDS	Neural networks
	Witte H. et al.	Epilepsy	Neural networks
	Yoshida K. et al.	Hepatobiliary disease	Neural networks Fuzzy rules
	Ichimura T. et al.	Hepatobiliary disease	Neural networks Fuzzy rules
	Tsumoto S. et al.	Headache and facial pain	Probabilitic rule-based reasoning
	Tong D.A. et al.	Cardiology	Telemedicine system
	Dore L. et al. (CPR)	Hypertension	Object oriented reasoning
	Ambrosino R. et al.	Cost-effective health care	Rule-based reasoning
	Ryder R.M. et al.	Cardiovascular rehabilitation	Rule-based reasoning
	Hogan W.R. et al.	Medicine	Belief network (For encoding reminder rules)
	Haddawy P. et al. (BNG)	Cardiology	Bayesian networks
	Hadzikadic M. et al.	Trauma	Standard logistic regression
	Kuperman G.J. et al.	Pharmacy	Rule-based reasoning
	Boon-Ralleur A.L. et al.	Hyperthyroid	Rule-based reasoning
	Smart J.R. et al.	Pathology	Rule-based reasoning
	Hosseini-Nezhad S.M. et al.	Pediatric	Neural networks
	Spyropoulos B. et al.	Nosology	Case-based reasoning
	Astion M.L. et al.	Rheumatic disease	Neural networks
	Ozkarahan I.	Health care costs in operation room	Rule-based reasoning
	Place J.F. et al.	Medicine	Neural networks
	Duong D.V. et al.	Semiotic	IAC neural networks
	Mayer-Ohly E. et al. (MEDRISK)	Insurance medical knowledge	Rule-based reasoning
	Shahar Y. et al. (RESUME)	Diabetes	Knowledge-based temporal abstraction
	Anderson J.D.	Clinical uncertainty	Case-based reasoning
	Boom R.A. (TICITL)	Jaundice, fever, acute high upper quadrant abdominal pain	Case-based reasoning
	Alendahl K.	Primary health care	Rule-based reasoning
	Cl ret M. (ADM[a])	Cardiology, pathologies	Rule-based reasoning
	Ferri F. (CADMIO)	Medicine	Rule-based reasoning
	Fiore M. (MUMPS)	Medicine	Rule-based reasoning
	Mann G.	Medicine	Object-oriented system
	Ohmann C.	Acute abdominal pain	Rule-based reasoning
	Schmidt R. (ICONS)	Antibiotics therapy	Case-based reasoning
	Baatar S. (RGT)	Medicine	Rule-based reasoning
	Hofest R. (METABOLICA)	Metabolic disease	Rule-based reasoning
	Kindler H. (FORMs)	Medicine	Rule-based reasoning
	Lau F.	ICU care	Case-based reasoning
	Narita Y. (3-AND-3-OR)	Medicine	Rule-based reasoning
	Stelmann F.	Toxoplasmasis	Rule-based reasoning
	Kovacs M. (Auctoriatas)	Psychiatry	Rule-based reasoning

APPENDIX *(continued)*
Medical Expert Systems Developed from 1992 to 1996

Year	System	Domain	Knowledge representation
	Nguyen H.P. (CHROMASSI[a])	Painful syndromes and chronic disease	Rule-based reasoning
	Balas E.A. (QFES)	Diabetes	Rule-based reasoning
	Edwards G.A. (PEIRS)	Pathology	Rule-based reasoning
	Frize M.	Intensive care	Case-based reasoning
	Schriger D.L. (EDECS)	Clinical guidelines	Rule-based reasoning
	Safran C.	HIV	Case-based reasoning
	Richards B.	Drug therapy in intensive care	Rule-based reasoning
	Brai A. (ALERT)	Anthrax, plague, smallpox	Case-based reasoning
	Sternberg M.J. et al.	Protein	STAMP algorithm
	Evans C.D.	Dysmorphology	Case-based reasoning
	Li Y.C. et al.	The behavior of physicians	Rule-based reasoning
	Seroussi B. et al.	Hemato-oncology	Rule-based reasoning
	Siregar P. (CAI)	Cardiology	Rule-based reasoning
	Ito M. (SAPIEN-Tx)	Renal disease	Rule-based reasoning
	Park H.A.	Stomach cancer	Neural networks
	Schriger D.L. (EDECS)	Emergency patient	Rule-based reasoning
1996	Thews O. et al.	Leukemia	Semantic networks
	Derks E.P. (PCV)	Chemical information	Neural networks
	Brickley M.R. et al.	Dentistry	Neural networks
	Sabbatini R.M.	Electrocardiograms Electroencephalograms	Neural networks
	Leao B.D. et al.	Medicine	Combinatorial neural networks Fuzzy ARTMAP model Semantic ART
	Wallner F.	Ophthalmology	Fuzzy
	Davenprot J.C. et al.	Dentistry	Rule-based reasoning
	Miao J. et al.	Hematology	Bayes Gaussia classification
	Dojat M. et al.	Ventilation	Rule-based reasoning
	White S.C.	Dentistry	Rule-based reasoning Bayesian conditional probability
	Michiko H. et al.	Diabetes mellitus	Rule-based reasoning Fuzzy
	Kim S.K.	Headache	Fuzzy Neural networks
	Peter S. et al. (FHDSS)	Fetal health	Rule-based reasoning Object-oriented method
	Garibaldi J.M. et al.	Umbilical cord blood	Fuzzy logic Rule-based reasoning
	Mcalister M.J. et al.	Color blindness	Rule-based reasoning Multimedia system
	Chae Y.M. et al.	Asthma	Neural networks Case-based reasoning Discriminant analysis
	Takahashi E. et al.	Hypertension	Rule-based reasoning
	Mann G. et al.	Collagen disease	Rule-based reasoning
	Godard P. et al. (Asthmaexpert)	Asthma	Rule-based reasoning Statistical method

APPENDIX   *(continued)*
Medical Expert Systems Developed from 1992 to 1996

Year	System	Domain	Knowledge representation
	Zbigniew S. et al. (SEKSDIAM)	Orthodontia	Neural networks
	Alexander R. et al.	Ischemia heart disease	Fuzzy set theory
	John L.N. et al.	Diabetes	Rule-based reasoning
	Kristian G. et al.	Diagnosis of multiple diseases	Causal probabilistic networks
	Wiesman F. et al.	Biomedical literature	Neural networks
	Gongxian C. et al.	Optic nerve diseases	Neural networks (SOM)
	David B. et al.	Radiology (Image retrieval)	Case-based reasoning Heuristic rules
	Paulescu N. et al. (FITOTER)	Phytotherapy	Rule-based reasoning
	Kokol P.Z. et al. (RO²SE)	Cardiology	Object-oriented method
	Meeking D.R. et al. (DIAS)	Diabetes	Causal probabilistic network
	Erkki P.	Acute abdominal pain	Neural networks
	Marek W.K. et al.	Acute renal failure	Rule-based reasoning
	Frauendienst G. et al.	Inborn error	Causal probabilistic networks Rule-based reasoning
	McCullagh P.J. et al.	Brainstem auditory evoked potentials	Neural networks
	Ankica B. et al.	Chronic hepatitis C	Rule-based reasoning
	Gudrun Z. et al.	Claucoma	Fuzzy rules Neural networks
	Iaid B. et al.	Clinical decision	Rule-based reasoning
	Gogou G. et al. (DBIRA)	Diabetes	Rule-based reasoning
	Rainer S. et al.	Kidney function	Case-based reasoning
	Fatima T. et al.	Hypertension	Rule-based reasoning
	Mann G. et al.	Lupus erythematosus	Rule-based reasoning
	Emilia S. et al. (MetEnerg)	Metabolic emergencies	Rule-based reasoning
	Gogou G. et al. (AntibiolS)	Antibiosis (Antibiotic prescription)	Rule-based reasoning (DELPHI language)
	Simona A. et al.	Alternative medicine	Traditional chinese methods (CompAc)
	Park H.A. et al.	Nursing scheduling	Neural networks
	Park K.S. et al.	Leukemia	Case-based reasoning

ᵃ Clinical use.

Source: Medline database; *Proceedings of the Medical Informatics Europe '96; Proceedings of the 3rd World Congress on Expert Systems; Proceedings of the 8th World Congress on Medical Informatics.*

33 Non-Defense Government Services and Operations

Amelia A. Baldwin, Paul L. Bowen, and Linda Gammill

CONTENTS

1. INTRODUCTION

Comparatively little attention has been given to the development and use of expert systems by governmental bodies or for governmental applications. Governmental-related expert systems are motivated by the regulatory role of government and pressure to reduce the size of government while increasing the quality of the services provided.

Due to their size and the unique characteristics of their environments, governments may reap more of the benefits associated with implementation of expert systems than organizations in the private sector. These benefits include managing complexity, promoting consistent responses, providing effective training, retaining organizational knowledge, and sharing and disseminating scarce expertise. Unfortunately, governments face difficult challenges in developing, implementing, and updating expert systems, e.g., short-term orientation of government officials, short-term view of voters, and many activities competing for limited funds.

This chapter reviews the motivation, benefits, development, and use of expert systems in the public sector, specifically for services and operations. This chapter first discusses the background of expert systems development in government, including factors that motivate and inhibit such development and the strategy of developing expert systems for government. Then, examples of governmental expert systems are illustrated. Research issues are addressed, followed by a brief discussion of future trends.

2.   BACKGROUND

Many areas of government can benefit from the proper development and use of expert systems technology. The possibilities are practically endless. Expert systems can be used to overcome some of the unique problems faced by governments. For example, expert systems can help overcome inconsistencies in government service caused by periodic changes in personnel due to political changes or scheduled rotation of personnel. Expert systems can help smooth the transition from one administration to another by reducing the learning curve for newly elected officials and political appointees.

Diplomats who change posts on a frequent basis can learn about the unique characteristics of their new host country using an expert system tutor. Expert systems can train unskilled or under-privileged citizens to prepare them for employment in government or the private sector. Expert system tutors can also be used to train government workers for new job tasks.

The regulatory role of government is immense. Much of government is characterized by a plethora of rules and regulations that must be followed. Expert systems can be used as knowledge compliance systems, which insure that actions comply with complex government rules and regulations.

Expert systems can be used to provide information to citizens through either manned or unmanned help desks. For example, the IRS often has difficulty during the height of tax season handling the many requests for tax assistance and information. A shortage of knowledgeable technicians is particularly trying at this time of the year. An expert information system cannot only provide consistent service to the public, but can decrease the work overload on IRS personnel at tax time. Only a handful of people have an in-depth knowledge of some sections of the tax code. Expert systems can facilitate the knowledge sharing and dissemination of that specialized knowledge and expertise.

2.1.   STRATEGY OF DEVELOPMENT

Organizations, including government entities, develop expert systems because they expect these systems to have an impact on the success of the organization. The organizational strategy process may be modeled with six steps, as shown in Figure 1. This process usually involves an assessment of the state of the organization and a recognition that the organization (or some part of it) can be or must be improved. Expert systems are then developed and used as a part of the organization's strategy for changing itself. Characteristics of the organization, such as technology orientation, may impact the development of expert systems. Ultimately, the development and use of expert systems affect the state of the organization, creating a positive change, such as improved productivity. To illustrate this process, the organizational strategy process that resulted in the MAGIC system of Merced County, California, is described in Table 1.

There are a few examples of measuring results of the reinvention efforts (Kellam, 1995). For example, Sunnyvale, California, measures performance to reward successful managers. A manager can receive up to a 10% bonus when his/her program exceeds its objectives for quality and productivity. The state of Oregon sets benchmarks to judge how it is doing in such areas as reducing the crime rate, improving basic student skills, etc. While few expert systems include detailed performance measurements, such measurements are vital to governments to assess whether individual expert systems in government have been or will be a success.

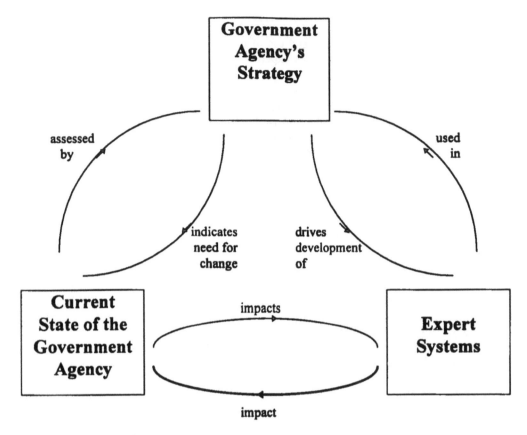

FIGURE 1 Organizational strategy process.

TABLE 1
The Relationship Between Organization, Strategy, and Expert System Development

The MAGIC Expert System

1	The state of the organization is assessed in light of the organization's strategy	Merced County's (California) Human Services Agency (HSA) delivers social services, which include welfare, food stamps, medicaid, and foster care. The services must be delivered while numerous rules and policies are followed.
2	Change is desired in the state of the organization	HSA desired to improve the delivery of these social services while at the same time reduce their costs.
3	Expert systems are developed	MAGIC (Merced Automated Global Information Control) was developed.
4	Expert systems used in the organization's strategy	MAGIC is used by agency workers to determine client eligibility at the first interview.
5	The organization impacts the expert systems	Pressures on HSA to cut costs and improve service quality and timing impacted the design of the MAGIC expert system.
6	The expert systems impact the state of the organization	Use of the MAGIC expert system has resulted in a 28% reduction in staff, an 85% reduction in the time needed to process an application, and $1.5 million in cost savings in the first year alone.

2.2.   Factors Motivating Expert System Development

The factors motivating the development and use of expert systems by governmental entities are similar to the reasons businesses engage in expert systems development. Governmental entities, however, must take into consideration the unique characteristics and challenges associated with public institutions. Specifically, conditions that motivate the use of expert systems in government include pressure to shrink the size of government and increase productivity, the role of government as an information provider, the complexity of regulation, the volume of information that must be processed, the scarcity of experts, and citizen dissatisfaction.

Shrinking government. A number of factors contribute to the attrition of experienced staff in both the private and public sectors. Expert systems encode and store the knowledge and experience of an expert within a software program. Facts, relationships, and judgmental knowledge of human experts are incorporated into the expert system. Thus, the expert system application is an invaluable resource that makes an organization less vulnerable to staff attrition by encapsulating knowledge into a tangible system that can be owned, retained, and improved by an entity.

Quest for productivity. Expert systems can be used to increase the productivity and effectiveness of experienced as well as novice personnel. Merced County, California, uses an expert system designed to make the provision of social services more efficient and effective (Kidd and Carlson, 1992). Because welfare and social services often get bogged down in the mass of rules and regulations, a similar system is being developed for the State of Pennsylvania Welfare Department. Tulare County, California, uses a similar expert system to manage the 6000 frequently changing rules that govern welfare and social service payments. Previously, employees were unable to apply all the rules correctly; the expert system has reduced the error rate from 38% to virtually zero (Betts, 1993).

Nature of regulation. Expert systems applications are well suited to iterative tasks that require frequent interpretation of standard sets of rules or procedures, as is often the case with governmental regulations. High task frequency and a continuing task need are indicators of sufficient demand to motivate expert system development. Taxation and social services, for example, involve iterative tasks that use rules and procedures and must be done in volume. Expert systems can assist in handling the high volume of such tasks and improving the consistency of performance.

Volume of information. The implementation of expert systems can aid in handling problems requiring the filtering, interpretation, and cross-referencing of large volumes of information that are common to governmental applications. The U.S. federal tax code and regulations alone are comprised of over 7 million words of complex and incomprehensible legalese. In addition, the U.S. Internal Revenue Service sends about 15 million letters to taxpayers each year. The IRS now uses an expert system to generate these letters.

Providing information services. Government workers spend a great deal of time engaged in information-related tasks, suggesting that one of the roles of government is as an information service provider. Expert systems, making use of the knowledge of some of the best organizational experts, are particularly well suited for information service operations and governmental organizations for a number of reasons. First, expert system applications have quicker response times than their human counterparts. Second, the systems can be designed to provide highly interactive and user-friendly information for ease in understanding and interpreting information. Finally, artificial intelligence implementations provide organizations with round-the-clock expert service for both consumers and government officials.

Scarcity of experts. The demand for expert systems is related to the lack of accessibility to experts on a dependable and consistent basis. In government, this problem is aggravated by the phenomenon that the most expert and experienced employees may be lured away from government to potentially more lucrative jobs in the private sector. In addition, some areas of government service are so unique that alternate sources of expertise may not even exist. For example, government activities such as tax compliance, welfare and social services, and law enforcement have no real equivalents in the business world.

Citizen dissatisfaction. The 1994 American Consumer Satisfaction Index survey revealed that Americans rate the public sector (including trash collection, police, and the Internal Revenue Service) lowest overall for quality of goods and service used by Americans. Dissatisfaction with government services is almost universal. Unlike the private sector, in which the payer and the consumer are generally assumed to be the same, governmental consumers can be divided into two types, which are not mutually exclusive. Those receiving the benefit of the services (citizens) and those paying for the services (taxpayers) are unique kinds of customers — most of whom are also voters.

In the private sector, organizations face the discipline of the competitive free market. Governments, however, usually hold monopoly positions. Dissatisfaction with a business product or service is shown by either complaints or by consumers not purchasing the product or services again. Of course, choosing *not* to purchase a governmental service is not generally an option — taxes, municipal services, and police protection, for example. In most countries and localities, governmental consumers show their dissatisfaction for governmental service through complaints, and more important, at the ballot box. Voters demand improved governmental services. Expert systems may be at least a partial solution.

2.3. FACTORS INHIBITING EXPERT SYSTEM DEVELOPMENT

While some of the factors that inhibit expert systems development in government are similar to those in business, others are unique to the circumstances surrounding government activities. The major impediments to governmental development of expert systems include cost, knowledge engineering difficulties, technology orientation, time frame of government officials, voter attitude, and competing activities for limited funds.

Cost. The costs of developing expert systems can be high, depending on the complexity of the domain, availability of experts, etc. Unfortunately, many, if not most, governmental agencies do not have access to the large research and development budgets of some business organizations. The Internal Revenue Service (IRS), for example, began an artificial intelligence development program in 1983. Because the IRS had no previous experience, a considerable investment in training and technology was required, and the annual budget now exceeds $5 million (Rogers and Beckman, 1990).

Fortunately, the cost of the necessary computer hardware and software has been falling and expert system shells and tools are providing quicker development. Furthermore, given the size of government, significant economies of scale can often be achieved by government organizations, i.e., more people may use an expert system than in the private sector where several organizations perform the same function but do not share an expert system for competitive reasons.

Knowledge engineering difficulties. In the public sector, the scarcity of knowledge engineers is a major factor inhibiting expert systems development. In addition, in some areas of government where an expert system could be most useful, communication between knowledge engineers and domain experts can be quite difficult, e.g. diplomats in far-flung regions. Also, the need to update systems for changing environments in such domains as diplomacy could be onerous.

Technology orientation (or lack of it). For an organization to effectively develop and use expert systems, its people must be willing to adapt to new ideas and new technologies. Organizations without a technology orientation are more likely to experience expert systems development failure. Predictably, many of the governmental agencies that have already successfully implemented expert systems are those that had a forward-looking technology attitude even before the expert systems development was begun, such as military and defense departments and space exploration agencies.

Time frame of government officials. One of the characteristics that defines public institutions is the short time perspective of its top managers, sometimes averaging as little as 18 months. This relatively short time horizon that shapes governmental unit culture is a result of political constraints. One of the casualties of this short time frame is technological innovation and investment, especially those like expert systems that take a considerable amount to time to develop. Because of the pressure to see results immediately, more short- term, highly visible projects have a higher priority.

Short-term voter view. Expert systems development is not accomplished overnight. Because governmental bodies are altered as voter' preferences change, voters' evaluation of an expert system project may be crucial to its long-term success. Unfortunately, voters tend to have a short-term view. As today's society becomes accustomed to almost instant information and feedback, voters are likely to adopt an even shorter term focus. Therefore, expert systems are most appropriate for governmental tasks that are not radically transformed by a change in elected officials.

Competing activities for limited funds. Taxation and budgetary allocatoins provide the monetary resources for public institutions to perform their activities and accomplish their mission and goals. Most information resource management (IRM) expenditures in the public sector are lower than in the private sector, as low as 1 or 2% of budget. Because of limited resources in the public sector, many projects are competing for them. In fact, most dollars spent on information technology go into maintaining existing applications rather than developing new systems, including expert systems. Hence, the non-committed resource available to develop expert systems can be severely limited.

In analyzing where states are choosing to expend resources, the major portion of them are building their infrastructure to improve transaction processing and communication, especially with the states' citizens. If the public sector follows the pattern of information technology implementation that the private sector has, only after their infrastructures for transaction processing and management information systems have been well developed will they recognize the usefulness of expert systems.

3.   APPLICATIONS

While expert systems development has occurred in a wide variety of government agencies, only five principle domains are addressed in this section. Some areas involve security and defense and therefore have limited publicly available information. Other areas are so specialized that they do not provide useful examples to promote expert systems development in other government departments or countries. The five areas that are discussed below are environment and pollution, construction and planning, law and law enforcement, social services, and taxation. These areas are particularly suited to expert systems development because they are highly regulated tasks, are important to voters, and are generally applicable to most nations, states, and localities.

3.1.   ENVIRONMENTAL APPLICATIONS

Many areas relating to measuring the quality of the environment and enforcement of environmental legislation are appropriate for expert systems development. The development of expert systems for examining pollution and contamination is growing. Environmental expert systems are being developed and used in a number of countries.

The SIRENAS expert system, developed by a department of the Industry, Commerce and Tourism Ministry of Spain, simulates the results of a release of hazardous material and assesses the risks posed by the accident. A similar system that assesses pollution sources and exposure has been developed in Russia (Liebowitz, 1994). The U.S. Nuclear Regulatory Commission's Reactor Safety Assessment System helps a nuclear reactor safety team respond to a power plant accident. The Expert Disclosure Analysis and Avoidance System helps the U.S. Environmental Protection Agency determine what information concerning toxic chemical releases may be released to the public without compromising information that it is legally obligated to protect from public disclosure (Karna, 1985).

Expert-system-based ecologist workstations are used in Russia to perform environmental protection tasks in industrial areas (Kuzmin and Solovyov, 1993). The SAFE prototype expert system determines causes for poor indoor air quality in Italy (Liebowitz, 1994). The SEPIC expert system aids the Travis County, Texas, Heath Department in assessing applications for installing sewers (Karna, 1985).

3.2. Construction and Planning Applications

Structural engineering and planning applications involve numerous mathematical methods and calculations that would normally have to be mastered before proceeding to the planning stages of structural development. Through the use of well-defined rules, often involving symbolic representations, expert systems relieve engineers of some of the planning/inspection and design difficulties. The regulation and enforcement of building codes is a primary function of local governments. This area involves a large number of complex regulations and the plan checkers who administer them often have little experience.

A prototype expert system used by the City of Vancouver, British Columbia, Canada, aids in the review of compliance within the fire separation component of Vancouver's building bylaws. The system increases the productivity of plan checkers and improves the accuracy and consistency of regulation enforcement (Heikkila and Blewett, 1992). The NORM expert system evaluates architectural applications submitted to a local city planning agency in Italy to identify any part of the application that does not comply with building laws and rules (Liebowitz, 1994).

The Mexican Federal Electric Commission's SE-Viento expert system guides and assists the calculation of wind loads on buildings during the design stage (Liebowitz, 1994). The Computerized Highway Noise Analyst is a rule-based expert system that is used to control a highway noise barrier design model called OPTIMA. AUGERPILE is an expert system being developed to aid in the field inspection of augured concrete cast-in-place pile installation (Karna, 1985).

3.3. Law and Law Enforcement Applications

Legal and law enforcement applications of artificial intelligence and expert systems are not found as often as in other areas. This may be due in part to lawyers' traditional distrust of new information technologies. Implementations of expert systems in the legal arena, however, are growing.

The Police Officer Large Expert System assists police authorities in their day-to-day handling of law enforcement activities. This system provides coordination of quick reaction and order in sudden events, organization of information about police situations, and assistance in decisions applying Chinese policy and law. The Computer Aided Crime Investigation Tool expert system supports crime scene reconstruction in Taiwan (Liebowitz, 1994). PSR-Advisor helps probation officers make sentence recommendations to U.K. Magistrate's Courts (Copley, 1994). EVIDENT is a prototype expert system for determining the admissibility of evidence under U.S. federal rules (Zeide and Liebowitz, 1994).

3.4. Social Services Applications

In the U.S., welfare and social services assistance is provided by state departments of public welfare through the administration of a number of welfare programs. Rules and regulations governing welfare and social service programs are the responsibility of federal and state governments. Relatively few expert systems applications exist in the social services and public welfare sector of government because of the difficulty in gathering the knowledge needed to implement systems. Increased development in the social services and public welfare arena is needed.

The Foster Care Expert System (FOCES) is a system being developed to provide advice to social workers at the Roanoke City, Virginia, Department of Social Services. The primary goal of the system is to match children with possible foster care homes (Karna, 1985). The Tulare County, California, Department of Public Social Services has placed an expert system in the county's rural areas. The system explains the county's welfare services in six languages to the neediest citizens and leads them through the application process (Betts, 1993).

An expert system at the Human Services Agency in California's Merced County helped the agency make some needed improvements. MAGIC (Merced Automated Global Information Control) helps integrate Aid to Dependent Children, Food Stamps, Medi-Cal, Foster Care, and Refugee Cash Assistance programs into one system. The integration of these programs into one system has enabled the agency to fully automate the process of determining eligibility and availability of benefits as well as assist in tracking, scheduling, monitoring, and reporting case-management information. MAGIC allows caseworkers to become more productive by eliminating tedious filing and manual tracking procedures. Before MAGIC, an applicant would complete a 12–14 page form before an initial meeting (Kidd and Carlson, 1992).

3.5.   TAXATION

Taxation usually involves mega-volumes of complex regulations. Taxation agencies are traditionally rated in the basement for citizen satisfaction. Expert systems are one way to handle the complexity and improve both productivity and service quality.

HM Customs & Excise agency collects the value added tax (VAT) on supplies of goods and services. Businesses must comply with numerous, complex, and changing regulations or face harsh civil penalties. General auditors review client VAT systems as part of an annual audit. A U.K. auditing firm developed VAT Intelligent Assistant to help auditors appraise clients' VAT systems and procedures.

In the early 1980s, the U.S. Internal Revenue Service determined that artificial intelligence techniques could be used to solve some of its information processing problems. The shear volume of information processing needed to process tax information for the individual and corporate taxpayers in a populous country was overwhelming the federal agency. The IRS began an AI project that has grown substantially over the past dozen years and now includes a number of expert systems in use (Rogers and Beckman, 1990).

The IRS now uses the Correspondex expert system to generate its 15 million letter to taxpayers each year. The system not only reduced the error rate from 30% to less than 10%, but also ensures that every letter is grammatically correct and begins with a polite paragraph. The IRS's Automated Issues Identification System decides which issues should be investigated in a tax return audit. The Taxpayer Service Assistant helped the IRS provide correct tax information to taxpayers who call in their questions by phone.

Other systems are in use or development. The Link Analysis System is used to identify criminal tax activity. The Reasonable Cause Determination expert system helps determine when late payment penalties should not be enforced. The International Section 482 expert system will analyze multinational corporations' income and expense calculations (Rogers and Beckman, 1990).

Clearly, taxation is a domain that is well-suited for expert systems applications. Tax authorities can use expert systems to improve productivity, taxpayer satisfaction, and collections. The IRS serves as an exemplar of expert systems development and application that other government agencies should model.

4.   RESEARCH ISSUES

Areas for development in governmental services and operations are numerous. Some of the type of tasks that are appropriate for expert systems development are discussed below. Research questions are also identified.

4.1. TRANSITIONING

Expert systems can be developed to provide an organizational or functional memory in periods of transition. Governments, even more so than the private sector, are often characterized by periodic and frequent changes in personnel, particularly the politically elected or appointed. In addition, the diplomatic corps usually involves continuous rotation of duties from one country to another, causing diplomatic personnel to experience a learning curve each time a new post begins. Expert systems can serve as tutors to help them through the transition period more successfully and quickly. These systems will insure that the organizational knowledge is not lost with each transition or change, but is retained and made easily available for use by succeeding personnel.

A number of research issues of importance are apparent. How should the required organizational intelligence be identified, captured, stored, and updated? What organizational structures are required to insure that the knowledge base is updated in a timely, effective, and cost-efficient manner? How should out-of-date knowledge be identified and purged or replaced? This last issue is particularly germane for diplomats who enter new foreign settings in which major upheavals of government have occurred. Much of the information in the knowledge base will be useless, if not dysfunctional, under those circumstances.

4.2. TRAINING AND JOB ISSUES

Expert systems should be designed for use in training, identifying available jobs, forecasting skill requirements for jobs, and matching people with the appropriate jobs. As job skill requirements are identified, expert system technology can be used to train workers with the appropriate skills. Research issues to be addressed include: How is knowledge concerning job skills and needs gathered? How is such a knowledge base to be maintained properly?

4.3. TECHNICAL ASSISTANCE

One of the most onerous tasks of government and for citizens is dealing with the many rules and regulations that affect daily living. Expert systems can be used to serve as automated or semi-automated help desks. Specific applications include answering tax compliance questions, addressing compliance with health and safety regulations, identifying paperwork required to start a small business, and determining rules for obtaining permits for construction. Relevant research issues include: How can conflicts and ambiguities in laws and regulations be resolved for inclusion in a knowledge base? How are changes to regulations or laws identified and appropriate updates made to a knowledge base? How is the complexity of regulations and laws designed into a knowledge base and/or inference engine?

4.4. FRAUD, WASTE, AND ABUSE

Expert systems can be developed to spot fraud, waste, and abuse caused through government contractors, inappropriate welfare recipients, or social security payments made to deceased individuals. Expert systems can also be used to examine large volumes of information in which small errors can be critical, such as criminal system records. Previous research in auditing and compliance can assist in addressing such questions as: How are likely frauds or errors identified? What data are most likely to provide evidence of errors or wrongdoing?

4.5. PLANNING

The planning function of government is one of its largest and most complex functions. Roads, sewers, schools, and other public services require massive amounts of planning. Expert systems to assist in planning will necessarily involve large amounts of data. How is such data controlled and organized? Furthermore, how are experts needed for development of knowledge bases identified? Do experts really exist for this purpose? Or, should the expert systems development process itself be part of the expertise creation function?

4.6. FORECASTING AND MEASUREMENT

Can expert systems be used to forecast and measure the effects of laws and regulations? Laws are usually passed in order to achieve a specific goal or set of goals. Often, the actual outcomes are neither desired nor predicted in advance. This research involves modeling and forecasting human behavior in a complex environment. An expert system, for example, that predicts the effect of a change in tax law must make inferences on a wide range of behavioral and environmental factors. Are such expert systems currently too complex for development?

5. FUTURE TRENDS AND SUMMARY

Due to the increased necessity of handling vast amounts of knowledge and data, expert systems and artificial intelligence applications have grown considerably in a number of fields. The ability to use expert system technology to train new experts, reduce costs, and retain greater amounts of knowledge and data have led to arguments for the incorporation of expert systems into governmental and public sector institutions. Clearly, the use of expert systems in the corporate world has led the way for introduction and further implementation of a wide variety of intelligent systems in government. Government agencies must investigate the utility of expert systems to assist with their assigned functions.

> A good government implies two things; first, fidelity to the object of government, which is the happiness of the people; secondly, a knowledge of the means by which that object can be best attained.
>
> James Madison

Expert systems may be the means of achieving the reinvention of many government services. Specific areas in public institutions that have been identified as targeted areas of improvement and for which expert systems have been successfully utilized in the private sector are as follows. At the federal level, the reinvention of human resources management at the U.S. Office of Personnel Management is central to the government reinvention efforts. Expert systems could be used successfully in matching personnel skill sets with newly established job descriptions, right-sizing the workforce, identifying job positions no longer needed, establishing training plans that match needed job skills, performance appraisals, etc. Another major area of reinvention is procurement not only at the federal level, but also at the state level. Expert systems could assist decision-making in RFP creation, RFP evaluations, vendor evaluations, etc.

Many opportunities for expert system consideration exist in revamping state services. Arizona's efforts to increase productivity in the entire civil service system, Idaho's efforts to reengineer its risk management area, Massachusetts' welfare determination that will be going from specialized caseworkers to generic caseworkers, Mississippi's review of the tax collection process, and Texas' department consolidation efforts are some examples of expert system opportunities.

This chapter has discussed expert systems developed in nine countries on three continents. Development of expert systems should be encouraged in more government agencies and in more countries. Countries and agencies with more experience in expert systems development should assist other countries and agencies in improving their services with this technology. Technological innovation and knowledge sharing in government have many possibilities, including economies of scale, fewer errors and frustrations, and reduced overall cost of government.

REFERENCES

Betts, M. (1993a). Reinventing government. *Computerworld,* 27(16:April 19) 20.

Copley, M.G. (1994). PSR-Advisor: an expert system to aid probation officers in sentence recommendation. *International Journal of Applied Expert Systems,* 2(1) 22–38.

Heikkila, E. and E. Blewett (1992). Using expert systems to check compliance with municipal building codes. *Journal of the American Planning Association,* 58(1) 72–80.

Karna, K., Editor (1985). *Expert Systems in Government Symposium* (Washington D.C.: IEEE Computer Society Press), 423–430.

Kellam, S. (1995). Reinventing Government. *CQ Researcher,* 5(7) 147–167.

Kidd. R.C. and R.J. Carlson (1992). A truly magic solution. In (Scott and Klahr, Editors), *Innovative Applications of Artificial Intelligence,* 4 (AAAI Press: Menlo Park, CA) 237–247.

Kuzmin, S.M. and V.D. Solovyov (1993). Expert-system-based ecologists' workstations. *International Journal of Applied Expert Systems,* 1(1) 75–85.

Liebowitz, J., editor (1994). *Moving Towards Expert Systems Globally in the 21st Century* (New York: Cognizant Communications Corporation).

Rogers, T. and T. J. Beckman (1990). The IRS artificial intelligence laboratory. *The Tax Advisor,* 21(1) 51–54.

Zeide, J. and J. Liebowitz (1994). An applications experience of introducing EVIDENT to law professors. In (J. Liebowitz, Editor), *Moving Toward Expert Systems Globally in the 21st Century* (New York: Cognizant Communications Corporation) 1396–1398.

34 Military Expert Systems Applications

Thomas P. Galvin

CONTENTS

1. INTRODUCTION

The U.S. military is an extraordinarily complex organization. It is self-sustaining with respect to its personnel, intelligence, and logistical needs. Its elements range from the strategic planners at the Pentagon to combat units scattered throughout the world. Its mission and requirements change constantly, spurred by external events such as conflict, terrorism, humanitarian needs, and the election process.

Few events have affected the military like the fall of the Soviet Union and subsequent end of the Cold War. Immediately, voters' cries to reduce the American defense establishment translated into manpower and equipment downsizing. Yet, military requirements have not reduced in kind. Without the Soviet presence, smaller nations and groups have resumed old rivalries. Peacekeeping and peace enforcement missions have increased, as have military-supported humanitarian and economic assistance programs. "Do more with less" has become a mantra.

Expert system technologies have helped the military meet this mantra. At the highest levels, expert systems are providing strategic planners with "what-if" capabilities, saving time and manpower in implementing political mandates. In the field, expert systems are helping to reduce the amount of equipment a soldier must carry on the battlefield. Through all echelons, expert systems are working to integrate and synthesize the vast amounts of information produced on the battlefield.

This chapter is organized as follows. First, it will describe the U.S. military's artificial intelligence (AI) program, including a comparison of the different ways the services implement their programs. Second, it will present a series of expert systems applications present and recent past. These applications will range from lab experiments to fully employed systems. Finally, it will present the military's vision of expert systems as the military enters the 21st century.

2.   THE AI PROGRAM IN THE U.S. MILITARY

With respect to introducing AI into large organizations, there is value in reviewing the AI programs among the Navy, Air Force, and Army. Each has organized and staffed its AI effort to suit its needs, and each has been tremendously successful.

The military took notice of AI as it came out of the lab and into the corporate world during the late 1970s. To help foster and manage the introduction of expert systems and other AI technologies, each service established central oversight agencies. In 1982, the Navy established the Navy Center for Applied Research in Artificial Intelligence (NCARAI). The NCARAI provides oversight for both the Navy and the Marines. The Army established the U.S. Army Artificial Intelligence Center (USAAIC) in 1984. The Air Force's Office of Scientific Research (AFOSR) established oversight for the Air Force's AI program that same year.

Each of the service's oversight agencies has similar missions — to serve as a proponent of artificial intelligence for their respective services. All three manage the awarding of external contracts for expert system software. The difference lies in how in-house development of expert systems is managed.

- The Navy and Air Force programs are somewhat centralized. The Navy's in-house development teams are primarily in the Naval Research Lab facilities and the Naval Postgraduate School in Monterey, CA. The Air Force's program is similarly centralized, operating out of the main Air Force laboratories (Rome, Wright, Armstrong, and Phillips) and the Air Force Institute of Technology at Wright-Patternson AFB in Dayton, OH. Most Navy and Air Force AI personnel are civilian, although both send officers to their respective post-graduate schools for AI degrees.
- The Army's program is more decentralized. In 1988, the USAAIC established the Knowledge Engineering Group (KEG) concept, and has established over 30 KEGs in Department of the Army agencies, schools, and some corps headquarters. The purpose of a KEG is to provide their commander with direct access to expert systems technologies. Most KEGs are composed of two to four AI-trained uniformed officers and civilians. KEGs are located in several Department of the Army agencies, schools, and tactical commands. The Army has established a special career track for AI-trained officers, and these officers are assigned AI-related jobs by the USAAIC.

There are advantages and disadvantages to both approaches:

- The clear advantage to the Army's decentralized approach is that it makes the technology directly visible to the customer. KEGs are accessible and generally have an easier time gaining access to domain experts. KEGs can also focus on integrating expert system solutions into the overall solution to a problem. The disadvantage is that KEGs are only manned for prototype development and can rarely sustain a system or knowledge base. Also, KEGs can only handle small short-term projects. Larger projects require outside assistance.
- The Navy and Air Force's centralized approach is better suited for long-term or large projects. As you will see in the applications portion of this chapter, many of the Navy and Air Force technology efforts require a long-term focus — especially in the areas of robotics and logistics. The two disadvantages are the comparative lack of visibility and the danger of projects becoming lab experiments not suitable for the field.

3.   CURRENT AND RECENT APPLICATIONS

Military expert system applications span a wide range. Expert systems have found their way into such functional areas as resource allocation, personnel, operations, logistics, training and education, intelligence, and others. Many applications are local to a specific headquarters, but some have been expanded for use across the U.S. Department of Defense. This section presents successful applications for each of the above functions.

The services' respective oversight agencies and laboratories maintain listings of active and recent projects. The projects described below were selected from these lists. Some project managers have published journal or magazine articles and/or conference papers describing their work. These are cited in the text and listed in the References section of this chapter. The Acknowledgments section provides the location and points of contact for all nonpublished projects or those published in military-only magazines.

3.1.   STRATEGIC DECISION-MAKING AND PLANNING

The volatile and uncertain nature of the post-Cold War era has shown that major crises can surface anywhere in the world. In some cases, the U.S. military will respond — either as a deterrent, a peacekeeping or peace enforcement force, a disaster relief force, or, in the worst case, a combat force. Their composition depends on the nature of the crisis, available units, and available transportation to deploy and sustain the units.

Responding to an emergency is an incredibly complex and time-consuming problem. U.S. military units are stationed all over the world. Some units face significant equipment or personnel shortages. Many specialized support units, such as civil affairs groups, are reserve units that would have to be activated. Political considerations often restrict the planners' options. The planners must weigh hundreds of such variables when preparing their plans. Compounding the problem is that much of the process is manual. Consequently, preparing a plan for a response is expensive, averaging 19 people and 9 days. A 9-day delay could mean significant loss of life or property at the crisis location.

This section discusses two related USAAIC projects that help planners study a national emergency and build an operation plan to handle it. They are Blacksmith and SABRE, and together they won the American Defense Preparedness Association (ADPA) award at the 1994 ADPA AI Conference.

3.1.1.   Strategic Decision-Making Based
on Organizational Behavior — Blacksmith

Translation of political objectives and policy decisions into military operations is a difficult and dangerous task, both in peace and in war. The second- and third-order effects of a policy decision are almost impossible to measure ahead of time. Policy decisions do not affect personnel, equipment, and facilities equally. Sometimes adverse effects come unexpectedly. Explaining anticipated effects to Congress is difficult without some hard supporting data.

Blacksmith (USAAIC, 1996) uses expert system and blackboard technologies to model policy decisions and report their impact to the Army's senior leadership. Blacksmith is a distributed system consisting of six separate models: personnel, logistics, installations, force structure (units), dollars, and the integrating blackboard model. These models run on separate computers within the Pentagon. Theoretically, personnel officers manage the expertise in the personnel model, etc. Examples of policy decisions to be tested might be the following:

- What is the impact of various reorganizations? What happens to those soldiers who must be reclassified in their job specialty?
- What is the impact of shifting units from overseas to the continental U.S.?
- What is the cost of implementing a policy decision? Are there any real savings?

The blackboard architecture provides the link among the models. Results of one policy model will clearly affect the results of other models. The output to the CSA is through a single graphical interface that combines the results. This gives the CSA the needed ammunition to justify to, or combat, Congress on policy decisions.

3.1.2. Resource Allocation —
SABRE (Single Army Battlefield Requirements Evaluator)

Military planners have hundreds of plans available for various types of national emergencies. These plans are generic, based on a general class of emergency in some part of the world. When an actual emergency arises, the plan must be adjusted and actual units selected to resource it. SABRE (Branley, 1995) is a decision aid that allows planners to quickly choose specific Army units to employ during a national emergency. With SABRE, one planner can prepare an error-free contingency plan in only 3 hours. Deploying units get greater preparation time. Resolution to the crisis is speedier and usually more peaceful.

The general statement of the problem is very simple. Given the following,

- A pool of military units, each uniquely identifiable
- A proposed plan containing requirements for types and quantities of units
- A set of weighted constraints, with minimum values indicated,

there is an attempt to satisfy all requirements with units that have the most desirable attribute values. The typical size of a SABRE problem involves over 8000 units and 1000 requirements in the proposed plan.

The SABRE database contains a description of all military units. Each unit is listed with a set of attributes describing its *component, location, availability, status,* and *readiness. Component* refers to active, reserve, or National Guard status. *Availability* describes whether or not the unit is currently deployed on a mission. *Status* describes if the unit is activating, deactivating, or reorganizing. All units submit monthly assessments of their equipment, personnel, training, and logistics readiness in accordance with regulations.

The planners provide the requirements and constraints. They list requirements strictly by type and quantity of unit based on planning guidance. Constraints will often come from the political leadership. Examples are, "Reserve forces will not be used unless absolutely necessary," or "Minimize the use of units stationed in the continental U.S." Sometimes the constraints will be highly restrictive, such as "Reserve forces will not be used." The planner must translate this guidance into constraints on the unit attributes.

SABRE, a Common LISP and X-Motif-based system, builds its database from the output of existing systems. The planner uses X-Motif dialog boxes to specify the requirements and constraints and then launches SABRE's analysis submodule.

The analysis submodule, called the Alternatives Analyzer, Comparer, Editor, and Sourcer (AACES) performs two steps. First, heuristics help AACES reduce the number of units to study. One example is eliminating all units that cannot meet any of the requirements. Another example is not considering a unit from Europe to a contingency in South Korea when like units in the Pacific are available.

Second, AACES sources units that best suit the requirement. AACES uses a suitability function, incorporating the constraints, readiness of the unit, etc. The output of this step is a report of the units sourced, requirements that could not be met, and requirements that might need additional actions to take place (such as activation of reserve units). AACES supplements the output with narrative explanations of its reasoning.

The planner is not isolated from the sourcing process. The Army AI Center recognized that planners must make subjective trade-offs when declaring the final sources. For example, some subunits might have extensive experience in crises similar to the on-going one. Also, sometimes deploying a unit might have adverse side-effects (as happened when the activation of reserve units for the Persian Gulf War caused serious shortfalls of policemen and doctors in some U.S. counties). SABRE behaves more as a partner in the process, and allows the planner to exercise these trade-offs as needed.

Another SABRE submodule formats the reports for use in other existing systems. This allows SABRE to be part of a total planning and deployment package.

SABRE was fielded to FORSCOM Headquarters at Fort McPherson, GA in 1993. As part of the fielding, the AI Center updated the knowledge base to include rapid deployment and crisis action planning considerations. Exercises showed that a planning process that previously took 9 days was reduced to 9 hours. Currently, a prototype client-server version of SABRE is underway. Also, SABRE is being installed into the Department of Defense's Global Command and Control System (GCCS). This installation will mean that SABRE will be available to most major Department of Defense headquarters for contingency planning.

3.2. LOGISTICS

Military logistics is highly complex. There are over 20,000 different equipment systems in use, each with its own set of spare parts and maintenance procedures. The Army supply system alone has over 10 million items in its supply system. A deployed unit can ill afford to have damaged equipment awaiting parts or tied up in lengthy diagnostic repairs. ES have helped contribute to making the logistics system work better.

3.2.1.   Unit-Level Maintenance — Turbine Engine Diagnosis (TED) System and Others

A seemingly simple process such as preventive maintenance on equipment can actually be quite daunting for an individual soldier. Each system, such as a tank, weapon, or telecommunications, has a stack of manuals describing the maintenance procedures and parts lists. Simple diagnosis and repair can therefore become a time-consuming task.

The military has had several successful expert systems in the diagnosis and repair arena. Among them are PRIDE (Keller, 1990) for the Army's HAWK missile system and the Expert Missile Maintenance Aid from the Air Force's Phillips Laboratory for the GBU-15 missile system. A more recent success is the TED project, which won the 1993 ADPA award.

TED, sponsored by the U.S. Army Ordnance Center and School in Aberdeen, MD, provides expert assistance to tank mechanics for the M-1 Abrams tank power pack unit (known as an FUPP).

FIGURE 1   An Army maintenance soldier in front of an M-1 Abrams tank. A laptop computer with Turbine Engine Diagnostics (TED) software replaces the stacks of technical manuals and test equipment flanking the soldier. (Photo courtesy of the U.S. Army Artificial Intelligence Center, Pentagon.)

The TED knowledge base contains all the information contained in the Abrams' technical manuals and provides rule-based interaction with the mechanic. The output is a repair parts requirement list printed on standard Army requisition forms.

Supplementing user interaction, TED uses sensors that listen to the engine while running. A multiplexer converts the analog sounds from the transmission into digital form, analyzes them for abnormalities, and reports them to the mechanic. The reports contain the probable cause, parts needed, time required to perform the repair, and special tools that the mechanic must acquire to do the job.

The return on investment for TED has been dramatic. The photograph in Figure 1 shows a mechanic with the stacks of technical manuals and diagnostic equipment. This mechanic is holding a TED laptop that effectively replaces it all. As of this writing, TED is being fielded to all Army tank maintenance units, and TED is being upgraded to include neural networks.

3.2.2.   Large Unit Supply — Knowledge-Based Logistics Planning Shell (KBLPS)

The Persian Gulf War illustrates the complexity of large unit supply. During the build-up, suppliers had to distribute massive quantities of food, ammunition, fuel, construction materials, and especially water to Army, Marine, and Air Force units on the ground.

Each unit has different consumption rates of supply based on the type of supply and the unit's equipment. Some supplies such as food, fuel, and water are consumed regularly and must be constantly replenished. Others, such as construction materials, repair parts, and personal care items, can be replenished on a regular basis. Ammunition resupply depends greatly on the situation. Units must maintain a minimum of certain types of ammunition while there is no fighting. If fighting occurs, then the ammunition requirements increase.

Military units prepare huge manuals containing only tabular information about consumption rates. However, these manuals are often rendered obsolete quickly. New equipment often causes units to reorganize. Major deployments, such as the Persian Gulf War, involve the mixing and matching of not only Army, Marine, and Air Force units, but also units from allied nations.

Expert systems clearly can help streamline the process. Expert systems can piece together a resupply plan much more quickly than using the large stacks of manuals. Also, expert systems can identify potential problem areas before they arise.

Developed by Carnegie Group, Inc., and sponsored by the Combined Arms Support Command (CASCOM), KBLPS takes a war plan and develops and tests supply plans to support it. KBLPS combines a rule-based plan development shell with a simulation model. The simulation helps determine the logistical feasibility of the war plan and identify areas of risk.

As of this writing, KBLPS is in its fourth prototype version. This version has a well-developed knowledge base for bulk fuel (gasoline, diesel, and aircraft fuel) and ammunition. It has the capability to analyze food, personal care items, construction items, major equipment systems, and packaged fuel (oil, grease, and other petroleum products) for corps units and below. The project's goal is to handle all classes of supply throughout the theater.

CASCOM is also involved in two other logistics planning projects:

- The Planning Assistant for Logistical Systems (PALOS) studies the issues concerning support relationships. As described above, the make-up of forces is determined by the situation. Consequently, units would have to support unfamiliar units from other services or countries. PALOS evaluates the impact and feasibility of these unusual support relationships.
- SIMUlation of LOGistics Systems (SIMULOGS) develops and simulates logistical concepts for strategic contingency plans.

3.3. TRAINING AND EDUCATION

Training and education are very important to a professional military. The American public expects the military to be prepared for any situation and serve as a deterrent from aggression. In peacetime, military training must be realistic, thorough, and rigorous. All the services establish high and exacting standards of performance that can only be met by practice and study. They set these standards for individuals and units of all sizes from a seven-man squad to an entire 100,000-man corps.

However, the price of meeting these training and educational requirements is extremely high. Field training of units requires the expenditure of vast amounts of resources. Many units, especially reserves, must travel great distances to conduct a field exercise. Training places wear and tear on equipment. Most Army and Marine bases have insufficient land for large-scale maneuvers, meaning regular large-unit training is impractical. Individual education requirements require attendance at specialized schools across the country, involving heavy moving and tuition costs. Finally, field training causes environmental and collateral damage — all of which the military must provide compensation.

For much of the 1990s, various military organizations have looked to simulation and distance education technologies to offset these costs. Simulation provides the capability to train units and individual equipment operators while reducing equipment wear and tear. Distance education allows students to take courses at an individual pace while staying at their home base. These applications often involve expert systems, intelligent agent technologies, and intelligent computer-aided instruction over the Internet.

3.3.1. Education

Officers of all services will spend at least 4, and as many as 7, years in school. The school environment provides opportunities for officers to study lessons learned from recent conflicts and deployments, to share knowledge of other theaters, and a worry-free environment to hone command and staff skills.

The services recognize the importance of these schools, but:

- Sending students to schools involves taking students out of their regular jobs for up to a year. It involves heavy relocation costs.
- The curriculum of most military schools goes beyond the collective expertise of its faculty.
- Schools required of all officers have the option to take the course by correspondence, thus involving shipping lots of books and administering exams using marksense forms. Unlike the resident students, correspondence students perform no collaborative work. Clearly, there is some loss of quality in the education value.

Consequently, there have been numerous efforts throughout the military to use intelligent technologies to improve both the quality and availability of military education. Some notable examples follow.

- The Army Research Institute of Infectious Diseases (USAMRIID) teaches a course in Medical Defense Against Biological Warfare Agents. This course is expensive because of the travel and facility costs. However, by using the Internet and intelligent tutoring methods, the course is readily available and tailored to the individual students' needs (USAAIC, 1996).
- The Army and Air Force academies offer Internet-based intelligent tutorials for classes in freshman chemistry and evaluating a satellite's ground tracks. By using computerized instruction for entry-level or basic courses, their respective faculty are able to devote more time to their advanced courses or research efforts (USAAIC, 1996).
- The Magidan Army Medical Center (MAMC) provides an example of an intelligent tutor to improve medical service. They developed an expert system for headache diagnosis in the early 1990s and later converted it into an intelligent training system for patients. The purpose is not to teach patients how to self-diagnose headaches, but to provide a means for informing the patient of causes, side-effects, and treatments when a physician is not available (USAAIC, 1996).
- One military research effort is *Stat Lady*, a project at the U.S. Air Force's Armstrong Laboratory (Shute, 1994). The goal of the research effort is to improve both the effectiveness of intelligent tutors and the speed at which effective tutors for new material can be written. One phase of the project compared intelligent and nonintelligent versions of the same tutor (for statistics and algebra). The intelligent version represents a student's conceptual knowledge, symbolic knowledge, and procedural skills, and applies that information toward individualizing the feedback. Another phase focuses on using *Stat Lady* for research in knowledge acquisition methods for intelligent tutorials.

3.3.2.   Wargaming and Simulation — Soar/IFOR (Intelligent Forces)

Without question, wargaming and simulation are critical to modern military training. Computer-based wargames have been prevalent since the 1970s. Yes, despite the very clear benefit they would bring, expert systems and other intelligent technologies have been comparatively slow in getting involved (Estvanik, 1994). Only now is the processing speed and power permitting viable intelligent computerized wargaming. With advances in hardware come several highly advanced projects in distributed wargaming — using expert systems, intelligent agents, and complex computer networks. The Defense Advanced Research Projects Agency (DARPA) and all three services have sponsored several intelligent wargaming projects.

Among them is Soar/IFOR (Rosenbloom, et al., 1993), a collaborative effort of the Universities of Michigan and Southern California along with Carnegie-Mellon University in Pittsburgh. The Soar research group is developing intelligent agents for tactical air simulation. This will allow computerized pilots to participate in a simulation and behave exactly like real pilots. Such agents are especially useful when programmed to behave like a true enemy force, using Soviet-style or other doctrines. A sufficient number of pilots can be added according to the actual size of the force being simulated. The realism of the training improves greatly.

NPSNet, based at the Naval Postgraduate School in Monterey, CA, is a leading research project in virtual reality simulations and wargames. NPSNet's project goal is to achieve an interactive wargame with over 100,000 players. However, the current Distributed Interactive Simulation (DIS) standards do not provide the bandwidth to handle such a player load. NPSNet is researching the use of intelligent agents and "smart networks" to speed up message traffic. The agents would provide a filtering and combining capability that would reduce the number of messages. The smart networks would recognize which entities in the wargame are visible to the entity being updated. They will route the update messages solely to those other entities (Stone, 1996).

3.4. ROBOTICS

Each military service must perform duties that are unduly hazardous or are extremely difficult for humans to do. Among them are entrance into chemically or nuclear contaminated areas, survey of ocean floors, explosive ordnance disarming and disposal, and reconnaissance/surveillance activities behind enemy lines. The first two describe situations where the soldiers' or sailors' performance clearly deteriorates over time and their health is at risk. The latter two describe situations where lives are at tremendous and potentially unnecessary risk. The military is looking toward robotics as providing a safer means to perform these tasks. Many robotics applications have expert system and symbolic reasoning components.

The Naval Postgraduate School has an Autonomous Underwater Vehicle (AUV) research group, whose significant on-going research effort involves the Phoenix AUV. Phoenix is primarily a research effort that studies how AUVs can perform countermine operations and coastal environmental studies. The Phoenix performs its assigned missions using a Rational Behavior Model (RBM), consisting of three layers of software. The execution layers govern the Phoenix reactive real-time control mechanisms. The tactical layer provides the Phoenix with near-real-time sensor analysis and operation. The strategic layer manages the Phoenix long-term mission planning and mission control. The RBM helps the Phoenix perform its tasks similarly to crew members aboard ships (Brutzman, 1997).

The Army has several on-going Unmanned Ground Vehicle (UGV) projects managed by the UGV Systems Joint Project Office (USAAIC, 1996). Included among them are tactical vehicles, vehicles to breach enemy minefields, perform environmental restoration activities, neutralize explosive ordinance, and perform area security and patrolling functions. The vision of the office is to eventually provide a robotic tank platoon consisting of two soldiers and four tanks. All the soldiers would ride in one tank, leaving the other tanks unmanned. The unmanned tanks would have full capability to move and to load and fire its weapons. The plans include rule-based systems to allow the tanks to recognize and avoid obstacles, stay in formation during maneuver, and engage enemy targets.

However, the military's interests in robotics extends beyond supporting conventional warfare. The Colorado School of Mines recently announced some success in robot-assisted Urban Search and Rescue (USAR). Rescue teams can deploy small intelligent robots that are able to seek out trapped victims in a collapsed building. The expert system component encodes the knowledge of the building's pre-collapse structure and deduces likely locations of void spaces. These spaces would have the greatest chance of housing survivors of the collapse. (Blitch, 1996). As the military continues to perform foreign humanitarian aid and disaster relief missions, using intelligent robots for dangerous missions such as USAR will be a factor in savings lives and resources.

3.5.   INTELLIGENCE APPLICATIONS

Intelligence gathering and interpretation are complex and difficult. Depending on areas of responsibility and expertise, an analyst might have to sift through over 700 messages daily. The analyst does not know up front for what he is looking. Many of these messages are unformatted narrative text. Often on short suspense, the analyst must search for and extract important information, establish spatial and temporal relationships when possible, and provide a concise analysis to superiors.

Research into expert systems and emerging Natural Language Understanding (NLU) techniques is beginning to provide useful synthesis tools to the analyst. The Intelligent Analyst Associate (IAA) project at the U.S. Air Force Rome Laboratory is one example. By extracting and visualizing simple entity and event data from text, IAA provides visual cues to the analyst. These cues help narrow down what the analyst must read and pinpoint related pieces of information. IAA is in its early stages of development, in part because NLU is still only an emerging technology. As the state-of-the-art of NLU rises, IAA will be better able to handle the identification of more complex events.

Another project that is not specifically military in nature but has military implications is a NASA project to identify violations to nuclear treaties (Mason, 1995). Obviously, countries intending to violate a ban on nuclear testing will go to great lengths to conceal that fact. Nuclear testing still leaves important seismic clues that sensors can isolate. The rule base performs two interpretations:

- The "partial interpretation" helps identify that an interesting event has occurred. This helps weed out the regular seismic activity that constantly occurs throughout the world. This is done by employing a belief system that looks at input from various seismograms and indicates that it believes or disbelieves that they constitute the same event. As more information comes in, the strength of belief increases or new information can contradict what is already believed.
- The "full interpretation" takes the interesting events and tries to identify the likely cause and narrow down the source of the event. Seismic events consist of a series of segments where the intensity of the waves increase and decrease. Expert system rules identify the segments, and subsequently identify the likely event.

This concept is applicable to other intelligence applications — such as those that seek to interpret troop movements and other activities on satellite photograph.

3.6.   QUALITY OF LIFE APPLICATIONS — BUDGET BASED ANALYSIS, EUROPE (BBAE)

Quality of Life (QOL) concerns are very important and very peculiar to the military vs. the corporate world. The military not only provides a work environment, but also provides its own community-like services for its soldiers, airmen, and sailors. These include family housing, commissaries (grocery stores), exchange services (department stores, gas stations, military clothing, dry cleaning), hospitals, schools, daycare facilities, and morale, welfare, and recreation activities (i.e., MWR — sports facilities, youth clubs, automotive shops, arts and crafts facilities). Providing these services is critical to the military for maintaining soldier and family morale — which directly impact the military's readiness.

The United States Army, Europe (USAREUR) has published QOL standards that "define and quantify the minimum level of services that soldiers, civilians, and family members can expect, regardless of duty station." When the Cold War ended and the U.S. military began reducing its forces in Europe, there was great concern that the QOL programs would degrade to unacceptable levels. Unfortunately, it is impossible to cut QOL in a purely proportional manner. For example, one unit might have had to travel 20 minutes to reach the nearest daycare center. If that daycare center closes but the unit remains, the soldiers in that unit might have to travel greater distances to reach the next nearest center. This clearly would affect the soldier's morale and job performance.

In 1993, USAREUR requested assistance in studying the impact of budget constraints and closing of units and facilities on QOL. Eventually, the U.S. Military Academy's KEG became involved and helped to construct a decision support system. The system, called Budget Based Analysis, Europe (BBAE), allows USAREUR leaders to perform "what-if" analysis concerning budget reductions, shutdown of facilities, and deactivation or movement of units.

Constructing BBAE's knowledge base was an arduous task. USAREUR provided detailed information about the current units, soldier demographics, and QOL facilities. Each facility was analyzed for location, capacity, current customer base, and financial impact. The Army staff was consulted for projected changes in the force structure in the USAREUR area of operations. With this knowledge base, and a simple user-interface, BBAE users can build queries to satisfy questions like the following:

- Compare the costs of operating and maintaining QOL assets in <present date> to those of <some future date>.
- Do all family housing areas in <location> meet the QOL standard for proximity to <type of facility>? If not, which ones do not? What travel time standard is met?
- What is the closest medical facility to <unit or housing area>?
- What timetable will <unit> have to move from Germany to Italy?

BBAE was completed and delivered in 1994. The developers released a second version for American forces in the Republic of Korea a year later.

4. RESEARCH ISSUES

Because of its numerous successes in expert systems applications, the military has invested heavily in expert systems research. The intent is to facilitate expert system development for a wider range of applications. Two notable research efforts involve conceptual mapping for knowledge acquisition and validation and verification.

4.1. KNOWLEDGE ACQUISITION — ADVANCED KNOWLEDGE ACQUISITION AND DESIGN ACQUISITION METHODS (AKADAM)

Traditional knowledge acquisition techniques tend to restrict the domain to being expressed in strict rules of logic so that the decision process can be readily encoded. AKADAM (McNeese, 1995) is a research effort into employing a more expert-centered approach with the help of more advanced knowledge acquisition techniques. AKADAM will allow the domain expert to retrieve and elaborate on situated knowledge using conceptual models. AKADAM converts these models internally to implementable rules.

AKADAM uses three types of knowledge representations: knowledge as concepts (using conceptual maps), knowledge as functions (using IDEF models), and knowledge as designs (storyboards). The combination of these representations allows greater flexibility in expressing the domain. The AKADEM prototype has been applied in several complex Air Force projects.

4.2. VERIFICATION AND VALIDATION

The military is especially concerned about verification and validation because expert system errors can be costly in lives and equipment. The Army Research Institute for the Behavioral and Social

Sciences compiled a handbook for the managing the life cycle of an expert system (Adelman, 1996). This book discusses several issues common to locally developed expert systems, such as how to properly progress an expert system out of the prototype stage and into full usage. Although this research effort is now concluded, there is a need for translating this work into automated verification and validation means.

5. FUTURE TRENDS

There is little question that applications similar to those presented in this chapter will continue to flourish. The increased pace of the modern battlefield and the need to minimize casualties will only increase the demand for the ability to synthesize large amounts of information in an intelligent manner. As unmanned vehicles leave the laboratory and enter the field, expert systems will play an important role in their ability to perform their mission. Simulations will continue to increase their use of expert systems.

"Joint" applications will increase. "Joint" refers to an integrated Army, Navy, and Air Force operation or activity. The U.S. military has emphasized "joint" capabilities since the Goldwater-Nicholls Act of 1986, when the Department of Defense was reorganized. Before this act, the services had very different ways of doing business. This led to redundancy, and sometimes incompatibility. Expert systems will help bridge communication gaps among the services and eliminate the redundancy.

The role of expert systems in training and education will certainly increase. The use of simulations for training will certainly increase as the availability and expendability of resources decrease. Military education will make greater use of intelligent tutorials with Internet-based collaborative systems in order to reduce travel costs and provide quality education to all its soldiers, sailors, and airmen.

6. SUMMARY

The U.S. military is a good example of how expert systems can play an important role in a large and complex organization. It has properly resourced and manned itself sufficiently for expert system development. It has ensured that expert systems are properly integrated into the total solution to a problem, not treated as a solution in itself. Most importantly, the applications provide a return on investment throughout the organization. Because of this, the military has been, and will continue to be, a strong proponent for intelligent technologies.

ACKNOWLEDGEMENTS

The author acknowledges the following for their assistance in researching this chapter: LTC Steve Woffinden, Major Bill Atkinson, Major Bruce Simpson, and Major Dave Roberts (SABRE and Blacksmith) of the U.S. Army Artificial Intelligence Center, Pentagon; Mr. Northrup Fowler and Ms. Cynthia Pine (IAA), Rome Laboratory, U.S. Air Force; Dr. Michael D. McNeese (AKADAM), Armstong Laboratory, U.S. Air Force; Dr. Robert McGhee (Phoenix and Aquarobot) and Mr. Don Brutzman (NPSNet), Naval Postgraduate School; Major Larry Campbell (BBAE), U.S. Military Academy at West Point; and Thomas R. Knutilla (PRIDE), LESCO, Inc. The author also acknowledges Dr. Jay Liebowitz, George Washington University, and Dr. Ed Feigenbaum, Chief Scientist, U.S. Air Force, for their help in the search for points of contact.

REFERENCES

Adelman, Leonard and Riedel, Sharon. *Handbook for Evaluating Knowledge-Based Systems: Conceptual Framework and Compendium of Methods.* Kluwer Academic Publishers, 1996.

Blitch, John. "Artificial Intelligence Technologies for Robot Assisted Urban Search and Rescue," *Expert Systems with Applications,* Volume 11, Number 2, pp. 109–125.

Branley, William and Harris, Ernest. "SABRE." *Proceedings of the 1995 Innovative Applications of Artificial Intelligence Conference,* AAAI Press, Menlo Park, NJ, 1995.

Brutzman, Don, Healey, Tony, Marco, Dave and McGhee, Bob, "The Phoenix Autonomous Underwater Vehicle," AI-Based Mobile Robots, editors David Kortenkamp, Pete Bonasso, and Robin Murphy, MIT/AAAI Press, Cambridge MA, to be published 1997.

Estvanik, Steve. "Artificial Intelligence in Wargames," *AI Expert,* Miller Freeman, Inc., San Francisco, CA, May 1994, pp. 23–31.

Keller, Brian and Knutilla, Thomas. "U.S. Army Builds An AI Diagnostic Expert System, By Soldiers for Soldiers," *Industrial Engineer Magazine,* Institute for Industrial Engineering, Norcross, GA, September 1990, pp. 38–41.

Mason, Cindy. "An Intelligent Assistant for Nuclear Test Ban Treaty Verification," *IEEE Expert,* December 1995, pp. 42–49.

McNeese, M., Zaff, B., Citera, M., Brown, C., Whitaker, R., "AKADAM: Eliciting User Knowledge to Support Participatory Ergonomics," *International Journal of Industrial Ergonomics 15,* Special Issue on Cognitive Mapping, Elsevier Science, New York, NY, 1995, pp. 345–363.

Rosenbloom, Paul, Laird, John, and Newell, Allen (Eds.), *The Soar Papers: Research on Integrated Intelligence.* MIT Press: Artificial Intelligence Series, Cambridge, MA, 1993.

Shute, Valerie. "Regarding the I in ITS: Student Modeling," *Proceedings of the 1994 World Conference of Educational Multimedia and Hypermedia,* Association for the Advancement of Computing in Education, Charlottesville, VA, 1994.

Stone, S., Zyda, M., Brutzman, D., and Falby, John "Mobile Agents and Smart Networks for Distributed Simulations," *Proceedings of the 14th Distributed Simulations Conference,* Orlando, FL, March 11–15, 1996.

United States Army Artificial Intelligence Center. *Project Summary — Blacksmith. Proceedings of the 1995 U.S. Army Artificial Intelligence Proponency Conference,* USAAIC, Washington, D.C., 1995.

United States Army Artificial Intelligence Center. *Proceedings of the 1996 U.S. Army Artificial Intelligence Proponency Conference,* USAAIC, Washington, D.C., 1996.

35 Agriculture

Ahmed Rafea

CONTENTS

1. INTRODUCTION

An expert system can be defined as a tool for information generation from knowledge. Information is either found in various forms or generated from data and/or knowledge. Text, images, video, and audio are forms of media from which information can be found, and the role of information technology is to invent and devise tools to store and retrieve this information. Statistical information is a good example of information generated from data while advice generated by an expert system is a good example of information generated from knowledge.

At the beginning, the concentration was mainly on textual information. Information technology used for textual information ranged from paper archiving tool to the sophisticated electronic computer software tools such as database management systems and hypertext tools. Images were very difficult to be included in an information system just few years ago until scanner technology was advanced, as well as the invention of the optical storage devices that have the capacity to store hundreds of megabytes. This technology has enabled the developers to include images in their systems. Input peripherals to capture video and audio information have been commercialized also and are now available on the market. Storage of audio and video would be impossible had large storage media not been invented.

The advances in data processing have led to generating information efficiently from data. Software tools and methodologies have been developed in the field of statistics and data analysis to process data and to allow these data more to be informative to users who need them. Database management systems have also contributed to efficient data storage, processing, and retrieval.

The information is sometimes generated from knowledge and experience. When an expert in a specific area gives advice to a less experienced person, he/she actually uses his/her knowledge and experience to generate this piece of information. This is a very precious piece of information because it is generated after many hours of work and experience, and interaction with other experts and practitioners. Sometimes, this piece of information is not included in any form: text, audio, video, etc. Even if it is included, it is not linked with its scientific origin, especially if it is a combination of different domains and methods. This piece of information gets more precious if it is the result of solving a problem that different specialists have participated in deriving its solution. In this case, it is rare to find this piece of information in any text. Expert systems technology can play a very important role in generating information from knowledge.

This chapter is written to present different aspects related to agricultural expert systems, namely: why expert systems in agriculture, what applications have been developed, how these application have been developed, and what research issues should be addressed.

2.   NEED FOR EXPERT SYSTEMS IN AGRICULTURE

The need for expert systems for technical information transfer in agriculture can be identified by recognizing the problems in using the traditional system for technical information transfer, and by proving that expert systems can help overcome the problems addressed and be feasibly developed.

2.1.   INFORMATION TRANSFER PROBLEMS

Static information: Examining the information stored and available in the agriculture domain revealed that this information is static and may not respond to the growers' needs. All extension documentations give general recommendations because there are many factors to be taken into consideration; thus, many different recommendations should be included in the document.

Specialties integration: Most of the extension documents handle problems related to a certain specialty: for example, plant pathology, entomology, nutrition, or any other specialty. In real situations, the problem may be due to more than one cause and may need the integration of the knowledge behind the information included in the different extension documents and books.

Combination of more than one information source: Images may sometimes need an expert to combine other factors to reach an accurate diagnosis; and even if a diagnosis is reached, the treatment of the diagnosed disorder should be provided through the extension document.

Updating: Changes in chemicals, their doses, and their effects on the environment should be considered. Updating this information in documents and distributing them takes long time. The same arguments can be made for audio tapes, which are another form of extension documents but in voice instead of written words. Video tapes are more stable than other media, as the information provided through the tape describes usually well-established agricultural operations. However, if the tape includes information as to what is commonly included in documents and audio tapes, this information should be updated.

Information unavailability: Information may not be available in any form of media. It may only be available from human experts, extensionists, and/or experienced growers. In addition, the information transfer from specialists and scientists to extensionists and farmers, represents a bottleneck for the development of agriculture on the national level. The current era is witnessing a vast development in all fields of agriculture. Therefore, there is a need to transfer the information of experts in certain domains to the general public of farmers, especially that the number of experts in new technologies is lesser than their demand.

2.2.   Suitability and Feasibility of Expert Systems

The problems already raised can, to a large extent, be solved using expert systems to generate the information to the growers by using its knowledge base and reasoning mechanism acquired from human experts and other sources.

The expert system generates the advice based on the knowledge base and reasoning mechanism that are actually behind all developed extension documents, and more. Consequently, when a user enters the data of his/her plantation to the system, the appropriate advice is generated. There are no limitations as to the number of generated recommendations. Therefore, the expert system overcomes the problem of static information provided in extension documents.

The knowledge acquisition process for building an expert system facilitates the integration of knowledge and experiences of different specialties. For example, an agricultural diagnostic expert system requires the integration of specialists in nutrition, plant pathology, entomology, breeding, and production. Therefore, when a problem occurs, the system can help the user in identifying the cause of the problem in a much more efficient way than consulting a document that handles a specific problem.

Expert systems can be integrated with other information sources, such as image bases and/or textual bases, to make use of these sources. For example, images can be used for describing symptoms, as it is very difficult and very confusing to describe them in words. Images can also be used for confirming the diagnosis of the cause of a certain disorder. Expert systems can also be integrated with textual databases that may be the extension documents related to the specialty and/or commodity handled by an expert system. This textual database can be used for explanation purposes of basic terms and operations. It can also be used to confirm the reached conclusion in some situations.

The updating problem is also found in expert systems. However, the knowledge base can be maintained more efficiently than maintaining manual documents. The problem of updating the versions in the field can be eliminated in case the expert systems are stored on a central computer and accessed through a computer network. The undocumented experience and knowledge can be acquired and stored in the knowledge base of an expert system for a certain specialty and/or commodity. This experience can be available to all growers using the system. The feedback from the usage of the system can be used as a source of information when analyzed by researchers, the knowledge behind it can be identified, and the knowledge base can be updated continuously. Expert systems can also help in overcoming the problem of the relatively few numbers of experts relative to the demand from the growers. Expert systems technology can help transfer the information of experts, and experienced growers, to farmers through the extension system.

3.   HISTORICAL ACCOUNT

Knowledge-based expert system technology has been applied to a variety of agricultural problems since the early 1980s. The following paragraphs present how expert systems were considered in agriculture in the 1980s. The papers have been selected to represent different applications and to be easily obtained by interested readers.

The expert system applied to the problems of diagnosing soybean diseases (Michalski et al., 1983) is one of the earliest expert systems developed in agriculture. A unique feature of the system is that it uses two types of decision rules: (1) the rules representing expert diagnostic knowledge, and (2) the rules obtained through inductive learning from several hundred cases of disease. Experimental testing of the system has indicated a high level of correctness of the system's advice (in an experiment involving a few hundred cases , approximately 98% of the diagnosis were correct).

POMME (Roach et al,, 1985) is an expert system for apple orchid management. POMME advises growers about when and what to spray on their apples to avoid infestations. The system also provides advice regarding treatment of winter injuries, drought control, and multiple insect problems.

COMAX (Lemon, 1986) is a crop management expert system for cotton that can predict crop growth and yield in response to external weather variables, physical soil parameters, soil fertility, and pest damage. The expert system is integrated with a computer model, Gossym, that simulates the growth of the cotton plant. This was the first integration of an expert system with a simulation model for daily use in farm management.

In 1987, expert system technology was identified as an appropriate technology to speed up agricultural desert development in Egypt (Rafea and El-Beltagy, 1987). The paper discussed the importance of applying expert systems in agricultural desert development in Egypt and suggested an integrated structure of an R&D unit to develop and maintain an efficient use of these systems.

CALEX system (Plant, 1989) was developed for agriculture management. It is domain independent and can be used with any commodity. CALEX consists of three separate modules: an executive, a scheduler, and an expert system shell. The executive serves as the primary interface to the user, to models, and to the disk. The scheduler generates a sequence of management activities by repeatedly activating the expert system. The expert system makes the actual management decisions. Initial development of the system has focused on the development of a package of modules for California cotton and another package for peaches.

In the 1990s, several expert systems have also been developed. A sampling of these expert systems has also been selected as examples. The selected examples demonstrate trends in the 1990s and their accessibility by the reader is also considered.

An agroforestry expert system (UNU-AES) was designed to support land-use officials, research scientists, farmers, and other individuals interested in maximizing benefits gained from applying agroforestry management techniques in developing countries (Warkentin et al., 1990). UNU-AES is a first attempt to apply expert systems technology to agroforestry. This system addresses the option for alley cropping, a promising agroforestry technology that has potential applicability when used under defined conditions in the tropics and subtropics. Alley cropping involves the planting of crops in alleys or interspaces between repeatedly hedgerows of fast-growing, preferably leguminous, woody perennials. With the inclusion of more climatic and socioeconomic data and improved advisory recommendations, UNU-AES can be expanded to provide advice on alley cropping in more diverse geographical and ecological conditions and eventually address other agroforestry techniques.

In 1991, serious efforts have been started in Egypt to develop crop management expert systems for different crops. A prototype for an expert system for cucumber seedlings productions has been developed. This prototype has six functions: seed cultivation, media preparation, control of environmental growth factors, diagnosis, treatment, and protection. The implementation has used the Hypertext facility included in the EXSYS shell. The overall control was implemented using the language provided by the tool, and consequently, the rule base was divided into modules according to the system functions (Rafea et al., 1991). Another expert system for cucumber production management under plastic tunnel (CUPTEX) was developed to be used by the agricultural extension service within the Egyptian Ministry of Agriculture and by the private sector. The main objective of developing such systems is to transfer new technology in agromanagement to farmers through packaging this technology using expert systems. This will lead to increasing the production and hence the national income, on the one hand, to reducing the production cost, on the other hand. CUPTEX is composed of three expert systems for fertigation, plant care, and disorder remediation. The validation of CUPTEX has revealed that it over-performs a group of experts in different specialties. Although the direct payoff is not the main objective of the development, experimentation with CUPTEX in two research sites has revealed an approximately 26% increase in the production and a 15% decrease in direct cost. These results show that CUPTEX could pay off approximately 60% of the development cost in 4 months if it is used to manage the plastic tunnels cultivating cucumber in the five sites in which it was deployed (Rafea et al., 1995). This system is the first deployed agricultural expert system to be selected in the conference of innovative application for artificial intelligence. It is also the first deployed expert system in developing countries — not only in agriculture, but in other fields as well.

In Italy, an expert system for integrated pest management of apple orchards (Gerevini et al., 1992), POMI, has been developed. Integrated pest management is definable as the reasoned application of agronomic methods products as well as chemicals, to allow optimal productive factors, while respecting the farm worker, the environment, and the consumer. POMI addresses the first preliminary phase of the complex process of apple orchard integrated control, namely the detection of the insect populations in the field and approximate the populations dimensions. The system consists of two parts: classification of user findings and explanation of these findings using abductive reasoning.

In India, an intelligent front-end for selecting evapotranspiration estimation methods (Mohan and Arumugam, 1995) has been integrated with methods that calculate the evapotranspiration factor. Evapotranspiration (ET) is an important parameter needed by water managers for the design, operation and management of irrigation systems. Since there are many methods to compute ET, based on climatic data, an inexperienced engineer or hydrologist is perplexed with the selection of an appropriate method. An intelligent front end expert system (ETES) has been developed to select suitable ET estimation methods under South Indian climatic conditions. Ten meteorological stations located in different climatic regions and thirteen ET estimation methods have been considered in this ES. Along with the recommended method, ETES also suggests suitable correction factors for converting the resulting ET values to those of methods that result in accurate estimation.

A picture-based expert system for weed identification (Schulthess et al., 1996) has been developed. Most current expert systems for weed identification are rule based and use text that contains a large number of botanical terms. In this system, the hierarchical classification generic task was used and the text descriptions were replaced with pictures to minimize the use of technical terms. Hypotheses are established or ruled out on the basis of the user's choices among options presented as pictures.

4.   METHODOLOGIES AND APPLICATIONS

In this section, it is not the intention to describe in detail different expert system methodologies, as this should be covered elsewhere. The attempt here is to analyze the examples given in the previous section from two aspects: the methodological aspect and the domain application aspect. The two main methodology categories are first-generation and second-generation expert systems. The first-generation expert system methodology is based on using commercial expert system shells after acquiring the knowledge through traditional knowledge acquisition techniques and using rapid prototyping methods. The second-generation expert system methodology is primarily based on the principle of knowledge level, which means developing a knowledge model at the human level, problem-solving approach, not at the computational level approach. The domain application aspect will be analyzed taking the agriculture area and the task type to classify the given application. A domain-specific methodology will be presented in the last subsection .

4.1.   METHODOLOGICAL ASPECTS

Most of the expert systems developed in agriculture apply the first-generation expert system methodology. Examples of this methodology can be found in Warkentin et al. (1990), Rafea et al. (1991), and Mohan and Arumugam (1995). The first two applications use the EXSYS shell, and a documentation of this methodology based on a modified Waterfall method is described in (Rafea et al. 1993). The third example application uses the CLIPS shell while the fourth example uses the VP-Expert shell.

Another approach that can be considered as an intermediate between the first- and second-generation expert systems is the usage of expert system shells in the implementation of a higher level of reasoning. An example of this approach can be found in Gerevini et al. (1992). In this application, the shell KEE is used but the system is explicitly divided into two parts. The first part is concerned with helping the user in classifying the findings, whereas the second part is an interactive abductive module that suggests explanation of those findings.

Few applications have been developed following the second-generation expert system approach. The two methodologies used are the KADS methodology and the generic task methodology. The KADS methodology was used for developing expert systems for cucumber and citrus management (Rafea et al. 1994; 1995), whereas the generic task methodology was used for developing an expert system for wheat management (Schroeder et al., 1994; Schulthess et al., 1996). In the second-generation expert systems methodology, there are generic models for different types of tasks such as diagnosis, planning, design, etc. In the agriculture domain, we find that two main generic models are used, namely: the diagnosis (or more broadly the classification), and the scheduling tasks. In KADS methodology, there is a library of expertise model for each one of these two tasks (Rafea et al., 1994), whereas in the generic task methodology, the hierarchical classification model is found suitable for the diagnosis applications and the routine design model is found suitable for the scheduling application (Kamel et al., 1994).

4.2.   DOMAIN APPLICATION ASPECTS

The agriculture domain can be classified into subdomains, namely: plant production, animal production, and management of natural resources related to the agricultural operations such as soil and water. Expert systems have been applied in the three subdomains; however, the concentration here is on the plant production part, as most of the expert systems in agriculture have been developed in this subdomain.

Expert systems for field crops are implemented for: diagnosis of soybean diseases (Michalski et al., 1983), crop management for cotton (Lemon, 1986; Plant, 1989), and weed identification for wheat (Schulthess et.al., 1996). Expert systems were also implemented for horticulture crops: apple orchard management (Roach et al., 1985; Gerevini et al., 1992), and cucumber production management (Rafea et al., 1995). Agroforestry is another area in plant production where expert systems have been developed (Warkentin et al., 1990). Some other applications cannot be categorized commodity wise, for example, the expert system developed for selecting evapotranspiration estimation methods (Mohan and Arumugam, 1995).

Another way of classifying agricultural expert systems is the domain-specific task that this system performs, such as: irrigation, fertilization, pest management, diagnosis of plant diseases, etc. There is mapping between the domain-specific tasks and the generic tasks. For example, irrigation application is mainly a special case of scheduling, whereas diagnosis is a special case of classification.

4.3.   A PROPOSED DOMAIN SPECIFIC METHODOLOGY

The methodology proposed here is based on our experience during the last 7 years in developing expert systems in agriculture. It is not intended to be a comprehensive methodology but it will give some thoughts on domain-specific task architectures in agriculture. Generally, we can classify agricultural operations into precultivation operations and during cultivation operations. Precultivation operations are interested in preparing the field for growing a particular crop. During cultivation operations can be further classified into diagnosis operations (which concern finding a reasonable explanation for undesired phenomenon), and scheduling operations (which include irrigation, fertilization, and treatment operations). We will concentrate in this section on scheduling in the agriculture domain as an example.

Our methodology is based on two principles that have emerged during the last decade of AI research:

- Knowledge-level modeling: Knowledge should be modeled on a higher level than that of exploited knowledge representation formalisms, to avoid premature design decisions and to facilitate communication with domain experts.
- Reusability of task and domain knowledge: This principle implies that the complexity of KBS development can be relieved by the construction of reusable components libraries, just as any other engineering activity.

Following the model-driven approach, the KBS development process is composed of two phases. In the first phase, an epistemological model is constructed, representing the conceptual model for the application problem. In the second phase, this model is transformed into a computational model, implemented on computer, and preserving the structure of the epistemological model.

An epistemological model in CommonKADS consists of three main components, namely: task knowledge, inference knowledge, and domain knowledge. Generating one generic model for each task (irrigation, fertilization, and treatment), will increase the model reusability among many different crop types, which minimizes the effort and the cost of knowledge-based systems development. The following subsection describes the inference model of irrigation as an example of this methodology.

The main goal of this task is to design an irrigation schedule for a particular crop in a particular farm. The output schedule is simply a plan of water quantities to be applied and the time of application, according to the requirements of the plant, and the affecting factors like soil type, climate, source of water, etc.

Figure 1 shows the constructed generic inference structure for the irrigation task. As illustrated in Figure 1, the irrigation task starts with acquiring a *case description*, which includes parameters that affect the irrigation process, such as soil, water, and climate data. The *expand* inference step uses these initial parameters to derive other parameters needed in the subsequent inference steps. The knowledge required for this inference step is the derivation model that can be represented as

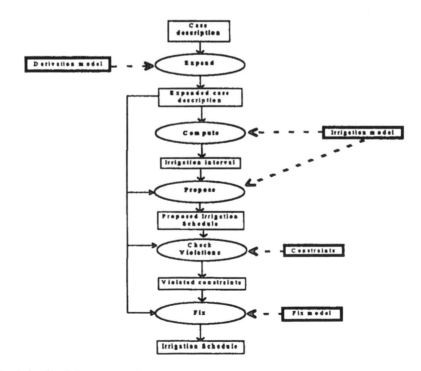

FIGURE 1   Irrigation inference structure.

object hierarchies, rules, facts, and mathematical functions, according to the nature of knowledge. The *compute* inference step, calculates the irrigation interval using the input and derived parameters. The knowledge required by this step is represented in the form of mathematical functions. The *propose* step generates a preliminary irrigation schedule depending on a set of fixed mathematical functions regardless of any additional environmental constraints, which includes all circumstances that are not covered by the irrigation model. The *check violation* step evaluates the proposed irrigation schedule with regard to some environmental constraints (e.g., the existence of certain disorders in the farm) and reports these violations to be fixed by the *fix inference* step, to produce the final, acceptable *irrigation schedule.*

5.   RESEARCH ISSUES

The research issues to be addressed in this section are: the integration of other software components with agricultural expert systems, agricultural knowledge sharing and reuse, intelligent retrieval of agricultural data, and automatic knowledge acquisition.

5.1.   INTEGRATION OF SOFTWARE COMPONENTS WITH AGRICULTURAL EXPERT SYSTEMS

Some existing expert systems are integrated with other software components such as crop simulation models (Kamel et al., 1994), GIS (Loh et al., 1994), and multimedia (Rafea et al., 1995). An agent-based approach can be used to integrate distributed heterogeneous systems and hence solve the integration problems in addition to other problems related to distributed components in different environments. However, more research is needed, as described in the following subsections.

5.1.1.   Crop Simulation Models and Expert Systems

The integration of numerical simulation models into the crop management expert system is receiving widespread attention. The reason is largely due to the perceived "naturalness" of an interaction between "experience" to quickly center on a part of a large search space, and numerical methods to select the correct exact solution from the narrowed possibilities. This mode of interaction leverages strengths of both expert systems and simulation models, using the expert system to quickly limit the search space, then using simulation-based methods to find the best candidate within the current focus. For example, the simulation model CERES wheat takes as input boundary conditions, such as planting date and irrigation regime, and then predicts (among other items) grain output at harvest. Although quite accurate in its output, one difficulty in the production use of CERES is the level of expertise that must be employed to set the initial input parameters. A scheme has been given by Kamel et al. (1994), that uses a compiled-level problem solver to determine the initial planting parameters (seed variety, planting date, planting and land preparation methods). These values are used to parameterize the CERES wheat model. The model is then used to predict iteratively the water and nutrient needs of the crop.

The example given has proved to be very useful in integrating numerical and symbolic methods to solve specific problems. This may encourage the integration of other types of simulation models such as pests infestation and economic models with expert systems. There remains further research to be done on the best ways of integration and interfaces between the expert system and the simulation model.

5.1.2.   GIS and Expert Systems

An example of integrating GIS and expert systems is given by Loh et al. (1994). In this example involving the USDA Forest Service , both expert systems, GIS and relational database management systems (RDBMS), have been introduced for maintaining resource inventories, GIS for organizing and analyzing spatially referenced data, and expert systems for capturing the essence of standards and guidelines of management plans and the accumulated knowledge of experts in the Service. To achieve this objective, some problems have been identified, namely: data sharing between the GIS and expert system components, and fitting the two components into a common problem-solving framework. The example application has succeeded in solving these problems using ARC/INFO for GIS, CLIPS for the expert system, and ORACLE for RDBMS. However, some other issues have been raised that require more research: the enhancement of the expert systems components to reason on spatial rules. This necessitates the inclusion of a spatial operator such as "intersect with" or "adjacent to." To accommodate such operators, a macro would have to be developed on the GIS side to communicate with the expert system shell. The integration of GIS and the expert system is fairly new, and more problems will be envisaged when more applications using both technologies are performed.

5.1.3.   Multimedia and Expert Systems

Integrating multimedia with expert systems is a hot topic that is booming currently. The integration with images was frequently done to more efficiently acquire the user inputs, whereas other types of media such as sound and video are also addressed. An example of integrating multimedia with expert systems is given by Rafea et al. (1995).

It was found that describing symptoms in words is very difficult and sometimes very confusing. Therefore, images are identified to be used for two main purposes: describing a disorder symptom, and confirming the diagnosis of the cause of a certain disorder. Detailed images for all symptoms, and unique images that confirm the occurrence of disorders at different stages, should be collected.

Although images are very useful in acquiring the user inputs, the uncertainty problem is still there. Therefore, giving the user the option to select an image with a degree of certainty should be provided. Providing more than one picture for the same symptom can reduce the user uncertainty, but this will lead to exerting more effort in collecting and classifying the images.

As the output of an expert system for crop production management is a set of agricultural operations, describing how to perform an agricultural operation in words is very hard, and one can never guarantee that the user can understand what has been written. Displaying a video for a professional doing the recommended operation would be very educational.

The sound is essential because sometimes it is not easy to write terminology used by growers in daily life. In addition, combining the video with sound is also recommended in order to comment on how the operation is done.

Although the given example proved the possibility of integrating multimedia with expert systems, there are still some problems that need further research: the intelligent selection of the appropriate media for presentation, taking into consideration the user level; getting input data from images, for example providing the expert system with an infected leaf of a plant for diagnosis; and/or enhancements of all input devices interfaces, which is a general research issue, in order to provide expert system with data in different forms.

5.2.   KNOWLEDGE SHARING AND REUSE

Knowledge sharing and reuse is one of the topics that has attracted the attention of the AI researchers in the last few years. The research in knowledge sharing in agriculture can be directed toward identifying common knowledge that can be shared among different expert systems such as identification of agriculture ontology, knowledge related to common resources, namely: soil, water and climate, knowledge related to the same taxonomic category of a set of crops, etc. The research in knowledge reuse can be directed toward building a library of domain-specific tasks in agriculture such as: irrigation, fertilization, integrated pest management, etc.

5.3. Intelligent Retrieval of Agricultural Data

Meteorological data are very important for agronomists as forecasting weather data helps in giving recommendations to growers. A system that serves as an intelligent assistant for meteorologists to locate and analyze historical situations of interest has been developed using case-based reasoning (Jones and Roydhouse, 1995). This work was oriented to be used by meteorologists, but not agronomists. The basic idea could be investigated to retrieve historical situations that are important for managing different crops.

5.4. Automatic Knowledge Acquisition

Automatic knowledge acquisition is a general research issue in expert systems development. In agriculture, research can be directed toward using the knowledge models developed for specific tasks in building tools to acquire the domain knowledge interactively with the domain experts. Another approach is to use machine learning to automatically generate and refine knowledge bases. Although this approach was one of the first approaches in building expert systems (Michalski et al., 1983), no elaboration on this approach was pursued. A recent application that uses machine learning to generate agriculture data is given by McQueen et al. (1995). This approach can be very useful when data sets are available in certain areas.

6. FUTURE TRENDS

In effect, the future trends are highly related to the research issues discussed in the previous section. It is expected that the agent-based approach will be extensively used in solving the problems resulting from the integration of expert systems with other software components. The agent-based approach will address other issues related to heterogeneous components that are distributed on different platforms. The agent-based approach is a general approach suitable for any domain. In agriculture, we can see its usage in integrating GIS, multimedia, and simulation models with expert systems.

Developing domain-specific tasks in agriculture is a very important future trend that will help in knowledge sharing and reuse and in automating the knowledge acquisition process. Successful results in these two directions will expedite the development procedure of expert systems. Machine learning will help also in automating the knowledge acquisition process and more attention will be given to it in the near future.

Sophisticated user interfaces for different media types are expected to be an important issue. Different user interface models will also be investigated in as much as agricultural expert systems have different types of users: researchers, extensionists, and growers. Their requirements and needs are different.

More sophisticated explanations facilities will be provided once domain-specific models are well established. An explanation facility should not match what expert systems are providing now — the why and how primitives, but it should be intelligent enough to generate the explanation based on the user level. Intelligent agent-based approach may also be used in developing such an explanation facility.

Another issue that will play an important role is the usage of the Internet to access expert systems developed in different locations. There is a trend now to develop tools to facilitate the dissemination of expert systems through the WorldWide Web. It is expected in the near future that shells and tools will enable developers to put their expert systems on the Web.

SUMMARY

This chapter has discussed the needs of expert systems in agriculture and revealed their importance as tools for information transfer through information generation from knowledge and expertise.

The advantages of an expert system over traditional methods include: providing the growers with dynamic information related to their actual situations, taking into consideration different specialties and different sources of information; shortening the update time of information, especially if the expert system is centralized and accessible from different locations; and transferring real experience that is not documented in any form of media by acquiring it from its sources: extensionists, highly experienced growers, and/or researchers.

The expert systems selected to demonstrate applications in the 1980s revealed that these systems actually addressed issues that need further research. The usage of machine learning to generate the knowledge base was addressed in the soybean diagnosis system. The integration of simulation model with expert system was considered and implemented in the cotton expert system. The concept of a task-specific package was raised in the CALEX system. The importance of an expert system as an appropriate technology to expedite agricultural desert development was emphasized in the late 1980s by Rafea and El-Beltagy (1987).

In the 1990s, expert systems have been expanded to include other commodities and disciplines such as agroforestry and meteorology. The second-generation expert systems methodologies have been applied. More sophisticated expert system shells were used, such as NEXPERT/OBJECT and KEE. Programming languages such as Prolog and Small Talk were also used. The integration of multimedia was first addressed due to the advances made in this technology. Expert systems in the field for real use have been deployed.

Research issues in agricultural expert systems are categorized under these topics: integration of software components with agricultural expert systems, knowledge sharing and reuse, intelligent retrieval of agricultural data, and automatic knowledge acquisition. The future trends in research and development of agricultural expert systems are expected to be: using agent-based approaches to solve the integration problem of different software components, developing domain-specific tasks that will contribute to knowledge sharing and reuse, and automatic knowledge acquisition. Sophisticated user interfaces and explanation facilities that depend on the user level are expected to be seriously considered. The dissemination of expert systems through the Internet is also anticipated.

REFERENCES

Gerevini, A., Perini, A., Ricci, F., Forti, D., Ioratti, C., and Mattedi, L. (1992). POMI: an expert system for integrated pest management of apple orchards, *AI Applications*, 6(3): 51–62.
Jones, E. and Roydhouse, A. (1995). Intelligent retrieval of archived meteorological data, *IEEE Expert*, 10(6): 50–57.
Kamel, A., Schroeder, K., Sticklen, J., Rafea,A., Salah,A., Schulthess,U., Ward, R., and Ritchie, J. (1994). Integrated wheat crop management system based on generic task knowledge based systems and CERES numerical simulation. *AI Applications*, 9(1): 17–27.
Lemmon, H. (1986). COMAX: an expert system for cotton crop management. *Science*, 233: 29–33.
Loh, D., Hsieh, Y., Choo, Y., and Holtfrerich, D. (1994). Integration of a rule-based expert system with GIS through a relational database management system for forest resource management. *Computers and Electronics in Agriculture*, 11(2): 215–228.
McQueen, R., Garner, S., Manning, C., and Witten, I. (1995). Applying machine learning to agricultural data. *Computers and Electronics in Agriculture*, 12(4): 275–293.
Michalski, R., Davis, J., Visht, V., and Sinclair, J. (1983). A computer-based advisory system for diagnosing soybean diseases in Illinois. *Plant Disease*, 67: 459–463.
Mohan, S. and Arumugam, N. (1995). An intelligent front-end for selecting evapotranspiration estimation methods. *Computers and Electronics in Agriculture*, 12(4): 295–309.
Warkentin, M., Nair, P., Ruth, S., and Sprague, K. (1990). A knowledge-based expert system for planning and design of agroforestry systems. *Agroforestry Systems*, 11(1): 71–83.
Plant, R. (1989). An integrated expert decision support system for agricultural management. *Agricultural Systems*, 29: 49–66.

Rafea, A. and El-Beltagy, A. (1987). Expert systems as an appropriate technology to speed up agriculture desert development in Egypt. *Proceedings of the Second International Desert Development Conference*, Harwood Academic Publisher. 47–57.

Rafea, A., Warkentin, M., and Ruth, S. (1991). Knowledge engineering: creating expert systems for crop production management in Egypt. Chapter 7: 89–104 in *Expert Systems in Developing Countries: Practice and Promise*, Stephen R. Ruth and Chip Mann (eds.), Boulder, CO: Westview Press, ISBN0-8133-8397-8.

Rafea, A., El-Dessouki A., Hassan H., and Mohammed, S. (1993). Development and implementation of a knowledge acquisition methodology for crop management expert systems. *Computers and Electronics in Agriculture*, 8(2): 129–146.

Rafea, A., Edrees, S., El-Azhari, S., and Mahmoud M. (1994). A development methodology for agricultural expert systems based on KADS. *Proceedings of the Second World Congress on Expert Systems*.

Rafea, A., El-Azhari, S., and Hassan, E. (1995). Integrating multimedia with expert systems for crop production management. *Proceedings of the Second International IFAC Workshop on Artificial Intelligence in Agriculture*, Wageningen, The Netherlands.

Rafea, A., El-Azhari, S., Ibrahim, I., Edres, S., and Mahmoud, M. (1995). Experience with the development and deployment of expert systems in agriculture. *Proceedings of IAAI-95*.

Roach, J., Virkar, R., Weaver M., and Drake, C. (1985). POMME: a computer-based consultation system for apple orchard management using Prolog. *Expert Systems*, 2(2): 56–69.

Schroeder, K., Kamel, A., Sticklen, J., Ward, R., Ritchie, J., Schulthess, U., Rafea, A., and Salah, A. (1994). Guiding object-oriented design via the knowledge level architecture: the irrigated wheat testbed. *Mathl. Comput. Modeling*, 20(8): 1–16.

Schulthess, U. et al. (1996). NEPER-Weed: a picture-based expert system for weed identification. *Agron. J.*, 88: 423–427.

Index